Sir Walter Scott

The Works of
Sir Walter Scott

with an Introduction and Bibliography

Wordsworth Poetry Library

ISBN 1-85326-437-7

Printed and bound in Denmark by Nørhaven.

INTRODUCTION

SIR WALTER SCOTT entered literature through poetry and, absorbed as he was in folklore and the supernatural, he started his literary career by anonymously publishing in 1796 an adaptation of *Ballads* by G.A. Burger, which he followed in 1801 by contributions to M.G. Lewis's 'hobgoblin repast' better known as *Tales of Wonder*. At about this time he translated Goethe's *Goetz von Berlichingen* and, in 1802-3, put out the *Minstrelsy of the Scottish Border*, an edition of old and new ballads. A metrical version of the romance *Sir Tristrem* appeared in 1804. Scott's poetic writing so far was dominated by a blend of Gothic-Germanic sorcery and antiquarian enthusiasm.

It was in 1805, with the publication of *The Lay of the Last Minstrel*, based on an old border narrative, that his name became more widely known. Supposedly recited by an aged minstrel to the Duchess of Buccleuch and her ladies at Newark Castle, the sequence of old Border scenes and incidents is elaborated with an admirable combination of antique lore, clan enthusiasm and vividly picturesque art. By nature, Scott was a great improviser; he created his impression more by the ardour and vividness of his presentation than by the charm of a subtle and finished art. His next poetical story, *Marmion* (1808), is so full of heroic matter on a large scale that its form seems almost unimportant. The culmination of the story is Flodden, and the fortunes of his faulty hero, Lord Marmion, are simply the means of approaching the great theme. In *The Lay of the Last Minstrel*, said Scott, the force is laid on style; in *Marmion*, on description. The opening picture of Norham Castle in the setting sun gives the keynote, and scene after scene follows, culminating in the dramatic picture of the stress and tumult of the Flodden conflict. Some of its details are among the best-known passages of Scott's poetry; but the story does not flow quite so freely as the happy improvisation in *The Lay*. In *The Lady of the Lake* (1810) the force is laid on incident. The poem sets before us an almost continuous succession of exciting occurrences, yet it lives chiefly by its enchanting descriptions of scenery. It made Loch Katrine part of everyone's romantic geography. In construction it is simple; introductory stanzas of Spenserian form lead to cantos in octosyllabics, with interspersed songs that are among the most familiar of lyrics. In *Rokeby* (1813) the force is laid on character, but the poem has never been really popular because we want Scott to write more about Loch Katrine, not about Marston Moor; though it has to be admitted that in *Rokeby* he included two of his most delightful songs. In *The Lord of the Isles* (1818), again the historic interest is powerful – almost too powerful; but the pageantry of the poem is admirably managed. Of the less important romances – *The Vision of Don Roderick* (1811) *The Bridal of Trierman* (1813) and *Harold the Dauntless* (1817) – little need be said; nor need we do more than chronicle Scott's well-meant dramatic efforts – *Halidon Hill* (1822), *Macduff's Cross* (1822) *The Doom of Devorgoil* (1830) and *The Tragedy of Auchindrane* (1830). The genius of Scott was too Homeric for drama, but his power as a writer of pure lyric is underestimated. In the poetic romances there are lyrical strains of exquisite quality – even Burns could not have achieved the haunting suggestion of *Proud Maisie*.

It should be remembered that throughout the writing of his poetry, Scott was also involved in prose writing and editorial work on a grand scale, and that he was one of the leading lights in establishing *The Quarterly Review* in 1809. His poetic romances represent only a fraction of his endowments, and, ultimately, he found that they limited his expression in scope and range. From 1814, with *Waverley*, Scott turned his attention to the writing of novels, and, ironically, some of his most memorable poems are to be found in these. Scott remains a giant among Scottish writers, who contributed an intellectual foundation to the revival of the Scottish consciousness that was more respectable than the poetry of the less disciplined Robert Burns. He still has the power to move the modern reader who braves the length of the dramatic poems. His command of the lyrical turn of phrase and the drama of historical event have ensured a timely revival of interest in his work.

BIOGRAPHICAL NOTE

Walter Scott (1771-1832) was born in College Wynd, Edinburgh, the son of a Writer to the Signet (a solicitor in Scotland). He was educated at Edinburgh High School and Edinburgh University, became apprenticed to his father and qualified in 1793. His family roots were in the Borders and he became passionately devoted to that area. He married a French woman, Margaret Charlotte Charpentier from Lyon, in 1797 and was appointed sheriff-depute of Selkirkshire in 1799. He became a partner in James Ballantyne's printing business and, in 1809, a partner in the booksellers John Ballantyne & Co., moves that subsequently caused him great financial distress and ruined his health. In 1811 he purchased Abbotsford on the River Tweed where he built a country house. In 1813 Scott declined the offer of the Poet Laureatship, recommending instead Southey for the honour. Scott was created a baronet in 1820, at the height of his fame. In 1826 James Ballantyne became involved in the bankruptcy of Constable & Co. and Scott found himself personally liable for the then huge sum of around £130,000. He worked prodigiously to pay off the creditors, and all his outstanding debts were honourably discharged in full after his death, from the proceeds of his writing.

FURTHER READING

W.E.K. Anderson (ed.): *Journal of Sir Walter Scott* (1972).
J. Buchan: *Life of Sir Walter Scott* (1932).
J.O. Hayden: *Scott: The Critical Heritage.*
E. Johnson: *Sir Walter Scott: the Great Unknown* (2 vols) (1970).
J.G. Lockhart: *Sir Walter Scott: A Life* (1837/8).
J. Sutherland: *The Life of Sir Walter Scott* (1995).

Acknowledgement

The Publishers gratefully acknowledge the kind permission of the Syndics of the Cambridge University Press for allowing them to quote liberally from the *Concise Cambridge History of English Literature* and the *Cambridge Guide to Literature in English* in the above Introduction.

CONTENTS.

THE LAY OF THE LAST MINSTREL.

TO THE

RIGHT HONOURABLE

CHARLES EARL OF DALKEITH,

THIS POEM IS INSCRIBED BY

THE AUTHOR.

PREFACE TO THE FIRST EDITION.

The Poem, now offered to the Public, is intended to illustrate the customs and manners which anciently prevailed on the Borders of England and Scotland. The inhabitants living in a state partly pastoral and partly warlike, and combining habits of constant depredation with the influence of a rude spirit of chivalry, were often engaged in scenes highly susceptible of poetical ornament. As the description of scenery and manners was more the object of the Author than a combined and regular narrative, the plan of the Ancient Metrical Romance was adopted, which allows greater latitude, in this respect, than would be consistent with the dignity of a regular Poem. The same model offered other facilities, as it permits an occasional alteration of measure, which, in some degree, authorizes the change of rhythm in the text. The machinery, also, adopted from popular belief, would have seemed puerile in a Poem which did not partake of the rudeness of the old Ballad, or Metrical Romance.

For these reasons, the Poem was put into the mouth of an ancient Minstrel, the last of the race, who, as he is supposed to have survived the Revolution, might have caught somewhat of the refinement of modern poetry, without losing the simplicity of his original model. The date of the Tale itself is about the middle of the sixteenth century, when most of the personages actually flourished. The time occupied by the action is Three Nights and Three Days.

THE LAY OF THE LAST MINSTREL.

INTRODUCTION.

THE way was long, the wind was cold,
The Minstrel was infirm and old ;
His wither'd cheek, and tresses gray,
Seem'd to have known a better day ;
The harp, his sole remaining joy,
Was carried by an orphan boy.
The last of all the Bards was he,
Who sung of Border chivalry ;
For, welladay ! their date was fled,
His tuneful brethren all were dead ;
And he, neglected and oppress'd,
Wish'd to be with them, and at rest.
No more on prancing palfrey borne,
He caroll'd, light as lark at morn ;
No longer courted and caress'd,
High placed in hall, a welcome guest,
He pour'd, to lord and lady gay,
The unpremeditated lay :
Old times were changed, old manners gone ;
A stranger filled the Stuarts' throne ;
The bigots of the iron time
Had call'd his harmless art a crime.
A wandering Harper, scorn'd and poor,
He begg'd his bread from door to door.
And tuned, to please a peasant's ear,
The harp, a king had loved to hear.

He pass'd where Newark's* stately
    tower
Looks out from Yarrow's birchen bower:
The Minstrel gazed with wishful eye—
No humbler resting-place was nigh,

With hesitating step at last,
The embattled portal arch he pass'd,
Whose ponderous grate and massy bar
Had oft roll'd back the tide of war,
But never closed the iron door
Against the desolate and poor.
The Duchess† marked his weary pace,
His timid mien, and reverend face,
And bade her page the menials tell,
That they should tend the old man well:
For she had known adversity,
Though born in such a high degree ;
In pride of power, in beauty's bloom,
Had wept o'er Monmouth's bloody tomb !

When kindness had his wants supplied,
And the old man was gratified,
Began to rise his minstrel pride :
And he began to talk anon,
Of good Earl Francis,‡ dead and gone,
And of Earl Walter,§ rest him, God !
A braver ne'er to battle rode ;
And how full many a tale he knew,
Of the old warriors of Buccleuch :
And, would the noble Duchess deign
To listen to an old man's strain,
Though stiff his hand, his voice though
    weak,
He thought even yet, the sooth to speak,

---

* *Newark's stately tower.* A ruined tower
now ; situated three miles from Selkirk, on the
banks of the Yarrow.

---

† *The Duchess.* Anne, the heiress of Buccleuch, who had been married to the unhappy
Duke of Monmouth, son of Charles II. He
was beheaded for rebellion against James II.
1685.
‡ *Earl Francis.* The Duchess's late father.
§ Walter, Earl of Buccleuch, grandfather
of the Duchess, and a celebrated warrior.

That, if she loved the harp to hear,
He could make music to her ear.

The humble boon was soon obtain'd;
The Aged Minstrel audience gain'd.
But, when he reach'd the room of state,
Where she, with all her ladies, sate,
Perchance he wished his boon denied:
For, when to tune his harp he tried,
His trembling hand had lost the ease,
Which marks security to please;
And scenes, long past, of joy and pain,
Came wildering o'er his aged brain—
He tried to tune his harp in vain!
The pitying Duchess praised its chime,
And gave him heart, and gave him time,
Till every string's according glee
Was blended into harmony.
And then, he said, he would full fain
He could recall an ancient strain,
He never thought to sing again.
It was not framed for village churls,
But for high dames and mighty earls;
He had play'd it to King Charles the Good,
When he kept court in Holyrood;
And much he wish'd, yet fear'd to try
The long-forgotten melody
Amid the strings his fingers stray'd,
And an uncertain warbling made,
And oft he shook his hoary head.
But when he caught the measure wild,
The old man raised his face, and smiled;
And lighten'd up his faded eye,
With all a poet's ecstasy!
In varying cadence, soft or strong,
He swept the sounding chords along:
The present scene, the future lot,
His toils, his wants, were all forgot:
Cold diffidence, and age's frost,
In the full tide of song were lost;
Each blank in faithless memory void,
The poet's glowing thought supplied;
And, while his harp responsive rung,
'Twas thus the LATEST MINSTREL sung.

CANTO FIRST.

I.

The feast was over in Branksome tower,[1]
And the Ladye had gone to her secret
    bower;
Her bower that was guarded by word
    and by spell,
Deadly to hear, and deadly to tell—
Jesu Maria, shield us well!
No living wight, save the Ladye alone,
Had dared to cross the threshold stone.

II.

The tables were drawn, it was idlesse all;
    Knight, and page, and household squire,
Loiter'd through the lofty hall,
    Or crowded round the ample fire:
The staghounds, weary with the chase,
    Lay stretch'd upon the rushy floor,
And urged, in dreams, the forest race,
    From Teviot-stone to Eskdale-moor

III.

Nine-and-twenty knights of fame
    Hung their shields in Branksome-Hall;[2]
Nine-and-twenty squires of name
    Brought them their steeds to bower from
        stall;
        Nine-and-twenty yeomen tall
        Waited, duteous, on them all;
        They were all knights of mettle true,
        Kinsmen to the bold Buccleuch.

IV.

Ten of them were sheathed in steel,
With belted sword, and spur on heel:
They quitted not their harness bright,
Neither by day, nor yet by night:
        They lay down to rest,
        With corslet laced,
Pillow'd on buckler cold and hard;
        They carved at the meal
        With gloves of steel,
And they drank the red wine through the
    helmet barr'd.

V.

Ten squires, ten yeomen, mail-clad men,
Waited the beck of the warders ten ;
Thirty steeds, both fleet and wight,
Stood saddled in stable day and night,
Barbed with frontlet of steel, I trow,
And with Jedwood-axe at saddlebow ;[3]
A hundred more fed free in stall :—
Such was the custom of Branksome-Hall.

VI.

Why do these steeds stand ready dight ?
Why watch these warriors, arm'd, by
  night?—
They watch, to hear the blood-hound
  baying ?
They watch to hear the war-horn braying;
To see St. George's red cross streaming,
To see the midnight beacon gleaming :
They watch, against Southern force and
  guile,
  Lest Scroop, or Howard, or Percy's
  powers,
  Threaten Branksome's lordly towers,
From Warkwork, or Naworth, or merry
  Carlisle.[4]

VII.

Such is the custom of Branksome-Hall—
  Many a valiant knight is here ;
But he, the chieftain of them all,
His sword hangs rusting on the wall,
  Beside his broken spear.
  Bards long shall tell
  How Lord Walter fell![5]
When startled burghers fled, afar,
The furies of the Border war ;
When the streets of high Dunedin *
Saw lances gleam and falchions redden,
And heard the slogan's † deadly yell—
Then the Chief of Branksome fell.

VIII.

Can piety the discord heal,
  Or stanch the death-feud's enmity ?
Can Christian lore, can patriot zeal,
  Can love of blessed charity ?

---

* Edinburgh.
 † The war-cry, or gathering word, of a
Border clan.

No ! vainly to each holy shrine,
  In mutual pilgrimage they drew ;
Implored, in vain, the grace divine
  For chiefs, their own red falchions slew:
While Cessford owns the rule of Carr,
  While Ettrick boasts the line of Scott,
The slaughter'd chiefs, the mortal jar,
The havoc of the feudal war,
  Shall never, never be forgot ![6]

IX.

In sorrow o'er Lord Walter's bier
  The warlike foresters had bent ;
And many a flower, and many a tear,
  Old Teviot's maids and matrons lent:
But o'er her warrior's bloody bier
The Ladye dropp'd nor flower nor tear !
Vengeance, deep-brooding o'er the slain,
  Had lock'd the source of softer woe ;
And burning pride, and high disdain,
  Forbade the rising tear to flow ·
Until, amid his sorrowing clan,
  Her son lisp'd from the nurse's knee—
" And if I live to be a man,
  My father's death revenged shall be !"
Then fast the mother's tears did seek
To dew the infant's kindling cheek.

X.

All loose her negligent attire,
  All loose her golden hair,
Hung Margaret o'er her slaughter'd sire,
  And wept in wild despair,
But not alone the bitter tear
  Had filial grief supplied ;
For hopeless love, and anxious fear,
  Had lent their mingled tide :
Nor in her mother's alter'd eye
Dared she to look for sympathy.
Her lover, 'gainst her father's clan,
  With Carr in arms had stood,[7]
When Mathouse-burn to Melrose ran,
  All purple with their blood ;
And well she knew, her mother dread,
Before Lord Cranstoun[8] she should wed,
Would see her on her dying bed.

XI.

Of noble race the Ladye came,
  Her father was a clerk of fame,

Of Bethune's line of Picardie:[9]
He learn'd the art that none may name,
    In Padua, far beyond the sea.[10]
Men said, he changed his mortal frame
    By feat of magic mystery;
For when, in studious mode, he paced
    St. Andrew's cloister'd hall,
His form no darkening shadow traced
    Upon the sunny wall![11]

XII.

And of his skill, as bards avow,
    He taught that Ladye fair,
Till to her bidding she could bow
    The viewless forms of air.
And now she sits in secret bower,
In old Lord David's western tower,
And listens to a heavy sound,
That moans the mossy turrets round.
Is it the roar of Teviot's tide,
That chafes against the scaur's* red side?
Is it the wind that swings the oaks?
Is it the echo from the rocks?
What may it be, the heavy sound,
That moans old Branksome's turrets
    round?

XIII.

At the sullen, moaning sound,
    The ban-dogs bay and howl;
And, from the turrets round,
    Loud whoops the startled owl.
In the hall, both squire and knight
Swore that a storm was near,
And looked forth to view the night?
    But the night was still and clear!

XIV.

From the sound of Teviot's tide,
Chafing with the mountain's side,
From the groan of the wind-swung oak,
From the sullen echo of the rock,
From the voice of the coming storm,
    The Ladye knew it well!
It was the Spirit of the Flood that spoke,
    And he called on the Spirit of the Fell.

XV.

RIVER SPIRIT.

" Sleep'st thou, brother!"—

MOUNTAIN SPIRIT.

            —" Brother, nay—
On my hills the moon-beams play.
From Craik-cross to Skelfhill-pen,
By every rill, in every glen,
    Merry elves their morris pacing,
        To aërial minstrelsy,
    Emerald rings on brown heath tracing,
        Trip it deft and merrily.
    Up, and mark their nimble feet!
    Up, and list their music sweet!"—

XVI.

RIVER SPIRIT.

" Tears of an imprisoned maiden
    Mix with my polluted stream;
Margaret of Branksome, sorrow-laden,
    Mourns beneath the moon's pale beam.
Tell me, thou, who view'st the stars,
When shall cease these feudal jars?
What shall be the maiden's fate?
Who shall be the maiden's mate?"

XVII.

MOUNTAIN SPIRIT.

" Arthur's slow wain his course doth roll,
In utter darkness round the pole;
The Northern Bear lowers black and grim;
Orion's studded belt is dim;
Twinkling faint, and distant far,
Shimmers through mist each planet star;
    Ill may I read their high decree!
But no kind influence deign they shower
On Teviot's tide, and Branksome's tower,
    Till pride be quell'd, and love be free."

XVIII.

The unearthly voices ceast,
    And the heavy sound was still;
It died on the river's breast,
    It died on the side of the hill.
But round Lord David's tower
    The sound still floated near;
For it rung in the Ladye's bower,
    And it rung in the Ladye's ear.

---

* A steep embankment.

She raised her stately head,
 And her heart throbb'd high with
  pride:—
" Your mountains shall bend,
 And your streams ascend,
Ere Margaret be our foeman's bride !"

XIX.

The Lady sought the lofty hall,
 Where many a bold retainer lay,
And, with jocund din, among them all,
 Her son pursued his infant play.
A fancied moss-trooper,* the boy
 The truncheon of a spear bestrode,
And round the hall, right merrily,
 In mimic foray rode,
Even bearded knights, in arms grown old,
 Share in his frolic gambols bore,
Albeit their hearts of rugged mould,
 Were stubborn as the steel they wore.
For the grey warriors prophesied,
 How the brave boy, in future war,
Should tame the Unicorn's pride,†
 Exalt the Crescent and the Star.‡

XX.

The Ladye forgot her purpose high,
 One moment, and no more ;
One moment gazed with a mother's eye,
 As she paused at the arched door :
Then from amid the armed train,
She call'd to her William of Deloraine.

XXI.

A stark moss-trooping Scott was he,
As e'er couch'd Border lance by knee ;
Through Solway sands, through Tarras
 moss,
Blindfold, he knew the paths to cross ;

By wily turns, by desperate bounds,
Had baffled Percy's best blood-hounds ;[12]
In Eske or Liddel, fords were none,
But he would ride them, one by one ;
Alike to him was time or tide,
December's snow, or July's pride ;
Alike to him was tide or time,
Moonless midnight, or matin prime ;
Steady of heart, and stout of hand,
As ever drove prey from Cumberland ;
Five times outlawed had he been,
By England's King, and Scotland's Queen.

XXII.

" Sir William of Deloraine, good at need,
Mount thee on the wightest steed ;
Spare not to spur, nor stint to ride,
Until thou come to fair Tweedside ;
And in Melrose's holy pile
Seek thou the Monk of St. Mary's aisle.
 Greet the Father well from me ;
  Say that the fated hour is come,
 And to-night he shall watch with thee,
  To win the treasure of the tomb ·
For this will be St. Michael's night,
And, though stars be dim, the moon is
 bright ;
And the Cross, of bloody red,
Will point to the grave of the mighty dead.

XXIII.

" What he gives thee, see thou keep ;
Stay not thou for food or sleep :
Be it scroll, or be it book,
Into it, Knight, thou must not look ;
If thou readest, thou art lorn !
Better hadst thou ne'er been born."—

XXIV.

"O swiftly can speed my dapple-grey steed,
 Which drinks of the Teviot clear ;
Ere break of day," the Warrior 'gan say,
 " Again will I be here :
And safer by none may thy errand be done,
 Than, noble dame, by me ;
Letter nor line know I never a one,
 Wer't my neck-verse at Hairibee."§

---

* Moss-trooper, a borderer, whose profession was pillage of the English. These
marauders were called *moss-troopers* because
they dwelt in the mosses, and rode, on their
incursions, in troops.

† The Unicorn Head was the crest of the
Carrs, or Kerrs, of Cessford, the enemies of
the child's late father.

‡ The Crescent and the Star were armorial
bearings of the Scotts of Buccleuch.

§ *Hairibee,* the place on Carlisle wall where

XXV.

Soon in his saddle sate he fast,
And soon the steep descent he past,
Soon cross'd the sounding barbican,*
And soon the Teviot side he won.
Eastward the wooded path he rode,
Green hazels o'er his basnet nod;
He passed the Peel of Goldiland,†
And cross'd old Borthwick's roaring
    strand;
Dimly he view'd the Moat-hill's mound,
Where Druid shades still flitted round;
In Hawick twinkled many a light;
Behind him soon they set in night;
And soon he spurr'd his courser keen
Beneath the tower of Hazeldean.

XXVI.

The clattering hoofs the watchmen
    mark;—
"Stand, ho! thou courier of the dark."—
"For Branksome, ho!" the knight rejoin'd,
And left the friendly tower behind.
    He turn'd him now from Teviotside,
    And, guided by the tinkling rill,
    Northward the dark ascent did ride,
    And gained the moor at Horsliehill;
Broad on the left before him lay,
For many a mile, the Roman way.‡

XXVII.

A moment now he slack'd his speed,
A moment breathed his panting steed;
Drew saddle-girth and corslet-band,
And loosen'd in the sheath his brand.

---

the moss-troopers, if caught, were hung.
The neck-verse was the first verse of Psalm
51. If a criminal claimed on the scaffold
"benefit of his clergy," a priest instantly
presented him with a Psalter, and he read his
neck-verse. The power of reading it entitled
him to his life, which was spared; but he
was banished the kingdom. See Palgrave's
"Merchant and Friar."

* *Barbican*, the defence of the outer gate
of a feudal castle.

† *Peel*, a Border tower.

‡ An ancient Roman road, crossing through
part of Roxburghshire.

On Minto-crags the moonbeams glint,
Where Barnhill hew'd his bed of flint;
Who flung his outlaw'd limbs to rest,
Where falcons hang their giddy nest,
Mid cliffs, from whence his eagle eye
For many a league his prey could spy;
Cliffs, doubling, on their echoes borne,
The terrors of the robber's horn?
Cliffs, which, for many a later year,
The warbling Doric reed shall hear,
When some sad swain shall teach the grove,
Ambition is no cure for love!

XXVIII.

Unchallenged, thence pass'd Deloraine,
To ancient Riddel's fair domain,
    Where Aill, from mountains freed,
Down from the lakes did raving come;
Each wave was crested with tawny foam,
    Like the mane of a chestnut steed.
In vain! no torrent, deep or broad,
Might bar the bold moss-trooper's road.

XXIX.

At the first plunge the horse sunk low,
And the water broke o'er the saddlebow;
Above the foaming tide, I ween,
Scarce half the charger's neck was seen;
For he was barded§ from counter to tail,
And the rider was armed complete in mail;
Never heavier man and horse
Stemm'd a midnight torrent's force.
The warrior's very plume, I say
Was daggled by the dashing spray;
Yet, through good heart, and Our Ladye's
    grace,
At length he gain'd the landing place.

XXX.

Now Bowden Moor the march-man won,
    And sternly shook his plumed head,
As glanced his eye o'er Halidon;‖
    For on his soul the slaughter red
Of that unhallow'd morn arose,
When first the Scott and Carr were foes;

---

§ *Barded*, or barbed, applied to a horse
accoutred with defensive armour.

‖ Halidon was an ancient seat of the Kerrs
of Cessford, now demolished.

When royal James beheld the fray,
Prize to the victor of the day;
When Home and Douglas, in the van,
Bore down Buccleuch's retiring clan,
Till gallant Cessford's heart-blood dear
Reek'd on dark Elliot's Border spear.

XXXI.

In bitter mood he spurred fast,
And soon the hated heath was past;
And far beneath, in lustre wan,
Old Melros' rose, and fair Tweed ran:
Like some tall rock with lichens grey,
Seem'd dimly huge, the dark Abbaye.
When Hawick he pass'd, had curfew rung,
Now midnight lauds * were in Melrose
    sung.
The sound, upon the fitful gale,
In solemn wise did rise and fail,
Like that wild harp, whose magic tone
Is waken'd by the winds alone.
But when Melrose he reach'd, 'twas silence
    all;
He meetly stabled his steed in stall,
And sought the convent's lonely wall.[13]

HERE paused the harp; and with its swell
The Master's fire and courage fell;
Dejectedly, and low, he bow'd,
And, gazing timid on the crowd,
He seem'd to seek, in every eye,
If they approved his minstrelsy;
And, diffident of present praise,
Somewhat he spoke of former days,
And how old age, and wand'ring long,
Had done his hand and harp some wrong.
The Duchess, and her daughters fair,
And every gentle lady there,
Each after each, in due degree,
Gave praises to his melody;
His hand was true, his voice was clear,
And much they long'd the rest to hear.
Encouraged thus, the Aged Man,
After meet rest, again began.

---

* *Lauds*, the midnight service of the
Catholic church.

CANTO SECOND.

I.

IF thou would'st view fair Melrose aright,
Go visit it by the pale moonlight;
For the gay beams of lightsome day
Gild, but to flout, the ruins grey.
When the broken arches are black in night,
And each shafted oriel glimmers white;
When the cold light's uncertain shower
Streams on the ruin'd central tower;
When buttress and buttress, alternately,
Seem framed of ebon and ivory;
When silver edges the imagery,
And the scrolls that teach thee to live and
    die;[11]
When distant Tweed is heard to rave,
And the owlet to hoot o'er the dead man's
    grave,
Then go—but go alone the while—
Then view St. David's ruin'd pile;
And, home returning, soothly swear,
Was never scene so sad and fair!

II.

Short halt did Deloraine make there;
Little reck'd he of the scene so fair;
With dagger's hilt, on the wicket strong,
He struck full loud, and struck full long.
The porter hurried to the gate—
" Who knocks so loud, and knocks so
    late?"
" From Branksome I," the warrior cried;
And straight the wicket open'd wide:
For Branksome's Chiefs had in battle
    stood,
    To fence the rights of fair Melrose;
And lands and livings, many a rood,
    Had gifted the shrine for their souls'
    repose.

III.

Bold Deloraine his errand said;
The porter bent his humble head;
With torch in hand, and feet unshod,
And noiseless step, the path he trod,
The arched cloister, far and wide,
Rang to the warrior's clanking stride,

Till, stooping low his lofty crest,
He enter'd the cell of the ancient priest,
And lifted his barred aventayle,*
To hail the Monk of St. Mary's aisle.

IV.

"The Ladye of Branksome greets thee by
        me,
    Says, that the fated hour is come,
And that to-night I shall watch with thee,
    To win the treasure of the tomb."
From sackcloth couch the Monk arose,
    With toil his stiffen'd limbs he rear'd;
A hundred years had flung their snows
    On his thin locks and floating beard.

V.

And strangely on the Knight look'd he,
    And his blue eyes gleam'd wild and wide;
"And, darest thou, Warrior! seek to see
    What heaven and hell alike would hide?
My breast, in belt of iron pent,
    With shirt of hair and scourge of thorn;
For threescore years, in penance spent,
    My knees those flinty stones have worn:
Yet all too little to atone
For knowing what should ne'er be known.
    Would'st thou thy every future year
    In ceaseless prayer and penance drie,
    Yet wait thy latter end with fear—
    Then, daring Warrior, follow me!—

VI.

"Penance, father, will I none;
Prayer know I hardly one;
For mass or prayer can I rarely tarry,
Save to patter an Ave Mary,
When I ride on a Border foray.
Other prayer can I none;
So speed me my errand, and let me be
    gone."—

VII.

Again on the Knight look'd the Church-
    man old,
    And again he sighed heavily;
For he had himself been a warrior bold,
    And fought in Spain and Italy.

---

*   Aventayle, visor of the helmet.

And he thought on the days that were
    long since by,
When his limbs were strong, and his
    courage was high:—
Now, slow and faint, he led the way,
Where, cloister'd round, the garden lay;
The pillar'd arches were over their head,
And beneath their feet were the bones of
    the dead.

VIII.

Spreading herbs, and flowerets bright,
Glisten'd with the dew of night;
Nor herb, nor floweret, glisten'd there,
But was carved in the cloister-arches as fair.
    The monk gazed long on the lovely
        moon,
    Then into the night he looked forth;
And red and bright the streamers light
    Were dancing in the glowing north.
So had he seen, in fair Castille,
    The youth in glittering squadrons
        start;
Sudden the flying jennet wheel,
    And hurl the unexpected dart.
He knew, by the streamers that shot so
    bright,
That spirits were riding the northern light.

IX.

By a steel-clenched postern door,
    They enter'd now the chancel tall;
The darken'd roof rose high aloof
    On pillars lofty and light and small:
The key-stone, that lock'd each ribbed
    aisle,
Was a fleur-de-lys, or a quatre-feuille,
The corbells were carved grotesque and
    grim;
And the pillars, with cluster'd shafts so
    trim,
With base and with capital flourish'd
    around,
Seem'd bundles of lances which garlands
    had bound.

X.

Full many a scutcheon and banner riven,
Shook to the cold night-wind of heaven,

Around the screenèd altar's pale ;
And there the dying lamps did burn,
Before thy low and lonely urn,
O gallant Chief of Otterburne ! [15]
  And thine, dark Knight of Liddesdale ! [6]
O fading honours of the dead !
O high ambition, lowly laid !

XI.

The moon on the east oriel shone
Through slender shafts of shapely stone,
  By foliaged tracery combined ;
Thou wouldst have thought some fairy's hand
'Twixt poplars straight the ozier wand,
  In many a freakish knot, had twined ;
Then framed a spell, when the work was done,
And changed the willow-wreaths to stone.
The silver light, so pale and faint,
Shew'd many a prophet, and many a saint,
  Whose image on the glass was dyed ;
Full in the midst, his Cross of Red
Triumphant Michael brandishèd,
  And trampled the Apostate's pride.
The moon-beam kiss'd the holy pane,
And threw on the pavement a bloody
    stain.

XII.

They sate them down on a marble stone,
  (A Scottish monarch slept below ;)*
Thus spoke the Monk, in solemn tone :—
  " I was not always a man of woe ;
For Paynim countries I have trod,
And fought beneath the Cross of God :
Now, strange to my eyes thine arms appear,
  And their iron clang sounds strange to
    my ear.

XIII.

" In these far climes it was my lot
To meet the wondrous Michael Scott, [17]
  A wizard, of such dreaded fame,
That when, in Salamanca's cave,
Him listed his magic wand to wave,
  The bells would ring in Notre Dame !
Some of his skill he taught to me ;

And, Warrior, I could say to thee
The words that cleft Eildon hills in three, [18]
  And bridled the Tweed with a curb of
    stone :
But to speak them were a deadly sin ;
And for having but thought them my
    heart within,
  A treble penance must be done.

XIV.

" When Michael lay on his dying bed,
His conscience was awakened :
He bethought him of his sinful deed,
And he gave me a sign to come with speed ;
I was in Spain when the morning rose,
But I stood by his bed ere evening close.
The words may not again be said,
That he spoke to me, on death-bed laid ;
They would rend this Abbaye's massy
    nave,
And pile it in heaps above his grave.

XV.

" I swore to bury his Mighty Book,
That never mortal might therein look ;
And never to tell where it was hid,
Save at his Chief of Branksome's need :
And when that need was past and o'er,
Again the volume to restore.
I buried him on St. Michael's night,
When the bell toll'd one, and the moon
    was bright,
And I dug his chamber among the dead,
When the floor of the chancel was stained
    red,
That his patron's cross might over him
    wave,
And scare the fiends from the Wizard's
    grave.

XVI.

" It was a night of woe and dread,
When Michael in the tomb I laid !
Strange sounds along the chancel pass'd,
The banners waved without a blast ;"—
—Still spoke the Monk, when the bell
    toll'd one !—
I tell you, that a braver man
Than William of Deloraine, good at need,
Against a foe ne'er spurr'd a steed ;

---

* Alexander II.

Yet somewhat was he chill'd with dread,
And his hair did bristle upon his head.

XVII.

"Lo, Warrior! now, the Cross of Red
Points to the grave of the mighty dead;
Within it burns a wondrous light,
To chase the spirits that love the night:
That lamp shall burn unquenchably,
Until the eternal doom shall be."*—
Slow moved the Monk to the broad flag-
    stone,
Which the bloody Cross was traced upon:
He pointed to a secret nook;
An iron bar the Warrior took;
And the Monk made a sign with his
    wither'd hand,
The grave's huge portal to expand.

XVIII.

With beating heart to the task he went;
His sinewy frame o'er the grave-stone
    bent;
With bar of iron heaved amain,
Till the toil-drops fell from his brows,
    like rain.
It was by dint of passing strength,
That he moved the massy stone at length.
I would you had been there, to see
How the light broke forth so gloriously,
Stream'd upward to the chancel roof,
And through the galleries far aloof!
No earthly flame blazed e'er so bright:
It shone like heaven's own blessed light,
    And, issuing from the tomb,
Show'd the Monk's cowl, and visage pale,
Danced on the dark-brow'd Warrior's
    mail,
And kiss'd his waving plume.

XIX.

Before their eyes the Wizard lay,
As if he had not been dead a day.
His hoary beard in silver roll'd,
He seem'd some seventy winters old;

A palmer's amice wrapp'd him round,
With a wrought Spanish baldric bound,
    Like a pilgrim from beyond the sea;
His left hand held his Book of Might;
A silver cross was in his right;
    The lamp was placed beside his knee;
High and majestic was his look,
At which the fellest fiends had shook,
And all unruffled was his face:
They trusted his soul had gotten grace.

XX.

Often had William of Deloraine
Rode through the battle's bloody plain,
And trampled down the warriors slain,
    And neither known remorse nor awe;
Yet now remorse and awe he own'd;
His breath came thick, his head swam
    round,
    When this strange scene of death he saw,
Bewilder'd and unnerved he stood,
And the priest pray'd fervently and loud:
With eyes averted prayed he;
He might not endure the sight to see,
Of the man he had loved so brotherly.

XXI.

And when the priest his death-prayer had
    pray'd,
Thus unto Deloraine he said:—
"Now, speed thee what thou hast to do,
Or, Warrior, we may dearly rue;
For those, thou may'st not look upon,
Are gathering fast round the yawning
    stone!"—
Then Deloraine, in terror, took
From the cold hand the Mighty Book,
With iron clasp'd, and with iron bound:
He thought, as he took it, the dead man
    frown'd;
But the glare of the sepulchral light,
Perchance, had dazzled the warrior's sight.

XXII.

When the huge stone sunk o'er the tomb,
The night return'd in double gloom;
For the moon had gone down, and the
    stars were few;
And, as the Knight and Priest withdrew,

---

* It was a belief of the Middle Ages, that
eternal lamps were to be found burning in
ancient sepulchres.

With wavering steps and dizzy brain,
They hardly might the postern gain.
'Tis said, as through the aisles they
    pass'd,
They heard strange noises on the blast ;
And through the cloister-galleries small,
Which at mid-height thread the chancel
    wall,
Loud sobs, and laughter louder, ran,
And voices unlike the voice of man ;
As if the fiends kept holiday,
Because these spells were brought to day.
I cannot tell how the truth may be ;
I say the tale as 'twas said to me.

XXIII.

" Now, hie thee hence," the Father said,
" And when we are on death-bed laid,
O may our dear Ladye, and sweet St.
    John,
Forgive our souls for the deed we have
    done !"
    The Monk return'd him to his cell,
    And many a prayer and penance sped ;
    When the convent met at the noontide
      bell—
      The Monk of St. Mary's aisle was
      dead !
Before the cross was the body laid,
With hands clasp'd fast, as if still he pray'd.

XXIV

The Knight breathed free in the morning
    wind,
And strove his hardihood to find :
He was glad when he pass'd the tomb-
    stones grey,
Which girdle round the fair Abbaye ;
For the mystic Book, to his bosom prest,
Felt like a load upon his breast ;
And his joints, with nerves of iron twined,
Shook, like the aspen leaves in wind.
Full fain was he when the dawn of day
Began to brighten Cheviot grey ;
He joy'd to see the cheerful light,
And he said Ave Mary, as well as he
    might.

XXV.

The sun had brighten'd Cheviot grey,
    The sun had brighten'd the Carter's*
    side ;
And soon beneath the rising day
    Smiled Branksome Towers and Teviot's
    tide.
The wild birds told their warbling tale,
    And waken'd every flower that blows ;
And peeped forth the violet pale,
    And spread her breast the mountain rose.
And lovelier than the rose so red,
    Yet paler than the violet pale,
She early left her sleepless bed,
    The fairest maid of Teviotdale

XXVI.

Why does fair Margaret so early awake ?
    And don her kirtle so hastilie ;
And the silken knots, which in hurry she
    would make,
    Why tremble her slender fingers to tie ;
Why does she stop, and look often around,
    As she glides down the secret stair ;
And why does she pat the shaggy blood-
    hound,
    As he rouses him up from his lair ;
And, though she passes the postern alone,
Why is not the watchman's bugle blown ?

XXVII.

The ladye steps in doubt and dread,
Lest her watchful mother hear her tread ;
The lady caresses the rough blood-hound,
Lest his voice should waken the castle
    round,
The watchman's bugle is not blown,
For he was her foster-father's son ;
And she glides through the greenwood at
    dawn of light
To meet Baron Henry her own true knight.

XXVIII.

The Knight and ladye fair are met,
And under the hawthorn's boughs are set.

---

* A mountain on the Border of England,
above Jedburgh.

A fairer pair were never seen
To meet beneath the hawthorn green.
He was stately, and young, and tall;
Dreaded in battle, and loved in hall:
And she, when love, scarce told, scarce hid,
Lent to her cheek a livelier red;
When the half sigh her swelling breast
Against the silken ribbon prest;
When her blue eyes their secret told,
Though shaded by her locks of gold—
Where would you find the peerless fair,
With Margaret of Branksome might compare!

XXIX.

And now, fair dames, methinks I see
You listen to my minstrelsy;
Your waving locks ye backward throw,
And sidelong bend your necks of snow;
Ye ween to hear a melting tale,
Of two true lovers in a dale;
　And how the Knight, with tender fire,
　　To paint his faithful passion strove;
Swore he might at her feet expire,
　But never, never, cease to love;
And how she blush'd, and how she sigh'd.
And, half consenting, half denied,
And said that she would die a maid;—
Yet, might the bloody feud be stay'd,
Henry of Cranstoun, and only he,
Margaret of Branksome's choice should be.

XXX.

Alas! fair dames, your hopes are vain!
My harp has lost the enchanting strain;
　Its lightness would my age reprove:
My hairs are grey, my limbs are old,
My heart is dead, my veins are cold:
　I may not, must not, sing of love.

XXXI.

Beneath an oak, moss'd o'er by eld,
The Baron's Dwarf his courser held,[19]
　And held his crested helm and spear:
That Dwarf was scarce an earthly man,
If the tales were true of him ran
　Through all the Border far and near.
'Twas said, when the Baron a-hunting rode,
Through Reedsdale's glens, but rarely trod,

He heard a voice cry, "Lost! lost!
　　lost!"
And, like tennis-ball by racket toss'd,
　A leap, of thirty feet and three,
Made from the gorse this elfin shape,
Distorted like some dwarfish ape,
　And lighted at Lord Cranstoun's
　　knee.
Lord Cranstoun was some whit dismay'd;
'Tis said that five good miles he rade,
　To rid him of his company;
But where he rode one mile, the Dwarf
　ran four,
And the Dwarf was first at the castle door.

XXXII.

Use lessens marvel, it is said:
This elvish Dwarf with the Baron staid;
Little he ate, and less he spoke,
Nor mingled with the menial flock:
And oft apart his arms he toss'd,
And often mutter'd "Lost! lost! lost!"
　He was waspish, arch, and litherlie,*
　But well Lord Cranstoun served he:
And he of his service was full fain;
For once he had been ta'en or slain,
　An it had not been for his ministry.
All between Home and Hermitage,
Talk'd of Lord Cranstoun's Goblin-Page.

XXXIII.

For the Baron went on Pilgrimage,
And took with him this elvish Page,
　To Mary's Chapel of the Lowes·
For there beside our Ladye's lake,
An offering he had sworn to make,
　And he would pay his vows.
But the Ladye of Branksome gather'd a
　band
Of the best that would ride at her command:
　The trysting place was Newark Lee.
Wat of Harden came thither amain,
And thither came John of Thirlestane,
And thither came William of Deloraine;
　They were three hundred spears and
　　three.

---

* Idle.

Through Douglas-burn, up Yarrow
   stream,
Their horses prance, their lances gleam.
They came to St. Mary's lake ere day;
But the chapel was void, and the Baron
   away.
They burn'd the chapel for very rage,
And cursed Lord Cranstoun's Goblin-
   Page.

XXXIV.

And now, in Branksome's good green
   wood,
As under the aged oak he stood,
The Baron's courser pricks his ears,
As if a distant noise he hears.
The Dwarf waves his long lean arm on
   high,
And signs to the lovers to part and fly;
No time was then to vow or sigh.
Fair Margaret through the hazel grove,
Flew like the startled cushat-dove:
The Dwarf the stirrup held and rein;
Vaulted the Knight on his steed amain,
And, pondering deep that morning's
   scene,
Rode eastward through the hawthorns
   green.

     —————

WHILE thus he pour'd the lengthen'd tale
The Minstrel's voice began to fail:
Full slyly smiled the observant page,
And gave the wither'd hand of age
A goblet crown'd with mighty wine,
The blood of Velez' scorched vine.
He raised the silver cup on high,
And, while the big drop fill'd his eye,
Pray'd God to bless the Duchess long,
And all who cheer'd a son of song.
The attending maidens smiled to see
How long, how deep, how zealously,
The precious juice the Minstrel quaff'd;
And he, embolden'd by the draught,
Look'd gaily back to them, and laugh'd.
The cordial nectar of the bowl
Swell'd his old veins, and cheer'd his soul;
A lighter, livelier prelude ran,
Ere thus his tale again began.

CANTO THIRD.

I.

AND said I that my limbs were old,
And said I that my blood was cold,
And that my kindly fire was fled,
And my poor wither'd heart was dead,
   And that I might not sing of love?—
How could I to the dearest theme,
That ever warm'd a minstrel's dream,
  So foul, so false a recreant prove!
How could I name love's very name,
Nor wake my heart to notes of flame!

II.

In peace, Love tunes the shepherd's reed;
In war, he mounts the warrior's steed;
In halls, in gay attire is seen,
In hamlets, dances on the green.
Love rules the court, the camp, the grove,
And men below, and saints above;
For love is heaven, and heaven is love.

III.

So thought Lord Cranstoun, as I ween,
While, pondering deep the tender scene,
He rode through Branksome's hawthorn
   green.
   But the Page shouted wild and shrill,
    And scarce his helmet could he don,
   When downward from the shady hill
    A stately knight came pricking on.
That warrior's steed, so dapple-gray,
Was dark with sweat, and splashed with
   clay;
   His armour red with many a stain;
He seem'd in such a weary plight,
As if he had ridden the live-long night;
   For it was William of Deloraine.

IV.

But no whit weary did he seem,
When, dancing in the sunny beam,
He mark'd the crane on the baron's crest;*
For his ready spear was in his rest.

    —————

* The crest of the Cranstouns, in allusion
to their name, is a crane, dormant, holding a

Few were the words, and stern and high,
 That mark'd the foemen's feudal
  hate;
For question fierce, and proud reply,
 Gave signal soon of dire debate.
Their very coursers seemed to know
That each was other's mortal foe,
And snorted fire, when wheel'd around,
To give each knight his vantage-ground.

V.

In rapid round the Baron bent;
 He sigh'd a sigh, and pray'd a prayer;
The prayer was to his patron saint,
 The sigh was to his ladye fair.
Stout Deloraine nor sigh'd nor pray'd,
Nor saint, nor ladye, call'd to aid;
But he stoop'd his head, and couch'd his
  spear,
And spurred his steed to full career.
The meeting of these champions proud
Seem'd like the bursting thunder-cloud.

VI.

Stern was the dint the Borderer lent!
The stately Baron backwards bent;
Bent backwards to his horse's tail,
And his plumes went scattering on the gale.
The tough ash spear, so stout and true,
Into a thousand flinders flew.
But Cranstoun's lance, of more avail,
Pierced through, like silk, the Borderer's
  mail;
Through shield, and jack, and acton,
  past,
Deep in his bosom, broke at last.—
Still sate the warrior saddle-fast,
Till, stumbling in the mortal shock,
Down went the steed, the girthing broke,
Hurl'd on a heap lay man and horse.
The Baron onward pass'd his course;
Nor knew—so giddy roll'd his brain—
His foe lay stretch'd upon the plain.

VII.

But when he rein'd his courser round,
And saw his foeman on the ground
 Lie senseless as the bloody clay,
He bade his page to stanch the wound,
 And there beside the warrior stay,
And tend him in his doubtful state,
And lead him to Branksome castle-gate:
His noble mind was inly moved
For the kinsman of the maid he loved.
"This shalt thou do without delay:
No longer here myself may stay;
Unless the swifter I speed away,
Short shrift will be at my dying day."

VIII.

Away in speed Lord Cranstoun rode;
The Goblin Page behind abode;
His lord's command he ne'er withstood,
Though small his pleasure to do good.
As the corslet off he took,
The dwarf espied the Mighty Book!
Much he marvell'd a knight of pride,
Like a book-bosom'd priest should ride;*
He thought not to search or stanch the
  wound,
Until the secret he had found.

IX.

The iron band, the iron clasp,
Resisted long the elfin grasp:
For when the first he had undone,
It closed as he the next begun.
Those iron clasps, that iron band,
Would not yield to unchristen'd hand,
Till he smear'd the cover o'er
With the Borderer's curdled gore;
A moment then the volume spread,
And one short spell therein he read,
It had much of glamour† might,
Could make a ladye seem a knight;
The cobwebs on a dungeon wall
Seem tapestry in lordly hall;

---

stone in his foot, with an emphatic Border
motto, *Thou shalt want ere I want.* Arms
thus punning on the name, are said heral-
dically to be "canting."

* Priests were wont to carry their mass-
book, for burying and marrying, &c., in their
bosoms.
 † Magical delusion.

A nut-shell seem a gilded barge,
A sheeling* seem a palace large,
And youth seem age, and age seem youth—
All was delusion, nought was truth.²⁰

X.

He had not read another spell,
When on his cheek a buffet fell,
So fierce, it stretch'd him on the plain,
Beside the wounded Deloraine.
From the ground he rode dismay'd,
And shook his huge and matted head ;
One word he mutter'd, and no more,
"Man of age, thou smitest sore !"—
No more the Elfin Page durst try
Into the wondrous Book to pry ;
The clasps, though smear'd with Christian gore,
Shut faster than they were before.
He hid it underneath his cloak.—
Now, if you ask who gave the stroke,
I cannot tell, so mot I thrive ;
It was not given by man alive.

XI.

Unwillingly himself he address'd,
To do his master's high behest :
He lifted up the living corse,
And laid it on the weary horse ;
He led him into Branksome Hall,
Before the beards of the warders all ;
And each did after swear and say,
There only pass'd a wain of hay.
He took him to Lord David's tower,
Even to the Ladye's secret bower ;
And, but that stronger spells were spread,
And the door might not be opened,
He had laid him on her very bed.
Whate'er he did of gramarye,†
Was always done maliciously ;
He flung the warrior on the ground,
And the blood well'd freshly from the wound.

XII.

As he repass'd the outer court,
He spied the fair young child at sport ;

He thought to train him to the wood ;
For, at a word, be it understood,
He was always for ill, and never for good.
Seem'd to the boy, some comrade gay
Led him forth to the woods to play ;
On the drawbridge the warders stout
Saw a terrier and lurcher passing out.

XIII.

He led the boy o'er bank and fell,
    Until they came to a woodland brook ;²¹
The running stream dissolved the spell,
    And his own elvish shape he took.
Could he have had his pleasure vilde,
He had crippled the joints of the noble child ;
Or, with his fingers long and lean,
Had strangled him in fiendish spleen ;
But his awful mother he had in dread,
And also his power was limited ;
So he but scowl'd on the startled child,
And darted through the forest wild ;
The woodland brook he bounding cross'd,
And laugh'd, and shouted, "Lost ! lost ! lost !"—

XIV.

Full sore amazed at the wondrous change,
    And frighten'd as a child might be,
At the wild yell and visage strange,
    And the dark words of gramarye,
The child, amidst the forest bower,
Stood rooted like a lily flower ;
    And when, at length, with trembling pace,
        He sought to find where Branksome lay,
    He fear'd to see that grisly face
        Glare from some thicket on his way.
Thus, starting oft, he journey'd on,
And deeper in the wood is gone,—
For aye the more he sought his way,
The farther still he went astray,—
Until he heard the mountains round
Ring to the baying of a hound.

XV.

And hark ! and hark ! the deep-mouth'd bark
    Comes nigher still, and nigher :

---

* A shepherd's hut.   † Magic.

Bursts on the path a dark blood-hound,
His tawny muzzle track'd the ground,
  And his red eye shot fire.
Soon as the wilder'd child saw he
He flew at him right furiouslie.
I ween you would have seen with joy
The bearing of the gallant boy,
When, worthy of his noble sire,
His wet cheek glow'd 'twixt fear and ire!
He faced the blood-hound manfully,
And held his little bat on high;
So fierce he struck, the dog, afraid,
At cautious distance hoarsely bay'd,
  But still in act to spring;
When dash'd an archer through the glade,
And when he saw the hound was stay'd,
  He drew his tough bow-string;
But a rough voice cried, "Shoot not, hoy!
Ho! shoot not, Edward—'Tis a boy!"

XVI.

The speaker issued from the wood,
And check'd his fellow's surely mood,
  And quell'd the ban-dog's ire:
He was an English yeoman good,
  And born in Lancashire.
Well could he hit a fallow-deer
  Five hundred feet him fro;
With hand more true, and eye more clear,
  No archer bended bow.
His coal-black hair, shorn round and close,
  Set off his sun-burn'd face:
Old England's sign, St. George's cross,
  His barret-cap did grace;
His bugle-horn hung by his side,
  All in a wolf-skin baldric tied;
And his short falchion, sharp and clear,
Had pierced the throat of many a deer.

XVII.

His kirtle, made of forest green,
  Reach'd scantly to his knee;
And, at his belt, of arrows keen
  A furbish'd sheaf bore he;
His buckler, scarce in breadth a span,
  No larger fence had he;
He never counted him a man,
  Would strike below the knee;[22]

His slacken'd bow was in his hand,
And the leash, that was his blood-hound's
  band.

XVIII.

He would not do the fair child harm,
But held him with his powerful arm,
That he might neither fight nor flee;
For when the Red-Cross spied he,
The boy strove long and violently.
"Now, by St. George," the archer cries,
"Edward, methinks we have a prize!
This boy's fair face, and courage free,
Show he is come of high degree."—

XIX.

"Yes! I am come of high degree,
  For I am the heir of bold Buccleuch;
And, if thou dost not set me free,
  False Southron, thou shalt dearly rue!
For Walter of Harden shall come with
  speed,
And William of Deloraine, good at need,
And every Scott, from Esk to Tweed;
And, if thou dost not let me go,
Despite thy arrows, and thy bow,
I'll have thee hang'd to feed the crow!"—

XX.

"Gramercy,* for thy good-will, fair boy!
My mind was never set so high;
But if thou art chief of such a clan,
And art the son of such a man,
And ever comest to thy command,
  Our wardens had need to keep good
    order;
My bow of yew to a hazel wand,
  Thou'lt make them work upon the
    Border.
Meantime, be pleased to come with me,
For good Lord Dacre shalt thou see;
I think our work is well begun,
When we have taken thy father's son."

XXI.

Although the child was led away,
In Branksome still he seem'd to stay,

Grand merci, thanks.

For so the Dwarf his part did play ;
And, in the shape of that young boy,
He wrought the castle much annoy.
The comrades of the young Buccleuch
He pinch'd, and beat, and overthrew ;
Nay, some of them he wellnigh slew.
He tore Dame Maudlin's silken tire,
And, as Sym Hall stood by the fire,
He lighted the match of his bandelier,*
And wofully scorch'd the hackbuteer.†
It may be hardly thought or said,
The mischief that the urchin made,
Till many of the castle guess'd
That the young Baron was possess'd !

XXII.

Well I ween the charm he held
The noble Ladye had soon dispell'd ;
But she was deeply busied then
To tend the wounded Deloraine.
   Much she wonder'd to find him lie,
     On the stone threshold stretch'd
      along ;
   She thought some spirit of the sky
     Had done the bold moss-trooper
      wrong ;
Because, despite her precept dread,
Perchance he in the Book had read ;
But the broken lance in his bosom stood,
And it was earthly steel and wood.

XXIII.

She drew the splinter from the wound,
   And with a charm she stanch'd the
     blood ;
She bade the gash be cleansed and bound ;
   No longer by his couch she stood ;
But she has ta'en the broken lance,
   And wash'd it from the clotted gore,
   And salved the splinter o'er and o'er.‡
William of Deloraine, in trance,
   Whene'er she turn'd it round and round,
   Twisted as if she gall'd his wound.

---

* *Bandelier*, belt for carrying ammunition.
† *Hackbuteer*, musketeer.
  ‡ This was called the cure by sympathy.
Sir Kenelm Digby was wont occasionally to
practise it.

Then to her maidens she did say,
   That he should be whole man and sound,
     Within the course of a night and day.
Full long she toil'd ; for she did rue
Mishap to friend so stout and true.

XXIV.

So pass'd the day—the evening fell,
'Twas near the time of curfew bell ;
The air was mild, the wind was calm,
The stream was smooth, the dew was balm;
E'en the rude watchman, on the tower,
Enjoy'd and bless'd the lovely hour.
Far more fair Margaret loved and bless'd
The hour of silence and of rest.
On the high turret sitting lone,
She waked at times the lute's soft tone ;
Touch'd a wild note, and all between
Thought of the bower of hawthorns green.
Her golden hair stream'd free from band,
Her fair cheek rested on her hand,
Her blue eyes sought the west afar,
For lovers love the western star.

XXV.

Is yon the star, o'er Penchryst Pen,
That rises slowly to her ken,
And, spreading broad its wavering light,
Shakes its loose tresses on the night ?
Is yon red glare the western star ?—
O, 'tis the beacon-blaze of war !
Scarce could she draw her tighten'd breath,
For well she knew the fire of death !

XXVI.

The Warder view'd it blazing strong,
And blew his war-note loud and long,
Till, at the high and haughty sound,
Rock, wood, and river rung around.
The blast alarm'd the festal hall,
And startled forth the warriors all ;
Far downward, in the castle-yard,
Full many a torch and cresset glared ;
And helms and plumes, confusedly toss'd,
Were in the blaze half-seen, half-lost ;
And spears in wild disorder shook,
Like reeds beside a frozen brook.

XXVII.

The Seneschal, whose silver hair
Was redden'd by the torches' glare,
Stood in the midst, with gesture proud,
And issued forth his mandates loud:—
"On Penchryst glows a bale* of fire,
And three are kindling on Pricsthaugh-
    swire;
      Ride out, ride out,
      The foe to scout!
Mount, mount for Branksome,† every
    man!
Thou, Todrig, warn the Johnstone clan,
    That ever are true and stout—
Ye need not send to Liddesdale;
For when they see the blazing bale,
Elliots and Armstrongs never fail.—
Ride, Alton, ride, for death and life!
And warn the Warder of the strife,
Young Gilbert, let our beacon blaze,
Our kin, and clan, and friends to raise."

XXVIII

Fair Margaret from the turret head,
Heard, far below, the coursers' tread,
    While loud the harness rung,
As to their seats, with clamour dread,
    The ready horsemen sprung:
And trampling hoofs, and iron coats,
And leaders' voices, mingled notes,
    And out! and out!
    In hasty route,
The horsemen gallop'd forth;
Dispersing to the south to scout,
    And east, and west, and north,
To view their coming enemies,
And warn their vassals and allies.

XXIX.

The ready page, with hurried hand,
Awaked the need-fire's‡ slumbering brand,
    And ruddy blush'd the heaven:
For a sheet of flame, from the turret high,
Waved like a blood-flag on the sky,
    All flaring and uneven;

And soon a score of fires, I ween,
From height, and hill, and cliff, were seen;
Each with warlike tidings fraught;
Each from each the signal caught;
Each after each they glanced to sight,
As stars arise upon the night.
They gleamed on many a dusky tarn,§
Haunted by the lonely earn; ||
On many a cairn's grey pyramid,
Where urns of mighty chiefs lie hid;²³
Till high Dunedin the blazes saw,
From Soltra and Dumpender Law;
And Lothian heard the Regent's order,
That all should bowne¶ them for the
    Border.

XXX.

The livelong night in Branksome rang
    The ceaseless sound of steel;
The castle-bell, with backward clang,
    Sent forth the larum peal;
Was frequent heard the heavy jar,
Where massy stone and iron bar
Were piled on echoing keep and tower,
To whelm the foe with deadly shower;
Was frequent heard the changing guard,
And watchword from the sleepless ward;
While, wearied by the endless din,
Blood-hound and ban-dog yell'd within.

XXXI.

The noble Dame, amid the broil,
Shared the grey Seneschal's high toil,
And spoke of danger with a smile;
    Cheer'd the young knights, and council
    sage
Held with the chiefs of riper age.
No tidings of the foe were brought,
Nor of his numbers knew they aught,
Nor what in time of truce he sought.
    Some said, that there were thousands ten;
And others ween'd that it was nought
    But Leven Clans, or Tynedale men,
Who came to gather in black-mail;**

---

* A Border beacon.
† *Mount for Branksome* was the gathering word of the Scotts.
‡ *Need-fire,* beacon.

§ *Tarn,* a mountain lake.
|| *Earn,* a Scottish eagle.
¶ *Bowne,* make ready.
** Protection money exacted by freebooters.

And Liddesdale, with small avail,
  Might drive them lightly back agen.
So pass'd the anxious night away,
And welcome was the peep of day.

———

CEASED the high sound—the listening
  throng
Applaud the Master of the Song;
And marvel much, in helpless age,
So hard should be his pilgrimage.
Had he no friend—no daughter dear,
His wandering toil to share and cheer;
No son to be his father's stay,
And guide him on the rugged way?
" Ay, once he had—but he was dead !"—
Upon the harp he stoop'd his head,
And busied himself the strings withal,
To hide the tear that fain would fall.
In solemn measure, soft and slow,
Arose a father's notes of woe.

———

CANTO FOURTH.

I.

SWEET Teviot ! on thy silver tide
  The glaring bale-fires blaze no more;
No longer steel-clad warriors ride
  Along thy wild and willow'd shore;
Where'er thou wind'st, by dale or hill,
All, all is peaceful, all is still,
  As if thy waves, since Time was born,
Since first they roll'd upon the Tweed,
Had only heard the shepherd's reed,
  Nor started at the bugle-horn.

II.

Unlike the tide of human time,
  Which, though it change in ceaseless flow,
Retains each grief, retains each crime
  Its earliest course was doom'd to know;
And, darker as it downward bears,
Is stain'd with past and present tears,
  Low as that tide has ebb'd with me,
It still reflects to Memory's eye

The hour my brave, my only boy,
  Fell by the side of great Dundee.*
Why, when the volleying musket play'd
Against the bloody Highland blade,
Why was not I beside him laid !—
Enough—he died the death of fame !
Enough—he died with conquering Græme.

III.

Now over Border, dale, and fell,
  Full wide and far was terror spread;
For pathless march, and mountain cell,
  The peasant left his lowly shed.[24]
The frighten'd flocks and herds were pent
Beneath the peel's rude battlement;
And maids and matrons dropp'd the tear,
While ready warriors seized the spear.
From Branksome's towers, the watch-
  man's eye
Dun wreaths of distant smoke can spy,
Which, curling in the rising sun,
Show'd southern ravage was begun.

IV.

Now loud the heedful gate-ward cried—
  " Prepare ye all for blows and blood !
Watt Tinlinn,[25] from the Liddel-side,
  Comes wading through the flood.
Full oft the Tynedale snatchers knock
At his lone gate, and prove the lock;
It was but last St. Barnabright†
They sieged him a whole summer night,
But fled at morning; well they knew,
In vain he never twang'd the yew.
Right sharp has been the evening shower,
That drove him from his Liddel tower;
And by my faith," the gate-ward said,
" I think 'twill prove a Warden-Raid."‡

V.

While thus he spoke, the bold yeoman
Enter'd the echoing barbican.

———

* Claverhouse, Viscount of Dundee, slain in
the battle of Killicrankie.
† St. Barnabas's day, June 11. It is still
called Barnaby Bright in Hants, from its being
generally a bright sunshiny day.
‡ An inroad commanded by the Warden in
person.

He led a small and shaggy nag,
That through a bog, from hag to hag,*
Could bound like any Billhope stag.
It bore his wife and children twain ;
A half-clothed serf† was all their train ;
His wife, stout, ruddy, and dark-brow'd,
Of silver brooch and bracelet proud,
Laugh'd to her friends among the crowd.
He was of stature passing tall,
But sparely form'd, and lean withal ;
A batter'd morion on his brow ;
A leather jack, as fence enow,
On his broad shoulders loosely hung ;
A border axe behind was slung ;
  His spear, six Scottish ells in length,
    Seem'd newly dyed with gore ;
  His shafts and bow, of wondrous
    strength,
    His hardy partner bore.

VI.

Thus to the Ladye did Tinlinn show
The tidings of the English foe :—
" Belted Will Howard²⁶ is marching here,
And hot Lord Dacre²⁷ with many a spear,
And all the German hackbut-men,²⁸
Who have long lain at Askerten :
They cross'd the Liddel at curfew hour,
And burn'd my little lonely tower :
The fiend receive their souls therefor !
It had not been burnt this year and more.
Barn-yard and dwelling, blazing bright,
Served to guide me on my flight ;
But I was chased the livelong night.
Black John of Akeshaw, and Fergus
    Græme,
Fast upon my traces came,
Until I turn'd at Priesthaugh Scrogg,
And shot their horses in the bog,
Slew Fergus with my lance outright—
I had him long at high despite :
He drove my cows last Fastern's night.‡

VII.

Now weary scouts from Liddesdale,
Fast hurrying in, confirm'd the tale ;

---

* The broken ground in a bog.
  † Bondsman.
  ‡ Shrove Tuesday, the eve of the great
Spring fast.

As far as they could judge by ken,
  Three hours would bring to Teviot's
    strand
Three thousand armed Englishmen—
  Meanwhile, full many a warlike band,
From Teviot, Aill, and Ettrick shade,
Came in, their Chief's defence to aid.
There was saddling and mounting in
    haste,
  There was pricking o'er moor and lea ;
He that was last at the trysting place
  Was but lightly held of his gaye ladye.

VIII.

From fair St. Mary's silver wave,
  From dreary Gamescleugh's dusky
    height,
His ready lances Thirlestane brave
  Array'd beneath a banner bright.
The treasured fleur-de-luce he claims,
To wreathe his shield, since royal James,
Encamp'd by Fala's mossy wave,
The proud distinction grateful gave,
  For faith 'mid feudal jars ;
What time, save Thirlestane alone,
Of Scotland's stubborn barons none
  Would march to southern wars ;
And hence, in fair remembrance worn,
Yon sheaf of spears his crest has borne ;
Hence his high motto shines reveal'd—
" Ready, aye ready," for the field.²⁹

IX.

An aged Knight, to danger steel'd,
  With many a moss-trooper, came on :
And azure in a golden field,
  The stars and crescent graced his shield,
    Without the bend of Murdieston.
Wide lay his lands round Oakwood tower,
And wide round haunted Castle-Ower ;
High over Borthwick's mountain flood,
His wood-embosom'd mansion stood,
In the dark glen, so deep below,
The herds of plunder'd England low ;
His bold retainers' daily food,
And bought with danger, blows, and
    blood.
Marauding chief ! his sole delight
The moonlight raid, the morning fight ;

Not even the Flower of Yarrow's charms,
In youth, might tame his rage for arms;
And still, in age, he spurn'd at rest,
And still his brows the helmet press'd,
Albeit the blanched locks below
Were white as Dinlay's spotless snow;
     Five stately warriors drew the sword
       Before their father's band;
     A braver knight than Harden's lord
       Ne'er belted on a brand.*

X.

Scotts of Eskdale, a stalwart band,
  Came trooping down the Todshawhill;
By the sword they won their land,
  And by the sword they hold it still.
Harken, Ladye, to the tale,
How thy sires won fair Eskdale.—
Earl Morton was lord of that valley fair,
The Beattisons were his vassals there.
The Earl was gentle, and mild of mood,
The vassals were warlike, and fierce, and
    rude;
High of heart, and haughty of word,
Little they reck'd of a tame liege lord.
The Earl into fair Eskdale came,
Homage and seignory to claim:
Of Gilbert the Galliard a heriot† he sought,
Saying, "Give thy best steed, as a vassal
    ought."
—"Dear to me is my bonny white steed,
Oft has he help'd me at pinch of need;
Lord and Earl though thou be, I trow,
I can rein Bucksfoot better than thou."
Word on word gave fuel to fire,
Till so highly blazed the Beattisons' ire,
But that the Earl the flight had ta'en,
The vassals there their lord had slain.
Sore he plied both whip and spur,
As he urged his steed through Eskdale
    muir;
And it fell down a weary weight,
Just on the threshold of Branksome gate.

* This knight was the ancestor of Sir
Walter Scott.

† The feudal superior, in certain cases, was
entitled to the best horse of the vassal, in
name of Heriot, or Herezeld.

XI.

The Earl was a wrathful man to see,
Full fain avenged would he be,
In haste to Branksome's Lord he spoke,
Saying—"Take these traitors to thy yoke;
For a cast of hawks, and a purse of gold,
All Eskdale I'll sell thee, to have and hold:
Beshrew thy heart, of the Beattisons' clan
If thou leavest on Eske a landed man;
But spare Woodkerrick's lands alone,
For he lent me his horse to escape upon."
A glad man then was Branksome bold,
Down he flung him the purse of gold;
To Eskdale soon he spurr'd amain,
And with him five hundred riders has
    ta'en.
He left his merrymen in the mist of the
    hill,
And bade them hold them close and still;
And alone he wended to the plain,
To meet with the Galliard and all his train.
To Gilbert the Galliard thus he said:—
"Know thou me for thy liege-lord and
    head,
Deal not with me as with Morton tame,
For Scotts play best at the roughest game.
Give me in peace my heriot due,
Thy bonny white steed, or thou shalt rue,
If my horn I three times wind,
Eskdale shall long have the sound in mind."

XII.

Loudly the Beattison laugh'd in scorn;
"Little care we for thy winded horn.
Ne'er shall it be the Galliard's lot,
To yield his steed to a haughty Scott.
Wend thou to Branksome back on foot,
With rusty spur and miry boot."—
He blew his bugle so loud and hoarse,
That the dun deer started at fair Craik-
    cross:
He blew again so loud and clear,
Through the grey mountain-mist there
    did lances appear:
And the third blast rang with such a din,
That the echoes answer'd from Pentoun-
    linn,
And all his riders came lightly in.

Then had you seen a gallant shock,
When saddles were emptied, and lances
    broke !
For each scornful word the Galliard had
    said,
A Beattison on the field was laid.
His own good sword the Chieftain drew,
And he bore the Galliard through and
    through :
Where the Beattison's blood mix'd with
    the rill,
The Galliard's-Haugh men call it still.
The Scotts have scatter'd the Beattison
    clan,
In Eskdale they left but one landed man.
The valley of Eske, from the mouth to
    the source,
Was lost and won for that bonny white
    horse.

XIII.

Whitslade the Hawk, and Headshaw
    came,
And warriors more than I may name ;
From Yarrow-cleugh to Hindhaugh-
    swair,
From Woodhouselie to Chester-glen.
Troop'd man and horse, and bow and
    spear ;
    Their gathering word was Bellenden.[30]
And better hearts o'er Border sod
To siege or rescue never rode.
    The Ladye mark'd the aids come in,
    And high her heart of pride arose :
She bade her youthful son attend,
That he might know his father's friend,
    And learn to face his foes.
" The boy is ripe to look on war ;
    I saw him draw a cross-bow stiff,
And his true arrow struck afar
    The raven's nest upon the cliff ;
The red cross, on a southern breast,
Is broader than the raven's nest :
Thou, Whitslade, shalt teach him his
    weapon to wield,
And o'er him hold his father's shield."

XIV.

Well may you think, the wily page
Cared not to face the Ladye sage.

He counterfeited childish fear,
And shriek'd, and shed full many a tear,
    And moan'd and plain'd in manner wild.
    The attendants to the Ladye told,
    Some fairy, sure, had changed the child,
    That wont to be so free and bold.
Then wrathful was the noble dame ;
She blush'd blood-red for very shame :—
" Hence ! ere the clan his faintness view ;
Hence with the weakling to Buccleuch !—
Wat Tinlinn, thou shalt be his guide
To Rangleburn's lonely side.—
Sure some fell fiend has cursed our line,
That coward should e'er be son of mine !"—

XV.

A heavy task Watt Tinlinn had,
To guide the counterfeited lad.
Soon as the palfrey felt the weight
Of that ill-omen'd elfish freight,
He bolted, sprung, and rear'd amain,
Nor heeded bit, nor curb, nor rein.
    It cost Watt Tinlinn mickle toil
    To drive him but a Scottish mile ;
    But as a shallow brook they cross'd,
The elf, amid the running stream,
His figure changed, like form in dream,
    And fled, and shouted, " Lost ! lost !
        lost !"
Full fast the urchin ran and laugh'd,
But faster still a cloth-yard shaft
Whistled from startled Tinlinn's yew,
And pierced his shoulder through and
    through.
Although the imp might not be slain,
And though the wound soon heal'd again,
Yet, as he ran, he yell'd for pain ;
And Watt of Tinlinn, much aghast,
Rode back to Branksome fiery fast.

XVI.

Soon on the hill's steep verge he stood,
That looks o'er Branksome's towers and
    wood ;
And martial murmurs, from below,
Proclaim'd the approaching southern foe.
Through the dark wood, in mingled tone,
Were Border pipes and bugles blown ;
The coursers' neighing he could ken,
A measured tread of marching men ;

While broke at times the solemn hum,
The Almayn's sullen kettle-drum;
  And banners tall, of crimson sheen,
    Above the copse appear;
  And, glistening through the hawthorns
    green,
  Shine helm, and shield, and spear.

XVII.

Light forayers, first, to view the ground,
Spurr'd their fleet coursers loosely round;
  Behind, in close array, and fast,
    The Kendal archers, all in green,
  Obedient to the bugle blast,
    Advancing from the wood were seen.
To back and guard the archer band,
Lord Dacre's bill-men were at hand:
A hardy race, on Irthing bred,
With kirtles white, and crosses red,
Array'd beneath the banner tall,
That stream'd o'er Acre's conquer'd wall;
And minstrels, as they march'd in order,
Play'd " Noble Lord Dacre, he dwells on
  the Border."

XVIII.

Behind the English bill and bow,
The mercenaries, firm and slow,
  Moved on to fight, in dark array,
By Conrad led of Wolfenstein,
Who brought the band from distant Rhine,
  And sold their blood for foreign pay.
The camp their home, their law the sword,
They knew no country, own'd no lord:
They were not arm'd like England's sons,
But bore the levin-darting guns,
Buff coats, all frounced and 'broider'd o'er,
And morsin-horns* and scarfs they wore;
Each better knee was bared, to aid
The warriors in the escalade;
All, as they march'd, in rugged tongue,
Songs of Teutonic feuds they sung.

XIX.

But louder still the clamour grew,
And louder still the minstrels blew,
When, from beneath the greenwood tree,
Rode forth Lord Howard's chivalry;

* Powder flasks.

His men-at-arms, with glaive and spear,
Brought up the battle's glittering rear,
There many a youthful knight, full keen
To gain his spurs, in arms was seen;
With favour in his crest, or glove,
Memorial of his ladye-love.
So rode they forth in fair array,
Till full their lengthen'd lines display;
Then call'd a halt, and made a stand,
And cried, " St. George, for merry
  England !"

XX.

Now every English eye, intent
On Branksome's armed towers was bent;
So near they were, that they might know
The straining harsh of each cross-bow;
On battlement and bartizan
Gleam'd axe, and spear, and partisan;
Falcon and culver,† on each tower,
Stood prompt their deadly hail to shower;
And flashing armour frequent broke
From eddying whirls of sable smoke,
Where upon tower and turret head,
The seething pitch and molten lead
Reek'd, like a witch's caldron red.
While yet they gaze, the bridges fall,
The wicket opes, and from the wall
Rides forth the hoary Seneschal.

XXI.

Armed he rode, all save the head,
His white beard o'er his breast-plate
  spread;
Unbroke by age, erect his seat,
He ruled his eager courser's gait;
Forced him, with chasten'd fire, to prance,
And, high curvetting, slow advance:
In sign of truce, his better hand
Display'd a peeled willow wand;
His squire, attending in the rear,
Bore high a gauntlet on a spear.‡

† Ancient pieces of artillery.
‡ A glove upon a lance was the emblem of
faith among the ancient Borderers, who were
wont, when any one broke his word, to ex-
pose this emblem, and proclaim him a faithless villain at the first Border meeting. This
ceremony was much dreaded.—*See* LESLEY.

When they espied him riding out,
Lord Howard and Lord Dacre stout
Sped to the front of their array,
To hear what this old knight should say.

XXII.

" Ye English warden lords, of you
Demands the Ladye of Buccleuch,
Why, 'gainst the truce of Border tide,
In hostile gu se ye dare to ride,
With Kendal bow, and Gilsland brand,
And all yon mercenary band,
Upon the bounds of fair Scotland?
My Ladye redes you swith* return;
And, if but one poor straw you burn,
Or do our towers so much molest,
As scare one swallow from her nest,
St. Mary! but we'll light a brand
Shall warm your hearths in Cumber-
    land."—

XXIII.

A wrathful man was Dacre's lord,
But calmer Howard took the word:
" May't please thy Dame, Sir Seneschal,
To seek the castle's outward wall,
Our pursuivant-at-arms shall show
Both where we came, and when we go."—
The message sped, the noble Dame
To the wall's outward circle came;
Each chief around lean'd on his spear,
To see the pursuivant appear.
All in Lord Howard's livery dress'd,
The lion argent deck'd his breast;
He led a boy of blooming hue—
O sight to meet a mother's view!
It was the heir of great Buccleuch.
Obeisance meet the herald made,
And thus his master's will he said:—

XXIV.

" It irks, high Dame, my noble Lords,
'Gainst ladye fair to draw their swords;
But yet they may not tamely see,
All through the Western Wardenry,
Your law-contemn ng kinsmen ride,
And burn and spoil the Border-side;

And ill beseems your rank and birth
To make your towers a flemens-firth.†
We claim from thee William of Deloraine,
That he may suffer march-treason[31] pain.
It was but last St. Cuthbert's even
He prick'd to Stapleton on Leven,
Harried‡ the lands of Richard Musgrave,
And slew his brother by dint of glaive.
Then, since a lone and widow'd Dame
These restless riders may not tame,
Either receive within thy towers
Two hundred of my master's powers,
Or straight they sound their warrison,§
And storm and spoil thy garrison:
And this fair boy, to London led,
Shall good King Edward's page be bred."

XXV.

He ceased—and loud the boy did cry,
And stretch'd his little arms on high;
Implored for aid each well-known face,
And strove to seek the Dame's embrace.
A moment changed that Ladye's cheer,
Gush'd to her eye the unbidden tear;
She gazed upon the leaders round,
And dark and sad each warrior frown'd;
Then, deep within her sobbing breast
She lock'd the struggling sigh to rest;
Unalter'd and collected stood,
And thus replied, in dauntless mood:—

XXVI.

" Say to your Lords of high emprize,
Who war on women and on boys,
That either William of Deloraine
Will cleanse him, by oath, of march-
    treason stain.
Or else he will the combat take
'Gainst Musgrave, for his honour's sake,
No knight in Cumberland so good,
But William may count with him kin
    and blood.
Knighthood he took of Douglas' sword,[32]
When English blood swell'd Ancram's
    ford;[33]

---

* *Swith*, instantly.

† An asylum for outlaws.
Plundered.   § Note of assault.

And but Lord Dacre's steed was wight,
And bare him ably in the flight,
Himself had seen him dubb'd a knight.
For the young heir of Branksome's line,
God be his aid, and God be mine;
Through me no friend shall meet his doom;
Here, while I live, no foe finds room.
  Then, if thy Lords their purpose urge,
  Take our defiance loud and high;
  Our slogan is their lyke-wake* dirge,
    Our moat, the grave where they
      shall lie."

XXVII.

Proud she look'd round, applause to
  claim—
Then lighten'd Thirlestane's eye of flame;
  His bugle Wat of Harden blew;
Pensils and pennons wide were flung,
To heaven the Border slogan rung,
  "St. Mary for the young Buccleuch!"
The English war-cry answer'd wide,
  And forward bent each southern spear;
Each Kendal archer made a stride,
  And drew the bowstring to his ear;
Each minstrel's war-note loud was
  blown:—
But, ere a gray-goose shaft had flown,
  A horseman gallop'd from the rear.

XXVIII.

"Ah! noble Lords!" he breathless said,
"What treason has your march betray'd?
What make you here, from aid so far,
Before you walls, around you war?
Your foemen triumph in the thought,
That in the toils the lion's caught.
Already on dark Ruberslaw
The Douglas holds his weapon-schaw;†
The lances, waving in his train,
Clothe the dun heath like autumn grain;
And on the Liddel's northern strand,
To bar retreat to Cumberland,
Lord Maxwell ranks his merry-men good,
Beneath the eagle and the rood;

---

* Watching a corpse all night.
† *Weapon-schaw*—military gathering of a chief's followers, or the army of a county.

And Jedwood, Eske, and Teviotdale,
  Have to proud Angus come,
And all the Merse and Lauderdale
  Have risen with haughty Home.
An exile from Northumberland,
  In Liddesdale I've wander'd long;
But still my heart was with merry
  England,
    And cannot brook my country's
      wrong;
And hard I've spurr'd all night to show
The mustering of the coming foe."

XXIX.

"And let them come!" fierce Dacre cried;
"For soon yon crest, my father's pride,
That swept the shores of Judah's sea,
And waved in gales of Galilee,
From Branksome's highest towers dis-
  play'd,
Shall mock the rescue's lingering aid!—
Level each harquebuss on row;
Draw, merry archers, draw the bow;
Up, bill-men, to the walls, and cry,
Dacre for England, win or die!"—

XXX.

"Yet hear," quoth Howard, "calmly
  hear,
Nor deem my words the words of fear:
For who, in field or foray slack,
Saw the blanche lion e'er fall back?³¹
But thus to risk our Border flower
In strife against a kingdom's power,
Ten thousand Scots 'gainst thousands
  three,
Certes, were desperate policy.
Nay, take the terms the Ladye made,
Ere conscious of the advancing aid:
Let Musgrave meet fierce Deloraine
In single fight, and, if he gain,
He gains for us; but if he's cross'd,
'Tis but a single warrior lost:
The rest, retreating as they came,
Avoid defeat, and death, and shame."

XXXI.

Ill could the haughty Dacre brook
His brother Warden's sage rebuke;

And yet his forward step he staid,
And slow and sullenly obey'd.
But ne'er again the Border side
Did these two lords in friendship ride;
And this slight discontent, men say,
Cost blood upon another day.

XXXII.

The pursuivant-at-arms again
    Before the castle took his stand;
His trumpet call'd, with parleying strain,
    The leaders of the Scottish band;
And he defied, in Musgrave's right,
Stout Deloraine to single fight;
A gauntlet at their feet he laid,
And thus the terms of fight he said :—
" If in the lists good Musgrave's sword
    Vanquish the Knight of Deloraine,
Your youthful chieftain, Branksome's
        Lord,
    Shall hostage for his clan remain :
If Deloraine foil good Musgrave,
The boy his liberty shall have,
    Howe'er it falls, the English band,
Unharming Scots, by Scots unharm'd,
In peaceful march, like men unarm'd,
    Shall straight retreat to Cumberland."

XXXIII.

Unconscious of the near relief,
The proffer pleased each Scottish chief,
    Though much the Ladye sage gainsay'd;
For though their hearts were brave and
        true,
From Jedwood's recent sack they knew,
    How tardy was the Regent's aid:
And you may guess the noble Dame
    Durst not the secret prescience own,
Sprung from the art she might not name,
    By which the coming help was known.
Closed was the compact, and agreed
That lists should be enclosed with speed,
    Beneath the castle, on a lawn :
They fix'd the morrow for the strife,
On foot, with Scottish axe and knife,
    At the fourth hour from peep of dawn;
When Deloraine, from sickness freed,
Or else a champion in his stead,
Should for himself and chieftain stand,
Against stout Musgrave, hand to hand.

XXXIV.

I know right well, that, in their lay,
Full many minstrels sing and say,
    Such combat should be made on horse,
On foaming steed, in full career,
With brand to aid, when as the spear
    Should shiver in the course :
But he, the jovial Harper, taught
Me, yet a youth, how it was fought,
    In guise which now I say;
He knew each ordinance and clause
Of Black Lord Archibald's battle-laws,
    In the old Douglas' day.
He brook'd not, he, that scoffing tongue
Should tax his minstrelsy with wrong,
    Or call his song untrue :
For this, when they the goblet plied,
And such rude taunt had chafed his pride,
    The Bard of Reull he slew.
On Teviot's side, in fight they stood,
And tuneful hands were stain'd with
        blood ;
Where still the thorn's white branches
        wave,
Memorial o'er his rival's grave.

XXXV.

Why should I tell the rigid doom,
That dragg'd my master to his tomb;
    How Ousenam's maidens tore their hair,
Wept till their eyes were dead and dim,
And wrung their hands for love of him,
    Who died at Jedwood Air?
He died !—his scholars, one by one,
To the cold silent grave are gone;
And I, alas ! survive alone,
To muse o'er rivalries of yore,
And grieve that I shall hear no more
The strains, with envy heard before;
For, with my minstrel brethren fled,
My jealousy of song is dead.

————

He paused: the listening dames again
Applaud the hoary Minstrel's strain.
With many a word of kindly cheer,—
In pity half, and half sincere,—
Marvell'd the Duchess how so well
His legendary song could tell—

Of ancient deeds, so long forgot ;
Of feuds, whose memory was not ;
Of forests, now laid waste and bare ;
Of towers, which harbour now the hare;
Of manners, long since changed and gone;
Of chiefs, who under their grey stone
So long had slept, that fickle Fame
Had blotted from her rolls their name,
And twined round some new minion's head
The fading wreath for which they bled ;
In sooth, 'twas strange, this old man's verse
Could call them from their marble hearse.

The Harper smiled, well-pleased; for
  ne'er
Was flattery lost on poet's ear :
A simple race ! they waste their toil
For the vain tribute of a smile ;
E'en when in age their flame expires,
Her dulcet breath can fan its fires :
Their drooping fancy wakes at praise,
And strives to trim the short-lived blaze.

Smiled then, well-pleased, the Aged Man,
And thus his tale continued ran.

———◆———

CANTO FIFTH.

I.

CALL it not vain :—they do not err,
  Who say, that when the Poet dies,
Mute Nature mourns her worshipper,
  And celebrates his obsequies :
Who say, tall cliff, and cavern lone,
For the departed Bard make moan ;
That mountains weep in crystal rill ;
That flowers in tears of balm distil ;
Through his loved groves that breezes sigh,
And oaks, in deeper groan, reply ;
And rivers teach their rushing wave
To murmur dirges round his grave.

II.

Not that, in sooth, o'er mortal urn
Those things inanimate can mourn ;
But that the stream, the wood, the gale,
Is vocal with the plaintive wail
Of those, who, else forgotten long,
Lived in the poet's faithful song,

And, with the poet's parting breath,
Whose memory feels a second death.
The Maid's pale shade, who wails her lot,
That love, true love, should be forgot,
From rose and hawthorn shakes the tear
Upon the gentle Minstrel's bier :
The phantom Knight, his glory fled,
Mourns o'er the field he heap'd with dead ;
Mounts the wild blast that sweeps amain,
And shrieks along the battle-plain.
The Chief, whose antique crownlet long
Still sparkled in the feudal song,
Now, from the mountain's misty throne,
Sees, in the thanedom once his own,
His ashes undistinguish'd lie,
His place, his power, his memory die :
His groans the lonely caverns fill,
His tears of rage impel the rill :
All mourn the Minstrel's harp unstrung,
Their name unknown, their praise unsung.

III.

Scarcely the hot assault was staid,
The terms of truce were scarcely made,
When they could spy from Branksome's
  towers,
The advancing march of martial powers.
Thick clouds of dust afar appear'd,
And trampling steeds were faintly heard;
Bright spears, above the columns dun,
Glanced momentary to the sun ;
And feudal banners fair display'd
The bands that moved to Branksome's aid.

IV.

Vails not to tell each hardy clan,
  From the fair Middle Marches came ;
The Bloody Heart blazed in the van,
  Announcing Douglas, dreaded name![3]
Vails not to tell what steeds did spurn,
Where the Seven Spears of Wedderburne*
  Their men in battle-order set ;
And Swinton laid the lance in rest,
That tamed of yore the sparkling crest
  Of Clarence's Plantagenet.[35]

---

* Sir David Home of Wedderburn, who
was slain in the fatal battle of Flodden, left
seven sons, who were called the Seven Spears
of Wedderburne.

Nor list I say what hundreds more,
From the rich Merse and Lammermore,
And Tweed's fair borders, to the war,
Beneath the crest of Old Dunbar,
  And Hepburn's mingled banners come,
Down the steep mountain glittering far,
  And shouting still, " A Home ! a
    Home !"[37]

V.

Now squire and knight, from Branksome
    sent,
On many a courteous message went ;
To every chief and lord they paid
Meet thanks for prompt and powerful aid ;
And told them,—how a truce was made,
  And how a day of fight was ta'en
    'Twixt Musgrave and stout Deloraine ;
    And how the Ladye pray'd them dear,
  That all would stay the fight to see,
  And deign, in love and courtesy,
    To taste of Branksome cheer.
Nor, while they bade to feast each Scot,
Were England's noble Lords forgot.
Himself, the hoary Seneschal
Rode forth, in seemly terms to call
Those gallant foes to Branksome Hall.
Accepted Howard, than whom knight
Was never dubb'd, more bold in fight ;
Nor, when from war and armour free,
More famed for stately courtesy :
But angry Dacre rather chose
In his pavilion to repose.

VI.

Now, noble Dame, perchance you ask,
  How these two hostile armies met ?
Deeming it were no easy task
  To keep the truce which here was set ;
Where martial spirits, all on fire,
Breathed only blood and mortal ire.—
By mutual inroads, mutual blows,
By habit, and by nation, foes,
  They met on Teviot's strand ;
They met and sate them mingled down,
Without a threat, without a frown,
  As brothers meet in foreign land :
The hands, the spear that lately grasp'd,
Still in the mailed gauntlet clasp'd,
  Were interchanged in greeting dear ;

Visors were raised, and faces shown,
And many a friend, to friend made known,
  Partook of social cheer.
Some drove the jolly bowl about ;
  With dice and craughts some chased
    the day ;
And some, with many a merry shout,
In riot, revelry, and rout,
  Pursued the foot-ball play.

VII.

Yet, be it known, had bugles blown,
  Or sign of war be seen,
Those bands, so fair together ranged,
Those hands, so frankly interchanged,
  Had dyed with gore the green :
The merry shout by Teviot-side
Had sunk in war-cries wild and wide,
  And in the groan of death :
And whingers* now in friendship bare,
The social meal to part and share,
  Had found a bloody sheath.
'Twixt truce and war, such sudden
    change
Was not infrequent, nor held strange,
  In the old Border-day :[38]
But yet on Branksome's towers and town,
In peaceful merriment, sunk down
  The sun's declining ray.

VIII.

The blithesome signs of wassel gay
Decay'd not with the dying day ;
Soon through the latticed windows tall
Of lofty Branksome's lordly hall,
Divided square by shafts of stone,
Huge flakes of ruddy lustre shone ;
Nor less the gilded rafters rang
With merry harp and beakers' clang :
  And frequent, on the darkening plain,
    Loud hollo, whoop, or whistle ran,
   As bands, their stragglers to regain,
    Give the shrill watchword of their
      clan ;[39]
And revellers, o'er their bowls, proclaim
Douglas or Dacre's conquering name.

---

* Large knives.

IX.

Less frequent heard, and fainter still,
　At length the various clamours died:
And you might hear, from Branksome hill,
　No sound but Teviot's rushing tide;
Save when the changing sentinel
The challenge of his watch could tell;
And save, where, through the dark profound,
The clanging axe and hammer's sound
　Rung from the nether lawn;
For many a busy hand toil'd there,
Strong pales to shape, and beams to square,
The lists' dread barriers to prepare
　Against the morrow's dawn.

X.

Margaret from hall did soon retreat,
　Despite the Dame's reproving eye;
Nor mark'd she, as she left her seat,
　Full many a stifled sigh;
For many a noble warrior strove
To win the Flower of Teviot's love,
　And many a bold ally.—
With throbbing head and anxious heart,
All in her lonely bower apart,
　In broken sleep she lay;
By times, from silken couch she rose;
While yet the banner'd hosts repose,
　She view'd the dawning day;
Of all the hundreds sunk to rest,
First woke the loveliest and the best.

XI.

She gazed upon the inner court,
　Which in the tower's tall shadow lay;
Where coursers' clang, and stamp, and snort,
　Had rung the livelong yesterday;
Now still as death; till stalking slow,—
　The jingling spurs announced his tread,
A stately warrior pass'd below;
　But when he raised his plumed head—
　Blessed Mary! can it be?—
Secure, as if in Ousenam bowers,
He walks through Branksome's hostile towers,
　With fearless step and free.
She dared not sign, she dared not speak—

Oh! if one page's slumbers break,
　His blood the price must pay!
Not all the pearls Queen Mary wears,
Not Margaret's yet more precious tears,
　Shall buy his life a day.

XII.

Yet was his hazard small; for well
You may bethink you of the spell
　Of that sly urchin page;
This to his lord he did impart,
And made him seem, by glamour art,
　A knight from Hermitage.
Unchallenged thus, the warder's post,
The court, unchallenged, thus he cross'd,
　For all the vassalage:
But O! what magic's quaint disguise
Could blind fair Margaret's azure eyes!
　She started from her seat;
While with surprise and fear she strove,
And both could scarcely master love—
　Lord Henry's at her feet.

XIII.

Oft have I mused, what purpose bad
That foul malicious urchin had
　To bring this meeting round,
For happy love's a heavenly sight,
And by a vile malignant sprite
　In such no joy is found;
And oft I've deem'd, perchance he thought
Their erring passion might have wrought
　Sorrow, and sin, and shame;
And death to Cranstoun's gallant Knight,
And to the gentle ladye bright,
　Disgrace, and loss of fame.
But earthly spirit could not tell
The heart of them that loved so well.
True love's the gift which God has given
To man alone beneath the heaven:
　It is not fantasy's hot fire,
　　Whose wishes, soon as granted, fly;
　It liveth not in fierce desire,
　　With dead desire it doth not die;
It is the secret sympathy,
The silver link, the silken tie,
Which heart to heart, and mind to mind,
In body and in soul can bind.—
Now leave we Margaret and her Knight,
To tell you of the approaching fight.

XIV.

Their warning blasts the bugles blew,
  The pipe's shrill port* aroused each clan;
In haste, the deadly strife to view,
  The trooping warriors eager ran:
Thick round the lists their lances stood,
Like blasted pines in Ettrick wood;
To Branksome many a look they threw,
The combatants' approach to view,
And bandied many a word of boast,
About the knight each favour'd most.

XV.

Meantime full anxious was the Dame;
For now arose disputed claim,
Of who should fight for Deloraine,
'Twixt Harden and 'twixt Thirlestaine:
  They 'gan to reckon kin and rent,
And frowning brow on brow was bent;
  But yet not long the strife—for, lo!
Himself, the Knight of Deloraine,
Strong, as it seem'd, and free from pain,
  In armour sheath'd from top to toe,
Appear'd, and craved the combat due.
The Dame her charm successful knew,
And the fierce chiefs their claims withdrew.

XVI.

When for the lists they sought the plain,
The stately Ladye's silken rein
  Did noble Howard hold;
Unarmed by her side he walk'd,
And much, in courteous phrase, they talk'd
  Of feats of arms of old.
Costly his garb—his Flemish ruff
Fell o'er his doublet, shaped of buff,
  With satin slash'd and lined;
Tawny his boot, and gold his spur,
His cloak was all of Poland fur,
  His hose with silver twined;
His Bilboa blade, by Marchmen felt,
Hung in a broad and studded belt;
Hence, in rude phrase, the Borderers still
Call'd noble Howard, Belted Will.

XVII.

Behind Lord Howard and the Dame,
Fair Margaret on her palfrey came,

---

* A martial piece of music, adapted to the bagpipes.

Whose foot-cloth swept the ground:
White was her whimple, and her veil,
And her loose locks a chaplet pale
  Of whitest roses bound;
The lordly Angus, by her side,
In courtesy to cheer her tried;
Without his aid, her hand in vain
Had strove to guide her broider'd rein.
He deem'd she shudder'd at the sight
Of warriors met for mortal fight;
But cause of terror, all unguess'd,
Was fluttering in her gentle breast,
When, in their chairs of crimson placed,
The Dame and she the barriers graced.

XVIII.

Prize of the field, the young Buccleuch,
An English knight led forth to view;
Scarce rued the boy his present plight,
So much he longed to see the fight.
Within the lists, in knightly pride,
High Home and haughty Dacre ride;
Their leading staffs of steel they wield,
As marshals of the mortal field;
While to each knight their care assign'd
Like vantage of the sun and wind.
The heralds hoarse did loud proclaim,
In King and Queen, and Warden's name,
  That none, while lasts the strife,
Should dare, by look, or sign, or word,
Aid to a champion to afford,
  On peril of his life;
And not a breath the silence broke,
Till thus the alternate Herald spoke:

XIX.

ENGLISH HERALD.

" Here standeth Richard of Musgrave,
  Good knight and true, and freely born,
Amends from Deloraine to crave,
  For foul despiteous scathe and scorn.
He sayeth, that William of Deloraine
  Is traitor false by Border laws;
This with his sword he will maintain,
  So help him God, and his good cause!"

XX.

SCOTTISH HERALD.

" Here standeth William of Deloraine,
Good knight and true, of noble strain,

Who sayeth, that foul treason's stain,
  Since he bore arms, ne'er soil'd his coat;
    And that, so help him God above!
    He will on Musgrave's body prove,
  He lies most foully in his throat."

LORD DACRE.

" Forward, brave champions, to the
    fight!
Sound trumpets!"——

LORD HOME.

——" God defend the right!"—
Then, Teviot! how thine echoes rang,
When bugle-sound and trumpet clang
  Let loose the martial foes,
And in mid list with shield poised high,
And measured step and wary eye,
  The combatants did close.

XXI.

Ill would it suit your gentle ear,
  Ye lovely listeners to hear
How to the axe the helms did sound,
And blood pour'd down from many a
    wound;
For desperate was the strife and long,
And either warrior fierce and strong.
But, were each dame a listening knight,
I well could tell how warriors fight!
For I have seen war's lightning flashing,
Seen the claymore with bayonet clashing,
Seen through red blood the war-horse
    dashing,
And scorn'd, amid the reeling strife,
To yield a step for death or life.—

XXII.

'Tis done, 'tis done! that fatal blow
  Has stretch'd him on the bloody plain!
. He strives to rise—Brave Musgrave, no!
  Thence never shalt thou rise again!
He chokes in blood—some friendly hand
Undo the visor's barred band,
Unfix the gorget's iron clasp,
And give him room for life to gasp!—
O, bootless aid!—haste holy Friar,
Haste, ere the sinner shall expire!
Of all his guilt let him be shriven,
And smooth his path from earth to heaven!

XXIII.

In haste the holy Friar sped;—
His naked foot was dyed with red,
  As through the lists he ran;
Unmindful of the shouts on high,
That hail'd the conqueror's victory,
  He raised the dying man;
Loose waved his silver beard and hair,
As o'er him he kneel'd down in prayer:
And still the crucifix on high
He holds before his darkening eye;
And still he bends an anxious ear,
His faltering penitence to hear;
  Still props him from the bloody sod,
Still, even when soul and body part,
Pours ghostly comfort on his heart,
  And bids him trust in God!
Unheard he prays;—the death-pang's o'er!
Richard of Musgrave breathes no more.

XXIV.

As if exhausted in the fight,
Or musing o'er the piteous sight,
  The silent victor stands;
His beaver did he not unclasp,
Mark'd not the shouts, felt not the grasp
  Of gratulating hands.
When lo! strange cries of wild surprise,
Mingled with seeming terror, rise
  Among the Scottish bands;
And all, amid the throng'd array,
In panic haste gave open way
To a half-naked ghastly man,
Who downward from the castle ran:
He cross'd the barriers at a bound,
And wild and haggard look'd around,
  As dizzy, and in pain;
And all, upon the armed ground,
  Knew William of Deloraine!
Each ladye sprung from seat with speed,
Vaulted each marshal from his steed;
  " And who art thou," they cried,
" Who hast this battle fought and won?"—
His plumed helm was soon undone—
  " Cranstoun of Teviot-side!
For this fair prize I've fought and won,"—
And to the Ladye led her son.

XXV.

Full oft the rescued boy she kiss'd,
And often press'd him to her breast;
For, under all her dauntless show,
Her heart had throbb'd at every blow;
Yet not Lord Cranstoun deign'd she greet,
Though low he kneeled at her feet.
Me lists not tell what words were made,
What Douglas, Home, and Howard,
    said—
—For Howard was a generous foe—
And how the clan united pray'd
    The Ladye would the feud forego,
And deign to bless the nuptial hour
Of Cranstoun's Lord and Teviot's Flower.

XXV

She look'd to river, look'd to hill,
    Thought on the Spirit's prophecy,
Then broke her silence stern and still,—
    " Not you, but Fate, has vanquish'd me.
Their influence kindly stars may shower
On Teviot's tide and Branksome's tower,
    For pride is quell'd, and love is free."—
She took fair Margaret by the hand,
Who, breathless, trembling, scarce might
    stand
    That hand to Cranstoun's lord gave
    she:—
" As I am true to thee and thine,
Do thou be true to me and mine!
    This clasp of love our bond shall be;
For this is your betrothing day,
And all these noble lords shall stay,
    To grace it with their company."

XXVII.

All as they left the listed plain,
Much of the story she did gain;
How Cranstoun fought with Deloraine,
And of his page, and of the Book
Which from the wounded knight he took;
And how he sought her castle high,
That morn, by help of gramarye;
How, in Sir William's armour dight,
Stolen by his page, while slept the knight,
He took on him the single fight.
But half his tale he left unsaid,
And linger'd till he join'd the maid.—

Cared not the Ladye to betray
Her mystic arts in view of day;
But well she thought, ere midnight came,
Of that strange page the pride to tame,
From his foul hands the Book to save,
And send it back to Michael's grave.—
Needs not to tell each tender word
'Twixt Margaret and 'twixt Cranstoun's
    iord;
Nor how she told of former woes,
And how her bosom fell and rose,
While he and Musgrave bandied blows.—
Needs not these lover's' joys to tell:
One day, fair maids, you'll know them well.

XXVIII.

William of Deloraine, some chance
Had waken'd from his death-like trance;
    And taught that, in the listed plain,
Another, in his arms and shield,
Against fierce Musgrave axe did wield,
    Under the name of Deloraine.
Hence, to the field, unarm'd, he ran,
And hence his presence scared the clan,
Who held him for some fleeting wraith.[*]
And not a man of blood and breath.
    Not much this new ally he loved,
    Yet, when he saw what hap had proved,
        He greeted him right heartilie:
He would not waken old debate,
For he was void of rancorous hate,
    Though rude and scant of courtesy;
In raids he spilt but seldom blood,
Unless when men-at-arms withstood,
Or, as was meet for deadly feud,
He ne'er bore grudge for stalwart blow,
Ta'en in fair fight from gallant foe;
    And so 'twas seen of him, e'en now,
        When on dead Musgrave he look'd
        down;
    Grief darken'd on his rugged brow,
        Though half disguised with a frown;
And thus, while sorrow bent his head,
His foeman's epitaph he made.

XXIX.

" Now, Richard Musgrave, liest thou here!
    I ween my deadly enemy;

---

[*] The spectral apparition of a living person.

For, if I slew thy brother dear,
  Thou slew'st a sister's son to me;
And when I lay in dungeon dark,
  Of Naworth Castle, long months three,
Till ransom'd for a thousand mark,
  Dark Musgrave, it was long of thee.
And, Musgrave, could our fight be tried,
  And thou wert now alive as I,
No mortal man should us divide,
  Till one, or both of us, did die:
Yet rest thee God! for well I know
I ne'er shall find a nobler foe.
In all the northern counties here,
Whose word is Snaffle, spur, and spear,
Thou wert the best to follow gear!
'Twas pleasure, as we look'd behind,
To see how thou the chase could'st wind,
Cheer the dark blood-hound on his way,
And with the bugle rouse the fray!
I'd give the lands of Deloraine,
Dark Musgrave were alive again."

XXX.

So mourn'd he, till Lord Dacre's band
Were bowning back to Cumberland.
They raised brave Musgrave from the field,
And laid him on his bloody shield;
On levell'd lances, four and four,
By turns the noble burden bore.
Before, at times, upon the gale,
Was heard the Minstrel's plaintive wail;
Behind, four priests, in sable stole,
Sung requiem for the warrior's soul:
Around, the horsemen slowly rode;
With trailing pikes the spearmen trode;
And thus the gallant knight they bore,
Through Liddesdale to Leven's shore,
Thence to Holme Coltrame's lofty nave,
And laid him in his father's grave.

THE harp's wild notes, though hush'd the song,
The mimic march of death prolong;
Now seems it far, and now a-near,
Now meets, and now eludes the ear;
Now seems some mountain side to sweep,
Now faintly dies in valley deep;
Seems now as if the Minstrel's wail,
Now the sad requiem, loads the gale;

Last, o'er the warrior's closing grave,
Rung the full choir in choral stave.

After due pause, they bade him tell,
Why he, who touch'd the harp so well,
Should thus, with ill-rewarded toil,
Wander a poor and thankless soil,
When the more generous Southern Land
Would well requite his skilful hand.

The Aged Harper, howsoe'er
His only friend, his harp, was dear,
Liked not to hear it ranked so high
Above his flowing poesy:
Less liked he still, that scornful jeer
Misprised the land he loved so dear;
High was the sound, as thus again
The Bard resumed his minstrel strain.

CANTO SIXTH.

I.

BREATHES there the man, with soul so dead,
Who never to himself hath said,
  This is my own, my native land!
Whose heart hath ne'er within him burn'd,
As home his footsteps he hath turn'd,
  From wandering on a foreign strand!
If such there breathe, go, mark him well;
For him no Minstrel raptures swell;
High though his titles, proud his name,
Boundless his wealth as wish can claim;
Despite those titles, power, and pelf,
The wretch, concentred all in self,
Living, shall forfeit fair renown,
And, doubly dying, shall go down
To the vile dust, from whence he sprung,
Unwept, unhonour'd, and unsung.

II.

O Caledonia! stern and wild,
Meet nurse for a poetic child!
Land of brown heath and shaggy wood,
Land of the mountain and the flood,
Land of my sires! what mortal hand
Can e'er untie the filial band,
That knits me to thy rugged strand!

Still, as I view each well-known scene,
Think what is now, and what hath been,
Seems as, to me, of all bereft,
Sole friends thy woods and streams were
    left;
And thus I love them better still,
Even in extremity of ill.
By Yarrow's streams still let me stray,
Though none should guide my feeble way;
Still feel the breeze down Ettrick break,
Although it chill my wither'd cheek;
Still lay my head by Teviot Stone,
Though there, forgotten and alone,
The Bard may draw his parting groan.

III.

Not scorn'd like me! to Branksome Hall
The Minstrels came, at festive call;
Trooping they came, from near and far,
The jovial priests of mirth and war;
Alike for feast and fight prepared,
Battle and banquet both they shared.
Of late, before each martial clan,
They blew their death-note in the van,
But now, for every merry mate,
Rose the portcullis' iron grate;
They sound the pipe, they strike the string,
They dance, they revel, and they sing,
Till the rude turrets shake and ring.

IV.

Me lists not at this tide declare
    The splendour of the spousal rite,
How muster'd in the chapel fair
    Both maid and matron, squire and
        knight;
Me lists not tell of owches rare,
Of mantles green, and braided hair,
And kirtles furr'd with miniver;
What plumage waved the altar round,
How spurs and ringing chainlets sound;
And hard it were for bard to speak
The changeful hue of Margaret's cheek;
That lovely hue which comes and flies,
As awe and shame alternate rise!

V.

Some bards have sung, the Ladye high
Chapel or altar came not nigh;

Nor durst the rights of spousal grace,
So much she fear'd each holy place.
False slanders these:—I trust right well
She wrought not by forbidden spell;[40]
For mighty words and signs have power
O'er sprites in planetary hour:
Yet scarce I praise their venturous part,
Who tamper with such dangerous art.
    But this for faithful truth I say,
    The Ladye by the altar stood,
    Of sable velvet her array,
    And on her head a crimson hood,
With pearls embroider'd and entwined,
Guarded with gold, with ermine lined;
A merlin sat upon her wrist[41]
Held by a leash of silken twist

VI.

The spousal rites were ended soon:
'Twas now the merry hour of noon,
And in the lofty arched hall
Was spread the gorgeous festival.
Steward and squire, with heedful haste,
Marshall'd the rank of every guest;
Pages, with ready blade, were there,
The mighty meal to carve and share:
O'er canon, heron-shew, and crane,
And princely peacock's gilded train,[42]
And o'er the boar-head, garnish'd brave,
And cygnet from St. Mary's wave;*
O'er ptarmigan and venison,
The priest had spoke his benison.
Then rose the riot and the din,
Above, beneath, without, within!
For, from the lofty balcony,
Rung trumpet, shalm, and psaltery:
Their clanging bowls old warriors quaff'd,
Loudly they spoke, and loudly laugh'd;
Whisper'd young knights, in tone more
        mild;
To ladies fair, and ladies smiled.
The hooded hawks, high perch'd on beam,
The clamour join'd with whistling scream,
And flapp'd their wings, and shook their
        bells,
In concert with the stag-hound's yells.

---

* Flights of wild swans are often seen on
St. Mary's Lake, which is at the head of the
Yarrow,

Round go the flasks of ruddy wine,
From Bourdeaux, Orleans, or the Rhine;
Their tasks the busy sewers ply
And all is mirth and revelry.

VII.

The Goblin Page, omitting still
No opportunity of ill,
Strove now, while blood ran hot and high,
To rouse debate and jealousy;
Till Conrad, Lord of Wolfenstein,
By nature fierce, and warm with wine,
And now in humour highly cross'd,
About some steeds his band had lost,
High words to words succeeding still,
Smote, with his gauntlet, stout Hunthill;[43]
A hot and hardy Rutherford,
Whom men called Dickon Draw-the-
   sword.

He took it on the page's saye,
Hunthill had driven these steeds away.
Then Howard, Home, and Douglas rose,
The kindling discord to compose:
Stern Rutherford right little said,
But bit his glove,[44] and shook his head.—
A fortnight thence, in Inglewood,
Stout Conrade, cold, and drench'd in
   blood,
His bosom gored with many a wound,
Was by a woodman's lyme-dog found;
Unknown the manner of his death,
Gone was his brand, both sword and
   sheath;
But ever from that time, 'twas said,
That Dickon wore a Cologne blade.

VIII.

The dwarf, who fear'd his master's eye
Might his foul treachery espie,
Now sought the castle buttery,
Where many a yeoman, bold and free,
Revell'd as merrily and well
As those that sat in lordly selle.
Watt Tinlinn, there, did frankly raise
The pledge to Arthur Fire-the-Braes;*

* The person bearing this redoubtable *nom
de guerre* was an Elliott, and resided at
Thorleshope, in Liddesdale. He occurs in
the list of Border riders, in 1597.

And he, as by his breeding bound,
To Howard's merry-men sent it round.
To quit them, on the English side,
Red Roland Forster loudly cried,
" A deep carouse to yon fair bride !"—
At every pledge, from vat and pail,
Foam'd forth in floods the nut-brown ale;
While shout the riders every one;
Such day of mirth ne'er cheer'd their
   clan,
Since old Buccleuch the name did gain,
When in the cleuch the buck was ta'en.

IX.

The wily page, with vengeful thought,
   Remember'd him of Tinlinn's yew,
And swore, it should be dearly bought
   That ever he the arrow drew.
First, he the yeoman did molest,
With bitter gibe and taunting jest;
Told, how he fled at Solway strife,
And how Hob Armstrong cheer'd his
   wife;
Then, shunning still his powerful arm,
At unawares he wrought him harm;
From trencher stole his choicest cheer,
Dash'd from his lips his can of beer;
Then, to his knee sly creeping on,
With bodkin pierced him to the bone:
The venom'd wound, and festering joint,
Long after rued that bodkin's point.
The startled yeoman swore and spurn'd,
And board and flagons overturn'd.
Riot and clamour wild began;
Back to the hall the Urchin ran;
Took in a darkling nook his post,
And grinn'd, and mutter'd, " Lost! lost!
   lost !"

X.

By this, the Dame, lest farther fray
Should mar the concord of the day,
Had bid the Minstrels tune their lay.
And first stept forth old Albert Græme,
The Minstrel of that ancient name:[45]
Was none who struck the harp so well,
Within the Land Debateable
Well friended, too, his hardy kin,
Whoever lost, were sure to win;

They sought the beeves that made their broth,
In Scotland and in England both.
In homely guise, as nature bade,
His simple song the Borderer said.

XI.

ALBERT GRÆME.

It was an English ladye bright,
  (The sun shines fair on Carlisle wall,*)
And she would marry a Scottish knight,
  For Love will still be lord of all.

Blithely they saw the rising sun,
  When he shone fair on Carlisle wall;
But they were sad ere day was done,
  Though Love was still the lord of all.

Her sire gave brooch and jewel fine,
  Where the sun shines fair on Carlisle wall;
Her brother gave but a flask of wine,
  For ire that Love was lord of all.

For she had lands, both meadow and lea,
  Where the sun shines fair on Carlisle wall,
And he swore her death, ere he would see
  A Scottish knight the lord of all!

XII.

That wine she had not tasted well,
  (The sun shines fair on Carlisle wall,)
When dead, in her true love's arms, she fell,
  For Love was still the lord of all!

He pierced her brother to the heart,
  Where the sun shines fair on Carlisle wall:—
So perish all would true love part,
  That Love may still be lord of all!

And then he took the cross divine,
  (Where the sun shines fair on Carlisle wall,)
And died for her sake in Palestine,
  So Love was still the lord of all.

---

* This burden is from an old Scottish song.

Now all ye lovers, that faithful prove,
  (The sun shines fair on Carlisle wall,)
Pray for their souls who died for love,
  For Love shall still be lord of all!

XIII.

As ended Albert's simple lay,
  Arose a bard of loftier port;
For sonnet, rhyme, and roundelay,
  Renown'd in haughty Henry's court:
There rung thy harp, unrivall'd long,
Fitztraver of the silver song!
  The gentle Surrey loved his lyre—
    Who has not heard of Surrey's fame?[16]
  His was the hero's soul of fire,
    And his the bard's immortal name,
And his was love, exalted high
By all the glow of chivalry.

XIV.

They sought, together, climes afar,
  And oft, within some olive grove,
When even came with twinkling star,
  They sung of Surrey's absent love.
His step the Italian peasant stay'd,
  And deem'd, that spirits from on high,
Round where some hermit saint was laid,
  Were breathing heavenly melody;
So sweet did harp and voice combine,
To praise the name of Geraldine.

XV.

Fitztraver! O what tongue may say
  The pangs thy faithful bosom knew,
When Surrey, of the deathless lay,
  Ungrateful Tudor's sentence slew?
Regardless of the tyrant's frown,
His harp call'd wrath and vengeance down.
He left, for Naworth's iron towers,
Windsor's green glades, and courtly bowers,
And faithful to his patron's name,
With Howard still Fitztraver came;
Lord William's foremost favourite he,
And chief of all his minstrelsy.

XVI.

FITZTRAVER.

'Twas all-souls' eve, and Surrey's heart
beat high;
He heard the midnight bell with anxious
start,
Which told the mystic hour, approaching
nigh,
When wise Cornelius promised, by his
art,
To show to him the ladye of his heart,
Albeit betwixt them roar'd the ocean
grim;
Yet so the sage had hight to play his part,
That he should see her form in life and
limb,
And mark, if still she loved, and still she
thought of him.

XVII.

Dark was the vaulted room of gramarye,
To which the wizard led the gallant
Knight,
Save that before a mirror, huge and high,
A hallow'd taper shed a glimmering light
On mystic implements of magic might;
On cross, and character, and talisman,
And almagest, and altar, nothing bright:
For fitful was the lustre, pale and wan,
As watchlight by the bed of some depart-
ing man.

XVIII.

But soon, within that mirror huge and
high,
Was seen a self-emitted light to gleam;
And forms upon its breast the Earl 'gan
spy,
Cloudy and indistinct, as feverish dream;
Till, slow arranging, and defined, they
seem
To form a lordly and a lofty room,
Part lighted by a lamp with silver beam,
Placed by a couch of Agra's silken
loom,
And part by moonshine pale, and part was
hid in gloom.

XIX.

Fair all the pageant—but how passing
fair
The slender form, which lay on couch
of Ind!
O'er her white bosom stray'd her hazel
hair,
Pale her dear cheek, as if for love she
pined;
All in her night-robe loose she lay reclined,
And, pensive, read from tablet ebur-
nine,
Some strain that seem'd her inmost soul
to find;—
That favour'd strain was Surrey's
raptured line,
That fair and lovely form, the Lady Geraldine!

XX.

Slow roll'd the clouds upon the lovely
form,
And swept the goodly vision all
away—
So royal envy roll'd the murky storm
O'er my beloved Master's glorious
day.
Thou jealous, ruthless tyrant! Heaven
repay
On thee, and on thy children's latest
line,
The wild caprice of thy despotic sway,
The gory bridal bed, the plunder'd
shrine,
The murder'd Surrey's blood, the tears
of Geraldine!

XXI.

Both Scots, and Southern chiefs prolong
Applauses of Fitztraver's song;
These hated Henry's name as death,
And those still held the ancient faith.—
Then, from his seat, with lofty air,
Rose Harold, bard of brave St. Clair;
St. Clair, who, feasting high at Home,
Had with that lord to battle come.
Harold was born where restless seas
Howl round the storm-swept Orcades;

Where erst St. Clairs held princely sway
O'er isle and islet, strait and bay;—
Still nods their palace to its fall,
Thy pride and sorrow, fair Kirkwall!—
Thence oft he mark'd fierce Pentland
      rave,
As if grim Odin rode her wave;
And watch'd, the whilst, with visage pale,
And throbbing heart, the struggling sail;
For all of wonderful and wild
Had rapture for the lonely child.

XXII.

And much of wild and wonderful
In these rude isles might fancy cull;
For thither came, in times afar,
Stern Lochlin's sons of roving war,
The Norsemen, train'd to spoil and blood,
Skill'd to prepare the raven's food;
Kings of the main their leaders brave,
Their barks the dragons of the wave.
And there, in many a stormy vale,
The Scald had told his wondrous tale;
And many a Runic column high
Had witness'd grim idolatry.
And thus had Harold, in his youth,
Learn'd many a Saga's rhyme uncouth,—
Of that Sea-Snake* tremendous curl'd,
Whose monstrous circle girds the world;
Of those dread Maids† whose hideous yell
Maddens the battle's bloody swell;
Of Chiefs, who, guided through the gloom,
By the pale death-lights of the tomb,
Ransack'd the graves of warriors old,
Their falchions wrench'd from corpses'
      hold,
Waked the deaf tomb with war's alarms,
And bade the dead arise to arms!
With war and wonder all on flame,
To Roslin's bowers young Harold came,
Where, by sweet glen and greenwood tree,
He learn'd a milder minstrelsy;
Yet something of the Northern spell
Mix'd with the softer numbers well.

---

* For the Sea-Snake, see the "Edda," or
Mallet's "Northern Antiquities," p. 445.
    † The Valkyrior or Scandinavian Fates, or
Fatal Sisters.

XXIII.

HAROLD.

O listen, listen, ladies gay!
    No haughty feat of arms I tell;
Soft is the note, and sad the lay,
    That mourns the lovely Rosabelle;

—"Moor, moor the barge, ye gallant crew!
    And, gentle ladye, deign to stay,
Rest thee in Castle Ravensheuch,
    Nor tempt the stormy firth to-day.

"The blackening wave is edged with white:
    To inch‡ and rock the sea-mews fly;
The fishers have heard the Water-Sprite,
    Whose screams forbode that wreck is
      nigh

"Last night the gifted Seer did view
    A wet shroud swathed round ladye gay;
Then stay thee, Fair, in Ravensheuch:
    "Why cross the gloomy firth to-day?"—

"'Tis not because Lord Lindesay's heir
    To-night at Roslin leads the ball,
But that my ladye-mother there
    Sits lonely in her castle-hall.

"'Tis not because the ring they ride,
    And Lindesay at the ring rides well,
But that my sire the wine will chide,
    If 'tis not fill'd by Rosabelle."—

O'er Roslin all that dreary night
    A wondrous blaze was seen to gleam;
'Twas broader than the watch-fire's light,
    And redder than the bright moon-beam.

It glared on Roslin's castled rock,
    It ruddied all the copse-wood glen,
'Twas seen from Dryden's groves of oak,
    And seen from cavern'd Hawthornden.

Seem'd all on fire that chapel proud,
    Where Roslin's chiefs uncoffin'd lie,
Each Baron, for a sable shroud,
    Sheathed in his iron panoply.

---

‡ *Inch.* an island.

Seem'd all on fire, within, around,
  Deep sacristy and altar's pale,
Shone every pillar foliage-bound,
  And glimmer'd all the dead men's mail.

Blazed battlement and pinnet high,
  Blazed every rose-carved buttress fair—
So still they blaze, when fate is nigh
  The lordly line of high St. Clair.

There are twenty of Roslin's barons bold
  Lie buried within that proud chapelle;
Each one the holy vault doth hold—
  But the sea holds lovely Rosabelle!

And each St. Clair was buried there,
  With candle, with book, and with knell;
But the sea-caves rung, and the wild winds
      sung,
  The dirge of lovely Rosabelle.

XXIV.

So sweet was Harold's piteous lay,
  Scarce mark'd the guests the darken'd
      hall,
Though, long before the sinking day,
  A wondrous shade involv'd them all;
It was not eddying mist or fog,
Drain'd by the sun from fen or bog;
  Of no eclipse had sages told;
And yet, as it came on apace,
Each one could scarce his neighbour's face,
  Could scarce his own stretch'd hand
      behold.
A secret horror check'd the feast;
And chill'd the soul of every guest;
Even the high Dame stood half aghast,
The elfish page fell to the ground,
And, shuddering, mutter'd, "Found!
  found! found!"

XXV.

Then sudden, through the darken'd air,
  A flash of lightning came;
So broad, so bright, so red the glare,
  The castle seem'd on flame.
Glanced every rafter of the hall,
Glanced every shield upon the wall;

Each trophied beam, each sculptured stone,
Were instant seen, and instant gone;
Full through the guests' bedazzled band
Resistless flash'd the levin-brand,
And fill'd the hall with smouldering smoke,
As on the elfish page it broke.
  It broke, with thunder long and loud,
  Dismay'd the brave, appall'd the
      proud,—
    From sea to sea the larum rung;
  On Berwick wall, and at Carlisle withal,
    To arms the startled warders sprung,
When ended was the dreadful roar,
The elvish dwarf was seen no more.

XXVI.

Some heard a voice in Branksome Hall,
Some saw a sight, not seen by all;
That dreadful voice was heard by some,
Cry, with loud summons, "GYLBIN,
  COME!"
  And on the spot where burst the brand,
    Just where the page had flung him
      down,
  Some saw an arm, and some a hand,
    And some the waving of a gown.
The guests in silence pray'd and shook,
And terror dimm'd each lofty look.
But none of all the astonish'd train
Was so dismay'd as Deloraine;
His blood did freeze, his brain did burn,
'Twas fear'd his mind would ne'er return;
For he was speechless, ghastly, wan,
Like him of whom the story ran,
  Who spoke the spectre-hound in Man.
At length, by fits, he darkly told,
With broken hint, and shuddering cold—
  That he had seen, right certainly,
A shape with amice wrapp'd around,
With a wrought Spanish baldric bound,
  Like pilgrim from beyond the sea;
And knew—but how it matter'd not—
It was the wizard, Michael Scott.

XXVII.

The anxious crowd, with horror pale,
All trembling heard the wondrous tale;
  No sound was made, no word was spoke,
  Till noble Angus silence broke;

And he a solemn sacred plight
Did to St. Bride of Douglas make,
That he a pilgrimage would take
To Melrose Abbey, for the sake
Of Michael's restless sprite.
Then each, to ease his troubled breast,
To some bless'd saint his prayers address'd:
Some to St. Modan made their vows,
Some to St. Mary of the Lowes,
Some to the Holy Rood of Lisle,
Some to our Ladye of the Isle;
Each did his patron witness make,
That he such pilgrimage would take,
And monks should sing, and bells should toll,
All for the weal of Michael's soul.
While vows were ta'en, and prayers were pray'd,
'Tis said the noble dame, dismay'd,
Renounced, for aye, dark magic's aid.

XXVIII.

Nought of the bridal will I tell,
Which after in short space befell;
Nor how brave sons and daughters fair
Bless'd Teviot's Flower, and Cranstoun's heir:
After such dreadful scene, 'twere vain
To wake the note of mirth again.
    More meet it were to mark the day
    Of penitence and prayer divine,
    When pilgrim chiefs, in sad array,
    Sought Melrose' holy shrine.

XXIX

With naked foot, and sackcloth vest,
And arms enfolded on his breast,
    Did every pilgrim go;
The standers-by might hear uneath,*
Footstep, or voice, or high-drawn breath,
    Through all the lengthen'd row:
No lordly look, nor martial stride,
Gone was their glory, sunk their pride,
    Forgotten their renown;
Silent and slow, like ghosts they glide
To the high altar's hallow'd side,
    And there they knelt them down:

---

* Scarcely hear.

Above the suppliant chieftains wave
The banners of departed brave;
Beneath the letter'd stones were laid
The ashes of their fathers dead;
From many a garnish'd niche around,
Stern saints and tortured martyrs frown'd.

XXX.

And slow up the dim aisle afar,
With sable cowl and scapular,
And snow-white stoles, in order due,
The holy Fathers, two and two,
    In long procession came;
Taper and host, and book they bare,
And holy banner, flourish'd fair
    With the Redeemer's name.
Above the prostrate pilgrim band
The mitred Abbot stretch'd his hand,
    And bless'd them as they kneel'd;
With holy cross he sign'd them all,
And pray'd they might be sage in hall,
    And fortunate in field.
Then mass was sung, and prayers were said,
And solemn requiem for the dead;
And bells toll'd out their mighty peal,
For the departed spirit's weal;
And ever in the office close
The hymn of intercession rose;
And far the echoing aisles prolong
The awful burthen of the song,—
    DIES IRÆ, DIES ILLA,
    SOLVET SÆCLUM IN FAVILLA;
While the pealing organ rung.
    Were it meet with sacred strain
    To close my lay, so light and vain,
Thus the holy Fathers sung:—

XXXI.

HYMN FOR THE DEAD.

That day of wrath, that dreadful day,
When heaven and earth shall pass away,
What power shall be the sinner's stay?
How shall he meet that dreadful day?

When, shrivelling like a parched scroll,
The flaming heavens together roll;
When louder yet, and yet more dread,
Swells the high trump that wakes the dead,

Oh! on that day, that wrathful day,
When man to judgment wakes from clay,
Be THOU the trembling sinner's stay,
Though heaven and earth shall pass away!

———

HUSH'D is the harp—the Minstrel gone.
And did he wander forth alone?
Alone, in indigence and age,
To linger out his pilgrimage?
No; close beneath proud Newark's tower,
Arose the Minstrel's lowly bower;
A simple hut; but there was seen
The little garden hedged with green,
The cheerful hearth, and lattice clean.
There shelter'd wanderers, by the blaze,
Oft heard the tale of other days;

For much he loved to ope his door,
And give the aid he begg'd before.
So pass'd the winter's day; but still,
When summer smiled on sweet Bowhill,
And July's eve, with balmy breath,
Waved the blue-bells on Newark heath;
When throstles sung in Harehead-shaw,
And corn was green on Carterhaugh,
And flourish'd, broad, Blackandro's oak,
The aged Harper's soul awoke!
Then would he sing achievements high,
And circumstance of chivalry,
Till the rapt traveller would stay,
Forgetful of the closing day;
And noble youths, the strain to hear,
Forsook the hunting of the deer;
And Yarrow, as he roll'd along,
Bore burden to the Minstrel's song.

MARMION.

TO THE

RIGHT HONOURABLE

HENRY LORD MONTAGU,

&c. &c. &c.

THIS ROMANCE IS INSCRIBED BY

THE AUTHOR.

ADVERTISEMENT TO THE FIRST EDITION.

It is hardly to be expected, that an Author whom the Public have honoured with some degree of applause, should not be again a trespasser on their kindness. Yet the Author of MARMION must be supposed to feel some anxiety concerning its success, since he is sensible that he hazards, by this second intrusion, any reputation which his first Poem may have procured him. The present story turns upon the private adventures of a fictitious character; but is called a Tale of Flodden Field, because the hero's fate is connected with that memorable defeat, and the causes which led to it. The design of the Author was, if possible, to apprize his readers, at the outset, of the date of his Story, and to prepare them for the manners of the Age in which it is laid. Any Historical Narrative, far more an attempt at Epic composition, exceeded his plan of a Romantic Tale; yet he may be permitted to hope, from the popularity of THE LAY OF THE LAST MINSTREL, that an attempt to paint the manners of the feudal times, upon a broader scale, and in the course of a more interesting story, will not be unacceptable to the Public.

The Poem opens about the commencement of August, and concludes with the defeat of Flodden, 9th September, 1513.

ASHESTIEL, 1808.

MARMION.

Alas! that Scottish maid should sing
The combat where her lover fell!
That Scottish bard should wake the string,
The triumph of our foes to tell!

LEYDEN.

~~~~~~~~~~~~~~~~~~~~

INTRODUCTION TO CANTO FIRST.

TO

WILLIAM STEWART ROSE, ESQ.

Ashestiel, Ettrick Forest.

NOVEMBER's sky is chill and drear,
November's leaf is red and sear:
Late, gazing down the steepy linn,
That hems our little garden in,
Low in its dark and narrow glen,
You scarce the rivulet might ken,
So thick the tangled greenwood grew,
So feeble trill'd the streamlet through:
Now murmuring hoarse, and frequent seen
Through bush and brier, no longer green,
An angry brook, it sweeps the glade,
Brawls over rock and wild cascade,
And, foaming brown with doubled speed,
Hurries its waters to the Tweed.

No longer Autumn's glowing red
Upon our Forest hills is shed;
No more, beneath the evening beam,
Fair Tweed reflects their purple gleam;
Away hath pass'd the heather-bell
That bloom'd so rich on Needpath-fell;
Sallow his brow, and russet bare
Are now the sister-heights of Yair.
The sheep, before the pinching heaven,
To shelter'd dale and down are driven,
Where yet some faded herbage pines,
And yet a watery sunbeam shines:
In meek despondency they eye
The wither'd sward and wintry sky,
And far beneath their summer hill,
Stray sadly by Glenkinnon's rill:
The shepherd shifts his mantle's fold,
And wraps him closer from the cold;
His dogs, no merry circles wheel,
But, shivering, follow at his heel;
A cowering glance they often cast,
As deeper moans the gathering blast.

My imps, though hardy, bold, and wild,
As best befits the mountain child,
Feel the sad influence of the hour,
And wail the daisy's vanished flower;
Their summer gambols tell, and mourn,
And anxious ask,—Will spring return,
And birds and lambs again be gay,
And blossoms clothe the hawthorn spray?

Yes, prattlers, yes. The daisy's flower
Again shall paint your summer bower;
Again the hawthorn shall supply
The garlands you delight to tie;
The lambs upon the lea shall bound,
The wild birds carol to the round,
And while you frolic light as they,
Too short shall seem the summer day

To mute and to material things
New life revolving summer brings;

The genial call dead Nature hears,
And in her glory reappears.
But oh! my country's wintry state
What second spring shall renovate?
What powerful call shall bid arise
The buried warlike and the wise;
The mind that thought for Britain's weal,
The hand that grasp'd the victor steel?
The vernal sun new life bestows
Even on the meanest flower that blows;
But vainly, vainly may he shine,
Where glory weeps o'er NELSON's shrine;
And vainly pierce the solemn gloom,
That shrouds, O PITT, thy hallowed
    tomb!

Deep graved in every British heart,
O never let those names depart!
Say to your sons,—Lo, here his grave,
Who victor died on Gadite wave;*
To him, as to the burning levin,
Short, bright, resistless course was given.
Where'er his country's foes were found,
Was heard the fated thunder's sound,
Till burst the bolt on yonder shore,
Roll'd, blazed, destroy'd,—and was no
    more.

Nor mourn ye less his perish'd worth,
Who bade the conqueror go forth,
And launch'd that thunderbolt of war
On Egypt, Hafnia,† Trafalgar;
Who, born to guide such high emprize,
For Britain's weal was early wise;
Alas! to whom the Almighty gave,
For Britain's sins, an early grave!
His worth, who, in his mightiest hour
A bauble held the pride of power,
Spurn'd at the sordid lust of pelf,
And served his Albion for herself;
Who, when the frantic crowd amain
Strain'd at subjection's bursting rein,
O'er their wild mood full conquest gain'd,
The pride, he would not crush, restrain'd,
Show'd their fierce zeal a worthier cause,
And brought the freeman's arm, to aid
    the freeman's laws.

---

* Nelson. *Gadite wave*, sea of Cadiz, or
Gades.
  † Copenhagen.

Had'st thou but lived, though stripp'd
    of power,
A watchman on the lonely tower,
Thy thrilling trump had roused the land,
When fraud or danger were at hand;
By thee, as by the beacon-light,
Our pilots had kept course aright;
As some proud column, though alone,
Thy strength had propp'd the tottering
    throne:
Now is the stately column broke,
The beacon-light is quench'd in smoke,
The trumpet's silver sound is still,
The warder silent on the hill!

Oh think, how to his latest day,
When Death, just hovering, claim'd his
    prey,
With Palinure's unalter'd mood,
Firm at his dangerous post he stood;
Each call for needful rest repell'd,
With dying hand the rudder held,
Till, in his fall, with fateful sway,
The steerage of the realm gave way!
Then, while on Britain's thousand plains,
One unpolluted church remains,
Whose peaceful bells ne'er sent around
The bloody tocsin's maddening sound,
But still, upon the hallow'd day,
Convoke the swains to praise and pray;
While faith and civil peace are dear,
Grace this cold marble with a tear,—
He, who preserved them, PITT, lies here!

Nor yet suppress the generous sigh,
Because his rival slumbers nigh;
Nor be thy *requiescat* dumb,
Lest it be said o'er Fox's tomb.
For talents mourn, untimely lost,
When best employ'd, and wanted most;
Mourn genius high, and lore profound,
And wit that loved to play, not wound;
And all the reasoning powers divine,
To penetrate, resolve, combine;
And feelings keen, and fancy's glow,—
They sleep with him who sleeps below:
And, if thou mourn'st they could not save
From error him who owns this grave,
Be every harsher thought suppress'd,
And sacred be the last long rest.

Here, where the end of earthly things
Lays heroes, patriots, bards, and kings;
Where stiff the hand, and still the tongue,
Of those who fought, and spoke, and sung;
Here, where the fretted aisles prolong
The distant notes of holy song,
As if some angel spoke agen,
" All peace on earth, good-will to men;"
If ever from an English heart,
O, *here* let prejudice depart,
And, partial feeling cast aside,
Record, that Fox a Briton died!
When Europe crouch'd to France's yoke,
And Austria bent, and Prussia broke,
And the firm Russian's purpose brave,
Was barter'd by a timorous slave,
Even then dishonour's peace he spurn'd,
The sullied olive-branch return'd,
Stood for his country's glory fast,
And nail'd her colours to the mast!
Heaven, to reward his firmness, gave
A portion in this honour'd grave,
And ne'er held marble in its trust
Of two such wondrous men the dust.

With more than mortal powers en-
        dow'd,
How high they soar'd above the crowd!
Theirs was no common party race,
Jostling by dark intrigue for place;
Like fabled Gods, their mighty war
Shook realms and nations in its jar;
Beneath each banner proud to stand,
Look'd up the noblest of the land,
Till through the British world were known
The names of PITT and FOX alone.
Spells of such force no wizard grave
E'er framed in dark Thessalian cave,
Though his could drain the ocean dry,
And force the planets from the sky.
These spells are spent, and, spent with
        these,
The wine of life is on the lees.
Genius, and taste, and talent gone,
For ever tomb'd beneath the stone,
Where—taming thought to human
        pride!—
The mighty chiefs sleep side by side.
Drop upon FOX's grave the tear,
'Twill trickle to his rival's bier;

O'er PITT's the mournful requiem sound,
And FOX's shall the notes rebound.
The solemn echo seems to cry,—
" Here let their discord with them die.
Speak not for those a separate doom,
Whom Fate made Brothers in the tomb;
But search the land of living men,
Where wilt thou find their like agen?"

Rest, ardent Spirits! till the cries
Of dying Nature bid you rise;
Not even your Britain's groans can pierce
The leaden silence of your hearse;
Then, O, how impotent and vain
This grateful tributary strain!
Though not unmark'd from northern
        clime,
Ye heard the Border Minstrel's rhyme:
His Gothic harp has o'er you rung;
The Bard you deign'd to praise, your
        deathless names has sung.

Stay yet, illusion, stay a while,
My wilder'd fancy still beguile!
From this high theme how can I part,
Ere half unloaded is my heart!
For all the tears e'er sorrow drew,
And all the raptures fancy knew,
And all the keener rush of blood,
That throbs through bard in bard-like
        mood,
Were here a tribute mean and low,
Though all their mingled streams could
        flow—
Woe, wonder, and sensation high,
In one spring-tide of ecstasy!—
It will not be—it may not last—
The vision of enchantment's past:
Like frostwork in the morning ray,
The fancied fabric melts away;
Each Gothic arch, memorial-stone,
And long, dim, lofty aisle, are gone;
And, lingering last, deception dear,
The choir's high sounds die on my ear.
Now slow return the lonely down,
The silent pastures bleak and brown,
The farm begirt with copsewood wild,
The gambols of each frolic child,
Mixing their shrill cries with the tone
Of Tweed's dark waters rushing on.

Prompt on unequal tasks to run,
Thus Nature disciplines her son:
Meeter, she says, for me to stray,
And waste the solitary day,
In plucking from yon fen the reed,
And watch it floating down the Tweed;
Or idly list the shrilling lay,
With which the milkmaid cheers her way,
Marking its cadence rise and fail,
As from the field, beneath her pail,
She trips it down the uneven dale:
Meeter for me, by yonder cairn,
The ancient shepherd's tale to learn;
Though oft he stop in rustic fear,
Lest his old legends tire the ear
Of one, who, in his simple mind,
May boast of book-learn'd taste refined.

But thou, my friend, canst fitly tell,
(For few have read romance so well),
How still the legendary lay
O'er poet's bosom holds its sway;
How on the ancient minstrel strain
Time lays his palsied hand in vain;
And how our hearts at doughty deeds,
By warriors wrought in steely weeds,
Still throb for fear and pity's sake;
As when the champion of the Lake
Enters Morgana's fated house,
Or in the Chapel Perilous,
Despising spells and demons' force,
Holds converse with the unburied corse;[1]
Or when, Dame Ganore's grace to move,
(Alas, that lawless was their love!)
He sought proud Tarquin in his den,
And freed full sixty knights; or when,
A sinful man, and unconfess'd,
He took the Sangreal's holy quest,
And, slumbering, saw the vision high,
He might not view with waking eye.[2]

The mightiest chiefs of British song
Scorn'd not such legends to prolong:
They gleam through Spenser's elfin dream,
And mix in Milton's heavenly theme;
And Dryden, in immortal strain,
Had raised the Table Round again,[3]
But that a ribald King and Court
Bade him toil on, to make them sport;
Demanded for their niggard pay,

Fit for their souls, a looser lay,
Licentious satire, song, and play;
The world defrauded of the high design,
Profaned the God-given strength, and
      marr'd the lofty line.

Warm'd by such names, well may we
      then,
Though dwindled sons of little men,
Essay to break a feeble lance
In the fair fields of old romance;
Or seek the moated castle's cell,
Where long through talisman and spell,
While tyrants ruled, and damsels wept,
Thy Genius, Chivalry, hath slept:
There sound the harpings of the North,
Till he awake and sally forth,
On venturous quest to prick again,
In all his arms, with all his train,
Shield, lance, and brand, and plume, and
      scarf,
Fay, giant, dragon, squire, and dwarf,
And wizard with his wand of might,
And errant maid on palfrey white.
Around the Genius weave their spells,
Pure Love, who scarce his passion tells;
Mystery, half veil'd and half reveal'd;
And Honour, with his spotless shield;
Attention, with fix'd eye; and Fear,
That loves the tale she shrinks to hear;
And gentle Courtesy; and Faith,
Unchanged by sufferings, time, or death;
And Valour, lion-mettled lord,
Leaning upon his own good sword.

Well has thy fair achievement shown,
A worthy meed may thus be won;
Ytene's* oaks—beneath whose shade
Their theme the merry minstrels made,
Of Ascapart, and Bevis bold,[4]
And that Red King,† who, while of old,
Through Boldrewood the chase he led,
By his loved huntsman's arrow bled—
Ytene's oaks have heard again
Renew'd such legendary strain;
For thou hast sung, how He of Gaul,
That Amadis so famed in hall,

---

* *Ytene*, ancient name of the New Forest,
Hants.

† William Rufus.

For Oriana, foil'd in fight
The Necromancer's felon might;
And well in modern verse hast wove
Partenopex's mystic love :*
Hear, then, attentive to my lay,
A knightly tale of Albion's elder day.

CANTO FIRST.

The Castle.

I.

Day set on Norham's castled steep,[5]
And Tweed's fair river, broad and deep,
  And Cheviot's mountains lone :
The battled towers, the donjon keep,[6]
The loophole grates, where captives weep,
The flanking walls that round it sweep,
  In yellow lustre shone.
The warriors on the turrets high,
Moving athwart the evening sky,
  Seem'd forms of giant height :
Their armour, as it caught the rays,
Flash'd back again the western blaze,
  In lines of dazzling light.

II.

Saint George's banner, broad and gay,
Now faded, as the fading ray
  Less bright, and less, was flung;
The evening gale had scarce the power
To wave it on the Donjon Tower,
  So heavily it hung.
The scouts had parted on their search,
  The Castle gates were barr'd;
Above the gloomy portal arch,
Timing his footsteps to a march,
  The Warder kept his guard;
Low humming, as he paced along,
Some ancient Border gathering song.

III.

A distant trampling sound he hears;
He looks abroad, and soon appears,

---

* *Partenopex*, a poem by W. S. Rose,

O'er Horncliff-hill a plump of spears,†
  Beneath a pennon gay;
A horseman, darting from the crowd,
Like lightning from a summer cloud,
Spurs on his mettled courser proud,
  Before the dark array.
Beneath the sable palisade,
That closed the Castle barricade,
  His bugle horn he blew;
The warder hasted from the wall,
And warn'd the Captain in the hall,
  For well the blast he knew;
And joyfully that knight did call,
To sewer, squire, and seneschal.

IV.

" Now broach ye a pipe of Malvoisie,‡
  Bring pasties of the doe,
And quickly make the entrance free,
And bid my heralds ready be,
And every minstrel sound his glee,
  And all our trumpets blow;
And, from the platform, spare ye not
To fire a noble salvo-shot;
  Lord Marmion waits below !"
Then to the Castle's lower ward
  Sped forty yeomen tall,
The iron-studded gates unbarr'd,
Raised the portcullis' ponderous guard,
The lofty palisade unsparr'd
  And let the drawbridge fall.

V.

Along the bridge Lord Marmion rode,
Proudly his red-roan charger trode,
His helm hung at the saddlebow;
Well by his visage you might know
He was a stalworth knight, and keen,
And had in many a battle been;
The scar on his brown cheek reveal'd
A token true of Bosworth field;
His eyebrow dark, and eye of fire,
Show'd spirit proud, and prompt to ire;
Yet lines of thought upon his cheek
Did deep design and counsel speak.

---

† Body of men-at-arms.
‡ Malmsey.

His forehead, by his casque worn bare,
His thick moustache, and curly hair,
Coal-black, and grizzled here and there,
    But more through toil than age;
His square-turn'd joints, and strength of limb,
Show'd him no carpet knight so trim,
But in close fight a champion grim,
    In camps a leader sage.

VI.

Well was he arm'd from head to heel,
In mail and plate of Milan steel;[7]
But his strong helm, of mighty cost,
Was all with burnish'd gold emboss'd;
Amid the plumage of the crest,
A falcon hover'd on her nest,
With wings outspread, and forward breast;
E'en such a falcon, on his shield,
Soar'd sable in an azure field:
The golden legend bore aright,
Who checks at me, to death is dight.[9]
Blue was the charger's broider'd rein;
Blue ribbons deck'd his arching mane;
The knightly housing's ample fold
Was velvet blue, and trapp'd with gold.

VII.

Behind him rode two gallant squires,
Of noble name, and knightly sires;
They burn'd the gilded spurs to claim;
For well could each a war-horse tame,
Could draw the bow, the sword could sway,
And lightly bear the ring away;
Nor less with courteous precepts stored,
Could dance in hall, and carve at board,
And frame love-ditties passing rare,
And sing them to a lady fair.

VIII.

Four men-at-arms came at their backs,
With halbert, bill, and battle-axe;
They bore Lord Marmion's lance so strong,
And led his sumpter-mules along,
And ambling palfrey, when at need
Him listed ease his battle-steed.

The last and trustiest of the four,
On high his forky pennon bore;
Like swallow's tail, in shape and hue,
Flutter'd the streamer glossy blue,
Where, blazon'd sable, as before,
The towering falcon seem'd to soar.
Last, twenty yeomen, two and two,
In hosen black, and jerkins blue,
With falcons broider'd on each breast,
Attended on their lord's behest.
Each, chosen for an archer good,
Knew hunting-craft by lake or wood;
Each one a six-foot bow could bend,
And far a cloth-yard shaft could send;
Each held a boar-spear tough and strong,
And at their belts their quivers rung.
Their dusty palfreys, and array,
Show'd they had march'd a weary way.

IX.

'Tis meet that I should tell you now,
How fairly arm'd, and order'd how,
    The soldiers of the guard,
With musket, pike, and morion,
To welcome noble Marmion,
    Stood in the Castle-yard;
Minstrels and trumpeters were there,
The gunner held his linstock yare,
    For welcome-shot prepared:
Enter'd the train, and such a clang,
As then through all his turrets rang,
    Old Norham never heard.

X

The guards their morrice-pikes advanced,
    The trumpets flourish'd brave,
The cannon from the ramparts glanced,
    And thundering welcome gave.
A blithe salute, in martial sort,
    The minstrels well might sound,
For, as Lord Marmion cross'd the court,
    He scatter'd angels* round.
" Welcome to Norham, Marmion!
    Stout heart, and open hand!
Well dost thou brook thy gallant roan,
    Thou flower of English land!"

---

* A gold coin of the period, value about ten shillings.

XI.

Two pursuivants, whom tabarts* deck,
With silver scutcheon round their neck,
Stood on the steps of stone,
By which you reach the donjon gate,
And there, with herald pomp and state,
They hail'd Lord Marmion:
They hail'd him Lord of Fontenaye,
Of Lutterward, and Scrivelbaye,
Of Tamworth tower and town;⁹
And he, their courtesy to requite,
Gave them a chain of twelve marks' weight,
All as he lighted down.
" Now, largesse, largesse,† Lord Marmion,
Knight of the crest of gold !
A blazon'd shield, in battle won,
Ne'er guarded heart so bold."

XII.

They marshall'd him to the Castle-hall,
Where the guests stood all aside,
And loudly flourish'd the trumpet-call,
And the heralds loudly cried,
—" Room, lordings, room for Lord Marmion,
With the crest and helm of gold !
Full well we know the trophies won
In the lists of Cottiswold:
There, vainly Ralph de Wilton strove
'Gainst Marmion's force to stand;
To him he lost his lady-love,
And to the King his land.
Ourselves beheld the listed field,
A sight both sad and fair;
We saw Lord Marmion pierce his shield,
And saw his saddle bare;
We saw the victor win the crest
He wears with worthy pride;
And on the gibbet-tree, reversed,
His foeman's scutcheon tied.

Place, nobles, for the Falcon-Knight !
Room, room, ye gentles gay,
For him who conquer'd in the right,
Marmion of Fontenaye !"

XIII.

Then stepp'd to meet that noble Lord,
Sir Hugh the Heron bold,
Baron of Twisell, and of Ford,
And Captain of the Hold.¹⁰
He led Lord Marmion to the deas,
Raised o'er the pavement high,
And placed him in the upper place—
They feasted full and high:
The whiles a Northern harper rude
Chanted a rhyme of deadly feud,
  "How the fierce Thirwalls, and Ridleys all,
    Stout Willimondswick,
    And Hardriding Dick,
  And Hughie of Hawdon, and Will o' the Wall,
Have set on Sir Albany Featherstonhaugh,
And taken his life at the Deadman's-shaw."
Scantly Lord Marmion's ear could brook
The harper's barbarous lay;
Yet much he prais'd the pains he took,
And well those pains did pay:
For lady's suit, and minstrel's strain,
By knight should ne'er be heard in vain.

XIV.

" Now, good Lord Marmion," Heron says,
  " Of your fair courtesy,
I pray you bide some little space
  In this poor tower with me.
Here may you keep your arms from rust,
  May breathe your war-horse well;
Seldom hath pass'd a week but giust
  Or feat of arms befell:
The Scots can rein a mettled steed;
  And love to couch a spear;—
Saint George ! a stirring life they lead,
  That have such neighbours near.
Then stay with us a little space,
  Our northern wars to learn;
I pray you, for your lady's grace !"
Lord Marmion's brow grew stern.

---

* The embroidered overcoat of the heralds, &c.

† The cry by which the bounty of knights and nobles was thanked. The word is still used in the hop gardens of Kent and Sussex, as a demand for payment from strangers entering them.

XV.

The Captain mark'd his alter'd look,
  And gave a squire the sign;
A mighty wassail-bowl he took,
  And crown'd it high in wine.
"Now pledge me here, Lord Marmion:
  But first I pray thee fair,
Where hast thou left that page of thine,
That used to serve thy cup of wine,
  Whose beauty was so rare?
When last in Raby towers we met,
  The boy I closely eyed,
And often mark'd his cheeks were wet,
  With tears he fain would hide:
His was no rugged horse-boy's hand,
To burnish shield or sharpen brand,
  Or saddle battle-steed;
But meeter seem'd for lady fair,
To fan her cheek, or curl her hair,
Or through embroidery, rich and rare,
  The slender silk to lead;
His skin was fair, his ringlets gold,
  His bosom—when he sigh'd,
The russet doublet's rugged fold
  Could scarce repel its pride!
Say, hast thou given that lovely youth
  To serve in lady's bower?
Or was the gentle page, in sooth,
  A gentle paramour?"

XVI.

Lord Marmion ill could brook such jest;
  He roll'd his kindling eye,
With pain his rising wrath suppress'd,
  Yet made a calm reply:
"That boy thou thought'st so goodly fair,
He might not brook the northern air,
More of his fate if thou wouldst learn,
I left him sick in Lindisfarn:
Enough of him.—But, Heron, say,
Why does thy lovely lady gay
Disdain to grace the hall to-day?
Or has that dame, so fair and sage,
Gone on some pious pilgrimage?"—
He spoke in covert scorn, for fame
Whisper'd light tales of Heron's dame.

XVII.

Unmark'd, at least unreck'd, the taunt,
  Careless the Knight replied,

"No bird, whose feathers gaily flaunt,
  Delights in cage to bide:
Norham is grim and grated close,
Hemm'd in by battlement and fosse,
  And many a darksome tower;
And better loves my lady bright
To sit in liberty and light,
  In fair Queen Margaret's bower.
We hold our greyhound in our hand,
  Our falcon on our glove;
But where shall we find leash or band,
  For dame that loves to rove?
Let the wild falcon soar her swing,
She'll stoop when she has tired her wing."—

XVIII.

"Nay, if with Royal James's bride,
The lovely Lady Heron bide,
Behold me here a messenger,
Your tender greetings prompt to bear;
For, to the Scottish court address'd,
I journey at our King's behest,
And pray you, of your grace, provide
For me, and mine, a trusty guide.
I have not ridden in Scotland since
James back'd the cause of that mock prince
Warbeck, that Flemish counterfeit,
Who on the gibbet paid the cheat.
Then did I march with Surrey's power,
What time we razed old Ayton tower."[11]

XIX.

"For such-like need, my lord, I trow,
Norham can find you guides enow;
For here be some have prick'd as far,
On Scottish ground, as to Dunbar;
Have drunk the monks of St. Bothan's ale,
And driven the beeves of Lauderdale;
Harried the wives of Greenlaw's goods,
And given them light to set their hoods."[12]

XX.

"Now, in good sooth," Lord Marmion
  cried,
"Were I in warlike wise to ride,
A better guard I would not lack,
Than your stout forayers at my back,
But, as in form of peace I go,
A friendly messenger, to know,

Why through all Scotland, near and far,
Their King is mustering troops for war,
The sight of plundering border spears
Might justify suspicious fears,
And deadly feud, or thirst of spoil,
Break out in some unseemly broil:
A herald were my fitting guide;
Or friar, sworn in peace to bide;
Or pardoner, or travelling priest,
Or strolling pilgrim, at the least."

XXI.

The Captain mused a little space,
And pass'd his hand across his face.
—" Fain would I find the guide you
    want,
But ill may spare a pursuivant,
The only men that safe can ride
Mine errands on the Scottish side:
And though a bishop built this fort,
Few holy brethren here resort;
Even our good chaplain, as I ween,
Since our last siege, we have not seen:
The mass he might not sing or say,
Upon one stinted meal a-day;
So, safe he sat in Durham aisle,
And pray'd for our success the while.
Our Norham vicar, woe betide,
Is all too well in case to ride;
The priest of Shoreswood[13]—he could rein
The wildest war-horse in your train;
But then, no spearman in the hall
Will sooner swear, or stab, or brawl.
Friar John of Tillmouth were the man:
A blithesome brother at the can,
A welcome guest in hall and bower,
He knows each castle, town, and tower,
In which the wine and ale is good,
'Twixt Newcastle and Holy-Rood.
But that good man, as ill befalls,
Hath seldom left our castle walls,
Since, on the vigil of St. Bede,
In evil hour, he cross'd the Tweed,
To teach Dame Alison her creed.
Old Bughtrig found him with his wife;
And John, an enemy to strife,
Sans frock and hood, fled for his life.
The jealous churl hath deeply swore,
That, if again he venture o'er,
He shall shrieve penitent no more.

Little he loves such risks, I know;
Yet, in your guard, perchance will go."

XXII.

Young Selby, at the fair hall-board,
Carved to his uncle and that lord,
And reverently took up the word.
" Kind uncle, woe were we each one,
If harm should hap to brother John.
He is a man of mirthful speech,
Can many a game and gambol teach;
Full well at tables can he play,
And sweep at bowls the stake away.
None can a lustier carol bawl,
The needfullest among us all,
When time hangs heavy in the hall,
And snow comes thick at Christmas tide,
And we can neither hunt, nor ride
A foray on the Scottish side.
The vow'd revenge of Bughtrig rude,
May end in worse than loss of hood.
Let Friar John, in safety, still
In chimney-corner snore his fill,
Roast hissing crabs, or flagons swill:
Last night, to Norham there came one,
Will better guide Lord Marmion."—
" Nephew," quoth Heron, " by my fay,
Well hast thou spoke; say forth thy say."

XXIII.

" Here is a holy Palmer come,
From Salem first, and last from Rome;
One, that hath kiss'd the blessed tomb,
And visited each holy shrine
In Araby and Palestine;
On hills of Armenie hath been,
Where Noah's ark may yet be seen;
By that Red Sea, too, hath he trod,
Which parted at the prophet's rod;
In Sinai's wilderness he saw
The Mount, where Israel heard the law,
'Mid thunder-dint, and flashing levin,
And shadows, mists, and darkness, given.
He shows Saint James's cockle-shell,
Of fair Montserrat, too, can tell;
    And of that Grot where Olives nod,
Where, darling of each heart and eye,
From all the youth of Sicily,
    Saint Rosalie retired to God.[14]

XXIV.

"To stout Saint George of Norwich
        merry,
Saint Thomas, too, of Canterbury,
Cuthbert of Durham and Saint Bede,
For his sins' pardon hath he pray'd.
He knows the passes of the North,
And seeks far shrines beyond the Forth ;
Little he eats, and long will wake,
And drinks but of the stream or lake.
This were a guide o'er moor and dale ;
But, when our John hath quaff'd his ale,
As little as the wind that blows,
And warms itself against his nose,
Kens he, or cares, which way he goes."—

XXV.

" Gramercy !" quoth Lord Marmion,
" Full loth were I, that Friar John,
That venerable man, for me,
Were placed in fear or jeopardy.
If this same Palmer will me lead
    From hence to Holy-Rood,
Like his good saint, I'll pay his meed,
Instead of cockle-shell, or bead,
    With angels fair and good.
I love such holy ramblers ; still
They know to charm a weary hill,
    With song, romance, or lay :
Some jovial tale, or glee, or jest,
Some lying legend, at the least,
    They bring to cheer the way."—

XXVI.

" Ah ! noble sir," young Selby said,
And finger on his lip he laid,
" This man knows much, perchance e'en
        more
Than he could learn by holy lore.
Still to himself he's muttering,
And shrinks as at some unseen thing.
Last night we listen'd at his cell ;
Strange sounds we heard, and, sooth to
        tell,
He murmur'd on till morn, howe'er
No living mortal could be near.
Sometimes I thought I heard it plain,
As other voices spoke again,

I cannot tell—I like it not—
Friar John hath told us it is wrote,
No conscience clear, and void of wrong,
Can rest awake, and pray so long.
Himself still sleeps before his beads
Have mark'd ten aves, and two creeds."[15]

XXVII.

—" Let pass," quoth Marmion ; " by
        my fay,
This man shall guide me on my way,
Although the great arch-fiend and he
Had sworn themselves of company.
So please you, gentle youth, to call
This Palmer to the Castle-hall."
The summon'd Palmer came in place ;[16]
His sable cowl o'erhung his face ;
In his black mantle was he clad,
With Peter's keys, in cloth of red,
    On his broad shoulders wrought ;
The scallop shell his cap did deck ;
The crucifix around his neck
    Was from Loretto brought ;
His sandals were with travel tore,
Staff, budget, bottle, scrip, he wore ;
The faded palm-branch in his hand
Show'd pilgrim from the Holy Land.

XXVIII.

When as the Palmer came in hall,
No lord, nor knight, was there more tall,
Nor had a statelier step withal,
    Or look'd more high and keen ;
For no saluting did he wait,
But strode across the hall of state,
And fronted Marmion where he sate,
    As he his peer had been.
But his gaunt frame was worn with toil ;
His cheek was sunk, alas the while !
And when he struggled at a smile,
    His eye look'd haggard wild :
Poor wretch ! the mother that him bare,
If she had been in presence there,
In his wan face, and sun-burn'd hair,
    She had not known her child.
Danger, long travel, want, or woe,
Soon change the form that best we know—
For deadly fear can time outgo,
    And blanch at once the hair·

Hard toil can roughen form and face,
And want can quench the eye's bright
    grace,
Nor does old age a wrinkle trace
    More deeply than despair.
Happy whom none of these befall,
But this poor Palmer knew them all.

XXIX.

Lord Marmion then his boon did ask;
The Palmer took on him the task,
So he would march with morning tide,
To Scottish court to be his guide.
" But I have solemn vows to pay,
And may not linger by the way,
    To fair St. Andrews bound,
Within the ocean-cave to pray,
Where good Saint Rule his holy lay,
From midnight to the dawn of day,
    Sung to the billows' sound;[17]
Thence to Saint Fillan's blessed well,
Whose spring can frenzied dreams dispel,
    And the crazed brain restore:[18]
Saint Mary grant, that cave or spring
Could back to peace my bosom bring,
    Or bid it throb no more!"

XXX.

And now the midnight draught of sleep,
Where wine and spices richly steep,
In massive bowl of silver deep,
    The page presents on knee.
Lord Marmion drank a fair good rest,
The Captain pledged his noble guest,
The cup went through among the rest,
    Who drain'd it merrily;
Alone the Palmer pass'd it by,
Though Selby press'd him courteously.
This was a sign the feast was o'er;
It hush'd the merry wassel roar,
    The minstrels ceased to sound.
Soon in the castle nought was heard,
But the slow footstep of the guard,
    Pacing his sober round.

XXXI.

With early dawn Lord Marmion rose:
And first the chapel doors unclose;
Then, after morning rites were done,
(A hasty mass from Friar John,)

And knight and squire had broke their fast,
On rich substantial repast,
Lord Marmion's bugles blew to horse:
Then came the stirrup-cup in course:
Between the Baron and his host,
No point of courtesy was lost;
High thanks were by Lord Marmion paid,
Solemn excuse the Captain made,
Till, filing from the gate, had pass'd
That noble train, their Lord the last.
Then loudly rung the trumpet call;
Thunder'd the cannon from the wall,
    And shook the Scottish shore;
Around the castle eddied slow,
Volumes of smoke as white as snow,
    And hid its turrets hoar;
Till they roll'd forth upon the air,
And met the river breezes there,
Which gave again the prospect fair.

INTRODUCTION TO CANTO SECOND.

TO

THE REV. JOHN MARRIOTT, A.M.

Ashestiel, Ettrick Forest.

THE scenes are desert now, and bare,
Where flourish'd once a forest fair,[19]
When these waste glens with copse were
    lined,
And peopled with the hart and hind.
Yon Thorn—perchance whose prickly
    spears
Have fenced him for three hundred years,
While fell around his green compeers—
Yon lonely Thorn, would he could tell
The changes of his parent dell,
Since he, so grey and stubborn now,
Waved in each breeze a sapling bough;
Would he could tell how deep the shade
A thousand mingled branches made;
How broad the shadows of the oak,
How clung the rowan* to the rock,
And through the foliage show'd his head,
With narrow leaves and berries red;

---

* Mountain ash.

What pines on every mountain sprung,
O'er every dell what birches hung,
In every breeze what aspens shook,
What alders shaded every brook!

"Here, in my shade," methinks he'd say,
"The mighty stag at noon-tide lay:
The wolf I've seen, a fiercer game,
(The neighbouring dingle bears his name,)
With lurching step around me prowl,
And stop, against the moon to howl;
The mountain-boar, on battle set,
His tusks upon my stem would whet;
While doe, and roe, and red-deer good,
Have bounded by, through gay green-
    wood.
Then oft, from Newark's riven tower,
Sallied a Scottish monarch's power:
A thousand vassals muster'd round,
With horse, and hawk, and horn, and
    hound;
And I might see the youth intent,
Guard every pass with crossbow bent;
And through the brake the rangers stalk,
And falc'ners hold the ready hawk;
And foresters, in green-wood trim,
Lead in the leash the gazehounds grim,
Attentive, as the bratchet's* bay
From the dark covert drove the prey,
To slip them as he broke away.
The startled quarry bounds amain,
As fast the gallant greyhounds strain
Whistles the arrow from the bow,
Answers the harquebuss below;
While all the rocking hills reply,
To hoof-clang, hound, and hunters' cry,
And bugles ringing lightsomely."

Of such proud huntings, many tales
Yet linger in our lonely dales,
Up pathless Ettrick and on Yarrow,
Where erst the outlaw drew his arrow.†
But not more blithe that silvan court,
Than we have been at humbler sport;
Though small our pomp, and mean our
    game,
Our mirth, dear Marriott, was the same.

Remember'st thou my greyhounds true?
O'er holt or hill there never flew,
From slip or leash there never sprang,
More fleet of foot, or sure of fang.
Nor dull, between each merry chase,
Pass'd by the intermitted space;
For we had fair resource in store,
In Classic and in Gothic lore:
We mark'd each memorable scene,
And held poetic talk between;
Nor hill, nor brook, we paced along,
But had its legend or its song.
All silent now—for now are still
Thy bowers, untenanted Bowhill!‡
No longer, from thy mountains dun,
The yeoman hears the well-known gun,
And while his honest heart glows warm,
At thought of his paternal farm,
Round to his mates a brimmer fills,
And drinks, "The Chieftain of the Hills!"
No fairy forms, in Yarrow's bowers,
Trip o'er the walks, or tend the flowers,
Fair as the elves whom Janet saw
By moonlight dance on Carterhaugh;
No youthful Baron's left to grace
The Forest-Sheriff's lonely chase,
And ape, in manly step and tone,
The majesty of Oberon:
And she is gone, whose lovely face
Is but her least and lowest grace;
Though if to Sylphid Queen 'twere given,
To show our earth the charms of Heaven,
She could not glide along the air,
With form more light, or face more fair.
No more the widow's deafen'd ear
Grows quick that lady's step to hear:
At noontide she expects her not,
Nor busies her to trim the cot;
Pensive she turns her humming wheel,
Or pensive cooks her orphans' meal;
Yet blesses, ere she deals their bread,
The gentle hand by which they're fed.

From Yair,—which hills so closely bind,
Scarce can the Tweed his passage find,
Though much he fret, and chafe, and toil,
Till all his eddying currents boil,—

---

* Slowhound.
† Murray, the Robin Hood of Ettrick, but
inferior in good qualities to our archer.

‡ A seat of the Duke of Buccleuch on the
Yarrow.

Her long-descended lord is gone,
And left us by the stream alone.
And much I m.ss those sportive boys,
Companions of my mountain joys,
Just at the age 'twixt boy and youth,
When thought is speech, and speech is
    truth.
Close to my side, with what delight
They press'd to hear of Wallace wight,
When, pointing to his airy mound,
I call'd his ramparts holy ground!
Kindled their brows to hear me speak;
And have smiled, to feel my cheek,
Despite the difference of our years,
Return again the glow of theirs.
Ah, happy boys! such feelings pure,
They will not, cannot, long endure;
Condemn'd to stem the world's rude tide,
You may not linger by the side;
For Fate shall thrust you from the shore,
And Passion ply the sail and oar.
Yet cherish the remembrance still,
Of the lone mountain, and the rill;
For trust, dear boys, the time will come,
When fiercer transport shall be dumb,
And you will think right frequently,
But, well, I hope, without a sigh,
On the free hours that we have spent
Together, on the brown hill's bent.

When, musing on companions gone,
We doubly feel ourselves alone,
Something, my friend, we yet may gain;
There is a pleasure in this pain:
It soothes the love of lonely rest,
Deep in each gentler heart impress'd.
'Tis silent amid worldly toils,
And stifled soon by mental broils;
But in a bosom thus prepared,
Its still small voice is often heard,
Whispering a mingled sentiment,
'Twixt resignation and content.
Oft in my mind such thoughts awake,
By lone St. Mary's silent lake;[20]
Thou know'st it well,—nor fen, nor sedge,
Pollute the pure lake's crystal edge;
Abrupt and sheer, the mountains sink
At once upon the level brink;
And just a trace of silver sand
Marks where the water meets the land.

Far in the mirror, bright and blue,
Each hill's huge outline you may view;
Shaggy with heath, but lonely bare,
Nor tree, nor bush, nor brake, is there,
Save where, of land, yon slender line
Bears thwart the lake the scatter'd pine.
Yet even this nakedness has power,
And aids the feeling of the hour:
Nor thicket, dell, nor copse you spy,
Where living thing conceal'd might lie;
Nor point, retiring, hides a dell,
Where swain, or woodman lone, might
    dwell;
There's nothing left to fancy's guess,
You see that all is loneliness:
And silence aids—though the steep hills
Send to the lake a thousand rills;
In summer tide, so soft they weep,
The sound but lulls the ear asleep;
Your horse's hoof-tread sounds too rude,
So stilly is the solitude.

Nought living meets the eye or ear,
But well I ween the dead are near;
For though, in feudal strife, a foe
Hath laid Our Lady's chapel low,[21]
Yet still, beneath the hallow'd soil,
The peasant rests him from his toil,
And, dying, bids his bones be laid,
Where erst his simple fathers pray'd.

If age had tamed the passions' strife,
And fate had cut my ties to life,
Here, have I thought, 'twere sweet to
    dwell,
And rear again the chaplain's cell,
Like that same peaceful hermitage,
Where Milton long'd to spend his age.
'Twere sweet to mark the setting day,
On Bourhope's lonely top decay;
And, as it faint and feeble died
On the broad lake, and mountain's
    side,
To say, "Thus pleasures fade away;
Youth, talents, beauty, thus decay,
And leave us dark, forlorn, and grey;"
Then gaze on Dryhope's ruin'd tower,
And think on Yarrow's faded Flower:
And when that mountain-sound I heard,
Which bids us be for storm prepared,

The distant rustling of his wings,
As up his force the Tempest brings,
'Twere sweet, ere yet his terrors rave,
To sit upon the Wizard's grave;
That Wizard Priest's, whose bones are
 thrust
From company of holy dust;[22]
On which no sunbeam ever shines—
(So superstition's creed divines)—
Thence view the lake, with sullen roar,
Heave her broad billows to the shore;
And mark the wild-swans mount the gale,
Spread wide through mist their snowy sail,
And ever stoop again, to lave
Their bosoms on the surging wave:
Then, when against the driving hail
No longer might my plaid avail,
Back to my lonely home retire,
And light my lamp, and trim my fire;
There ponder o'er some mystic lay,
Till the wild tale had all its sway.
And, in the bittern's distant shriek,
I heard unearthly voices speak,
And thought the Wizard Priest was come,
To claim again his ancient home!
And bade my busy fancy range,
To frame him fitting shape and strange,
Till from the task my brow I clear'd,
And smiled to think that I had fear'd.

But chief, 'twere sweet to think such
 life,
(Though but escape from fortune's strife,)
Something most matchless good and wise,
A great and grateful sacrifice;
And deem each hour to musing given,
A step upon the road to heaven.

Yet him, whose heart is ill at ease,
Such peaceful solitudes displease:
He loves to drown his bosom's jar
Amid the elemental war:
And my black Palmer's choice had been
Some ruder and more savage scene,
Like that which frowns round dark Loch-
 skene.[23]
There eagles scream from isle to shore;
Down all the rocks the torrents roar;
O'er the black waves incessant driven,
Dark mists infect the summer heaven;

Through the rude barriers of the lake,
Away its hurrying waters break,
Faster and whiter dash and curl,
Till down yon dark abyss they hurl.
Rises the fog-smoke white as snow,
Thunders the viewless stream below,
Diving, as if condemned to lave
Some demon's subterranean cave,
Who, prison'd by enchanter's spell,
Shakes the dark rock with groan and yell.
And well that Palmer's form and mien
Had suited with the stormy scene,
Just on the edge, straining his ken
To view the bottom of the den,
Where, deep deep down, and far within,
Toils with the rocks the roaring linn;
Then, issuing forth one foamy wave,
And wheeling round the Giant's Grave,
White as the snowy charger's tail,
Drives down the pass of Moffatdale.

Marriott, thy harp, on Isis strung,
To many a Border theme has rung:
Then list to me, and thou shalt know
Of this mysterious Man of Woe.

———◆———

CANTO SECOND.

The Convent.

I.

THE breeze which swept away the smoke,
 Round Norham Castle roll'd,
When all the loud artillery spoke,
With lightning-flash and thunder-stroke,
 As Marmion left the Hold.
It curl'd not Tweed alone, that breeze,
For, far upon Northumbrian seas,
 It freshly blew, and strong,
Where, from high Whitby's cloister'd
 pile,
Bound to St. Cuthbert's Holy Isle,[24]
 It bore a bark along.
Upon the gale she stoop'd her side,
And bounded o'er the swelling tide,
 As she were dancing home;
The merry seamen laugh'd, to see

Their gallant ship so lustily
  Furrow the green sea-foam.
Much joy'd they in their honour'd freight;
For, on the deck, in chair of state,
The Abbess of Saint Hilda placed,
With five fair nuns, the galley graced.

II.

'Twas sweet to see these holy maids,
Like birds escaped to green-wood shades,
  Their first flight from the cage,
How timid, and how curious too,
For all to them was strange and new,
And all the common sights they view,
  Their wonderment engage.
One eyed the shrouds and swelling sail,
  With many a benedicite;
One at the rippling surge grew pale,
  And would for terror pray;
Then shriek'd, because the sea-dog, nigh,
His round black head, and sparkling eye,
  Rear'd o'er the foaming spray;
And one would still adjust her veil,
Disorder'd by the summer gale,
Perchance lest some more worldly eye
Her dedicated charms might spy;
Perchance, because such action graced
Her fair-turn'd arm and slender waist.
Light was each simple bosom there,—
Save two, who ill might pleasure share,—
The Abbess and the Novice Clare.

III.

The Abbess was of noble blood,
But early took the veil and hood,
Ere upon life she cast a look,
Or knew the world that she forsook.
Fair too she was, and kind had been
As she was fair, but ne'er had seen
For her a timid lover sigh,
Nor knew the influence of her eye.
Love, to her ear, was but a name,
Combined with vanity and shame;
Her hopes, her fears, her joys, were all
Bounded within the cloister wall:
The deadliest sin her mind could reach,
Was of monastic rule the breach;
And her ambition's highest aim
To emulate Saint Hilda's fame.

For this she gave her ample dower,
To raise the convent's eastern tower;
For this, with carving rare and quaint,
She deck'd the chapel of the saint,
And gave the relic-shrine of cost,
With ivory and gems emboss'd.
The poor her Convent's bounty blest,
The pilgrim in its halls found rest.

IV.

Black was her garb, her rigid rule
Reform'd on Benedictine school;
Her cheek was pale, her form was spare;
Vigils, and penitence austere,
Had early quench'd the light of youth,
But gentle was the dame, in sooth;
Though vain of her religious sway,
She loved to see her maids obey.
Yet nothing stern was she in cell,
And the nuns loved their Abbess well.
Sad was this voyage to the dame;
Summon'd to Lindisfarne, she came,
There, with Saint Cuthbert's Abbot old,
And Tynemouth's Prioress, to hold
A chapter of St. Benedict,
For inquisition stern and strict,
On two apostates from the faith,
And, if need were, to doom to death.

V.

Nought say I here of Sister Clare,
Save this, that she was young and fair;
As yet, a novice unprofess'd,
Lovely and gentle, but distress'd.
She was betroth'd to one now dead,
Or worse, who had dishonour'd fled.
Her kinsmen bade her give her hand
To one, who loved her for her land:
Herself, almost heart-broken now,
Was bent to take the vestal vow,
And shroud within Saint Hilda's gloom,
Her blasted hopes and wither'd bloom.

VI

She sate upon the galley's prow,
And seem'd to mark the waves below;
Nay, seem'd, so fix'd her look and eye,
To count them as they glided by.
She saw them not—'twas seeming all—
Far other scene her thoughts recall,—

A sun-scorch'd desert, waste and bare,
Nor waves, nor breezes, murmur'd there;
There saw she, where some careless hand
O'er a dead corpse had heap'd the sand,
To hide it till the jackals come,
To tear it from the scanty tomb.—
See what a woful look was given,
As she raised up her eyes to heaven!

VII.

Lovely, and gentle, and distress'd—
These charms might tame the fiercest
   breast;
Harpers have sung, and poets told,
That he, in fury uncontroll'd,
The shaggy monarch of the wood,
Before a virgin, fair and good,
Hath pacified his savage mood.
But passions in the human frame,
Oft put the lion's rage to shame:
And jealousy, by dark intrigue,
With sordid avarice in league,
Had practised with their bowl and knife,
Against the mourner's harmless life.
This crime was charged 'gainst those who
   lay
Prison'd in Cuthbert's islet grey.

VIII

And now the vessel skirts the strand
Of mountainous Northumberland;
Towns, towers, and halls, successive rise,
And catch the nuns' delighted eyes.
Monk-Wearmouth soon behind them lay;
And Tynemouth's priory and bay;
They mark'd, amid her trees. the hall
Of lofty Seaton-Delaval;
They saw the Blythe and Wansbeck floods
Rush to the sea through sounding woods;
They pass'd the tower of Widderington,
Mother of many a valiant son;
At Coquet-isle their beads they tell
To the good Saint who own'd the cell;
Then did the Alne attention claim,
And Warkworth, proud of Percy's name;
And next, they cross'd themselves, to hear
The whitening breakers sound so near,
Where, boiling through the rocks, they
   roar,
On Dunstanborough's cavern'd shore;

Thy tower, proud Bamborough, mark'd
   they there,
King Ida's castle, huge and square,
From its tall rock look grimly down,
And on the swelling ocean frown;
Then from the coast they bore away,
And reach'd the Holy Island's bay.

IX.

The tide did now its flood-mark gain,
And girdled in the Saint's domain:
For, with the flow and ebb, its style
Varies from continent to isle;
Dry-shod, o'er sands, twice every day,
The pilgrims to the shrine find way;
Twice every day, the waves efface
Of staves and sandall'd feet the trace.
As to the port the galley flew,
Higher and higher rose to view
The Castle with its battled walls,
The ancient Monastery's halls,
A solemn, huge, and dark-red pile,
Placed on the margin of the isle.

X.

In Saxon strength that abbey frown'd,
With massive arches broad and round,
   That rose alternate, row and row,
     On ponderous columns, short and low,
     Built ere the art was known,
   By pointed aisle, and shafted stalk,
   The arcades of an alley'd walk
     To emulate in stone.
On the deep walls, the heathen Dane
Had pour'd his impious rage in vain;
And needful was such strength to these,
Exposed to the tempestuous seas,
Scourged by the winds' eternal sway,
Open to rovers fierce as they,
Which could twelve hundred years with-
   stand
Winds, waves, and northern pirates' hand.
Not but that portions of the pile,
Rebuilded in a later style,
Show'd where the spoiler's hand had been;
Not but the wasting sea-breeze keen
Had worn the pillar's carving quaint,
And moulder'd in his niche the saint,
And rounded, with consuming power,
The pointed angles of each tower;

Yet still entire the Abbey stood,
Like veteran, worn, but unsubdued.

XI.

Soon as they near'd his turrets strong,
The maidens raised Saint Hilda's song,
  And with the sea-wave and the wind,
  Their voices, sweetly shrill, combined,
    And made harmonious close;
  Then, answering from the sandy shore,
  Half drown'd amid the breakers' roar,
    According chorus rose:
Down to the haven of the Isle,
The monks and nuns in order file,
From Cuthbert's cloisters grim;
Banner, and cross, and relics there,
To meet St. Hilda's maids, they bare;
And, as they caught the sounds on air,
  They echoed back the hymn.
The islanders, in joyous mood,
Rush'd emulously through the flood,
  To hale the bark to land;
Conspicuous by her veil and hood,
Signing the cross, the Abbess stood,
  And bless'd them with her hand.

XII.

Suppose we now the welcome said,
Suppose the Convent banquet made:
  All through the holy dome,
Through cloister, aisle, and gallery,
Wherever vestal maid might pry,
Nor risk to meet unhallow'd eye,
  The stranger sisters roam:
Till fell the evening damp with dew,
And the sharp sea-breeze coldly blew,
For there, even summer night is chill.
Then, having stray'd and gazed their fill,
  They closed around the fire;
And all, in turn, essay'd to paint,
The rival merits of their saint,
  A theme that ne'er can tire
A holy maid; for, be it known,
That their saint's honour is their own.

XIII.

Then Whitby's nuns exulting told,
How to their house three Barons bold
  Must menial service do;
While horns blow out a note of shame,

And monks cry " Fye upon your name!
In wrath, for loss of sylvan game,
  Saint Hilda's priest ye slew."—
" This, on Ascension-day, each year,
While labouring on our harbour-pier,
Must Herbert, Bruce, and Percy hear."—
They told, how in their convent cell
A Saxon princess once did dwell,
  The lovely Edelfled;²⁵
And how, of thousand snakes, each one
Was changed into a coil of stone,
  When holy Hilda pray'd;
Themselves, within their holy bound,
Their stony folds had often found.
They told, how sea-fowls' pinions fail
As over Whitby's towers they sail,²⁶
And, sinking down, with flutterings faint,
They do their homage to the saint.

XIV.

Nor did St. Cuthbert's daughters fail,
To vie with these in holy tale;
His body's resting-place, of old,
How oft their patron changed, they told;²⁷
How, when the rude Dane burn'd their
  pile,
The monks fled forth from Holy Isle;
O'er northern mountain, marsh, and moor,
From sea to sea, from shore to shore,
Seven years Saint Cuthbert's corpse they
  bore.
  They rested them in fair Melrose;
  But though, alive, he loved it well,
  Not there his relics might repose ·
  For, wondrous tale to tell!
In his stone coffin forth he rides,
A ponderous bark for river tides,
Yet light as gossamer it glides,
  Downward to Tilmouth cell.
Nor long was his abiding there,
For southward did the saint repair;
Chester-le-Street, and Rippon saw
His holy corpse, ere Wardilaw
  Hail'd him with joy and fear;
And, after many wanderings past,
He chose his lordly seat at last,
Where his cathedral, huge and vast,
  Looks down upon the Wear:
There, deep in Durham's Gothic shade,
His relics are in secret laid;

But none may know the place,
Save of his holiest servants three,
Deep sworn to solemn secrecy,
    Who share that wondrous grace.

XV.

Who may his miracles declare!
Even Scotland's dauntless king, and heir,
    (Although with them they led
Galwegians, wild as ocean's gale,
And Lodon's knights, all sheathed in mail,
And the bold men of Teviotdale,)
    Before his standard fled.[28]
'Twas he, to vindicate his reign,
Edged Alfred's falchion on the Dane,
And turn'd the Conqueror back again,[29]
When, with his Norman bowyer band,
He came to waste Northumberland.

XVI.

But fain Saint Hilda's nuns would learn
If, on a rock by Lindisfarne,
Saint Cuthbert sits, and toils to frame
The sea-born beads that bear his name:[30]
Such tales had Whitby's fishers told,
And said they might his shape behold,
    And hear his anvil sound;
A deaden'd clang,—a huge dim form,
Seen but, and heard, when gathering
    storm
    And night were closing round.
But this, as tale of idle fame,
The nuns of Lindisfarne disclaim.

XVII.

While round the fire such legends go,
Far different was the scene of woe,
Where, in a secret aisle beneath,
Council was held of life and death.
    It was more dark and lone that vault,
    Than the worst dungeon cell:
    Old Colwulf[31] built it, for his fault,
        In penitence to dwell,
When he, for cowl and beads, laid down
The Saxon battle-axe and crown.
This den, which, chilling every sense
    Of feeling, hearing, sight,
Was call'd the Vault of Penitence,
    Excluding air and light,

Was, by the prelate Sexhelm, made
A place of burial for such dead,
As, having died in mortal sin,
Might not be laid the church within.
'Twas now a place of punishment;
Whence if so loud a shriek were sent,
    As reach'd the upper air,
The hearers blessed themselves, and said,
The spirits of the sinful dead
    Bemoan'd their torments there.

XVIII.

But though, in the monastic pile,
Did of this penitential aisle
    Some vague tradition go,
Few only, save the Abbot, knew
Where the place lay; and still more few
Were those, who had from him the clew
    To that dread vault to go.
Victim and executioner
Were blindfold when transported there.
In low dark rounds the arches hung,
From the rude rock the side-walls sprung;
The grave-stones, rudely sculptured o'er,
Half sunk in earth, by time half wore,
Were all the pavement of the floor;
The mildew-drops fell one by one,
With tinkling plash, upon the stone.
A cresset,* in an iron chain,
Which served to light this drear domain,
With damp and darkness seem'd to strive,
As if it scarce might keep alive;
And yet it dimly served to show
The awful conclave met below.

XIX.

There, met to doom in secrecy,
Were placed the heads of convents three:
All servants of Saint Benedict,
The statutes of whose order strict
    On iron table lay;
In long black dress, on seats of stone,
Behind were these three judges shown
    By the pale cresset's ray:
The Abbess of Saint Hilda's, there,
Sat for a space with visage bare,
Until, to hide her bosom's swell,

---

* Antique chandelier.

And tear-drops that for pity fell,
    She closely drew her veil:
Yon shrouded figure, as I guess,
By her proud mien and flowing dress,
Is Tynemouth's haughty Prioress,[32]
    And she with awe looks pale:
And he, that Ancient Man, whose sight
Has long been quench'd by age's night,
Upon whose wrinkled brow alone,
Nor ruth, nor mercy's trace, is shown,
    Whose look is hard and stern,—
Saint Cuthbert's Abbot is his style;
For sanctity call'd, through the isle,
    The Saint of Lindisfarne.

XX.

Before them stood a guilty pair;
But, though an equal fate they share,
    Yet one alone deserves our care.
Her sex a page's dress belied;
The cloak and doublet, loosely tied,
Obscured her charms, but could not hide.
    Her cap down o'er her face she drew;
        And, on her doublet breast,
    She tried to hide the badge of blue,
        Lord Marmion's falcon crest.
But, at the Prioress' command,
A Monk undid the silver band,
    That tied her tresses fair,
And raised the bonnet from her head,
And down her slender form they spread,
    In ringlets rich and rare.
Constance de Beverley they know,
Sister profess'd of Fontevraud,
Whom the church number'd with the
        dead,
For broken vows, and convent fled.

XXI.

When thus her face was given to view,
(Although so pallid was her hue,
It did a ghastly contrast bear
To those bright ringlets glistering fair,)
Her look composed, and steady eye,
Bespoke a matchless constancy;
And there she stood so calm and pale,
That, but her breathing did not fail,
And motion slight of eye and head,
And of her bosom, warranted

That neither sense nor pulse she lacks,
You might have thought a form of wax,
Wrought to the very life, was there;
So still she was, so pale, so fair.

XXII.

Her comrade was a sordid soul,
    Such as does murder for a meed;
Who, but of fear, knows no control,
Because his conscience, sear'd and foul,
    Feels not the import of his deed;
One, whose brute-feeling ne'er aspires
Beyond his own more brute desires.
Such tools the Tempter ever needs,
To do the savagest of deeds;
For them no vision'd terrors daunt,
Their nights no fancied spectres haunt,
One fear with them, of all most base,
The fear of death,—alone finds place.
This wretch was clad in frock and cowl,
And shamed not loud to moan and howl,
His body on the floor to dash,
And crouch, like hound beneath the lash;
While his mute partner, standing near,
Waited her doom without a tear.

XXIII.

Yet well the luckless wretch might shriek,
Well might her paleness terror speak!
For there were seen in that dark wall,
Two niches, narrow, deep and tall;—
Who enters at such grisly door,
Shall ne'er, I ween, find exit more.
In each a slender meal was laid,
Of roots, of water, and of bread:
By each, in Benedictine dress,
Two haggard monks stood motionless;
Who, holding high a blazing torch,
Show'd the grim entrance of the porch:
Reflecting back the smoky beam,
The dark-red walls and arches gleam.
Hewn stones and cement were display'd,
And building tools in order laid.

XXIV.

These executioners were chose,
As men who were with mankind foes,
And with despite and envy fired,
Into the cloister had retired;

Or who, in desperate doubt of grace,
Strove, by deep penance, to efface
' Of some foul crime the stain ;
For, as the vassals of her will,
Such men the Church selected still,
As either joy'd in doing ill,
Or thought more grace to gain,
If, in her cause, they wrestled down
Feelings their nature strove to own.
By strange device were they brought there,
They knew not how, nor knew not where.

XXV.

And now that blind old Abbot rose,
To speak the Chapter's doom,
On those the wall was to enclose,
Alive, within the tomb,[33]
But stopp'd, because that woful Maid,
Gathering her powers, to speak essay'd.
Twice she essay'd, and twice in vain ;
Her accents might no utterance gain ;
Nought but imperfect murmurs slip
From her convulsed and quivering lip ;
'Twixt each attempt all was so still,
You seem'd to hear a distant rill—
'Twas ocean's swells and falls ;
For though this vault of sin and fear
Was to the sounding surge so near,
A tempest there you scarce could hear,
So massive were the walls.

XXVI.

At length, an effort sent apart
The blood that curdled to her heart,
And light came to her eye,
And colour dawn'd upon her cheek,
A hectic and a flutter'd streak,
Like that left on the Cheviot peak,
By Autumn's stormy sky ;
And when her silence broke at length,
Still as she spoke she gather'd strength,
And arm'd herself to bear.
It was a fearful sight to see
Such high resolve and constancy,
In form so soft and fair.

XXVII.

" I speak not to implore your grace,
Well know I, for one minute's space
Successless might I sue :

Nor do I speak your prayers to gain ;
For if a death of lingering pain,
To cleanse my sins, be penance vain,
Vain are your masses too.—
I listen'd to a traitor's tale,
I left the convent and the veil ;
For three long years I bow'd my pride,
A horse-boy in his train to ride ;
And well my folly's meed he gave,
Who forfeited, to be his slave,
All here, and all beyond the grave.—
He saw young Clara's face more fair,
He knew her of broad lands the heir,
Forgot his vows, his faith foreswore,
And Constance was beloved no more.—
'Tis an old tale, and often told ;
But did my fate and wish agree,
Ne'er had been read, in story old,
Of maiden true betray'd for gold,
That loved, or was avenged, like me!

XXVIII.

" The King approved his favourite's aim ;
In vain a rival barr'd his claim,
Whose fate with Clare's was plight,
For he attaints that rival's fame
With treason's charge—and on they came,
In mortal lists to fight.
Their oaths are said,
Their prayers are pray'd,
Their lances in the rest are laid,
They meet in mortal shock ;
And, hark ! the throng, with thundering
cry,
Shout ' Marmion, Marmion ! to the sky,
De Wilton to the block !'
Say ye, who preach Heaven shall decide
When in the lists two champions ride,
Say, was Heaven's justice here !
When, loyal in his love and faith,
Wilton found overthrow or death,
Beneath a traitor's spear ?
How false the charge, how true he fell,
This guilty packet best can tell."—
Then drew a packet from her breast,
Paused, gather'd voice, and spoke the rest.

XXIX.

" Still was false Marmion's bridal staid ;
To Whitby's convent fled the maid,

The hated match to shun.
' Ho! shifts she thus?' King Henry cried,
' Sir Marmion, she shall be thy bride,
    If she were sworn a nun.'
One way remain'd—the King's command
Sent Marmion to the Scottish land:
I linger'd here, and rescue plann'd
    For Clara and for me:
This caitiff Monk, for gold, did swear,
He would to Whitby's shrine repair,
And, by his drugs, my rival fair
    A saint in heaven should be.
But ill the dastard kept his oath,
Whose cowardice has undone us both.

XXX.

" And now my tongue the secret tells,
Not that remorse my bosom swells,
But to assure my soul that none
Shall ever wed with Marmion.
Had fortune my last hope betray'd,
This packet, to the King convey'd,
Had given him to the headsman's stroke,
Although my heart that instant broke.—
Now, men of death, work forth your will,
For I can suffer, and be still;
And come he slow, or come he fast,
It is but Death who comes at last.

XXXI.

" Yet dread me, from my living tomb,
Ye vassal slaves of bloody Rome!
If Marmion's late remorse should wake,
Full soon such vengeance will he take,
That you shall wish the fiery Dane
Had rather been your guest again.
Behind, a darker hour ascends!
The altars quake, the crosier bends,
The ire of a despotic King
Rides forth upon destruction's wing;
Then shall these vaults, so strong and deep
Burst open to the sea-winds' sweep;
Some traveller then shall find my bones
Whitening amid disjointed stones,
And, ignorant of priests' cruelty,
Marvel such relics here should be."

XXXII.

Fix'd was her look, and stern her air:
Back from her shoulders stream'd her hair;
The locks, that wont her brow to shade,
Stared up erectly from her head;
Her figure seem'd to rise more high;
Her voice, despair's wild energy
Had given a tone of prophecy.
Appall'd the astonish'd conclave sate;
With stupid eyes, the men of fate
Gazed on the light inspired form,
And listen'd for the avenging storm;
The judges felt the victim's dread;
No hand was moved, no word was said,
Till thus the Abbot's doom was given,
Raising his sightless balls to heaven:—
" Sister, let thy sorrows cease;
Sinful brother, part in peace!"
    From that dire dungeon, place of doom,
    Of execution too, and tomb,
        Paced forth the judges three;
    Sorrow it were, and shame, to tell
    The butcher-work that there befell,
    When they had glided from the cell
        Of sin and misery.

XXXIII.

An hundred winding steps convey
That conclave to the upper day;
But, ere they breathed the fresher air,
They heard the shriekings of despair,
    And many a stifled groan:
With speed their upward way they take,
(Such speed as age and fear can make,)
And cross'd themselves for terror's sake,
    As hurrying, tottering on:
Even in the vesper's heavenly tone,
They seem'd to hear a dying groan,
And bade the passing knell to toll
For welfare of a parting soul.
Slow o'er the midnight wave it swung,
Northumbrian rocks in answer rung;
To Warkworth cell the echoes roll'd,
His beads the wakeful hermit told,
The Bamborough peasant raised his head,
But slept ere half a prayer he said;
So far was heard the mighty knell,
The stag sprung up on Cheviot Fell,
Spread his broad nostril to the wind,
Listed before, aside, behind,
Then couch'd him down beside the hind,
And quaked among the mountain fern,
To hear that sound so dull and stern.

INTRODUCTION TO CANTO THIRD.

TO

WILLIAM ERSKINE, ESQ.*

Ashestiel, Ettrick Forest.

LIKE April morning clouds, that pass,
With varying shadow, o'er the grass,
And imitate, on field and furrow,
Life's chequer'd scene of joy and sorrow ;
Like streamlet of the mountain north,
Now in a torrent racing forth,
Now winding slow its silver train,
And almost slumbering on the plain ;
Like breezes of the autumn day,
Whose voice inconstant dies away,
And ever swells again as fast,
When the ear deems its murmur past ;
Thus various, my romantic theme
Flits, winds, or sinks, a morning dream.
Yet pleased, our eye pursues the trace
Of Light and Shade's inconstant race ;
Pleased, views the rivulet afar,
Weaving its maze irregular ;
And pleased, we listen as the breeze
Heaves its wild sigh through Autumn
　　　trees ;
Then, wild as cloud, or stream, or gale,
Flow on, flow unconfined, my Tale !

Need I to thee, dear Erskine, tell
I love the license all too well,
In sounds now lowly, and now strong,
To raise the desultory song ?—
Oft, when 'mid such capricious chime,
Some transient fit of lofty rhyme
To thy kind judgment seem'd excuse
For many an error of the muse,
Oft hast thou said, " If, still mis-spent,
Thine hours to poetry are lent,
Go, and to tame thy wandering course,
Quaff from the fountain at the source ;
Approach those masters, o'er whose tomb
Immortal laurels ever bloom :
Instructive of the feebler bard,
Still from the grave their voice is heard ;

From them, and from the paths they
　　　show'd
Choose honour'd guide and practised road ;
Nor ramble on through brake and maze,
With harpers rude, of barbarous days.

" Or deem'st thou not our later time
Yields topic meet for classic rhyme ?
Hast thou no elegiac verse
For Brunswick's venerable hearse ?
What, not a line, a tear, a sigh,
When valour bleeds for liberty ?—
Oh, hero of that glorious time,
When, with unrivall'd light sublime,—
Though martial Austria, and though all
The might of Russia, and the Gaul,
Though banded Europe stood her foes—
The star of Brandenburgh arose !
Thou could'st not live to see her beam
For ever quench'd in Jena's stream.
Lamented chief !—it was not given
To thee to change the doom of Heaven,
And crush that dragon in its birth,
Predestined scourge of guilty earth.
Lamented chief !—not thine the power,
To save in that presumptuous hour,
When Prussia hurried to the field,
And snatch'd the spear, but left the shield ;
Valour and skill 'twas thine to try,
And, tried in vain, 'twas thine to die.
Ill had it seem'd thy silver hair
The last, the bitterest pang to share,
For princedoms reft, and scutcheons riven,
And birthrights to usurpers given ;
Thy land's, thy children's wrongs to feel,
And witness woes thou couldst not heal !
On thee relenting Heaven bestows
For honour'd life an honour'd close ;
And when revolves, in time's sure change,
The hour of Germany's revenge,
When, breathing fury for her sake,
Some new Arminius shall awake,
Her champion, ere he strike, shall come
To whet his sword on BRUNSWICK's tomb.

" Or of the Red-Cross hero† teach,
Dauntless in dungeon as on breach :
Alike to him, the sea, the shore,
The brand, the bridle, or the oar :

---

* A Judge of the Court of Session, afterwards, by title, Lord Kinnedder. He died
in 1822.

† Sir Sidney Smith.

Alike to him the war that calls
Its votaries to the shatter'd walls,
Which the grim Turk, besmear'd with
    blood,
Against the Invincible made good ;
Or that, whose thundering voice could
    wake
The silence of the polar lake,
When stubborn Russ, and metal'd Swede,
On the warp'd wave their death-game
    play'd ;
Or that, where Vengeance and Affright
Howl'd round the father of the fight,
Who snatch'd, on Alexandria's sand,
The conqueror's wreath with dying hand.*

  " Or, if to touch such chord be thine,
Restore the ancient tragic line,
And emulate the notes that wrung
From the wild harp, which silent hung
By silver Avon's holy shore,
Till twice an hundred years roll'd o'er ;
When she, the bold Enchantress† came,
With fearless hand and heart on flame !
From the pale willow snatch'd the treasure,
And swept it with a kindred measure,
Till Avon's swans, while rung the grove
With Montfort's hate and Basil's love,
Awakening at the inspired strain,
Deem'd their own Shakspeare lived again."

  Thy friendship thus thy judgment
    wronging,
With praises not to me belonging,
In task more meet for mightiest powers,
Wouldst thou engage my thriftless hours.
But say, my Erskine, hast thou weigh'd
That secret power by all obey'd,
Which warps not less the passive mind,
Its source conceal'd or undefined ;
Whether an impulse, that has birth
Soon as the infant wakes on earth,
One with our feelings and our powers,
And rather part of us than ours ;
Or whether fitlier term'd the sway
Of habit form'd in early day ?
Howe'er derived, its force confest
Rules with despotic sway the breast,

---

        * Sir Ralph Abercromby.
        † Joanna Baillie.

And drags us on by viewless chain,
While taste and reason plead in vain.
Look east, and ask the Belgian why,
Beneath Batavia's sultry sky,
He seeks not eager to inhale
The freshness of the mountain gale,
Content to rear his whiten'd wall
Beside the dank and dull canal ?
He'll say, from youth he loved to see
The white sail gliding by the tree.
Or see yon weatherbeaten hind,
Whose sluggish herds before him wind,
Whose tatter'd plaid and rugged cheek
His northern clime and kindred speak ;
Through England's laughing meads he
    goes,
And England's wealth around him flows;
Ask, if it would content him well,
At ease in those gay plains to dwell,
Where hedge-rows spread a verdant screen,
And spires and forests intervene,
And the neat cottage peeps between ?
No ! not for these will he exchange
His dark Lochaber's boundless range :
Not for fair Devon's meads forsake
Bennevis grey, and Garry's lake.

  Thus, while I ape the measure wild
Of tales that charm'd me yet a child,
Rude though they be, still with the chime
Return the thoughts of early time ;
And feelings, roused in life's first day,
Glow in the line, and prompt the lay.
Then rise those crags, that mountain tower,
Which charm'd my fancy's wakening
    hour.
Though no broad river swept along,
To claim, perchance, heroic song ;
Though sigh'd no groves in summer gale,
To prompt of love a softer tale ;
Though scarce a puny streamlet's speed
Claim'd homage from a shepherd's reed ;
Yet was poetic impulse given,
By the green hill and clear blue heaven.
It was a barren scene, and wild,
Where naked cliffs were rudely piled ;
But ever and anon between
Lay velvet tufts of loveliest green ;
And well the lonely infant knew
Recesses where the wall-flower grew,

And honey-suckle loved to crawl
Up the low crag and ruin'd wall.
I deem'd such nooks the sweetest shade
The sun in all its round survey'd;
And still I thought that shatter'd tower *
The mightiest work of human power;
And marvell'd as the aged hind
With some strange tale bewitch'd my mind,
Of forayers, who, with headlong force,
Down from that strength had spurr'd their
horse,
Their southern rapine to renew,
Far in the distant Cheviots blue,
And, home returning, fill'd the hall
With revel, wassel-rout, and brawl.
Methought that still with trump and clang,
The gateway's broken arches rang;
Methought grim features, seam'd with
scars,
Glared through the window's rusty bars,
And ever, by the winter hearth,
Old tales I heard of woe or mirth,
Of lovers' slights, of ladies' charms,
Of witches' spells, of warriors' arms;
Of patriot battles, won of old
By Wallace wight and Bruce the bold;
Of later fields of feud and fight,
When, pouring from their Highland
height,
The Scottish clans, in headlong sway,
Had swept the scarlet ranks away.
While stretch'd at length upon the floor,
Again I fought each combat o'er,
Pebbles and shells, in order laid,
The mimic ranks of war display'd;
And onward still the Scottish Lion bore,
And still the scatter'd Southron fled before.

Still, with vain fondness, could I trace,
Anew, each kind familiar face,
That brighten'd at our evening fire!
From the thatch'd mansion's grey-hair'd
Sire,†
Wise without learning, plain and good,
And sprung of Scotland's gentler blood;
Whose eye, in age, quick, clear, and keen,
Show'd what in youth its glance had been;

Whose doom discording neighbours
sought,
Content with equity unbought;
To him the venerable Priest,
Our frequent and familiar guest,
Whose life and manners well could paint
Alike the student and the saint;
Alas! whose speech too oft I broke
With gambol rude and timeless joke:
For I was wayward, bold, and wild,
A self-will'd imp, a grandame's child;
But half a plague, and half a jest,
Was still endured, beloved, caress'd.

For me, thus nurtured, dost thou ask
The classic poet's well-conn'd task?
Nay, Erskine, nay—On the wild hill
Let the wild heath-bell flourish still;
Cherish the tulip, prune the vine,
But freely let the woodbine twine,
And leave, untrimm'd the eglantine:
Nay, my friend, nay—Since oft thy praise
Hath given fresh vigour to my lays;
Since oft thy judgment could refine
My flatten'd thought, or cumbrous line;
Still kind, as is thy wont, attend,
And in the minstrel spare the friend.
Though wild as cloud, as stream, as gale,
Flow forth, flow unrestrain'd, my Tale!

CANTO THIRD.

The Hostel, or Inn.

I.

THE livelong day Lord Marmion rode:
The mountain path the Palmer show'd,
By glen and streamlet winded still,
Where stunted birches hid the rill.
They might not choose the lowland road,
For the Merse forayers were abroad,
Who, fired with hate and thirst of prey,
Had scarcely fail'd to bar their way.
Oft on the trampling band, from crown
Of some tall cliff, the deer look'd down;
On wing of jet, from his repose
In the deep heath, the black-cock rose;

---

* Smailholm tower, in Berwickshire.

† Robert Scott of Sandyknows, the grandfather of the poet.

Sprung from the gorse the timid roe,
Nor waited for the bending bow ;
And when the stony path began,
By which the naked peak they wan,
Up flew the snowy ptarmigan.
The noon had long been pass'd before
They gain'd the height of Lammermoor;
Thence winding down the northern way
Before them, at the close of day,
Old Gifford's towers and hamlet lay.

II.

No summons calls them to the tower,
To spend the hospitable hour.
To Scotland's camp the Lord was gone;
His cautious dame, in bower alone,
Dreaded her castle to unclose,
So late, to unknown friends or foes.
On through the hamlet as they paced,
Before a porch, whose front was graced
With bush and flagon trimly placed,
  Lord Marmion drew his rein :
The village inn seem'd large, though
    rude ;[31]
Its cheerful fire and hearty food
  Might well relieve his train.
Down from their seats the horsemen
    sprung,
With jingling spurs the court-yard rung;
They bind their horses to the stall,
For forage, food, and firing call,
And various clamour fills the hall :
Weighing the labour with the cost,
Toils everywhere the bustling host.

III.

Soon, by the chimney's merry blaze,
Through the rude hostel might you gaze;
Might see, where, in dark nook aloof,
The rafters of the sooty roof
  Bore wealth of winter cheer ;
Of sea-fowl dried, and solands store,
And gammons of the tusky boar,
  And savoury haunch of deer.
The chimney arch projected wide ;
Above, around it, and beside,
  Were tools for housewives' hand ;
Nor wanted, in that martial day,
The implements of Scottish fray,
  The buckler, lance, and brand.

Beneath its shade, the place of state,
On oaken settle Marmion sate,
And view'd around the blazing hearth.
His followers mix in noisy mirth ;
Whom with brown ale, in jolly tide,
From ancient vessels ranged aside,
Full actively their host supplied.

IV.

Theirs was the glee of martial breast,
And laughter theirs at little jest ;
And oft Lord Marmion deign'd to aid,
And mingle in the mirth they made;
For though, with men of high degree,
The proudest of the proud was he,
Yet, train'd in camps, he knew the art
To win the soldier's hardy heart.
They love a captain to obey,
Boisterous as March, yet fresh as May;
With open hand, and brow as free,
Lover of wine and minstrelsy ;
Ever the first to scale a tower,
As venturous in a lady's bower :—
Such buxom chief shall lead his host
From India's fires to Zembla's frost.

V.

Resting upon his pilgrim staff,
  Right opposite the Palmer stood ;
His thin dark visage seen but half,
    Half hidden by his hood.
Still fix'd on Marmion was his look,
Which he, who ill such gaze could brook,
    Strove by a frown to quell ;
But not for that, though more than once
Full met their stern encountering glance,
    The Palmer's visage fell.

VI.

By fits less frequent from the crowd
Was heard the burst of laughter loud ;
For still, as squire and archer stared
    On that dark face and matted beard,
    Their glee and game declined.
All gazed at length in silence drear,
Unbroke, save when in comrade's ear
Some yeoman, wondering in his fear,
    Thus whisper'd forth his mind :—
" Saint Mary ! saw'st thou e'er such sight?
How pale his cheek, his eye how bright,

Whene'er the firebrand's fickle light
  Glances beneath his cowl!
Full on our Lord he sets his eye;
For his best palfrey, would not I
  Endure that sullen scowl."

VII.

But Marmion, as to chase the awe
Which thus had quell'd their hearts, who
      saw
The ever-varying fire-light show
That figure stern and face of woe,
  'Now call'd upon a squire:—
"Fitz-Eustace, know'st thou not some lay,
To speed the lingering night away?
  We slumber by the fire."—

VIII.

"So please you," thus the youth rejoin'd,
"Our choicest minstrel's left behind.
Ill may we hope to please your ear,
Accustom'd Constant's strains to hear.
The harp full deftly can he strike,
And wake the lover's lute alike;
To dear Saint Valentine, no thrush
Sings livelier from a spring-tide bush,
No nightingale her love-lorn tune
More sweetly warbles to the moon.
Woe to the cause, whate'er it be,
Detains from us his melody,
Lavish'd on rocks, and billows stern,
Or duller monks of Lindisfarne.
Now must I venture, as I may,
To sing his favourite roundelay."

IX.

A mellow voice Fitz-Eustace had,
The air he chose was wild and sad;
Such have I heard, in Scottish land,
Rise from the busy harvest band,
When falls before the mountaineer,
On Lowland plains, the ripen'd ear.
Now one shrill voice the notes prolong,
Now a wild chorus swells the song:
Oft have I listen'd, and stood still,
As it came soften'd up the hill,
And deem'd it the lament of men
Who languish'd for their native glen;
And thought how sad would be such sound
On Susquehana's swampy ground,

Kentucky's wood-encumber'd brake,
Or wild Ontario's boundless lake,
Where heart-sick exiles, in the strain,
Recall'd fair Scotland's hills again!

X.

SONG.

Where shall the lover rest,
  Whom the fates sever
From his true maiden's breast,
  Parted for ever!
Where, through groves deep and high,
  Sounds the far billow,
Where early violets die,
  Under the willow.

CHORUS.

Eleu loro, &c. Soft shall be his pillow.

There, through the summer day,
  Cool streams are laving;
There, while the tempests sway,
  Scarce are boughs waving;
There, thy rest shalt thou take,
  Parted for ever,
Never again to wake,
  Never, O never!

CHORUS.

Eleu loro, &c. Never, O never!

XI.

Where shall the traitor rest,
  He, the deceiver,
Who could win maiden's breast,
  Ruin, and leave her?
In the lost battle,
  Borne down by the flying,
Where mingles war's rattle
  With groans of the dying.

CHORUS.

Eleu loro, &c. There shall he be lying.

Her wing shall the eagle flap
  O'er the false-hearted;
His warm blood the wolf shall lap,
  Ere life be parted.

Shame and dishonour sit
  By his grave ever;
Blessing shall hallow it,—
  Never, O never!

CHORUS.

Eleu loro, &c.   Never. O never!

XII.

It ceased, the melancholy sound;
And silence sunk on all around.
The air was sad; but sadder still
  It fell on Marmion's ear,
And plain'd as if disgrace and ill,
  And shameful death, were near.
He drew his mantle past his face,
  Between it and the band,
And rested with his head a space,
  Reclining on his hand.
His thoughts I scan not; but I ween,
That, could their import have been seen,
The meanest groom in all the hall,
That e'er tied courser to a stall,
Would scarce have wish'd to be their prey,
For Lutterward and Fontenaye.

XIII.

High minds, of native pride and force,
Most deeply feel thy pangs, Remorse!
Fear, for their scourge, mean villains have,
Thou art the torturer of the brave!
Yet fatal strength they boast to steel
Their minds to bear the wounds they feel,
Even while they writhe beneath the smart
Of civil conflict in the heart.
For soon Lord Marmion raised his head,
And, smiling, to Fitz-Eustace said,—
" Is it not strange, that, as ye sung,
Seem'd in mine ear a death-peal rung,
Such as in nunneries they toll
For some departing sister's soul?
  Say, what may this portend?"—
Then first the Palmer silence broke,
(The livelong day he had not spoke,)
" The death of a dear friend."³⁵

XIV.

Marmion, whose steady heart and eye
Ne'er changed in worst extremity;

Marmion, whose soul could scantly brook,
Even from his King, a haughty look;
Whose accent of command controll'd,
In camps, the boldest of the bold—
Thought, look, and utterance failed him
    now,
Fall'n was his glance, and flush'd his brow;
  For either in the tone,
Or something in the Palmer's look,
So full upon his conscience strook,
  That answer he found none.
Thus oft it haps, that when within
They shrink at sense of secret sin,
  A feather daunts the brave;
A fool's wild speech confounds the wise,
And proudest princes vail their eyes
  Before their meanest slave.

XV.

Well might he falter!—By his aid
Was Constance Beverley betray'd.
Not that he augur'd of the doom,
Which on the living closed the tomb:
But, tired to hear the desperate maid
Threaten by turns, beseech, upbraid;
And wroth, because in wild despair,
She practised on the life of Clare;
Its fugitive the Church he gave,
Though not a victim, but a slave;
And deem'd restraint in convent strange
Would hide her wrongs, and her revenge.
Himself, proud Henry's favourite peer,
Held Romish thunders idle fear,
Secure his pardon he might hold,
For some slight mulct of penance-gold.
Thus judging, he gave secret way,
When the stern priests surprised their prey.
His train but deem'd the favourite page
Was left behind, to spare his age;
Or other if they deem'd, none dared
To mutter what he thought and heard:
Woe to the vassal, who durst pry
Into Lord Marmion's privacy!

XVI.

His conscience slept—he deem'd her well,
And safe secured in distant cell;
But, waken'd by her favourite lay,
And that strange Palmer's boding say,

That fell so ominous and drear,
Full on the object of his fear,
To aid remorse's venom'd throes,
Dark tales of convent-vengeance rose ;
And Constance, late betray'd and scorn'd,
All lovely on his soul return'd ;
Lovely as when, at treacherous call,
She left her convent's peaceful wall,
Crimson'd with shame, with terror mute,
Dreading alike escape, pursuit,
Till love, victorious o'er alarms,
Hid fears and blushes in his arms.

XVII.

" Alas!" he thought, "how changed that
    mien !
How changed these timid looks have been,
Since years of guilt, and of disguise,
Have steel'd her brow, and arm'd her eyes !
No more of virgin terror speaks
The blood that mantles in her cheeks ;
Fierce, and unfeminine, are there,
Frenzy for joy, for grief despair ;
And I the cause—for whom were given
Her peace on earth, her hopes in heaven !—
Would," thought he, as the picture grows,
"I on its stalk had left the rose !
Oh, why should man's success remove
The very charms that wake his love !
Her convent's peaceful solitude
Is now a prison harsh and rude.
And, pent within the narrow cell,
How will her spirit chafe and swell !
How brook the stern monastic laws !
The penance how—and I the cause !
Vigil and scourge—perchance even
    worse !"—
And twice he rose to cry, " To horse!"—
And twice his Sovereign's mandate came,
Like damp upon a kindling flame ;
And twice he thought, " Gave I not charge
She should be safe, though not at large ?
They durst not, for their island, shred
One golden ringlet from her head."

XVIII.

While thus in Marmion's bosom strove
Repentance and reviving love,
Like whirlwinds, whose contending sway
I've seen Loch Vennachar obey,

Their Host the Palmer's speech had heard,
And, talkative, took up the word :
    " Ay, reverend Pilgrim, you, who stray
From Scotland's simple land away,
    To visit realms afar,
Full often learn the art to know
Of future weal, or future woe,
    By word, or sign, or star ;
Yet might a knight his fortune hear,
If, knight-like, he despises fear,
Not far from hence ;—if fathers old
Aright our hamlet legend told."—
These broken words the menials move,
(For marvels still the vulgar love,)
And, Marmion giving license cold,
His tale the host thus gladly told :—

XIX.

The Host's Tale.

" A Clerk could tell what years have flown
Since Alexander fill'd our throne,
(Third monarch of that warlike name,)
And eke the time when here he came
To seek Sir Hugo, then our lord :
A braver never drew a sword ;
A wiser never, at the hour
Of midnight, spoke the word of power :
The same, whom ancient records call
The founder of the Goblin-Hall.[36]
I would, Sir Knight, your longer stay
Gave you that cavern to survey.
Of lofty roof, and ample size,
Beneath the castle deep it lies :
To hew the living rock profound,
The floor to pave, the arch to round,
There never toil'd a mortal arm,
It all was wrought by word and charm ;
And I have heard my grandsire say,
That the wild clamour and affray
Of those dread artisans of hell,
Who labour'd under Hugo's spell,
Sounded as loud as ocean's war,
Among the caverns of Dunbar.

XX.

" The King Lord Gifford's castle sought.
Deep labouring with uncertain thought ;
Even then he muster'd all his host,
To meet upon the western coast :

For Norse and Danish galleys plied
Their oars within the frith of Clyde.
There floated Haco's banner trim,[37]
Above Norweyan warriors grim,
Savage of heart, and large of limb;
Threatening both continent and isle,
Bute, Arran, Cunninghame, and Kyle.
Lord Gifford, deep beneath the ground,
Heard Alexander's bugle sound,
And tarried not his garb to change,
But, in his wizard habit strange,
Came forth,—a quaint and fearful sight;
His mantle lined with fox-skins white;
His high and wrinkled forehead bore
A pointed cap, such as of yore
Clerks say that Pharaoh's Magi wore:
His shoes were mark'd with cross and
   spell,
Upon his breast a pentacle;[38]
His zone, of virgin parchment thin,
Or, as some tell, of dead man's skin,
Bore many a planetary sign,
Combust, and retrograde, and trine;
And in his hand he held prepared,
A naked sword without a guard.

XXI.

" Dire dealings with the fiendish race
Had mark'd strange lines upon his face;
Vigil and fast had worn him grim,
His eyesight dazzled seem'd and dim,
As one unused to upper day;
Even his own menials with dismay
Beheld, Sir Knight, the grisly Sire,
In his unwonted wild attire;
Unwonted, for traditions run,
He seldom thus beheld the sun.—
' I know,' he said—his voice was hoarse,
And broken seem'd its hollow force,—
' I know the cause, although untold,
Why the King seeks his vassal's hold:
Vainly from me my liege would know
His kingdom's future weal or woe;
But yet, if strong his arm and heart,
His courage may do more than art.

XXII.

" ' Of middle air the demons proud,
Who ride upon the racking cloud,
Can read, in fix'd or wandering star,
The issue of events afar;
But still their sullen aid withhold,
Save when by mightier force controll'd.
Such late I summon'd to my hall;
And though so potent was the call,
That scarce the deepest nook of hell
I deem'd a refuge from the spell,
Yet, obstinate in silence still,
The haughty demon mocks my skill.
But thou—who little know'st thy might,
As born upon that blessed night[39]
When yawning graves, and dying groan,
Proclaim'd hell's empire overthrown,—
With untaught valour shalt compel
Response denied to magic spell.'
' Gramercy,' quoth our Monarch free,
' Place him but front to front with me,
And, by this good and honour'd brand,
The gift of Cœur-de-Lion's hand,
Soothly I swear, that, tide what tide,
The demon shall a buffet bide.'—
His bearing bold the wizard view'd,
And thus, well pleased, his speech re-
   new'd:—
' There spoke the blood of Malcolm!—
   mark:
Forth pacing hence, at midnight dark,
The rampart seek, whose circling crown
Crests the ascent of yonder down:
A southern entrance shalt thou find;
There halt, and there thy bugle wind,
And trust thine elfin foe to see,
In guise of thy worst enemy:
Couch then thy lance, and spur thy steed—
Upon him! and Saint George to speed!
If he go down, thou soon shalt know
Whate'er these airy sprites can show;—
If thy heart fail thee in the strife,
I am no warrant for thy life.'

XXIII.

" Soon as the midnight bell did ring,
Alone, and arm'd, forth rode the King
To that old camp's deserted round:
Sir Knight, you well might mark the
   mound,
Left hand the town,—the Pictish race,
The trench, long since, in blood did trace;

The moor around is brown and bare,
The space within is green and fair.
The spot our village children know,
For there the earliest wild-flowers grow ;
But woe betide the wandering wight,
That treads its circle in the night !
The breadth across, a bowshot clear,
Gives ample space for full career :
Opposed to the four points of heaven,
By four deep gaps are entrance given.
The southernmost our Monarch past,
Halted, and blew a gallant blast ;
And on the north, within the ring,
Appear'd the form of England's King,
Who then, a thousand leagues afar,
In Palestine waged holy war :
Yet arms like England's did he wield,
Alike the leopards in the shield,
Alike his Syrian courser's frame,
The rider's length of limb the same :
Long afterwards did Scotland know,
Fell Edward* was her deadliest foe.

XXIV.

" The vision made our Monarch start,
But soon he mann'd his noble heart,
And in the first career they ran,
The Elfin Knight fell, horse and man ;
Yet did a splinter of his lance
Through Alexander's visor glance,
And razed the skin—a puny wound.
The King, light leaping to the ground,
With naked blade his phantom foe
Compell'd the future war to show.
Of Largs he saw the glorious plain,
Where still gigantic bones remain,
    Memorial of the Danish war ;
Himself he saw, amid the field,
On high his brandish'd war-axe wield,
    And strike proud Haco from his car,
While all around the shadowy Kings
Denmark's grim ravens cower'd their
        wings.
 Tis said, that, in that awful night,
Remoter visions met his sight,
Foreshowing future conquests far,
When our sons' sons wage northern war :

---

* Edward I. of England.

A royal city, tower and spire,
Redden'd the midnight sky with fire,
And shouting crews her navy bore,
Triumphant, to the victor shore.†
Such signs may learned clerks explain,
They pass the wit of simple swain.

XXV.

" The joyful King turn'd home again,
Headed his host, and quell'd the Dane ;
But yearly, when return'd the night
Of his strange combat with the sprite,
    His wound must bleed and smart ;
Lord Gifford then would gibing say,
' Bold as ye were, my liege, ye pay
    The penance of your start.'
Long since, beneath Dunfermline's nave,
King Alexander fills his grave,
    Our Lady give him rest !
Yet still the knightly spear and shield
The Elfin Warrior doth wield,
    Upon the brown hill's breast ;10
And many a knight hath proved his chance,
In the charm'd ring to break a lance,
    But all have foully sped ;
Save two, as legends tell, and they
Were Wallace wight, and Gilbert Hay.—
Gentles, my tale is said."

XXVI.

The quaighs ‡ were deep, the liquor
        strong,
And on the tale the yeoman-throng
Had made a comment sage and long,
    But Marmion gave a sign :
And, with their lord, the squires retire ;
The rest, around the hostel fire,
    Their drowsy limbs recline ;
For pillow, underneath each head,
The quiver and the targe were laid.
Deep slumbering on the hostel floor,
Oppress'd with toil and ale, they snore :
The dying flame, in fitful change,
Threw on the group its shadows strange.

---

† An allusion to the battle of Copenhagen.
1801.
‡ Quaigh, a wooden cup.

XXVII.

Apart, and nestling in the hay
Of a waste loft, Fitz-Eustace lay;
Scarce, by the pale moonlight, were seen
The foldings of his mantle green:
Lightly he dreamt, as youth will dream,
Of sport by thicket, or by stream.
Of hawk or hound, of ring or glove,
Or, lighter yet, of lady's love.
A cautious tread his slumber broke,
And, close beside him, when he woke,
In moonbeam half, and half in gloom,
Stood a tall form, with nodding plume;
But, ere his dagger Eustace drew,
His master Marmion's voice he knew.

XXVIII.

—" Fitz-Eustace! rise, I cannot rest;
Yon churl's wild legend haunts my breast,
And graver thoughts have chafed my
    mood:
The air must cool my feverish blood;
And fain would I ride forth, to see
The scene of Elfin chivalry.
Arise, and saddle me my steed;
And, gentle Eustace, take good heed
Thou dost not rouse these drowsy slaves;
I would not, that the prating knaves
Had cause for saying, o'er their ale,
That I could credit such a tale."—
Then softly down the steps they slid,
Eustace the stable door undid,
And, darkling, Marmion's steed array'd,
While, whispering, thus the Baron said:—

XXIX.

" Did'st never, good my youth, hear tell,
    That on the hour when I was born,
Saint George, who graced my sire's
    chapelle,
Down from his steed of marble fell,
    A weary wight forlorn?
The flattering chaplains all agree,
The champion left his steed to me.
I would, the omen's truth to show,
That I could meet this Elfin Foe!
Blithe would I battle, for the right
To ask one question at the sprite:—

Vain thought! for elves, if elves there be,
An empty race, by fount or sea,
To dashing waters dance and sing,
Or round the green oak wheel their ring."
Thus speaking, he his steed bestrode,
And from the hostel slowly rode

XXX.

Fitz-Eustace followed him abroad,
And mark'd him pace the village road,
    And listen'd to his horse's tramp,
        Till, by the lessening sound,
    He judged that of the Pictish camp
        Lord Marmion sought the round.
Wonder it seem'd, in the squire's eyes,
That one, so wary held, and wise,—
Of whom 'twas said, he scarce received
For gospel, what the church believed,—
    Should, stirr'd by idle tale,
Ride forth in silence of the night,
As hoping half to meet a sprite,
    Array'd in plate and mail.
For little did Fitz-Eustace know,
That passions, in contending flow,
    Unfix the strongest mind;
Wearied from doubt to doubt to flee,
We welcome fond credulity,
    Guide confident, though blind.

XXXI.

Little for this Fitz-Eustace cared,
But, patient, waited till he heard,
At distance, prick'd to utmost speed,
The foot-tramp of a flying steed,
    Come town-ward rushing on;
First, dead, as if on turf it trode,
Then, clattering on the village road,—
In other pace than forth he yode,*
    Return'd Lord Marmion.
Down hastily he sprung from selle,
And, in his haste, wellnigh he fell;
To the squire's hand the rein he threw,
And spoke no word as he withdrew:
But yet the moonlight did betray,
The falcon-crest was soil'd with clay;
And plainly might Fitz-Eustace see,
By stains upon the charger's knee,

---

* *Yode,* used by old poets for *went.*

And his left side, that on the moor
He had not kept his footing sure.
Long musing on these wondrous signs,
At length to rest the squire reclines,
Broken and short; for still, between,
Would dreams of terror intervene:
Eustace did ne'er so blithely mark
The first notes of the morning lark.

INTRODUCTION TO CANTO FOURTH.

TO

JAMES SKENE, ESQ.*

Ashestiel, Ettrick Forest.

An ancient Minstrel sagely said,
" Where is the life which late we led?"
That motley clown in Arden wood,
Whom humorous Jacques with envy
    view'd,
Not even that clown could amplify,
On this trite text, so long as I.
Eleven years we now may tell,
Since we have known each other well;
Since, riding side by side, our hand
First drew the voluntary brand,
And sure, through many a varied scene,
Unkindness never came between.
Away these winged years have flown,
To join the mass of ages gone;
And though deep mark'd, like all below,
With chequer'd shades of joy and woe;
Though thou o'er realms and seas hast
    ranged,
Mark'd cities lost, and empires changed,
While here, at home, my narrower ken
Somewhat of manners saw, and men;
Though varying wishes, hopes, and fears,
Fever'd the progress of these years,
Yet now, days, weeks, and months, but
    seem
The recollection of a dream,
So still we glide down to the sea
Of fathomless eternity.

---

* James Skene, Esq., of Rubislaw, Aberdeenshire.

Even now it scarcely seems a day,
Since first I tuned this idle lay;
A task so often thrown aside,
When leisure graver cares denied,
That now, November's dreary gale,
Whose voice inspired my opening tale,
That same November gale once more
Whirls the dry leaves on Yarrow shore.
Their vex'd boughs streaming to the sky,
Once more our naked birches sigh,
And Blackhouse heights, and Ettrick Pen,
Have donn'd their wintry shrouds again:
And mountain dark, and flooded mead,
Bid us forsake the banks of Tweed,
Earlier than wont along the sky,
Mix'd with the rack, the snow mists fly;
The shepherd, who in summer sun,
Had something of our envy won,
As thou with pencil, I with pen,
The features traced of hill and glen;—
He who, outstretch'd the livelong day,
At ease among the heath-flowers lay,
View'd the light clouds with vacant look,
Or slumber'd o'er his tatter'd book,
Or idly busied him to guide
His angle o'er the lessen'd tide;—
At midnight now, the snowy plain
Finds sterner labour for the swain.

When red hath set the beamless sun,
Through heavy vapours dark and dun;
When the tired ploughman, dry and warm,
Hears, half asleep, the rising storm
Hurling the hail, and sleeted rain,
Against the casement's tinkling pane;
The sounds that drive wild deer, and fox,
To shelter in the brake and rocks,
Are warnings which the shepherd ask
To dismal and to dangerous task.
Oft he looks forth, and hopes, in vain,
The blast may sink in mellowing rain;
Till, dark above, and white below,
Decided drives the flaky snow,
And forth the hardy swain must go.
Long, with dejected look and whine,
To leave the hearth his dogs repine;
Whistling and cheering them to aid,
Around his back he wreathes the plaid:
His flock he gathers, and he guides,
To open downs, and mountain-sides,

Where fiercest though the tempest blow,
Least deeply lies the drift below.
The blast, that whistles o'er the fells,
Stiffens his locks to icicles;
Oft he looks back, while streaming far,
His cottage window seems a star,—
Loses its feeble gleam,—and then
Turns patient to the blast again,
And, facing to the tempest's sweep,
Drives through the gloom his lagging sheep.
If fails his heart, if his limbs fail,
Benumbing death is in the gale:
His paths, his landmarks, all unknown,
Close to the hut, no more his own,
Close to the aid he sought in vain,
The morn may find the stiffen'd swain:[41]
The widow sees, at dawning pale,
His orphans raise their feeble wail;
And, close beside him, in the snow,
Poor Yarrow, partner of their woe,
Couches upon his master's breast,
And licks his cheek to break his rest.

Who envies now the shepherd's lot,
His healthy fare, his rural cot,
His summer couch by greenwood tree,
His rustic kirn's* loud revelry,
His native hill-notes, tuned on high,
To Marion of the blithesome eye;
His crook, his scrip, his oaten reed,
And all Arcadia's golden creed?

Changes not so with us, my Skene,
Of human life the varying scene?
Our youthful summer oft we see
Dance by on wings of game and glee,
While the dark storm reserves its rage,
Against the winter of our age:
As he, the ancient Chief of Troy,
His manhood spent in peace and joy;
But Grecian fires, and loud alarms,
Call'd ancient Priam forth to arms.
Then happy those, since each must drain
His share of pleasure, share of pain,—
Then happy those, beloved of Heaven,
To whom the mingled cup is given;
Whose lenient sorrows find relief,
Whose joys are chasten'd by their grief.

* Scottish harvest-home.

And such a lot, my Skene, was thine,
When thou of late, wert doom'd to
    twine,—
Just when thy bridal hour was by,—
The cypress with the myrtle tie.
Just on thy bride her Sire had smiled,
And bless'd the union of his child,
When love must change its joyous cheer,
And wipe affection's filial tear.
Nor did the actions next his end,
Speak more the father than the friend:
Scarce had lamented Forbes[42] paid
The tribute to his Minstrel's shade;
The tale of friendship scarce was told,
Ere the narrator's heart was cold—
Far may we search before we find
A heart so manly and so kind!
But not around his honour'd urn,
Shall friends alone and kindred mourn;
The thousand eyes his care had dried,
Pour at his name a bitter tide;
And frequent falls the grateful dew,
For benefits the world ne'er knew.
If mortal charity dare claim
The Almighty's attributed name,
Inscribe above his mouldering clay,
"The widow's shield, the orphan's stay.
Nor, though it wake thy sorrow, deem
My verse intrudes on this sad theme;
For sacred was the pen that wrote,
"Thy father's friend forget thou not:"
And grateful title may I plead,
For many a kindly word and deed,
To bring my tribute to his grave:—
'Tis little—but 'tis all I have.

To thee, perchance, this rambling strain
Recalls our summer walks again;
When, doing nought,—and, to speak true,
Not anxious to find aught to do,—
The wild unbounded hills we ranged,
While oft our talk its topic changed,
And, desultory as our way,
Ranged, unconfined, from grave to gay.
Even when it flagg'd, as oft will chance,
No effort made to break its trance,
We could right pleasantly pursue
Our sports in social silence too;
Thou bravely labouring to portray
The blighted oak's fantastic spray;

I spelling o'er, with much delight,
The legend of that antique knight,
Tirante by name, yclep'd the White.
At either's feet a trusty squire,
Pandour and Camp,* with eyes of fire,
Jealous, each other's motions view'd
And scarce suppress'd their ancient feud.
The laverock† whistled from the cloud;
The stream was lively, but not loud;
From the whitethorn the May-flower shed
Its dewy fragrance round our head:
Not Ariel lived more merrily
Under the blossom'd bough, than we.

And blithesome nights, too, have been
　　　　ours,
When Winter stript the summer's bowers.
Careless we heard, what now I hear,
The wild blast sighing deep and drear,
When fires were bright, and lamps beam'd
　　　　gay,
And ladies tuned the lovely lay;
And he was held a laggard soul,
Who shunn'd to quaff the sparkling bowl.
Then he, whose absence we deplore,‡
Who breathes the gales of Devon's shore,
The longer miss'd, bewail'd the more;
And thou, and I, and dear loved R——,§
And one whose name I may not say,—
For not Mimosa's tender tree
Shrinks sooner from the touch than he,—
In merry chorus well combined,
With laughter drown'd the whistling wind.
Mirth was within; and Care without
Might gnaw her nails to hear our shout.
Not but amid the buxom scene
Some grave discourse might intervene—
Of the good horse that bore him best,
His shoulder, hoof, and arching crest:
For, like mad Tom's‖ our chiefest care,
Was horse to ride, and weapon wear.
Such nights we've had; and, though the
　　　　game
Of manhood be more sober tame,

* A favourite bull terrier of Sir Walter's.
† *Laverock*, the lark.
‡ Colin Mackenzie, of Portmore.
§ Sir William Rae, Bart., of St. Catharine's.
‖ Common name for an idiot; assumed by
Edgar in King Lear.

And though the field-day, or the drill,
Seem less important now—yet still
Such may we hope to share again.
The sprightly thought inspires my strain!
And mark, how, like a horseman true,
Lord Marmion's march I thus renew.

————

CANTO FOURTH.

The Camp.

I.

EUSTACE, I said, did blithely mark
The first notes of the merry lark.
The lark sang shrill, the cock he crew,
And loudly Marmion's bugles blew,
And with their light and lively call,
Brought groom and yeoman to the stall.
　　Whistling they came, and free of heart,
　　　　But soon their mood was changed;
　　Complaint was heard on every part,
　　　　Of something disarranged.
Some clamoured loud for armour lost;
Some brawl'd and wrangled with the
　　　　host;
" By Becket's bones," cried one, " I fear,
That some false Scot has stolen my
　　　　spear!"—
Young Blount, Lord Marmion's second
　　　　squire,
Found his steed wet with sweat and mire;
Although the rated horse-boy sware,
Last night he dress'd him sleek and fair.
While chafed the impatient squire like
　　　　thunder,
Old Hubert shouts, in fear and wonder,—
" Help, gentle Blount! help, comrades all!
Bevis lies dying in his stall:
To Marmion who the plight dare tell,
Of the good steed he loves so well?"
Gaping for fear and ruth, they saw
The charger panting on his straw;
Till one, who would seem wisest, cried,—
" What else but evil could betide,
With that cursed Palmer for our guide?
Better we had through mire and bush
Been lantern-led by Friar Rush."*

II.

Fitz-Eustace, who the cause but guess'd'
Nor wholly understood,
His comrades' clamorous plaints sup-
press'd ;
He knew Lord Marmion's mood.
Him, ere he issued forth, he sought,
And found deep plunged in gloomy
thought,
And did his tale display
Simply as if he knew of nought
To cause such disarray.
Lord Marmion gave attention cold,
Nor marvell'd at the wonders told,—
Pass'd them as accidents of course,
And bade his clarions sound to horse.

III.

Young Henry Blount, meanwhile, the cost
Had reckon'd with their Scottish host ;
And, as the charge he cast and paid,
" Ill thou deserv'st thy hire," he said ;
" Dost see, thou knave, my horse's plight ?
Fairies have ridden him all the night,
And left him in a foam !
I trust that soon a conjuring band,
With English cross and blazing brand,
Shall drive the devils from this land,
To their infernal home:
For in this haunted den, I trow,
All night they trample to and fro."
The laughing host looked on the hire,—
" Gramercy, gentle southern squire,
And if thou comest among the rest,
With Scottish broadsword to be blest,
Sharp be the brand, and sure the blow,
And short the pang to undergo."
Here stay'd their talk,—for Marmion
Gave now the signal to set on.
The Palmer showing forth the way,
They journey'd all the morning day.

IV.

The green-sward way was smooth and
good,
Through Humbie's and through Saltoun's
wood ;
A forest glade, which, varying still,
Here gave a view of dale and hill.

There narrower closed, till over head,
A vaulted screen the branches made.
" A pleasant path," Fitz-Eustace said ;
" Such as where errant-knights might see
Adventures of high chivalry ;
Might meet some damsel flying fast,
With hair unbound and looks aghast ;
And smooth and level course were here,
In her defence to break a spear.
Here, too, are twilight nooks and dells ;
And oft, in such, the story tells,
The damsel kind, from danger freed,
Did grateful pay her champion's meed."
He spoke to cheer Lord Marmion's mind :
Perchance to show his lore design'd ;
For Eustace much had pored
Upon a huge romantic tome,
In the hall window of his home,
Imprinted at the antique dome
Of Caxton, or De Worde.*
Therefore he spoke,—but spoke in vain,
For Marmion answer'd nought again.

V.

Now sudden, distant trumpets shrill,
In notes prolong'd by wood and hill,
Were heard to echo far ;
Each ready archer grasp'd his bow,
But by the flourish soon they know,
They breathed no point of war.
Yet cautious, as in foeman's land,
Lord Marmion's order speeds the band,
Some opener ground to gain ;
And scarce a furlong had they rode,
When thinner trees, receding, show'd
A little woodland plain.
Just in that advantageous glade,
The halting troop a line had made,
As forth from the opposing shade
Issued a gallant train.

VI.

First came the trumpets at whose clang
So late the forest echoes rang ;
On prancing steeds they forward press'd,
With scarlet mantle, azure vest ;

---

* William Caxton was the earliest English
printer ; born in Kent, A.D. 1412 ; Wynken
de Worde was his successor.

Each at his trump a banner wore,
Which Scotland's royal scutcheon bore:
Heralds and pursuivants, by name
Bute, Islay, Marchmount, Rothsay, came,
In painted tabards, proudly showing
Gules, Argent, Or, and Azure glowing,
Attendant on a King-at-arms,
Whose hand the armorial truncheon held
That feudal strife had often quell'd,
When wildest its alarms.

VII.

He was a man of middle age;
In aspect manly, grave, and sage,
As on King's errand come;
But in the glances of his eye,
A penetrating, keen, and sly
Expression found its home;
The flash of that satiric rage,
Which, bursting on the early stage,
Branded the vices of the age,
And broke the keys of Rome.
On milk-white palfrey forth he paced;
His cap of maintenance was graced
With the proud heron-plume.
From his steed's shoulder, loin, and
breast,
Silk housings swept the ground,
With Scotland's arms, device, and
crest,
Embroider'd round and round.
The double tressure might you see,
First by Achaius borne,
The thistle and the fleur-de-lis,
And gallant unicorn.
So bright the King's armorial coat,
That scarce the dazzled eye could note,
In living colours, blazon'd brave,
The Lion, which his title gave;
A train which well beseem'd his state,
But all unarm'd, around him wait.
Still is thy name in high account,
And still thy verse has charms,
Sir David Lindesay of the Mount,
Lord Lion King-at-arms![44]

VIII.

Down from his horse did Marmion spring,
Soon as he saw the Lion-King;
For well the stately Baron knew
To him such courtesy was due,
Whom royal James himself had crown'd,
And on his temples placed the round
Of Scotland's ancient diadem:
And wet his brow with hallow'd wine,
And on his finger given to shine
The emblematic gem.
Their mutual greetings duly made,
The Lion thus his message said:—
"Though Scotland's King hath deeply
swore
Ne'er to knit faith with Henry more,
And strictly hath forbid resort
From England to his royal court;
Yet, for he knows Lord Marmion's name,
And honours much his warlike fame,
My liege hath deem'd it shame, and lack
Of courtesy, to turn him back;
And, by his order, I, your guide,
Must lodging fit and fair provide,
Till finds King James meet time to see
The flower of English chivalry."

IX.

Though inly chafed at this delay,
Lord Marmion bears it as he may,
The Palmer, his mysterious guide,
Beholding thus his place supplied,
Sought to take leave in vain;
Strict was the Lion-King's command,
That none, who rode in Marmion's band,
Should sever from the train:
"England has here enow of spies
In Lady Heron's witching eyes;"
To Marchmount thus, apart, he said,
But fair pretext to Marmion made.
The right hand path they now decline,
And trace against the stream the Tyne.

X.

At length up that wild dale they wind,
Where Crichtoun Castle[45] crowns the
bank;
For there the Lion's care assigned
A lodging meet for Marmion's rank.
That Castle rises on the steep
Of the green vale of Tyne:
And far beneath, where slow they creep,
From pool to eddy, dark and deep,
Where alders moist, and willows weep,

You hear her streams repine.
The towers in different ages rose;
Their various architecture shows
    The builders' various hands;
A mighty mass, that could oppose,
When deadliest hatred fired its foes,
    The vengeful Douglas bands.

XI.

Crichtoun! though now thy miry court
    But pens the lazy steer and sheep,
    Thy turrets rude, and totter'd Keep,
Have been the minstrel's loved resort.
Oft have I traced, within thy fort,
    Of mouldering shields the mystic sense,
    Scutcheons of honour, or pretence,
Quarter'd in old armorial sort,
    Remains of rude magnificence.
Nor wholly yet had time defaced
    Thy lordly gallery fair;
Nor yet the stony cord unbraced,
Whose twisted knots, with roses laced,
    Adorn thy ruin'd stair.
Still rises unimpair'd below,
The court-yard's graceful portico;
Above its cornice, row and row
    Of fair hewn facets richly show
        Their pointed diamond form,
    Though there but houseless cattle go,
        To shield them from the storm.
And, shuddering, still may we explore,
    Where oft whilom were captives pent,
    The darkness of thy Massy More;
    Or, from thy grass-grown battlement,
May trace, in undulating line,
The sluggish mazes of the Tyne.

XII.

Another aspect Crichtoun show'd,
As through its portal Marmion rode;
But yet 'twas melancholy state
Received him at the outer gate;
For none were in the Castle then,
But women, boys, or aged men.
With eyes scarce dried, the sorrowing
        dame,
To welcome noble Marmion, came;
Her son, a stripling twelve years old,
Proffer'd the Baron's rein to hold;

For each man that could draw a sword
Had march'd that morning with their lord,
Earl Adam Hepburn,[46] he who died
On Flodden, by his sovereign's side.
Long may his Lady look in vain!
She ne'er shall see his gallant train,
Come sweeping back through Crichtoun-
        Dean.
'Twas a brave race, before the name
Of hated Bothwell stain'd their fame.

XIII.

And here two days did Marmion rest,
    With every rite that honour claims,
Attended as the King's own guest:—
    Such the command of Royal James,
Who marshall'd then his land's array,
Upon the Borough-moor that lay.
Perchance he would not foeman's eye
Upon his gathering host should pry,
Till full prepared was every band
To march against the English land.
Here while they dwelt, did Lindesay's wit
Oft cheer the Baron's moodier fit;
And, in his turn, he knew to prize
Lord Marmion's powerful mind, and
        wise.—
Train'd in the lore of Rome and Greece,
And policies of war and peace.

XIV.

It chanced, as fell the second night,
    That on the battlements they walk'd,
And, by the slowly fading light,
    Of varying topics talked;
And, unaware, the Herald-bard
Said, Marmion might his toil have spared,
    In travelling so far;
For that a messenger from heaven
In vain to James had counsel given
    Against the English war;[47]
And, closer question'd, thus he told
A tale, which chronicles of old
In Scottish story have enroll'd:—

XV.

Sir David Lindesay's Tale.

" Of all the palaces so fair,
    Built for the royal dwelling,

In Scotland, far beyond compare
  Linlithgow is excelling;
And in its park in joyal June,
How sweet the merry linnet's tune,
  How blithe the blackbird's lay!
The wild-buckbells[48] from ferny brake,
The coot dives merry on the lake,
The saddest heart might pleasure take
  To see all nature gay.
But June is to our sovereign dear
The heaviest month in all the year:
Too well his cause of grief you know,
June saw his father's overthrow.[49]
Woe to the traitors, who could bring
The princely boy against his King!
Still in his conscience burns the sting.
In offices as strict as Lent,
King James's June is ever spent

XVI.

" When last this ruthful month was come,
And in Linlithgow's holy dome
  The King, as wont, was praying;
While, for his royal father's soul,
The chanters sung, the bells did toll,
  The Bishop mass was saying—
For now the year brought round again
The day the luckless king was slain—
In Katharine's aisle the Monarch knelt,
With sackcloth-shirt, and iron belt,
  And eyes with sorrow streaming;
Around him in their stalls of state,
The Thistle's Knight-Companions sate,
  Their banners o'er them beaming.
I too was there, and, sooth to tell,
Bedeafen'd with the jangling knell,
Was watching where the sunbeams fell,
  Through the stain'd casement gleaming;
But, while I mark'd what next befell,
  It seem'd as I were dreaming.
Stepp'd from the crowd a ghostly wight,
In azure gown, with cincture white;
His forehead bald, his head was bare,
Down hung at length his yellow hair.—
Now, mock me not, when, good my Lord,
I pledge to you my knightly word,
That, when I saw his placid grace,
His simple majesty of face,
His solemn bearing, and his pace

So stately gliding on,—
Seem'd to me ne'er did limner paint
So just an image of the Saint,
Who propp'd the Virgin in her faint,—
  The loved Apostle John!

XVII.

" He stepp'd before the Monarch's chair,
And stood with rustic plainness there,
  And little reverence made;
Nor head, nor body, bow'd nor bent,
But on the desk his arm he leant,
  And words like these he said,
In a low voice, but never tone,
So thrill'd through vein, and nerve and
    bone:—
' My mother sent me from afar,
Sir King, to warn thee not to war,—
  Woe waits on thine array;
If war thou wilt, of woman fair,
Her witching wiles and wanton snare,
James Stuart, doubly warn'd, beware:
  God keep thee as he may!'
    The wondering Monarch seem'd to
      seek
      For answer, and found none;
    And when he raised his head to speak,
      The monitor was gone.
The Marshal and myself had cast
To stop him as he outward pass'd;
But, lighter than the whirlwind's blast,
  He vanish'd from our eyes,
Like sunbeam on the billow cast,
  That glances but, and dies."

XVIII.

While Lindesay told his marvel
    strange,
  The twilight was so pale,
He mark'd not Marmion's colour
    change,
  While listening to the tale;
But, after a suspended pause,
The Baron spoke:—" Of Nature's
    laws
  So strong I held the force,
That never superhuman cause
  Could e'er control their course.

And, three days since, had judged your
  aim
Was but to make your guest your game.
But I have seen, since past the Tweed,
What much has changed my sceptic creed,
And made me credit aught."—He staid,
And seem'd to wish his words unsaid:
But, by that strong emotion press'd,
Which prompts us to unload our breast,
  Even when discovery's pain,
To Lindesay did at length unfold
The tale his village host had told,
  At Gifford, to his train.
Nought of the Palmer says he there,
And nought of Constance, or of Clare;
The thoughts, which broke his sleep, he
  seems
To mention but as feverish dreams.

XIX.

"In vain," said he, "to rest I spread
My burning limbs, and couch'd my head:
  Fantastic thoughts return'd;
And, by their wild dominion led,
  My heart within me burn'd.
So sore was the delirious goad,
I took my steed, and forth I rode,
And, as the moon shone bright and cold,
Soon reach'd the camp upon the wold.
The southern entrance I pass'd through,
And halted, and my bugle blew.
Methought an answer met my ear,—
Yet was the blast so low and drear,
So hollow, and so faintly blown,
It might be echo of my own.

XX.

"Thus judging, for a little space
I listen'd, ere I left the place;
  But scarce could trust my eyes,
Nor yet can think they served me true,
When sudden in the ring I view,
In form distinct of shape and hue,
  A mounted champion rise.—
I've fought, Lord-Lion, many a day,
In single fight, and mix'd affray,
And ever, I myself may say,
  Have borne me as a knight;
But when this unexpected foe

Seem'd starting from the gulf below,—
I care not though the truth I show,—
  I trembled with affright;
And as I placed in rest my spear,
My hand so shook for very fear,
  I scarce could couch it right.

XXI.

"Why need my tongue the issue tell?
We ran our course,—my charger fell;—
What could he 'gainst the shock of hell?—
  I roll'd upon the plain.
High o'er my head, with threatening hand,
The spectre shook his naked brand,—
  Yet did the worst remain:
My dazzled eyes I upward cast,—
Not opening hell itself could blast
  Their sight, like what I saw!
Full on his face the moonbeam strook,—
A face could never be mistook!
I knew the stern vindictive look,
  And held my breath for awe.
I saw the face of one who, fled
To foreign climes, has long been dead,—
  I well believe the last;
For ne'er, from vizor raised, did stare
A human warrior, with a glare
  So grimly and so ghast.
Thrice o'er my head he shook the blade;
But when to good Saint George I pray'd,
(The first time e'er I ask'd his aid,)
  He plunged it in the sheath;
And, on his courser mounting light,
He seem'd to vanish from my sight:
The moonbeam droop'd, and deepest night
  Sunk down upon the heath.—
'Twere long to tell what cause I have
  To know his face, that met me there,
Call'd by his hatred from the grave,
  To cumber upper air:
Dead or alive, good cause had he
To be my mortal enemy."

XXII.

Marvell'd Sir David of the Mount;
Then, learn'd in story, 'gan recount
  Such chance had happ'd of old,
When once, near Norham, there did fight
A spectre fell of fiendish might,
  In likeness of a Scottish knight,

With Brian Bulmer bold,
And train'd him nigh to disallow
The aid of his baptismal vow.
" And such a phantom, too, 'tis said,
With Highland broadsword, targe, and
　　plaid,
　And fingers, red with gore,
Is seen in Rothiemurcus glade,
Or where the sable pine-trees shade
Dark Tomantoul, and Auchnaslaid,
　Dromouchty, or Glenmore.
And yet, whate'er such legends say,
Of warlike demon, ghost, or fay,
　On mountain, moor, or plain,
Spotless in faith, in bosom bold,
True son of chivalry should hold,
　These midnight terrors vain ;
For seldom have such spirits power
To harm, save in the evil hour,
When guilt we meditate within,
Or harbour unrepented sin."—
Lord Marmion turn'd him half aside,
And twice to clear his voice he tried,
　Then press'd Sir David's hand,—
But nought, at length, in answer said ;
And here their farther converse staid,
　Each ordering that his band
Should bowne them with the rising day,
To Scotland's camp to take their way.—
　Such was the King's command.

XXIII.

Early they took Dun-Edin's road,
And I could trace each step they trode.
Hill, brook, nor dell, nor rock, nor stone,
Lies on the path to me unknown.
Much might it boast of storied lore ;
But, passing such digression o'er,
Suffice it that the route was laid
Across the furzy hills of Braid.
They pass'd the glen and scanty rill,
And climb'd the opposing bank, until
They gain'd the top of Blackford Hill.

XXIV.

Blackford ! on whose uncultured
　　breast,
　Among the broom, and thorn, and
　　whin,

A truant-boy, I sought the nest,
Or listed, as I lay at rest,
　While rose, on breezes thin,
The murmur of the city crowd,
And, from his steeple jangling loud,
　Saint Giles's mingling din.
Now, from the summit to the plain,
Waves all the hill with yellow grain ;
　And o'er the landscape as I look,
Nought do I see unchanged remain,
　Save the rude cliffs and chiming brook.
To me they make a heavy moan,
Of early friendships past and gone.

XXV.

But different far the change has been,
　Since Marmion, from the crown
Of Blackford, saw that martial scene
　Upon the bent so brown :
Thousand pavilions, white as snow,
Spread all the Borough-moor[30] below,
　Upland, and dale, and down :—
A thousand did I say ?　I ween,
Thousands on thousands there were seen,
That chequer'd all the heath between
　The streamlet and the town ;
In crossing ranks extending far,
Forming a camp irregular ;
Oft giving way, where still there stood
Some relics of the old oak wood,
That darkly huge did intervene,
And tamed the glaring white with green :
In these extended lines there lay
A martial kingdom's vast array.

XXVI.

For from Hebudes, dark with rain,
To eastern Lodon's fertile plain,
And from the Southern Redswire edge,
To farthest Rosse's rocky ledge ;
From west to east, from south to north,
Scotland sent all her warriors forth.
Marmion might hear the mingled hum
Of myriads up the mountain come ;
The horses' tramp, and tingling clank,
Where chiefs review'd their vassal rank,
　And charger's shrilling neigh ;
And see the shifting lines advance,

While frequent flash'd, from shield and
    lance,
The sun's reflected ray.

XXVII.

Thin curling in the morning air,
The wreaths of failing smoke declare
To embers now the brands decay'd,
Where the night-watch their fires had
    made.
They saw, slow rolling on the plain,
Full many a baggage-cart and wain,
And dire artillery's clumsy car,
By sluggish oxen tugg'd to war;
And there were Borthwick's Sisters
    Seven,*
And culverins which France had given.
Ill-omen'd gift! the guns remain
The conqueror's spoil on Flodden plain.

XXVIII.

Nor mark'd they less, where in the air
A thousand streamers flaunted fair;
    Various in shape, device, and hue,
    Green, sanguine, purple, red, and blue,
Broad, narrow, swallow-tail'd, and
    square,
Scroll, pennon, pensil, bandrol, there
    O'er the pavilions flew.
Highest and midmost, was descried
The royal banner floating wide;
    The staff, a pine-tree, strong and
        straight,
Pitch'd deeply in a massive stone,
Which still in memory is shown,
    Yet bent beneath the standard's weight
    Whene'er the western wind unroll'd,
With toil, the huge and cumbrous fold,
And gave to view the dazzling field,
Where, in proud Scotland's royal shield,
    The ruddy lion ramp'd in gold.[51]

XXIX.

Lord Marmion view'd the landscape
    bright,—
He view'd it with a chief's delight,—
    Until within him burn'd his heart,
    And lightning from his eye did part,

* Seven culverins, so called from him who
cast them.

As on the battle-day;
    Such glance did falcon never dart,
    When stooping on his prey.
" Oh! well, Lord-Lion, hast thou said,
Thy King from warfare to dissuade
    Were but a vain essay:
For, by St. George, were that host mine,
Not power infernal nor divine,
Should once to peace my soul incline,
Till I had dimm'd their armour's shine
    In glorious battle-fray!"
Answer'd the Bard, of milder mood:
" Fair is the sight,—and yet 'twere good,
    That kings would think withal,
When peace and wealth their land has
        bless'd,
'Tis better to sit still at rest,
    Than rise, perchance to fall."

XXX.

Still on the spot Lord Marmion stay'd,
For fairer scene he ne'er survey'd.
    When sated with the martial show
    That peopled all the plain below,
    The wandering eye could o'er it go,
    And mark the distant city glow
        With gloomy splendour red;
    For on the smoke-wreaths, huge and
        slow,
    That round her sable turrets flow,
        The morning beams were shed,
    And tinged them with a lustre proud,
    Like that which streaks a thunder-cloud.
Such dusky grandeur clothed the height,
Where the huge Castle holds its state,
    And all the steep slope down,
Whose ridgy back heaves to the sky,
Piled deep and massy, close and high,
    Mine own romantic town!
But northward far, with purer blaze,
On Ochil mountains fell the rays,
And as each heathy top they kissed,
It gleam'd a purple amethyst.
Yonder the shores of Fife you saw;
Here Preston-Bay and Berwick-Law:
    And, broad between them roll'd,
The gallant Frith the eye might note,
Whose islands on its bosom float,
    Like emeralds chased in gold.
Fitz-Eustace' heart felt closely pent;

As if to give his rapture vent,
The spur he to his charger lent,
    And raised his bridle hand,
And, making demi-volte in air,
Cried, " Where's the coward that would
        not dare
    To fight for such a land ?"
The Lindesay smiled his joy to see ;
Nor Marmion's frown repress'd his glee.

XXXI.

Thus while they look'd, a flourish proud,
Where mingled trump and clarion loud,
    And fife, and kettle-drum,
And sackbut deep, and psaltery,
And war-pipe with discordant cry,
And cymbal clattering to the sky,
Making wild music bold and high,
    Did up the mountain come ;
The whilst the bells, with distant chime,
Merrily told the hour of prime,
And thus the Lindesay spoke :
" Thus clamour still the war-notes when
The king to mass his way has ta'en,
Or to St. Katharine's of Sienne,
    Or Chapel of Saint Rocque.
To you they speak of martial fame ;
But me remind of peaceful game,
    When blither was their cheer,
Thrilling in Falkland-woods the air,
In signal none his steed should spare,
But strive which foremost might repair
    To the downfall of the deer.

XXXII.

"Nor less," he said,—"when looking forth,
I view yon Empress of the North
    Sit on her hilly throne ;
Her palace's imperial bowers,
Her castle, proof to hostile powers,
Her stately halls and holy towers—
    Nor less," he said, " I moan,
To think what woe mischance may bring,
And how these merry bells may ring
The death-dirge of our gallant king ;
    Or with the larum call
The burghers forth to watch and ward,
'Gainst Southern sack and fires to guard
    Dun-Edin's leaguer'd wall.—

But not for my presaging thought,
Dream conquest sure, or cheaply bought !
    Lord Marmion, I say nay :
God is the guider of the field,
He breaks the champion's spear and
        shield,—
    But thou thyself shalt say,
When joins yon host in deadly stowre,
That England's dames must weep in bower,
    Her monks the death-mass sing ;
For never saw'st thou such a power
    Led on by such a King."—
And now, down winding to the plain,
The barriers of the camp they gain,
    And there they made a stay.—
There stays the Minstrel, till he fling
His hand o'er every Border string,
And fit his harp the pomp to sing,
Of Scotland's ancient Court and King,
    In the succeeding lay.

INTRODUCTION TO CANTO FIFTH.

TO

GEORGE ELLIS, ESQ.[*]

Edinburgh.

WHEN dark December glooms the day,
And takes our autumn joys away ;
When short and scant the sunbeam throws,
Upon the weary waste of snows,
A cold and profitless regard,
Like patron on a needy bard ;
When silvan occupation's done,
And o'er the chimney rests the gun,
And hang, in idle trophy, near,
The game-pouch, fishing-rod, and spear ;
When wiry terrier, rough and grim,
And greyhound, with his length of limb,
And pointer, now employ'd no more,
Cumber our parlour's narrow floor ;
When in his stall the impatient steed
Is long condemn'd to rest and feed ;

---

[*] The learned editor of the "Specimens of
Ancient English Romances."

When from our snow-encircled home,
Scarce cares the hardiest step to roam,
Since path is none, save that to bring
The needful water from the spring ;
When wrinkled news-page, thrice conn'd
 o'er,
Beguiles the dreary hour no more,
And darkling politician, cross'd,
Inveighs against the lingering post,
And answering housewife sore complains
Of carriers' snow-impeded wains ;
When such the country cheer, I come,
Well pleased, to seek our city home ;
For converse, and for books, to change
The Forest's melancholy range,
And welcome, with renew'd delight,
The busy day and social night.

Not here need my desponding rhyme
Lament the ravages of time,
As erst by Newark's riven towers,
And Ettrick stripp'd of forest bowers.
True,—Caledonia's Queen is changed,[52]
Since on her dusky summit ranged,
Within its steepy limits pent,
By bulwark, line, and battlement,
And flanking towers, and laky flood,
Guarded and garrison'd she stood,
Denying entrance or resort,
Save at each tall embattled port ;
Above whose arch, suspended, hung
Portcullis spiked with iron prong.
That long is gone,—but not so long
Since, early closed, and opening late,
Jealous revolved the studded gate,
Whose task, from eve to morning tide,
A wicket churlishly supplied.
Stern then, and steel-girt was thy brow,
Dun-Edin ! O, how alter'd now,
When safe amid thy mountain court
Thou sit'st, like Empress at her sport,
And liberal, unconfined, and free,
Flinging thy white arms to the sea.
For thy dark cloud, with umber'd lower,
That hung o'er cliff, and lake, and tower,
Thou gleam'st against the western ray
Ten thousand lines of brighter day.

Not she, the Championess of old,
In Spenser's magic tale enroll'd,
She, for the charmed spear renown'd,
Which forced each knight to kiss the
 ground,—
Not she more changed, when placed at rest,
What time she was Malbecco's guest,
She gave to flow her maiden vest ;
When from the corslet's grasp relieved,
Free to the sight her bosom heaved ;
Sweet was her blue eye's modest smile,
Erst hidden by the aventayle ;
And down her shoulders graceful roll'd
Her locks profuse, of paly gold.
They who whilom, in midnight fight,
Had marvell'd at her matchless might,
No less her maiden charms approved,
But looking liked, and liking loved.
The sight could jealous pangs beguile,
And charm Malbecco's cares a while ;
And he, the wandering Squire of Dames,
Forgot his Columbella's claims,
And passion, erst unknown, could gain
The breast of blunt Sir Satyrane ;
Nor durst light Paridel advance,
Bold as he was, a looser glance.
She charm'd, at once, and tamed the heart,
Incomparable Britomarte !*

So thou, fair City ! disarray'd
Of battled wall, and rampart's aid,
As stately seem'st, but lovelier far
Than in that panoply of war.
Nor deem that from thy fenceless throne
Strength and security are flown ;
Still, as of yore, Queen of the North !
Still canst thou send thy children forth.
Ne'er readier at alarm-bell's call
Thy burghers rose to man thy wall,
Than now, in danger, shall be thine,
Thy dauntless voluntary line ;
For fosse and turret proud to stand,
Their breasts the bulwarks of the land.
Thy thousands, train'd to martial toil,
Full red would stain their native soil,
Ere from thy mural crown there fell
The slightest knosp, or pinnacle.
And if it come,—as come it may,
Dun-Edin ! that eventful day,—

---

* The Maiden Knight in Spenser's "Fairy Queen," book iii. canto 9.

Renown'd for hospitable deed,
That virtue much with Heaven may plead,
In patriarchal times whose care
Descending angels deign'd to share;
That claim may wrestle blessings down
On those who fight for The Good Town,
Destined in every age to be
Refuge of injured royalty;
Since first, when conquering York arose,
To Henry meek she gave repose,*
Till late, with wonder, grief, and awe,
Great Bourbon's relics, sad she saw.

Truce to these thoughts!—for, as they
    rise,
How gladly I avert mine eyes,
Bodings, or true or false, to change,
For Fiction's fair romantic range,
Or for tradition's dubious light,
That hovers 'twixt the day and night:
Dazzling alternately and dim,
Her wavering lamp I'd rather trim,
Knights, squires, and lovely dames to see,
Creation of my fantasy,
Than gaze abroad on reeky fen,
And make of mists invading men.
Who loves not more the night of June
Than dull December's gloomy noon?
The moonlight than the fog of frost?
And can we say, which cheats the most?

But who shall teach my harp to gain
A sound of the romantic strain,
Whose Anglo-Norman tones whilere
Could win the royal Henry's ear,
Famed Beauclerc call'd, for that he loved
The minstrel† and his lay approved?
Who shall these lingering notes redeem,
Decaying on Oblivion's stream;
Such notes as from the Breton tongue
Marie‡ translated, Blondel sung?—
O! born, Time's ravage to repair,
And make the dying muse thy care;

Who, when his scythe her hoary foe
Was poising for the final blow,
The weapon from his hand could wring,
And break his glass, and shear his wing,
And bid, reviving in his strain,
The gentle poet live again;
Thou, who canst give to lightest lay
An unpedantic moral gay,
Nor less the dullest theme bid flit
On wings of unexpected wit;
In letters as in life approved,
Example honour'd, and beloved,—
Dear ELLIS! to the bard impart
A lesson of thy magic art,
To win at once the head and heart,—
At once to charm, instruct and mend,
My guide, my pattern, and my friend!

Such minstrel lesson to bestow
Be long thy pleasing task,—but, O!
No more by thy example teach,
—What few can practise, all can preach,—
With even patience to endure
Lingering disease, and painful cure,
And boast affliction's pangs subdued
By mild and manly fortitude.
Enough, the lesson has been given:
Forbid the repetition, Heaven!

Come listen, then! for thou hast
    known,
And loved the Minstrel's varying tone,
Who, like his Border sires of old,
Waked a wild measure rude and bold,
Till Windsor's oaks, and Ascot plain,
With wonder heard the northern strain.
Come listen! bold in thy applause,
The bard shall scorn pedantic laws;
And, as the ancient art could stain
Achievements on the storied pane,
Irregularly traced and plann'd,
But yet so glowing and so grand,—
So shall he strive, in changeful hue,
Field, feast, and combat, to renew,
And loves, and arms, and harpers' glee,
And all the pomp of chivalry.

* Henry VI. of England, who sought re-
fuge in Scotland after the fatal battle of
Towton. "The Meek Usurper," *see* Gray.
† Philip de Than.
‡ Marie of France, who translated the
"Lais" of Brittany into French. She re-
sided at the Court of Henry III. of England,
to whom she dedicated her book.

CANTO FIFTH.

The Court.

I.

THE train has left the hills of Braid;
The barrier guard have open made
(So Lindesay bade) the palisade,
    That closed the tented ground;
Their men the warders backward drew,
And carried pikes as they rode through,
    Into its ample bound.
Fast ran the Scottish warriors there,
Upon the Southern band to stare,
And envy with their wonder rose,
To see such well-appointed foes;
Such length of shafts, such mighty bows,
So huge, that many simply thought,
But for a vaunt such weapons wrought;
And little deem'd their force to feel,
Through links of mail, and plates of steel,
When rattling upon Flodden vale,
The cloth-yard arrows flew like hail.[53]

II.

Nor less did Marmion's skilful view
Glance every line and squadron through;
And much he marvell'd one small land
Could marshal forth such various band:
    For men-at-arms were here,
Heavily sheathed in mail and plate,
Like iron towers for strength and weight,
On Flemish steeds of bone and height,
    With battle-axe and spear.
Young knights and squires, a lighter train,
Practised their chargers on the plain,
By aid of leg, of hand, and rein,
    Each warlike feat to show,
To pass, to wheel, the croupe to gain,
And high curvett, that not in vain
The sword sway might descend amain
    On foeman's casque below.
He saw the hardy burghers there
March arm'd, on foot, with faces bare,[54]
    For vizor they wore none,
Nor waving plume, nor crest of knight;
But burnished were their corslets bright,
Their brigantines, and gorgets light,
    Like very silver shone.

Long pikes they had for standing fight,
    Two-handed swords they wore,
And many wielded mace of weight,
    And bucklers bright they bore.

III.

On foot the yeoman too, but dress'd
In his steel-jack, a swarthy vest,
    With iron quilted well;
Each at his back (a slender store)
His forty days' provision bore,
    As feudal statutes tell.
His arms were halbert, axe, or spear,[55]
A crossbow there, a hagbut here,
    A dagger-knife, and brand.
Sober he seem'd, and sad of cheer,
As loth to leave his cottage dear,
And march to foreign strand;
Or musing, who would guide his steer,
    To till the fallow land.
Yet deem not in his thoughtful eye
Did aught of dastard terror lie;
    More dreadful far his ire,
Than theirs, who, scorning danger's name,
In eager mood to battle came,
Their valour like light straw on flame,
    A fierce but fading fire.

IV.

Not so the Borderer:—bred to war,
He knew the battle's din afar,
    And joy'd to hear it swell.
His peaceful day was slothful ease;
Nor harp, nor pipe, his ear could please
    Like the loud slogan yell.
On active steed, with lance and blade,
The light-arm'd pricker plied his trade,—
    Let nobles fight for fame;
Let vassals follow where they lead,
Burghers to guard their townships bleed,
    But war's the Borderer's game.
Their gain, their glory, their delight,
To sleep the day, maraud the night,
    O'er mountain, moss, and moor;
Joyful to fight they took their way,
Scarce caring who might win the day,
    Their booty was secure.
These, as Lord Marmion's train pass'd by,
Look'd on at first with careless eye,

Nor marvell'd aught, well taught to know
The form and force of English bow.
But when they saw the Lord array'd
In splendid arms and rich brocade,
Each Borderer to his kinsman said,—
  " Hist, Ringan ! seest thou there !
Canst guess which road they'll home-
    ward ride ?—
O ! could we but on Border side,
By Eusedale glen, or Liddell's tide,
  Beset a prize so fair !
That fangless Lion, too, their guide,
Might chance to lose his glistering h de ;
Brown Maudlin, of that doublet pied,
  Could make a kirtle rare."

V.

Next, Marmion mark'd the Celtic race,
Of different language, form, and face,
  A various race of man ;
Just then the Chiefs their tribes array'd,
And wild and garish semblance made,
The chequer'd trews, and belted plaid,
And varying notes the war-pipes bray'd,
  To every varying clan ;
Wild through their red or sable hair
Look'd out their eyes with savage stare,
  On Marmion as he pass'd ;
Their legs above the knee were bare ;
Their frame was sinewy, short, and spare,
  And harden'd to the blast ;
Of taller race, the chiefs they own
Were by the eagle's plumage known.
The hunted red-deer's undress'd hide
Their hairy buskins well supplied ;
The graceful bonnet deck'd their head :
Back from their shoulders hung the plaid ;
A broadsword of unwieldy length,
A dagger proved for edge and strength,
  A studded targe they wore,
And quivers, bows, and shafts,—but, O !
Short was the shaft, and weak the bow,
  To that which England bore.
The Isles-men carried at their backs
The ancient Danish battle-axe.
They raised a wild and wondering cry,
As with his guide rode Marmion by.
Loud were their clamouring tongues, as
    when
The clanging sea-fowl leave the fen,

And, with their cries discordant mix'd,
Grumbled and yell'd the pipes betwixt.

VI.

Thus through the Scottish camp they
    pass'd,
And reach'd the City gate at last,
Where all around, a wakeful guard,
Arm'd burghers kept their watch and ward.
Well had they cause of jealous fear,
When lay encamp'd, in field so near,
The Borderer and the Mountaineer.
As through the bustling streets they go,
All was alive with martial show :
At every turn, with dinning clang,
The armourer's anvil clash'd and rang ;
Or toil'd the swarthy smith, to wheel
The bar that arms the charger's heel ;
Or axe, or falchion, to the side
Of jarring grindstone was applied.
Page, groom, and squire, with hurrying
    pace,
Through street, and lane, and market-
    place,
  Bore lance, or casque, or sword ;
While burghers, with important face,
  Described each new-come lord,
Discuss'd his lineage, told his name,
His following, and his warlike fame.
The Lion led to lodging meet,
Which high o'erlook'd the crowded street ;
  There must the Baron rest,
Till past the hour of vesper tide,
And then to Holy-Rood must ride,—
  Such was the King's behest.
Meanwhile the Lion's care assigns
A banquet rich, and costly wines,
  To Marmion and his train ;[16]
And when the appointed hour succeeds,
The Baron dons his peaceful weeds,
And following Lindesay as he leads,
  The palace-halls they gain.

VII.

Old Holy-Rood rung merrily,
That night, with wassell, mirth, and glee ;
King James within her princely bower,
Feasted the Chiefs of Scotland's power,
Summon'd to spend the parting hour ;
For he had charged, that his array

Should southward march by break of day.
Well loved that splendid monarch aye
   The banquet and the song,
By day the tourney, and by night
The merry dance, traced fast and light,
The maskers quaint, the pageant bright,
   The revel loud and long.
This feast outshone his banquets past,
It was his blithest—and his last
The dazzling lamps, from gallery gay,
Cast on the Court a dancing ray;
Here to the harp did minstrels sing;
There ladies touch'd a softer string;
With long-ear'd cap, and motley vest,
The licensed fool retail'd his jest;
His magic tricks the juggler plied;
At dice and draughts the gallants vied;
While some, in close recess apart,
Courted the ladies of their heart,
   Nor courted them in vain;
For often, in the parting hour,
Victorious Love asserts his power
   O'er coldness and disdain;
And flinty is her heart, can view
To battle march a lover true—
Can hear, perchance, his last adieu,
   Nor own her share of pain.

VIII.

Through this mix'd crowd of glee and game,
The King to greet Lord Marmion came,
   While, reverent, all made room.
An easy task it was, I trow,
King James's manly form to know.
Although, his courtesy to show,
He doff'd to Marmion bending low,
   His broider'd cap and plume.
For royal was his garb and mien,
   His cloak, of crimson velvet piled,
   Trimm'd with the fur of martin wild;
His vest of changeful satin sheen,
   The dazzled eye beguiled;
His gorgeous collar hung adown,
Wrought with the badge of Scotland's
      crown,
The thistle brave, of old renown:
His trusty blade, Toledo right,
Descended from a baldric bright;
White were his buskins, on the heel
His spurs inlaid of gold and steel;

His bonnet, all of crimson fair,
Was button'd with a ruby rare:
And Marmion deem'd he ne'er had seen
A prince of such a noble mien.

IX.

The monarch's form was middle size;
For feat of strength, or exercise,
   Shaped in proportion fair;
And hazel was his eagle eye,
And auburn of the darkest dye,
   His short curl'd beard and hair.
Light was his footstep in the dance,
   And firm his stirrup in the lists;
And, oh! he had that merry glance,
   That seldom lady's heart resists.
Lightly from fair to fair he flew,
And loved to plead, lament, and sue;—
Suit lightly won, and short-lived pain,
For monarchs seldom sigh in vain.
   I said he joy'd in banquet bower;
But, 'mid his mirth, 'twas often strange,
How suddenly his cheer would change,
   His look o'ercast and lower,
If, in a sudden turn, he felt
The pressure of his iron belt,
That bound his breast in penance pain,
In memory of his father slain.[37]
Even so 'twas strange how, evermore,
Soon as the passing pang was o'er
Forward he rush'd, with double glee,
Into the stream of revelry:
Thus, dim-seen object of affright
Startles the courser in his flight,
And half he halts, half springs aside;
But feels the quickening spur applied,
And, straining on the tighten'd rein,
Scours doubly swift o'er hill and plain.

X.

O'er James's heart, the courtiers say,
Sir Hugh the Heron's wife held sway:[38]
   To Scotland's Court she came,
To be a hostage for her lord,
Who Cessford's gallant heart had gored,
And with the King to make accord,
   Had sent his lovely dame.
Nor to that lady free alone
Did the gay King allegiance own;

For the fair Queen of France
Sent him a turquois ring and glove,
And charged him, as her knight and love,
  For her to break a lance;[59]
And strike three strokes with Scottish
  brand,
And march three miles on Southron land,
And bid the banners of his band
  In English breezes dance.
And thus, for France's Queen he drest
His manly limbs in mailed vest;
And thus admitted English fair
His inmost counsels still to share;
And thus for both, he madly plann'd
The ruin of himself and land!
  And yet, the sooth to tell,
Nor England's fair, nor France's Queen,
Were worth one pearl-drop, bright and
   sheen,
From Margaret's eyes that fell,—
His own Queen Margaret, who, in Lith-
  gow's bower,
All lonely sat, and wept the weary hour.

XI.

The Queen sits lone in Lithgow pile,
  And weeps the weary day,
The war against her native soil,
Her Monarch's risk in battle broil:—
And in gay Holy-Rood, the while
Dame Heron rises with a smile
  Upon the harp to play.
Fair was her rounded arm, as o'er
  The strings her fingers flew;
And as she touch'd and tuned them all,
Even her bosom's rise and fall
  Was plainer given to view;
For, all for heat, was laid aside
Her wimple, and her hood untied.
And first she pitch'd her voice to sing,
Then glanced her dark eye on the King,
And then around the silent ring;
And laugh'd, and blush'd, and oft did
  say
Her pretty oath, by Yea, and Nay,
She could not, would not, durst not play!
At length, upon the harp, with glee,
Mingled with arch simplicity,
A soft, yet lively air she rung,
While thus the wily lady sung:—

XII.

LOCHINVAR.

Lady Heron's Song.

O, young Lochinvar is come out of the
  west,
Through all the wide Border his steed
  was the best;
And save his good broadsword he wea-
  pons had none,
He rode all unarm'd, and he rode all alone.
So faithful in love, and so dauntless in war,
There never was knight like the young
  Lochinvar.

He staid not for brake, and he stopp'd not
  for stone,
He swam the Eske river where ford there
  was none;
But ere he alighted at Netherby gate,
The bride had consented, the gallant
  came late:
For a laggard in love, and a dastard in war,
Was to wed the fair Ellen of brave
  Lochinvar.

So boldly he enter'd the Netherby Hall,
Among bride's-men, and kinsmen, and
  brothers, and all:
Then spoke the bride's father, his hand on
  his sword,
(For the poor craven bridegroom said
  never a word,)
"O come ye in peace here, or come ye
  in war,
Or to dance at our bridal, young Lord
  Lochinvar?"—

"I long woo'd your daughter, my suit
  you denied;—
Love swells like the Solway, but ebbs like
  its tide—
And now am I come, with this lost love
  of mine,
To lead but one measure, drink one cup
  of wine.
There are maidens in Scotland more lovely
  by far,
That would gladly be bride to the young
  Lochinvar."

The bride kiss'd the goblet: the knight
   took it up,
He quaff'd off the wine, and he threw
   down the cup.
She look'd down to blush, and she look'd
   up to sigh,
With a smile on her lips, and a tear in
   her eye.
He took her soft hand, ere her mother
   could bar,—
" Now tread we a measure !" said young
   Lochinvar.

So stately his form, and so lovely her face,
That never a hall such a galliard did grace;
While her mother did fret, and her father
   did fume,
And the bridegroom stood dangling his
   bonnet and plume ;
And the bride-maidens whisper'd, "'Twere
   better by far,
To have match'd our fair cousin with
   young Lochinvar."

One touch to her hand, and one word in
   her ear,
When they reach'd the hall-door, and the
   charger stood near ;
So light to the croupe the fair lady he
   swung,
So light to the saddle before her he sprung !
" She is won ! we are gone, over bank,
   bush, and scaur ;
They'll have fleet steeds that follow,"
   quoth young Lochinvar.

There was mounting 'mong Græmes of
   the Netherby clan ;
Forsters, Fenwicks, and Musgraves, they
   rode and they ran :
There was racing and chasing, on Cannobie
   Lee,
But the lost bride of Netherby ne'er did
   they see.
So daring in love, and so dauntless in war,
Have ye e'er heard of gallant like young
   Lochinvar ?

XIII.

The Monarch o'er the siren hung
  And beat the measure as she sung ;

And, pressing closer, and more near,
He whisper'd praises in her ear.
In loud applause the courtiers vied ;
And ladies wink'd, and spoke aside.
  The witching dame to Marmion threw
    A glance, where seem'd to reign
  The pride that claims applauses due,
    And of her royal conquest too,
    A real or feign'd disdain :
Familiar was the look, and told,
Marmion and she were friends of old.
The King observed their meeting eyes,
With something like displeased surprise ;
For monarchs ill can rivals brook,
Even in a word, or smile, or look.
Straight took he forth the parchment
   broad,
Which Marmion's high commission
   show'd :
" Our Borders sack'd by many a raid,
Our peaceful liege-men robb'd," he said :
" On day of truce our Warden slain,
Stout Barton kill'd, his vassals ta'en—
Unworthy were we here to reign,
Should these for vengeance cry in vain ;
Our full defiance, hate, and scorn,
Our herald has to Henry borne."

XIV.

He paused, and led where Douglas stood,
And with stern eye the pageant view'd :
I mean that Douglas, sixth of yore,
Who coronet of Angus bore,
And, when his blood and heart were high,
Did the third James in camp defy,
And all his minions led to die
  On Lauder's dreary flat :
Princes and favourites long grew tame,
And trembled at the homely name
  Of Archibald Bell-the-Cat ; [60]
The same who left the dusky vale
Of Hermitage in Liddisdale,
  Its dungeons, and its towers,
Where Bothwell's turrets brave the air,
And Bothwell bank is blooming fair,
  To fix his princely bowers.
Though now, in age, he had laid down
His armour for the peaceful gown
  And for a staff his brand.

Yet often would flash forth the fire,
That could, in youth, a monarch's ire
    And minion's pride withstand ;
And even that day, at council board,
    Unapt to soothe his sovereign's mood,
    Against the war had Angus stood,
And chafed his royal lord.[61]

XV.

His giant-form, like ruin'd tower,
Though fall'n its muscles' brawny vaunt,
Huge-boned, and tall, and grim, and gaunt,
    Seem'd o'er the gaudy scene to lower :
His locks and beard in silver grew ;
His eyebrows kept their sable hue.
Near Douglas when the Monarch stood,
His bitter speech he thus pursued :
" Lord Marmion, since these letters say
That in the North you needs must stay,
    While slightest hopes of peace remain,
Uncourteous speech it were, and stern,
To say—Return to Lindisfarne,
    Until my herald come again.—
Then rest you in Tantallon Hold ;[62]
Your host shall be the Douglas bold,—
A chief unlike his sires of old.
He wears their motto on his blade,[63]
Their blazon o'er his towers display'd ;
Yet loves his sovereign to oppose,
More than to face his country's foes.
And, I bethink me, by St. Stephen,
But e'en this morn to me was given
A prize, the first fruits of the war,
Ta'en by a galley from Dunbar,
    A bevy of the maids of Heaven.
Under your guard, these holy maids
Shall safe return to cloister shades,
And, while they at Tantallon stay,
Requiem for Cochran's soul may say."
And, with the slaughter'd favourite's
        name,
Across the Monarch's brow there came
A cloud of ire, remorse and shame.

XVI.

In answer nought could Angus speak ;
His proud heart swell'd wellnigh to break :
He turn'd aside, and down his cheek
    A burning tear there stole,

His hand the Monarch sudden took,
That sight his kind heart could not brook :
    " Now, by the Bruce's soul,
Angus, my hasty speech forgive !
For sure as doth his spirit live,
As he said of the Douglas old,
    I well may say of you,—
That never king did subject hold,
In speech more free, in war more bold,
    More tender and more true :
Forgive me, Douglas, once again."—
And, while the King his hand did strain,
The old man's tears fell down like rain.
To seize the moment Marmion tried,
And whisper'd to the King aside :
" Oh ! let such tears unwonted plead
For respite short from dubious deed !
A child will weep a bramble's smart,
A maid to see her sparrow part,
A stripling for a woman's heart :
But woe awaits a country, when
She sees the tears of bearded men.
Then, oh ! what omen, dark and high,
When Douglas wets his manly eye !"

XVII.

Displeased was James, that stranger view'd
And tamper'd with his changing mood.
" Laugh those that can, weep those that
        may,"
Thus did the fiery Monarch say,
" Southward I march by break of day ;
And if within Tantallon strong,
The good Lord Marmion tarries long,
Perchance our meeting next may fall
At Tamworth, in his castle-hall."—
The haughty Marmion felt the taunt,
And answer'd, grave, the royal vaunt :
" Much honour'd were my humble home,
If in its halls King James should come ;
But Nottingham has archers good,
And Yorkshire men are stern of mood ;
Northumbrian prickers wild and rude.
On Derby Hills the paths are steep ;
In Ouse and Tyne the fords are deep ;
And many a banner will be torn,
And many a knight to earth be borne,
And many a sheaf of arrows spent,
Ere Scotland's King shall cross the Trent,

Yet pause, brave Prince, while yet you
    may!"—
The Monarch lightly turn'd away,
And to his nobles loud did call,—
" Lords, to the dance,—a hall! a hall!"*
Himself his cloak and sword flung by,
And led Dame Heron gallantly;
And minstrels, at the royal order,
Rung out—" Blue Bonnets o'er the
    Border."

XVIII.

Leave we these revels now, to tell
What to Saint Hilda's maids befell,
Whose galley, as they sail'd again
To Whitby, by a Scot was ta'en.
Now at Dun-Edin did they bide,
Till James should of their fate decide;
    And soon, by his command,
Were gently summon'd to prepare
To journey under Marmion's care,
As escort honour'd, safe, and fair,
    Again to English land.
The Abbess told her chaplet o'er,
Nor knew which saint she should implore;
For, when she thought of Constance, sore
    She fear'd Lord Marmion's mood.
And judge what Clara must have felt!
The sword, that hung in Marmion's belt,
    Had drunk De Wilton's blood.
Unwittingly, King James had given,
    As guard to Whitby's shades,
The man most dreaded under Heaven
    By these defenceless maids:
Yet what petition could avail,
Or who would listen to the tale
Of woman, prisoner, and nun,
'Mid bustle of a war begun?
They deem'd it hopeless to avoid
The convoy of their dangerous guide.

XIX.

Their lodging, so the King assign'd,
To Marmion's, as their guardian, join'd;
And thus it fell, that, passing nigh,
The Palmer caught the Abbess' eye,

---

* The ancient cry to make room for a
dance, or pageant.

Who warn'd him by a scroll,
She had a secret to reveal,
That much concern'd the Church's weal,
    And health of sinner's soul;
And, with deep charge of secrecy,
    She named a place to meet,
Within an open balcony,
That hung from dizzy pitch, and high,
    Above the stately street;
To which, as common to each home,
At night they might in secret come.

XX.

At night, in secret, there they came,
The Palmer and the holy Dame.
The moon among the clouds rose high,
And all the city hum was by.
Upon the street, where late before
Did din of war and warriors roar,
    You might have heard a pebble fall,
A beetle hum, a cricket sing,
An owlet flap his boding wing
    On Giles's steeple tall.
The antique buildings, climbing high,
Whose Gothic frontlets sought the sky,
    Were here wrapt deep in shade;
There on their brows the moon-beam
    broke,
Through the faint wreaths of silvery smoke,
    And on the casements play'd.
    And other light was none to see,
      Save torches gliding far,
    Before some chieftain of degree,
    Who left the royal revelry
      To bowne him for the war.—
A solemn scene the Abbess chose;
A solemn hour, her secret to disclose.

XXI.

" O, holy Palmer!" she began,—
" For sure he must be sainted man,
Whose blessed feet have trod the ground
Where the Redeemer's tomb is found,—
For His dear Church's sake, my tale
Attend, nor deem of light avail,
Though I must speak of worldly love,—
How vain to those who wed above!—
De Wilton and Lord Marmion woo'd
Clara de Clare, of Gloster's blood;

(Idle it were of Whitby's dame,
To say of that same blood I came;)
And once, when jealous rage was high,
Lord Marmion said despiteously,
Wilton was traitor in his heart,
And had made league with Martin Swart,[64]
When he came here on Simnel's part;
And only cowardice did restrain
His rebel aid on Stokefield's plain,—
And down he threw his glove:—the thing
Was tried, as wont, before the King;
Where frankly did De Wilton own,
That Swart in Gueldres he had known;
And that between them then there went
Some scroll of courteous compliment.
For this he to his castle sent;
But when his messenger return'd,
Judge how De Wilton's fury burn'd!
For in his packet there were laid
Letters that claim'd disloyal aid,
And proved King Henry's cause betray'd.
His fame, thus blighted, in the field
He strove to clear, by spear and shield;—
To clear his fame in vain he strove,
For wondrous are His ways above!
Perchance some form was unobserved;
Perchance in prayer, or faith, he swerved;
Else how could guiltless champion quail,
Or how the blessed ordeal fail?

XXII.

" His squire, who now De Wilton saw
As recreant doom'd to suffer law,
　Repentant, own'd in vain,
That, while he had the scrolls in care,
A stranger maiden, passing fair,
Had drench'd him with a beverage rare;
　His words no faith could gain.
With Clare alone he credence won,
Who, rather than wed Marmion,
Did to Saint Hilda's shrine repair,
To give our house her livings fair
And die a vestal vot'ress there.
The impulse from the earth was given,
But bent her to the paths of heaven.
A purer heart, a lovelier maid,
Ne'er shelter'd her in Whitby's shade,
No, not since Saxon Edelfled;
　Only one trace of earthly strain,
　　That for her lover's loss

She cherishes a sorrow vain,
　And murmurs at the cross.—
And then her heritage;—it goes
　Along the banks of Tame;
Deep fields of grain the reaper mows,
In meadows rich the heifer lows,
The falconer and huntsman knows
　Its woodlands for the game.
Shame were it to Saint Hilda dear,
And I, her humble vot'ress here,
　Should do a deadly sin,
Her temple spoil'd before mine eyes,
If this false Marmion such a prize
　By my consent should win;
Yet hath our boisterous monarch sworn
That Clare shall from our house be torn,
And grievous cause have I to fear
Such mandate doth Lord Marmion bear.

XXIII.

" Now, prisoner, helpless, and betray'd
To evil power, I claim thine aid,
　By every step that thou hast trod
To holy shrine and grotto dim,
By every martyr's tortured limb,
By angel, saint, and seraphim,
　And by the Church of God!
For mark:—When Wilton was betray'd,
And with his squire forged letters laid,
She was, alas! that sinful maid,
　By whom the deed was done,—
O! shame and horror to be said!—
　She was a perjured nun!
No clerk in all the land, like her,
Traced quaint and varying character.
Perchance you may a marvel deem,
　That Marmion's paramour
(For such vile thing she was) should scheme
　Her lover's nuptial hour;
But o'er him thus she hoped to gain,
As privy to his honour's stain,
　Illimitable power:
For this she secretly retain'd
　Each proof that might the plot reveal,
　Instructions with his hand and seal;
And thus Saint Hilda deign'd,
　Through sinner's perfidy impure,
　Her house's glory to secure,
And Clare's immortal weal.

XXIV.

" 'Twere long, and needless, here to tell,
How to my hand these papers fell;
  With me they must not stay.
Saint Hilda keep her Abbess true!
Who knows what outrage he might do,
  While journeying by the way?—
O, blessed Saint, if e'er again
I venturous leave thy calm domain,
To travel or by land or main,
  Deep penance may I pay!—
Now, saintly Palmer, mark my prayer:
I give this packet to thy care,
For thee to stop they will not dare;
  And O! with cautious speed,
To Wolsey's hand the papers bring,
That he may show them to the King:
  And, for thy well-earn'd meed,
Thou holy man, at Whitby's shrine
A weekly mass shall still be thine,
  While priests can sing and read.—
What ail'st thou?—Speak!" For as he took
The charge, a strong emotion shook
  His frame; and, ere reply,
They heard a faint, yet shrilly tone,
Like distant clarion feebly blown,
  That on the breeze did die;
And loud the Abbess shriek'd in fear,
" Saint Withold, save us!—What is here?
  Look at yon City Cross!
See on its battled tower appear
Phantoms, that scutcheons seem to rear,
  And blazon'd banners toss!"

XXV.

Dun-Edin's Cross, a pillar'd stone,[65]
Rose on a turret octagon;
(But now is razed that monument,
  Whence royal edict rang,
And voice of Scotland's law was sent
  In glorious trumpet-clang
O! be his tomb as lead to lead,
Upon its dull destroyer's head!
A minstrel's malison* is said.)
Then on its battlements they saw
A vision, passing Nature's law,
  Strange, wild, and dimly seen;

---

* Curse.

Figures that seem'd to rise and die,
Gibber and sign, advance and fly,
While nought confirm'd could ear or eye
  Discern of sound or mien.
Yet darkly did it seem, as there
Heralds and Pursuivants prepare,
With trumpet sound and blazon fair,
  A summons to proclaim;
But indistinct the pageant proud,
As fancy forms of midnight cloud,
When flings the moon upon her shroud
  A wavering tinge of flame;
It flits, expands, and shifts, till loud,
From midmost of the spectre crowd,
  This awful summons came:[66]—

XXVI.

" Prince, prelate, potentate, and peer,
  Whose names I now shall call,
Scottish, or foreigner, give ear;
Subjects of him who sent me here,
At his tribunal to appear,
  I summon one and all:
I cite you by each deadly sin,
That e'er hath soil'd your hearts within:
I cite you by each brutal lust,
That e'er defiled your earthly dust,—
  By wrath, by pride, by fear,
By each o'er-mastering passion's tone,
By the dark grave, and dying groan!
When forty days are pass'd and gone,
I cite you, at your Monarch's throne,
  To answer and appear."
Then thunder'd forth a roll of names:
The first was thine, unhappy James!
  Then all thy nobles came;
Crawford, Glencairn, Montrose, Argyle,
Ross, Bothwell, Forbes, Lennox, Lyle,—
Why should I tell their separate style?
  Each chief of birth and fame,
Of Lowland, Highland, Border, Isle,
Fore-doom'd to Flodden's carnage pile,
  Was cited there by name;
And Marmion, Lord of Fontenaye,
Of Lutterward, and Scrivelbaye;
De Wilton, erst of Aberley,
The self-same thundering voice did say.—
  But then another spoke:
" Thy fatal summons I deny,

And thine infernal Lord defy,
Appealing me to Him on High,
  Who burst the sinner's yoke."
At that dread accent, with a scream,
Parted the pageant like a dream,
  The summoner was gone.
Prone on her face the Abbess fell,
And fast, and fast, her beads did tell;
Her nuns came, startled by the yell,
  And found her there alone.
She mark'd not, at the scene aghast,
What time, or how, the Palmer pass'd.

XXVII.

Shift we the scene.—The camp doth move,
  Dun-Edin's streets are empty now,
Save when, for weal of those they love,
  To pray the prayer, and vow the vow,
The tottering child, the anxious fair,
The grey-hair'd sire, with pious care,
To chapels and to shrines repair—
Where is the Palmer now? and where
The Abbess, Marmion, and Clare?—
Bold Douglas! to Tantailon fair
  They journey in thy charge:
Lord Marmion rode on his right hand,
The Palmer still was with the band;
Angus, like Lindesay, did command,
  That none should roam at large.
But in that Palmer's altered mien
A wondrous change might now be seen,
  Freely he spoke of war,
Of marvels wrought by single hand,
When lifted for a native land;
And still look'd high, as if he plann'd
  Some desperate deed afar.
His courser would he feed and stroke,
And, tucking up his sable frocke,
Would first his mettle bold provoke,
  Then soothe or quell his pride.
Old Hubert said, that never one
He saw, except Lord Marmion,
  A steed so fairly ride.

XXVIII.

Some half-hour's march behind, there
    came,
  By Eustace govern'd fair,
A troop escorting Hilda's Dame,
  With all her nuns, and Clare.

No audience had Lord Marmion sought;
  Ever he fear'd to aggravate
  Clara de Clare's suspicious hate;
And safer 'twas, he thought,
  To wait till, from the nuns removed,
  The influence of kinsmen loved,
  And suit by Henry's self approved,
Her slow consent had wrought.
  His was no flickering flame, that dies
  Unless when fann'd by looks and sighs,
  And lighted oft at lady's eyes;
  He long'd to stretch his wide command
  O'er luckless Clara's ample land:
  Besides, when Wilton with him vied,
  Although the pang of humbled pride
  The place of jealousy supplied,
Yet conquest by that meanness won
He almost loath'd to think upon,
Led him, at times, to hate the cause,
Which made him burst through honour's
    laws.
If e'er he lov'd, 'twas her alone,
Who died within that vault of stone.

XXIX.

And now, when close at hand they saw
North Berwick's town, and lofty Law,
Fitz-Eustace bade them pause awhile,
Before a venerable pile,*
  Whose turrets view'd, afar,
The lofty Bass, the Lambie Isle,
  The ocean's peace or war.
At tolling of a bell, forth came
The convent's venerable Dame,
And pray'd Saint Hilda's Abbess rest
With her, a loved and honour'd guest,
Till Douglas should a bark prepare
To waft her back to Whitby fair.
Glad was the Abbess, you may guess,
And thank'd the Scottish Prioress;
And tedious were to tell, I ween,
The courteous speech that pass'd between.
  O'erjoy'd the nuns their palfreys leave;
But when fair Clara did intend,
Like them, from horseback to descend,
  Fitz-Eustace said,—"I grieve,

---

* A convent of Cistertian nuns, founded by
the Earl of Fife in 1216.

Fair lady, grieve e'en from my heart,
Such gentle company to part,—
    Think not discourtesy,
But lords' commands must be obey'd;
And Marmion and the Douglas said,
    That you must wend with me.
Lord Marmion hath a letter broad,
Which to the Scottish Earl he show'd,
Commanding that, beneath his care,
Without delay, you shall repair
To your good kinsman, Lord Fitz-Clare."

XXX.

The startled Abbess loud exclaim'd;
But she, at whom the blow was aim'd,
Grew pale as death, and cold as lead,—
She deem'd she heard her death-doom read.
"Cheer thee, my child!" the Abbess said,
"They dare not tear thee from my hand,
To ride alone with armed band."
    "Nay, holy mother, nay,"
Fitz-Eustace said, "the lovely Clare
Will be in Lady Angus' care,
    In Scotland while we stay;
And, when we move, an easy ride
Will bring us to the English side,
Female attendance to provide
Befitting Gloster's heir:
Nor thinks nor dreams my noble lord,
By slightest look, or act, or word,
    To harass Lady Clare.
Her faithful guardian he will be,
Nor sue for slightest courtesy
That e'en to stranger falls,
Till he shall place her, safe and free,
    Within her kinsman's halls."
He spoke, and blush'd with earnest grace;
His faith was painted on his face,
    And Clare's worst fear relieved.
The Lady Abbess loud exclaim'd
On Henry, and the Douglas blamed,
    Entreated, threaten'd, grieved;
To martyr, saint, and prophet pray'd,
Against Lord Marmion inveigh'd,
And call'd the Prioress to aid,
To curse with candle, bell, and book.
Her head the grave Cistertian shook:
"The Douglas, and the King," she said,
"In their commands will be obey'd;

Grieve not, nor dream that harm can fall
The maiden in Tantallon hall."

XXXI.

The Abbess, seeing strife was vain,
Assumed her wonted state again,—
    For much of state she had,—
Composed her veil, and raised her head,
And—"Bid," in solemn voice she said,
    "Thy master, bold and bad,
The records of his house turn o'er,
    And, when he shall there written see,
    That one of his own ancestry
    Drove the Monks forth of Coventry,
Bid him his fate explore!
    Prancing in pride of earthly trust,
    His charger hurl'd him to the dust,
    And, by a base plebeian thrust,.
He died his band before.
    God judge 'twixt Marmion and me;
    He is a Chief of high degree,
And I a poor recluse:
    Yet oft, in holy writ, we see
    Even such weak minister as me
May the oppressor bruise:
    For thus, inspired, did Judith slay
    The mighty in his sin,
    And Jael thus, and Deborah"——
    Here hasty Blount broke in:
"Fitz-Eustace, we must march our band;
St. Anton' fire thee! wilt thou stand
All day, with bonnet in thy hand,
    To hear the lady preach?
By this good light! if thus we stay,
Lord Marmion, for our fond delay,
    Will sharper sermon teach.
Come, don thy cap, and mount thy horse;
The Dame must patience take perforce."—

XXXII.

"Submit we then to force," said Clare,
"But let this barbarous lord despair
    His purposed aim to win;
Let him take living, land, and life:
But to be Marmion's wedded wife
    In me were deadly sin:
And if it be the King's decree
That I must find no sanctuary,
    In that inviolable dome,
Where even a homicide might come,

And safely rest his head,
Though at its open portals stood,
Thirsting to pour forth blood for blood,
  The kinsmen of the dead;
Yet one asylum is my own
  Against the dreaded hour;
A low, a silent, and a lone,
  Where kings have little power.
One victim is before me there.—
Mother, your blessing, and in prayer,
Remember your unhappy Clare!"
Loud weeps the Abbess, and bestows
  Kind blessings many a one:
Weeping and wailing loud arose,
Round patient Clare, the clamorous
    woes
  Of every simple nun.
His eyes the gentle Eustace dried,
And scarce rude Blount the sight could
    bide.
  Then took the squire her rein,
And gently led away her steed,
And, by each courteous word and deed,
  To cheer her strove in vain.

XXXIII.

But scant three miles the band had rode,
  When o'er a height they pass'd,
And, sudden, close before them show'd
  His towers, Tantallon vast;
Broad, massive, high, and stretching far,
And held impregnable in war.
On a projecting rock they rose,
And round three sides the ocean flows,
The fourth did battled walls enclose,
  And double mound and fosse.
By narrow drawbridge, outworks strong,
Through studded gates, an entrance long,
  To the main court they cross.
It was a wide and stately square:
Around were lodgings, fit and fair,
  And towers of various form,
Which on the court projected far,
And broke its lines quadrangular.
Here was square keep, there turret high,
Or pinnacle that sought the sky,
Whence oft the warder could descry
  The gathering ocean storm.

XXXIV.

Here did they rest.—The princely care
Of Douglas, why should I declare,
Or say they met reception fair?
  Or why the tidings say,
Which, varying, to Tantallon came,
By hurrying posts or fleeter fame,
  With ever varying day?
And, first they heard King James had
    won
  Etall, and Wark, and Ford; and then,
  That Norham Castle strong was ta'en.
At that sore marvell'd Marmion;—
And Douglas hoped his Monarch's hand
Would soon subdue Northumberland:
  But whisper'd news there came,
That, while his host inactive lay,
And melted by degrees away,
King James was dallying off the day
  With Heron's wily dame.—
Such acts to chronicles I yield;
  Go seek them there, and see:
Mine is a tale of Flodden Field,
  And not a history.—
At length they heard the Scottish host
On that high ridge had made their post,
  Which frowns o'er Millfield Plain;
And that brave Surrey many a band
Had gather'd in the Southern land,
And march'd into Northumberland,
  And camp at Wooler ta'en.
Marmion, like charger in the stall,
That hears, without, the trumpet-call,
  Began to chafe, and swear:—
" A sorry thing to hide my head
In castle, like a fearful maid,
  When such a field is near!
Needs must I see this battle-day:
Death to my fame if such a fray
Were fought, and Marmion away!
The Douglas, too, I wot not why,
Hath 'bated of his courtesy:
No longer in his halls I'll stay."
Then bade his band they should array
For march against the dawning day.

INTRODUCTION TO CANTO SIXTH.

TO

RICHARD HEBER, ESQ.

Mertoun-House, Christmas.

HEAP on more wood!—the wind is chill;
But let it whistle as it will,
We'll keep our Christmas merry still.
Each age has deem'd the new-born year
The fittest time for festal cheer:
Even, heathen yet, the savage Dane
At Iol more deep the mead did drain; [68]
High on the beach his galleys drew,
And feasted all his pirate crew;
Then in his low and pine-built hall,
Where shields and axes deck'd the wall,
They gorged upon the half dress'd steer;
Caroused in seas of sable beer;
While round, in brutal jest, were thrown
The half-gnaw'd rib, and marrow-bone:
Or listen'd all, in grim delight,
While Scalds yell'd out the joys of fight.
Then forth, in frenzy, would they hie,
While, wildly-loose their red locks fly,
And dancing round the blazing pile,
They make such barbarous mirth the while,
As best might to the mind recall
The boisterous joys of Odin's hall.

And well our Christian sires of old
Loved when the year its course had roll'd,
And brought blithe Christmas back again,
With all his hospitable train.
Domestic and religious rite
Gave honour to the holy night;
On Christmas eve the bells were rung;
On Christmas eve the mass was sung:
That only night in all the year,
Saw the stoled priest the chalice rear.
The damsel donn'd her kirtle sheen;
The hall was dress'd with holy green;
Forth to the wood did merry-men go,
To gather in the mistletoe.
Then open'd wide the Baron's hall
To vassal, tenant, serf, and all;
Power laid his rod of rule aside,
And Ceremony doff'd his pride.

The heir, with roses in his shoes,
That night might village partner choose;
The Lord, underogating, share
The vulgar game of "post and pair."*
All hail'd, with uncontroll'd delight,
And general voice, the happy night,
That to the cottage, as the crown,
Brought tidings of salvation down.

The fire, with well-dried logs supplied,
Went roaring up the chimney wide;
The huge hall-table's oaken face,
Scrubb'd till it shone, the day to grace,
Bore then upon its massive board
No mark to part the squire and lord.
Then was brought in the lusty brawn,
By old blue-coated serving-man;
Then the grim boar's head frown'd on high,
Crested with bays and rosemary.
Well can the green-garb'd ranger tell,
How, when, and where, the monster fell;
What dogs before his death he tore,
And all the baiting of the boar.
The wassel round, in good brown bowls,
Garnish'd with ribbons, blithely trowls.
There the huge sirloin reek'd; hard by
Plum-porridge stood, and Christmas pie;
Nor fail'd old Scotland to produce,
At such high tide, her savoury goose.
Then came the merry maskers in,
And carols roar'd with blithesome din;
If unmelodious was the song,
It was a hearty note, and strong.
Who lists may in their mumming see
Traces of ancient mystery; [69]
White shirts supplied the masquerade,
And smutted cheeks the visors made;
But, O! what maskers, richly dight,
Can boast of bosoms half so light!
England was merry England, when
Old Christmas brought his sports again.
'Twas Christmas broach'd the mightiest ale;
'Twas Christmas told the merriest tale;
A Christmas gambol oft could cheer
The poor man's heart through half the year.

---

* An old game at cards.

Still linger, in our northern clime,
Some remnants of the good old time;
And still, within our valleys here,
We hold the kindred title dear,
Even when, perchance, its far-fetch'd
    claim
To Southron ear sounds empty name;
For course of blood, our proverbs deem,
Is warmer than the mountain-stream.*
And thus, my Christmas still I hold
Where my great grandsire came of old,
With amber beard, and flaxen hair,
And reverend apostolic air—
The feast and holy-tide to share,
And mix sobriety with wine,
And honest mirth with thoughts divine:
Small thought was his, in after time
E'er to be hitch'd into a rhyme.
The simple sire could only boast,
That he was loyal to his cost;
The banish'd race of kings revered,
And lost his land,—but kept his beard.

In these dear halls, where welcome kind
Is with fair liberty combined;
Where cordial friendship gives the hand,
And flies constraint the magic wand
Of the fair dame that rules the land.
Little we heed the tempest drear,
While music, mirth, and social cheer,
Speed on their wings the passing year.
And Mertoun's halls are fair e'en now,
When not a leaf is on the bough.
Tweed loves them well, and turns again,
As loath to leave the sweet domain,
And holds his mirror to her face,
And clips her with a close embrace:—
Gladly as he, we seek the dome,
And as reluctant turn us home.

How just that, at this time of glee,
My thoughts should, Heber, turn to thee!
For many a merry hour we've known,
And heard the chimes of midnight's tone.
Cease, then, my friend! a moment cease,
And leave these classic tomes in peace!
Of Roman and of Grecian lore,
Sure mortal brain can hold no more.

These ancients, as Noll Bluff might say,
" Were pretty fellows in their day;"
But time and tide o'er all prevail—
On Christmas eve a Christmas tale—
Of wonder and of war—" Profane!
What! leave the lofty Latian strain,
Her stately prose, her verse's charms,
To hear the clash of rusty arms:
In Fairy Land or Limbo lost,
To jostle conjurer and ghost,
Goblin and witch!"—Nay, Heber dear,
Before you touch my charter, hear:
Though Leyden aids, alas! no more,
My cause with many-languaged lore,
This may I say:—in realms of death
Ulysses meets Alcides' *wraith;*
Æneas, upon Thracia's shore,
The ghost of murder'd Polydore;
For omens, we in Livy cross,
At every turn, *locutus Bos.*
As grave and duly speaks that ox,
As if he told the price of stocks;
Or held, in Rome republican,
The place of common-councilman.

All nations have their omens drear,
Their legends wild of woe and fear.
To Cambria look—the peasant see,
Bethink him of Glendowerdy,
And shun " the spirit's Blasted Tree."†
The Highlander, whose red claymore
The battle turn'd on Maida's shore,
Will, on a Friday morn, look pale,
If ask'd to tell a fairy tale:70
He fears the vengeful Elfin King,
Who leaves that day his grassy ring:
Invisible to human ken,
He walks among the sons of men.

Didst e'er, dear Heber, pass along
Beneath the towers of Franchémont,
Which, like an eagle's nest in air,
Hang o'er the stream and hamlet fair?
Deep in their vaults, the peasants say,
A mighty treasure buried lay,

---

* " Blood is warmer than water."

† Alluding to the Welsh tradition of Howel
Sell and Owen Glendwr. Howel fell in single
combat against Glendwr, and his body was
concealed in a hollow oak.

Amass'd through rapine and through
    wrong
By the last Lord of Franchémont[71]
The iron chest is bolted hard,
A huntsman sits, its constant guard;
Around his neck his horn is hung,
His hanger in his belt is slung;
Before his feet his blood-hounds lie.
An 'twere not for his gloomy eye,
Whose withering glance no heart can
    brook,
As true a huntsman doth he look,
As bugle e'er in brake did sound,
Or ever holloo'd to a hound.
To chase the fiend, and win the prize
In that same dungeon ever tries
An aged necromantic priest;
It is an hundred years at least,
Since 'twixt them first the strife begun,
And neither yet has lost nor won.
And oft the Conjurer's words will make
The stubborn Demon groan and quake;
And oft the bands of iron break,
Or bursts one lock, that still amain,
Fast as 'tis open'd, shuts again.
That magic strife within the tomb
May last until the day of doom,
Unless the adept shall learn to tell
The very word that clench'd the spell,
When Franch'mont lock'd the treasure
    cell.
An hundred years are pass'd and gone,
And scarce three letters has he won.

Such general superstition may
Excuse for old Pitscottie say;
Whose gossip history has given
My song the messenger from Heaven,
That warn'd, in Lithgow, Scotland's King,
Nor less the infernal summoning;
May pass the Monk of Durham's tale,
Whose demon fought in Gothic mail;
May pardon plead for Fordun grave,
Who told of Gifford's Goblin-Cave.
But why such instances to you,
Who, in an instant, can renew
Your treasured hoards of various lore,
And furnish twenty thousand more;
Hoards, not like theirs whose volumes rest
Like treasures in the Franch'mont chest,

While gripple owners still refuse
To others what they cannot use;
Give them the priest's whole century,
They shall not spell you letters three;
Their pleasure in the books the same
The magpie takes in pilfer'd gem.
Thy volumes, open as thy heart,
Delight, amusement, science, art,
To every ear and eye impart;
Yet who of all who thus employ them,
Can like the owner's self enjoy them?—
But, hark! I hear the distant drum!
The day of Flodden Field is come.—
Adieu, dear Heber! life and health,
And store of literary wealth.

———◆———

CANTO SIXTH.

The Battle.

I.

WHILE great events were on the gale,
And each hour brought a varying tale,
And the demeanour, changed and cold,
Of Douglas, fretted Marmion bold,
And, like the impatient steed of war,
He snuff'd the battle from afar;
And hopes were none, that back again
Herald should come from Terouenne,
Where England's King in leaguer lay,
Before decisive battle-day;
Whilst these things were, the mournful
    Clare
Did in the Dame's devotions share:
For the good Countess ceaseless pray'd
To Heaven and Saints, her sons to aid,
And, with short interval, did pass
From prayer to book, from book to mass,
And all in high Baronial pride,—
A life both dull and dignified;—
Yet as Lord Marmion nothing press'd
Upon her intervals of rest,
Dejected Clara well could bear
The formal state, the lengthen'd prayer,
Though dearest to her wounded heart
The hours that she might spend apart.

II.

I said, Tantallon's dizzy steep
Hung o'er the margin of the deep.
Many a rude tower and rampart there
Repell'd the insult of the air,
Which, when the tempest vex'd the sky,
Half breeze, half spray, came whistling by.
Above the rest, a turret square
Did o'er its Gothic entrance bear,
Of sculpture rude, a stony shield;
The Bloody Heart was in the Field,
And in the chief three mullets stood,
The cognizance of Douglas blood.
The turret held a narrow stair,
Which, mounted, gave you access where
A parapet's embattled row
Did seaward round the castle go.
Sometimes in dizzy steps descending,
Sometimes in narrow circuit bending,
Sometimes in platform broad extending,
Its varying circle did combine
Bulwark, and bartizan, and line,
And bastion, tower, and vantage-coign;
Above the booming ocean leant
The far-projecting battlement;
The billows burst, in ceaseless flow,
Upon the precipice below.
Where'er Tantallon faced the land,
Gate-works, and walls, were strongly
     mann'd;
No need upon the sea-girt side;
The steepy rock, and frantic tide,
Approach of human step denied;
And thus these lines and ramparts rude,
Were left in deepest solitude.

III.

And, for they were so lonely, Clare
Would to these battlements repair,
And muse upon her sorrows there,
     And list the sea-bird's cry;
Or slow, like noontide ghost, would glide
Along the dark-grey bulwarks' side,
And ever on the heaving tide
     Look down with weary eye.
Oft did the cliff and swelling main,
Recall the thoughts of Whitby's fane,—
A home she ne'er might see again;
     For she had laid adown,

So Douglas bade, the hood and veil,
And frontlet of the cloister pale,
     And Benedictine gown:
It were unseemly sight, he said,
A novice out of convent shade.—
Now her bright locks, with sunny glow,
Again adorn'd her brow of snow;
Her mantle rich, whose borders, round,
A deep and fretted broidery bound,
In golden foldings sought the ground;
Of holy ornament, alone
Remain'd a cross with ruby stone;
     And often did she look
On that which in her hand she bore,
With velvet bound, and broider'd o'er,
     Her breviary book.
In such a place, so lone, so grim,
At dawning pale, or twilight dim,
     It fearful would have been
To meet a form so richly dress'd,
With book in hand, and cross on breast,
     And such a woeful mien.
Fitz-Eustace, loitering with his bow,
To practise on the gull and crow,
Saw her, at distance, gliding slow,
     And did by Mary swear,—
Some love-lorn Fay she might have been,
Or, in Romance, some spell-bound Queen;
For ne'er, in work-day world, was seen
     A form so witching fair.

IV.

Once walking thus, at evening tide,
It chanced a gliding sail she spied,
And, sighing, thought—"The Abbess,
     there,
Perchance, does to her home repair;
Her peaceful rule, where Duty, free,
Walks hand in hand with Charity;
Where oft Devotion's tranced glow
Can such a glimpse of heaven bestow,
That the enraptured sisters see
High vision and deep mystery;
The very form of Hilda fair,
Hovering upon the sunny air,
And smiling on her votaries' prayer.
O! wherefore, to my duller eye,
Did still the Saint her form deny!
Was it, that, sear'd by sinful scorn,
My heart could neither melt nor burn?

Or lie my warm affections low,
With him, that taught them first to glow?
Yet, gentle Abbess, well I knew,
To pay thy kindness grateful due,
And well could brook the mild command,
That ruled thy simple maiden band.
How different now! condemn'd to bide
My doom from this dark tyrant's pride.—
But Marmion has to learn, ere long,
That constant mind, and hate of wrong,
Descended to a feeble girl,
From Red De Clare, stout Gloster's Earl:
Of such a stem, a sapling weak,
He ne'er shall bend, although he break.

V.

"But see! what makes this armour
    here?"—
    For in her path there lay
Targe, corslet, helm;—she view'd them
    near.—
"The breast-plate pierced!—Ay, much
    I fear,
Weak fence wert thou 'gainst foeman's
    spear,
That hath made fatal entrance here,
    As these dark blood-gouts say.—
Thus Wilton!—Oh! not corslet's ward,
Not truth, as diamond pure and hard,
Could be thy manly bosom's guard,
    On yon disastrous day!"—
She raised her eyes in mournful mood,—
Wilton himself before her stood!
It might have seem'd his passing ghost,
For every youthful grace was lost;
And joy unwonted, and surprise,
Gave their strange wildness to his eyes.—
Expect not, noble dames and lords,
That I can tell such scene in words:
What skilful limner e'er would choose
To paint the rainbow's varying hues,
Unless to mortal it were given
To dip his brush in dyes of heaven?
Far less can my weak line declare
    Each changing passion's shade;
Brightening to rapture from despair,
Sorrow, surprise, and pity there,
And joy, with her angelic air,
And hope, that paints the future fair,
    Their varying hues display'd:

Each o'er its rival's ground extending,
Alternate conquering, shifting, blending,
Till all, fatigued, the conflict yield,
And mighty Love retains the field.
Shortly I tell what then he said,
By many a tender word delay'd,
And modest blush, and bursting sigh,
And question kind, and fond reply:—

VI.

De Wilton's History.

"Forget we that disastrous day,
When senseless in the lists I lay.
    Thence dragg'd,—but how I cannot
    know,
    For sense and recollection fled,—
I found me on a pallet low,
    Within my ancient beadsman's shed.
Austin,—remember'st thou, my Clare,
How thou didst blush, when the old man,
When first our infant love began,
    Said we would make a matchless pair?—
Menials, and friends, and kinsmen fled
From the degraded traitor's bed,—
He only held my burning head,
And tended me for many a day,
While wounds and fever held their sway.
But far more needful was his care,
When sense return'd to wake despair;
    For I did tear the closing wound,
    And dash me frantic on the ground,
If e'er I heard the name of Clare.
At length, to calmer reason brought,
Much by his kind attendance wrought,
    With him I left my native strand,
And, in a palmer's weeds array'd,
My hated name and form to shade,
    I journey'd many a land;
No more a lord of rank and birth,
But mingled with the dregs of earth.
Oft Austin for my reason fear'd,
When I would sit, and deeply brood
On dark revenge, and deeds of blood,
    Or wild mad schemes uprear'd.
My friend at length fell sick, and said,
    God would remove him soon:
And, while upon his dying bed,
    He begg'd of me a boon—

If e'er my deadliest enemy
Beneath my brand should conquer'd lie,
Even then my mercy should awake,
And spare his life for Austin's sake.

VII.

"Still restless as a second Cain,
To Scotland next my route was ta'en,
    Full well the paths I knew.
Fame of my fate made various sound,
That death in pilgrimage I found,
That I had perish'd of my wound,
    None cared which tale was true;
And living eye could never guess
De Wilton in his Palmer's dress;
For now that sable slough is shed,
And trimm'd my shaggy beard and head,
I scarcely know me in the glass.
A chance most wondrous did provide,
That I should be that Baron's guide—
    I will not name his name!—
Vengeance to God alone belongs;
But, when I think on all my wrongs,
    My blood is liquid flame!
And ne'er the time shall I forget,
When, in a Scottish hostel set,
    Dark looks we did exchange:
What were his thoughts I cannot tell;
But in my bosom muster'd Hell
    Its plans of dark revenge.

VIII.

"A word of vulgar augury,
That broke from me, I scarce knew why,
    Brought on a village tale;
Which wrought upon his moody sprite,
And sent him armed forth by night.
    I borrow'd steed and mail,
And weapons, from his sleeping band;
    And, passing from a postern door,
We met, and 'counter'd hand to hand,—
    He fell on Gifford moor.
For the death-stroke my brand I drew,
(O then my helmed head he knew,
    The Palmer's cowl was gone,)
Then had three inches of my blade
The heavy debt of vengeance paid,—
My hand the thought of Austin staid,
    I left him there alone,—

O good old man! even from the grave
Thy spirit could thy master save:
If I had slain my foeman, ne'er
Had Whitby's Abbess, in her fear,
Given to my hand this packet dear,
Of power to clear my injured fame,
And vindicate De Wilton's name.—
Perchance you heard the Abbess tell
Of the strange pageantry of Hell,
    That broke our secret speech—
It rose from the infernal shade,
Or featly was some juggle play'd,
    A tale of peace to teach.
Appeal to Heaven I judged was best,
When my name came among the rest.

IX.

"Now here, within Tantallon Hold,
To Douglas late my tale I told,
To whom my house was known of old.
Won by my proofs, his falchion bright
This eve anew shall dub me knight.
These were the arms that once did turn
The tide of fight on Otterburne,
And Harry Hotspur forced to yield,
When the Dead Douglas won the field.*
These Angus gave—his armourer's care,
Ere morn shall every breach repair;
For nought, he said, was in his halls,
But ancient armour on the walls,
And aged chargers in the stalls,
And women, priests, and grey-hair'd men;
The rest were all in Twisel glen.†
And now I watch my armour here,
By law of arms, till midnight's near;
Then, once again a belted knight,
Seek Surrey's camp with dawn of light.

X.

"There soon again we meet, my Clare!
This Baron means to guide thee there:
Douglas reveres his King's command,
Else would he take thee from his band.
And there thy kinsman, Surrey, too,
Will give De Wilton justice due.

---

* See the ballad of Otterbourne, in the
"Border Minstrelsy," vol. i. p. 345.
† Where James encamped before taking
post on Flodden.

Now meeter far for martial broil,
Firmer my limbs, and strung by toil,
Once more "—" O Wilton! must we
    then
Risk new-found happiness again,
  Trust fate of arms once more?
And is there not an humble glen,
  Where we, content and poor,
Might build a cottage in the shade,
A shepherd thou, and I to aid
  Thy task on dale and moor?—
That reddening brow!—too well I know,
Not even thy Clare can peace bestow,
  While falsehood stains thy name;
Go then to fight! Clare bids thee go!
Clare can a warrior's feelings know,
  And weep a warrior's shame;
Can Red Earl Gilbert's spirit feel,
Buckle the spurs upon thy heel,
And belt thee with thy brand of steel,
  And send thee forth to fame!"

XI.

That night, upon the rocks and bay,
The midnight moon-beam slumbering lay,
And pour'd its silver light, and pure,
Through loop-hole, and through em-
    brazure,
Upon Tantallon tower and hall;
But chief where arched windows wide
Illuminate the chapel's pride,
  The sober glances fall.
Much was their need; though seam'd with
    scars,
Two veterans of the Douglas' wars,
  Though two grey priests were there,
And each a blazing torch held high,
You could not by their blaze descry
  The chapel's carving fair.
Amid that dim and smoky light,
Chequering the silver moon-shine bright,
  A bishop by the altar stood,*
  A noble lord of Douglas blood,
With mitre sheen, and rocquet white.

---

* The well-known Gawain Douglas, Bishop of Dunkeld, son of Archibald Bell-the-Cat, Earl of Angus. He was author of a Scottish metrical version of the Æneid, and of many other poetical pieces of great merit. He had not at this period attained the mitre.

Yet show'd his meek and thoughtful eye
  But little pride of prelacy;
More pleased that, in a barbarous age,
He gave rude Scotland Virgil's page,
Than that beneath his rule he held
The bishopric of fair Dunkeld.
Beside him ancient Angus stood,
Doff'd his furr'd gown, and sable hood:
O'er his huge form and visage pale,
He wore a cap and shirt of mail;
And lean'd his large and wrinkled hand
Upon the huge and sweeping brand
Which wont of yore, in battle fray,
His foeman's limbs to shred away,
As wood-knife lops the sapling spray.[72]
  He seem'd as, from the tombs around
    Rising at judgment-day,
  Some giant Douglas may be found
    In all his old array;
So pale his face, so huge his limb,
So old his arms, his look so grim.

XII.

Then at the altar Wilton kneels,
And Clare the spurs bound on his heels;
And think what next he must have felt,
At buckling of the falchion belt!
  And judge how Clara changed her hue,
While fastening to her lover's side
A friend, which, though in danger tried,
  He once had found untrue!
Then Douglas struck him with his blade:
" Saint Michael and St. Andrew aid,
  I dub thee knight.
Arise, Sir Ralph, De Wilton's heir!
For King, for Church, for Lady fair,
  See that thou fight."—
And Bishop Gawain, as he rose,
Said—" Wilton! grieve not for thy woes,
  Disgrace, and trouble:
For He, who honour best bestows,
  May give thee double."
De Wilton sobb'd, for sob he must—
" Where'er I meet a Douglas, trust
  That Douglas is my brother!"—
" Nay, nay," old Angus said, "not so;
To Surrey's camp thou now must go,
  Thy wrongs no longer smother.
I have two sons in yonder field;
And, if thou meet'st them under shield,

Upon them bravely—do thy worst ;
And foul fall him that blenches first !"

XIII.

Not far advanced was morning day,
When Marmion did his troop array
  To Surrey's camp to ride ;
He had safe conduct for his band,
Beneath the royal seal and hand,
  And Douglas gave a guide :
The ancient Earl, with stately grace,
Would Clara on her palfrey place,
And whisper'd in an under tone,
" Let the hawk stoop, his prey is flown."
The train from out the castle drew,
But Marmion stopp'd to bid adieu :—
  " Though something I might plain,"
    he said,
" Of cold respect to stranger guest,
Sent hither by your King's behest,
  While in Tantallon's towers I staid ;
Part we in friendship from your land,
And, noble Earl, receive my hand."—
But Douglas round him drew his cloak,
Folded his arms, and thus he spoke :—
" My manors, halls, and bowers, shall still
Be open, at my Sovereign's will,
To each one whom he lists, howe'er
Unmeet to be the owner's peer.
My castles are my King's alone,
From turret to foundation-stone—
The hand of Douglas is his own ;
And never shall in friendly grasp
The hand of such as Marmion clasp."—

XIV.

Burn'd Marmion's swarthy cheek like fire,
And shook his very frame for ire,
  And—" This to me !" he said,—
" An 'twere not for thy hoary beard,
Such hand as Marmion's had not spared
  To cleave the Douglas' head !
And, first, I tell thee, haughty Peer,
He, who does England's message here,
Although the meanest in her state,
May well, proud Angus, be thy mate :
And, Douglas, more I tell thee here,
  Even in thy pitch of pride,
Here in thy hold, thy vassals near,

(Nay, never look upon your lord,
And lay your hands upon your sword,)
  I tell thee, thou'rt defied !
And if thou said'st I am not peer
To any lord in Scotland here,
Lowland or Highland, far or near,
  Lord Angus, thou hast lied !"
On the Earl's cheek the flush of rage
O'ercame the ashen hue of age :
Fierce he broke forth,—" And darest
    thou, then,
To beard the lion in his den,
  The Douglas in his hall ?
And hopest thou hence unscathed to go ?—
No, by Saint Bride of Bothwell, no !
Up drawbridge, grooms—what, Warder,
    ho !
  Let the portcullis fall."⁷³
Lord Marmion turn'd,—well was his
    need,
And dash'd the rowels in his steed,
Like arrow through the archway sprung,
The ponderous grate behind him rung :
To pass there was such scanty room,
The bars, descending, razed his plume.

XV.

The steed along the drawbridge flies,
Just as it trembled on the rise ;
Nor lighter does the swallow skim
Along the smooth lake's level brim :
And when Lord Marmion reach'd his
    band,
He halts, and turns with clenched hand,
And shout of loud defiance pours,
And shook his gauntlet at the towers.
" Horse ! horse !" the Douglas cried,
    " and chase !"
But soon he rein'd his fury's pace :
" A royal messenger he came,
Though most unworthy of the name.—
A letter forged ! Saint Jude to speed !
Did ever knight so foul a deed !⁷⁴
At first in heart it liked me ill,
When the King praised his clerkly skill.
Thanks to Saint Bothan, son of mine,
Save Gawain, ne'er could pen a line.
So swore I, and I swear it still,
Let my boy-bishop fret his fill.—

Saint Mary mend my fiery mood:
Old age ne'er cools the Douglas blood,
I thought to slay him where he stood.
'Tis pity of him too," he cried:
" Bold can he speak, and fairly ride,
I warrant him a warrior tried."
With this his mandate he recalls,
And slowly seeks his castle halls.

XVI.

The day in Marmion's journey wore;
Yet, ere his passion's gust was o'er,
They cross'd the heights of Stanrig-moor.
His troop more closely there he scann'd,
And missed the Palmer from the band.—
" Palmer or not," young Blount did say,
" He parted at the peep of day;
Good sooth, it was in strange array."—
" In what array?" said Marmion, quick.
" My lord, I ill can spell the trick;
But all night long, with clink and bang,
Close to my couch did hammers clang;
At dawn the falling drawbridge rang,
And from a loop-hole while I peep,
Old Bell-the-Cat came from the Keep,
Wrapped in a gown of sables fair,
As fearful of the morning air;
Beneath, when that was blown aside,
A rusty shirt of mail I spied,
By Archibald won in bloody work,
Against the Saracen and Turk:
Last night it hung not in the hall;
I thought some marvel would befall.
And next I saw them saddled lead
Old Cheviot forth, the Earl's best steed;
A matchless horse, though something
    old,
Prompt in his paces, cool and bold.
I heard the Sheriff Sholto say,
The Earl did much the Master* pray
To use him on the battle-day;
But he preferr'd—" " Nay, Henry, cease!
Thou sworn horse-courser, hold thy
    peace.—
Eustace, thou bear'st a brain—I pray
What did Blount see at break of day?"—

---

* His eldest son, the Master of Angus.

XVII.

" In brief, my lord, we both descried
(For then I stood by Henry's side)
The Palmer mount, and outwards ride,
    Upon the Earl's own favourite steed:
All sheathed he was in armour bright,
And much resembled that same knight,
Subdued by you in Cotswold fight:
    Lord Angus wished him speed."—
The instant that Fitz-Eustace spoke,
A sudden light on Marmion broke;—
" Ah! dastard fool, to reason lost!"
He mutter'd; " 'Twas nor fay nor ghost
I met upon the moonlight wold,
But living man of earthly mould.—
    O dotage blind and gross!
Had I but fought as wont, one thrust
Had laid De Wilton in the dust,
    My path no more to cross.—
How stand we now?—he told his tale
To Douglas; and with some avail;
'Twas therefore gloom'd his rugged
    brow.—
Will Surrey dare to entertain,
'Gainst Marmion, charge disproved and
    vain?
    Small risk of that, I trow
Yet Clare's sharp questions must I shun;
Must separate Constance from the Nun—
O, what a tangled web we weave,
When first we practise to deceive!
A Palmer too!—no wonder why
I felt rebuked beneath his eye:
I might have known there was but one
Whose look could quell Lord Marmion."

XVIII.

Stung with these thoughts, he urged to
    speed
His troop, and reach'd, at eve, the Tweed,
Where Lennel's convent closed their
    march;
(There now is left but one frail arch;
    Yet mourn thou not its cells;
Our time a fair exchange has made;
Hard by, in hospitable shade,
    A reverend pilgrim dwells,
Well worth the whole Bernardine brood,
That e'er wore sandal, frock, or hood.)

Yet d.d Saint Bernard's Abbot there
Give Marmion entertainment fair,
And lodging for his train and Clare.
Next morn the Baron climb'd the tower,
To view afar the Scottish power,
  Encamp'd on Flodden edge:
The white pavilions made a show,
Like remnants of the winter snow,
  Along the dusky ridge.
Long Marmion look'd :—at length his eye
Unusual movement might descry
  Amid the shifting lines :
The Scottish host drawn out appears,
For, flashing on the hedge of spears
  The eastern sunbeam shines.
Their front now deepening, now extending ;
Their flank inclining, wheeling, bending,
Now drawing back, and now descending,
The skilful Marmion well could know,
They watch'd the motions of some foe,
Who traversed on the plain below.

XIX.

Even so it was.   From Flodden ridge
  The Scots beheld the English host
  Leave Barmore-wood, their evening post,
  And heedful watch'd them as they cross'd
The Till by Twisel Bridge.[75]
  High sight it is, and haughty, while
  They dive into the deep defile ;
  Beneath the cavern'd cliff they fall,
  Beneath the castle's airy wall.
By rock, by oak, by hawthorn-tree,
  Troop after troop are disappearing ;
  Troop after troop their banners rearing,
Upon the eastern bank you see.
Still pouring down the rocky den,
  Where flows the sullen Till,
And rising from the dim-wood glen,
Standards on standards, men on men,
  In slow succession still,
And, sweeping o'er the Gothic arch,
And pressing on, in ceaseless march,
  To gain the opposing hill.
That morn, to many a trumpet clang,
Twisel! thy rock's deep echo rang ;

And many a chief of birth and rank,
Saint Helen! at thy fountain drank.
Thy hawthorn glade, which now we see
In spring-tide bloom so lavishly.
Had then from many an axe its doom,
To give the marching columns room.

XX.

And why stands Scotland idly now,
Dark Flodden! on thy airy brow,
Since England gains the pass the while,
And struggles through the deep defile?
What checks the fiery soul of James?
Why sits that champion of the dames
  Inactive on his steed,
And sees, between him and his land,
Between him and Tweed's southern strand,
  His host Lord Surrey lead?
What 'vails the vain knight-errant's brand?
—O, Douglas, for thy leading wand!
  Fierce Randolph, for thy speed!
O for one hour of Wallace wight,
Or well-skill'd Bruce, to rule the fight,
And cry—" Saint Andrew and our right!"
Another sight had seen that morn,
From Fate's dark book a leaf been torn,
And Flodden had been Bannockbourne!—
The precious hour has pass'd in vain,
And England's host has gain'd the plain ;
Wheeling their march, and circling still,
Around the base of Flodden hill.

XXI.

Ere yet the bands met Marmion's eye,
Fitz-Eustace shouted loud and high,
" Hark! hark! my lord, an English drum!
And see ascending squadrons come
  Between Tweed's river and the hill,
Foot, horse, and cannon :—hap what hap,
My basnet to a prentice cap,
  Lord Surrey's o'er the Till!
Yet more! yet more!—how far array'd
They file from out the hawthorn shade,
  And sweep so gallant by :
With all their banners bravely spread,
  And all their armour flashing high,
St. George might waken from the dead,
  To see fair England's standards fly."—
" Stint in thy prate," quoth Blount,
  " thou'dst best,

And listen to our lord's behest."—
With kindling brow Lord Marmion
   said,—
" This instant be our band array'd;
The river must be quickly cross'd,
That we may join Lord Surrey's host.
If fight King James,—as well I trust,
That fight he will, and fight he must,—
The Lady Clare behind our lines
Shall tarry, while the battle joins."

XXII.

Himself he swift on horseback threw,
Scarce to the Abbot bade adieu;
Far less would listen to his prayer,
To leave behind the helpless Clare.
Down to the Tweed his band he drew,
And mutter'd as the flood they view,
" The pheasant in the falcon's claw,
He scarce will yield to please a daw ·
Lord Angus may the Abbot awe,
   So Clare shall bide with me."
Then on that dangerous ford, and deep,
Where to the Tweed Leat's eddies
   creep,
   He ventured desperately:
And not a moment will he bide,
Till squire, or groom, before him ride;
Headmost of all he stems the tide;
   And stems it gallantly.
Eustace held Clare upon her horse,
   Old Hubert led her rein,
Stoutly they braved the current's course,
And, though far downward driven per
   force,
   The southern bank they gain;
Behind them straggling, came to shore,
   As best they might, the train:
Each o'er his head his yew-bow bore,
   A caution not in vain;
Deep need that day that every string,
By wet unharm'd, should sharply ring.
A moment then Lord Marmion staid,
And breathed his steed, his men array'd,
   Then forward moved his band,
Until, Lord Surrey's rear-guard won,
He halted by a Cross of Stone,
That, on a hillock standing lone,
   Did all the field command.

XXIII.

Hence might they see the full array
Of either host, for deadly fray ;[76]
Their marshall'd lines stretch'd east and
   west,
   And fronted north and south,
And distant salutation pass'd
   From the loud cannon mouth;
Not in the close successive rattle,
That breathes the voice of modern battle,
   But slow and far between.—
The hillock gain'd, Lord Marmion staid:
" Here, by this Cross," he gently said,
   " You well may view the scene.
Here shalt thou tarry, lovely Clare:
O! think of Marmion in thy prayer!—
Thou wilt not?—well,—no less my care
Shall, watchful, for thy weal prepare.—
You, Blount and Eustace, are her guard,
   With ten pick'd archers of my train ;
With England if the day go hard,
   To Berwick speed amain.—
But if we conquer, cruel maid,
My spoils shall at your feet be laid,
   When here we meet again."
He waited not for answer there,
And would not mark the maid's despair,
   Nor heed the discontented look
From either squire; but spurr'd amain,
And, dashing through the battle plain,
   His way to Surrey took.

XXIV.

"—— The good Lord Marmion, by my
   life!
Welcome to danger's hour!—
Short greeting serves in time of strife!
   Thus have I ranged my power:—
Myself will rule this central host,
   Stout Stanley fronts their right,
My sons command the vaward post,
   With Brian Tunstall, stainless knight,[77]
Lord Dacre, with his horsemen light,
   Shall be in rear-ward of the fight,
And succour those that need it most.
   Now, gallant Marmion, well I know,
   Would gladly to the vanguard go;
Edmund, the Admiral, Tunstall there,
With thee their charge will blithely share;

There fight thine own retainers too,
Beneath De Burg, thy steward true."
" Thanks, noble Surrey !" Marmion said,
Nor farther greeting there he paid ;
But, parting like a thunderbolt,
First in the vanguard made a halt,
  Where such a shout there rose
Of " Marmion ! Marmion !" that the cry,
Up Flodden mountain shrilling high,
  Startled the Scottish foes.

XXV.

Blount and Fitz-Eustace rested still
With Lady Clare upon the hill !
On which (for far the day was spent)
The western sunbeams now were bent.
The cry they heard, its meaning knew,
Could plain their distant comrades view ;
Sadly to Blount did Eustace say,
" Unworthy office here to stay !
No hope of gilded spurs to-day.—
But see ! look up—on Flodden bent
The Scottish foe has fired his tent."

  And sudden, as he spoke,
From the sharp ridges of the hill,
All downward to the banks of Till,
  Was wreathed in sable smoke.
Volumed and fast, and rolling far,
The cloud enveloped Scotland's war,
  As down the hill they broke ;
Nor martial shout, nor minstrel tone,
Announced their march ; their tread alone,
At times one warning trumpet blown,
  At times a stifled hum,
Told England, from his mountain-throne
King James did rushing come.—
Scarce could they hear, or see their foes,
  Until at weapon-point they close.—
They close, in clouds of smoke and dust,
With sword-sway, and with lance's thrust ;
  And such a yell was there,
Of sudden and portentous birth,
As if men fought upon the earth,
  And fiends in upper air ;
O life and death were in the shout,
Recoil and rally, charge and rout,
  And triumph and despair.
Long look'd the anxious squires ; their eye
Could in the darkness nought descry.

XXVI.

At length the freshening western blast
Aside the shroud of battle cast ;
And, first, the ridge of mingled spears
Above the brightening cloud appears ;
And in the smoke the pennons flew,
As in the storm the white sea-mew.
Then mark'd they, dashing broad and far,
The broken billows of the war,
And plumed crests of chieftains brave,
Floating like foam upon the wave ;
  But nought distinct they see :
Wide raged the battle on the plain ;
Spears shook, and falchions flash'd amain ;
Fell England's arrow-flight like rain ;
Crests rose, and stoop'd, and rose again,
  Wild and disorderly.
Amid the scene of tumult, high
They saw Lord Marmion's falcon fly :
And stainless Tunstall's banner white,
And Edmund Howard's lion bright,
Still bear them bravely in the fight :
  Although against them come,
Of gallant Gordons many a one,
And many a stubborn Highlandman,
And many a rugged Border clan,
  With Huntly, and with Home.

XXVII.

Far on the left, unseen the while,
Stanley broke Lennox and Argyle ;
Though there the western mountaineer
Rush'd with bare bosom on the spear,
And flung the feeble targe aside,
And with both hands the broadsword plied.
'Twas vain :—But Fortune, on the right,
With fickle smile, cheer'd Scotland's fight.
Then fell that spotless banner white,
  The Howard's lion fell ;
Yet still Lord Marmion's falcon flew
With wavering flight, while fiercer grew
  Around the battle-yell.
The Border slogan rent the sky !
A Home ! a Gordon ! was the cry :
  Loud were the clanging blows ;
Advanced,—forced back,—now low, now
  high,
  The pennon sunk and rose ;

As bends the bark's mast in the gale,
When rent are rigging, shrouds, and sail,
  It waver'd 'mid the foes.
No longer Blount the view could bear:
" By Heaven, and all its saints! I swear
  I will not see it lost!
Fitz-Eustace, you with Lady Clare
May bid your beads, and patter prayer,—
  I gallop to the host."
And to the fray he rode amain,
Follow'd by all the archer train.
The fiery youth, with desperate charge,
Made, for a space, an opening large,—
  The rescued banner rose,—
But darkly closed the war around,
Like pine-tree, rooted from the ground,
  It sunk among the foes.
Then Eustace mounted too:—yet staid
As loath to leave the helpless maid,
  When, fast as shaft can fly,
Blood-shot his eyes, his nostrils spread,
The loose rein dangling from his head,
Housing and saddle bloody red,
  Lord Marmion's steed rush'd by;
And Eustace, maddening at the sight,
  A look and sign to Clara cast
To mark he would return in haste,
Then plunged into the fight.

XXVIII.

Ask me not what the maiden feels,
  Left in that dreadful hour alone:
Perchance her reason stoops, or reels;
  Perchance a courage, not her own,
  Braces her mind to desperate tone.—
The scatter'd van of England wheels:—
  She only said, as loud in air
The tumult roar'd, " Is Wilton
  there?"—
  They fly, or, madden'd by despair,
Fight but to die,—" Is Wilton there?"
With that, straight up the hill there rode
Two horsemen drench'd with gore,
And in their arms, a helpless load,
  A wounded knight they bore.
His hand still strain'd the broken brand;
His arms were smear'd with blood and
  sand.
Dragg'd from among the horses' feet,
With dinted shield, and helmet beat,

The falcon-crest and plumage gone,
Can that be haughty Marmion! . . .
Young Blount his armour did unlace,
And, gazing on his ghastly face,
  Said—" By Saint George, he's gone!
That spear-wound has our master sped,
And see the deep cut on his head!
  Good-night to Marmion."—
" Unnurtured Blount! thy brawling cease:
He opes his eyes," said Eustace; " peace!"

XXIX.

When, doff'd his casque, he felt free air,
Around 'gan Marmion wildly stare:—
" Where's Harry Blount? Fitz-Eustace
  where?
Linger ye here, ye hearts of hare!
Redeem my pennon,—charge again!
Cry—' Marmion to the rescue!'—Vain!
Last of my race, on battle-plain
That shout shall ne'er be heard again!—
Yet my last thought is England's—fly,
  To Dacre bear my signet-ring:
  Tell him his squadrons up to bring.—
Fitz-Eustace, to Lord Surrey hie;
  Tunstall lies dead upon the field,
  His life-blood stains the spotless shield:
  Edmund is down:—my life is reft;
  The Admiral alone is left.
  Let Stanley charge with spur of fire,—
  With Chester charge, and Lancashire,
  Full upon Scotland's central host,
  Or victory and England's lost.—
  Must I bid twice?—hence, varlets! fly!
  Leave Marmion here alone—to die."
  They parted, and alone he lay;
  Clare drew her from the sight away,
Till pain wrung forth a lowly moan,
And half he murmur'd,—" Is there none,
  Of all my halls have nurst,
Page, squire, or groom, one cup to bring
Of blessed water from the spring,
  To slake my dying thirst!"

XXX.

O, Woman! in our hours of ease,
Uncertain, coy, and hard to please,
  And variable as the shade
By the light quivering aspen made;

When pain and anguish wring the brow,
A ministering angel thou!—
Scarce were the piteous accents said,
When, with the Baron's casque, the maid
  To the nigh streamlet ran:
Forgot were hatred, wrongs, and fears;
The plaintive voice alone she hears,
Sees but the dying man.

She stoop'd her by the runnel's side,
  But in abhorrence backward drew;
For, oozing from the mountain's side,
Where raged the war, a dark-red tide
  Was curdling in the streamlet blue.
Where shall she turn?—behold her mark
  A little fountain cell,
Where water, clear as diamond-spark,
  In a stone basin fell.
Above, some half-worn letters say,
𝔇rink. wearp. pilgrim. drink and. prap.
𝔣or. the. kind. soul. of. Spbil. 𝔊rep.
𝔚ho built. this. cross. and. well.
She fill'd the helm, and back she hied,
And with surprise and joy espied
  A monk supporting Marmion's head:
A pious man, whom duty brought
To dubious verge of battle fought,
  To shrieve the dying, bless the dead.

XXXI.

Deep drank Lord Marmion of the wave,
And, as she stoop'd his brow to lave—
  "Is it the hand of Clare," he said,
"Or injured Constance, bathes my head?"
  Then, as remembrance rose,—
"Speak not to me of shrift or prayer!
  I must redress her woes.
Short space, few words, are mine to spare;
Forgive and listen, gentle Clare!"
  "Alas!" she said, "the while,—
O, think of your immortal weal!
In vain for Constance is your zeal;
  She——died at Holy Isle."—
Lord Marmion started from the ground,
As light as if he felt no wound;
Though in the action burst the tide,
In torrents, from his wounded side.
"Then it was truth,"—he said—"I knew
That the dark presage must be true.—
I would the Fiend, to whom belongs
The vengeance due to all her wrongs,

Would spare me but a day!
For wasting fire, and dying groan,
And priests slain on the altar-stone,
  Might bribe him for delay.
It may not be!—this dizzy trance—
Curse on yon base marauder's lance,
And doubly cursed my failing brand!
A sinful heart makes feeble hand."
Then, fainting, down on earth he sunk,
Supported by the trembling Monk.

XXXII.

With fruitless labour, Clara bound,
And strove to stanch the gushing wound:
The Monk, with unavailing cares,
Exhausted all the Church's prayers,
Ever, he said, that, close and near,
A lady's voice was in his ear,
And that the priest he could not hear,
  For that she ever sung,
"*In the lost battle, borne down by the flying,*
Where mingles war's rattle with groans
    of the dying!"
  So the notes rung;—
"Avoid thee, Fiend!—with cruel hand,
Shake not the dying sinner's sand!—
O, look, my son, upon yon sign
Of the Redeemer's grace divine;
  O, think on faith and bliss!—
By many a death-bed I have been,
And many a sinner's parting seen,
  But never aught like this."—
The war, that for a space did fail,
Now trebly thundering swell'd the gale,
  And—STANLEY! was the cry;
A light on Marmion's visage spread,
  And fired his glazing eye;
With dying hand, above his head,
He shook the fragment of his blade,
  And shouted "Victory!—
Charge, Chester, charge! On, Stanley,
  on!"
Were the last words of Marmion.

XXXIII.

By this, though deep the evening fell,
Still rose the battle's deadly swell,
For still the Scots, around their King,
Unbroken, fought in desperate ring.
Where's now their victor vaward wing,

Where Huntly, and where Home ?—
O, for a blast of that dread horn,
On Fontarabian echoes borne,
   That to King Charles did come,
When Rowland brave, and Olivier,
And every paladin and peer,
   On Roncesvalles died !
Such blast might warn them, not in vain,
To quit the plunder of the slain,
And turn the doubtful day again,
   While yet on Flodden side,
Afar, the Royal Standard flies,
And round it toils, and bleeds, and dies,
   Our Caledonian pride !
In vain the wish—for far away,
While spoil and havock mark their way,
Near Sybil's Cross the plunderers stray.—
" O, Lady," cried the Monk, " away !"
   And placed her on her steed,
And led her to the chapel fair,
   Of Tillmouth upon Tweed.
There all the night they spent in prayer,
And at the dawn of morning, there
She met her kinsman, Lord Fitz-Clare.

XXXIV

But as they left the dark'ning heath,
More desperate grew the strife of death.
The English shafts in volleys hail'd,
In headlong charge their horse assail'd ;
Front, flank, and rear, the squadrons
      sweep
To break the Scottish circle deep,
   That fought around their King.
But yet, though thick the shafts as snow,
Though charging knights like whirl-
      winds go,
Though bill-men ply the ghastly blow,
   Unbroken was the ring ;
The stubborn spear-men still made good
   Their dark impenetrable wood,
Each stepping where his comrade stood,
   The instant that he fell.
No thought was there of dastard flight ;
Link'd in the serried phalanx tight,
Groom fought like noble, squire like
      knight,
   As fearlessly and well ;
Till utter darkness closed her wing
O'er their thin host and wounded King.

Then skilful Surrey's sage commands
Led back from strife his shatter'd bands ;
And from the charge they drew,
As mountain-waves, from wasted lands,
   Sweep back to ocean blue.
Then did their loss his foemen know ;
Their King, their Lords, their mightiest
      low,
They melted from the field as snow,
When streams are swoln and south winds
      blow,
   Dissolves in silent dew.
Tweed's echoes heard the ceaseless plash,
While many a broken band,
Disorder'd, through her currents dash,
   To gain the Scottish land ;
To town and tower, to down and dale,
To tell red Flodden's dismal tale,
And raise the universal wail.
Tradition, legend, tune, and song,
Shall many an age that wail prolong :
Still from the sire the son shall hear
Of the stern strife, and carnage drear,
   Of Flodden's fatal field,
Where shiver'd was fair Scotland's spear,
   And broken was her shield !

XXXV.

Day dawns upon the mountain's side :—
There, Scotland ! lay thy bravest pride,
Chiefs, knights, and nobles, many a one :
The sad survivors all are gone —
View not that corpse mistrustfully,
Defaced and mangled though it be ;
Nor to yon Border Castle high,
Look northward with upbraiding eye ;
   Nor cherish hope in vain,
That, journeying far on foreign strand,
The Royal Pilgrim to his land
   May yet return again.
He saw the wreck his rashness wrought ;
Reckless of life, he desperate fought,
   And fell on Flodden plain ;
And well in death his trusty brand,
Firm clench'd within his manly hand,
   Beseem'd the monarch slain.[78]
But, O ! how changed since yon blithe
      night !—
Gladly I turn me from the sight,
   Unto my tale again

XXXVI.

Short is my tale:—Fitz-Eustace' care
A pierced and mangled body bare
To moated Lichfield's lofty pile ;
And there, beneath the southern aisle,
A tomb, with Gothic sculpture fair,
Did long Lord Marmion's image bear,
(Now vainly for its sight you look ;
'Twas levell'd when fanatic Brook
The fair cathedral storm'd and took ;[79]
But, thanks to Heaven and good Saint
   Chad,
A guerdon meet the spoiler had !)
There erst was martial Marmion found,
His feet upon a couchant hound,
   His hands to heaven upraised ;
And all around, on scutcheon rich,
And tablet carved, and fretted niche,
   His arms and feats were blazed.
And yet, though all was carved so fair,
And priest for Marmion breathed the
   prayer,
The last Lord Marmion lay not there.
From Ettrick woods a peasant swain
Follow'd his lord to Flodden plain,—
One of those flowers, whom plaintive lay
In Scotland mourns as " wede away:"
Sore wounded, Sybil's Cross he spied,
And dragg'd him to its foot, and died,
Close by the noble Marmion's side.
The spoilers stripp'd and gash'd the slain,
And thus their corpses were mista'en ;
And thus, in the proud Baron's tomb,
The lowly woodsman took the room.

XXXVII.

Less easy task it were, to show
Lord Marmion's nameless grave, and
   low.
   They dug his grave e'en where he lay,
   But every mark is gone ;
   Time's wasting hand has done away
   The simple Cross of Sybil Grey,
   And broke her font of stone :
But yet from out the little hill
Oozes the slender springlet still.
   Oft halts the stranger there,
   For thence may best his curious eye

The memorable field descry ;
   And shepherd boys repair
To seek the water-flag and rush,
And rest them by the hazel bush,
   And plait their garlands fair ;
Nor dream they sit upon the grave,
That holds the bones of Marmion brave.—
When thou shalt find the little hill,
With thy heart commune, and be still.
If ever, in temptation strong,
Thou left'st the right path for the wrong ;
If every devious step, thus trod,
Still led thee farther from the road ;
Dread thou to speak presumptuous doom
On noble Marmion's lowly tomb ;
But say, " He died a gallant knight,
With sword in hand, for England's right."

XXXVIII.

I do not rhyme to that dull elf,
Who cannot image to himself,
That all through Flodden's dismal night,
Wilton was foremost in the fight ;
That, when brave Surrey's steed was slain,
'Twas Wilton mounted him again ;
'Twas Wilton's brand that deepest hew'd,
Amid the spearmen's stubborn wood ;
Unnamed by Hollinshed or Hall,
He was the living soul of all :
That, after fight, his faith made plain,
He won his rank and lands again ;
And charged his old paternal shield
With bearings won on Flodden Field.
Nor sing I to that simple maid,
To whom it must in terms be said,
That King and kinsmen did agree,
To bless fair Clara's constancy ;
Who cannot, unless I relate,
Paint to her mind the bridal's state ;
That Wolsey's voice the blessing spoke,
More, Sands, and Denny, pass'd the joke,
That bluff King Hal the curtain drew,
And Catherine's hand the stocking threw ;
And afterwards, for many a day,
That it was held enough to say,
In blessing to a wedded pair,
" Love they like Wilton and like Clare !"

L'Envoy.

TO THE READER.

WHY then a final note prolong,
Or lengthen out a closing song,
Unless to bid the gentles speed,
Who long have listed to my rede ?*
To Statesmen grave, if such may deign
To read the Minstrel's idle strain,
Sound head, clean hand, and piercing wit,
And patriotic heart—as PITT !

---

* Story.

A garland for the hero's crest,
And twined by her he loves the best;
To every lovely lady bright,
What can I wish but faithful knight?
To every faithful lover too,
What can I wish but lady true?
And knowledge to the studious sage;
And pillow to the head of age.
To thee, dear school-boy, whom my
    lay
Has cheated of thy hour of play,
Light task, and merry holiday!
To all, to each, a fair good night,
And pleasing dreams, and slumbers light!

THE LADY OF THE LAKE.

TO THE

MOST NOBLE

JOHN JAMES MARQUIS OF ABERCORN,

&c. &c. &c.

THIS POEM IS INSCRIBED BY

THE AUTHOR.

ARGUMENT.

———◆———

The Scene of the following Poem is laid chiefly in the vicinity of Loch Katrine, in the Western Highlands of Perthshire. The time of action includes six days, and the transactions of each day occupy a Canto.

THE LADY OF THE LAKE.

CANTO FIRST.

The Chase.

Harp of the North! that mouldering
    long hast hung
On the witch-elm that shades Saint
    Fillan's spring,
And down the fitful breeze thy numbers
    flung,
    Till envious ivy did around thee cling,
Muffling with verdant ringlet every
    string,—
    O minstrel Harp, still must thine accents
    sleep?
Mid rustling leaves and fountains murmur-
    ing,
    Still must thy sweeter sounds their
    silence keep,
Nor bid a warrior smile, nor teach a maid
    to weep?

Not thus, in ancient days of Caledon,
    Was thy voice mute amid the festal
    crowd,
When lay of hopeless love, or glory won,
    Aroused the fearful, or subdued the
    proud.
At each according pause, was heard
    aloud
    Thine ardent symphony sublime and
    high!
Fair dames and crested chiefs attention
    bow'd;
    For still the burden of thy minstrelsy
Was Knighthood's dauntless deed, and
    Beauty's matchless eye.

O wake once more! how rude soe'er the
    hand
    That ventures o'er thy magic maze to
    stray;
O wake once more! though scarce my
    skill command
    Some feeble echoing of thine earlier lay:
Though harsh and faint, and soon to die
    away,
    And all unworthy of thy nobler strain,
Yet if one heart throb higher at its sway,
    The wizard note has not been touch'd
    in vain.
Then silent be no more! Enchantress,
    wake again!

I.

The stag at eve had drunk his fill,
Where danced the moon on Monan's rill,
And deep his midnight lair had made
In lone Glenartney's hazel shade;
But, when the sun his beacon red
Had kindled on Benvoirlich's head,*
The deep-mouth'd bloodhound's heavy
    bay
Resounded up the rocky way,
And faint, from farther distance borne,
Were heard the clanging hoof and horn.

II.

As Chief, who hears his warder call,
"To arms! the foemen storm the wall,"

---

* One of the Grampian chain of mountains
at the head of the Valley of the Garry.

The antler'd monarch of the waste
Sprung from his heathery couch in haste.
But, ere his fleet career he took,
The dew-drops from his flanks he shook;
Like crested leader proud and high,
Toss'd his beam'd frontlet to the sky;
A moment gazed adown the dale,
A moment snuff'd the tainted gale,
A moment listen'd to the cry,
That thicken'd as the chase drew nigh;
Then, as the headmost foes appear'd,
With one brave bound the copse he clear'd,
And, stretching forward free and far,
Sought the wild heaths of Uam-Var.

III

Yell'd on the view the opening pack;
Rock, glen, and cavern, paid them back;
To many a mingled sound at once
The awaken'd mountain gave response.
A hundred dogs bay'd deep and strong,
Clatter'd a hundred steeds along,
Their peal the merry horns rung out,
A hundred voices join'd the shout;
With hark and whoop and wild halloo,
No rest Benvoirlich's echoes knew.
Far from the tumult fled the roe,
Close in her covert cower'd the doe,
The falcon, from her cairn on high,
Cast on the rout a wondering eye,
Till far beyond her piercing ken
The hurricane had swept the glen.
Faint and more faint, its failing din
Return'd from cavern, cliff, and linn,
And silence settled, wide and still,
On the lone wood and mighty hill.

IV.

Less loud the sounds of sylvan war
Disturb'd the heights of Uam-Var,
And roused the cavern, where 'tis told,
A giant made his den of old;[1]
For ere that steep ascent was won,
High in his pathway hung the sun,
And many a gallant, stay'd perforce,
Was fain to breathe his faltering horse,
And of the trackers of the deer,
Scarce half the lessening pack was near;
So shrewdly on the mountain side
Had the bold burst their mettle tried.

V.

The noble stag was pausing now,
Upon the mountain's southern brow,
Where broad extended, far beneath,
The varied realms of fair Menteith.
With anxious eye he wander'd o'er
Mountain and meadow, moss and moor,
And ponder'd refuge from his toil,
By far Lochard or Aberfoyle.
But nearer was the copsewood grey,
That waved and wept on Loch-Achray,
And mingled with the pine-trees blue
On the bold cliffs of Benvenue.
Fresh vigour with the hope return'd,
With flying foot the heath he spurn'd,
Held westward with unwearied race,
And left behind the panting chase.

VI.

'Twere long to tell what steeds gave o'er,
As swept the hunt through Cambus-more;
What reins were tighten'd in despair,
When rose Benledi's ridge in air;[*]
Who flagg'd upon Bochastle's heath,
Who shun'd to stem the flooded Teith,[†]—
For twice that day, from shore to shore,
The gallant stag swam stoutly o'er.
Few were the stragglers, following far,
That reach'd the lake of Venachar;
And when the Brigg[‡] of Turk was won,
The headmost horseman rode alone.

VII.

Alone, but with unbated zeal,
That horseman plied the scourge and steel;
For jaded now, and spent with toil,
Emboss'd with foam, and dark with soil,
While every gasp with sobs he drew,
The labouring stag strain'd full in view.
Two dogs of black Saint Hubert's breed,
Unmatch'd for courage, breath, and speed,
Fast on his flying traces came
And all but won that desperate game;

---

* Benledi is a high mountain on the north-
west of Callender. Its name signifies the
mountain of God.
† A river which gives its name to the terri-
tory of Menteith.
‡ *Brigg*, a bridge.

For, scarce a spear's length from his
   haunch,
Vindictive toil'd the bloodhounds staunch;
Nor nearer might the dogs attain,
Nor farther might the quarry strain.
Thus up the margin of the lake,
Between the precipice and brake,
O'er stock and rock their race they take.

VIII.

The Hunter mark'd that mountain high,
The lone lake's western boundary,
And deem'd the stag must turn to bay,
Where that huge rampart barr'd the way;
Already glorying in the prize,
Measured his antlers with his eyes;
For the death-wound and death-halloo,
Muster'd his breath, his whinyard drew;[b]—
But thundering as he came prepared,
With ready arm and weapon bared,
The wily quarry shunn'd the shock,
And turn'd him from the opposing rock;
Then, dashing down a darksome glen,
Soon lost to hound and hunter's ken,
In the deep Trosach's wildest nook
His solitary refuge took.
There, while close couch'd, the thicket
   shed
Cold dews and wild-flowers on his head,
He heard the baffled dogs in vain
Rave through the hollow pass amain.
Chiding the rocks that yell'd again.

IX.

Close on the hounds the hunter came,
To cheer them on the vanish'd game;
But, stumbling in the rugged dell,
The gallant horse exhausted fell.
The impatient rider strove in vain
To rouse him with the spur and rein,
For the good steed, his labours o'er,
Stretch'd his stiff limbs, to rise no more;
Then, touch'd with pity and remorse,
He sorrow'd o'er the expiring horse.
"I little thought, when first thy rein
I slack'd upon the banks of Seine,
That Highland eagle e'er should feed
On thy fleet limbs, my matchless steed!

Woe worth the chase, woe worth the day,
That costs thy life, my gallant grey!"

X.

Then through the dell his horn resounds,
From vain pursuit to call the hounds.
Back limp'd, with slow and crippled pace,
The sulky leaders of the chase;
Close to their master's side they press'd,
With drooping tail and humbled crest;
But still the dingle's hollow throat
Prolong'd the swelling bugle-note.
The owlets started from their dream,
The eagles answered with their scream,
Round and around the sounds were cast,
Till echo seem'd an answering blast;
And on the hunter hied his way,
To join some comrades of the day;
Yet often paused, so strange the road,
So wondrous where the scenes it show'd

XI.

The western waves of ebbing day
Roll'd o'er the glen their level way;
Each purple peak, each flinty spire,
Was bathed in floods of living fire.
But not a setting beam could glow
Within the dark ravines below,
Where twined the path in shadow hid,
Round many a rocky pyramid,
Shooting abruptly from the dell
Its thunder-splinter'd pinnacle;
Round many an insulated mass,
The native bulwarks of the pass,
Huge as the tower* which builders vain
Presumptuous piled on Shinar's plain.
The rocky summits, split and rent,
Form'd turret, dome, or battlement,
Or seem'd fantastically set
With cupola or minaret,
Wild crests as pagod ever deck'd,
Or mosque of Eastern architect.
Nor were these earth-born castles bare,
Nor lack'd they many a banner fair;
For, from their shiver'd brows display'd,
Far o'er the unfathomable glade,
All twinkling with the dewdrops sheen,
The brier-rose fell in streamers green,

---

* The Tower of Babel.—Genesis xi. 1—9.

And creeping shrubs, of thousand dyes,
Waved in the west-wind's summer sighs.

XII.

Boon nature scatter'd, free and wild,
Each plant or flower, the mountain's child,
Here eglantine embalm'd the air,
Hawthorn and hazel mingled there;
The primrose pale and violet flower,
Found in each cliff a narrow bower;
Fox-glove and night-shade, side by side,
Emblems of punishment and pride,
Group'd their dark hues with every stain
The weather-beaten crags retain.
With boughs that quaked at every breath,
Grey birch and aspen wept beneath;
Aloft, the ash and warrior oak
Cast anchor in the rifted rock;
And, higher yet, the pine-tree hung
His shatter'd trunk, and frequent flung,
Where seem'd the cliffs to meet on high,
His boughs athwart the narrow'd sky.
Highest of all, where white peaks glanced,
Where glist'ning streamers waved and
    danced,
The wanderer's eye could barely view
The summer heaven's delicious blue;
So wondrous wild, the whole might seem
The scenery of a fairy dream.

XIII.

Onward, amid the copse 'gan peep
A narrow inlet, still and deep,
Affording scarce such breadth of brim,
As served the wild duck's brood to swim,
Lost for a space, through thickets veering,
But broader when again appearing,
Tall rocks and tufted knolls their face
Could on the dark-blue mirror trace;
And farther as the hunter stray'd,
Still broader sweeps its channels made.
The shaggy mounds no longer stood,
Emerging from entangled wood,
But, wave-encircled, seem'd to float,
Like castle girdled with its moat;
Yet broader floods extending still
Divide them from their parent hill,
Till each, retiring, claims to be
An islet in an inland sea.

XIV.

And now, to issue from the glen,
No pathway meets the wanderer's ken,
Unless he climb, with footing nice,
A far projecting precipice.[1]
The broom's tough roots his ladder made,
The hazel saplings lent their aid;
And thus an airy point he won,
Where, gleaming with the setting sun,
One burnish'd sheet of living gold,
Loch Katrine lay beneath him roll'd,
In all her length far winding lay,
With promontory, creek, and bay,
And islands that, empurpled bright,
Floated amid the livelier light,
And mountains, that like giants stand,
To sentinel enchanted land.
High on the south, huge Benvenue
Down on the lake in masses threw
Crags, knolls and mounds, confusedly
    hurl'd,
The fragments of an earlier world;
A wildering forest feather'd o'er
His ruin'd sides and summit hoar,
While on the north, through middle air,
Ben-an heaved high his forehead bare.

XV.

From the steep promontory gazed
The stranger, raptured and amazed.
And, " What a scene were here," he cried,
" For princely pomp, or churchman's
    pride!
On this bold brow, a lordly tower;
In that soft vale, a lady's bower;
On yonder meadow, far away,
The turrets of a cloister grey;
How blithely might the bugle-horn
Chide, on the lake, the lingering morn!
How sweet, at eve, the lover's lute
Chime, when the groves were still and
    mute!
And, when the midnight moon should lave
Her forehead in the silver wave,
How solemn on the ear would come
The holy matins' distant hum,
While the deep peal's commanding tone
Should wake, in yonder islet lone,

A sainted hermit from his cell,
To drop a bead with every knell—
And bugle, lute, and bell, and all,
Should each bewilder'd stranger call
To friendly feast, and lighted hall.

XVI.

" Blithe were it then to wander here !
But now,—beshrew yon nimble deer,—
Like that same hermit's, thin and spare,
The copse must give my evening fare ;
Some mossy bank my couch must be,
Some rustling oak my canopy.
Yet pass we that ; the war and chase
Give little choice of resting-place ;—
A summer night, in greenwood spent,
Were but to-morrow's merriment :
But hosts may in these wilds abound,
Such as are better miss'd than found ;
To meet with Highland plunderers here,
Were worse than loss of steed or deer.—
I am alone ;—my bugle strain
May call some straggler of the train ;
Or, fall the worst that may betide,
Ere now this falchion has been tried."

XVII.

But scarce again his horn he wound,
When lo ! forth starting at the sound,
From underneath an aged oak,
That slanted from the islet rock,
A damsel guider of its way,
A little skiff shot to the bay,
That round the promontory steep
Led its deep line in graceful sweep,
Eddying in almost viewless wave,
The weeping willow-twig to lave,
And kiss, with whispering sound and slow,
The beach of pebbles bright as snow.
The boat had touch'd this silver strand,
Just as the Hunter left his stand,
And stood conceal'd amid the brake,
To view this Lady of the Lake.
The maiden paused, as if again
She thought to catch the distant strain.
With head up-raised, and look intent,
And eye and ear attentive bent,
And locks flung back, and lips apart,
Like monument of Grecian art,

In listening mood, she seem'd to stand,
The guardian Naiad of the strand.

XVIII.

And ne'er did Grecian chisel trace
A Nymph, a Naiad, or a Grace,
Of finer form, or lovelier face !
What though the sun, with ardent frown,
Had slightly tinged her cheek with
brown,—
The sportive toil, which, short and light,
Had dyed her glowing hue so bright,
Served too in hastier swell to show
Short glimpses of a breast of snow :
What though no rule of courtly grace
To measured mood had train'd her pace,—
A foot more light, a step more true,
Ne'er from the heath-flower dash'd the
dew ;
E'en the slight harebell raised its head,
Elastic from her airy tread :
What though upon her speech there hung
The accents of the mountain tongue,—
Those silver sounds, so soft, so dear,
The listener held his breath to hear !

XIX.

A Chieftain's daughter seem'd the maid ;
Her satin snood,* her silken plaid,
Her golden brooch, such birth betray'd.
And seldom was a snood amid
Such wild luxuriant ringlets hid,
Whose glossy black to shame might bring
The plumage of the raven's wing ;
And seldom o'er a breast so fair,
Mantled a plaid with modest care,
And never brooch the folds combined
Above a heart more good and kind.
Her kindness and her worth to spy,
You need but gaze on Ellen's eye ;
Not Katrine, in her mirror blue,
Gives back the shaggy banks more true,
Than every free-born glance confess'd
The guileless movements of her breast ;
Whether joy danced in her dark eye,
Or woe or pity claim'd a sigh,

---

* *Snood*, the fillet worn round the hair of
maidens.

Or filial love was glowing there,
Or meek devotion pour'd a prayer,
Or tale of injury call'd forth
The indignant spirit of the North.
One only passion unreveal'd,
With maiden pride the maid conceal'd,
Yet not less purely felt the flame;—
O need I tell that passion's name!

XX.

Impatient of the silent horn,
Now on the gale her voice was borne;—
"Father!" she cried; the rocks around
Loved to prolong the gentle sound.
Awhile she paused, no answer came,—
"Malcolm, was thine the blast?" the name
Less resolutely utter'd fell,
The echoes could not catch the swell.
"A stranger I," the Huntsman said,
Advancing from the hazel shade.
The maid, alarmed, with hasty oar,
Push'd her light shallop from the shore,
And when a space was gain'd between,
Closer she drew her bosom's screen;
(So forth the startled swan would swing,
So turn to prune his ruffled wing.)
Then safe, though flutter'd and amazed,
She paused, and on the stranger gazed.
Not his the form, nor his the eye,
That youthful maidens wont to fly.

XXI.

On his bold visage middle age
Had slightly press'd its signet sage
Yet had not quench'd the open truth
And fiery vehemence of youth;
Forward and frolic glee was there,
The will to do, the soul to dare,
The sparkling glance, soon blown to fire,
Of hasty love, or headlong ire.
His limbs were cast in manly mould,
For hardy sports or contest bold;
And though in peaceful garb array'd,
And weaponless, except his blade,
His stately mien as well implied
A high-born heart, a martial pride,
As if a Baron's crest he wore,
And sheathed in armour trode the shore.

Slighting the petty need he show'd,
He told of his benighted road;
His ready speech flow'd fair and free,
In phrase of gentlest courtesy;
Yet seem'd that tone, and gesture bland,
Less used to sue than to command.

XXII.

A while the maid the stranger eyed,
And, reassured, at length replied,
That Highland halls were open still
To wilder'd wanderers of the hill.
"Nor think you unexpected come
To yon lone isle, our desert home;
Before the heath had lost the dew,
This morn, a couch was pull'd for you;
On yonder mountain's purple head
Have ptarmigan and heath-cock bled,
And our broad nets have swept the mere,
To furnish forth your evening cheer."—
"Now, by the rood, my lovely maid,
Your courtesy has err'd," he said;
"No right have I to claim, misplaced,
The welcome of expected guest.
A wanderer, here by fortune tost,
My way, my friends, my courser lost,
I ne'er before, believe me, fair,
Have ever drawn your mountain air,
Till on this lake's romantic strand,
I found a fay in fairy land!"—

XXIII.

"I well believe," the maid replied,
As her light skiff approach'd the side,—
"I well believe, that ne'er before
Your foot has trod Loch Katrine's shore;
But yet, as far as yesternight,
Old Allan-bane foretold your plight,—
A gray-hair'd sire, whose eye intent
Was on the vision'd future bent.[6]
He saw your steed, a dapp'ed grey,
Lie dead beneath the birchen way;
Painted exact your form and mien,
Your hunting suit of Lincoln green,
That tassell'd horn so gaily gilt,
That falchion's crooked blade and hilt,
That cap with heron plumage trim,
And yon two hounds so dark and grim.

He bade that all should ready be,
To grace a guest of fair degree;
But light I held his prophecy,
And deem'd it was my father's horn,
Whose echoes o'er the lake were borne."

XXIV.

The stranger smiled:—"Since to your
   home
A destined errant-knight I come,
Announced by prophet sooth and old,
Doom'd, doubtless, for achievement bold,
I'll lightly front each high emprise,
For one kind glance of those bright eyes.
Permit me, first, the task to guide
Your fairy frigate o'er the tide."
The maid, with smile suppress'd and sly,
The toil unwonted saw him try;
For seldom sure, if e'er before,
His noble hand had grasp'd an oar:
Yet with main strength his strokes he drew,
And o'er the lake the shallop flew;
With heads erect, and whimpering cry,
The hounds behind their passage ply.
Nor frequent does the bright oar break
The dark'ning mirror of the lake,
Until the rocky isle they reach,
And moor their shallop on the beach.

XXV.

The stranger view'd the shore around,
'Twas all so close with copsewood bound,
Nor track nor pathway might declare
That human foot frequented there,
Until the mountain-maiden show'd
A clambering unsuspected road,
That winded through the tangled screen,
And open'd on a narrow green,
Where weeping birch and willow round
With their long fibres swept the ground.
Here, for retreat in dangerous hour,
Some chief had framed a rustic bower.[7]

XXVI.

It was a lodge of ample size,
But strange of structure and device;
Of such materials, as around
The workman's hand had readiest found.
Lopp'd off their boughs, their hoar trunks
   bared,
And by the hatchet rudely squared,
To give the walls their destined height,
The sturdy oak and ash unite;
While moss and clay and leaves combined
To fence each crevice from the wind.
The lighter pine-trees, over-head,
Their slender length for rafters spread,
And wither'd heath and rushes dry
Supplied a russet canopy.
Due westward, fronting to the green,
A rural portico was seen,
Aloft on native pillars borne,
Of mountain fir, with bark unshorn,
Where Ellen's hand had taught to twine
The ivy and Idæan vine,
The clematis, the favour'd flower
Which boasts the name of virgin-bower,
And every hardy plant could bear
Loch Katrine's keen and searching air.
An instant in this porch she staid,
And gaily to the stranger said,
"On heaven and on thy lady call,
And enter the enchanted hall!"

XXVII.

"My hope, my heaven, my trust must be,
My gentle guide, in following thee."
He cross'd the threshold—and a clang
Of angry steel that instant rang.
To his bold brow his spirit rush'd,
But soon for vain alarm he blush'd,
When on the floor he saw display'd,
Cause of the din, a naked blade
Dropp'd from the sheath, that careless
   flung
Upon a stag's huge antlers swung;
For all around, the walls to grace,
Hung trophies of the fight or chase:
A target there, a bugle here,
A battle-axe, a hunting-spear,
And broadswords, bows, and arrows store,
With the tusk'd trophies of the boar.
Here grins the wolf as when he died,
And there the wild-cat's brindled hide
The frontlet of the elk adorns,
Or mantles o'er the bison's horns;
Pennons and flags defaced and stain'd,
That blackening streaks of blood retain'd,

And deer-skins, dappled, dun, and white,
With otter's fur and seal's unite,
In rude and uncouth tapestry all,
To garnish forth the sylvan hall.

XXVIII.

The wondering stranger round him gazed,
And next the fallen weapon raised:—
Few were the arms whose sinewy strength
Sufficed to stretch it forth at length,
And as the brand he poised and sway'd,
" I never knew but one," he said,
" Whose stalwart arm might brook to
    wield
A blade like this in battle-field.
She sigh'd, then smiled and took the word:
" You see the guardian champion's sword:
As light it trembles in his hand,
As in my grasp a hazel wand;
My sire's tall form might grace the part
Of Ferragus or Ascabart;[8]
But in the absent giant's hold
Are women now, and menials old."

XXIX.

The mistress of the mansion came,
Mature of age, a graceful dame;
Whose easy step and stately port
Had well become a princely court,
To whom, though more than kindred
    knew,
Young Ellen gave a mother's due.
Meet welcome to her guest she made,
And every courteous rite was paid,
That hospitality could claim,
Though all unask'd his birth and name.[9]
Such then the reverence to a guest,
That fellest foe might join the feast,
And from his deadliest foeman's door
Unquestion'd turn, the banquet o'er.
At length his rank the stranger names,
" The Knight of Snowdoun, James Fitz-
    James;
Lord of a barren heritage,
Which his brave sires, from age to age,
By their good swords had held with toil;
His sire had fallen in such turmoil,
And he, God wot, was forced to stand
Oft for his right with blade in hand.

This morning, with Lord Moray's train,
He chased a stalwart stag in vain,
Outstripp'd his comrades, miss'd the deer,
Lost his good steed, and wander'd here."

XXX.

Fain would the knight in turn require
The name and state of Ellen's sire.
Well show'd the elder lady's mien,
That courts and cities she had seen;
Ellen, though more her looks display'd
The simple grace of sylvan maid,
In speech and gesture, form and face,
Show'd she was come of gentle race.
'Twere strange, in ruder rank to find,
Such looks, such manners, and such mind.
Each hint the Knight of Snowdoun gave,
Dame Margaret heard with silence grave;
Or Ellen, innocently gay,
Turn'd all inquiry light away:—
" Weird women we! by dale and down
We dwell, afar from tower and town.
We stem the flood, we ride the blast,
On wandering knights our spells we cast;
While viewless minstrels touch the string,
'Tis thus our charmed rhymes we sing."
She sung, and still a harp unseen
Fill'd up the symphony between.

XXXI.

Song.

" Soldier, rest! thy warfare o er,
   Sleep the sleep that knows not breaking;
Dream of battled fields no more,
   Days of danger, nights of waking.
In our isle's enchanted hall,
   Hands unseen thy couch are strewing,
Fairy strains of music fall,
   Every sense in slumber dewing.
Soldier, rest! thy warfare o'er,
Dream of fighting fields no more:
Sleep the sleep that knows not breaking,
Morn of toil, nor night of waking.

" No rude sound shall reach thine ear,
   Armour's clang, or war-steed champing,
Trump nor pibroch summon here
   Mustering clan, or squadron tramping,

Yet the lark's shrill fife may come
　At the day-break from the fallow,
And the bittern sound his drum,
　Booming from the sedgy shallow.
Ruder sounds shall none be near
Guards nor warders challenge here,
Here's no war-steed's neigh and champing,
Shouting clans, or squadrons stamping."

XXXII.

She paused—then, blushing, led the lay
To grace the stranger of the day.
Her mellow notes awhile prolong
The cadence of the flowing song,
Till to her lips in measured frame
The minstrel verse spontaneous came.

Song continued.

" Huntsman, rest ! thy chase is done,
　While our slumbrous spells assail ye,
Dream not, with the rising sun,
　Bugles here shall sound reveillé.
Sleep ! the deer is in his den ;
　Sleep ! thy hounds are by thee lying ;
Sleep ! nor dream in yonder glen,
　How thy gallant steed lay dying.
Huntsman, rest ! thy chase is done,
Think not of the rising sun,
For at dawning to assail ye,
Here no bugles sound reveillé."

XXXIII.

The hall was clear'd—the stranger's bed
Was there of mountain heather spread,
Where oft a hundred guests had lain,
And dream'd their forest sports again.
But vainly did the heath-flower shed
Its moorland fragrance round his head ;
Not Ellen's spell had lull'd to rest
The fever of his troubled breast.
In broken dreams the image rose
Of varied perils, pains, and woes :
His steed now flounders in the brake,
Now sinks his barge upon the lake ;
Now leader of a broken host,
His standard falls, his honour's lost.
Then,—from my couch may heavenly might
Chase that worst phantom of the night !—

Again return'd the scenes of youth,
Of confident undoubting truth ;
Again his soul he interchanged
With friends whose hearts were long
　estranged.
They come, in dim procession led,
The cold, the faithless, and the dead ;
As warm each hand, each brow as gay,
As if they parted yesterday.
And doubt distracts him at the view
O were his senses false or true !
Dream'd he of death, or broken vow,
Or is it all a vision now ?

XXXIV.

At length, with Ellen in a grove
He seem'd to walk, and speak of love ;
She listen'd with a blush and sigh,
His suit was warm, his hopes were high.
He sought her yielded hand to clasp,
And a cold gauntlet met his grasp :
The phantom's sex was changed and gone,
Upon its head a helmet shone ;
Slowly enlarged to giant size,
With darken'd cheek and threatening eyes,
The grisly visage, stern and hoar,
To Ellen still a likeness bore.—
He woke, and panting with affright,
Recall'd the vision of the night.
The hearth's decaying brands were red,
And deep and dusky lustre shed,
Half showing, half concealing, all
The uncouth trophies of the hall.
'Mid those the stranger fixed his eye,
Where that huge falchion hung on high,
And thoughts on thoughts, a countless
　throng,
Rush'd, chasing countless thoughts along,
Until, the giddy whirl to cure,
He rose, and sought the moonshine pure.

XXXV.

The wild-rose, eglantine, and broom,
Wasted around their rich perfume :
The birch-trees wept in fragrant balm,
The aspens slept beneath the calm ;
The silver light, with quivering glance,
Play'd on the water's still expanse,—

Wild were the heart whose passions'
  sway
Could rage beneath the sober ray !
He felt its calm, that warrior guest,
While thus he communed with his
  breast :—
" Why is it, at each turn I trace
Some memory of that exiled race !
Can I not mountain-maiden spy,
But she must bear the Douglas eye ?
Can I not view a Highland brand,
But it must match the Douglas hand ?
Can I not frame a fever'd dream,
But still the Douglas is the theme ?
I'll dream no more—by manly mind
Not even in sleep is will resign'd.
My midnight orisons said o'er,
I'll turn to rest, and dream no more."
His midnight orisons he told,
A prayer with every bead of gold,
Consign'd to heaven his cares and woes,
And sunk in undisturb'd repose ;
Until the heath-cock shrilly crew,
And morning dawn'd on Benvenue.

------◆------

CANTO SECOND.

The Island.

I.

AT morn the black-cock trims his jetty
  wing,
  'Tis morning prompts the linnet's
    blithest lay,
All Nature's children feel the matin spring
Of life reviving, with reviving day ;
And while yon little bark glides down the
  bay,
  Wafting the stranger on his way again,
Morn's genial influence roused a minstrel
  grey,
  And sweetly o'er the lake was heard
    thy strain,
Mix'd with the sounding harp, O white-
  hair'd Allan-Bane !⁰

II.

Song.

" Not faster yonder rowers' might
  Flings from their oars the spray,
Not faster yonder rippling bright,
That tracks the shallop's course in light,
  Melts in the lake away,
Than men from memory erase
The benefits of former days ;
Then, stranger, go ! good speed the while,
Nor think again of the lonely isle.

" High place to thee in royal court,
  High place in battle line,
Good hawk and hound for sylvan sport,
Where beauty sees the brave resort,
  The honour'd meed be thine !
True be thy sword, thy friend sincere,
Thy lady constant, kind, and dear,
And lost in love and friendship's smile
Be memory of the lonely isle.

III.

Song continued.

" But if beneath yon southern sky
  A plaided stranger roam,
Whose drooping crest and stifled sigh,
And sunken cheek and heavy eye,
  Pine for his Highland home ;
Then, warrior, then be thine to show
The care that soothes a wanderer's woe ;
Remember then thy hap ere while,
A stranger in the lonely isle.

" Or if on life's uncertain main
  Mishap shall mar thy sail ;
If faithful, wise, and brave in vain,
Woe, want, and exile thou sustain
  Beneath the fickle gale ;
Waste not a sigh on fortune changed,
On thankless courts, or friends estranged,
But come where kindred worth shall smile,
To greet thee in the lonely isle."

IV.

As died the sounds upon the tide,
The shallop reach'd the mainland side,

And ere his onward way he took,
The stranger cast a lingering look,
Where easily his eye might reach
The Harper on the islet beach,
Reclined against a blighted tree,
As wasted, grey, and worn as he.
To minstrel meditation given,
His reverend brow was raised to heaven,
As from the rising sun to claim
A sparkle of inspiring flame.
His hand, reclined upon the wire,
Seem'd watching the awakening fire;
So still he sate, as those who wait
Till judgment speak the doom of fate;
So still, as if no breeze might dare
To lift one lock of hoary hair;
So still, as life itself were fled,
In the last sound his harp had sped.

V.

Upon a rock with lichens wild,
Beside him Ellen sate and smiled.—
Smiled she to see the stately drake
Lead forth his fleet upon the lake,
While her vex'd spaniel from the beach,
Bay'd at the prize beyond his reach?
Yet tell me, then, the maid who knows,
Why deepen'd on her cheek the rose?—
Forgive, forgive, Fidelity!
Perchance the maiden smiled to see
Yon parting lingerer wave adieu,
And stop and turn to wave anew;
And, lovely ladies, ere your ire
Condemn the heroine of my lyre,
Show me the fair would scorn to spy,
And prize such conquest of her eye!

VI.

While yet he loiter'd on the spot,
It seem'd as Ellen mark'd him not;
But when he turn'd him to the glade,
One courteous parting sign she made;
And after, oft the knight would say,
That not when prize of festal day
Was dealt him by the brightest fair,
Who e'er wore jewel in her hair,
So highly did his bosom swell,
As at that simple mute farewell.
Now with a trusty mountain-guide,
And his dark stag-hounds by his side,

He parts—the maid, unconscious still,
Watch'd him wind slowly round the hill;
But when his stately form was hid,
The guardian in her bosom chid—
" Thy Malcolm! vain and selfish maid!"
'Twas thus upbraiding conscience said,—
" Not so had Malcolm idly hung
On the smooth phrase of southern tongue;
Not so had Malcolm strain'd his eye,
Another step than thine to spy.
Wake, Allan-Bane," aloud she cried,
To the old Minstrel by her side,—
" Arouse thee from thy moody dream!
I'll give thy harp heroic theme,
And warm thee with a noble name;
Pour forth the glory of the Græme!"[11]
Scarce from her lip the word had rush'd,
When deep the conscious maiden blush'd;
For of his clan, in hall and bower,
Young Malcolm Græme was held the
  flower.

VII.

The Minstrel waked his harp—three times
Arose the well-known martial chimes,
And thrice their high heroic pride
In melancholy murmurs died.
" Vainly thou bid'st, O noble maid,"
Clasping his wither'd hands, he said,
" Vainly thou bid'st me wake the strain,
Though all unwont to bid in vain.
Alas! than mine a mightier hand
Has tuned my harp, my strings has
  spann'd!
I touch the chords of joy, but low
And mournful answer notes of woe;
And the proud march, which victors tread,
Sinks in the wailing for the dead.
O well for me, if mine alone
That dirge's deep prophetic tone!
If, as my tuneful fathers said,
This harp, which erst Saint Modan
  sway'd,[12]
Can thus its master's fate foretell,
Then welcome be the minstrel's knell!

VIII.

" But ah! dear lady, thus it sigh'd
The eve thy sainted mother died;

And such the sounds which, while I strove
To wake a lay of war or love,
Came marring all the festal mirth,
Appalling me who gave them birth,
And, disobedient to my call,
Wail'd loud through Bothwell's banner'd
    hall,
Ere Douglasses, to ruin driven,[13]
Were exiled from their native heaven.—
Oh! if yet worse mishap and woe,
My master's house must undergo,
Or aught but weal to Ellen fair,
Brood in these accents of despair,
No future bard, sad Harp! shall fling
Triumph or rapture from thy string;
One short, one final strain shall flow,
Fraught with unutterable woe,
Then shiver'd shall thy fragments lie,
Thy master cast him down and die!"

IX.

Soothing she answer'd him, "Assuage,
Mine honour'd friend, the fears of age;
All melodies to thee are known,
That harp has rung, or pipe has blown,
In Lowland vale or Highland glen,
From Tweed to Spey—what marvel, then,
At times, unbidden notes should rise,
Confusedly bound in memory's ties,
Entangling, as they rush along,
The war-march with the funeral song?—
Small ground is now for boding fear;
Obscure, but safe, we rest us here.
My sire, in native virtue great,
Resigning lordship, lands, and state,
Not then to fortune more resign'd,
Than yonder oak might give the wind;
The graceful foliage storms may reave,
The noble stem they cannot grieve.
For me,"—she stoop'd, and, looking
    round,
Pluck'd a blue hare-bell from the
    ground,—
"For me, whose memory scarce conveys
An image of more splendid days,
This little flower, that loves the lea,
May well my simple emblem be;
It drinks heaven's dew as blithe as rose
That in the king's own garden grows;
And when I place it in my hair,

Allan, a bard is bound to swear
He ne'er saw coronet so fair."
Then playfully the chaplet wild
She wreath'd in her dark locks, and
    smiled.

X.

Her smile, her speech, with winning sway,
Wiled the old harper's mood away.
With such a look as hermits throw,
When angels stoop to soothe their woe,
He gazed, till fond regret and pride
Thrill'd to a tear, then thus replied:
"Loveliest and best! thou little know'st
The rank, the honours, thou hast lost!
O might I live to see thee grace,
In Scotland's court, thy birth-right place,
To see my favourite's step advance,
The lightest in the courtly dance,
The cause of every gallant's sigh,
And leading star of every eye,
And theme of every minstrel's art,
The Lady of the Bleeding Heart!"*—

XI.

"Fair dreams are these," the maiden
    cried,
(Light was her accent, yet she sigh'd;)
"Yet is this mossy rock to me
Worth splendid chair and canopy;
Nor would my footsteps spring more gay
In courtly dance than blithe strathspey,
Nor half so pleased mine ear incline
To royal minstrel's lay as thine.
And then for suitors proud and high,
To bend before my conquering eye,—
Thou, flattering bard! thyself wilt say,
That grim Sir Roderick owns its sway.
The Saxon scourge, Clan-Alpine's pride,
The terror of Loch Lomond's side,
Would, at my suit, thou know'st, delay
A Lennox foray—for a day."—

XII.

The ancient bard his glee repress'd:
"Ill hast thou chosen theme for jest!

* The cognizance of the Douglas family.

For who, through all this western wild,
Named Black Sir Roderick e'er, and
    smiled !
In Holy-Rood a knight he slew ;[14]
I saw, when back the dirk he drew,
Courtiers give place before the stride
Of the undaunted homicide;
And since, though outlaw'd, hath his hand
Full sternly kept his mountain land.
Who else dared give—ah ! woe the day,
That I such hated truth should say—
The Douglas, like a stricken deer,
Disown'd by every noble peer,[15]
Even the rude refuge we have here?
Alas, this wild marauding Chief
Alone might hazard our relief,
And now thy maiden charms expand,
Looks for his guerdon in thy hand;
Full soon may dispensation sought,
To back his suit, from Rome be brought.
Then, though an exile on the hill,
Thy father, as the Douglas, still
Be held in reverence and fear;
And though to Roderick thou'rt so dear,
That thou mightst guide with silken
    thread,
Slave of thy will, this chieftain dread ;
Yet, O loved maid, thy mirth refrain !
Thy hand is on a lion's mane."—

XIII.

"Minstrel," the maid replied, and high
Her father's soul glanced from her eye,
" My debts to Roderick's house I know:
All that a mother could bestow,
To Lady Margaret's care I owe,
Since first an orphan in the wild
She sorrow'd o'er her sister's child ;
To her brave chieftain son, from ire
Of Scotland's king who shrouds my sire,
A deeper, holier debt is owed;
And, could I pay it with my blood,
Allan ! Sir Roderick should command
My blood, my life,—but not my hand.
Rather will Ellen Douglas dwell
A votaress in Maronnan's cell;[16]
Rather through realms beyond the sea,
Seeking the world's cold charity,
Where ne'er was spoke a Scottish word,
And ne'er the name of Douglas heard,

An outcast pilgrim will she rove,
Than wed the man she cannot love.

XIV.

"Thou shakest, good friend, thy tresses
    grey,—
That pleading look, what can it say
But what I own ?—I grant him brave,
But wild as Bracklinn's thundering
    wave ;[17]
And generous—save vindictive mood,
Or jealous transport, chafe his blood :
I grant him true to friendly band,
As his claymore is to his hand ;
But O ! that very blade of steel
More mercy for a foe would feel:
I grant him liberal, to fling
Among his clan the wealth they bring,
When back by lake and glen they wind,
And in the Lowland leave behind,
Where once some pleasant hamlet stood,
A mass of ashes slaked with blood.
The hand that for my father fought,
I honour, as his daughter ought ;
But can I clasp it reeking red,
From peasants slaughter'd in their shed?
No ! wildly while his virtues gleam,
They make his passions darker seem,
And flash along his spirit high,
Like lightning o'er the midnight sky.
While yet a child,—and children know,
Instinctive taught, the friend and foe,—
I shudder'd at his brow of gloom,
His shadowy plaid, and sable plume ;
A maiden grown, I ill could bear
His haughty mien and lordly air:
But, if thou join'st a suitor's claim,
In serious mood, to Roderick's name,
I thrill with anguish ! or, if e'er
A Douglas knew the word, with fear.
To change such odious theme were best,—
What think'st thou of our stranger
    guest ?"—

XV.

"What think I of him ?—woe the while
That brought such wanderer to our isle !
Thy father's battle-brand, of yore
For Tine-man forged by fairy lore,[18]

What time he leagued, no longer foes,
His Border spears with Hotspur's bows,
Did, self-unscabbarded, foreshow
The footstep of a secret foe.[19]
If courtly spy hath harbour'd here,
What may we for the Douglas fear?
What for this island, deem'd of old
Clan-Alpine's last and surest hold?
If neither spy nor foe, I pray
What yet may jealous Roderick say?
—Nay, wave not thy disdainful head,
Bethink thee of the discord dread
That kindled, when at Beltane game
Thou ledst the dance with Malcolm
　　Græme;
Still, though thy sire the peace renew'd,
Smoulders in Roderick's breast the feud;
Beware!—But hark, what sounds are
　　these?
My dull ears catch no faltering breeze,
No weeping birch, nor aspens wake,
Nor breath is dimpling in the lake,
Still is the canna's* hoary beard,
Yet, by my minstrel faith, I heard—
And hark again! some pipe of war
Sends the bold pibroch from afar."

XVI.

Far up the lengthen'd lake were spied
Four darkening specks upon the tide,
That, slow enlarging on the view,
Four mann'd and masted barges grew,
And, bearing downwards from Glengyle,
Steer'd full upon the lonely isle;
The point of Brianchoil they pass'd,
And, to the windward as they cast,
Against the sun they gave to shine
The bold Sir Roderick's banner'd Pine.
Nearer and nearer as they bear,
Spear, pikes, and axes flash in air.
Now might you see the tartans brave,
And plaids and plumage dance and wave:
Now see the bonnets sink and rise,
As his tough oar the rower plies;
See, flashing at each sturdy stroke,
The wave ascending into smoke;
See the proud pipers on the bow,
And mark the gaudy streamers flow

From their loud chanters† down, and sweep
The furrow'd bosom of the deep,
As, rushing through the lake amain,
They plied the ancient Highland strain.

XVII.

Ever, as on they bore, more loud
And louder rung the pibroch proud.
At first the sound, by distance tame,
Mellow'd along the waters came,
And, lingering long by cape and bay,
Wail'd every harsher note away;
Then bursting bolder on the ear,
The clan's shrill Gathering they could
　　hear;
Those thrilling sounds, that call the might
Of old Clan-Alpine to the fight.[20]
Thick beat the rapid notes, as when
The mustering hundreds shake the glen,
And, hurrying at the signal dread,
The batter'd earth returns their tread.
Then prelude light, of livelier tone,
Express'd their merry marching on,
Ere peal of closing battle rose,
With mingled outcry, shrieks, and blows;
And mimic din of stroke and ward,
As broad sword upon target jarr'd;
And groaning pause, ere yet again,
Condensed, the battle yell'd amain;
The rapid charge, the rallying shout,
Retreat borne headlong into rout,
And bursts of triumph, to declare
Clan-Alpine's conquest—all were there.
Nor ended thus the strain; but slow,
Sunk in a moan prolong'd and low,
And changed the conquering clarion swell,
For wild lament o'er those that fell.

XVIII.

The war-pipes ceased; but lake and hill
Were busy with their echoes still;
And, when they slept, a vocal strain
Bade their hoarse chorus wake again,
While loud a hundred clansmen raise
Their voices in their Chieftain's praise.
Each boatman, bending to his oar,
With measured sweep the burden bore,

---

* Cotton grass.　　　　　　　† The pipe of the bagpipe.

In such wild cadence, as the breeze
Makes through December's leafless trees.
The chorus first could Allan know,
" Roderick Vich Alpine, ho! iro!"
And near, and nearer as they row'd,
Distinct the martial ditty flow'd.

XIX.

Boat Song.

Hail to the Chief who in triumph advances!
  Honour'd and bless'd be the ever-green
    Pine!
Long may the tree, in his banner that
    glances,
  Flourish, the shelter and grace of our
    line!
      Heaven send it happy dew,
      Earth lend it sap anew,
  Gayly to bourgeon, and broadly to
    grow,
      While every Highland glen
      Sends our shout back agen,
  " Roderigh Vich Alpine dhu, ho!
    ieroe!"[21]

Ours is no sapling, chance-sown by the
    fountain,
Blooming at Beltane, in winter to fade;
When the whirlwind has stripp'd every
    leaf on the mountain,
  The more shall Clan-Alpine exult in
    her shade.
      Moor'd in the rifted rock,
      Proof to the tempest's shock,
  Firmer he roots him the ruder it blow;
      Menteith and Breadalbane, then,
      Echo his praise agen,
  " Roderigh Vich Alpine dhu, ho!
    ieroe!"

XX.

Proudly our pibroch* has thrill'd in
    Glen Fruin,
  And Bannochar's groans to our slogan†
    replied;

---

* Bagpipe air belonging to a clan.
† *Slogan,* a war-cry.

Glen Luss and Ross-dhu, they are smok-
    ing in ruin,
  And the best of Loch Lomond lie dead
    on her side.
      Widow and Saxon maid
      Long shall lament our raid,
  Think of Clan-Alpine with fear and
    with woe;
      Lennox and Leven-glen
      Shake when they hear agen,
  " Roderigh Vich Alpine dhu, ho!
    ieroe!"

Row, vassals, row, for the pride of the
    Highlands!
  Stretch to your oars, for the ever-green
    Pine!
O! that the rose-bud that graces yon
    islands,
  Were wreathed in a garland around
    him to twine!
      O that some seedling gem,
      Worthy such noble stem,
  Honour'd and bless'd in their shadow
    might grow!
      Loud should Clan-Alpine then
      Ring from the deepmost glen,
  " Roderigh Vich Alpine dhu, ho!
    ieroe!"

XXI.

With all her joyful female band,
Had Lady Margaret sought the strand,
Loose on the breeze their tresses flew,
And high their snowy arms they threw,
As echoing back with shrill acclaim,
And chorus wild, the Chieftain's name;
While, prompt to please, with mother's
    art,
The darling passion of his heart,
The Dame call'd Ellen to the strand,
To greet her kinsman ere he land:
" Come, loiterer, come! a Douglas thou,
And shun to wreathe a victor's brow?"—
Reluctantly and slow, the maid
The unwelcome summoning obey'd,
And, when a distant bugle rung,
In the mid-path aside she sprung:—
" List, Allan-Bane! From mainland cast,
I hear my father's signal blast,

Be ours," she cried, " the skiff to guide,
And waft him from the mountain side."
Then, like a sunbeam, swift and bright,
She darted to her shallop light,
And, eagerly while Roderick scann'd,
For her dear form, his mother's band,
The islet far behind her lay,
And she had landed in the bay.

XXII.

Some feelings are to mortals given,
With less of earth in them than heaven:
And if there be a human tear
From passion's dross refined and clear,
A tear so limpid and so meek,
It would not stain an angel's cheek,
'Tis that which pious fathers shed
Upon a duteous daughter's head!
And as the Douglas to his breast
His darling Ellen closely press'd,
Such holy drops her tresses steep'd,
Though 'twas a hero's eye that weep'd,
Nor while on Ellen's faltering tongue
Her filial welcomes crowded hung,
Mark'd she, that fear (affection's proof)
Still held a graceful youth aloof;
No! not till Douglas named his name,
Although the youth was Malcolm Græme.

XXIII.

Allan, with wistful look the while,
Mark'd Roderick landing on the isle;
His master piteously he eyed,
Then gazed upon the Chieftain's pride.
Then dash'd, with hasty hand, away
From his dimm'd eye the gathering spray;
And Douglas, as his hand he laid
On Malcolm's shoulder, kindly said,
" Canst thou, young friend, no meaning spy
In my poor follower's glistening eye?
I'll tell thee:—he recalls the day,
When in my praise he led the lay
O'er the arch'd gate of Bothwell proud,
While many a minstrel answer'd loud,
When Percy's Norman pennon, won
In bloody field, before me shone,
And twice ten knights, the least a name

As mighty as yon Chief may claim,
Gracing my pomp, behind me came.
Yet trust me, Malcolm, not so proud
Was I of all that marshall'd crowd,
Though the waned crescent own'd my might,
And in my train troop'd lord and knight,
Though Blantyre hymn'd her holiest lays,
And Bothwell's bards flung back my praise,
As when this old man's silent tear,
And this poor maid's affection dear,
A welcome give more kind and true,
Then aught my better fortunes knew.
Forgive, my friend, a father's boast,
O! it out-beggars all I lost!"

XXIV.

Delightful praise!—Like summer rose,
That brighter in the dew-drop glows,
The bashful maiden's cheek appear'd,
For Douglas spoke, and Malcolm heard.
The flush of shame-faced joy to hide,
The hounds, the hawk, her cares divide;
The loved caresses of the maid
The dogs with crouch and whimper paid;
And, at her whistle, on her hand
The falcon took her favourite stand,
Closed his dark wing, relax'd his eye,
Nor, though unhooded, sought to fly.
And, trust, while in such guise she stood,
Like fabled Goddess of the wood,
That if a father's partial thought
O'erweigh'd her worth and beauty aught,
Well might the lover's judgment fail
To balance with a juster scale;
For with each secret glance he stole,
The fond enthusiast sent his soul.

XXV.

Of stature tall, and slender frame,
But firmly knit, was Malcolm Græme.
The belted plaid and tartan hose
Did ne'er more graceful limbs disclose;
His flaxen hair of sunny hue,
Curl'd closely round his bonnet blue.
Train'd to the chase, his eagle eye
The ptarmigan in snow could spy:
Each pass, by mountain, lake, and heath,
He knew, through Lennox and Menteith;

Vain was the bound of dark-brown doe,
When Malcolm bent his sounding bow,
And scarce that doe, though wing'd
　　with fear,
Outstripp'd in speed the mountaineer:
Right up Ben-Lomond could he press,
And not a sob his toil confess.
His form accorded with a mind
Lively and ardent, frank and kind;
A blither heart, till Ellen came,
Did never love nor sorrow tame;
It danced as lightsome in his breast,
As play'd the feather on his crest.
Yet friends, who nearest knew the youth
His scorn of wrong, his zeal for truth,
And bards, who saw his features bold,
When kindled by the tales of old,
Said, were that youth to manhood grown,
Not long should Roderick Dhu's renown
Be foremost voiced by mountain fame,
But quail to that of Malcolm Græme.

XXVI.

Now back they wend their watery way,
And, "O my sire!" did Ellen say,
" Why urge thy chase so far astray?
And why so late return'd? And why—"
The rest was in her speaking eye.
" My child, the chase I follow far,
'Tis mimicry of noble war;
And with that gallant pastime reft
Were all of Douglas I have left.
I met young Malcolm as I stray'd,
Far eastward, in Glenfinlas' shade,
Nor stray'd I safe; for, all around,
Hunters and horsemen scour'd the ground.
This youth, though still a royal ward,
Risk'd life and land to be my guard,
And through the passes of the wood,
Guided my steps, not unpursued;
And Roderick shall his welcome make,
Despite old spleen, for Douglas' sake.
Then must he seek Strath-Endrick glen,
Nor peril aught for me agen."

XXVII.

Sir Roderick, who to meet them came,
Redden'd at sight of Malcolm Græme,
Yet, not in action, word, or eye,
Fail'd aught in hospitality.

In talk and sport they wiled away
The morning of that summer day;
But at high noon a courier light
Held secret parley with the knight,
Whose moody aspect soon declared,
That evil were the news he heard.
Deep thought seem'd toiling in his head;
Yet was the evening banquet made,
Ere he assembled round the flame,
His mother, Douglas, and the Græme,
And Ellen, too; then cast around
His eyes, then fix'd them on the ground,
As studying phrase that might avail
Best to convey unpleasant tale.
Long with his dagger's hilt he play'd,
Then raised his haughty brow, and said:—

XXVIII.

" Short be my speech;—nor time affords,
Nor my plain temper, glozing words.
Kinsman and father,—if such name
Douglas vouchsafe to Roderick's claim;
Mine honour'd mother;—Ellen—why,
My cousin, turn away thine eye?—
And Græme; in whom I hope to know
Full soon a noble friend or foe,
When age shall give thee thy command,
And leading in thy native land,—
List all!—The King's vindictive pride
Boasts to have tamed the Border-side,
Where chiefs, with hound and hawk who
　　came
To share their monarch's sylvan game,
Themselves in bloody toils were snared;
And when the banquet they prepared,
And wide their loyal portals flung,
O'er their own gateway struggling hung.
Loud cries their blood from Meggat's
　　mead,
From Yarrow braes, and banks of Tweed,
Where the lone streams of Ettrick glide,
And from the silver Teviot's side;
The dales, where martial clans did ride,
Are now one sheep-walk, waste and wide.
This tyrant of the Scottish throne,
So faithless and so ruthless known,
Now hither comes; his end the same,
The same pretext of sylvan game.
What grace for Highland Chiefs, judge ye
By fate of Border chivalry.

Yet more ; amid Glenfinlas green,
Douglas, thy stately form was seen.
This by espial sure I know ;
Your counsel in the streight I show."

XXIX.

Ellen and Margaret fearfully
Sought comfort in each other's eye,
Then turn'd their ghastly look, each one,
This to her sire—that to her son.
The hasty colour went and came
In the bold cheek of Malcolm Græme ;
But from his glance it well appear'd,
'Twas but for Ellen that he fear'd ;
While, sorrowful, but undismay'd,
The Douglas thus his counsel said :—
" Brave Roderick, though the tempest roar,
It may but thunder and pass o'er ;
Nor will I here remain an hour,
To draw the lightning on thy bower ;
For well thou know'st, at this grey head
The royal bolt were fiercest sped.
For thee, who, at thy King's command,
Canst aid him with a gallant band,
Submission, homage, humbled pride,
Shall turn the Monarch's wrath aside.
Poor remnants of the Bleeding Heart,
Ellen and I will seek, apart,
The refuge of some forest cell,
There, like the hunted quarry, dwell,
Till on the mountain and the moor,
The stern pursuit be pass'd and o'er."—

XXX.

" No, by mine honour," Roderick said,
" So help me, heaven, and my good blade !
No, never ! Blasted be yon Pine,
My fathers' ancient crest and mine,
If from its shade in danger part
The lineage of the Bleeding Heart !
Hear my blunt speech : Grant me this maid
To wife, thy counsel to mine aid ;
To Douglas, leagued with Roderick Dhu,
Will friends and allies flock enow ;
Like cause of doubt, distrust, and grief,
Will bind to us each Western Chief.
When the loud pipes my bridal tell,
The Links of Forth shall hear the knell,

The guards shall start in Stirling's porch ;
And, when I light the nuptial torch,
A thousand villages in flames,
Shall scare the slumbers of King James !
—Nay, Ellen, blench not thus away,
And, mother. cease these signs, I pray ;
I meant not all my heart might say.—
Small need of inroad, or of fight,
When the sage Douglas may unite
Each mountain clan in friendly band,
To guard the passes of their land,
Till the foil'd king, from pathless glen,
Shall bootless turn him home agen."

XXXI.

There are who have, at midnight hour,
In slumber scaled a dizzy tower,
And, on the verge that beetled o'er
The ocean-tide's incessant roar,
Dream'd calmly out their dangerous dream,
Till waken'd by the morning beam ;
When, dazzled by the eastern glow,
Such startler cast his glance below,
And saw unmeasured depth around,
And heard unintermitted sound,
And thought the battled fence so frail,
It waved like cobweb in the gale ;—
Amid his senses' giddy wheel,
Did he not desperate impulse feel,
Headlong to plunge himself below,
And meet the worst his fears foreshow ?—
Thus, Ellen, dizzy and astound,
As sudden ruin yawn'd around,
By crossing terrors wildly toss'd,
Still for the Douglas fearing most,
Could scarce the desperate thought withstand
To buy his safety with her hand.

XXXII.

Such purpose dread could Malcolm spy
In Ellen's quivering lip and eye,
And eager rose to speak—but ere
His tongue could hurry forth his fear,
Had Douglas mark'd the hectic strife,
Where death seemed combating with life;
For to her cheek, in feverish flood,
One instant rush'd the throbbing blood,

Then ebbing back, with sudden sway,
Left its domain as wan as clay.
"Roderick, enough! enough!" he cried,
"My daughter cannot be thy bride;
Not that the blush to wooer dear,
Nor paleness that of maiden fear.
It may not be—forgive her, Chief,
Nor hazard aught for our relief.
Against his sovereign, Douglas ne'er
Will level a rebellious spear.
'Twas I that taught his youthful hand
To rein a steed and wield a brand;
I see him yet, the princely boy!
Not Ellen more my pride and joy;
I love him still, despite my wrongs,
By hasty wrath, and slanderous tongues.
O seek the grace you well may find,
Without a cause to mine combined."

XXXIII.

Twice through the hall the Chieftain
 strode;
The waving of his tartans broad,
And darken'd brow, where wounded pride
With ire and disappointment vied,
Seem'd, by the torch's gloomy light,
Like the ill Demon of the night.
Stooping his pinions' shadowy sway
Upon the nighted pilgrim's way:
But, unrequited Love! thy dart
Plunged deepest its envenom'd smart,
And Roderick, with thine anguish stung,
At length the hand of Douglas wrung,
While eyes, that mock'd at tears before,
With bitter drops were running o'er.
The death-pangs of long-cherish'd hope
Scarce in that ample breast had scope,
But, struggling with his spirit proud,
Convulsive heaved its chequer'd shroud,
While every sob—so mute were all—
Was heard distinctly through the hall.
The son's despair, the mother's look,
Ill might the gentle Ellen brook;
She rose, and to her side there came,
To aid her parting steps, the Græme.

XXXIV.

Then Roderick from the Douglas broke—
As flashes flame through sable smoke,
Kindling its wreaths, long, dark, and low,
To one broad blaze of ruddy glow,
So the deep anguish of despair
Burst, in fierce jealousy, to air.
With stalwart grasp his hand he laid
On Malcolm's breast and belted plaid:
"Back, beardless boy!" he sternly said,
"Back, minion! hold'st thou thus at
 naught
The lesson I so lately taught?
This roof, the Douglas, and that maid,
Thank thou for punishment delay'd."
Eager as greyhound on his game,
Fiercely with Roderick grappled Græme.
"Perish my name, if aught afford
Its Chieftain safety save his sword!"
Thus as they strove, their desperate hand
Griped to the dagger or the brand,
And death had been—but Douglas rose,
And thrust between the struggling foes
His giant strength:—"Chieftains, forego!
I hold the first who strikes, my foe.—
Madmen, forbear your frantic jar!
What! is the Douglas fall'n so far,
His daughter's hand is doom'd the spoil
Of such dishonourable broil!"
Sullen and slowly they unclasp,
As struck with shame, their desperate
 grasp,
And each upon his rival glared,
With foot advanced, and blade half bared.

XXXV.

Ere yet the brands aloft were flung,
Margaret on Roderick's mantle hung,
And Malcolm heard his Ellen's scream,
As, falter'd through terrific dream.
Then Roderick plunged in sheath his
 sword,
And veil'd his wrath in scornful word:
"Rest safe till morning; pity 'twere
Such cheek should feel the midnight air!
Then mayest thou to James Stuart tell,
Roderick will keep the lake and fell,
Nor lackey, with his freeborn clan,
The pageant pomp of earthly man.
More would he of Clan-Alpine know,
Thou canst our strength and passes
 show,—

Malise, what ho!"—his henchman came;*
" Give our safe-conduct to the Græme."
Young Malcolm answer'd, calm and bold,
" Fear nothing for thy favourite hold ;
The spot, an angel deigned to grace,
Is bless'd, though robbers haunt the place.
Thy churlish courtesy for those
Reserve, who fear to be thy foes.
As safe to me the mountain way
At midnight as in blaze of day,
Though with his boldest at his back
Even Roderick Dhu beset the track.—
Brave Douglas,—lovely Ellen,—nay,
Nought here of parting will I say.
Earth does not hold a lonesome glen,
So secret, but we meet agen.—
Chieftain! we too shall find an hour."
He said, and left the sylvan bower.

XXXVI.

Old Allan follow'd to the strand,
(Such was the Douglas's command,)
And anxious told, how, on the morn,
The stern Sir Roderick deep had sworn,
The Fiery Cross should circle o'er
Dale, glen, and valley, down, and moor.
Much were the peril to the Græme,
From those who to the signal came ;
Far up the lake 'twere safest land,
Himself would row him to the strand.
He gave his counsel to the wind,
While Malcolm did, unheeding, bind,
Round dirk and pouch and broadsword roll'd,
His ample plaid in tighten'd fold,
And stripp'd his limbs to such array,
As best might suit the watery way,—

XXXVII.

Then spoke abrupt : " Farewell to thee,
Pattern of old fidelity !"
The Minstrel's hand he kindly press'd,—
" O ! could I point a place of rest !
My sovereign holds in ward my land,
My uncle leads my vassal band ;

* A henchman was the confidential attendant or gilly of a chief. His standing behind
his lord at festivals originated the name of
haunch-man or henchman.

To tame his foes, his friends to aid,
Poor Malcolm has but heart and blade.
Yet, if there be one faithful Græme,
Who loves the Chieftain of his name,
Not long shall honour'd Douglas dwell,
Like hunted stag in mountain cell ;
Nor, ere yon pride-swoll'n robber dare—
I may not give the rest to air !
Tell Roderick Dhu, I owed him nought,
Not the poor service of a boat,
To waft me to yon mountain-side.'
Then plunged he in the flashing tide.
Bold o'er the flood his head he bore,
And stoutly steer'd him from the shore ;
And Allan strain'd his anxious eye,
Far 'mid the lake his form to spy.
Darkening across each puny wave
To which the moon her silver gave,
Fast as the cormorant could skim,
The swimmer plied each active limb ;
Then landing in the moonlight dell,
Loud shouted of his weal to tell.
The Minstrel heard the far halloo,
And joyful from the shore withdrew.

CANTO THIRD.

The Gathering.

I.

TIME rolls his ceaseless course. The race
of yore,
  Who danced our infancy upon their
  knee,
And told our marvelling boyhood legends
store,
  Of their strange ventures happ'd by land
  or sea,
How are they blotted from the things
that be!
  How few, all weak and wither'd of
  their force,
Wait on the verge of dark eternity,
  Like stranded wrecks, the tide returning hoarse,
To sweep them from our sight! Time
rolls his ceaseless course.

Yet live there still who can remember
    well,
    How, when a mountain chief his bugle
        blew,
Both field and forest, dingle, cliff, and dell,
    And solitary heath, the signal knew;
And fast the faithful clan around him drew,
    What time the warning note was keenly
        wound,
What time aloft their kindred banner flew,
    While clamorous war-pipes yell'd the
        gathering sound.
And while the Fiery Cross glanced like a
    meteor round.[22]

II.

The Summer dawn's reflected hue
To purple changed Loch Katrine blue;
Mildly and soft the western breeze
Just kiss'd the lake, just stirr'd the trees,
And the pleased lake, like maiden coy,
Trembled but dimpled not for joy;
The mountain-shadows on her breast
Were neither broken nor at rest;
In bright uncertainty they lie,
Like future joys to Fancy's eye.
The water-lily to the light
Her chalice rear'd of silver bright;
The doe awoke, and to the lawn,
Begemm'd with dew-drops, led her fawn;
The grey mist left the mountain side,
The torrent show'd its glistening pride;
Invisible in flecked sky,
The lark sent down her revelry;
The blackbird and the speckled thrush
Good-morrow gave from brake and bush;
In answer coo'd the cushat dove
Her notes of peace, and rest, and love.

III.

No thought of peace, no thought of rest,
Assuaged the storm in Roderick's breast.
With sheathed broadsword in his hand,
Abrupt he paced the islet strand,
And eyed the rising sun, and laid
His hand on his impatient blade.
Beneath a rock, his vassals' care
Was prompt the ritual to prepare,
With deep and deathful meaning fraught;
For such Antiquity had taught

Was preface meet, ere yet abroad
The Cross of Fire should take its road.
The shrinking band stood oft aghast
At the impatient glance he cast;—
Such glance the mountain eagle threw,
As from the cliffs of Benvenue,
She spread her dark sails on the wind,
And, high in middle heaven, reclined,
With her broad shadow on the lake,
Silenced the warblers of the brake.

IV.

A heap of wither'd boughs was piled,
Of juniper and rowan wild,
Mingled with shivers from the oak,
Rent by the lightning's recent stroke.
Brian, the Hermit, by it stood,
Barefooted, in his frock and hood.
His grisled beard and matted hair
Obscured a visage of despair;
His naked arms and legs, seam'd o'er,
The scars of frantic penance bore.
That monk, of savage form and face,[23]
The impending danger of his race
Had drawn from deepest solitude,
Far in Benharrow's bosom rude.
Not his the mien of Christian priest,
But Druid's, from the grave released,
Whose harden'd heart and eye might brook
On human sacrifice to look;
And much, 'twas said, of heathen lore
Mix'd in the charms he mutter'd o'er.
The hallow'd creed gave only worse
And deadlier emphasis of curse;
No peasant sought that Hermit's prayer,
His cave the pilgrim shunn'd with care,
The eager huntsman knew his bound,
And in mid chase call'd off his hound;
Or if, in lonely glen or strath,
The desert-dweller met his path,
He pray'd, and sign'd the cross between,
While terror took devotion's mien.

V.

Of Brian's birth strange tales were told:[24]
His mother watch'd a midnight fold,
Built deep within a dreary glen,
Where scatter'd lay the bones of men,
In some forgotten battle slain,
And bleach'd by drifting wind and rain.

It might have tamed a warrior's heart,
To view such mockery of his art!
The knot-grass fetter'd there the hand,
Which once could burst an iron band;
Beneath the broad and ample bone,
That buckler'd heart to fear unknown,
A feeble and a timorous guest,
The field-fare framed her lowly nest,
There the slow blind-worm left his slime,
On the fleet limbs that mock'd at time;
And there, too, lay the leader's skull,
Still wreathed with chaplet, flush'd and full,
For heath-bell with her purple bloom,
Supplied the bonnet and the plume.
All night, in this sad glen, the maid
Sate, shrouded in her mantle's shade:
—She said, no shepherd sought her side,
No hunter's hand her snood untied,
Yet ne'er again to braid her hair
The virgin snood did Alice wear;[25]
Gone was her maiden glee and sport,
Her maiden girdle all too short,
Nor sought she, from that fatal night,
Or holy church or blessed rite,
But lock'd her secret in her breast,
And died in travail, unconfess'd.

VI.

Alone, among his young compeers,
Was Brian from his infant years;
A moody and heart-broken boy,
Estranged from sympathy and joy,
Bearing each taunt which careless tongue
On his mysterious lineage flung.
Whole nights he spent by moonlight pale,
To wood and stream his hap to wail,
Till, frantic, he as truth received
What of his birth the crowd believed,
And sought, in mist and meteor fire,
To meet and know his Phantom Sire!
In vain, to soothe his wayward fate,
The cloister oped her pitying gate;
In vain, the learning of the age
Unclasp'd the sable-letter'd page;
Even in its treasures he could find
Food for the fever of his mind.
Eager he read whatever tells
Of magic, cabala, and spells,
And every dark pursuit allied
To curious and presumptuous pride;

Till with fired brain and nerves o'erstrung,
And heart with mystic horrors wrung,
Desperate he sought Benharrow's den,
And hid him from the haunts of men.

VII.

The desert gave him visions wild,
Such as might suit the spectre's child.
Where with black cliffs the torrents toil,
He watch'd the wheeling eddies boil,
Till, from their foam, his dazzled eyes
Beheld the River Demon rise;
The mountain mist took form and limb,
Of noontide hag, or goblin grim;
The midnight wind came wild and dread,
Swell'd with the voices of the dead;
Far on the future battle-heath
His eye beheld the ranks of death:
Thus the lone Seer, from mankind hurl'd,
Shaped forth a disembodied world.
One lingering sympathy of mind
Still bound him to the mortal kind;
The only parent he could claim
Of ancient Alpine's lineage came.
Late had he heard, in prophet's dream,
The fatal Ben-Shie's boding scream;[26]
Sounds, too, had come in midnight blast,
Of charging steeds, careering fast
Along Benharrow's shingly side,
Where mortal horsemen ne'er might ride;[27]
The thunderbolt had split the pine,—
All augur'd ill to Alpine's line.
He girt his loins, and came to show
The signals of impending woe,
And now stood prompt to bless or ban,
As bade the Chieftain of his clan.

VIII.

'Twas all prepared;—and from the rock,
A goat, the patriarch of the flock,
Before the kindling pile was laid,
And pierced by Roderick's ready blade.
Patient the sickening victim eyed
The life-blood ebb in crimson tide,
Down his clogg'd beard and shaggy limb,
Till darkness glazed his eyeballs dim.
The grisly priest, with murmuring prayer,
A slender crosslet form'd with care,
A cubit's length in measure due;
The shaft and limbs were rods of yew,

Whose parents in Inch-Cailliach wave
Their shadows o'er Clan-Alpine's grave,
And, answering Lomond's breezes deep,
Soothe many a chieftain's endless sleep.
The Cross, thus form'd, he held on high,
With wasted hand, and haggard eye,
And strange and mingled feelings woke,
While his anathema he spoke.

IX.

"Woe to the clansman, who shall view
This symbol of sepulchral yew,
Forgetful that its branches grew
Where weep the heavens their holiest dew,
On Alpine's dwelling low!
Deserter of his Chieftain's trust,
He ne'er shall mingle with their dust,
But, from his sires and kindred thrust,
Each clansman's execration just
      Shall doom him wrath and woe!"
He paused;—the word the vassals took,
With forward step and fiery look,
On high their naked brands they shook,
Their clattering targets wildly strook;
      And first in murmur low,
Then, like the billow in his course,
That far to seaward finds his source,
And flings to shore his muster'd force,
Burst, with loud roar, their answer hoarse,
      "Woe to the traitor, woe!"
Ben-an's grey scalp the accents knew,
The joyous wolf from covert drew,
The exulting eagle scream'd afar,—
They knew the voice of Alpine's war.

X.

The shout was hush'd on lake and fell,
The monk resumed his mutter'd spell:
Dismal and low its accents came,
The while he scathed the Cross with flame;
And the few words that reach'd the air,
Although the holiest name was there,
Had more of blasphemy than prayer.
But when he shook above the crowd
Its kindled points, he spoke aloud:—
"Woe to the wretch who fails to rear
At this dread sign the ready spear!
For, as the flames this symbol sear,

Her home, the refuge of his fear,
      A kindred fate shall know;
Far o'er its roof the volumed flame
Clan-Alpine's vengeance shall proclaim,
While maids and matrons on his name
Shall call down wretchedness and shame,
      And infamy and woe."
Then rose the cry of females, shrill
As goss-hawk's whistle on the hill,
Denouncing misery and ill,
Mingled with childhood's babbling trill
      Of curses stammer'd slow;
Answering, with imprecation dread,
"Sunk be his home in embers red!
And cursed be the meanest shed
That e'er shall hide the houseless head,
      We doom to want and woe!"
A sharp and shrieking echo gave,
Coir-Uriskin, thy goblin cave!
And the grey pass where birches wave,
      On Beala-nam-bo.

XI.

Then deeper paused the priest anew,
And hard his labouring breath he drew,
While, with set teeth and clenched hand,
And eyes that glow'd like fiery brand,
He meditated curse more dread,
And deadlier, on the clansman's head,
Who, summon'd to his Chieftain's a.d,
The signal saw and disobey'd.
The crosslet's points of sparkling wood,
He quench'd among the bubbling blood,
And, as again the sign he rear'd,
Hollow and hoarse his voice was heard:
"When flits this Cross from man to man,
Vich-Alpine's summons to his clan,
Burst be the ear that fails to heed!
Palsied the foot that shuns to speed!
May ravens tear the careless eyes,
Wolves make the coward heart their prize!
As sinks that blood-stream in the earth,
So may his heart's-blood drench his hearth!
As dies in hissing gore the spark,
Quench thou his light, Destruction dark,
And be the grace to him denied,
Bought by this sign to all beside!"
He ceased; no echo gave agen
The murmur of the deep Amen.

XII.

Then Roderick, with impatient look,
From Brian's hand the symbol took:
" Speed, Malise, speed !" he said, and gave
The crosslet to his henchman brave.
" The muster-place be Lanrick mead—
Instant the time—speed, Malise, speed !"
Like heath-bird, when the hawks pursue,
A barge across Loch Katrine flew ;
High stood the henchman on the prow ;
So rapidly the barge-men row,
The bubbles, where they launch'd the boat,
Were all unbroken and afloat,
Dancing in foam and ripple still,
When it had near'd the mainland hill ;
And from the silver beach's side
Still was the prow three fathom wide,
When lightly bounded to the land
The messenger of blood and brand.

XIII.

Speed, Malise, speed ! the dun deer's hide
On fleeter foot was never tied.[28]
Speed, Malise, speed ! such cause of haste
Thine active sinews never braced.
Bend 'gainst the steepy hill thy breast,
Burst down like torrent from its crest ;
With short and springing footstep pass
The trembling bog and false morass ;
Across the brook like roebuck bound,
And thread the brake like questing hound ;
The crag is high, the scaur is deep,
Yet shrink not from the desperate leap :
Parch'd are thy burning lips and brow,
Yet by the fountain pause not now ;
Herald of battle, fate, and fear,
Stretch onward in thy fleet career !
The wounded hind thou track'st not now,
Pursuest not maid through greenwood
        bough,
Nor pliest thou now thy flying pace,
With rivals in the mountain race ;
But danger, death, and warrior deed,
Are in thy course—speed, Malise, speed !

XIV.

Fast as the fatal symbol flies,
In arms the huts and hamlets rise ;
From winding glen, from upland brown,
They pour'd each hardy tenant down.
Nor slack'd the messenger his pace ;
He show'd the sign, he named the place,
And, pressing forward like the wind,
Left clamour and surprise behind.
The fisherman forsook the strand,
The swarthy smith took dirk and brand ;
With changed cheer, the mower blithe
Left in the half-cut swathe the scythe ;
The herds without a keeper stray'd,
The plough was in mid-furrow staid,
The falc'ner toss'd his hawk away,
The hunter left the stag at bay ;
Prompt at the signal of alarms,
Each son of Alpine rush'd to arms ;
So swept the tumult and affray
Along the margin of Achray.
Alas ! thou lovely lake ! that e'er
Thy banks should echo sounds of fear !
The rocks, the bosky thickets, sleep
So stilly on thy bosom deep,
The lark's blithe carol, from the cloud,
Seems for the scene too gaily loud

XV.

Speed, Malise, speed ! the lake is past,
Duncraggan's huts appear at last,
And peep, like moss-grown rocks, half
        seen,
Half hidden in the copse so green ;
There mayest thou rest, thy labour done,
Their Lord shall speed the signal on.—
As stoops the hawk upon his prey,
The henchman shot him down the way.
—What woeful accents load the gale ?
The funeral yell, the female wail !
A gallant hunter's sport is o'er,
A valiant warrior fights no more.
Who, in the battle or the chase,
At Roderick's side shall fill his place !—
Within the hall, where torches' ray
Supplies the excluded beams of day,
Lies Duncan on his lowly bier,
And o'er him streams his widow's tear.
His stripling son stands mournful by,
His youngest weeps, but knows not why ;
The village maids and matrons round
The dismal coronach resound.[29]

XVI.

Coronach.

He is gone on the mountain,
   He is lost to the forest,
Like a summer-dried fountain,
   When our need was the sorest.
The font, reappearing,
   From the rain-drops shall borrow,
But to us comes no cheering,
   To Duncan no morrow!
The hand of the reaper
   Takes the ears that are hoary,
But the voice of the weeper
   Wails manhood in glory.
The autumn winds rushing
   Waft the leaves that are searest,
But our flower was in flushing,
   When blighting was nearest.

Fleet foot on the correi,*
   Sage counsel in cumber,
Red hand in the foray,
   How sound is thy slumber!
Like the dew on the mountain,
   Like the foam on the river,
Like the bubble on the fountain,
   Thou art gone, and for ever!

XVII.

See Stumah,† who, the bier beside,
His master's corpse with wonder eyed,
Poor Stumah! whom his least halloo
Could send like lightning o'er the dew,
Bristles his crest, and points his ears,
As if some stranger step he hears.
'Tis not a mourner's muffled tread,
Who comes to sorrow o'er the dead,
But headlong haste, or deadly fear,
Urge the precipitate career.
All stand aghast:—unheeding all,
The henchman bursts into the hall;
Before the dead man's bier he stood;
Held forth the Cross besmear'd with
   blood;

---

* *Correi*, the hollow side of the hill where
game usually lies.

† The name of a dog. The word is Celtic
for "faithful."

"The muster-place is Lanrick mead;
Speed forth the signal! clansmen, speed!"

XVIII.

Angus, the heir of Duncan's line,
Sprung forth and seized the fatal sign.
In haste the stripling to his side
His father's dirk and broadsword tied;
But when he saw his mother's eye
Watch him in speechless agony,
Back to her open'd arms he flew,
Press'd on her lips a fond adieu—
"Alas!" she sobb'd,—"and yet, be gone,
And speed thee forth, like Duncan's son!"
One look he cast upon the bier,
Dash'd from his eye the gathering tear,
Breathed deep to clear his labouring breast,
And toss'd aloft his bonnet crest,
Then, like the high-bred colt, when, freed,
First he essays his fire and speed,
He vanish'd, and o'er moor and moss
Sped forward with the Fiery Cross.
Suspended was the widow's tear,
While yet his footsteps she could hear;
And when she mark'd the henchman's eye
Wet with unwonted sympathy,
"Kinsman," she said, "his race is run,
That should have sped thine errand on;
The oak has fall'n,—the sapling bough
Is all Duncraggan's shelter now.
Yet trust I well, his duty done,
The orphan's God will guard my son.—
And you, in many a danger true,
At Duncan's hest your blades that drew,
To arms, and guard that orphan's head!
Let babes and women wail the dead."
Then weapon-clang, and martial call,
Resounded through the funeral hall,
While from the walls the attendant band
Snatch'd sword and targe, with hurried
   hand;
And short and flitting energy
Glanced from the mourner's sunken eye,
As if the sounds to warrior dear,
Might rouse her Duncan from his bier.
But faded soon that borrow'd force
Grief claim'd his right, and tears their
   course.

XIX.

Benledi saw the Cross of Fire,
It glanced like lightning up Strath-Ire.
O'er dale and hill the summons flew,
Nor rest nor pause young Angus knew;
The tear that gather'd in his eye
He left the mountain breeze to dry;
Until, where Teith's young waters roll,
Betwixt nim and a wooded knoll,
That graced the sable strath with green,
The chapel of St. Bride was seen.
Swoln was the stream, remote the bridge,
But Angus paused not on the edge;
Though the dark waves danced dizzily,
Though reel'd his sympathetic eye,
He dash'd amid the torrent's roar:
His right hand high the crosslet bore,
His left the pole-axe grasp'd, to guide
And stay his footing in the tide.
He stumbled twice—the foam splash'd
    high,
With hoarser swell the stream raced by;
And had he fall'n,—for ever there,
Farewell Duncraggan's orphan heir!
But still, as if in parting life,
Firmer he grasp'd the Cross of strife,
Until the opposing bank he gain'd,
And up the chapel pathway strain'd.

XX.

A blithesome rout, that morning tide,
Had sought the chapel of St. Bride.
Her troth Tombea's Mary gave
To Norman, heir of Armandave.
And, issuing from the Gothic arch,
The bridal now resumed their march.
In rude, but glad procession, came
Bonneted sire and coif-clad dame;
And plaided youth, with jest and jeer,
Which snooded maiden would not hear;
And children, that, unwitting why,
Lent the gay shout their shrilly cry;
And minstrels, that in measures vied
Before the young and bonny bride,
Whose downcast eye and cheek disclose
The tear and blush of morning rose.
With virgin step, and bashful hand,
She held the 'kerchief's snowy band;

The gallant bridegroom by her side,
Beheld his prize with victor's pride,
And the glad mother in her ear
Was closely whispering word of cheer.

XXI.

Who meets them at the churchyard gate!
The messenger of fear and fate!
Haste in his hurried accent lies,
And grief is swimming in his eyes.
All dripping from the recent flood,
Panting and travel-soil'd he stood,
The fatal sign of fire and sword
Held forth, and spoke the appointed
    word:
"The muster-place is Lanrick mead;
Speed forth the signal! Norman, speed!"
And must he change so soon the hand,
Just link'd to his by holy band,
For the fell Cross of blood and brand?
And must the day, so blithe that rose,
And promised rapture in the close,
Before its setting hour, divide
The bridegroom from the plighted bride!
O fatal doom!—it must! it must!
Clan-Alpine's cause, her Chieftain's trust,
Her summons dread, brook no delay;
Stretch to the race—away! away!

XXII.

Yet slow he laid his plaid aside,
And, lingering, eyed his lovely bride,
Until he saw the starting tear
Speak woe he might not stop to cheer;
Then, trusting not a second look,
In haste he sped him up the brook,
Nor backward glanced, till on the heath
Where Lubnaig's lake supplies the Teith.
—What in the racer's bosom stirr'd?
The sickening pang of hope deferr'd,
And memory, with a torturing train
Of all his morning visions vain.
Mingled with love's impatience, came
The manly thirst for martial fame;
The stormy joy of mountaineers,
Ere yet they rush upon the spears;
And zeal for Clan and Chieftain burning,
And hope, from well-fought field return-
    ing,

With war's red honours on his crest,
To clasp his Mary to his breast.
Stung by such thoughts, o'er bank and brae,
Like fire from flint he glanced away,
While high resolve, and feeling strong,
Burst into voluntary song.

XXIII.

Song.

The heath this night must be my bed,
The bracken* curtain for my head,
My lullaby the warder's tread,
　　Far, far from love and thee, Mary;
To-morrow eve, more stilly laid,
My couch may be my bloody plaid,
My vesper song, thy wail, sweet maid!
　　It will not waken me, Mary!

I may not, dare not, fancy now
The grief that clouds thy lovely brow,
I dare not think upon thy vow,
　　And all it promised me, Mary.
No fond regret must Norman know;
When bursts Clan-Alpine on the foe,
His heart must be like bended bow,
　　His foot like arrow free, Mary.

A time will come with feeling fraught,
For, if I fall in battle fought,
Thy hapless lover's dying thought
　　Shall be a thought on thee, Mary.
And if return'd from conquer'd foes,
How blithely will the evening close,
How sweet the linnet sing repose,
　　To my young bride and me, Mary!

XXIV.

Not faster o'er thy heathery braes,
Balquidder, speeds the midnight blaze,[30]
Rushing, in conflagration strong,
Thy deep ravines and dells along,
Wrapping thy cliffs in purple glow,
And reddening the dark lakes below;
Nor faster speeds it, nor so far,
As o'er thy heaths the voice of war.
The signal roused to martial coil
The sullen margin of Loch Voil,

Waked still Loch Doine, and to the source
Alarm'd, Balvaig, thy swampy course;
Thence southward turn'd its rapid road
Adown Strath-Gartney's valley broad,
Till rose in arms each man might claim
A portion in Clan-Alpine's name,
From the grey sire, whose trembling hand
Could hardly buckle on his brand,
To the raw boy, whose shaft and bow
Were yet scarce terror to the crow.
Each valley, each sequester'd glen,
Muster'd its little horde of men,
That met as torrents from the height
In Highland dales their streams unite,
Still gathering, as they pour along,
A voice more loud, a tide more strong,
Till at the rendezvous they stood
By hundreds prompt for blows and blood;
Each train'd to arms since life began,
Owning no tie but to his clan,
No oath, but by his chieftain's hand,
No law, but Roderick Dhu's command.

XXV.

That summer morn had Roderick Dhu
Survey'd the skirts of Benvenue,
And sent his scouts o'er hill and heath,
To view the frontiers of Menteith.
All backward came with news of truce;
Still lay each martial Græme and Bruce,
In Rednoch courts no horsemen wait,
No banner waved on Cardross gate,
On Duchray's towers no beacon shone,
Nor scared the herons from Loch Con;
All seem'd at peace.—Now, wot ye why
The Chieftain, with such anxious eye,
Ere to the muster he repair,
This western frontier scann'd with care?—
In Benvenue's most darksome cleft,
A fair, though cruel, pledge was left;
For Douglas, to his promise true,
That morning from the isle withdrew,
And in a deep sequester'd dell
Had sought a low and lonely cell.
By many a bard, in Celtic tongue,
Has Coir-nan-Uriskin been sung;[31]
A softer name the Saxons gave,
And call'd the grot the Goblin-cave.

---

* Fern.

XXVI.

It was a wild and strange retreat,
As e'er was trod by outlaw's feet.
The dell, upon the mountain's crest,
Yawn'd like a gash on warrior's breast;
Its trench had staid full many a rock,
Hurl'd by primeval earthquake shock
From Benvenue's grey summit wild,
And here, in random ruin piled,
They frown'd incumbent o'er the spot,
And form'd the rugged silvan grot.
The oak and birch, with mingled shade,
At noontide there a twilight made,
Unless when short and sudden shone
Some straggling beam on cliff or stone,
With such a glimpse as prophet's eye
Gains on thy depth, Futurity.
No murmur waked the solemn still,
Save tinkling of a fountain rill;
But when the wind chafed with the lake,
A sullen sound would upward break,
With dashing hollow voice, that spoke
The incessant war of wave and rock.
Suspended cliffs with hideous sway,
Seem'd nodding o'er the cavern grey.
From such a den the wolf had sprung,
In such the wild-cat leaves her young;
Yet Douglas and his daughter fair
Sought for a space their safety there.
Grey Superstition's whisper dread
Debarr'd the spot to vulgar tread;
For there, she said, did fays resort,
And satyrs* hold their silvan court,
By moonlight tread their mystic maze,
And blast the rash beholder's gaze.

XXVII.

Now eve, with western shadows long,
Floated on Katrine bright and strong,
When Roderick, with a chosen few,
Repass'd the heights of Benvenue.
Above the Goblin-cave they go,
Through the wild pass of Beal-nam-bo:
The prompt retainers speed before,
To launch the shallop from the shore,
For cross Loch Katrine lies his way

---

* The Highlanders had a mythological satyr or urisk.

To view the passes of Achray,
And place his clansmen in array.
Yet lags the chief in musing mind,
Unwonted sight, his men behind.
A single page, to bear his sword,
Alone attended on his lord;
The rest their way through thickets
break,
And soon await him by the lake.
It was a fair and gallant sight,
To view them from the neighbouring
height,
By the low-levell'd sunbeams light !
For strength and stature, from the clan
Each warrior was a chosen man,
As even afar might well be seen,
By their proud step and martial mien.
Their feathers dance, their tartans float,
Their targets gleam, as by the boat
A wild and warlike group they stand,
That well became such mountain-strand.

XXVIII.

Their Chief, with step reluctant, still
Was lingering on the craggy hill,
Hard by where turn'd apart the road
To Douglas's obscure abode.
It was but with that dawning morn,
That Roderick Dhu had proudly sworn
To drown his love in war's wild roar,
Nor think of Ellen Douglas more;
But he who stems a stream with sand,
And fetters flame with flaxen band,
Has yet a harder task to prove—
By firm resolve to conquer love !
Eve finds the Chief, like restless ghost,
Still hovering near his treasure lost;
For though his haughty heart deny
A parting meeting to his eye,
Still fondly strains his anxious ear,
The accents of her voice to hear,
And inly did he curse the breeze
That waked to sound the rustling trees.
But hark ! what mingles in the strain?
It is the harp of Allan-Bane,
That wakes its measure slow and high,
Attuned to sacred minstrelsy.
What melting voice attends the strings?
'Tis Ellen, or an angel, sings.

XXIX.

Hymn to the Virgin.

Ave Maria! maiden mild!
  Listen to a maiden's prayer!
Thou canst hear though from the wild,
  Thou canst save amid despair.
Safe may we sleep beneath thy care,
  Though banish'd, outcast, and reviled—
Maiden! hear a maiden's prayer;
  Mother, hear a suppliant child!
               Ave Maria!

Ave Maria! undefiled!
  The flinty couch we now must share
Shall seem with down of eider piled,
  If thy protection hover there.
The murky cavern's heavy air
  Shall breathe of balm if thou hast smiled;
Then, Maiden! hear a maiden's prayer;
  Mother, list a suppliant child!
               Ave Maria!

Ave Maria! stainless styled!
  Foul demons of the earth and air,
From this their wonted haunt exiled,
  Shall flee before thy presence fair.
We bow us to our lot of care,
  Beneath thy guidance reconciled;
Hear for a maid a maiden's prayer,
  And for a father hear a child!
               Ave Maria!

XXX.

Died on the harp the closing hymn—
Unmoved in attitude and limb,
As list'ning still, Clan-Alpine's lord
Stood leaning on his heavy sword,
Until the page, with humble sign,
Twice pointed to the sun's decline.
Then while his plaid he round him cast,
"It is the last time—'tis the last,"
He mutter'd thrice,—"the last time e'er
That angel voice shall Roderick hear!"
It was a goading thought—his stride
Hied hastier down the mountain-side;
Sullen he flung him in the boat,
And instant 'cross the lake it shot.
They landed in that silvery bay,
And eastward held their hasty way,

Till, with the latest beams of light,
The band arrived on Lanrick height,
Where muster'd, in the vale below,
Clan-Alpine's men in martial show.

XXXI.

A various scene the clansmen made,
Some sate, some stood, some slowly
    stray'd;
But most with mantles folded round,
Were couch'd to rest upon the ground,
Scarce to be known by curious eye,
From the deep heather where they lie,
So well was match'd the tartan screen
With heath-bell dark and brackens green;
Unless where, here and there, a blade,
Or lance's point, a glimmer made,
Like glow-worm twinkling through the
    shade.
But when, advancing through the gloom,
They saw the Chieftain's eagle plume,
Their shout of welcome, shrill and wide,
Shook the steep mountain's steady side.
Thrice it arose, and lake and fell
Three times return'd the martial yell;
It died upon Bochastle's plain,
And Silence claim'd her evening reign.

CANTO FOURTH.

The Prophecy.

I.

"The rose is fairest when 'tis budding new,
  And hope is brightest when it dawns
    from fears;
The rose is sweetest wash'd with morning
    dew,
  And love is loveliest when embalm'd in
    tears.
O wilding rose, whom fancy thus endears,
  I bid your blossoms in my bonnet wave,
Emblem of hope and love through future
    years!"
Thus spoke young Norman, heir of
    Armandave,
What time the sun arose on Vennachar's
    broad wave.

II.

Such fond conceit, half said, half sung,
Love prompted to the bridegroom's
    tongue.
All while he stripp'd the wild-rose spray,
His axe and bow beside him lay,
For on a pass 'twixt lake and wood,
A wakeful sentinel he stood.
Hark! on the rock a footstep rung,
And instant to his arms he sprung.
"Stand, or thou diest!—What, Malise?
    —soon
Art thou return'd from Braes of Doune.
By thy keen step and glance I know,
Thou bring'st us tidings of the foe." —
(For while the Fiery Cross hied on,
On distant scout had Malise gone.)
" Where sleeps the Chief?" the hench-
    man said.—
" Apart, in yonder misty glade;
To his lone couch I'll be your guide."—
Then call'd a slumberer by his side,
And stirr'd him with his slacken'd bow—
" Up, up, Glentarkin! rouse thee, ho!
We seek the Chieftain; on the track,
Keep eagle watch till I come back."

III.

Together up the pass they sped:
" What of the foemen?" Norman said.—
"Varying reports from near and far;
This certain—that a band of war
Has for two days been ready boune,
At prompt command, to march from
    Doune;
King James, the while, with princely
    powers,
Holds revelry in Stirling towers.
Soon will this dark and gathering cloud
Speak on our glens in thunder loud.
Inured to bide such bitter bout,
The warrior's plaid may bear it out;
But, Norman, how wilt thou provide
A shelter for thy bonny bride?"
" What! know ye not that Roderick's care
To the lone isle hath caused repair
Each maid and matron of the clan,
And every child and aged man
Unfit for arms; and given his charge,

Nor skiff nor shallop, boat nor barge,
Upon these lakes shall float at large,
But all beside the islet moor,
That such dear pledge may rest secure?"—

IV.

" 'Tis well advised—the Chieftain's plan
Bespeaks the father of his clan.
But wherefore sleeps Sir Roderick Dhu
Apart from all his followers true?"—
" It is because last evening-tide
Brian an augury hath tried,
Of that dread kind which must not be
Unless in dread extremity,
The Taghairm call'd; by which, afar,
Our sires foresaw the events of war.[32]
Duncraggan's milk-white bull they slew."

MALISE.

" Ah! well the gallant brute I knew!
The choicest of the prey we had,
When swept our merry-men Gallangad.
His hide was snow, his horns were dark,
His red eye glow'd like fiery spark;
So fierce, so tameless, and so fleet,
Sore did he cumber our retreat,
And kept our stoutest kernes in awe,
Even at the pass of Beal 'maha.
But steep and flinty was the road,
And sharp the hurrying pikemen's goad,
And when we came to Dennan's Row,
A child might scatheless stroke his
    brow."—

V.

NORMAN.

" That bull was slain: his reeking hide
They stretch'd the cataract beside,
Whose waters their wild tumult toss
Adown the black and craggy boss
Of that huge cliff, whose ample verge
Tradition calls the Hero's Targe.[33]
Couch'd on a shelve beneath its brink,
Close where the thundering torrents sink,
Rocking beneath their headlong sway,
And drizzled by the ceaseless spray,
Midst groan of rock, and roar of stream,
The wizard waits prophetic dream.
Nor distant rests the Chief;—but hush!
See, gliding slow through mist and bush,

The hermit gains yon rock, and stands
To gaze upon our slumbering bands.
Seems he not, Malise, like a ghost,
That hovers o'er a slaughter'd host?
Or raven on the blasted oak,
That, watching while the deer is broke,
His morsel claims with sullen croak?"

MALISE.

—" Peace! peace! to other than to me,
Thy words were evil augury;
But still I hold Sir Roderick's blade
Clan-Alpine's omen and her aid,
Not aught that, glean'd from heaven or hell,
Yon fiend-begotten monk can tell.
The Chieftain joins him, see—and now,
Together they descend the brow."

VI.

And as they came, with Alpine's Lord
The Hermit Monk held solemn word :—
" Roderick! it is a fearful strife,
For man endow'd with mortal life,
Whose shroud of sentient clay can still
Feel feverish pang and fainting chill,
Whose eye can stare in stony trance,
Whose hair can rouse like warrior's
          lance,—
'Tis hard for such to view, unfurl'd,
The curtain of the future world.
Yet, witness every quaking limb,
My sunken pulse, my eyeballs dim,
My soul, with harrowing anguish torn,—
This for my Chieftain have I borne!—
The shapes that sought my fearful couch,
A human tongue may ne'er avouch;
No mortal man,—save he, who, bred
Between the living and the dead,
Is gifted beyond nature's law,—
Had e'er survived to say he saw.
At length the fatal answer came,
In characters of living flame!
Not spoke in word, nor blazed in scroll,
But borne and branded on my soul ;—
WHICH SPILLS THE FOREMOST FOE-
    MAN'S LIFE,
THAT PARTY CONQUERS IN THE
    STRIFE!"[31]

VII.

" Thanks, Brian, for thy zeal and care!
Good is thine augury, and fair,

Clan-Alpine ne'er in battle stood,
But first our broadswords tasted blood.
A surer victim still I know,
Self-offer'd to the auspicious blow;
A spy has sought my land this morn,—
No eye shall witness his return!
My followers guard each pass's mouth,
To east, to westward, and to south;
Red Murdoch, bribed to be his guide,
Has charge to lead his steps aside,
Till, in deep path or dingle brown,
He light on those shall bring him down.
—But see, who comes his news to show!
Malise! what tidings of the foe?"—

VIII.

" At Doune, o'er many a spear and glaive
Two Barons proud their banners wave.
I saw the Moray's silver star,
And mark'd the sable pale of Mar."—
" By Alpine's soul, high tidings those!
I love to hear of worthy foes.
When move they on?"—" To-morrow's
          noon
Will see them here for battle boune."—
" Then shall it see a meeting stern!—
But, for the place—say, couldst thou learn
Nought of the friendly clans of Earn?
Strengthen'd by them, we well might bide
The battle on Benledi's side.
Thou couldst not?—Well! Clan-Alpine's
          men
Shall man the Trosach's shaggy glen;
Within Loch Katrine's gorge we'll fight,
All in our maids' and matrons' sight,
Each for his hearth and household fire,
Father for child, and son for sire,—
Lover for maid beloved!—But why—
Is it the breeze affects mine eye?
Or dost thou come, ill-omen'd tear!
A messenger of doubt or fear?
No! sooner may the Saxon lance
Unfix Benledi from his stance,
Than doubt or terror can pierce through
The unyielding heart of Roderick Dhu!
'Tis stubborn as his trusty targe.—
Each to his post!—all know their charge."
The pibroch sounds, the bands advance,
The broadswords gleam, the banners
          dance,

Obedient to the Chieftain's glance.
—I turn me from the martial roar,
And seek Coir-Uriskin once more.

IX.

Where is the Douglas ?—he is gone ;
And Ellen sits on the grey stone
Fast by the cave, and makes her moan
While vainly Allan's words of cheer
Are pour'd on her unheeding ear.—
" He will return—Dear lady, trust !—
With joy return ;—he will—he must
Well was it time to seek, afar,
Some refuge from impending war,
When e'en Clan-Alpine's rugged swarm
Are cow'd by the approaching storm.
I saw their boats, with many a light,
Floating the live-long yesternight,
Shifting like flashes darted forth
By the red streamers of the north ;
I mark'd at morn how close they ride,
Thick moor'd by the lone islet's side,
Like wild-ducks couching in the fen,
When stoops the hawk upon the glen.
Since this rude race dare not abide
The peril on the mainland side,
Shall not thy noble father's care
Some safe retreat for thee prepare ?"—

X.

ELLEN.

" No, Allan, no ! Pretext so kind
My wakeful terrors could not blind.
When in such tender tone, yet grave,
Douglas a parting blessing gave,
The tear that glisten'd in his eye
Drown'd not his purpose fix'd on high.
My soul, though feminine and weak,
Can image his ; e'en as the lake,
Itself disturb'd by slightest stroke,
Reflects the invulnerable rock.
He hears report of battle rife,
He deems himself the cause of strife.
I saw him redden, when the theme
Turn'd, Allan, on thine idle dream,
Of Malcolm Græme, in fetters bound,
Which I, thou saidst, about him wound.
Think'st thou he trow'd thine omen aught ?
Oh no ! twas apprehensive thought

For the kind youth,—for Roderick too—
(Let me be just) that friend so true ;
In danger both, and in our cause !
Minstrel, the Douglas, dare not pause.
Why else that solemn warning given,
' If not on earth, we meet in heaven !'
Why else, to Cambus-kenneth's fane,
If eve return him not again,
Am I to hie, and make me known ?
Alas ! he goes to Scotland's throne,
Buys his friend's safety with his own ;—
He goes to do—what I had done,
Had Douglas' daughter been his son !"—

XI.

" Nay, lovely Ellen !—dearest, nay !
If aught should his return delay,
He only named yon holy fane
As fitting place to meet again.
Be sure he's safe ; and for the Græme,—
Heaven's blessing on his gallant name !—
My vision'd sight may yet prove true,
Nor bode of ill to him or you.
When did my gifted dream beguile ?
Think of the stranger at the isle,
And think upon the harpings slow,
That presaged this approaching woe ?
Sooth was my prophecy of fear ;
Believe it when it augurs cheer.
Would we had left this dismal spot !
Ill luck still haunts a fairy grot.
Of such a wondrous tale I know—
Dear lady, change that look of woe,
My harp was wont thy grief to cheer."—

ELLEN.

" Well, be it as thou wilt ; I hear,
But cannot stop the bursting tear."
The Minstrel tried his simple art,
But distant far was Ellen's heart.

XII.

Ballad.

ALICE BRAND.

Merry it is in the good greenwood,
  Where the mavis* and merlet are
    singing,

---

* *Mavis*, a thrush,   † *Merle*, a blackbird,

When the deer sweeps by, and the hounds
  are in cry,
And the hunter's horn is ringing.

"O Alice Brand, my native land
  Is lost for love of you;
And we must hold by wood and wold,
  As outlaws wont to do.

"O Alice, 'twas all for thy locks so
  bright,
And 'twas all for thine eyes so blue,
That on the night of our luckless flight,
  Thy brother bold I slew.

"Now must I teach to hew the beech
  The hand that held the glaive,
For leaves to spread our lowly bed,
  And stakes to fence our cave.

"And for vest of pall, thy fingers small,
  That wont on harp to stray,
A cloak must sheer from the slaughter'd
  deer,
  To keep the cold away."—

"O Richard! if my brother died,
  'Twas but a fatal chance,
For darkling was the battle tried,
  And fortune sped the lance.

"If pall and vair no more I wear,
  Nor thou the crimson sheen,
As warm, we'll say, is the russet grey,
  As gay the forest green.

"And, Richard, if our lot be hard,
  And lost thy native land,
Still Alice has her own Richard,
  And he his Alice Brand."

XIII.

Ballad continued.

'Tis merry, 'tis merry, in good greenwood,
  So blithe Lady Alice is singing;
On the beech's pride, and oak's brown
  side,
  Lord Richard's axe is ringing.

Up spoke the moody Elfin King,
  Who wonn'd within the hill,—
Like wind in the porch of a ruin'd church,
  His voice was ghostly shrill.

"Why sounds yon stroke on beech and
  oak,
  Our moonlight circle's screen?
Or who comes here to chase the deer,
  Beloved of our Elfin Queen?[35]
Or who may dare on wold to wear
  The fairies' fatal green?[36]

"Up, Urgan, up! to yon mortal hie,
  For thou wert christen'd man;[37]
For cross or sign thou wilt not fly,
  For mutter'd word or ban.

"Lay on him the curse of the wither'd
  heart,
  The curse of the sleepless eye;
Till he wish and pray that his life would
  part,
  Nor yet find leave to die."

XIV.

Ballad continued.

'Tis merry, 'tis merry, in good greenwood,
  Though the birds have still'd their
  singing;
The evening blaze doth Alice raise,
  And Richard is fagots bringing.

Up Urgan starts, that hideous dwarf
  Before Lord Richard stands,
And, as he cross'd and bless'd himself,
  "I fear not sign," quoth the grisly elf,
  "That is made with bloody hands."

But out then spoke she, Alice Brand,
  That woman void of fear,—
"And if there's blood upon his hand,
  'Tis but the blood of deer."—

"Now loud thou liest, thou bold of mood!
  It cleaves unto his hand,
The stain of thine own kindly blood,
  The blood of Ethert Brand."

Then forward stepp'd she, Alice Brand,
  And made the holy sign,—
" And if there's blood on Richard's hand,
  A spotless hand is mine.

" And I conjure thee, Demon elf,
  By Him whom Demons fear,
To show us whence thou art thyself,
  And what thine errand here ?"—

XV.

Ballad continued.

" 'Tis merry, 'tis merry in Fairy-land,
  When fairy birds are singing,
When the court doth ride by their
    monarch's side,
  With bit and bridle ringing :

" And gaily shines the Fairy-land—
  But all is glistening show,
Like the idle gleam that December's beam
  Can dart on ice and snow.

" And fading, like that varied gleam,
  Is our inconstant shape,
Who now like knight and lady seem,
  And now like dwarf and ape.

" It was between the night and day,
  When the Fairy King has power,
That I sunk down in a sinful fray,
And 'twixt life and death, was snatch'd
    away
  To the joyless Elfin bower.

" But wist I of a woman bold,
  Who thrice my brow durst sign,
I might regain my mortal mold,
  As fair a form as thine."

She cross'd him once—she cross'd him
    twice—
  That lady was so brave ;
The fouler grew his goblin hue,
  The darker grew the cave.

She cross'd him thrice, that lady bold ;
  He rose beneath her hand
The fairest knight on Scottish mold,
  Her brother, Ethert Brand !

Merry it is in good greenwood,
  When the mavis and merle are singing,
But merrier were they in Dunfermline
    grey,
  When all the bells were ringing.

XVI.

Just as the minstrel sounds were staid,
A stranger climb'd the steepy glade :
His martial step, his stately mien,
His hunting suit of Lincoln green,
His eagle glance, remembrance claims—
'Tis Snowdoun's Knight, 'tis James Fitz-
    James.
Ellen beheld as in a dream,
Then, starting, scarce suppress'd a scream :
" O stranger ! in such hour of fear,
What evil hap has brought thee here ?"—
" An evil hap how can it be,
That bids me look again on thee ?
By promise bound, my former guide
Met me betimes this morning tide,
And marshall'd, over bank and bourne,
The happy path of my return."—
" The happy path !—what ! said he nought
Of war, of battle to be fought,
Of guarded pass ?"—" No, by my faith !
Nor saw I aught could augur scathe."—
" O haste thee, Allan, to the kern,
—Yonder his tartans I discern ;
Learn thou his purpose, and conjure
That he will guide the stranger sure !—
What prompted thee, unhappy man ?
The meanest serf in Roderick's clan
Had not been bribed by love or fear,
Unknown to him to guide thee here."—

XVII.

" Sweet Ellen, dear my life must be,
Since it is worthy care from thee ;
Yet life I hold but idle breath,
When love or honour's weigh'd with
    death.
Then let me profit by my chance,
And speak my purpose bold at once.
I come to bear thee from a wild,
Where ne'er before such blossom smiled ;
By this soft hand to lead thee far
From frantic scenes of feud and war.

Near Bochastle my horses wait;
They bear us soon to Stirling gate.
I'll place thee in a lovely bower,
I'll guard thee like a tender flower "——
"O! hush, Sir Knight! 'twere female art,
To say I do not read thy heart;
Too much, before, my selfish ear
Was idly soothed my praise to hear.
That fatal bait hath lured thee back,
In deathful hour, o'er dangerous track;
And how, O how, can I atone
The wreck my vanity brought on!—
One way remains—I'll tell him all—
Yes! struggling bosom, forth it shall!
Thou, whose light folly bears the blame,
Buy thine own pardon with thy shame!
But first—my father is a man
Outlaw'd and exiled, under ban;
The price of blood is on his head,
With me 'twere infamy to wed.—
Still wouldst thou speak?—then hear the
    truth!
Fitz-James, there is a noble youth,—
If yet he is!—exposed for me
And mine to dread extremity—
Thou hast the secret of my heart:
Forgive, be generous, and depart!"

XVIII.

Fitz-James knew every wily train
A lady's fickle heart to gain;
But here he knew and felt them vain.
There shot no glance from Ellen's eye,
To give her steadfast speech the lie;
In maiden confidence she stood,
Though mantled in her cheek the blood,
And told her love with such a sigh
Of deep and hopeless agony,
As death had seal'd her Malcolm's doom,
And she sat sorrowing on his tomb.
Hope vanish'd from Fitz-James's eye,
But not with hope fled sympathy.
He proffer'd to attend her side,
As brother would a sister guide.—
"O! little know'st thou Roderick's heart!
Safer for both we go apart.
O haste thee, and from Allan learn,
If thou may'st trust yon wily kern."
With hand upon his forehead laid,

The conflict of his mind to shade,
A parting step or two he made;
Then, as some thought had cross'd his
    brain,
He paused, and turn'd, and came again.

XIX.

"Hear, lady, yet, a parting word!—
It chanced in fight that my poor sword
Preserved the life of Scotland's lord.
This ring the grateful monarch gave,
And bade when I had boon to crave,
To bring it back, and boldly claim
The recompense that I would name.
Ellen, I am no courtly lord,
But one who lives by lance and sword,
Whose castle is his helm and shield,
His lordship the embattled field.
What from a prince can I demand,
Who neither reck of state nor land?
Ellen, thy hand—the ring is thine;
Each guard and usher knows the sign.
Seek thou the king without delay;
This signet shall secure thy way;
And claim thy suit, whate'er it be,
As ransom of his pledge to me."
He placed the golden circlet on,
Paused—kiss'd her hand—and then was
    gone.
The aged Minstrel stood aghast,
So hastily Fitz-James shot past.
He join'd his guide, and wending down
The ridges of the mountain brown,
Across the stream they took their way,
That joins Loch Katrine to Achray.

XX.

All in the Trosach's glen was still,
Noontide was sleeping on the hill;
Sudden his guide whoop'd loud and high—
"Murdoch! was that a signal cry?"—
He stammer'd forth,—"I shout to scare
Yon raven from his dainty fare."
He look'd—he knew the raven's prey,
His own brave steed:—"Ah! gallant
    grey!
For thee—for me, perchance—'twere well
We ne'er had seen the Trosach's dell.—
Murdoch, move first—but silently;
Whistle or whoop, and thou shalt die!"

Jealous and sullen on they fared,
Each silent, each upon his guard.

XXI.

Now wound the path its dizzy ledge
Around a precipice's edge,
When lo! a wasted female form,
Blighted by wrath of sun and storm,
In tatter'd weeds and wild array,
Stood on a cliff beside the way,
And glancing round her restless eye,
Upon the wood, the rock, the sky,
Seem'd nought to mark, yet all to spy.
Her brow was wreath'd with gaudy broom;
With gesture wild she waved a plume
Of feathers, which the eagles fling
To crag and cliff from dusky wing;
Such spoils her desperate step had sought,
Where scarce was footing for the goat.
The tartan plaid she first descried,
And shriek'd till all the rocks replied;
As loud she laugh'd when near they drew,
For then the Lowland garb she knew;
And then her hands she wildly wrung,
And then she wept, and then she sung—
She sung!—the voice, in better time,
Perchance to harp or lute might chime;
And now, though strain'd and roughen'd, still
Rung wildly sweet to dale and hill.

XXII.

Song.

They bid me sleep, they bid me pray,
  They say my brain is warp'd and wrung—
I cannot sleep on Highland brae,
  I cannot pray in Highland tongue.
But were I now where Allan* glides,
Or heard my native Devan's tides,
So sweetly would I rest, and pray
That Heaven would close my wintry day!

'Twas thus my hair they bade me braid,
  They made me to the church repair;

---

* *Allan* and *Devan,* two rivers running through Stirling Plain.

It was my bridal morn they said,
  And my true love would meet me there.
But woe betide the cruel guile,
That drown'd in blood the morning smile!
And woe betide the fairy dream!
I only waked to sob and scream.

XXIII.

" Who is this maid? what means her lay?
She hovers o'er the hollow way,
And flutters wide her mantle grey,
As the lone heron spreads his wing,
By twilight, o'er a haunted spring."—
" 'Tis Blanche of Devan," Murdoch said,
" A crazed and captive Lowland maid,
Ta'en on the morn she was a bride,
When Roderick foray'd Devan-side.
The gay bridegroom resistance made,
And felt our Chief's unconquer'd blade,
I marvel she is now at large,
But oft she 'scapes from Maudlin's charge.—
Hence, brain-sick fool!"—He raised his bow:—
" Now, if thou strikest her but one blow,
I'll pitch thee from the cliff as far
As ever peasant pitch'd a bar!"—
"Thanks, champion, thanks!" the Maniac cried,
And press'd her to Fitz-James's side.
" See the grey pennons I prepare,
To seek my true-love through the air;
I will not lend that savage groom,
To break his fall, one downy plume!
No!—deep amid disjointed stones,
The wolves shall batten on his bones,
And then shall his detested plaid,
By bush and brier in mid air staid,
Wave forth a banner fair and free,
Meet signal for their revelry."—

XXIV.

" Hush thee, poor maiden, and be still!"—
" O! thou look'st kindly, and I will.—
Mine eye has dried and wasted been,
But still it loves the Lincoln green,
And, though mine ear is all unstrung,
Still, still it loves the Lowland tongue.

"For O my sweet William was
  forester true,
 He stole poor Blanche's heart away!
 His coat it was all of the greenwood
  hue,
  And so blithely he trill'd the Lowland lay!

"It was not that I meant to tell
But thou art wise and guessest well."
Then, in a low and broken tone,
And hurried note, the song went on.
Still on the Clansman, fearfully,
She fix'd her apprehensive eye;
Then turn'd it on the Knight, and then
Her look glanced wildly o'er the glen.

XXV.

 "The toils are pitch'd, and the stakes
  are set,
 Ever sing merrily, merrily;
 The bows they bend, and the knives
  they whet,
  Hunters live so cheerily.

 "It was a stag, a stag of ten,*
  Bearing its branches sturdily;
 He came stately down the glen,
  Ever sing hardily, hardily.

 "It was there he met with a wounded
  doe,
 She was bleeding deathfully;
 She warn'd him of the toils below,
  O, so faithfully, faithfully!

 "He had an eye, and he could heed,
  Ever sing warily, warily;
 He had a foot, and he could speed—
  Hunters watch so narrowly."

XXVI.

Fitz-James's mind was passion-toss'd,
When Ellen's hints and fears were lost;
But Murdoch's shout suspicion wrought,
And Blanche's song conviction brought.—
Not like a stag that spies the snare,
But lion of the hunt aware,

---

* Of ten branches to his antlers; a royal or
noble deer.

He waved at once his blade on high,
 "Disclose thy treachery, or die!"
Forth at full speed the Clansman flew,
But in his race his bow he drew.
The shaft just grazed Fitz-James's crest,
And thrill'd in Blanche's faded breast,—
Murdoch of Alpine! prove thy speed,
For ne'er had Alpine's son such need!
With heart of fire, and foot of wind,
The fierce avenger is behind!
Fate judges of the rapid strife—
The forfeit death—the prize is life!
Thy kindred ambush lies before,
Close couch'd upon the heathery moor;
Them couldst thou reach—it may not
 be—
Thine ambush'd kin thou ne'er shalt see,
The fiery Saxon gains on thee!
—Resistless speeds the deadly thrust,
As lightning strikes the pine to dust;
With foot and hand Fitz-James must
 strain,
Ere he can win his blade again.
Bent o'er the fall'n, with falcon eye,
He grimly smiled to see him die;
Then slower wended back his way,
Where the poor maiden bleeding lay.

XXVII.

She sate beneath the birchen-tree,
Her elbow resting on her knee;
She had withdrawn the fatal shaft,
And gazed on it, and feebly laugh'd;
Her wreath of broom and feathers grey,
Daggled with blood, beside her lay.
The Knight to stanch the life-stream
 tried,—
"Stranger, it is in vain!" she cried.
"This hour of death has given me
 more
Of reason's power than years before;
For, as these ebbing veins decay,
My frenzied visions fade away.
A helpless injured wretch I die,
And something tells me in thine eye,
That thou wert mine avenger born.—
Seest thou this tress?—O! still I've worn
This little tress of yellow hair,
Through danger, frenzy, and despair!

It once was bright and clear as thine,
But blood and tears have dimm'd its
    shine.
I will not tell thee when 'twas shred,
Nor from what guiltless victim's head—
My brain would turn!—but it shall wave
Like plumage on thy helmet brave,
Till sun and wind shall bleach the stain,
And thou wilt bring it me again.—
I waver still.—O God! more bright
Let reason beam her parting light!—
O! by thy knighthood's honour'd sign,
And for thy life preserved by mine,
When thou shalt see a darksome man,
Who boasts him Chief of Alpine's Clan,
With tartans broad and shadowy plume,
And hand of blood, and brow of gloom,
Be thy heart bold, thy weapon strong,
And wreak poor Blanche of Devan's
    wrong!—
They watch for thee by pass and fell . . .
Avoid the path . . . . O God! . . . .
    farewell."

XXVIII.

A kindly heart had brave Fitz-James;
Fast pour'd his eyes at pity's claims,
And now with mingled grief and ire,
He saw the murder'd maid expire.
" God, in my need, be my relief,
As I wreak this on yonder Chief!"
A lock from Blanche's tresses fair
He blended with her bridegroom's hair;
The mingled braid in blood he dyed,
And placed it on his bonnet-side:
" By Him whose word is truth! I swear,
No other favour will I wear,
Till this sad token I imbrue
In the best blood of Roderick Dhu!
—But hark! what means yon faint halloo?
The chase is up,—but they shall know,
The stag at bay 's a dangerous foe."
Barr'd from the known but guarded
    way,
Through copse and cliffs Fitz-James
    must stray,
And oft must change his desperate track,
By stream and precipice turn'd back.
Heartless, fatigued, and faint, at length,
From lack of food and loss of strength,

He couch'd him in a thicket hoar,
And thought his toils and perils o'er:—
" Of all my rash adventures past,
This frantic feat must prove the last!
Who e'er so mad but might have guess'd,
That all this Highland hornet's nest
Would muster up in swarms so soon
As e'er they heard of bands at Doune?—
Like bloodhounds now they search me
    out,—
Hark, to the whistle and the shout!—
If farther through the wilds I go,
I only fall upon the foe:
I'll couch me here till evening grey,
Then darkling try my dangerous way."

XXIX.

The shades of eve come slowly down,
The woods are wrapt in deeper brown,
The owl awakens from her dell,
The fox is heard upon the fell;
Enough remains of glimmering light
To guide the wanderer's steps aright.
Yet not enough from far to show
His figure to the watchful foe.
With cautious step, and ear awake,
He climbs the crag and threads the brake;
And not the summer solstice, there,
Temper'd the midnight mountain air,
But every breeze, that swept the wold,
Benumb'd his drenched limbs with cold.
In dread, in danger, and alone,
Famish'd and chill'd, through ways un-
    known,
Tangled and steep, he journey'd on;
Till, as a rock's huge point he turn'd,
A watch-fire close before him burn'd.

XXX.

Beside its embers red and clear,
Bask'd, in his plaid, a mountaineer;
And up he sprung with sword in hand,—
" Thy name and purpose! Saxon,
    stand!"—
" A stranger." — " What dost thou
    require?"—
" Rest and a guide, and food and fire.
My life's beset, my path is lost,
The gale has chill'd my limbs with
    frost."—

" Art thou a friend to Roderick ?"—
" No."—
" Thou darest not call thyself a foe ?"—
" I dare ! to him and all the band
He brings to aid his murderous hand."—
" Bold words !—but, though the beast of
    game
The privilege of chase may claim,
Though space and law the stag we lend,
Ere hound we slip, or bow we bend,
Who ever reck'd, where, how, or when,
The prowling fox was trapp'd or slain ?[38]
Thus treacherous scouts,—yet sure they
    lie,
Who say thou camest a secret spy !"—
" They do, by heaven !—Come Roderick
    Dhu,
And of his clan the boldest two,
And let me but till morning rest,
I write the falsehood on their crest."—
" If by the blaze I mark aright,
Thou bear'st the belt and spur of
    Knight."—
" Then by these tokens mayest thou know
Each proud oppressor's mortal foe."—
" Enough, enough ; sit down and share
A soldier's couch, a soldier's fare."

XXXI.

He gave him of his Highland cheer,
The harden'd flesh of mountain deer ;[39]
Dry fuel on the fire he laid,
And bade the Saxon share his plaid.
He tended him like welcome guest,
Then thus his farther speech address'd.
" Stranger, I am to Roderick Dhu
A clansman born, a kinsman true ;
Each word against his honour spoke,
Demands of me avenging stroke ;
Yet more,—upon thy fate, 'tis said,
A mighty augury is laid,
It rests with me to wind my horn,—
Thou art with numbers overborne ;
It rests with me, here, brand to brand,
Worn as thou art, to bid thee stand :
But, not for clan, nor kindred's cause,
Will I depart from honour's laws ;
To assail a wearied man were shame,
And stranger is a holy name ;

Guidance and rest, and food and fire,
In vain he never must require.
Then rest thee here till dawn of day ;
Myself will guide thee on the way,
O'er stock and stone, through watch and
    ward,
Till past Clan-Alpine's outmost guard,
As far as Coilantogle's ford ;
From thence thy warrant is thy sword."—
" I take thy courtesy, by heaven,
As freely as 'tis nobly given !"
" Well, rest thee ; for the bittern's cry
Sings us the lake's wild lullaby."
With that he shook the gather'd heath,
And spread his plaid upon the wreath ;
And the brave foemen, side by side,
Lay peaceful down, like brothers tried,
And slept until the dawning beam
Purpled the mountain and the stream.

———◆———

CANTO FIFTH.

The Combat.

I.

FAIR as the earliest beam of eastern light,
    When first, by the bewilder'd pilgrim
        spied,
It smiles upon the dreary brow of night,
    And silvers o'er the torrent's foaming
        tide,
And lights the fearful path on mountain
        side,
    Fair as that beam, although the fairest
        far,
Giving to horror grace, to danger pride,
    Shine martial Faith, and Courtesy's
        bright star,
Through all the wreckful storms that
        cloud the brow of War.

II.

That early beam, so fair and sheen,
Was twinkling through the hazel screen,
When, rousing at its glimmer red,
The warriors left their lowly bed,
Look'd out upon the dappled sky,
Mutter'd their soldier matins by,

And then awaked their fire, to steal,
As short and rude, their soldier meal.
That o'er, the Gael* around him threw
His graceful plaid of varied hue,
And, true to promise, led the way,
By thicket green and mountain grey.
A wildering path!—they winded now
Along the precipice's brow,
Commanding the rich scenes beneath,
The windings of the Forth and Teith,
And all the vales beneath that lie,
Till Stirling's turrets melt in sky;
Then, sunk in copse, their farthest glance
Gain'd not the length of horseman's lance.
'Twas oft so steep, the foot was fain
Assistance from the hand to gain;
So tangled oft, that, bursting through,
Each hawthorn shed her showers of dew,—
That diamond dew, so pure and clear,
It rivals all but Beauty's tear!

III.

At length they came where, stern and steep,
The hill sinks down upon the deep.
Here Vennachar in silver flows,
There, ridge on ridge, Benledi rose;
Ever the hollow path twined on,
Beneath steep bank and threatening stone;
An hundred men might hold the post
With hardihood against a host.
The rugged mountain's scanty cloak
Was dwarfish shrubs of birch and oak,
With shingles bare, and cliffs between,
And patches bright of bracken green,
And heather black, that waved so high,
It held the copse in rivalry.
But where the lake slept deep and still,
Dank osiers fringed the swamp and hill;
And oft both path and hill were torn,
Where wintry torrents down had borne,
And heap'd upon the cumber'd land
Its wreck of gravel, rocks, and sand.
So toilsome was the road to trace,
The guide, abating of his pace,
Led slowly through the pass's jaws,
And ask'd Fitz-James, by what strange
        cause

---

* *Gael*, the ancient or Celtic name of a
Highlander.

He sought these wilds? traversed by few,
Without a pass from Roderick Dhu.

IV.

" Brave Gael, my pass in danger tried,
Hangs in my belt and by my side;
Yet, sooth to tell," the Saxon said,
" I dreamt not now to claim its aid.
When here, but three days since, I came,
Bewilder'd in pursuit of game,
All seem'd as peaceful and as still,
As the mist slumbering on yon hill;
Thy dangerous Chief was then afar,
Nor soon expected back from war.
Thus said, at least, my mountain-guide,
Though deep, perchance, the villain
        lied."—
" Yet why a second venture try?"
" A warrior thou, and ask me why!—
Moves our free course by such fix'd cause,
As gives the poor mechanic laws:
Enough, I sought to drive away
The lazy hours of peaceful day:
Slight cause will then suffice to guide
A Knight's free footsteps far and wide—
A falcon flown, a greyhound stray'd,
The merry glance of mountain maid:
Or, if a path be dangerous known,
The danger's self is lure alone."

V.

" Thy secret keep, I urge thee not;—
Yet, ere again ye sought this spot,
Say, heard ye nought of Lowland war,
Against Clan-Alpine, raised by Mar?"
—" No, by my word;—of bands prepared
To guard King James's sports I heard;
Nor doubt I aught, but, when they hear
This muster of the mountaineer,
Their pennons will abroad be flung,
Which else in Doune had peaceful hung."—
" Free be they flung!—for we were loth
Their silken folds should feast the moth.
Free be they flung!—as free shall wave
Clan-Alpine's pine in banner brave.
But, Stranger, peaceful since you came,
Bewilder'd in the mountain game,
Whence the bold boast by which you show
Vich-Alpine's vow'd and mortal foe?"—

" Warrior, but yester-morn, I knew
Nought of thy Chieftain, Roderick Dhu,
Save as an outlaw'd desperate man,
The chief of a rebellious clan,
Who, in the Regent's court and sight,
With ruffian dagger stabb'd a knight:
Yet this alone might from his part
Sever each true and loyal heart."

VI.

Wrothful at such arraignment foul,
Dark lower'd the clansman's sable scowl,
A space he paused, then sternly said,
"And heard'st thou why he drew his blade?
Heard'st thou that shameful word and blow
Brought Roderick's vengeance on his foe?
What reck'd the Chieftain if he stood
On Highland heath, or Holy-Rood?
He rights such wrong where it is given,
If it were in the court of heaven."—
" Still was it outrage;—yet, 'tis true,
Not then claim'd sovereignty his due;
While Albany, with feeble hand,
Held borrow'd truncheon of command, 40
The young King, mew'd in Stirling tower,
Was stranger to respect and power.
But then, thy Chieftain's robber life!—
Winning mean prey by causeless strife,
Wrenching from ruin'd Lowland swain
His herds and harvest rear'd in vain.—
Methinks a soul, like thine, should scorn
The spoils from such foul foray borne."

VII.

The Gael beheld him grim the while,
And answer'd with disdainful smile,—
" Saxon, from yonder mountain high,
I mark'd thee send delighted eye,
Far to the south and east, where lay,
Extended in succession gay,
Deep waving fields and pastures green,
With gentle slopes and groves between:—
These fertile plains, that soften'd vale,
Were once the birthright of the Gael;
The stranger came with iron hand,
And from our fathers reft the land.
Where dwell we now? See, rudely swell
Crag over crag, and fell o'er fell.
Ask we this savage hill we tread,
For fatten'd steer or household bread;

Ask we for flocks these shingles dry,
And well the mountain might reply,—
' To you, as to your sires of yore,
Belong the target and claymore!
I give you shelter in my breast,
Your own good blades must win the rest.'
Pent in this fortress of the North,
Think'st thou we will not sally forth,
To spoil the spoiler as we may,
And from the robber rend the prey?
Ay, by my soul!—While on yon plain
The Saxon rears one shock of grain;
While, of ten thousand herds, there strays
But one along yon river's maze,—
The Gael, of plain and river heir,
Shall, with strong hand, redeem his share.
Where live the mountain chiefs who hold,
That plundering Lowland field and fold
Is aught but retribution true?
Seek other cause 'gainst Roderick Dhu."—

VIII.

Answer'd Fitz-James,—" And, if I
    sought,
Think'st thou no other could be brought?
What deem ye of my path waylaid?
My life given o'er to ambuscade?"—
" As of a meed to rashness due:
Hadst thou sent warning fair and true,—
I seek my hound, or falcon stray'd,
I seek, good faith, a Highland maid,—
Free hadst thou been to come and go;
But secret path marks secret foe.
Nor yet, for this, even as a spy,
Hadst thou, unheard, been doom'd to
    die,
Save to fulfil an augury."—
" Well, let it pass; nor will I now
Fresh cause of enmity avow,
To chafe thy mood and cloud thy brow,
Enough, I am by promise tied
To match me with this man of pride:
Twice have I sought Clan-Alpine's glen
In peace; but when I come agen,
I come with banner, brand, and bow,
As leader seeks his mortal foe.
For love-lorn swain, in lady's bower,
Ne'er panted for the appointed hour,
As I, until before me stand
This rebel Chieftain and his band!"—

IX.

" Have, then, thy wish !"—he whistled
　　shrill,
And he was answer'd from the hill ;
Wild as the scream of the curlew,
From crag to crag the signal flew.
Instant, through copse and heath, arose
Bonnets and spears and bended bows ;
On right, on left, above, below,
Sprung up at once the lurking foe ;
From shingles grey their lances start,
The bracken bush sends forth the dart,
The rushes and the willow-wand
Are bristling into axe and brand,
And every tuft of broom gives life
To plaided warrior arm'd for strife.
That whistle garrison'd the glen
At once with full five hundred men,
As if the yawning hill to heaven
A subterranean host had given.
Watching their leader's beck and will,
All silent there they stood, and still.
Like the loose crags, whose threatening
　　mass
Lay tottering o'er the hollow pass,
As if an infant's touch could urge
Their headlong passage down the verge,
With step and weapon forward flung,
Upon the mountain-side they hung.
The Mountaineer cast glance of pride
Along Benledi's living side,
Then fix'd his eye and sable brow
Full on Fitz-James—" How say'st thou
　　now ?
These are Clan-Alpine's warriors true ;
And, Saxon,—I am Roderick Dhu !"

X.

Fitz-James was brave :—Though to his
　　heart
The life-blood thrill'd with sudden start,
He mann'd himself with dauntless air,
Return'd the chief his haughty stare,
His back against a rock he bore,
And firmly placed his foot before :—
" Come one, come all ! this rock shall fly
From its firm base as soon as I,"
Sir Roderick mark'd—and in his eyes
Respect was mingled with surprise,

And the stern joy which warriors feel
In foemen worthy of their steel.
Short space he stood—then waved his
　　hand :
Down sunk the disappearing band ;
Each warrior vanish'd where he stood,
In broom or bracken, heath or wood ;
Sunk brand and spear and bended bow,
In osiers pale and copses low ;
It seem'd as if their mother Earth
Had swallow'd up her warlike birth.
The wind's last breath had toss'd in air,
Pennon, and plaid, and plumage fair,—
The next but swept a lone hill-side,
Where heath and fern were waving wide :
The sun's last glance was glinted back
From spear and glaive, from targe and
　　jack,—
The next, all unreflected, shone
On bracken green, and cold grey stone.

XI.

Fitz-James look'd round—yet scarce
　　believed
The witness that his sight received ;
Such apparition well might seem
Delusion of a dreadful dream.
Sir Roderick in suspense he eyed,
And to his look the Chief replied,
" Fear nought—nay, that I need not say—
But—doubt not aught from mine array.
Thou art my guest ;—I pledged my word
As far as Coilantogle ford :
Nor would I call a clansman's brand
For aid against one valiant hand,
Though on our strife lay every vale
Rent by the Saxon from the Gael.
So move we on ;—I only meant
To show the reed on which you leant,
Deeming this path you might pursue
Without a pass from Roderick Dhu."[41]
They moved :—I said Fitz-James was
　　brave,
As ever knight that belted glaive ;
Yet dare not say, that now his blood
Kept on its wont and temper'd flood,
As, following Roderick's stride, he drew
That seeming lonesome pathway through,
Which yet, by fearful proof, was rife
With lances, that, to take his life,

Waited but signal from a guide,
So late dishonour'd and defied.
Ever, by stealth, his eye sought round
The vanish'd guardians of the ground,
And still, from copse and heather deep,
Fancy saw spear and broadsword peep,
And in the plover's shrilly strain,
The signal whistle heard again.
Nor breathed he free till far behind
The pass was left; for then they wind
Along a wide and level green,
Where neither tree nor tuft was seen,
Nor rush, nor bush of broom was near,
To hide a bonnet or a spear.

XII

The Chief in silence strode before,
And reach'd that torrent's sounding shore,
Which, daughter of three mighty lakes,
From Vennachar in silver breaks,
Sweeps through the plain, and ceaseless
    mines
On Bochastle the mouldering lines,
Where Rome, the Empress of the world,
Of yore her eagle wings unfurl'd.[42]
And here his course the Chieftain staid,
Threw down his target and his plaid,
And to the Lowland warrior said:—
" Bold Saxon! to his promise just,
Vich-Alpine has discharged his trust.
This murderous Chief, this ruthless man,
This head of a rebellious clan,
Hath led thee safe through watch and
    ward,
Far past Clan-Alpine's outmost guard.
Now, man to man, and steel to steel,
A Chieftain's vengeance thou shalt feel.
See here, all vantageless I stand,
Arm'd, like thyself, with single brand :[43]
For this is Coilantogle ford,
And thou must keep thee with thy sword."

XIII.

The Saxon paused:—" I ne'er delay'd,
When foeman bade me draw my blade;
Nay, more, brave Chief, I vow'd thy
    death;
Yet sure thy fair and generous faith,
And my deep debt for life preserved,
A better meed have well deserved:

Can nought but blood our feud atone ?
Are there no means?"—" No, Stranger,
    none !
And hear,—to fire thy flagging zeal,—
The Saxon cause rests on thy steel;
For thus spoke Fate, by prophet bred
Between the living and the dead :
' Who spills the foremost foeman's life,
His party conquers in the strife.' "—
" Then, by my word," the Saxon said,
" The riddle is already read.
Seek yonder brake beneath the cliff,—
There lies Red Murdoch, stark and stiff.
Thus Fate has solved her prophecy,
Then yield to Fate, and not to me.
To James, at Stirling, let us go,
When, if thou wilt be still his foe,
Or if the King shall not agree
To grant thee grace and favour free,
I plight mine honour, oath, and word,
That, to thy native strengths restored,
With each advantage shalt thou stand,
That aids thee now to guard thy land."

XIV.

Dark lightning flash'd from Roderick's
    eye—
" Soars thy presumption, then, so high,
Because a wretched kern ye slew,
Homage to name to Roderick Dhu ?
He yields not, he, to man nor Fate !
Thou add'st but fuel to my hate:—
My clansman's blood demands revenge.
Not yet prepared ?—By heaven, I change
My thought, and hold thy valour light
As that of some vain carpet knight,
Who ill deserved my courteous care,
And whose best boast is but to wear
A braid of his fair lady's hair."—
" I thank thee, Roderick, for the word !
It nerves my heart, it steels my sword;
For I have sworn this braid to stain
In the best blood that warms thy vein.
Now, truce, farewell! and, ruth, begone!—
Yet think not that by thee alone,
Proud Chief! can courtesy be shown !
Though not from copse, or heath, or cairn,
Start at my whistle clansmen stern,
Of this small horn one feeble blast
Would fearful odds against thee cast.

But fear not—doubt not—which thou
  wilt—
We try this quarrel hilt to hilt."—
Then each at once his falchion drew,
Each on the ground his scabbard threw,
Each look'd to sun, and stream, and plain,
As what they ne'er might see again;
Then foot, and point, and eye opposed,
In dubious strife they darkly closed.

XV.

Ill fared it then with Roderick Dhu,
That on the field his targe he threw,[44]
Whose brazen studs and tough bull-hide
Had death so often dash'd aside;
For, train'd abroad his arms to wield,
Fitz-James's blade was sword and shield.
He practised every pass and ward,
To thrust, to strike, to feint, to guard;
While less expert, though stronger far,
The Gael maintain'd unequal war.
Three times in closing strife they stood,
And thrice the Saxon blade drank blood;
No stinted draught, no scanty tide,
The gushing flood the tartans dyed.
Fierce Roderick felt the fatal drain,
And shower'd his blows like wintry rain;
And, as firm rock, or castle-roof,
Against the winter shower is proof,
The foe, invulnerable still,
Foil'd his wild rage by steady skill:
Till, at advantage ta'en, his brand
Forced Roderick's weapon from his hand,
And backward borne upon the lea,
Brought the proud chieftain to his knee.

XVI.

"Now, yield thee, or by Him who made
The world, thy heart's blood dyes my
  blade!"
"Thy threats, thy mercy, I defy!
Let recreant yield, who fears to die."
—Like adder darting from his coil,
Like wolf that dashes through the toil,
Like mountain-cat who guards her young,
Full at Fitz-James's throat he sprung;
Received, but reck'd not of a wound,
And lock'd his arms his foeman round.—
Now, gallant Saxon, hold thine own!
No maiden's hand is round thee thrown!

That desperate grasp thy frame might
  feel,
Through bars of brass and triple steel!—
They tug, they strain! down, down they go,
The Gael above, Fitz-James below:
The Chieftain's gripe his throat compress'd,
His knee was planted on his breast;
His clotted locks he backward threw,
Across his brow his hand he drew,
From blood and mist to clear his sight,
Then gleam'd aloft his dagger bright!—
—But hate and fury ill supplied
The stream of life's exhausted tide,
And all too late the advantage came,
To turn the odds of deadly game;
For, while the dagger gleam'd on high,
Reel'd soul and sense, reel'd brain and eye,
Down came the blow! but in the heath
The erring blade found bloodless sheath.
The struggling foe may now unclasp
The fainting Chief's relaxing grasp;
Unwounded from the dreadful close,
But breathless all, Fitz-James arose.

XVII.

He falter'd thanks to Heaven for life,
Redeem'd, unhoped, from desperate strife;
Next on his foe his look he cast,
Whose every gasp appear'd his last;
In Roderick's gore he dipt the braid,—
"Poor Blanche! thy wrongs are dearly
  paid:
Yet with thy foe must die, or live,
The praise that Faith and Valour give."
With that he blew a bugle-note,
Undid the collar from his throat,
Unbonneted, and by the wave
Sate down his brow and hands to lave.
Then faint afar are heard the feet
Of rushing steeds in gallop fleet;
The sounds increase, and now are seen
Four mounted squires in Lincoln green:
Two who bear lance, and two who lead,
By loosen'd rein, a saddled steed:
Each onward held his headlong course,
And by Fitz-James rein'd up his horse,—
With wonder view'd the bloody spot—
—"Exclaim not, gallants! question not.—
You, Herbert and Luffness, alight,
And bind the wounds of yonder knight;

Let the grey palfrey bear his weight,
We destined for a fairer freight,
And bring him on to Stirling straight:
I will before at better speed,
To seek fresh horse and fitting weed.
The sun rides high;—I must be boune,*
To see the archer-game at noon:
But lightly Bayard clears the lea.—
De Vaux and Herries, follow me.

XVIII.

"Stand, Bayard, stand!"—the steed
obey'd,
With arching neck and bending head,
And glancing eye and quivering ear
As if he loved his lord to hear.
No foot Fitz-James in stirrup staid,
No grasp upon the saddle laid,
But wreath'd his left hand in the mane,
And lightly bounded from the plain,
Turn'd on the horse his armed heel,
And stirr'd his courage with the steel.
Bounded the fiery steed in air,
The rider sate erect and fair,
Then like a bolt from steel crossbow
Forth launch'd, along the plain they go.
They dash'd that rapid torrent through,
And up Carhonie's hill they flew;
Still at the gallop prick'd the Knight,
His merry-men follow'd as they might.
Along thy banks, swift Teith! they ride,
And in the race they mock'd thy tide;
Torry and Lendrick now are past,
And Deanstown lies behind them cast:
They rise, the banner'd towers of Doune,
They sink in distant woodland soon;
Blair-Drummond sees the hoof strike
fire,
They sweep like breeze through Ochter-
tyre;
They mark just glance and disappear
The lofty brow of ancient Kier;
They bathe their courser's sweltering sides,
Dark Forth! amid thy sluggish tides,
And on the opposing shore take ground,
With plash, with scramble, and with
bound.

---

* *Boune*, prepared.

Right-hand they leave thy cliffs, Craig-
Forth!
And soon the bulwark of the North,
Grey Stirling, with her towers and town,
Upon their fleet career look'd down.

XIX.

As up the flinty path they strain'd
Sudden his steed the leader rein'd;
A signal to his squire he flung,
Who instant to his stirrup sprung:—
"Seest thou, De Vaux, yon woodsman
grey,
Who town-ward holds the rocky way,
Of stature tall and poor array?
Mark'st thou the firm, yet active stride,
With which he scales the mountain-side?
Know'st thou from whence he comes, or
whom?"—
"No, by my word;—a burly groom
He seems, who in the field or chase
A baron's train would nobly grace."—
"Out, out, De Vaux! can fear supply,
And jealousy, no sharper eye?
Afar, ere to the hill he drew,
That stately form and step I knew;
Like form in Scotland is not seen,
Treads not such step on Scottish green.
'Tis James of Douglas, by Saint Serle!
The uncle of the banish'd Earl.
Away, away, to court, to show
The near approach of dreaded foe:
The King must stand upon his guard:
Douglas and he must meet prepared."
Then right-hand wheel'd their steeds, and
straight
They won the castle's postern gate.

XX.

The Douglas, who had bent his way
From Cambus-Kenneth's abbey grey,
Now, as he climb'd the rocky shelf,
Held sad communion with himself!—
"Yes! all is true my fears could frame:
A prisoner lies the noble Græme,
And fiery Roderick soon will feel
The vengeance of the royal steel.
I, only I, can ward their fate,—
God grant the ransom come not late!

The Abbess hath her promise given,
My child shall be the bride of Heaven;—
—Be pardon'd one repining tear!
For He, who gave her, knows how dear,
How excellent! but that is by,
And now my business is—to die.
—Ye towers! within whose circuit dread
A Douglas by his sovereign bled;
And thou, O sad and fatal mound!*
That oft hast heard the death-axe sound,
As on the noblest of the land
Fell the stern headsman's bloody hand,—
The dungeon, block, and nameless tomb
Prepare—for Douglas seeks his doom!
—But hark! what blithe and jolly peal
Makes the Franciscan steeple reel?
And see! upon the crowded street,
In motley groups what masquers meet!
Banner and pageant, pipe and drum,
And merry morrice-dancers come.
I guess, by all this quaint array,
The burghers hold their sports to-day.[45]
James will be there; he loves such show,
Where the good yeoman bends his bow,
And the tough wrestler foils his foe,
As well as where, in proud career,
The high-born tilter shivers spear.
I'll follow to the Castle-park,
And play my prize;—King James shall mark,
If age has tamed these sinews stark,
Whose force so oft, in happier days,
His boyish wonder loved to praise."

XXI.

The Castle gates were open flung,
The quivering drawbridge rock'd and rung,
And echo'd loud the flinty street
Beneath the coursers' clattering feet,
As slowly down the steep descent
Fair Scotland's King and nobles went,
While all along the crowded way
Was jubilee and loud huzza.
And ever James was bending low,
To his white jennet's saddle-bow,

Doffing his cap to city dame,
Who smiled and blush'd for pride and shame.
And well the simperer might be vain,—
He chose the fairest of the train.
Gravely he greets each city sire,
Commends each pageant's quaint attire,
Gives to the dancers thanks aloud,
And smiles and nods upon the crowd,
Who rend the heavens with their acclaims,
"Long live the Commons' King, King James!"
Behind the King throng'd peer and knight,
And noble dame and damsel bright,
Whose fiery steeds ill brook'd the stay
Of the steep street and crowded way.
—But in the train you might discern
Dark lowering brow and visage stern;
There nobles mourn'd their pride restrain'd,
And the mean burgher's joys disdain'd;
And chiefs, who, hostage for their clan,
Were each from home a banish'd man,
There thought upon their own grey tower,
Their waving woods, their feudal power,
And deem'd themselves a shameful part
Of pageant which they cursed in heart.

XXII.

Now, in the Castle-park, drew out
Their chequer'd bands the joyous rout.
There morricers, with bell at heel,
And blade in hand, their mazes wheel;
But chief, beside the butts, there stand
Bold Robin Hood[46] and all his band,—
Friar Tuck with quarterstaff and cowl,
Old Scathelocke with his surly scowl,
Maid Marion, fair as ivory bone,
Scarlet, and Mutch, and Little John;
Their bugles challenge all that will,
In archery to prove their skill.
The Douglas bent a bow of might,—
His first shaft centered in the white,
And when in turn he shot again,
His second split the first in twain.
From the King's hand must Douglas take
A silver dart, the archer's stake;

* A mound on the N.E. of Stirling Castle, where State criminals were executed.

Fondly he watch'd, with watery eye,
Some answering glance of sympathy,—
No kind emotion made reply !
Indifferent as to archer wight,
The monarch gave the arrow bright.

XXIII.

Now, clear the ring ! for, hand to hand,
The manly wrestlers take their stand.
Two o'er the rest superior rose,
And proud demanded mightier foes,
Nor call'd in vain ; for Douglas came.
—For life is Hugh of Larbert lame ;
Scarce better John of Alloa's fare,
Whom senseless home his comrades bear.
Prize of the wrestling match, the King
To Douglas gave a golden ring,[47]
While coldly glanced his eye of blue,
As frozen drop of wintry dew.
Douglas would speak, but in his breast
His struggling soul his words suppress'd ;
Indignant then he turn'd him where
Their arms the brawny yeomen bare,
To hurl the massive bar in air.
When each his utmost strength had
    shown,
The Douglas rent an earth-fast stone
From its deep bed, then heaved it high,
And sent the fragment through the sky,
A rood beyond the farthest mark ;—
And still in Stirling's royal park,
The grey-hair'd sires, who know the past,
To strangers point the Douglas-cast,
And moralize on the decay
Of Scottish strength in modern day.

XXIV.

The vale with loud applauses rang,
The Ladies' Rock sent back the clang.
The King, with look unmoved, bestow'd
A purse well-fill'd with pieces broad.
Indignant smiled the Douglas proud,
And threw the gold among the crowd,
Who now, with anxious wonder, scan,
And sharper glance, the dark grey man ;
Till whispers rose among the throng,
That heart so free, and hand so strong,
Must to the Douglas blood belong ;
The old men mark'd, and shook the head,
To see his hair with silver spread,

And wink'd aside, and told each son,
Of feats upon the English done,
Ere Douglas of the stalwart hand
Was exiled from his native land.
The women praised his stately form,
Though wreck'd by many a winter's
    storm !
The youth with awe and wonder saw
His strength surpassing Nature's law.
Thus judged, as is their wont, the crowd,
Till murmur rose to clamours loud.
But not a glance from that proud ring
Of peers who circled round the King,
With Douglas held communion kind,
Or call'd the banish'd man to mind ;
No, not from those who, at the chase,
Once held his side the honour'd place,
Begirt his board, and, in the field,
Found safety underneath his shield ;
For he, whom royal eyes disown,
When was his form to courtiers known !

XXV.

The Monarch saw the gambols flag,
And bade let loose a gallant stag,
Whose pride, the holiday to crown,
Two favourite greyhounds should pull
    down,
That venison free, and Bordeaux wine,
Might serve the archery to dine.
But Lufra,—whom from Douglas' side
Nor bribe nor threat could e'er divide,
The fleetest hound in all the North,—
Brave Lufra saw, and darted forth.
She left the royal hounds mid-way,
And dashing on the antler'd prey,
Sunk her sharp muzzle in his flank,
And deep the flowing life-blood drank.
The King's stout huntsman saw the sport
By strange intruder broken short,
Came up, and with his leash unbound,
In anger struck the noble hound.
—The Douglas had endured, that morn,
The King's cold look, the nobles' scorn,
And last, and worst to spirit proud,
Had borne the pity of the crowd ;
But Lufra had been fondly bred,
To share his board, to watch his bed,
And oft would Ellen Lufra's neck
In maiden glee with garlands deck ;

They were such playmates, that with name
Of Lufra, Ellen's image came.
His stifled wrath is brimming high,
In darken'd brow and flashing eye:
As waves before the bark divide,
The crowd gave way before his stride;
Needs but a buffet and no more,
The groom lies senseless in his gore.
Such blow no other hand could deal,
Though gauntleted in glove of steel.

XXVI.

Then clamour'd loud the royal train,
And brandish'd swords and staves amain.
But stern the Baron's warning—" Back!
Back, on your lives, ye menial pack!
Beware the Douglas.—Yes! behold,
King James! the Douglas, doom'd of old,
And vainly sought for near and far,
A victim to atone the war,
A willing victim, now attends,
Nor craves thy grace but for his friends."—
" Thus is my clemency repaid?
Presumptuous Lord!" the monarch said;
" Of thy misproud ambitious clan,
Thou, James of Bothwell, wert the man,
The only man, in whom a foe
My woman-mercy would not know:
But shall a Monarch's presence brook
Injurious blow, and haughty look?—
What ho! the Captain of our Guard!
Give the offender fitting ward,—
Break off the sports!"—for tumult rose,
And yeomen 'gan to bend their bows,—
" Break off the sports!" he said, and
    frown'd,
" And bid our horsemen clear the ground."

XXVII.

Then uproar wild and misarray
Marr'd the fair form of festal day.
The horsemen prick'd among the crowd,
Repell'd by threats and insult loud;
To earth are borne the old and weak,
The timorous fly, the women shriek;
With flint, with shaft, with staff, with bar,
The hardier urge tumultuous war.
At once round Douglas darkly sweep
The royal spears in circle deep,
And slowly scale the pathway steep;

While on the rear in thunder pour
The rabble with disordered roar.
With grief the noble Douglas saw
The Commons rise against the law,
And to the leading soldier said,—
" Sir John of Hyndford! 'twas my blade
That knighthood on thy shoulder laid;
For that good deed, permit me then
A word with these misguided men.

XXVIII.

" Hear, gentle friends! ere yet for me
Ye break the bands of fealty.
My life, my honour, and my cause,
I tender free to Scotland's laws.
Are these so weak as must require
The aid of your misguided ire!
Or, if I suffer causeless wrong,
Is then my selfish rage so strong,
My sense of public weal so low,
That, for mean vengeance on a foe,
Those cords of love I should unbind,
Which knit my country and my kind?
Oh no! Believe, in yonder tower
It will not soothe my captive hour,
To know those spears our foes should
    dread,
For me in kindred gore are red;
To know, in fruitless brawl begun,
For me, that mother wails her son;
For me, that widow's mate expires;
For me, that orphans weep their sires:
That patriots mourn insulted laws;
And curse the Douglas for the cause.
O let your patience ward such ill,
And keep your right to love me still!"

XXIX.

The crowd's wild fury sunk again
In tears, as tempests melt in rain.
With lifted hands and eyes, they pray'd
For blessings on his generous head,
Who for his country felt alone,
And prized her blood beyond his own.
Old men, upon the verge of life,
Bless'd him who staid the civil strife;
And mothers held their babes on high,
The self-devoted Chief to spy,
Triumphant over wrongs and ire,
To whom the prattlers owed a sire:

Even the rough soldier's heart was moved;
As if behind some bier beloved,
With trailing arms and drooping head,
The Douglas up the hill he led,
And at the Castle's battled verge
With sighs resign'd his honour'd charge.

XXX.

The offended Monarch rode apart,
With bitter thought and swelling heart,
And would not now vouchsafe again
Through Stirling streets to lead his train.
" O Lennox, who would wish to rule
This changeling crowd, this common fool?
Hear'st thou," he said, " the loud acclaim,
With which they shout the Douglas' name!
With like acclaim, the vulgar throat
Strain'd for King James their morning
    note;
With like acclaim they hail'd the day
When first I broke the Douglas' sway;
And like acclaim would Douglas greet,
If he could hurl me from my seat.
Who o'er the herd would wish to reign,
Fantastic, fickle, fierce, and vain!
Vain as the leaf upon the stream,
And fickle as a changeful dream;
Fantastic as a woman's mood,
And fierce as Frenzy's fever'd blood.
Thou many-headed monster-thing,
O who would wish to be thy king!

XXXI.

" But soft! what messenger of speed
Spurs hitherward his panting steed?
I guess his cognizance afar—
What from our cousin, John of Mar?"—
" He prays, my liege, your sports keep
    bound
Within the safe and guarded ground:
For some foul purpose yet unknown,—
Most sure for evil to the throne,—
The outlaw'd Chieftain, Roderick Dhu,
Has summoned his rebellious crew;
'Tis said, in James of Bothwell's aid
These loose banditti stand array'd.
The Earl of Mar, this morn, from Doune,
To break their muster march'd, and soon
Your grace will hear of battle fought;
But earnestly the Earl besought,

Till for such danger he provide,
With scanty train you will not ride."—

XXXII.

" Thou warn'st me I have done amiss,—
I should have earlier look'd to this:
I lost it in this bustling day.
—Retrace with speed thy former way;
Spare not for spoiling of thy steed,
The best of mine shall be thy meed.
Say to our faithful Lord of Mar,
We do forbid the intended war:
Roderick, this morn, in single fight,
Was made our prisoner by a knight;
And Douglas hath himself and cause
Submitted to our kingdom's laws.
The tidings of their leaders lost
Will soon dissolve the mountain host,
Nor would we that the vulgar feel,
For their Chief's crimes, avenging steel.
Bear Mar our message, Braco: fly!"—
He turn'd his steed,—" My liege, I hie.—
Yet, ere I cross this lily lawn,
I fear the broadswords will be drawn."
The turf the flying courser spurn'd,
And to his towers the King return'd.

XXXIII.

Ill with King James's mood that day,
Suited gay feast and minstrel lay;
Soon were dismiss d the courtly throng,
And soon cut short the festal song.
Nor less upon the sadden'd town
The evening sunk in sorrow down.
The burghers spoke of civil jar,
Of rumour'd feuds and mountain war,
Of Moray, Mar, and Roderick Dhu,
All up in arms:—the Douglas too,
They mourn'd him pent within the hold,
" Where stout Earl William was of
    old"*—
And there his word the speaker staid,
And finger on his lip he laid,
Or pointed to his dagger blade.
But jaded horsemen, from the west,
At evening to the Castle press'd;

---

* He had been stabbed by James II. in
Stirling Castle.

And busy talkers said they bore
Tidings of fight on Katrine's shore;
At noon the deadly fray begun,
And lasted till the set of sun.
Thus giddy rumour shook the town,
Till closed the Night her pennons brown.

———◆———

CANTO SIXTH.

The Guard-Room.

I.

THE sun, awakening, through the smoky
    air
Of the dark city casts a sullen glance,
Rousing each caitiff to his task of care,
    Of sinful man the sad inheritance;
Summoning revellers from the lagging
    dance,
  Scaring the prowling robber to his den ;
Gilding on battled tower the warder's lance,
    And warning student pale to leave his
      pen,
  And yield his drowsy eyes to the kind
      nurse of men.

What various scenes, and, O ! what
    scenes of woe,
  Are witness'd by that red and struggling
    beam !
The fever'd patient, from his pallet low,
    Through crowded hospital beholds it
    stream ;
The ruin'd maiden trembles at its gleam,
    The debtor wakes to thought of gyve
    and jail,
The love-lorn wretch starts from tor-
    menting dream ;
    The wakeful mother, by the glimmer-
     ing pale,
Trims her sick infant's couch, and soothes
    his feeble wail.

II.

At dawn the towers of Stirling rang
With soldier-step and weapon-clang,

While drums, with rolling note, foretell
Relief to weary sentinel.
Through narrow loop and casement barr'd,
The sunbeams sought the Court of Guard,
And, struggling with the smoky air,
Deaden'd the torches' yellow glare.
In comfortless alliance shone
The lights through arch of blacken'd stone,
And show'd wild shapes in garb of war,
Faces deform'd with beard and scar,
All haggard from the midnight watch,
And fever'd with the stern debauch ;
For the oak table's massive board,
Flooded with wine, with fragments stored,
And beakers drain'd, and cups o'er-
    thrown,
Show'd in what sport the night had flown.
Some, weary, snored on floor and bench,
Some labour'd still their thirst to quench;
Some, chill'd with watching, spread their
    hands
O'er the huge chimney's dying brands,
While round them, or beside them flung,
At every step their harness rung.

III.

These drew not for their fields the sword,
Like tenants of a feudal lord,
Nor own'd the patriarchal claim
Of chieftain in their leader's name ;
Adventurers they, from far who roved,
To live by battle which they loved.[48]
There the Italian's clouded face,
The swarthy Spaniard's there you trace ;
The mountain-loving Switzer there
More freely breathed in mountain-air ;
The Fleming there despised the soil,
That paid so ill the labourer's toil ;
Their rolls show'd French and German
    name ;
And merry England's exiles came,
To share, with ill conceal'd disdain,
Of Scotland's pay the scanty gain.
All brave in arms, well train'd to wield
The heavy halberd, brand, and shield ;
In camps licentious, wild, and bold ;
In pillage fierce and uncontroll'd ;
And now, by holytide and feast,
From rules of discipline released.

IV

They held debate of bloody fray,
Fought 'twixt Loch Katrine and Achray,
Fierce was their speech, and, 'mid their
    words,
Their hands oft grappled to their
    swords;
Nor sunk their tone to sparc the ear
Of wounded comrades groaning near,
Whose mangled limbs, and bodies gored,
Bore token of the mountain sword,
Though, neighbouring to the Court of
    Guard,
Their prayers and feverish wails were
    heard;.
Sad burden to the ruffian joke,
And savage oath by fury spoke!—
At length up-started John of Brent,
A yeoman from the banks of Trent;
A stranger to respect or fear,
In peace a chaser of the deer,
In host a hardy mutineer,
But still the boldest of the crew,
When deed of danger was to do.
He grieved, that day, their games cut
    short,
And marr'd the dicer's brawling sport,
And shouted loud, "Renew the bowl!
And, while a merry catch I troll,
Let each the buxom chorus bear,
Like brethren of the brand and spear."

V.

Soldier's Song.

Our vicar still preaches that Peter and
    Poule
Laid a swinging long curse on the bonny
    brown bowl,
That there's wrath and despair in the
    bonny black-jack,
And the seven deadly sins in a flagon of
    sack;
Yet whoop, Barnaby! off with thy liquor,
Drink upsees* out, and a fig for the vicar!

---

* A Dutch health, or drinking word.

Our vicar he calls it damnation to sip
The ripe ruddy dew of a woman's dear
    lip,
Says, that Beelzebub lurks in her kerchief
    so sly,
And Apollyon shoots darts from her merry
    black eye.
Yet whoop, Jack! kiss Gillian the quicker,
Till she bloom like a rose, and a fig for
    the vicar!

Our vicar thus preaches—and why should
    he not?
For the dues of his cure are the placket
    and pot;
And 'tis right of his office poor laymen to
    lurch,
Who infringe the domains of our good
    Mother Church.
Yet whoop, bully-boys! off with your
    liquor,
Sweet Marjorie's the word, and a fig for
    the vicar!

VI.

The warder's challenge, heard without,
Staid in mid-roar the merry shout.
A soldier to the portal went,—
" Here is old Bertram, sirs, of Ghent,
And,—beat for jubilee the drum!
A maid and minstrel with him come."
Bertram, a Fleming, grey and scarr'd,
Was entering now the Court of Guard,
A harper with him, and in plaid
All muffled close, a mountain maid,
Who backward shrunk to 'scape the
    view
Of the loose scene and boisterous crew.
" What news?" they roar'd:—" I only
    know,
From noon till eve we fought with foe,
As wild and as untameable
As the rude mountains where they
    dwell;
On both sides store of blood is lost,
Nor much success can either boast."—
" But whence thy captives, friend? such
    spoil
As theirs must needs reward thy toil.

Old dost thou wax, and wars grow
   sharp;
Thou now hast glee-maiden and harp!
Get thee an ape, and trudge the land,
The leader of a juggler band."—⁴⁹

VII.

" No, comrade;—no such fortune mine,
After the fight these sought our line,
That aged harper and the girl,
And, having audience of the Earl,
Mar bade I should purvey them steed,
And bring them hitherward with speed,
Forbear your mirth and rude alarm,
Nor none shall do them shame or
   harm."—
" Hear ye his boast?" cried John of
   Brent,
Ever to strife and jangling bent;
" Shall he strike doe beside our lodge,
And yet the jealous niggard grudge
To pay the forester his fee?
I'll have my share, howe'er it be,
Despite of Moray, Mar, or thee."
Bertram his forward step withstood;
And, burning with his vengeful mood,
Old Allan, though unfit for strife,
Laid hand upon his dagger-knife;
But Ellen boldly stepp'd between,
And dropp'd at once the tartan
   screen:—
So, from his morning cloud, appears
The sun of May, through summer tears.
The savage soldiery, amazed,
As on descended angel gazed;
Even hardy Brent, abash'd and tamed,
Stood half admiring, half ashamed.

VIII.

Boldly she spoke,—" Soldiers, attend!
My father was the soldier's friend;
Cheer'd him in camps, in marches led,
And with him in the battle bled.
Not from the valiant, or the strong,
Should exile's daughter suffer wrong.'—
Answer'd De Brent, most forward still
In every feat or good or ill,
" I shame me of the part I play'd:
And thou an outlaw's child, poor maid!

An outlaw I by forest laws,
And merry Needwood knows the cause.
Poor Rose,—if Rose be living now,"—
He wiped his iron eye and brow,—
" Must bear such age, I think, as thou.—
Hear ye, my mates; I go to call
The Captain of our watch to hall:
There lies my halberd on the floor;
And he that steps my halberd o'er,
To do the maid injurious part,
My shaft shall quiver in his heart!—
Beware loose speech, or jesting rough:
Ye all know John de Brent. Enough."

IX.

Their Captain came, a gallant young.—
(Of Tullibardine's house he sprung),
Nor wore he yet the spurs of knight;
Gay was his mien, his humour light,
And, though by courtesy controll'd,
Forward his speech, his bearing bold.
The high-born maiden ill could brook
The scanning of his curious look
And dauntless eye;—and yet, in sooth,
Young Lewis was a generous youth;
But Ellen's lovely face and mien,
Ill suited to the garb and scene,
Might lightly bear construction strange,
And give loose fancy scope to range.
" Welcome to Stirling towers, fair maid!
Come ye to seek a champion's aid,
On palfrey white, with harper hoar,
Like errant damosel of yore?
Does thy high quest a knight require,
Or may the venture suit a squire?"—
Her dark eye flash'd;—she paused and
   sigh'd,—
" O what have I to do with pride!—
Through scenes of sorrow, shame, and
   strife,
A suppliant for a father's life,
I crave an audience of the King.
Behold, to back my suit, a ring,
The royal pledge of grateful claims,
Given by the Monarch to Fitz-James."

X.

The signet-ring young Lewis took,
With deep respect and alter'd look;

And said,—"This ring our duties own;
And pardon, if to worth unknown,
In semblance mean obscurely veil'd,
Lady, in aught my folly fail'd.
Soon as the day flings wide his gates,
The King shall know what suitor waits.
Please you, meanwhile, in fitting bower
Repose you till his waking hour;
Female attendance shall obey
Your hest, for service or array.
Permit I marshall you the way."
But, ere she followed, with the grace
And open bounty of her race,
She bade her slender purse be shared
Among the soldiers of the guard.
The rest with thanks their guerdon took;
But Brent, with shy and awkward look,
On the reluctant maiden's hold
Forced bluntly back the proffer'd gold;—
"Forgive a haughty English heart,
And O forget its ruder part!
The vacant purse shall be my share,
Which in my barret-cap I'll bear,
Perchance, in jeopardy of war,
Where gayer crests may keep afar."
With thanks—'twas all she could—the maid
His rugged courtesy repaid.

XI.

When Ellen forth with Lewis went,
Allan made suit to John of Brent:—
"My lady safe, O let your grace
Give me to see my master's face!
His minstrel I,—to share his doom
Bound from the cradle to the tomb.
Tenth in descent, since first my sires
Waked for his noble house their lyres,
Nor one of all the race was known
But prized its weal above their own.
With the Chief's birth begins our care;
Our harp must soothe the infant heir,
Teach the youth tales of fight, and grace
His earliest feat of field or chase;
In peace, in war, our rank we keep,
We cheer his board, we soothe his sleep,
Nor leave him till we pour our verse—
A doleful tribute!—o'er his hearse.
Then let me share his captive lot;
It is my right—deny it not!"—

"Little we reck," said John of Brent,
"We Southern men, of long descent;
Nor wot we how a name—a word—
Makes clansmen vassals to a lord:
Yet kind my noble landlord's part,—
God bless the house of Beaudesert!
And, but I loved to drive the deer,
More than to guide the labouring steer,
I had not dwelt an outcast here.
Come, good old Minstrel, follow me;
Thy Lord and Chieftain shalt thou see."

XII.

Then, from a rusted iron hook,
A bunch of ponderous keys he took,
Lighted a torch, and Allan led
Through grated arch and passage dread.
Portals they pass'd, where, deep within,
Spoke prisoner's moan, and fetters' din;
Through rugged vaults, where, loosely stored,
Lay wheel, and axe, and headsman's sword,
And many an hideous engine grim,
For wrenching joint, and crushing limb,
By artist form'd, who deem'd it shame
And sin to give their work a name.
They halted at a low-brow'd porch,
And Brent to Allan gave the torch,
While bolt and chain he backward roll'd,
And made the bar unhasp its hold.
They enter'd:—'twas a prison-room
Of stern security and gloom,
Yet not a dungeon; for the day
Through lofty gratings found its way,
And rude and antique garniture
Deck'd the sad walls and oaken floor;
Such as the rugged days of old
Deem'd fit for captive noble's hold.
"Here," said De Brent, "thou mayst remain
Till the Leech visit him again.
Strict is his charge, the warders tell,
To tend the noble prisoner well."
Retiring then, the bolt he drew,
And the lock's murmurs growl'd anew.
Roused at the sound, from lowly bed
A captive feebly raised his head;

The wondering Minstrel look'd, and
knew—
Not his dear lord, but Roderick Dhu!
For, come from where Clan-Alpine
fought,
They, erring, deem'd the Chief he sought.

XIII.

As the tall ship, whose lofty prore
Shall never stem the billows more,
Deserted by her gallant band,
Amid the breakers lies astrand,—
So, on his couch, lay Roderick Dhu!
And oft his fever'd limbs he threw
In toss abrupt, as when her sides
Lie rocking in the advancing tides,
That shake her frame with ceaseless beat,
Yet cannot heave her from her seat;—
O! how unlike her course at sea!
Or his free step on hill and lea!—
Soon as the Minstrel he could scan,
"What of thy lady?—of my clan?—
My mother?—Douglas?—tell me all!
Have they been ruin'd in my fall?
Ah, yes! or wherefore art thou here?
Yet speak,—speak boldly,—do not
fear."—
(For Allan, who his mood well knew,
Was choked with grief and terror too.)—
"Who fought—who fled?—Old man,
be brief;—
Some might—for they had lost their
Chief.
Who basely live?—who bravely died?"—
"O calm thee, Chief!" the Minstrel
cried,
"Ellen is safe;"—"For that, thank
Heaven!"—
"And hopes are for the Douglas given;—
The Lady Margaret, too, is well;
And, for thy clan,—on field or fell,
Has never harp of minstrel told,
Of combat fought so true and bold.
Thy stately Pine is yet unbent,
Though many a goodly bough is rent."

XIV.

The Chieftain rear'd his form on high,
And fever's fire was in his eye;

But ghastly, pale, and livid streaks
Chequer'd his swarthy brow and cheeks.
—"Hark, Minstrel! I have heard thee
play,
With measure bold, on festal day,
In yon lone isle, . . . again where ne'er
Shall harper play, or warrior hear! . . .
That stirring air that peels on high,
O'er Dermid's race our victory.—
Strike it![50]—and then, (for well thou
canst,)
Free from thy minstrel-spirit glanced,
Fling me the picture of the fight,
When met my clan the Saxon might.
I'll listen, till my fancy hears
The clang of swords, the crash of
spears!
These grates, these walls, shall vanish
then,
For the fair field of fighting men,
And my free spirit burst away,
As if it soar'd from battle fray"
The trembling Bard with awe obey'd,—
Slow on the harp his hand he laid;
But soon remembrance of the sight
He witness'd from the mountain's height,
With what old Bertram told at night,
Awaken'd the full power of song,
And bore him in career alone;—
As shallop launch'd on river's tide,
That slow and fearful leaves the side,
But, when it feels the middle stream,
Drives downward swift as lightning's
beam.

XV.

Battle of Beal' an Duine.[51]

"The Minstrel came once more to view
The eastern ridge of Benvenue,
For, ere he parted, he would say
Farewell to lovely Loch Achray—
Where shall he find, in foreign land,
So lone a lake, so sweet a strand!
There is no breeze upon the fern,
Nor ripple on the lake,
Upon her eyry nods the erne,
The deer has sought the brake;
The small birds will not sing aloud,
The springing trout lies still,

So darkly glooms yon thunder cloud,
That swathes, as with a purple shroud,
   Benledi's distant hill.
Is it the thunder's solemn sound
  That mutters deep and dread,
Or echoes from the groaning ground
  The warrior's measured tread?
Is it the lightning's quivering glance
  That on the thicket streams,
Or do they flash on spear and lance
  The sun's retiring beams?
—I see the dagger-crest of Mar,
I see the Moray's silver star,
Wave o'er the cloud of Saxon war,
That up the lake comes winding far!
To hero bound for battle-strife,
  Or bard of martial lay,
'Twere worth ten years of peaceful life,
  One glance at their array!

XVI.

" Their light-arm'd archers far and near
  Survey'd the tangled ground,
Their centre ranks, with pike and spear,
  A twilight forest frown'd,
Their barbed horsemen, in the rear,
  The stern battalia crown'd.
No cymbal clash'd, no clarion rang,
  Still were the pipe and drum;
Save heavy tread, and armour's clang,
  The sullen march was dumb.
There breathed no wind their crests to
    shake,
  Or wave their flags abroad;
Scarce the frail aspen seem'd to quake,
  That shadow'd o'er their road.
Their vaward scouts no tidings bring,
  Can rouse no lurking foe,
Nor spy a trace of living thing,
  Save when they stirr'd the roe;
The host moves like a deep-sea wave,
Where rise no rocks its pride to brave,
  High-swelling, dark, and slow.
The lake is pass'd, and now they gain
A narrow and a broken plain,
Before the Trosach's rugged jaws;
And here the horse and spearmen pause,
While to explore the dangerous glen,
Dive through the pass the archer-men.

XVII.

" At once there rose so wild a yell
Within that dark and narrow dell,
As all the fiends, from heaven that fell,
Had peal'd the banner-cry of hell!
  Forth from the pass in tumult driven,
  Like chaff before the wind of heaven,
    The archery appear,
  For life! for life! their plight they ply—
  And shriek, and shout, and battle-cry,
  And plaids and bonnets waving high,
  And broadswords flashing to the sky,
    Are maddening in the rear.
Onward they drive, in dreadful race,
  Pursuers and pursued;
Before that tide of flight and chase,
How shall it keep its rooted place,
  The spearmen's twilight wood?—
' Down, down,' cried Mar, ' your
    lances down!
  Bear back both friend and foe!'—
Like reeds before the tempest's frown,
That serried grove of lances brown
  At once lay levell'd low;
And closely shouldering side to side,
The bristling ranks the onset bide.—
' We'll quell the savage mountaineer,
  As their Tinchel* cows the game!
They come as fleet as forest deer,
  We'll drive them back as tame.'—

XVIII.

" Bearing before them, in their course,
The relics of the archer force,
Like wave with crest of sparkling foam,
Right onward did Clan-Alpine come.
  Above the tide, each broadsword bright
  Was brandishing like beam of light,
    Each targe was dark below;
  And with the ocean's mighty swing,
  When heaving to the tempest's wing,
    They hurl'd them on the foe.
I heard the lance's shivering crash,
As when the whirlwind rends the ash,

---

* A circle of sportsmen, who, by surrounding a great space, and gradually narrowing, brought immense quantities of deer together, which usually made desperate efforts to break through the *Tinchel.*

I heard the broadsword's deadly clang,
As if an hundred anvils rang!
But Moray wheel'd his rearward rank
Of horsemen on Clan-Alpine's flank,
    —' My banner-man, advance!
I see,' he cried, ' their column shake.—
Now, gallants! for your ladies' sake,
Upon them with the lance !'—
The horsemen dash'd among the rout,
    As deer break through the broom ;
Their steeds are stout, their swords
    are out,
    They soon make lightsome room.
Clan - Alpine's best are backward
    borne—
Where, where was Roderick then !
One blast upon his bugle-horn
    Were worth a thousand men !
And refluent through the pass of fear
    The battle's tide was pour'd ;
Vanish'd the Saxon's struggling spear,
    Vanish'd the mountain-sword.
As Bracklinn's chasm, so black and
    steep,
    Receives her roaring linn,
As the dark caverns of the deep
    Suck the wild whirlpool in,
So did the deep and darksome pass
Devour the battle's mingled mass :
None linger now upon the plain,
Save those who ne'er shall fight again.

XIX.

"Now westward rolls the battle's din,
That deep and doubling pass within,
—Minstrel, away, the work of fate
Is bearing on: its issue wait,
Where the rude Trosach's dread defile
Opens on Katrine's lake and isle.—
Grey Benvenue I soon repass'd,
Loch Katrine lay beneath me cast.
    The sun is set ;—the clouds are met,
    The lowering scowl of heaven
    An inky view of vivid blue
    To the deep lake has given ;
Strange gusts of wind from mountain-glen
Swept o'er the lake, then sunk agen.
I heeded not the eddying surge,
Mine eye but saw the Trosach's gorge,

Mine ear but heard the sullen sound,
Which like an earthquake shook the
    ground,
And spoke the stern and desperate strife
That parts not but with parting life,
Seeming, to minstrel ear, to toll
The dirge of many a passing soul.
Nearer it comes—the dim-wood glen
The martial flood disgorged agen,
    But not in mingled tide ;
The plaided warriors of the North
High on the mountain thunder forth
    And overhang its side ;
While by the lake below appears
The dark'ning cloud of Saxon spears.
At weary bay each shatter'd band,
Eyeing their foemen, sternly stand ;
Their banners stream like tatter'd sail,
That flings its fragments to the gale,
And broken arms and disarray
Mark'd the fell havoc of the day.

XX.

"Viewing the mountain's ridge askance,
The Saxon stood in sullen trance,
Till Moray pointed with his lance,
    And cried—' Behold yon isle!—
See! none are left to guard its strand,
But women weak, that wring the hand:
'Tis there of yore the robber band
    Their booty wont to pile ;
My purse, with bonnet-pieces store,
To him will swim a bow-shot o'er,
And loose a shallop from the shore.
Lightly we'll tame the war-wolf then,
Lords of his mate, and brood, and den.'
Forth from the ranks a spearman sprung,
On earth his casque and corslet rung,
    He plunged him in the wave :—
All saw the deed—the purpose knew,
And to their clamours Benvenue
    A mingled echo gave ;
The Saxons shout, their mate to cheer,
The helpless females scream for fear,
And yells for rage the mountaineer.
'Twas then, as by the outcry riven,
Pour'd down at once the lowering heaven ;
A whirlwind swept Loch Katrine's breast,
Her billows rear'd their snowy crest.

Well for the swimmer swell'd they high,
To mar the Highland marksman's eye;
For round him shower'd, 'mid rain and
    hail,
The vengeful arrows of the Gael.—
In vain—He nears the isle—and lo!
His hand is on a shallop's bow.
—Just then a flash of lightning came,
It tinged the waves and strand with
    flame;—
I mark'd Duncraggan's widow'd dame,
Behind an oak I saw her stand,
A naked dirk gleam'd in her hand:
It darken'd,—but amid the moan
Of waves, I heard a dying groan;
Another flash!—the spearman floats
A weltering corse beside the boats,
And the stern matron o'er him stood,
Her hand and dagger streaming blood.

XXI.

"'Revenge! revenge!' the Saxons cried,
The Gaels' exulting shout replied.
Despite the elemental rage,
Again they hurried to engage;
But, er' they closed in desperate fight,
Bloody with spurring came a knight,
Sprung from his horse, and, from a crag,
Waved 'twixt the hosts a milk-white flag.
Clarion and trumpet by his side
Rung forth a truce-note high and wide,
While, in the Monarch's name, afar
An herald's voice forbade the war,
For Bothwell's lord, and Roderick bold,
Were both, he said, in captive hold."
—But here the lay made sudden stand!—
The harp escaped the Minstrel's hand!—
Oft had he stolen a glance, to spy
How Roderick brook'd his minstrelsy:
At first, the Chieftain, to the chime,
With lifted hand kept feeble time;
That motion ceased,—yet feeling strong,
Varied his look as changed the song;
At length, no more his deafen'd ear
The minstrel melody can hear;
His face grows sharp,—his hands are
    clench'd,
As if some pang his heart-strings wrench'd,
Set are his teeth, his fading eye
Is sternly fix'd on vacancy;

Thus, motionless, and moanless, drew
His parting breath, stout Roderick
    Dhu!—
Old Allan-Bane look'd on aghast,
While grim and still his spirit pass'd:
But when he saw that life was fled,
He pour'd his wailing o'er the dead.

XXII.

Lament.

"And art thou cold and lowly laid,
Thy foeman's dread, thy people's aid,
Breadalbane's boast, Clan-Alpine's shade!
For thee shall none a requiem say?
—For thee,—who loved the minstrel's lay,
For thee, of Bothwell's house the stay,
The shelter of her exiled line,
E'en in this prison-house of thine,
I'll wail for Alpine's honour'd Pine!

"What groans shall yonder valleys fill!
What shrieks of grief shall rend yon hill!
What tears of burning rage shall thrill,
When mourns thy tribe thy battles done,
Thy fall before the race was won,
Thy sword ungirt ere set of sun!
There breathes not clansman of thy line,
But would have given his life for thine.—
O woe for Alpine's honour'd Pine!

"Sad was thy lot on mortal stage!—
The captive thrush may brook the cage,
The prison'd eagle dies for rage.
Brave spirit, do not scorn my strain!
And, when its notes awake again,
Even she, so long beloved in vain,
Shall with my harp her voice combine,
And mix her woe and tears with mine,
To wail Clan-Alpine's honour'd Pine."

XXIII.

Ellen, the while, with bursting heart,
Remain'd in lordly bower apart,
Where play'd with many-colour'd gleams,
Through storied pane the rising beams.
In vain on gilded roof they fall,
And lighten'd up a tapestried wall,
And for her use a menial train
A rich collation spread in vain.

The banquet proud, the chamber gay,
Scarce drew one curious glance astray;
Or, if she look'd, 'twas but to say,
With better omen dawn'd the day
In that lone isle, where waved on high
The dun-deer's hide for canopy;
Where oft her noble father shared
The simple meal her care prepared,
While Lufra, crouching by her side,
Her station claim'd with jealous pride,
And Douglas, bent on woodland game,
Spoke of the chase to Malcolm Græme,
Whose answer, oft at random made,
The wandering of his thoughts betray'd.—
Those who such simple joys have known,
Are taught to prize them when they're
     gone.
But sudden, see, she lifts her head!
The window seeks with cautious tread.
What distant music has the power
To win her in this woful hour!
'Twas from a turret that o'erhung
Her latticed bower, the strain was sung.

XXIV.

Lay of the Imprisoned Huntsman.

" My hawk is tired of perch and hood,
My idle greyhound loathes his food,
My horse is weary of his stall,
And I am sick of captive thrall.
I wish I were, as I have been,
Hunting the hart in forest green,
With bended bow and bloodhound free,
For that's the life is meet for me.
I hate to learn the ebb of time,
From yon dull steeple's drowsy chime,
Or mark it as the sunbeams crawl,
Inch after inch along the wall.
The lark was wont my matins ring,
The sable rook my vespers sing,
These towers, although a king's they be,
Have not a hall of joy for me.
No more at dawning morn I rise,
And sun myself in Ellen's eyes,
Drive the fleet deer the forest through,
And homeward wend with evening dew;
A blithesome welcome blithely meet,
And lay my trophies at her feet,

While fled the eve on wing of glee,—
That life is lost to love and me!"

XXV.

The heart-sick lay was hardly said,
The list'ner had not turn'd her head,
It trickled still, the starting tear,
When light a footstep struck her ear,
And Snowdoun's graceful knight was near.
She turn'd the hastier, lest again
The prisoner should renew his strain.—
" O welcome, brave Fitz-James!" she
     said;
" How may an almost orphan maid
Pay the deep debt "—" O say not so!
To me no gratitude you owe.
Not mine, alas! the boon to give,
And bid thy noble father live;
I can but be thy guide, sweet maid,
With Scotland's king thy suit to aid.
No tyrant he, though ire and pride
May lay his better mood aside.
Come, Ellen, come! 'tis more than time,
He holds his court at morning prime."
With beating heart, and bosom wrung,
As to a brother's arm she clung.
Gently he dried the falling tear,
And gently whisper'd hope and cheer;
Her faltering steps half led, half staid,
Through gallery fair, and high arcade,
Till, at its touch, its wings of pride
A portal arch unfolded wide.

XXVI.

Within 'twas brilliant all and light,
A thronging scene of figures bright;
It glow'd on Ellen's dazzled sight,
As when the setting sun has given
Ten thousand hues to summer even,
And from their tissue, fancy frames
Aërial knights and fairy dames.
Still by Fitz-James her footing staid;
A few faint steps she forward made,
Then slow her drooping head she raised,
And fearful round the presence gazed;
For him she sought, who own'd this state,
The dreaded prince whose will was fate.
She gazed on many a princely port,
Might well have ruled a royal court;

On many a splendid garb she gazed,
Then turn'd bewilder'd and amazed,
For all stood bare; and, in the room,
Fitz-James alone wore cap and plume.
To him each lady's look was lent;
On him each courtier's eye was bent;
Midst furs and silks, and jewels sheen,
He stood, in simple Lincoln green,
The centre of the glittering ring.
And Snowdoun's Knight is Scotland's
    King.[52]

XXVII.

As wreath of snow, on mountain-breast,
Slides from the rock that gave it rest,
Poor Ellen glided from her stay,
And at the Monarch's feet she lay;
No word her choking voice commands,—
She show'd the ring, she clasp'd her hands.
O ! not a moment could he brook,
The generous prince, that suppliant look !
Gently he raised her; and, the while,
Check'd with a glance the circle's smile;
Graceful, but grave, her brow he kiss'd,
And bade her terrors be dismiss'd :—
" Yes, Fair ; the wandering poor Fitz-
    James
The fealty of Scotland claims.
To him thy woes, thy wishes, bring ;
He will redeem his signet ring.
Ask nought for Douglas ; yester even,
His prince and he have much forgiven.
Wrong hath he had from slanderous
    tongue,
I, from his rebel kinsmen, wrong.
We would not, to the vulgar crowd,
Yield what they craved with clamour
    loud;
Calmly we heard and judged his cause,
Our council aided, and our laws.
I stanch'd thy father's death-feud stern,
With stout De Vaux and Grey Glencairn;
And Bothwell's Lord henceforth we own
The friend and bulwark of our Throne.
But, lovely infidel, how now ?
What clouds thy misbelieving brow ?
Lord James of Douglas, lend thine
    aid ;
Thou must confirm this doubting maid."

XXVIII.

Then forth the noble Douglas sprung,
And on his neck his daughter hung.
The Monarch drank, that happy hour,
The sweetest, holiest, draught of Power,—
When it can say, with godlike voice,
Arise, sad Virtue, and rejoice !
Yet would not James the general eye
On Nature's raptures long should pry ;
He stepp'd between—" Nay, Douglas, nay,
Steal not my proselyte away !
The riddle 'tis my right to read,
That brought this happy chance to speed.
Yes, Ellen, when disguised I stray
In life's more low but happier way,
'Tis under name which veils my power,
Nor falsely veils—for Stirling's tower
Of yore the name of Snowdoun claims,[53]
And Normans call me James Fitz-James.
Thus watch I o'er insulted laws,
Thus learn to right the injured cause."—
Then, in a tone apart and low,—
" Ah, little traitress ! none must know
What idle dream, what lighter thought,
What vanity full dearly bought,
Join'd to thine eye's dark witchcraft, drew
My spell-bound steps to Benvenue,
In dangerous hour, and all but gave
Thy Monarch's life to mountain glaive !"—
Aloud he spoke—" Thou still dost hold
That little talisman of gold,
Pledge of my faith, Fitz-James's ring—
What seeks fair Ellen of the King ?"

XXIX.

Full well the conscious maiden guess'd
He probed the weakness of her breast ;
But, with that consciousness, there came
A lightening of her fears for Græme,
And more she deem'd the Monarch's ire
Kindled 'gainst him, who, for her sire,
Rebellious broadsword boldly drew ;
And, to her generous feeling true,
She craved the grace of Roderick Dhu.
" Forbear thy suit :—the King of Kings
Alone can stay life's parting wings,
I know his heart, I know his hand,
Have shared his cheer, and proved his
    brand :—

My fairest earldom would I give
To bid Clan-Alpine's Chieftain live!
Hast thou no other boon to crave?
No other captive friend to save?"
Blushing, she turn'd her from the King,
And to the Douglas gave the ring,
As if she wish'd her sire to speak
The suit that stain'd her glowing cheek.—
" Nay, then, my pledge has lost its force,
And stubborn justice holds her course.—
Malcolm, come forth!"—And, at the word,
Down kneel'd the Græme to Scotland's Lord.·
" For thee, rash youth, no suppliant sues,
From thee may Vengeance claim her dues,
Who, nurtured underneath our smile,
Hast paid our care by treacherous wile,
And sought amid thy faithful clan,
A refuge for an outlaw'd man,
Dishonouring thus thy loyal name.—
Fetters and warder for the Græme!"—
His chain of gold the King unstrung,
The links o'er Malcolm's neck he flung,
Then gently drew the glittering band,
And laid the clasp on Ellen's hand.

———

HARP of the North, farewell! The hills
grow dark,
On purple peaks a deeper shade descending;
In twilight copse the glow-worm lights her
spark,
The deer, half-seen, are to the covert
wending.
Resume thy wizard elm! the fountain
lending,
And the wild breeze, thy wilder minstrelsy;
Thy numbers sweet with nature's vespers
blending,
With distant echo from the fold and lea,
And herd-boy's evening pipe, and hum
of housing bee.

Yet, once again, farewell, thou Minstrel
harp!
Yet, once again, forgive my feeble sway,
And little reck I of the censure sharp
May idly cavil at an idle lay.
Much have I owed thy strains on life's
long way,
Through secret woes the world has
never known,
When on the weary night dawn'd wearier
day,
And bitterer was the grief devour'd
alone.
That I o'erlive such woes, Enchantress!
is thine own.

Hark! as my lingering footsteps slow
retire,
Some Spirit of the Air has waked thy
string!
'Tis now a seraph bold, with touch of fire,
'Tis now the brush of Fairy's frolic wing.
Receding now, the dying numbers ring
Fainter and fainter down the rugged dell,
And now the mountain breezes scarcely
bring
A wandering witch-note of the distant
spell—
And now, 'tis silent all!—Enchantress,
fare thee well!

THE VISION OF DON RODERICK.

TO

JOHN WHITMORE, Esq.

AND TO THE

COMMITTEE OF SUBSCRIBERS FOR RELIEF OF THE PORTUGUESE
SUFFERERS IN WHICH HE PRESIDES,

THIS POEM,

(THE VISION OF DON RODERICK,)

COMPOSED FOR THE BENEFIT OF THE FUND UNDER THEIR
MANAGEMENT,

IS RESPECTFULLY INSCRIBED BY

WALTER SCOTT.

PREFACE.

The following Poem is founded upon a Spanish Tradition, particularly detailed in the Notes ; but bearing, in general, that Don Roderick, the last Gothic King of Spain, when the Invasion of the Moors was impending, had the temerity to descend into an ancient vault, near Toledo, the opening of which had been denounced as fatal to the Spanish Monarchy. The legend adds, that his rash curiosity was mortified by an emblematical representation of those Saracens who, in the year 714, *defeated him in battle, and reduced Spain under their dominion. I have presumed to prolong the Vision of the Revolutions of Spain down to the present eventful crisis of the Peninsula ; and to divide it, by a supposed change of scene, into* THREE PERIODS. *The* FIRST *of these represents the Invasion of the Moors, the Defeat and Death of Roderick, and closes with the peaceful occupation of the country by the Victors. The* SECOND PERIOD *embraces the state of the Peninsula, when the conquests of the Spaniards and Portuguese in the East and West Indies had raised to the highest pitch the renown of their arms ; sullied, however, by superstition and cruelty. An allusion to the inhumanities of the Inquisition terminates this picture. The* LAST PART *of the Poem opens with the state of Spain previous to the unparalleled treachery of* BUONAPARTE ; *gives a sketch of the usurpation attempted upon that unsuspicious and friendly kingdom, and terminates with the arrival of the British succours. It may be farther proper to mention, that the object of the Poem is less to commemorate or detail particular incidents, than to exhibit a general and impressive picture of the several periods brought upon the stage.*

I am too sensible of the respect due to the Public, especially by one who has already experienced more than ordinary indulgence, to offer any apology for the inferiority of the poetry to the subject it is chiefly designed to commemorate. Yet I think it proper to mention, that while I was hastily executing a work, written for a temporary purpose, and on passing events, the task was most cruelly interrupted by the successive deaths of LORD PRESIDENT BLAIR, *and* LORD VISCOUNT MELVILLE. *In those distinguished characters, I had not only to regret persons whose lives were most important to Scotland, but also whose notice and patronage honoured my entrance upon active life ; and, I may add, with melancholy pride, who permitted my more advanced age to claim no common share in their friendship. Under such interruptions, the following verses, which my best and happiest efforts must have left far unworthy of their theme, have, I am myself sensible, an appearance of negligence and incoherence, which, in other circumstances, I might have been able to remove.*

EDINBURGH, *June* 24, 1811.

THE VISION OF DON RODERICK.

Quid dignum memorare tuis, Hispania, terris,
Vox humana valet !—CLAUDIAN.

~~~~~~~~~~~~~~~~~~~~~

INTRODUCTION.

I.

LIVES there a strain, whose sounds of
    mounting fire
  May rise distinguish'd o'er the din of
    war ;
Or died it with yon Master of the Lyre,
  Who sung beleaguer'd Ilion's evil
    star ?
Such, WELLINGTON, might reach thee
    from afar,
  Wafting its descant wide o'er Ocean's
    range ;
Nor shouts, nor clashing arms, its mood
    could mar,
  All as it swell'd 'twixt each loud
    trumpet-change,
That clangs to Britain victory, to Portugal
    revenge !

II.

Yes ! such a strain, with all o'er-pour-
    ing measure,
  Might melodize with each tumul-
    tuous sound,
Each voice of fear or triumph, woe or
    pleasure,
  That rings Mondego's ravaged shores
    around ;
The thundering cry of hosts with con-
    quest crown'd,
  The female shriek, the ruin'd pea-
    sant's moan,
The shout of captives from their chains
    unbound,

The foil'd oppressor's deep and sullen
    groan,
A Nation's choral hymn for tyranny o'er-
    thrown.

III.

But we, weak minstrels of a laggard
    day,
  Skill'd but to imitate an elder page,
Timid and raptureless, can we repay
  The debt thou claim'st in this ex-
    hausted age ?
Thou givest our lyres a theme, that
    might engage
  Those that could send thy name o'er
    sea and land,
While sea and land shall last; for
    Homer's rage
  A theme; a theme for Milton's
    mighty hand—
How much unmeet for us, a faint de-
    generate band !

IV.

Ye mountains stern ! within whose
    rugged breast
  The friends of Scottish freedom
    found repose ;
Ye torrents ! whose hoarse sounds have
    soothed their rest,
  Returning from the field of vanquish'd
    foes ;
Say have ye lost each wild majestic
    close,
  That erst the choir of Bards or Druids
    flung ;

What time their hymn of victory arose,
And Cattraeth's glens with voice of
    triumph rung,
And mystic Merlin harp'd, and grey-
    hair'd Llywarch sung![1]

V.

O! if your wilds such minstrelsy retain,
    As sure your changeful gales seem
        oft to say,
When sweeping wild and sinking soft
        again,
    Like trumpet-jubilee, or harp's wild
        . sway;
If ye can echo such triumphant lay,
    Then lend the note to him has loved
        you long!
Who pious gather'd each tradition
        grey,
    That floats your solitary wastes
        along,
And with affection vain gave them new
    voice in song.

VI.

For not till now, how oft soe'er the
        task
    Of truant verse hath lighten'd graver
        care,
From Muse or Sylvan was he wont to
        ask,
    In phrase poetic, inspiration fair;
Careless he gave his numbers to the air,
    They came unsought for, if applauses
        came;
Nor for himself prefers he now the
        prayer;
    Let but his verse befit a hero's fame,
Immortal be the verse!—forgot the poet's
    name.

VII.

Hark, from yon misty cairn their
        answer tost:
    "Minstrel! the fame of whose
        romantic lyre,
Capricious-swelling now, may soon be
        lost,
    Like the light flickering of a cottage
        fire;

If to such task presumptuous thou
        aspire,
    Seek not from us the meed to warrior
        due:
Age after age has gather'd son to
        sire,
    Since our grey cliffs the din of con-
        flict knew,
Or, pealing through our vales, victorious
    bugles blew.

VIII.

"Decay'd our old traditionary lore,
    Save where the lingering fays renew
        their ring,
By milk-maid seen beneath the haw-
        thorn hoar,
    Or round the marge of Minchmore's
        haunted spring:[2]
Save where their legends grey-hair'd
        shepherds sing,
    That now scarce win a listening ear
        but thine,
Of feuds obscure, and Border ravaging,
    And rugged deeds recount in rugged
        line,
Of moonlight foray made on Teviot,
    Tweed, or Tyne.

IX.

"No! search romantic lands, where
        the near Sun
    Gives with unstinted boon ethereal
        flame,
Where the rude villager, his labour
        done,
    In verse spontaneous[3] chants some
        favour'd name.
Whether Olalia's charms his tribute
        claim,
    Her eye of diamond, and her locks
        of jet;
Or whether, kindling at the deeds of
        Græme,[4]
    He sing, to wild Morisco measure set,
Old Albin's red claymore, green Erin's
    bayonet!

X.

" Explore those regions, where the flinty crest
Of wild Nevada ever gleams with snows,
Where in the proud Alhambra's ruin'd breast
Barbaric monuments of pomp repose;
Or where the banners of more ruthless foes
Than the fierce Moor, float o'er Toledo's fane,
From whose tall towers even now the patriot throws
An anxious glance, to spy upon the plain
The blended ranks of England, Portugal, and Spain.

XI.

" There, of Numantian fire a swarthy spark
Still lightens in the sun-burnt native's eye;
The stately port, slow step, and visage dark,
Still mark enduring pride and constancy.
And, if the glow of feudal chivalry
Beam not, as once, thy nobles' dearest pride,
Iberia! oft thy crestless peasantry
Have seen the plumed Hidalgo quit their side,
Have seen, yet dauntless stood—'gainst fortune fought and died.

XII.

" And cherish'd still by that unchanging race,
Are themes for minstrelsy more high than thine;
Of strange tradition many a mystic trace,
Legend and vision, prophecy and sign;
Where wonders wild of Arabesque combine
With Gothic imagery of darker shade,
Forming a model meet for minstrel line.
Go, seek such theme!"—The Mountain Spirit said:
With filial awe I heard—I heard, and I obey'd.

I.

REARING their crests amid the cloudless skies,
And darkly clustering in the pale moonlight,
Toledo's holy towers and spires arise,
As from a trembling lake of silver white.
Their mingled shadows intercept the sight
Of the broad burial-ground outstretch'd below,
And nought disturbs the silence of the night;
All sleeps in sullen shade, or silver glow,
All save the heavy swell of Teio's ceaseless flow.

II.

All save the rushing swell of Teio's tide,
Or, distant heard, a courser's neigh or tramp;
Their changing rounds as watchful horsemen ride,
To guard the limits of King Roderick's camp.
For, through the river's night-fog rolling damp,
Was many a proud pavilion dimly seen,
Which glimmer'd back against the moon's fair lamp,
Tissues of silk and silver twisted sheen,
And standards proudly pitch'd, and warders arm'd between.

III.

But of their Monarch's person keeping
    ward,
  Since last the deep-mouth'd bell of
    vespers toll'd,
The chosen soldiers of the royal guard
  The post beneath the proud Cathe-
    dral hold;
A band unlike their Gothic sires of old,
  Who, for the cap of steel and iron
    mace,
Bear slender darts, and casques be-
    deck'd with gold,
  While silver-studded belts their
    shoulders grace,
Where ivory quivers ring in the broad
  falchion's place.

IV.

In the light language of an idle court,
  They murmur'd at their master's
    long delay,
And held his lengthen'd orisons in
  sport:—
" What! will Don Roderick here
  till morning stay,
To wear in shrift and prayer the night
  away?
  And are his hours in such dull
    penance past,
For fair Florinda's plunder'd charms to
  pay?"⁵
  Then to the east their weary eyes
    they cast,
And wish'd the lingering dawn would
  glimmer forth at last.

V.

But, far within, Toledo's Prelate lent
  An ear of fearful wonder to the
    King;
The silver lamp a fitful lustre sent,
  So long that sad confession wit-
    nessing:
For Roderick told of many a hidden
  thing,
  Such as are lothly utter'd to the air,
When Fear, Remorse, and Shame the
  bosom wring,

And Guilt his secret burden cannot
  bear,
And Conscience seeks in speech a respite
  from Despair.

VI.

Full on the Prelate's face, and silver hair,
  The stream of failing light was feebly
    roll'd:
But Roderick's visage, though his head
  was bare,
  Was shadow'd by his hand and
    mantle's fold.
While of his hidden soul the sins he told,
  Proud Alaric's descendant could not
    brook,
That mortal man his bearing should
  behold,
  Or boast that he had seen, when
    Conscience shook,
Fear tame a monarch's brow, Remorse a
  warrior's look.

VII.

The old man's faded cheek wax'd yet
  more pale,
  As many a secret sad the King be-
    wray'd;
As sign and glance eked out the unfinish'd
  tale,
  When in the midst his faltering
    whisper staid.—
" Thus royal Witiza* was slain,"—he
  said;
  " Yet, holy Father, deem not it was I."
Thus still Ambition strives her crimes to
  shade.—
  " Oh! rather deem 'twas stern neces-
    sity!
Self-preservation bade, and I must kill
  or die.

VIII.

" And if Florinda's shrieks alarm'd the
  air,
  If she invoked her absent sire in vain,

---

* Witiza was Roderick's predecessor on the
Spanish throne. He was slain by Roderick's
connivance.

And on her knees implored that I
    would spare,
  Yet, reverend priest, thy sentence
    rash refrain!—
All is not as it seems—the female train
  Know by their bearing to disguise
    their mood:"—
But Conscience here, as if in high disdain,
  Sent to the Monarch's cheek the
    burning blood—
He stay'd his speech abrupt—and up the
    Prelate stood.

IX.

" O harden'd offspring of an iron race!
  What of thy crimes, Don Roderick,
    shall I say?
What alms, or prayers, or penance
    can efface
  Murder's dark spot, wash treason's
    stain away!
For the foul ravisher how shall I pray,
  Who, scarce repentant, makes his
    crime his boast?
How hope Almighty vengeance shall
    delay,
  Unless in mercy to yon Christian
    host,
He spare the shepherd, lest the guiltless
    sheep be lost."

X.

Then kindled the dark Tyrant in his
    mood,
  And to his brow return'd its daunt-
    less gloom;
" And welcome then," he cried, " be
    blood for blood,
  For treason treachery, for dishonour
    doom!
Yet will I know whence come they, or
    by whom.
  Show, for thou canst—give forth the
    fated key,
And guide me, Priest, to that mys-
    terious room,
  Where, if aught true in old tradition
    be,
His nation's future fates a Spanish King
    shall see,"—

XI

" Ill-fated Prince! recall the desperate
    word,
  Or pause ere yet the omen thou obey?
Bethink, yon spell-bound portal would
    afford
  Never to former Monarch entrance-
    way;
Nor shall it ever ope, old records say,
  Save to a King, the last of all his
    line,
What time his empire totters to decay,
  And treason digs, beneath, her fatal
    mine,
And, high above, impends avenging wrath
    divine."—

XII.

" Prelate! a Monarch's fate brooks no
    delay;
  Lead on!"—The ponderous key the
    old man took,
And held the winking lamp, and led
    the way,
  By winding stair, dark aisle, and
    secret nook,
Then on an ancient gateway bent his
    look;
  And, as the key the desperate King
    essay'd,
Low mutter'd thunders the Cathedral
    shook,
  And twice he stopp'd, and twice
    new effort made,
Till the huge bolts roll'd back, and the
    loud hinges bray'd.

XIII.

Long, large, and lofty, was that vaulted
    hall;
  Roof, walls, and floor, were all of
    marble stone,
Of polish'd marble, black as funeral pall,
  Carved o'er with signs and characters
    unknown.
A paly light, as of the dawning, shone
  Through the sad bounds, but
    whence they could not spy;
For window to the upper air was none:

Yet, by that light, Don Roderick
  could descry
Wonders that ne'er till then were seen
  by mortal eye.

XIV.

Grim sentinels, against the upper wall,
  Of molten bronze, two Statues held
  their place;
Massive their naked limbs, their stature
  tall,
  Their frowning foreheads golden
  circles grace.
Moulded they seem'd for kings of giant
  race,
  That lived and sinn'd before the
  avenging flood;
This grasp'd a scythe, that rested on a
  mace;
  This spread his wings for flight, that
  pondering stood,
Each stubborn seem'd and stern, immu-
  table of mood.

XV.

Fix'd was the right-hand Giant's brazen
  look
  Upon his brother's glass of shifting
  sand,
As if its ebb he measured by a book,
  Whose iron volume loaded his huge
  hand;
In which was wrote of many a fallen
  land,
  Of empires lost, and kings to exile
  driven:
And o'er that pair their names in scroll
  expand—
  "Lo, DESTINY and TIME! to
  whom by Heaven
The guidance of the earth is for a season
  given."—

XVI.

Even while they read, the sand-glass
  wastes away;
  And, as the last and lagging grains
  did creep,
That right-hand Giant 'gan his club
  upsway,

As one that startles from a heavy
  sleep.
Full on the upper wall the mace's sweep
  At once descended with the force of
  thunder,
And hurtling down at once, in crumbled
  heap,
  The marble boundary was rent
  asunder,
And gave to Roderick's view new
  sights of fear and wonder.

XVII.

For they might spy, beyond that mighty
  breach,
  Realms as of Spain in vision'd prospect laid,
Castles and towers, in due proportion
  each,
  As by some skilful artist's hand portray'd ·
Here, crossed by many a wild Sierra's
  shade,
  And boundless plains that tire the
  traveller's eye;
There, rich with vineyard and with
  olive glade,
  Or deep-embrown'd by forests huge
  and high,
Or wash'd by mighty streams, that slowly
  murmur'd by.

XVIII.

And here, as erst upon the antique stage,
  Pass'd forth the band of masquers
  trimly led,
In various forms, and various equipage,
  While fitting strains the hearer's
  fancy fed;
So, to sad Roderick's eye in order
  spread,
  Successive pageants fill'd that mystic
  scene,
Showing the fate of battles ere they
  bled,
  And issue of events that had not
  been;
And, ever and anon, strange sounds
  were heard between.

XIX.

First shrill'd an unrepeated female
  shriek!—
  It seemed as if Don Roderick knew
  the call,
For the bold blood was blanching in
  his cheek.—
  Then answer'd kettle-drum and ata-
  bal,
Gong-peal and cymbal-clank the ear
  appal,
  The Tecbir war-cry, and the Lelie's
  yell,[6]
Ring wildly dissonant along the hall.
  Needs not to Roderick their dread
  import tell—
" The Moor!" he cried, " the Moor!—
  ring out the Tocsin bell!

XX.

" They come! they come! 1 see the
  groaning lands
  White with the turbans of each
  Arab horde;
Swart Zaarah joins her misbelieving
  bands,
  Alla and Mahomet their battle-word,
The choice they yield, the Koran or
  the Sword—
  See how the Christians rush to arms
  amain!—
In yonder shout the voice of conflict
  roar'd,
  The shadowy hosts are closing on
  the plain—
Now, God and Saint Iago strike, for the
  good cause of Spain!

XXI.

" By Heaven, the Moors prevail! the
  Christians yield!
  Their coward leader gives for flight
  the sign!
The sceptred craven mounts to quit
  the field—
  Is not yon steed Orelio?—Yes, 'tis
  mine!7
But never was she turn'd from battle-
  line:

Lo! where the recreant spurs o'er
  stock and stone!
Curses pursue the slave, and wrath
  divine!
  Rivers ingulph him!"—" Hush," in
  shuddering tone,
The Prelate said;—"rash Prince, yon
  vision'd form's thine own."

XXII.

Just then, a torrent cross'd the flier's
  course;
  The dangerous ford the Kingly Likeness tried;
But the deep eddies whelm'd both man
  and horse,
  Swept like benighted peasant down
  the tide;
And the proud Moslemah spread far
  and wide,
  As numerous as their native locust
  band;
Berber and Ismael's sons the spoils
  divide,
  With naked scimitars mete out the
  land,
And for the bondsmen base the freeborn
  natives brand.

XXIII.

Then rose the grated Harem, to enclose
  The loveliest maidens of the Christian
  line;
Then, menials, to their misbelieving
  foes,
  Castile's young nobles held forbidden
  wine;
Then, too, the holy Cross, salvation's
  sign,
  By impious hands was from the altar
  thrown,
And the deep aisles of the polluted
  shrine
  Echo'd, for holy hymn and organ-
  tone
The Santon's frantic dance, the Fakir's
  gibbering moan.

XXIV.

How fares Don Roderick?—E'en as
    one who spies
  Flames dart their glare o'er midnight's
    sable woof,
And hears around his children's pierc-
    ing cries,
  And sees the pale assistants stand
    aloof;
While cruel Conscience brings him
    bitter proof,
  His folly or his crime have caused
    his grief;
And while above him nods the crum-
    bling roof,
  He curses earth and Heaven—him-
    self in chief—
Desperate of earthly aid, despairing
    Heaven's relief!

XXV.

That scythe-arm'd Giant turn'd his
    fatal glass
  And twilight on the landscape closed
    her wings;
Far to Asturian hills the war-sounds
    pass,
  And in their stead rebeck or timbrel
    rings;
And to the sound the bell-deck'd
    dancer springs,
  Bazaars resound as when their marts
    are met,
In tourney light the Moor his jerrid*
    flings,
  And on the land as evening seem'd
    to set,
The Imaum's chant was heard from
    mosque or minaret.

XXVI.

So pass'd that pageant. Ere another
    came,
  The visionary scene was wrapp'd in
    smoke,
Whose sulph'rous wreaths were cross'd
    by sheets of flame;

With every flash a bolt explosive
    broke,
Till Roderick deem'd the fiends had
    burst their yoke,
  And waved 'gainst heaven the in-
    fernal gonfalone?
For War a new and dreadful language
    spoke,
  Never by ancient warrior heard or
    known;
Lightning and smoke her breath, and
    thunder was her tone.

XXVII.

From the dim landscape roll the clouds
    away—
  The Christians have regain'd their
    heritage;
Before the Cross has waned the Cres-
    cent's ray
  And many a monastery decks the
    stage,
And lofty church, and low-brow'd
    hermitage.
  The land obeys a Hermit and a
    Knight,—
The Genii those of Spain for many an
    age;
  This clad in sackcloth, that in armour
    bright,
And that was VALOUR named, this
    BIGOTRY was hight.

XXVIII.

VALOUR was harness'd like a Chief of
    old,
  Arm'd at all points, and prompt for
    knightly gest;
His sword was temper'd in the Ebro
    cold,
  Morena's eagle plume adorn'd his
    crest,
The spoils of Afric's lion bound his
    breast.
  Fierce he stepp'd forward and flung
    down his gage;
As if of mortal kind to brave the
    best.

---

* *Jerrid*, javelin.

† *Gonfalone*, banner.

Him follow'd his Companion, dark
  and sage,
As he, my Master, sung the dangerous
  Archimage.

XXIX.

Haughty of heart and brow the Warrior
  came,
  In look and language proud as proud
  might be,
Vaunting his lordship, lineage, fights,
  and fame:
  Yet was that barefoot monk more
  proud than he:
And as the ivy climbs the tallest tree,
  So round the loftiest soul his toils he
  wound,
And with his spells subdued the fierce
  and free,
  Till ermined Age and Youth in arms
  renown'd,
Honouring his scourge and hair-cloth,
  meekly kiss'd the ground.

XXX.

And thus it chanced that VALOUR,
  peerless knight,
  Who ne'er to King or Kaiser veil'd
  his crest,
Victorious still in bull-feast or in fight,
  Since first his limbs with mail he did
  invest,
Stoop'd ever to that Anchoret's behest;
  Nor reason'd of the right, nor of the
  wrong,
But at his bidding laid the lance in rest,
  And wrought fell deeds the troubled
  world along,
For he was fierce as brave, and pitiless as
  strong.

XXXI.

Oft his proud galleys sought some new-
  found world,
  That latest sees the sun, or first the
  morn;
Still at that Wizard's feet their spoils
  he hurl'd,—
Ingots of ore from rich Potosi borne.

Crowns by Caciques,* aigrettes by
  Omrahs worn,
Wrought of rare gems, but broken,
  rent, and foul;
Idols of gold from heathen temples
  torn,
  Bedabbled all with blood.—With
  grisly scowl
The Hermit mark'd the stains, and smiled
  beneath his cowl.

XXXII.

Then did he bless the offering, and
  bade make
  Tribute to Heaven of gratitude and
  praise:
And at his word the choral hymns
  awake,
  And many a hand the silver censer
  sways.
But with the incense-breath these
  censers raise,
  Mix steams from corpses smouldering in the fire;
The groans of prison'd victims mar the
  lays,
  And shrieks of agony confound the
  quire;
While, 'mid the mingled sounds, the
  darken'd scenes expire.

XXXIII.

Preluding light, were strains of music
  heard,
  As once again revolved that measured
  sand;
Such sounds as when, for sylvan dance
  prepared,
  Gay Xeres summons forth her vin-
  tage band;
When for the light bolero ready stand
  The mozo blithe, with gay muchacha met,[8]
He conscious of his broider'd cap and
  band,

---

* *Caciques and Omrahs*, Peruvian and
Mexican chiefs or nobles.

She of her netted locks and light
    corsette,
Each tiptoe perch'd to spring, and shake
    the castanet.

XXXIV.

And well such strains the opening
    scene became,
    For VALOUR had relax'd his ardent
    look,
And at a lady's feet, like lion tame,
    Lay stretch'd, full loth the weight
    of arms to brook;
And soften'd BIGOTRY, upon his book,
    Patter'd a task of little good or ill:
But the blithe peasant plied his prun-
    ing-hook,
    Whistled the muleteer o'er vale and
    hill,
And rung from village-green the merry
    seguidille.

XXXV.

Grey Royalty, grown impotent of toil,
    Let the grave sceptre slip his lazy
    hold;
And, careless, saw his rule become the
    spoil
    Of a loose Female and her minion
    bold.
But peace was on the cottage and the
    fold,
    From court intrigue, from bickering
    faction far;
Beneath the chestnut-tree Love's tale
    was told,
    And to the tinkling of the light
    guitar,
Sweet stoop'd the western sun, sweet rose
    the evening star.

XXXVI.

As that sea-cloud, in size like human
    hand,
    When first from Carmel by the
    Tishbite* seen,

* Elijah the Prophet. *See* 1 Kings,
chap. xviii.

Came slowly overshadowing Israel's
    land,
    A while, perchance, bedeck'd with
    colours sheen,
While yet the sunbeams on its skirts
    had been,
    Limning with purple and with gold
    its shroud,
Till darker folds obscured the blue
    serene,
    And blotted heaven with one broad
    sable cloud,
Then sheeted rain burst down, and whirl-
    winds howl'd aloud:—

XXXVII.

Even so, upon that peaceful scene was
    pour'd,
    Like gathering clouds, full many a
    foreign band,
And HE, their Leader, wore in sheath
    his sword,
    And offer'd peaceful front and open
    hand,
Veiling the perjured treachery he
    plann'd,
    By friendship's zeal and honour's
    specious guise,
Until he won the passes of the land;
    Then burst were honour's oath, and
    friendship's ties!
He clutch'd his vulture-grasp, and call'd
    fair Spain his prize.

XXXVIII.

An Iron Crown his anxious forehead
    bore;
    And well such diadem his heart
    became.
Who ne'er his purpose for remorse
    gave o'er,
    Or check'd his course for piety or
    shame;
Who, train'd a soldier, deem'd a sol-
    dier's fame
    Might flourish in the wreath of
    battles won,
Though neither truth nor honour
    deck'd his name;

Who, placed by fortune on a
   Monarch's throne,
Reck'd not of Monarch's faith, or Mercy's
   kingly tone.

XXXIX.

From a rude isle his ruder lineage came,
   The spark, that, from a suburb-
    hovel's hearth
Ascending, wraps some capital in flame,
   Hath not a meaner or more sordid
    birth.
And for the soul that bade him waste
   the earth—
   The sable land-flood from some
    swamp obscure,
That poisons the glad husband-field
   with dearth,
   And by destruction bids its fame
    endure,
Hath not a source more sullen, stagnant,
   and impure.*

XL.

Before that Leader strode a shadowy
   Form;
   Her limbs like mist, her torch like
    meteor show'd,
With which she beckon'd him through
   fight and storm,
   And all he crush'd that cross'd his
    desperate road,
Nor thought, nor fear'd, nor look'd on
   what he trode.
   Realms could not glut his pride,
    blood could not slake,
So oft as e'er she shook her torch
   abroad—
   It was AMBITION bade her terrors
    wake,
Nor deign'd she, as of yore, a milder form
   to take.

XLI.

No longer now she spurn'd at mean
   revenge,
   Or staid her hand for conquer'd
    foeman's moan;

---

* In historical truth, Napoleon I.'s family
was not plebeian.

As when, the fates of aged Rome to
   change,
   By Cæsar's side she cross'd the
    Rubicon.
Nor joy'd she to bestow the spoils she
   won,
   As when the banded powers of Greece
    were task'd
To war beneath the Youth of Macedon:
   No seemly veil her modern minion
    ask'd,
He saw her hideous face, and loved the
   fiend unmask'd.

XLII.

That Prelate mark'd his march—On
   banners blazed
   With battles won in many a distant
    land,
On eagle-standards and on arms he
   gazed;
   " And hopest thou then," he said,
    " thy power shall stand?
O, thou hast builded on the shifting
   sand,
   And thou hast temper'd it with
    slaughter's flood;
And know, fell scourge in the Al-
   mighty's hand,
   Gore-moisten'd trees shall perish in
    the bud,
And by a bloody death shall die the Man
   of Blood!"

XLIII.

The ruthless Leader beckon'd from his
   train
   A wan fraternal Shade, and bade
    him kneel,
And paled his temples with the crown
   of Spain,
   While trumpets rang, and heralds
    cried, " Castile!"9
Not that he loved him—No!—In no
   man's weal,
   Scarce in his own, e'er joy'd that
    sullen heart;
Yet round that throne he bade his
   warriors wheel,

That the poor Puppet might perform
  his part,
And be a sceptred slave, at his stern beck
  to start.

XLIV.

But on the Natives of that Land misused,
  Not long the silence of amazement
  hung,
Nor brook'd they long their friendly
  faith abused;
  For, with a common shriek, the
  general tongue
Exclaim'd, "To arms!" and fast to
  arms they sprung.
  And VALOUR woke, that Genius of
  the Land!
Pleasure, and ease, and sloth, aside he
  flung,
  As burst th' awakening Nazarite his
  band,
When 'gainst his treacherous foes he
  clench'd his dreadful hand.*

XLV.

That Mimic Monarch now cast anxious
  eye
  Upon the Satraps that begirt him
  round,
Now doff'd his royal robe in act to fly,
  And from his brow the diadem
  unbound.
So oft, so near, the Patriot bugle wound,
  From Tarick's walls to Bilboa's
  mountains blown,
These martial satellites hard labour
  found,
  To guard a while his substituted
  throne—
Light recking of his cause, but battling
  for their own.

XLVI.

From Alpuhara's peak that bugle rung,
  And it was echo'd from Corunna's
  wall;
Stately Seville responsive war-shot flung,

Grenada caught it in her Moorish
  hall;
Galicia bade her children fight or
  fall,
  Wild Biscay shook his mountain-
  coronet,
Valencia roused her at the battle-call,
  And, foremost still where Valour's
  sons are met,
First started to his gun each fiery Miquelet.

XLVII.

But unappall'd and burning for the fight,
  The Invaders march, of victory
  secure;
Skilful their force to sever or unite,
  And train'd alike to vanquish or
  endure.
Nor skilful less, cheap conquest to
  ensure,
  Discord to breathe, and jealousy to
  sow,
To quell by boasting, and by bribes to
  lure;
  While nought against them bring the
  unpractised foe,
Save hearts for Freedom's cause, and hands
  for Freedom's blow.

XLVIII.

Proudly they march—but, O! they
  march not forth
  By one hot field to crown a brief
  campaign,
As when their Eagles, sweeping through
  the North,
  Destroy'd at every stoop an ancient
  reign!
Far other fate had Heaven decreed for
  Spain;
  In vain the steel, in vain the torch
  was plied,
New Patriot armies started from the
  slain,
  High blazed the war, and long, and
  far, and wide,[10]
And oft the God of Battles blest the
  righteous side.

---

* Samson. *See* Judges, chap. xv. 9—16.

XLIX.

Nor unatoned, where Freedom's foes
    prevail,
  Remain'd their savage waste. With
    blade and brand,
By day the Invaders ravaged hill and
    dale,
  But, with the darkness, the Guerilla
    band
Came like night's tempest, and avenged
    the land,
  And claim'd for blood the retribu-
    tion due,
Probed the hard heart, and lopp'd the
    murd'rous hand;
  And Dawn, when o'er the scene her
    beams she threw,
Midst ruins they had made, the spoilers'
    corpses knew.

L.

What minstrel verse may sing, or
    tongue may tell,
  Amid the vision'd strife from sea to
    sea,
How oft the Patriot banners rose or fell,
  Still honour'd in defeat as victory!
For that sad pageant of events to be,
  Show'd every form of fight by field
    and flood;
Slaughter and Ruin, shouting forth
    their glee,
  Beheld, while riding on the tempest
    scud,
The waters choked with slain, the earth
    bedrench'd with blood!

LI.

Then Zaragoza—blighted be the tongue
  That names thy name without the
    honour due!
For never hath the harp of Minstrel rung
  Of faith so felly proved, so firmly true!
Mine, sap, and bomb, thy shatter'd
    ruins knew,
  Each art of war's extremity had room,
Twice from thy half-sack'd streets the
    foe withdrew,

And when at length stern fate decreed
    thy doom,
They won not Zaragoza, but her children's
    bloody tomb.[11]

LII.

Yet raise thy head, sad city! Though
    in chains,
  Enthrall'd thou canst not be! Arise,
    and claim
Reverence from every heart where
    Freedom reigns,
  For what thou worshippest!—thy
    sainted dame,
  She of the Column, honour'd be her
    name,
  By all, whate'er their creed, who
    honour love!
And like the sacred relics of the flame,
  That gave some martyr to the bless'd
    above,
To every loyal heart may thy sad embers
    prove!

LIII.

Nor thine alone such wreck. Gerona
    fair!
  Faithful to death thy heroes shall be
    sung,
Manning the towers while o'er their
    heads the air
  Swart as the smoke from raging
    furnace hung;
Now thicker dark'ning where the mine
    was sprung,
  Now briefly lighten'd by the cannon's
    flare,
Now arch'd with fire-sparks as the
    bomb was flung,
  And redd'ning now with conflagra-
    tion's glare,
While by the fatal light the foes for storm
    prepare.

LIV.

While all around was danger, strife,
    and fear,
  While the earth shook, and darken'd
    was the sky,

And wide Destruction stunn'd the
listening ear,
Appall'd the heart, and stupified the
eye,—
Afar was heard that thrice-repeated
cry,
In which old Albion's heart and
tongue unite,
Whene'er her soul is up, and pulse
beats high,
Whether it hail the wine cup or the
fight,
And bid each arm be strong, or bid each
heart be light.

LV.

Don Roderick turn'd him as the shout
grew loud—
A varied scene the changeful vision
show'd,
For, where the ocean mingled with the
cloud,
A gallant navy stemm'd the billows
broad.
From mast and stern St. George's
symbol flow'd,
Blent with the silver cross to Scotland
dear;
Mottling the sea their landward barges
row'd.
And flash'd the sun on bayonet,
brand, and spear,
And the wild beach return'd the seaman's
jovial cheer.

LVI.

It was a dread, yet spirit-stirring sight!
The billows foam'd beneath a thousand oars,
Fast as they land the red-cross ranks
unite,
Legions on legions bright'ning all the
shores.
Then banners rise, and cannon-signal
roars,
Then peals the warlike thunder of
the drum,
Thrills the loud fife, the trumpet-
flourish pours,
And patriot hopes awake, and doubts
are dumb,
For, bold in Freedom's cause, the bands
of Ocean come!

LVII.

A various host they came—whose
ranks display
Each mode in which the warrior
meets the fight,
The deep battalion locks its firm array,
And meditates his aim the marksman light;
Far glance the light of sabres flashing
bright,
Where mounted squadrons shake
the echoing mead,
Lacks not artillery breathing flame and
night,
Nor the fleet ordnance whirl'd by
rapid steed,
That rivals lightning's flash in ruin and in
speed.

LVIII.

A various host—from kindred realms
they came,
Brethren in arms, but rivals in
renown—
For yon fair bands shall merry England
claim,
And with their deeds of valour deck
her crown.
Hers their bold port, and hers their
martial frown,
And hers their scorn of death in
freedom's cause,
Their eyes of azure, and their locks of
brown,
And the blunt speech that bursts
without a pause,
And freeborn thoughts, which league the
Soldier with the Laws.

LIX.

And, O! loved warriors of the Minstrel's land!
Yonder your bonnets nod, your
tartans wave!

The rugged form may mark the moun-
    tain band,
    And harsher features, and a mien
      more grave;
But ne'er in battle-field throbbed heart
    so brave,
    As that which beats beneath the
      Scottish plaid;
And when the pibroch bids the battle
    rave,
    And level for the charge your arms
      are laid,
Where lives the desperate foe that for
    such onset staid!

LX.

Hark! from yon stately ranks what
    laughter rings,
    Mingling wild mirth with war's stern
      minstrelsy,
His jest while each blithe comrade
    round him flings,
    And moves to death with military
      glee:
Boast, Erin, boast them! tameless,
    frank, and free,
    In kindness warm, and fierce in
      danger known,
Rough nature's children, humorous as
    she:
    And HE, yon Chieftain—strike the
      proudest tone
Of thy bold harp, green Isle!—the Hero
    is thine own.

LXI.

Now on the scene Vimeira* should be
    shown,
    On Talavera's fight should Roderick
      gaze,
And hear Corunna wail her battle won,
    And see Busaco's crest with lightning
      blaze:—
But shall fond fable mix with heroes'
    praise?

---

* The battle of Vimeira was fought August
21st, 1808; Corunna, January 16th, 1809;
Talavera, July 28th, 1809, Busaco, September 27th, 1810.

Hath Fiction's stage for Truth's
    long triumphs room?
And dare her wild-flowers mingle with
    the bays,
    That claim a long eternity to bloom
Around the warrior's crest, and o'er the
    warrior's tomb!

LXII.

Or may I give adventurous Fancy
    scope,
    And stretch a bold hand to the awful
      veil
That hides futurity from anxious hope,
    Bidding beyond it scenes of glory
      hail,
And painting Europe rousing at the
    tale
    Of Spain's invaders from her confines
      hurl'd,
While kindling nations buckle on their
    mail,
    And Fame, with clarion-blast and
      wings unfurl'd,
To Freedom and Revenge awakes an
    injured World?

LXIII.

O vain, though anxious, is the glance I
    cast,
    Since Fate has mark'd futurity her
      own:
Yet fate resigns to worth the glorious
    past,
    The deeds recorded, and the laurels
      won.
Then, though the Vault of Destiny be
    gone,
    King, Prelate, all the phantasms of
      my brain,
Melted away like mist-wreaths in the
    sun,
    Yet grant for faith, for valour, and
      for Spain,
One note of pride and fire, a Patriot's
    parting strain!

Conclusion.

I.

" WHO shall command Estrella's moun-
    tain tide
    Back to the source, when tempest-
    chafed, to hie?
Who, when Gascogne's vex'd gulf is
    raging wide,
    Shall hush it as a nurse her infant's cry?
His magic power let such vain boaster
    try,
    And when the torrent shall his voice
    obey,
And Biscay's whirlwinds list his lullaby,
    Let him stand forth and bar mine
    eagles' way,
And they shall heed his voice, and at his
    bidding stay.

II.

" Else ne'er to stoop, till high on
    Lisbon's towers
    They close their wings, the symbol
    of our yoke,
And their own sea hath whelm'd yon
    red-cross Powers!"
    Thus, on the summit of Alverca's
    rock,
To Marshal, Duke, and Peer, Gaul's
    Leader spoke.
    While downward on the land his
    legions press,
Before them it was rich with vine and
    flock,
    And smiled like Eden in her summer
    dress;
Behind their wasteful march, a reeking
    wilderness.[3]

III.

And shall the boastful Chief maintain
    his word,
    Though Heaven hath heard the wail-
    ings of the land,
Though Lusitania whet her vengeful
    sword,
    Though Britons arm, and WEL-
    LINGTON command!
No! grim Busaco's iron ridge shall stand

An adamantine barrier to his force;
And from its base shall wheel his shat-
    ter'd band,
As from the unshaken rock the tor-
    rent hoarse
Bears off its broken waves, and seeks a
    devious course.

IV.

Yet not because Alcoba's mountain-
    hawk
    Hath on his best and bravest made
    her food,
In numbers confident, yon Chief shall
    balk
    His Lord's imperial thirst for spoil
    and blood:
For full in view the promised conquest
    stood,
    And Lisbon's matrons from their
    walls might sum
The myriads that had half the world
    subdued,
    And hear the distant thunders cf the
    drum,
That bids the bands of France to storm
    and havoc come.

V.

Four moons have heard these thunders
    idly roll'd,
    Have seen these wistful myriads eye
    their prey,
As famish'd wolves survey a guarded
    fold—
    But in the middle path a Lion lay!
At length they move—but not to battle-
    fray,
    Nor blaze yon fires where meets the
    manly fight;
Beacons of infamy, they light the way
    Where cowardice and cruelty unite
To damn with double shame their igno-
    minious flight!

VI.

O triumph for the Fiends of Lust and
    Wrath!
    Ne'er to be told, yet ne'er to be
    forgot,

What wanton horrors mark'd their
 wreckful path!
 The peasant butcher'd in his ruin'd
  cot,
The hoary priest even at the altar shot,
 Childhood and age given o'er to
  sword and flame,
Woman to infamy;—no crime forgot,
 By which inventive demons might
  proclaim
Immortal hate to man, and scorn of God's
 great name!

VII.

The rudest sentinel, in Britain born,
 With horror paused to view the
  havoc done,
Gave his poor crust to feed some wretch
 forlorn,[14]
 Wiped his stern eye, then fiercer
  grasp'd his gun.
Nor with less zeal shall Britain's peace-
 ful son
 Exult the debt of sympathy to pay;
Riches nor poverty the tax shall shun,
 Nor prince nor peer, the wealthy
  nor the gay,
Nor the poor peasant's mite, nor bard's
 more worthless lay.

VIII.

But thou—unfoughten wilt thou yield
 to Fate,
 Minion of Fortune, now miscall'd
  in vain!
Can vantage-ground no confidence
 create,
 Marcella's pass, nor Guarda's mountain chain?
Vainglorious fugitive![15] yet turn again!
 Behold, where, named by some prophetic Seer,
Flows Honour's Fountain,* as fore-
 doom'd the stain
 From thy dishonour'd name and
  arms to clear—
Fallen Child of Fortune, turn, redeem
 her favour here!

---

* The literal translation of *Fuentes d'Honoro.*

IX.

Yet, ere thou turn'st, collect each dis-
 tant aid;
 Those chief that never heard the
  lion roar!
Within whose souls lives not a trace
 portray'd
 Of Talavera, or Mondego's shore!
Marshal each band thou hast, and
 summon more;
 Of war's fell stratagems exhaust the
  whole;
Rank upon rank, squadron on squadron
 pour,
 Legion on legion on thy foeman roll,
And weary out his arm—thou canst not
 quell his soul.

X.

O vainly gleams with steel Agueda's
 shore,
 Vainly thy squadrons hide Assuava's
  plain,
And front the flying thunders as they
 roar,
 With frantic charge and tenfold
  odds, in vain![16]
And what avails thee that, for CAMERON
 slain,[17]
 Wild from his plaided ranks the yell
  was given—
Vengeance and grief gave mountain-
 rage the rein,
 And, at the bloody spear-point headlong driven,
Thy Despot's giant guards fled like the
 rack of heaven.

XI.

Go, baffled boaster! teach thy haughty
 mood
 To plead at thine imperious master's
  throne,
Say, thou hast left his legions in their
 blood,
 Deceived his hopes, and frustrated
  thine own;
Say, that thine utmost skill and valour
 shown,

By British skill and valour were
    outvied;
Last say, thy conqueror was WEL-
    LINGTON!
    And if he chafe, be his own fortune
      tried—
God and our cause to friend, the venture
    we'll abide.

XII.

But you, ye heroes of that well-fought
    day,
    How shall a bard, unknowing and
      unknown,
His meed to each victorious leader pay,
    Or bind on every brow the laurels won?
Yet fain my harp would wake its
    boldest tone,
    O'er the wide sea to hail CADOGAN
      brave ;
And he, perchance, the minstrel-note
    might own,
    Mindful of meeting brief that For-
      tune gave
Mid yon far western isles that hear the
    Atlantic rave.

XIII.

Yes! hard the task, when Britons
    wield the sword,
    To give each Chief and every field
      its fame:
Hark! Albuera thunders BERESFORD,
    And Red Barosa shouts for dauntless
      GRÆME!
O for a verse of tumult and of flame,
    Bold as the bursting of their cannon
      sound,
To bid the world re-echo to their fame!
    For never, upon gory battle-ground,
With conquest's well-bought wreath were
    braver victors crown'd!

XIV.

O who shall grudge him Albuera's bays,
    Who brought a race regenerate to
    the field,
Roused them to emulate their fathers'
    praise,

Temper'd their headlong rage, their
    courage steel'd,[18]
And raised fair Lusitania's fallen shield,
    And gave new edge to Lusitania's
    sword,
And taught her sons forgotten arms to
    wield—
    Shiver'd my harp, and burst its every
    chord,
If it forget thy worth, victorious BERES-
    FORD!

XV.

Not on that bloody field of battle
    won,
    Though Gaul's proud legions roll'd
    like mist away,
Was half his self-devoted valour
    shown,—
    He gaged but life on that illustrious
    day ;
But when he toil'd those squadrons to
    array,
    Who fought like Britons in the
    bloody game,
Sharper than Polish pike or assagay,
    He braved the shafts of censure and
    of shame,
And, dearer far than life, he pledged a
    soldier's fame.

XVI.

Nor be his praise o'erpast who strove
    to hide
    Beneath the warrior's vest affection's
    wound,
Whose wish Heaven for his country's
    weal denied ;
    Danger and fate he sought, but
    glory found.
From clime to clime, where'er war's
    trumpets sound,
    The wanderer went; yet, Caledonia!
    still
Thine was his thought in march and
    tented ground ;
    He dream'd 'mid Alpine cliffs of
    Athole's hill,
And heard in Ebro's roar his Lyndoch's
    lovely rill.

XVII.

O hero of a race renown'd of old,
    Whose war-cry oft has waked the
        battle-swell,
Since first distinguish'd in the onset
        bold,
    Wild sounding when the Roman
        rampart fell!
By Wallace' side it rung the Southron's
        knell,
    Alderne, Kilsythe, and Tibber,
        own'd its fame,
Tummell's rude pass can of its terrors
        tell,
    But ne'er from prouder field arose
        the name,
Than when wild Ronda learn'd the con-
    quering shout of GRÆME![19]

XVIII.

But all too long, through seas unknown
    and dark,
    (With Spenser's parable I close my
        tale,)
By shoal and rock hath steer'd my
    venturous bark,
    And landward now I drive before
        the gale.
And now the blue and distant shore I
    hail,
    And nearer now I see the port
        expand,
And now I gladly furl my weary sail,
    And as the prow light touches on
        the strand,
I strike my red-cross flag and bind my
    skiff to land.

ROKEBY.

TO

JOHN B. S. MORRITT, Esq.

THIS POEM,

THE SCENE OF WHICH IS LAID IN HIS BEAUTIFUL DEMESNE OF ROKEBY,

IS INSCRIBED, IN TOKEN OF SINCERE FRIENDSHIP, BY

WALTER SCOTT.

ADVERTISEMENT.

The Scene of this Poem is laid at Rokeby, near Greta Bridge, in Yorkshire, and shifts to the adjacent fortress of Barnard Castle, and to other places in that Vicinity.

The Time occupied by the Action is a space of Five Days, Three of which are supposed to elapse between the end of the Fifth and beginning of the Sixth Canto.

The date of the supposed events is immediately subsequent to the great battle of Marston Moor, 3rd July, 1644. This period of public confusion has been chosen, without any purpose of combining the Fable with the Military or Political Events of the Civil War, but only as affording a degree of probability to the Fictitious Narrative now presented to the Public.

ROKEBY.

CANTO FIRST.

I.

THE Moon is in her summer glow,
But hoarse and high the breezes blow,
And, racking o'er her face, the cloud
Varies the tincture of her shroud;
On Barnard's towers, and Tees's stream,[1]
She changes as a guilty dream,
When conscience, with remorse and fear,
Goads sleeping Fancy's wild career.
Her light seems now the blush of shame,
Seems now fierce anger's darker flame,
Shifting that shade, to come and go,
Like apprehension's hurried glow;
Then sorrow's livery dims the air,
And dies in darkness, like despair.
Such varied hues the warder sees
Reflected from the woodland Tees,
Then from old Baliol's tower looks forth,
Sees the clouds mustering in the north,
Hears, upon turret-roof and wall,
By fits the plashing rain-drop fall,
Lists to the breeze's boding sound,
And wraps his shaggy mantle round.

II.

Those towers, which in the changeful gleam
Throw murky shadows on the stream,
Those towers of Barnard hold a guest,
The emotions of whose troubled breast,
In wild and strange confusion driven,
Rival the flitting rack of heaven.
Ere sleep stern OSWALD's senses tied,
Oft had he changed his weary side,
Composed his limbs, and vainly sought
By effort strong to banish thought.
Sleep came at length, but with a train
Of feelings true and fancies vain,
Mingling, in wild disorder cast,
The expected future with the past.
Conscience, anticipating time,
Already rues the enacted crime,
And calls her furies forth, to shake
The sounding scourge and hissing snake;
While her poor victim's outward throes
Bear witness to his mental woes,
And show what lesson may be read
Beside a sinner's restless bed.

III.

Thus Oswald's labouring feelings trace
Strange changes in his sleeping face,
Rapid and ominous as these
With which the moonbeams tinge the Tees.
There might be seen of shame the blush,
There anger's dark and fiercer flush,
While the perturbed sleeper's hand
Seem'd grasping dagger-knife, or brand.
Relax'd that grasp, the heavy sigh,
The tear in the half-opening eye,
The pallid cheek and brow, confess'd
That grief was busy in his breast;
Nor paused that mood—a sudden start
Impell'd the life-blood from the heart:
Features convulsed, and mutterings dread,
Show terror reigns in sorrow's stead.
That pang the painful slumber broke,
And Oswald with a start awoke.

IV.

He woke, and fear'd again to close
His eyelids in such dire repose;
He woke,—to watch the lamp, and tell
From hour to hour the castle-bell.
Or listen to the owlet's cry,
Or the sad breeze that whistles by,
Or catch, by fits, the tuneless rhyme
With which the warder cheats the time,
And envying think, how, when the sun
Bids the poor soldier's watch be done,
Couch'd on his straw, and fancy-free,
He sleeps like careless infancy.

V.

Far townward sounds a distant tread,
And Oswald, starting from his bed,
Hath caught it, though no human ear,[2]
Unsharpen'd by revenge and fear,
Could e'er distinguish horse's clank,
Until it reach'd the castle bank.
Now nigh and plain the sound appears,
The warder's challenge now he hears,
Then clanking chains and levers tell,
That o'er the moat the drawbridge fell,
And, in the castle court below,
Voices are heard, and torches glow,
As marshalling the stranger's way,
Straight for the room where Oswald lay;
The cry was,—" Tidings from the host,
Of weight—a messenger comes post."
Stifling the tumult of his breast,
His answer Oswald thus express'd—
" Bring food and wine, and trim the fire;
Admit the stranger, and retire."

VI.

The stranger came with heavy stride,
The morion's plumes his visage hide,
And the buff-coat, an ample fold,
Mantles his form's gigantic mould.[3]
Full slender answer deigned he
To Oswald's anxious courtesy,
But mark'd, by a disdainful smile,
He saw and scorn'd the petty wile,
When Oswald changed the torch's place,
Anxious that on the soldier's face
Its partial lustre might be thrown,
To show his looks, yet hide his own.

His guest, the while, laid low aside
The ponderous cloak of tough bull's hide,
And to the torch glanced broad and clear
The corslet of a cuirassier;
Then from his brows the casque he drew,
And from the dank plume dash'd the dew,
From gloves of mail relieved his hands,
And spread them to the kindling brands,
And, turning to the genial board,
Without a health, or pledge, or word
Of meet and social reverence said,
Deeply he drank, and fiercely fed;
As free from ceremony's sway,
As famish'd wolf that tears his prey.

VII.

With deep impatience, tinged with fear,
His host beheld him gorge his cheer,
And quaff the full carouse, that lent
His brow a fiercer hardiment.
Now Oswald stood a space aside,
Now paced the room with hasty stride
In feverish agony to learn
Tidings of deep and dread concern,
Cursing each moment that his guest
Protracted o'er his ruffian feast.
Yet, viewing with alarm, at last,
The end of that uncouth repast,
Almost he seem'd their haste to rue,
As, at his sign, his train withdrew,
And left him with the stranger, free
To question of his mystery.
Then did his silence long proclaim
A struggle between fear and shame.

VIII.

Much in the stranger's mien appears,
To justify suspicious fears.
On his dark face a scorching clime,[4]
And toil, had done the work of time,
Roughen'd the brow, the temples bared,
And sable hairs with silver shared,
Yet left—what age alone could tame—
The lip of pride, the eye of flame;
The full-drawn lip that upward curl'd,
The eye, that seem'd to scorn the world.
That lip had terror never blench'd;
Ne'er in that eye had tear-drop quench'd
The flash severe of swarthy glow,
That mock'd at pain, and knew not woe.

Inured to danger's direst form,
Tornade and earthquake, flood and storm,
Death had he seen by sudden blow,
By wasting plague, by tortures slow,
By mine or breach, by steel or ball,
Knew all his shapes, and scorn'd them all.

IX.

But yet, though BERTRAM's harden'd
    look,
Unmoved, could blood and danger brook,
Still worse than apathy had place
On his swart brow and callous face;
For evil passions, cherish'd long,
Had plough'd them with impressions
    strong.
All that gives gloss to sin, all gay
Light folly, past with youth away,
But rooted stood, in manhood's hour,
The weeds of vice without their flower.
And yet the soil in which they grew,
Had it been tamed when life was new,
Had depth and vigour to bring forth
The hardier fruits of virtuous worth.
Not that, e'en then, his heart had known
The gentler feelings' kindly tone;
But lavish waste had been refined
To bounty in his chasten'd mind,
And lust of gold, that waste to feed,
Been lost in love of glory's meed,
And, frantic then no more, his pride
Had ta'en fair virtue for its guide.

X.

Even now, by conscience unrestrain'd,
Clogg'd by gross vice, by slaughter stain'd,
Still knew his daring soul to soar,
And mastery o'er the mind he bore;
For meaner guilt, or heart less hard,
Quail'd beneath Bertram's bold regard
And this felt Oswald, while in vain
He strove, by many a winding train,
To lure his sullen guest to show,
Unask'd, the news he long'd to know,
While on far other subject hung
His heart, than falter'd from his tongue.
Yet nought for that his guest did deign
To note or spare his secret pain,
But still, in stern and stubborn sort,
Return'd him answer dark and short,

Or started from the theme, to range
In loose digression wild and strange,
And forced the embarrass'd host to buy,
By query close, direct reply.

XI.

A while he glozed upon the cause
Of Commons, Covenant, and Laws,
And Church Reform'd—but felt rebuke
Beneath grim Bertram's sneering look,
Then stammer'd—" Has a field been
    fought?
Has Bertram news of battle brought?
For sure a soldier, famed so far
In foreign fields for feats of war,
On eve of fight ne'er left the host,
Until the field were won and lost."
" Here, in your towers by circling Tees,
You, Oswald Wycliffe, rest at ease;
Why deem it strange that others come
To share such safe and easy home,
From fields where danger, death, and toil,
Are the reward of civil broil?"—
" Nay, mock not, friend! since well we
    know
The near advances of the foe,
To mar our northern army's work,
Encamp'd before beleaguer'd York;
Thy horse with valiant Fairfax lay,
And must have fought—how went the
    day?"

XII.

" Wouldst hear the tale?—On Marston
    heath⁵
Met, front to front, the ranks of death;
Flourish'd the trumpets fierce, and now
Fired was each eye, and flush'd each brow;
On either side loud clamours ring,
' God and the Cause!'—' God and the
    King!'
Right English all, they rush'd to blows,
With nought to win, and all to lose.
I could have laugh'd—but lack'd the
    time—
To see, in phrenesy sublime,
How the fierce zealots fought and bled,
For king or state, as humour led
Some for a dream of public good,
Some for church-tippet, gown and hood,

Draining their veins, in death to claim
A patriot's or a martyr's name.—
Led Bertram Risingham the hearts,
That counter'd there on adverse parts,
No superstitious fool had I
Sought El Dorados in the sky!
Chili had heard me through her states,
And Lima oped her silver gates,
Rich Mexico I had march'd through,
And sack'd the splendours of Peru,
Till sunk Pizarro's daring name,
And, Cortez, thine, in Bertram's fame."—
" Still from the purpose wilt thou stray!
Good gentle friend, how went the day?"—

XIII.

" Good am I deem'd at trumpet-sound,
And good where goblets dance the round,
Though gentle ne'er was join'd, till now,
With rugged Bertram's breast and
    brow.—
But I resume. The battle's rage
Was like the strife which currents wage,
Where Orinoco, in his pride,
Rolls to the main no tribute tide,
But 'gainst broad ocean urges far
A rival sea of roaring war;
While, in ten thousand eddies driven,
The billows fling their foam to heaven,
And the pale pilot seeks in vain,
Where rolls the river, where the main.
Even thus upon the bloody field,
The eddying tides of conflict wheel'd
Ambiguous, till that heart of flame,
Hot Rupert, on our squadrons came,
Hurling against our spears a line
Of gallants, fiery as their wine;
Then ours, though stubborn in their zeal,
In zeal's despite began to reel.
What wouldst thou more?—in tumult
    tost,
Our leaders fell, our ranks were lost.
A thousand men, who drew the sword
For both the Houses and the Word,
Preach'd forth from hamlet, grange, and
    down,
To curb the crosier and the crown,
Now, stark and stiff, lie stretch'd in gore,
And ne'er shall rail at mitre more.—

Thus fared it, when I left the fight,
With the good Cause and Commons'
    right."—

XIV.

" Disastrous news!" dark Wycliffe said;
Assumed despondence bent his head,
While troubled joy was in his eye,
The well-feign'd sorrow to belie.—
" Disastrous news!—when needed most,
Told ye not that your chiefs were lost?
Complete the woful tale and say,
Who fell upon that fatal day;
What leaders of repute and name
Bought by their death a deathless fame.
If such my direst foeman's doom,
My tears shall dew his honour'd tomb.—
No answer?—Friend, of all our host,
Thou know'st whom I should hate the
    most,
Whom thou, too, once wert wont to
    hate,
Yet leavest me doubtful of his fate."
With look unmoved,—" Of friend or foe,
Aught," answer'd Bertram, " would'st
    thou know
Demand in simple terms and plain,
A soldier's answer shalt thou gain;—
For question dark, or riddle high,
I have nor judgment nor reply."

XV.

The wrath his art and fear suppress'd,
Now blazed at once in Wycliffe's breast;
And brave, from man so meanly born,
Roused his hereditary scorn.
" Wretch! hast thou paid thy bloody
    debt?
PHILIP OF MORTHAM, lives he yet?
False to thy patron or thine oath,
Trait'rous or perjured, one or both.
Slave! hast thou kept thy promise plight,
To slay thy leader in the fight?"—
Then from his seat the soldier sprung,
And Wycliffe's hand he strongly wrung;
His grasp, as hard as glove of mail,
Forced the red blood-drop from the nail—
" A health!" he cried; and, ere he quaff'd,
Flung from him Wycliffe's hand, and
    laugh'd:

—"Now, Oswald Wycliffe, speaks thy
    heart!
Now play'st thou well thy genuine part!
Worthy, but for thy craven fear,
Like me to roam a bucanier.
What reck'st thou of the Cause divine,
If Mortham's wealth and lands be thine?
What carest thou for beleaguer'd York,
If this good hand have done its work?
Or what, though Fairfax and his best
Are reddening Marston's swarthy breast,
If Philip Mortham with them lie,
Lending his life-blood to the dye?—
Sit, then! and as 'mid comrades free
Carousing after victory,
When tales are told of blood and fear,
That boys and women shrink to hear,
From point to point I frankly tell
The deed of death as it befell.

XVI.

" When purposed vengeance I forego,
Term me a wretch, nor deem me foe;
And when an insult I forgive,
Then brand me as a slave, and live!—
Philip of Mortham is with those
Whom Bertram Risingham calls foes;
Or whom more sure revenge attends,
If number'd with ungrateful friends.
As was his wont, ere battle glow'd,
Along the marshall'd ranks he rode,
And wore his vizor up the while.
I saw his melancholy smile,
When, full opposed in front, he knew
Where ROKEBY's kindred banner flew.
' And thus,' he said, ' will friends
    divide!'—
I heard, and thought how, side by side,
We two had turn'd the battle's tide,
In many a well-debated field,
Where Bertram's breast was Philip's
    shield.
I thought on Darien's deserts pale,
Where death bestrides the evening gale,
How o'er my friend my cloak I threw,
And fenceless faced the deadly dew;
I thought on Quariana's cliff,
Where, rescued from our foundering skiff,
Through the white breakers' wrath I bore
Exhausted Mortham to the shore;

And when his side an arrow found,
I suck'd the Indian's venom'd wound.
These thoughts like torrents rush'd along,
To sweep away my purpose strong.

XVII.

" Hearts are not flint, and flints are rent;
Hearts are not steel, and steel is bent.
When Mortham bade me, as of yore,
Be near him in the battle's roar,
I scarcely saw the spears laid low,
I scarcely heard the trumpets blow;
Lost was the war in inward strife,
Debating Mortham's death or life.
'Twas then I thought, how, lured to
    come,
As partner of his wealth and home,
Years of piratic wandering o'er,
With him I sought our native shore.
But Mortham's lord grew far estranged
From the bold heart with whom he
    ranged;
Doubts, horrors, superstitious fears,
Sadden'd and dimm'd descending years;
The wily priests their victim sought,
And damn'd each free-born deed and
    thought.
Then must I seek another home,
My license shook his sober dome;
If gold he gave, in one wild day
I revell'd thrice the sum away.
An idle outcast then I stray'd,
Unfit for tillage or for trade.
Deem'd, like the steel of rusted lance,
Useless and dangerous at once.
The women fear'd my hardy look,
At my approach the peaceful shook;
The merchant saw my glance of flame,
And lock'd his hoards when Bertram
    came;
Each child of coward peace kept far
From the neglected son of war.

XVIII.

" But civil discord gave the call,
And made my trade the trade of all.
By Mortham urged, I came again
His vassals to the fight to train.
What guerdon waited on my care?
I could not cant of creed or prayer;

Sour fanatics each trust obtain'd,
And I, dishonour'd and disdain'd,
Gain'd but the high and happy lot,
In these poor arms to front the shot!—
All this thou know'st, thy gestures tell;
Yet hear it o'er, and mark it well.
'Tis honour bids me now relate
Each circumstance of Mortham's fate.

XIX.

"Thoughts, from the tongue that slowly part,
Glance quick as lightning through the heart.
As my spur press'd my courser's side,
Philip of Mortham's cause was tried,
And, ere the charging squadrons mix'd,
His plea was cast, his doom was fix'd.
I watch'd him through the doubtful fray,
That changed as March's moody day,
Till, like a stream that bursts its bank,
Fierce Rupert thunder'd on our flank.
'Twas then, 'midst tumult, smoke, and strife,
Where each man fought for death or life,
'Twas then I fired my petronel,
And Mortham, steed and rider, fell.
One dying look he upward cast,
Of wrath and anguish—'twas his last.
Think not that there I stopp'd, to view
What of the battle should ensue;
But ere I clear'd that bloody press,
Our northern horse ran masterless;
Monckton and Mitton told the news,
How troops of roundheads choked the Ouse,
And many a bonny Scot, aghast,
Spurring his palfrey northward, past,
Cursing the day when zeal or meed
First lured their Lesley o'er the Tweed.[6]
Yet when I reach'd the banks of Swale,
Had rumour learn'd another tale;
With his barb'd horse, fresh tidings say,
Stout Cromwell has redeem'd the day:[7]
But whether false the news, or true,
Oswald, I reck as light as you."

XX.

Not then by Wycliffe might be shown,
How his pride startled at the tone

In which his complice, fierce and free,
Asserted guilt's equality.
In smoothest terms his speech he wove,
Of endless friendship, faith, and love;
Promised and vow'd in courteous sort,
But Bertram broke professions short.
"Wycliffe, be sure not here I stay,
No, scarcely till the rising day;
Warn'd by the legends of my youth,
I trust not an associate's truth.
Do not my native dales prolong
Of Percy Rede the tragic song,
Train'd forward to his bloody fall,
By Girsonfield, that treacherous Hall?[8]
Oft, by the Pringle's haunted side,
The shepherd sees his spectre glide.
And near the spot that gave me name,
The moated mound of Risingham,
Where Reed upon her margin sees
Sweet Woodburne's cottages and trees,
Some ancient sculptor's art has shown
An outlaw's image on the stone;[9]
Unmatch'd in strength, a giant he,
With quiver'd back, and kirtled knee.
Ask how he died, that hunter bold,
The tameless monarch of the wold,
And age and infancy can tell,
By brother's treachery he fell.
Thus warn'd by legends of my youth,
I trust to no associate's truth.

XXI.

"When last we reason'd of this deed,
Nought, I bethink me, was agreed,
Or by what rule, or when, or where,
The wealth of Mortham we should share
Then list, while I the portion name,
Our differing laws give each to claim.
Thou, vassal sworn to England's throne,
Her rules of heritage must own;
They deal thee, as to nearest heir,
Thy kinsman's lands and livings fair,
And these I yield:—do thou revere
The statutes of the Bucanier.[10]
Friend to the sea, and foeman sworn
To all that on her waves are borne,
When falls a mate in battle broil,
His comrade heirs his portion'd spoil;
When dies in fight a daring foe,
He claims his wealth who struck the blow;

And either rule to me assigns
Those spoils of Indian seas and mines,
Hoarded in Mortham's caverns dark ;
Ingot of gold and diamond spark,
Chalice and plate from churches borne,
And gems from shrieking beauty torn,
Each string of pearl, each silver bar,
And all the wealth of western war.
I go to search, where, dark and deep,
Those Trans-atlantic treasures sleep.
Thou must along—for, lacking thee,
The heir will scarce find entrance free ;
And then farewell.   I haste to try
Each varied pleasure wealth can buy ;
When cloyed each wish, those wars afford
Fresh work for Bertram's restless sword."

XXII.

An undecided answer hung
On Oswald's hesitating tongue.
Despite his craft, he heard with awe
This ruffian stabber fix the law ;
While his own troubled passions veer
Through hatred, joy, regret, and fear :—
Joy'd at the soul that Bertram flies,
He grudged the murderer's mighty prize,
Hated his pride's presumptuous tone,
And fear'd to wend with him alone.
At length, that middle course to steer,
To cowardice and craft so dear,
" His charge," he said, " would ill allow
His absence from the fortress now ;
WILFRID on Bertram should attend,
His son should journey with his friend."

XXIII.

Contempt kept Bertram's anger down,
And wreathed to savage smile his frown.
" Wilfrid, or thou—'tis one to me,
Whichever bears the golden key.
Yet think not but I mark, and smile
To mark, thy poor and selfish wile !
It injury from me you fear,
What, Oswald Wycliffe, shields thee
    here ?
I've sprung from walls more high than
    these,
I've swam through deeper streams than
    Tees.

Might I not stab thee, ere one yell
Could rouse the distant sentinel ?
Start not—it is not my design,
But, if it were, weak fence were thine ;
And, trust me, that, in time of need,
This hand hath done more desperate deed.
Go, haste and rouse thy slumbering son ;
Time calls, and I must needs be gone."

XXIV.

Nought of his sire's ungenerous part
Polluted Wilfrid's gentle heart ;
A heart too soft from early life
To hold with fortune needful strife.
His sire, while yet a hardier race
Of numerous sons were Wycliffe's grace,
On Wilfrid set contemptuous brand,
For feeble heart and forceless hand ;
But a fond mother's care and joy
Were centred in her sickly boy.
No touch of childhood's frolic mood
Show'd the elastic spring of blood ;
Hour after hour he loved to pore
On Shakspeare's rich and varied lore,
But turn'd from martial scenes and light,
From Falstaff's feast and Percy's fight,
To ponder Jaques' moral strain,
And muse with Hamlet, wise in vain ;
And weep himself to soft repose
O'er gentle Desdemona's woes.

XXV.

In youth he sought not pleasures found
By youth in horse, and hawk, and hound,
But loved the quiet joys that wake
By lonely stream and silent lake ;
In Deepdale's solitude to lie,
Where all is cliff and copse and sky ;
To climb Catcastle's dizzy peak,
Or lone Pendragon's mound to seek.
Such was his wont ; and there his dream
Soar'd on some wild fantastic theme,
Of faithful love, or ceaseless spring,
Till Contemplation's wearied wing
The enthusiast could no more sustain,
And sad he sunk to earth again.

XXVI.

He loved—as many a lay can tell,
Preserved in Stanmore's lonely dell ;

For his was minstrel's skill, he caught
The art unteachable, untaught;
He loved—his soul did nature frame
For love, and fancy nursed the flame;
Vainly he loved—for seldom swain
Of such soft mould is loved again ;
Silent he loved—in every gaze
Was passion, friendship in his phrase.
So mused his life away—till died
His brethren all, their father's pride.
Wilfrid is now the only heir
Of all his stratagems and care,
And destined, darkling, to pursue
Ambition's maze by Oswald's clue.

XXVII.

Wilfrid must love and woo the bright
Matilda, heir of Rokeby's knight.
To love her was an easy hest,
The secret empress of his breast;
To woo her was a harder task
To one that durst not hope or ask.
Yet all Matilda could, she gave
In pity to her gentle slave ;
Friendship, esteem, and fair regard,
And praise, the poet's best reward !
She read the tales his taste approved,
And sung the lays he framed or loved ;
Yet, loth to nurse the fatal flame
Of hopeless love in friendship's name,
In kind caprice she oft withdrew
The favouring glance to friendship due,
Then grieved to see her victim's pain,
And gave the dangerous smiles again.

XXVIII.

So did the suit of Wilfrid stand,
When war's loud summons waked the land.
Three banners, floating o'er the Tees,
The wo-forboding peasant sees ;
In concert oft they braved of old
The bordering Scot's incursion bold ;
Frowning defiance in their pride,
Their vassals now and lords divide.
From his fair hall on Greta banks,
The Knight of Rokeby led his ranks,
To aid the valiant northern Earls,
Who drew the sword for royal Charles.
Mortham, by marriage near allied,—
His sister had been Rokeby's bride,

Though long before the civil fray,
In peaceful grave the lady lay,—
Philip of Mortham raised his band,
And march'd at Fairfax's command ;
While Wycliffe, bound by many a train
Of kindred art with wily Vane,
Less prompt to brave the bloody field,
Made Barnard's battlements his shield,
Secured them with his Lunedale powers,
And for the Commons held the towers.

XXIX.

The lovely heir of Rokeby's Knight
Waits in his halls the event of fight ;
For England's war revered the claim
Of every unprotected name,
And spared, amid its fiercest rage,
Childhood and womanhood and age.
But Wilfrid, son to Rokeby's foe,
Must the dear privilege forego,
By Greta's side, in evening grey,
To steal upon Matilda's way,
Striving, with fond hypocrisy,
For careless step and vacant eye ;
Calming each anxious look and glance,
To give the meeting all to chance,
Or framing, as a fair excuse,
The book, the pencil, or the muse :
Something to give, to sing, to say,
Some modern tale, some ancient lay.
Then, while the long'd-for minutes last,—
Ah ! minutes quickly over-past !
Recording each expression free,
Of kind or careless courtesy,
Each friendly look, each softer tone,
As food for fancy when alone.
All this is o'er—but still unseen,
Wilfrid may lurk in Eastwood green,
To watch Matilda's wonted round,
While springs his heart at every sound.
She comes !—'tis but a passing sight,
Yet serves to cheat his weary night ;
She comes not—He will wait the hour,
When her lamp lightens in the tower ;
'Tis something yet, if, as she past,
Her shade is o'er the lattice cast.
" What is my life, my hope?" he said ;
" Alas ! a transitory shade."

XXX.

Thus wore his life, though reason strove
For mastery in vain with love,
Forcing upon his thoughts the sum
Of present woe and ills to come,
While still he turn'd impatient ear
From Truth's intrusive voice severe.
Gentle, indifferent, and subdued,
In all but this, unmoved he view'd
Each outward change of ill and good:
But Wilfrid, docile, soft, and mild,
Was Fancy's spoil'd and wayward child;
In her bright car she bade him ride,
With one fair form to grace his side,
Or, in some wild and lone retreat,
Flung her high spells around his seat,
Bathed in her dews his languid head,
Her fairy mantle o'er him spread,
For him her opiates gave to flow,
Which he who tastes can ne'er forego,
And placed him in her circle, free
From every stern reality,
Till, to the Visionary, seem
Her day-dreams truth, and truth a dream.

XXXI.

Woe to the youth whom fancy gains,
Winning from Reason's hand the reins,
Pity and woe! for such a mind
Is soft, contemplative, and kind;
And woe to those who train such youth,
And spare to press the rights of truth,
The mind to strengthen and anneal,
While on the stithy glows the steel!
O teach him, while your lessons last,
To judge the present by the past;
Remind him of each wish pursued,
How rich it glow'd with promised good;
Remind him of each wish enjoy'd,
How soon his hopes possession cloy'd!
Tell him, we play unequal game,
Whene'er we shoot by Fancy's aim;
And, ere he strip him for her race,
Show the conditions of the chase.
Two sisters by the goal are set,
Cold Disappointment and Regret;
One disenchants the winner's eyes,
And strips of all its worth the prize.

While one augments its gaudy show,
More to enhance the loser's woe.
The victor sees his fairy gold,
Transform'd, when won, to drossy mold,
But still the vanquish'd mourns his loss,
And rues, as gold, that glittering dross.

XXXII.

More wouldst thou know—yon tower survey,
Yon couch unpress'd since parting day,
Yon untrimm'd lamp, whose yellow gleam
Is mingling with the cold moonbeam,
And yon thin form!—the hectic red
On his pale cheek unequal spread;
The head reclined, the loosen'd hair,
The limbs relax'd, the mournful air.—
See, he looks up;—a woful smile
Lightens his wo-worn cheek a while,—
'Tis fancy wakes some idle thought,
To gild the ruin she has wrought;
For, like the bat of Indian brakes,
Her pinions fan the wound she makes,
And soothing thus the dreamer's pain,
She drinks his life-blood from the vein.
Now to the lattice turn his eyes,
Vain hope! to see the sun arise.
The moon with clouds is still o'ercast,
Still howls by fits the stormy blast;
Another hour must wear away,
Ere the East kindle into day,
And hark! to waste that weary hour,
He tries the minstrel's magic power.

XXXIII.

Song.

TO THE MOON.

Hail to thy cold and clouded beam,
  Pale pilgrim of the troubled sky!
Hail, though the mists that o'er thee stream
  Lend to thy brow their sullen dye!
How should thy pure and peaceful eye
  Untroubled view our scenes below,
Or how a tearless beam supply
  To light a world of war and woe!

Fair Queen! I will not blame thee now,
  As once by Greta's fairy side

Each little cloud that dimm'd thy brow
　Did then an angel's beauty hide.
And of the shades I then could chide,
　Still are the thoughts to memory dear,
For, while a softer strain I tried,
　They hid my blush, and calm'd my fear.

Then did I swear thy ray serene
　Was form'd to light some lonely dell,
By two fond lovers only seen,
　Reflected from the crystal well,
　Or sleeping on their mossy cell,
　Or quivering on the lattice bright,
Or glancing on their couch, to tell
　How swiftly wanes the summer night!

XXXIV.

He starts—a step at this lone hour!
A voice!—his father seeks the tower,
With haggard look and troubled sense,
Fresh from his dreadful conference.
" Wilfrid!—what, not to sleep address'd?
Thou hast no cares to chase thy rest.
Mortham has fall'n on Marston-moor;
Bertram brings warrant to secure
His treasures, bought by spoil and blood,
For the State's use and public good.
The menials will thy voice obey;
Let his commission have its way,
In every point, in every word."—
Then, in a whisper,—" Take thy sword!
Bertram is—what I must not tell.
I hear his hasty step—farewell!"

CANTO SECOND.

I.

FAR in the chambers of the west,
The gale had sigh'd itself to rest;
The moon was cloudless now and clear,
But pale, and soon to disappear.
The thin grey clouds wax dimly light
On Brusleton and Houghton height;
And the rich dale, that eastward lay,
Waited the wakening touch of day,
To give its woods and cultured plain,
And towers and spires, to light again.

But, westward, Stanmore's shapeless swell,
And Lunedale wild, and Kelton-fell,
And rock-begirdled Gilmanscar,
And Arkingarth, lay dark afar;
While, as a livelier twilight falls,
Emerge proud Barnard's banner'd walls.
High crown'd he sits, in dawning pale,
The sovereign of the lovely vale.

II.

What prospects, from his watch-tower
　high,
Gleam gradual on the warder's eye!—
Far sweeping to the east, he sees
Down his deep woods the course of Tees,[11]
And tracks his wanderings by the steam
Of summer vapours from the stream;
And ere he paced his destined hour
By Brackenbury's dungeon-tower,
These silver mists shall melt away,
And dew the woods with glittering spray.
Then in broad lustre shall be shown
That mighty trench of living stone,
And each huge trunk that, from the side,
Reclines him o'er the darksome tide,
Where Tees, full many a fathom low,
Wears with his rage no common foe;
For pebbly bank, nor sand-bed here,
Nor clay-mound, checks his fierce career,
Condemn'd to mine a channell'd way,
O'er solid sheets of marble grey.

III.

Nor Tees alone, in dawning bright,
Shall rush upon the ravish'd sight;
But many a tributary stream
Each from its own dark dell shall gleam:
Staindrop, who, from her silvan bowers,
Salutes proud Raby's battled towers;
The rural brook of Egliston,
And Balder, named from Odin's son;
And Greta, to whose banks ere long
We lead the lovers of the song;
And silver Lune, from Stanmore wild,
And fairy Thorsgill's murmuring child,
And last and least, but loveliest still,
Romantic Deepdale's slender rill.
Who in that dim-wood glen hath stray'd,
Yet long'd for Roslin's magic glade?

Who, wandering there, hath sought to
 change
Even for that vale so stern and strange,
Where Cartland's Crags, fantastic rent,
Through her green copse like spires are
 sent?
Yet, Albin, yet the praise be thine,
Thy scenes and story to combine!
Thou bid'st him, who by Roslin strays,
List to the deeds of other days;
'Mid Cartland's Crags thou show'st the
 cave,
The refuge of thy champion brave;
Giving each rock its storied tale,
Pouring a lay for every dale,
Knitting, as with a moral band,
Thy native legends with thy land,
To lend each scene the interest high
Which genius beams from Beauty's eye.

IV.

Bertram awaited not the sight
Which sun-rise shows from Barnard's
 height,
But from the towers, preventing day,
With Wilfrid took his early way,
While misty dawn, and moonbeam pale,
Still mingled in the silent dale.
By Barnard's bridge of stately stone,
The southern bank of Tees they won;
Their winding path then eastward cast,
And Egliston's grey ruins pass'd;[12]
Each on his own deep visions bent,
Silent and sad they onward went.
Well may you think that Bertram's mood,
To Wilfrid savage seem'd and rude;
Well may you think bold Risingham
Held Wilfrid trivial, poor, and tame;
And small the intercourse, I ween,
Such uncongenial souls between.

V.

Stern Bertram shunn'd the nearer way,
Through Rokeby's park and chase that
 lay,
And, skirting high the valley's ridge,
They cross'd by Greta's ancient bridge,
Descending where her waters wind
Free for a space and unconfined,

As, 'scaped from Brignall's dark-wood
 glen,
She seeks wild Mortham's deeper den.
There, as his eye glanced o'er the mound,
Raised by that Legion[13] long renown'd,
Whose votive shrine asserts their claim,
Of pious, faithful, conquering fame,
" Stern sons of war!" sad Wilfrid sigh'd,
" Behold the boast of Roman pride!
What now of all your toils are known?
A grassy trench, a broken stone!"—
This to himself; for moral strain
To Bertram were address'd in vain.

VI.

Of different mood, a deeper sigh
Awoke, when Rokeby's turrets high[14]
Were northward in the dawning seen
To rear them o'er the thicket green.
O then, though Spenser's self had stray'd
Beside him through the lovely glade,
Lending his rich luxuriant glow
Of fancy, all its charms to show,
Pointing the stream rejoicing free,
As captive set at liberty,
Flashing her sparkling waves abroad,
And clamouring joyful on her road;
Pointing where, up the sunny banks,
The trees retire in scatter'd ranks,
Save where, advanced before the rest,
On knoll or hillock rears his crest,
Lonely and huge, the giant Oak,
As champions, when their band is broke,
Stand forth to guard the rearward post,
The bulwark of the scatter'd host—
All this, and more, might Spenser say,
Yet waste in vain his magic lay,
While Wilfrid eyed the distant tower,
Whose lattice lights Matilda's bower.

VII.

The open vale is soon passed o'er,
Rokeby, though nigh, is seen no more;
Sinking 'mid Greta's thickets deep,
A wild and darker course they keep,
A stern and lone, yet lovely road,
As e'er the foot of Minstrel trode![15]
Broad shadows o'er their passage fell,
Deeper and narrower grew the dell;

It seem'd some mountain, rent and riven,
A channel for the stream had given,
So high the cliffs of limestone grey
Hung beetling o'er the torrent's way,
Yielding, along their rugged base,
A flinty footpath's niggard space,
Where he, who winds 'twixt rock and
    wave,
May hear the headlong torrent rave,
And like a steed in frantic fit,
That flings the froth from curb and bit,
May view her chafe her waves to spray,
O'er every rock that bars her way,
Till foam-globes on her eddies ride,
Thick as the schemes of human pride
That down life's current drive amain,
As frail, as frothy, and as vain!

VIII.

The cliffs that rear their haughty head
High o'er the river's darksome bed,
Were now all naked, wild, and grey,
Now waving all with greenwood spray;
Here trees to every crevice clung,
And o'er the dell their branches hung;
And there, all splinter'd and uneven,
The shiver'd rocks ascend to heaven;
Oft, too, the ivy swath'd their breast,
And wreathed its garland round their crest,
Or from the spires bade loosely flare
Its tendrils in the middle air.
As pennons wont to wave of old
O'er the high feast of Baron bold,
When revell'd loud the feudal rout,
And the arch'd halls return'd their shout;
Such and more wild is Greta's roar,
And such the echoes from her shore,
And so the ivied banners' gleam,
Waved wildly o'er the brawling stream.

IX.

Now from the stream the rocks recede,
But leave between no sunny mead,
No, nor the spot of pebbly sand,
Oft found by such a mountain strand;
Forming such warm and dry retreat,
As fancy deems the lonely seat,
Where hermit wandering from his cell,
His rosary might love to tell.

But here, 'twixt rock and river, grew
A dismal grove of sable yew,
With whose sad tints were mingled seen
The blighted fir's sepulchral green.
Seem'd that the trees their shadows cast,
The earth that nourish'd them to blast;
For never knew that swarthy grove
The verdant hue that fairies love;
Nor wilding green, nor woodland flower,
Arose within its baleful bower:
The dank and sable earth receives
Its only carpet from the leaves,
That, from the withering branches cast,
Bestrew'd the ground with every blast.
Though now the sun was o'er the hill,
In this dark spot 'twas twilight still,
Save that on Greta's farther side
Some straggling beams through copse-
    wood glide;
And wild and savage contrast made
That dingle's deep and funeral shade,
With the bright tints of early day,
Which, glimmering through the ivy spray,
On the opposing summit lay.

X.

The lated peasant shunn'd the dell;
For Superstition wont to tell
Of many a grisly sound and sight,
Scaring its path at dead of night.
When Christmas logs blaze high and wide,
Such wonders speed the festal tide;
While Curiosity and Fear,
Pleasure and Pain, sit crouching near,
Till childhood's cheek no longer glows,
And village maidens lose the rose.
The thrilling interest rises higher,
The circle closes nigh and nigher,
And shuddering glance is cast behind,
As louder moans the wintry wind.
Believe, that fitting scene was laid
For such wild tales in Mortham glade;
For who had seen, on Greta's side,
By that dim light fierce Bertram stride,
In such a spot, at such an hour,—
If touch'd by Superstition's power,
Might well have deem'd that Hell had
    given
A murderer's ghost to upper Heaven,

While Wilfrid's form had seem'd to glide
Like his pale victim by his side.

XI.

Nor think to village swains alone
Are these unearthly terrors known;
For not to rank nor sex confined
Is this vain ague of the mind:
Hearts firm as steel, as marble hard,
'Gainst faith, and love, and pity barr'd,
Have quaked, like aspen leaves in May,
Beneath its universal sway.
Bertram had listed many a tale
Of wonder in his native dale,
That in his secret soul retain'd
The credence they in childhood gain'd:
Nor less his wild adventurous youth
Believed in every legend's truth;
Learn'd when, beneath the tropic gale,
Full swell'd the vessel's steady sail,
And the broad Indian moon her light
Pour'd on the watch of middle night,
When seamen love to hear and tell
Of portent, prodigy, and spell:
What gales are sold on Lapland's shore,
How whistle rash bids tempests roar,[16]
Of witch, of mermaid, and of sprite,
Of Erick's cap and Elmo's light;[17]
Or of that Phantom Ship, whose form
Shoots like a meteor through the storm;
When the dark scud comes driving hard,
And lower'd is every topsail yard,
And canvass, wove in earthly looms,
No more to brave the storm presumes!
Then, 'mid the war of sea and sky,
Top and top-gallant hoisted high,
Full spread and crowded every sail,
The Demon Frigate braves the gale;[18]
And well the doom'd spectators know
The harbinger of wreck and woe.

XII.

Then, too, were told, in stifled tone,
Marvels and omens all their own;
How, by some desert isle or key,[19]
Where Spaniards wrought their cruelty,
Or where the savage pirate's mood
Repaid it home in deeds of blood,
Strange nightly sounds of woe and fear
Appall'd the listening Bucanier,

Whose light-arm'd shallop anchor'd lay
In ambush by the lonely bay.
The groan of grief, the shriek of pain
Ring from the moonlight groves of cane;
The fierce adventurer's heart they scare,
Who wearies memory for a prayer,
Curses the road-stead, and with gale
Of early morning lifts the sail,
To give, in thirst of blood and prey,
A legend for another bay.

XIII.

Thus, as a man, a youth, a child,
Train'd in the mystic and the wild,
With this on Bertram's soul at times
Rush'd a dark feeling of his crimes;
Such to his troubled soul their form,
As the pale Death-ship to the storm,
And such their omen dim and dread,
As shrieks and voices of the dead,—
That pang, whose transitory force
Hover'd 'twixt horror and remorse;
That pang, perchance, his bosom press'd,
As Wilfrid sudden he address'd:—
" Wilfrid, this glen is never trode
Until the sun rides high abroad;
Yet twice have I beheld to-day
A Form, that seem'd to dog our way;
Twice from my glance it seem'd to flee,
And shroud itself by cliff or tree.
How think'st thou?—Is our path way-laid?
Or hath thy sire my trust betray'd?
If so"——Ere, starting from his dream,
That turn'd upon a gentler theme,
Wilfrid had roused him to reply,
Bertram sprung forward, shouting high,
"Whate'er thou art, thou now shalt
        stand!"
And forth he darted, sword in hand.

XIV.

As bursts the levin in his wrath,
He shot him down the sounding path;
Rock, wood, and stream, rang wildly out,
To his loud step and savage shout.
Seems that the object of his race
Hath scaled the cliffs; his frantic chase
Sidelong he turns, and now 'tis bent
Right up the rock's tall battlement;

Straining each sinew to ascend,
Foot, hand, and knee, their aid must lend.
Wilfrid, all dizzy with dismay,
Views from beneath, his dreadful way:
Now to the oak's warp'd roots he clings,
Now trusts his weight to ivy strings,
Now, like the wild-goat, must he dare
An unsupported leap in air;
Hid in the shrubby rain-course now,
You mark him by the crashing bough.
And by his corslet's sullen clank,
And by the stones spurn'd from the bank,
And by the hawk scared from her nest,
And ravens croaking o'er their guest,
Who deem his forfeit limbs shall pay
The tribute of his bold essay.

XV.

See! he emerges!—desperate now
All farther course—Yon beetling brow,
In craggy nakedness sublime,
What heart or foot shall dare to climb?
It bears no tendril for his clasp,
Presents no angle to his grasp:
Sole stay his foot may rest upon,
Is yon earth-bedded jetting stone.
Balanced on such precarious prop,
He strains his grasp to reach the top.
Just as the dangerous stretch he makes,
By Heaven, his faithless footstool shakes!
Beneath his tottering bulk it bends,
It sways, . . it loosens, . . it descends!
And downward holds its headlong way,
Crashing o'er rock and copsewood spray.
Loud thunders shake the echoing dell!—
Fell it alone?—alone it fell.
Just on the very verge of fate,
The hardy Bertram's falling weight
He trusted to his sinewy hands,
And on the top unharm'd he stands!—

XVI.

Wilfrid a safer path pursued;
At intervals where, roughly hew'd,
Rude steps ascending from the dell
Render'd the cliffs accessible.
By circuit slow he thus attain'd
The height that Risingham had gain'd,
And when he issued from the wood,
Before the gate of Mortham stood.[20]

'Twas a fair scene! the sunbeam lay
On battled tower and portal grey:
And from the grassy slope he sees
The Greta flow to meet the Tees;
Where, issuing from her darksome bed,
She caught the morning's eastern red,
And through the softening vale below
Roll'd her bright waves, in rosy glow,
All blushing to her bridal bed,
Like some shy maid in convent bred;
While linnet, lark, and blackbird gay,
Sing forth her nuptial roundelay.

XVII.

'Twas sweetly sung that roundelay;
That summer morn shone blithe and gay;
But morning beam, and wild-bird's call,
Awaked not Mortham's silent hall.
No porter, by the low-brow'd gate,
Took in the wonted niche his seat;
To the paved court no peasant drew;
Waked to their toil no menial crew;
The maiden's carol was not heard,
As to her morning task she fared:
In the void offices around,
Rung not a hoof, nor bay'd a hound;
Nor eager steed, with shrilling neigh,
Accused the lagging groom's delay;
Untrimm'd, undress'd, neglected now,
Was alley'd walk and orchard bough;
All spoke the master's absent care,
All spoke neglect and disrepair.
South of the gate, an arrow flight,
Two mighty elms their limbs unite,
As if a canopy to spread
O'er the lone dwelling of the dead;
For their huge boughs in arches bent
Above a massive monument,
Carved o'er in ancient Gothic wise,
With many a scutcheon and device;
There, spent with toil and sunk in gloom,
Bertram stood pondering by the tomb.

XVIII.

" It vanish'd, like a flitting ghost!
Behind this tomb," he said, " 'twas lost—
This tomb, where oft I deem'd lies stored
Of Mortham's Indian wealth the hoard.
'Tis true, the aged servants said
Here his lamented wife is laid;

But weightier reasons may be guess'd
For their lord's strict and stern behest,
That none should on his steps intrude,
Whene'er he sought this solitude.—
An ancient mariner I knew,
What time I sail'd with Morgan's crew,
Who oft, 'mid our carousals, spake
Of Raleigh, Frobisher, and Drake;
Adventurous hearts! who barter'd, bold,
Their English steel for Spanish gold.
Trust not, would his experience say,
Captain or comrade with your prey;
But seek some charnel, when, at full,
The moon gilds skeleton and skull·
There dig, and tomb your precious heap;
And bid the dead your treasure keep;[1]
Sure stewards they, if fitting spell
Their service to the task compel.
Lacks there such charnel?—kill a slave,
Or prisoner, on the treasure-grave;
And bid his discontented ghost
Stalk nightly on his lonely post.—
Such was his tale. Its truth, I ween,
Is in my morning vision seen."—

XIX.

Wilfrid, who scorn'd the legend wild,
In mingled mirth and pity smiled,
Much marvelling that a breast so bold
In such fond tale belief should hold;
But yet of Bertram sought to know
The apparition's form and show.—
The power within the guilty breast,
Oft vanquish'd, never quite suppress'd,
That unsubdued and lurking lies
To take the felon by surprise,
And force him, as by magic spell,
In his despite his guilt to tell,—[22]
That power in Bertram's breast awoke;
Scarce conscious he was heard, he spoke;
" 'Twas Mortham's form, from foot to
    head!
His morion, with the plume of red,
His shape, his mien—'twas Mortham, right
As when I slew him in the fight."—
" Thou slay him?—thou?"—With con-
    scious start
He heard, then mann'd his haughty heart—
" I slew him?—I!—I had forgot
Thou, stripling, knew'st not of the plot.

But it is spoken—nor will I
Deed done, or spoken word, deny.
I slew him; I! for thankless pride;
'Twas by this hand that Mortham died

XX.

Wilfrid, of gentle hand and heart,
Averse to every active part,
But most averse to martial broil,
From danger shrunk, and turn'd from toil,
Yet the meek lover of the lyre
Nursed one brave spark of noble fire,
Against injustice, fraud, or wrong,
His blood beat high, his hand wax'd strong.
Not his the nerves that could sustain
Unshaken, danger, toil, and pain;
But, when that spark blazed forth to flame,
He rose superior to his frame.
And now it came, that generous mood:
And, in full current of his blood,
On Bertram he laid desperate hand,
Placed firm his foot, and drew his brand.
" Should every fiend, to whom thou'rt
    sold,
Rise in thine aid, I keep my hold.—
Arouse there, ho! take spear and sword!
Attach the murderer of your Lord!"

XXI.

A moment, fix'd as by a spell,
Stood Bertram—It seem'd miracle,
That one so feeble, soft, and tame
Set grasp on warlike Risingham.
But when he felt a feeble stroke,
The fiend within the ruffian woke!
To wrench the sword from Wilfrid's
    hand,
To dash him headlong on the sand,
Was but one moment's work,—one more
Had drench'd the blade in Wilfrid's gore;
But, in the instant it arose,
To end his life, his love, his woes,
A warlike form, that mark'd the scene,
Presents his rapier sheathed between,
Parries the fast-descending blow,
And steps 'twixt Wilfrid and his foe;
Nor then unscabbarded his brand,
But, sternly pointing with his hand,
With monarch's voice forbade the fight,
And motion'd Bertram from his sight.

" Go, and repent," he said, " while time
Is given thee; add not crime to crime."

XXII.

Mute, and uncertain, and amazed,
As on a vision Bertram gazed !
'Twas Mortham's bearing, bold and high,
His sinewy frame, his falcon eye,
His look and accent of command,
The martial gesture of his hand,
His stately form, spare-built and tall,
His war-bleach'd locks—'twas Mortham
all.
Through Bertram's dizzy brain career
A thousand thoughts, and all of fear;
His wavering faith received not quite
The form he saw as Mortham's sprite,
But more he fear'd it, if it stood
His lord, in living flesh and blood.—
What spectre can the charnel send,
So dreadful as an injured friend ?
Then, too, the habit of command,
Used by the leader of the band,
When Risingham, for many a day,
Had march'd and fought beneath his sway,
Tamed him—and, with reverted face,
Backwards he bore his sullen pace;
Oft stopp'd, and oft on Mortham stared,
And dark as rated mastiff glared;
But when the tramp of steeds was heard,
Plunged in the glen, and disappear'd;—
Nor longer there the warrior stood,
Retiring eastward through the wood;
But first to Wilfrid warning gives,
" Tell thou to none that Mortham lives."

XXIII.

Still rung these words in Wilfrid's ear,
Hinting he knew not what of fear;
When nearer came the coursers' tread,
And, with his father at their head,
Of horsemen arm'd a gallant power
Rein'd up their steeds before the tower.
" Whence these pale looks, my son ?" he
said:
" Where's Bertram?—Why that naked
blade ?"
Wilfrid ambiguously replied,
(For Mortham's charge his honour tied,)

" Bertram is gone—the villain's word
Avouch'd him murderer of his lord !
Even now we fought—but, when your
tread
Announced you nigh, the felon fled."
In Wycliffe's conscious eye appear
A guilty hope, a guilty fear;
On his pale brow the dewdrop broke,
And his lip quiver'd as he spoke:—

XXIV.

" A murderer!—Philip Mortham died
Amid the battle's wildest tide.
Wilfrid, or Bertram raves, or you !
Yet, grant such strange confession true,
Pursuit were vain—let him fly far—
Justice must sleep in civil war."
A gallant Youth rode near his side,
Brave Rokeby's page, in battle tried;
That morn, an embassy of weight
He brought to Barnard's castle gate,
And follow'd now in Wycliffe's train,
An answer for his lord to gain.
His steed, whose arch'd and sable neck
An hundred wreaths of foam bedeck,
Chafed not against the curb more high
Than he at Oswald's cold reply;
He bit his lip, implored his saint,
(His old faith)—then burst restraint.

XXV.

" Yes ! I beheld his bloody fall
By that base traitor's dastard ball,
Just when I thought to measure sword,
Presumptuous hope! with Mortham's lord
And shall the murderer 'scape, who slew
His leader, generous, brave, and true ?
Escape, while on the dew you trace
The marks of his gigantic pace?
No! ere the sun that dew shall dry,
False Risingham shall yield or die.—
Ring out the castle 'larum bell !
Arouse the peasants with the knell !
Meantime disperse—ride, gallants, ride !
Beset the wood on every side.
But if among you one there be,
That honours Mortham's memory,
Let him dismount and follow me !
Else on your crests sit fear and shame,
And foul suspicion dog your name !"

XXVI.

Instant to earth young REDMOND sprung;
Instant on earth the harness rung
Of twenty men of Wycliffe's band,
Who waited not their lord's command.
Redmond his spurs from buskins drew,
His mantle from his shoulders threw,
His pistols in his belt he placed,
The green-wood gain'd, the footsteps
    traced,
Shouted like huntsman to his hounds,
"To cover, hark!"—and in he bounds.
Scarce heard was Oswald's anxious cry,
"Suspicion! yes—pursue him, fly—
But venture not, in useless strife,
On ruffian desperate of his life,
Whoever finds him, shoot him dead!
Five hundred nobles for his head!"

XXVII.

The horsemen gallop'd, to make good
Each path that issued from the wood.
Loud from the thickets rung the shout
Of Redmond and his eager rout;
With them was Wilfrid, stung with ire,
And envying Redmond's martial fire,
And emulous of fame.—But where
Is Oswald, noble Mortham's heir?
He, bound by honour, law, and faith,
Avenger of his kinsman's death?—
Leaning against the elmin tree,
With drooping head and slacken'd knee,
And clenched teeth, and close-clasp'd
    hands,
In agony of soul he stands!
His downcast eye on earth is bent,
His soul to every sound is lent;
For in each shout that cleaves the air,
May ring discovery and despair.

XXVIII.

What vail'd it him, that brightly play'd
The morning sun on Mortham's glade?
All seems in giddy round to ride,
Like objects on a stormy tide,
Seen eddying by the moonlight dim,
Imperfectly to sink and swim.
What 'vail'd it, that the fair domain,
Its battled mansion, hill, and plain,

On which the sun so brightly shone,
Envied so long, was now his own?
The lowest dungeon, in that hour,
Of Brackenbury's dismal tower,[23]
Had been his choice, could such a doom
Have open'd Mortham's bloody tomb!
Forced, too, to turn unwilling ear
To each surmise of hope or fear,
Murmur'd among the rustics round,
Who gather'd at the 'larum sound;
He dared not turn his head away,
E'en to look up to heaven to pray,
Or call on hell, in bitter mood,
For one sharp death-shot from the wood!

XXIX.

At length, o'erpast that dreadful space,
Back straggling came the scatter'd chase:
Jaded and weary, horse and man,
Return'd the troopers one by one.
Wilfrid, the last, arrived to say,
All trace was lost of Bertram's way,
Though Redmond still, up Brignall wood,
The hopeless quest in vain pursued.—
O, fatal doom of human race!
What tyrant passions passions chase!
Remorse from Oswald's brow is gone,
Avarice and pride resume their throne;
The pang of instant terror by,
They dictate thus their slave's reply:—

XXX.

"Ay—let him range like hasty hound!
And if the grim wolf's lair be found,
Small is my care how goes the game
With Redmond, or with Risingham.—
Nay, answer not, thou simple boy!
Thy fair Matilda, all so coy
To thee, is of another mood
To that bold youth of Erin's blood.
Thy ditties will she freely praise,
And pay thy pains with courtly phrase;
In a rough path will oft command—
Accept at least—thy friendly hand;
His she avoids, or, urged and pray'd,
Unwilling takes his proffer'd aid,
While conscious passion plainly speaks
In downcast look and blushing cheeks.
Whene'er he sings, will she glide nigh,
And all her soul is in her eye;

Yet doubts she still to tender free
The wonted words of courtesy.
These are strong signs!—yet wherefore
    sigh,
And wipe, effeminate, thine eye?
Thine shall she be, if thou attend
The counsels of thy sire and friend.

XXXI.

" Scarce wert thou gone, when peep of
    light
Brought genuine news of Marston's fight.
Brave Cromwell turn'd the doubtful tide,
And conquest bless'd the rightful side;
Three thousand cavaliers lie dead,
Rupert and that bold Marquis fled;
Nobles and knights, so proud of late,
Must fine for freedom and estate.
Of these, committed to my charge,
Is Rokeby, prisoner at large;
Redmond, his page, arrived to say
He reaches Barnard's towers to-day.
Right heavy shall his ransom be,
Unless that maid compound with thee!²⁴
Go to her now—be bold of cheer,
While her soul floats 'twixt hope and
    fear;
It is the very change of tide,
When best the female heart is tried—
Pride, prejudice, and modesty,
Are in the current swept to sea;
And the bold swain, who plies his oar,
May lightly row his bark to shore."

CANTO THIRD.

I.

THE hunting tribes of air and earth
Respect the brethren of their birth;
Nature, who loves the claim of kind,
Less cruel chase to each assign'd.
The falcon, poised on soaring wing,
Watches the wild-duck by the spring;
The slow-hound wakes the fox's lair;
The greyhound presses on the hare;
The eagle pounces on the lamb;
The wolf devours the fleecy dam:

Even tiger fell, and sullen bear,
Their likeness and their lineage spare,
Man, only, mars kind Nature's plan,
And turns the fierce pursuit on man;
Plying war's desultory trade,
Incursion, flight, and ambuscade,
Since Nimrod, Cush's mighty son,
At first the bloody game begun.

II.

The Indian, prowling for his prey,
Who hears the settlers track his way,²⁵
And knows in distant forest far
Camp his red brethren of the war;
He, when each double and disguise
To baffle the pursuit he tries,
Low crouching now his head to hide,
Where swampy streams through rushes
    glide,
Now covering with the wither'd leaves
The foot-prints that the dew receives:
He, skill'd in every silvan guile,
Knows not, nor tries, such various wile,
As Risingham, when on the wind
Arose the loud pursuit behind.
In Redesdale his youth had heard
Each art her wily dalesmen dared,
When Rooken-edge, and Redswair high,
To bugle rung and blood-hound's cry,²⁶
Announcing Jedwood-axe and spear,
And Lid'sdale riders in the rear;
And well his venturous life had proved,
The lessons that his childhood loved.

III.

Oft had he shown, in climes afar,
Each attribute of roving war;
The sharpen'd ear, the piercing eye,
The quick resolve in danger nigh;
The speed, that in the flight or chase,
Outstripp'd the Charib's rapid race;
The steady brain, the sinewy limb,
To leap, to climb, to dive, to swim;
The iron frame, inured to bear
Each dire inclemency of air,
Nor less confirm'd to undergo
Fatigue's faint chill, and famine's throe.
These arts he proved, his life to save,
In peril oft by land and wave,

On Arawaca's desert shore,
Or where La Plata's billows roar,
When oft the sons of vengeful Spain
Track'd the marauder's steps in vain.
These arts, in Indian warfare tried,
Must save him now by Greta's side.

IV.

'Twas then, in hour of utmost need,
He proved his courage, art, and speed.
Now slow he stalk'd with stealthy pace,
Now started forth in rapid race,
Oft doubling back in mazy train,
To blind the trace the dews retain;
Now clomb the rocks projecting high,
To baffle the pursuer's eye;
Now sought the stream, whose brawling
    sound
The echo of his footsteps drown'd.
But if the forest verge he nears,
There trample steeds, and glimmer spears;
If deeper down the copse he drew,
He heard the rangers' loud halloo,
Beating each cover while they came,
As if to start the silvan game.
'Twas then—like tiger close beset
At every pass with toil and net,
'Counter'd, where'er he turns his glare,
By clashing arms and torches' flare,
Who meditates, with furious bound,
To burst on hunter, horse, and hound,—
'Twas then that Bertram's soul arose,
Prompting to rush upon his foes:
But as that crouching tiger, cow'd
By brandish'd steel and shouting crowd,
Retreats beneath the jungle's shroud,
Bertram suspends his purpose stern,
And couches in the brake and fern,
Hiding his face, lest foemen spy,
The sparkle of his swarthy eye.[27]

V.

Then Bertram might the bearing trace
Of the bold youth who led the chase;
Who paused to list for every sound,
Climb every height to look around,
Then rushing on with naked sword,
Each dingle's bosky depths explored.
'Twas Redmond—by the azure eye;
'Twas Redmond—by the locks that fly

Disorder'd from his glowing cheek;
Mien, face, and form, young Redmond
    speak.
A form more active, light, and strong,
Ne'er shot the ranks of war along;
The modest, yet the manly mien,
Might grace the court of maiden queen;
A face more fair you well might find,
For Redmond's knew the sun and wind,
Nor boasted, from their tinge when free,
The charm of regularity;
But every feature had the power
To aid the expression of the hour:
Whether gay wit, and humour sly,
Danced laughing in his light-blue eye;
Or bended brow, and glance of fire,
And kindling cheek, spoke Erin's ire;
Or soft and sadden'd glances show
Her ready sympathy with woe;
Or in that wayward mood of mind,
When various feelings are combined,
When joy and sorrow mingle near,
And hope's bright wings are check'd by
    fear,
And rising doubts keep transport down,
And anger lends a short-lived frown;
In that strange mood which maids approve
Even when they dare not call it love;
With every change his features play'd,
As aspens show the light and shade.

VI.

Well Risingham young Redmond knew:
And much he marvell'd that the crew,
Roused to revenge bold Mortham dead,
Were by that Mortham's foeman led;
For never felt his soul the woe,
That wails a generous foeman low,
Far less that sense of justice strong,
That wreaks a generous foeman's wrong.
But small his leisure now to pause;
Redmond is first, whate'er the cause;
And twice that Redmond came so near
Where Bertram couch'd like hunted deer,
The very boughs his steps displace,
Rustled against the ruffian's face,
Who, desperate, twice prepared to start,
And plunge his dagger in his heart!
But Redmond turn'd a different way,
And the bent boughs resumed their sway,

And Bertram held it wise, unseen,
Deeper to plunge in coppice green.
Thus, circled in his coil, the snake,
When roving hunters beat the brake,
Watches with red and glistening eye,
Prepared, if heedless step draw nigh,
With forked tongue and venom'd fang
Instant to dart the deadly pang;
But if the intruders turn aside,
Away his coils unfolded glide,
And through the deep savannah wind,
Some undisturb'd retreat to find.

VII.

But Bertram, as he backward drew,
And heard the loud pursuit renew,
And Redmond's hollo on the wind,
Oft mutter'd in his savage mind—
"Redmond O'Neale! were thou and I
Alone this day's event to try,
With not a second here to see,
But the grey cliff and oaken tree,—
That voice of thine, that shouts so loud,
Should ne'er repeat its summons proud!
No! nor e'er try its melting power
Again in maiden's summer bower."
Eluded, now behind him die,
Faint and more faint, each hostile cry;
He stands in Scargill wood alone,
Nor hears he now a harsher tone
Than the hoarse cushat's plaintive cry,
Or Greta's sound that murmurs by;
And on the dale, so lone and wild,
The summer sun in quiet smiled.

VIII.

He listen'd long with anxious heart,
Ear bent to hear, and foot to start,
And, while his stretch'd attention glows,
Refused his weary frame repose.
'Twas silence all—he laid him down,
Where purple heath profusely strown,
And throatwort, with its azure bell,
And moss and thyme his cushion swell.
There, spent with toil, he listless eyed
The course of Greta's playful tide;
Beneath, her banks now eddying dun,
Now brightly gleaming to the sun,
As, dancing over rock and stone,
In yellow light her currents shone,

Matching in hue the favourite gem
Of Albin's mountain-diadem.
Then, tired to watch the current's play,
He turn'd his weary eyes away,
To where the bank opposing show'd
Its huge, square cliffs through shaggy
     wood.
One, prominent above the rest,
Rear'd to the sun its pale grey breast;
Around its broken summit grew
The hazel rude, and sable yew;
A thousand varied lichens dyed
Its waste and weather-beaten side;
And round its rugged basis lay,
By time or thunder rent away,
Fragments, that, from its frontlet torn,
Were mantled now by verdant thorn.
Such was the scene's wild majesty,
That fill'd stern Bertram's gazing eye.

IX.

In sullen mood he lay reclined,
Revolving, in his stormy mind,
The felon deed, the fruitless guilt,
His patron's blood by treason spilt;
A crime, it seem'd, so dire and dread,
That it had power to wake the dead.
Then, pondering on his life betray'd
By Oswald's art to Redmond's blade,
In treacherous purpose to withhold,
So seem'd it, Mortham's promised gold,
A deep and full revenge he vow'd
On Redmond, forward, fierce, and proud;
Revenge on Wilfrid—on his sire
Redoubled vengeance, swift and dire!—
If, in such mood, (as legends say,
And well believed that simple day,)
The Enemy of man has power
To profit by the evil hour,
Here stood a wretch, prepared to change
His soul's redemption for revenge![24]
But though his vows, with such a fire
Of earnest and intense desire
For vengeance dark and fell, were made,
As well might reach hell's lowest shade,
No deeper clouds the grove embrown'd,
No nether thunders shook the ground;—
The demon knew his vassal's heart,
And spared temptation's needless art.

X.

Oft, mingled with the direful theme,
Came Mortham's form—Was it a dream?
Or had he seen, in vision true,
That very Mortham whom he slew?
Or had in living flesh appear'd
The only man on earth he fear'd?—
To try the mystic cause intent,
His eyes, that on the cliff were bent,
'Counter'd at once a dazzling glance,
Like sunbeam flash'd from sword or
    lance.
At once he started as for fight,
But not a foeman was in sight;
He heard the cushat's murmur hoarse,
He heard the river's sounding course;
The solitary woodlands lay,
As slumbering in the summer ray.
He gazed, like lion roused, around,
Then sunk again upon the ground.
'Twas but, he thought, some fitful beam,
Glanced sudden from the sparkling
    stream;
Then plunged him from his gloomy train
Of ill-connected thoughts again,
Until a voice behind him cried,
" Bertram! well met on Greta side."

XI.

Instant his sword was in his hand,
As instant sunk the ready brand;
Yet, dubious still, opposed he stood
To him that issued from the wood:
" Guy Denzil!—is it thou?" he said;
" Do we two meet in Scargill shade?—
Stand back a space!—thy purpose show,
Whether thou comest as friend or foe.
Report hath said, that Denzil's name
From Rokeby's band was razed with
    shame."—
" A shame I owe that hot O'Neale,
Who told his knight, in peevish zeal,
Of my marauding on the clowns
Of Calverley and Bradford downs.[29]
I reck not. In a war to strive,
Where, save the leaders, none can thrive,
Suits ill my mood; and better game
Awaits us both, if thou'rt the same
Unscrupulous, bold Risingham,

Who watched with me in midnight dark,
To snatch a deer from Rokeby-park.
How think'st thou?"—" Speak thy pur-
    pose out;
I love not mystery or doubt."—

XII.

" Then, list.—Not far there lurk a crew
Of trusty comrades, stanch and true,
Glean'd from both factions—Roundheads,
    freed
From cant of sermon and of creed;
And Cavaliers, whose souls, like mine,
Spurn at the bonds of discipline.
Wiser, we judge, by dale and wold,
A warfare of our own to hold,
Than breathe our last on battle-down,
For cloak or surplice, mace or crown.
Our schemes are laid, our purpose set,
A chief and leader lack we yet.—
Thou art a wanderer, it is said;
For Mortham's death, thy steps way-laid,
Thy head at price—so say our spies,
Who range the valley in disguise.
Join then with us:—though wild debate
And wrangling rend our infant state,
Each to an equal loth to bow,
Will yield to chief renown'd as thou."—

XIII.

" Even now," thought Bertram, passion-
    stirr'd,
" I call'd on hell, and hell has heard!
What lack I, vengeance to command,
But of stanch comrades such a band?
This Denzil, vow'd to every evil,
Might read a lesson to the devil.
Well, be it so! each knave and fool
Shall serve as my revenge's tool."—
Aloud, " I take thy proffer, Guy,
But tell me where thy comrades lie?"—
" Not far from hence," Guy Denzil said;
" Descend, and cross the river's bed,
Where rises yonder cliff so grey."—
" Do thou," said Bertram, " lead the way."
Then mutter'd, " It is best make sure;
Guy Denzil's faith was never pure."
He follow'd down the steep descent,
Then through the Greta's streams they
    went;

And, when they reach'd the farther shore,
They stood the lonely cliff before.

XIV

With wonder Bertram heard within
The flinty rock a murmur'd din;
But when Guy pull'd the wilding spray,
And brambles, from its base away,
He saw, appearing to the air,
A little entrance, low and square,
Like opening cell of hermit lone,
Dark, winding through the living stone.
Here enter'd Denzil, Bertram here;
And loud and louder on their ear,
As from the bowels of the earth,
Resounded shouts of boisterous mirth.
Of old, the cavern strait and rude,
In slaty rock the peasant hew'd;
And Brignall's woods, and Scargill's, wave,
E'en now, o'er many a sister cave,[30]
Where, far within the darksome rift,
The wedge and lever ply their thrift.
But war had silenced rural trade,
And the deserted mine was made
The banquet-hall and fortress too,
Of Denzil and his desperate crew.—
There Guilt his anxious revel kept;
There, on his sordid pallet, slept
Guilt-born Excess, the goblet drain'd
Still in his slumbering grasp retain'd;
Regret was there, his eye still cast
With vain rep'ning on the past;
Among the feasters waited near
Sorrow, and unrepentant Fear,
And Blasphemy, to frenzy driven,
With his own crimes reproaching heaven;
While Bertram show'd, amid the crew,
The Master-Fiend that Milton drew.

XV.

Hark! the loud revel wakes again,
To greet the leader of the train.
Behold the group by the pale lamp,
That struggles with the earthy damp.
By what strange features Vice hath known,
To single out and mark her own!
Yet some there are, whose brows retain
Less deeply stamp'd her brand and stain.
See yon pale stripling! when a boy,
A mother's pride, a father's joy!

Now, 'gainst the vault's rude walls reclined,
An early image fills his mind:
The cottage, once his sire's, he sees,
Embower'd upon the banks of Tees;
He views sweet Winston's woodland
    scene,
And shares the dance on Gainford-green.
A tear is springing—but the zest
Of some wild tale, or brutal jest,
Hath to loud laughter stirr'd the rest.
On him they call, the aptest mate
For jovial song and merry feat.
Fast flies his dream—with dauntless air,
As one victorious o'er Despair,
He bids the ruddy cup go round,
Till sense and sorrow both are drown'd:
And soon, in merry wassail, he,
The life of all their revelry,
Peals his loud song!—The muse has found
Her blossoms on the wildest ground,
'Mid noxious weeds at random strew'd,
Themselves all profitless and rude.—
With desperate merriment he sung,
The cavern to the chorus rung;
Yet mingled with his reckless glee
Remorse's bitter agony.

XVI.

Song.

O, Brignall banks are wild and fair,
    And Greta woods are green,
And you may gather garlands there,
    Would grace a summer queen.
And as I rode by Dalton-hall,
    Beneath the turrets high,
A Maiden on the castle wall
    Was singing merrily,—

CHORUS.

"O, Brignall banks are fresh and fair
    And Greta woods are green;
I'd rather rove with Edmund there,
    Than reign our English queen."—

"If, Maiden, thou wouldst wend with me,
    To leave both tower and town,
Thou first must guess what life lead we,
    That dwell by dale and down?

And if thou canst that riddle read,
　As read full well you may,
Then to the greenwood shalt thou speed,
　As blithe as Queen of May."—

Yet sung she, " Brignall banks are fair,
　And Greta woods are green;
I'd rather rove with Edmund there,
　Than reign our English queen.

XVII.

" I read you, by your bugle-horn,
　And by your palfrey good,
I read you for a ranger sworn,
　To keep the king's greenwood."—
" A Ranger, lady, winds his horn,
　And 'tis at peep of light;
His blast is heard at merry morn,
　And mine at dead of night."—

Yet sung she, " Brignall banks are fair,
　And Greta woods are gay;
I would I were with Edmund there,
　To reign his Queen of May!

" With burnish'd brand and musketoon,
　So gallantly you come,
I read you for a bold Dragoon,
　That lists the tuck of drum."—
" I list no more the tuck of drum,
　No more the trumpet hear;
But when the beetle sounds his hum,
　My comrades take the spear.

" And, O! though Brignall banks be fair,
　And Greta woods be gay,
Yet mickle must the maiden dare,
　Would reign my Queen of May!

XVIII.

" Maiden! a nameless life I lead,
　A nameless death I'll die!
The fiend, whose lantern lights the mead,
　Were better mate than I!
And when I'm with my comrades met,
　Beneath the greenwood bough,
What once we were we all forget,
　Nor think what we are now.

" Yet Brignall banks are fresh and fair,
　And Greta woods are green,
And you may gather garlands there
　Would grace a summer queen."

When Edmund ceased his simple song,
Was silence on the sullen throng,
Till waked some ruder mate their glee
With note of coarser minstrelsy.
But, far apart, in dark divan,
Denzil and Bertram many a plan,
Of import foul and fierce, design'd,
While still on Bertram's grasping mind
The wealth of murder'd Mortham hung;
Though half he fear'd his daring tongue,
When it should give his wishes birth,
Might raise a spectre from the earth!

XIX.

At length his wondrous tale he told:
When, scornful, smiled his comrade bold;
For, train'd in license of a court,
Religion's self was Denzil's sport;
Then judge in what contempt he held
The visionary tales of eld!
His awe for Bertram scarce repress'd
The unbeliever's sneering jest.
" 'Twere hard," he said, " for sage or seer,
To spell the subject of your fear;
Nor do I boast the art renown'd,
Vision and omen to expound.
Yet, faith if I must needs afford
To spectre watching treasured hoard,
As bandog keeps his master's roof,
Bidding the plunderer stand aloof,
This doubt remains—thy goblin gaunt
Hath chosen ill his ghostly haunt;
For why his guard on Mortham hold,
When Rokeby castle hath the gold
Thy patron won on Indian soil,
By stealth, by piracy, and spoil?"

XX.

At this he paused—for angry shame
Lower'd on the brow of Risingham.
He blush'd to think, that he should seem
Assertor of an airy dream,
And gave his wrath another theme.

"Denzil," he says, "though lowly laid,
Wrong not the memory of the dead;
For, while he lived, at Mortham's look
Thy very soul, Guy Denzil, shook!
And when he tax'd thy breach of word
To yon fair Rose of Allenford,
I saw thee crouch like chasten'd hound,
Whose back the huntsman's lash hath
    found.
Nor dare to call his foreign wealth
The spoil of piracy or stealth;
He won it bravely with his brand,
When Spain waged warfare with our
    land,[31]
Mark, too—I brook no idle jeer,
Nor couple Bertram's name with fear;
Mine is but half the demon's lot,
For I believe, but tremble not.—
Enough of this.—Say, why this hoard
Thou deem'st at Rokeby castle stored;
Or think'st that Mortham would bestow
His treasure with his faction's foe?"

XXI.

Soon quench'd was Denzil's ill-timed
    mirth;
Rather he would have seen the earth
Give to ten thousand spectres birth,
Than venture to awake to flame
The deadly wrath of Risingham.
Submiss he answer'd,—"Mortham's mind,
Thou know'st, to joy was ill inclined.
In youth, 'tis said, a gallant free,
A lusty reveller was he;
But since return'd from over sea,
A sullen and a silent mood
Hath numb'd the current of his blood.
Hence he refused each kindly call
To Rokeby's hospitable hall,
And our stout knight, at dawn of morn
Who loved to hear the bugle-horn,
Nor less, when eve his oaks embrown'd,
To see the ruddy cup go round,
Took umbrage that a friend so near
Refused to share his chase and cheer;
Thus did the kindred barons jar,
Ere they divided in the war.
Yet, trust me, friend, Matilda fair
Of Mortham's wealth is destined heir,—

XXII.

"Destined to her! to yon slight maid!
The prize my life had wellnigh paid,
When 'gainst Laroche, by Cayo's wave,
I fought, my patron's wealth to save!—
Denzil, I knew him long, yet ne'er
Knew him that joyous cavalier,
Whom youthful friends and early fame
Call'd soul of gallantry and game.
A moody man, he sought our crew,
Desperate and dark, whom no one knew;
And rose, as men with us must rise,
By scorning life and all its ties.
On each adventure rash he roved,
As danger for itself he loved;
On his sad brow nor mirth nor wine
Could e'er one wrinkled knot untwine;
Ill was the omen if he smiled,
For 'twas in peril stern and wild;
But when he laugh'd, each luckless mate
Might hold our fortune desperate.
Foremost he fought in every broil,
Then scornful turned him from the spoil;
Nay, often strove to bar the way
Between his comrades and their prey;
Preaching, even then, to such as we,
Hot with our dear-bought victory,
Of mercy and humanity.

XXIII.

"I loved him well—His fearless part,
His gallant leading, won my heart.
And after each victorious fight,
'Twas I that wrangled for his right,
Redeem'd his portion of the prey
That greedier mates had torn away:
In field and storm thrice saved his life,
And once amid our comrades' strife.—[32]
Yes, I have loved thee! Well hath proved
My toil, my danger, how I loved!
Yet will I mourn no more thy fate,
Ingrate in life, in death ingrate.
Rise if thou canst!" he look'd around,
And sternly stamp'd upon the ground—
"Rise, with thy bearing proud and high,
Even as this morn it met mine eye,
And give me, if thou darest, the lie!"
He paused—then, calm and passion-freed,
Bade Denzil with his tale proceed.

XXIV.

"Bertram, to thee I need not tell,
What thou hast cause to wot so well,
How Superstition's nets were twined
Around the Lord of Mortham's mind!
But since he drove thee from his tower,
A maid he found in Greta's bower,
Whose speech, like David's harp, had
    sway,
To charm his evil fiend away.
I know not if her features moved
Remembrance of the wife he loved;
But he would gaze upon her eye,
Till his mood soften'd to a sigh.
He, whom no living mortal sought
To question of his secret thought,
Now every thought and care confess'd
To his fair niece's faithful breast;
Nor was there aught of rich and rare,
In earth, in ocean, or in air,
But it must deck Matilda's hair.
Her love still bound him unto life;
But then awoke the civil strife,
And menials bore, by his commands,
Three coffers, with their iron bands,
From Mortham's vault, at midnight deep,
To her lone bower in Rokeby-Keep,
Ponderous with gold and plate of pride,
His gift, if he in battle died."—

XXV.

"Then, Denzil, as I guess, lays train,
These iron-banded chests to gain;
Else, wherefore should he hover here,
Where many a peril waits him near,
For all his feats of war and peace,
For plunder'd boors, and harts of greese?
Since through the hamlets as he fared,
What hearth has Guy's marauding spared,
Or where the chase that hath not rung
With Denzil's bow, at midnight
    strung?"—
"I hold my wont—my rangers go,
Even now to track a milk-white doe.
By Rokeby-hall she takes her lair,
In Greta wood she harbours fair,
And when my huntsman marks her way,
What think'st thou, Bertram, of the prey?
Were Rokeby's daughter in our power,
We rate her ransom at her dower."

XXVI.

"'Tis well!—there's vengeance in the
    thought,
Matilda is by Wilfrid sought;
And hot-brain'd Redmond, too, 'tis said,
Pays lover's homage to the maid.
Bertram she scorn'd—If met by chance,
She turn'd from me her shuddering glance,
Like a nice dame, that will not brook
On what she hates and loathes to look;
She told to Mortham she could ne'er
Behold me without secret fear,
Foreboding evil;—She may rue
To find her prophecy fall true!—
The war has weeded Rokeby's train,
Few followers in his halls remain;
If thy scheme miss, then, brief and bold,
We are enow to storm the hold;
Bear off the plunder, and the dame,
And leave the castle all in flame."—

XXVII.

"Still art thou Valour's venturous son!
Yet ponder first the risk to run:
The menials of the castle, true,
And stubborn to their charge, though few;
The wall to scale—the moat to cross—
The wicket-grate—the inner fosse"—
—"Fool! if we blench for toys like these,
On what fair guerdon can we seize?
Our hardiest venture, to explore
Some wretched peasant's fenceless door,
And the best prize we bear away,
The earnings of his sordid day."—
"A while thy hasty taunt forbear:
In sight of road more sure and fair,
Thou wouldst not choose, in blindfold
    wrath,
Or wantonness, a desperate path?
List, then;—for vantage or assault,
From gilded vane to dungeon-vault,
Each pass of Rokeby-house I know:
There is one postern, dark and low,
That issues at a secret spot,
By most neglected or forgot.
Now, could a spial of our train
On fair pretext admittance gain,
That sally-port might be unbarr'd:
Then, vain were battlement and ward!"—

XXVIII.

"Now speak'st thou well:—to me the same,
If force or art shall urge the game;
Indifferent, if like fox I wind,
Or spring like tiger on the hind.—
But, hark! our merry-men so gay
Troll forth another roundelay."—

Song.

"A weary lot is thine, fair maid,
    A weary lot is thine!
To pull the thorn thy brow to braid,
    And press the rue for wine!
A lightsome eye, a soldier's mien,
    A feather of the blue,
A doublet of the Lincoln green,—
    No more of me you knew,
                        My love!
No more of me you knew.

"This morn is merry June, I trow,
    The rose is budding fain;
But she shall bloom in winter snow,
    Ere we two meet again."
He turn'd his charger as he spake,
    Upon the river shore,
He gave his bridle-reins a shake,
    Said, "Adieu for evermore,
                        My love!
And adieu for evermore."—[33]

XXIX.

"What youth is this, your band among,
The best for minstrelsy and song?
In his wild notes seem aptly met
A strain of pleasure and regret."—
"Edmund of Winston is his name;
The hamlet sounded with the fame
Of early hopes his childhood gave,—
Now center'd all in Brignall cave!
I watch him well—his wayward course
Shows oft a tincture of remorse.
Some early love-shaft grazed his heart,
And oft the scar will ache and smart.
Yet is he useful:—of the rest,
By fits, the darling and the jest,
His harp, his story, and his lay,
Oft aid the idle hours away.

When unemploy'd, each fiery mate
Is ripe for mutinous debate.
He tuned his strings e'en now—again
He wakes them, with a blither strain."

XXX.

Song.

ALLEN-A-DALE.

Allen-a-Dale has no fagot for burning,
Allen-a-Dale has no furrow for turning,
Allen-a-Dale has no fleece for the spinning,
Yet Allen-a-Dale has red gold for the
    winning.
Come, read me my riddle! come, hearken
    my tale!
And tell me the craft of bold Allen-a-Dale.

The Baron of Ravensworth* prances in
    pride,
And he views his domains upon Arkindale
    side,
The mere for his net, and the land for his
    game,
The chase for the wild, and the park for
    the tame,
Yet the fish of the lake, and the deer of
    the vale,
Are less free to Lord Dacre than Allen-a-
    Dale!

Allen-a-Dale was ne'er belted a knight,
Though his spur be as sharp, and his blade
    be as bright;
Allen-a-Dale is no baron or lord,
Yet twenty tall yeomen will draw at his
    word;
And the best of our nobles his bonnet will
    vail,
Who at Rere-cross[31] on Stanmore meets
    Allen-a-dale.

---

* The ruins of Ravensworth Castle stand
in the North Riding of Yorkshire, about three
miles from the town of Richmond, and adjoining to the waste called the Forest of
Arkingarth. It belonged originally to the
powerful family of Fitz-Hugh, from whom it
passed to the Lords Dacre of the South.

Allen-a-Dale to his wooing is come;
The mother, she ask'd of his household
  and home:
"Though the castle of Richmond stand
  fair on the hill,
My hall," quoth bold Allen, " shows gal-
  lanter still;
'Tis the blue vault of heaven, with its
  crescent so pale,
And with all its bright spangles!" said
  Allen-a-Dale.

The father was steel, and the mother was
  stone;
They lifted the latch, and they bade him
  be gone;
But loud, on the morrow, their wail and
  their cry:
He had laugh'd on the lass with his bonny
  black eye.
And she fled to the forest to hear a love-
  tale,
And the youth it was told by was Allen-
  a-Dale!

XXXI.

"Thou see'st that, whether sad or gay.
Love mingles ever in his lay.
But when his boyish wayward fit
Is o'er, he hath address and wit;
O! 'tis a brain of fire, can ape
Each dialect, each various shape."
"Nay, then, to aid thy project, Guy—
Soft! who comes here?"—"My trusty spy.
Speak, Hamlin! hast thou lodged our
  deer?"—³⁵
"I have—but two fair stags are near.
I watch'd her, as she slowly stray'd
From Egliston up Thorsgill glade;
But Wilfrid Wycliffe sought her side,
And then young Redmond, in his pride,
Shot down to meet them on their way:
Much, as it seem'd, was theirs to say:
There's time to pitch both toil and net,
Before their path be homeward set."
A hurried and a whisper'd speech
Did Bertram's will to Denzil teach;
Who, turning to the robber band,
Bade four, the bravest, take the brand.

CANTO FOURTH.

I.

WHEN Denmark's raven soar'd on high,
Triumphant through Northumbrian sky,
Till, hovering near, her fatal croak
Bade Reged's Britons dread the yoke,³⁶
And the broad shadow of her wing
Blacken'd each cataract and spring,
Where Tees in tumult leaves his source,
Thundering o'er Ca'dron and High-Force:
Beneath the shade the Northmen came,
Fix'd on each vale a Runic name,³⁷
Rear'd high their altar's rugged stone,
And gave their Gods the land they won.
Then, Balder, one bleak garth was thine,
And one sweet brooklet's silver line,
And Woden's Croft did title gain
From the stern Father of the Slain;
But to the Monarch of the Mace,
That held in fight the foremost place,
To Odin's son, and Sifia's spouse,
Near Stratfortn high they paid their vows,
Remember'd Thor's victorious fame,
And gave the dell the Thunderer's name.

II.

Yet Scald or Kemper err'd, I ween,
Who gave that soft and quiet scene,
With all its varied light and shade,
And every little sunny glade,
And the blithe brook that strolls along
Its pebbled bed with summer song,
To the grim God of blood and scar,
The grisly King of Northern War.
O, better were its banks assign'd
To spirits of a gentler kind!
For where the thicket groups recede,
And the rath primrose decks the mead,
The velvet grass seems carpet meet
For the light fairies' lively feet.
Yon tufted knoll, with daisies strown,
Might make proud Oberon a throne,
While, hidden in the thicket nigh,
Puck should brood o'er his frolic sly;
And where profuse the wood-vetch clings
Round ash and elm, in verdant rings,
Its pale and azure-pencill'd flower
Should canopy Titania's bower.

III.

Here rise no cliffs the vale to shade;
But, skirting every sunny glade,
In fair variety of green
The woodland lends its silvan screen.
Hoary, yet haughty, frowns the oak,
Its boughs by weight of ages broke;
And towers erect, in sable spire,
The pine-tree scathed by lightning fire;
The drooping ash and birch, between,
Hang their fair tresses o'er the green,
And all beneath, at random grow
Each coppice dwarf of varied show,
Or, round the stems profusely twined,
Fling summer odours on the wind.
Such varied group Urbino's hand
Round Him of Tarsus nobly plann'd,
What time he bade proud Athens own
On Mars's Mount the God unknown!
Then grey Philosophy stood nigh,
Though bent by age, in spirit high:
Then rose the scar-seam'd veteran's spear,
There Grecian Beauty bent to hear,
While Childhood at her foot was placed,
Or clung delighted to her waist.

IV.

" And rest we here," Matilda said,
And sat her in the varying shade.
" Chance-met, we well may steal an hour,
To friendship due, from fortune's power.
Thou, Wilfrid, ever kind, must lend
Thy counsel to thy sister-friend;
And, Redmond, thou, at my behest,
No farther urge thy desperate 'quest.
For to my care a charge is left,
Dangerous to one of aid bereft;
Wellnigh an orphan, and alone,
Captive her sire, her house o'erthrown."
Wilfrid, with wonted kindness graced,
Beside her on the turf she placed;
Then paused, with downcast look and
  eye,
Nor bade young Redmond seat him nigh.
Her conscious diffidence he saw,
Drew backward, as in modest awe,
And sat a little space removed,
Unmark'd to gaze on her he loved.

V.

Wreathed in its dark-brown rings, her
  hair
Half hid Matilda's forehead fair,
Half hid and half reveal'd to view
Her full dark eye of hazel hue.
The rose, with faint and feeble streak,
So slightly tinged the maiden's cheek,
That you had said her hue was pale;
But if she faced the summer gale,
Or spoke, or sung, or quicker moved,
Or heard the praise of those she loved,
Or when of interest was express'd
Aught that waked feeling in her breast,
The mantling blood in ready play
Rivall'd the blush of rising day.
There was a soft and pensive grace,
A cast of thought upon her face,
That suited well the forehead high,
The eyelash dark, and downcast eye;
The mild expression spoke a mind
In duty firm, composed, resign'd;
'Tis that which Roman art has given,
To mark their maiden Queen of Heaven
In hours of sport, that mood gave way
To Fancy's light and frolic play;
And when the dance, or tale, or song,
In harmless mirth sped time along,
Full oft her doating sire would call
His Maud the merriest of them all.
But days of war and civil crime,
Allow'd but ill such festal time,
And her soft pensiveness of brow
Had deepen'd into sadness now.
In Marston field her father ta'en,
Her friends dispersed, brave Mortham
  slain,
While every ill her soul foretold,
From Oswald's thirst of power and gold,
And boding thoughts that she must part
With a soft vision of her heart,—
All lower'd around the lovely maid,
To darken her dejection's shade.

VI.

Who has not heard—while Erin yet
Strove 'gainst the Saxon's iron bit—
Who has not heard how brave O'Neale
In English blood imbrued his steel,[38]

Against St. George's cross blazed high
The banners of his Tanistry,
To fiery Essex gave the foil,
And reign'd a prince on Ulster's soil?
But chief arose his victor pride,
When that brave Marshal fought and
    died,[39]
And Avon-Duff to ocean bore
His billows red with Saxon gore.
'Twas first in that disastrous fight,
Rokeby and Mortham proved their might.
There had they fallen 'mongst the rest,
But pity touch'd a chieftain's breast;
The Tanist he to great O'Neale;[40]
He check'd his followers' bloody zeal,
To quarter took the kinsmen bold,
And bore them to his mountain-hold,
Gave them each silvan joy to know,
Slieve-Donard's cliffs and woods could
    show,
Shared with them Erin's festal cheer,
Show'd them the chase of wolf and deer,
And, when a fitting time was come,
Safe and unransom'd sent them home,
Loaded with many a gift, to prove
A generous foe's respect and love.

VII.

Years speed away. On Rokeby's head
Some touch of early snow was shed;
Calm he enjoy'd, by Greta's wave,
The peace which James the Peaceful gave,
While Mortham, far beyond the main,
Waged his fierce wars on Indian Spain.—
It chanced upon a wintry night,
That whiten'd Stanmore's stormy height,
The chase was o'er, the stag was kill'd,
In Rokeby hall the cups were fill'd,
And by the huge stone chimney sate
The Knight in hospitable state.
Moonless the sky, the hour was late,
When a loud summons shook the gate,
And sore for entrance and for aid
A voice of foreign accent pray'd.
The porter answer'd to the call,
And instant rushed into the hall
A Man, whose aspect and attire
Startled the circle by the fire.

VIII.

His plaited hair in elf-locks spread
Around his bare and matted head;
On leg and thigh, close stretch'd and
    trim,
His vesture show'd the sinewy limb;
In saffron dyed, a linen vest
Was frequent folded round his breast;
A mantle long and loose he wore,
Shaggy with ice, and stain'd with gore.
He clasp'd a burden to his heart,
And, resting on a knotted dart,
The snow from hair and beard he shook,
And round him gazed with wilder'd look.
Then up the hall, with staggering pace,
He hasten'd by the blaze to place,
Half lifeless from the bitter air,
His load, a Boy of beauty rare.
To Rokeby, next, he louted low,
Then stood erect his tale to show,
With wild majestic port and tone,
Like envoy of some barbarous throne.[41]
" Sir Richard, Lord of Rokeby, hear!
Turlough O'Neale salutes thee dear;
He graces thee, and to thy care
Young Redmond gives, his grandson fair.
He bids thee breed him as thy son,
For Turlough's days of joy are done;
And other lords have seized his land,
And faint and feeble is his hand;
And all the glory of Tyrone
Is like a morning vapour flown.
To bind the duty on thy soul,
He bids thee think on Erin's bowl!
If any wrong the young O'Neale,
He bids thee think of Erin's steel.
To Mortham first this charge was due,
But, in his absence, honours you.—
Now is my master's message by,
And Ferraught will contented die."

IX.

His look grew fix'd, his cheek grew pale,
He sunk when he had told his tale;
For, hid beneath his mantle wide,
A mortal wound was in his side.
Vain was all aid—in terror wild,
And sorrow, scream'd the orphan Child

Poor Ferraught raised his wistful eyes,
And faintly strove to soothe his cries;
All reckless of his dying pain,
He blest and blest him o'er again!
And kiss'd the little hands outspread,
And kiss'd and cross'd the infant head,
And, in his native tongue and phrase,
Pray'd to each Saint to watch his days;
Then all his strength together drew,
The charge to Rokeby to renew.
When half was falter'd from his breast,
And half by dying signs express'd,
" Bless the O'Neale!" he faintly said,
And thus the faithful spirit fled.

X.

'Twas long ere soothing might prevail
Upon the Child to end the tale;
And then he said, that from his home
His grandsire had been forced to roam,
Which had not been if Redmond's hand
Had but had strength to draw the brand,
The brand of Lenaugh More the Red,
That hung beside the grey wolf's head.—
'Twas from his broken phrase descried,
His foster-father was his guide,[42]
Who, in his charge, from Ulster bore
Letters and gifts a goodly store:
But ruffians met them in the wood,
Ferraught in battle boldly stood,
Till wounded and o'erpower'd at length,
And stripp'd of all, his failing strength
Just bore him here—and then the child
Renew'd again his moaning wild.

XI.

The tear down childhood's cheek that
        flows,
Is like the dewdrop on the rose;
When next the summer breeze comes by,
And waves the bush, the flower is dry.
Won by their care, the orphan Child
Soon on his new protector smiled,
With dimpled cheek and eye so fair,
Through his thick curls of flaxen hair,
But blithest laugh'd that cheek and eye,
When Rokeby's little Maid was nigh;
'Twas his, with elder brother's pride,
Matilda's tottering steps to guide;

His native lays in Irish tongue,
To soothe her infant ear he sung,
And primrose twined with daisy fair,
To form a chaplet for her hair.
By lawn, by grove, by brooklet's strand,
The children still were hand in hand,
And good Sir Richard smiling eyed
The early knot so kindly tied.

XII.

But summer months bring wilding shoot
From bud to bloom, from bloom to fruit;
And years draw on our human span,
From child to boy, from boy to man;
And soon in Rokeby's woods is seen
A gallant boy in hunter's green.
He loves to wake the felon boar,
In his dark haunt on Greta's shore,
And loves, against the deer so dun,
To draw the shaft, or lift the gun,
Yet more he loves, in autumn prime,
The hazel's spreading boughs to climb,
And down its cluster'd stores to hail,
Where young Matilda holds her veil.
And she, whose veil receives the shower,
Is alter'd too, and knows her power;
Assumes a monitress's pride,
Her Redmond's dangerous sports to chide;
Yet listens still to hear him tell
How the grim wild-boar fought and fell,
How at his fall the bugle rung,
Till rock and greenwood answer flung;
Then blesses her, that man can find
A pastime of such savage kind!

XIII.

But Redmond knew to weave his tale
So well with praise of wood and dale,
And knew so well each point to trace,
Gives living interest to the chase,
And knew so well o'er all to throw
His spirit's wild romantic glow,
That, while she blamed, and while she
        fear'd,
She loved each venturous tale she heard.
Oft, too, when drifted snow and rain
To bower and hall their steps restrain,
Together they explored the page
Of glowing bard or gifted sage;

Oft, placed the evening fire beside,
The minstrel art alternate tried,
While gladsome harp and lively lay
Bade winter-night flit fast away:
Thus, from their childhood, blending still
Their sport, their study, and their skill,
An union of the soul they prove,
But must not think that it was love.
But though they dared not, envious Fame
Soon dared to give that union name;
And when so often, side by side,
From year to year the pair she eyed,
She sometimes blamed the good old
        Knight,
As dull of ear and dim of sight,
Sometimes his purpose would declare,
That young O'Neale should wed his heir.

XIV.

The suit of Wilfrid rent disguise
And bandage from the lovers' eyes;
'Twas plain that Oswald, for his son,
Had Rokeby's favour well nigh won.
Now must they meet with change of cheer,
With mutual looks of shame and fear;
Now must Matilda stray apart,
To school her disobedient heart:
And Redmond now alone must rue
The love he never can subdue.
But factions rose, and Rokeby sware
No rebel's son should wed his heir;
And Redmond, nurtured while a child
In many a bard's traditions wild,
Now sought the lonely wood or stream,
To cherish there a happier dream,
Of maiden won by sword or lance,
As in the regions of romance;
And count the heroes of his line,
Great Nial of the Pledges Nine,[43]
Shane-Dymas[44] wild, and Geraldine,[45]
And Connan-more, who vowed his race,
For ever to the fight and chase,
And cursed him, of his lineage born,
Should sheathe the sword to reap the
        corn,
Or leave the mountain and the wold,
To shroud himself in castled hold.
From such examples hope he drew,
And brighten'd as the trumpet blew.

XV

If brides were won by heart and blade,
Redmond had both his cause to aid,
And all beside of nurture rare
That might beseem a baron's heir.
Turlough O'Neale, in Erin's strife,
On Rokeby's Lord bestow'd his life,
And well did Rokeby's generous Knight
Young Redmond for the deed requite.
Nor was his liberal care and cost
Upon the gallant stripling lost;
Seek the North-Riding broad and wide,
Like Redmond none could steed bestride;
From Tynemouth search to Cumberland,
Like Redmond none could wield a brand;
And then, of humour kind and free,
And bearing him to each degree
With frank and fearless courtesy,
There never youth was form'd to steal
Upon the heart like brave O'Neale.

XVI.

Sir Richard loved him as his son;
And when the days of peace were done,
And to the gales of war he gave
The banner of his sires to wave,
Redmond, distinguish'd by his care,
He chose that honour'd flag to bear,
And named his page, the next degree,
In that old time, to chivalry.[46]
In five pitch'd fields he well maintain'd
The honour'd place his worth obtain'd,
And high was Redmond's youthful name
Blazed in the roll of martial fame.
Had fortune smiled on Marston fight,
The eve had seen him dubb'd a knight;
Twice, 'mid the battle's doubtful strife,
Of Rokeby's Lord he saved the life.
But when he saw him prisoner made,
He kiss'd and then resign'd his blade,
And yielded him an easy prey
To those who led the Knight away;
Resolved Matilda's sire should prove
In prison, as in fight, his love.

XVII.

When lovers meet in adverse hour,
'Tis like a sun-glimpse through a shower,

A watery ray, an instant seen
The darkly closing clouds between.
As Redmond on the turf reclined,
The past and present fill'd his mind:
"It was not thus," Affection said,
"I dream'd of my return, dear maid!
Not thus, when from thy trembling hand,
I took the banner and the brand,
When round me, as the bugles blew,
Their blades three hundred warriors drew,
And, while the standard I unroll'd,
Clash'd their bright arms, with clamour
　　　　　bold.
Where is that banner now?—its pride
Lies 'whelm'd in Ouse's sullen tide!
Where now these warriors?—in their gore,
They cumber Marston's dismal moor!
And what avails a useless brand,
Held by a captive's shackled hand,
That only would his life retain,
To aid thy sire to bear his chain!"
Thus Redmond to himself apart;
Nor lighter was his rival's heart;
For Wilfrid, while his generous soul
Disdain'd to profit by control,
By many a sign could mark too plain,
Save with such aid, his hopes were vain.—
But now Matilda's accents stole
On the dark visions of their soul,
And bade their mournful musing fly,
Like mist before the zephyr's sigh.

XVIII.

"I need not to my friends recall,
How Mortham shunn'd my father's hall;
A man of silence and of woe,
Yet ever anxious to bestow
On my poor self whate'er could prove
A kinsman's confidence and love.
My feeble aid could sometimes chase
The clouds of sorrow for a space:
But oftener, fix'd beyond my power,
I mark'd his deep despondence lower.
One dismal cause, by all unguess'd,
His fearful confidence confess'd;
And twice it was my hap to see
Examples of that agony,
Which for a season can o'erstrain
And wreck the structure of the brain.

He had the awful power to know
The approaching mental overthrow,
And while his mind had courage yet
To struggle with the dreadful fit,
The victim writhed against its throes,
Like wretch beneath a murderer's blows.
This malady, I well could mark,
Sprung from some direful cause and dark;
But still he kept its source conceal'd,
Till arming for the civil field;
Then in my charge he bade me hold
A treasure huge of gems and gold,
With this disjointed dismal scroll,
That tells the secret of his soul,
In such wild words as oft betray
A mind by anguish forced astray."—

XIX.

MORTHAM'S HISTORY.

"Matilda! thou hast seen me start,
As if a dagger thrill'd my heart,
When it has hap'd some casual phrase
Waked memory of my former days.
Believe, that few can backward cast
Their thoughts with pleasure on the past;
But I !—my youth was rash and vain,
And blood and rage my manhood stain,
And my grey hairs must now descend
To my cold grave without a friend!
Even thou, Matilda, wilt disown
Thy kinsman, when his guilt is known.
And must I lift the bloody veil,
That hides my dark and fatal tale!
I must—I will—Pale phantom, cease!
Leave me one little hour in peace!
Thus haunted, think'st thou I have skill
Thine own commission to fulfil?
Or, while thou point'st with gesture fierce,
Thy blighted cheek, thy bloody hearse,
How can I paint thee as thou wert,
So fair in face, so warm in heart!

XX.

"Yes, she was fair!—Matilda, thou
Hast a soft sadness on thy brow;
But hers was like the sunny glow,
That laughs on earth and all below!
We wedded secret—there was need—
Differing in country and in creed;

And, when to Mortham's tower she came,
We mentioned not her race and name,
Until thy sire, who fought afar,
Should turn him home from foreign war,
On whose kind influence we relied
To soothe her father's ire and pride.
Few months we lived retired, unknown,
To all but one dear friend alone,
One darling friend—I spare his shame,
I will not write the villain's name!
My trespasses I might forget,
And sue in vengeance for the debt
Due by a brother worm to me,
Ungrateful to God's clemency,
That spared me penitential time,
Nor cut me off amid my crime.—

XXI.

" A kindly smile to all she lent,
But on her husband's friend 'twas bent
So kind, that from its harmless glee,
The wretch misconstrued villany.
Repulsed in his presumptuous love,
A vengeful snare the traitor wove.
Alone we sat—the flask had flow'd,
My blood with heat unwonted glow'd.
When through the alley'd walk we spied
With hurried step my Edith glide,
Cowering beneath the verdant screen,
As one unwilling to be seen.
Words cannot paint the fiendish smile,
That curl'd the traitor's cheek the while!
Fiercely I question'd of the cause;
He made a cold and artful pause,
Then pray'd it might not chafe my mood—
'There was a gallant in the wood!'
We had been shooting at the deer;
My cross-bow (evil chance!) was near:
That ready weapon of my wrath
I caught, and, hasting up the path,
In the yew grove my wife I found,
A stranger's arms her neck had bound!
I mark'd his heart—the bow I drew—
I loosed the shaft—'twas more than true!
I found my Edith's dying charms
Lock'd in her murder'd brother's arms!
He came in secret to enquire
Her state, and reconcile her sire.

XXII.

" All fled my rage—the villain first,
Whose craft my jealousy had nursed;
He sought in far and foreign clime
To 'scape the vengeance of his crime.
The manner of the slaughter done
Was known to few, my guilt to none;
Some tale my faithful steward framed—
I know not what—of shaft mis-aim'd;
And even from those the act who knew,
He hid the hand from which it flew.
Untouch'd by human laws I stood,
But God had heard the cry of blood!
There is a blank upon my mind,
A fearful vision ill-defined,
Of raving till my flesh was torn,
Of dungeon-bolts and fetters worn—
And when I waked to woe more mild,
And question'd of my infant child—
(Have I not written, that she bare
A boy, like summer morning fair?)—
With looks confused my menials tell
That armed men in Mortham dell
Beset the nurse's evening way,
And bore her, with her charge, away.
My faithless friend, and none but he,
Could profit by this villany;
Him then, I sought, with purpose dread
Of treble vengeance on his head!
He 'scaped me—but my bosom's wound
Some faint relief from wandering found;
And over distant land and sea
I bore my load of misery.

XXIII.

" 'Twas then that fate my footsteps led
Among a daring crew and dread,
With whom full oft my hated life
I ventured in such desperate strife,
That even my fierce associates saw
My frantic deeds with doubt and awe.
Much then I learn'd, and much can
show,
Of human guilt and human woe,
Yet ne'er have, in my wanderings, known
A wretch, whose sorrows match'd my
own!—
It chanced, that after battle fray,
Upon the bloody field we lay;

The yellow moon her lustre shed
Upon the wounded and the dead,
While, sense in toil and wassail drown'd,
My ruffian comrades slept around,
There came a voice—its silver tone
Was soft, Matilda, as thine own—
' Ah, wretch!' it said, ' what makest thou
    here,
While unavenged my bloody bier,
While unprotected lives mine heir,
Without a father's name and care?'

XXIV.

"I heard—obey'd—and homeward drew;
The fiercest of our desperate crew
I brought at time of need to aid
My purposed vengeance, long delay'd.
But, humble be my thanks to Heaven,
That better hopes and thoughts has given,
And by our Lord's dear prayer has
    taught,
Mercy by mercy must be bought!—
Let me in misery rejoice—
I've seen his face—I've heard his voice—
I claim'd of him my only child—
As he disown'd the theft, he smiled!
That very calm and callous look,
That fiendish sneer his visage took,
As when he said, in scornful mood,
' There is a gallant in the wood!'—
I did not slay him as he stood—
All praise be to my Maker given!
Long suffrance is one path to heaven."

XXV.

Thus far the woful tale was heard,
When something in the thicket stirr'd.
Up Redmond sprung; the villain Guy,
(For he it was that lurk'd so nigh,)
Drew back—he durst not cross his steel
A moment's space with brave O'Neale,
For all the treasured gold that rests
In Mortham's iron-banded chests.
Redmond resumed his seat ;—he said,
Some roe was rustling in the shade.
Bertram laugh'd grimly when he saw
His timorous comrade backward draw;
" A trusty mate art thou, to fear
A single arm, and aid so near!
Yet have I seen thee mark a deer.

Give me thy carabine—I'll show
An art that thou wilt gladly know,
How thou mayst safely quell a foe."

XXVI.

On hands and knees fierce Bertram drew
The spreading birch and hazels through,
Till he had Redmond full in view ;
The gun he levell'd—Mark like this
Was Bertram never known to miss,
When fair opposed to aim there sate
An object of his mortal hate.
That day young Redmond's death had
    seen,
But twice Matilda came between
The carabine and Redmond's breast,
Just ere the spring his finger press'd.
A deadly oath the ruffian swore,
But yet his fell design forbore:
" It ne'er," he mutter'd, " shall be said,
That thus I scath'd thee, haughty maid!"
Then moved to seek more open aim,
When to his side Guy Denzil came:
" Bertram, forbear!—we are undone
For ever, if thou fire the gun.
By all the fiends, an armed force
Descends the dell, of foot and horse!
We perish if they hear a shot—
Madman! we have a safer plot—
Nay, friend, be ruled, and bear thee back!
Behold, down yonder hollow track,
The warlike leader of the band
Comes, with his broadsword in his hand."
Bertram look'd up ; he saw, he knew
That Denzil's fears had counsell'd true,
Then cursed his fortune and withdrew,
Threaded the woodlands undescried,
And gained the cave on Greta side.

XXVII.

They whom dark Bertram, in his wrath,
Doom'd to captivity or death,
Their thoughts to one sad subject lent,
Saw not nor heard the ambushment.
Heedless and unconcern'd they sate,
While on the very verge of fate;
Heedless and unconcern'd remain'd,
When Heaven the murderer's arm re-
    strain'd;

As ships drift darkling down the tide,
Nor see the shelves o'er which they
    glide.
Uninterrupted thus they heard
What Mortham's closing tale declared.
He spoke of wealth as of a load,
By Fortune on a wretch bestow'd,
In bitter mockery of hate,
His cureless woes to aggravate;
But yet he pray'd Matilda's care
Might save that treasure for his heir—
His Edith's son—for still he raved
As confident his life was saved;
In frequent vision, he averr'd,
He saw his face, his voice he heard;
Then argued calm—had murder been,
The blood, the corpses, had been seen;
Some had pretended, too, to mark
On Windermere a stranger bark,
Whose crew, with jealous care, yet mild,
Guarded a female and a child.
While these faint proofs he told and
    press'd,
Hope seem'd to kindle in his breast;
Though inconsistent, vague, and vain,
It warp'd his judgment, and his brain.

XXVIII.

These solemn words his story close:—
" Heaven witness for me, that I chose
My part in this sad civil fight,
Moved by no cause but England's right.
My country's groans have bid me draw
My sword for Gospel and for law;—
These righted, I fling arms aside,
And seek my son through Europe wide,
My wealth, on which a kinsman nigh
Already casts a grasping eye,
With thee may unsuspected lie.
When of my death Matilda hears,
Let her retain her trust three years;
If none, from me, the treasure claim,
Perish'd is Mortham's race and name.
Then let it leave her generous hand,
And flow in bounty o'er the land;
Soften the wounded prisoner's lot,
Rebuild the peasant's ruin'd cot;
So spoils, acquired by fight afar,
Shall mitigate domestic war."

XXIX.

The generous youths, who well had
    known
Of Mortham's mind the powerful tone,
To that high mind, by sorrow swerved,
Gave sympathy his woes deserved;
But Wilfrid chief, who saw reveal'd
Why Mortham wish'd his life conceal'd,
In secret, doubtless, to pursue
The schemes his wilder'd fancy drew.
Thoughtful he heard Matilda tell,
That she would share her father's cell,
His partner of captivity,
Where'er his prison-house should be;
Yet grieved to think that Rokeby hall,
Dismantled, and forsook by all,
Open to rapine and to stealth,
Had now no safe-guard for the wealth
Intrusted by her kinsman kind,
And for such noble use design'd.
" Was Barnard Castle then her choice,"
Wilfrid enquired with hasty voice,
" Since there the victor's laws ordain,
Her father must a space remain?"
A flutter'd hope his accents shook,
A flutter'd joy was in his look.
Matilda hasten'd to reply,
For anger flash'd in Redmond's eye;—
" Duty," she said, with gentle grace,
" Kind Wilfrid, has no choice of place;
Else had I for my sire assign'd
Prison less galling to his mind,
Than that his wild-wood haunts which
    sees
And hears the murmur of the Tees,
Recalling thus, with every glance,
What captive's sorrow can enhance;
But where those woes are highest, there
Needs Rokeby most his daughter's care."

XXX.

He felt the kindly check she gave,
And stood abash'd—then answer'd grave:
" I sought thy purpose, noble maid,
Thy doubts to clear, thy schemes to aid.
I have beneath mine own command,
So wills my sire, a gallant band,
And well could send some horseman wight
To bear the treasure forth by night,

And so bestow it as you deem
In these ill days may safest seem."—
"Thanks, gentle Wilfrid, thanks," she
  said :
"O, be it not one day delay'd !
And, more, thy sister-friend to aid,
Be thou thyself content to hold,
In thine own keeping, Mortham's gold,
Safest with thee."—While thus she spoke,
Arm'd soldiers on their converse broke,
The same of whose approach afraid,
The ruffians left their ambuscade.
Their chief to Wilfrid bended low,
Then look'd around as for a foe.
"What mean'st thou, friend," young
  Wycliffe said,
"Why thus in arms beset the glade ?"—
"That would I gladly learn from you :
For up my squadron as I drew,
To exercise our martial game
Upon the moor of Barninghame,
A stranger told you were waylaid,
Surrounded, and to death betray'd.
He had a leader's voice, I ween,
A falcon glance, a warrior's mien.
He bade me bring you instant aid;
I doubted not, and I obey'd."

XXXI.

Wilfrid changed colour, and, amazed,
Turn'd short, and on the speaker gazed;
While Redmond every thicket round
Track'd earnest as a questing hound,
And Denzil's carabine he found ;
Sure evidence, by which they knew
The warning was as kind as true.
Wisest it seem'd, with cautious speed
To leave the dell. It was agreed,
That Redmond, with Matilda fair,
And fitting guard, should home repair ;
At nightfall Wilfrid should attend,
With a strong band, his sister-friend,
To bear with her from Rokeby's bowers
To Barnard Castle's lofty towers,
Secret and safe the banded chests,
In which the wealth of Mortham rests.
This hasty purpose fix'd, they part,
Each with a grieved and anxious heart.

CANTO FIFTH.

I.

The sultry summer day is done,
The western hills have hid the sun,
But mountain peak and village spire
Retain reflection of his fire.
Old Barnard's towers are purple still,
To those that gaze from Toller-hill ;
Distant and high, the tower of Bowes
Like steel upon the anvil glows ;
And Stanmore's ridge, behind that lay,
Rich with the spoils of parting day,
In crimson and in gold array'd,
Streaks yet a while the closing shade,
Then slow resigns to darkening heaven
The tints which brighter hours had given.
Thus aged men, full loth and slow,
The vanities of life forego,
And count their youthful follies o'er,
Till Memory lends her light no more.

II.

The eve, that slow on upland fades,
Has darker closed on Rokeby's glades,
Where, sunk within their banks profound,
Her guardian streams to meeting wound.
The stately oaks, whose sombre frown
Of noontide made a twilight brown,
Impervious now to fainter light,
Of twilight make an early night.
Hoarse into middle air arose
The vespers of the roosting crows,
And with congenial murmurs seem
To wake the Genii of the stream ;
For louder clamour'd Greta's tide,
And Tees in deeper voice replied.
And fitful waked the evening wind,
Fitful in sighs its breath resign'd.
Wilfrid, whose fancy-nurtured soul
Felt in the scene a soft control,
With lighter footstep press'd the ground,
And often paused to look around ;
And, though his path was to his love,
Could not but linger in the grove,
To drink the thrilling interest dear,
Of awful pleasure check'd by fear.
Such inconsistent moods have we,
Even when our passions strike the key.

III.

Now, through the wood's dark mazes past,
The opening lawn he reach'd at last,
Where, silver'd by the moonlight ray,
The ancient Hall before him lay.
Those martial terrors long were fled,
That frown'd of old around its head:
The battlements, the turrets grey,
Seem'd half abandon'd to decay;[47]
On barbican and keep of stone
Stern Time the foeman's work had done.
Where banners the invader braved,
The harebell now and wallflower waved;
In the rude guard-room, where of yore
Their weary hours the warders wore,
Now, while the cheerful fagots blaze,
On the paved floor the spindle plays;
The flanking guns dismounted lie,
The moat is ruinous and dry,
The grim portcullis gone—and all
The fortress turn'd to peaceful Hall.

IV

But yet precautions, lately ta'en,
Show'd danger's day revived again;
The court-yard wall show'd marks of care,
The fall'n defences to repair,
Lending such strength as might withstand,
The insult of marauding band.
The beams once more were taught to bear
The trembling drawbridge into air,
And not, till question'd o'er and o'er,
For Wilfrid oped the jealous door,
And when he entered, bolt and bar
Resumed their place with sullen jar;
Then, as he cross'd the vaulted porch,
The old grey porter raised his torch,
And view'd him o'er, from foot to head,
Ere to the hall his steps he led.
That huge old hall, of knightly state,
Dismantled seem'd and desolate.
The moon through transom-shafts of stone,
Which cross'd the latticed oriels, shone,
And by the mournful light she gave,
The Gothic vault seem'd funeral cave.
Pennon and banner waved no more
O'er beams of stag and tusks of boar,
Nor glimmering arms were marshall'd
    seen,
To glance those silvan spoils between.

Those arms, those ensigns, borne away,
Accomplish'd Rokeby's brave array,
But all were lost on Marston's day!
Yet here and there the moonbeams fall
Where armour yet adorns the wall,
Cumbrous of size, uncouth to sight,
And useless in the modern fight!
Like veteran relic of the wars,
Known only by neglected scars.

V.

Matilda soon to greet him came,
And bade them light the evening flame;
Said, all for parting was prepared,
And tarried but for Wilfrid's guard.
But then, reluctant to unfold
His father's avarice of gold,
He hinted, that lest jealous eye
Should on their precious burden pry,
He judged it best the castle gate
To enter when the night wore late;
And therefore he had left command
With those he trusted of his band,
That they should be at Rokeby met,
What time the midnight-watch was set.
Now Redmond came, whose anxious care
Till then was busied to prepare
All needful, meetly to arrange
The mansion for its mournful change.
With Wilfrid's care and kindness pleased,
His cold unready hand he seized,
And press'd it, till his kindly strain
The gentle youth return'd again.
Seem'd as between them this was said,
" A while let jealousy be dead;
And let our contest be, whose care
Shall best assist this helpless fair."

VI.

There was no speech the truce to bind,
It was a compact of the mind,—
A generous thought, at once impress'd
On either rival's generous breast.
Matilda well the secret took,
From sudden change of mien and look;
And—for not small had been her fear
Of jealous ire and danger near—
Felt, even in her dejected state,
A joy beyond the reach of fate.

They closed beside the chimney's blaze,
And talk'd and hoped for happier days,
And lent their spirits' rising glow
A while to gild impending woe;—
High privilege of youthful time,
Worth all the pleasures of our prime!
The bickering fagot sparkled bright,
And gave the scene of love to sight,
Bade Wilfrid's cheek more lively glow,
Play'd on Matilda's neck of snow,
Her nut-brown curls and forehead high,
And laugh'd in Redmond's azure eye.
Two lovers by the maiden sate,
Without a glance of jealous hate;
The maid her lovers sat between,
With open brow and equal mien;—
It is a sight but rarely spied,
Thanks to man's wrath and woman's pride.

VII.

While thus in peaceful guise they sate,
A knock alarm'd the outer gate,
And ere the tardy porter stirr'd,
The tinkling of a harp was heard.
A manly voice of mellow swell,
Bore burden to the music well.

Song.

"Summer eve is gone and past,
Summer dew is falling fast;—
I have wander'd all the day,
Do not bid me farther stray!
Gentle hearts, of gentle kin,
Take the wandering harper in!"

But the stern porter answer gave,
With "Get thee hence, thou strolling
knave
The king wants soldiers; war, I trow,
Were meeter trade for such as thou."
At this unkind reproof, again
Answer'd the ready Minstrel's strain.

Song resumed.

"Bid not me, in battle-field,
Buckler lift, or broadsword wield!
All my strength and all my art
Is to touch the gentle heart,
With the wizard notes that ring
From the peaceful minstrel-string."

The porter, all unmoved, replied,—
"Depart in peace, with Heaven to guide;
If longer by the gate thou dwell,
Trust me, thou shalt not part so well."

VIII.

With somewhat of appealing look,
The harper's part young Wilfrid took:
"These notes so wild and ready thrill,
They show no vulgar minstrel's skill;
Hard were his task to seek a home
More distant, since the night is come;
And for his faith I dare engage—
Your Harpool's blood is sour'd by age;
His gate, once readily display'd,
To greet the friend, the poor to aid,
Now even to me, though known of old,
Did but reluctantly unfold."
"O blame not, as poor Harpool's crime,
An evil of this evil time.
He deems dependent on his care
The safety of his patron's heir,
Nor judges meet to ope the tower
To guest unknown at parting hour,
Urging his duty to excess
Of rough and stubborn faithfulness.
For this poor harper, I would fain
He may relax:—Hark to his strain!"—

IX.

Song resumed.

"I have song of war for knight,
Lay of love for lady bright,
Fairy tale to lull the heir,
Goblin grim the maids to scare.
Dark the night, and long till day,
Do not bid me farther stray!

"Rokeby's lords of martial fame,
I can count them name by name;
Legends of their line there be,
Known to few, but known to me;
If you honour Rokeby's kin,
Take the wandering harper in!

"Rokeby's lords had fair regard
For the harp, and for the bard:
Baron's race throve never well,
Where the curse of minstrel fell.

If you love that noble kin,
Take the weary harper in !"—

" Hark ! Harpool parleys — there is
hope,"
Said Redmond, "that the gate will ope."—
—" For all thy brag and boast, I trow,
Nought know'st thou of the Felon Sow,"[48]
Quoth Harpool, " nor how Greta-side
She roam'd, and Rokeby forest wide ;
Nor how Ralph Rokeby gave the beast
To Richmond's friars to make a feast.
Of Gilbert Griffinson the tale
Goes, and of gallant Peter Dale,
That well could strike with sword amain,
And of the valiant son of Spain,
Friar Middleton, and blithe Sir Ralph :
There were a jest to make us laugh !
If thou canst tell it, in yon shed
Thou'st won thy supper and thy bed."

X.

Matilda smiled ; " Cold hope," said she,
" From Harpool's love of minstrelsy !
But, for this harper, may we dare,
Redmond, to mend his couch and fare ?"—
" O, ask me not !—At minstrel-string
My heart from infancy would spring ;
Nor can I hear its simplest strain,
But it brings Erin's dream again,
When placed by Owen Lysagh's knee.
(The Filea of O'Neale was he,[49]
A blind and bearded man, whose eld
Was sacred as a prophet's held,)
I've seen a ring of rugged kerne,
With aspects shaggy, wild, and stern,
Enchanted by the master's lay,
Linger around the livelong day,
Shift from wild rage to wilder glee,
To love, to grief, to ecstacy,
And feel each varied change of soul
Obedient to the bard's control.—
Ah, Clandeboy ! thy friendly floor
Slieve-Donard's oak shall light no more ;[50]
Nor Owen's harp, beside the blaze,
Tell maiden's love, or hero's praise !
The mantling brambles hide thy hearth,
Centre of hospitable mirth ;
All undistinguish'd in the glade,
My sires' glad home is prostrate laid,

Their vassals wander wide and far,
Serve foreign lords in distant war,
And now the stranger's sons enjoy
The lovely woods of Clandeboy !"
He spoke, and proudly turn'd aside,
The starting tear to dry and hide.

XI.

Matilda's dark and soften'd eye
Was glistening ere O'Neale's was dry.
Her hand upon his arm she laid,—
" It is the will of Heaven," she said.
" And think'st thou, Redmond, I can part
From this loved home with lightsome
     heart,
Leaving to wild neglect whate'er
Even from my infancy was dear ?
For in this calm domestic bound
Were all Matilda's pleasures found.
That hearth, my sire was wont to grace,
Full soon may be a stranger's place ;
This hall, in which a child I play'd,
Like thine, dear Redmond, lowly laid,
The bramble and the thorn may braid ;
Or, pass'd for aye from me and mine,
It ne'er may shelter Rokeby's line.
Yet is this consolation given,
My Redmond—'tis the will of Heaven."
Her word, her action, and her phrase,
Were kindly as in early days ;
For cold reserve had lost its power,
In sorrow's sympathetic hour.
Young Redmond dared not trust his voice ;
But rather had it been his choice
To share that melancholy hour,
Than, arm'd with all a chieftain's power,
In full possession to enjoy
Slieve-Donard wide, and Clandeboy.

XII.

The blood left Wilfrid's ashen cheek ;
Matilda sees, and hastes to speak.—
" Happy in friendship's ready aid,
Let all my murmurs here be staid !
And Rokeby's Maiden will not part
From Rokeby's hall with moody heart.
This night at least, for Rokeby's fame,
The hospitable hearth shall flame,
And, ere its native heir retire,
Find for the wanderer rest and fire,

While this poor harper, by the blaze,
Recounts the tale of other days.
Bid Harpool ope the door with speed,
Admit him, and relieve each need.—
Meantime, kind Wycliffe, wilt thou try
Thy minstrel skill ?—Nay, no reply—
And look not sad !—I guess thy thought,
Thy verse with laurels would be bought ;
And poor Matilda, landless now,
Has not a garland for thy brow.
True, I must leave sweet Rokeby's glades,
Nor wander more in Greta's shades ;
But sure, no rigid jailer, thou
Wilt a short prison-walk allow,
Where summer flowers grow wild at
    will,
On Marwood-chase and Toller Hill ;[51]
Then holly green and lily gay
Shall twine in guerdon of thy lay."
The mournful youth, a space aside,
To tune Matilda's harp applied ;
And then a low sad descant rung,
As prelude to the lay he sung.

XIII.

The Cypress Wreath.

O, Lady, twine no wreath for me,
Or twine it of the cypress-tree !
Too lively glow the lilies light,
The varnish'd holly 's all too bright,
The May-flower and the eglantine
May shade a brow less sad than mine;
But, Lady, weave no wreath for me,
Or weave it of the cypress-tree !

Let dimpled Mirth his temples twine
With tendrils of the laughing vine;
The manly oak, the pensive yew,
To patriot and to sage be due;
The myrtle bough bids lovers live,
But that Matilda will not give ;
Then, Lady, twine no wreath for me,
Or twine it of the cypress-tree !

Let merry England proudly rear
Her blended roses, bought so dear;
Let Albin bind her bonnet blue
With heath and harebell dipp'd in dew;

On favour'd Erin's crest be seen
The flower she loves of emerald green—
But, Lady, twine no wreath for me,
Or twine it of the cypress-tree.

Strike the wild harp, while maids pre-
    pare
The ivy meet for minstrel's hair ;
And, while his crown of laurel-leaves,
With bloody hand the victor weaves,
Let the loud trump his triumph tell ;
But, when you hear the passing-bell,
Then, Lady, twine a wreath for me,
And twine it of the cypress-tree.

Yes ! twine for me the cypress bough ;
But, O Matilda, twine not now !
Stay till a few brief months are past,
And I have look'd and loved my last !
When villagers my shroud bestrew
With panzies, rosemary, and rue,—
Then, Lady, weave a wreath for me,
And weave it of the cypress-tree.

XIV.

O'Neale observed the starting tear,
And spoke with kind and blithesome
    cheer—
" No, noble Wilfrid ! ere the day
When mourns the land thy silent lay,
Shall many a wreath be freely wove
By hand of friendship and of love.
I would not wish that rigid Fate
Had doom'd thee to a captive's state,
Whose hands are bound by honour's
    law,
Who wears a sword he must not draw ;
But were it so, in minstrel pride
The land together would we ride,
On prancing steeds, like harpers old,
Bound for the halls of barons bold,
Each lover of the lyre we'd seek,
From Michael's Mount to Skiddaw's
    Peak,
Survey wild Albin's mountain strand,
And roam green Erin's lovely land,
While thou the gentler souls should move,
With lay of pity and of love,
And I, thy mate, in rougher strain,
Would sing of war and warriors slain,

Old England's bards were vanquish'd then,
And Scotland's vaunted Hawthornden,
And, silenced on Iernian shore,
M'Curtin's harp should charm no more!"
In lively mood he spoke, to wile
From Wilfrid's wo-worn cheek a smile.

XV.

" But," said Matilda, " ere thy name,
Good Redmond, gain its destined fame,
Say, wilt thou kindly deign to call
Thy brother-minstrel to the hall?
Bid all the household, too, attend,
Each in his rank a humble friend;
I know their faithful hearts will grieve,
When their poor Mistress takes her leave;
So let the horn and beaker flow
To mitigate their parting woe."
The harper came,—in youth's first prime
Himself; in mode of olden time
His garb was fashion'd, to express
The ancient English minstrel's dress,⁵²
A seemly gown of Kendal green,
With gorget closed of silver sheen;
His harp in silken scarf was slung,
And by his side an anlace hung.
It seem'd some masquer's quaint array,
For revel or for holiday.

XVI.

He made obeisance with a free
Yet studied air of courtesy.
Each look and accent, framed to please,
Seem'd to affect a playful ease;
His face was of that doubtful kind,
That wins the eye, but not the mind;
Yet harsh it seem'd to deem amiss
Of brow so young and smooth as this.
His was the subtle look and sly,
That, spying all, seems nought to spy;
Round all the group his glances stole,
Unmark'd themselves, to mark the whole.
Yet sunk beneath Matilda's look,
Nor could the eye of Redmond brook.
To the suspicious, or the old,
Subtile and dangerous and bold
Had seem'd this self-invited guest;
But young our lovers,—and the rest,
Wrapt in their sorrow and their fear
At parting of their Mistress dear,

Tear-blinded to the Castle-hall,
Came as to bear her funeral pall.

XVII.

All that expression base was gone,
When waked the guest his minstrel tone;
It fled at inspiration's call,
As erst the demon fled from Saul.
More noble glance he cast around,
More free-drawn breath inspired the sound,
His pulse beat bolder and more high,
In all the pride of minstrelsy!
Alas! too soon that pride was o'er,
Sunk with the lay that bade it soar!
His soul resumed, with habit's chain,
Its vices wild and follies vain,
And gave the talent, with him born,
To be a common curse and scorn.
Such was the youth whom Rokeby's Maid,
With condescending kindness, pray'd
Here to renew the strains she loved,
At distance heard and well approved.

XVIII.

Song.

THE HARP.

I was a wild and wayward boy,
My childhood scorn'd each childish toy,
Retired from all, reserved and coy,
To musing prone,
I woo'd my solitary joy,
My Harp alone.

My youth, with bold Ambition's mood,
Despised the humble stream and wood,
Where my poor father's cottage stood,
To fame unknown;—
What should my soaring views make good?
My Harp alone!

Love came with all his frantic fire,
And wild romance of vain desire:
The baron's daughter heard my lyre,
And praised the tone;—
What could presumptuous hope inspire?
My Harp alone!

At manhood's touch the bubble burst,
And manhood's pride the vision curst;

And all that had my folly nursed
    Love's sway to own;
Yet spared the spell that lull'd me first,
    My Harp alone!

Woe came with war, and want with woe;
And it was mine to undergo
Each outrage of the rebel foe:—
    Can aught atone
My fields laid waste, my cot laid low?
    My Harp alone!

Ambition's dreams I've seen depart,
Have rued of penury the smart,
Have felt of love the venom'd dart,
    When hope was flown;
Yet rests one solace to my heart,—
    My Harp alone!

Then over mountain, moor, and hill,
My faithful Harp, I'll bear thee still;
And when this life of want and ill
    Is wellnigh gone,
Thy strings mine elegy shall thrill,
    My Harp alone!

XIX.

" A pleasing lay!" Matilda said;
But Harpool shook his old grey head,
And took his baton and his torch,
To seek his guard-room in the porch.
Edmund observed; with sudden change,
Among the strings his fingers range,
Until they waked a bolder glee
Of military melody;
Then paused amid the martial sound,
And look'd with well-feign'd fear
    around;—
" None to this noble housebelong,"
He said, " that would a Minstrel
    wrong,
Whose fate has been, through good and
    ill,
To love his Royal Master still;
And with your honour'd leave, would fain
Rejoice you with a loyal strain."
Then, as assured by sign and look,
The warlike tone again he took;
And Harpool stopp'd, and turn'd to hear
A ditty of the Cavalier.

XX.

Song.

THE CAVALIER.

While the dawn on the mountain was
    misty and grey,
My true love has mounted his steed and
    away
Over hill, over valley, o'er dale, and o'er
    down;
Heaven shield the brave Gallant that fights
    for the Crown!

He has doff'd the silk doublet the breast-
    plate to bear,
He has placed the steel-cap o'er his long
    flowing hair,
From his belt to his stirrup his broad-
    sword hangs down;
Heaven shield the brave Gallant that fights
    for the Crown!

For the rights of fair England that broad-
    sword he draws,
Her King is his leader, her Church is his
    cause;
His watchword is honour, his pay is
    renown,—
GOD strike with the Gallant that strikes
    for the Crown!

They may boast of their Fairfax, their
    Waller, and all
The roundheaded rebels of Westminster
    Hall;
But tell these bold traitors of London's
    proud town,
That the spears of the North have en-
    circled the Crown.

There's Derby and Cavendish, dread of
    their foes;
There's Erin's high Ormond, and Scot-
    land's Montrose!
Would you match the base Skippon, and
    Massey, and Brown,
With the Barons of England, that fight
    for the Crown?

Now joy to the crest of the brave Ca-
    valier!
Be his banner unconquer'd, resistless his
    spear,
Till in peace and in triumph his toils he
    may drown,
In a pledge to fair England, her Church,
    and her Crown.

XXI.

"Alas!" Matilda said, "that strain,
Good harper, now is heard in vain!
The time has been, at such a sound,
When Rokeby's vassals gather'd round,
An hundred manly hearts would bound;
But now the stirring verse we hear,
Like trump in dying soldier's ear!
Listless and sad the notes we own,
The power to answer them is flown.
Yet not without his meet applause,
Be he that sings the rightful cause,
Even when the crisis of its fate
To human eye seems desperate.
While Rokeby's Heir such power retains,
Let this slight guerdon pay thy pains:—
And, lend thy harp; I fain would try,
If my poor skill can aught supply,
Ere yet I leave my father's hall,
To mourn the cause in which we fall."

XXII.

The harper, with a downcast look,
And trembling hand, her bounty took.—
As yet, the conscious pride of art
Had steel'd him in his treacherous part;
A powerful spring, of force unguess'd,
That hath each gentler mood suppress'd,
And reign'd in many a human breast;
From his that plans the red campaign,
To his that wastes the woodland reign.
The failing wing, the blood-shot eye,—
The sportsman marks with apathy,
Each feeling of his victim's ill
Drown'd in his own successful skill.
The veteran, too, who now no more
Aspires to head the battle's roar,
Loves still the triumph of his art,
And traces on the pencill'd chart
Some stern invader's destined way,
Through blood and ruin, to his prey;

Patriots to death, and towns to flame,
He dooms, to raise another's name,
And shares the guilt, though not the fame.
What pays him for his span of time
Spent in premeditating crime?
What against pity arms his heart?—
It is the conscious pride of art.

XXIII.

But principles in Edmund's mind
Were baseless, vague, and undefined.
His soul, like bark with rudder lost,
On Passion's changeful tide was tost,
Nor Vice nor Virtue had the power
Beyond the impression of the hour;
And, O! when Passion rules, how rare
The hours that fall to Virtue's share!
Yet now she roused her—for the pride,
That lack of sterner guilt supplied,
Could scarce support him when arose
The lay that mourned Matilda's woes.

Song.

THE FAREWELL.

The sound of Rokeby's woods I hear,
    They mingle with the song:
Dark Greta's voice is in mine ear,
    I must not hear them long.
From every loved and native haunt
    The native Heir must stray,
And, like a ghost whom sunbeams daunt,
    Must part before the day.

Soon from the halls my fathers rear'd,
    Their scutcheons may descend.
A line so long beloved and fear'd
    May soon obscurely end.
No longer here Matilda's tone
    Shall bid those echoes swell;
Yet shall they hear her proudly own
    The cause in which we fell.

The Lady paused, and then again
Resumed the lay in loftier strain.

XXIV.

Let our halls and towers decay,
    Be our name and line forgot,

Lands and manors pass away,—
　　We but share our Monarch's lot.
If no more our annals show
　　Battles won and banners taken,
Still in death, defeat, and woe,
　　Ours be loyalty unshaken!

Constant still in danger's hour,
　　Princes own'd our fathers' aid;
Lands and honours, wealth and power,
　　Well their loyalty repaid.
Perish wealth, and power, and pride!
　　Mortal boons by mortals given;
But let constancy abide,—
　　Constancy's the gift of Heaven.

XXV.

While thus Matilda's lay was heard,
A thousand thoughts in Edmund stirr'd.
In peasant life he might have known
As fair a face, as sweet a tone;
But village notes could ne'er supply
That rich and varied melody;
And ne'er in cottage-maid was seen
The easy dignity of mien,
Claiming respect, yet waving state,
That marks the daughters of the great.
Yet not, perchance, had these alone
His scheme of purposed guilt o'erthrown;
But while her energy of mind
Superior rose to griefs combined,
Lending its kindling to her eye,
Giving her form new majesty,—
To Edmund's thought Matilda seem'd
The very object he had dream'd;
When, long ere guilt his soul had known,
In Winston bowers he mused alone,
Taxing his fancy to combine
The face, the air, the voice divine,
Of princess fair, by cruel fate
Reft of her honours, power, and state,
Till to her rightful realm restored
By destined hero's conquering sword.

XXVI.

"Such was my vision!" Edmund thought;
" And have I, then, the ruin wrought
Of such a maid, that fancy ne'er
In fairest vision form'd her peer?

Was it my hand that could unclose
The postern to her ruthless foes?
Foes, lost to honour, law, and faith,
Their kindest mercy sudden death!
Have I done this? I! who have swore,
That if the globe such angel bore,
I would have traced its circle broad,
To kiss the ground on which she trode!—
And now—O! would that earth would
　　rive
And close upon me while alive!—
Is there no hope?　Is all then lost?—
Bertram's already on his post!
Even now, beside the Hall's arch'd door,
I saw his shadow cross the floor!
He was to wait my signal strain—
A little respite thus we gain:
By what I heard the menials say,
Young Wycliffe's troop are on their way—
Alarm precipitates the crime!
My harp must wear away the time."—
And then, in accents faint and low,
He falter'd forth a tale of woe.

XXVII.

Ballad.

" And whither would you lead me then?"
　　Quoth the Friar of orders grey;
And the Ruffians twain replied again,
　　" By a dying woman to pray."

" I see," he said, " a lovely sight,
　　A sight bodes little harm,
A lady as a lily bright,
　　With an infant on her arm."—

" Then do thine office, Friar grey,
　　And see thou shrive her free?
Else shall the sprite, that parts to-night,
　　Fling all its guilt on thee,

" Let mass be said, and trentals read,
　　When thou'rt to convent gone,
And bid the bell of St. Benedict
　　Toll out its deepest tone."

The shrift is done, the Friar is gone,
　　Blindfolded as he came—
Next morning, all in Littlecot Hall[13]
　　Were weeping for their dame.

Wild Darrell is an alter'd man,
  The village crones can tell;
He looks pale as clay, and strives to
    pray,
  If he hears the convent bell.

If prince or peer cross Darrell's way,
  He'll beard him in his pride—
If he meet a Friar of orders grey,
  He droops and turns aside.

XXVIII.

" Harper! methinks thy magic lays,"
Matilda said, " can goblins raise!
Wellnigh my fancy can discern,
Near the dark porch, a visage stern;
E'en now, in yonder shadowy nook,
I see it!—Redmond, Wilfrid, look!—
A human form distinct and clear—
God for thy mercy!—It draws near!"
She saw too true. Stride after stride,
The centre of that chamber wide
Fierce Bertram gain'd; then made a stand,
And, proudly waving with his hand,
Thunder'd—" Be still, upon your lives!—
He bleeds who speaks, he dies who strives."
Behind their chief, the robber crew
Forth from the darken'd portal drew
In silence—save that echo dread
Return'd their heavy measured tread.
The lamp's uncertain lustre gave
Their arms to gleam, their plumes to
    wave;
File after file in order pass,
Like forms on Banquo's mystic glass.
Then, halting at their leader's sign,
At once they form'd and curved their line,
Hemming within its crescent drear
Their victims, like a herd of deer.
Another sign, and to the aim
Levell'd at once their muskets came,
As waiting but their chieftain's word,
To make their fatal volley heard.

XXIX.

Back in a heap the menials drew;
Yet, even in mortal terror, true,
Their pale and startled group oppose
Between Matilda and the foes.

" O, haste thee, Wilfrid!" Redmond
    cried;
" Undo that wicket by thy side!
Bear hence Matilda—gain the wood—
The pass may be a while made good—
Thy band, ere this, must sure be nigh—
O speak not—dally not—but fly!"
While yet the crowd their motions hide,
Through the low wicket door they glide.
Through vaulted passages they wind,
In Gothic intricacy twined;
Wilfrid half led, and half he bore,
Matilda to the postern-door,
And safe beneath the forest tree,
The Lady stands at liberty.
The moonbeams, the fresh gale's caress,
Renew'd suspended consciousness;—
" Where's Redmond?" eagerly she cries;
" Thou answer'st not—he dies! he dies!
And thou hast left him, all bereft
Of mortal aid—with murderers left!
I know it well—he would not yield
His sword to man—his doom is seal'd!
For my scorn'd life, which thou hast
    bought
At price of his, I thank thee not."

XXX.

The unjust reproach, the angry look,
The heart of Wilfrid could not brook.
" Lady," he said, " my band so near,
In safety thou mayst rest thee here.
For Redmond's death thou shalt not
    mourn,
If mine can buy his safe return."
He turn'd away—his heart throbb'd high,
The tear was bursting from his eye;
The sense of her injustice press'd
Upon the Maid's distracted breast,—
" Stay, Wilfrid, stay! all aid is vain!"
He heard, but turn'd him not again;
He reaches now the postern-door,
Now enters—and is seen no more.

XXXI.

With all the agony that e'er
Was gender'd 'twixt suspense and fear,
She watch'd the line of windows tall,
Whose Gothic lattice lights the Hall,

Distinguish'd by the paly red
The lamps in dim reflection shed,
While all beside in wan moonlight
Each grated casement glimmer'd white.
No sight of harm, no sound of ill,
It is a deep and midnight still.
Who look'd upon the scene, had guess'd
All in the Castle were at rest:
When sudden on the windows shone
A lightning flash, just seen and gone!
A shot is heard—Again the flame
Flash'd thick and fast—a volley came!
Then echo'd wildly, from within,
Of shout and scream the mingled din,
And weapon-crash and maddening cry,
Of those who kill, and those who die!—
As fill'd the Hall with sulphurous smoke,
More red, more dark, the death-flash
    broke;
And forms were on the lattice cast,
That struck, or struggled, as they past.

XXXII.

What sounds upon the midnight wind
Approach so rapidly behind?
It is, it is, the tramp of steeds,
Matilda hears the sound, she speeds,
Seizes upon the leader's rein—
" O, haste to aid, ere aid be vain!
Fly to the postern—gain the Hall!"
From saddle spring the troopers all;
Their gallant steeds, at liberty,
Run wild along the moonlight lea.
But, ere they burst upon the scene,
Full stubborn had the conflict been.
When Bertram mark'd Matilda's flight,
It gave the signal for the fight;
And Rokeby's veterans, seam'd with scars
Of Scotland's and of Erin's wars,
Their momentary panic o'er,
Stood to the arms which then they bore;
(For they were weapon'd, and prepared
Their Mistress on her way to guard.)
Then cheer'd them to the fight O'Neale,
Then peal'd the shot, and clash'd the steel;
The war-smoke soon with sable breath
Darken'd the scene of blood and death,
While on the few defenders close
The Bandits, with redoubled blows,

And, twice driven back, yet fierce and fell
Renew the charge with frantic yell.

XXXIII.

Wilfrid has fall'n—but o'er him stood
Young Redmond, soil'd with smoke and
    blood,
Cheering his mates with heart and hand
Still to make good their desperate stand.
" Up, comrades, up! In Rokeby halls
Ne'er be it said our courage falls.
What! faint ye for their savage cry,
Or do the smoke-wreaths daunt your eye?
These rafters have return'd a shout
As loud at Rokeby's wassail rout,
As thick a smoke these hearths have given
At Hallow-tide or Christmas-even.[54]
Stand to it yet! renew the fight,
For Rokeby's and Matilda's right!
These slaves! they dare not, hand to hand,
Bide buffet from a true man's brand."
Impetuous, active, fierce, and young,
Upon the advancing foes he sprung.
Woe to the wretch at whom is bent
His brandish'd falchion's sheer descent!
Backward they scatter'd as he came,
Like wolves before the levin flame,
When, 'mid their howling conclave driven,
Hath glanced the thunderbolt of heaven.
Bertram rush'd on—but Harpool clasp'd
His knees, although in death he gasp'd,
His falling corpse before him flung,
And round the trammell'd ruffian clung.
Just then, the soldiers fill'd the dome,
And, shouting, charged the felons home
So fiercely, that, in panic dread,
They broke, they yielded, fell, or fled.
Bertram's stern voice they heed no more,
Though heard above the battle's roar;
While, trampling down the dying man,
He strove, with volley'd threat and ban,
In scorn of odds, in fate's despite,
To rally up the desperate fight.

XXXIV.

Soon murkier clouds the Hall enfold
Than e'er from battle-thunders roll'd;
So dense, the combatants scarce know
To aim or to avoid the blow,

Smothering and blindfold grows the
    fight—
But soon shall dawn a dismal light!
'Mid cries, and clashing arms, there came
The hollow sound of rushing flame;
New horrors on the tumult dire
Arise—the Castle is on fire!
Doubtful, if chance had cast the brand,
Or frantic Bertram's desperate hand.
Matilda saw—for frequent broke
From the dim casements gusts of smoke.
Yon tower, which late so clear defined
On the fair hemisphere reclined,
That, pencill'd on its azure pure,
The eye could count each embrazure,
Now, swath'd within the sweeping cloud,
Seems giant-spectre in his shroud;
Till, from each loop-hole flashing light,
A spout of fire shines ruddy bright,
And, gathering to united glare,
Streams high into the midnight air;
A dismal beacon, far and wide
That waken'd Greta's slumbering side.
Soon all beneath, through gallery long,
And pendant arch the fire flash'd strong,
Snatching whatever could maintain,
Raise, or extend, its furious reign;
Startling, with closer cause of dread,
The females who the conflict fled,
And now rush'd forth upon the plain,
Filling the air with clamours vain.

XXXV.

But ceased not yet, the Hall within,
The shriek, the shout, the carnage-din,
Till bursting lattices give proof
The flames have caught the rafter'd roof.
What! wait they till its beams amain
Crash on the slayers and the slain?
The alarm is caught—the drawbridge falls,
The warriors hurry from the walls,
But, by the conflagration's light,
Upon the lawn renew the fight.
Each struggling felon down was hew'd,
Not one could gain the sheltering wood;
But forth the affrighted harper sprung,
And to Matilda's robe he clung.
Her shriek, entreaty, and command,
Stopp'd the pursuer's lifted hand.

Denzil and he alive were ta'en;
The rest, save Bertram, all are slain.

XXXVI.

And where is Bertram?—Soaring high
The general flame ascends the sky;
In gather'd group the soldiers gaze
Upon the broad and roaring blaze,
When, like infernal demon, sent,
Red from his penal element,
To plague and to pollute the air,—
His face all gore, on fire his hair,
Forth from the central mass of smoke
The giant form of Bertram broke!
His brandish'd sword on high he rears,
Then plung'd among opposing spears;
Round his left arm his mantle truss'd,
Received and foil'd three lances' thrust;
Nor these his headlong course withstood,
Like reeds he snapp'd the tough ash-
    wood.
In vain his foes around him clung;
With matchless force aside he flung
Their boldest,—as the bull, at bay,
Tosses the ban-dogs from his way,
Through forty foes his path he made,
And safely gain'd the forest glade.

XXXVII.

Scarce was this final conflict o'er,
When from the postern Redmond bore
Wilfrid, who, as of life bereft,
Had in the fatal Hall been left,
Deserted there by all his train:
But Redmond saw, and turn'd again.—
Beneath an oak he laid him down,
That in the blaze gleam'd ruddy brown,
And then his mantle's clasp undid;
Matilda held his drooping head,
Till, given to breathe the freer air,
Returning life repaid their care.
He gazed on them with heavy sigh,—
"I could have wish'd even thus to die!"
No more he said—for now with speed
Each trooper had regain'd his steed;
The ready palfreys stood array'd,
For Redmond and for Rokeby's Maid;
Two Wilfrid on his horse sustain,
One leads his charger by the rein.

But oft Matilda look'd behind,
As up the Vale of Tees they wind,
Where far the mansion of her sires
Beacon'd the dale with midnight fires.
In gloomy arch above them spread,
The clouded heaven lower'd bloody red;
Beneath, in sombre light, the flood
Appear'd to roll in waves of blood.
Then, one by one, was heard to fall
The tower, the donjon-keep, the hall.
Each rushing down with thunder sound,
A space the conflagration drown'd;
Till, gathering strength, again it rose,
Announced its triumph in its close,
Shook wide its light the landscape o'er,
Then sunk—and Rokeby was no more!

CANTO SIXTH.

I.

The summer sun, whose early power
Was wont to gild Matilda's bower,
And rouse her with his matin ray
Her duteous orisons to pay,—
That morning sun has three times seen
The flowers unfold on Rokeby green,
But sees no more the slumbers fly
From fair Matilda's hazel eye;
That morning sun has three times broke
On Rokeby's glades of elm and oak,
But, rising from their silvan screen,
Marks no grey turrets glance between.
A shapeless mass lie keep and tower,
That, hissing to the morning shower,
Can but with smouldering vapour pay
The early smile of summer day.
The peasant, to his labour bound,
Pauses to view the blacken'd mound,
Striving, amid the ruin'd space,
Each well-remember'd spot to trace.
That length of frail and fire-scorch'd
    wall
Once screen'd the hospitable hall;
When yonder broken arch was whole,
'Twas there was dealt the weekly dole;
And where yon tottering columns nod,
The chapel sent the hymn to God.—

So flits the world's uncertain span!
Nor zeal for God, nor love for man,
Gives mortal monuments a date
Beyond the power of Time and Fate.
The towers must share the builder's doom;
Ruin is theirs, and his a tomb:
But better boon benignant Heaven
To Faith and Charity has given,
And bids the Christian hope sublime
Transcend the bounds of Fate and Time.

II.

Now the third night of summer came,
Since that which witness'd Rokeby's flame.
On Brignall cliffs and Scargill brake
The owlet's homilies awake,
The bittern scream'd from rush and flag,
The raven slumber'd on his crag,
Forth from his den the otter drew,—
Grayling and trout their tyrant knew,
As between reed and sedge he peers,
With fierce round snout and sharpen'd ears,
Or, prowling by the moonbeam cool,
Watches the stream or swims the pool;—
Perch'd on his wonted eyrie high,
Sleep seal'd the tercelet's wearied eye,
That all the day had watch'd so well
The cushat dart across the dell.
In dubious beam reflected shone
That lofty cliff of pale grey stone,
Beside whose base the secret cave
To rapine late a refuge gave.
The crag's wild crest of copse and yew
On Greta's breast dark shadows threw;
Shadows that met or shunn'd the sight,
With every change of fitful light;
As hope and fear alternate chase
Our course through life's uncertain race.

III.

Gliding by crag and copsewood green,
A solitary form was seen
To trace with stealthy pace the wold,
Like fox that seeks the midnight fold,
And pauses oft, and cowers dismay'd,
At every breath that stirs the shade.
He passes now the ivy bush,—
The owl has seen him, and is hush;
He passes now the dodder'd oak,—
Ye heard the startled raven croak;

Lower and lower he descends,
Rustle the leaves, the brushwood bends;
The otter hears him tread the shore,
And dives, and is beheld no more;
And by the cliff of pale grey stone
The midnight wanderer stands alone.
Methinks that by the moon we trace
A well-remember'd form and face!
That stripling shape, that cheek so pale,
Combine to tell a rueful tale,
Of powers misused, of passion's force,
Of guilt, of grief, and of remorse!
'Tis Edmund's eye, at every sound
That flings that guilty glance around;
'Tis Edmund's trembling haste divides
The brushwood that the cavern hides;
And, when its narrow porch lies bare,
'Tis Edmund's form that enters there.

IV.

His flint and steel have sparkled bright,
A lamp hath lent the cavern light.
Fearful and quick his eye surveys
Each angle of the gloomy maze.
Since last he left that stern abode,
It seem'd as none its floor had trode;
Untouch'd appear'd the various spoil,
The purchase of his comrades' toil;
Masks and disguises grim'd with mud,
Arms broken and defiled with blood,
And all the nameless tools that aid
Night-felons in their lawless trade,
Upon the gloomy walls were hung,
Or lay in nooks obscurely flung.
Still on the sordid board appear
The relics of the noontide cheer;
Flagons and emptied flasks were there,
And bench o'erthrown, and shatter'd chair,
And all around the semblance show'd,
As when the final revel glow'd,
When the red sun was setting fast,
And parting pledge Guy Denzil past.
"To Rokeby treasure-vaults!" they
    quaff'd,
And shouted loud and wildly laugh'd,
Pour'd maddening from the rocky door,
And parted—to return no more!
They found in Rokeby vaults their
    doom,—
A bloody death, a burning tomb!

V.

There his own peasant dress he spies,
Doff'd to assume that quaint disguise;
And, shuddering, thought upon his glee,
When prank'd in garb of minstrelsy.
" O, be the fatal art accurst,"
He cried, "that moved my folly first;
Till, bribed by bandits' base applause,
I burst through God's and Nature's laws!
Three summer days are scantly past
Since I have trod this cavern last,
A thoughtless wretch, and prompt to err—
But, O, as yet no murderer!
Even now I list my comrades' cheer,
That general laugh is in mine ear,
Which raised my pulse and steel'd my
    heart,
As I rehearsed my treacherous part—
And would that all since then could seem
The phantom of a fever's dream !
But fatal Memory notes too well
The horrors of the dying yell
From my despairing mates that broke,
When flash'd the fire and roll'd the smoke;
When the avengers shouting came,
And hemm'd us 'twixt the sword and
    flame !
My frantic flight,—the lifted brand,—
That angel's interposing hand ?—
If, for my life from slaughter freed,
I yet could pay some grateful meed !
Perchance this object of my quest
May aid"—he turn'd, nor spoke the rest

VI.

Due northward from the rugged hearth,
With paces five he metes the earth,
Then toil'd with mattock to explore
The entrails of the cabin floor,
Nor paused till, deep beneath the ground,
His search a small steel casket found.
Just as he stoop'd to loose its hasp,
His shoulder felt a giant grasp;
He started, and look'd up aghast,
Then shriek'd!—'Twas Bertram held
    him fast.
" Fear not!" he said; but who could hear
That deep stern voice, and cease to fear

"Fear not!—By Heaven, he shakes as
        much
As partridge in the falcon's clutch:"—
He raised him, and unloosed his hold,
While from the opening casket roll'd
A chain and reliquaire of gold.
Bertram beheld it with surprise,
Gazed on its fashion and device,
Then, cheering Edmund as he could,
Somewhat he smooth'd his rugged mood:
For still the youth's half-lifted eye
Quiver'd with terror's agony,
And sidelong glanced, as to explore,
In meditated flight, the door.
"Sit," Bertram said, "from danger free:
Thou canst not, and thou shalt not, flee.
Chance brings me hither; hill and plain
I've sought for refuge-place in vain.
And tell me now, thou aguish boy,
What makest thou here? what means
        this toy?
Denzil and thou, I mark'd, were ta'en;
What lucky chance unbound your chain?
I deem'd, long since on Baliol's tower,
Your heads were warp'd with sun and
        shower.
Tell me the whole—and, mark! nought
        e'er
Chafes me like falsehood, or like fear."
Gathering his courage to his aid,
But trembling still, the youth obey'd.

VII.

"Denzil and I two nights pass'd o'er
In fetters on the dungeon floor.
A guest the third sad morrow brought;
Our hold dark Oswald Wycliffe sought,
And eyed my comrade long askance,
With fix'd and penetrating glance.
'Guy Denzil art thou call'd?'—'The
        same.'—
'At Court who served wild Buckinghame;
Thence banish'd, won a keeper's place,
So Villiers will'd, in Marwood-chase;
That lost—I need not tell thee why—
Thou madest thy wit thy wants supply,
Then fought for Rokeby:—Have I guess'd
My prisoner right?'—'At thy behest.'—
He paused a while, and then went on
With low and confidential tone;—

Me, as I judge, not then he saw,
Close nestled in my couch of straw.—
'List to me, Guy. Thou know'st the
        great
Have frequent need of what they hate;
Hence, in their favour oft we see
Unscrupled, useful men like thee.
Were I disposed to bid thee live,
What pledge of faith hast thou to give?'

VIII.

"The ready Fiend, who never yet
Hath failed to sharpen Denzil's wit,
Prompted his lie—'His only child
Should rest his pledge.'—The Baron
        smiled,
And turn'd to me—'Thou art his son?'
I bowed—our fetters were undone,
And we were led to hear apart
A dreadful lesson of his art.
Wilfrid, he said, his heir and son,
Had fair Matilda's favour won;
And long since had their union been,
But for her father's bigot spleen,
Whose brute and blindfold party-rage
Would, force per force, her hand engage
To a base kern of Irish earth,
Unknown his lineage and his birth,
Save that a dying ruffian bore
The infant brat to Rokeby door.
Gentle restraint, he said, would lead
Old Rokeby to enlarge his creed;
But fair occasion he must find
For such restraint well-meant and kind,
The Knight being rendered to his charge
But as a prisoner at large.

IX.

"He school'd us in a well-forged tale,
Of scheme the Castle walls to scale,
To which was leagued each Cavalier
That dwells upon the Tyne and Wear;
That Rokeby, his parole forgot,
Had dealt with us to aid the plot.
Such was the charge, which Denzil's zeal
Of hate to Rokeby and O'Neale
Proffer'd as witness, to make good,
Even though the forfeit were their blood.

I scrupled, until o'er and o'er
His prisoners' safety Wycliffe swore ;
And then—alas! what needs there more?
I knew I should not live to say
The proffer I refused that day ;
Ashamed to live, yet loth to die,
I soil'd me with their infamy !"—
" Poor youth," said Bertram, " wavering
    still,
Unfit alike for good or ill !
But what fell next ?"—" Soon as at large
Was scroll'd and sign'd our fatal charge,
There never yet, on tragic stage,
Was seen so well a painted rage
As Oswald's show'd ! With loud alarm
He call'd his garrison to arm ;
From tower to tower, from post to post,
He hurried as if all were lost ;
Consign'd to dungeon and to chain
The good old Knight and all his train ;
Warn'd each suspected Cavalier,
Within his limits, to appear
To-morrow, at the hour of noon,
In the high church at Egliston."—

X.

" Of Egliston !—Even now I pass'd,"
Said Bertram, " as the night closed fast ;
Torches and cressets gleam'd around,
I heard the saw and hammer sound,
And I could mark they toil'd to raise
A scaffold, hung with sable baize,
Which the grim headsman's scene display'd,
Block, axe, and sawdust ready laid.
Some evil deed will there be done,
Unless Matilda wed his son ;—
She loves him not—'tis shrewdly guess'd
That Redmond rules the damsel's breast.
This is a turn of Oswald's skill ;
But I may meet, and foil him still !——
How camest thou to thy freedom ?"—
    " There
Lies mystery more dark and rare.
In midst of Wycliffe's well-feign'd rage,
A scroll was offer'd by a page,
Who told, a muffled horseman late
Had left it at the Castle-gate.
He broke the seal—his cheek show'd
    change,
Sudden, portentous, wild, and strange ;

The mimic passion of his eye
Was turn'd to actual agony ;
His hand like summer sapling shook,
Terror and guilt were in his look.
Denzil he judged, in time of need,
Fit counsellor for evil deed ;
And thus apart his counsel broke,
While with a ghastly smile he spoke :—

XI.

" ' As in the pageants of the stage,
The dead awake in this wild age,
Mortham—whom all men deem'd decreed
In his own deadly snare to bleed,
Slain by a bravo, whom, o'er sea,
He train'd to aid in murdering me,—
Mortham has 'scaped ! The coward shot
The steed, but harm'd the rider not.' "
Here, with an execration fell,
Bertram leap'd up, and paced the cell :—
" Thine own grey head, or bosom dark,"
He mutter'd, " may be surer mark !"
Then sat, and sign'd to Edmund, pale
With terror, to resume his tale.
" Wycliffe went on :—' Mark with what
    flights
Of wilder'd reverie he writes :—

The Letter.

" ' Ruler of Mortham's destiny !
Though dead, thy victim lives to thee.
Once had he all that binds to life,
A lovely child, a lovelier wife ;
Wealth, fame, and friendship, were his
    own—
Thou gavest the word, and they are
    flown.
Mark how he pays thee :—To thy hand
He yields his honours and his land,
One boon premised ;—Restore his child !
And, from his native land exiled,
Mortham no more returns to claim
His lands, his honours, or his name ;
Refuse him this, and from the slain
Thou shalt see Mortham rise again.'—

XII.

" This billet while the Baron read,
His faltering accents show'd his dread ;

He press'd his forehead with his palm,
Then took a scornful tone and calm ;
' Wild as the winds, as billows wild !
What wot I of his spouse or child ?
Hither he brought a joyous dame,
Unknown her lineage or her name :
Her, in some frantic fit, he slew ;
The nurse and child in fear withdrew.
Heaven be my witness ! wist I where
To find this youth, my kinsman's heir,—
Unguerdon'd, I would give with joy
The father's arms to fold his boy,
And Mortham's lands and towers resign
To the just heirs of Mortham's line.'—
Thou know'st that scarcely e'en his fear
Suppresses Denzil's cynic sneer ;—
' Then happy is thy vassal's part,'
He said, ' to ease his patron's heart !
In thine own jailer's watchful care
Lies Mortham's just and rightful heir ;
Thy generous wish is fully won,—
Redmond O'Neale is Mortham's son.'—

XIII.

" Up starting with a frenzied look,
His clenched hand the Baron shook :
' Is Hell at work ? or dost thou rave,
Or darest thou palter with me, slave !
Perchance thou wot'st not, Barnard's
        towers
Have racks, of strange and ghastly powers.'
Denzil, who well his safety knew,
Firmly rejoin'd, ' I tell thee true.
Thy racks could give thee but to know
The proofs, which I, untortured, show.—
It chanced upon a winter night,
When early snow made Stanmore
        white,
That very night, when first of all
Redmond O'Neale saw Rokeby hall,
It was my goodly lot to gain
A reliquary and a chain,
Twisted and chased of massive gold.
—Demand not how the prize I hold !
It was not given, nor lent, nor sold.—
Gilt tablets to the chain were hung,
With letters in the Irish tongue.
I hid my spoil, for there was need
That I should leave the land with speed ;

Nor then I deem'd it safe to bear
On mine own person gems so rare.
Small heed I of the tablets took,
But since have spell'd them by the book,
When some sojourn in Erin's land
Of their wild speech had given com-
        mand.
But darkling was the sense ; the phrase
And language those of other days,
Involved of purpose, as to foil
An interloper's prying toil.
The words, but not the sense, I knew,
Till fortune gave the guiding clue.

XIV.

" ' Three days since, was that clue re-
        veal'd,
In Thorsgill as I lay conceal'd,
And heard at full when Rokeby's Maid
Her uncle's history display'd ;
And now I can interpret well
Each syllable the tablets tell.
Mark, then : Fair Edith was the joy
Of old O'Neale of Clandeboy ;
But from her sire and country fled,
In secret Mortham's Lord to wed.
O'Neale, his first resentment o'er,
Despatch'd his son to Greta's shore,
Enjoining he should make him known
(Until his farther will were shown)
To Edith, but to her alone.
What of their ill-starr'd meeting fell,
Lord Wycliffe knows, and none so well.

XV.

" O'Neale it was, who, in despair,
Robb'd Mortham of his infant heir ;
He bred him in their nurture wild,
And call'd him murder'd Connel's child.
Soon died the nurse ; the Clan believed
What from their Chieftain they received.
His purpose was, that ne'er again
The boy should cross the Irish main ;
But, like his mountain sires, enjoy
The woods and wastes of Clandeboy.
Then on the land wild troubles came,
And stronger Chieftains urged a claim,
And wrested from the old man's hands
His native towers, his father's lands.

Unable then, amid the strife,
To guard young Redmond's rights or
      life,
Late and reluctant he restores
The infant to his native shores,
With goodly gifts and letters stored,
With many a deep conjuring word,
To Mortham and to Rokeby's Lord.
Nought knew the clod of Irish earth,
Who was the guide, of Redmond's birth;
But deem'd his Chief's commands were
      laid
On both, by both to be obey'd.
How he was wounded by the way,
I need not, and I list not say.'—

XVI.

'" A wondrous tale! and, grant it true,
What,' Wycliffe answer'd, ' might I do?
Heaven knows, as willingly as now
I raise the bonnet from my brow,
Would I my kinsman's manors fair
Restore to Mortham, or his heir;
But Mortham is distraught—O'Neale
Has drawn for tyranny his steel,
Malignant to our rightful cause,
And train'd in Rome's delusive laws.
Hark thee apart!'—They whisper'd long,
Till Denzil's voice grew bold and strong;—
' My proofs! I never will,' he said,
' Show mortal man where they are laid.
Nor hope discovery to foreclose,
By giving me to feed the crows;
For I have mates at large, who know
Where I am wont such toys to stow.
Free me from peril and from band,
These tablets are at thy command:
Nor were it hard to form some train,
To wile old Mortham o'er the main.
Then, lunatic's nor papist's hand
Should wrest from thine the goodly land.'—
—' I like thy wit,' said Wycliffe, ' well;
But here in hostage shalt thou dwell.
Thy son, unless my purpose err,
May prove the trustier messenger.
A scroll to Mortham shall he bear
From me, and fetch these tokens rare.
Gold shalt thou have, and that good store,
And freedom, his commission o'er;

But if his faith should chance to fail,
The gibbet frees thee from the jail.'—

XVII.

" Mesh'd in the net himself had twined,
What subterfuge could Denzil find?
He told me, with reluctant sigh,
That hidden here the tokens lie;
Conjured my swift return and aid,
By all he scoff'd and disobey'd,
And look'd as if the noose were tied,
And I the priest who left his side.
This scroll for Mortham Wycliffe gave,
Whom I must seek by Greta's wave;
Or in the hut where chief he hides,
Where Thorsgill's forester resides.
(Then chanced it, wandering in the glade,
That he descried our ambuscade.)
I was dismiss'd as evening fell,
And reach'd but now this rocky cell."—
" Give Oswald's letter."—Bertram read,
And tore it fiercely shred by shred:—
" All lies and villany! to blind
His noble kinsman's generous mind,
And train him on from day to day,
Till he can take his life away.—
And now, declare thy purpose, youth,
Nor dare to answer, save the truth;
If aught I mark of Denzil's art,
I'll tear the secret from thy heart!"—

XVIII.

" It needs not. I renounce," he said,
" My tutor and his deadly trade.
Fix'd was my purpose to declare
To Mortham, Redmond is his heir;
To tell him in what risk he stands,
And yield these tokens to his hands.
Fix'd was my purpose to atone,
Far as I may, the evil done;
And fix'd it rests—if I survive
This night, and leave this cave alive."
" And Denzil?"—" Let them ply the rack
Even till his joints and sinews crack!
If Oswald tear him limb from limb,
What ruth can Denzil claim from him,
Whose thoughtless youth he led astray,
And damn'd to this unhallow'd way?

He school'd me faith and vows were vain;
Now let my master reap his gain."—
"True," answer'd Bertram, "'tis his
    meed ;
There's retribution in the deed.
But thou—thou art not for our course,
Hast fear, hast pity, hast remorse :
And he with us the gale who br ves,
Must heave such cargo to the waves,
Or lag with overloaded prore,
While barks unburden'd reach the shore."

XIX.

He paused, and, stretching him at length,
Seem'd to repose his bulky strength.
Communing with his secret mind,
As half he sat, and half reclined,
One ample hand his forehead press'd,
And one was dropp'd across his breast.
The shaggy eyebrows deeper came
Above his eyes of swarthy flame ;
His lip of pride a while forbore
The haughty curve till then it wore ;
The unaltered fierceness of his look
A shade of darken'd sadness took,—
For dark and sad a presage press'd,
Resistlessly on Bertram's breast,—
And when he spoke, his wonted tone,
So fierce, abrupt, and brief was gone.
His voice was steady, low, and deep,
Like distant waves, when breezes sleep ;
And sorrow mix'd with Edmund's fear,
Its low unbroken depth to hear.

XX.

" Edmund, in thy sad tale I find
The woe that warp'd my patron's mind :
'Twould wake the fountains of the eye
In other men, but mine are dry.
Mortham must never see the fool,
That sold himself base Wycliffe's tool ;
Yet less from thirst of sordid gain,
Than to avenge supposed disdain.
Say, Bertram rues his fault ;—a word,
Till now, from Bertram never heard :
Say, too, that Mortham's Lord he prays
To think but on their former days ;
On Quariana's beach and rock,
On Cayo's bursting battle-shock ;

On Darien's sands and deadly dew,
And on the dart Tlatzeca threw ;—
Perchance my patron yet may hear
More that may grace his comrade's
    bier.
My soul hath felt a secret weight,
A warning of approaching fate ;
A priest had said, ' Return, repent !'
As well to bid that rock be rent.
Firm as that flint I face mine end ;
My heart may burst, but cannot bend.

XXI.

" The dawning of my youth, with awe
And prophecy, the Dalesmen saw ;
For over Redesdale it came,
As bodeful as their beacon-flame.
Edmund, thy years were scarcely mine,
When, challenging the Clans of Tyne,
To bring their best my brand to prove,
O'er Hexham's altar hung my glove ;⁵⁵
But Tynedale, nor in tower nor town,
Held champion meet to take it down.
My noontide, India may declare ;
Like her fierce sun, I fired the air !
Like him, to wood and cave bade fly
Her natives, from mine angry eye.
Panama's maids shall long look pale
When Risingham inspires the tale ;
Chili's dark matrons long shall tame
The froward child with Bertram's name.
And now, my race of terror run,
Mine be the eve of tropic sun !
No pale gradations quench his ray,
No twilight dews his wrath allay ;
With disk like battle-target red,
He rushes to his burning bed,
Dyes the wide wave with bloody light,
Then sinks at once—and all is night.—

XXII.

" Now to thy mission, Edmund. Fly,
Seek Mortham out, and bid him hie
To Richmond, where his troops are laid,
And lead his force to Redmond's aid.
Say, till he reaches Egliston,
A friend will watch to guard his son.
Now, fare-thee-well ; for night draws on,
And I would rest me here alone."

Despite his ill dissembled fear,
There swam in Edmund's eye a tear;
A tribute to the courage high,
Which stoop'd not in extremity,
But strove, irregularly great,
To triumph o'er approaching fate!
Bertram beheld the dewdrop start,
It almost touch'd his iron heart:—
" I did not think there lived," he said,
"One, who would tear for Bertram
    shed."
He loosen'd then his baldric's hold,
A buckle broad of massive gold;—
" Of all the spoil that paid his pains,
But this with Risingham remains;
And this, dear Edmund, thou shalt take,
And wear it long for Bertram's sake.
Once more—to Mortham speed amain;
Farewell! and turn thee not again."

XXIII.

The night has yielded to the morn,
And far the hours of prime are worn.
Oswald, who, since the dawn of day,
Had cursed his messenger's delay,
Impatient question'd now his train,
" Was Denzil's son return'd again?"
It chanced there answer'd of the crew,
A menial, who young Edmund knew:
" No son of Denzil this,"—he said;
"A peasant boy from Winston glade,
For song and minstrelsy renown'd,
And knavish pranks, the hamlets
    round."—
" Not Denzil's son!—From Winston
    vale!—
Then it was false, that specious tale:
Or, worse—he hath despatch'd the youth
To show to Mortham's Lord its truth.
Fool that I was!—but 'tis too late:—
This is the very turn of fate!—
The tale, or true or false, relies
On Denzil's evidence! He dies!
Ho! Provost Marshal! instantly
Lead Denzil to the gallows-tree!
Allow him not a parting word;
Short be the shrift, and sure the cord!
Then let his gory head appal
Marauders from the Castle-wall.

Lead forth thy guard, that duty done,
With best despatch to Egliston.—
—Basil, tell Wilfrid he must straight
Attend me at the Castle-gate."

XXIV.

" Alas!" the old domestic said,
And shook his venerable head,
" Alas, my lord! full ill to-day
May my young master brook the way!
The leech has spoke with grave alarm,
Of unseen hurt, of secret harm,
Of sorrow lurking at the heart,
That mars and lets his healing art."—
" Tush, tell not me!—Romantic boys
Pine themselves sick for airy toys,
I will find cure for Wilfrid soon;
Bid him for Egliston be boune,
And quick!—I hear the dull death-drum
Tell Denzil's hour of fate is come."
He paused with scornful smile, and then
Resumed his train of thought agen.
" Now comes my fortune's crisis near!
Entreaty boots not—instant fear,
Nought else, can bend Matilda's pride,
Or win her to be Wilfrid's bride.
But when she sees the scaffold placed,
With axe and block and headsman graced,
And when she deems, that to deny
Dooms Redmond and her sire to die,
She must give way.—Then, were the line
Of Rokeby once combined with mine,
I gain the weather-gage of fate!
If Mortham come, he comes too late,
While I, allied thus and prepared,
Bid him defiance to his beard.—
—If she prove stubborn, shall I dare
To drop the axe!—Soft! pause we there.
Mortham still lives—yon youth may tell
His tale—and Fairfax loves him well;—
Else, wherefore should I now delay
To sweep this Redmond from my way?
But she to piety perforce
Must yield—Without there! Sound to
    horse."

XXV.

'Twas bustle in the court below,—
" Mount, and march forward!"—Forth
    they go;

Steeds neigh and trample all around,
Steel rings, spears glimmer, trumpets
.....sound.—
Just then was sung his parting hymn;
And Denzil turn'd his eyeballs dim,
And, scarcely conscious what he sees,
Follows the horsemen down the Tees;
And scarcely conscious what he hears,
The trumpets tingle in his ears.
O'er the long bridge they're sweeping now,
The van is hid by greenwood bough;
But ere the rearward had passed o'er,
Guy Denzil heard and saw no more!
One stroke, upon the Castle bell,
To Oswald rung his dying knell.

XXVI.

O, for that pencil, erst profuse
Of chivalry's emblazon'd hues,
That traced of old, in Woodstock bower,
The pageant of the Leaf and Flower,
And bodied forth the tourney high,
Held for the hand of Emily!
Then might I paint the tumult loud,
That to the crowded abbey flow'd,
And pour'd, as with an ocean's sound,
Into the church's ample bound!
Then might I show each varying mien,
Exulting, woeful, or serene;
Indifference, with his idiot stare,
And Sympathy, with anxious air;
Paint the dejected Cavalier,
Doubtful, disarm'd, and sad of cheer;
And his proud foe, whose formal eye
Claim'd conquest now and mastery;
And the brute crowd, whose envious zeal
Huzzas each turn of Fortune's wheel,
And loudest shouts when lowest lie
Exalted worth and station high.
Yet what may such a wish avail?
'Tis mine to tell an onward tale,
Hurrying, as best I can, along,
The hearers and the hasty song;—
Like traveller when approaching home,
Who sees the shades of evening come,
And must not now his course delay,
Or choose the fair, but winding way;
Nay, scarcely may his pace suspend,
Where o'er his head the wildings bend,

To bless the breeze that cools his brow,
Or snatch a blossom from the bough.

XXVII.

The reverend pile lay wild and waste,
Profaned, dishonour'd, and defaced.
Through storied lattices no more
In soften'd light the sunbeams pour,
Gilding the Gothic sculpture rich
Of shrine, and monument, and niche.
The Civil fury of the time
Made sport of sacrilegious crime;
For dark Fanaticism rent
Altar, and screen, and ornament,
And peasant hands the tombs o'erthrew
Of Bowes, of Rokeby, and Fitz-Hugh.
And now was seen, unwonted sight,
In holy walls a scaffold dight;
Where once the priest, of grace divine
Dealt to his flock the mystic sign,
There stood the block display'd, and there
The headsman grim his hatchet bare,
And for the word of Hope and Faith,
Resounded loud a doom of death.
Thrice the fierce trumpet's breath was
.....heard,
And echo'd thrice the herald's word,
Dooming, for breach of martial laws,
And treason to the Commons' cause,
The Knight of Rokeby and O'Neale
To stoop their heads to block and steel.
The trumpets flourish'd high and shrill,
Then was a silence dead and still;
And silent prayers to heaven were cast,
And stifled sobs were bursting fast,
Till from the crowd begun to rise
Murmurs of sorrow or surprise,
And from the distant aisles there came
Deep-mutter'd threats, with Wycliffe's
.....name.

XXVIII.

But Oswald, guarded by his band,
Powerful in evil, waved his hand,
And bade Sedition's voice be dead,
On peril of the murmurer's head.
Then first his glance sought Rokeby's
.....Knight;
Who gazed on the tremendous sight,

As calm as if he came a guest
To kindred Baron's feudal feast,
As calm as if that trumpet-call
Were summons to the banner'd hall;
Firm in his loyalty he stood,
And prompt to seal it with his blood.
With downcast look drew Oswald nigh,—
He durst not cope with Rokeby's eye!—
And said, with low and faltering breath,
" Thou know'st the terms of life and
death."
The Knight then turn'd, and sternly
smiled;
" The maiden is mine only child,
Yet shall my blessing leave her head,
If with a traitor's son she wed."
Then Redmond spoke: " The life of one
Might thy malignity atone,
On me be flung a double guilt!
Spare Rokeby's blood, let mine be spilt!"
Wycliffe had listen'd to his suit,
But dread prevail'd, and he was mute.

XXIX.

And now he pours his choice of fear
In secret on Matilda's ear;
" An union form'd with me and mine,
Ensures the faith of Rokeby's line.
Consent, and all this dread array,
Like morning dream, shall pass away;
Refuse, and, by my duty press'd,
I give the word—thou know'st the rest."
Matilda, still and motionless,
With terror heard the dread address,
Pale as the sheeted maid who dies
To hopeless love a sacrifice;
Then wrung her hands in agony,
And round her cast bewilder'd eye.
Now on the scaffold glanced, and now
On Wycliffe's unrelenting brow.
She veil'd her face, and, with a voice
Scarce audible,—" I make my choice!
Spare but their lives!—for aught beside,
Let Wilfrid's doom my fate decide.
He once was generous!"—As she spoke,
Dark Wycliffe's joy in triumph broke:—
" Wilfrid, where loiter'd ye so late?
Why upon Basil rest thy weight?—
Art spell-bound by enchanter's wand?—
Kneel, kneel, and take her yielded hand;

Thank her with raptures, simple boy!
Should tears and trembling speak thy
joy?"—
" O hush, my sire! To prayer and tear
Of mine thou hast refused thine ear;
But now the awful hour draws on,
When truth must speak in loftier tone."

XXX.

He took Matilda's hand: " Dear maid,
Couldst thou so injure me," he said,
" Of thy poor friend so basely deem,
As blend with him this barbarous scheme?
Alas! my efforts made in vain,
Might well have saved this added pain.
But now, bear witness earth and heaven,
That ne'er was hope to mortal given,
So twisted with the strings of life,
As this—to call Matilda wife!
I bid it now for ever part,
And with the effort bursts my heart!"
His feeble frame was worn so low,
With wounds, with watching, and with
woe,
That nature could no more sustain
The agony of mental pain.
He kneel'd—his lip her hand had press'd,—
Just then he felt the stern arrest.
Lower and lower sunk his head,—
They raised him,—but the life was fled!
Then, first alarm'd, his sire and train
Tried every aid, but tried in vain.
The soul, too soft its ills to bear,
Had left our mortal hemisphere,
And sought in better world the meed,
To blameless life by Heaven decreed.

XXXI.

The wretched sire beheld, aghast,
With Wilfrid all his projects past,
All turn'd and centred on his son,
On Wilfrid all—and he was gone.
" And I am childless now," he said,
" Childless, through that relentless maid!
A lifetime's arts, in vain essay'd,
Are bursting on their artist's head!
Here lies my Wilfrid dead—and there
Comes hated Mortham for his heir,

Eager to knit in happy band
With Rokeby's heiress Redmond's hand.
And shall their triumph soar o'er all
The schemes deep-laid to work their
fall?
No!—deeds, which prudence might not
dare,
Appal not vengeance and despair.
The murd'ress weeps upon his bier—
I'll change to real that feigned tear!
They all shall share destruction's shock;—
Ho! lead the captives to the block!"—
But ill his Provost could divine
His feelings, and forbore the sign.
" Slave! to the block!—or I, or they,
Shall face the judgment-seat this day!"

XXXII.

The outmost crowd have heard a sound,
Like horse's hoof on harden'd ground:
Nearer it came, and yet more near,—
The very death's-men paused to hear.
'Tis in the churchyard now—the tread
Hath waked the dwelling of the dead!
Fresh sod, and old sepulchral stone,
Return the tramp in varied tone.
All eyes upon the gateway hung,
When through the Gothic arch there
sprung
A horseman arm'd, at headlong speed—
Sable his cloak, his plume, his steed.⁵⁶
Fire from the flinty floor was spurn'd,
The vaults unwonted clang return'd!—
One instant's glance around he threw,
From saddlebow his pistol drew.
Grimly determined was his look!
His charger with the spurs he strook—
All scatter'd backward as he came,
For all knew Bertram Risingham!
Three bounds that noble courser gave;
The first has reach'd the central nave,
The second clear'd the chancel wide,
The third—he was at Wycliffe's side.
Full levell'd at the Baron's head,
Rung the report—the bullet sped—
And to his long account, and last,
Without a groan dark Oswald past!
All was so quick that it might seem
A flash of lightning, or a dream.

XXXIII.

While yet the smoke the deed conceals,
Bertram his ready charger wheels;
But flounder'd on the pavement-floor
The steed, and down the rider bore,
And, bursting in the headlong sway,
The faithless saddle-girths gave way.
'Twas while he toil'd him to be freed,
And with the rein to raise the steed,
That from amazement's iron trance
All Wycliffe's soldiers waked at once.
Sword, halbert, musket-but, their blows
Hail'd upon Bertram as he rose;
A score of pikes, with each a wound,
Bore down and pinn'd him to the ground;
But still his struggling force he rears,
'Gainst hacking brands and stabbing
spears;
Thrice from assailants shook him free,
Once gain'd his feet, and twice his knee.
By tenfold odds oppress'd at length,
Despite his struggles and his strength,
He took a hundred mortal wounds,
As mute as fox 'mongst mangling hounds;
And when he died, his parting groan
Had more of laughter than of moan!
—They gazed, as when a lion dies,
And hunters scarcely trust their eyes,
But bend their weapons on the slain,
Lest the grim king should rouse again!
Then blow and insult some renew'd,
And from the trunk, the head had hew'd,
But Basil's voice the deed forbade;
A mantle o'er the corse he laid:—
" Fell as he was in act and mind,
He left no bolder heart behind:
Then give him, for a soldier meet,
A soldier's cloak for winding sheet."

XXXIV.

No more of death and dying pang,
No more of trump and bugle clang,
Though through the sounding woods there
come
Banner and bugle, trump and drum.
Arm'd with such powers as well had freed
Young Redmond at his utmost need,
And back'd with such a band of horse,
As might less ample powers enforce;

Possess'd of every proof and sign
That gave an heir to Mortham's line,
And yielded to a father's arms
An image of his Edith's charms,—
Mortham is come, to hear and see
Of this strange morn the history.
What saw he?—not the church's floor,
Cumber'd with dead and stain'd with gore;
What heard he?—not the clamorous
    crowd,
That shout their gratulations loud:
Redmond he saw and heard alone,
Clasp'd him, and sobb'd, "My son! my
    son!"—

XXXV.

This chanced upon a summer morn,
When yellow waved the heavy corn:
But when brown August o'er the land
Call'd forth the reaper's busy band,
A gladsome sight the silvan road
From Egliston to Mortham show'd.

A while the hardy rustic leaves
The task to bind and pile the sheaves,
And maids their sickles fling aside,
To gaze on bridegroom and on bride,
And childhood's wondering group draws
    near,
And from the gleaner's hands the ear
Drops, while she folds them for a prayer
And blessing on the lovely pair.
'Twas then the Maid of Rokeby gave
Her plighted troth to Redmond brave;
And Teesdale can remember yet
How Fate to Virtue paid her debt,
And, for their troubles, bade them prove
A lengthen'd life of peace and love.

Time and Tide had thus their sway,
Yielding, like an April day,
Smiling noon for sullen morrow,
Years of joy for hours of sorrow!

THE BRIDAL OF TRIERMAIN,

OR,

THE VALE OF ST. JOHN.

A LOVER'S TALE.

PREFACE TO THE FIRST EDITION.

In the EDINBURGH ANNUAL REGISTER, *for the year* 1809, *Three Fragments were inserted, written in imitation of Living Poets. It must have been apparent, that by these prolusions, nothing burlesque, or disrespectful to the authors, was intended, but that they were offered to the public as serious, though certainly very imperfect, imitations of that style of composition, by which each of the writers is supposed to be distinguished. As these exercises attracted a greater degree of attention than the author anticipated, he has been induced to complete one of them, and present it as a separate publication.*

It is not in this place that an examination of the works of the master whom he has here adopted as his model, can, with propriety, be introduced; since his general acquiescence in the favourable suffrage of the public must necessarily be inferred from the attempt he has now made. He is induced, by the nature of his subject, to offer a few remarks on what has been called ROMANTIC POETRY;—*the popularity of which has been revived in the present day, under the auspices, and by the unparalleled success, of one individual.*

The original purpose of poetry is either religious or historical, or, as must frequently happen, a mixture of both. To modern readers, the poems of Homer have many of the features of pure romance; but in the estimation of his contemporaries, they probably derived their chief value from their supposed historical authenticity. The same may be generally said of the poetry of all early ages. The marvels and miracles which the poet blends with his song, do not exceed in number or extravagance the figments of the historians of the same period of society; and, indeed, the difference betwixt poetry and prose, as the vehicles of historical truth, is always of late introduction. Poets, under various denominations of Bards, Scalds, Chroniclers, and so forth, are the first historians of all nations. Their intention is to relate the events they have witnessed, or the traditions that have reached them; and they clothe the relation in rhyme, merely as the means of rendering it more solemn in the narrative or more easily committed to memory. But as the poetical historian improves in the art of conveying information, the authenticity of his narrative unavoidably declines. He is tempted to dilate and dwell upon the events that are interesting to his imagination, and, conscious how indifferent his audience is to the naked truth of his poem, his history gradually becomes a romance.

It is in this situation that those epics are found, which have been generally regarded as the standards of poetry ; and it has happened somewhat strangely, that the moderns have pointed out as the characteristics and peculiar excellencies of narrative poetry, the very circumstances which the authors themselves adopted, only because their art involved the duties of the historian as well as the poet. It cannot be believed, for example, that Homer selected the siege of Troy as the most appropriate subject for poetry ; his purpose was to write the early history of his country ; the event he has chosen, though not very fruitful in varied incident, nor perfectly well adapted for poetry, was nevertheless combined with traditionary and genealogical anecdotes extremely interesting to those who were to listen to him ; and this he has adorned by the exertions of a genius, which, if it has been equalled, has certainly been never surpassed. It was not till comparatively a late period that the general accuracy of his narrative, or his purpose in composing it was brought into question. Δοκεῖ πρῶτος [ὁ Αναξαγόρας] (καθά φησι Φαβορῖνος εν παντοδαπῇ Ἱστορίᾳ) τὴν Ὁμήρου ποίησιν ἀποφήνασθαι εἶναι περὶ ἀρετῆς καὶ δικαιοσύνης. *But whatever theories might be framed by speculative men, his work was of an historical, not of an allegorical nature.* Εναντίλλετο μετὰ τοῦ Μέντεω καὶ ὅπου ἑκάστοτε αφίκοιτο, πάντα τὰ επιχώρια διερωτᾶτο, καὶ ἱστορέων επυνθάνετο· εἰκὸς δέ μιν ην καὶ μνημοσυνα πάντων γράφεσθαι. *Instead of recommending the choice of a subject similar to that of Homer, it was to be expected that critics should have exhorted the poets of these latter days to adopt or invent a narrative in itself more susceptible of poetical ornament, and to avail themselves of that advantage in order to compensate, in some degree, the inferiority of genius. The contrary course has been inculcated by almost all the writers upon the* Εpopœia *; with what success, the fate of Homer's numerous imitators may best show. The ultimum supplicium of criticism was inflicted on the author if he did not choose a subject which at once deprived him of all claim to originality, and placed him, if not in actual contest, at least in fatal comparison, with those giants in the land whom it was most his interest to avoid. The celebrated receipt for writing an epic poem, which appeared in the " Guardian," was the first instance in which common sense was applied to this department of poetry ; and, indeed, if the question be considered on its own merits, we must be satisfied that narrative poetry, if strictly confined to the great occurrences of history, would be deprived of the individual interest which it is so well calculated to excite.*

Modern poets may therefore be pardoned in seeking simpler subjects of verse, more interesting in proportion to their simplicity. Two or three figures, well grouped, suit the artist better than a crowd, for whatever purpose assembled. For the same reason a scene immediately presented to the imagination, and directly brought home to the feelings, though involving the fate of but one or two persons, is more favourable for poetry than the political struggles and convulsions which influence the fate of kingdoms. The former are within the reach and comprehension of all, and, if depicted with vigour, seldom fail to fix attention: The other, if more sublime, are more vague and distant, less capable of being distinctly understood, and infinitely less capable of exciting those sentiments which it is the very purpose of poetry to inspire. To generalize is always to destroy effect. We would, for example, be more interested in the fate of an individual soldier in combat, than in the grand event of a general action; with the happiness of two lovers raised from misery and anxiety to peace and union, than with the successful exertions of a whole nation. From what causes this may originate, is a separate and obviously an immaterial consideration. Before ascribing this peculiarity to causes decidedly and odiously selfish, it is proper to recollect, that while men see only a limited space, and while their affections and conduct are regulated, not by aspiring to an universal good, but by exerting their power of making themselves and others happy within the limited scale allotted to each individual, so long will individual history and individual virtue be the readier and more accessible road to general interest and attention; and, perhaps, we may add, that it is the more useful, as well as the more accessible, inasmuch as it affords an example capable of being easily imitated.

According to the author's idea of Romantic Poetry, as distinguished from Epic, the former comprehends a fictitious narrative, framed and combined at the pleasure of the writer; beginning and ending as he may judge best: which neither exacts nor refuses the use of supernatural machinery; which is free from the technical rules of the Epic; and is subject only to those which good sense, good taste, and good morals, apply to every species of poetry without exception. The date may be in a remote age, or in the present; the story may detail the adventures of a prince or of a peasant. In a word, the author is absolute master of his country and its inhabitants, and every thing is permitted to him, excepting to be heavy or prosaic, for which, free and unembarrassed as he is, he has no manner of apology. Those, it is probable, will be found the peculiarities of this species of composition; and before joining the outcry against the vitiated taste that fosters and encourages it, the justice and grounds of it ought to be made perfectly apparent. If the want of sieges, and battles, and great military evolutions, in our poetry, is complained of, let us reflect, that the campaigns and heroes of our days are perpetuated in a record that neither requires nor admits of the aid of fiction: and if the complaint refers to the inferiority of our bards, let us pay a just tribute to their modesty, limiting them, as it does, to subjects which, however indifferently treated, have still the interest and charm of novelty, and which thus prevents them from adding insipidity to their other more insuperable defects.

THE BRIDAL OF TRIERMAIN

INTRODUCTION.

I.

COME, LUCY! while 'tis morning hour,
 The woodland brook we needs must
 pass;
So, ere the sun assume his power,
We shelter in our poplar bower,
Where dew lies long upon the flower,
 Though vanish'd from the velvet grass
Curbing the stream, this stony ridge
May serve us for a silvan bridge;
 For here compell'd to disunite,
 Round petty isles the runnels glide,
And chafing off their puny spite,
The shallow murmurers waste their might,
 Yielding to footstep free and light
 A dry-shod pass from side to side.

II.

Nay, why this hesitating pause?
And, Lucy, as thy step withdraws,
Why sidelong eye the streamlet's brim?
 Titania's foot without a slip,
Like thine, though timid, light, and slim,
 From stone to stone might safely trip,
 Nor risk the glow-worm clasp to dip
That binds her slipper's silken rim.
Or trust thy lover's strength: nor fear
 That this same stalwart arm of mine,
Which could yon oak's prone trunk
 uprear,
Shall shrink beneath the burden dear
 Of form so slender, light, and fine—
So,—now, the danger dared at last,
Look back, and smile at perils past!

III.

And now we reach the favourite glade,
 Paled in by copsewood, cliff, and stone,
Where, never harsher sounds invade,
 To break affection's whispering tone,
Than the deep breeze that waves the shade,
 Than the small brooklet's feeble moan.
Come! rest thee on thy wonted seat;
 Moss'd is the stone, the turf is green,
A place where lovers best may meet,
 Who would that not their love be seen.
The boughs, that dim the summer sky,
Shall hide us from each lurking spy,
 That fain would spread the invidious
 tale,
How Lucy of the lofty eye,
Noble in birth, in fortunes high,
She for whom lords and barons sigh,
 Meets her poor Arthur in the dale.

IV.

How deep that blush!—how deep that
 sigh!
And why does Lucy shun mine eye?
Is it because that crimson draws
Its colour from some secret cause,
Some hidden movement of the breast,
She would not that her Arthur guess'd!
O! quicker far is lover's ken
Than the dull glance of common men,
And, by strange sympathy, can spell
The thoughts the loved one will not tell!
And mine, in Lucy's blush, saw met
The hues of pleasure and regret;
 Pride mingled in the sigh her voice,
 And shared with Love the crimson
 glow;

Well pleased that thou art Arthur's
　　choice,
　　Yet shamed thine own is placed so
　　　low:
Thou turn'st thy self-confessing cheek,
　　As if to meet the breeze's cooling;
Then, Lucy, hear thy tutor speak,
　　For Love, too, has his hours of
　　　schooling.

V.

Too oft my anxious eye has spied
That secret grief thou fain wouldst hide,
The passing pang of humbled pride;
　　Too oft, when through the splendid hall,
　　　The load-star of each heart and eye,
　My fair one leads the glittering ball,
　Will her stol'n glance on Arthur fall,
　　With such a blush and such a sigh!
　Thou would'st not yield, for wealth or
　　　rank,
　　The heart thy worth and beauty won,
　Nor leave me on this mossy bank,
　　To meet a rival on a throne:
Why, then, should vain repinings rise,
That to thy lover fate denies
A nobler name, a wide domain,
A Baron's birth, a menial train,
Since Heaven assign'd him, for his part,
A lyre, a falchion, and a heart?

VI.

My sword—its master must be dumb;
　　But, when a soldier names my name,
　Approach, my Lucy! fearless come,
　　Nor dread to hear of Arthur's shame.
　My heart—'mid all yon courtly crew,
　　Of lordly rank and lofty line,
　Is there to love and honour true,
　　That boasts a pulse so warm as mine?
They praised thy diamonds' lustre rare—
　Match'd with thine eyes, I thought it
　　faded;
They praised the pearls that bound thy
　　hair—
I only saw the locks they braided;
They talk'd of wealthy dower and land,
　And titles of high birth the token—
I thought of Lucy's heart and hand,
　Nor knew the sense of what was spoken.

And yet, if rank'd in Fortune's roll,
　I might have learn'd their choice unwise,
Who rate the dower above the soul,
　And Lucy's diamonds o'er her eyes.

VII.

My lyre—it is an idle toy,
　That borrows accents not its own,
Like warbler of Colombian sky,
　That sings but in a mimic tone.*
Ne'er did it sound o'er sainted well,
Nor boasts it aught of Border spell;
　Its strings no feudal slogan pour,
　Its heroes draw no broad claymore;
　No shouting clans applauses raise.
　Because it sung their father's praise;
　On Scottish moor, or English down,
　It ne'er was graced by fair renown;
　Nor won,—best meed to minstrel true,—
　One favouring smile from fair Buc-
　　cleuch!
By one poor streamlet sounds its tone,
And heard by one dear maid alone.

VIII.

But, if thou bid'st, these tones shall tell
Of errant knight, and damozelle;
Of the dread knot a Wizard tied,
In punishment of maiden's pride,
In notes of marvel and of fear,
That best may charm romantic ear.
For Lucy loves,—like COLLINS, ill-
　starred name!
Whose lay's requital was that tardy fame,
Who bound no laurel round his living head,
Should hang it o'er his monument when
　dead,—
For Lucy loves to tread enchanted strand,
And thread, like him, the maze of fairy
　land;
Of golden battlements to view the gleam,
And slumber soft by some Elysian stream;
Such lays she loves,—and, such my Lucy's
　choice,
What other song can claim her Poet's
　voice?

---

* The Mocking Bird.

CANTO FIRST.

I.

WHERE is the Maiden of mortal strain,
That may match wi*t* the Baron of Trier-
    main?[1]
She must be lovely, and constant, and
    kind,
Holy and pure, and humble of mind,
Blithe of cheer, and gentle of mood,
Courteous, and generous, and noble of
    blood—
Lovely as the sun's first ray,
When it breaks the clouds of an April day;
Constant and true as the widow'd dove,
Kind as a minstrel that sings of love;
Pure as the fountain in rocky cave,
Where never sunbeam kiss'd the wave:
Humble as maiden that loves in vain,
Holy as hermit's vesper strain;
Gentle as breeze that but whispers and
    dies,
Yet blithe as the light leaves that dance
    in its sighs;
Courteous as monarch the morn he is
    crown'd,
Generous as spring-dews that bless the
    glad ground;
Noble her blood as the currents that met
In the veins of the noblest Plantagenet—
Such must her form be, her mood, and
    her strain,
That shall match with Sir Roland of
    Triermain.

II.

Sir Roland de Vaux he hath laid him to
    sleep,
His blood it was fever'd, his breathing
    was deep.
He had been pricking against the Scot,
The foray was long, and the skirmish hot;
His dinted helm and his buckler's plight
Bore token of a stubborn fight.
    All in the castle must hold them still,
Harpers must lull him to his rest,
With the slow soft tunes he loves the best,
Till sleep sink down upon his breast,
    Like the dew on a summer hill.

III.

It was the dawn of an autumn day;
The sun was struggling with frost-fog grey,
That like a silvery cape was spread
Round Skiddaw's dim and distant head,
And faintly gleam'd each painted pane
Of the lordly halls of Triermain.
    When that Baron bold awoke.
Starting he woke, and loudly did call.
Rousing his menials in bower and hall,
    While hastily he spoke.

IV.

" Hearken, my minstrels! Which of ye all
Touch'd his harp with that dying fall,
    So sweet, so soft, so faint,
It seem'd an angel's whisper'd call
    To an expiring saint?
And hearken, my merry-men! What
    time or where
    Did she pass, that maid with her
        heavenly brow,
With her look so sweet and her eyes so fair,
And her graceful step and her angel air,
And the eagle plume in her dark-brown
    hair,
    That pass'd from my bower e'en
        now?"

V.

Answer'd him Richard de Bretville; he
Was chief of the Baron's minstrelsy,—
" Silent, noble chieftain, we
    Have sat since midnight close,
When such lulling sounds as the brooklet
    sings,
Murmur'd from our melting strings,
    And hush'd you to repose.
Had a harp-note sounded here,
    It had caught my watchful ear,
Although it fell as faint and shy
As bashful maiden's half-form'd sigh,
    When she thinks her lover near."—
Answer'd Philip of Fasthwaite tall,
He kept guard in the outer-hall,—
" Since at eve our watch took post,
Not a foot has thy portal cross'd;

Else had I heard the steps, though
low
And light they fell, as when earth receives,
In morn of frost, the wither'd leaves,
  That drop when no winds blow."—

VI.

"Then come thou hither, Henry, my
  page,
Whom I saved from the sack of Hermitage,
When that dark castle, tower, and spire,
Rose to the skies a pile of fire,
  And redden'd all the Nine-stane Hill,
And the shrieks of death that wildly broke
Through devouring flame and smothering
  smoke,
  Made the warrior's heart-blood chill.
The trustiest thou of all my train,
My fleetest courser thou must rein,
  And ride to Lyulph's tower,
And from the Baron of Triermain
  Greet well that sage of power.
He is sprung from Druid sires,
And British bards that tuned their lyres
To Arthur's and Pendragon's praise,
And his who sleeps at Dunmailraise.*
Gifted like his gifted race,
He the characters can trace,
Graven deep in elder time
Upon Helvellyn's cliffs sublime;
Sign and sigil well doth he know
And can bode of weal and woe,
Of kingdoms' fall, and fate of wars,
From mystic dreams and course of stars.
He shall tell if middle earth
To that enchanting shape gave birth,
Or if 'twas but an airy thing,
Such as fantastic slumbers bring,
Framed from the rainbow's varying dyes,
Or fading tints of western skies.
For, by the Blessed Rood I swear,
If that fair form breathe vital air,
No other maiden by my side
Shall ever rest De Vaux's bride!"

* Dunmailraise is one of the grand passes
from Cumberland into Westmoreland. There
is a cairn on it said to be the monument of
Dunmail, the last King of Cumberland.

VII.

The faithful Page he mounts his steed,
And soon he cross'd green Irthing's mead,
Dash'd o'er Kirkoswald's verdant plain,
And Eden barr'd his course in vain.
He pass'd red Penrith's Table Round,[2]
For feats of chivalry renown'd,
Left Mayburgh's mound[3] and stones of
  power,
By Druids raised in magic hour,
And traced the Eamont's winding way,
Till Ulfo's† lake beneath him lay.

VIII.

Onward he rode, the pathway still
Winding betwixt the lake and hill;
Till, on the fragment of a rock,
Struck from its base by lightning shock,
  He saw the hoary Sage:
The silver moss and lichen twined,
With fern and deer-hair check'd and
  lined,
  A cushion fit for age;
And o'er him shook the aspin-tree,
  A restless rustling canopy.
Then sprung young Henry from his selle,
  And greeted Lyulph grave,
And then his master's tale did tell,
  And then for counsel crave.
The Man of Years mused long and deep,
Of time's lost treasures taking keep,
And then, as rousing from a sleep,
  His solemn answer gave.

IX.

" That maid is born of middle earth,
  And may of man be won,
Though there have glided since her birth
  Five hundred years and one.
But where's the Knight in all the north,
That dare the adventure follow forth,
So perilous to knightly worth,
  In the valley of St. John?
Listen, youth, to what I tell,
And bind it on thy memory well;

† Ulswater.

Nor muse that I commence the rhyme
Far distant 'mid the wrecks of time.
The mystic tale, by bard and sage,
Is handed down from Merlin's age.

X.

Lyulph's Tale.

" KING ARTHUR has ridden from merry
 Carlisle
 When Pentecost was o'er:
He journey'd like errant-knight the while,
And sweetly the summer sun did smile
 On mountain, moss, and moor.
Above his solitary track
Rose Glaramara's ridgy back,
Amid whose yawning gulfs the sun
Cast umber'd radiance red and dun,
Though never sunbeam could discern
The surface of that sable tarn,[1]
In whose black mirror you may spy
The stars, while noontide lights the sky.
The gallant King he skirted still
The margin of that mighty hill;
Rock upon rocks incumbent hung,
And torrents, down the gullies flung,
Join'd the rude river that brawl'd on,
Recoiling now from crag and stone,
Now diving deep from human ken,
And raving down its darksome glen.
The Monarch judged this desert wild,
With such romantic ruin piled,
Was theatre by Nature's hand
For feat of high achievement plann'd.

XI.

" O rather he chose, that Monarch bold,
 On vent'rous quest to ride,
In plate and mail, by wood and wold,
Than, with ermine trapp'd and cloth of
 · gold,
 In princely bower to bide;
The bursting crash of a foeman's spear
 As it shiver'd against his mail,
Was merrier music to his ear
 Than courtier's whisper'd tale:
And the clash of Caliburn* more dear,

* King Arthur's sword, called by Tennyson
Excalibur.

When on the hostile casque it rung,
 Than all the lays
  To their monarch's praise
That the harpers of Reged sung.
He loved better to rest by wood or river,
Than in bower of his bride, Dame
 Guenever,
For he left that lady, so lovely of cheer,
To follow adventures of danger and fear;
And the frank-hearted Monarch full little
 did wot,
That she smiled, in his absence, on brave
 Lancelot.

XII.

" He rode, till over down and dell
The shade more broad and deeper fell;
And though around the mountain's head
Flow'd streams of purple, and gold, and
 red,
Dark at the base, unblest by beam,
Frown'd the black rocks, and roar'd the
 stream.
With toil the King his way pursued
By lonely Threlkeld's waste and wood,
Till on his course obliquely shone
The narrow valley of SAINT JOHN,
Down sloping to the western sky,
Where lingering sunbeams love to lie.
Right glad to feel those beams again,
The King drew up his charger's rein;
With gauntlet raised he screen'd his
 sight,
As dazzled with the level light,
And, from beneath his glove of mail,
Scann'd at his ease the lovely vale,
While gainst the sun his armour bright
Gleam'd ruddy like the beacon's light.

XIII.

" Paled in by many a lofty hill,
The narrow dale lay smooth and still,
And, down its verdant bosom led,
A winding brooklet found its bed.
But, midmost of the vale, a mound
Arose with airy turrets crown'd,
Buttress, and rampire's circling bound,
 And mighty keep and tower;

Seem'd some primeval giant's hand,
The castle's massive walls had plann'd,
A ponderous bulwark to withstand
    Ambitious Nimrod's power.
Above the moated entrance slung,
The balanced drawbridge trembling hung,
    As jealous of a foe;
Wicket of oak, as iron hard,
With iron studded, clench'd, and barr'd,
And prong'd portcullis, join'd to guard
    The gloomy pass below.
But the grey walls no banners crown'd,
Upon the watch-tower's airy round
No warder stood his horn to sound,
No guard beside the bridge was found,
And where the Gothic gateway frown'd,
    Glanced neither bill nor bow.

XIV.

" Beneath the castle's gloomy pride
In ample round did Arthur ride
Three times; nor living thing he spied,
    Nor heard a living sound,
Save that, awakening from her dream,
The owlet now began to scream,
In concert with the rushing stream,
    That wash'd the battled mound.
He lighted from his goodly steed,
And he left him to graze on bank and
    mead;
And slowly he climb'd the narrow way,
That reach'd the entrance grim and
    grey,
And he stood the outward arch below,
And his bugle-horn prepared to blow,
    In summons blithe and bold,
Deeming to rouse from iron sleep
The guardian of this dismal Keep,
    Which well he guess'd the hold
Of wizard stern, or goblin grim,
Or pagan of gigantic limb,
    The tyrant of the wold.

XV.

" The ivory bugle's golden tip
Twice touch'd the monarch's manly lip,
    And twice his hand withdrew.

—Think not but Arthur's heart was
    good!
His shield was cross'd by the blessed rood.
Had a pagan host before him stood,
    He had charged them through and
      through;
Yet the silence of that ancient place
Sunk on his heart, and he paused a space
    Ere yet his horn he blew.
But, instant as its 'larum rung,
The castle gate was open flung,
Portcullis rose with crashing groan
Full harshly up its groove of stone;
The balance-beams obey'd the blast,
And down the trembling drawbridge
    cast
The vaulted arch before him lay,
With nought to bar the gloomy way,
And onward Arthur paced, with hand
On Caliburn's resistless brand.

XVI.

" A hundred torches, flashing bright,
Dispell'd at once the gloomy night
    That lour'd along the walls,
And show'd the King's astonish'd sight
    The inmates of the halls.
Nor wizard stern, nor goblin grim,
Nor giant huge of form and limb,
    Nor heathen knight, was there;
But the cressets, which odours flung aloft,
Show'd by their yellow light and soft,
    A band of damsels fair.
Onward they came, like summer wave
    That dances to the shore;
An hundred voices welcome gave,
    And welcome o'er and o'er!
An hundred lovely hands assail
The bucklers of the monarch's mail,
And busy labour'd to unhasp
Rivet of steel and iron clasp.
One wrapp'd him in a mantle fair,
And one flung odours on his hair;
His short curl'd ringlets one smooth'd
    down,
One wreathed them with a myrtle crown.
A bride upon her wedding-day,
Was tended ne'er by troop so gay.

XVII.

" Loud laugh'd they all,—the King, in
vain,
With questions task'd the giddy train ;
Let him entreat, or crave, or call,
Twas one reply—loud laugh'd they all.
Then o'er him mimic chains they fling,
Framed of the fairest flowers of spring.
While some their gentle force unite,
Onward to drag the wondering knight,
Some, bolder, urge his pace with blows,
Dealt with the lily or the rose.
Behind him were in triumph borne
The warlike arms he late had worn.
Four of the train combined to rear
The terrors of Tintagel's spear ;⁵
Two, laughing at their lack of strength,
Dragg'd Caliburn in cumbrous length ;
One, while she aped a martial stride,
Placed on her brows the helmet's pride ;
Then scream'd, 'twixt laughter and sur-
prise,
To feel its depth o'erwhelm her eyes.
With revel-shout, and triumph-song,
Thus gaily march'd the giddy throng.

XVIII.

" Through many a gallery and hall
They led, I ween, their royal thrall ;
At length, beneath a fair arcade
Their march and song at once they staid.
The eldest maiden of the band,
    (The lovely maid was scarce eighteen,)
Raised, with imposing air her hand,
And reverent silence did command,
On entrance of their Queen,
And they were mute.—But as a glance
They steal on Arthur's countenance
    Bewilder'd with surprise,
Their smother'd mirth again 'gan speak,
In archly dimpled chin and cheek,
    And laughter-lighted eyes.

XIX.

" The attributes of those high days
Now only live in minstrel-lays ;
For Nature, now exhausted, still
Was then profuse of good and ill.

Strength was gigantic, valour high,
And wisdom soar'd beyond the sky,
And beauty had such matchless beam
As lights not now a lover's dream.
Yet e'en in that romantic age,
    Ne'er were such charms by mortal seen,
As Arthur's dazzled eyes engage,
When forth on that enchanted stage,
With glittering train of maid and page,
    Advanced the castle's Queen !
While up the hall she slowly pass'd,
Her dark eye on the King she cast,
    That flash'd expression strong ;
The longer dwelt that lingering look,
Her cheek the livelier colour took,
And scarce the shame-faced King could
    brook
The gaze that lasted long.
A sage, who had that look espied,
Where kindling passion strove with pride,
Had whisper'd, ' Prince, beware !
From the chafed tiger rend the prey,
Rush on the lion when at bay,
Bar the fell dragon's blighted way,
    But shun that lovely snare !'—

XX.

" At once that inward strife suppress'd,
The dame approach'd her warlike guest,
With greeting in that fair degree,
Where female pride and courtesy
Are blended with such passing art
As awes at once and charms the heart.
A courtly welcome first she gave,
Then of his goodness 'gan to crave
    Construction fair and true
Of her light maidens' idle mirth,
Who drew from lonely glens their birth,
Nor knew to pay to stranger worth
    And dignity their due ;
And then she pray'd that he would rest
That night her castle's honour'd guest.
The Monarch meetly thanks express'd ;
The banquet rose at her behest,
With lay and tale, and laugh and jest,
    Apace the evening flew.

XXI.

" The Lady sate the Monarch by,
Now in her turn abash'd and shy,

And with indifference seem'd to hear
The toys he whispered in her ear.
Her bearing modest was and fair,
Yet shadows of constraint were there,
That show'd an over-cautious care
    Some inward thought to hide ;
Oft did she pause in full reply,
And oft cast down her large dark eye,
Oft check'd the soft voluptuous sigh,
    That heaved her bosom's pride.
Slight symptoms these, but shepherds
    know
How hot the mid-day sun shall glow,
    From the mist of morning sky ;
And so the wily Monarch guess'd,
That this assumed restraint express'd
More ardent passions in the breast,
    Than ventured to the eye.
Closer he press'd, while beakers rang,
While maidens laughed and minstrels
    sang,
    Still closer to her ear—
But why pursue the common tale ?
Or wherefore show how knights prevail
    When ladies dare to hear ?
Or wherefore trace from what slight
    cause
Its source one tyrant passion draws,
    Till, mastering all within,
Where lives the man that has not tried,
How mirth can into folly glide,
    And folly into sin ?"

CANTO SECOND.

I.

Lyulph's Tale, continued.

" ANOTHER day, another day,
And yet another glides away !
The Saxon stern, the pagan Dane,
Maraud on Britain's shores again.
Arthur, of Christendom the flower,
Lies loitering in a lady's bower ;
The horn, that foemen wont to fear,
Sounds but to wake the Cumbrian deer,
And Caliburn, the British pride,
Hangs useless by a lover's side.

II.

" Another day, another day,
And yet another, glides away !
Heroic plans in pleasure drown'd,
He thinks not of the Table Round ;
In lawless love dissolved his life,
He thinks not of his beauteous wife :
Better he loves to snatch a flower
From bosom of his paramour,
Than from a Saxon knight to wrest
The honours of his heathen crest !
Better to wreathe, 'mid tresses brown,
The heron's plume her hawk struck down,
Than o'er the altar give to flow
The banners of a Paynim foe.
Thus, week by week, and day by day,
His life inglorious glides away :
But she, that soothes his dream, with fear
Beholds his hour of waking near !

III.

" Much force have mortal charms to
    stay
Our peace in Virtue's toilsome way ;
But Guendolen's might far outshine
Each maid of merely mortal line.
Her mother was of human birth,
Her sire a Genie of the earth,
In days of old deem'd to preside
O'er lovers' wiles and beauty's pride,
By youths and virgins worshipp'd long,
With festive dance and choral song,
Till, when the cross to Britain came,
On heathen altars died the flame.
Now, deep in Wastdale solitude,
The downfall of his rights he rued,
And, born of his resentment heir,
He train'd to guile that lady fair,
To sink in slothful sin and shame
The champions of the Christian name.
Well skill'd to keep vain thoughts alive,
And all to promise, nought to give,—
The timid youth had hope in store,
The bold and pressing gain'd no more.
As wilder'd children leave their home,
After the rainbow's arch to roam,
Her lovers barter'd fair esteem,
Faith, fame, and honour, for a dream.

IV.

" Her sire's soft arts the soul to tame
She practised thus—till Arthur came;
Then, frail humanity had part,
And all the mother claim'd her heart.
Forgot each rule her father gave,
Sunk from a princess to a slave,
Too late must Guendolen deplore,
He, that has all, can hope no more!
Now must she see her lover strain,
At every turn her feeble chain;
Watch, to new-bind each knot, and shrink
To view each fast-decaying link.
Art she invokes to Nature's aid,
Her vest to zone, her locks to braid;
Each varied pleasure heard her call,
The feast, the tourney, and the ball:
Her storied lore she next applies,
Taxing her mind to aid her eyes;
Now more than mortal wise, and then
In female softness sunk again:
Now, raptured, with each wish complying,
With feign'd reluctance now denying;
Each charm she varied, to retain
A varying heart—and all in vain!

V.

" Thus in the garden's narrow bound,
Flank'd by some castle's Gothic round,
Fain would the artist's skill provide,
The limits of his realms to hide.
The walks in labyrinths he twines,
Shade after shade with skill combines,
With many a varied flowery knot,
And copse, and arbour, decks the spot,
Tempting the hasty foot to stay,
And linger on the lovely way——
Vain art! vain hope! 'tis fruitless all!
At length we reach the bounding wall,
And, sick of flower and trim-dress'd tree,
Long for rough glades and forest free.

VI.

"Three summer months had scantly flown,
When Arthur, in embarrass'd tone,
Spoke of his liegemen and his throne;
Said, all too long had been his stay,
And duties, which a Monarch sway,

Duties, unknown to humbler men,
Must tear her knight from Guendolen.—
She listen'd silently the while,
Her mood express'd in bitter smile;
Beneath her eye must Arthur quail,
And oft resume the unfinish'd tale,
Confessing, by his downcast eye,
The wrong he sought to justify.
He ceased.   A moment mute she gazed,
And then her looks to heaven she raised;
One palm her temples veiled, to hide
The tear that sprung in spite of pride!
The other for an instant press'd
The foldings of her silken vest!

VII.

" At her reproachful sign and look,
The hint the Monarch's conscience took.
Eager he spoke—' No, lady, no!
Deem not of British Arthur so,
Nor think he can deserter prove
To the dear pledge of mutual love.
I swear by sceptre and by sword,
As belted knight and Britain's lord,
That if a boy shall claim my care,
That boy is born a kingdom's heir;
But, if a maiden Fate allows,
To choose that maid a fitting spouse,
A summer-day in lists shall strive
My knights,—the bravest knights alive,—
And he, the best and bravest tried,
Shall Arthur's daughter claim for bride.'—
He spoke, with voice resolved and high—
The lady deign'd him not reply.

VIII.

" At dawn of morn, ere on the brake
His matins did a warbler make,
Or stirr'd his wing to brush away
A single dew-drop from the spray,
Ere yet a sunbeam through the mist,
The castle-battlements had kiss'd,
The gates revolve, the drawbridge falls,
And Arthur sallies from the walls.
Doff'd his soft garb of Persia's loom,
And steel from spur to helmet-plume,
His Lybian steed full proudly trode,
And joyful neigh'd beneath his load.

The Monarch gave a passing sigh
To penitence and pleasures by,
When, lo! to his astonish'd ken
Appear'd the form of Guendolen.

IX.

" Beyond the outmost wall she stood,
Attired like huntress of the wood:
Sandall'd her feet, her ankles bare,
And eagle-plumage deck'd her hair;
Firm was her look, her bearing bold,
And in her hand a cup of gold.
' Thou goest,' she said, ' and ne'er again
Must we two meet, in joy or pain.
Full fain would I this hour delay,
Though weak the wish—yet, wilt thou
      stay?
—No! thou look'st forward. Still at-
      tend,—
Part we like lover and like friend.'
She raised the cup—' Not this the juice
The sluggish vines of earth produce;
Pledge we, at parting, in the draught
Which Genii love!'—she said, and quaff'd;
And strange unwonted lustres fly
From her flush'd cheek and sparkling eye.

X.

" The courteous Monarch bent him low,
And, stooping down from saddlebow,
Lifted the cup, in act to drink.
A drop escaped the goblet's brink—
Intense as liquid fire from hell,
Upon the charger's neck it fell.
Screaming with agony and fright,
He bolted twenty feet upright—
—The peasant still can show the dint,
Where his hoofs lighted on the flint.—
From Arthur's hand the goblet flew,
Scattering a shower of fiery dew,[6]
That burn'd and blighted where it fell!
The frantic steed rush'd up the dell,
As whistles from the bow the reed;
Nor bit nor rein could check his speed,
      Until he gain'd the hill;
Then breath and sinew fail'd apace,
And, reeling from the desperate race,
      He stood, exhausted, still.

The Monarch, breathless and amazed,
Back on the fatal castle gazed——
Nor tower nor donjon could he spy,
Darkening against the morning sky;[7]
But, on the spot where once they frown'd,
The lonely streamlet brawl'd around
A tufted knoll, where dimly shone
Fragments of rocks and rifted stone.
Musing on this strange hap the while,
The king wends back to fair Carlisle:
And cares, that cumber royal sway,
Wore memory of the past away.

XI.

" Full fifteen years, and more, were sped,
Each brought new wreaths to Arthur's
      head.
Twelve bloody fields, with glory fought,[8]
The Saxons to subjection brought:
Rython, the mighty giant, slain
By his good brand, relieved Bretagne:
The Pictish Gillamore in fight,
And Roman Lucius own'd his might;
And wide were through the world re-
      nown'd
The glories of his Table Round.
Each knight who sought adventurous fame,
To the bold court of Britain came,
And all who suffer'd causeless wrong,
From tyrant proud, or faitour strong,
Sought Arthur's presence to complain,
Nor there for aid implored in vain.

XII.

" For this the King with pomp and pride,
Held solemn court at Whitsuntide,
      And summon'd Prince and Peer,
All who owed homage for their land,
Or who craved knighthood from his hand,
Or who had succour to demand,
      To come from far and near.
At such high tide, were glee and game
Mingled with feats of martial fame,
For many a stranger champion came,
      In lists to break a spear;
And not a knight of Arthur's host,
Save that he trode some foreign coast,
But at this feast of Pentecost
      Before him must appear.

Ah, Minstrels! when the Table Round
Arose, with all its warriors crown'd,
There was a theme for bards to sound
    In triumph to their string!
Five hundred years are past and gone,
But time shall draw his dying groan,
Ere he behold the British throne
    Begirt with such a ring!

XIII.

" The heralds named the appointed spot,
As Caerleon or Camelot,
    Or Carlisle fair and free.
At Penrith, now, the feast was set,
And in fair Eamont's vale were met
    The flower of Chivalry.
There Galaad sate with manly grace,
Yet maiden meekness in his face;
There Morolt of the iron mace,
    And love-lorn Tristrem there:[9]
And Dinadam with lively glance,
And Lanval with the fairy lance,
And Mordred with his look askance,
    Brunor and Bevidere.
Why should I tell of numbers more?
Sir Cay, Sir Bannier, and Sir Bore,
    Sir Carodac the keen,
The gentle Gawain's courteous lore,
Hector de Mares and Pellinore,
And Lancelot, that ever more
    Look'd stol'n-wise on the Queen.[10]

XIV.

" When wine and mirth did most abound,
And harpers play'd their blithest round,
A shrilly trumpet shook the ground,
    And marshals clear'd the ring;
A maiden, on a palfrey white,
Heading a band of damsels bright,
Paced through the circle, to alight
    And kneel before the King.
Arthur, with strong emotion, saw
Her graceful boldness check'd by awe,
Her dress, like huntress of the wold,
Her bow and baldric trapp'd with gold,
Her sandall'd feet, her ankles bare,
And the eagle-plume that deck'd her hair.
Graceful her veil she backward flung——
The King, as from his seat he sprung,
    Almost cried, ' Guendolen!'

But 'twas a face more frank and wild,
Betwixt the woman and the child,
Where less of magic beauty smiled
    Than of the race of men;
And in the forehead's haughty grace,
The lines of Britain's royal race,
    Pendragon's you might ken.

XV.

" Faltering, yet gracefully, she said—
' Great Prince! behold an orphan maid,
In her departed mother's name,
A father's vow'd protection claim!
The vow was sworn in desert lone,
In the deep valley of St. John.'
At once the King the suppliant raised,
And kiss'd her brow, her beauty praised;
His vow, he said, should well be kept,
Ere in the sea the sun was dipp'd,—
Then, conscious, glanced upon his queen;
But she, unruffled at the scene
Of human frailty, construed mild,
Look'd upon Lancelot and smiled.

XVI.

"'Up! up! each knight of gallant crest
    Take buckler, spear, and brand!
He that to-day shall bear him best,
    Shall win my Gyneth's hand.
And Arthur's daughter, when a bride,
    Shall bring a noble dower;
Both fair Strath-Clyde and Reged wide,
    And Carlisle town and tower.'
Then might you hear each valiant knight,
    To page and squire that cried,
' Bring my armour bright, and my courser
    wight!
'Tis not each day that a warrior's might
    May win a royal bride.'
Then cloaks and caps of maintenance
    In haste aside they fling;
The helmets glance, and gleams the lance,
    And the steel-weaved hauberks ring.
Small care had they of their peaceful
    array,
    They might gather it that wolde;
For brake and bramble glitter'd gay,
    With pearls and cloth of gold.

XVII.

" Within trumpet sound of the Table
　　Round
　　Were fifty champions free,
And they all arise to fight that prize,—
　　They all arise but three.
Nor love's fond troth, nor wedlock's oath,
　　One gallant could withhold,
For priests will allow of a broken vow,
　　For penance or for gold.
But sigh and glance from ladies bright
　　Among the troop were thrown,
To plead their right, and true-love
　　plight,
　　And 'plain of honour flown.
The knights they busied them so fast,
　　With buckling spur and belt,
That sigh and look, by ladies cast,
　　Were neither seen nor felt.
From pleading, or upbraiding glance,
　　Each gallant turns aside,
And only thought, ' If speeds my lance,
　　A queen becomes my bride !
She has fair Strath-Clyde, and Reged
　　wide,
　　And Carlisle tower and town ;
She is the loveliest maid, beside,
　　That ever heir'd a crown.'
So in haste their coursers they bestride,
　　And strike their visors down.

XVIII.

" The champions, arm'd in martial sort,
　　Have throng'd into the list,
And but three knights of Arthur's court
　　Are from the tourney miss'd.
And still these lovers' fame survives
　　For faith so constant shown,—
There were two who loved their neigh-
　　bour's wives,
　　And one who loved his own.[11]
The first was Lancelot de Lac,
　　The second Tristrem bold,
The third was valiant Carodac,
　　Who won the cup of gold,[12]
What time, of all King Arthur's crew,
　　(Thereof came jeer and laugh,)
He, as the mate of lady true,
　　Alone the cup could quaff.

Though envy's tongue would fain sur-
　　mise,
　　That but for very shame,
Sir Carodac, to fight that prize,
　　Had given both cup and dame ;
Yet, since but one of that fair court
　　Was true to wedlock's shrine,
Brand him who will with base report,—
　　He shall be free from mine.

XIX.

" Now caracoled the steeds in air,
Now plumes and pennons wanton'd fair,
As all around the lists so wide
In panoply the champions ride.
King Arthur saw with startled eye,
The flower of chivalry march by,
The bulwark of the Christian creed,
The kingdom's shield in hour of need.
Too late he thought him of the woe
Might from their civil conflict flow ;
For well he knew they would not part
Till cold was many a gallant heart.
His hasty vow he 'gan to rue,
And Gyneth then apart he drew ;
To her his leading-staff resign'd,
But added caution grave and kind.

XX.

" ' Thou seest, my child, as promise-
　　bound,
I bid the trump for tourney sound.
Take thou my warder as the queen
And umpire of the martial scene ;
But mark thou this :—as Beauty bright
Is polar star to valiant knight,
As at her word his sword he draws,
His fairest guerdon her applause,
So gentle maid should never ask
Of knighthood vain and dangerous task ;
And Beauty's eyes should ever be
Like the twin stars that soothe the sea,
And Beauty's breath shall whisper peace,
And bid the storm of battle cease.
I tell thee this, lest all too far,
These knights urge tourney into war.
Blithe at the trumpet let them go,
And fairly counter blow for blow ;—

No striplings these, who succour need
For a razed helm or falling steed.
But, Gyneth, when the strife grows warm,
And threatens death or deadly harm,
Thy sire entreats, thy king commands,
Thou drop the warder from thy hands.
Trust thou thy father with thy fate,
Doubt not he choose thee fitting mate;
Nor be it said, through Gyneth's pride
A rose of Arthur's chaplet died.'

XXI.

" A proud and discontented glow
O'ershadow'd Gyneth's brow of snow;
   She put the warder by:—
'Reserve thy boon, my liege,' she said,
'Thus chaffer'd down and limited,
Debased and narrow'd for a maid
   Of less degree than I.
No petty chief but holds his heir
At a more honour'd price and rare
   Than Britain's King holds me!
Although the sun-burn'd maid, for dower,
Has but her father's rugged tower,
   His barren hill and lee.'—
King Arthur swore, " By crown and
   sword,
As belted knight and Britain's lord,
That a whole summer's day should strive
His knights, the bravest knights alive!"
Recall thine oath! and to her glen
Poor Gyneth can return agen!
Not on thy daughter will the stain,
That soils thy sword and crown remain.
But think not she will e'er be bride
Save to the bravest, proved and tried;
Pendragon's daughter will not fear
For clashing sword or splinter'd spear,
   Nor shrink though blood should
      flow;
And all too well sad Guendolen
Hath taught the faithlessness of men,
That child of hers should pity, when
   Their meed they undergo.'—

XXII.

" He frown'd and sigh'd, the Monarch
   bold:—
'I give—what I may not withhold;

For, not for danger, dread, or death,
Must British Arthur break his faith.
Too late I mark, thy mother's art
Hath taught thee this relentless part.
I blame her not, for she had wrong,
But not to these my faults belong.
Use, then, the warder as thou wilt;
But trust me, that, if life be spilt,
In Arthur's love, in Arthur's grace,
Gyneth shall lose a daughter's place.
With that he turn'd his head aside,
Nor brook'd to gaze upon her pride,
As, with the truncheon raised, she sate
The arbitress of mortal fate:
Nor brook'd to mark, in ranks disposed,
How the bold champions stood opposed,
For shrill the trumpet-flourish fell
Upon his ear like passing bell!
Then first from sight of martial fray
Did Britain's hero turn away.

XXIII.

" But Gyneth heard the clangour high,
As hears the hawk the partridge cry.
Oh, blame her not! the blood was hers,
That at the trumpet's summons stirs!—
And e'en the gentlest female eye
Might the brave strife of chivalry
   A while untroubled view;
So well accomplish'd was each knight,
To strike and to defend in fight,
Their meeting was a goodly sight,
   While plate and mail held true.
The lists with painted plumes were strewn,
Upon the wind at random thrown,
But helm and breastplate bloodless shone,
It seem'd their feather'd crests alone
   Should this encounter rue.
And ever, as the combat grows,
The trumpet's cheery voice arose,
Like lark's shrill song the flourish flows,
Heard while the gale of April blows
   The merry greenwood through.

XXIV.

" But soon to earnest grew their game,
The spears drew blood, the swords struck
   flame,
And, horse and man, to ground there came
   Knights, who shall rise no more!

Gone was the pride the war that graced,
Gay shields were cleft, and crests defaced,
And steel coats riven, and helms unbraced,
    And pennons stream'd with gore.
Gone, too, were fence and fair array,
And desperate strength made deadly way
At random through the bloody fray,
And blows were dealt with headlong sway,
    Unheeding where they fell;
And now the trumpet's clamours seem
Like the shrill sea-bird's wailing scream,
Heard o'er the whirlpool's gulfing stream,
    The sinking seaman's knell!

XXV

"Seem'd in this dismal hour, that Fate
Would Camlan's ruin antedate,
    And spare dark Mordred's crime;
Already gasping on the ground
Lie twenty of the Table Round,
    Of chivalry the prime.
Arthur, in anguish, tore away
From head and beard his tresses grey,
And she, proud Gyneth, felt dismay,
    And quaked with ruth and fear;
But still she deem'd her mother's shade
Hung o'er the tumult, and forbade
The sign that had the slaughter staid,
    And chid the rising tear.
Then Brunor, Taulas, Mador, fell,
Helias the White, and Lionel,
    And many a champion more;
Rochemont and Dinadam are down,
And Ferrand of the Forest Brown
    Lies gasping in his gore.
Vanoc, by mighty Morolt press'd
Even to the confines of the list,
Young Vanoc of the beardless face,
(Fame spoke the youth of Merlin's
    race,)
O'erpower'd at Gyneth's footstool bled,
His heart's-blood dyed her sandals red.
But then the sky was overcast,
Then howl'd at once a whirlwind's blast,
    And, rent by sudden throes,
Yawn'd in mid lists the quaking earth,
And from the gulf,—tremendous birth!—
    The form of Merlin rose.

XXVI.

" Sternly the Wizard Prophet eyed
The dreary lists with slaughter dyed,
    And sternly raised his hand:—
' Madmen,' he said, ' your strife forbear;
And thou, fair cause of mischief, hear
    The doom thy fates demand!
Long shall close in stony sleep
Eyes for ruth that would not weep;
Iron lethargy shall seal
Heart that pity scorn'd to feel.
Yet, because thy mother's art
Warp'd thine unsuspicious heart,
And for love of Arthur's race,
Punishment is blent with grace,
Thou shalt bear thy penance lone
In the Valley of Saint John,
And this weird* shall overtake thee;
Sleep, until a knight shall wake thee,
For feats of arms as far renown'd
As warrior of the Table Round.
Long endurance of thy slumber
Well may teach the world to number
All their woes from Gyneth's pride,
When the Red Cross champions died.

XXVII.

" As Merlin speaks, on Gyneth's eye
Slumber's load begins to lie;
Fear and anger vainly strive
Still to keep its light alive.
Twice, with effort and with pause,
O'er her brow her hand she draws;
Twice her strength in vain she tries,
From the fatal chair to rise,
Merlin's magic doom is spoken,
Vanoc's death must now be wroken.
Slow the dark-fringed eyelids fall,
Curtaining each azure ball,
Slowly as on summer eves
Violets fold their dusky leaves.
The weighty baton of command
Now bears down her sinking hand,
On her shoulder droops her head;
Net of pearl and golden thread,

---

* Doom.

Bursting, gave her locks to flow
O'er her arm and breast of snow.
And so lovely seem'd she there,
Spell-bound in her ivory chair,
That her angry sire, repenting,
Craved stern Merlin for relenting,
And the champions, for her sake,
Would again the contest wake;
Till, in necromantic night,
Gyneth vanish'd from their sight.

XXVIII.

" Still she bears her weird alon,
In the Valley of Saint John;
And her semblance oft will seem,
Mingling in a champion's dream,
Of her weary lot to 'plain,
And crave his aid to burst her chain
While her wondrous tale was new,
Warriors to her rescue drew,
Fast and west, and south and north,
From the Liffy, Thames, and Forth.
Most have sought in vain the glen,
Tower nor castle could they ken;
Not at every time or tide,
Nor by every eye, descried.
Fast and vigil must be borne,
Many a night in watching worn,
Ere an eye of mortal powers
Can discern those magic towers.
Of the persevering few,
Some from hopeless task withdrew,
When they read the dismal threat
Graved upon the gloomy gate.
Few have braved the yawning door,
And those few return'd no more.
In the lapse of time forgot,
Wellnigh lost is Gyneth's lot;
Sound her sleep as in the tomb,
Till waken'd by the trump of doom."

 END OF LYULPH'S TALE.

Here pause my tale; for all too soon,
My Lucy, comes the hour of noon.
Already from thy lofty dome
Its courtly inmates 'gin to roam,
And each, to kill the goodly day
That God has granted them, his way

Of lazy sauntering has sought;
Lordlings and witlings not a few,
Incapable of doing aught,
Yet ill at ease with nought to do.
Here is no longer place for me;
For, Lucy, thou wouldst blush to see
Some phantom fashionably thin,
With limb of lath and kerchief'd
chin,
And lounging gape, or sneering grin,
Steal sudden on our privacy.
And how should I, so humbly born,
Endure the graceful spectre's scorn?
Faith! ill, I fear, while conjuring wand
Of English oak is hard at hand.

II.

Or grant the hour be all too soon
For Hessian boot and pantaloon,
And grant the lounger seldom strays
Beyond the smooth and gravell'd maze,
Laud we the gods, that Fashion's train
Folds hearts of more adventurous strain.
Artists are hers, who scorn to trace
Their rules from Nature's boundless
grace,
But their right paramount assert
To limit her by pedant art,
Damning whate'er of vast and fair
Exceeds a canvass three feet square.
This thicket, for their *gumption* fit,
May furnish such a happy *bit*.
Bards, too, are hers, wont to recite
Their own sweet lays by waxen light,
Half in the salver's tingle drown'd,
While the *chasse-café* glides around;
And such may hither secret stray,
To labour an extempore:
Or sportsman, with his boisterous hollo
May here his wiser spaniel follow,
Or stage-struck Juliet may presume
To choose this bower for tiring-room;
And we alike must shun regard,
From painter, player, sportsman, bard.
Insects that skim in Fashion's sky,
Wasp, blue-bottle, or butterfly,
Lucy, have all alarms for us,
For all can hum and all can buzz.

III.

But oh, my Lucy, say how long
We still must dread this trifling throng,
And stoop to hide, with coward art,
The genuine feelings of the heart!
No parents thine whose just command
Should rule their child's obedient hand;
Thy guardians, with contending voice,
Press each his individual choice.
And which is Lucy's?—Can it be
That puny top, trimm'd cap-a-pee,
Who loves in the saloon to show
The arms that never knew a foe;
Whose sabre trails along the ground,
Whose legs in shapeless boots are
     drown'd;
A new Achilles, sure,—the steel
Fled from his breast to fence his heel;
One, for the simple manly grace
That wont to deck our martial race,
   Who comes in foreign trashery
     Of tinkling chain and spur,
   A walking haberdashery,
     Of feathers, lace, and fur:
In Rowley's antiquated phrase,
Horse-milliner[13] of modern days?

IV.

Or is it he, the wordy youth,
   So early train'd for statesman's part,
Who talks of honour, faith, and truth,
   As themes that he has got by heart;
Whose ethics Chesterfield can teach,
Whose logic is from Single-speech;
Who scorns the meanest thought to vent,
Save in the phrase of Parliament;
Who, in a tale of cat and mouse,
Calls " order," and " divides the house,"
Who " craves permission to reply,"
Whose " noble friend is in his eye;"
Whose loving tender some have reckon'd
A motion, you should gladly second?

V.

What, neither? Can there be a third,
To such resistless swains preferr'd?—
O why, my Lucy, turn aside,
With that quick glance of injured pride?

Forgive me, love, I cannot bear
That alter'd and resentful air.
Were all the wealth of Russel mine,
And all the rank of Howard's line,
All would I give for leave to dry
That dewdrop trembling in thine eye.
Think not I fear such fops can wile
From Lucy more than careless smile;
But yet if wealth and high degree
Give gilded counters currency,
Must I not fear, when rank and birth
Stamp the pure ore of genuine worth?
Nobles there are, whose martial fires
Rival the fame that raised their sires,
And patriots, skill'd through storms of
     fate
To guide and guard the reeling state.
Such, such there are—If such should come,
Arthur must tremble and be dumb,
Self-exiled seek some distant shore,
And mourn till life and grief are o'er.

VI.

What sight, what signal of alarm,
That Lucy clings to Arthur's arm?
Or is it, that the rugged way
Makes Beauty lean on lover's stay?
Oh, no! for on the vale and brake,
Nor sight nor sounds of danger wake,
And this trim sward of velvet green,
Were carpet for the Fairy Queen.
That pressure slight was but to tell,
That Lucy loves her Arthur well,
And fain would banish from his mind
Suspicious fear and doubt unkind.

VII.

But wouldst thou bid the demons fly
Like mist before the dawning sky,
There is but one resistless spell—
Say, wilt thou guess, or must I tell?
'Twere hard to name, in minstrel phrase,
A landaulet and four blood-bays,
But bards agree this wizard band
Can but be bound in Northern land.
'Tis there—nay, draw not back thy
     hand!—
'Tis there this slender finger round
Must golden amulet be bound,

Which, bless'd with many a holy prayer,
Can change to rapture lovers' care,
And doubt and jealousy shall die,
And fears give place to ecstasy.

VIII.

Now, trust me, Lucy, all too long
Has been thy lover's tale and song.
O, why so silent, love, I pray?
Have I not spoke the livelong day?
And will not Lucy deign to say
 One word her friend to bless?
I ask but one—a simple sound,
Within three little letters bound,
 O, let the word be YES!

CANTO THIRD.

INTRODUCTION.

I.

Long loved, long woo'd, and lately won,
My life's best hope, and now mine own!
Doth not this rude and Alpine glen
Recall our favourite haunts agen?
A wild resemblance we can trace,
Though reft of every softer grace,
As the rough warrior's brow may bear
A likeness to a sister fair.
Full well advised our Highland host,
That this wild pass on foot be cross'd,
While round Ben-Cruach's mighty base
Wheel the slow steeds and lingering chaise.
The keen old carle, with Scottish pride,
He praised his glen and mountains wide;
An eye he bears for nature's face,
Ay, and for woman's lovely grace.
Even in such mean degree we find
The subtle Scot's observing mind;
For, nor the chariot nor the train
Could gape of vulgar wonder gain,
But when old Allan would expound
Of Beal-na-paish* the Celtic sound,
His bonnet doff'd, and bow, applied
His legend to my bonny bride;

---

* *Beal-na-paish*, in English the Vale of the Bridal.

While Lucy blush'd beneath his eye,
Courteous and cautious, shrewd and sly.

II.

Enough of him.—Now, ere we lose,
Plunged in the vale, the distant views,
Turn thee, my love! look back once more
To the blue lake's retiring shore.
On its smooth breast the shadows seem
Like objects in a morning dream,
What time the slumberer is aware
He sleeps, and all the vision's air:
Even so, on yonder liquid lawn,
In hues of bright reflection drawn,
Distinct the shaggy mountains lie,
Distinct the rocks, distinct the sky;
The summer-clouds so plain we note,
That we might count each dappled spot:
We gaze and we admire, yet know
The scene is all delusive show.
Such dreams of bliss would Arthur draw,
When first his Lucy's form he saw;
Yet sigh'd and sicken'd as he drew,
Despairing they could e'er prove true!

III.

But, Lucy, turn thee now, to view
 Up the fair glen, our destined way:
The fairy path that we pursue,
Distinguish'd but by greener hue,
 Winds round the purple brae,
While Alpine flowers of varied dye
For carpet serve, or tapestry.
See how the little runnels leap,
In threads of silver, down the steep,
 To swell the brooklet's moan!
Seems that the Highland Naiad grieves,
Fantastic while her crown she weaves,
Of rowan, birch, and alder-leaves,
 So lovely, and so lone.
There's no illusion there; these flowers,
That wailing brook, these lovely bowers,
 Are, Lucy, all our own;
And, since thine Arthur call'd thee wife,
Such seems the prospect of his life,
A lovely path, on-winding still,
By gurgling brook and sloping hill.
'Tis true, that mortals cannot tell
What waits them in the distant dell;

But be it hap, or be it harm,
We tread the pathway arm in arm.

IV.

And now, my Lucy, wot'st thou why
I could thy bidding twice deny,
When twice you pray'd I would again
Resume the legendary strain
Of the bold knight of Triermain?
At length yon peevish vow you swore,
That you would sue to me no more,
Until the minstrel fit drew near,
And made me prize a listening ear.
But, loveliest, when thou first didst pray
Continuance of the knightly lay,
Was it not on the happy day
    That made thy hand mine own?
When, dizzied with mine ecstasy,
Nought past, or present, or to be,
Could I or think on, hear, or see,
    Save, Lucy, thee alone!
A giddy draught my rapture was,
As ever chemist's magic gas.

V.

Again the summons I denied
In yon fair capital of Clyde:
My Harp—or let me rather choose
The good old classic form—my Muse,
(For Harp's an over-scutched phrase,
Worn out by bards of modern days,)
My Muse, then—seldom will she wake,
Save by dim wood and silent lake;
She is the wild and rustic Maid,
Whose foot unsandall'd loves to tread
Where the soft greensward is inlaid
    With varied moss and thyme;
And, lest the simple lily-braid,
That coronets her temples, fade,
She hides her still in greenwood shade,
    To meditate her rhyme.

VI.

And now she comes! The murmur dear
Of the wild brook hath caught her ear,
    The glade hath won her eye,
She longs to join with each blithe rill
That dances down the Highland hill,
    Her blither melody.

And now, my Lucy's way to cheer,
She bids Ben-Cruach's echoes hear
How closed the tale, my love whilere
    Loved for its chivalry.
List how she tells, in notes of flame,
" Child Roland to the dark tower came."

CANTO THIRD.

I.

BEWCASTLE now must keep the Hold,
    Speir-Adam's steeds must bide in stall,
Of Hartley-burn the bowmen bold
    Must only shoot from battled wall;
And Liddesdale may buckle spur,
    And Teviot now may belt the brand,
Tarras and Ewes keep nightly stir,
    And Eskdale foray Cumberland.
Of wasted fields and plundered flocks
    The Borderers bootless may complain;
They lack the sword of brave de Vaux,
    There comes no aid from Triermain.
That lord, on high adventure bound,
    Hath wander'd forth alone,
And day and night keeps watchful round
    In the valley of Saint John.

II.

When first began his vigil bold,
The moon twelve summer nights was old,
    And shone both fair and full;
High in the vault of cloudless blue,
O'er streamlet, dale, and rock, she threw
    Her light composed and cool.
Stretch'd on the brown hill's heathy breast,
    Sir Roland eyed the vale;
Chief where, distinguish'd from the rest,
Those clustering rocks uprear'd their crest,
The dwelling of the fair distress'd,
    As told grey Lyulph's tale.
Thus as he lay the lamp of night
Was quivering on his armour bright,
    In beams that rose and fell,
And danced upon his buckler's boss,
That lay beside him on the moss,
    As on a crystal well.

III.

Ever he watch'd, and oft he deem'd,
While on the mound the moonlight
    stream'd,
    It alter'd to his eyes ;
Fain would he hope the rocks 'gan
    change
To buttress'd walls their shapeless range,
Fain think, by transmutation strange,
    He saw grey turrets rise.
But scarce his heart with hope throbb'd
    high,
Before the wild illusions fly,
    Which fancy had conceived,
Abetted by an anxious eye
    That long'd to be deceived.
It was a fond deception all,
Such as, in solitary hall,
    Beguiles the musing eye,
When, gazing on the sinking fire,
Bulwark, and battlement, and spire,
    In the red gulf we spy.
For, seen by moon of middle night,
Or by the blaze of noontide bright,
Or by the dawn of morning light,
    Or evening's western flame,
In every tide, at every hour,
In mist, in sunshine, and in shower,
    The rocks remain'd the same.

IV.

Oft has he traced the charmed mound,
Oft climb'd its crest, or paced it round,
    Yet nothing might explore,
Save that the crags so rudely piled,
At distance seen, resemblance wild
    To a rough fortress bore.
Yet still his watch the Warrior keeps,
Feeds hard and spare, and seldom
    sleeps,
    And drinks but of the well :
Ever by day he walks the hill,
And when the evening gale is chill,
    He seeks a rocky cell,
Like hermit poor to bid his bead,
And tell his Ave and his Creed,
Invoking every saint at need,
    For aid to burst his spell.

V.

And now the moon her orb has hid,
And dwindled to a silver thread,
    Dim seen in middle heaven,
While o'er its curve careering fast,
Before the fury of the blast
    The midnight clouds are driven.
The brooklet raved, for on the hills,
The upland showers had swoln the rills,
    And down the torrents came ;
Mutter'd the distant thunder dread,
And frequent o'er the vale was spread
    A sheet of lightning flame.
De Vaux, within his mountain cave,
(No human step the storm durst brave,)
    To moody meditation gave
    Each faculty of soul,
Till, lull'd by distant torrent sound,
And the sad winds that whistled round,
Upon his thoughts, in musing drown'd,
    A broken slumber stole.

VI.

'Twas then was heard a heavy sound,
    (Sound, strange and fearful there to
    hear,
'Mongst desert hills, where, leaguer
    around,
    Dwelt but the gorcock and the deer :)
As, starting from his couch of fern,
Again he heard in clangour stern,
    That deep and solemn swell,—
Twelve times, in measured tone, it spoke,
Like some proud minster's pealing clock,
    Or city's 'larum-bell.
What thought was Roland's first when
    fell,
In that deep wilderness, the knell
    Upon his startled ear ?
To slander warrior were I loth,
Yet must I hold my minstrel troth,—
    It was a thought of fear.

VII.

But lively was the mingled thrill
That chased that momentary chill,
    For Love's keen wish was there,
And eager Hope, and Valour high,
And the proud glow of Chivalry,
    That burn'd to do and dare.

Forth from the cave the Warrior rush'd,
Long ere the mountain-voice was hush'd,
   That answer'd to the knell;
For long and far the unwonted sound,
Eddying in echoes round and round,
   Was toss'd from fell to fell;
And Glaramara answer flung,
And Grisdale-pike responsive rung,
And Legbert heights their echoes swung,
   As far as Derwent's dell.

VIII.

Forth upon trackless darkness gazed
The Knight, bedeafen'd and amazed,
   Till all was hush'd and still,
Save the swoln torrent's sullen roar,
And the night-blast that wildly bore
   Its course along the hill.
Then on the northern sky there came
A light, as of reflected flame,
   And over Legbert-head,
As if by magic art controll'd,
A mighty meteor slowly roll'd
   Its orb of fiery red;
Thou wouldst have thought some demon dire
Came mounted on that car of fire,
   To do his errand dread.
Far on the sloping valley's course,
On thicket, rock, and torrent hoarse,
Shingle and Scrae,* and Fell and Force,†
   A dusky light arose:
Display'd, yet alter'd was the scene;
Dark rock, and brook of silver sheen,
Even the gay thicket's summer green,
   In bloody tincture glows.

IX.

De Vaux had mark'd the sunbeams set,
At eve, upon the coronet
   Of that enchanted mound,
And seen but crags at random flung,
That, o'er the brawling torrent hung,
   In desolation frown'd.
What sees he by that meteor's lour?—
A banner'd Castle, keep, and tower,
   Return the lurid gleam,

With battled walls and buttress fast,
And barbican‡ and ballium§ vast,
And airy flanking towers, that cast
   Their shadows on the stream.
'Tis no deceit!—distinctly clear
Crenell‖ and parapet appear,
While o'er the pile that meteor drear
   Makes momentary pause;
Then forth its solemn path it drew,
And fainter yet and fainter grew
Those gloomy towers upon the view,
   As its wild light withdraws.

X.

Forth from the cave did Roland rush,
O'er crag and stream, through brier and
   bush,
   Yet far he had not sped,
Ere sunk was that portentous light
Behind the hills, and utter night
   Was on the valley spread.
He paused perforce, and blew his horn,
And, on the mountain-echoes borne,
   Was heard an answering sound,
A wild and lonely trumpet-note,—
In middle air it seem'd to float
   High o'er the battled mound;
And sounds were heard, as when a guard,
Of some proud castle, holding ward,
   Pace forth their nightly round.
The valiant Knight of Triermain
Rung forth his challenge-blast again,
   But answer came there none;
And 'mid the mingled wind and rain,
Darkling he sought the vale in vain,
   Until the dawning shone;
And when it dawn'd, that wondrous sight,
Distinctly seen by meteor light,
   It all had pass'd away!
And that enchanted mount once more
A pile of granite fragments bore,
   As at the close of day.

XI.

Steel'd for the deed, De Vaux's heart,
Scorn'd from his vent'rous quest to part,

---

* Bank of loose stones.   † Waterfall.

‡ The outer defence of a castle gate.
§ A fortified court.
‖ Apertures for shooting arrows.

He walks the vale once more;
But only sees, by night or day,
That shatter'd pile of rocks so grey,
    Hears but the torrent's roar.
Till when, through hills of azure borne,
The moon renew'd her silver horn,
Just at the time her waning ray
Had faded in the dawning day,
    A summer mist arose:
Adown the vale the vapours float,
And cloudy undulations moat
That tufted mound of mystic note,
    As round its base they close.
And higher now the fleecy tide
Ascends its stern and shaggy side,
Until the airy billows hide
    The rock's majestic isle;
It seem'd a veil of filmy lawn,
By some fantastic fairy drawn
    Around enchanted pile.

XII.

The breeze came softly down the brook,
    And, sighing as it blew,
The veil of silver mist it shook,
And to De Vaux's eager look
    Renew'd that wondrous view.
For, though the loitering vapour braved
The gentle breeze, yet oft it waved
    Its mantle's dewy fold;
And still, when shook that filmy screen,
Were towers and bastions dimly seen,
And Gothic battlements between
    Their gloomy length unroll'd.
Speed, speed, De Vaux, ere on thine
    eye
Once more the fleeting vision die!
    —The gallant knight 'gan speed
As prompt and light as, when the hound
Is opening, and the horn is wound,
    Careers the hunter's steed.
Down the steep dell his course amain
    Hath rivall'd archer's shaft;
But ere the mound he could attain,
The rocks their shapeless form regain,
And, mocking loud his labour vain,
    The mountain spirits laugh'd.
Far up the echoing dell was borne
Their wild unearthly shout of scorn.

XIII.

Wroth wax'd the Warrior.—"Am I then
Fool'd by the enemies of men,
Like a poor hind, whose homeward way
Is haunted by malicious fay!
Is Triermain become your taunt,
De Vaux your scorn? False fiends,
    avaunt!"
A weighty curtal-axe he bare;
The baleful blade so bright and square,
And the tough shaft of heben wood,
Were oft in Scottish gore imbrued.
Backward his stately form he drew,
And at the rocks the weapon threw,
Just where one crag's projected crest
Hung proudly balanced o'er the rest.
Hurl'd with main force, the weapon's
    shock
Rent a huge fragment of the rock.
If by mere strength, 'twere hard to tell,
Or if the blow dissolved some spell,
But down the headlong ruin came,
With cloud of dust and flash of flame.
Down bank, o'er bush, its course was
    borne,
Crush'd lay the copse, the earth was torn,
Till staid at length, the ruin dread
Cumber'd the torrent's rocky bed,
And bade the water's high-swoln tide
Seek other passage for its pride.

XIV.

When ceased that thunder, Triermain
Survey'd the mound's rude front again;
And lo! the ruin had laid bare,
Hewn in the stone, a winding stair,
Whose moss'd and fractured steps might
    lend
The means the summit to ascend;
And by whose aid the brave De Vaux
Began to scale these magic rocks,
    And soon a platform won,
Where, the wild witchery to close,
Within three lances' length arose
    The Castle of Saint John!
No misty phantom of the air,
No meteor-blazon'd show was there;
In morning splendour, full and fair,
    The massive fortress shone.

XV.

Embattled high and proudly tower'd,
Shaded by pond'rous flankers, lower'd
    The portal's gloomy way.
Though for six hundred years and more,
Its strength had brook'd the tempest's roar,
The scutcheon'd emblems which it bore
    Had suffer'd no decay:
But from the eastern battlement
A turret had made sheer descent,
And, down in recent ruin rent,
    In the mid torrent lay.
Else, o'er the Castle's brow sublime,
Insults of violence or of time
    Unfelt had pass'd away.
In shapeless characters of yore,
The gate this stern inscription bore:—

XVI.

Inscription.

"Patience waits the destined day,
Strength can clear the cumber'd way.
Warrior, who hast waited long,
Firm of soul, of sinew strong,
It is given thee to gaze
On the pile of ancient days.
Never mortal builder's hand
This enduring fabric plann'd;
Sign and sigil, word of power,
From the earth raised keep and tower.
View it o'er, and pace it round,
Rampart, turret, battled mound.
Dare no more!   To cross the gate
Were to tamper with thy fate;
Strength and fortitude were vain,
View it o'er—and turn again."

XVII.

"That would I," said the Warrior bold,
"If that my frame were bent and old,
And my thin blood dropp'd slow and cold,
    As icicle in thaw;
But while my heart can feel it dance,
Blithe as the sparkling wine of France,
And this good arm wields sword or lance,
I mock these words of awe!"

He said; the wicket felt the sway
Of his strong hand, and straight gave way,
And, with rude crash and jarring bray,
    The rusty bolts withdraw;
But o'er the threshold as he strode,
And forward took the vaulted road,
An unseen arm, with force amain,
The ponderous gate flung close again,
    And rusted bolt and bar
Spontaneous took their place once more,
While the deep arch with sullen roar
    Return'd their surly jar.
" Now closed is the gin and the prey within
    By the rood of Lanercost !
But he that would win the war-wolf's skin,
    May rue him of his boast."
Thus muttering, on the Warrior went,
By dubious light down deep descent.

XVIII.

Unbarr'd, unlock'd, unwatch'd, a port
Led to the Castle's outer court:
There the main fortress, broad and tall,
Spread its long range of bower and hall,
    And towers of varied size,
Wrought with each ornament extreme,
That Gothic art, in wildest dream
    Of fancy, could devise;
But full between the Warrior's way
And the main portal arch, there lay
    An inner moat;
    Nor bridge nor boat
Affords De Vaux the means to cross
The clear, profound, and silent fosse.
His arms aside in haste he flings,
Cuirass of steel and hauberk rings,
And down falls helm, and down the shield,
Rough with the dints of many a field.
Fair was his manly form, and fair
His keen dark eye, and close curl'd hair,
When, all unarm'd, save that the brand
Of well-proved metal graced his hand,
With nought to fence his dauntless breast
But the close gipon's* under-vest,
Whose sullied buff the sable stains
Of hauberk and of mail retains,—

---

* A sort of doublet worn beneath the armour.

Roland De Vaux upon the brim
Of the broad moat stood prompt to swim.

XIX.

Accoutred thus he dared the tide,
And soon he reach'd the farther side,
   And enter'd soon the Hold,
And paced a hall, whose walls so wide
Were blazon'd all with feats of pride,
   By warriors done of old.
In middle lists they counter'd here,
   While trumpets seem'd to blow;
And there, in den or desert drear,
   They quell'd gigantic foe,
Braved the fierce griffon in his ire,
Or faced the dragon's breath of fire.
Strange in their arms, and strange in face,
Heroes they seem'd of ancient race,
Whose deeds of arms, and race, and name,
Forgotten long by later fame,
   Were here depicted, to appal
Those of an age degenerate,
Whose bold intrusion braved their fate,
   In this enchanted hall.
For some short space the venturous knight
With these high marvels fed his sight,
Then sought the chamber's upper end,
Where three broad easy steps ascend
   To an arch'd portal door,
In whose broad folding leaves of state
Was framed a wicket window-grate,
   And, ere he ventured more,
The gallant Knight took earnest view
The grated wicket-window through.

XX.

O, for his arms! Of martial weed
Had never mortal Knight such need!
He spied a stately gallery; all
Of snow-white marble was the wall,
   The vaulting, and the floor;
And, contrast strange, on either hand
There stood array'd in sable band
   Four Maids whom Afric bore.
And each a Libyan tiger led,
Held by as bright and frail a thread
   As Lucy's golden hair,—
For the leash that bound these monsters dread
   Was but of gossamer.

Each Maiden's short barbaric vest
Left all unclosed the knee and breast,
   And limbs of shapely jet;
White was their vest and turban's fold,
On arms and ankles rings of gold
   In savage pomp were set;
A quiver on their shoulders lay,
And in their hand an assagay.
Such and so silent stood they there,
   That Roland wellnigh hoped
He saw a band of statues rare,
Station'd the gazer's soul to scare;
   But when the wicket oped,
Each grisly beast 'gan upward draw,
Roll'd his grim eye, and spread his claw,
Scented the air, and licked his jaw;
While these weird maids, in Moorish tongue,
A wild and dismal warning sung.

XXI.

" Rash Adventurer, bear thee back!
   Dread the spell of Dahomay!
Fear the race of Zaharak,*
   Daughters of the burning day!

" When the whirlwind's gusts are wheeling,
   Ours it is the dance to braid;
Zarah's sands in pillars reeling,
   Join the measure that we tread,
When the Moon has donn'd her cloak,
   And the stars are red to see,
Shrill when pipes the sad Siroc,
   Music meet for such as we.

" Where the shatter'd columns lie,
   Showing Carthage once had been,
If the wandering Santon's eye
   Our mysterious rites hath seen,—
Oft he cons the prayer of death,
   To the nations preaches doom,
' Azrael's brand hath left the sheath!
   Moslems, think upon the tomb!'

" Ours the scorpion, ours the snake,
   Ours the hydra of the fen,

---

* The Arab name of the Great Desert.

Ours the tiger of the brake,
   All that plague the sons of men.
Ours the tempest's midnight wrack,
   Pestilence that wastes by day—
Dread the race of Zaharak!
   Fear the spell of Dahomay!"

XXII.

Uncouth and strange the accents shrill
   Rung those vaulted roofs among,
Long it was ere, faint and still,
   Died the far resounding song.
While yet the distant echoes roll,
The Warrior communed with his soul.
"When first I took this venturous quest,
   I swore upon the rood,
Neither to stop, nor turn, nor rest,
   For evil or for good.
My forward path too well I ween,
Lies yonder fearful ranks between!
For man unarm'd, 'tis bootless hope
With tigers and with fiends to cope—
Yet, if I turn, what waits me there,
Save famine dire and fell despair?—
Other conclusion let me try,
Since, choose howe'er I list, I die.
Forward, lies faith and knightly fame;
Behind, are perjury and shame.
In life or death I hold my word!"
With that he drew his trusty sword,
Caught down a banner from the wall,
And enter'd thus the fearful hall.

XXIII.

On high each wayward Maiden threw
Her swarthy arm, with wild halloo!
On either side a tiger sprung—
Against the leftward foe he flung
The ready banner, to engage
With tangling folds the brutal rage;
The right-hand monster in mid air
He struck so fiercely and so fair,
Through gullet and through spinal bone,
The trenchant blade had sheerly gone.
His grisly brethren ramp'd and yell'd,
But the slight leash their rage withheld,
Whilst, 'twixt their ranks, the dangerous
   road
Firmly, though swift, the champion
   strode,

Safe to the gallery's bound he drew,
Safe pass'd an open portal through;
And when against pursuit he flung
The gate, judge if the echoes rung!
Onward his daring course he bore,
While, mix'd with dying growl and roar,
Wild jubilee and loud hurra
Pursued him on his venturous way.

XXIV.

"Hurra, hurra! Our watch is done!
We hail once more the tropic sun.
Pallid beams of northern day,
Farewell, farewell! Hurra, hurra!

"Five hundred years o'er this cold glen
Hath the pale sun come round agen;
Foot of man, till now, hath ne'er
Dared to cross the Hall of Fear.

"Warrior! thou, whose dauntless heart
Gives us from our ward to part,
Be as strong in future trial,
Where resistance is denial.

"Now for Afric's glowing sky,
Zwenga wide and Atlas high,
Zaharak and Dahomay!—
Mount the winds! Hurra, hurra!"

XXV.

The wizard song at distance died,
   As if in ether borne astray,
While through waste halls and chambers
   wide
   The Knight pursued his steady way,
Till to a lofty dome he came,
That flash'd with such a brilliant flame,
As if the wealth of all the world
Were there in rich confusion hurl'd.
For here the gold, in sandy heaps,
With duller earth, incorporate, sleeps;
Was there in ingots piled, and there
Coin'd badge of empery it bare;
Yonder, huge bars of silver lay,
Dimm'd by the diamond's neighbouring
   ray,
Like the pale moon in morning day;
And in the midst four Maidens stand,
The daughters of some distant land.

Their hue was of the dark-red dye,
That fringes oft a thunder sky;
Their hands palmetto baskets bare,
And cotton fillets bound their hair;
Slim was their form, their mien was
shy,
To earth they bent the humbled eye,
Folded their arms, and suppliant
kneel'd,
And thus their proffer'd gifts reveal'd.

XXVI.

CHORUS.

" See the treasures Merlin piled,
Portion meet for Arthur's child.
Bathe in Wealth's unbounded stream,
Wealth that Avarice ne'er could dream!"

FIRST MAIDEN.

" See these clots of virgin gold!
Sever'd from the sparry mould,
Nature's mystic alchemy
In the mine thus bade them lie;
And their orient smile can win
Kings to stoop, and saints to sin."—

SECOND MAIDEN.

" See these pearls, that long have slept;
These were tears by Naiads wept
For the loss of Marinel.
Tritons in the silver shell
Treasured them, till hard and white
As the teeth of Amphitrite."—

THIRD MAIDEN.

" Does a livelier hue delight?
Here are rubies blazing bright,
Here the emerald's fairy green,
And the topaz glows between;
Here their varied hues unite,
In the changeful chrysolite."—

FOURTH MAIDEN.

" Leave these gems of poorer shine,
Leave them all, and look on mine!
While their glories I expand,
Shade thine eyebrows with thy hand.
Mid-day sun and diamond's blaze
Blind the rash beholder's gaze."—

CHORUS.

" Warrior, seize the splendid store;
Would 'twere all our mountains bore!
We should ne'er in future story,
Read, Peru, thy perish'd glory!"

XXVII.

Calmly and unconcern'd, the Knight
Waved aside the treasures bright:—
" Gentle Maidens, rise, I pray!
Bar not thus my destined way.
Let these boasted brilliant toys
Braid the hair of girls and boys!
Bid your streams of gold expand
O'er proud London's thirsty land.
De Vaux of wealth saw never need,
Save to purvey him arms and steed,
And all the ore he deign'd to hoard
Inlays his helm, and hilts his sword."
Thus gently parting from their hold,
He left, unmoved, the dome of gold.

XXVIII.

And now the morning sun was high,
De Vaux was weary, faint, and dry;
When, lo! a plashing sound he hears,
A gladsome signal that he nears
        Some frolic water-run;
And soon he reach'd a court-yard square,
Where, dancing in the sultry air,
Toss'd high aloft, a fountain fair
        Was sparkling in the sun.
On right and left, a fair arcade,
In long perspective view display'd
Alleys and bowers, for sun or shade:
        But, full in front, a door,
Low-brow'd and dark, seem'd as it led
To the lone dwelling of the dead,
        Whose memory was no more.

XXIX.

Here stopp'd De Vaux an instant's space,
To bathe his parched lips and face,
        And mark'd with well-pleased eye,
Refracted on the fountain stream,
In rainbow hues the dazzling beam
        Of that gay summer sky.
His senses felt a mild control,
Like that which lulls the weary soul,

From contemplation high
Relaxing, when the ear receives
The music that the greenwood leaves
　　Make to the breezes' sigh.

XXX.

And oft in such a dreamy mood,
　　The half-shut eye can frame
Fair apparitions in the wood
As if the nymphs of field and flood
　　In gay procession came.
Are these of such fantastic mov'd,
　　Seen distant down the fair arcade,
These Maids enlink'd in sister-fold,
　　Who, late at bashful distance staid,
　　Now tripping from the greenwood
　　　shade,
Nearer the musing champion draw,
And, in a pause of seeming awe,—
　　Again stand doubtful now?—
Ah, that sly pause of witching powers!
That seems to say, "To please be ours,
　　Be yours to tell us how."
Their hue was of the golden glow
That suns of Candahar bestow,
O'er which in slight suffusion flows
A frequent tinge of paly rose;
Their limbs were fashion'd fair and free,
In nature's justest symmetry;
And, wreathed with flowers, with odours
　　graced,
Their raven ringlets reach'd the waist:
In eastern pomp, its gilding pale
'The hennah lent each shapely nail,
And the dark sumah gave the eye
More liquid and more lustrous dye.
The spotless veil of misty lawn,
In studied disarrangement, drawn
　　The form and bosom o'er,
To win the eye, or tempt the touch,
For modesty show'd all too much—
　　Too much—yet promised more.

XXXI.

"Gentle Knight, a while delay,"
Thus they sung, "thy toilsome way,
　　While we pay the duty due
　　To our Master and to you.

Over Avarice, over Fear,
Love triumphant led thee here;
Warrior, list to us, for we
Are slaves to Love, are friends to thee.
Though no treasured gems have we,
To proffer on the bended knee,
Though we boast nor arm nor heart,
For the assagay or dart,
Swains allow each simple girl
Ruby lip and teeth of pearl;
Or, if dangers more you prize,
Flatterers find them in our eyes.

"Stay, then, gentle Warrior, stay,
Rest till evening steal on day;
Stay, O, stay!—in yonder bowers
We will braid thy locks with flowers,
Spread the feast and fill the wine,
Charm thy ear with sounds divine,
Weave our dances till delight
Yield to languor, day to night.

"Then shall she you most approve,
Sing the lays that best you love,
Soft thy mossy couch shall spread,
Watch thy pillow, prop thy head,
Till the weary night be o'er—
Gentle Warrior, wouldst thou more?
Wouldst thou more, fair Warrior,—she
Is slave to Love and slave to thee."

XXXII.

O, do not hold it for a crime
In the bold hero of my rhyme,
　　For Stoic look,
　　And meet rebuke,
He lack'd the heart or time;
As round the band of sirens trip,
He kiss'd one damsel's laughing lip,
And press'd another's proffer'd hand.
Spoke to them all in accents bland,
But broke their magic circle through;
"Kind Maids," he said, "adieu, adieu!
My fate, my fortune, forward lies."
He said, and vanish'd from their eyes;
But, as he dared that darksome way,
Still heard behind their lovely lay:—
"Fair Flower of Courtesy, depart!
Go, where the feelings of the heart
With the warm pulse in concord move;
Go, where Virtue sanctions Love!"

XXXIII.

Downward De Vaux through darksome
    ways
  And ruin'd vaults has gone,
Till issue from their wilder'd maze,
  Or safe retreat, seem'd none,—
And e'en the dismal path he strays
  Grew worse as he went on.
For cheerful sun, for living air,
Foul vapours rise and mine-fires glare,
Whose fearful light the dangers show'd
That dogg'd him on that dreadful road.
Deep pits, and lakes of waters dun,
They show'd, but show'd not how to shun.
These scenes of desolate despair,
These smothering clouds of poison'd air;
How gladly had De Vaux exchanged,
Though 'twere to face yon tigers ranged!
  Nay, soothful bards have said
So perilous his state seem'd now,
He wish'd him under arbour bough
  With Asia's willing maid.
When, joyful sound! at distance near
A trumpet flourish'd loud and clear,
  And as it ceased, a lofty lay
Seem'd thus to chide his lagging way.

XXXIV.

" Son of Honour, theme of story,
Think on the reward before ye!
Danger, darkness, toil despise;
'Tis Ambition bids thee rise.

" He that would her heights ascend,
Many a weary step must wend;
Hand and foot and knee he tries;
Thus Ambition's minions rise.

" Lag not now, though rough the way,
Fortune's mood brooks no delay;
Grasp the boon that's spread before ye,
Monarch's power, and Conqueror's
    glory!"

It ceased. Advancing on the sound,
A steep ascent the Wanderer found,
  And then a turret stair:
Nor climb'd he far its steepy round
  Till fresher blew the air,

And next a welcome glimpse was given,
That cheer'd him with the light of heaven.
  At length his toil had won
A lofty hall with trophies dress'd,
Where, as to greet imperial guest,
Four Maidens stood, whose crimson vest
  Was bound with golden zone.

XXXV.

Of Europe seem'd the damsels all;
The first a nymph of lively Gaul,
Whose easy step and laughing eye
Her borrow'd air of awe belie;
  The next a maid of Spain,
Dark-eyed, dark-hair'd, sedate, yet bold;
White ivory skin and tress of gold,
Her shy and bashful comrade told
  For daughter of Almaine.
These maidens bore a royal robe,
With crown, with sceptre, and with globe,
  Emblems of empery;
The fourth a space behind them stood,
And leant upon a harp, in mood
  Of minstrel ecstasy.
Of merry England she, in dress
Like ancient British Druidess.
Her hair an azure fillet bound,
Her graceful vesture swept the ground,
  And, in her hand display'd,
A crown did that fourth Maiden hold,
But unadorn'd with gems and gold,
  Of glossy laurel made.

XXXVI.

At once to brave De Vaux knelt down
  These foremost Maidens three,
And proffer'd sceptre, robe, and crown,
  Liegedom and seignorie,
O'er many a region wide and fair,
Destined, they said, for Arthur's heir;
  But homage would he none:—
" Rather," he said, " De Vaux would
    ride,
A Warden of the Border-side,
In plate and mail, than, robed in pride,
  A monarch's empire own;
Rather, far rather, would he be
A free-born knight of England free,
  Than sit on Despot's throne."

So pass'd he on, when that fourth Maid,
　　As starting from a trance,
Upon the harp her finger laid;
Her magic touch the chords obey'd,
　　Their soul awaked at once!

SONG OF THE FOURTH MAIDEN.

"Quake to your foundations deep,
Stately Towers, and Banner'd Keep,
Bid your vaulted echoes moan,
As the dreaded step they own.

"Fiends, that wait on Merlin's spell,
Hear the foot-fall! mark it well!
Spread your dusky wings abroad,
Boune ye for your homeward road!

"It is HIS, the first who e'er
Dared the dismal Hall of Fear;
HIS, who hath the snares defied
Spread by Pleasure, Wealth, and Pride.

Quake to your foundations deep,
Bastion huge, and Turret steep!
Tremble, Keep! and totter, Tower!
This is Gyneth's waking hour."

XXXVII.

Thus while she sung, the venturous Knight
Has reach'd a bower, where milder light
　　Through crimson curtains fell;
Such soften'd shade the hill receives,
Her purple veil when twilight leaves
　　Upon its western swell.
That bower, the gazer to bewitch,
Hath wondrous store of rare and rich
　　As e'er was seen with eye;
For there by magic skill, I wis,
Form of each thing that living is
　　Was limn'd in proper dye.
All seem'd to sleep—the timid hare
On form, the stag upon his lair,
The eagle in her eyrie fair
　　Between the earth and sky.
But what of pictured rich and rare
Could win De Vaux's eye-glance, where,
Deep slumbering in the fatal chair,
　　He saw King Arthur's child!
Doubt, and anger, and dismay,
From her brow had pass'd away,

Forgot was that fell tourney-day,
　　For, as she slept, she smiled:
It seem'd, that the repentant Seer
Her sleep of many a hundred year
　　With gentle dreams beguiled.

XXXVIII.

That form of maiden loveliness,
　　'Twixt childhood and 'twixt youth,
That ivory chair, that silvan dress,
The arms and ankles bare, express
　　Of Lyulph's tale the truth.
Still upon her garment's hem
Vanoc's blood made purple gem,
And the warder of command
Cumber'd still her sleeping hand;
Still her dark locks dishevell'd flow
From net of pearl o'er breast of snow;
And so fair the slumberer seems,
That De Vaux impeach'd his dreams,
Vapid all and void of might,
Hiding half her charms from sight.
Motionless a while he stands,
Folds his arms and clasps his hands,
Trembling in his fitful joy,
Doubtful how he should destroy
　　Long-enduring spell;
Doubtful, too, when slowly rise
Dark-fringed lids of Gyneth's eyes,
　　What these eyes shall tell.—
"St. George! St. Mary! can it be,
That they will kindly look on me!"

XXXIX

Gently, lo! the Warrior kneels,
Soft that lovely hand he steals,
Soft to kiss, and soft to clasp—
But the warder leaves her grasp;
　　Lightning flashes, rolls the thunder,
Gyneth startles from her sleep,
Totters Tower, and trembles Keep,
　　Burst the Castle-walls asunder!
Fierce and frequent were the shocks,—
　　Melt the magic halls away;
—— But beneath their mystic rocks,
In the arms of bold De Vaux,
　　Safe the princess lay;
Safe and free from magic power,
Blushing like the rose's flower
　　Opening to the day;

And round the Champion's brows were
        bound
The crown that Druidess had wound,
        Of the green laurel-bay.
And this was what remain'd of all
The wealth of each enchanted hall,
        The Garland and the Dame:
But where should Warrior seek the meed,
Due to high worth for daring deed,
        Except from Love and Fame![14]

CONCLUSION.

I.

My Lucy, when the Maid is won,
The Minstrel's task, thou know'st, is
        done;
        And to require of bard
That to his dregs the tale should run,
        Were ordinance too hard.
Our lovers, briefly be it said,
Wedded as lovers wont to wed,
        When tale or play is o'er;
Lived long and blest, loved fond and true,
And saw a numerous race renew
        The honours that they bore.
Know, too, that when a pilgrim strays,
In morning mist or evening maze,
        Along the mountain lone,
That fairy fortress often mocks
His gaze upon the castled rocks
        Of the Valley of St. John;
But never man since brave De Vaux
        The charmed portal won.

'Tis now a vain illusive snow,
That melts whene'er the sunbeams glow
        Or the fresh breeze hath blown.

II.

But see, my love, where far below
Our lingering wheels are moving slow,
        The whiles, up-gazing still,
Our menials eye our steepy way,
Marvelling, perchance, what whim can
        stay
Our steps, when eve is sinking grey,
        On this gigantic hill.
So think the vulgar—Life and time
Ring all their joys in one dull chime
        Of luxury and ease;
And, O! beside these simple knaves,
How many better born are slaves
        To such coarse joys as these,—
Dead to the nobler sense that glows
When Nature's grander scenes unclose!
But, Lucy, we will love them yet,
The mountain's misty coronet,
        The greenwood, and the wold;
And love the more, that of their maze
Adventure high of other days
        By ancient bards is told,
Bringing, perchance, like my poor tale,
Some moral truth in fiction's veil:
Nor love them less, that o'er the hill
The evening breeze, as now, comes chill;—
        My love shall wrap her warm,
And, fearless of the slippery way,
While safe she trips the heathy brae,
        Shall hang on Arthur's arm.

THE LORD OF THE ISLES.

〜〜〜〜〜〜〜〜〜〜〜

ADVERTISEMENT TO THE FIRST EDITION.

The scene of this Poem lies, at first, in the Castle of Artornish, on the coast of Argyleshire; and, afterwards, in the Islands of Skye and Arran, and upon the coast of Ayrshire. Finally, it is laid near Stirling. The story opens in the spring of the year 1307, when Bruce, who had been driven out of Scotland by the English, and the Barons who adhered to that foreign interest, returned from the Island of Rachrin on the coast of Ireland, again to assert his claims to the Scottish crown. Many of the personages and incidents introduced are of historical celebrity. The authorities used are chiefly those of the venerable Lord Hailes, as well entitled to be called the restorer of Scottish history, as Bruce the restorer of Scottish monarchy; and of Archdeacon Barbour, a correct edition of whose Metrical History of Robert Bruce will soon, I trust, appear, under the care of my learned friend the Rev. Dr. Jamieson.

ABBOTSFORD, 10th December, 1814.

THE LORD OF THE ISLES.

~~~~~~~~~~~~~~~~~~~~~~

CANTO FIRST.

AUTUMN departs—but still his mantle's
    fold
Rests on the groves of noble Somerville,*
Beneath a shroud of russet dropp'd
    with gold
Tweed and his tributaries mingle still;
Hoarser the wind, and deeper sounds
    the rill,
Yet lingering notes of silvan music
    swell,
The deep-toned cushat, and the red-
    breast shrill;
And yet some tints of summer splendour
    tell
When the broad sun sinks down on
    Ettrick's western fell.

Autumn departs—from Gala's fields no
    more
Come rural sounds our kindred banks
    to cheer;
Blent with the stream, and gale that
    wafts it o'er,
No more the distant reaper's mirth we
    hear.
The last blithe shout hath died upon
    our ear,
And harvest-home hath hush'd the
    clanging wain,
On the waste hill no forms of life appear,

Save where, sad laggard of the autumnal
    train,
Some age-struck wanderer gleans few ears
    of scatter'd grain.

Deem'st thou these sadden'd scenes have
    pleasure still,
Lovest thou through Autumn's fading
    realms to stray,
To see the heath-flower wither'd on
    the hill,
To listen to the wood's expiring lay,
To note the red leaf shivering on the
    spray,
To mark the last bright tints the
    mountain stain,
On the waste fields to trace the gleaner's
    way,
And moralize on mortal joy and pain?—
O! if such scenes thou lovest, scorn not
    the minstrel strain.

No! do not scorn, although its hoarser
    note
Scarce with the cushat's homely song
    can vie,
Though faint its beauties as the tints
    remote
That gleam through mist in autumn's
    evening sky,
And few as leaves that tremble, sear
    and dry,
When wild November hath his bugle
    wound;
Nor mock my toil—a lonely gleaner I,
Through fields time-wasted, on sad
    inquest bound,
Where happier bards of yore have richer
    harvest found.

* The Pavilion, the residence of Lord
Somerville, situated on the Tweed, over
against Melrose, and in sight of Abbotsford.

So shalt thou list, and haply not un-
    moved,
To a wild tale of Albyn's warrior day;
In distant lands, by the rough West
    reproved,
Still live some relics of the ancient lay.
For, when on Coolin's hills the lights
    decay,
With such the Seer of Skye the eve
    beguiles;
'Tis known amid the pathless wastes
    of Reay,
In Harries known, and in Iona's piles,
Where rest from mortal coil the Mighty
    of the Isles.

I.

"Wake, Maid of Lorn!" the Minstrels
    sung.
Thy rugged halls, Artornish! rung,[1]
And the dark seas, thy towers that lave,
Heaved on the beach a softer wave,
As 'mid the tuneful choir to keep
The diapason of the Deep.
Lull'd were the winds on Inninmore,
And green Loch-Alline's woodland shore,
As if wild woods and waves had pleasure
In listing to the lovely measure.
And ne'er to symphony more sweet
Gave mountain echoes answer meet,
Since, met from mainland and from isle,
Ross, Arran, Ilay, and Argyle,
Each minstrel's tributary lay
Paid homage to the festal day.
Dull and dishonour'd were the bard,
Worthless of guerdon and regard,
Deaf to the hope of minstrel fame,
Or lady's smiles, his noblest aim,
Who on that morn's resistless call
Were silent in Artornish hall.

II.

"Wake, Maid of Lorn!" 'twas thus
    they sung,
And yet more proud the descant rung,
"Wake, Maid of Lorn! high right is
    ours,
To charm dull sleep from Beauty's
    bowers;

Earth, Ocean, Air, have nought so shy
But owns the power of minstrelsy.
In Lettermore the timid deer
Will pause, the harp's wild chime to hear;
Rude Heiskar's seal through surges dark
Will long pursue the minstrel's bark;[2]
To list his notes, the eagle proud
Will poise him on Ben-Cailliach's cloud;
Then let not Maiden's ear disdain
The summons of the minstrel train,
But while our harps wild music make,
Edith of Lorn, awake, awake!

III.

"O wake, while Dawn, with dewy shine,
Wakes Nature's charms to vie with thine!
She bids the mottled thrush rejoice
To mate thy melody of voice;
The dew that on the violet lies
Mocks the dark lustre of thine eyes;
But, Edith, wake, and all we see
Of sweet and fair shall yield to thee!"—
"She comes not yet," grey Ferrand cried;
"Brethren, let softer spell be tried,
Those notes prolong'd, that soothing
    theme,
Which best may mix with Beauty's dream,
And whisper, with their silvery tone,
The hope she loves, yet fears to own."
He spoke, and on the harp-strings died
The strains of flattery and of pride;
More soft, more low, more tender fell
The lay of love he bade them tell.

IV.

"Wake, Maid of Lorn! the moments fly,
Which yet that maiden-name allow;
Wake, Maiden, wake! the hour is nigh
When Love shall claim a plighted vow
By Fear, thy bosom's fluttering guest,
By Hope, that soon shall fears remove,
We bid thee break the bonds of rest,
And wake thee at the call of Love!

"Wake, Edith, wake! in yonder bay
Lies many a galley gaily mann'd,
We hear the merry pibrochs play,
We see the streamers' silken band.
What Chieftain's praise these pibrochs
    swell,
What crest is on these banners wove,

The harp, the minstrel, dare not tell—
　The riddle must be read by Love."

V.

Retired her maiden train among,
Edith of Lorn received the song,
But tamed the minstrel's pride had been
That had her cold demeanour seen;
For not upon her cheek awoke
The glow of pride when Flattery spoke,
Nor could their tenderest numbers bring
One sigh responsive to the string.
As vainly had her maidens vied
In skill to deck the princely bride.
Her locks, in dark-brown length array'd,
Cathleen of Ulne, 'twas thine to braid;
Young Eva with meet reverence drew
On the light foot the silken shoe,
While on the ankle's slender round
Those strings of pearl fair Bertha wound,
That, bleach'd Lochryan's depths within,
Seem'd dusky still on Edith's skin.
But Einion, of experience old,
Had weightiest task—the mantle's fold
In many an artful plait she tied,
To show the form it seem'd to hide,
Till on the floor descending roll'd
Its waves of crimson blent with gold.

VI.

O! lives there now so cold a maid,
Who thus in beauty's pomp array'd,
In beauty's proudest pitch of power,
And conquest won—the bridal hour—
With every charm that wins the heart,
By Nature given, enhanced by Art,
Could yet the fair reflection view,
In the bright mirror pictured true,
And not one dimple on her cheek
A tell-tale consciousness bespeak?—
Lives still such maid?—Fair damsels, say,
For further vouches not my lay,
Save that such lived in Britain's isle,
When Lorn's bright Edith scorn'd to
　　smile.

VII.

But Morag, to whose fostering care
Proud Lorn had given his daughter fair,
Morag, who saw a mother's aid
By all a daughter's love repaid,
(Strict was that bond—most kind of all—
Inviolate in Highland hall)—
Grey Morag sate a space apart,
In Edith's eyes to read her heart.
In vain the attendants' fond appeal
To Morag's skill, to Morag's zeal;
She mark'd her child receive their care,
Cold as the image sculptured fair,
(Form of some sainted patroness,)
Which cloister'd maids combine to dress;
She mark'd—and knew her nursling's
　　heart
In the vain pomp took little part.
Wistful a while she gazed—then press'd
The maiden to her anxious breast
In finish'd loveliness—and led
To where a turret's airy head,
Slender and steep, and battled round,
O'erlook'd, dark Mull! thy mighty
　　Sound,[3]
Where thwarting tides, with mingled roar,
Part thy swarth hills from Morven's shore.

VIII.

"Daughter," she said, "these seas behold,
Round twice a hundred islands roll'd,
From Hirt, that hears their northern roar,
To the green Ilay's fertile shore;
Or mainland turn, where many a tower
Owns thy bold brother's feudal power,
Each on its own dark cape reclined,
And listening to its own wild wind,
From where Mingarry, sternly placed,
O'erawes the woodland and the waste,
To where Dunstaffnage hears the raging
Of Connal with his rocks engaging.
Think'st thou, amid this ample round,
A single brow but thine has frown'd,
To sadden this auspicious morn,
That bids the daughter of high Lorn
Impledge her spousal faith to wed
The heir of mighty Somerled![4]
Ronald, from many a hero sprung,
The fair, the valiant, and the young,
LORD OF THE ISLES, whose lofty name[5]
A thousand bards have given to fame,

The mate of monarchs, and allied
On equal terms with England's pride.—
From chieftain's tower to bondsman's cot,
Who hears the tale, and triumphs not?
The damsel dons her best attire,
The shepherd lights his beltane fire,
Joy, joy! each warder's horn hath sung,
Joy, joy! each matin bell hath rung;
The holy priest says grateful mass,
Loud shouts each hardy galla-glass,
No mountain den holds outcast boor,
Of heart so dull, of soul so poor,
But he hath flung his task aside,
And claim'd this morn for holy-tide;
Yet, empress of this joyful day,
Edith is sad while all are gay."—

IX.

Proud Edith's soul came to her eye,
Resentment check'd the struggling sigh.
Her hurrying hand indignant dried
The burning tears of injured pride—
"Morag, forbear! or lend thy praise
To swell yon hireling harpers' lays;
Make to yon maids thy boast of power,
That they may waste a wondering hour,
Telling of banners proudly borne,
Of pealing bell and bugle-horn,
Or, theme more dear, of robes of price,
Crownlets and gauds of rare device.
But thou, experienced as thou art,
Think'st thou with these to cheat the heart,
That, bound in strong affection's chain,
Looks for return and looks in vain?
No! sum thine Edith's wretched lot
In these brief words—He loves her not!

X.

"Debate it not—too long I strove
To call his cold observance love,
All blinded by the league that styled
Edith of Lorn,—while yet a child,
She tripp'd the heath by Morag's side,—
The brave Lord Ronald's destined bride.
Ere yet I saw him, while afar
His broadsword blazed in Scotland's war,
Train'd to believe our fates the same,
My bosom throbb'd when Ronald's name
Came gracing Fame's heroic tale,
Like perfume on the summer gale.

What pilgrim sought our halls, nor told
Of Ronald's deeds in battle bold;
Who touch'd the harp to heroes' praise,
But his achievements swell'd the lays?
Even Morag—not a tale of fame
Was her's but closed with Ronald's name.
He came! and all that had been told
Of his high worth seem'd poor and cold,
Tame, lifeless, void of energy,
Unjust to Ronald and to me!

XI.

"Since then, what thought had Edith's
    heart
And gave not plighted love its part!—
And what requital? cold delay—
Excuse that shunn'd the spousal day—
It dawns, and Ronald is not here!—
Hunts he Bentalla's nimble deer,
Or loiters he in secret dell
To bid some lighter love farewell,
And swear, that though he may not scorn
A daughter of the House of Lorn,[6]
Yet, when these formal rites are o'er,
Again they meet, to part no more?"

XII.

—"Hush, daughter, hush! thy doubts
    remove,
More nobly think of Ronald's love.
Look, where beneath the castle grey
His fleet unmoor from Aros bay!
See'st not each galley's topmast bend,
As on the yards the sails ascend?
Hiding the dark-blue land, they rise
Like the white clouds on April skies;
The shouting vassals man the oars,
Behind them sink Mull's mountain shores,
Onward their merry course they keep,
Through whistling breeze and foaming
    deep.
And mark the headmost, seaward cast,
Stoop to the freshening gale her mast,
As if she veil'd its banner'd pride,
To greet afar her prince's bride!
Thy Ronald comes, and while in speed
His galley mates the flying steed,
He chides her sloth!"—Fair Edith sigh'd,
Blush'd, sadly smiled, and thus replied:—

XIII.

" Sweet thought, but vain !—No, Morag!
    mark,
Type of his course, yon lonely bark,
That oft hath shifted helm and sail,
To win its way against the gale.
Since peep of morn, my vacant eyes
Have view'd by fits the course she tries;
Now, though the darkening scud comes on,
And dawn's fair promises be gone,
And though the weary crew may see
Our sheltering haven on their lee,
Still closer to the rising wind
They strive her shivering sail to bind,
Still nearer to the shelves' dread verge
At every tack their course they urge,
As if they fear'd Artornish more
Than adverse winds and breakers' roar."

XIV.

Sooth spoke the maid.—Amid the tide
    The skiff she mark'd lay tossing sore,
And shifted oft her stooping side,
    In weary tack from shore to shore.
Yet on her destined course no more
    She gain'd, of forward way,
Than what a minstrel may compare
To the poor meed which peasants share,
    Who toil the livelong day;
And such the risk her pilot braves,
    That oft, before she wore,
Her boltsprit kiss'd the broken waves,
Where in white foam the ocean raves
    Upon the shelving shore.
Yet, to their destined purpose true,
Undaunted toil'd her hardy crew,
    Nor look'd where shelter lay,
Nor for Artornish Castle drew,
    Nor steer'd for Aros bay.

XV.

Thus while they strove with wind and
    seas,
Borne onward by the willing breeze,
    Lord Ronald's fleet swept by,
Streamer'd with silk, and trick'd with gold,
Mann'd with the noble and the bold
    Of Island chivalry,

Around their prows the ocean roars,
And chafes beneath their thousand oars,
    Yet bears them on their way:
So chafes the war-horse in his might,
That fieldward bears some valiant knight,
Champs, till both bit and boss are white,
    But, foaming, must obey.
On each gay deck they might behold
Lances of steel and crests of gold,
And hauberks with their burnish'd fold,
    That shimmer'd fair and free;
And each proud galley, as she pass'd,
To the wild cadence of the blast
    Gave wilder minstrelsy.
Full many a shrill triumphant note
Saline and Scallastle bade float
    Their misty shores around;
And Morven's echoes answer'd well,
And Duart heard the distant swell
    Come down the darksome Sound.

XVI.

So bore they on with mirth and pride,
And if that labouring bark they spied,
    'Twas with such idle eye
As nobles cast on lowly boor,
When, toiling in his task obscure,
    They pass him careless by.
Let them sweep on with heedless eyes !
But, had they known what mighty prize
    In that frail vessel lay,
The famish'd wolf, that prowls the wold,
Had scatheless pass'd the unguarded fold,
Ere, drifting by these galleys bold,
    Unchallenged were her way !
And thou, Lord Ronald, sweep thou on,
With mirth, and pride, and minstrel tone !
But hadst thou known who sail'd so nigh,
Far other glance were in thine eye !
Far other flush were on thy brow,
That, shaded by the bonnet, now
Assumes but ill the blithesome cheer
Of bridegroom when the bride is near !

XVII.

Yes, sweep they on !—We will not leave
For them that triumph, those who grieve,
    With that armada gay

Be laughter loud and jocund shout,
And bards to cheer the wassail route,
  With tale, romance, and lay ;
And of wild mirth each clamorous art
Which, if it cannot cheer the heart,
May stupify and stun its smart,
  For one loud busy day.
Yes, sweep they on!—But with that skiff
  Abides the minstrel tale,
Where there was dread of surge and cliff,
Labour that strain'd each sinew stiff,
  And one sad Maiden's wail.

XVIII.

All day with fruitless strife they toil'd,
With eve the ebbing currents boil'd
  More fierce from strait and lake ;
And midway through the channel met
Conflicting tides that foam and fret,
And high their mingled billows jet,
  As spears, that, in the battle set,
  Spring upward as they break.
Then, too, the lights of eve were past,
And louder sung the western blast
  On rocks of Innimore ;
Rent was the sail, and strain'd the mast,
And many a leak was gaping fast,
And the pale steersman stood aghast,
  And gave the conflict o'er.

XIX.

'Twas then that One, whose lofty look
Nor labour dull'd nor terror shook,
  Thus to the Leader spoke ;—
" Brother, how hopest thou to abide
The fury of this wilder'd tide,
Or how avoid the rock's rude side,
  Until the day has broke ?
Didst thou not mark the vessel reel,
With quivering planks, and groaning keel,
  At the last billow's shock ?
Yet how of better counsel tell,
Though here thou see'st poor Isabel
  Half dead with want and fear ;
For look on sea, or look on land,
Or yon dark sky—on every hand
  Despair and death are near.
For her alone I grieve,—on me
Danger sits light, by land and sea,
  I follow where thou wilt ;

Either to bide the tempest's lour,
Or wend to yon unfriendly tower,
Or rush amid their naval power,
With war-cry wake their wassail-hour,
  And die with hand on hilt."—

XX.

That elder Leader's calm reply
  In steady voice was given,
" In man's most dark extremity
  Oft succour dawns from Heaven.
Edward, trim thou the shatter'd sail,
The helm be mine, and down the gale
  Let our free course be driven ;
So shall we 'scape the western bay,
The hostile fleet, the unequal fray,
So safely hold our vessel's way
  Beneath the Castle wall ;
For if a hope of safety rest,
'Tis on the sacred name of guest,
Who seeks for shelter, storm-distress'd,
  Within a chieftain's hall.
If not—it best beseems our worth,
Our name, our right, our lofty birth,
  By noble hands to fall."

XXI.

The helm, to his strong arm consign'd,
Gave the reef'd sail to meet the wind,
  And on her alter'd way,
Fierce bounding, forward sprung the ship,
Like greyhound starting from the slip
  To seize his flying prey.
Awaked before the rushing prow,
The mimic fires of ocean glow,
  Those lightnings of the wave ;
Wild sparkles crest the broken tides,
And, flashing round, the vessel's sides
  With elvish lustre lave,
While, far behind, their livid light
To the dark billows of the night
  A gloomy splendour gave.
It seems as if old Ocean shakes
From his dark brow the lucid flakes
  In envious pageantry,
To match the meteor-light that streaks
  Grim Hecla's midnight sky.

XXII.

Nor lack'd they steadier light to keep
Their course upon the darken'd deep;—
Artornish, on her frowning steep
  'Twixt cloud and ocean hung,
Glanced with a thousand lights of glee,
And landward far, and far to sea,
  Her festal radiance flung.
By that blithe beacon-light they steer'd,
  Whose lustre mingled well
With the pale beam that now appear'd,
As the cold moon her head uprear'd
  Above the eastern fell.

XXIII.

Thus guided, on their course they bore,
Until they near'd the mainland shore,
When frequent on the hollow blast
Wild shouts of merriment were cast,
And wind and wave and sea-birds' cry
With wassail sounds in concert vie,
Like funeral shrieks w.th revelry,
  Or like the battle-shout
By peasants heard from cliffs on high,
When Triumph, Rage, and Agony,
  Madden the fight and route.
Now nearer yet, through mist and storm
Dimly arose the Castle's form,
  And deepen'd shadow made,
Far lengthen'd on the main below,
Where, dancing in reflected glow,
  A hundred torches play'd,
Spangling the wave with lights as vain
As pleasures in this vale of pain,
  That dazzle as they fade.

XXIV.

Beneath the Castle's sheltering lee,
They staid their course in quiet sea.
Hewn in the rock, a passage there
Sought the dark fortress by a stair,
  So straight, so high, so steep,
With peasant's staff one valiant hand
Might well the dizzy pass have mann'd,
'Gainst hundreds arm'd with spear and
    brand,
  And plunged them in the deep.

His bugle then the helmsman wound;
Loud answer'd every echo round,
  From turret, rock, and bay,
The postern's hinges crash and groan,
And soon the warder's cresset shone
On those rude steps of slippery stone,
  To light the upward way.
" Thrice welcome, holy Sire!" he said;
" Full long the spousal train have staid,
  And, vex'd at thy delay,
Fear'd lest, amidst these wildering seas,
The darksome night and freshening breeze
  Had driven thy bark astray."—

XXV.

" Warder," the younger stranger said,
" Thine erring guess some mirth had made
In mirthful hour; but nights like these,
When the rough winds wake western seas,
Brook not of glee.   We crave some aid
And needful shelter for this maid
  Until the break of day;
For, to ourselves, the deck's rude plank
Is easy as the mossy bank
  That's breath'd upon by May.
And for our storm-toss'd skiff we seek
Short shelter in this leeward creek,
Prompt when the dawn the east shall
    streak
  Again to bear away."—
Answered the Warder,—" In what name
Assert ye hospitable claim?
  Whence come, or whither bound?
Hath Erin seen your parting sails?
Or come ye on Norweyan gales?
And seek ye England's fertile vales,
  Or Scotland's mountain ground?"—

XXVI.

" Warriors—for other title none
For some brief space we list to own,
Bound by a vow—warriors are we;
In strife by land, and storm by sea,
  We have been known to fame;
And these brief words have import dear,
When sounded in a noble ear,
To harbour safe, and friendly cheer,
  That gives us rightful claim.

Grant us the trivial boon we seek,
And we in other realms will speak
  Fair of your courtesy;
Deny—and be your niggard Hold
Scorn'd by the noble and the bold,
Shunn'd by the pilgrim on the wold,
  And wanderer on the lea!"—

XXVII.

" Bold stranger, no—'gainst claim like
    thine,
No bolt revolves by hand of mine,
Though urged in tone that more express'd
A monarch than a suppliant guest.
Be what ye will, Artornish Hall
On this glad eve is free to all.
Though ye had drawn a hostile sword
'Gainst our ally, great England's Lord,
Or mail upon your shoulders borne,
To battle with the Lord of Lorn,
Or, outlaw'd, dwelt by greenwood tree
With the fierce Knight of Ellerslie,*
Or aided even the murderous strife,
When Comyn fell beneath the knife
Of that fell homicide The Bruce,
This night had been a term of truce.—
Ho, vassals! give these guests your care,
And show the narrow postern stair."

XXVIII.

To land these two bold brethren leapt,
(The weary crew their vessel kept,)
And, lighted by the torches' flare,
That seaward flung their smoky glare,
The younger knight that maiden bare
-Half lifeless up the rock;
On his strong shoulder lean'd her head,
And down her long dark tresses shed,
As the wild vine in tendrils spread,
  Droops from the mountain oak.
Him follow'd close that elder Lord,
And in his hand a sheathed sword,
  Such as few arms could wield;
But when he boun'd him to such task,
Well could it cleave the strongest casque,
  And rend the surest shield.

---

* Sir William Wallace.

XXIX.

The raised portcullis' arch they pass,
The wicket with its bars of brass,
  The entrance long and low,
Flank'd at each turn by loop-holes strait,
Where bowmen might in ambush wait,
(If force or fraud should burst the gate,)
  To gall an entering foe.
But every jealous post of ward
Was now defenceless and unbarr'd,
  And all the passage free
To one low-brow'd and vaulted room,
Where squire and yeoman, page and
   groom,
  Plied their loud revelry.

XXX.

And " Rest ye here," the Warder bade,
" Till to our Lord your suit is said.—
And, comrades, gaze not on the maid,
And on these men who ask our aid,
  As if ye ne'er had seen
A damsel tired of midnight bark,
Or wanderers of a moulding stark,
  And bearing martial mien."
But not for Eachin's reproof
Would page or vassal stand aloof,
  But crowded on to stare,
As men of courtesy untaught,
Till fiery Edward roughly caught,
  From one the foremost there,
His chequer'd plaid, and in its shroud,
To hide her from the vulgar crowd,
  Involved his sister fair.
His brother, as the clansman bent
His sullen brow in discontent,
  Made brief and stern excuse;—
" Vassal, were thine the cloak of pall
That decks thy Lord in bridal hall,
  'Twere honour'd by her use."

XXXI.

Proud was his tone, but calm; his eye
Had that compelling dignity,
His mien that bearing haught and high,
  Which common spirits fear!

Needed nor word nor signal more,
Nod, wink, and laughter, all were o'er;
Upon each other back they bore,
  And gazed like startled deer.
But now appear'd the Seneschal,
Commission'd by his lord to call
The strangers to the Baron's hall,
  Where feasted fair and free
  That Island Prince in nuptial tide,
  With Edith there his lovely bride,
  And her bold brother by her side,
  And many a chief, the flower and pride
    Of Western land and sea.

Here pause we, gentles, for a space;
And, if our tale hath won your grace,
Grant us brief patience, and again
We will renew the minstrel strain.

CANTO SECOND.

FILL the bright goblet, spread the
  festive board!
Summon the gay, the noble, and the
  fair!
Through the loud hall in joyous concert pour'd,
Let mirth and music sound the dirge
  of Care!
But ask thou not if Happiness be there,
If the loud laugh disguise convulsive
  throe,
Or if the brow the heart's true livery
  wear;
Lift not the festal mask!—enough to
  know,
No scene of mortal life but teems with
  mortal woe.

II.

With beakers' clang, with harpers' lay,
With all that olden time deem'd gay,
The Island Chieftain feasted high;
But there was in his troubled eye
A gloomy fire, and on his brow,
Now sudden flush'd, and faded now,

Emotions such as draw their birth
From deeper source than festal mirth.
By fits he paused, and harper's strain
And jester's tale went round in vain,
Or fell but on his idle ear
Like distant sounds which dreamers hear.
Then would he rouse him, and employ
Each art to aid the clamorous joy,
  And call for pledge and lay,
And, for brief space, of all the crowd,
As he was loudest of the loud,
  Seem gayest of the gay.

III.

Yet nought amiss the bridal throng
Mark'd in brief mirth, or musing long;
The vacant brow, the unlistening ear,
They gave to thoughts of raptures near,
And his fierce starts of sudden glee
Seem'd bursts of bridegroom's ecstasy.
Nor thus alone misjudged the crowd,
Since lofty Lorn, suspicious, proud,
And jealous of his honour'd line,
And that keen knight, De Argentine,[8]
(From England sent on errand high,
The western league more firm to tie,)
Both deem'd in Ronald's mood to find
A lover's transport-troubled mind.
But one sad heart, one tearful eye,
Pierced deeper through the mystery,
And watch'd, with agony and fear,
Her wayward bridegroom's varied cheer.

IV.

She watch'd—yet fear'd to meet his glance,
And he shunn'd hers;—till when by chance
They met, the point of foeman's lance
  Had given a milder pang!
Beneath the intolerable smart
He writhed—then sternly mann'd his
    heart
To play his hard but destined part,
  And from the table sprang.
"Fill me the mighty cup!" he said,
"Erst own'd by royal Somerled:[9]
Fill it, till on the studded brim
In burning gold the bubbles swim,
And every gem of varied shine
Glow doubly bright in rosy wine!

To you, brave lord, and brother mine,
Of Lorn, this pledge I drink—
The union of Our House with thine,
By this fair bridal-link !"—

V.

" Let it pass round !" quoth He of Lorn,
" And in good time—that winded horn
Must of the Abbot tell ;
The laggard monk is come at last."
Lord Ronald heard the bugle-blast,
And on the floor at random cast,
The untasted goblet fell.
But when the warder in his ear
Tells other news, his blither cheer
Returns like sun of May,
When through a thunder-cloud it
beams !—
Lord of two hundred isles, he seems
As glad of brief delay,
As some poor criminal might feel,
When, from the gibbet or the wheel,
Respited for a day.

VI.

" Brother of Lorn," with hurried voice
He said, " and you, fair lords, rejoice !
Here, to augment our glee,
Come wandering knights from travel far,
Well proved, they say, in strife of war,
And tempest on the sea.—
Ho ! give them at your board such place
As best their presences may grace,
And bid them welcome free !"
With solemn step, and silver wand,
The Seneschal the presence scann'd
Of these strange guests; and well he knew
How to assign their rank its due ;
For though the costly furs
That erst had deck'd their caps were torn,
And their gay robes were over-worn,
And soil'd their gilded spurs,
Yet such a high commanding grace
Was in their mien and in their face,
As suited best the princely dais,*
And royal canopy ;
And there he marshall'd them their place,
First of that company.

---

* Dais—the great hall-table—elevated a
step or two above the rest of the room.

VII.

Then lords and ladies spake aside,
And angry looks the error chide,
That gave to guests unnamed, unknown
A place so near their prince's throne ;
But Owen Erraught said,
" For forty years a seneschal,
To marshal guests in bower and hall
Has been my honour'd trade.
Worship and birth to me are known,
By look, by bearing, and by tone,
Not by furr'd robe or broider'd zone;
And 'gainst an oaken bough
I'll gage my silver wand of state,
That these three strangers oft have sate
In higher place than now."—

VIII.

" I, too," the aged Ferrand said,
" Am qualified by minstrel trade
Of rank and place to tell ;—
Mark'd ye the younger stranger's eye,
My mates, how quick, how keen, how
high,
How fierce its flashes fell,
Glancing among the noble rout
As if to seek the noblest out,
Because the owner might not brook
On any save his peers to look ?
And yet it moves me more,
That steady, calm, majestic brow,
With which the elder chief even now
Scann'd the gay presence o'er,
Like being of superior kind,
In whose high-toned impartial mind
Degrees of mortal rank and state
Seem objects of indifferent weight.
The lady too—though closely tied
The mantle veil both face and eye,
Her motions' grace it could not hide,
Nor could her form's fair symmetry."

IX.

Suspicious doubt and lordly scorn
Lour'd on the haughty front of Lorn.
From underneath his brows of pride,
The stranger guests he sternly eyed,
And whisper'd closely what the ear
Of Argentine alone might hear ;
Then question'd, high and brief,

If, in their voyage, aught they knew
Of the rebellious Scottish crew,
Who to Rath-Erin's shelter drew,
  With Carrick's outlaw'd Chief![10]
And if, their winter's exile o'er,
They harbour'd still by Ulster's shore,
Or launch'd their galleys on the main,
To vex their native land again?

X.

That younger stranger, fierce and high,
At once confronts the Chieftain's eye
  With look of equal scorn;—
"Of rebels have we nought to show;
But if of Royal Bruce thou'dst know,
  I warn thee he has sworn,
Ere thrice three days shall come and go,
His banner Scottish winds shall blow,
Despite each mean or mighty foe,
From England's every bill and bow,
  To Allaster of Lorn."
Kindled the mountain Chieftain's ire,
But Ronald quench'd the rising fire:
"Brother, it better suits the time
To chase the night with Ferrand's rhyme,
Than wake, 'midst mirth and wine, the
    jars
That flow from these unhappy wars."—
"Content," said Lorn; and spoke apart
With Ferrand, master of his art,
  Then whisper'd Argentine,—
"The lay I named will carry smart
To these bold strangers' haughty heart,
  If right this guess of mine."
He ceased, and it was silence all,
Until the minstrel waked the hall.

XI.

The Broach of Lorn.[11]

"Whence the broach of burning gold,
That clasps the Chieftain's mantle-fold,
Wrought and chased with rare device,
Studded fair with gems of price,
On the varied tartans beaming,
As, through night's pale rainbow gleam-
    ing,
Fainter now, now seen afar,
Fitful shines the northern star!

"Gem! ne'er wrought on Highland
    mountain,
Did the fairy of the fountain,
Or the mermaid of the wave,
Frame thee in some coral cave?
Did, in Iceland's darksome mine,
Dwarf's swart hands thy metal twine?
Or, mortal-moulded, comest thou here,
From England's love, or France's fear?

XII.

Song continued.

"No!—thy splendours nothing tell
Foreign art or faëry spell.
Moulded thou for monarch's use,
By the overweening Bruce,
When the royal robe he tied
O'er a heart of wrath and pride;
Thence in triumph wert thou torn,
By the victor hand of Lorn!

"When the gem was won and lost,
Widely was the war-cry toss'd!
Rung aloud Bendourish fell,
Answer'd Douchart's sounding dell,
Fled the deer from wild Teyndrum,
When the homicide, o'ercome,
Hardly 'scaped, with scathe and scorn,
Left the pledge with conquering Lorn!

XIII.

Song concluded.

"Vain was then the Douglas brand,
Vain the Campbell's vaunted hand,
Vain Kirkpatrick's bloody dirk,
Making sure of murder's work;[12]
Barendown fled fast away,
Fled the fiery De la Haye,[13]
When this broach, triumphant borne,
Beam'd upon the breast of Lorn.

"Farthest fled its former Lord,
Left his men to brand and cord,
Bloody brand of Highland steel,
English gibbet, axe, and wheel.
Let him fly from coast to coast,
Dogg'd by Comyn's vengeful ghost,
While his spoils, in triumph worn,
Long shall grace victorious Lorn!"

XIV.

As glares the tiger on his foes,
Hemm'd in by hunters, spears, and bows,
And, ere he bounds upon the ring,
Selects the object of his spring,—
Now on the Bard, now on his Lord,
So Edward glared and grasp'd his sword—
But stern his brother spoke,—"Be still.
What! art thou yet so wild of will,
After high deeds and sufferings long,
To chafe thee for a menial's song?—
Well hast thou framed, Old Man, thy
    strains,
To praise the hand that pays thy pains!
Yet something might thy song have told
Of Lorn's three vassals, true and bold,
Who rent their Lord from Bruce's hold,
As underneath his knee he lay,
And died to save him in the fray.
I've heard the Bruce's cloak and clasp
Was clench'd within their dying grasp,
What time a hundred foemen more
Rush'd in, and back the victor bore,
Long after Lorn had left the strife,
Full glad to 'scape with limb and life.—
Enough of this—And, Minstrel, hold,
As minstrel hire, this chain of gold,
For future lays a fair excuse,
To speak more nobly of the Bruce."

XV.

"Now, by Columba's shrine, I swear,
And every saint that's buried there,
'Tis he himself!" Lorn sternly cries,
"And for my kinsman's death he dies."
As loudly Ronald calls,—"Forbear!
Not in my sight while brand I wear,
O'ermatched by odds, shall warrior fall,
Or blood of stranger stain my hall!
This ancient fortress of my race
Shall be misfortune's resting-place,
Shelter and shield of the distress'd,
No slaughter-house for shipwreck'd
    guest."—
"Talk not to me," fierce Lorn replied,
"Of odds or match!—when Comyn died,
Three daggers clash'd within his side!
Talk not to me of sheltering hall,
The Church of GOD saw Comyn fall!

On God's own altar stream'd his blood,
While o'er my prostrate kinsman stood
The ruthless murderer—e'en as now—
With armed hand and scornful brow!—
Up, all who love me! blow on blow!
And lay the outlaw'd felons low!"

XVI.

Then up sprang many a mainland Lord,
Obedient to their Chieftain's word.
Barcaldine's arm is high in air,
And Kinloch-Alline's blade is bare,
Black Murthok's dirk has left its sheath,
And clench'd is Dermid's hand of death.
Their mutter'd threats of vengeance swell
Into a wild and warlike yell;
Onward they press with weapons high,
The affrighted females shriek and fly,
And, Scotland, then thy brightest ray
Had darken'd ere its noon of day,—
But every chief of birth and fame,
That from the Isles of Ocean came,
At Ronald's side that hour withstood
Fierce Lorn's relentless thirst for blood.

XVII.

Brave Torquil from Dunvegan high,
Lord of the misty hills of Skye,
Mac-Niel, wild Bara's ancient thane,
Duart, of bold Clan-Gillian's strain,
Fergus, of Canna's castled bay,
Mac-Duffith, Lord of Colonsay,
Soon as they saw the broadswords glance,
With ready weapons rose at once,
More prompt, that many an ancient feud,
Full oft suppress'd, full oft renew'd,
Glow'd 'twixt the chieftains of Argyle,
And many a lord of ocean's isle.
Wild was the scene—each sword was
    bare,
Back stream'd each chieftain's shaggy hair,
In gloomy opposition set,
Eyes, hands, and brandish'd weapons
    met;
Blue gleaming o'er the social board,
Flash'd to the torches many a sword;
And soon those bridal lights may shine
On purple blood for rosy wine.

XVIII.

While thus for blows and death prepared,
Each heart was up, each weapon bared,
Each foot advanced,—a surly pause
Still reverenced hospitable laws.
All menaced violence, but alike
Reluctant each the first to strike,
(For aye accursed in minstrel line
Is he who brawls 'mid song and wine,)
And, match'd in numbers and in might,
Doubtful and desperate seem'd the fight.
Thus threat and murmur died away,
Till on the crowded hall there lay
Such silence, as the deadly still,
Ere bursts the thunder on the hill.
With blade advanced, each Chieftain bold
Show'd like the Sworder's form of old,
As wanting still the torch of life,
To wake the marble into strife.

XIX.

That awful pause the stranger maid,
And Edith, seized to pray for aid.
As to De Argentine she clung,
Away her veil the stranger flung,
And, lovely 'mid her wild despair,
Fast stream'd her eyes, wide flow'd her
    hair.
" O thou, of knighthood once the flower,
Sure refuge in distressful hour,
Thou, who in Judah well hast fought
For our dear faith, and oft hast sought
Renown in knightly exercise,
When this poor hand has dealt the prize,
Say, can thy soul of honour brook
On the unequal strife to look,
When, butcher'd thus in peaceful hall,
Those once thy friends, my brethren, fall!"
To Argentine she turn'd her word,
But her eye sought the Island Lord.
A flush like evening's setting flame
Glow'd on his cheek ; his hardy frame,
As with a brief convulsion, shook :
With hurried voice and eager look,—
" Fear not," he said, " my Isabel !
What said I—Edith !—all is well—
Nay, fear not—I will well provide
The safety of my lovely bride—

My bride ?"—but there the accents clung
In tremor to his faltering tongue.

XX.

Now rose De Argentine, to claim
The prisoners in his sovereign's name,
To England's crown, who, vassals sworn,
'Gainst their liege lord had weapon
    borne—
(Such speech, I ween, was but to hide
His care their safety to provide ;
For knight more true in thought and deed
Than Argentine ne'er spurr'd a steed)—
And Ronald, who his meaning guess'd,
Seem'd half to sanction the request.
This purpose fiery Torquil broke :—
" Somewhat we've heard of England's
    yoke,"
He said, " and, in our islands, Fame
Hath whisper'd of a lawful claim,
That calls the Bruce fair Scotland's Lord;
Though dispossess'd by foreign sword.
This craves reflection—but though right
And just the charge of England's Knight,
Let England's crown her rebels seize
Where she has power ;—in towers like
    these,
'Midst Scottish Chieftains summon'd here
To bridal mirth and bridal cheer,
Be sure, with no consent of mine,
Shall either Lorn or Argentine
With chains of violence, in our sight,
Oppress a brave and banish'd Knight."

XXI.

Then waked the wild debate again,
With brawling threat and clamour vain.
Vassals and menials, thronging in,
Lent their brute rage to swell the din ;
When, far and wide, a bugle-clang
From the dark ocean upward rang.
    " The Abbot comes!" they cry at once,
    " The holy man, whose favour'd glance
        Hath sainted visions known ;
    Angels have met him on the way,
    Beside the blessed martyrs' bay,
        And by Columba's stone.

His monks have heard their hymnings
    high
Sound from the summit of Dun-Y,
    To cheer his penance lone,
When at each cross, on girth and wold,
(Their number thrice a hundred-fold,)
His prayer he made, his beads he told,
    With Aves many a one—
He comes our feuds to reconcile,
A sainted man from sainted isle;
We will his holy doom abide,
The Abbot shall our strife decide."

XXII.

Scarcely this fair accord was o'er,
When through the wide revolving door
    The black-stoled brethren wind;
Twelve sandall'd monks, who relics bore,
With many a torch-bearer before,
    And many a cross behind.
Then sunk each fierce uplifted hand,
And dagger bright and flashing brand
    Dropp'd swiftly at the sight;
They vanish'd from the Churchman's eye,
As shooting stars, that glance and die,
    Dart from the vault of night.

XXIII.

The Abbot on the threshold stood,
And in his hand the holy rood;
Back on his shoulders flow'd his hood,
    The torch's glaring ray
Show'd, in its red and flashing light,
His wither'd cheek and amice white,
His blue eye glistening cold and bright,
    His tresses scant and grey.
"Fair Lords," he said, "Our Lady's
    love,
And peace be with you from above,
    And Benedicite!—
—But what means this? no peace is
    here!—
Do dirks unsheathed suit bridal cheer?
    Or are these naked brands
A seemly show for Churchman's sight,
When he comes summon'd to unite
    Betrothed hearts and hands?"

XXIV.

Then, cloaking hate with fiery zeal,
Proud Lorn first answer'd the appeal ;—
    " Thou comest, O holy Man,
True sons of blessed church to greet,
But little deeming here to meet
    A wretch, beneath the ban
Of Pope and Church, for murder done
Even on the sacred altar-stone!—
Well mayest thou wonder we should
    know
Such miscreant here, nor lay him low,
Or dream of greeting, peace, or truce,
With excommunicated Bruce!
Yet well I grant, to end debate,
Thy sainted voice decide his fate."

XXV.

Then Ronald pled the stranger's cause,
And knighthood's oath and honour's laws;
And Isabel, on bended knee,
Brought pray'rs and tears to back the
    plea;
And Edith lent her generous aid,
And wept, and Lorn for mercy pray'd.
" Hence," he exclaim'd, " degenerate
    maid !
Was't not enough to Ronald's bower
I brought thee, like a paramour,"
Or bond-maid at her master's gate,
His careless cold approach to wait ?—
But the bold Lord of Cumberland,
The gallant Clifford, seeks thy hand;
His it shall be—Nay, no reply !
Hence! till those rebel eyes be dry."
With grief the Abbot heard and saw,
Yet nought relax'd his brow of awe.

XXVI.

Then Argentine, in England's name,
So highly urged his sovereign's claim,
He waked a spark, that, long suppress'd,
Had smoulder'd in Lord Ronald's breast;
And now, as from the flint the fire,
Flash'd forth at once his generous ire.
" Enough of noble blood," he said,
" By English Edward had been shed,

Since matchless Wallace first had been
In mock'ry crown'd with wreaths of
    green,[15]
And done to death by felon hand,
For guarding well his father's land.
Where's Nigel Bruce? and De la Haye,
And valiant Seton—where are they?
Where Somerville, the kind and free?
And Fraser, flower of chivalry?
Have they not been on gibbet bound,
Their quarters flung to hawk and hound,
And hold we here a cold debate,
To yield more victims to their fate?
What! can the English Leopard's mood
Never be gorged with northern blood?
Was not the life of Athole shed,
To soothe the tyrant's sicken'd bed?[13]
And must his word, till dying day,
Be nought but quarter, hang, and slay!—
Thou frown'st, De Argentine,—My gage
Is prompt to prove the strife I wage."—

XXVII.

"Nor deem," said stout Dunvegan's
    knight,
"That thou shalt brave alone the fight!
By saints of isle and mainland both,
By Woden wild, (my grandsire's oath,)*
Let Rome and England do their worst,
Howe'er attainted or accursed.
If Bruce shall e'er find friends again,
Once more to brave a battle-plain,
If Douglas couch again his lance,
Or Randolph dare another chance,
Old Torquil will not be to lack
With twice a thousand at his back.—
Nay, chafe not at my bearing bold,
Good Abbot! for thou know'st of old,
Torquil's rude thought and stubborn will
Smack of the wild Norwegian still:
Nor will I barter Freedom's cause
For England's wealth, or Rome's ap-
    plause."

XXVIII.

The Abbot seem'd with eye severe
The hardy Chieftain's speech to hear;

---

* The Macleods were of Scandinavian
descent—the ancient worshippers of Thor and
Woden.

Then on King Robert turn'd the Monk,
But twice his courage came and sunk,
Confronted with the hero's look;
Twice fell his eye, his accents shook;
At length, resolved in tone and brow,
Sternly he question'd him—"And thou,
Unhappy! what hast thou to plead,
Why I denounce not on thy deed
That awful doom which canons tell
Shuts paradise, and opens hell?
Anathema of power so dread,
It blends the living with the dead,
Bids each good angel soar away,
And every ill one claim his prey;
Expels thee from the church's care,
And deafens Heaven against thy prayer;
Arms every hand against thy life,
Bans all who aid thee in the strife,
Nay, each whose succour, cold and scant,
With meanest alms relieves thy want;
Haunts thee while living,—and, when dead,
Dwells on thy yet devoted head,
Rends Honour's scutcheon from thy
    hearse,
Stills o'er thy bier the holy verse,
And spurns thy corpse from hallow'd
    ground,
Flung like vile carrion to the hound;
Such is the dire and desperate doom
For sacrilege, decreed by Rome;
And such the well-deserved meed
Of thine unhallow'd, ruthless deed."

XXIX.

"Abbot!" the Bruce replied, "thy
    charge
It boots not to dispute at large.
This much, howe'er, I bid thee know,
No selfish vengeance dealt the blow,
For Comyn died his country's foe.
Nor blame I friends whose ill-timed speed
Fulfill'd my soon-repented deed,
Nor censure those from whose stern tongue
The dire anathema has rung.
I only blame mine own wild ire,
By Scotland's wrongs incensed to fire.
Heaven knows my purpose to atone,
Far as I may, the evil done,
And hears a penitent's appeal
From papal curse and prelate's zeal.

My first and dearest task achieved,
Fair Scotland from her thrall relieved,
Shall many a priest in cope and stole
Say requiem for Red Comyn's soul,
While I the blessed cross advance,
And expiate this unhappy chance
In Palestine, with sword and lance.[17]
But, while content the Church should
   know
My conscience owns the debt I owe,
Unto De Argentine and Lorn
The name of traitor I return,
Bid them defiance stern and high,
And give them in their throats the lie!
These brief words spoke, I speak no more.
Do what thou wilt; my shrift is o'er."

XXX.

Like man by prodigy amazed,
Upon the King the Abbot gazed;
Then o'er his pallid features glance
Convulsions of ecstatic trance.
His breathing came more thick and fast,
And from his pale blue eyes were cast
Strange rays of wild and wandering light;
Uprise his locks of silver white,
Flush'd is his brow, through every vein
In azure tide the currents strain,
And undistinguish'd accents broke
The awful silence ere he spoke.

XXXI.

"De Bruce! I rose with purpose dread
To speak my curse upon thy head,[18]
And give thee as an outcast o'er
To him who burns to shed thy gore;
But, like the Midianite of old,
Who stood on Zophim, heaven-controll'd,
I feel within mine aged breast
A power that will not be repress'd.
It prompts my voice, it swells my veins,
It burns, it maddens, it constrains!—
De Bruce, thy sacrilegious blow
Hath at God's altar slain thy foe:
O'ermaster'd yet by high behest,
I bless thee, and thou shalt be bless'd!"
He spoke, and o'er the astonish'd throng
Was silence, awful, deep, and long.

XXXII

Again that light has fired his eye,
Again his form swells bold and high,
The broken voice of age is gone,
'Tis vigorous manhood's lofty tone:—
"Thrice vanquish'd on the battle-plain,
Thy followers slaughter'd, fled, or ta'en,
A hunted wanderer on the wild,
On foreign shores a man exiled, [19]
Disown'd, deserted, and distress'd,
I bless thee, and thou shalt be bless'd!
Bless'd in the hall and in the field,
Under the mantle as the shield.
Avenger of thy country's shame
Restorer of her injured fame,
Bless'd in thy sceptre and thy sword,
De Bruce, fair Scotland's rightful Lord,
Bless'd in thy deeds and in thy fame,
What lengthen'd honours wait thy name!
In distant ages, sire to son
Shall tell thy tale of freedom won,
And teach his infants, in the use
Of earliest speech, to falter Bruce.
Go, then, triumphant! sweep along
Thy course, the theme of many a song!
The Power, whose dictates swell my
   breast,
Hath bless'd thee, and thou shalt be
   bless'd!—
Enough—my short-lived strength decays,
And sinks the momentary blaze.—
Heaven hath our destined purpose broke,
Not here must nuptial vow be spoke;
Brethren, our errand here is o'er,
Our task discharged.—Unmoor, unmoor!"
His priests received the exhausted Monk,
As breathless in their arms he sunk.
Punctual his orders to obey,
The train refused all longer stay,
Embark'd, raised sail, and bore away.

CANTO THIRD.

I.

HAST thou not mark'd, when o'er thy
   startled head
Sudden and deep the thunder-peal has
   roll'd,

I.

How, when its echoes fell, a silence
 dead
Sunk on the wood, the meadow, and
 the wold?
The rye-grass shakes not on the sod-
 built fold,
The rustling aspen's leaves are mute
 and still,
The wall-flower waves not on the ruin'd
 hold,
Till, murmuring distant first, then near
 and shrill,
The savage whirlwind wakes, and sweeps
 the groaning hill.

II.

Artornish! such a silence sunk
Upon thy halls, when that grey Monk
 His prophet-speech had spoke;
And his obedient brethren's sail
Was stretch'd to meet the southern gale
 Before a whisper woke.
Then murmuring sounds of doubt and
 fear,
Close pour'd in many an anxious ear,
 The solemn stillness broke;
And still they gazed with eager guess,
Where, in an oriel's deep recess,
The Island Prince seem'd bent to press
What Lorn, by his impatient cheer,
And gesture fierce, scarce deign'd to hear.

III.

Starting at length, with frowning look,
His hand he clench'd, his head he shook,
 And sternly flung apart;—
"And deem'st thou me so mean of mood,
As to forget the mortal feud,
And clasp the hand with blood imbrued
 From my dear Kinsman's heart?
Is this thy rede?—a due return
For ancient league and friendship sworn!
But well our mountain proverb shows
The faith of Islesmen ebbs and flows.
Be it even so—believe, ere long,
He that now bears shall wreak the
 wrong.—
Call Edith—call the Maid of Lorn!
My sister, slaves!—for further scorn,

Be sure nor she nor I will stay.—
Away, De Argentine, away!—
We nor ally nor brother know,
In Bruce's friend, or England's foe."

IV.

But who the Chieftain's rage can tell,
When, sought from lowest dungeon cell
To highest tower the castle round,
No Lady Edith was there found!
He shouted, "Falsehood!—treachery!—
Revenge and blood!—a lordly meed
To him that will avenge the deed!
A Baron's lands!"—His frantic mood
Was scarcely by the news withstood,
That Morag shared his sister's flight,
And that, in hurry of the night,
'Scaped noteless, and without remark,
Two strangers sought the Abbot's bark.—
"Man every galley!—fly—pursue!
The priest his treachery shall rue!
Ay, and the time shall quickly come,
When we shall hear the thanks that Rome
Will pay his feigned prophecy!"
Such was fierce Lorn's indignant cry;
And Cormac Doil in haste obey'd,
Hoisted his sail, his anchor weigh'd,
(For, glad of each pretext for spoil,
A pirate sworn was Cormac Doil.)
But others, lingering, spoke apart,—
"The Maid has given her maiden heart
 To Ronald of the Isles,
And, fearful lest her brother's word
Bestow her on that English Lord,
 She seeks Iona's piles,
And wisely deems it best to dwell
A votaress in the holy cell,
Until these feuds so fierce and fell
 The Abbot reconciles."

V.

As, impotent of ire, the hall
Echo'd to Lorn's impatient call,
"My horse, my mantle, and my train!
Let none who honours Lorn remain!"—
Courteous, but stern, a bold request
To Bruce De Argentine express'd.
"Lord-Earl," he said,—"I cannot chuse
But yield such title to the Bruce,

Though name and earldom both are gone,
Since he braced rebel's armour on—
But, Earl or Serf—rude phrase was thine
Of late, and launch'd at Argentine;
Such as compels me to demand
Redress of honour at thy hand.
We need not to each other tell,
That both can wield their weapons well;
   Then do me but the soldier grace,
   This glove upon thy helm to place
      Where we may meet in fight;
   And I will say, as still I've said,
   Though by ambition far misled,
      Thou art a noble knight."—

VI.

" And I," the princely Bruce replied,
" Might term it stain on knighthood's pride
That the bright sword of Argentine
Should in a tyrant's quarrel shine;
But, for your brave request,
Be sure the honour'd pledge you gave
In every battle-field shall wave
Upon my helmet-crest:
Believe, that if my hasty tongue
Hath done thine honour causeless wrong,
It shall be well redress'd.
Not dearer to my soul was glove,
Bestow'd in youth by lady's love,
   Than this which thou hast given!
Thus, then, my noble foe I greet;
Health and high fortune till we meet,
   And then—what pleases Heaven."

VII.

Thus parted they—for now, with sound
Like waves roll'd back from rocky ground,
   The friends of Lorn retire;
Each mainland chieftain, with his train,
Draws to his mountain towers again,
Pondering how mortal schemes prove vain,
   And mortal hopes expire.
But through the castle double guard,
By Ronald's charge, kept wakeful ward,
Wicket and gate were trebly barr'd,
   By beam and bolt and chain;
Then of the guests, in courteous sort,
He pray'd excuse for mirth broke short,
And bade them in Artornish fort
   In confidence remain.

Now torch and menial tendance led
Chieftain and knight to bower and bed,
And beads were told, and Aves said,
   And soon they sunk away
Into such sleep, as wont to shed
Oblivion on the weary head,
   After a toilsome day.

VIII.

But soon uproused, the Monarch cried
To Edward slumbering by his side,
   " Awake, or sleep for aye!
Even now there jarr'd a secret door—
A taper-light gleams on the floor—
   Up, Edward, up, I say!
Some one glides in like midnight ghost—
Nay, strike not! 'tis our noble Host."
Advancing then his taper's flame,
Ronald stept forth, and with him came
   Dunvegan's chief—each bent the knee
   To Bruce in sign of fealty,
      And proffer'd him his sword,
   And hail'd him, in a monarch's style,
   As king of mainland and of isle,
      And Scotland's rightful lord.
" And O," said Ronald, " Own'd of
      Heaven!
Say, is my erring youth forgiven,
By falsehood's arts from duty driven,
   Who rebel falchion drew,
Yet ever to thy deeds of fame,
Even while I strove against thy claim,
   Paid homage just and true?"—
" Alas! dear youth, the unhappy time,"
Answer'd the Bruce, " must bear the
      crime,
   Since, guiltier far than you,
Even I"—he paused; for Falkirk's woes
Upon his conscious soul arose.[20]
The Chieftain to his breast he press'd,
And in a sigh conceal'd the rest.

IX.

They proffer'd aid, by arms and might,
To repossess him in his right;
But well their counsels must be weigh'd,
Ere banners raised and musters made.
For English hire and Lorn's intrigues
Bound many chiefs in southern leagues.

In answer, Bruce his purpose bold
To his new vassals frankly told.
" The winter worn in exile o'er,
I long'd for Carrick's kindred shore.
I thought upon my native Ayr,
And long'd to see the burly fare
That Clifford makes, whose lordly call
Now echoes through my father's hall.
But first my course to Arran led,
Where valiant Lennox gathers head,
And on the sea, by tempest toss'd,
Our barks dispersed, our purpose cross'd,
Mine own, a hostile sail to shun,
Far from her destined course had run,
When that wise will, which masters ours,
Compell'd us to your friendly towers."

X.

Then Torquil spoke:—" The time craves
　　speed !
We must not linger in our deed,
But instant pray our Sovereign Liege,
To shun the perils of a siege.
The vengeful Lorn, with all his powers,
Lies but too near Artornish towers,
And England's light-arm'd vessels ride,
Not distant far, the waves of Clyde,
Prompt at these tidings to unmoor,
And sweep each strait, and guard each
　　shore.
Then, till this fresh alarm pass by,
Secret and safe my Liege must lie
In the far bounds of friendly Skye,
Torquil thy pilot and thy guide."—
" Not so, brave Chieftain," Ronald cried;
" Myself will on my Sovereign wait,
And raise in arms the men of Sleate,
Whilst thou, renow'd where chiefs debate,
Shalt sway their souls by council sage,
And awe them by thy locks of age."
—" And if my words in weight shall fail,
This ponderous sword shall turn the scale."

XI.

—" The scheme," said Bruce, " contents
　　me well ;
Meantime, 'twere best that Isabel,
For safety, with my bark and crew,
Again to friendly Erin drew.

There Edward, too, shall with her wend,
In need to cheer her and defend,
And muster up each scatter'd friend."—
Here seem'd it as Lord Ronald's ear
Would other counsel gladlier hear ;
But, all achieved as soon as plann'd,
Both barks, in secret arm'd and mann'd,
　　From out the haven bore ;
On different voyage forth they ply,
This for the coast of winged Skye,
　　And that for Erin's shore.

XII

With Bruce and Ronald bides the tale.—
To favouring winds they gave the sail,
Till Mull's dark headlands scarce they
　　knew,
And Ardnamurchan's hills were blue.
But then the squalls blew close and hard,
And, fain to strike the galley's yard,
　　And take them to the oar,
With these rude seas, in weary plight,
They strove the livelong day and night,
Nor till the dawning had a sight
　　Of Skye's romantic shore.
Where Coolin stoops him to the west,
They saw upon his shiver'd crest
　　The sun's arising gleam ;
But such the labour and delay,
Ere they were moor'd in Scavigh bay,
(For calmer heaven compell'd to stay,)
　　He shot a western beam.
Then Ronald said, " If true mine eye,
These are the savage wilds that lie
North of Strathnardill and Dunskye ;[21]
　　No human foot comes here,
And, since these adverse breezes blow,
If my good Liege love hunter's bow,
What hinders that on land we go,
　　And strike a mountain-deer?
Allan, my page, shall with us wend ;
A bow full deftly can he bend,
And, if we meet a herd, may send
　　A shaft shall mend our cheer."
Then each took bow and bolts in hand,
Their row-boat launch'd and leapt to land,
　　And left their skiff and train,
Where a wild stream, with headlong shock,
Came brawling down its bed of rock,
　　To mingle with the main.

XIII.

A while their route they silent made,
  As men who stalk for mountain-
    deer,
Till the good Bruce to Ronald said,
  "St. Mary! what a scene is here!—
I've traversed many a mountain-strand,
  Abroad and in my native land,
And it has been my lot to tread
Where safety more than pleasure led;
Thus, many a waste I've wander'd o'er,
Clombe many a crag, cross'd many a moor,
  But, by my halidome,
A scene so rude, so wild as this,
Yet so sublime in barrenness,
Ne'er did my wandering footsteps press,
  Where'er I happ'd to roam."

XIV.

No marvel thus the Monarch spake;
  For rarely human eye has known
A scene so stern as that dread lake,
  With its dark ledge of barren stone
Seems that primeval earthquake's sway
Hath rent a strange and shatter'd way
  Through the rude bosom of the hill,
And that each naked precipice,
Sable ravine, and dark abyss,
  Tells of the outrage still.
The wildest glen, but this, can show
Some touch of Nature's genial glow;
On high Benmore green mosses grow,
And heath-bells bud in deep Glencroe,
  And copse on Cruchan-Ben;
But here,—above, around, below,
  On mountain or in glen,
Nor tree, nor shrub, nor plant, nor flower,
Nor aught of vegetative power,
  The weary eye may ken.
For all is rocks at random thrown,
Black waves, bare crags, and banks of
    stone.
  As if were here denied
The summer sun, the spring's sweet dew,
That clothe with many a varied hue
  The bleakest mountain-side.

XV.

And wilder, forward as they wound,
Were the proud cliffs and lake profound.
Huge terraces of granite black
Afforded rude and cumber'd track;
  For from the mountain hoar,
Hurl'd headlong in some night of fear,
When yell'd the wolf and fled the deer,
  Loose crags had toppled o'er;
And some, chance-poised and balanced,
    lay,
So that a stripling arm might sway
  A mass no host could raise,
In Nature's rage at random thrown,
Yet trembling like the Druid's stone
  On its precarious base.
The evening mists, with ceaseless change,
Now clothed the mountains' lofty range,
  Now left their foreheads bare,
And round the skirts their mantle furl'd,
Or on the sable waters curl'd,
Or on the eddying breezes whirl'd,
  Dispersed in middle air.
And oft, condensed, at once they lower,
When, brief and fierce, the mountain
    shower
Pours like a torrent down,
And when return the sun's glad beams,
Whiten'd with foam a thousand streams
  Leap from the mountain's crown.

XVI.

"This lake," said Bruce, "whose barriers
    drear
Are precipices sharp and sheer,
Yielding no track for goat or deer,
  Save the black shelves we tread,
How term you its dark waves? and how
Yon northern mountain's pathless brow,
  And yonder peak of dread,
That to the evening sun uplifts
The griesly gulfs and slaty rifts,
  Which seam its shiver'd head?"—
"Coriskin call the dark lake's name,
Coolin the ridge, as bards proclaim,
From old Cuchullin, chief of fame.
But bards, familiar in our isles
Rather with Nature's frowns than smiles,
Full oft their careless humours please
By sportive names from scenes like these.
I would old Torquil were to show
His maidens with their breasts of snow,

Or that my noble Liege were nigh
To hear his Nurse sing lullaby!
(The Maids—tall cliffs with breakers white,
The Nurse—a torrent's roaring might,)
Or that your eye could see the mood
Of Corryvrekin's whirlpool rude,
When dons the Hag her whiten'd hood—
'Tis thus our islesmen's fancy frames,
For scenes so stern, fantastic names."

XVII.

Answer'd the Bruce, " And musing mind
Might here a graver moral find.
These mighty cliffs, that heave on high
Their naked brows to middle sky,
Indifferent to the sun or snow,
Where nought can fade, and nought can
  blow,
May·they not mark a Monarch's fate,—
Raised high 'mid storms of strife and state,
Beyond life's lowlier pleasures placed,
His soul a rock, his heart a waste?
O'er hope and love and fear aloft
High rears his crowned head—But soft!
Look, underneath yon jutting crag
Are hunters and a slaughter'd stag.
Who may they be? But late you said
No steps these desert regions tread."—

XVIII.

"So said I—and believed in sooth,"
Ronald replied, "I spoke the truth.
Yet now I spy, by yonder stone,
Five men—they mark us, and come on;
And by their badge on bonnet borne,
I guess them of the land of Lorn,
Foes to my Liege."—"So let it be;
I've faced worse odds than five to three;
—But the poor page can little aid;
Then be our battle thus array'd,
If our free passage they contest;
Cope thou with two, I'll match the rest."—
"Not so, my Liege—for, by my life,
This sword shall meet the treble strife;
My strength, my skill in arms, more small,
And less the loss should Ronald fall.
But islemen soon to soldiers grow,
Allan has sword as well as bow,
And were my Monarch's order given,
Two shafts should make our number
  even,"

" No! not to save my life !" he said;
" Enough of blood rests on my head,
Too rashly spill'd—we soon shall know,
Whether they come as friend or foe"

XIX.

Nigh came the strangers, and more nigh;—
Still less they pleased the Monarch's eye.
Men were they all of evil mien,
Down-look'd, unwilling to be seen;
They moved with half-resolved pace,
And bent on earth each gloomy face.
The foremost two were fair array'd,
With brogue and bonnet, trews and plaid,
And bore the arms of mountaineers,
Daggers and broadswords, bows and
     spears.
The three, that lagg'd small space behind,
Seem'd serfs of more degraded kind;
Goat-skins or deer-hides o'er them cast,
Made a rude fence against the blast;
Their arms and feet and heads were bare,
Matted their beards, unshorn their hair;
For arms, the caitiffs bore in hand,
A club, an axe, a rusty brand.

XX.

Onward, still mute, they kept the track;—
"Tell who ye be, or else stand back,"
Said Bruce; "In deserts when they meet,
Men pass not as in peaceful street."
Still, at his stern command, they stood,
And proffer'd greeting brief and rude,
But acted courtesy so ill,
As seem'd of fear, and not of will.
" Wanderers we are, as you may be;
Men hither driven by wind and sea,
Who, if you list to taste our cheer,
Will share with you this fallow deer."—
" If from the sea, where lies your bark?"—
" Ten fathom deep in ocean dark!
Wreck'd yesternight: but we are men,
Who little sense of peril ken.
The shades come down—the day is shut—
Will you go with us to our hut?"—
" Our vessel waits us in the bay;
Thanks for your proffer—have good-
    day,"—

" Was that your galley, then, which rode
Not far from shore when evening
 glow'd ?"—
"It was."—"Then spare your needless
 pain,
There will she now be sought in vain.
We saw her from the mountain head,
When, with St. George's blazon red,
A southern vessel bore in sight,
And yours raised sail, and took to flight."—

XXI.

" Now, by the rood, unwelcome news !"
Thus with Lord Ronald communed Bruce;
" Nor rests there light enough to show
If this their tale be true or no.
The men seem bred of churlish kind,
Yet mellow nuts have hardest rind;
We will go with them—food and fire
And sheltering roof our wants require.
Sure guard 'gainst treachery will we keep,
And watch by turns our comrades' sleep.—
Good fellows, thanks; your guests we'll be,
And well will pay the courtesy.
Come, lead us where your lodging lies,—
—Nay, soft ! we mix not companies.—
Show us the path o'er crag and stone,
And we will follow you;—lead on."

XXII.

They reach'd the dreary cabin, made
Of sails against a rock display'd,
 And there, on entering, found
A slender boy, whose form and mien
Ill suited with such savage scene,
In cap and cloak of velvet green,
 Low seated on the ground.
His garb was such as minstrels wear,
Dark was his hue, and dark his hair,
His youthful cheek was marr'd by care,
 His eyes in sorrow drown'd.
" Whence this poor boy ?"—As Ronald
 spoke,
The voice his trance of anguish broke;
As if awaked from ghastly dream,
He raised his head with start and scream,
 And wildly gazed around;
Then to the wall his face he turn'd,
And his dark neck with blushes burn'd.

XXIII.

" Whose is the boy ?" again he said.—
" By chance of war our captive made;
He may be yours, if you should hold
That music has more charms than gold;
For, though from earliest childhood mute,
The lad can deftly touch the lute,
 And on the rote and viol play,
 And well can drive the time away
  For those who love such glee;
For me, the favouring breeze, when
 loud
It pipes upon the galley's shroud,
 Makes blither melody."—
" Hath he, then, sense of spoken sound ?"—
 "Aye; so his mother bade us know,
A crone in our late shipwreck drown'd,
 And hence the silly stripling's woe.
More of the youth I cannot say,
Our captive but since yesterday;
When wind and weather wax'd so grim,
We little listed think of him.—
But why waste time in idle words?
Sit to your cheer—unbelt your swords."
Sudden the captive turn'd his head,
And one quick glance to Ronald sped.
It was a keen and warning look,
And well the Chief the signal took.

XXIV.

" Kind host," he said, " our needs require
A separate board and separate fire;
For know, that on a pilgrimage
Wend I, my comrade, and this page.
And, sworn to vigil and to fast,
Long as this hallow'd task shall last,
We never doff the plaid or sword,
Or feast us at a stranger's board;
And never share one common sleep,
But one must still his vigil keep.
Thus, for our separate use, good friend,
We'll hold this hut's remoter end."—
" A churlish vow," the eldest said,
" And hard, methinks, to be obey'd.
How say you, if, to wreak the scorn
That pays our kindness harsh return,
We should refuse to share our meal ?"
" Then say we, that our swords are steel !

And our vow binds us not to fast,
Where gold or force may buy repast."—
Their host's dark brow grew keen and fell,
His teeth are clench'd, his features swell;
Yet sunk the felon's moody ire
Before Lord Ronald's glance of fire,
Nor could his craven courage brook
The Monarch's calm and dauntless look.
With laugh constrain'd,—" Let every man
Follow the fashion of his clan!
Each to his separate quarters keep,
And feed or fast, or wake or sleep."

XXV.

Their fire at separate distance burns,
By turns they eat, keep guard by turns;
For evil seem'd that old man's eye,
Dark and designing, fierce yet shy.
Still he avoided forward look,
But slow and circumspectly took
A circling, never-ceasing glance,
By doubt and cunning mark'd at once,
Which shot a mischief-boding ray,
From under eyebrows shagg'd and grey.
The younger, too, who seem'd his son,
Had that dark look the timid shun;
The half-clad serfs behind them sate,
And scowl'd a glare 'twixt fear and hate—
Till all, as darkness onward crept,
Couch'd down, and seem'd to sleep or slept.
Nor he, that boy, whose powerless tongue
Must trust his eyes to wail his wrong,
A longer watch of sorrow made,
But stretch'd his limbs to slumber laid.

XXVI.

Not in his dangerous host confides
The King, but wary watch provides.
Ronald keeps ward till midnight past,
Then wakes the King, young Allan last;
Thus rank'd, to give the youthful page
The rest required by tender age.
What is Lord Ronald's wakeful thought,
To chase the languor toil had brought?—
(For deem not that he deign'd to throw
Much care upon such coward foe,)—
He thinks of lovely Isabel,
When at her foeman's feet she fell,
Nor less when, placed in princely selle,

She glanced on him with favouring eyes,
At Woodstock when he won the prize,
Nor, fair in joy, in sorrow fair,
In pride of place as 'mid despair,
Must she alone engross his care.
His thoughts to his betrothed bride,
To Edith, turn—O how decide,
When here his love and heart are given,
And there his faith stands plight to Heaven!
No drowsy ward 'tis his to keep,
For seldom lovers long for sleep.
Till sung his midnight hymn the owl,
Answer'd the dog-fox with his howl,
Then waked the King—at his request,
Lord Ronald stretch'd himself to rest.

XXVII.

What spell was good King Robert's, say,
To drive the weary night away?
His was the patriot's burning thought,
Of Freedom's battle bravely fought,
Of castles storm'd, of cities freed,
Of deep design and daring deed,
Of England's roses reft and torn,
And Scotland's cross in triumph worn,
Of rout and rally, war and truce,—
As heroes think, so thought the Bruce.
No marvel, 'mid such musings high,
Sleep shunn'd the Monarch's thoughtful
   eye.
Now over Coolin's eastern head
The greyish light begins to spread,
The otter to his cavern drew,
And clamour'd shrill the wakening mew;
Then watch'd the page—to needful rest
The King resign'd his anxious breast

XXVIII.

To Allan's eyes was harder task,
The weary watch their safeties ask.
He trimm'd the fire, and gave to shine
With bickering light the splinter'd pine;
Then gazed awhile, where silent laid
Their hosts were shrouded by the plaid.
But little fear waked in his mind,
For he was bred of martial kind,
And, if to manhood he arrive,
May match the boldest knight alive.
Then thought he of his mother's tower,
His little sisters' greenwood bower,

How there the Easter-gambols pass,
And of Dan Joseph's lengthen'd mass.
But still before his weary eye
In rays prolong'd the blazes die—
Again he roused him—on the lake
Look'd forth, where now the twilight-
    flake
Of pale cold dawn began to wake.
On Coolin's cliffs the mist lay furl'd,
The morning breeze the lake had curl'd,
The short dark waves, heaved to the land,
With ceaseless plash kiss'd cliff or sand ;—
It was a slumbrous sound—he turn'd
To tales at which his youth had burn'd,
Of pilgrim's path by demon cross'd,
Of sprightly elf or yelling ghost,
Of the wild witch's baneful cot,
And mermaid's alabaster grot,
Who bathes her limbs in sunless well,
Deep in Strathaird's enchanted cell.²²
Thither in fancy rapt he flies,
And on his sight the vaults arise ;
That hut's dark walls he sees no more,
His foot is on the marble floor,
And o'er his head the dazzling spars
Gleam like a firmament of stars !
—Hark ! hears he not the sea-nymph speak
Her anger in that thrilling shriek !—
No ! all too late, with Allan's dream
Mingled the captive's warning scream.
As from the ground he strives to start,
A ruffian's dagger finds his heart !
Upward he casts his dizzy eyes, . . .
Murmurs his master's name, . . . and dies!

XXIX.

Not so awoke the King ! his hand
Snatch'd from the flame a knotted brand,
The nearest weapon of his wrath ;
With this he cross'd the murderer's path,
    And venged young Allan well !
The spatter'd brain and bubbling blood
Hiss'd on the half-extinguish'd wood,
    The miscreant gasp'd and fell !
Nor rose in peace the Island Lord ;
One caitiff died upon his sword,
And one beneath his grasp lies prone,
In mortal grapple overthrown.
But while Lord Ronald's dagger drank
The life-blood from his panting flank,

The Father-ruffian of the band
Behind him rears a coward hand !
    —O for a moment's aid,
Till Bruce, who deals no double blow,
Dash to the earth another foe,
    Above his comrade laid !—
And it is gain'd—the captive sprung
On the raised arm, and closely clung,
    And, ere he shook him loose,
The master'd felon press'd the ground,
And gasp'd beneath a mortal wound,
    While o'er him stands the Bruce.

XXX.

" Miscreant ! while lasts thy flitting spark,
Give me to know the purpose dark,
That arm'd thy hand with murderous knife,
Against offenceless stranger's life ?"—
" No stranger thou !" with accent fell,
Murmur'd the wretch ; " I know thee well ;
And know thee for the foeman sworn
Of my high Chief, the mighty Lorn."—
" Speak yet again, and speak the truth
For thy soul's sake !—from whence this
    youth?
His country, birth, and name declare,
And thus one evil deed repair."—
—" Vex me no more ! . . . my blood
    runs cold . . .
No more I know than I have told.
We found him in a bark we sought
With different purpose . . . and I
    thought" . . .
Fate cut him short ; in blood and broil,
As he had lived, died Cormac Doil.

XXXI.

Then resting on his bloody blade,
The valiant Bruce to Ronald said,
" Now shame upon us both !—that boy
    Lifts his mute face to heaven,
And clasps his hands, to testify
His gratitude to God on high,
    For strange deliverance given.
His speechless gesture thanks hath paid,
Which our free tongues have left unsaid !"
He raised the youth with kindly word,
But mark'd him shudder at the sword :
He cleansed it from its hue of death,
And plunged the weapon in its sheath.

" Alas, poor child! unfitting part
Fate doom'd, when with so soft a heart,
  And form so slight as thine,
She made thee first a pirate's slave,
Then, in his stead, a patron gave
  Of wayward lot like mine;
A landless prince, whose wandering life
Is but one scene of blood and strife—
Yet scant of friends the Bruce shall be,
But he'll find resting-place for thee.—
Come, noble Ronald! o'er the dead
Enough thy generous grief is paid,
And well has Allan's fate been wroke;
Come, wend we hence—the day has broke.
Seek we our bark—I trust the tale
Was false, that she had hoisted sail."

XXXII.

Yet, ere they left that charnel-cell,
The Island Lord bade sad farewell
To Allan:—" Who shall tell this tale,"
He said, " in halls of Donagaile!
Oh, who his widow'd mother tell,
That, ere his bloom, her fairest fell!—
Rest thee, poor youth! and trust my care
For mass and knell and funeral prayer;
While o'er those caitiffs, where they lie,
The wolf shall snarl, the raven cry!"
And now the eastern mountain's head
On the dark lake threw lustre red;
Bright gleams of gold and purple streak
Ravine and precipice and peak—
(So earthly power at distance shows;
Reveals his splendour, hides his woes.)
O'er sheets of granite, dark and broad,
Rent and unequal, lay the road.
In sad discourse the warriors wind,
And the mute captive moves behind.

———————

CANTO FOURTH

I.

STRANGER! if e'er thine ardent step
    hath traced
The northern realms of ancient
    Caledon,

Where the proud Queen of Wilder-
    ness hath placed
By lake and cataract, her lonely throne;
Sublime but sad delight thy soul hath
    known,
Gazing on pathless glen and mountain
    high,
Listing where from the cliffs the torrents
    thrown
Mingle their echoes with the eagle's
    cry,
And with the sounding lake, and with the
    moaning sky.

Yes! 'twas sublime, but sad.—The lone-
    liness
Loaded thy heart, the desert tired thine
    eye;
And strange and awful fears began to
    press
Thy bosom with a stern solemnity.
Then hast thou wish'd some woodman's
    cottage nigh,
Something that show'd of life, though
    low and mean;
Glad sight, its curling wreath of smoke
    to spy,
Glad sound, its cock's blithe carol
    would have been,
Or children whooping wild beneath the
    willows green.

Such are the scenes, where savage gran-
    deur wakes
An awful thrill that softens into sighs;
Such feelings rouse them by dim Ran-
    noch's lakes,
In dark Glencoe such gloomy raptures
    rise:
Or farther, where, beneath the northern
    skies,
Chides wild Loch-Eribol his caverns
    hoar—
But, be the minstrel judge, they yield
    the prize
Of desert dignity to that dread shore,
That sees grim Coolin rise, and hears
    Coriskin roar.

II.

Through such wild scenes, the champion
    pass'd,
When bold halloo and bugle-blast
Upon the oreeze came loud and fast.
"There," said the Bruce, "rung Edward's
    horn!
What can have caused such brief return?
And see, brave Ronald,—see him dart
O'er stock and stone like hunted hart,
Precipitate, as is the use,
In war or sport, of Edward Bruce.
—He marks us, and his eager cry
Will tell his news ere he be nigh."

III.

Loud Edward shouts, " What make ye
    here,
Warring upon the mountain-deer,
    When Scotland wants her King?
A bark from Lennox cross'd our track,
With her in speed I hurried back,
    These joyful news to bring—
The Stuart stirs in Teviotdale,
And Douglas wakes his native vale;
Thy storm-toss'd fleet hath won its way
With little loss to Brodick-Bay,
And Lennox, with a gallant band,
Waits but thy coming and command
To waft them o'er to Carrick strand.
There are blithe news!—but mark the
    close!
Edward, the deadliest of our foes,
As with his host he northward pass'd,
Hath on the Borders breathed his last."

IV.

Still stood the Bruce—his steady cheek
Was little wont his joy to speak,
    But then his colour rose:
" Now, Scotland! shortly shalt thou see
With God's high will, thy children free,
    And vengeance on thy foes!
Yet to no sense of selfish wrongs,
Bear witness with me, Heaven, belongs
    My joy o'er Edward's bier;[23]
I took my knighthood at his hand,
And lordship held of him, and land,
    And well may vouch it here,

That, blot the story from his page,
Of Scotland ruin'd in his rage,
You read a monarch brave and sage,
    And to his people dear."—
" Let London's burghers mourn her Lord,
And Croydon monks his praise record,"
    The eager Edward said;
" Eternal as his own, my hate
Surmounts the bounds of mortal fate,
    And dies not with the dead!
Such hate was his on Solway's strand,
When vengeance clench'd his palsied hand,
That pointed yet to Scotland's land,
    As his last accents pray'd
Disgrace and curse upon his heir,
If he one Scottish head should spare,
Till stretch'd upon the bloody lair
    Each rebel corpse was laid!
Such hate was his, when his last breath,
Renounced the peaceful house of death,
And bade his bones to Scotland's coast
Be borne by his remorseless host,
    As if his dead and stony eye
Could still enjoy her misery!
Such hate was his—dark, deadly, long;
Mine,—as enduring, deep, and strong!"—

V.

" Let women, Edward, war with words,
With curses monks, but men with swords:
Nor doubt of living foes, to sate
Deepest revenge and deadliest hate.
Now, to the sea! behold the beach,
And see the galleys' pendants stretch
Their fluttering length down favouring
    gale!
Aboard, aboard! and hoist the sail.
Hold we our way for Arran first,
Where meet in arms our friends dispersed;
Lennox the loyal, De la Haye,
And Boyd the bold in battle fray.
I long the hardy band to head,
And see once more my standard spread.—
Does noble Ronald share our course,
Or stay to raise his island force?"—
" Come weal, come woe, by Bruce's side,"
Replied the Chief, " will Ronald bide.
And since two galleys yonder ride,
Be mine, so please my liege, dismiss'd
To wake to arms the clans of Uist,

And all who hear the Minche's roar,
On the Long Island's lonely shore.
The nearer Isles, with slight delay,
Ourselves may summon in our way;
And soon on Arran's shore shall meet,
With Torquil's aid, a gallant fleet,
If aught avails their Chieftain's hest
Among the islesmen of the west."

VI.

Thus was their venturous council said.
But, ere their sails the galleys spread,
Coriskin dark and Coolin high
Echoed the dirge's doleful cry.
Along that sable lake pass' slow,—
Fit scene for such a sight of woe,—
The sorrowing islesmen, as they bore
The murder'd Allan to the shore.
At every pause, with dismal shout,
Their coronach of grief rung out,
And ever, when they moved again,
The pipes resumed their clamorous strain,
And, with the pibroch's shrilling wail,
Mourn'd the young heir of Donagaile.
Round and around, from cliff and cave,
His answer stern old Coolin gave,
Till high upon his misty side
Languish'd the mournful notes, and died.
For never sounds, by mortal made,
Attain'd his high and haggard head,
That echoes but the tempest's moan,
Or the deep thunder's rending groan.

VII.

Merrily, merrily bounds the bark,
  She bounds before the gale,
The mountain breeze from Ben-na-darch
  Is joyous in her sail!
With fluttering sound like laughter hoarse,
  The cords and canvass strain,
The waves, divided by her force,
In rippling eddies chased her course,
  As if they laugh'd again.
Not down the breeze more blithely flew,
Skimming the wave, the light sea-mew,
  Than the gay galley bore
Her course upon that favouring wind,
And Coolin's crest has sunk behind,
  And Slapin's cavern'd shore.

'Twas then that warlike signals wake
Dunscaith's dark towers and Eisord's
  lake,
And soon, from Cavilgarrigh's head,
Thick wreaths of eddying smoke were
  spread;
A summons these of war and wrath
To the brave clans of Sleat and Strath,
  And, ready at the sight,
Each warrior to his weapons sprung,
And targe upon his shoulder flung,
  Impatient for the fight.
Mac-Kinnon's chief, in warfare grey,
Had charge to muster their array,
And guide their barks to Brodick-Bay

VIII.

Signal of Ronald's high command,
A beacon gleam'd o'er sea and land,
From Canna's tower, that, steep and grey,
Like falcon-nest o'erhangs the bay.
Seek not the giddy crag to climb,
To view the turret scathed by time,
It is a task of doubt and fear
To aught but goat or mountain-deer.
  But rest thee on the silver beach,
  And let the aged herdsman teach
    His tale of former day;
  His cur's wild clamour he shall chide,
  And for thy seat by ocean's side,
    His varied plaid display;
  Then tell, how with their Chieftain
    came,
  In ancient times, a foreign dame
    To yonder turret grey.
Stern was her Lord's suspicious mind,
Who in so rude a jail confined
  So soft and fair a thrall!
And oft, when moon on ocean slept,
That lovely lady sate and wept
  Upon the castle-wall,
And turn'd her eye to southern climes,
And thought perchance of happier times,
And touch'd her lute by fits, and sung
Wild ditties in her native tongue.
And still, when on the cliff and bay
Placid and pale the moonbeams play,
  And every breeze is mute,

Upon the lone Hebridean's ear
Steals a strange pleasure mix'd with fear,
While from that cliff he seems to hear
    The murmur of a lute,
And sounds, as of a captive lone,
That mourns her woes in tongue un-
    known.—
Strange is the tale—but all too long
Already hath it staid the song—
    Yet who may pass them by,
That crag and tower in ruins grey,
Nor to their hapless tenant pay
    The tribute of a sigh!

IX.

Merrily, merrily bounds the bark
    O'er the broad ocean driven,
Her path by Ronin's mountains dark
    The steersman's hand hath given.
And Ronin's mountains dark have sent
    Their hunters to the shore,[24]
And each his ashen bow unbent,
    And gave his pastime o'er,
And at the Island Lord's command,
For hunting spear took warrior's brand.
On Scooreigg next a warning light
Summon'd her warriors to the fight;
A numerous race, ere stern MacLeod
O'er their bleak shores in vengeance
    strode,[25]
When all in vain the ocean-cave
Its refuge to his victims gave.
The Chief, relentless in his wrath,
With blazing heath blockades the path;
In dense and stifling volumes roll'd,
The vapour fill'd the cavern'd hold!
The warrior-threat, the infant's plain,
The mother's screams, were heard in vain!
The vengeful Chief maintains his fires,
Till in the vault a tribe expires!
The bones which strew that cavern's
    gloom,
Too well attest their dismal doom.

X.

Merrily, merrily goes the bark
    On a breeze from the northward free,
So shoots through the morning sky the lark,
    Or the swan through the summer sea.

The shores of Mull on the eastward lay,
And Ulva dark and Colonsay,
And all the group of islets gay
    That guard famed Staffa round.
Then all unknown its columns rose,
Where dark and undisturb'd repose
    The cormorant had found,
And the shy seal had quiet home,
And welter'd in that wondrous dome,
Where, as to shame the temples deck'd
By skill of earthly architect,
Nature herself, it seem'd would raise
A Minster to her Maker's praise!
Not for a meaner use ascend
Her columns, or her arches bend;
Nor of a theme less solemn tells
That mighty surge that ebbs and swells,
And still, between each awful pause,
From the high vault an answer draws,
In varied tone prolong'd and high,
That mocks the organ's melody.
Nor doth its entrance front in vain
To old Iona's holy fane,
That Nature's voice might seem to say,
"Well hast thou done, frail Child of clay!
Thy humble powers that stately shrine
Task'd high and hard—but witness
    mine!"

XI.

Merrily, merrily goes the bark,
    Before the gale she bounds;
So darts the dolphin from the shark,
    Or the deer before the hounds.
They left Loch-Tua on their lee,
And they waken'd the men of the wild
    Tiree,
And the Chief of the sandy Coll;
They paused not at Columba's isle,
Though peal'd the bells from the holy pile
    With long and measured toll;
No time for matin or for mass,
And the sounds of the holy summons pass
    Away in the billow's roll.
Lochbuie's fierce and warlike Lord
Their signal saw, and grasp'd his sword,
And verdant Islay call'd her host,
And the clans of Jura's rugged coast
    Lord Ronald's call obey,

And Scarba's isle, whose tortured shore
Still rings to Cornevreken's roar,
    And lonely Colonsay;
—Scenes sung by him who sings no more![26]
His bright and brief career is o'er,
    And mute his tuneful strains;
Quench'd is his lamp of varied lore,
That loved the light of song to pour;
A distant and a deadly shore
    Has LEYDEN'S cold remains!

XII.

Ever the breeze blows merrily,
But the galley ploughs no more the sea.
Lest, rounding wild Cantyre, they meet
The southern foemen's watchful fleet,
    They held unwonted way;—
Up Tarbat's western lake they bore,
Then dragg'd their bark the isthmus o'er,[27]
As far as Kilmaconnel's shore,
    Upon the eastern bay.
It was a wondrous sight to see
Topmast and pennon glitter free,
High raised above the greenwood tree,
As on dry land the galley moves,
By cliff and copse and alder groves.
Deep import from that selcouth sign,
Did many a mountain Seer divine,
For ancient legends told the Gael,
That when a royal bark should sail
    O'er Kilmaconnel moss,
Old Albyn should in fight prevail,
And every foe should faint and quail
    Before her silver Cross.

XIII.

Now launch'd once more, the inland sea
They furrow with fair augury,
    And steer for Arran's isle;
The sun, ere yet he sunk behind
Ben-Ghoil, "the Mountain of the Wind,"
Gave his grim peaks a greeting kind,
    And bade Loch Ranza smile.[28]
Thither their destined course they drew;
It seem'd the isle her monarch knew,
So brilliant was the landward view,
    The ocean so serene;
Each puny wave in diamonds roll'd
O'er the calm deep, where hues of gold

With azure strove and green.
The hill, the vale, the tree, the tower,
Glow'd with the tints of evening's hour,
    The beach was silver sheen,
The wind breathed soft as lover's sigh,
And, oft renew'd, seem'd oft to die,
    With breathless pause between.
O who, with speech of war and woes,
Would wish to break the soft repose
    Of such enchanting scene!

XIV.

Is it of war Lord Ronald speaks?
The blush that dyes his manly cheeks,
The timid look and downcast eye,
And faltering voice the theme deny.
    And good King Robert's brow ex-
        press'd,
    He ponder'd o'er some high request,
        As doubtful to approve;
    Yet in his eye and lip the while,
    Dwelt the half-pitying glance and smile,
    Which manhood's graver mood beguile,
        When lovers talk of love.
Anxious his suit Lord Ronald pled;
—" And for my bride betrothed," he said,
" My Liege has heard the rumour spread,
Of Edith from Artornish fled.
Too hard her fate—I claim no right
'To blame her for her hasty flight;
Be joy and happiness her lot!—
But she hath fled the bridal knot,
And Lorn recall'd his promised plight,
In the assembled chieftains' sight.—
    When, to fulfil our fathers' band,
    I proffer'd all I could—my hand—
        I was repulsed with scorn;
    Mine honour I should ill assert,
    And worse the feelings of my heart,
    If I should play a suitor's part
        Again, to pleasure Lorn."

XV.

" Young Lord," the royal Bruce replied,
" That question must the Church decide;
Yet seems it hard, since rumours state
Edith takes Clifford for her mate,
The very tie, which she hath broke,
To thee should still be binding yoke.

But, for my sister Isabel—
The mood of woman who can tell?
I guess the Champion of the Rock,
Victorious in the tourney shock,
That knight unknown, to whom the prize
She dealt,—had favour in her eyes;
But since our brother Nigel's fate,
Our ruin'd house and hapless state,
From worldly joy and hope estranged,
Much is the hapless mourner changed.
Perchance," here smiled the noble King,
" This tale may other musings bring.
Soon shall we know—yon mountains hide
The little convent of Saint Bride;
There, sent by Edward, she must stay,
Till fate shall give more prosperous day;
And thither will I bear thy suit,
Nor will thine advocate be mute."

XVI.

As thus they talk'd in earnest mood,
That speechless boy beside them stood.
He stoop'd his head against the mast,
And bitter sobs came thick and fast,
A grief that would not be repress'd,
But seem'd to burst his youthful breast.
His hands, against his forehead held,
As if by force his tears repell'd,
But through his fingers, long and slight,
Fast trill'd the drops of crystal bright.
Edward, who walk'd the deck apart,
First spied this conflict of the heart.
Thoughtless as brave, with bluntness kind
He sought to cheer the sorrower's mind;
By force the slender hand he drew
From those poor eyes that stream'd with
   dew.
As in his hold the stripling strove,—
('Twas a rough grasp, though meant in
   love,)
Away his tears the warrior swept,
And bade shame on him that he wept.
" I would to Heaven, thy helpless tongue
Could tell me who hath wrought thee
   wrong!
For, were he of our crew the best,
The insult went not unredress'd.
Come, cheer thee; thou art now of age
To be a warrior's gallant page;

Thou shalt be mine!—a palfrey fair
O'er hill and holt my boy shall bear,
To hold my bow in hunting grove,
Or speed on errand to my love;
For well I wot thou wilt not tell
The temple where my wishes dwell."

XVII.

Bruce interposed,—" Gay Edward, no,
This is no youth to hold thy bow,
To fill thy goblet, or to bear
Thy message light to lighter fair.
Thou art a patron all too wild
And thoughtless, for this orphan child.
See'st thou not how apart he steals,
Keeps lonely couch, and lonely meals?
Fitter by far in yon calm cell
To tend our sister Isabel,
With Father Augustin to share
The peaceful change of convent prayer,
Than wander wild adventures through,
With such a reckless guide as you."—
"Thanks, brother!" Edward answer'd
   gay,
" For the high laud thy words convey!
But we may learn some future day,
If thou or I can this poor boy
Protect the best, or best employ.
Meanwhile, our vessel nears the strand;
Launch we the boat, and seek the land."

XVIII.

To land King Robert lightly sprung,
And thrice aloud his bugle rung
With note prolong'd and varied strain,
Till bold Ben-Ghoil replied again.
Good Douglas then, and De la Haye,
Had in a glen a hart at bay,
And Lennox cheer'd the laggard hounds,
When waked that horn the greenwood
   bounds.
" It is the foe!" cried Boyd who came
In breathless haste with eye of flame,—
" It is the foe!—Each valiant lord
Fling by his bow, and grasp his sword!"—
" Not so," replied the good Lord James,
" That blast no English bugle claims.
Oft have I heard it fire the fight,
Cheer the pursuit, or stop the flight.

Dead were my heart, and deaf mine ear,
If Bruce should call, nor Douglas hear !
Each to Loch Ranza's margin spring ;
That blast was winded by the King !"29

XIX.

Fast to their mates the tidings spread,
And fast to shore the warriors sped.
Bursting from glen and greenwood tree,
High waked their loyal jubilee !
Around the royal Bruce they crowd,
And clasp'd his hands, and wept aloud.
Veterans of early fields were there,
Whose helmets press'd their hoary hair,
Whose swords and axes bore a stain
From life-blood of the red-hair'd Dane ;
And boys, whose hands scarce brook'd
    to wield
The heavy sword or bossy shield.
Men too were there, that bore the scars
Impress'd in Albyn's woful wars,
At Falkirk's fierce and fatal fight,
Teyndrum's dread rout, and Methven's
    flight ;
The might of Douglas there was seen,
There Lennox with his graceful mien ;
Kirkpatrick, Closeburn's dreaded Knight;
The Lindsay, fiery, fierce, and light ;
The Heir of murder'd De la Haye,
And Boyd the grave, and Seton gay.
Around their King regain'd they press'd,
Wept, shouted, clasp'd him to their breast,
And young and old, and serf and lord,
And he who ne'er unsheathed a sword,
And he in many a peril tried,
Alike resolved the brunt to bide,
And live or die by Bruce's side !

XX.

Oh, War ! thou hast thy fierce delight,
Thy gleams of joy, intensely bright !
Such gleams, as from thy polish'd shield
Fly dazzling o'er the battle-field !
Such transports wake, severe and high,
Amid the pealing conquest-cry ;
Scarce less, when, after battle lost,
Muster the remnants of a host,
And as each comrade's name they tell,
Who in the well-fought conflict fell,

Knitting stern brow o'er flashing eye,
Vow to avenge them or to die !—
Warriors ! — and where are warriors
    found,
If not on martial Britain's ground ?
And who, when waked with note of fire,
Love more than they the British
    lyre ?—
Know ye not,—hearts to honour dear !
That joy, deep-thrilling, stern, severe,
At which the heartstrings vibrate high,
And wake the fountains of the eye ?
And blame ye, then, the Bruce, if trace
Of tear is on his manly face,
When, scanty relics of the train
That hail'd at Scone his early reign,
This patriot band around him hung,
And to his knees and bosom clung ?—
Blame ye the Bruce ?—his brother blamed,
But shared the weakness, while ashamed,
With haughty laugh his head he turn'd,
And dash'd away the tear he scorn'd.30

XXI.

'Tis morning, and the Convent bell
Long time had ceased its matin knell,
    Within thy walls, Saint Bride !
An aged Sister sought the cell
Assign'd to Lady Isabel,
    And hurriedly she cried,
" Haste, gentle Lady, haste—there waits
A noble stranger at the gates ;
Saint Bride's poor vot'ress ne'er has seen
A Knight of such a princely mien ;
His errand, as he bade me tell,
Is with the Lady Isabel."
The princess rose,—for on her knee
Low bent she told her rosary,—
" Let him by thee his purpose teach :
I may not give a stranger speech."—
" Saint Bride forefend, thou royal Maid !"
The portress cross'd herself, and said,
" Not to be prioress might I
Debate his will, his suit deny."—
" Has earthly show then, simple fool,
Power o'er a sister of thy rule ?
And art thou, like the worldly train,
Subdued by splendours light and vain ?"—

XXII.

"No, Lady! in old eyes like mine,
Gauds have no glitter, gems no shine;
Nor grace his rank attendants vair,
One youthful page is all his train.
It is the form, the eye, the word,
The bearing of that stranger Lord;
His stature, manly, bold, and tall,
Built like a castle's battled wall,
Yet moulded in such just degrees,
His giant-strength seems lightsome ease.
Close as the tendrils of the vine
His locks upon his forehead twine,
Jet-black, save where some touch of grey
Has ta'en the youthful hue away.
Weather and war their rougher trace
Have left on that majestic face;—
But 'tis his dignity of eye!
There, if a suppliant, would I fly,
Secure, 'mid danger, wrongs, and grief,
Of sympathy, redress, relief—
That glance, if guilty, would I dread
More than the doom that spoke me
     dead!'"—
" Enough, enough," the princess cried,
"'Tis Scotland's hope, her joy, her pride!
To meaner front was ne'er assign'd
Such mastery o'er the common mind—
Bestow'd thy high designs to aid,
How long, O Heaven! how long de-
     lay'd!—
Haste, Mona, haste, to introduce
My darling brother, royal Bruce!"

XXIII.

They met like friends who part in pain,
And meet in doubtful hope again.
But when subdued that fitful swell,
The Bruce survey'd the humble cell;—
" And this is thine, poor Isabel!—
That pallet-couch, and naked wall,
For room of state, and bed of pall;
For costly robes and jewels rare,
A string of beads and zone of hair;
And for the trumpet's sprightly call
To sport or banquet, grove or hall,
The bell's grim voice divides thy care,
'Twixt hours of penitence and prayer!—

O ill for thee, my royal claim
From the First David's sainted name!
O woe for thee, that while he sought
His right, thy brother feebly fought!"—

XXIV.

" Now lay these vain regrets aside,
And be the unshaken Bruce!" she cried.
" For more I glory to have shared
The woes thy venturous spirit dared,
When raising first thy valiant band
In rescue of thy native land,
Than had fair Fortune set me down
The partner of an empire's crown.
And grieve not that on Pleasure's stream
No more I drive in giddy dream,
For Heaven the erring pilot knew,
And from the gulf the vessel drew,
Tried me with judgments stern and great,
My house's ruin, thy defeat,
Poor Nigel's death, till, tamed, I own,
My hopes are fix'd on Heaven alone;
Nor e'er shall earthly prospects win
My heart to this vain world of sin."—

XXV.

" Nay, Isabel, for such stern choice,
First wilt thou wait thy brother's voice;
Then ponder if in convent scene
No softer thoughts might intervene—
Say they were of that unknown Knight,
Victor in Woodstock's tourney-fight—
Nay, if his name such blush you owe,
Victorious o'er a fairer foe!"
Truly his penetrating eye
Hath caught that blush's passing dye,—
Like the last beam of evening thrown
On a white cloud,—just seen and gone.
Soon with calm cheek and steady eye,
The princess made composed reply:—
" I guess my brother's meaning well;
For not so silent is the cell,
But we have heard the islesmen all
Arm in thy cause at Ronald's call,
And mine eye proves that Knight unknown
And the brave Island Lord are one.—
Had then his suit been earlier made,
In his own name, with thee to aid, .
(But that his plighted faith forbade,)

I know not . . . But thy page so near?—
This is no tale for menial's ear."

XXVI.

Still stood that page, as far apart
    As the small cell would space afford;
With dizzy eye and bursting heart,
    He leant his weight on Bruce's sword,
The monarch's mantle too he bore,
And drew the fold his visage o'er.
" Fear not for him—in murderous strife,"
Said Bruce, " his warning saved my life;
Full seldom parts he from my side,
And in his silence I confide,
Since he can tell no tale again.
He is a boy of gentle strain,
And I have purposed he shall dwell
In Augustin the chaplain's cell,
And wait on thee, my Isabel.—
Mind not his tears; I've seen them flow,
As in the thaw dissolves the snow.
'Tis a kind youth, but fanciful,
Unfit against the tide to pull,
And those that with the Bruce would sail,
Must learn to strive with stream and gale.—
But forward, gentle Isabel—
My answer for Lord Ronald tell."—

XXVII.

" This answer be to Ronald given—
The heart he asks is fix'd on heaven.
My love was like a summer flower,
That wither'd in the wintry hour,
Born but of vanity and pride,
And with these sunny visions died.
If further press his suit—then say,
He should his plighted troth obey,
Troth plighted both with ring and word,
And sworn on crucifix and sword.—
Oh, shame thee, Robert! I have seen
Thou hast a woman's guardian been!
Even in extremity's dread hour,
When press'd on thee the Southern power,
And safety, to all human sight,
Was only found in rapid flight,
Thou heard'st a wretched female plain
In agony of travail-pain,
And thou didst bid thy little band
Upon the instant turn and stand,

And dare the worst the foe might do,
Rather than, like a knight untrue,
Leave to pursuers merciless
A woman in her last distress.[31]
And wilt thou now deny thine aid
To an oppress'd and injured maid.
Even plead for Ronald's perfidy,
And press his fickle faith on me?—
So witness Heaven, as true I vow,
Had I those earthly feelings now,
Which could my former bosom move
Ere taught to set its hopes above,
I'd spurn each proffer he could bring,
Till at my feet he laid the ring,
The ring and spousal contract both,
And fair acquittal of his oath,
By her who brooks his perjured scorn,
The ill-requited Maid of Lorn!"

XXVIII.

With sudden impulse forward sprung
The page, and on her neck he hung;
Then, recollected instantly,
His head he stoop'd, and bent his knee,
Kiss'd twice the hand of Isabel,
Arose, and sudden left the cell.—
The princess, loosen'd from his hold,
Blush'd angry at his bearing bold;
    But good King Robert cried,
" Chafe not—by signs he speaks his
        mind,
He heard the plan my care design'd,
    Nor could his transports hide.—
But, sister, now bethink thee well;
No easy choice the convent cell;
Trust, I shall play no tyrant part,
Either to force thy hand or heart,
Or suffer that Lord Ronald scorn,
Or wrong for thee, the Maid of Lorn.
But think,—not long the time has been,
That thou wert wont to sigh unseen,
And wouldst the ditties best approve,
That told some lay of hapless love.
Now are thy wishes in thy power,
And thou art bent on cloister bower!
O! if our Edward knew the change,
How would his busy satire range,
With many a sarcasm varied still
On woman's wish, and woman's will!"—

XXIX.

" Brother, I well believe," she said,
" Even so would Edward's part be play'd.
Kindly in heart, in word severe,
A foe to thought, and grief, and fear,
He holds his humour uncontroll'd;
But thou art of another mould.
Say then to Ronald, as I say,
Unless before my feet he lay
The ring which bound the faith he swore,
By Edith freely yielded o'er,
He moves his suit to me no more.
Nor do I promise, even if now
He stood absolved of spousal vow,
That I would change my purpose made
To shelter me in holy shade.—
Brother, for little space, farewell !
To other duties warns the bell !"—

XXX.

" Lost to the world," King Robert said,
When he had left the royal maid,
" Lost to the world by lot severe,
O what a gem lies buried here,
Nipp'd by misfortune's cruel frost,
The buds of fair affection lost !—
But what have I with love to do ?
Far sterner cares my lot pursue.
—Pent in this isle we may not lie,
Nor would it long our wants supply.
Right opposite, the mainland towers
Of my own Turnberry court our powers—
—Might not my father's beadsman hoar,
Cuthbert, who dwells upon the shore,
Kindle a signal-flame, to show
The time propitious for the blow ?
It shall be so—some friend shall bear
Our mandate with despatch and care;
—Edward shall find the messenger.
That fortress ours, the island fleet
May on the coast of Carrick meet.—
O Scotland ! shall it e'er be mine
To wreak thy wrongs in battle-line,
To raise my victor-head, and see
Thy hills, thy dales, thy people free,—
That glance of bliss is all I crave,
Betwixt my labours and my grave !"
Then down the hill he slowly went,
Oft pausing on the steep descent,

And reach'd the spot where his bold train
Held rustic camp upon the plain.

CANTO FIFTH.

I.

On fair Loch-Ranza stream'd the early
    day,
Thin wreaths of cottage-smoke are
    upward curl'd
From the lone hamlet, which her inland
    bay
And circling mountains sever from the
    world.
And there the fisherman his sail unfurl'd,
The goat-herd drove his kids to steep
    Ben-Ghoil,
Before the hut the dame her spindle
    twirl'd,
Courting the sunbeam as she plied her
    toil,—
For, wake where'er he may, Man wakes
    to care and coil.

But other duties call'd each convent
    maid,
Roused by the summons of the moss-
    grown bell;
Sung were the matins, and the mass
    was said,
And every sister sought her separate
    cell,
Such was the rule, her rosary to tell.
And Isabel has knelt in lonely prayer;
The sunbeam, through the narrow
    lattice, fell
Upon the snowy neck and long dark
    hair,
As stoop'd her gentle head in meek
    devotion there.

II.

She raised her eyes, that duty done,
When glanced upon the pavement-stone,
Gemm'd and enchased, a golden ring,
Bound to a scroll with silken string,

With few brief words inscribed to tell,
" This for the Lady Isabel."
Within, the writing further bore,—
" 'Twas with this ring his plight he swore,
With this his promise I restore;
To her who can the heart command,
Well may I yield the plighted hand.
And O! for better fortune born,
Grudge not a passing sigh to mourn
Her who was Edith once of Lorn!"
One single flash of glad surprise
Just glanced from Isabel's dark eyes,
But vanish'd in the blush of shame,
That, as its penance, instant came.
" O thought unworthy of my race!
Selfish, ungenerous, mean, and base,
A moment's throb of joy to own,
That rose upon her hopes o'erthrown!—
Thou pledge of vows too well believed,
Of man ingrate and maid deceived,
Think not thy lustre here shall gain
Another heart to hope in vain!
For thou shalt rest, thou tempting gaud,
Where worldly thoughts are overawed,
And worldly splendours sink debased."
Then by the cross the ring she placed.

III.

Next rose the thought,—its owner far,
How came it here through bolt and
  bar?—
But the dim lattice is ajar.—
She looks abroad, the morning dew
A light short step had brush'd anew,
  And there were foot-prints seen
On the carved buttress rising still,
Till on the mossy window-sill,
  Their track effaced the green.
The ivy twigs were torn and fray'd,
As if some climber's steps to aid.—
But who the hardy messenger,
Whose venturous path these signs infer?—
" Strange doubts are mine!—Mona, draw
  nigh;
—Nought 'scapes old Mona's curious eye—
What strangers, gentle mother, say,
Have sought these holy walls to-day?"
" None, Lady, none of note or name;
Only your brother's foot-page came,

At peep of dawn—I pray'd him pass
To chapel where they said the mass;
But like an arrow he shot by,
And tears seem'd bursting from his eye."

IV.

The truth at once on Isabel,
As darted by a sunbeam, fell,—
" 'Tis Edith's self! — her speechless
  woe,
Her form, her looks, the secret show!
—Instant, good Mona, to the bay,
And to my royal brother say,
I do conjure him seek my cell,
With that mute page he loves so well."—
" What! know'st thou not his warlike
  host
At break of day has left our coast?
My old eyes saw them from the tower.
At eve they couch'd in greenwood bower,
At dawn a bugle signal, made
By their bold Lord, their ranks array'd;
Up sprung the spears through bush and
  tree,
No time for benedicite!
Like deer, that, rousing from their lair,
Just shake the dewdrops from their hair,
And toss their armed crests aloft,
Such matins theirs!"—" Good mother,
  soft—
Where does my brother bend his way?"
" As I have heard, for Brodick-Bay,
Across the isle—of barks a score
Lie there, 'tis said, to waft them o'er,
On sudden news, to Carrick-shore."—
" If such their purpose, deep the need,"
Said anxious Isabel, " of speed!
Call Father Augustin, good dame."
The nun obey'd, the Father came.

V.

" Kind Father, hie without delay,
Across the hills to Brodick-Bay.
This message to the Bruce be given;
I pray him, by his hopes of Heaven,
That, till he speak with me, he stay!—
Or, if his haste brook no delay,
That he deliver, on my suit,
Into thy charge that stripling mute.

Thus prays his sister Isabel,
For causes more than she may tell—
Away, good father! and take heed,
That life and death are on thy speed."
His cowl the good old priest did on,
Took his piked staff and sandall'd shoon,
And, like a palmer bent by eld,
O'er moss and moor his journey held.

VI.

Heavy and dull the foot of age,
And rugged was the pilgrimage;
But none was there beside, whose care
Might such important message bear.
Through birchen copse he wander'd slow,
Stunted and sapless, thin and low;
By many a mountain stream he pass'd,
From the tall cliffs in tumult cast,
Dashing to foam their waters dun,
And sparkling in the summer sun.
Round his grey head the wild curlew
In many a fearless circle flew.
O'er chasms he pass'd, where fractures wide
Craved wary eye and ample stride;[32]
He cross'd his brow beside the stone
Where Druids erst heard victims groan,
And at the cairns upon the wild,
O'er many a heathen hero piled,
He breathed a timid prayer for those
Who died ere Shiloh's sun arose.
Beside Macfarlane's Cross he staid,
There told his hours within the shade,
And at the stream his thirst allay'd.
Thence onward journeying, slowly still,
As evening closed he reach'd the hill,
Where, rising through the woodland green,
Old Brodick's gothic towers were seen,
From Hastings, late their English lord,
Douglas had won them by the sword.[33]
The sun that sunk behind the isle,
Now tinged them with a parting smile.

VII.

But though the beams of light decay,
'Twas bustle all in Brodick-Bay.
The Bruce's followers crowd the shore,
And boats and barges some unmoor,
Some raise the sail, some seize the oar;
Their eyes oft turn'd where glimmer'd far
What might have seem'd an early star
On heaven's blue arch, save that its light
Was all too flickering, fierce, and bright.
Far distant in the south, the ray
Shone pale amid retiring day,
But as, on Carrick shore,
Dim seen in outline faintly blue,
The shades of evening closer drew,
It kindled more and more.
The monk's slow steps now press the sands,
And now amid a scene he stands,
Full strange to churchman's eye;
Warriors, who, arming for the fight,
Rivet and clasp their harness light,
And twinkling spears, and axes bright,
And helmets flashing high.
Oft, too, with unaccustom'd ears,
A language much unmeet he hears,[34]
While, hastening all on board,
As stormy as the swelling surge
That mix'd its roar, the leaders urge
Their followers to the ocean verge,
With many a haughty word.

VIII.

Through that wild throng the Father pass'd,
And reach'd the Royal Bruce at last.
He leant against a stranded boat,
That the approaching tide must float,
And counted every rippling wave,
As higher yet her sides they lave,
And oft the distant fire he eyed,
And closer yet his hauberk tied,
And loosen'd in its sheath his brand.
Edward and Lennox were at hand,
Douglas and Ronald had the care
The soldiers to the barks to share.—
The Monk approach'd and homage paid;
" And art thou come," King Robert said,
" So far to bless us ere we part?"—
—" My Liege, and with a loyal heart!—
But other charge I have to tell,"—
And spoke the hest of Isabel,
—" Now by Saint Giles," the monarch cried,
" This moves me much!—this morning tide,

I sent the stripling to Saint Bride,
With my commandment there to bide."—
—" Thither he came the portress show'd,
But there, my Liege, made brief abode."—

IX.

" 'Twas I," said Edward, "found employ
Of nobler import for the boy.
Deep pondering in my anxious mind,
A fitting messenger to find,
To bear thy written mandate o'er
To Cuthbert on the Carrick shore,
I chanced, at early dawn, to pass
The chapel gate to snatch a mass.
I found the stripling on a tomb
Low-seated, weeping for the doom
That gave his youth to convent gloom.
I told my purpose, and his eyes
Flash'd joyful at the glad surprise.
He bounded to the skiff, the sail
Was spread before a prosperous gale,
And well my charge he hath obey'd;
For, see! the ruddy signal made,
That Clifford, with his merry-men all,
Guards carelessly our father's hall."—

X.

" O wild of thought, and hard of heart!"
Answer'd the Monarch, " on a part
Of such deep danger to employ
A mute, an orphan, and a boy!
Unfit for flight, unfit for strife,
Without a tongue to plead for life!
Now, were my right restored by Heaven,
Edward, my crown I would have given,
Ere, thrust on such adventure wild,
I perill'd thus the helpless child."—
—Offended half, and half submiss,
" Brother and Liege, of blame like this,"
Edward replied, " I little dream'd.
A stranger messenger, I deem'd,
Might safest seek the beadsman's cell,
Where all thy squires are known so well.
Noteless his presence, sharp his sense,
His imperfection his defence.
If seen, none can his errand guess;
If ta'en, his words no tale express—
Methinks, too, yonder beacon's shine
Might expiate greater fault than mine."—

" Rash," said King Robert, " was the
deed—
But it is done.—Embark with speed!—
Good Father, say to Isabel
How this unhappy chance befell;
If well we thrive on yonder shore,
Soon shall my care her page restore.
Our greeting to our sister bear,
And think of us in mass and prayer."—

XI.

" Aye!" said the Priest, " while this poor
hand
Can chalice raise or cross command,
While my old voice has accents' use,
Can Augustin forget the Bruce!"
Then to his side Lord Ronald press'd,
And whisper'd, " Bear thou this request,
That when by Bruce's side I fight,
For Scotland's crown and freedom's right,
The princess grace her knight to bear
Some token of her favouring care;
It shall be shown where England's best
May shrink to see it on my crest.
And for the boy—since weightier care
For royal Bruce the times prepare,
The helpless youth is Ronald's charge,
His couch my plaid, his fence my targe."
He ceased; for many an eager hand
Had urged the barges from the strand.
Their number was a score and ten,
They bore thrice threescore chosen men.
With such small force did Bruce at last
The die for death or empire cast!

XII.

Now on the darkening main afloat,
Ready and mann'd rocks every boat,
Beneath their oars the ocean's might
Was dash'd to sparks of glimmering light;
Faint and more faint, as off they bore,
Their armour glanced against the shore,
And, mingled with the dashing tide,
Their murmuring voices distant died.—
" God speed them!" said the Priest, as dark
On distant billows glides each bark;
" O Heaven! when swords for freedom
shine,
And monarch's right, the cause is thine!

Edge doubly every patriot blow!
Beat down the banners of the foe!
And be it to the nations known,
That Victory is from God alone!"
As up the hill his path he drew,
He turn'd his blessings to renew,
Oft turn'd, till on the darken'd coast
All traces of their course were lost;
Then slowly bent to Brodick tower,
To shelter for the evening hour.

XIII.

In night the fairy prospects sink,
Where Cumray's isles with verdant link
Close the fair entrance of the Clyde;
The woods of Bute, no more descried,
Are gone—and on the placid sea
The rowers ply their task with glee,
While hands that knightly lances bore
Impatient aid the labouring oar.
The half-faced moon shone dim and pale,
And glanced against the whiten'd sail;
But on that ruddy beacon-light
Each steersman kept the helm aright,
And oft, for such the King's command,
That all at once might reach the strand,
From boat to boat loud shout and hail
Warn'd them to crowd or slacken sail.
South and by west the armada bore,
And near at length the Carrick shore.
As less and less the distance grows,
High and more high the beacon rose;
The light, that seem'd a twinkling star,
Now blazed portentous, fierce, and far.
Dark-red the heaven above it glow'd,
Dark-red the sea beneath it flow'd,
Red rose the rocks on ocean's brim,
In blood-red light her islets swim;
Wild scream the dazzled sea-fowl gave,
Dropp'd from their crags on plashing
    wave.
The deer to distant covert drew,
The black-cock deem'd it day, and crew.
Like some tall castle given to flame,
O'er half the land the lustre came.
"Now, good my Liege, and brother sage,
What think ye of mine elfin page?"—
"Row on!" the noble King replied,
"We'll learn the truth whate'er betide;

Yet sure the beadsman and the child
Could ne'er have waked that beacon wild.'

XIV.

With that the boats approach'd the land,
But Edward's grounded on the sand;
The eager Knight leap'd in the sea
Waist-deep, and first on shore was he,
Though every barge's hardy band
Contended which should gain the land,
When that strange light, which, seen afar,
Seem'd steady as the polar star,
Now, like a prophet's fiery chair,
Seem'd travelling the realms of air.
Wide o'er the sky the splendour glows,
As that portentous meteor rose;
Helm, axe, and falchion glitter'd bright,
And in the red and dusky light
His comrade's face each warrior saw,
Nor marvell'd it was pale with awe.
Then high in air the beams were lost,
And darkness sunk upon the coast.—
Ronald to Heaven a prayer address'd,
And Douglas cross'd his dauntless breast;
"Saint James protect us!" Lennox cried,
But reckless Edward spoke aside,
"Deem'st thou, Kirkpatrick, in that flame,
Red Comyn's angry spirit came,
Or would thy dauntless heart endure
Once more to make assurance sure?"—
"Hush!" said the Bruce, "we soon shall
    know,
If this be sorcerer's empty show,
Or stratagem of southern foe.
The moon shines out—upon the sand
Let every leader rank his band."

XV.

Faintly the moon's pale beams supply
That ruddy light's unnatural dye;
The dubious cold reflection lay
On the wet sands and quiet bay.
Beneath the rocks King Robert drew
His scatter'd files to order due,
Till shield compact and serried spear
In the cool light shone blue and clear.
Then down a path that sought the tide,
That speechless page was seen to glide;
He knelt him lowly on the sand,
And gave a scroll to Robert's hand,

" A torch," the Monarch cried, " What,
    ho !
Now shall we Cuthbert's tidings know."
But evil news the letters bare,
The Clifford's force was strong and ware,
Augmented, too, that very morn,
By mountaineers who came with Lorn.
Long harrow'd by oppressor's hand,
Courage and faith had fled the land,
And over Carrick, dark and deep,
Had sunk dejection's iron sleep.—
Cuthbert had seen that beacon-flame,
Unwitting from what source it came.
Doubtful of perilous event,
Edward's mute messenger he sent,
If Bruce deceived should venture o'er,
To warn him from the fatal shore.

XVI.

As round the torch the leaders crowd,
Bruce read these chilling news aloud.
" What council, nobles, have we now ?—
To ambush us in greenwood bough,
And take the chance which fate may send
To bring our enterprise to end,
Or shall we turn us to the main
As exiles, and embark again ?"—
Answer'd fierce Edward, " Hap what may,
In Carrick, Carrick's Lord must stay.
I would not minstrels told the tale,
Wildfire or meteor made us quail."—
Answer'd the Douglas, " If my Liege
May win yon walls by storm or siege,
Then were each brave and patriot heart
Kindled of new for loyal part."—
Answer'd Lord Ronald, " Not for shame
Would I that aged Torquil came,
And found, for all our empty boast,
Without a blow we fled the coast.
I will not credit that this land,
So famed for warlike heart and hand,
The nurse of Wallace and of Bruce,
Will long with tyrants hold a truce."—
" Prove we our fate—the brunt we'll bide !"
So Boyd and Haye and Lennox cried;
So said, so vow'd, the leaders all;
So Bruce resolved : " And in my hall
Since the Bold Southern make their home,
The hour of payment soon shall come,

When with a rough and rugged host
Clifford may reckon to his cost.
Meantime, through well-known bosk and
    dell,
I'll lead where we may shelter well."

XVII.

Now ask you whence that wondrous light,
Whose fairy glow beguiled their sight !—
It ne'er was known [35]—yet grey-hair'd eld
A superstitious credence held,
That never did a mortal hand
Wake its broad glare on Carrick strand;
Nay, and that on the self-same night
When Bruce cross'd o'er, still gleams the
    light.
Yearly it gleams o'er mount and moor,
And glittering wave and crimson'd shore—
But whether beam celestial, lent
By Heaven to aid the King's descent,
Or fire hell-kindled from beneath,
To lure him to defeat and death,
Or were it but some meteor strange,
Of such as oft through midnight range,
Startling the traveller late and lone,
I know not—and it ne'er was known.

XVIII.

Now up the rocky pass they drew,
And Ronald, to his promise true,
Still made his arm the stripling's stay,
To aid him on the rugged way.
" Now cheer thee, simple Amadine!
Why throbs that silly heart of thine ?"—
—That name the pirates to their slave
(In Gaelic 'tis the Changeling) gave—
" Dost thou not rest thee on my arm ?
Do not my plaid-folds hold thee warm ?
Hath not the wild bull's treble hide
This targe for thee and me supplied ?
Is not Clan-Colla's sword of steel ?
And, trembler, can'st thou terror feel !
Cheer thee, and still that throbbing heart;
From Ronald's guard thou shalt not part."
—O ! many a shaft, at random sent,
Finds mark the archer little meant !
And many a word, at random spoken,
May soothe or wound a heart that's
    broken !

Half soothed, half grieved, half terrified,
Close drew the page to Ronald's side;
A wild delirious thrill of joy
Was in that hour of agony,
As up the steepy pass he strove,
Fear, toil, and sorrow, lost in love!

XIX.

The barrier of that iron shore,
The rock's steep ledge, is now climb'd o'er;
And from the castle's distant wall,
From tower to tower the warders call:
The sound swings over land and sea,
And marks a watchful enemy.—
They gain'd the Chase, a wide domain
Left for the Castle's silvan reign,
(Seek not the scene—the axe, the plough,
The boor's dull fence, have marr'd it now,)
But then, soft swept in velvet green
The plain with many a glade between,
Whose tangled alleys far invade
The depth of the brown forest shade.
Here the tall fern obscured the lawn,
Fair shelter for the sportive fawn;
There, tufted close with copsewood green,
Was many a swelling hillock seen;
And all around was verdure meet
For pressure of the fairies' feet.
The glossy holly loved the park,
The yew-tree lent its shadow dark,
And many an old oak, worn and bare,
With all its shiver'd boughs, was there.
Lovely between, the moonbeams fell
On lawn and hillock, glade and dell.
The gallant Monarch sigh'd to see
These glades so loved in childhood free.
Bethinking that, as outlaw now,
He ranged beneath the forest bough.

XX.

Fast o'er the moonlight Chase they sped.
Well knew the band that measured tread,
When, in retreat or in advance,
The serried warriors move at once;
And evil were the luck, if dawn
Descried them on the open lawn.
Copses they traverse, brooks they cross,
Strain up the bank and o'er the moss.

From the exhausted page's brow
Cold drops of toil are streaming now;
With effort faint and lengthen'd pause,
His weary step the stripling draws.
"Nay, droop not yet!" the warrior said;
"Come, let me give thee ease and aid!
Strong are mine arms, and little care
A weight so slight as thine to bear.—
What! wilt thou not?—capricious boy!
Then thine own limbs and strength employ.
Pass but this night, and pass thy care,
I'll place thee with a lady fair,
Where thou shalt tune thy lute to tell
How Ronald loves fair Isabel!"
Worn out, dishearten'd, and dismay'd,
Here Amadine let go the plaid:
His trembling limbs their aid refuse,
He sunk among the midnight dews!

XXI.

What may be done?—the night is gone—
The Bruce's band moves swiftly on—
Eternal shame, if at the brunt
Lord Ronald grace not battle's front!—
"See yonder oak, within whose trunk
Decay a darken'd cell hath sunk;
Enter, and rest thee there a space,
Wrap in my plaid thy limbs, thy face.
I will not be, believe me, far;
But must not quit the ranks of war.
Well will I mark the bosky bourne,
And soon, to guard thee hence, return.—
Nay, weep not so, thou simple boy!
But sleep in peace, and wake in joy."
In silvan lodging close bestow'd,
He placed the page, and onward strode
With strength put forth, o'er moss and
       brook,
And soon the marching band o'ertook.

XXII.

Thus strangely left, long sobb'd and wept
The page, till, wearied out, he slept—
A rough voice waked his dream—"Nay,
       here,
Here by this thicket, passed the deer—
Beneath that oak old Ryno staid—
What have we here?—a Scottish plaid,
And in its folds a stripling laid?—

Come forth ! thy name and business tell !—
What, silent ?—then I guess thee well,
The spy that sought old Cuthbert's cell,
Wafted from Arran yester morn—
Come, comrades, we will straight return.
Our Lord may choose the rack should teach
To this young lurcher use of speech.
Thy bow-string till I bind him fast."—
" Nay, but he weeps and stands aghast;
Unbound we'll lead him, fear it not ;
'Tis a fair stripling, though a Scot."
The hunters to the castle sped,
And there the hapless captive led.

XXIII.

Stout Clifford in the castle-court
Prepared him for the morning sport;
And now with Lorn held deep discourse,
Now gave command for hound and horse.
War-steeds and palfreys paw'd the ground,
And many a deer-dog howl'd around.
To Amadine, Lorn's well-known word
Replying to that Southern Lord,
Mix'd with this clanging din, might seem
The phantasm of a fever'd dream.
The tone upon his ringing ears
Came like the sounds which fancy hears,
When in rude waves or roaring winds
Some words of woe the muser finds,
Until more loudly and more near,
Their speech arrests the page's ear.

XXIV.

" And was she thus," said Clifford, " lost ?
The priest should rue it to his cost !
What says the monk ?"—" The holy Sire
Owns, that in masquer's quaint attire
She sought his skiff, disguised, unknown
To all except to him alone.
But, says the priest, a bark from Lorn
Laid them aboard that very morn,
And pirates seized her for their prey.
He proffer'd ransom-gold to pay,
And they agreed—but ere told o'er,
The winds blow loud, the billows roar;
They sever'd, and they met no more.
He deems—such tempest vex'd the coast—
Ship, crew, and fugitive, were lost.

So let it be, with the disgrace
And scandal of her lofty race !
Thrice better she had ne'er been born,
Than brought her infamy on Lorn !"

XXV.

Lord Clifford now the captive spied ;—
" Whom, Herbert, hast thou there ?" he cried.
" A spy we seized within the Chase,
A hollow oak his lurking place "—
" What tidings can the youth afford ?"—
" He plays the mute."—" Then noose a cord—
Unless brave Lorn reverse the doom
For his plaid's sake."—" Clan-Colla's loom,"
Said Lorn, whose careless glances trace
Rather the vesture than the face,
" Clan-Colla's dames such tartans twine;
Wearer nor plaid claims care of mine.
Give him, if my advice you crave,
His own scathed oak ; and let him wave
In air, unless, by terror wrung,
A frank confession find his tongue.—
Nor shall he die without his rite;
—Thou, Angus Roy, attend the sight,
And give Clan-Colla's dirge thy breath,
As they convey him to his death."—
" O brother ! cruel to the last !"
Through the poor captive's bosom pass'd
The thought, but, to his purpose true,
He said not, though he sigh'd, " Adieu !"

XXVI.

And will he keep his purpose still,
In sight of that last closing ill,
When one poor breath, one single word,
May freedom, safety, life afford ?
Can he resist the instinctive call,
For life that bids us barter all?—
Love, strong as death, his heart hath steel'd,
His nerves hath strung—he will not yield!
Since that poor breath, that little word,
May yield Lord Ronald to the sword.—
Clan-Colla's dirge is pealing wide,
The griesly headsman's by his side;

Along the greenwood Chase they bend,
And now their march has ghastly end!
That old and shatter'd oak beneath,
They destine for the place of death.
—What thoughts are his, while all in vain
His eye for aid explores the plain?
What thoughts, while, with a dizzy ear,
He hears the death-prayer mutter'd near?
And must he die such death accurst,
Or will that bosom-secret burst?
Cold on his brow breaks terror's dew,
His trembling lips are livid blue;
The agony of parting life
Has nought to match that moment's strife!

XXVII.

But other witnesses are nigh,
Who mock at fear, and death defy!
Soon as the dire lament was play'd,
It waked the lurking ambuscade.
The Island Lord look'd forth, and spied
The cause, and loud in fury cried,
" By Heaven, they lead the page to die,
And mock me in his agony!
They shall abye it!"—On his arm
Bruce laid strong grasp, " They shall not harm
A ringlet of the stripling's hair;
But, till I give the word, forbear.
—Douglas, lead fifty of our force
Up yonder hollow water-course,
And couch thee midway on the wold,
Between the flyers and their hold:
A spear above the copse display'd,
Be signal of the ambush made.
— Edward, with forty spearmen, straight
Through yonder copse approach the gate,
And, when thou hear'st the battle-din,
Rush forward, and the passage win,
Secure the drawbridge—storm the port,
And man and guard the castle-court.—
The rest move slowly forth with me,
In shelter of the forest-tree,
Till Douglas at his post I see."

XXVIII.

Like war-dogs eager to rush on,
Compell'd to wait the signal blown,
Hid, and scarce hid, by greenwood bough,
Trembling with rage, stands Ronald now,
And in his grasp his sword gleams blue,
Soon to be dyed with deadlier hue.—
Meanwhile the Bruce, with steady eye,
Sees the dark death-train moving by,
And, heedful, measures oft the space
The Douglas and his band must trace,
Ere they can reach their destined ground.
Now sinks the dirge's wailing sound,
Now cluster round the direful tree
That slow and solemn company,
While hymn mistuned and mutter'd prayer
The victim for his fate prepare.—
What glances o'er the greenwood shade?
The spear that marks the ambuscade.
" Now, noble Chief! I leave thee loose;
Upon them, Ronald!" said the Bruce.

XXIX.

" The Bruce, the Bruce!" to well-known cry
His native rocks and woods reply.
" The Bruce, the Bruce!" in that dread word
The knell of hundred deaths was heard.
The astonish'd Southern gazed at first,
Where the wild tempest was to burst,
That waked in that presaging name.
Before, behind, around it came!
Half-arm'd, surprised on every side
Hemm'd in, hew'd down, they bled and died.
Deep in the ring the Bruce engaged,
And fierce Clan-Colla's broadsword raged!
Full soon the few who fought were sped,
Nor better was their lot who fled,
And met, 'mid terror's wild career,
The Douglas's redoubted spear!
Two hundred yeomen on that morn
The castle left, and none return.

XXX.

Not on their flight press'd Ronald's brand,
A gentler duty claim'd his hand.
He raised the page, where on the plain
His fear had sunk him with the slain:
And twice, that morn, surprise well near
Betray'd the secret kept by fear;

Once, when, with life returning, came
To the boy's lip Lord Ronald's name,
And hardly recollection drown'd
The accents in a murmuring sound;
And once, when scarce he could resist
The Chieftain's care to loose the vest,
Drawn tightly o'er his labouring breast.
But then the Bruce's bugle blew,
For martial work was yet to do.

XXXI.

A harder task fierce Edward waits,
Ere signal given, the castle gates
    His fury had assail'd;
Such was his wonted reckless mood,
Yet desperate valour oft made good,
Even by its daring, venture rude,
    Where prudence might have fail'd.
Upon the bridge his strength he threw,
And struck the iron chain in two,
    By which its planks arose;
The warder next his axe's edge
Struck down upon the threshold ledge,
'Twixt door and post a ghastly wedge!
    The gate they may not close.
Well fought the Southern in the fray,
Clifford and Lorn fought well that day,
But stubborn Edward forced his way
    Against a hundred foes.
Loud came the cry, "The Bruce, the
    Bruce!"
No hope or in defence or truce,
    Fresh combatants pour in;
Mad with success, and drunk with gore,
They drive the struggling foe before,
    And ward on ward they win.
Unsparing was the vengeful sword,
And limbs were lopp'd and life-blood
    pour'd,
The cry of death and conflict roar'd,
    And fearful was the din!
The startling horses plunged and flung,
Clamour'd the dogs till turrets rung,
    Nor sunk the fearful cry,
Till not a foeman was there found
Alive, save those who on the ground
    Groan'd in their agony!

XXXII.

The valiant Clifford is no more:
On Ronald's broadsword stream'd his gore
But better hap had he of Lorn,
Who, by the foemen backward borne,
Yet gain'd with slender train the port,
Where lay his bark beneath the fort,
    And cut the cable loose.
Short were his shrift in that debate,
That hour of fury and of fate,
    If Lorn encounter'd Bruce!
Then long and loud the victor shout
From turret and from tower rung out,
    The rugged vaults replied;
And from the donjon tower on high,
The men of Carrick may descry
Saint Andrew's cross, in blazonry
    Of silver, waving wide!

XXXIII.

The Bruce hath won his father's hall![36]
—"Welcome, brave friends and comrades
    all,
    Welcome to mirth and joy!
The first, the last, is welcome here,
From lord and chieftain, prince and peer,
    To this poor speechless boy.
Great God! once more my sire's abode
Is mine—behold the floor I trode
    In tottering infancy!
And there the vaulted arch, whose sound
Echoed my joyous shout and bound
In boyhood, and that rung around
    To youth's unthinking glee!
O first, to thee, all-gracious Heaven,
Then to my friends, my thanks be
    given!"—
He paused a space, his brow he cross'd—
Then on the board his sword he toss'd,
Yet steaming hot; with Southern gore
From hilt to point 'twas crimson'd o'er.

XXXIV.

"Bring here," he said, "the mazers four,*
My noble fathers loved of yore.

---

* *The mazers four*, large drinking cups, or
goblets.

Thrice let them circle round the board,
The pledge, fair Scotland's rights restored!
And he whose lip shall touch the wine,
Without a vow as true as mine,
To hold both lands and life at nought,
Until her freedom shall be bought,—
Be brand of a disloyal Scot,
And lasting infamy his lot!
Sit, gentle friends! our hour of glee
Is brief, we'll spend it joyously!
Blithest of all the sun's bright beams,
When betwixt storm and storm he gleams.
Well is our country's work begun,
But more, far more, must yet be done.
Speed messengers the country through;
Arouse old friends, and gather new;
Warn Lanark's knights to gird their mail,
Rouse the brave sons of Teviotdale,
Let Ettrick's archers sharp their darts,
The fairest forms, the truest hearts!
Call all, call all! from Reedswair-Path!
To the wild confines of Cape-Wrath;
Wide let the news through Scotland ring,—
The Northern Eagle claps his wing!"

CANTO SIXTH.

I.

O who, that shared them, ever shall
    forget
The emotions of the spirit-rousing time,
When breathless in the mart the
    couriers met,
Early and late, at evening and at prime;
When the loud cannon and the merry
    chime
Hail'd news on news, as field on field
    was won!
When Hope, long doubtful, soar'd at
    length sublime,
And our glad eyes, awake as day begun,
Watch'd Joy's broad banner rise, to meet
    the rising sun!

O these were hours, when thrilling joy
    repaid
A long, long course of darkness, doubts,
    and fears!

The heart-sick faintness of the hope
    delay'd,
The waste, the woe, the bloodshed, and
    the tears,
That track'd with terror twenty rolling
    years,
All was forgot in that blithe jubilee!
Her downcast eye even pale Affliction
    rears,
To sigh a thankful prayer, amid the glee,
That hail'd the Despot's fall, and peace
    and liberty!

Such news o'er Scotland's hills trium-
    phant rode,
When 'gainst the invaders turn'd the
    battle's scale,
When, Bruce's banner had victorious
    flow'd
O'er Loudoun's mountain, and in Ury's
    vale;[37]
When English blood oft deluged
    Douglas-dale,[38]
And fiery Edward routed stout St.
    John,[39]
When Randolph's war-cry swell'd the
    southern gale,[40]
And many a fortress, town, and tower,
    was won,
And Fame still sounded forth fresh deeds
    of glory done.

II.

Blithe tidings flew from baron's tower,
To peasant's cot, to forest bower,
And waked the solitary cell,
Where lone Saint Bride's recluses dwell.
Princess no more, fair Isabel,
    A vot'ress of the order now,
Say, did the rule that bid thee wear
Dim veil and woollen scapulaire,
And reft thy locks of dark-brown hair,
    That stern and rigid vow,
Did it condemn the transport high,
Which glisten'd in thy watery eye,
When minstrel or when palmer told
Each fresh exploit of Bruce the bold?—
And whose the lovely form, that shares
Thy anxious hopes, thy fears, thy prayers?

No sister she of convent shade;
So say these locks in lengthen'd braid,
So say the blushes and the sighs,
The tremors that unbidden rise,
When, mingled with the Bruce's fame,
The brave Lord Ronald's praises came.

III.

Believe, his father's castle won,
And his bold enterprise begun,
That Bruce's earliest cares restore
The speechless page to Arran's shore:
Nor think that long the quaint disguise
Conceal'd her from a sister's eyes;
And sister-like in love they dwell
In that lone convent's silent cell.
There Bruce's slow assent allows
Fair Isabel the veil and vows;
And there, her sex's dress regain'd,
The lovely Maid of Lorn remain'd,
Unnamed, unknown, while Scotland far
Resounded with the din of war;
And many a month, and many a day.
In calm seclusion wore away.

IV.

These days, these months, to years had
   worn,
When tidings of high weight were borne
  To that lone island's shore;
Of all the Scottish conquests made
By the First Edward's ruthless blade,
  His son retain'd no more,
Northward of Tweed, but Stirling's
   towers,
Beleaguer'd by King Robert's powers;
  And they took term of truce,[41]
If England's King should not relieve
The siege ere John the Baptist's eve,
  To yield them to the Bruce.
England was roused—on every side
Courier and post and herald hied,
  To summon prince and peer,
At Berwick-bounds to meet their Liege,
Prepared to raise fair Stirling's siege,
  With buckler, brand, and spear.
The term was nigh—they muster'd fast,
By beacon and by bugle-blast
  Forth marshall'd for the field;

There rode each knight of noble name,
There England's hardy archers came,
The land they trode seem'd all on flame,
  With banner, blade, and shield!
And not famed England's powers alone,
Renown'd in arms, the summons own;
  For Neustria's knights obey'd,
Gascogne hath lent her horsemen good,
And Cambria, but of late subdued,
Sent forth her mountain multitude,[42]
And Connoght pour'd from waste and
  wood
Her hundred tribes, whose sceptre rude
  Dark Eth O'Connor sway'd.[43]

V

Right to devoted Caledon
The storm of war rolls slowly on,
  With menace deep and dread:
So the dark clouds, with gathering power,
Suspend awhile the threaten'd shower,
Till every peak and summit lower
  Round the pale pilgrim's head
Not with such pilgrim's startled eye
King Robert mark'd the tempest nigh!
  Resolved the brunt to bide,
His royal summons warn'd the land,
That all who own'd their King's com
   mand
Should instant take the spear and brand,
  To combat at his side.
O who may tell the sons of fame,
That at King Robert's bidding came,
  To battle for the right!
From Cheviot to the shores of Ross,
From Solway-Sands to Marshal's-Moss,
  All boun'd them for the fight.
Such news the royal courier tells,
Who came to rouse dark Arran's dells;
But farther tidings must the ear
Of Isabel in secret hear.
These in her cloister walk, next morn,
Thus shared she with the Maid of Lorn.

VI.

" My Edith, can I tell how dear
Our intercourse of hearts sincere
  Hath been to Isabel ?—

Judge then the sorrow or my heart,
When I must say the words, We part!
  The cheerless convent-cell
Was not, sweet maiden, made for thee;
Go thou where thy vocation free
  On happier fortunes fell.
Nor, Edith, judge thyself betray'd
Though Robert knows that Lorn's high
    Maid
And his poor silent page were one.
Versed in the fickle heart of man,
Earnest and anxious hath he look'd
How Ronald's heart the message brook'd
That gave him, with her last farewell,
The charge of Sister Isabel,
To think upon thy better right,
And keep the faith his promise plight.
Forgive him for thy sister's sake,
At first if vain repinings wake—
  Long since that mood is gone:
Now dwells he on thy juster claims,
And oft his breach of faith he blames—
  Forgive him for thine own!"—

VII.

" No! never to Lord Ronald's bower
Will I again as paramour "——
" Nay, hush thee, too impatient maid,
Until my final tale be said!—
The good King Robert would engage
Edith once more his elfin page,
By her own heart, and her own eye,
Her lover's penitence to try—
Safe in his royal charge, and free,
Should such thy final purpose be,
Again unknown to seek the cell,
And live and die with Isabel."
Thus spoke the maid—King Robert's
    eye
Might have some glance of policy;
Dunstaffnage had the monarch ta'en,
And Lorn had own'd King Robert's
    reign,
Her brother had to England fled,
And there in banishment was dead;
Ample, through exile, death, and flight,
O'er tower and land was Edith's right;
This ample right o'er tower and land
Were safe in Ronald's faithful hand.

VIII.

Embarrass'd eye and blushing cheek
Pleasure and shame, and fear bespeak.
Yet much the reasoning Edith made!
" Her sister's faith she must upbraid,
Who gave such secret, dark and dear,
In council to another's ear.
Why should she leave the peaceful cell?—
How should she part with Isabel?—
How wear that strange attire agen?—
How risk herself 'midst martial men?—
And how be guarded on the way?—
At least she might entreat delay."
Kind Isabel, with secret smile,
Saw and forgave the maiden's wile,
Reluctant to be thought to move
At the first call of truant love.

IX.

Oh, blame her not!—when zephyrs wake,
The aspen's trembling leaves must shake;
When beams the sun through April's
    shower,
It needs must bloom, the violet flower;
And Love, howe'er the maiden strive,
Must with reviving hope revive!
A thousand soft excuses came,
To plead his cause 'gainst virgin shame.
Pledged by their sires in earliest youth,
He had her plighted faith and truth—
Then, 'twas her Liege's strict command,
And she, beneath his royal hand,
A ward in person and in land:—
And, last, she was resolved to stay
Only brief space—one little day—
Close hidden in her safe disguise
From all, but most from Ronald's eyes—
But once to see him more!—nor blame
Her wish—to hear him name her name!—
Then, to bear back to solitude
The thought he had his falsehood rued!
But Isabel, who long had seen
Her pallid cheek and pensive mien,
And well herself the cause might know,
Though innocent, of Edith's woe,
Joy'd, generous, that revolving time
Gave means to expiate the crime.
High glow'd her bosom as she said,
" Well shall her sufferings be repaid!"

Now came the parting hour—a band
From Arran's mountains left the land;
Their chief, Fitz-Louis, had the care
The speechless Amadine to bear
To Bruce, with honour, as behoved
To page the monarch dearly loved.

X.

The King had deem'd the maiden bright
Should reach him long before the fight,
But storms and fate her course delay:
It was on eve of battle-day:
When o'er the Gillie's-hill she rode.
The landscape like a furnace glow'd,
And far as e'er the eye was borne,
The lances waved like autumn-corn.
In battles four beneath their eye,
The forces of King Robert lie.
And one below the hill was laid,
Reserved for rescue and for aid;
And three, advanced, form'd vaward-line,
'Twixt Bannock's brook and Ninian's
    shrine.
Detach'd was each, yet each so nigh
As well might mutual aid supply.
Beyond, the Southern host appears,
A boundless wilderness of spears,
Whose verge or rear the anxious eye
Strove far, but strove in vain, to spy.
Thick flashing in the evening beam,
Glaives, lances, bills, and banners gleam;
And where the heaven join'd with the hill,
Was distant armour flashing still,
So wide, so far, the boundless host
Seem'd in the blue horizon lost.

XI.

Down from the hill the maiden pass'd,
At the wild show of war aghast;
And traversed first the rearward host,
Reserved for aid where needed most.
The men of Carrick and of Ayr,
Lennox and Lanark, too, were there,
    And all the western land;
With these the valiant of the Isles
Beneath their chieftains rank'd their files,
    In many a plaided band.
There, in the centre, proudly raised,
The Bruce's royal standard blazed,

And there Lord Ronald's banner bore
A galley driven by sail and oar.
A wild, yet pleasing contrast, made
Warriors in mail and plate array'd,
With the plumed bonnet and the plaid
    By these Hebrideans worn;
But O! unseen for three long years,
Dear was the garb of mountaineers
    To the fair Maid of Lorn!
For one she look'd—but he was far
Busied amid the ranks of war—
Yet with affection's troubled eye
She mark'd his banner boldly fly,
Gave on the countless foe a glance,
And thought on battle's desperate
    chance.

XII.

To centre of the vaward-line
Fitz-Louis guided Amadine.
Arm'd all on foot, that host appears
A serried mass of glimmering spears.
There stood the Marchers' warlike band,
The warriors there of Lodon's land;
Ettrick and Liddell bent the yew,
A band of archers fierce, though few;
The men of Nith and Annan's vale,
And the bold Spears of Teviotdale;—
The dauntless Douglas these obey,
And the young Stuart's gentle sway.
North-eastward by Saint Ninian's shrine,
Beneath fierce Randolph's charge, combine
The warriors whom the hardy North
From Tay to Sutherland sent forth.
The rest of Scotland's war-array
With Edward Bruce to westward lay,
Where Bannock, with his broken bank
And deep ravine, protects their flank.
Behind them, screen'd by sheltering
    wood,
The gallant Keith, Lord Marshal, stood:
His men-at-arms bear mace and lance,
And plumes that wave, and helms that
    glance.
Thus fair divided by the King,
Centre, and right, and left-ward wing,
Composed his front; nor distant far
Was strong reserve to aid the war.
And 'twas to front of this array,
Her guide and Edith made their way.

XIII.

Here must they pause ; for, in advance
As far as one might pitch a lance,
The monarch rode along the van,
The foe's approaching force to scan,
His line to marshal and to range,
And ranks to square, and fronts to change,
Alone he rode—from head to heel
Sheathed in his ready arms of steel ;
Nor mounted yet on war-horse wight,
But, till more near the shock of fight,
Reining a palfrey low and light.
A diadem of gold was set
Above his bright steel basinet,
And clasp'd within its glittering twine
Was seen the glove of Argentine ;
Truncheon or leading staff he lacks,
Bearing, instead, a battle-axe.
He ranged his soldiers for the fight,
Accoutred thus, in open sight
Of either host.—Three bowshots far,
Paused the deep front of England's war,
And rested on their arms awhile,
To close and rank their warlike file,
And hold high council, if that night
Should view the strife, or dawning light.

XIV.

O gay, yet fearful to behold,
Flashing with steel and rough with gold,
    And bristled o'er with bills and spears,
With plumes and pennons waving fair,
Was that bright battle-front ! for there
    Rode England's King and peers:
And who, that saw that monarch ride,
His kingdom battled by his side,
Could then his direful doom foretell !—
Fair was his seat in knightly selle,
And in his sprightly eye was set
Some spark of the Plantagenet.
Though light and wandering was his
        glance,
It flash'd at sight of shield and lance.
"Know'st thou," he said, "De Argentine,
Yon knight who marshals thus their
        line?"—
'The tokens on his helmet tell
The Bruce, my Liege: I know him well."—

"And shall the audacious traitor brave
The presence where our banners wave?"—
"So please my Liege," said Argentine,
"Were he but horsed on steed like mine,
To give him fair and knightly chance,
I would adventure forth my lance."—
"In battle-day," the King replied,
"Nice tourney rules are set aside.
—Still must the rebel dare our wrath?
Set on him—sweep him from our path!"—
And, at King Edward's signal, soon
Dash'd from the ranks Sir Henry Boune.

XV.

Of Hereford's high blood he came,
A race renown'd for knightly fame.
He burn'd before his Monarch's eye
To do some deed of chivalry.
He spurr'd his steed, he couch'd his lance,
And darted on the Bruce at once.
—As motionless as rocks, that bide
The wrath of the advancing tide,
The Bruce stood fast.—Each breast beat
        high,
And dazzled was each gazing eye—
The heart had hardly time to think,
The eyelid scarce had time to wink,
While on the King, like flash of flame,
Spurr'd to full speed the war-horse came !
The partridge may the falcon mock,
If that slight palfrey stand the shock—
But, swerving from the knight's career,
Just as they met, Bruce shunn'd the spear,
Onward the baffled warrior bore
His course—but soon his course was
        o'er !—
High in his stirrups stood the King,
And gave his battle-axe the swing.
Right on De Boune, the whiles he pass'd,
Fell that stern dint—the first—the last!—
Such strength upon the blow was put,
The helmet crash'd like hazel-nut ;
The axe-shaft, with its brazen clasp,
Was shiver'd to the gauntlet grasp.
Springs from the blow the startled horse,
Drops to the plain the lifeless corse ;
—First of that fatal field, how soon,
How sudden, fell the fierce De Boune !

XVI.

One pitying glance the Monarch sped,
Where on the field his foe lay dead;
Then gently turn'd his palfrey's head,
And, pacing back his sober way,
Slowly he gain'd his own array.
There round their King the leaders crowd,
And blame his recklessness aloud,
That risk'd 'gainst each adventurous spear,
A life so valued and so dear.
His broken weapon's shaft survey'd
The King, and careless answer made,—
" My loss may pay my folly's tax;
I've broke my trusty battle-axe."
'Twas then Fitz-Louis, bending low,
Did Isabel's commission show;
Edith, disguised at distance stands,
And hides her blushes with her hands.
The Monarch's brow has changed its hue,
Away the gory axe he threw,
While to the seeming page he drew,
    Clearing war's terrors from his eye.
Her hand with gentle ease he took,
With such a kind protecting look,
    As to a weak and timid boy
Might speak, that elder brother's care
And elder brother's love were there.

XVII.

" Fear not," he said, " young Amadine!"
Then whisper'd, "Still that name be thine.
Fate plays her wonted fantasy,
Kind Amadine, with thee and me,
And sends thee here in doubtful hour.
But soon we are beyond her power;
For on this chosen battle-plain,
Victor or vanquish'd, I remain.
Do thou to yonder hill repair;
The followers of our host are there,
And all who may not weapons bear.—
Fitz-Louis, have him in thy care.—
Joyful we meet, if all go well;
If not in Arran's holy cell
Thou must take part with Isabel;
For brave Lord Ronald, too, hath sworn,
Not to regain the Maid of Lorn,
(The bliss on earth he covets most,)
Would he forsake his battle-post,

Or shun the fortune that may fall
To Bruce, to Scotland, and to all.—
But, hark! some news these trumpets
    tell
Forgive my haste — farewell ! — fare-
    well !"—
And in a lower voice he said,
" Be of good cheer — farewell, sweet
    maid !"—

XVIII.

" What train of dust, with trumpet-sound
And glimmering spears, is wheeling round
Our leftward flank?"—the Monarch cried,
To Moray's Earl who rode beside.
" Lo! round thy station pass the foes !
Randolph, thy wreath has lost a rose;"
The Earl his visor closed, and said,
" My wreath shall bloom, or life shall
    fade.—
Follow, my household !"—And they go
Like lightning on the advancing foe.
" My Liege," said noble Douglas then,
" Earl Randolph has but one to ten:
Let me go forth his band to aid !"—
—" Stir not. The error he hath made,
Let him amend it as he may ;
I will not weaken mine array."
Then loudly rose the conflict-cry,
And Douglas's brave heart swell'd high,—
" My Liege," he said, "with patient ear
I must not Moray's death-knell hear!"—
" Then go—but speed thee back again."—
Forth sprung the Douglas with his train:
But, when they won a rising hill,
He bade his followers hold them still.—
" See, see! the routed Southern fly !
The Earl hath won the victory.
Lo! where yon steeds run masterless,
His banner towers above the press.
Rein up; our presence would impair
The fame we come too late to share."
Back to the host the Douglas rode,
And soon glad tidings are abroad,
That, Dayncourt by stout Randolph
    slain,
His followers fled with loosen'd rein.—
That skirmish closed the busy day,
And couch'd in battle's prompt array,
Each army on their weapons lay.

XIX.

It was a night of lovely June,
High rode in cloudless blue the moon,
  Demayet smiled beneath her ray ;
Old Stirling's towers arose in light,
And, twined in links of silver bright,
  Her winding river lay.
Ah, gentle planet ! other sight
Shall greet thee next returning night,
  Of broken arms and banners tore,
And marshes dark with human gore,
And piles of slaughter'd men and horse,
And Forth that floats the frequent corse,
And many a wounded wretch to plain
Beneath thy silver light in vain !
But now, from England's host, the cry
Thou hear'st of wassail revelry,
While from the Scottish legions pass
The murmur'd prayer, the early mass !—
Here, numbers had presumption given ;
There, bands o'er-match'd sought aid
    from Heaven.

XX.

On Gillie's hill, whose height commands
The battle-field, fair Edith stands,
With serf and page unfit for war,
To-eye the conflict from afar,
O ! with what doubtful agony
She sees the dawning tint the sky !—
Now on the Ochils gleams the sun,
And glistens now Demayet dun ;
  Is it the lark that carols shrill ?
    Is it the bittern's early hum ?
No !—distant, but increasing still,
  The trumpet's sound swells up the hill,
    With the deep murmur of the drum.
Responsive from the Scottish host,
Pipe-clang and bugle sound were toss'd,[45]
His breast and brow each soldier cross'd,
  And started from the ground ;
Arm'd and array'd for instant fight,
Rose archer, spearman, squire and knight,
And in the pomp of battle bright
  The dread battalia frown'd.

XXI.

Now onward, and in open view,
The countless ranks of England drew,

Dark rolling like the ocean-tide,
When the rough west nath chafed his pride,
And his deep roar sends challenge wide
  To all that bars his way !
In front the gallant archers trode,
The men-at-arms behind them rode,
And midmost of the phalanx broad
  The Monarch held his sway.
Beside him many a war-horse fumes,
Around him waves a sea of plumes,
Where many a knight in battle known,
And some who spurs had first braced on,
And deem'd that fight should see them
    won,
  King Edward's hests obey.
De Argentine attends his side,
With stout De Valence, Pembroke's
  pride,
Selected champions from the train,
To wait upon his bridle-rein.
Upon the Scottish foe he gazed—
  —At once, before his sight amazed,
    Sunk banner, spear, and shield ;
Each weapon-point is downward sent,
Each warrior to the ground is bent.
" The rebels, Argentine, repent !
  For pardon they have kneel'd."—
" Aye !—but they bend to other powers,
And other pardon sue than ours !
See where yon bare-foot Abbot stands,
And blesses them with lifted hands ![46]
Upon the spot where they have kneel'd,
These men will die or win the field."—
—" Then prove we if they die or win !
Bid Gloster's Earl the fight begin."

XXII.

Earl Gilbert waved his truncheon high,
  Just as the Northern ranks arose,
Signal for England's archery
  To halt and bend their bows.
Then stepp'd each yeoman forth a pace,
Glanced at the intervening space,
  And raised his left hand high ;
To the right ear the cords they bring
—At once ten thousand bow-strings ring,
  Ten thousand arrows fly !
Nor paused on the devoted Scot
The ceaseless fury of their shot ;
  As fiercely and as fast,

Forth whistling came the grey-goose wing
As the wild hailstones pelt and ring
  Adown December's blast.
Nor mountain targe of tough bull-hide,
Nor lowland mail, that storm may bide;
Woe, woe to Scotland's banner'd pride,
  If the fell shower may last!
Upon the right, behind the wood,
Each by his steed dismounted, stood
  The Scottish chivalry;—
With foot in stirrup, hand on mane,
Fierce Edward Bruce can scarce restrain
His own keen heart, his eager train,
Until the archers gained the plain;
  Then, "Mount, ye gallants free!"
He cried; and, vaulting from the ground,
His saddle every horseman found.
On high their glittering crests they toss,
As springs the wild-fire from the moss;
The shield hangs down on every breast,
Each ready lance is in the rest,
  And loud shouts Edward Bruce,—
" Forth, Marshal! on the peasant foe!
We'll tame the terrors of their bow,
  And cut the bow-string loose!"[47]

XXIII.

Then spurs were dash'd in chargers' flanks,
They rushed among the archer ranks.
No spears were there the shock to let,
No stakes to turn the charge were set,
And how shall yeoman's armour slight,
Stand the long lance and mace of might?
Or what may their short swords avail,
'Gainst barbed horse and shirt of mail?
Amid their ranks the chargers sprung,
High o'er their heads the weapons swung,
And shriek and groan and vengeful shout
Give note of triumph and of rout!
Awhile, with stubborn hardihood,
Their English hearts the strife made good.
Borne down at length on every side,
Compell'd to flight, they scatter wide.—
Let stags of Sherwood leap for glee,
And bound the deer of Dallom-Lee!
The broken bows of Bannock's shore
Shall in the greenwood ring no more!
Round Wakefield's merry May-pole now,
The maids may twine the summer bough,

May northward look with longing glance,
For those that wont to lead the dance,
For the blithe archers look in vain!
Broken, dispersed, in flight o'erta'en,
Pierced through, trode down, by thousands
  slain,
They cumber Bannock's bloody plain.

XXIV.

The King with scorn beheld their flight.
" Are these," he said, " our yeomen wight?
Each braggart churl could boast before,
Twelve Scottish lives his baldric bore![48]
Fitter to plunder chase or park,
Than make a manly foe their mark.—
Forward, each gentleman and knight!
Let gentle blood show generous might,
And chivalry redeem the fight!"
To rightward of the wild affray,
The field show'd fair and level way;
  But, in mid-space, the Bruce's care
Had bored the ground with many a pit,
With turf and brushwood hidden yet,
  That form'd a ghastly snare.
Rushing, ten thousand horsemen came,
With spears in rest, and hearts on flame,
  That panted for the shock!
With blazing crests and banners spread,
And trumpet-clang and clamour dread,
The wide plain thunder'd to their tread,
  As far as Stirling rock.
Down! down! in headlong overthrow,
Horseman and horse, the foremost go,[49]
  Wild floundering on the field!
The first are in destruction's gorge,
Their followers wildly o'er them urge:—
  The knightly helm and shield,
The mail, the acton, and the spear,
Strong hand, high heart, are useless here!
Loud from the mass confused the cry
Of dying warriors swells on high,
And steeds that shriek in agony![50]
They came like mountain-torrent red,
That thunders o'er its rocky bed;
They broke like that same torrent's wave
When swallow'd by a darksome cave.
Billows on billows burst and boil,
Maintaining still the stern turmoil,
And to their wild and tortured groan
Each adds new terrors of his own!

XXV

Too strong in courage and in might
Was England yet, to yield the fight.
  Her noblest all are here;
Names that to fear were never known,
Bold Norfolk's Earl De Brotherton,
  And Oxford's famed De Vere.
There Gloster plied the bloody sword,
And Berkley, Grey, and Hereford,
  Bottetourt and Sanzavere,
Ross, Montague, and Mauley, came,
And Courtenay's pride, and Percy's
    fame—
Names known too well in Scotland's war,
At Falkirk, Methven, and Dunbar,
Blazed broader yet in after years,
At Cressy red and fell Poitiers.
Pembroke with these, and Argentine,
Brought up the rearward battle-line.
With caution o'er the ground they tread,
Slippery with blood and piled with dead,
Till hand to hand in battle set,
The bills with spears and axes met,
And, closing dark on every side,
Raged the full contest far and wide.
Then was the strength of Douglas tried,
Then proved was Randolph's generous
    pride,
And well did Stewart's actions grace
The sire of Scotland's royal race!
  Firmly they kept their ground;
As firmly England onward press'd,
And down went many a noble crest,
And rent was many a valiant breast,
  And Slaughter revell'd round.

XXVI.

Unflinching foot 'gainst foot was set,
Unceasing blow by blow was met;
  The groans of those who fell
Were drown'd amid the shriller clang
That from the blades and harness rang,
  And in the battle-yell.
Yet fast they fell, unheard, forgot,
Both Southern fierce and hardy Scot;
And O! amid that waste of life,
What various motives fired the strife!
The aspiring Noble bled for fame,
The Patriot for his country's claim;

This Knight his youthful strength to
    prove,
And that to win his lady's love;
Some fought from ruffian thirst of blood,
From habit some, or hardihood.
But ruffian stern, and soldier good,
  The noble and the slave,
From various cause the same wild road,
On the same bloody morning, trode,
  To that dark inn, the grave!

XXVII.

The tug of strife to flag begins,
Though neither loses yet nor wins.
High rides the sun, thick rolls the dust,
And feebler speeds the blow and thrust.
Douglas leans on his war-sword now,
And Randolph wipes his bloody brow;
Nor less had toil'd each Southern knight,
From morn till mid-day in the fight.
Strong Egremont for air must gasp,
Beauchamp undoes his visor-clasp,
And Montague must quit his spear,
And sinks thy falchion, bold De Vere!
The blows of Berkley fall less fast,
And gallant Pembroke's bugle-blast
  Hath lost its lively tone;
Sinks, Argentine, thy battle-word,
And Percy's shout was fainter heard,
  "My merry-men, fight on!"

XXVIII.

Bruce, with the pilot's wary eye,
The slackening of the storm could spy.
  "One effort more, and Scotland's
    free!
  Lord of the Isles, my trust in thee
    Is firm as Ailsa Rock;[51]
  Rush on with Highland sword and
    targe,
  I, with my Carrick spearmen charge;
    Now, forward to the shock!"
At once the spears were forward thrown,
Against the sun the broadswords
    shone;
The pibroch lent its maddening tone,
And loud King Robert's voice was
    known—

"Carrick, press on—they fail, they fail!
Press on, brave sons of Innisgail,
  The foe is fainting fast!
Each strike for parent, child, and wife,
For Scotland, liberty, and life,—
  The battle cannot last!"

XXIX.

The fresh and desperate onset bore
The foes three furlongs back and more,
Leaving their noblest in their gore.
  Alone, De Argentine
Yet bears on high his red-cross shield,
Gathers the relics of the field,
Renews the ranks where they have reel'd,
  And still makes good the line.
Brief strife, but fierce,—his efforts raise
A bright but momentary blaze.
Fair Edith heard the Southron shout,
Beheld them turning from the rout,
Heard the wild call their trumpets sent,
In notes 'twixt triumph and lament.
That rallying force, combined anew,
Appear'd in her distracted view,
  To hem the Islesmen round;
"O God! the combat they renew,
  And is no rescue found!
And ye that look thus tamely on,
And see your native land o'erthrown,
O! are your hearts of flesh or stone?"

XXX.

The multitude that watch'd afar,
Rejected from the ranks of war,
Had not unmoved beheld the fight,
When strove the Bruce for Scotland's
  right;
Each heart had caught the patriot spark,
Old man and stripling, priest and clerk,
Bondsman and serf; even female hand
Stretch'd to the hatchet or the brand;
But, when mute Amadine they heard
Give to their zeal his signal-word,
  A frenzy fired the throng;
"Portents and miracles impeach
Our sloth—the dumb our duties teach—
And he that gives the mute his speech,
  Can bid the weak be strong.

To us, as to our lords, are given
A native earth, a promised heaven;
To us, as to our lords, belongs
The vengeance for our nation's wrongs;
The choice 'twixt death or freedom,
  warms
Our breasts as theirs—To arms, to arms!"
To arms they flew,—axe, club, or spear,—
And mimic ensigns high they rear,[52]
And, like a banner'd host afar,
Bear down on England's wearied war.

XXXI.

Already scatter'd o'er the plain,
Reproof, command, and counsel vain,
The rearward squadrons fled amain,
  Or made but doubtful stay;
But when they mark'd the seeming show
Of fresh and fierce and marshall'd foe,
  The boldest broke array.
O give their hapless prince his due!
In vain the royal Edward threw
  His person 'mid the spears,
Cried, "Fight!" to terror and despair,
Menaced, and wept, and tore his hair,
  And cursed their caitiff fears;
Till Pembroke turn'd his bridle rein,
And forced him from the fatal plain.
With them rode Argentine, until
They gain'd the summit of the hill,
But quitted there the train:—
"In yonder field a gage I left,—
I must not live of fame bereft;
  I needs must turn again.
Speed hence, my Liege, for on your trace
The fiery Douglas takes the chase,
  I know his banner well.
God send my Sovereign joy and bliss,
And many a happier field than this!—
  Once more, my Liege, farewell."

XXXII.

Again he faced the battle-field,—
Wildly they fly, are slain, or yield.
"Now then," he said, and couch'd his
  spear,
"My course is run, the goal is near;
One effort more, one brave career,
  Must close this race of mine."

Then in his stirrups rising high,
He shouted loud his battle-cry,
   "Saint James for Argentine!"
And, of the bold pursuers, four
The gallant knight from saddle bore;
But not unharm'd—a lance's point
Has found his breastplate's loosen'd joint,
   An axe has razed his crest;
Yet still on Colonsay's fierce lord,
Who press'd the chase with gory sword,
   He rode with spear in rest,
And through his bloody tartans bored,
   And through his gallant breast.
Nail'd to the earth, the mountaineer
Yet writhed him up against the spear,
   And swung his broadsword round!
—Stirrup, steel-boot, and cuish gave way,
Beneath that blow's tremendous sway,
   The blood gush'd from the wound;
And the grim Lord of Colonsay
   Hath turn'd him on the ground,
And laugh'd in death-pang, that his blade
The mortal thrust so well repaid.

XXXIII.

Now toil'd the Bruce, the battle done,
To use his conquest boldly won;
And gave command for horse and spear
To press the Southron's scatter'd rear,
Nor let his broken force combine,
  —When the war-cry of Argentine
   Fell faintly on his ear;
" Save, save his life," he cried, " O save
The kind, the noble, and the brave!"
The squadrons round free passage gave,
   The wounded knight drew near;
He raised his red-cross shield no more,
Helm, cuish, and breastplate stream'd
   with gore,
Yet, as he saw the King advance,
He strove even then to couch his lance—
   The effort was in vain!
The spur-stroke fail'd to rouse the horse;
Wounded and weary, in mid course
   He stumbled on the plain.
Then foremost was the generous Bruce
To raise his head, his helm to loose;—
   " Lord Earl, the day is thine!

My Sovereign's charge, and adverse fate,
Have made our meeting all too late:
   Yet this may Argentine,
As boon from ancient comrade, crave—
A Christian's mass, a soldier's grave."

XXXIV.

Bruce press'd his dying hand—its grasp
Kindly replied; but, in his clasp,
   It stiffen'd and grew cold—
" And, O farewell!" the victor cried,
" Of chivalry the flower and pride,
   The arm in battle bold,
The courteous mien, the noble race,
The stainless faith, the manly face!—
Bid Ninian's convent light their shrine,
For late-wake of De Argentine.
O'er better knight on death-bier laid,
Torch never gleam'd nor mass was said!"

XXXV.

Nor for De Argentine alone,
Through Ninian's church these torches
   shone,
And rose the death-prayer's awful tone.
That yellow lustre glimmer'd pale,
On broken plate and bloodied mail,
Rent crest and shatter'd coronet,
Of Baron, Earl, and Banneret;
And the best names that England knew,
Claim'd in the death-prayer dismal due.
   Yet mourn not, Land of Fame!
Though ne'er the Leopards on thy shield
Retreated from so sad a field,
   Since Norman William came.
Oft may thine annals justly boast
Of battles stern by Scotland lost :
   Grudge not her victory,
When for her freeborn rights she strove;
Rights dear to all who freedom love,
   To none so dear as thee!

XXXVI.

Turn we to Bruce, whose curious ear
Must from Fitz-Louis tidings hear;
With him, a hundred voices tell
Of prodigy and miracle,
   " For the mute page had spoke."—

"Page!" said Fitz-Louis, "rather say,
An angel sent from realms of day,
  To burst the English yoke.
I saw his plume and bonnet drop,
When hurrying from the mountain top;
A lovely brow, dark locks that wave,
To his bright eyes new lustre gave,
A step as light upon the green,
As if his pinions waved unseen!"—
"Spoke he with none?"—"With none—
  one word
Burst when he saw the Island Lord,
Returning from the battle-field."—
"What answer made the Chief?"—"He
  kneel'd,
Durst not look up, but mutter'd low,
Some mingled sounds that none might
  know,
And greeted him 'twixt joy and fear,
As being of superior sphere."

XXXVII.

Even upon Bannock's bloody plain,
Heap'd then with thousands of the slain,
'Mid victor monarch's musings high,
Mirth laugh'd in good King Robert's
  eye.—
"And bore he such angelic air,
Such noble front, such waving hair?
Hath Ronald kneel'd to him?" he said,
"Then must we call the church to aid—
Our will be to the Abbot known,
Ere these strange news are wider blown,
To Cambuskenneth straight ye pass,
And deck the church for solemn mass,
To pay for high deliverance given,
A nation's thanks to gracious Heaven.
Let him array, besides, such state,
As should on princes' nuptials wait.

Ourself the cause, through fortune's spite,
That once broke short that spousal rite,
Ourself will grace, with early morn,
The bridal of the Maid of Lorn."

CONCLUSION.

Go forth, my Song, upon thy venturous way;
Go boldly forth; nor yet thy master
  blame,
Who chose no patron for his humble
  lay,
And graced thy numbers with no
  friendly name,
Whose partial zeal might smooth thy
  path to fame.
There was—and O! how many sorrows
  crowd
Into these two brief words!—*there was*
  a claim
By generous friendship given—had fate
  allow'd,
It well had bid thee rank the proudest
  of the proud!

All angel now—yet little less than all,
While still a pilgrim in our world below!
What 'vails it us that patience to recall,
Which hid its own to soothe all other
  woe;
What 'vails to tell, how Virtue's purest
  glow
Shone yet more lovely in a form so fair:
And, least of all, what 'vails the world
  should know,
That one poor garland, twined to deck
  thy hair,
Is hung upon thy hearse, to droop and
  wither there!

THE FIELD OF WATERLOO.

A POEM,

TO

HER GRACE THE

DUCHESS OF WELLINGTON,

PRINCESS OF WATERLOO.

&c. &c. &c.

THE FOLLOWING VERSES ARE MOST RESPECTFULLY

INSCRIBED BY

THE AUTHOR.

ADVERTISEMENT.

———————

It may be some apology for the imperfections of this poem, that it was composed hastily, and during a short tour upon the Continent, when the Author's labours were liable to frequent interruption; but its best apology is, that it was written for the purpose of assisting the Waterloo Subscription.

ABBOTSFORD, 1815.

THE FIELD OF WATERLOO:

Though Valois braved young Edward's gentle hand,
And Albert rush'd on Henry's way-worn band,
With Europe's chosen sons, in arms renown'd,
Yet not on Vere's bold archers long they look'd,
Nor Audley's squires, nor Mowbray's yeomen brook'd,—
They saw their standard fall, and left their monarch bound.

AKENSIDE.

I.

FAIR Brussels, thou art far behind,
Though, lingering on the morning wind,
  We yet may hear the hour
Peal'd over orchard and canal,
With voice prolong'd and measured fall,
  From proud St. Michael's tower;
Thy wood, dark Soignies, holds us now*
Where the tall beeches' glossy bough
  For many a league around,
With birch and darksome oak between,
Spreads deep and far a pathless screen,
  Of tangled forest ground.
Stems planted close by stems defy
The adventurous foot—the curious eye
  For access seeks in vain;
And the brown tapestry of leaves,
Strew'd on the blighted ground, receives
  Nor sun, nor air, nor rain.
No opening glade dawns on our way,
No streamlet, glancing to the ray,
  Our woodland path has cross'd;
And the straight causeway which we tread,
Prolongs a line of dull arcade,
Unvarying through the unvaried shade
  Until in distance lost.

* The wood of Soignies is a remnant of the forest of Ardennes, the scene of the charming and romantic incidents of Shakespeare's "As you Like it."

II.

A brighter, livelier scene succeeds;
In groups the scattering wood recedes,
Hedge-rows, and huts, and sunny meads,
  And corn-fields, glance between;
The peasant, at his labour blithe,
Plies the hook'd staff and shorten'd
  scythe:¹—
  But when these ears were green,
Placed close within destruction's scope,
Full little was that rustic's hope
  Their ripening to have seen!
And, lo, a hamlet and its fane:—
Let not the gazer with disdain
  Their architecture view;
For yonder rude ungraceful shrine,
And disproportion'd spire, are thine,
  Immortal WATERLOO!

III.

Fear not the heat, though full and high
The sun has scorch'd the autumn sky,
And scarce a forest straggler now
To shade us spreads a greenwood bough:
These fields have seen a hotter day
Than e'er was fired by sunny ray.
Yet one mile on—yon shatter'd hedge
Crests the soft hill whose long smooth
  ridge
  Looks on the field below,

And sinks so gently on the dale,
That not the folds of Beauty's veil
  In easier curves can flow.
Brief space from thence, the ground aga'n
Ascending slowly from the plain,
  Forms an opposing screen,
Which, with its crest of upland ground,
Shuts the horizon all around.
  The soften'd vale between
Slopes smooth and fair for courser's tread;
Not the most timid maid need dread
To give her snow-white palfrey head
  On that wide stubble-ground;
Nor wood, nor tree, nor bush, are there,
Her course to intercept or scare,
  Nor fosse nor fence are found,
Save where, from out her shatter'd bowers,
Rise Hougomont's dismantled towers.

IV.

Now, see'st thou aught in this lone scene
Can tell of that which late hath been?—
  A stranger might reply,
"The bare extent of stubble-plain
Seems lately lighten'd of its grain;
And yonder sable tracks remain
Marks of the peasant's ponderous wain,
  When harvest-home was nigh.
On these broad spots of trampled ground,
Perchance the rustics danced such round
  As Teniers loved to draw;
And where the earth seems scorch'd by
  flame,
To dress the homely feast they came,
And toil'd the kerchief'd village dame
  Around her fire of straw."

V.

So deem'st thou—so each mortal deems,
Of that which is from that which seems.—
  But other harvest here,
Than that which peasant's scythe demands,
Was gather'd in by sterner hands,
  With bayonet, blade, and spear.
No vulgar crop was theirs to reap,
No stinted harvest thin and cheap!
Heroes before each fatal sweep
  Fell thick as ripen'd grain;
And ere the darkening of the day,
Piled high as autumn shocks, there lay

The ghastly harvest of the fray,
  The corpses of the slain.

VI.

Ay, look again—that line, so black
And trampled, marks the bivouac,
Yon deep-graved ruts the artillery's track,
  So often lost and won;
And close beside, the harden'd mud
Still shows where, fetlock-deep in blood,
The fierce dragoon, through battle's flood,
  Dash'd the hot war-horse on.
These spots of excavation tell
The ravage of the bursting shell—
And feel'st thou not the tainted steam,
That reeks against the sultry beam,
  From yonder trenched mound?
The pestilential fumes declare
That Carnage has replenish'd there
  Her garner-house profound.

VII.

Far other harvest-home and feast,
Than claims the boor from scythe released,
  On these scorch'd fields were known!
Death hover'd o'er the maddening rout,
And, in the thrilling battle-shout,
Sent for the bloody banquet out
  A summons of his own.
Through rolling smoke the Demon's eye
Could well each destined guest espy,
Well could his ear in ecstasy
  Distinguish every tone
That fill'd the chorus of the fray—
From cannon-roar and trumpet-bray,
From charging squadrons' wild hurra,
From the wild clang that mark'd their
  way,—
Down to the dying groan,
And the last sob of life's decay,
  When breath was all but flown.

VIII.

Feast on, stern foe of mortal life,
Feast on!—but think not that a strife,
With such promiscuous carnage rife,
  Protracted space may last;
The deadly tug of war at length
Must limits find in human strength,
  And cease when these are past.

Vain hope!—that morn's o'erclouded sun
Heard the wild shout of fight begun
 Ere he attain'd his height,
And through the war-smoke, volumed
 high,
Still peals that unremitted cry,
 Though now he stoops to night.
For ten long hours of doubt and dread,
Fresh succours from the extended head
Of either hill the contest fed;
 Still down the slope they drew,
The charge of columns paused not,
Nor ceased the storm of shell and shot;
 For all that war could do
Of skill and force was proved that day,
And turn'd not yet the doubtful fray
 On bloody Waterloo.

IX.

Pale Brussels! then what thoughts were
 thine,[2]
When ceaseless from the distant line
 Continued thunders came!
Each burgher held his breath, to hear
These forerunners of havoc near,
 Of rapine and of flame.
What ghastly sights were thine to meet,
When roiling through thy stately street,
The wounded show'd their mangled
 plight
In token of the unfinish'd fight,
And from each anguish-laden wain
The blood-drops laid thy dust like rain!
How often in the distant drum
Heard'st thou the fell Invader come,
While Ruin, shouting to his band,
Shook high her torch and gory brand!—
Cheer thee, fair City! From yon stand,
Impatient, still his outstretch'd hand
 Points to his prey in vain,
While maddening in his eager mood,
And all unwont to be withstood,
 He fires the fight again.

X.

" On! On!" was still his stern exclaim;[3]
" Confront the battery's jaws of flame!
 Rush on the levell'd gun!
My steel-clad cuirassiers, advance!
Each Hulan forward with his lance.

My Guard—my Chosen—charge for
 France,
 France and Napoleon!"
Loud answer'd their acclaiming shout,
Greeting the mandate which sent out
Their bravest and their best to dare
The fate their leader shunn'd to share.[4]
But He, his country's sword and shield,
Still in the battle-front reveal'd,
Where danger fiercest swept the field,
 Came like a beam of light,
In action prompt, in sentence brief—
" Soldiers, stand firm," exclaim'd the Chief,
 " England shall tell the fight!"[5]

XI.

On came the whirlwind—like the last
But fiercest sweep of tempest-blast—
On came the whirlwind — steel-gleams
 broke
Like lightning through the rolling smoke;
 The war was waked anew,
Three hundred cannon-mouths roar'd
 loud,
And from their throats, with flash and
 cloud,
 Their showers of iron threw.
Beneath their fire, in full career,
Rush'd on the ponderous cuirassier,
The lancer couch'd his ruthless spear,
And hurrying as to havoc near,
 The cohorts' eagles flew.
In one dark torrent, broad and strong,
The advancing onset roll'd along,
Forth harbinger'd by fierce acclaim,
That, from the shroud of smoke and
 flame,
Peal'd wildly the imperial name.

XII.

But on the British heart were lost
The terrors of the charging host;
For not an eye the storm that view'd
Changed its proud glance of fortitude,
Nor was one forward footstep staid,
As dropp'd the dying and the dead.
Fast as their ranks the thunders tear,
Fast they renew'd each serried square;
And on the wounded and the slain
Closed their diminish'd files again,

Till from their line scarce spears' lengths
   three,
Emerging from the smoke they see
Helmet, and plume, and panoply,—
   Then waked their fire at once!
Each musketeer's revolving knell,
As fast, as regularly fell,
As when they practise to display
Their discipline on festal day.

   Then down went helm and lance,
Down were the eagle banners sent,
Down reeling steeds and riders went,
Corslets were pierced, and pennons rent;
   And, to augment the fray,
Wheel'd full against their staggering flanks,
The English horsemen's foaming ranks
   Forced their resistless way.
Then to the musket-knell succeeds
The clash of swords—the neigh of steeds—
As plies the smith his clanging trade,[6]
Against the cuirass rang the blade;
And while amid their close array
The well-served cannon rent their way,
And while amid their scatter'd band
Raged the fierce rider's bloody brand,
Recoil'd in common rout and fear,
Lancer and guard and cuirassier,
Horsemen and foot—a mingled host,
Their leaders fall'n, their standards lost.

XIII.

Then, WELLINGTON ! thy piercing eye
This crisis caught of destiny—
   The British host had stood
That morn 'gainst charge of sword and
   lance*
As their own ocean-rocks hold stance,
But when thy voice had said, " Advance!"
   They were their ocean's flood.—
O Thou, whose inauspicious aim
Hath wrought thy host this hour of shame,
Think'st thou thy broken bands will bide
The terrors of yon rushing tide ?

Or will thy chosen brook to feel
The British shock of levell'd steel,[7]
   Or dost thou turn thine eye
Where coming squadrons gleam afar,
And fresher thunders wake the war,
   And other standards fly ?—
Think not that in yon columns, file
Thy conquering troops from distant
   Dyle—
   Is Blucher yet unknown ?
Or dwells not in thy memory still,
(Heard frequent in thine hour of ill,)
What notes of hate and vengeance thrill
   In Prussia's trumpet tone ?—
What yet remains ?—shall it be thine
To head the relics of thy line
   In one dread effort more ?—
The Roman lore thy leisure loved,
And thou canst tell what fortune proved
   That Chieftain, who, of yore,
Ambition's dizzy paths essay'd,
And with the gladiators' aid
   For empire enterprised—
He stood the cast his rashness play'd,
Left not the victims he had made,
Dug his red grave with his own blade,
And on the field he lost was laid,
   Abhorr'd—but not despised.

XIV.

But if revolves thy fainter thought
On safety—howsoever bought,—
Then turn thy fearful rein and ride,
Though twice ten thousand men have died
   On this eventful day,
To gild the military fame
Which thou, for life, in traffic tame
   Wilt barter thus away.
Shall future ages tell this tale
Of inconsistence faint and frail ?
And art thou He of Lodi's bridge,
Marengo's field, and Wagram's ridge !
   Or is thy soul like mountain-tide,
That, swell'd by winter storm and shower,
Rolls down in turbulence of power,
   A torrent fierce and wide;
Reft of these aids, a rill obscure,
Shrinking unnoticed, mean and poor,
   Whose channel shows display'd

---

* "The British square stood unmoved, and
never gave fire until the cavalry were within
ten yards, when men rolled one way, horses
galloped another, and the cuirassiers were in
every instance driven back." — Life of
Bonaparte, vol. ix, p, 12,

The wrecks of its impetuous course,
But not one symptom of the force
　By which these wrecks were made!

XV

Spur on thy way!—since now thine ear
Has brook'd thy veterans' wish to hear,
　Who, as thy flight they eyed,
Exclaim'd,—while tears of anguish came,
Wrung forth by pride, and rage, and
　shame,—
"O, that he had but died!"
But yet, to sum this hour of ill,
Look, ere thou leavest the fatal hill,
　Back on yon broken ranks—
Upon whose wild confusion gleams
The moon, as on the troubled streams
　When rivers break their banks,
And, to the ruin'd peasant's eye,
Objects half seen roll swiftly by,
　Down the dread current hurl'd—
So mingle banner, wain, and gun,
Where the tumultuous flight rolls on
Of warriors, who, when morn begun,
　Defied a banded world.

XVI.

List—frequent to the hurrying rout,
The stern pursuers' vengeful shout
Tells, that upon their broken rear
Rages the Prussian's bloody spear.
　So fell a shriek was none,
When Beresina's icy flood
Redden'd and thaw'd with flame and blood,
And, pressing on thy desperate way,
Raised oft and long their wild hurra,
　The children of the Don.
Thine ear no yell of horror cleft
So ominous, when all bereft
Of aid, the valiant Polack left*—
Ay, left by thee—found soldier's grave
In Leipsic's corpse-encumber'd wave.
Fate, in those various perils past,
Reserved thee still some future cast;
On the dread die thou now hast thrown,
Hangs not a single field alone,

---

* For an account of the death of Ponia-
towski at Leipsic, see Sir Walter Scott's *Life
of Bonaparte.* vol. vii. p. 401.

Nor one campaign—thy martial fame,
Thy empire, dynasty, and name,
　Have felt the final stroke;
And now, o'er thy devoted head
The last stern vial's wrath is shed,
　The last dread seal is broke.

XVII.

Since live thou wilt—refuse not now
Before these demagogues to bow,
Late objects of thy scorn and hate,
Who shall thy once imperial fate
Make wordy theme of vain debate.—
Or shall we say, thou stoop'st less low
In seeking refuge from the foe,
Against whose heart, in prosperous life,
Thine hand hath ever held the knife?
　Such homage hath been paid
By Roman and by Grecian voice,
And there were honour in the choice,
　If it were freely made.
Then safely come—in one so low,—
So lost,—we cannot own a foe;
Though dear experience bid us end,
In thee we ne'er can hail a friend.—
Come, howsoe'er—but do not hide
Close in thy heart that germ of pride,
　Erewhile, by gifted bard espied,
　　That "yet imperial hope;"
Think not that for a fresh rebound,
To raise ambition from the ground,
　We yield thee means or scope.
In safety come—but ne'er again
Hold type of independent reign;
　No islet calls thee lord,
We leave thee no confederate band,
No symbol of thy lost command,
To be a dagger in the hand
　From which we wrench'd the sword.

XVIII.

Yet, even in yon sequester'd spot,
May worthier conquest be thy lot
　Than yet thy life has known;
Conquest, unbought by blood or harm,
That needs nor foreign aid nor arm,
　A triumph all thine own.
Such waits thee when thou shalt control
Those passions wild, that stubborn soul,
　That marr'd thy prosperous scene:—

Hear this—from no unmoved heart,
Which sighs, comparing what THOU ART
  With what thou MIGHT'ST HAVE
    BEEN!

XIX.

Thou, too, whose deeds of fame renew'd
Bankrupt a nation's gratitude,
To thine own noble heart must owe
More than the meed she can bestow.
For not a people's just acclaim,
Not the full hail of Europe's fame,
Thy Prince's smiles, thy State's decree,
The ducal rank, the garter'd knee,
Not these such pure delight afford
As that, when hanging up thy sword,
Well mays't thou think, "This honest steel
Was ever drawn for public weal;
And, such was rightful Heaven's decree,
Ne'er sheathed unless with victory!"

XX.

Look forth, once more, with soften'd
  heart,
Ere from the field of fame we part;
Triumph and Sorrow border near,
And joy oft melts into a tear.
Alas! what links of love that morn
Has War's rude hand asunder torn!
For ne'er was field so sternly fought,
And ne'er was conquest dearer bought.
Here piled in common slaughter sleep
Those whom affection long shall weep:
Here rests the sire, that ne'er shall strain
His orphans to his heart again;
The son, whom, on his native shore,
The parent's voice shall bless no more;
The bridegroom, who has hardly press'd
His blushing consort to his breast;
The husband, whom through many a year,
Long love and mutual faith endear.
Thou canst not name one tender tie,
But here dissolved its relics lie!
O! when thou see'st some mourner's veil
Shroud her thin form and visage pale,
Or mark'st the Matron's bursting tears
Stream when the stricken drum she hears;
Or see'st how manlier grief, suppress'd,
Is labouring in a father's breast,—

With no inquiry vain pursue
The cause, but think on Waterloo!

XXI.

Period of honour as of woes,
What bright careers 'twas thine to close![8]
Mark'd on thy roll of blood what names
To Briton's memory, and to Fame's,
Laid there their last immortal claims!
Thou saw'st in seas of gore expire
Redoubted PICTON's soul of fire—
Saw'st in the mingled carnage lie
All that of PONSONBY could die—
DE LANCEY change Love's bridal-wreath,
For laurels from the hand of Death[9]—
Saw'st gallant MILLER's failing eye[10]
Still bent where Albion's banners fly
And CAMERON,[11] in the shock of steel,
Die like the offspring of Lochiel;
And generous GORDON,[12] 'mid the strife,
Fall, while he watch'd his leader's life.—
Ah! though her guardian angel's shield
Fenced Britain's hero through the field,
Fate not the less her power made known,
Through his friends' hearts to pierce his
  own!*

XXII.

Forgive, brave Dead, the imperfect lay!
Who may your names, your numbers, say?
What high-strung harp, what lofty line,
To each the dear-earn'd praise assign,
From high-born chiefs of martial fame
To the poor soldier's lowlier name?
Lightly ye rose that dawning day,
From your cold couch of swamp and
  clay,
To fill, before the sun was low,
The bed that morning cannot know.—
Oft may the tear the green sod steep,
And sacred be the heroes' sleep,
  Till time shall cease to run;
And ne'er beside their noble grave,
May Briton pass and fail to crave
A blessing on the fallen brave
  Who fought with Wellington!

---

* The grief of the victor for the fate of his
friends is touchingly described by those who
witnessed it.

XXIII.

Farewell, sad Field! whose blighted face
Wears desolation's withering trace;
Long shall my memory retain
Thy shatter'd huts and trampled grain,
With every mark of martial wrong,
That scathe thy towers, fair Hougomont![13]
Yet though thy garden's green arcade
The marksman's fatal post was made,
Though on thy shatter'd beeches fell
The blended rage of shot and shell,
Though from thy blacken'd portals torn,
Their fall thy blighted fruit-trees mourn,
Has not such havoc bought a name
Immortal in the rolls of fame?
Yes—Agincourt may be forgot,
And Cressy be an unknown spot,
 And Blenheim's name be new;
But still in story and in song,
For many an age remember'd long,
Shall live the towers of Hougomont,
 And Field of Waterloo.

Conclusion.

Stern tide of human Time! that
 know'st not rest,
But sweeping from the cradle to the
 tomb,
Bear'st ever downward on thy dusky
 breast,
Successive generations to their doom;
While thy capacious stream has equal
 room
For the gay bark where Pleasure's
 streamers sport,
And for the prison-ship of guilt and
 gloom,
The fisher-skiff, and barge that bears a
 court,
Still wafting onward all to one dark silent
 port;—

Stern tide of Time! through what
 mysterious change
Of hope and fear have our frail barks
 been driven!

For ne'er, before, vicissitude so strange
Was to one race of Adam's offspring
 given.
And sure such varied change of sea
 and heaven,
Such unexpected bursts of joy and woe,
Such fearful strife as that where we have
 striven,
Succeeding ages ne'er again shall know,
Until the awful term when Thou shalt
 cease to flow!

Well hast thou stood, my Country!—
 the brave fight
Hast well maintain'd through good
 report and ill;
In thy just cause and in thy native
 might,
And in Heaven's grace and justice con‹
 stant still;
Whether the banded prowess, strength,
 and skill
Of half the world against thee stood
 array'd,
Or when, with better views and freer
 will,
Beside thee Europe's noblest drew the
 blade,
Each emulous in arms the Ocean Queen
 to aid.

Well art thou now repaid—though
 slowly rose,
And struggled long with mists thy
 blaze of fame,
While like the dawn that in the orient
 glows
On the broad wave its earlier lustre
 came;
Then eastern Egypt saw the growing
 flame,
And Maida's myrtles gleam'd beneath
 its ray,
Where first the soldier, stung with
 generous shame,
Rivall'd the heroes of the wat'ry way,
And wash'd in foeman's gore unjust
 reproach away.

Now, Island Empress, wave thy crest on high,
And bid the banner of thy Patron flow,
Gallant Saint George, the flower of Chivalry,
For thou hast faced, like him, a dragon foe,
And rescued innocence from overthrow,
And trampled down, like him, tyrannic might,
And to the gazing world mayst proudly show
The chosen emblem of thy sainted Knight,
Who quell'd devouring pride, and vindicated right.

Yet 'mid the confidence of just renown,
Renown dear-bought, but dearest thus acquired,
Write, Britain, write the moral lesson down:
'Tis not alone the heart with valour fired,
The discipline so dreaded and admired,
In many a field of bloody conquest known;
—Such may by fame be lured, by gold be hired—
'Tis constancy in the good cause alone,
Best justifies the meed thy valiant sons have won.

HAROLD THE DAUNTLESS:

A POEM, IN SIX CANTOS.

INTRODUCTION.

THERE is a mood of mind, we all have known
On drowsy eve, or dark and low'ring day,
When the tired spirits lose their sprightly tone,
And nought can chase the lingering hours away.
Dull on our soul falls Fancy's dazzling ray,
And wisdom holds his steadier torch in vain,
Obscured the painting seems, mistuned the lay,
Nor dare we of our listless load complain,
For who for sympathy may seek that cannot tell of pain?

The jolly sportsman knows such drearihood,
When bursts in deluge the autumnal rain,
Clouding that morn which threats the heath-cock's brood;
Of such, in summer's drought, the anglers plain,
Who hope the soft mild southern shower in vain;
But, more than all, the discontented fair,
Whom father stern, and sterner aunt, restrain

From county-ball, or race occurring rare,
While all her friends around their vestments gay prepare.

Ennui!—or, as our mothers call'd thee, Spleen!
To thee we owe full many a rare device;—
Thine is the sheaf of painted cards, I ween,
The rolling billiard-ball, the rattling dice,
The turning-lathe for framing gimcrack nice;
The amateur's blotch'd pallet thou mayst claim,
Retort, and air-pump, threatening frogs and mice,
(Murders disguised by philosophic name,)
And much of trifling grave, and much of buxom game.

Then of the books, to catch thy drowsy glance
Compiled, what bard the catalogue may quote!
Plays, poems, novels, never read but once;—
But not of such the tale fair Edgeworth wrote,
That bears thy name, and is thine antidote;

And not of such the strain my Thomson sung,
Delicious dreams inspiring by his note,
What time to Indolence his harp he strung;—
Oh! might my lay be rank'd that happier list among!

Each hath his refuge whom thy cares assail.
For me, I love my study-fire to trim,
And con right vacantly some idle tale,
Displaying on the couch each listless limb,
Till on the drowsy page the lights grow dim,
And doubtful slumber half supplies the theme;
While antique shapes of knight and giant grim,
Damsel and dwarf, in long procession gleam,
And the Romancer's tale becomes the Reader's dream.

'Tis thus my malady I well may bear,
Albeit outstretch'd, like Pope's own Paridel,
Upon the rack of a too-easy chair;
And find, to cheat the time, a powerful spell
In old romaunts of errantry that tell,
Or later legends of the Fairy-folk,
Or Oriental tale of Afrite fell,
Of Genii, Talisman, and broad-wing'd Roc,
Though taste may blush and frown, and sober reason mock.

Oft at such season too, will rhymes, unsought
Arrange themselves in some romantic lay;
The which, as things unfitting graver thought,
Are burnt or blotted on some wiser day.—
These few survive—and proudly let me say,

Court not the critic's smile, nor dread his frown;
They well may serve to wile an hour away,
Nor does the volume ask for more renown,
Than Ennui's yawning smile, what time she drops it down.

CANTO FIRST.

I.

LIST to the valorous deeds that were done
By Harold the Dauntless, Count Witikind's son!

Count Witikind came of a regal strain,
And roved with his Norsemen the land and the main.
Woe to the realms which he coasted! for there
Was shedding of blood, and rending of hair,
Rape of maiden, and slaughter of priest,
Gathering of ravens and wolves to the feast:
When he hoisted his standard black,
Before him was battle, behind him wrack,
And he burn'd the churches, that heathen Dane,
To light his band to their barks again.

II.

On Erin's shores was his outrage known,
The winds of France had his banners blown;
Little was there to plunder, yet still
His pirates had foray'd on Scottish hill:
But upon merry England's coast
More frequent he sail'd, for he won the most.
So wide and so far his ravage they knew,
If a sail but gleam'd white 'gainst the welkin blue,
Trumpet and bugle to arms did call,
Burghers hasten'd to man the wall,
Peasants fled inland his fury to 'scape,
Beacons were lighted on headland and cape,

Bells were toll'd out, and aye as they rung,
Fearful and faintly the grey brothers sung,
" Bless us, St. Mary, from flood and from fire,
From famine and pest, and Count Witikind's ire!"

III.

He liked the wealth of fair England so well,
That he sought in her bosom as native to dwell.
He enter'd the Humber in fearful hour,
And disembark'd with his Danish power.
Three Earls came against him with all their train,—
Two hath he taken, and one hath he slain.
Count Witikind left the Humber's rich strand,
And he wasted and warr'd in Northumberland.
But the Saxon King was a sire in age,
Weak in battle, in council sage;
Peace of that heathen leader he sought,
Gifts he gave, and quiet he bought;
And the Count took upon him the peaceable style
Of a vassal and liegeman of Britain's broad isle.

IV.

Time will rust the sharpest sword,
Time will consume the strongest cord;
That which moulders hemp and steel,
Mortal arm and nerve must feel.
Of the Danish band, whom Count Witikind led,
Many wax'd aged, and many were dead:
Himself found his armour full weighty to bear,
Wrinkled his brows grew, and hoary his hair;
He lean'd on a staff, when his step went abroad,
And patient his palfrey, when steed he bestrode.
As he grew feebler, his wildness ceased,
He made himself peace with prelate and priest;

Made his peace, and, stooping his head,
Patiently listed the counsel they said:
Saint Cuthbert's Bishop was holy and grave,
Wise and good was the counsel he gave.

V.

" Thou hast murder'd, robb'd, and spoil'd,
Time it is thy poor soul were assoil'd;
Priests didst thou slay, and churches burn,
Time it is now to repentance to turn;
Fiends hast thou worshipp'd, with fiendish rite,
Leave now the darkness, and wend into light:
O ! while life and space are given,
Turn thee yet, and think of Heaven !"
That stern old heathen his head he raised,
And on the good prelate he steadfastly gazed;
" Give me broad lands on the Wear and the Tyne,
My faith I will leave, and I'll cleave unto thine."

VI.

Broad lands he gave him on Tyne and Wear,
To be held of the church by bridle and spear;
Part of Monkwearmouth, of Tyndale part,
To better his will, and to soften his heart:
Count Witikind was a joyful man,
Less for the faith than the lands that he wan.
The high church of Durham is dress'd for the day,
The clergy are rank'd in their solemn array:
There came the Count, in a bear-skin warm,
Leaning on Hilda his concubine's arm.
He kneel'd before Saint Cuthbert's shrine,
With patience unwonted at rites divine;
He abjured the gods of heathen race,
And he bent his head at the font of grace.

But such was the grisly old proselyte's look,
That the priest who baptized him grew
    pale and shook ;
And the old monks mutter'd beneath their
    hood,
" Of a stem so stubborn can never spring
    good !"

VII.

Up then arose that grim convertite,
Homeward he hied him when ended the
    rite ;
The Prelate in honour will with him ride,
And feast in his castle on Tyne's fair side.
Banners and banderols danced in the wind,
Monks rode before them, and spearmen
    behind ;
Onward they pass'd, till fairly did shine
Pennon and cross on the bosom of Tyne;
And full in front did that fortress lower,
In darksome strength with its buttress
    and tower:
At the castle gate was young Harold there,
Count Witikind's only offspring and heir.

VIII.

Young Harold was fear'd for his hardi-
    hood,
His strength of frame, and his fury of
    mood.
Rude he was and wild to behold,
Wore neither collar nor bracelet of gold,
Cap of vair nor rich array,
Such as should grace that festal day:
His doublet of bull's hide was all un-
    braced,
Uncover'd his head, and his sandal un-
    laced:
His shaggy black locks on his brow hung
    low,
And his eyes glanced through them a
    swarthy glow;
A Danish club in his hand he bore,
The spikes were clotted with recent gore ;
At his back a she-wolf, and her wolf-
    cubs twain,
In the dangerous chase that morning slain.
Rude was the greeting his father he made,
None to the Bishop,—while thus he said:—

IX.

" What priest-led hypocrite art thou,
With thy humbled look and thy monkish
    brow,
Like a shaveling who studies to cheat his
    vow ?
Can'st thou be Witikind the Waster
    known,
Royal Eric's fearless son,
Haughty Gunhilda's haughtier lord,
Who won his bride by the axe and sword;
From the shrine of St. Peter the chalice
    who tore,
And melted to bracelets for Freya and
    Thor ;
With one blow of his gauntlet who burst
    the skull,
Before Odin's stone, of the Mountain
    Bull ?
Then ye worshipp'd with rites that to
    war-gods belong,
With the deed of the brave, and the blow
    of the strong ;
And now, in thine age to dotage sunk,
Wilt thou patter thy crimes to a shaven
    monk,—
Lay down thy mail-shirt for clothing of
    hair,—
Fasting and scourge, like a slave, wilt
    thou bear ?
Or, at best, be admitted in slothful bower
To batten with priest and with paramour?
Oh ! out upon thine endless shame !
Each Scald's high harp shall blast thy
    fame,
And thy son will refuse thee a father's
    name !"

X.

Ireful wax'd old Witikind's look,
His faltering voice with fury shook :—
" Hear me, Harold of harden'd heart !
Stubborn and wilful ever thou wert.
Thine outrage insane I command thee to
    cease,
Fear my wrath and remain at peace :—
Just is the debt of repentance I've paid,
Richly the church has a recompense made,
And the truth of her doctrines I prove
    with my blade,

But reckoning to none of my actions I
    owe,
And least to my son such accounting will
    show.
Why speak I to thee of repentance or
    truth,
Who ne'er from thy childhood knew
    reason or ruth?
Hence! to the wolf and the bear in her
    den;
These are thy mates, and not rational
    men."

XI.

Grimly smiled Harold, and coldly replied,
" We must honour our sires, if we fear
    when they chide.
For me, I am yet what thy lessons have
    made,
I was rock'd in a buckler and fed from a
    blade;
An infant, was taught to clasp hands and
    to shout
From the roofs of the tower when the
    flame had broke out;
In the blood of slain foemen my finger
    to dip,
And tinge with its purple my cheek and
    my lip.—
'Tis thou know'st not truth, that hast
    barter'd in eld,
For a price, the brave faith that thine
    ancestors held.
When this wolf,"—and the carcass he
    flung on the plain,—
" Shall awake and give food to her
    nurslings again,
The face of his father will Harold review;
Till then, aged Heathen, young Christian,
    adieu!"

XII.

Priest, monk, and prelate, stood aghast,
As through the pageant the heathen pass'd.
A cross-bearer out of his saddle he flung,
Laid his hand on the pommel, and into
    it sprung.
Loud was the shriek, and deep the groan,
When the holy sign on the earth was
    thrown!

The nerce old Count unsheathed his
    brand,
But the calmer Prelate stay'd his hand.
" Let him pass free!—Heaven knows its
    hour,—
But he must own repentance's power,
Pray and weep, and penance bear,
Ere he hold land by the Tyne and the
    Wear."
Thus in scorn and in wrath from his
    father is gone
Young Harold the Dauntless, Count
    Witikind's son.

XIII.

High was the feasting in Witikind's hall,
Revell'd priests, soldiers, and pagans, and
    all;
And e'en the good Bishop was fain to
    endure
The scandal, which time and instruction
    might cure:
It were dangerous, he deem'd, at the first
    to restrain,
In his wine and his wassail, a half-
    christen'd Dane.
The mead flow'd around, and the ale was
    drain'd dry,
Wild was the laughter, the song, and the
    cry;
With Kyrie Eleison, came clamorously in
The war-songs of Danesmen, Norweyan,
    and Finn.
Till man after man the contention gave
    o'er,
Outstretch'd on the rushes that strew'd
    the hall floor;
And the tempest within, having ceased its
    wild rout,
Gave place to the tempest that thunder'd
    without.

XIV.

Apart from the wassail, in turret alone,
Lay flaxen-hair'd Gunnar, old Ermen-
    garde's son;
In the train of Lord Harold that Page
    was the first,
For Harold in childhood had Ermengarde
    nursed;

And grieved was young Gunnar his
    master should roam,
Unhoused and unfriended, an exile from
    home.
He heard the deep thunder, the plashing
    of rain,
He saw the red lightning through shot-
    hole and pane;
" And oh !" said the Page, " on the
    shelterless wold
Lord Harold is wandering in darkness
    and cold !
What though he was stubborn, and way-
    ward, and wild,
He endured me because I was Ermen-
    garde's child,—
And often from dawn till the set of the sun,
In the chase, by his stirrup, unbidden I run ;
I would I were older, and knighthood
    could bear,
I would soon quit the banks of the Tyne
    and the Wear :
For my mother's command, with her last
    parting breath,
Bade me follow her nursling in life and to
    death.

XV.

" It pours and it thunders, it lightens
    amain,
As if Lok, the Destroyer, had burst from
    his chain !
Accursed by the Church, and expell'd by
    his sire,
Nor Christian nor Dane give him shelter
    or fire,
And this tempest what mortal may house-
    less endure ?
Unaided, unmantled, he dies on the moor,
Whate'er comes of Gunnar, he tarries not
    here."
He leapt from his couch and he grasp'd
    to his spear ;
Sought the hall of the feast.   Undisturb'd
    by his tread,
The wassailers slept fast as the sleep of
    the dead :
" Ungrateful and bestial !" his anger broke
    forth,
" To forget 'mid your goblets the pride
    of the North !

And you, ye cowl'd priests, who have
    plenty in store,
Must give Gunnar for ransom a palfrey
    and ore."

XVI.

Then, heeding full little of ban or of curse,
He has seized on the Prior of Jorvaux's
    purse :
Saint Meneholt's Abbot next morning has
    miss'd
His mantle, deep furr'd from the cape to
    the wrist :
The Seneschal's keys from his belt he has
    ta'en,
(Well drench'd on that eve was old
    Hildebrand's brain.)
To the stable-yard he made his way,
And mounted the Bishop's palfrey gay,
Castle and hamlet behind him has cast,
And right on his way to the moorland
    has pass'd.
Sore snorted the palfrey, unused to face
A weather so wild at so rash a pace ;
So long he snorted, so loud he neigh'd,
There answer'd a steed that was bound
    beside,
And the red flash of lightning show'd
    there where lay
His master, Lord Harold, outstretch'd
    on the clay.

XVII.

Up he started, and thunder'd out, "Stand !"
And raised the club in his deadly hand.
The flaxen-hair'd Gunnar his purpose told,
Show'd the palfrey and proffer'd the gold,
" Back, back, and home, thou simple boy !
Thou canst not share my grief or joy :
Have I not mark'd thee wail and cry
When thou hast seen a sparrow die?
And canst thou, as my follower should,
Wade ankle-deep through foeman's blood,
Dare mortal and immortal foe,
The gods above, the fiends below,
And man on earth, more hateful still,
The very fountain-head of ill ?
Desperate of life, and careless of death,
Lover of bloodshed, and slaughter, and
    scathe,

Such must thou be with me to roam,
And such thou canst not be—back, and
   home!"

XVIII.

Young Gunnar shook like an aspen bough,
As he heard the harsh voice and beheld
   the dark brow,
And half he repented his purpose and vow.
But now to draw back were bootless shame,
And he loved his master, so urged his
   claim:
"Alas! if my arm and my courage be weak,
Bear with me a while for old Ermengarde's
   sake;
Nor deem so lightly of Gunnar's faith,
As to fear he would break it for peril of
   death.
Have I not risk'd it to fetch thee this gold,
This surcoat and mantle to fence thee
   from cold?
And, did I bear a baser mind,
What lot remains if I stay behind?
The priests' revenge, thy father's wrath,
A dungeon, and a shameful death."

XIX.

With gentler look Lord Harold eyed
The Page, then turn'd his head aside;
And either a tear did his eyelash stain,
Or it caught a drop of the passing rain.
"Art thou an outcast, then?" quoth he;
"The meeter page to follow me."
'Twere bootless to tell what climes they
   sought,
Ventures achieved, and battles fought;
How oft with few, how oft alone,
Fierce Harold's arm the field hath won.
Men swore his eve, that flash'd so red
When each other glance was quench'd
   with dread,
Bore oft a light of deadly flame,
That ne'er from mortal courage came.
Those limbs so strong, that mood so stern,
That loved the couch of heath and fern,
Afar from hamlet, tower, and town,
More than to rest on driven down;
That stubborn frame, that sullen mood,
Men deem'd must come of aught but good;

And they whisper'd, the great Master
   Fiend was at one
With Harold the Dauntless, Count Witi-
   kind's son.

XX.

Years after years had gone and fled,
The good old Prelate lies lapp'd in lead;
In the chapel still is shown
His sculptured form on a marble stone,
With staff and ring and scapulaire,
And folded hands in the act of prayer.
Saint Cuthbert's mitre is resting now
On the haughty Saxon, bold Aldingar's
   brow;
The power of his crozier he loved to extend
O'er whatever would break, or whatever
   would bend;
And now hath he clothed him in cope
   and in pall,
And the Chapter of Durham has met at
   his call.
"And hear ye not, brethren," the proud
   Bishop said,
"That our vassal, the Danish Count
   Witikind's dead?
All his gold and his goods hath he given
To holy Church for the love of Heaven,
And hath founded a chantry with stipend
   and dole,
That priests and that beadsmen may pray
   for his soul:
Harold his son is wandering abroad,
Dreaded by man and abhorr'd by God;
Meet it is not, that such should heir
The lands of the church on the Tyne and
   the Wear,
And at her pleasure, her hallow'd hands
May now resume these wealthy lands."

XXI.

Answer'd good Eustace, a canon old,—
"Harold is tameless, and furious, and bold;
Ever Renown blows a note of fame,
And a note of fear, when she sounds his
   name;
Much of bloodshed and much of scathe
Have been their lot who have waked his
   wrath.

Leave him these lands and lordships still,
Heaven in its hour may change his will;
But if reft of gold, and of living bare,
An evil counsellor is despair."
More had he said, but the Prelate frown'd,
And murmur'd his brethren who sate
    around,
And with one consent have they given
    their doom,
That the Church should the lands of Saint
    Cuthbert resume.
So will'd the Prelate; and canon and dean
Gave to his judgment their loud amen.

CANTO SECOND.

I.

'Tis merry in greenwood,—thus runs the
    old lay,—
In the gladsome month of lively May,
When the wild birds' song on stem and
    spray
    Invites to forest bower;
Then rears the ash his airy crest,
Then shines the birch in silver vest,
And the beech in glistening leaves is drest,
And dark between shows the oak's proud
    breast,
    Like a chieftain's frowning tower;
Though a thousand branches join their
    screen,
Yet the broken sunbeams glance be-
    tween,
And tip the leaves with lighter green,
    With brighter tints the flower:
Dull is the heart that loves not then
The deep recess of the wildwood glen,
Where roe and red-deer find sheltering den,
    When the sun is in his power.

II.

Less merry, perchance, is the fading leaf
That follows so soon on the gather'd sheaf,
    When the greenwood loses the name;
Silent is then the forest bound,
Save the redbreast's note, and the rustling
    sound

Of frost-nipt leaves that are dropping
    round,
Or the deep-mouth'd cry of the distant
    hound
    That opens on his game:
Yet then, too, I love the forest wide,
Whether the sun in splendour ride,
And gild its many-colour'd side;
Or whether the soft and silvery haze,
In vapoury folds, o'er the landscape strays,
And half involves the woodland maze,
    Like an early widow's veil,
Where wimpling tissue from the gaze
The form half hides, and half betrays,
    Of beauty wan and pale.

III.

Fair Metelill was a woodland maid,
Her father a rover of greenwood shade,
By forest statutes undismay'd,
    Who lived by bow and quiver;
Well known was Wulfstane's archery,
By merry Tyne both on moor and lea,
Through wooded Weardale's glens so free,
Well beside Stanhope's wildwood tree,
    And well on Ganlesse river.
Yet free though he trespass'd on woodland
    game,
More known and more fear'd was the
    wizard fame
Of Jutta of Rookhope, the Outlaw's dame;
Fear'd when she frown'd was her eye of
    flame,
    More fear'd when in wrath she laugh'd;
For, then, 'twas said, more fatal true
To its dread aim her spell-glance flew
Than when from Wulfstane's bended yew
    Sprung forth the grey-goose shaft.

IV.

Yet had this fierce and dreaded pair,
So Heaven decreed, a daughter fair;
    None brighter crown'd the bed,
In Britain's bounds, of peer or prince,
Nor hath, perchance, a lovelier since,
    In this fair isle been bred.
And nought of fraud, or ire, or ill,
Was known to gentle Metelill,—
    A simple maiden she;

The spells in dimpled smile that lie,
And a downcast blush, and the darts
   that fly
With the sidelong glance of a hazel eye,
  Were her arms and witchery.
So young, so simple was she yet,
She scarce could childhood's joys forget,
And still she loved, in secret set
  Beneath the greenwood tree,
To plait the rushy coronet,
And braid with flowers her locks of jet,
  As when in infancy;—
Yet could that heart, so simple, prove
The early dawn of stealing love:
  Ah! gentle maid, beware!
The power who, now so mild a guest,
Gives dangerous yet delicious zest
To the calm pleasures of thy breast,
Will soon, a tyrant o'er the rest,
  Let none his empire share.

V.

One morn, in kirtle green array'd,
Deep in the wood the maiden stray'd,
  And, where a fountain sprung,
She sate her down, unseen, to thread
The scarlet berry's mimic braid,
  And while the beads she strung,
Like the blithe lark, whose carol gay
Gives a good-morrow to the day,
  So lightsomely she sung.

VI.

Song.

"LORD WILLIAM was born in gilded
  bower,
The heir of Wilton's lofty tower;
Yet better loves Lord William now
To roam beneath wild Rookhope's brow;
And William has lived where ladies fair
With gawds and jewels deck their hair,
Yet better loves the dewdrops still
That pearl the locks of Metelill.

"The pious Palmer loves, I wis,
Saint Cuthbert's hallow'd beads to kiss;
But I, though simple girl I be,
Might have such homage paid to me;

For did Lord William see me suit
This necklace of the bramble's fruit,
He fain—but must not have his will—
Would kiss the beads of Metelill.

"My nurse has told me many a tale,
How vows of love are weak and frail;
My mother says that courtly youth
By rustic maid means seldom sooth.
What should they mean? it cannot be,
That such a warning's meant for me,
For nought—oh! nought of fraud or ill
Can William mean to Metelill!"

VII.

Sudden she stops—and starts to feel
A weighty hand, a glove of steel,
Upon her shrinking shoulders laid;
Fearful she turn'd, and saw, dismay'd,
A Knight in plate and mail array'd,
His crest and bearing worn and fray'd,
  His surcoat soil'd and riven,
Form'd like that giant race of yore,
Whose long-continued crimes outwore
  The sufferance of Heaven.
Stern accents made his pleasure known,
Though then he used his gentlest tone:
"Maiden," he said, "sing forth thy glee,
Start not—sing on—it pleases me."

VIII.

Secured within his powerful hold,
To bend her knee, her hands to fold,
  Was all the maiden might;
And "Oh! forgive," she faintly said,
"The terrors of a simple maid,
  If thou art mortal wight!
But if—of such strange tales are told—
Unearthly warrior of the wold,
Thou comest to chide mine accents bold,
My mother, Jutta, knows the spell,
At noon and midnight pleasing well
  The disembodied ear.
Oh! let her powerful charms atone
For aught my rashness may have done,
  And cease thy grasp of fear."
Then laugh'd the Knight—his laughter's
  sound
Half in the hollow helmet drown'd;

His barred visor then he raised,
And steady on the maiden gazed.
He smooth'd his brows, as best he might,
To the dread calm of autumn night,
    When sinks the tempest roar;
Yet still the cautious fishers eye
The clouds, and fear the gloomy sky,
    And haul their barks on shore.

IX.

" Damsel," he said, " be wise and learn
Matters of weight and deep concern:
    From distant realms I come,
And, wanderer long, at length have plann'd
In this my native Northern land
    To seek myself a home.
Nor that alone—a mate I seek;
She must be gentle, soft, and meek,—
    No lordly dame for me;
Myself am something rough of mood,
And feel the fire of royal blood,
And therefore do not hold it good
    To match in my degree.
Then, since coy maidens say my face
Is harsh, my form devoid of grace,
For a fair lineage to provide,
'Tis meet that my selected bride
    In lineaments be fair;
I love thine well—till now I ne'er
Look'd patient on a face of fear,
But now that tremulous sob and tear
    Become thy beauty rare.
One kiss—nay, damsel, coy it not!—
And now go seek thy parents' cot,
And say, a bridegroom soon I come,
To woo my love, and bear her home."

X.

Home sprung the maid without a pause,
As leveret 'scaped from greyhound's jaws;
But still she lock'd, howe'er distress'd,
The secret in her boding breast;
Dreading her sire, who oft forbade
Her steps should stray to distant glade.
Night came—to her accustom'd nook
Her distaff aged Jutta took,
And by the lamp's imperfect glow,
Rough Wulfstane trimm'd his shafts and
    bow,

Sudden and clamorous, from the ground
Upstarted slumbering brach and hound;
Loud knocking next the lodge alarms,
And Wulfstane snatches at his arms,
When open flew the yielding door,
And that grim Warrior press'd the floor.

XI.

" All peace be here—What! none replies!
Dismiss your fears, and your surprise.
'Tis I—that Maid hath told my tale,—
Or, trembler, did thy courage fail?
It recks not—It is I demand
Fair Metelill in marriage band;
Harold the Dauntless I, whose name
Is brave men's boast and caitiff's shame."
The parents sought each other's eyes,
With awe, resentment, and surprise:
Wulfstane, to quarrel prompt, began
The stranger's size and thewes to scan;
But as he scann'd, his courage sunk,
And from unequal strife he shrunk,
Then forth, to blight and blemish, flies
The harmful curse from Jutta's eyes;
Yet, fatal howsoe'er, the spell
On Harold innocently fell!
And disappointment and amaze
Were in the witch's wilder gaze.

XII.

But soon the wit of woman woke,
And to the Warrior mild she spoke:
" Her child was all too young."—" A toy,
The refuge of a maiden coy."—
Again, " A powerful baron's heir
Claims in her heart an interest fair."—
" A trifle—whisper in his ear,
That Harold is a suitor here!"—
Baffled at length she sought delay:
" Would not the Knight till morning stay?
Late was the hour—he there might rest
Till morn, their lodge's honour'd guest."
Such were her words,—her craft might
    cast,
Her honour'd guest should sleep his last:
" No, not to-night—but soon," he swore,
" He would return, nor leave them more."
The threshold then his huge stride crost,
And soon he was in darkness lost.

XIII.

Appall'd a while the parents stood,
Then changed their fear to angry mood,
And foremost fell their words of ill
On unresisting Metelill:
Was she not caution'd and forbid,
Forewarn'd, implored, accused and chid,
And must she still to greenwood roam,
To marshal such misfortune home ?
"Hence, minion—to thy chamber hence—
There prudence learn and penitence."
She went—her lonely couch to steep
In tears which absent lovers weep ;
Or if she gain'd a troubled sleep,
Fierce Harold's suit was still the theme
And terror of her feverish dream.

XIV.

Scarce was she gone, her dame and sire
Upon each other bent their ire ;
" A woodsman thou, and hast a spear,
And couldst thou such an insult bear ?"
Sullen he said, " A man contends
With men, a witch with sprites and fiends;
Not to mere mortal wight belong
Yon gloomy brow and frame so strong.
But thou—is this thy promise fair,
That your Lord William, wealthy heir
To Ulrick, Baron of Witton-le-Wear,
Should Metelill to altar bear ?
Do all the spells thou boast'st as thine
Serve but to slay some peasant's kine,
His grain in autumn's storms to steep,
Or thorough fog and fen to sweep,
And hag-ride some poor rustic's sleep ?
Is such mean mischief worth the fame
Of sorceress and witch's name ?
Fame, which with all men's wish conspires,
With thy deserts and my desires,
To damn thy corpse to penal fires ?
Out on thee, witch! aroint! aroint!
What now shall put thy schemes in joint ?
What save this trusty arrow's point,
From the dark dingle when it flies,
And he who meets it gasps and dies."

XV.

Stern she replied, " I will not wage
War with thy folly or thy rage ;
But ere the morrow's sun be low,
Wulfstane of Rookhope, thou shalt know,
If I can venge me on a foe.
Believe the while, that whatsoe'er
I spoke, in ire, of bow and spear,
It is not Harold's destiny
The death of pilfer'd deer to die.
But he, and thou, and yon pale moon,
(That shall be yet more pallid soon,
Before she sink behind the dell,)
Thou, she, and Harold too, shall tell
What Jutta knows of charm or spell."
Thus muttering, to the door she bent
Her wayward steps, and forth she went,
And left alone the moody sire,
To cherish or to slake his ire.

XVI.

Far faster than belong'd to age
Has Jutta made her pilgrimage.
A priest has met her as she pass'd,
And cross'd himself and stood aghast:
She traced a hamlet—not a cur
His throat would ope, his foot would stir;
By crouch, by trembling, and by groan,
They made her hated presence known!
But when she trode the sable fell,
Were wilder sounds her way to tell,—
For far was heard the fox's yell,
The black-cock waked and faintly crew,
Scream'd o'er the moss the scared curlew;
Where o'er the cataract the oak
Lay slant, was heard the raven's croak;
The mountain-cat, which sought his prey,
Glared, scream'd, and started from her way.
Such music cheer'd her journey lone
To the deep dell and rocking stone:
There, with unhallow'd hymn of praise,
She called a God of heathen days.

XVII.

Invocation.

" From thy Pomeranian throne,
Hewn in rock of living stone,
Where, to thy godhead faithful yet,
Bend Esthonian, Finn, and Lett,
And their swords in vengeance whet,
That shall make thine altars wet,
Wet and red for ages more
With the Christians' hated gore,—

Hear me! Sovereign of the Rock,
Hear me! mighty Zernebock!

" Mightiest of the mighty known,
Here thy wonders have been shown;
Hundred tribes in various tongue
Oft have here thy praises sung;
Down that stone with Runic seam'd,
Hundred victims' blood hath stream'd!
Now one woman comes alone,
And but wets it with her own,
The last, the feeblest of thy flock,—
Hear—and be present, Zernebock!

" Hark! he comes! the night-blast cold
Wilder sweeps along the wold;
The cloudless moon grows dark and dim,
And bristling hair and quaking limb
Proclaim the Master Demon nigh,—
Those who view his form shall die!
Lo! I stoop and veil my head;
Thou who ridest the tempest dread,
Shaking hill and rending oak—
Spare me! spare me! Zernebock.

" He comes not yet! Shall cold delay
Thy votaress at her need repay?
Thou—shall I call thee god or fiend?—
Let others on thy mood attend
With prayer and ritual—Jutta's arms
Are necromantic words and charms;
Mine is the spell, that, utter'd once,
Shall wake Thy Master from his trance,
Shake his red mansion-house of pain,
And burst his seven-times-twisted chain!—
So! com'st thou ere the spell is spoke?
I own thy presence, Zernebock."—

XVIII.

"Daughter of dust," the Deep Voice said,
—Shook while it spoke the vale for dread,
Rock'd on the base that massive stone,
The Evil Deity to own,—
" Daughter of dust! not mine the power
Thou seek'st on Harold's fatal hour.
'Twixt heaven and hell there is a strife
Waged for his soul and for his life,
And fain would we the combat win,
And snatch him in his hour of sin.
There is a star now rising red,
That threats him with an influence dread:

Woman, thine arts of malice whet,
To use the space before it set.
Involve him with the church in strife,
Push on adventurous chance his life;
Ourself will in the hour of need,
As best we may thy counsels speed."
So ceased the Voice; for seven leagues round
Each hamlet started at the sound;
But slept again, as slowly died
Its thunders on the hill's brown side.

XIX.

And is this all," said Jutta stern,
"That thou canst teach and I can learn?
Hence! to the land of fog and waste,
There fittest is thine influence placed,
Thou powerless, sluggish Deity!
But ne'er shall Briton bend the knee
Again before so poor a god."
She struck the altar with her rod;
Slight was the touch, as when at need
A damsel stirs her tardy steed;
But to the blow the stone gave place,
And, starting from its balanced base,
Roll'd thundering down the moonlight
    dell,—
Re-echo'd moorland, rock, and fell;
Into the moonlight tarn it dash'd,
Their shores the sounding surges lash'd,
    And there was ripple, rage, and foam;
But on that lake, so dark and lone,
Placid and pale the moonbeam shone
    As Jutta hied her home.

——————

CANTO THIRD.

I.

GREY towers of Durham! there was
    once a time
I view'd your battlements with such
    vague hope,
As brightens life in its first dawning
    prime;
Not that e'en then came within fancy's
    scope
A vision vain of mitre, throne, or cope;
Yet, gazing on the venerable hall,
Her flattering dreams would in per-
    spective ope

Some reverend room, some prebendary's
    stall,—
And thus Hope me deceived as she de-
    ceiveth all.

Well yet I love thy mix'd and massive
    piles,
Half church of God, half castle 'gainst
    the Scot,
And long to roam these venerable aisles,
With records stored of deeds long since
    forgot;
There might I share my Surtees'
    happier lot,
Who leaves at will his patrimonial field
To ransack every crypt and hallow'd
    spot,
And from oblivion rend the spoils they
    yield,
Restoring priestly chant and clang of
    knightly shield.

Vain is the wish—since other cares
    demand
Each vacant hour, and in another
    clime;
But still that northern harp invites my
    hand,
Which tells the wonder of thine earlier
    time;
And fain its numbers would I now
    command
To paint the beauties of that dawning
    fair,
When Harold, gazing from its lofty
    stand
Upon the western heights of Beau-
    repaire,
Saw Saxon Eadmer's towers beg'rt by
    winding Wear.

II.

Fair on the half-seen stream the sun-
    beams danced,
Betraying it beneath the woodland bank,
And fair between the Gothic turrets
    glanced
Broad lights, and shadows fell on front
    and flank.

Where tower and buttress rose in
    martial rank,
And girdled in the massive donjon
    Keep,
And from their circuit peal'd o'er bush
    and bank
The matin bell with summons long
    and deep,
And echo answer'd still with long-re-
    sounding sweep.

III.

The morning mists rose from the ground,
Each merry bird awaken'd round,
    As if in revelry;
Afar the bugles' clanging sound
Call'd to the chase the lagging hound;
    The gale breathed soft and free,
And seem'd to linger on its way
To catch fresh odours from the spray,
And waved it in its wanton play
    So light and gamesomely.
The scenes which morning beams reveal,
Its sounds to hear, its gales to feel
In all their fragrance round him steal,
It melted Harold's heart of steel,
And, hardly wotting why,
He doff'd his helmet's gloomy pride,
And hung it on a tree beside,
    Laid mace and falchion by,
And on the greensward sate him down,
And from his dark habitual frown
    Relax'd his rugged brow—
Whoever hath the doubtful task
From that stern Dane a boon to ask,
    Were wise to ask it now.

IV.

His place beside young Gunnar took,
And mark'd his master's softening look,
And in his eye's dark mirror spied
The gloom of stormy thoughts subside,
And cautious watch'd the fittest tide
    To speak a warning word.
So when the torrent's billows shrink,
The timid pilgrim on the brink
Waits long to see them wave and sink,
    Ere he dare brave the ford,

And often, after doubtful pause,
His step advances or withdraws:
Fearful to move the slumbering ire
Of his stern lord, thus stood the squire,
  Till Harold raised his eye,
That glanced as when athwart the shroud
Of the dispersing tempest-cloud
  The bursting sunbeams fly.

V.

" Arouse thee, son of Ermengarde,
Offspring of prophetess and bard!
Take harp, and greet this lovely prime
With some high strain of Runic rhyme,
Strong, deep, and powerful! Peal it round
Like that loud bell's sonorous sound,
Yet wild by fits, as when tne lay
Of bird and bugle hail the day.
Such was my grandsire Eric's sport,
When dawn gleam'd on his martial court.
Heymar the Scald, with harp's high sound,
Summon'd the chiefs who slept around;
Couch'd on the spoils of wolf and bear,
They roused like lions from their lair,
Then rush'd in emulation forth
To enhance the glories of the North.—
Proud Eric, mightiest of thy race,
Where is thy shadowy resting-place?
In wild Valhalla hast thou quaff'd
From foeman's skull metheglin draught,
Or wanderest where thy cairn was piled
To frown o'er oceans wide and wild?
Or have the milder Christians given
Thy refuge in their peaceful heaven?
Where'er thou art, to thee are known
Our toils endured, our trophies won,
Our wars, our wanderings, and our woes."
He ceased, and Gunnar's song arose.

VI.

Song.

" HAWK and osprey scream'd for joy
O'er the beetling cliffs of Hoy,
Crimson foam the beach o'erspread,
The heath was dyed with darker red,
When o'er Eric, Inguar's son,
Dane and Northman piled the stone;

Singing wild the war-song stern,
' Rest thee, Dweller of the Cairn!'

" Where eddying currents foam and boil
By Bersa's burgh and Græmsay's isle,
The seaman sees a martial form
Half-mingled with the mist and storm.
In anxious awe he bears away
To moor his bark in Stromna's bay,
And murmurs from the bounding stern,
' Rest thee, Dweller of the Cairn!'

" What cares disturb the mighty dead?
Each honour'd rite was duly paid;
No daring hand thy helm unlaced,
Thy sword, thy shield, were near thee
    placed,—
Thy flinty couch no tear profaned,
Without, with hostile blood was stain'd;
Within, 'twas lined with moss and fern,—
Then rest thee, Dweller of the Cairn!"

" He may not rest: from realms afar
Comes voice of battle and of war,
Of conquest wrought with bloody hand
On Carmel's cliffs and Jordan's strand,
When Odin's warlike son could daunt ·
The turban'd race of Termagaunt."——

VII.

" Peace," said the Knight, " the noble
    Scald
Our warlike fathers' deeds recall'd,
But never strove to soothe the son
With tales of what himself had done.
At Odin's board the bard sits high
Whose harp ne'er stoop'd to flattery;
But highest he whose daring lay
Hath dared unwelcome truths to say."
With doubtful smile young Gunnar eyed
His master's looks, and nought replied—
But well that smile his master led
To construe what he left unsaid.
" Is it to me, thou timid youth,
Thou fear'st to speak unwelcome truth?
My soul no more thy censure grieves
Than frosts rob laurels of their leaves.
Say on—and yet—beware the rude
And wild distemper of my blood;
Loth were I that mine ire should wrong
The youth that bore my shield so long,

And who, in service constant still,
Though weak in frame, art strong in
    will."—
"Oh!" quoth the page, "even there
    depends
My counsel—there my warning tends—
Oft seems as of my master's breast
Some demon were the sudden guest;
Then at the first misconstrued word
His hand is on the mace and sword,
From her firm seat his wisdom driven,
His life to countless dangers given.—
O! would that Gunnar could suffice
To be the fiend's last sacrifice,
So that, when glutted with my gore,
He fled and tempted thee no more!"

VIII.

Then waved his hand, and shook his head
The impatient Dane, while thus he said:
"Profane not, youth—it is not thine
To judge the spirit of our line—
The bold Berserkar's rage divine,
Through whose inspiring, deeds are
    wrought
Past human strength and human thought.
When full upon his gloomy soul
The champion feels the influence roll,
He swims the lake, he leaps the wall—
Heeds not the depth, nor plumbs the fall—
Unshielded, mail-less, on he goes
Singly against a host of foes;
Their spears he holds like wither'd reeds,
Their mail like maiden's silken weeds;
One 'gainst a hundred will he strive,
Take countless wounds, and yet survive.
Then rush the eagles to his cry
Of slaughter and of victory,—
And blood he quaffs like Odin's bowl,
Deep drinks his sword,—deep drinks his
    soul;
And all that meet him in his ire
He gives to ruin, rout, and fire;
Then, like gorged lion, seeks some den,
And couches till he's man agen.—
Thou know'st the signs of look and limb,
When 'gins that rage to overbrim—
Thou know'st when I am moved, and why;
And when thou seest me roll mine eye,

Set my teeth thus, and stamp my foot,
Regard thy safety and be mute;
But else speak boldly out whate'er
Is fitting that a knight should hear.
I love thee, youth. Thy lay has power
Upon my dark and sullen hour;—
So Christian monks are wont to say
Demons of old were charm'd away;
Then fear not I will rashly deem
Ill of thy speech, whate'er the theme."

IX.

As down some strait in doubt and dread
The watchful pilot drops the lead,
And, cautious in the midst to steer,
The shoaling channel sounds with fear;
So, lest on dangerous ground he swerved.
The Page his master's brow observed,
Pausing at intervals to fling
His hand o'er the melodious string,
And to his moody breast apply
The soothing charm of harmony,
While hinted half, and half exprest,
This warning song convey'd the rest.—

Song.

I.

"Ill fares the bark with tackle riven,
And ill when on the breakers driven,—
Ill when the storm-sprite shrieks in air,
And the scared mermaid tears her hair;
But worse when on her helm the hand
Of some false traitor holds command.

2.

"Ill fares the fainting Palmer, placed
'Mid Hebron's rocks or Rana's waste,—
Ill when the scorching sun is high,
And the expected font is dry,—
Worse when his guide o'er sand and heath,
The barbarous Copt, has plann'd his death.

3.

"Ill fares the Knight with buckler cleft,
And ill when of his helm bereft,—
Ill when his steed to earth is flung,
Or from his grasp his falchion wrung;
But worse, if instant ruin token,
When he lists rede by woman spoken."—

X.

"How now, fond boy?—Canst thou
      think ill,"
Said Harold, "of fair Metelill?"—
"She may be fair," the Page replied,
   As through the strings he ranged,—
"She may be fair; but yet," he cried,
   And then the strain he changed,——

Song.

1.

"She may be fair," he sang, "but yet
   Far fairer have I seen
Than she, for all her locks of jet,
   And eyes so dark and sheen,
Were I a Danish knight in arms,
   As one day I may be,
My heart should own no foreign charms,—
   A Danish maid for me.

2.

"I love my fathers' northern land,
   Where the dark pine-trees grow,
And the bold Baltic's echoing strand
   Looks o'er each grassy oe.*
I love to mark the lingering sun,
   From Denmark loth to go,
And leaving on the billows bright,
To cheer the short-lived summer night,
   A path of ruddy glow.

3.

"But most the northern maid I love,
   With breast like Denmark's snow,
And form as fair as Denmark's pine,
Who loves with purple heath to twine
   Her locks of sunny glow;
And sweetly blends that shade of gold
   With the cheek's rosy hue,
And Faith might for her mirror hold
   That eye of matchless blue.

4.

"'Tis hers the manly sports to love
   That southern maidens fear,
To bend the bow by stream and grove,
   And lift the hunter's spear.

---

* Oe, Island.

She can her chosen champion's flight
   With eye undazzled see,
Clasp him victorious from the strife,
Or on his corpse yield up her life,—
   A Danish maid for me!"

XI.

Then smiled the Dane—"Thou canst so
      well
The virtues of our maidens tell,
Half could I wish my choice had been
Blue eyes, and hair of golden sheen,
And lofty soul;—yet what of ill
Hast thou to charge on Metelill?"—
"Nothing on her," young Gunnar said,
"But her base sire's ignoble trade.
Her mother, too—the general fame
Hath given to Jutta evil name,
And in her grey eye is a flame
Art cannot hide, nor fear can tame.—
That sordid woodman's peasant cot
Twice have thine honour'd footsteps
      sought,
And twice return'd with such ill rede
As sent thee on some desperate deed."—

XII.

"Thou errest; Jutta wisely said,
He that comes suitor to a maid,
Ere link'd in marriage, should provide
Lands and a dwelling for his bride—
My father's, by the Tyne and Wear,
I have reclaim'd."—"O, all too dear,
And all too dangerous the prize,
E'en were it won," young Gunnar
      cries;—
"And then this Jutta's fresh device,
That thou shouldst seek, a heathen Dane,
From Durham's priests a boon to gain,
When thou hast left their vassals slain
In their own halls!"—Flash'd Harold's
      eye,
Thunder'd his voice—"False Page, you
      lie!
The castle, hall and tower, is mine,
Built by old Witikind on Tyne.
The wild-cat will defend his den,
Fights for her nest the timid wren;

And think'st thou I'll forego my right
For dread of monk or monkish knight?
Up and away, that deepening bell
Doth of the Bishop's conclave tell.
Thither will I, in manner due,
As Jutta bade, my claim to sue;
And, if to right me they are loth,
Then woe to church and chapter both!"
Now shift the scene, and let the curtain
  fall,
And our next entry be Saint Cuthbert's
  hall.

CANTO FOURTH.

I.

FULL many a bard hath sung the solemn
  gloom
Of the long Gothic aisle and stone-
  ribb'd roof,
O'er-canopying shrine, and gorgeous
  tomb,
Carved screen, and altar glimmering far
  aloof,
And blending with the shade,—a
  matchless proof
Of high devotion, which hath now
  wax'd cold;
Yet legends say, that Luxury's brute
  hoof
Intruded oft within such sacred fold,
Like step of Bel's false priest, track'd in
  his fane of old.

Well pleased am I, howe'er, that when
  the rout
Of our rude neighbours whilome deign'd
  to come,
Uncall'd, and eke unwelcome, to sweep
  out
And cleanse our chancel from the rags
  of Rome,
They spoke not on our ancient fane the
  doom
To which their bigot zeal gave o'er
  their own,
But spared the martyr'd saint and
  storied tomb,

Though papal miracles had graced the
  stone,
And though the aisles still loved the organ's
  swelling tone.

And deem not, though 'tis now my
  part to paint
A Prelate sway'd by love of power
  and gold,
That all who wore the mitre of our Saint
Like to ambitious Aldingar I hold;
Since both in modern times and days of
  old
It sate on those whose virtues might
  atone
Their predecessors' frailties trebly told;
Matthew and Morton we as such may
  own—
And such (if fame speak truth) the
  honour'd Barrington.

II.

But now to earlier and to ruder times,
As subject meet, I tune my rugged
  rhymes,
Telling how fairly the chapter was met,
And rood and books in seemly order set;
Huge brass-clasp'd volumes, which the
  hand
Of studious priest but rarely scann'd,
Now on fair carved desk display'd,
'Twas theirs the solemn scene to aid.
O'erhead with many a scutcheon graced,
And quaint devices interlaced,
A labyrinth of crossing rows,
The roof in lessening arches shows;
Beneath its shade placed proud and high,
With footstool and with canopy,
Sate Aldingar,—and prelate ne'er
More haughty graced Saint Cuthbert's
  chair;
Canons and deacons were placed below,
In due degree and lengthen'd row.
Unmoved and silent each sat there,
Like image in his oaken chair;
Nor head, nor hand, nor foot they
  stirr'd,
Nor lock of hair, nor tress of beard;

And of their eyes severe alone
The twinkle show'd they were not stone.

III.

The Prelate was to speech address'd,
Each head sunk reverent on each breast;
But ere his voice was heard—without
Arose a wild tumultuous shout,
Offspring of wonder mix'd with fear,
Such as in crowded streets we hear
Hailing the flames, that, bursting out,
Attract yet scare the rabble rout.
Ere it had ceased, a giant hand
Shook oaken door and iron band,
Till oak and iron both gave way,
Clash'd the long bolts, the hinges bray,
And, ere upon angel or saint they can
    call,
Stands Harold the Dauntless in midst of
    the hall.

IV.

"Now save ye, my masters, both rochet
    and rood,
From Bishop with mitre to Deacon with
    hood!
For here stands Count Harold, old
    Witikind's son,
Come to sue for the lands which his
    ancestors won."
The Prelate look'd round him with sore
    troubled eye,
Unwilling to grant, yet afraid to deny;
While each Canon and Deacon who
    heard the Dane speak,
To be safely at home would have fasted
    a week:—
Then Aldingar roused him, and answer'd
    again,
"Thou suest for a boon which thou
    canst not obtain;
The Church hath no fiefs for an un-
    christen'd Dane.
Thy father was wise, and his treasure
    hath given,
That the priests of a chantry might hymn
    him to heaven;
And the fiefs which whilome he possess'd
    as his due,
Have lapsed to the Church, and been
    granted anew

To Anthony Conyers and Alberic Vere,
For the service Saint Cuthbert's bless'd
    banner to bear,
When the bands of the North come to
    foray the Wear;
Then disturb not our conclave with
    wrangling or blame,
But in peace and in patience pass hence
    as ye came."

V.

Loud laugh'd the stern Pagan,—"They're
    free from the care
Of fief and of service, both Conyers and
    Vere,—
Six feet of your chancel is all they will
    need,
A buckler of stone and a corslet of lead.—
Ho, Gunnar!—the tokens;"—and, sever'd
    anew,
A head and a hand on the altar he
    threw.
Then shudder'd with terror both Canon
    and Monk,
They knew the glazed eye and the coun-
    tenance shrunk,
And of Anthony Conyers the half-grizzled
    hair,
And the scar on the hand of Sir Alberic
    Vere.
There was not a churchman or priest
    that was there,
But grew pale at the sight, and betook
    him to prayer.

VI.

Count Harold laugh'd at their looks of
    fear:
"Was this the hand should your banner
    bear?
Was that the head should wear the casque
In battle at the Church's task?
Was it to such you gave the place
Of Harold with the heavy mace?
Find me between the Wear and Tyne
A knight will wield this club of mine,—
Give him my fiefs, and I will say
There's wit beneath the cowl of grey."

He raised it, rough with many a stain,
Caught from crush'd skull and spouting
    brain;
He wheel'd it that it shrilly sung,
And the aisles echo'd as it swung,
Then dash'd it down with sheer descent,
And split King Osric's monument.—
" How like ye this music! How trow
    ye the hand
That can wield such a mace may be reft
    of its land?
No answer?—I spare ye a space to agree,
And Saint Cuthbert inspire you, a saint
    if he be.
Ten strides through your chancel, ten
    strokes on your bell,
And again I am with you—grave fathers,
    farewell."

VII.

He turn'd from their presence, he clash'd
    the oak door,
And the clang of his stride died away on
    the floor;
And his head from his bosom the Prelate
    uprears
With a ghost-seer's look when the ghost
    disappears.
" Ye Priests of Saint Cuthbert, now give
    me your rede,
For never of counsel had Bishop more
    need!
Were the arch-fiend incarnate in flesh
    and in bone,
The language, the look, and the laugh
    were his own.
In the bounds of Saint Cuthbert there is
    not a knight
Dare confront in our quarrel yon goblin
    in fight;
Then rede me aright to his claim to reply,
'Tis unlawful to grant, and 'tis death to
    deny."

VIII.

On ven'son and malmsie that morning
    had fed
The Cellarer Vinsauf—'twas thus that he
    said:

" Delay till to-morrow the Chapter's
    reply;
Let the feast be spread fair, and the wine
    be pour'd high:
If he's mortal he drinks,—if he drinks, he
    is ours—
His bracelets of iron,—his bed in our
    towers."
This man had a laughing eye,
Trust not, friends, when such you spy;
A beaker's depth he well could drain,
Revel, sport, and jest amain—
The haunch of the deer and the grape's
    bright dye
Never bard loved them better than I;
But sooner than Vinsauf fill'd me my wine,
Pass'd me his jest, and laugh'd at mine,
Though the buck were of Bearpark, of
    Bordeaux the vine,
With the dullest hermit I'd rather dine
On an oaken cake and a draught of the
    Tyne.

IX.

Walwayn the leech spoke next—he knew
Each plant that loves the sun and dew,
But special those whose juice can gain
Dominion o'er the blood and brain;
The peasant who saw him by pale moon
    beam
Gathering such herbs by bank and stream,
Deem'd his thin form and soundless
    tread
Were those of wanderer from the dead.—
" Vinsauf, thy wine," he said, " hath
    power,
Our gyves are heavy, strong our tower,
Yet three drops from this flask of mine,
More strong than dungeons, gyves, or wine,
Shall give him prison under ground
More dark, more narrow, more profound.
Short rede, good rede, let Harold have—
A dog's death, and a heathen's grave."
I have lain on a sick man's bed,
Watching for hours for the leech's tread,
As if I deem'd that his presence alone
Were of power to bid my pain begone;
I have listed his words of comfort given,
As if to oracles from heaven;

I have counted his steps from my chamber
    door,
And bless'd them when they were heard
    no more;—
But sooner than Walwayn my sick couch
    should nigh,
My choice were, by leech-craft unaided,
    to die.

X.

" Such service done in fervent zeal
The Church may pardon and conceal,"
The doubtful Prelate said, " but ne'er
The counsel ere the act should hear.—
Anselm of Jarrow, advise us now,
The stamp of wisdom is on thy brow;
Thy days, thy nights, in cloister pent,
Are still to mystic learning lent;—
Anselm of Jarrow, in thee is my hope,
Thou well mayest give counsel to Prelate
    or Pope."

XI.

Answer'd the Prior—" 'Tis wisdom's use
Still to delay what we dare not refuse;
Ere granting the boon he comes hither to
    ask,
Shape for the giant gigantic task;
Let us see how a step so sounding can
    tread
In paths of darkness, danger, and dread;
He may not, he will not, impugn our
    decree,
That calls but for proof of his chivalry;
And were Guy to return, or Sir Bevis
    the Strong,
Our wilds have adventure might cumber
    them long—
The Castle of Seven Shields "——" Kind
    Anselm, no more!
The step of the Pagan approaches the
    door."
The churchmen were hush'd.—In his
    mantle of skin,
With his mace on his shoulder, Count
    Harold strode in.
There was foam on his lips, there was
    fire in his eye,
For, chafed by attendance, his fury was
    nigh.

" Ho! Bishop," he said, " dost thou
    grant me my claim?
Or must I assert it by falchion and
    flame?"—

XII.

" On thy suit, gallant Harold," the Bishop
    replied,
In accents which trembled, " we may not
    decide,
Until proof of your strength and your
    valour we saw—
'Tis not that we doubt them, but such is
    the law."—
" And would you, Sir Prelate, have
    Harold make sport
For the cowls and the shavelings that
    herd in thy court?
Say what shall he do?—From the shrine
    shall he tear
The lead bier of thy patron, and heave it
    in air,
And through the long chancel make
    Cuthbert take wing,
With the speed of a bullet dismiss'd from
    the sling?"—
" Nay, spare such probation," the Cellarer
    said,
" From the mouth of our minstrels thy
    task shall be read.
While the wine sparkles high in the
    goblet of gold,
And the revel is loudest, thy task shall be
    told;
And thyself, gallant Harold, shall, hear-
    ing it, tell
That the Bishop, his cowls, and his shave-
    lings, meant well."

XIII.

Loud revell'd the guests, and the goblets
    loud rang,
But louder the minstrel, Hugh Meneville,
    sang;
And Harold, the hurry and pride of
    whose soul,
E'en when verging to fury, own'd music's
    control,

Still bent on the harper his broad sable eye,
And often untasted the goblet pass'd by;
Than wine, or than wassail, to him was
   more dear
The minstrel's high tale of enchantment
   to hear;
And the Bishop that day might of Vinsauf
   complain
That his art had but wasted his wine-
   casks in vain.

XIV.

THE CASTLE OF THE SEVEN SHIELDS.

A Ballad.

THE Druid Urien had daughters seven,
Their skill could call the moon from
   heaven;
So fair their forms and so high their fame,
That seven proud kings for their suitors
   came.

King Mador and Rhys came from Powis
   and Wales,
Unshorn was their hair, and unpruned
   were their nails;
From Strath-Clwyde was Ewain, and
   Ewain was lame,
And the red-bearded Donald from Gal-
   loway came.

Lot, King of Lodon, was hunchback'd
   from youth;
Dunmail of Cumbria had never a tooth;
But Adolf of Bambrough, Northumberland's heir,
Was gay and was gallant, was young and
   was fair.

There was strife 'mongst the sisters, for
   each one would have
For husband King Adolf, the gallant and
   brave;
And envy bred hate, and hate urged them
   to blows,
When the firm earth was cleft, and the
   Arch-fiend arose!

He swore to the maidens their wish to
   fulfil—
They swore to the foe they would work
   by his will.
A spindle and distaff to each hath he
   given,
" Now hearken my spell," said the Outcast of heaven.

" Ye shall ply these spindles at midnight
   hour,
And for every spindle shall rise a tower,
Where the right shall be feeble, the
   wrong shall have power,
And there shall ye dwell with your
   paramour."

Beneath the pale moonlight they sate on
   the wold,
And the rhymes which they chanted must
   never be told;
And as the black wool from the distaff
   they sped,
With blood from their bosom they
   moisten'd the thread.

As light danced the spindles beneath the
   cold gleam,
The castle arose like the birth of a dream—
The seven towers ascended like mist from
   the ground,
Seven portals defend them, seven ditches
   surround.

Within that dread castle seven monarchs
   were wed,
But six of the seven ere the morning lay
   dead;
With their eyes all on fire, and their
   daggers all red,
Seven damsels surround the Northumbrian's bed.

" Six kingly bridegrooms to death we
   have done,
Six gallant kingdoms King Adolf hath
   won,
Six lovely brides all his pleasure to do,
Or the bed of the seventh shall be hus-
   bandless too."

Well chanced it that Adolf the night
when he wed,
Had confess'd and had sain'd him ere
boune to his bed;
He sprung from the couch and his broadsword he drew,
And there the seven daughters of Urien
he slew.

The gate of the castle he bolted and seal'd,
And hung o'er each arch-stone a crown
and a shield;
To the cells of Saint Dunstan then wended
his way,
And died in his cloister an anchorite grey.

Seven monarchs' wealth in that castle lies
stow'd,
The foul fiends brood o'er them like raven
and toad.
Whoever shall guesten these chambers
within,
From curfew till matins, that treasure
shall win.

But manhood grows faint as the world
waxes old!
There lives not in Britain a champion so
bold,
So dauntless of heart, and so prudent of
brain,
As to dare the adventure that treasure to
gain.

The waste ridge of Cheviot shall wave
with the rye,
Before the rude Scots shall Northumberland fly,
And the flint cliffs of Bambro' shall melt
in the sun,
Before that adventure be peril'd and won.

XV.

" And is this my probation?" wild Harold
he said,
" Within a lone castle to press a lone
bed?—
Good even, my Lord Bishop,—Saint
Cuthbert to borrow,
The Castle of Seven Shields receives me
to-morrow."

CANTO FIFTH.

I.

DENMARK'S sage courtier to her
princely youth,
Granting his cloud an ouzel or a whale,
Spoke, though unwittingly, a partial
truth;
For Fantasy embroiders Nature's veil.
The tints of ruddy eve, or dawning pale,
Of the swart thunder-cloud, or silver
haze,
Are but the ground-work of the rich
detail
Which Fantasy with pencil wild por-
trays,
Blending what seems and is, in the wrapt
muser's gaze.

Nor are the stubborn forms of earth and
stone
Less to the Sorceress's empire given;
For not with unsubstantial hues alone,
Caught from the varying surge, or
vacant heaven,
From bursting sunbeam, or from flash-
ing levin,
She limns her pictures: on the earth, as
air,
Arise her castles, and her car is driven;
And never gazed the eye on scene so
fair,
But of its boasted charms gave Fancy half
the share.

II.

Up a wild pass went Harold, bent to
prove,
Hugh Meneville, the adventure of thy
lay;
Gunnar pursued his steps in faith and
love,
Ever companion of his master's way.
Midward their path, a rock of granite
grey
From the adjoining cliff had made descent,—
A barren mass—yet with her drooping
spray

Had a young birch-tree crown'd its
    battlement,
Twisting her fibrous roots through
    cranny, flaw, and rent.

This rock and tree could Gunnar's
    thought engage
Till Fancy brought the tear-drop to his
    eye,
And at his master ask'd the timid Page,
" What is the emblem that a bard
    should spy
In that rude rock and its green canopy ?"
And Harold said, " Like to the helmet
    brave
Of warrior slain in fight it seems to lie,
And these same drooping boughs do
    o'er it wave
Not all unlike the plume his lady's favour
    gave."—

"Ah, no!" replied the Page; " the ill-
    starr'd love
Of some poor maid is in the emblem
    shown,
Whose fates are with some hero's in-
    terwove,
And rooted on a heart to love un-
    known :
And as the gentle dews of heaven alone
Nourish those drooping boughs, and as
    the scathe
Of the red lightning rends both tree
    and stone,
So fares it with her unrequited faith,—
Her sole relief is tears—her only refuge
    death."—

III.

"Thou art a fond fantastic boy,"
Harold replied, " to females coy,
    Yet prating still of love ;
Even so amid the clash of war
I know thou lovest to keep afar,
Though destined by thy evil star
    With one like me to rove,
Whose business and whose joys are found
Upon the bloody battle-ground.
Yet, foolish trembler as thou art,
Thou hast a nook of my rude heart,
And thou and I will never part ;—

Harold would wrap the world in flame
Ere injury on Gunnar came !"

IV.

The grateful Page made no reply,
But turn'd to Heaven his gentle eye,
And clasp'd his hands, as one who said,
" My toils—my wanderings are o'erpaid !"
Then in a gayer, lighter strain,
Compell'd himself to speech again ;
    And, as they flow'd along,
His words took cadence soft and slow,
And liquid, like dissolving snow,
    They melted into song.

V.

" What though through fields of carnage
    wide
I may not follow Harold's stride,
Yet who with faithful Gunnar's pride
    Lord Harold's feats can see ?
And dearer than the couch of pride,
He loves the bed of grey wolf's hide,
When slumbering by Lord Harold's side
    In forest, field, or lea."—

VI.

" Break off!" said Harold, in a tone
Where hurry and surprise were shown,
    With some slight touch of fear,—
" Break off! we are not here alone ;
A Palmer form comes slowly on !
By cowl, and staff, and mantle known,
    My monitor is near.
Now mark him, Gunnar, heedfully ;
He pauses by the blighted tree—
Dost see him, youth ?—Thou couldst not
    see
When in the vale of Galilee
    I first beheld his form,
Nor when we met that other while
In Cephalonia's rocky isle,
    Before the fearful storm,—
Dost see him now ?"—The Page, dis-
    traught
With terror, answer'd, " I see nought,
    And there is nought to see,

Save that the oak's scathed boughs fling
    down
Upon the path a shadow brown,
That, like a pilgrim's dusky gown,
    Waves with the waving tree."

VII.

Count Harold gazed upon the oak
As if his eyestrings would have broke,
    And then resolvedly said,—
" Be what it will yon phantom grey—
Nor heaven, nor hell shall ever say
That for their shadows from his way
    Count Harold turn'd dismay'd :
I'll speak him, though his accents fill
My heart with that unwonted thrill
    Which vulgar minds call fear.
I will subdue it !"—Forth he strode,
Paused where the blighted oak-tree show'd
Its sable shadow on the road,
And, folding on his bosom broad
    His arms, said, "Speak—I hear."

VIII.

The Deep Voice said, " O wild of will,
    Furious thy purpose to fulfil—
Heart-sear'd and unrepentant still,
How long, O Harold, shall thy tread
Disturb the slumbers of the dead ?
Each step in thy wild way thou makest,
The ashes of the dead thou wakest ;
And shout in triumph o'er thy path
The fiends of bloodshed and of wrath.
In this thine hour, yet turn and hear !
For life is brief and judgment near."

IX.

Then ceased The Voice.—The Dane
    replied
In tones where awe and inborn pride
For mastery strove,—" In vain ye chide
    The wolf for ravaging the flock,
Or with its hardness taunt the rock,—
I am as they—my Danish strain
Sends streams of fire through every vein.
Amid thy realms of goule and ghost,
Say, is the fame of Eric lost,
Or Witikind's the Waster, known
Where fame or spoil was to be won ;

Whose galleys ne'er bore off a shore
    They left not black with flame ?—
He was my sire,—and, sprung of him,
That rover merciless and grim,
    Can I be soft and tame ?
Part hence, and with my crimes no more
    upbraid me,
I am that Waster's son, and am but what
    he made me."

X.

The Phantom groan'd;—the mountain
    shook around,
The fawn and wild doe started at the
    sound,
The gorse and fern did wildly round
    them wave,
As if some sudden storm the impulse
    gave.
" All thou hast said is truth—Yet on the
    head
Of that bad sire let not the charge be laid,
That he, like thee, with unrelenting pace,
From grave to cradle ran the evil race:—
Relentless in his avarice and ire,
Churches and towns he gave to sword and
    fire ;
Shed blood like water, wasted every land,
Like the destroying angel's burning brand;
Fulfill'd whate'er of ill might be invented,
Yes—all these things he did—he did, but
    he REPENTED !
Perchance it is part of his punishment still,
That his offspring pursues his example
    of ill.
But thou, when thy tempest of wrath
    shall next shake thee,
Gird thy loins for resistance, my son, and
    awake thee ;
If thou yield'st to thy fury, how tempted
    soever,
The gate of repentance shall ope for thee
    NEVER !"—

XI.

" He is gone," said Lord Harold, and
    gazed as he spoke ;
"There is nought on the path but the
    shade of the oak,

He is gone, whose strange presence my
    feeling oppress'd,
Like the night-hag that sits on the
    slumberer's breast.
My heart beats as thick as a fugitive's
    tread,
And cold dews drop from my brow and
    my head.—
Ho! Gunnar, the flasket yon almoner
    gave;
He said that three drops would recall
    from the grave.
For the first time Count Harold owns
    leech-craft has power,
Or, his courage to aid, lacks the juice of
    a flower!"
The page gave the flasket, which Wal-
    wayn had fill'd
With the juice of wild roots that his art
    had distill'd—
So baneful their influence on all that had
    breath,
One drop had been frenzy, and two had
    been death.
Harold took it, but drank not; for jubilee
    shrill,
And music and clamour were heard on
    the hill,
And down the steep pathway, o'er stock
    and o'er stone,
The train of a bridal came blithesomely on;
There was song, there was pipe, there
    was timbrel, and still
The burden was, " Joy to the fair Mete-
    lill!"

XII.

Harold might see from his high stance,
Himself unseen, that train advance
    With mirth and melody ;—
On horse and foot a mingled throng,
Measuring their steps to bridal song
    And bridal minstrelsy ;
And ever when the blithsome rout
Lent to the song their choral shout,
Redoubling echoes roll'd about,
While echoing cave and cliff sent out
    The answering symphony
Of all those mimic notes which dwell
In hollow rock and sounding dell.

XIII.

Joy shook his torch above the band,
By many a various passion fann'd ;—
As elemental sparks can feed
On essence pure and coarsest weed,
Gentle, or stormy, or refined,
Joy takes the colours of the mind.
Lightsome and pure, but unrepress'd,
He fired the bridegroom's gallant breast ;
More feebly strove with maiden fear,
Yet still joy glimmer'd through the tear
On the bride's blushing cheek, that shows
Like dewdrop on the budding rose ;
While Wulfstane's gloomy smile declared
The glee that selfish avarice shared,
And pleased revenge and malice high
Joy's semblance took in Jutta's eye.
On dangerous adventure sped,
The witch deem'd Harold with the dead,
For thus that morn her Demon said :
" If, ere the set of sun, be tied
The knot 'twixt bridegroom and his bride,
The Dane shall have no power of ill
O'er William and o'er Metelill."
And the pleased witch made answer,
    " Then
Must Harold have pass'd from the paths
    of men!
Evil repose may his spirit have,—
May hemlock and mandrake find root in
    his grave,—
May his death-sleep be dogged by dreams
    of dismay,
And his waking be worse at the answer-
    ing day."

XIV.

Such was their various mood of glee
Blent in one shout of ecstasy.
But still when Joy is brimming highest,
Of Sorrow and Misfortune nighest,
Of Terror with her ague cheek,
And lurking Danger, sages speak :—
These haunt each path, but chief they lay
Their snares beside the primrose way.—
Thus found that bridal band their path
Beset by Harold in his wrath.
Trembling beneath his maddening mood,
High on a rock the giant stood ;

His shout was like the doom of death
Spoke o'er their heads that pass'd beneath.
His destined victims might not spy
The reddening terrors of his eye,—
The frown of rage that writhed his face,—
The lip that foam'd like boar's in chase;—
But all could see—and, seeing, all
Bore back to shun the threaten'd fall—
The fragment which their giant foe
Rent from the cliff and heaved to throw.

XV.

Backward they bore;—yet are there two
   For battle who prepare:
No pause of dread Lord William knew
   Ere his good blade was bare;
And Wulfstane bent his fatal yew,
But ere the silken cord he drew,
As hurl'd from Hecla's thunder, flew
   That ruin through the air!
Full on the outlaw's front it came,
And all that late had human name,
And human face, and human frame,
That lived, and moved, and had free will
To choose the path of good or ill,
   Is to its reckoning gone;
And nought of Wulfstane rests behind,
   Save that beneath that stone,
Half-buried in the dinted clay,
A red and shapeless mass there lay
   Of mingled flesh and bone!

XVI.

As from the bosom of the sky
   The eagle darts amain,
Three bounds from yonder summit high
   Placed Harold on the plain.
As the scared wild-fowl scream and fly,
   So fled the bridal train;
As 'gainst the eagle's peerless might
The noble falcon dares the fight,
   But dares the fight in vain,
So fought the bridegroom; from his hand
The Dane's rude mace has struck his
   brand,
Its glittering fragments strew the sand,
   Its lord lies on the plain.
Now, Heaven! take noble William's part,

And melt that yet unmelted heart,
Or, ere his bridal hour depart,
   The hapless bridegroom's slain!

XVII.

Count Harold's frenzied rage is high,
There is a death-fire in his eye,
Deep furrows on his brow are trench'd,
His teeth are set, his hand is clench'd,
The foam upon his lip is white,
His deadly arm is up to smite!
But as the mace aloft he swung,
To stop the blow young Gunnar sprung,
Around his master's knees he clung,
   And cried, " In mercy spare!
O, think upon the words of fear
Spoke by that visionary Seer,
The crisis he foretold is here,—
   Grant mercy,—or despair!"
This word suspended Harold's mood,
Yet still with arm upraised he stood,
And visage like the headsman's rude
   That pauses for the sign.
" O mark thee with the blessed rood,"
The page implored; " speak word of
   good,
Resist the fiend, or be subdued!"
   He sign'd the cross divine—
Instant his eye hath human light,
Less red, less keen, less fiercely bright,
His brow relax'd the obdurate frown,
The fatal mace sinks gently down,
   He turns and strides away;
Yet oft, like revellers who leave
Unfinish'd feast, looks back to grieve,
As if repenting the reprieve
   He granted to his prey.
Yet still of forbearance one sign hath he
   given,
And fierce Witikind's son made one step
   towards heaven.

XVIII.

But though his dreaded footsteps part,
Death is behind and shakes his dart;
Lord William on the plain is lying,
Beside him Metelill seems dying!—
Bring odours—essences in haste—
And lo! a flasket richly chased,—

But Jutta the elixir proves
Ere pouring it for those she loves.—
Then Walwayn's potion was not wasted,
For when three drops the hag had tasted,
 So dismal was her yell,
Each bird of evil omen woke,
The raven gave his fatal croak,
And shriek'd the night-crow from the oak,
The screech-owl from the thicket broke,
 And flutter'd down the dell!
So fearful was the sound and stern,
The slumbers of the full-gorged erne
Were startled, and from furze and fern
 Of forest and of fell,
The fox and famish'd wolf replied,
(For wolves then prowl'd the Cheviot
 side.)
From mountain head to mountain head
The unhallow'd sounds around were sped;
But when their latest echo fled,
The sorceress on the ground lay dead.

XIX.

Such was the scene of blood and woes,
With which the bridal morn arose
 Of William and of Metelill;
But oft, when dawning 'gins to spread,
The summer morn peeps dim and red
 Above the eastern hill,
Ere, bright and fair, upon his road
The King of Splendour walks abroad ;
So when this cloud had pass'd away,
Bright was the noontide of their day
And all serene its setting ray.

———

CANTO SIXTH.

I.

WELL do I hope that this my minstrel
 tale
Will tempt no traveller from southern
 fields,
Whether in tilbury, barouche, or mail,
To view the Castle of these Seven Proud
 Shields.
Small confirmation its condition yields

To Meneville's high lay,—No towers
 are seen
On the wild heath, but those that
 Fancy builds,
And, save a fosse that tracks the moor
 with green,
Is nought remains to tell of what may
 there have been.

And yet grave authors, with the no
 small waste
Of their grave time, have dignified the
 spot
By theories, to prove the fortress placed
By Roman bands, to curb the invading
 Scot.
Hutchinson, Horsley, Camden, I might
 quote,
But rather choose the theory less civil
Of boors, who, origin of things forgot,
Refer still to the origin of evil,
And for their master-mason choose that
 master-fiend the Devil.

II.

Therefore, I say, it was on fiend-built
 towers
That stout Count Harold bent his
 wondering gaze,
When evening dew was on the heather
 flowers,
And the last sunbeams made the mountain blaze,
And tinged the battlements of other
 days
With the bright level light ere sinking
 down.—
Illumined thus, the Dauntless Dane
 surveys
The Seven Proud Shields that o'er the
 portal frown,
And on their blazons traced high marks
 of old renown.

A wolf North Wales had on his ar-
 mour-coat,
And Rhys of Powis-land a couchant
 stag ;

Strath-Clwyde's strange emblem was a stranded boat,
Donald of Galloway's a trotting nag ;
A corn-sheaf gilt was fertile Lodon's brag ;
A dudgeon-dagger was by Dunmail worn ;
Northumbrian Adolf gave a sea-beat crag
Surmounted by a cross—such signs were borne
Upon these antique shields, all wasted now and worn.

III.

These scann'd, Count Harold sought the castle-door,
Whose ponderous bolts were rusted to decay ;
Yet till that hour adventurous knight forebore
The unobstructed passage to essay.
More strong than armed warders in array,
And obstacle more sure than bolt or bar,
Sate in the portal Terror and Dismay,
While Superstition, who forbade to war
With foes of other mould than mortal clay,
Cast spells across the gate, and barr'd the onward way.

Vain now these spells ; for soon with heavy clank
The feebly-fasten'd gate was inward push'd,
And, as it oped, through that emblazon'd rank
Of antique shields, the wind of evening rush'd
With sound most like a groan, and then was hush'd.
Is none who on such spot such sounds could hear
But to his heart the blood had faster rush'd ;
Yet to bold Harold's breast that throb was dear—
It spoke of danger nigh, but had no touch of fear.

IV.

Yet Harold and his Page no signs have traced
Within the castle, that of danger show'd ;
For still the halls and courts were wild and waste,
As through their precincts the adventurers trode.
The seven huge towers rose stately, tall, and broad,
Each tower presenting to their scrutiny
A hall in which a king might make abode,
And fast beside, garnish'd both proud and high,
Was placed a bower for rest in which a king might lie.

As if a bridal there of late had been,
Deck'd stood the table in each gorgeous hall ;
And yet it was two hundred years, I ween,
Since date of that unhallow'd festival.
Flagons, and ewers, and standing cups, were all
Of tarnish'd gold, or silver nothing clear,
With throne begilt, and canopy of pall,
And tapestry clothed the walls with fragments sear—
Frail as the spider's mesh did that rich woof appear.

V.

In every bower, as round a hearse, was hung
A dusky crimson curtain o'er the bed,
And on each couch in ghastly wise were flung
The wasted relics of a monarch dead ;
Barbaric ornaments around were spread,
Vests twined with gold, and chains of precious stone,
And golden circlets, meet for monarch's head ;
While grinn'd, as if in scorn amongst them thrown,
The wearer's fleshless skull, alike with dust bestrown.

For these were they who, drunken with
delight,
On pleasure's opiate pillow laid their
head,
For whom the bride's shy footsteps,
slow and light,
Was changed ere morning to the mur-
derer's tread.
For human bliss and woe in the frail
thread
Of human life are all so closely twined,
That till the shears of Fate the texture
shred,
The close succession cannot be disjoin'd,
Nor dare we, from one hour, judge that
which comes behind.

VI.

But where the work of vengeance had
been done,
In that seventh chamber, was a sterner
sight;
There of the witch-brides lay each
skeleton,
Still in the posture as to death when dight,
For this lay prone, by one blow slain
outright;
And that, as one who struggled long in
dying;
One bony hand held knife, as if to smite;
One bent on fleshless knees, as mercy
crying;
One lay across the door, as kill'd in act
of flying.

The stern Dane smiled this charnel-
house to see,—
For his chafed thought return'd to
Metelill;—
And "Well," he said, "hath woman's
perfidy,
Empty as air, as water volatile,
Been here avenged.—The origin of ill
Through woman rose, the Christian
doctrine saith:
Nor deem I, Gunnar, that thy minstrel
skill
Can show example where a woman's
breath
Hath made a true-love vow, and, tempted,
kept her faith."

VII.

The minstrel-boy half smiled, half sigh'd,
And his half-filling eyes he dried,
And said, "The theme I should but wrong,
Unless it were my dying song,
(Our Scalds have said, in dying hour
The northern harp has treble power,)
Else could I tell of woman's faith,
Defying danger, scorn, and death.
Firm was that faith,—as diamond stone
Pure and unflaw'd,—her love unknown,
And unrequited;—firm and pure,
Her stainless faith could all endure;
From clime to clime,—from place to place,
Through want, and danger, and disgrace,
A wanderer's wayward steps could trace.—
All this she did, and guerdon none
Required, save that her burial-stone
Should make at length the secret known,
'Thus hath a faithful woman done.'—
Not in each breast such truth is laid,
But Eivir was a Danish maid."—

VIII.

"Thou art a wild enthusiast," said
Count Harold, "for thy Danish maid;
And yet, young Gunnar, I will own
Hers were a faith to rest upon.
But Eivir sleeps beneath her stone,
And all resembling her are gone.
What maid e'er show'd such constancy
In plighted faith, like thine to me?
But couch thee, boy; the darksome shade
Falls thickly round, nor be dismay'd
   Because the dead are by.
They were as we; our little day
O'erspent, and we shall be as they.
Yet near me, Gunnar, be thou laid,
Thy couch upon my mantle made,
That thou mayst think, should fear invade,
   Thy master slumbers nigh."
Thus couch'd they in that dread abode,
Until the beams of dawning glow'd.

IX.

An alter'd man Lord Harold rose,
When he beheld that dawn unclose—
   There's trouble in his eyes,

And traces on his brow and cheek
Of mingled awe and wonder speak:
" My page," he said, " arise ;—
Leave we this place, my page."—No more
He utter'd till the castle door
They cross'd—but there he paused and
   said,
" My wildness hath awaked the dead—
  Disturb'd the sacred tomb !
Methought this night I stood on high,
Where Hecla roars in middle sky,
And in her cavern'd gulfs could spy
   The central place of doom ;
And there before my mortal eye
Souls of the dead came flitting by,
Whom fiends, with many a fiendish cry,
  Bore to that evil den !
My eyes grew dizzy, and my brain
Was wilder'd, as the elvish train,
With shriek and howl, dragg'd on amain
  Those who had late been men.

X.

" With haggard eyes and streaming hair,
Jutta the Sorceress was there,
And there pass'd Wulfstane, lately slain,
All crush'd and foul with bloody stain.—
More had I seen, but that uprose
A whirlwind wild, and swept the snows ;
And with such sound as when at need
A champion spurs his horse to speed,
Three arm'd knights rush on, who lead
Caparison'd a sable steed.
Sable their harness, and there came
Through their closed visors sparks of
  flame.
The first proclaim'd, in sounds of fear,
' Harold the Dauntless, welcome here !
The next cried, ' Jubilee ! we've won
Count Witikind the Waster's son !'
And the third rider sternly spoke,
' Mount, in the name of Zernebock !—
From us, O Harold, were thy powers,—
Thy strength, thy dauntlessness, are ours ;
Nor think, a vassal thou of hell,
With hell can strive.' The fiend spoke
  true !
My inmost soul the summons knew,
  As captives know the knell

That says the headsman's sword is bare,
And, with an accent of despair,
  Commands them quit their cell.
I felt resistance was in vain,
My foot had that fell stirrup ta'en,
My hand was on the fatal mane,
   When to my rescue sped
That Palmer's visionary form,
And—like the passing of a storm—
   The demons yell'd and fled !

XI.

" His sable cowl, flung back, reveal'd
The features it before conceal'd ;
  And, Gunnar, I could find
In him whose counsels strove to stay
So oft my course on wilful way,
   My father Witikind !
Doom'd for his sins, and doom'd for mine,
A wanderer upon earth to pine
Until his son shall turn to grace,
And smooth for him a resting-place.—
Gunnar, he must not haunt in vain
This world of wretchedness and pain :
I'll tame my wilful heart to live
In peace—to pity and forgive—
And thou, for so the Vision said,
Must in thy Lord's repentance aid.
Thy mother was a prophetess,
He said, who by her skill could guess
How close the fatal textures join
Which knit thy thread of life with mine ;
Then, dark, he hinted of disguise
She framed to cheat too curious eyes,
That not a moment might divide
Thy fated footsteps from my side.
Methought while thus my sire did teach,
I caught the meaning of his speech,
Yet seems its purport doubtful now."
His hand then sought his thoughtful brow,
Then first he mark'd, that in the tower
His glove was left at waking hour.

XII.

Trembling at first, and deadly pale,
Had Gunnar heard the vision'd tale ;
But when he learn'd the dubious close,
He blush'd like any opening rose,

And, glad to hide his tell-tale cheek,
Hied back that glove of mail to seek;
When soon a shriek of deadly dread
Summon'd his master to his aid.

XIII.

What sees Count Harold in that bower,
  So late his resting-place?—
The semblance of the Evil Power,
  Adored by all his race!
Odin in living form stood there,
His cloak the spoils of Polar bear;
For plumy crest a meteor shed
Its gloomy radiance o'er his head,
Yet veil'd its haggard majesty
To the wild lightnings of his eye.
Such height was his, as when in stone
O'er Upsal's giant altar shown:
  So flow'd his hoary beard;
Such was his lance of mountain-pine,
So did his sevenfold buckler shine;—
  But when his voice he rear'd,
Deep, without harshness, slow and strong,
The powerful accents roll'd along,
And, while he spoke, his hand was laid
On Captive Gunnar's shrinking head.

XIV.

" Harold," he said, " what rage is thine,
To quit the worship of thy line,
  To leave thy Warrior-God?—
With me is glory or disgrace,
Mine is the onset and the chase,
Embattled hosts before my face
  Are wither'd by a nod.
Wilt thou then forfeit that high seat
Deserved by many a dauntless feat,
Among the heroes of thy line,
Eric and fiery Thorarine?—
Thou wilt not. Only I can give
The joys for which the valiant live,
Victory and vengeance—only I
Can give the joys for which they die,
The immortal tilt—the banquet full,
The brimming draught from foeman's
  skull.
Mine art thou, witness this thy glove,
The faithful pledge of vassal's love."—

XV.

" Tempter," said Harold, firm of heart,
" I charge thee, hence! whate'er thou art,
I do defy thee—and resist
The kindling frenzy of my breast,
Waked by thy words; and of my mail,
Nor glove, nor buckler, splent, nor nail,
Shall rest with thee—that youth release,
And God, or Demon, part in peace."—
" Eivir," the Shape replied, " is mine,
Mark'd in the birth-hour with my sign.
Think'st thou that priest with drops of
  spray
Could wash that blood-red mark away?
Or that a borrow'd sex and name
Can abrogate a Godhead's claim?"
Thrill'd this strange speech through
  Harold's brain,
He clench'd his teeth in high disdain,
For not his new-born faith subdued
Some tokens of his ancient mood.—
" Now, by the hope so lately given
Of better trust and purer heaven,
I will assail thee, fiend!"—Then rose
His mace, and with a storm of blows
The mortal and the Demon close.

XVI.

Smoke roll'd above, fire flash'd around,
Darken'd the sky and shook the ground;
  But not the artillery of hell,
The bickering lightning, nor the rock
Of turrets to the earthquake's shock,
  Could Harold's courage quell.
Sternly the Dane his purpose kept,
And blows on blows resistless heap'd,
  Till quail'd that Demon Form,
And—for his power to hurt or kill
Was bounded by a higher will—
  Evanish'd in the storm.
Nor paused the Champion of the North,
But raised, and bore his Eivir forth,
From that wild scene of fiendish strife,
To light, to liberty, and life!

XVII.

He placed her on a bank of moss,
  A silver runnel bubbled by,

And new-born thoughts his soul en-
   gross,
And tremors yet unknown across
  His stubborn sinews fly,
The while with timid hand the dew
Upon her brow and neck he threw,
And mark'd how life with rosy hue
On her pale cheek revived anew,
  And glimmer'd in her eye.
Inly he said, "That silken tress,—
What blindness mine that could not
  guess!
Or how could page's rugged dress
  That bosom's pride belie?
O, dull of heart, through wild and wave
In search of blood and death to rave,
  With such a partner nigh!"

XVIII.

Then in the mirror'd pool he peer'd,
Blamed his rough locks and shaggy
  beard,
The stains of recent conflict clear'd,—
  And thus the Champion proved,
That he fears now who never fear'd,
  And loves who never loved.
And Eivir—life is on her cheek,
And yet she will not move or speak,
  Nor will her eyelid fully ope;
Perchance it loves, that half-shut eye,
Through its long fringe, reserved and
  shy,
Affection's opening dawn to spy;
And the deep blush, which bids its dye
O'er cheek, and brow, and bosom fly,
  speaks shame-facedness and hope.

XIX.

But vainly seems the Dane to seek
For terms his new-born love to speak,—
For words, save those of wrath and wrong,
Till now were strangers to his tongue;
So, when he raised the blushing maid,
In blunt and honest terms he said,
('Twere well that maids, when lovers woo,
Heard none more soft, were all as true,)
"Eivir! since thou for many a day
Hast follow'd Harold's wayward way,
It is but meet that in the line
Of after-life I follow thine.
To-morrow is Saint Cuthbert's tide,
And we will grace his altar's side,
A Christian knight and Christian bride;
And of Witikind's son shall the marvel be
  said,
That on the same morn he was christen'd
  and wed."

CONCLUSION.

And now, Ennui, what ails thee, weary
  maid?
And why these listless looks of yawning
  sorrow?
No need to turn the page, as if 'twere lead,
Or fling aside the volume till to-morrow.—
Be cheer'd—'tis ended—and I will not
  borrow,
To try thy patience more, one anecdote
From Bartholine, or Perinskiold, or
  Snorro.
Then pardon thou thy minstrel, who hath
  wrote
A Tale six cantos long, yet scorn'd to add
  a note.

CONTRIBUTIONS TO MINSTRELSY OF THE SCOTTISH BORDER.

Imitations of the Ancient Ballad.

THOMAS THE RHYMER.

IN THREE PARTS.

PART FIRST.—ANCIENT.

Few personages are so renowned in tradition as Thomas of Ercildoune, known by the appellation of *The Rhymer*. Uniting, or supposing to unite, in his person, the powers of poetical composition, and of vaticination, his memory, even after the lapse of five hundred years, is regarded with veneration by his countrymen. To give anything like a certain history of this remarkable man would be indeed difficult; but the curious may derive some satisfaction from the particulars here brought together.

It is agreed on all hands, that the residence, and probably the birthplace, of this ancient bard was Ercildoune, a village situated upon the Leader, two miles above its junction with the Tweed. The ruins of an ancient tower are still pointed out as the Rhymer's castle. The uniform tradition bears, that his sirname was Lermont, or Learmont; and that the appellation of *The Rhymer* was conferred on him in consequence of his poetical compositions. There remains, nevertheless, some doubt upon the subject.

We are better able to ascertain the period at which Thomas of Ercildoune lived, being the latter end of the thirteenth century. I am inclined to place his death a little farther back than Mr. Pinkerton, who supposes that he was alive in 1300.—(*List of Scottish Poets.*)

It cannot be doubted that Thomas of Ercildoune was a remarkable and important person in his own time, since, very shortly after his death, we find him celebrated as a prophet and as a poet. Whether he himself made any pretensions to the first of these characters, or whether it was gratuitously conferred upon him by the credulity of posterity, it seems difficult to decide. If we may believe Mackenzie, Learmont only versified the prophecies delivered by Eliza, an inspired nun of a convent at Haddington. But of this there seems not to be the most distant proof. On the contrary, all ancient authors, who quote the Rhymer's prophecies, uniformly suppose them to have been emitted by himself.

The popular tale bears, that Thomas was carried off, at an early age, to the Fairy Land, where he acquired all the knowledge, which made him afterwards so famous. After seven years' residence, he was permitted to return to the earth, to enlighten and astonish his countrymen by his prophetic powers; still, however, remaining bound to return to his royal mistress, when she should intimate her pleasure. Accordingly, while Thomas was making merry with his friends in the Tower of Ercildoune, a person came running in, and told, with marks of fear and astonishment, that a hart and hind had left the neighbouring forest, and were, composedly and slowly, parading the street of the village. The prophet instantly arose, left his habitation, and followed the wonderful animals to the forest, whence he was never seen to return. According to the popular belief, he still "drees his weird" in Fairy

Land, and is one day expected to revisit earth. In the meanwhile, his memory is held in the most profound respect. The Eildon Tree, from beneath the shade of which he delivered his prophecies, now no longer exists; but the spot is marked by a large stone, called Eildon Tree Stone. A neighbouring rivulet takes the name of the Bogle Burn (Goblin Brook) from the Rhymer's supernatural visitants.

It seemed to the Editor unpardonable to dismiss a person so important in Border traditions as the Rhymer, without some farther notice than a simple commentary upon the following ballad. It is given from a copy, obtained from a lady residing not far from Ercildoune, corrected and enlarged by one in Mrs. Brown's MSS. The former copy, however, as might be expected, is far more minute as to local description. To this old tale the Editor has ventured to add a Second Part, consisting of a kind of cento, from the printed prophecies vulgarly ascribed to the Rhymer; and a Third Part, entirely modern, founded upon the tradition of his having returned with the hart and hind, to the Land of Faëry. To make his peace with the more severe antiquaries, the Editor has prefixed to the Second Part some remarks on Learmont's prophecies.

TRUE THOMAS lay on Huntlie bank ;*
　A ferlie† he spied wi' his ee ;
And there he saw a ladye bright,
　Come riding down by the Eildon Tree.

Her shirt was o' the grass-green silk,
　Her mantle o' the velvet fyne ;
At ilka‡ tett of her horse's mane,
　Hung fifty siller bells and nine.

True Thomas, he pull'd aff his cap,
　And louted§ low down to his knee,
"All hail, thou mighty Queen of Heaven !
　For thy peer on earth I never did see."—

"O no, O no, Thomas," she said,
　"That name does not belang to me ;
I am but the Queen of fair Elfland,
　That am hither come to visit thee.

"Harp and carp, Thomas," she said ;
　"Harp and carp along wi' me ;
And if ye dare to kiss my lips,
　Sure of your bodie I will be."—

"Betide me weal, betide me woe,
　That weird‖ shall never daunton me."—
Syne he has kiss'd her rosy lips,
　All underneath the Eildon Tree.

"Now, ye maun go wi' me," she said ;
　"True Thomas, ye maun go wi' me ;
And ye maun serve me seven years,
　Thro' weal or woe as may chance to be."

She mounted on her milk-white steed ;
　She's ta'en true Thomas up behind :
And aye, whene'er her bridle rung,
　The steed flew swifter than the wind.

O they rade on, and farther on ;
　The steed gaed swifter than the wind ;
Until they reach'd a desert wide,
　And living land was left behind.

"Light down, light down, now, true Thomas,
　And lean your head upon my knee ;
Abide and rest a little space,
　And I will shew you ferlies¶ three.

"O see ye not yon narrow road,
　So thick beset with thorns and briers ?
That is the path of righteousness,
　Though after it but few enquires.

"And see ye not that braid braid road,
　That lies across that lily leven ?
That is the path of wickedness,
　Though some call it the road to heaven.

"And see not ye that bonny road,
　That winds about the fernie brae ?
That is the road to fair Elfland,
　Where thou and I this night maun gae.

* A spot afterwards included in the domain of Abbotsford.
† Wonder.　‡ Each.　§ Bowed.
‖ Destiny shall not alarm me.

¶ Wonders.

"But, Thomas, ye maun hold your
tongue,
Whatever ye may hear or see;
For, if ye speak word in Elflyn land,
Ye'll ne'er get back to your ain
countrie."

O they rade on, and farther on,
And they waded through rivers aboon
the knee,
And they saw neither sun nor moon,
But they heard the roaring of the sea.

It was mirk mirk night, and there was nae
stern light,
And they waded through red blude to
the knee,
For a' the blude that's shed on earth
Rins through the springs o' that
countrie.

Syne they came on to a garden green,
And she pu'd an apple frae a tree*—
"Take this for thy wages, true Thomas;
It will give thee the tongue that can
never lie."—

"My tongue is mine ain," true Thomas
said;
"A gudely gift ye wad gie to me!
I neither dought to buy nor sell,
At fair or tryst where I may be.

"I dought neither speak to prince or peer,
Nor ask of grace from fair ladye."—
"Now hold thy peace!" the lady said,
"For as I say, so must it be."—

He has gotten a coat of the even cloth,
And a pair of shoes of velvet green;
And till seven years were gane and past,
True Thomas on earth was never seen.

PART SECOND.—ALTERED FROM ANCIENT PROPHECIES.

The prophecies, ascribed to Thomas of Ercildoune, have been the principal means of
securing to him remembrance "amongst the sons of his people." The author of *Sir
Tristrem* would long ago have joined, in the vale of oblivion, "Clerk of Tranent, who wrote
the adventure of *Schir Gawain,*" if, by good hap, the same current of ideas respecting
antiquity, which causes Virgil to be regarded as a magician by the Lazaroni of Naples, had
not exalted the bard of Ercildoune to the prophetic character. Perhaps, indeed, he himself
affected it during his life. We know, at least, for certain, that a belief in his supernatural
knowledge was current soon after his death. His prophecies are alluded to by Barbour, by
Winton, and by Henry the Minstrel, or *Blind Harry*, as he is usually termed. None of
these authors, however, give the words of any of the Rhymer's vaticinations, but merely
narrate, historically, his having predicted the events of which they speak. The earliest of the
prophecies ascribed to him, which is now extant, is quoted by Mr. Pinkerton from a MS.
It is supposed to be a response from Thomas of Ercildoune to a question from the heroic
Countess of March, renowned for the defence of the Castle of Dunbar against the English,
and termed, in the familiar dialect of her time, *Black Agnes* of Dunbar. This prophecy is
remarkable, in so far as it bears very little resemblance to any verses published in the printed
copy of the Rhymer's supposed prophecies.

Corspatrick (Comes Patrick) Earl of March, but more commonly taking his title from
his castle of Dunbar, acted a noted part during the wars of Edward I. in Scotland. As
Thomas of Ercildoune is said to have delivered to him his famous prophecy of King
Alexander's death, the Editor has chosen to introduce him into the following ballad. All
the prophetic verses are selected from Hart's publication.†

---

* The traditional commentary upon this ballad informs us, that the apple was the produce
of the fatal Tree of Knowledge, and that the garden was the terrestrial paradise. The
repugnance of Thomas to be debarred the use of falsehood, when he might find it
convenient, has a comic effect.

† Prophecies supposed to have been delivered by True Thomas, Bede, Merlin, &c., published by Andro Hart, 1615.—[EDIT.]

When seven years were come and gane,
  The sun blink'd fair on pool and stream;
And Thomas lay on Huntlie Bank,
  Like one awaken'd from a dream.

He heard the trampling of a steed,
  He saw the flash of armour flee,
And he beheld a gallant knight
  Come riding down by the Eildon-tree.

He was a stalwart knight, and strong;
  Of giant make he 'pear'd to be:
He stirr'd his horse, as he were wode,
  Wi' gilded spurs, of faushion free.

Says—"Well met, well met, true Thomas!
  Some uncouth ferlies show to me."—
Says—"Christ thee save, Corspatrick
    brave!
'Thrice welcume, good Dunbar, to me!

"Light down, light down, Corspatrick
    brave!
  And I will show thee curses three,
Shall gar fair Scotland greet and grane,
  And change the green to the black livery.

"A storm shall roar this very hour,
  From Ross's hills to Solway sea."—
"Ye lied, ye lied, ye warlock hoar,
  For the sun shines sweet on fauld and
    lee."—

He put his hand on the Earlie's head;
  He show'd him a rock beside the sea,
Where a king lay stiff beneath his steed,*
  And steel-dight nobles wiped their ee.

"The neist curse lights on Branxton hills:
  By Flodden's high and heathery side,
Shall wave a banner red as blude,
  And chieftains throng wi' meikle pride.

"A Scottish King shall come full keen,
  The ruddy lion beareth he;
A feather'd arrow sharp, I ween,
  Shall make him wink and warre to see.

"When he is bloody, and all to bledde,
  Thus to his men he still shall say—
'For God's sake, turn ye back again,
  And give yon southern folk a fray!
Why should I lose, the right is mine?
  My doom is not to die this day.†

"Yet turn ye to the eastern hand,
  And woe and wonder ye sall see;
How forty thousand spearmen stand,
  Where yon rank river meets the sea.

"There shall the lion lose the gylte,
  And the libbards‡ bear it clean away;
At Pinkyn Cleuch there shall be spilt
  Much gentil bluid that day."—

"Enough, enough, of curse and ban;
  Some blessings show thou now to me,
Or, by the faith o' my bodie," Cors-
    patrick said,
  "Ye shall rue the day ye e'er saw
    me?"—

"The first of blessings I shall thee show,
  Is by a burn, that's call'd of bread;§
Where Saxon men shall tine the bow,
  And find their arrows lack the head.

"Beside that brigg, out ower that burn,
  Where the water bickereth bright and
    sheen,
Shall many a fallen courser spurn,
  And knights shall die in battle keen.

"Beside a headless cross of stone,
  The libbards there shall lose the gree:
The raven shall come, the erne shall go,
  And drink the Saxon bluid sae free.
The cross of stone they shall not know,
  So thick the corses there shall be."—

---

* King Alexander III., killed by a fall from his horse, near Kinghorn.

† The uncertainty which long prevailed in Scotland, concerning the fate of James IV., is well known.

‡ Leopards of Plantagenet. The Scottish banner is a lion on a field *gules:* the English banner then was the three leopards.

§ *Bannock,* or *Bread* Burn.

"But tell me, now," said brave Dunbar,
"True Thomas, tell now unto me,
What man shall rule the isle Britain,
Even from the north to the southern
sea?"—

"A French Queen shall bear the son,*
Shall rule all Britain to the sea;

He of the Bruce's blood shall come,
As near as in the ninth degree.

"The waters worship shall his race;
Likewise the waves of the farthest sea;
For they shall ride over ocean wide,
With hempen bridles, and horse of tree."

PART THIRD.—MODERN.

Thomas the Rhymer was renowned among his contemporaries, as the author of the celebrated romance of *Sir Tristrem*. Of this once-admired poem only one copy is now known to
exist, which is in the Advocates' Library. The Editor, in 1804, published a small edition of
this curious work ; which, if it does not revive the reputation of the bard of Ercildoune, is
at least the earliest specimen of Scottish poetry hitherto published. Some account of this
romance has already been given to the world in Mr. ELLIS's *Specimens of Ancient Poetry*,
vol. i. p. 165, iii. p. 410; a work to which our predecessors and our posterity are alike
obliged ; the former, for the preservation of the best-selected examples of their poetical taste;
and the latter, for a history of the English language, which will only cease to be interesting
with the existence of our mother-tongue, and all that genius and learning have recorded in
it. It is sufficient here to mention, that so great was the reputation of the romance of *Sir
Tristrem*, that few were thought capable of reciting it after the manner of the author.

The following attempt to commemorate the Rhymer's poetical fame, and the traditional
account of his marvellous return to Fairy Land, being entirely modern, would have been
placed with greater propriety among the class of Modern Ballads, had it not been for its
immediate connexion with the first and second parts of the same story.

When seven years more were come and
gone,
Was war through Scotland spread,
And Ruberslaw show'd high Dunyon†
His beacon blazing red.

Then all by bonny Coldingknow‡
Pitch'd palliouns§ took their room,
And crested helms, and spears a-rowe,
Glanced gaily through the broom.

The Leader, rolling to the Tweed,
Resounds the ensenzie; ∥
They roused the deer from Caddenhead,
To distant Torwoodlee.

The feast was spread in Ercildoune,
In Learmont's high and ancient hall:
And there were knights of great renown,
And ladies, laced in pall.

Nor lack'd they, while they sat at dine,
The music nor the tale,
Nor goblets of the blood-red wine,
Nor mantling quaighs¶ of ale.

True Thomas rose, with harp in hand,
When as the feast was done:
(In minstrel strife, in Fairy Land,
The elfin harp he won.)

Hush'd were the throng, both limb and
tongue,
And harpers for envy pale;
And armed lords lean'd on their swords,
And hearken'd to the tale.

In numbers high, the witching tale
The prophet pour'd along;
No after bard might e'er avail
Those numbers to prolong.

---

* James VI., son of Mary Queen of *France*
and Scotland.
† Hills near Jedburgh.
‡ A tower near Ercildoune.
§ Tents.
∥ *Ensenzie*—War-cry, or gathering word.

¶ *Quaighs*—Wooden cups, composed of
staves hooped together.

Yet fragments of the lofty strain
  Float down the tide of years,
As, buoyant on the stormy main,
  A parted wreck appears.

He sung King Arthur's Table Round:
  The Warrior of the Lake;
How courteous Gawaine met the wound,
  And bled for ladies' sake.

But chief, in gentle Tristrem's praise,
  The notes melodious swell;
Was none excell'd in Arthur's days,
  The knight of Lionelle.

For Marke, his cowardly uncle's right,
  A venom'd wound he bore;
When fierce Morholde he slew in fight,
  Upon the Irish shore.

No art the poison might withstand;
  No medicine could be found,
Till lovely Isolde's lily hand
  Had probed the rankling wound.

With gentle hand and soothing tongue
  She bore the leech's part;
And, while she o'er his sick-bed hung,
  He paid her with his heart.

O fatal was the gift, I ween!
  For, doom'd in evil tide,
The maid must be rude Cornwall's queen,
  His cowardly uncle's bride.

Their loves, their woes, the gifted bard,
  In fairy tissue wove;
Where lords, and knights, and ladies bright,
  In gay confusion strove.

The Garde Joyeuse, amid the tale,
  High rear'd its glittering head;
And Avalon's enchanted vale
  In all its wonders spread.

Brangwain was there, and Segramore,
  And fiend-born Merlin's gramarye;
Of that famed wizard's mighty lore,
  O who could sing but he?

Through many a maze the winning song
  In changeful passion led,
Till bent at length the listening throng
  O'er Tristrem's dying bed.

His ancient wounds their scars expand,
  With agony his heart is wrung:
O where is Isolde's lilye hand,
  And where her soothing tongue?

She comes! she comes!—like flash of flame
  Can lovers' footsteps fly:
She comes! she comes!—she only came
  To see her Tristrem die.

She saw him die; her latest sigh
  Join'd in a kiss his parting breath,
The gentlest pair, that Britain bare,
  United are in death.

There paused the harp: its lingering sound
  Died slowly on the ear;
The silent guests still bent around,
  For still they seem'd to hear.

Then woe broke forth in murmurs weak:
  Nor ladies heaved alone the sigh;
But half ashamed, the rugged cheek
  Did many a gauntlet dry.

On Leader's stream, and Learmont's tower,
  The mists of evening close;
In camp, in castle, or in bower,
  Each warrior sought repose.

Lord Douglas, in his lofty tent,
  Dream'd o'er the woeful tale;
When footsteps light, across the bent,
  The warrior's ears assail.

He starts, he wakes;—"What, Richard, ho!
  Arise, my page, arise!
What venturous wight, at dead of night,
  Dare step where Douglas lies."—

Then forth they rush'd: by Leader's tide,
  A selcouth* sight they see—
A hart and hind pace side by side,
  As white as snow on Fairnalie.

---

* Wondrous.

Beneath the moon, with gesture proud,
   They stately move and slow;
Nor scare they at the gathering crowd,
   Who marvel as they go.

To Learmont's tower a message sped,
   As fast as page might run;
And Thomas started from his bed,
   And soon his clothes did on.

First he woxe pale, and then woxe red;
   Never a word he spake but three;—
" My sand is run; my thread is spun;
   This sign regardeth me."

The elfin harp his neck around,
   In minstrel guise, he hung;
And on the wind, in doleful sound,
   Its dying accents rung.

Then forth he went; yet turn'd him oft
   To view his ancient hall:
On the grey tower, in lustre soft,
   The autumn moonbeams fall;

And Leader's waves, like silver sheen,
   Danced shimmering in the ray;
In deepening mass, at distance seen,
   Broad Soltra's mountains lay.

" Farewell, my fathers' ancient tower!
   A long farewell," said he:
" The scene of pleasure, pomp, or power,
   Thou never more shalt be.

" To Learmont's name no foot of earth
   Shall here again belong,
And, on thy hospitable hearth,
   The hare shall leave her young.

" Adieu! adieu!" again he cried,
   All as he turn'd him roun'—
" Farewell to Leader's silver tide!
   Farewell to Ercildoune!"

The hart and hind approach'd the place,
   As lingering yet he stood;
And there, before Lord Douglas' face,
   With them he cross'd the flood.

Lord Douglas leap'd on his berry-brown
   steed,
   And spurr'd him the Leader o'er;
But, though he rode with lightning speed,
   He never saw them more.

Some said to hill, and some to glen,
   Their wondrous course had been;
But ne'er in haunts of living men
   Again was Thomas seen.

GLENFINLAS; OR, LORD RONALD'S CORONACH.*

   The simple tradition, upon which the following stanzas are founded, runs thus: While two Highland hunters were passing the night in a solitary *bothy* (a hut, built for the purpose of hunting), and making merry over their venison and whisky, one of them expressed a wish that they had pretty lasses to complete their party. The words were scarcely uttered, when two beautiful young women, habited in green, entered the hut, dancing and singing. One of the hunters was seduced by the siren who attached herself particularly to him, to leave the hut: the other remained, and, suspicious of the fair seducers, continued to play upon a trump, or Jew's harp, some strain, consecrated to the Virgin Mary. Day at length came, and the temptress vanished. Searching in the forest, he found the bones of his unfortunate friend, who had been torn to pieces and devoured by the fiend into whose toils he had fallen. The place was from thence called the Glen of the Green Women.
   Glenfinlas is a tract of forest-ground, lying in the Highlands of Perthshire, not far from Callender in Menteith. It was formerly a royal forest, and now belongs to the Earl of

---

* *Coronach*—is the lamentation for a deceased warrior, sung by the aged of the clan.

Moray. This country, as well as the adjacent district of Balquidder, was, in times of yore, chiefly inhabited by the Macgregors. To the west of the Forest of Glenfinlas lies Loch Katrine, and its romantic avenue, called the Trosachs. Benledi, Benmore, and Benvoirlich, are mountains in the same district, and at no great distance from Glenfinlas. The river Teith passes Callender and the Castle of Doune, and joins the Forth near Stirling. The Pass of Lenny is immediately above Callender, and is the principal access to the Highlands, from that town. Glenartney is a forest, near Benvoirlich. The whole forms a sublime tract of alpine scenery.

This ballad first appeared in the *Tales of Wonder*, by Lewis.

> For them the viewless forms of air obey,
>   Their bidding heed, and at their beck repair;
> They know what spirit brews the stormful day,
>   And heartless oft, like moody madness stare,
> To see the phantom-train their secret work prepare.
> COLLINS.

"O HONE a rie'! O hone a rie'!*
    The pride of Albin's line is o'er,
And fall'n Glenartney's stateliest tree;
    We ne'er shall see Lord Ronald
        more!"—

O, sprung from great Macgillianore,
    The chief that never fear'd a foe,
How matchless was thy broad claymore,
    How deadly thine unerring bow!

Well can the Saxon widows tell,†
    How, on the Teith's resounding shore,
The boldest Lowland warriors fell,
    As down from Lenny's pass you bore.

But o'er his hills, in festal day,
    How blazed Lord Ronald's beltane-
        tree,[1]
While youths and maids the light strath-
        spey
    So nimbly danced with Highland glee!

Cheer'd by the strength of Ronald's shell,
    E'en age forgot his tresses hoar;
But now the loud lament we swell,
    O ne'er to see Lord Ronald more;

From distant isles a chieftain came,
    The joys of Ronald's halls to find,

And chase with him the dark-brown
        game,
    That bounds o'er Albin's hills of wind.

'Twas Moy; whom in Columba's isle
    The seer's prophetic spirit found,[2]
As, with a minstrel's fire the while,
    He waked his harp's harmonious sound,

Full many a spell to him was known,
    Which wandering spirits shrink to
        hear;
And many a lay of potent tone,
    Was never meant for mortal ear.

For there, 'tis said, in mystic mood,
    High converse with the dead they hold,
And oft espy the fated shroud,
    That shall the future corpse enfold.

O so it fell, that on a day,
    To rouse the red deer from their den,
The Chiefs have ta'en their distant way,
    And scour'd the deep Glenfinlas glen.

No vassals wait their sports to aid,
    To watch their safety, deck their board;
Their simple dress, the Highland plaid,
    Their trusty guard, the Highland
        sword.

Three summer days, through brake and
        dell,
    Their whistling shafts successful flew;
And still, when dewy evening fell,
    The quarry to their hut they drew.

---

* *O hone a rie'*—"Alas for the Chief!"
† The term Sassenach, or Saxon, is applied by the Highlanders to their Low-Country neighbours.

In grey Glenfinlas' deepest nook
  The solitary cabin stood,
Fast by Moneira's sullen brook,
    Which murmurs through that lonely
    wood.

Soft fell the night, the sky was calm,
    When three successive days had flown;
And summer mist in dewy balm
    Steep'd heathy bank and mossy stone.

The moon, half-hid in silvery flakes,
    Afar her dubious radiance shed,
Quivering on Katrine's distant lakes,
    And resting on Benledi's head.

Now in their hut, in social guise,
    Their silvan fare the Chiefs enjoy;
And pleasure laughs in Ronald's eyes,
    As many a pledge he quaffs to Moy.

" What lack we here to crown our bliss,
    While thus the pulse of joy beats high?
What, but fair woman's yielding kiss,
    Her panting breath and melting eye?

" To chase the deer of yonder shades,
    This morning left their father's pile
The fairest of our mountain maids,
    The daughters of the proud Glengyle.

" Long have I sought sweet Mary's heart,
    And dropp'd the tear, and heaved the
    sigh:
But vain the lover's wily art,
    Beneath a sister's watchful eye.

" But thou mayst teach that guardian fair,
    While far with Mary I am flown,
Of other hearts to cease her care,
    And find it hard to guard her own.

"Touch but thy harp, thou soon shalt
    see
The lovely Flora of Glengyle,
Unmindful of her charge and me,
    Hang on thy notes, 'twixt tear and
    smile.

" Or, if she choose a melting tale,
    All underneath the greenwood bough,
Will good St. Oran's rule prevail,[3]
    Stern huntsman of the rigid brow!"—

"Since Enrick's fight, since Morna's
    death,
    No more on me shall rapture rise,
Responsive to the panting breath,
    Or yielding kiss, or melting eyes.

" E'en then, when o'er the heath of woe,
    Where sunk my hopes of love and
    fame,
I bade my harp's wild wailings flow,
    On me the Seer's sad spirit came.

" The last dread curse of angry heaven,
    With ghastly sights and sounds of woe,
To dash each glimpse of joy was given—
    The gift, the future ill to know.

" The bark thou saw'st, yon summer
    morn,
    So gaily part from Oban's bay,
My eye beheld her dash'd and torn,
    Far on the rocky Colonsay.

"Thy Fergus too—thy sister's son,
    Thou saw'st, with pride, the gallant's
    power,
As marching 'gainst the Lord of Downe,
    He left the skirts of huge Benmore.

" Thou only saw'st their tartans* wave,
    As down Benvoirlich's side they wound,
Heard'st but the pibroch,† answering
    brave
To many a target clanking round.

" I heard the groans, I mark'd the tears,
    I saw the wound his bosom bore,
When on the serried Saxon spears
    He pour'd his clan's resistless roar.

" And thou, who bidst me think of bliss,
    And bidst my heart awake to glee,
And court, like thee, the wanton kiss—
    That heart, O Ronald, bleeds for thee!

---

* *Tartans*—the full Highland dress, made
of the chequered stuff so termed.
† *Pibroch*—a piece of martial music, adapted
to the Highland bagpipe.

"I see the death-damps chill thy brow;
  I hear thy Warning Spirit cry;
The corpse-lights dance—they're gone,
      and now. . . .
  No more is given to gifted eye!"——

" Alone enjoy thy dreary dreams,
  Sad prophet of the evil hour!
Say, should we scorn joy's transient
      beams,
  Because to-morrow's storm may lour?

" Or false, or sooth, thy words of woe,
  Clangillian's Chieftain ne'er shall fear;
His blood shall bound at rapture's glow,
  Though doom'd to stain the Saxon
      spear.

" E'en now, to meet me in yon dell,
  My Mary's buskins brush the dew."
He spoke, nor bade the Chief farewell,
  But called his dogs, and gay withdrew.

Within an hour return'd each hound;
  In rush'd the rousers of the deer;
They howl'd in melancholy sound,
  Then closely couch'd beside the Seer.

No Ronald yet; though midnight came,
  And sad were Moy's prophetic dreams,
As, bending o'er the dying flame,
  He fed the watch-fire's quivering
      gleams.

Sudden the hounds erect their ears,
  And sudden cease their moaning howl;
Close press'd to Moy, they mark their fears
  By shivering limbs and stifled growl.

Untouch'd, the harp began to ring,
  As softly, slowly, oped the door;
And shook responsive every string,
  As light a footstep press'd the floor.

And by the watch-fire's glimmering light,
  Close by the minstrel's side was seen
An huntress maid, in beauty bright,
  All dropping wet her robes of green.

All dropping wet her garments seem;
  Chill'd was her cheek, her bosom bare,
As, bending o'er the dying gleam,
  She wrung the moisture from her hair.

With maiden blush, she softly said,
  " O gentle huntsman, hast thou seen,
In deep Glenfinlas' moonlight glade,
  A lovely maid in vest of green:

" With her a Chief in Highland pride ·
  His shoulders bear the hunter's bow,
The mountain dirk adorns his side,
  Far on the wind his tartans flow?"—

" And who art thou? and who are they?"
  All ghastly gazing, Moy replied:
" And why, beneath the moon's pale ray,
  Dare ye thus roam Glenfinlas' side?"—

" Where wild Loch Katrine pours her tide,
  Blue, dark, and deep, round many an
      isle,
Our father's towers o'erhang her side,
  The castle of the bold Glengyle.

" To chase the dun Glenfinlas deer,
  Our woodland course this morn we
      bore,
And haply met, while wandering here,
  The son of great Macgillianore.

" O aid me, then, to seek the pair,
  Whom, loitering in the woods, I lost;
Alone, I dare not venture there,
  Where walks, they say, the shrieking
      ghost."—

" Yes, many a shrieking ghost walks
      there;
  Then, first, my own sad vow to keep,
Here will I pour my midnight prayer,
  Which still must rise when mortals
      sleep."—

" O first, for pity's gentle sake,
  Guide a lone wanderer on her way!
For I must cross the haunted brake,
  And reach my father's towers ere
      day."—

" First, three times tell each Ave-bead,
  And thrice a Pater-noster say;
Then kiss with me the holy rede;
  So shall we safely wend our way."—

"O shame to knighthood, strange and
    foul!
  Go, doff the bonnet from thy brow,
And shroud thee in the monkish cowl,
    Which best befits thy sullen vow.

"Not so, by high Dunlathmon's fire,
    Thy heart was froze to love and joy,
When gaily rung thy raptured lyre
    To wanton Morna's melting eye."

Wild stared the minstrel's eyes of flame,
    And high his sable locks arose,
And quick his colour went and came,
    As fear and rage alternate rose.

"And thou! when by the blazing oak
    I lay, to her and love resign'd,
Say, rode ye on the eddying smoke,
    Or sail'd ye on the midnight wind?

"Not thine a race of mortal blood,
    Nor old Glengyle's pretended line;
Thy dame, the Lady of the Flood—
    Thy sire, the Monarch of the Mine."

He mutter'd thrice St. Oran's rhyme,
    And thrice St. Fillan's powerful prayer;[1]
Then turn'd him to the eastern clime,
    And sternly shook his coal-black hair.

And, bending o'er his harp, he flung
    His wildest witch-notes on the wind;
And loud, and high, and strange, they rung,
    As many a magic change they find.

Tall wax'd the Spirit's altering form,
    Till to the roof her stature grew;
Then, mingling with the rising storm,
    With one wild yell away she flew.

Rain beats, hail rattles, whirlwinds tear:
    The slender hut in fragments flew;
But not a lock of Moy's loose hair
    Was waved by wind, or wet by dew.

Wild mingling with the howling gale,
    Loud bursts of ghastly laughter rise;
High o'er the minstrel's head they sail,
    And die amid the northern skies.

The voice of thunder shook the wood,
    As ceased the more than mortal yell;
And, spattering foul, a shower of blood
    Upon the hissing firebrands fell.

Next dropp'd from high a mangled arm;
    The fingers strain'd an half-drawn blade:
And last, the life-blood streaming warm,
    Torn from the trunk, a gasping head.

Oft o'er that head, in battling field,
    Stream'd the proud crest of high Ben-
        more;
That arm the broad claymore could wield,
    Which dyed the Teith with Saxon gore.

Woe to Moneira's sullen rills!
    Woe to Glenfinlas' dreary glen!
There never son of Albion's hills
    Shall draw the hunter's shaft agen.

E'en the tired pilgrim's burning feet
    At noon shall shun that sheltering den,
Lest, journeying in their rage, he meet
    The wayward Ladies of the Glen.

And we—behind the Chieftain's shield,
    No more shall we in safety dwell;
None leads the people to the field—
    And we the loud lament must swell.

O hone a rie'! O hone a rie'!
    The pride of Albin's line is o'er!
And fall'n Glenartney's stateliest tree;
    We ne'er shall see Lord Ronald more!

"Lewis's collection produced also what
Scott justly calls his 'first serious attempts in
verse;' and of these the earliest appears to
have been the Glenfinlas. Here the scene is
laid in the most favourite district of his
favourite Perthshire Highlands; and the
Gaelic tradition on which it is founded was
far more likely to draw out the secret strength
of his genius, as well as to arrest the feelings
of his countrymen, than any subject with
which the stores of German *diablerie* could
have supplied him."—*Life of Scott*, vol. ii.
p. 25.

THE EVE OF ST. JOHN.

Smaylho'me, or Smallholm Tower, the scene of the following ballad, is situated on the northern boundary of Roxburghshire, among a cluster of wild rocks, called Sandiknow-Crags, the property of Hugh Scott, Esq., of Harden, [Lord Polwarth.] The tower is a high square building, surrounded by an outer wall, now ruinous. The circuit of the outer court, being defended on three sides, by a precipice and morass, is accessible only from the west, by a steep and rocky path. The apartments, as is usual in a Border keep, or fortress, are placed one above another, and communicate by a narrow stair; on the roof are two barti-zans, or platforms, for defence or pleasure. The inner door of the tower is wood, the outer an iron gate; the distance between them being nine feet, the thickness, namely, of the wall. From the elevated situation of Smaylho'me Tower, it is seen many miles in every direction. Among the crags by which it is surrounded, one, more eminent, is called the _Watchfold_, and is said to have been the station of a beacon, in the times of war with England. Without the tower-court is a ruined chapel. Brotherstone is a heath, in the neighbourhood of Smayl-ho'me Tower.

This ballad was first printed in Mr. Lewis's _Tales of Wonder_. It is here published, with some additional illustrations, particularly an account of the battle of Ancram Moor; which seemed proper in a work upon Border antiquities. The catastrophe of the tale is founded upon a well-known Irish tradition. This ancient fortress and its vicinity formed the scene of the Editor's infancy, and seemed to claim from him this attempt to celebrate them in a Border tale.

THE Baron of Smaylho'me rose with day,
  He spurr'd his courser on,
Without stop or stay down the rocky way,
  That leads to Brotherstone.

He went not with the bold Buccleuch,
  His banner broad to rear;
He went not 'gainst the English yew,
  To lift the Scottish spear.

Yet his plate-jack* was braced, and his
    helmet was laced,
  And his vaunt-brace of proof he wore:
At his saddle-gerthe was a good steel
    sperthe,
  Full ten pound weight and more.

The Baron return'd in three days space,
  And his looks were sad and sour;
And weary was his courser's pace,
  As he reach'd his rocky tower.

He came not from where Ancram Moor[1]
  Ran red with English blood;
Where the Douglas true, and the bold
    Buccleuch,
  'Gainst keen Lord Evers stood.

Yet was his helmet hack'd and hew'd,
  His acton pierced and tore,
His axe and his dagger with blood im-
    brued,—
  But it was not English gore.

He lighted at the Chapellage,
  He held him close and still;
And he whistled thrice for his little foot-
    page,
  His name was English Will.

"Come thou hither, my little foot-page,
  Come hither to my knee;
Though thou art young and tender of age,
  I think thou art true to me.

"Come, tell me all that thou hast seen,
  And look thou tell me true!
Since I from Smaylho'me tower have been,
  What did thy lady do?"—

"My lady, each night, sought the lonely
    light,
  That burns on the wild Watchfold;
For, from height to height, the beacons
    bright
  Of the English foemen told.

---

* The plate-jack is coat-armour; the vaunt-brace or wam-brace, armour for the body: the sperthe, a battle-axe.

"The bittern clamour'd from the moss,
 The wind blew loud and shrill;
Yet the craggy pathway she did cross
 To the eiry Beacon Hill.

"I watch'd her steps, and silent came
 Where she sat her on a stone;—
No watchman stood by the dreary flame,
 It burned all alone.

"The second night I kept her in sight,
 Till to the fire she came,
And, by Mary's might! an Armed Knight
 Stood by the lonely flame.

"And many a word that warlike lord
 Did speak to my lady there;
But the rain fell fast, and loud blew the
  blast,
 And I heard not what they were.

"The third night there the sky was fair,
 And the mountain-blast was still,
As again I watch'd the secret pair,
 On the lonesome Beacon Hill.

"And I heard her name the midnight hour,
 And name this holy eve;
And say, 'Come this night to thy lady's
  bower;
Ask no bold Baron's leave.

"'He lifts his spear with the bold Buc-
  cleuch;
 His lady is all alone;
The door she'll undo, to her knight so true,
 On the eve of good St. John.'—

"'I cannot come; I must not come;
 I dare not come to thee;
On the eve of St. John I must wander alone:
 In thy bower I may not be.'—

"'Now, out on thee, fainthearted knight!
 Thou shouldst not say me nay;
For the eve is sweet, and when lovers meet,
 Is worth the whole summer's day.

"'And I'll chain the blood-hound, and
 the warder shall not sound,
And rushes shall be strew'd on the stair;

So, by the black rood-stone,* and by holy
 St. John,
 I conjure thee, my love, to be there!"—

"'Though the blood-hound be mute,
 and the rush beneath my foot,
And the warder his bugle should not
  blow,
Yet there sleepeth a priest in a chamber
  to the east,
 And my footstep he would know.'—

"'O fear not the priest, who sleepeth to
  the east!
For to Dryburgh† the way he has ta'en;
And there to say mass, till three days do
  pass,
For the soul of a knight that is slayne.'—

"He turn'd him around, and grimly he
 frown'd;
 Then he laughed right scornfully—
"He who says the mass-rite for the soul
 of that knight,
 May as well say mass for me:

"'At the lone midnight hour, when bad
 spirits have power,
 In thy chamber will I be.'—
With that he was gone, and my lady left
  alone,
 And no more did I see."

Then changed, I trow, was that bold
 Baron's brow,
 From the dark to the blood-red high;
"Now, tell me the mien of the knight
 thou hast seen,
 For, by Mary, he shall die!"—

"His arms shone full bright, in the
 beacon's red light:
 His plume it was scarlet and blue;

---

* The black-rood of Melrose was a crucifix of black marble, and of superior sanctity.

† Dryburgh Abbey stands on the banks of the Tweed. After its dissolution, it became the property of the Halliburtons of Newmains, and afterwards the seat of the Earls of Buchan.

On his shield was a hound, in a silver
    leash bound,
  And his crest was a branch of the
    yew."—

"Thou liest, thou liest, thou little foot-
    page,
  Loud dost thou lie to me!
For that knight is cold, and low laid in
    the mould,
  All under the Eildon-tree."*—

" Yet hear but my word, my noble lord!
  For I heard her name his name;
And that lady bright, she called the knight
  Sir Richard of Coldinghame."—

The bold Baron's brow then changed, I
    trow,
  From high blood-red to pale—
"The grave is deep and dark—and the
    corpse is stiff and stark—
  So I may not trust thy tale.

Where fair Tweed flows round holy
    Melrose,
  And Eildon slopes to the plain,
Full three nights ago, by some secret foe,
  That gay gallant was slain.

" The varying light deceived thy sight,
  And the wild winds drown'd the name;
For the Dryburgh bells ring, and the white
    monks do sing,
  For Sir Richard of Coldinghame!"

He pass'd the court-gate, and he oped the
    tower-gate,
  And he mounted the narrow stair,
To the bartizan-seat, where, with maids
    that on her wait,
  He found his lady fair.

That lady sat in mournful mood
  Look'd over hill and vale;

---

* Eildon is a high hill, terminating in three
conical summits, immediately above the town
of Melrose, where are the admired ruins of a
magnificent monastery. Eildon-tree is said to
be the spot where Thomas the Rhymer uttered
his prophecies.

Over Tweed's fair flood, and Mertoun's
    wood,
  And all down Teviotdale.

" Now hail, now hail, thou lady bright!"—
  " Now hail, thou Baron true!
What news, what news, from Ancram
    fight?
What news from the bold Buc-
    cleuch?"—

" The Ancram Moor is red with gore,
  For many a Southron fell;
And Buccleuch has charged us, evermore,
  To watch our beacons well."—

The lady blush'd red, but nothing she said:
  Nor added the Baron a word:
Then she stepp'd down the stair to her
    chamber fair,
  And so did her moody lord.

In sleep the lady mourn'd, and the Baron
    toss'd and turn'd,
  And oft to himself he said,—
" The worms around him creep, and his
    bloody grave is deep . . . . .
  It cannot give up the dead!"—

It was near the ringing of matin-bell,
  The night was well-nigh done,
When a heavy sleep on that Baron fell,
  On the eve of good St. John.

The lady look'd through the chamber fair,
  By the light of a dying flame;
And she was aware of a knight stood there—
  Sir Richard of Coldinghame!

" Alas! away, away!" she cried,
  " For the holy Virgin's sake!"—
" Lady, I know who sleeps by thy side;
  But, lady, he will not awake.

" By Eildon-tree, for long nights three,
  In bloody grave have I lain;
The mass and the death-prayer are said
    for me,
  But, lady, they are said in vain.

" By the Baron's brand, near Tweed's
    fair strand,
Most foully slain, I fell;
And my restless sprite on the beacon's
    height,
For a space is doom'd to dwell.

" At our trysting-place, for a certain space'
    I must wander to and fro;
But I had not had power to come to thy
    bower
Had'st thou not conjured me so. —

Love master'd fear— her brow she cross'd;
    " How, Richard, hast thou sped ?
And art thou saved, or art thou lost ?"—
    The vision shook his head !

" Who spilleth life, shall forfeit life;
    So bid thy lord believe:

That lawless love is guilt above,
    This awful sign receive."

He laid his left palm on an oaken beam :
    His right upon her hand;
The lady shrunk, and fainting sunk,
    For it scorch'd like a fiery brand.

The sable score, of fingers four,
    Remains on that board impress'd;
And for evermore that lady wore
    A covering on her wrist.[2]

There is a nun in Dryburgh bower,
    Ne'er looks upon the sun;
There is a monk in Melrose tower
    He speaketh word to none.

That nun, who ne'er beholds the day,[3]
    That monk, who speaks to none—
That nun was Smaylho'me's Lady gay,
    That monk the bold Baron.

CADYOW CASTLE.

The ruins of Cadyow, or Cadzow Castle, the ancient baronial residence of the family of Hamilton, are situated upon the precipitous banks of the river Evan, about two miles above its junction with the Clyde. It was dismantled, in the conclusion of the Civil Wars, during the reign of the unfortunate Mary, to whose cause the house of Hamilton devoted themselves with a generous zeal, which occasioned their temporary obscurity, and, very nearly their total ruin. The situation of the ruins, embosomed in wood, darkened by ivy and creeping shrubs, and overhanging the brawling torrent, is romantic in the highest degree. In the immediate vicinity of Cadyow is a grove of immense oaks, the remains of the Caledonian Forest, which anciently extended through the south of Scotland, from the eastern to the Atlantic Ocean. Some of these trees measure twenty-five feet, and upwards, in circumference; and the state of decay, in which they now appear, shows that they have witnessed the rites of the Druids. The whole scenery is included in the magnificent and extensive park of the Duke of Hamilton. There was long preserved in this forest the breed of the Scottish wild cattle, until their ferocity occasioned their being extirpated, about forty years ago. Their appearance was beautiful, being milk-white, with black muzzles, horns, and hoofs. The bulls are described by ancient authors as having white manes; but those of latter days had lost that peculiarity, perhaps by intermixture with the tame breed.*

In detailing the death of the Regent Murray, which is made the subject of the following ballad, it would be injustice to my readers to use other words than those of Dr. Robertson, whose account of that memorable event forms a beautiful piece of historical painting.

"Hamilton of Bothwellhaugh was the person who committed this barbarous action. He had been condemned to death soon after the battle of Langside, as we have already related, and owed his life to the Regent's clemency. But part of his estate had been bestowed upon one of the Regent's favourites,† who seized his house, and turned out his wife, naked,in a cold night, into the open fields, where, before next morning, she became furiously mad. This injury made

---

* They were formerly kept in the park at Drumlanrig, and are still to be seen at Chillingham Castle, in Northumberland.

† This was Sir James Bellenden, Lord Justice-Clerk, whose shameful and inhuman rapacity occasioned the catastrophe in the text,—SPOTTISWOODE.

a deeper impression on him than the benefit he had received, and from that moment he vowed to be revenged of the Regent. Party rage strengthened and inflamed his private resentment. His kinsmen, the Hamiltons, applauded the enterprise. The maxims of that age justified the most desperate course he could take to obtain vengeance. He followed the Regent for some time, and watched for an opportunity to strike the blow. He resolved at last to wait till his enemy should arrive at Linlithgow, through which he was to pass in his way from Stirling to Edinburgh. He took his stand in a wooden gallery,* which had a window towards the street; spread a feather-bed on the floor, to hinder the noise of his feet from being heard; hung up a black cloth behind him, that his shadow might not be observed from without; and, after all this preparation, calmly expected the Regent's approach, who had lodged, during the night, in a house not far distant. Some indistinct information of the danger which threatened him had been conveyed to the Regent, and he paid so much regard to it, that he resolved to return by the same gate through which he had entered, and to fetch a compass round the town. But, as the crowd about the gate was great, and he himself unacquainted with fear, he proceeded directly along the street; and the throng of people obliging him to move very slowly, gave the assassin time to take so true an aim, that he shot him, with a single bullet, through the lower part of his belly, and killed the horse of a gentleman who rode on his other side. His followers instantly endeavoured to break into the house whence the blow had come; but they found the door strongly barricaded, and, before it could be forced open, Hamilton had mounted a fleet horse,† which stood ready for him at a back passage, and was got far beyond their reach. The Regent died the same night of his wound."—*History of Scotland*, book v.

Bothwellhaugh rode straight to Hamilton, where he was received in triumph; for the ashes of the houses in Clydesdale, which had been burned by Murray's army, were yet smoking; and party prejudice, the habits of the age, and the enormity of the provocation, seemed to his kinsmen to justify the deed. After a short abode at Hamilton, this fierce and determined man left Scotland, and served in France, under the patronage of the family of Guise, to whom he was doubtless recommended by having avenged the cause of their niece, Queen Mary, upon her ungrateful brother. De Thou has recorded that an attempt was made to engage him to assassinate Gaspar de Coligni, the famous Admiral of France, and the buckler of the Huguenot cause. But the character of Bothwellhaugh was mistaken. He was no mercenary trader in blood, and rejected the offer with contempt and indignation. He had no authority, he said, from Scotland to commit murders in France; he had avenged his own just quarrel, but he would neither, for price nor prayer, avenge that of another man.—*Thuanus*, cap. 46.

The Regent's death happened 23rd January, 1569. It is applauded or stigmatized, by contemporary historians, according to their religious or party prejudices. The triumph of Blackwood is unbounded. He not only extols the pious feat of Bothwellhaugh, "who," he observes, "satisfied with a single ounce of lead, him whose sacrilegious avarice had stripped the metropolitan church of St. Andrews of its covering;" but he ascribes it to immediate divine inspiration, and the escape of Hamilton to little less than the miraculous interference of the Deity.—JEBB, vol. ii. p. 263. With equal injustice, it was, by others, made the ground of a general national reflection; for, when Mather urged Berney to assassinate Burleigh, and quoted the examples of Poltrot and Bothwellhaugh, the other conspirator answered, " that neyther Poltrot nor Hambleton did attempt their enterpryse without some reason or consideration to lead them to it; as the one, by hyre, and promise of preferment or rewarde; the other, upon desperate mind of revenge, for a lyttle wrong done unto him, as the report goethe, according to the vyle trayterous dysposysyon of the hoole natyon of the Scottes."—MURDIN's *State Papers*, vol. i. p. 197.

---

* The house to which this projecting gallery was attached was the property of the Archbishop of St. Andrews, a natural brother to the Duke of Chatelherault, and uncle to Bothwellhaugh. This, among many other circumstances, seems to evince the aid which Bothwellhaugh received from his clan in effecting his purpose.

† The gift of Lord John Hamilton, Commendator of Arbroath.

Addressed to the Right Honourable Lady Anne Hamilton.

WHEN princely Hamilton's abode
  Ennobled Cadyow's Gothic towers,
The song went round, the goblet flow'd,
  And revel sped the laughing hours.

Then, thrilling to the harp's gay sound,
  So sweetly rung each vaulted wall,
And echoed light the dancer's bound,
  As mirth and music cheer'd the hall.

But Cadyow's towers, in ruins laid,
  And vaults, by ivy-mantled o'er,
Thrill to the music of the shade,
  Or echo Evan's hoarser roar.

Yet still, of Cadyow's faded fame,
  You bid me tell a minstrel tale,
And tune my harp, of Border frame,
  On the wild banks of Evandale.

For thou, from scenes of courtly pride,
  From pleasure's lighter scenes, canst turn,
To draw oblivion's pall aside
  And mark the long-forgotten urn.

Then, noble maid! at thy command,
  Again the crumbled halls shall rise;
Lo! as on Evan's banks we stand,
  The past returns—the present flies.

Where, with the rock's wood cover'd side,
  Were blended late the ruins green,
Rise turrets in fantastic pride,
  And feudal banners flaunt between:

Where the rude torrent's brawling course
  Was shagg'd with thorn and tangling sloe,
The ashler buttress braves its force,
  And ramparts frown in battled row.

'Tis night—the shade of keep and spire
  Obscurely dance on Evan's stream;
And on the wave the warder's fire
  Is chequering the moonlight beam.

Fades slow their light; the east is grey;
  The weary warder leaves his tower;
Steeds snort; uncoupled stag-hounds bay,
  And merry hunters quit the bower.

The drawbridge falls—they hurry out—
  Clatters each plank and swinging chain,
As, dashing o'er, the jovial rout
  Urge the shy steed, and slack the rein.

First of his troop, the Chief rode on ;*
  His shouting merry-men throng behind;
The steed of princely Hamilton
  Was fleeter than the mountain wind.

From the thick copse the roebucks bound,
  The startled red-deer scuds the plain,
For the hoarse bugle's warrior-sound
  Has roused their mountain haunts again.

Through the huge oaks of Evandale,
  Whose limbs a thousand years have worn,
What sullen roar comes down the gale,
  And drowns the hunter's pealing horn!

Mightiest of all the beasts of chase,
  That roam in woody Caledon,
Crashing the forest in his race,
  The Mountain Bull comes thundering on.

Fierce, on the hunter's quiver'd band,
  He rolls his eyes of swarthy glow,
Spurns, with black hoof and horn, the sand,
  And tosses high his mane of snow.

---

* The head of the family of Hamilton, at this period, was James, Earl of Arran, Duke of Chatelherault, in France, and first peer of the Scottish realm. In 1569 he was appointed by Queen Mary her lieutenant-general in Scotland, under the singular title of her adopted father.

Aim'd well, the Chieftain's lance has
   flown;
Struggling in blood the savage lies;
His roar is sunk in hollow groan—
   Sound, merry huntsmen! sound the
    pryse[n]

'Tis noon—against the knotted oak
   The hunters rest the idle spear;
Curls through the trees the slender smoke,
   Where yeomen dight the woodland
    cheer.

Proudly the Chieftain mark'd his clan,
   On greenwood lap all careless thrown,
Yet miss'd his eye the boldest man
   That bore the name of Hamilton

" Why fills not Bothwellhaugh his place,
   Still wont our weal and woe to share?
Why comes he not our sport to grace?
   Why shares he not our hunter's
    fare?"—

Stern Claud replied,[2] with darkening face,
   (Grey Paisley's haughty lord was he,)
" At merry feast, or buxom chase,
   No more the warrior wilt thou see.

" Few suns have set since Woodhouse-
    lee[3]
Saw Bothwellhaugh's bright goblets
    foam
When to his hearths, in social glee,
   The war-worn soldier turn'd him home.

" There, wan from her maternal throes,
   His Margaret, beautiful and mild,
Sate in her bower, a pallid rose,
   And peaceful nursed her new-born child.

" O change accursed! past are those days;
   False Murray's ruthless spoilers came,
And, for the hearth's domestic blaze,
   Ascends destruction's volumed flame.

" What sheeted phantom wanders wild,
   Where mountain Eske through wood-
    land flows,
Her arms enfold a shadowy child—
   Oh! is it she, the pallid rose?

" The wilder'd traveller sees her glide,
   And hears her feeble voice with awe—
'Revenge,' she cries, 'on Murray's pride!
   And woe for injured Bothwellhaugh!'"

He ceased—and cries of rage and grief
   Burst mingling from the kindred band,
And half arose the kindling Chief,
   And half unsheathed his Arran brand.

But who, o'er bush, o'er stream and rock,
   Rides headlong, with resistless speed,
Whose bloody poniard's frantic stroke
   Drives to the leap his jaded steed;[4]

Whose cheek is pale, whose eyeballs glare,
   As one some vision'd sight that saw,
Whose hands are bloody, loose his hair?—
   'Tis he! 'tis he! 'tis Bothwellhaugh.

From gory selle,* and reeling steed,
   Sprung the fierce horseman with a
    bound,
And, reeking from the recent deed,
   He dash'd his carbine on the ground.

Sternly he spoke—" 'Tis sweet to hear
   In good greenwood the bugle blown,
But sweeter to Revenge's ear,
   To drink a tyrant's dying groan.

" Your slaughter'd quarry proudly trode,
   At dawning morn, o'er dale and down,
But prouder base-born Murray rode
   Through old Linlithgow's crowded
    town.

" From the wild Border's humbled side,[5]
   In haughty triumph marched he,
While Knox relax'd his bigot pride,
   And smiled, the traitorous pomp to see.

" But can stern Power, with all his vaunt,
   Or Pomp, with all her courtly glare,
The settled heart of Vengeance daunt,
   Or change the purpose of Despair?

---

* *Selle*—saddle. A word used by Spenser,
and other ancient authors.

"With hackbut bent,[6] my secret stand,
 Dark as the purposed deed, I chose,
And mark'd, where, mingling in his band,
 Troop'd Scottish pikes and English
  bows.

"Dark Morton,* girt with many a spear,
 Murder's foul minion, led the van;
And clash'd their broadswords in the rear
 The wild Macfarlane's plaided clan.[7]

"Glencairn and stout Parkhead[8] were
  nigh,
Obsequious at their Regent's rein,
And haggard Lindesay's iron eye,
 That saw fair Mary weep in vain.[9]

"'Mid pennon'd spears, a steely grove,
 Proud Murray's plumage floated high;
Scarce could his trampling charger move,
 So close the minions crowded nigh.[10]

"From the raised vizor's shade, his eye,
 Dark-rolling, glanced the ranks along,
And his steel truncheon, waved on high,
 Seem'd marshalling the iron throng.

"But yet his sadden'd brow confess'd
 A passing shade of doubt and awe;
Some fiend was whispering in his breast;
 'Beware of injured Bothwellhaugh!'

"The death-shot parts—the charger
  springs—
 Wild rises tumult's startling roar!
And Murray's plumy helmet rings—
 —Rings on the ground, to rise no more.

"What joy the raptured youth can feel,
 To hear her love the loved one tell—
Or he, who broaches on his steel
 The wolf, by whom his infant fell!

"But dearer to my injured eye
 To see in dust proud Murray roll;
And mine was ten times trebled joy,
 To hear him groan his felon soul.

"My Margaret's spectre glided near;
 With pride her bleeding victim saw;
And shriek'd in his death-deafen'd ear,
 'Remember injured Bothwellhaugh!'

"Then speed thee, noble Chatlerault!
 Spread to the wind thy banner'd tree!†
Each warrior bend his Clydesdale bow!—
 Murray is fall'n, and Scotland free!'"

Vaults every warrior to his steed;
 Loud bugles join their wild acclaim—
"Murray is fall'n, and Scotland freed!
 Couch, Arran! couch thy spear of
  flame!"

But, see! the minstrel vision fails—
 The glimmering spears are seen no
  more;
The shouts of war die on the gales,
 Or sink in Evan's lonely roar.

For the loud bugle, pealing high,
 The blackbird whistles down the vale,
And sunk in ivied ruins lie
 The banner'd towers of Evandale.

For Chiefs, intent on bloody deed,
 And Vengeance shouting o'er the slain,
Lo! high-born Beauty rules the steed,
 Or graceful guides the silken rein.

And long may Peace and Pleasure own
 The maids who list the minstrel's tale;
Nor e'er a ruder guest be known
 On the fair banks of Evandale!

---

* Of this noted person, it is enough to say, that he was active in the murder of David Rizzio, and at least privy to that of Darnley.

† An oak, half-sawn, with the motto *through*, is an ancient cognizance of the family of Hamilton.

THE GRAY BROTHER.

A FRAGMENT.

The imperfect state of this ballad, which was written several years ago, is not a circumstance affected for the purpose of giving it that peculiar interest which is often found to arise from ungratified curiosity. On the contrary, it was the Editor's intention to have completed the tale, if he had found himself able to succeed to his own satisfaction. Yielding to the opinion of persons, whose judgment, if not biassed by the partiality of friendship, is entitled to deference, he has preferred inserting these verses as a fragment, to his intention of entirely suppressing them.

The tradition upon which the tale is founded, regards a house upon the barony of Gilmerton, near Lasswade, in Mid-Lothian. This building, now called Gilmerton Grange, was originally named Burndale, from the following tragic adventure. The barony of Gilmerton belonged, of yore, to a gentleman named Heron, who had one beautiful daughter. This young lady was seduced by the Abbot of Newbattle, a richly endowed abbey, upon the banks of the South Esk, now a seat of the Marquis of Lothian. Heron came to the knowledge of this circumstance, and learned also that the lovers carried on their guilty intercourse by the connivance of the lady's nurse, who lived at this house of Gilmerton Grange, or Burndale He formed a resolution of bloody vengeance, undeterred by the supposed sanctity of the clerical character, or by the stronger claims of natural affection. Choosing, therefore, a dark and windy night, when the objects of his vengeance were engaged in a stolen interview, he set fire to a stack of dried thorns, and other combustibles, which he had caused to be piled against the house, and reduced to a pile of glowing ashes the dwelling, with all its inmates.

The scene with which the ballad opens, was suggested by the following curious passage, extracted from the life of Alexander Peden, one of the wandering and persecuted teachers of the sect of Cameronians, during the reign of Charles II. and his successor, James. This person was supposed by his followers, and, perhaps, really believed himself, to be possessed of supernatural gifts; for the wild scenes which they frequented, and the constant dangers which were incurred through their proscription, deepened upon their minds the gloom of superstition, so general in that age.

"About the same time he [Peden] came to Andrew Normand's house, in the parish of Alloway, in the shire of Ayr, being to preach at night in his barn. After he came in, he halted a little, leaning upon a chair-back, with his face covered; when he lifted up his head, he said, 'They are in this house that I have not one word of salvation unto;' he halted a little again, saying, 'This is strange, that the devil will not go out, that we may begin our work!' Then there was a woman went out, ill-looked upon almost all her life, and to her dying hour, for a witch, with many presumptions of the same. It escaped me, in the former passages, what John Muirhead (whom I have often mentioned) told me, that when he came from Ireland to Galloway, he was at family worship, and giving some notes upon the Scripture read, when a very ill-looking man came, and sat down within the door, at the back of the *hallan*, [partition of the cottage:] immediately he halted and said, 'There is some unhappy body just now come into this house. I charge him to go out, and not stop my mouth!' This person went out, and he *insisted* [went on,] yet he saw him neither come in nor go out."—*The Life and Prophecies of Mr. Alexander Peden, late Minister of the Gospel at New Glenluce, in Galloway,* part ii. § 26.

A friendly correspondent remarks, "that the incapacity of proceeding in the performance of a religious duty, when a contaminated person is present, is of much higher antiquity than the era of the Reverend Mr. Alexander Peden."—*Vide Hygini Fabulas,* cap. 26. "*Medea Corintho exul, Athenas, ad Ægeum Pandionis filium devenit in hospitium, eique nupsit.*

—— "*Postea sacerdos Dianæ Medeam exagitare cœpit, regique negabat sacra caste facere posse, ɔo quod in ea civitate esset mulier venefica et scelerata; tunc exulatur.*"

The Pope he was saying the high, high mass,
　All on Saint Peter's day,
With the power to him given, by the saints in heaven,
　To wash men's sins away.

The Pope he was saying the blessed mass,
　And the people kneel'd around,
And from each man's soul his sins did pass,
　As he kiss'd the holy ground.

And all, among the crowded throng,
　Was still both limb and tongue,
While, through vaulted roof and aisles aloof,
　The holy accents rung.

At the holiest word he quiver'd for fear,
　And falter'd in the sound—
And, when he would the chalice rear,
　He dropp'd it to the ground.

" The breath of one of evil deed
　Pollutes our sacred day;
He has no portion in our creed,
　No part in what I say.

" A being, whom no blessed word
　To ghostly peace can bring;
A wretch, at whose approach abhorr'd,
　Recoils each holy thing.

" Up, up, unhappy! haste, arise!
　My adjuration fear!
I charge thee not to stop my voice,
　Nor longer tarry here!"

Amid them all a pilgrim kneel'd,
　In gown of sackcloth grey;
Far journeying from his native field,
　He first saw Rome that day.

For forty days and nights so drear,
　I ween he had not spoke,
And, save with bread and water clear,
　His fast he ne'er had broke.

Amid the penitential flock,
　Seem'd none more bent to pray;
But, when the Holy Father spoke,
　He rose and went his way.

Again unto his native land
　His weary course he drew,
To Lothian's fair and fertile strand,
　And Pentland's mountains blue.

His unblest feet his native seat,
　'Mid Eske's fair woods, regain;
Thro' woods more fair no stream more sweet
　Rolls to the eastern main.

And lords to meet the pilgrim came,
　And vassals bent the knee;
For all 'mid Scotland's chiefs of fame,
　Was none more famed than he.

And boldly for his country, still,
　In battle he had stood,
Ay, even when on the banks of Till
　Her noblest pour'd their blood.

Sweet are the paths, O passing sweet!
　By Eske's fair streams that run,
O'er airy steep, through copsewood deep,
　Impervious to the sun.

There the rapt poet's step may rove,
　And yield the muse the day;
There Beauty, led by timid Love,
　May shun the tell-tale ray;

From that fair dome, where suit is paid
　By blast of bugle free,[1]
To Auchendinny's hazel glade,[2]
　And haunted Woodhouselee.

Who knows not Melville's beechy grove,[3]
　And Roslin's rocky glen,[4]
Dalkeith, which all the virtues love,[5]
　And classic Hawthornden?[6]

Yet never a path, from day to day,
　The pilgrim's footsteps range,
Save but the solitary way
　To Burndale's ruin'd grange.

A woful place was that, I ween,
　As sorrow could desire;
For nodding to the fall was each crumbling wall,
　And the roof was scathed with fire.

It fell upon a summer's eve,
　While, on Carnethy's head,
The last faint gleams of the sun's low
　　beams
　Had streak'd the grey with red;

And the convent bell did vespers tell,
　Newbattle's oaks among,
And mingled with the solemn knell
　Our Ladye's evening song·

The heavy knell, the choir's faint swell,
　Came slowly down the wind,
And on the pilgrim's ear they fell,
　As his wonted path he did find.

Deep sunk in thought, I ween, he was,
　Nor ever raised his eye,
Until he came to that dreary place,
　Which did all in ruins lie.

He gazed on the walls, so scathed with fire,
　With many a bitter groan—
And there was aware of a Gray Friar,
　Resting him on a stone.

"Now, Christ thee save!" said the Gray
　　Brother;
　"Some pilgrim thou seemest to be."
But in sore amaze did Lord Albert gaze,
　Nor answer again made he.

"O come ye from east, or come ye from
　　west,
　Or bring reliques from over the sea;
Or come ye from the shrine of James the
　　divine,
　Or St. John of Beverley?"—

"I come not from the shrine of St. James
　　the divine,
　Nor bring reliques from over the sea;
I bring but a curse from our father, the
　　Pope,
　Which for ever will cling to me."—
"Now, woful pilgrim, say not so!
　But kneel thee down to me,
And shrive thee so clean of thy deadly sin,
　That absolved thou mayst be."—

"And who art thou, thou Gray Brother,
　That I should shrive to thee,
When He, to whom are given the keys
　　of earth and heaven,
　Has no power to pardon me?"—

"O I am sent from a distant clime,
　Five thousand miles away,
And all to absolve a foul, foul crime,
　Done *here* 'twixt night and day."

The pilgrim kneel'd him on the sand,
　And thus began his saye—
When on his neck an ice-cold hand
　Did that Gray Brother laye.

　　　*　　*　　*　　*　　*

BALLADS, TRANSLATED, OR IMITATED, FROM THE GERMAN, &c.

~~~~~~~~~~~~~~~

WILLIAM AND HELEN.

1796.

IMITATED FROM THE "LENORÉ" OF BÜRGER.

I.

FROM heavy dreams fair Helen rose,
  And eyed the dawning red:
" Alas, my love, thou tarriest long!
  O art thou false or dead?"—

II.

With gallant Fred'rick's princely power
  He sought the bold Crusade;
But not a word from Judah's wars
  Told Helen how he sped.

III.

With Paynim and with Saracen
  At length a truce was made,
And ev'ry knight return'd to dry
  The tears his love had shed.

IV.

Our gallant host was homeward bound
  With many a song of joy;
Green waved the laurel in each plume,
  The badge of victory.

V.

And old and young, and sire and son,
  To meet them crowd the way,
With shouts, and mirth, and melody,
  The debt of love to pay.

VI.

Full many a maid her true-love met,
  And sobb'd in his embrace,
And flutt'ring joy in tears and smiles
  Array'd full many a face.

VII.

Nor joy nor smile for Helen sad;
  She sought the host in vain;
For none could tell her William's fate,
  If faithless, or if slain.

VIII.

The martial band is past and gone;
  She rends her raven hair,
And in distraction's bitter mood
  She weeps with wild despair.

IX.

" O rise, my child," her mother said,
  " Nor sorrow thus in vain,
A perjured lover's fleeting heart
  No tears recall again."—

X.

" O mother, what is gone, is gone,
  What's lost for ever lorn:
Death, death alone can comfort me;
  O had I ne'er been born!

XI.

" O break, my heart,—O break at once!
  Drink my life-blood, Despair!
No joy remains on earth for me,
  For me in heaven no share."—

XII.

" O enter not in judgment, Lord!"
  The pious mother prays;
" Impute not guilt to thy frail child!
  She knows not what she says.

XIII.

"O say thy pater noster, child!
　O turn to God and grace!
His will, that turn'd thy bliss to bale,
　Can change thy bale to bliss."—

XIV.

" O mother, mother, what is bliss?
　O mother, what is bale?
My William's love was heaven on earth,
　Without it earth is hell.

XV.

" Why should I pray to ruthless Heaven,
　Since my loved William's slain?
I only pray'd for William's sake,
　And all my prayers were vain."—

XVI.

" O take the sacrament, my child,
　And check these tears that flow;
By resignation's humble prayer,
　O hallow'd be thy woe!"—

XVII.

" No sacrament can quench this fire,
　Or slake this scorching pain;
No sacrament can bid the dead
　Arise and live again.

XVIII.

" O break, my heart,—O break at once!
　Be thou my god, Despair!
Heaven's heaviest blow has fallen on me,
　And vain each fruitless prayer."—

XIX.

" O enter not in judgment, Lord,
　With thy frail child of clay!
She knows not what her tongue has spoke;
　Impute it not, I pray!

XX.

" Forbear, my child, this desperate woe,
　And turn to God and grace;
Well can devotion's heavenly glow
　Convert thy bale to bliss."—

XXI.

" O mother, mother, what is bliss?
　O mother, what is bale?
Without my William what were heaven,
　Or with him what were hell?"—

XXII.

Wild she arraigns the eternal doom,
　Upbraids each sacred power,
Till, spent, she sought her silent room,
　All in the lonely tower.

XXIII.

She beat her breast, she wrung her hands,
　Till sun and day were o'er,
And through the glimmering lattice shone
　The twinkling of the star.

XXIV.

Then, crash! the heavy drawbridge fell
　That o'er the moat was hung;
And, clatter! clatter! on its boards
　The hoof of courser rung.

XXV.

The clank of echoing steel was heard
　As off the rider bounded;
And slowly on the winding stair
　A heavy footstep sounded.

XXVI.

And hark! and hark! a knock—Tap!
　tap!
A rustling stifled noise;—
Door-latch and tinkling staples ring;—
　At length a whispering voice.

XXVII.

" Awake, awake, arise, my love!
　How, Helen, dost thou fare?
Wak'st thou, or sleep'st? laugh'st thou,
　or weep'st?
Hast thought on me, my fair?"—

XXVIII.

" My love! my love!—so late by night!—
　I waked, I wept for thee:
Much have I borne since dawn of morn;
　Where, William, couldst thou be!"—

XXIX.

" We saddle late—from Hungary
    I rode since darkness fell;
And to its bourne we both return
    Before the matin-bell."—

XXX.

" O rest this night within my arms,
    And warm thee in their fold !
Chill howls through hawthorn bush the
    wind:—
  My love is deadly cold."—

XXXI.

" Let the wind howl through hawthorn
    bush !
    This night we must away ;
The steed is wight, the spur is bright;
    I cannot stay till day.

XXXII.

" Busk, busk, and boune!* Thou mount'st
    behind
    Upon my black barb steed:
O'er stock and stile, a hundred miles,
    We haste to bridal bed."—

XXXIII.

" To-night—to-night a hundred miles !—
    O dearest William, stay !
The bell strikes twelve—dark, dismal
    hour !
    O wait, my love, till day !"—

XXXIV.

" Look here, look here—the moon shines
    clear—
    Full fast I ween we ride ;
Mount and away ! for ere the day
    We reach our bridal bed.

XXXV.

" The black barb snorts, the bridle rings ;
    Haste, busk, and boune, and seat thee !
The feast is made, the chamber spread,
    The bridal guests await thee."—

---

* *Busk*—to dress. *Boune*—to prepare one's
self for a journey.

XXXVI.

Strong love prevail'd: She busks, she
    bounes,
    She mounts the barb behind,
And round her darling William's waist
    Her lily arms she twined.

XXXVII.

And, hurry ! hurry ! off they rode,
    As fast as fast might be ;
Spurn'd from the courser's thundering
    heels
    The flashing pebbles flee.

XXXVIII.

And on the right, and on the left,
    Ere they could snatch a view,
Fast, fast each mountain, mead, and plain,
    And cot, and castle, flew.

XXXIX.

" Sit fast—dost fear ?—The moon shines
    clear—
    Fleet goes my barb—keep hold !
Fear'st thou ?"—" O no !" she faintly said ;
    " But why so stern and cold ?

XL.

" What yonder rings? what yonder
    sings?
    Why shrieks the owlet grey ?"—
" 'Tis death-bells' clang, 'tis funeral song,
    The body to the clay.

XLI.

" With song and clang, at morrow's
    dawn,
    Ye may inter the dead:
To-night I ride, with my young bride,
    To deck our bridal bed.

XLII.

" Come with thy choir, thou coffin'd
    guest,
    To swell our nuptial song !
Come, priest, to bless our marriage feast !
    Come all, come all along !"—

XLIII.

Ceased clang and song; down sunk the
   bier;
   The shrouded corpse arose:
And, hurry! hurry! all the train
   The thundering steed pursues.

XLIV.

And, forward! forward! on they go;
   High snorts the straining steed;
Thick pants the rider's labouring breath,
   As headlong on they speed.

XLV.

" O William, why this savage haste?
   And where thy bridal bed?"—
" 'Tis distant far, low, damp, and chill,
   And narrow, trustless maid."—

XLVI.

" No room for me?"—" Enough for
   both;—
   Speed, speed, my barb, thy course!"
O'er thundering bridge, through boiling
   surge,
   He drove the furious horse.

XLVII.

Tramp! tramp! along the land they rode,*
   Splash! splash! along the sea;
The scourge is wight, the spur is bright,
   The flashing pebbles flee.

XLVIII.

Fled past on right and left how fast
   Each forest, grove, and bower!
On right and left fled past how fast
   Each city, town, and tower!

XLIX.

" Dost fear? dost fear? The moon shines
   clear,
   Dost fear to ride with me?—
Hurrah! hurrah! the dead can ride!"
   " O William, let them be!—

L.

" See there, see there! What yonder
   swings
   And creaks 'mid whistling rain?"—
" Gibbet and steel, th' accursed wheel;
   A murderer in his chain.—

LI.

" Hollo! thou felon, follow here:
   To bridal bed we ride;
And thou shalt prance a fetter dance
   Before me and my bride."—

LII.

And, hurry! hurry! clash, clash, clash!
   The wasted form descends;
And fleet as wind through hazel bush
   The wild career attends.

LIII.

Tramp! tramp! along the land they rode,
   Splash! splash! along the sea;
The scourge is red, the spur drops blood,
   The flashing pebbles flee.

LIV.

How fled what moonshine faintly show'd!
   How fled what darkness hid!
How fled the earth beneath their feet,
   The heaven above their head!

---

* In the preface to the edition of " William
and Helen," published anonymously in 1796,
Sir Walter Scott says:—" The first two lines
of the forty-seventh stanza, descriptive of the
speed of the lovers, may perhaps bring to the
recollection of many a passage extremely
similar in a translation of " Leonora," which
first appeared in the *Monthly Magazine*.
In justice to himself, the translator thinks it
his duty to acknowledge that his curiosity was
first attracted to this truly romantic story by a

gentleman, who having heard " Leonora "
once read in manuscript, could only recollect
the general outlines, and part of a couplet
which, from the singularity of its structure
and frequent recurrence, had remained impressed upon his memory. If, from despair
of rendering the passage so happily, the
property of another has been invaded, the
translator makes the only atonement now in
his power by restoring it thus publicly to the
rightful owner.

LV.

"Dost fear? dost fear? The moon
    shines clear,
And well the dead can ride;
Does faithful Helen fear for them?"—
    "O leave in peace the dead!"—

LVI.

"Barb! Barb! methinks I hear the cock;
    The sand will soon be run:
Barb! Barb! I smell the morning air;
    The race is wellnigh done."—

LVII.

Tramp! tramp! along the land they rode;
    Splash! splash! along the sea;
The scourge is red, the spur drops blood,
    The flashing pebbles flee.

LVIII.

"Hurrah! hurrah! well ride the dead;
    The bride, the bride is come;
And soon we reach the bridal bed,
    For, Helen, here's my home."—

LIX.

Reluctant on its rusty hinge
    Revolved an iron door,
And by the pale moon's setting beam
    Were seen a church and tower.

LX.

With many a shriek and cry whiz round
    The birds of midnight, scared;
And rustling like autumnal leaves
    Unhallow'd ghosts were heard.

LXI.

O'er many a tomb and tombstone pale
    He spurr'd the fiery horse,
Till sudden at an open grave
    He check'd the wondrous course.

LXII.

The falling gauntlet quits the rein,
    Down drops the casque of steel,
The cuirass leaves his shrinking side,
    The spur his gory heel.

LXIII.

The eyes desert the naked skull,
    The mould'ring flesh the bone,
Till Helen's lily arms entwine
    A ghastly skeleton.

LXIV.

The furious barb snorts fire and foam,
    And, with a fearful bound,
Dissolves at once in empty air,
    And leaves her on the ground.

LXV.

Half seen by fits, by fits half heard,
    Pale spectres flit along,
Wheel round the maid in dismal dance,
    And howl the funeral song;

LXVI.

"E'en when the heart's with anguish cleft,
    Revere the doom of Heaven,
Her soul is from her body reft;
    Her spirit be forgiven!"

THE WILD HUNTSMAN.*

[1796.]

This is a translation, or rather an imitation, of the *Wilde Jäger* of the German poet Bürger. The tradition upon which it is founded bears, that formerly a Wildgrave, or keeper of a royal forest, named Faulkenberg, was so much addicted to the pleasures of the chase, and otherwise so extremely profligate and cruel, that he not only followed this unhallowed amusement on the Sabbath, and other days consecrated to religious duty, but accompanied it with the most unheard-of oppression upon the poor peasants who were under his vassalage. When this second Nimrod died, the people adopted a superstition, founded

---

* Published (1796) with "William and Helen," and entitled "THE CHASE."

probably on the many various uncouth sounds heard in the depth of a German forest, during the silence of the night. They conceived they still heard the cry of the Wildgrave's hounds; and the well-known cheer of the deceased hunter, the sounds of his horse's feet, and the rustling of the branches before the game, the pack, and the sportsmen, are also distinctly discriminated; but the phantoms are rarely, if ever, visible. Once, as a benighted *Chasseur* heard this infernal chase pass by him, at the sound of the halloo, with which the Spectre Huntsman cheered his hounds, he could not refrain from crying, " *Gluck zu Falkenlurgh!* " [Good sport to ye, Falkenburgh!] "Dost thou wish me good sport?" answered a hoarse voice; " thou shalt share the game;" and there was thrown at him what seemed to be a huge pie ce of foul carrion. The daring *Chasseur* lost two of his best horses soon after, and never perfectly recovered the personal effects of this ghostly greeting. This tale, th ough told with some variations, is universally believed all over Germany.

The French had a similar tradition concerning an aërial hunter, who infested the forest of Fountainbleau.

THE Wildgrave winds his bugle horn,
    To horse, to horse! halloo, halloo!
His fiery courser snuffs the morn,
    And thronging serfs their lord pursue.

The eager pack, from couples freed,
    Dash through the brush, the brier, the brake;
While answering hound, and horn, and steed,
    The mountain echoes startling wake.

The beams of God's own hallow'd day
    Had painted yonder spire with gold,
And, calling sinful man to pray,
    Loud, long, and deep the bell had toll'd:

But still the Wildgrave onward rides;
    Halloo, halloo! and, hark again!
When spurring from opposing sides,
    Two Stranger Horsemen join the train.

Who was each Stranger, left and right,
    Well may I guess, but dare not tell;
The right-hand steed was silver white,
    The left, the swarthy hue of hell.

The right-hand Horseman young and fair,
    His smile was like the morn of May;
The left, from eye of tawny glare,
    Shot midnight lightning's lurid ray.

He waved his huntsman's cap on high,
    Cried, "Welcome, welcome, noble lord!
What sport can earth, or sea, or sky,
    To match the princely chase, afford?"

"Cease thy loud bugle's changing knell,"
    Cried the fair youth, with silver voice;
"And for devotion's choral swell,
    Exchange the rude unhallow'd noise.

"To-day, the ill-omen'd chase forbear,
    Yon bell yet summons to the fane;
To-day the Warning Spirit hear,
    To-morrow thou mayst mourn in vain."—

"Away, and sweep the glades along!"
    The Sable Hunter hoarse replies;
"To muttering monks leave matin-song,
    And bells, and books, and mysteries."

The Wildgrave spurr'd his ardent steed,
    And, launching forward with a bound,
"Who, for thy drowsy priestlike rede,
    Would leave the jovial horn and hound?

"Hence, if our manly sport offend!
    With pious fools go chant and pray:—
Well hast thou spoke, my dark-brow'd friend;
    Halloo, halloo! and, hark away!"

The Wildgrave spurr'd his courser light,
    O'er moss and moor, o'er holt and hill;
And on the left and on the right,
    Each stranger Horseman follow'd still.

Up springs, from yonder tangled thorn,
    A stag more white than mountain snow;
And louder rung the Wildgrave's horn,
    "Hark forward, forward! holla, ho!"

A heedless wretch has cross'd the way;
  He gasps the thundering hoofs below;—
But, live who can, or die who may,
  Still, " Forward, forward !" on they go.

See, where yon simple fences meet,
  A field with Autumn's blessings
    crown'd;
See, prostrate at the Wildgrave's feet,
  A husbandman with toil embrown'd :

" O mercy, mercy, noble lord !
  Spare the poor's pittance," was his cry,
" Earn'd by the sweat these brows have
    pour'd,
  In scorching hour of fierce July."

Earnest the right-hand Stranger pleads,
  The left still cheering to the prey;
The impetuous Earl no warning heeds,
  But furious holds the onward way.

" Away, thou hound ! so basely born,
  Or dread the scourge's echoing blow!"—
Then loudly rung his bugle-horn,
  " Hark forward, forward, holla, ho !"

So said, so done :—A single bound
  Clears the poor labourer's humble pale ;
Wild follows man, and horse, and hound,
  Like dark December's stormy gale.

And man and horse, and hound and horn,
  Destructive sweep the field along ;
While, joying o'er the wasted corn,
  Fell Famine marks the maddening
    throng.

Again uproused, the timorous prey
  Scours moss and moor, and holt and hill;
Hard run, he feels his strength decay,
  And trusts for life his simple skill.

Too dangerous solitude appear'd ;
  He seeks the shelter of the crowd ;
Amid the flock's domestic herd
  His harmless head he hopes to shroud.

O'er mass and moor, and holt and hill,
  His track the steady blood-hounds trace ;
O'er moss and moor, unwearied still,
  The furious Earl pursues the chase.

Full lowly did the herdsman fall ;—
  " O spare, thou noble Baron, spare
These herds, a widow's little all ;
  These flocks, an orphan's fleecy
    care !"—

Earnest the right-hand Stranger pleads,
  The left still cheering to the prey;
The Earl nor prayer nor pity heeds,
  But furious keeps the onward way.

" Unmanner'd dog ! To stop my sport
  Vain were thy cant and beggar whine,
Though human spirits, of thy sort,
  Were tenants of these carrion kine !"—

Again he winds his bugle-horn,
  " Hark forward, forward, holla, ho !"
And through the herd, in ruthless scorn,
  He cheers his furious hounds to go.

In heaps the throttled victims fall ;
  Down sinks their mangled herdsman
    near;
The murderous cries the stag appal,—
  Again he starts, new-nerved by fear.

With blood besmear'd, and white with
    foam,
  While big the tears of anguish pour,
He seeks, amid the forest's gloom,
  The humble hermit's hallow'd bower.

But man and horse, and horn and hound,
  Fast rattling on his traces go ;
The sacred chapel rung around
  With, " Hark away ! and, holla, ho !"

All mild, amid the rout profane,
  The holy hermit pour'd his prayer ;
" Forbear with blood God's house to stain;
  Revere his altar, and forbear !

" The meanest brute has rights to plead,
  Which, wrong'd by cruelty, or pride,
Draw vengeance on the ruthless head :—
  Be warn'd at length, and turn aside."

Still the Fair Horseman anxious pleads ;
  The Black, wild whooping, points the
    prey :—
Alas ! the Earl no warning heeds,
  But frantic keeps the forward way.

"Holy or not, or right or wrong,
  Thy altar, and its rites, I spurn;
Not sainted martyrs' sacred song,
  Not God himself, shall make me turn!"

He spurs his horse, he winds his horn,
  "Hark forward, forward, holla, ho!"—
But off, on whirlwind's pinions borne,
  The stag, the hut, the hermit, go.

And horse and man, and horn and hound,
  And clamour of the chase, was gone;
For hoofs, and howls, and bugle-sound,
  A deadly silence reign'd alone.

Wild gazed the affrighted Earl around;
  He strove in vain to wake his horn,
In vain to call: for not a sound
  Could from his anxious lips be borne.

He listens for his trusty hounds;
  No distant baying reached his ears:
His courser rooted to the ground,
  The quickening spur unmindful bears.

Still dark and darker frown the shades,
  Dark as the darkness of the grave;
And not a sound the still invades,
  Save what a distant torrent gave.

High o'er the sinner's humbled head
  At length the solemn silence broke;
And, from a cloud of swarthy red,
  The awful voice of thunder spoke.

"Oppressor of creation fair!
  Apostate Spirits' harden'd tool!
Scorner of God! Scourge of the poor!
  The measure of thy cup is full.

"Be chased for ever through the wood;
  For ever roam the affrighted wild;
And let thy fate instruct the proud,
  God's meanest creature is his child."

'Twas hush'd:—One flash, of sombre
    glare,
  With yellow tinged the forests brown;
Uprose the Wildgrave's bristling hair,
  And horror chill'd each nerve and bone.

Cold pour'd the sweat in freezing rill;
  A rising wind began to sing;
And louder, louder, louder still,
  Brought storm and tempest on its wing.

Earth heard the call;—her entrails rend;
  From yawning rifts, with many a yell,
Mix'd with sulphureous flames, ascend
  The misbegotten dogs of hell.

What ghastly Huntsman next arose,
  Well may I guess, but dare not tell;
His eye like midnight lightning glows,
  His steed the swarthy hue of hell.

The Wildgrave flies o'er bush and thorn,
  With many a shriek of helpless woe;
Behind him hound, and horse, and horn,
  And, "Hark away, and holla, ho!"

With wild despair's reverted eye,
  Close, close behind, he marks the
    throng,
With bloody fangs and eager cry;
  In frantic fear he scours along.—

Still, still shall last the dreadful chase,
  Till time itself shall have an end;
By day, they scour earth's cavern'd space,
  At midnight's witching hour, ascend.

This is the horn, and hound, and horse,
  That oft the lated peasant hears;
Appall'd, he signs the frequent cross,
  When the wild din invades his ears.

The wakeful priest oft drops a tear
  For human pride, for human woe,
When, at his midnight mass, he hears
  The infernal cry of, "Holla, ho!"

THE FIRE-KING.

"The blessings of the evil Genii, which are curses, were upon him."—*Eastern Tale.*

[1801.]

This ballad was written at the request of Mr. Lewis, to be inserted in his *Tales of Wonder.** It is the third in a series of four ballads, on the subject of Elementary Spirits. The story is, however, partly historical; for it is recorded, that, during the struggles of the Latin kingdom of Jerusalem, a Knight-Templar, called Saint-Alban, deserted to the Saracens, and defeated the Christians in many combats, till he was finally routed and slain, in a conflict with King Baldwin, under the walls of Jerusalem.

Bold knights and fair dames, to my harp
   give an ear,
Of love, and of war, and of wonder to
   hear;
And you haply may sigh, in the midst of
   your glee,
At the tale of Count Albert, and fair
   Rosalie.

O see you that castle, so strong and so
   high?
And see you that lady, the tear in her
   eye?
And see you that palmer, from Palestine's
   land,
The shell on his hat, and the staff in his
   hand?—

"Now palmer, grey palmer, O tell unto
   me,
What news bring you home from the
   Holy Countrie?
And how goes the warfare by Galilee's
   strand?
And how fare our nobles, the flower of
   the land?"—

"O well goes the warfare by Galilee's
   wave,
For Gilead, and Nablous, and Ramah we
   have;
And well fare our nobles by Mount
   Lebanon,
For the Heathen have lost, and the Chris-
   tians have won."

A fair chain of gold 'mid her ringlets
   there hung;
O'er the palmer's grey locks the fair chain
   has she flung:
"O palmer, grey palmer, this chain be
   thy fee,
For the news thou hast brought from the
   Holy Countrie.

"And, palmer, good palmer, by Galilee's
   wave,
O saw ye Count Albert, the gentle and
   brave?
When the Crescent went back, and the
   Red-cross rush'd on,
O saw ye him foremost on Mount Le-
   banon?"—

"O lady, fair lady, the tree green it
   grows;
O lady, fair lady, the stream pure it
   flows;
Your castle stands strong, and your hopes
   soar on high;
But, lady, fair lady, all blossoms to die.

"The green boughs they wither, the
   thunderbolt falls,
It leaves of your castle but levin-scorch'd
   walls;
The pure stream runs muddy; the gay
   hope is gone;
Count Albert is prisoner on Mount Lebanon."

* Published in 1801.

O she's ta'en a horse, should be fleet at
    her speed;
And she's ta'en a sword, should be sharp
    at her need;
And she has ta'en shipping for Palestine's
    land,
To ransom Count Albert from Soldanrie's
    hand.

Small thought had Count Albert on fair
    Rosalie,
Small thought on his faith, or his knight-
    hood, had he:
A heathenish damsel his light heart had
    won,
The Soldan's fair daughter of Mount
    Lebanon.

"O Christian, brave Christian, my love
    wouldst thou be,
Three things must thou do ere I hearken
    to thee:
Our laws and our worship on thee shalt
    thou take;
And this thou shalt first do for Zulema's
    sake.

"And, next, in the cavern, where burns
    evermore
The mystical flame which the Curdmans
    adore,
Alone, and in silence, three nights shalt
    thou wake;
And this thou shalt next do for Zulema's
    sake.

"And, last, thou shalt aid us with coun-
    sel and hand,
To drive the Frank robber from Pales-
    tine's land;
For my lord and my love then Count
    Albert I'll take,
When all this is accomplish'd for Zulema's
    sake."

He has thrown by his helmet, and cross-
    handled sword,
Renouncing his knighthood, denying his
    Lord;
He has ta'en the green caftan, and turban
    put on,
For the love of the maiden of fair Lebanon.

And in the dread cavern, deep deep under
    ground,
Which fifty steel gates and steel portals
    surround,
He has watch'd until daybreak, but sight
    saw he none,
Save the flame burning bright on its altar
    of stone.

Amazed was the Princess, the Soldan
    amazed,
Sore murmur'd the priests as on Albert
    they gazed;
They search'd all his garments, and, under
    his weeds,
They found, and took from him, his rosary
    beads

Again in the cavern, deep deep under
    ground,
He watch'd the lone night, while the
    winds whistled round;
Far off was their murmur, it came not
    more nigh,
The flame burn'd unmoved, and nought
    else did he spy.

Loud murmur'd the priests, and amazed
    was the King,
While many dark spells of their witch-
    craft they sing;
They search'd Albert's body, and, lo! on
    his breast
Was the sign of the Cross, by his father
    impress'd.

The priests they erase it with care and
    with pain,
And the recreant return'd to the cavern
    again;
But, as he descended, a whisper there fell;
It was his good angel, who bade him
    farewell!

High bristled his hair, his heart flutter'd
    and beat,
And he turn'd him five steps, half resolved
    to retreat;
But his heart it was harden'd, his purpose
    was gone,
When he thought of the Maiden of fair
    Lebanon.

Scarce pass'd he the archway, the threshold scarce trode,
When the winds from the four points of heaven were abroad,
They made each steel portal to rattle and ring,
And, borne on the blast, came the dread Fire-King.

Full sore rock'd the cavern whene'er he drew nigh,
The fire on the altar blazed bickering and high;
In volcanic explosions the mountains proclaim
The dreadful approach of the Monarch of Flame.

Unmeasured in height, undistinguish'd in form,
His breath it was lightning, his voice it was storm;
I ween the stout heart of Count Albert was tame,
When he saw in his terrors the Monarch of Flame.

In his hand a broad falchion blue-glimmer'd through smoke,
And Mount Lebanon shook as the monarch he spoke:
"With this brand shalt thou conquer, thus long, and no more,
Till thou bend to the Cross, and the Virgin adore."

The cloud-shrouded Arm gives the weapon; and see!
The recreant receives the charm'd gift on his knee:
The thunders growl distant, and faint gleam the fires,
As, borne on the whirlwind, the phantom retires.

Count Albert has arm'd him the Paynim among,
Though his heart it was false, yet his arm it was strong;
And the Red-cross wax'd faint, and the Crescent came on,
From the day he commanded on Mount Lebanon.

From Lebanon's forests to Galilee's wave,
The sands of Samaar drank the blood of the brave;
Till the Knights of the Temple, and Knights of Saint John,
With Salem's King Baldwin, against him came on.

The war-cymbals clatter'd, the trumpets replied,
The lances were couch'd, and they closed on each side;
And horsemen and horses Count Albert o'erthrew,
Till he pierced the thick tumult King Baldwin unto.

Against the charm'd blade which Count Albert did wield,
The fence had been vain of the King's Red-cross shield;
But a Page thrust him forward the monarch before,
And cleft the proud turban the renegade wore.

So fell was the dint, that Count Albert stoop'd low
Before the cross'd shield, to his steel saddlebow;
And scarce had he bent to the Red-cross his head,—
"*Bonne Grace, Notre Dame!*" he unwittingly said.

Sore sigh'd the charm'd sword, for its virtue was o'er,
It sprung from his grasp, and was never seen more;
But true men have said, that the lightning's red wing
Did waft back the brand to the dread Fire-King.

He clench'd his set teeth, and his gauntleted hand;
He stretch'd, with one buffet, that Page on the strand;
As back from the stripling the broken casque roll'd,
You might see the blue eyes, and the ringlets of gold.

Short time had Count Albert in horror
   to stare
On those death-swimming eyeballs, and
   blood-clotted hair;
For down came the Templars, like Cedron
   in flood,
And dyed their long lances in Saracen
   blood.

The Saracens, Curdmans, and Ishmaelites
   yield
To the scallop, the saltier, and crossleted
   shield;
And the eagles were gorged with the
   infidel dead,
From Bethsaida's fountains to Naphthali's
   head.

The battle is over on Bethsaida's plain.—
Oh, who is yon Paynim lies stretch'd 'mid
   the slain?

And who is yon Page lying cold at his
   knee?—
Oh, who but Count Albert and fair
   Rosalie!

The Lady was buried in Salem's bless'd
   bound,
The Count he was left to the vulture and
   hound;
Her soul to high mercy Our Lady did
   bring;
His went on the blast to the dread Fire-
   King.

Yet many a minstrel, in harping, can tell,
How the Red-cross it conquer'd, the
   Crescent it fell:
And lords and gay ladies have sigh'd,
   'mid their glee,
At the tale of Count Albert and fair
   Rosalie.

FREDERICK AND ALICE.

[1801.]

This tale is imitated, rather than translated, from a fragment introduced in Goethe's
" Claudina von Villa Bella," where it is sung by a member of a gang of banditti, to engage
the attention of the family, while his companions break into the castle. It owes any little
merit it may possess to my friend MR. LEWIS, to whom it was sent in an extremely rude
state: and who, after some material improvements, published it in his *Tales of Wonder*.

FREDERICK leaves the land of France,
   Homeward hastes his steps to measure,
Careless casts the parting glance
   On the scene of former pleasure.

Joying in his prancing steed,
   Keen to prove his untried blade,
Hope's gay dreams the soldier lead
   Over mountain, moor, and glade.

Helpless, ruin'd, left forlorn,
   Lovely Alice wept alone;
Mourn'd o'er love's fond contract torn,
   Hope, and peace, and honour flown.

Mark her breast's convulsive throbs!
   See, the tear of anguish flows!—
Mingling soon with bursting sobs,
   Loud the laugh of frenzy rose.

Wild she cursed, and wild she pray'd
   Seven long days and nights are o'er
Death in pity brought his aid,
   As the village bell struck four.

Far from her, and far from France,
   Faithless Frederick onward rides;
Marking, blithe, the morning's glance
   Mantling o'er the mountain's sides.

Heard ye not the boding sound,
  As the tongue of yonder tower,
Slowly, to the hills around,
  Told the fourth, the fated hour?

Starts the steed, and snuffs the air,
  Yet no cause of dread appears;
Bristles high the rider's hair,
  Struck with strange mysterious fears.

Desperate, as his terrors rise,
  In the steed the spur he hides;
From himself in vain he flies;
  Anxious, restless, on he rides.

Seven long days, and seven long nights,
  Wild he wander'd, woe the while!
Ceaseless care, and causeless fright,
  Urge his footsteps many a mile.

Dark the seventh sad night descends;
  Rivers swell, and rain-streams pour;
While the deafening thunder lends
  All the terrors of its roar.

Weary, wet, and spent with toil,
  Where his head shall Frederick hide?
Where, but in yon ruin'd aisle,
  By the lightning's flash descried.

To the portal, dank and low,
  Fast his steed the wanderer bound:
Down a ruin'd staircase slow,
  Next his darkling way he wound.

Long drear vaults before him lie!
  Glimmering lights are seen to glide!—
" Blessed Mary, hear my cry!
  Deign a sinner's steps to guide!"

Often lost their quivering beam,
  Still the lights move slow before,
Till they rest their ghastly gleam
  Right against an iron door.

Thundering voices from within,
  Mix'd with peals of laughter, rose;
As they fell, a solemn strain
  Lent its wild and wondrous close!

'Midst the din, he seem'd to hear
  Voice of friends, by death removed;
Well he knew that solemn air,
  'Twas the lay that Alice loved.—

Hark! for now a solemn knell
  Four times on the still night broke:
Four times, at its deaden'd swell,
  Echoes from the ruins spoke.

As the lengthen'd clangours die,
  Slowly opes the iron door!
Straight a banquet met his eye,
  But a funeral's form it wore!

Coffins for the seats extend;
  All with black the board was spread;
Girt by parent, brother, friend,
  Long since number'd with the dead!

Alice, in her grave-clothes bound,
  Ghastly smiling, points a seat;
All arose, with thundering sound;
  All the expected stranger greet.

High their meagre arms they wave,
  Wild their notes of welcome swell;—
" Welcome, traitor, to the grave!
  Perjured, bid the light farewell!"

THE BATTLE OF SEMPACH.*

[1818.]

These verses are a literal translation of an ancient Swiss ballad upon the battle of Sempach, fought 9th July, 1386, being the victory by which the Swiss cantons established their independence; the author, Albert Tchudi, denominated the Souter, from his profession of a shoemaker. He was a citizen of Lucerne, esteemed highly among his countrymen, both for his powers as a *Meister-Singer*, or minstrel, and his courage as a soldier.

* First published in *Blackwood*, Feb. 1818.

The circumstance of their being written by a poet returning from the well-fought field he describes, and in which his country's fortune was secured, may confer on Tchudi's verses an interest which they are not entitled to claim from their poetical merit. But ballad poetry, the more literally it is translated, the more it loses its simplicity, without acquiring either grace or strength; and, therefore, some of the faults of the verses must be imputed to the translator's feeling it a duty to keep as closely as possible to his original. The various puns, rude attempts at pleasantry, and disproportioned episodes, must be set down to Tchudi's account, or to the taste of his age.

The military antiquary will derive some amusement from the minute particulars which the martial poet has recorded. The mode in which the Austrian men-at-arms received the charge of the Swiss, was by forming a phalanx, which they defended with their long lances. The gallant Winkelreid, who sacrificed his own life by rushing among the spears, clasping in his arms as many as he could grasp, and thus opening a gap in those iron battalions, is celebrated in Swiss history. When fairly mingled together, the unwieldy length of their weapons, and cumbrous weight of their defensive armour, rendered the Austrian men-at-arms a very unequal match for the light armed mountaineers. The victories obtained by the Swiss over the German chivalry, hitherto deemed as formidable on foot as on horseback, led to important changes in the art of war. The poet describes the Austrian knights and squires as cutting the peaks from their boots ere they could act upon foot, in allusion to an inconvenient piece of foppery, often mentioned in the Middle Ages. Leopold III., Archduke of Austria, called "the handsome man-at-arms," was slain in the battle of Sempach, with the flower of his chivalry.

'TWAS when among our linden-trees
  The bees had housed in swarms,
(And grey-hair'd peasants say that these
  Betoken foreign arms,)

Then look'd we down to Willisow,
  The land was all in flame;
We knew the Archduke Leopold
  With all his army came.

The Austrian nobles made their vow,
  So hot their heart and bold,
"On Switzer carles we'll trample now,
  And slay both young and old."

With clarion loud, and banner proud,
  From Zurich on the lake,
In martial pomp and fair array,
  Their onward march they make.

"Now list, ye lowland nobles all—
  Ye seek the mountain strand,
Nor wot ye what shall be your lot
  In such a dangerous land.

"I rede ye, shrive ye of your sins,
  Before ye farther go;
A skirmish in Helvetian hills
  May send your souls to woe."—

"But where now shall we find a priest
  Our shrift that he may hear?"—
"The Switzer priest* has ta'en the field,
  He deals a penance drear.

"Right heavily upon your head
  He'll lay his hand of steel;
And with his trusty partisan
  Your absolution deal."—

'Twas on a Monday morning then,
  The corn was steep'd in dew,
And merry maids had sickles ta'en,
  When the host to Sempach drew.

The stalwart men of fair Lucerne
  Together have they join'd;
The pith and core of manhood stern,
  Was none cast looks behind.

It was the Lord of Hare-castle,
  And to the Duke he said,
"Yon little band of brethren true
  Will meet us undismay'd."—

---

* All the Swiss priests able to bear arms fought in this strife for their native land.

"O Hare-castle, thou heart of hare!"
　Fierce Oxenstern replied.—
"Shalt see then how the game will fare,"
　The taunted knight replied.

There was lacing then of helmets bright,
　And closing ranks amain;
The peaks they hew'd from their boot-
　　points
Might wellnigh load a wain.*

And thus they to each other said,
　" Yon handful down to hew
Will be no boastful tale to tell,
　The peasants are so few."—

The gallant Swiss Confederates there
　They pray'd to God aloud,
And he display'd his rainbow fair
　Against a swarthy cloud.

Then heart and pulse throbb'd more and
　　more
With courage firm and high,
And down the good Confederates bore
　On the Austrian chivalry.

The Austrian Lion 'gan to growl,
　And toss his mane and tail;
And ball, and shaft, and crossbow bolt,
　Went whistling forth like hail.

Lance, pike, and halbert, mingled there,
　The game was nothing sweet;
The boughs of many a stately tree
　Lay shiver'd at their feet.

The Austrian men-at-arms stood fast,
　So close their spears they laid;
It chafed the gallant Winkelreid,
　Who to his comrades said—

"I have a virtuous wife at home,
　A wife and infant son;
I leave them to my country's care,—
　This field shall soon be won.

"These nobles lay their spears right thick,
　And keep full firm array,
Yet shall my charge their order break,
　And make my brethren way."

He rush'd against the Austrian band,
　In desperate career,
And with his body, breast, and hand,
　Bore down each hostile spear.

Four lances splinter'd on his crest,
　Six shiver'd in his side;
Still on the serried files he press'd—
　He broke their ranks, and died.

This patriot's self-devoted deed
　First tamed the Lion's mood,
And the four forest cantons freed
　From thraldom by his blood.

Right where his charge had made a lane,
　His valiant comrades burst,
With sword, and axe, and partisan,
　And hack, and stab, and thrust.

The daunted Lion 'gan to whine,
　And granted ground amain,
The Mountain Bull† he bent his brows,
　And gored his sides again.

Then lost was banner, spear, and shield,
　At Sempach, in the flight,
The cloister vaults at Konig's-field
　Hold many an Austrian knight.

It was the Archduke Leopold,
　So lordly would he ride,
But he came against the Switzer churls,
　And they slew him in his pride.

The heifer said unto the bull,
　" And shall I not complain?
There came a foreign nobleman,
　To milk me on the plain.

"One thrust of thine outrageous horn
　Has gall'd the knight so sore,
That to the churchyard he is borne
　To range our glens no more."

---

* The boots of this period had long points
at the toes; so long that in the time of our
Richard II. they were chained up to the knees.
Of course, they greatly impeded the wearer's
movements on foot.

† The Urus, or wild-bull, gave name to the
Canton of Uri.

An Austrian noble left the stour,
 And fast the flight 'gan take:
And he arrived in luckless hour
 At Sempach on the lake.

He and his squire a fisher call'd,
 (His name was Hans Von Rot,)
" For love, or meed, or charity,
 Receive us in thy boat !"

Their anxious call the fisher heard,
 And, glad the meed to win,
His shallop to the shore he steer'd,
 And took the flyers in.

And while against the tide and wind
 Hans stoutly row'd his way,
The noble to his follower sign'd
 He should the boatman slay.

The fisher's back was to them turn'd,
 The squire his dagger drew,
Hans saw his shadow in the lake,
 The boat he overthrew

He 'whelm'd the boat, and as they strove,
 He stunn'd them with his oar,

" Now, drink ye deep, my gentle sirs,
 You'll ne'er stab boatman more.

" Two gilded fishes in the lake
 This morning have I caught,
Their silver scales may much avail,
 Their carrion flesh is naught."

It was a messenger of woe
 Has sought the Austrian land:
" Ah ! gracious lady, evil news !
 My lord lies on the strand.

" At Sempach, on the battle-field,
 His bloody corpse lies there."—
" Ah, gracious God !" the lady cried,
 " What tidings of despair !"

Now would you know the minstrel wight
 Who sings of strife so stern,
Albert the Souter is he hight,
 A burgher of Lucerne.

A merry man was he, I wot,
 The night he made the lay,
Returning from the bloody spot,
 Where God had judged the day.

THE NOBLE MORINGER.*

AN ANCIENT BALLAD.

[1819.]

I.

O, WILL you hear a knightly tale of old
  Bohemian day,
It was the noble Moringer in wedlock
  bed he lay;
He halsed and kiss'd his dearest dame,
  that was as sweet as May,
And said, " Now, lady of my heart,
  attend the words I say.

II.

" 'Tis I have vow'd a pilgrimage unto a
  distant shrine,
And I must seek Saint Thomas-land,
  and leave the land that's mine ;

Here shalt thou dwell the while in state,
  so thou wilt pledge thy fay,
That thou for my return wilt wait seven
  twelvemonths and a day."

III.

Then out and spoke that Lady bright,
  sore troubled in her cheer,
" Now tell me true, thou noble knight,
  what order takest thou here ;
And who shall lead thy vassal band, and
  hold thy lordly sway,
And be thy lady's guardian true when
  thou art far away ?"

---

* Published in the *Edinburgh Annual Register*, 1819.

IV.

Out spoke the noble Moringer, "Of that
    have thou no care,
There's many a valiant gentleman of me
    holds living fair;
The trustiest shall rule my land, my
    vassals and my state,
And be a guardian tried and true to thee,
    my lovely mate.

V.

"As Christian-man, I needs must keep
    the vow which I have plight,
When I am far in foreign land, remember
    thy true knight;
And cease, my dearest dame, to grieve,
    for vain were sorrow now,
But grant thy Moringer his leave, since
    God hath heard his vow."

VI.

It was the noble Moringer from bed he
    made him boune,
And met him there his Chamberlain, with
    ewer and with gown:
He flung his mantle on his back, 'twas
    furr'd with miniver,
He dipp'd his hand in water cold, and
    bathed his forehead fair.

VII.

"Now hear," he said, "Sir Chamberlain,
    true vassal art thou mine,
And such the trust that I repose in that
    proved worth of thine,
For seven years shalt thou rule my towers,
    and lead my vassal train,
And pledge thee for my lady's faith till I
    return again."

VIII.

The Chamberlain was blunt and true,
    and sturdily said he,
"Abide, my lord, and rule your own, and
    take this rede from me:
That woman's faith's a brittle trust—
    Seven twelvemonths didst thou say?
I'll pledge me for no lady's truth beyond
    the seventh fair day."

IX.

The noble Baron turn'd him round, his
    heart was full of care,
His gallant Esquire stood him nigh, he
    was Marstetten's heir,
To whom he spoke right anxiously,
    "Thou trusty squire to me,
Wilt thou receive this weighty trust when
    I am o'er the sea?

X.

"To watch and ward my castle strong,
    and to protect my land,
And to the hunting or the host to lead
    my vassal band;
And pledge thee for my Lady's faith till
    seven long years are gone,
And guard her as Our Lady dear was
    guarded by Saint John."

XI.

Marstetten's heir was kind and true, but
    fiery, hot, and young,
And readily he answer made with too
    presumptuous tongue;
"My noble lord, cast care away, and on
    your journey wend,
And trust this charge to me until your
    pilgrimage have end.

XII.

"Rely upon my plighted faith, which
    shall be truly tried,
To guard your lands, and ward your
    towers, and with your vassals ride;
And for your lovely Lady's faith, so
    virtuous and so dear,
I'll gage my head it knows no change,
    be absent thirty year."

XIII.

The noble Moringer took cheer when
    thus he heard him speak,
And doubt forsook his troubled brow,
    and sorrow left his cheek;
A long adieu he bids to all—hoists top-
    sails, and away,
And wanders in Saint Thomas-land seven
    twelvemonths and a day.

XIV.

It was the noble Moringer within an
  orchard slept,
When on the Baron's slumbering sense a
  boding vision crept;
And whisper'd in his ear a voice, " 'Tis
  time, Sir Knight, to wake,
Thy lady and thy heritage another master
  take.

XV.

" Thy tower another banner knows, thy
  steeds another rein,
And stoop them to another's will thy
  gallant vassal train
And she, the Lady of thy love, so faithful
  once and fair,
This night within thy fathers' hall she
  weds Marstetten's heir."

XVI.

It is the noble Moringer starts up and
  tears his beard,
" O would that I had ne'er been born!
  what tidings have I heard!
To lose my lordship and my lands the less
  would be my care,
But, God! that e'er a squire untrue should
  wed my Lady fair.

XVII.

" O good Saint Thomas, hear," he pray'd,
  " my patron Saint art thou,
A traitor robs me of my land even while I
  pay my vow!
My wife he brings to infamy that was so
  pure of name,
And I am far in foreign land, and must
  endure the shame."

XVIII.

It was the good Saint Thomas, then, who
  heard his pilgrim's prayer,
And sent a sleep so deep and dead that it
  o'erpower'd his care;
He waked in fair Bohemian land outstretch'd beside a rill,
High on the right a castle stood, low on
  the left a mill.

XIX

The Moringer he started up as one from
  spell unbound,
And dizzy with surprise and joy gazed
  wildly all around;
" I know my fathers' ancient towers, the
  mill, the stream I know,
Now blessed be my patron Saint who
  cheer'd his pilgrim's woe!"

XX.

He leant upon his pilgrim staff, and to the
  mill he drew,
So alter'd was his goodly form that none
  their master knew;
The Baron to the miller said, " Good
  friend, for charity,
Tell a poor palmer in your land what
  tidings may there be?"

XXI.

The miller answered him again, " He
  knew of little news,
Save that the Lady of the land did a new
  bridegroom choose;
Her husband died in distant land, such is
  the constant word,
His death sits heavy on our souls, he was
  a worthy Lord.

XXII.

" Of him I held the little mill which wins
  me living free,
God rest the Baron in his grave, he stil
  was kind to me!
And when Saint Martin's tide comes
  round, and millers take their toll,
The priest that prays for Moringer shall
  have both cope and stole."

XXIII.

It was the noble Moringer to climb the
  hill began,
And stood before the bolted gate a woe
  and weary man;
" Now help me, every saint in heaven
  that can compassion take,
To gain the entrance of my hall this woful
  match to break."

XXIV.

His very knock it sounded sad, his call
　　was sad and slow,
For heart and head, and voice and hand,
　　were heavy all with woe;
And to the warder thus he spoke : "Friend,
　　to thy Lady say,
A pilgrim from Saint Thomas-land craves
　　harbour for a day.

XXV.

"I've wander'd many a weary step, my
　　strength is wellnigh done,
And if she turn me from her gate I'll see
　　no morrow's sun;
I pray, for sweet Saint Thomas' sake, a
　　pilgrim's bed and dole,
And for the sake of Moringer's, her once-
　　loved husband's soul."

XXVI.

It was the stalwart warder then he came
　　his dame before,
"A pilgrim, worn and travel-toil'd, stands
　　at the castle-door;
And prays, for sweet Saint Thomas' sake,
　　for harbour and for dole,
And for the sake of Moringer, thy noble
　　husband's soul."

XXVII.

The Lady's gentle heart was moved, "Do
　　up the gate," she said,
"And bid the wanderer welcome be to
　　banquet and to bed;
And since he names my husband's name,
　　so that he lists to stay,
These towers shall be his harbourage a
　　twelvemonth and a day."

XXVIII.

It was the stalwart warder then undid the
　　portal broad,
It was the noble Moringer that o'er the
　　threshold strode:
"And have thou thanks, kind heaven," he
　　said, "though from a man of sin,
That the true lord stands here once more
　　his castle-gate within."

XXIX.

Then up the halls paced Moringer, his
　　step was sad and slow;
It sat full heavy on his heart, none seem'd
　　their Lord to know;
He sat him on a lowly bench, oppress'd
　　with woe and wrong,
Short space he sat, but ne'er to him
　　seem'd little space so long.

XXX.

Now spent was day, and feasting o'er,
　　and come was evening hour,
The time was nigh when new-made brides
　　retire to nuptial bower;
"Our castle's wont," a brides-man said,
　　"hath been both firm and long,
No guest to harbour in our halls till he
　　shall chant a song."

XXXI.

Then spoke the youthful bridegroom
　　there as he sat by the bride,
"My merry minstrel folk," quoth he,
　　"lay shalm and harp aside;
Our pilgrim guest must sing a lay, the
　　castle's rule to hold,
And well his guerdon will I pay with
　　garment and with gold."—

XXXII.

"Chill flows the lay of frozen age,"
　　'twas thus the pilgrim sung,
"Nor golden meed nor garment gay,
　　unlocks his heavy tongue;
Once did I sit, thou bridegroom gay, at
　　board as rich as thine,
And by my side as fair a bride with all
　　her charms was mine.

XXXIII.

"But time traced furrows on my face,
　　and I grew silver-hair'd,
For locks of brown, and cheeks of youth,
　　she left this brow and beard;
Once rich, but now a palmer poor, I
　　tread life's latest stage,
And mingle with your bridal mirth the
　　lay of frozen age."

XXXIV

It was the noble Lady there this woful
    lay that hears,
And for the aged pilgrim's grief her eye
    was dimm'd with tears;
She bade her gallant cupbearer a golden
    beaker take,
And bear it to the palmer poor to quaff
    it for her sake.

XXXV.

It was the noble Moringer that dropp'd
    amid the wine
A bridal ring of burning gold so costly
    and so fine:
Now listen, gentles, to my song, it tells
    you but the sooth,
'Twas with that very ring of gold he
    pledged his bridal truth.

XXXVI.

Then to the cupbearer he said, " Do me
    one kindly deed,
And should my better days return, full
    rich shall be thy meed;
Bear back the golden cup again to yonder
    bride so gay,
And crave her of her courtesy to pledge
    the palmer grey."

XXXVII.

The cupbearer was courtly bred, nor
    was the boon denied,
The golden cup he took again, and bore
    it to the bride;
" Lady," he said, " your reverend guest
    sends this, and bids me pray,
That, in thy noble courtesy, thou pledge
    the palmer grey."

XXXVIII.

The ring hath caught the Lady's eye, she
    views it close and near,
Then might you hear her shriek aloud,
    " The Moringer is here !"
Then might you see her start from seat,
    while tears in torrents fell,
But whether 'twas for joy or woe, the
    ladies best can tell.

XXXIX.

But loud she utter'd thanks to Heaven,
    and every saintly power,
That had return'd the Moringer before
    the midnight hour;
And loud she utter'd vow on vow, that
    never was there bride,
That had like her preserved her troth, or
    been so sorely tried.

XL.

" Yes, here I claim the praise," she said,
    " to constant matrons due,
Who keep the troth that they have
    plight, so steadfastly and true;
For count the term howe'er you will, so
    that you count aright,
Seven twelve-months and a day are out
    when bells toll twelve to-night."

XLI.

It was Marstetten then rose up, his
    falchion there he drew,
He kneel'd before the Moringer, and
    down his weapon threw;
" My oath and knightly faith are broke,"
    these were the words he said,
" Then take, my liege, thy vassal's sword,
    and take thy vassal's head."

XLII.

The noble Moringer he smiled, and then
    aloud did say,
" He gathers wisdom that hath roam'd
    seven twelve-months and a day;
My daughter now hath fifteen years,
    fame speaks her sweet and fair,
I give her for the bride you lose, and
    name her for my heir.

XLII.

" The young bridegroom hath youthful
    bride, the old bridegroom the old,
Whose faith was kept till term and tide
    so punctually were told;
But blessings on the warder kind that
    oped my castle gate,
For had I come at morrow tide, I came
    a day too late."

THE ERL-KING.

FROM THE GERMAN OF GOETHE.

(The Erl-King is a goblin that haunts the Black Forest in Thuringia.—To be read by a candle particularly long in the snuff.)

O, WHO rides by night thro' the woodland so wild?
It is the fond father embracing his child;
And close the boy nestles within his loved arm,
To hold himself fast, and to keep himself warm.

"O father, see yonder! see yonder!" he says;
"My boy, upon what dost thou fearfully gaze?"—
"O, 'tis the Erl-King with his crown and his shroud."
"No, my son, it is but a dark wreath of the cloud."

(THE ERL-KING SPEAKS.)

"O come and go with me, thou loveliest child;
By many a gay sport shall thy time be beguiled;
My mother keeps for thee full many a fair toy,
And many a fine flower shall she pluck for my boy."

"O, father, my father, and did you not hear
The Erl-King whisper so low in my ear?"—
"Be still, my heart's darling—my child, be at ease;
It was but the wild blast as it sung thro' the trees."

ERL-KING.

"O wilt thou go with me, thou loveliest boy?
My daughter shall tend thee with care and with joy;
She shall bear thee so lightly thro' wet and thro' wild,
And press thee, and kiss thee, and sing to my child."

"O father, my father, and saw you not plain,
The Erl-King's pale daughter glide past thro' the rain?"—
"O yes, my loved treasure, I knew it full soon;
It was the grey willow that danced to the moon."

ERL-KING.

"O come and go with me, no longer delay,
Or else, silly child, I will drag thee away."—
"O father! O father! now, now keep your hold,
The Erl-King has seized me—his grasp is so cold!"—

Sore trembled the father; he spurr'd thro' the wild,
Clasping close to his bosom his shuddering child;
He reaches his dwelling in doubt and in dread,
But, clasp'd to his bosom, the infant was *dead!*"

MISCELLANEOUS POEMS.

[Amongst these poems will be found a few selected from the "Minstrelsy of the Scottish Border." They are marked (to distinguish them from the original poems) with an asterisk.]

THE VIOLET.

These lines were first published in the English Minstrelsy, 1810. They were written in 1797, on occasion of the poet's disappointment in love.—See *Life of Scott*, vol. i. p. 333.

THE violet in her greenwood bower,
  Where birchen boughs with hazels
    mingle,
May boast itself the fairest flower
  In glen, or copse, or forest dingle.

Though fair her gems of azure hue,
  Beneath the dewdrop's weight re-
    clining;
I've seen an eye of lovelier hue,
  More sweet through wat'ry lustre
    shining.

The summer sun that dew shall dry
  Ere yet the day be past its morrow;
Nor longer in my false love's eye
  Remain'd the tear of parting sorrow.

◆

TO A LADY.
WITH FLOWERS FROM A ROMAN WALL.
1797.

Written in 1797, on an excursion from Gillsland, in Cumberland. See *Life*, vol. i. p. 365.

TAKE these flowers which, purple
    waving,
  On the ruin'd rampart grew,
Where, the sons of freedom braving,
  Rome's imperial standards flew.

Warriors from the breach of danger
  Pluck no longer laurels there;
They but yield the passing stranger
  Wild-flower wreaths for Beauty's
    hair.

◆

BOTHWELL CASTLE.
1799.

The following fragment of a ballad written at Bothwell Castle, in the autumn of 1799, was first printed in the *Life of Sir Walter Scott*.

WHEN fruitful Clydesdale's apple-
    bowers
  Are mellowing in the noon;
When sighs round Pembroke's ruin'd
    towers
  The sultry breath of June;

When Clyde, despite his sheltering
    wood,
  Must leave his channel dry;
And vainly o'er the limpid flood
  The angler guides his fly;

If chance by Bothwell's lovely braes
  A wanderer thou hast been,
Or hid thee from the summer's blaze
  In Blantyre's bowers of green,

Full where the copsewood opens wild
  Thy pilgrim step hath staid,
Where Bothwell's towers, in ruin piled,
  O'erlook the verdant glade;

And many a tale of love and fear
  Hath mingled with the scene—
Of Bothwell's banks that bloom'd so
    dear,
  And Bothwell's bonny Jean.

O, if with rugged minstrel lays
  Unsated be thy ear,
And thou of deeds of other days
  Another tale wilt hear,—

Then all beneath the spreading beech,
  Flung careless on the lea,
The Gothic muse the tale shall teach
  Of Bothwell's sisters three.

Wight Wallace stood on Deckmont
  head,
He blew his bugle round,
Till the wild bull in Cadyow wood
  Has started at the sound.

St. George's cross, o'er Bothwell hung,
  Was waving far and wide,
And from the lofty turret flung
  Its crimson blaze on Clyde;

And rising at the bugle blast
  That marked the Scottish foe,
Old England's yeomen muster'd fast,
  And bent the Norman bow.

Tall in the midst Sir Aylmer rose,
  Proud Pembroke's Earl was he—
While . . . .

---◆---

THE SHEPHERD'S TALE.

1799.

"Another imperfect ballad, in which he
had meant to blend together two legends
familiar to every reader of Scottish history
and romance, has been found in the same
portfolio, and the handwriting proves it to
be of the same early date.—LOCKHART'S
Life of Scott.

*   *   *   *   *

AND ne'er but once, my son, he says,
  Was yon sad cavern trod,
In persecution's iron days,
  When the land was left by God.

From Bewlie bog, with slaughter red,
  A wanderer hither drew,
And oft he stopt and turn'd his head,
  As by fits the night wind blew;

For trampling round by Cheviot edge
  Were heard the troopers keen,
And frequent from the Whitelaw ridge
  The death-shot flash'd between.

The moonbeams through the misty
  shower
  On yon dark cavern fell;
Through the cloudy night the snow
  gleam'd white,
  Which sunbeam ne'er could quell.

"Yon cavern dark is rough and rude,
  And cold its jaws of snow;
But more rough and rude are the men
  of blood,
  That hunt my life below!

"Yon spell-bound den, as the aged tell,
  Was hewn by demons' hands;
But I had lourd* melle with the fiends
  of hell,
  Than with Clavers and his band."

He heard the deep-mouth'd bloodhound
  bark,
He heard the horses neigh,
He plunged him in the cavern dark,
  And downward sped his way.

Now faintly down the winding path
  Came the cry of the faulting hound,
And the mutter'd oath of baulkèd wrath
  Was lost in hollow sound.

He threw him on the flinted floor,
  And held his breath for fear;
He rose and bitter cursed his foes,
  As the sounds died on his ear.

"O bare thine arm, thou battling Lord,
  For Scotland's wandering band;
Dash from the oppressor's grasp the
  sword,
  And sweep him from the land!

"Forget not thou thy people's groans
  From dark Donnotter's tower,
Mix'd with the seafowl's shrilly moans,
  And ocean's bursting roar!

---

* *Lourd; i.e.,* liefer—rather.

" O, in fell Clavers' hour of pride,
  Even in his mightiest day,
As bold he strides through conquest's
    tide,
  O, stretch him on the clay!

" His widow and his little ones,
  O, may their tower of trust
Remove its strong foundation stones,
  And crush them in the dust!"—

" Sweet prayers to me," a voice replied,
  " Thrice welcome, guest of mine!"
And glimmering on the cavern side,
  A light was seen to shine.

An aged man, in amice brown,
  Stood by the wanderer's side,
By powerful charm, a dead man's arm
  The torch's light supplied.

From each stiff finger, stretch'd upright,
  Arose a ghastly flame,
That waved not in the blast of night
  Which through the cavern came.

O, deadly blue was that taper's hue,
  That flamed the cavern o'er,
But more deadly blue was the ghastly
    hue
  Of his eyes who the taper bore.

He laid on his head a hand like lead,
  As heavy, pale, and cold—
" Vengeance be thine, thou guest of
    mine,
  If thy heart be firm and bold.

" But if faint thy heart, and caitiff fear
  Thy recreant sinews know,
The mountain erne thy heart shall tear,
  Thy nerves the hooded crow."

The wanderer raised him undismay'd:
  " My soul, by dangers steel'd,
Is stubborn as my border blade,
  Which never knew to yield.

" And if thy power can speed the hour
  Of vengeance on my foes,
Theirs be the fate, from bridge and gate,
  To feed the hooded crows."

The Brownie look'd him in the face,
  And his colour fled with speed—
" I fear me," quoth he, "uneath it will be
  To match thy word and deed.

" In ancient days when English bands
  Sore ravaged Scotland fair,
The sword and shield of Scottish land
  Was valiant Halbert Kerr.

" A warlock loved the warrior well,
  Sir Michael Scott by name,
And he sought for his sake a spell to
    make,
  Should the Southern foemen tame.

" ' Look, thou,' he said, ' from Cessford
    head,
  As the July sun sinks low,
And when glimmering white on Che-
    viot's height
  Thou shalt spy a wreath of snow,
The spell is complete which shall bring
    to thy feet
  The haughty Saxon foe.'

" For many a year wrought the wizard
    here,
  In Cheviot's bosom low,
Till the spell was complete, and in July's
    heat
  Appear'd December's snow;
But Cessford's Halbert never came
  The wondrous cause to know.

" For years before in Bowden aisle
  The warrior's bones had lain,
And after short while, by female guile,
  Sir Michael Scott was slain.

" But me and my brethren in this cell
  His mighty charms retain,
And he that can quell the powerful spell
  Shall o'er broad Scotland reign."

He led him through an iron door
  And up a winding stair,
And in wild amaze did the wanderer
    gaze
  On the sight which open'd there.

Through the gloomy night flash'd ruddy
  light—
  A thousand torches glow;
The cave rose high, like the vaulted sky,
  O'er stalls in double row.

In every stall of that endless hall
  Stood a steed in barbing bright;
At the foot of each steed, all arm'd save
  the head,
  Lay stretch'd a stalwart knight.

In each mail'd hand was a naked brand;
  As they lay on the black bull's hide,
Each visage stern did upwards turn,
  With eyeballs fix'd and wide.

A launcegay strong, full twelve ells long,
  By every warrior hung;
At each pommel there, for battle yare,
  A Jedwood axe was slung.

The casque hung near each cavalier;
  The plumes waved mournfully
At every tread which the wanderer made
  Through the hall of gramarye.

The ruddy beam of the torches' gleam
  That glared the warriors on,
Reflected light from armour bright,
  In noontide splendour shone.

And onward seen in lustre sheen,
  Still lengthening on the sight,
Through the boundless hall stood steeds
  in stall,
  And by each lay a sable knight.

Still as the dead lay each horseman
  dread,
  And moved nor limb nor tongue;
Each steed stood stiff as an earthfast
  cliff,
  Nor hoof nor bridle rung.

No sounds through all the spacious hall
  The deadly still divide,
Save where echoes aloof from the
  vaulted roof
To the wanderer's step replied.

At length before his wondering eyes,
  On an iron column borne,
Of antique shape and giant size,
  Appear'd a sword and horn.

"Now choose thee here," quoth his
  leader,
  "Thy venturous fortune try;
Thy woe and weal, thy boot and bale,
  In yon brand and bugle lie."

To the fatal brand he mounted his hand,
  But his soul did quiver and quail;
The life-blood did start to his shudder-
  ing heart,
  And left him wan and pale.

The brand he forsook, and the horn he
  took
  To 'say a gentle sound;
But so wild a blast from the bugle brast,
  That the Cheviot rock'd around.

From Forth to Tees, from seas to seas,
  The awful bugle rung;
On Carlisle wall, and Berwick withal,
  To arms the warders sprung.

With clank and clang the cavern rang,
  The steeds did stamp and neigh;
And loud was the yell as each warrior
  fell
  Sterte up with hoop and cry.

"Woe, woe," they cried, "thou caitiff
  coward,
  That ever thou wert born!
Why drew ye not the knightly sword
  Before ye blew the horn?"

The morning on the mountain shone,
  And on the bloody ground
Hurl'd from the cave with shiver'd
  bone,
  The mangled wretch was found.

And still beneath the cavern dread,
  Among the glidders grey,
A shapeless stone with lichens spread
  Marks where the wanderer lay.

*   *   *   *   *

CHEVIOT.

1799.

* * * * *

Go sit old Cheviot's crest below,
And pensive mark the lingering snow
  In all his scaurs abide,
And slow dissolving from the hill
In many a sightless, soundless rill,
  Feed sparkling Bowmont's tide.

Fair shine the stream by bank and lea,
As wimpling to the eastern sea
  She seeks Till's sullen bed,
Indenting deep the fatal plain,
Where Scotland's noblest, brave in vain,
  Around their monarch bled.

And westward hills on hills you see,
Even as old Ocean's mightiest sea
  Heaves high her waves of foam,
Dark and snow-ridged from Cutsfeld's wold
To the proud foot of Cheviot roll'd,
  Earth's mountain billows come.

* * * * *

THE REIVER'S WEDDING.

1802.

O, WILL ye hear a mirthful bourd?
  Or will ye hear of courtesie?
Or will hear how a gallant lord
  Was wedded to a gay ladye?

"Ca' out the kye," quo' the village herd,
  As he stood on the knowe,
"Ca' this ane's nine and that ane's ten,
  And bauld Lord William's cow."—

"Ah! by my sooth," quoth William then,
  "And stands it that way now,
When knave and churl have nine and ten,
  That the lord hath but his cow?

"I swear by the light of the Michaelmas moon,
  And the might of Mary high,

And by the edge of my braidsword brown,
  They shall soon say Harden's kye."

He took a bugle frae his side,
  With names carved o'er and o'er—
Full many a chief of meikle pride
  That Border bugle bore—

He blew a note baith sharp and hie,
  Till rock and water rang around—
Threescore of moss-troopers and three
  Have mounted at that bugle sound.

The Michaelmas moon had enter'd then,
  And ere she wan the full,
Ye might see by her light in Harden glen
  A bow o' kye and a bassen'd bull.

And loud and loud in Harden tower
  The quaigh gaed round wi' meikle glee;
For the English beef was brought in bower
  And the English ale flow'd merrïlie.

And mony a guest from Teviotside
  And Yarrow's Braes was there;
Was never a lord in Scotland wide
  That made more dainty fare.

They ate, they laugh'd, they sang and quaff'd,
  Till nought on board was seen,
When knight and squire were boun to dine,
  But a spur of silver sheen.

Lord William has ta'en his berry-brown steed—
  A sore shent man was he;
"Wait ye, my guests, a little speed—
  Weel feasted ye shall be."

He rode him down by Falsehope burn,
  His cousin dear to see,
With him to take a riding turn—
  Wat-draw-the-sword was he.

And when he came to Falsehope glen,
  Beneath the trysting-tree,
On the smooth green was carved plain,
  "To Lochwood bound are we."

"O, if they be gane to dark Lochwood
  To drive the Warden's gear,
Betwixt our names, I ween, there's
    feud;
  I'll go and have my share:

"For little reck I for Johnstone's feud,
  The Warden though he be."
So Lord William is away to dark
    Lochwood,
  With riders barely three.

The Warden's daughters in Lochwood
    sate,
  Were all both fair and gay,
All save the Lady Margaret,
  And she was wan and wae.

The sister, Jean, had a full fair skin,
  And Grace was bauld and braw;
But the leal-fast heart her breast within
  It weel was worth them a'.

Her father's pranked her sisters twa
  With meikle joy and pride;
But Margaret maun seek Dundren-
    nan's wa'—
  She ne'er can be a bride.

On spear and casque by gallants gent
  Her sisters' scarfs were borne,
But never at tilt or tournament
  Were Margaret's colours worn.

Her sisters rode to Thirlstane bower,
  But she was left at hame
To wander round the gloomy tower,
  And sigh young Harden's name.

"Of all the knights, the knight most
    fair,
  From Yarrow to the Tyne,"
Soft sigh'd the maid, "is Harden's heir,
  But ne'er can he be mine;

"Of all the maids, the foulest maid
  From Teviot to the Dee,
Ah!" sighing sad, that lady said,
  "Can ne'er young Harden's be."—

She look'd up the briery glen,
  And up the mossy brae,

And she saw a score of her father's
    men
  Yclad in the Johnstone grey.

O, fast and fast they downwards sped
  The moss and briers among,
And in the midst the troopers led
  A shackled knight along.

*   *   *   *   *

THE BARD'S INCANTATION.

WRITTEN UNDER THE THREAT OF IN-
VASION IN THE AUTUMN OF 1804.

THE forest of Glenmore is drear,
  It is all of black pine and the dark
    oak-tree;
And the midnight wind, to the mountain
    deer,
  Is whistling the forest lullaby;
The moon looks through the drifting
    storm,
But the troubled lake reflects not her
    form,
For the waves roll whitening to the land,
And dash against the shelvy strand.
There is a voice among the trees
  That mingles with the groaning oak—
That mingles with the stormy breeze,
  And the lake-waves dashing against
    the rock;—
There is a voice within the wood,
  The voice of the bard in fitful mood;
His song was louder than the blast,
As the bard of Glenmore through the
    forest past.

"Wake ye from your sleep of death,
  Minstrels and bards of other days!
For the midnight wind is on the heath,
  And the midnight meteors dimly
    blaze:
The Spectre with his Bloody Hand,*
Is wandering through the wild wood-
    land;
The owl and the raven are mute for
    dread,
And the time is meet to awake the dead!

---

* The forest of Glenmore is haunted by a
spirit called Lhamdearg, or Red-hand.

"Souls of the mighty, wake and say,
 To what high strain your harps were
  strung,
When Lochlin plow'd her billowy way,
 And on your shores her Norsemen flung?
Her Norsemen train'd to spoil and blood,
Skill'd to prepare the Raven's food,
All, by your harpings, doom'd to die
On bloody Largs and Loncarty.*

"Mute are ye all? No murmurs strange
 Upon the midnight breeze sail by;
Nor through the pines, with whistling
  change
 Mimic the harp's wild harmony?
Mute are ye now?—Ye ne'er were mute,
When Murder with his bloody foot,
And Rapine with his iron hand,
Were hovering near yon mountain strand.

"O yet awake the strain to tell,
 By every deed in song enroll'd,
By every chief who fought or fell,
 For Albion's weal in battle bold:—
From Coilgach,† first who roll'd his car
Through the deep ranks of Roman war,
To him, of veteran memory dear,
Who victor died on Aboukir.

"By all their swords, by all their scars,
 By all their names, a mighty spell!
By all their wounds, by all their wars,
 Arise, the mighty strain to tell!
For fiercer than fierce Hengist's strain,
More impious than the heathen Dane,
More grasping than all-grasping Rome,
Gaul's ravening legions hither come!"—
The wind is hush'd, and still the lake—
 Strange murmurs fill my tingling ears,
Bristles my hair, my sinews quake,
 At the dread voice of other years—
"When targets clash'd, and bugles rung,
And blades round warriors' heads were
  flung,
The foremost of the band were we,
And hymn'd the joys of Liberty!"

---

* Where the Norwegian invader of Scotland received two bloody defeats.
 † The Galgacus of Tacitus.

HELVELLYN.

1805.

In the spring of 1805, a young gentleman
of talents, and of a most amiable disposition,
perished by losing his way on the mountain
Helvellyn. His remains were not discovered
till three months afterwards, when they were
found guarded by a faithful terrier-bitch, his
constant attendant during frequent solitary
rambles through the wilds of Cumberland and
Westmoreland.

I CLIMB'D the dark brow of the mighty
  Helvellyn,
 Lakes and mountains beneath me
  gleam'd misty and wide;
All was still, save by fits, when the eagle
  was yelling,
 And starting around me the echoes
  replied.
On the right, Striden-edge round the
  Red-tarn was bending,
And Catchedicam its left verge was de-
  fending,
One huge nameless rock in the front was
  ascending,
 When I mark'd the sad spot where the
  wanderer had died.

Dark green was that spot 'mid the brown
  mountain-heather,
 Where the Pilgrim of Nature lay
  stretch'd in decay,
Like the corpse of an outcast abandon'd
  to weather,
 Till the mountain winds wasted the
  tenantless clay.
Nor yet quite deserted, though lonely extended,
For, faithful in death, his mute favourite
  attended,
The much-loved remains of her master
  defended,
 And chased the hill-fox and the raven
  away.

How long didst thou think that his
  silence was slumber?
 When the wind waved his garment,
  how oft didst thou start?

How many long days and long weeks
   didst thou number,
  Ere he faded before thee, the friend of
    thy heart?
And, oh! was it meet, that—no requiem
   read o'er him—
No mother to weep, and no friend to de-
   plore him,
And thou, little guardian, alone stretch'd
   before him—
  Unhonour'd the Pilgrim from life
    should depart?

When a Prince to the fate of the Peasant
   has yielded,
  The tapestry waves dark round the
    dim-lighted hall;
With scutcheons of silver the coffin is
   shielded,
  And pages stand mute by the canopied
    pall:
Through the courts, at deep midnight,
   the torches are gleaming;
In the proudly-arch'd chapel the banners
   are beaming,
Far adown the long aisle sacred music is
   streaming,
  Lamenting a Chief of the people should
    fall.

But meeter for thee, gentle lover of
   nature,
  To lay down thy head like the meek
    mountain lamb,
When, wilder'd, he drops from some
   cliff huge in stature,
  And draws his last sob by the side of
    his dam.
And more stately thy couch by this de-
   sert lake lying,
Thy obsequies sung by the grey plover
   flying,
With one faithful friend but to witness
   thy dying,
  In the arms of Helvellyn and Catche-
    dicam.

THE DYING BARD.

1806.

AIR—*Daffydz Gangwen.*

The Welsh tradition bears, that a Bard, on his death-bed, demanded his harp, and played the air to which these verses are adapted; requesting that it might be performed at his funeral.

I.

DINAS EMLINN, lament; for the moment
  is nigh,
When mute in the woodlands thine echoes
  shall die:
No more by sweet Teivi Cadwallon shall
  rave,
And mix his wild notes with the wild
  dashing wave.

II.

In spring and in autumn thy glories of
  shade
Unhonour'd shall flourish, unhonour'd
  shall fade;
For soon shall be lifeless the eye and the
  tongue,
That view'd them with rapture, with
  rapture that sung.

III.

Thy sons, Dinas Emlinn, may march in
  their pride,
And chase the proud Saxon from Pres-
  tatyn's side;
But where is the harp shall give life to
  their name?
And where is the bard shall give heroes
  their fame?

IV.

And oh, Dinas Emlinn! thy daughters so
  fair,
Who heave the white bosom, and wave
  the dark hair;
What tuneful enthusiast shall worship
  their eye,
When half of their charms with Cadwallon shall die?

V.

Then adieu, silver Teivi! I quit thy
    loved scene,
To join the dim choir of the bards who
    have been;
With Lewarch, and Meilor, and Merlin
    the Old,
And sage Taliessin, high harping to hold.

VI.

And adieu, Dinas Emlinn! still green be
    thy shades,
Unconquer'd thy warriors, and match-
    less thy maids!
And thou, whose faint warblings my
    weakness can tell,
Farewell, my loved Harp, my last treasure,
    farewell!

THE NORMAN HORSE-SHOE.
1806.

AIR—*The War-Song of the Men of Glamorgan.*

The Welsh, inhabiting a mountainous
country, and possessing only an inferior breed
of horses, were usually unable to encounter
the shock of the Anglo-Norman cavalry.
Occasionally, however, they were successful
in repelling the invaders; and the following
verses are supposed to celebrate a defeat of
CLARE, Earl of Striguil and Pembroke, and of
NEVILLE, Baron of Chepstow, Lords-Marchers
of Monmouthshire. Rymny is a stream which
divides the counties of Monmouth and Glamorgan: Caerphili, the scene of the supposed
battle, is a vale upon its banks, dignified by
the ruins of a very ancient castle.

I.

RED glows the forge in Striguil's bounds,
And hammers din, and anvil sounds,
And armourers, with iron toil,
Barb many a steed for battle's broil.
Foul fall the hand which bends the steel
Around the courser's thundering heel,
That e'er shall dint a sable wound
On fair Glamorgan's velvet ground!

II.

From Chepstow's towers, ere dawn of
    morn,
Was heard afar the bugle horn;
And forth, in banded pomp and pride,
Stout Clare and fiery Neville ride.
They swore their banners broad should
    gleam,
In crimson light, on Rymny's stream;
They vow'd, Caerphili's sod should feel
The Norman charger's spurning heel.

III.

And sooth they swore—the sun arose,
And Rymny's wave with crimson glows!
For Clare's red banner, floating wide,
Roll'd down the stream to Severn's tide!
And sooth they vow'd—the trampled
    green
Show'd where hot Neville's charge had
    been:
In every sable hoof-tramp stood
A Norman horseman's curdling blood!

IV.

Old Chepstow's brides may curse the toil,
That arm'd stout Clare for Cambrian broil;
Their orphans long the art may rue,
For Neville's war-horse forged the shoe.
No more the stamp of armed steed
Shall dint Glamorgan's velvet mead;
Nor trace be there, in early spring,
Save of the Fairies' emerald ring.

THE MAID OF TORO.
1806.

O, LOW shone the sun on the fair lake of
    Toro,
    And weak were the whispers that waved
        the dark wood,
All as a fair maiden, bewilder'd in sorrow,
    Sorely sigh'd to the breezes, and wept
        to the flood.
"O saints! from the mansions of bliss
    lowly bending;
    Sweet Virgin! who hearest the sup-
        pliant's cry,

Now grant my petition, in anguish ascending,
  My Henry restore, or let Eleanor die!"

All distant and faint were the sounds of
the battle,
  With the breezes they rise, with the
  breezes they fail,
Till the shout, and the groan, and the
conflict's dread rattle,
  And the chase's wild clamour, came
  loading the gale.

Breathless she gazed on the woodlands so
dreary;
  Slowly approaching a warrior was seen;
Life's ebbing tide mark'd his footsteps so
weary,
  Cleft was his helmet, and woe was his
  mien.

" O save thee, fair maid, for our armies
are flying!
  O save thee, fair maid, for thy guardian
is low!
Deadly cold on yon heath thy brave Henry
is lying,
  And fast through the woodland approaches the foe."

Scarce could he falter the tidings of sorrow,
  And scarce could she hear them, be-
  numb'd with despair :
And when the sun sank on the sweet lake
of Toro,
  For ever he set to the Brave and the Fair.

THE PALMER.

1806.

" O open the door, some pity to show,
  Keen blows the northern wind !
The glen is white with the drifted snow,
  And the path is hard to find.

" No outlaw seeks your castle gate,
  From chasing the King's deer,
Though even an outlaw's wretched state
  Might claim compassion here.

" A weary Palmer, worn and weak,
  I wander for my sin;

O open, for Our Lady's sake !
  A pilgrim's blessing win !

" I'll give you pardons from the Pope,
  And reliques from o'er the sea;—
Or if for these you will not ope,
  Yet open for charity.

" The hare is crouching in her form,
  The hart beside the hind ;
An aged man, amid the storm,
  No shelter can I find.

" You hear the Ettrick's sullen roar,
  Dark, deep, and strong is he,
And I must ford the Ettrick o'er,
  Unless you pity me.

" The iron gate is bolted hard,
  At which I knock in vain ;
The owner's heart is closer barr'd,
  Who hears me thus complain.

" Farewell, farewell ! and Mary grant,
  When old and frail you be,
You never may the shelter want,
  That's now denied to me."

The Ranger on his couch lay warm,
  And heard him plead in vain ;
But oft amid December's storm,
  He'll hear that voice again :

For lo, when through the vapours dank,
  Morn shone on Ettrick fair,
A corpse amid the alders rank,
  The Palmer welter'd there.

---◆---

THE MAID OF NEIDPATH.

1806.

There is a tradition in Tweeddale, that,
when Neidpath Castle, near Peebles, was inhabited by the Earls of March, a mutual
passion subsisted between a daughter of that
noble family, and a son of the Laird of
Tushielaw, in Ettrick Forest. As the alliance was thought unsuitable by her parents,
the young man went abroad. During his
absence, the lady fell into a consump-
tion ; and at length, as the only means of

saving her life, her father consented that her lover should be recalled. On the day when he was expected to pass through Peebles, on the road to Tushielaw, the young lady, though much exhausted, caused herself to be carried to the balcony of a house in Peebles, belonging to the family, that she might see him as he rode past. Her anxiety and eagerness gave such force to her organs, that she is said to have distinguished his horse's footsteps at an incredible distance. But Tushielaw, unprepared for the change in her appearance, and not expecting to see her in that place, rode on without recognising her, or even slackening his pace. The lady was unable to support the shock; and, after a short struggle, died in the arms of her attendants. There is an incident similar to this traditional tale in Count Hamilton's "Fleur d'Epine."

O LOVERS' eyes are sharp to see,
    And lovers' ears in hearing;
And love, in life's extremity,
    Can lend an hour of cheering.
Disease had been in Mary's bower,
    And slow decay from mourning,
Though now she sits on Neidpath's tower,
    To watch her love's returning.

All sunk and dim her eyes so bright,
    Her form decay'd by pining,
Till through her wasted hand, at night,
    You saw the taper shining;
By fits, a sultry hectic hue
    Across her cheek was flying;
By fits, so ashy pale she grew,
    Her maidens thought her dying.

Yet keenest powers to see and hear,
    Seem'd in her frame residing;
Before the watch-dog prick'd his ear,
    She heard her lover's riding;
Ere scarce a distant form was kenn'd,
    She knew, and waved to greet him;
And o'er the battlement did bend,
    As on the wing to meet him.

He came—he pass'd—a heedless gaze,
    As o'er some stranger glancing;
Her welcome, spoke in faltering phrase,
    Lost in his courser's prancing—

The castle arch, whose hollow tone
    Returns each whisper spoken,
Could scarcely catch the feeble moan,
    Which told her heart was broken.

WANDERING WILLIE.

1806.

ALL joy was bereft me the day that you
        left me,
    And climb'd the tall vessel to sail yon
        wide sea;
O weary betide it! I wander'd beside it,
    And bann'd it for parting my Willie
        and me.

Far o'er the wave hast thou follow'd thy
        fortune,
    Oft fought the squadrons of France
        and of Spain;
Ae kiss of welcome's worth twenty at
        parting,
    Now I hae gotten my Willie again.

When the sky it was mirk, and the winds
        they were wailing,
    I sat on the beach wi' the tear in my ee,
And thought o' the bark where my Willie
        was sailing,
    And wish'd that the tempest could a'
        blaw on me.

Now that thy gallant ship rides at her
        mooring,
    Now that my wanderer's in safety at
        hame,
Music to me were the wildest winds'
        roaring,
    That e'er o'er Inch-Keith drove the
        dark ocean faem.

When the lights they did blaze, and the
        guns they did rattle,
    And blithe was each heart for the great
        victory,
In secret I wept for the dangers of battle,
    And thy glory itself was scarce comfort
        to me.

But now shalt thou tell, while I eagerly
    listen,
  Of each bold adventure, and every
    brave scar;
And trust me, I'll smile, though my een
    they may glisten;
  For sweet after danger's the tale of the
    war.

And oh, how we doubt when there's dis-
    tance 'tween lovers,
  When there's naething to speak to the
    heart thro' the ee;
How often the kindest and warmest prove
    rovers,
  And the love of the faithfullest ebbs
    like the sea.

Till, at times—could I help it?—I pined
    and I ponder'd
  If love could change notes like the bird
    on the tree—
Now I'll ne'er ask if thine eyes may hae
    wander'd,
  Enough, thy leal heart has been con-
    stant to me.

Welcome from sweeping o'er sea and
    through channel,
  Hardships and danger despising for
    fame,
Furnishing story for glory's bright annal,
  Welcome, my wanderer, to Jeanie
    and hame!

Enough, now thy story in annals of glory
  Has humbled the pride of France,
    Holland, and Spain;
No more shalt thou grieve me, no more
    shalt thou leave me,
  I never will part with my Willie again.

HUNTING SONG.*

1808.

WAKEN, lords and ladies gay,
On the mountain dawns the day,

---

* Published in the continuation of Strutt's
curious romance called "Queenhoo Hall,"
1808.

All the jolly chase is here,
With hawk, and horse, and hunting-spear!
Hounds are in their couples yelling,
Hawks are whistling, horns are knelling,
Merrily, merrily, mingle they,
"Waken, lords and ladies gay."

Waken, lords and ladies gay,
The mist has left the mountain grey,
Springlets in the dawn are steaming,
Diamonds on the brake are gleaming:
And foresters have busy been,
To track the buck in thicket green;
Now we come to chant our lay,
"Waken, lords and ladies gay."

Waken, lords and ladies gay,
To the green-wood haste away;
We can show you where he lies,
Fleet of foot, and tall of size;
We can show the marks he made,
When 'gainst the oak his antlers fray'd;
You shall see him brought to bay,
"Waken, lords and ladies gay."

Louder, louder chant the lay,
Waken, lords and ladies gay!
Tell them youth, and mirth, and glee,
Run a course as well as we;
Time, stern huntsman! who can baulk,
Stanch as hound, and fleet as hawk:
Think of this, and rise with day,
Gentle lords and ladies gay.

EPITAPH,

*Designed for a monument in Lichfield
Cathedral, at the burial-place of the family
of Miss Seward.*

AMID these aisles, where once his precepts
    show'd
The Heavenward pathway which in life
    he trod,
This simple tablet marks a Father's bier,
And those he loved in life, in death are
    near;
For him, for them, a Daughter bade it
    rise,
Memorial of domestic charities.

Still wouldst thou know why o'er the
    marble spread,
In female grace the willow droops her
    head;
Why on her branches silent and unstrung,
The minstrel harp is emblematic hung;
What poet's voice is smother'd here in dust,
Till waked to join the chorus of the
    just,——
Lo! one brief line an answer sad supplies,
Honour'd, beloved, and mourn'd, here
    SEWARD lies!
Her worth, her warmth of heart, let
    friendship say,—
Go seek her genius in her living lay.

PROLOGUE

TO MISS BAILLIE'S PLAY OF THE
FAMILY LEGEND.

1809.

'TIS sweet to hear expiring Summer's sigh,
Through forests tinged with russet, wail
    and die;
'Tis sweet and sad the latest notes to hear
Of distant music, dying on the ear;
But far more sadly sweet, on foreign strand,
We list the legends of our native land,
Link'd as they come with every tender tie,
Memorials dear of youth and infancy.

Chief, thy wild tales, romantic Caledon,
Wake keen remembrance in each hardy
    son.
Whether on India's burning coasts he toil,
Or till Acadia's winter-fetter'd soil,
He hears with throbbing heart and
    moisten'd eyes,
And, as he hears, what dear illusions rise!
It opens on his soul his native dell,
The woods wild waving, and the water's
    swell;
Tradition's theme, the tower that threats
    the plain,
The mossy cairn that hides the hero slain;
The cot, beneath whose simple porch
    were told,
By grey-hair'd patriarch, the tales of old,

The infant group, that hush'd their sports
    the while,
And the dear maid who listen'd with a
    smile.
The wanderer, while the vision warms his
    brain,
Is denizen of Scotland once again.

Are such keen feelings to the crowd
    confined,
And sleep they in the Poet's gifted mind?
Oh no! For She, within whose mighty
    page
Each tyrant Passion shows his woe and
    rage,
Has felt the wizard influence they inspire,
And to your own traditions tuned her lyre.
Yourselves shall judge—whoe'er has raised
    the sail
By Mull's dark coast, has heard this
    evening's tale.
The plaided boatman, resting on his oar,
Points to the fatal rock amid the roar
Of whitening waves, and tells whate'er to-
    night
Our humble stage shall offer to your sight;
Proudly preferr'd that first our efforts give
Scenes glowing from her pen to breathe
    and live;
More proudly yet, should Caledon approve
The filial token of a Daughter's love.

THE POACHER.

*Written in imitation of Crabbe, and pub-
lished in the Edinburgh Annual Register of
1809.*

WELCOME, grave Stranger, to our green
    retreats,
Where health with exercise and freedom
    meets!
Thrice welcome, Sage, whose philosophic
    plan
By nature's limits metes the rights of man!
Generous as he, who now for freedom
    bawls,
Now gives full value for true Indian
    shawls:

O'er court, o'er customhouse, his shoe
who flings,
Now bilks excisemen, and now bullies
kings!
Like his, I ween, thy comprehensive mind
Holds laws as mouse-traps baited for
mankind;
Thine eye, applausive, each sly vermin sees,
That baulks the snare, yet battens on the
cheese;
Thine ear has heard, with scorn instead
of awe,
Our buckskinn'd justices expound the law,
Wire-draw the acts that fix for wires the
pain,
And for the netted partridge noose the
swain;
And thy vindictive arm would fain have
broke
The last light fetter of the feudal yoke,
To give the denizens of wood and wild,
Nature's free race, to each her free-born
child.
Hence hast thou mark'd, with grief, fair
London's race
Mock'd with the boon of one poor Easter
chase,
And long'd to send them forth as free as
when
Pour'd o'er Chantilly the Parisian train,
When musket, pistol, blunderbuss, com-
bined,
And scarce the field-pieces were left
behind!
A squadron's charge each leveret's heart
dismay'd,
On every covey fired a bold brigade;
La Douce Humanité approved the sport,
For great the alarm indeed, yet small the
hurt;
Shouts patriotic solemnized the day,
And Seine re-echo'd *Vive la Liberté!*
But mad *Citoyen*, meek *Monsieur* again,
With some few added links resumes his
chain.
Then, since such scenes to France no
more are known,
Come, view with me a hero of thine own!
One, whose free actions vindicate the cause
Of silvan liberty o'er feudal laws.

Seek we yon glades, where the proud
oak o'ertops
Wide-waving seas of birch and hazel copse,
Leaving between deserted isles of land,
Where stunted heath is patch'd with
ruddy sand;
And lonely on the waste the yew is seen,
Or straggling hollies spread a brighter
green.
Here, little worn, and winding dark and
steep,
Our scarce mark'd path descends yon
dingle deep:
Follow—but heedful, cautious of a trip,—
In earthly mire philosophy may slip.
Step slow and wary o'er that swampy
stream,
Till, guided by the charcoal's smothering
steam,
We reach the frail yet barricaded door
Of hovel form'd for poorest of the poor;
No hearth the fire, no vent the smoke
receives,
The walls are wattles, and the covering
leaves;
For, if such hut, our forest statutes say,
Rise in the progress of one night and day,
(Though placed where still the Con-
queror's hests o'erawe,
And his son's stirrup shines the badge of
law,)
The builder claims the unenviable boon,
To tenant dwelling, framed as slight and
soon
As wigwam wild, that shrouds the native
frore
On the bleak coast of frost-barr'd La-
brador.*

Approach, and through the unlatticed
window peep—
Nay, shrink not back, the inmate is asleep;
Sunk 'mid yon sordid blankets, till the sun
Stoop to the west, the plunderer's toils
are done.
Loaded and primed, and prompt for des-
perate hand,
Rifle and fowling-piece beside him stand;

---

* The New Forest is now disforested, and
its laws, &c., become a thing of the past.

While round the hut are in disorder laid
The tools and booty of his lawless trade;
For force or fraud, resistance or escape,
The crow, the saw, the bludgeon, and
　　the crape.
His pilfer'd powder in yon nook he hoards,
And the filch'd lead the church's roof
　　affords—
(Hence shall the rector's congregation
　　fret,
That while his sermon's dry his walls are
　　wet.)
The fish-spear barb'd, the sweeping net
　　are there,
Doe-hides, and pheasant plumes, and
　　skins of hare,
Cordage for toils, and wiring for the snare.
Barter'd for game from chase or warren
　　won,
Yon cask holds moonlight,* run when
　　moon was none;
And late-snatch'd spoils lie stow'd in hutch
　　apart,
To wait the associate higgler's evening
　　cart.

Look on his pallet foul, and mark his
　　rest:
What scenes perturb'd are acting in his
　　breast!
His sable brow is wet and wrung with
　　pain,
And his dilated nostril toils in vain;
For short and scant the breath each effort
　　draws,
And 'twixt each effort Nature claims a
　　pause.
Beyond the loose and sable neckcloth
　　stretch'd,
His sinewy throat seems by convulsion
　　twitch'd,
While the tongue falters, as to utterance
　　loth,
Sounds of dire import—watchword,
　　threat, and oath.
Though, stupified by toil, and drugg'd
　　with gin,
The body sleep, the restless guest within

Now plies on wood and wold his lawless
　　trade,
Now in the fangs of justice wakes dis-
　　may'd.—

" Was that wild start of terror and
　　despair,
Those bursting eyeballs, and that wilder'd
　　air,
Signs of compunction for a murder'd hare?
Do the locks bristle and the eyebrows arch,
For grouse or partridge massacred in
　　March?"—

No, scoffer, no! Attend, and mark
　　with awe,
There is no wicket in the gate of law!
He, that would e'er so lightly set ajar
That awful portal, must undo each bar:
Tempting occasion, habit, passion, pride,
Will join to storm the breach, and force
　　the barrier wide.

That ruffian, whom true men avoid
　　and dread,
Whom bruisers, poachers, smugglers, call
　　Black Ned,
Was Edward Mansell once;—the lightest
　　heart
That ever play'd on holiday his part!
The leader he in every Christmas game,
The harvest-feast grew blither when he
　　came,
And liveliest on the chords the bow did
　　glance,
When Edward named the tune and led
　　the dance.
Kind was his heart, his passions quick and
　　strong,
Hearty his laugh, and jovial was his song;
And if he loved a gun, his father swore,
" 'Twas but a trick of youth would soon
　　be o'er,
Himself had done the same some thirty
　　years before."

But he whose humours spurn law's
　　awful yoke,
Must herd with those by whom law's
　　bonds are broke.

---

* A cant term for smuggled spirits.

The common dread of justice soon allies
The clown, who robs the warren, or
   excise,
With sterner felons train'd to act more
   dread,
Even with the wretch by whom his fellow
   bled.
Then,—as in plagues the foul contagions
   pass,
Leavening and festering the corrupted
   mass,—
Guilt leagues with guilt, while mutual
   motives draw,
Their hope impunity, their fear the
   law;
Their foes, their friends, their rendezvous
   the same,
Till the revenue baulk'd, or pilfer'd game,
Flesh the young culprit, and example
   leads
To darker villany, and direr deeds.

  Wild howl'd the wind the forest glades
   along,
And oft the owl renew'd her dismal song;
Around the spot where erst he felt the
   wound,
Red William's spectre walk'd his mid-
   night round.
When o'er the swamp he cast his blight-
   ing look,
From the green marshes of the stagnant
   brook
The bittern's sullen shout the sedges
   shook!
The waning moon, with storm-presaging
   gleam,
Now gave and now withheld her doubtful
   beam;
The old Oak stoop'd his arms, then flung
   them high,
Bellowing and groaning to the troubled
   sky—
'Twas then, that, couch'd amid the brush-
   wood sere,
In Malwood-walk young Mansell watch'd
   the deer:
The fattest buck received his deadly shot—
The watchful keeper heard, and sought
   the spot.

Stout were their hearts, and stubborn was
   their strife,
O'erpower'd at length the Outlaw drew
   his knife!
Next morn a corpse was found upon the
   fell—
The rest his waking agony may tell!

SONG.

OH, say not, my love, with that mortified
   air,
  That your spring-time of pleasure is
   flown,
Nor bid me to maids that are younger
   repair,
  For those raptures that still are thine
   own.

Though April his temples may wreathe
   with the vine,
  Its tendrils in infancy curl'd,
'Tis the ardour of August matures us the
   wine,
  Whose life-blood enlivens the world.

Though thy form, that was fashion'd as
   light as a fay's,
  Has assumed a proportion more round,
And thy glance, that was bright as a
   falcon's at gaze,
  Looks soberly now on the ground,—

Enough, after absence to meet me again,
  Thy steps still with ecstasy move;
Enough, that those dear sober glances
   retain
  For me the kind language of love.

THE BOLD DRAGOON;

OR, THE PLAIN OF BADAJOS.

1812.

'TWAS a Maréchal of France, and he fain
  would honour gain,
And he long'd to take a passing glance at
  Portugal from Spain;

With his flying guns this gallant gay,
And boasted corps d'armée—
O he fear'd not our dragoons, with their
    long swords, boldly riding,
Whack, fal de ral, &c.

To Campo Mayor come, he had quietly
    sat down,
Just a fricassee to pick, while his soldiers
    sack'd the town,
When, 'twas peste! morbleu! mon
    General,
Hear the English bugle-call!
And behold the light dragoons, with their
    long swords, boldly riding,
Whack, fal de ral, &c.

Right about went horse and foot, artillery
    and all,
And, as the devil leaves a house, they
    tumbled through the wall;
They took no time to seek the door,
But, best foot set before—
O they ran from our dragoons, with their
    long swords, boldly riding,
Whack, fal de ral, &c.

Those valiant men of France they had
    scarcely fled a mile,
When on their flank there sous'd at once
    the British rank and file;
For Long, De Grey, and Otway, then
    Ne'er minded one to ten,
But came on like light dragoons, with
    their long swords, boldly riding,
Whack, fal de ral, &c.

Three hundred British lads they made
    three thousand reel,
Their hearts were made of English oak,
    their swords of Sheffield steel,
Their horses were in Yorkshire bred,
And Beresford them led;
So huzza for brave dragoons, with their
    long swords, boldly riding,
Whack, fal de ral, &c.

Then here's a health to Wellington, to
    Beresford, to Long,
And a single word of Bonaparte before I
    close my song:

The eagles that to fight he brings
Should serve his men with wings,
When they meet the bold dragoons, with
    their long swords, boldly riding,
Whack, fal de ral, &c.

ON THE MASSACRE OF
GLENCOE.

1814.

"In the beginning of the year 1692, an
action of unexampled barbarity disgraced the
government of King William III. in Scotland.
In the August preceding, a proclamation
had been issued, offering an indemnity to
such insurgents as should take the oaths to
the King and Queen, on or before the last
day of December; and the chiefs of such
tribes as had been in arms for James, soon
after took advantage of the proclamation.
But Macdonald of Glencoe was prevented by
accident, rather than by design, from tendering his submission within the limited time.
In the end of December he went to Colonel
Hill, who commanded the garrison in Fort-
William, to take the oaths of allegiance to
the government; and the latter having furnished him with a letter to Sir Colin Campbell, sheriff of the county of Argyle, directed
him to repair immediately to Inverary, to
make his submission in a legal manner before
that magistrate. But the way to Inverary
lay through almost impassable mountains,
the season was extremely rigorous, and the
whole country was covered with a deep snow.
So eager, however, was Macdonald to take the
oaths before the limited time should expire,
that, though the road lay within half a mile
of his own house, he stopped not to visit his
family, and, after various obstructions, arrived
at Inverary. The time had elapsed, and the
sheriff hesitated to receive his submission;
but Macdonald prevailed by his importuni-
ties, and even tears, in inducing that functionary to administer to him the oath of allegiance,
and to certify the cause of his delay. At this
time Sir John Dalrymple, afterwards Earl of
Stair, being in attendance upon William as
Secretary of State for Scotland, took advantage of Macdonald's neglecting to take the

oath within the time prescribed, and procured from the king a warrant of military execution against that chief and his whole clan. This was done at the instigation of the Earl of Breadalbane, whose lands the Glencoe men had plundered, and whose treachery to government in negotiating with the Highland clans, Macdonald himself had exposed. The King was accordingly persuaded that Glencoe was the main obstacle to the pacification of the Highlands; and the fact of the unfortunate chief's submission having been concealed, the sanguinary orders for proceeding to military execution against his clan were in consequence obtained. The warrant was both signed and countersigned by the King's own hand, and the Secretary urged the officers who commanded in the Highlands to execute their orders with the utmost rigour. Campbell of Glenlyon, a captain in Argyle's regiment, and two subalterns, were ordered to repair to Glencoe on the first of February with a hundred and twenty men. Campbell, being uncle to young Macdonald's wife, was received by the father with all manner of friendship and hospitality. The men were lodged at free quarters in the houses of his tenants, and received the kindest entertainment. Till the 13th of the month the troops lived in the utmost harmony and familiarity with the people; and on the very night of the massacre the officers passed the evening at cards in Macdonald's house. In the night, Lieutenant Lindsay, with a party of soldiers, called in a friendly manner at his door, and was instantly admitted. Macdonald, while in the act of rising to receive his guest, was shot dead through the back with two bullets. His wife had already dressed; but she was stripped naked by the soldiers, who tore the rings off her fingers with their teeth. The slaughter now became general, and neither age nor infirmity was spared. Some women, in defending their children, were killed; boys imploring mercy were shot dead by officers on whose knees they hung. In one place nine persons, as they sat enjoying themselves at table, were butchered by the soldiers. In Inverriggon, Campbell's own quarters, nine men were first bound by the soldiers, and then shot at intervals, one by one. Nearly forty persons were massacred by the troops; and several who fled to the mountains perished by famine and the inclemency of the season.

Those who escaped owed their lives to a tempestuous night. Lieutenant-Colonel Hamilton, who had received the charge of the execution from Dalrymple, was on his march with four hundred men, to guard all the passes from the valley of Glencoe; but he was obliged to stop by the severity of the weather, which proved the safety of the unfortunate clan. Next day he entered the valley, laid the houses in ashes, and carried away the cattle and spoil, which were divided among the officers and soldiers."—*Article* "BRITAIN;" *Encyc. Britannica—New Edition.*

"O TELL me, Harper, wherefore flow
Thy wayward notes of wail and woe,
Far down the desert of Glencoe,
    Where none may list their melody?
Say, harp'st thou to the mists that fly,
Or to the dun-deer glancing by,
Or to the eagle, that from high
    Screams chorus to thy minstrelsy?"—

"No, not to these, for they have rest,—
The mist-wreath has the mountain-crest,
The stag his lair, the erne her nest,
    Abode of lone security.
But those for whom I pour the lay,
Not wild-wood deep, nor mountain grey,
Not this deep dell, that shrouds from day,
    Could screen from treach'rous cruelty.

"Their flag was furl'd, and mute their drum,
The very household dogs were dumb,
Unwont to bay at guests that come
    In guise of hospitality.
His blithest notes the piper plied,
Her gayest snood the maiden tied,
The dame her distaff flung aside,
    To tend her kindly housewifery.

"The hand that mingled in the meal,
At midnight drew the felon steel,
And gave the host's kind breast to feel
    Meed for his hospitality!
The friendly hearth which warm'd that hand,
At midnight arm'd it with the brand,
That bade destruction's flames expand
    Their red and fearful blazonry.

" Then woman's shriek was heard in vain,
Nor infancy's unpitied plain,
More than the warrior's groan, could gain
  Respite from ruthless butchery !
The winter wind that whistled shrill,
The snows that night that cloked the hill,
Though wild and pitiless, had still
  Far more than Southern clemency.

" Long have my harp's best notes been
    gone,
Few are its strings, and faint their tone,
They can but sound in desert lone
  Their grey-hair'd master's misery.
Were each grey hair a minstrel string,
Each chord should imprecations fling,
Till startled Scotland loud should ring,
  'Revenge for blood and treachery !' "

FOR A' THAT AN' A' THAT.

A NEW SONG TO AN OLD TUNE.

1814.

THOUGH right be aft put down by
    strength,
  As mony a day we saw that,
The true and leilfu' cause at length
  Shall bear the grie for a' that,
For a' that an' a' that,
  Guns, guillotines, and a' that,
The Fleur-de-lis, that lost her right,
  Is queen again for a' that !

We'll twine her in a friendly knot
  With England's Rose, and a' that,
The Shamrock shall not be forgot,
  For Wellington made braw that.
The Thistle, though her leaf be rude,
  Yet faith we'll no misca' that,
She shelter'd in her solitude
  The Fleur-de-lis, for a' that.

The Austrian Vine, the Prussian Pine
  (For Blucher's sake, hurra that,)
The Spanish Olive, too, shall join,
  And bloom in peace for a' that.
Stout Russia's Hemp, so surely twined
  Around our wreath we'll draw that,
And he that would the cord unbind,
  Shall have it for his cra-vat !

Or, if to choke sae puir a sot,
  Your pity scorn to thraw that,
The Devil's elbow be his lot,
  Where he may sit and claw that.
In spite of slight, in spite of might,
  In spite of brags, an' a' that,
The lads that battled for the right,
  Have won the day, an' a' that !

There's ae bit spot I had forgot,
  America they ca' that !
A coward plot her rats had got
  Their father's flag to gnaw that :
Now see it fly top-gallant high,
  Atlantic winds shall blaw that,
And Yankee loon, beware your croun,
  There 's kames in hand to claw that!

For on the land, or on the sea,
  Where'er the breezes blaw that,
The British Flag shall bear the grie,
  And win the day for a' that !

SONG,

FOR THE ANNIVERSARY MEETING OF THE PITT CLUB OF SCOTLAND.

1814.

O, DREAD was the time, and more
    dreadful the omen,
  When the brave on Marengo lay
    slaughter'd in vain,
And beholding broad Europe bow'd
    down by her foemen,
  PITT closed in his anguish the map of
    her reign !
Not the fate of broad Europe could bend
    his brave spirit
  To take for his country the safety of
    shame;
O, then in her triumph remember his
    merit,
  And hallow the goblet that flows to
    his name.

Round the husbandman's head, while he
    traces the furrow,
  The mists of the winter may mingle
    with rain,

He may plough it with labour, and sow
it in sorrow,
And sigh while he fears he has sow'd it
in vain;
He may die ere his children shall reap in
their gladness,
But the blithe harvest-home shall remember his claim;
And their jubilee-shout shall be soften'd
with sadness,
While they hallow the goblet that
flows to his name.

Though anxious and timeless his life was
expended,
In toils for our country preserved by
his care,
Though he died ere one ray o'er the
nations ascended,
To light the long darkness of doubt
and despair;
The storms he endured in our Britain's
December,
The perils his wisdom foresaw and o'er-
came,
In her glory's rich harvest shall Britain
remember,
And hallow the goblet that flows to
his name.

Nor forget HIS grey head, who, all dark
in affliction,
Is deaf to the tale of our victories won,
And to sounds the most dear to paternal
affection,
The shout of his people applauding his
SON;
By his firmness unmoved in success and
disaster,
By his long reign of virtue, remember
his claim!
With our tribute to PITT join the praise
of his Master,
Though a tear stain the goblet that
flows to his name.

Yet again fill the wine-cup, and change
the sad measure,
The rites of our grief and our gratitude
paid,

To our Prince, to our Heroes, devote
the bright treasure,
The wisdom that plann'd, and the zeal
that obey'd.
Fill WELLINGTON'S cup till it beam like
his glory,
Forget not our own brave DALHOUSIE
and GRÆME;
A thousand years hence hearts shall
bound at their story,
And hallow the goblet that flows
to their fame.

———◆———

LINES,

ADDRESSED TO RANALD MACDONALD, ESQ., OF STAFFA.

1814.

STAFFA, sprung from high Macdonald,
Worthy branch of old Clan-Ranald!
Staffa! king of all kind fellows!
Well befall thy hills and valleys,
Lakes and inlets, deeps and shallows—
Cliffs of darkness, caves of wonder,
Echoing the Atlantic thunder;
Mountains which the grey mist covers,
Where the Chieftain spirit hovers,
Pausing while his pinions quiver,
Stretch'd to quit our land for ever!
Each kind influence reign above thee!
Warmer heart, 'twixt this and Staffa
Beats not, than in heart of Staffa!

———◆———

HEALTH TO LORD MELVILLE.

Sung at a public dinner given in honour
of his acquittal after his trial in 1806.

SINCE here we are set in array round
the table,
Five hundred good fellows well met
in a hall,
Come listen, brave boys, and I'll sing
as I'm able
How innocence triumph'd and pride
got a fall.

But push round the claret—
Come, stewards, don't spare it—
With rapture you'll drink to the toast
    that I give:
    Here, boys,
    Off with it merrily—
MELVILLE for ever, and long may he
    live!

What were the Whigs doing, when
    boldly pursuing,
    PITT banish'd Rebellion, gave Trea-
    son a string?
Why, they swore on their honour, for
    ARTHUR O'CONNOR,
And fought hard for DESPARD
    against country and king.
    Well, then, we knew, boys,
    PITT and MELVILLE were true
    boys,
And the tempest was raised by the
    friends of Reform.
    Ah, woe!
    Weep to his memory;
Low lies the pilot that weather'd the
    storm!

And pray, don't you mind when the
    Blues were first raising,
    And we scarcely could think the
    house safe o'er our heads?
When villains and coxcombs, French
    politics praising,
    Drove peace from our tables and
    sleep from our beds?
    Our hearts they grew bolder,
    When, musket on shoulder,
Stepp'd forth our old Statesmen ex-
    ample to give.
    Come, boys, never fear,
    Drink the Blue grenadier—
Here's to old HARRY, and long may
    he live!

They would turn us adrift; though rely,
    sir, upon it—
    Our own faithful chronicles warrant
    us that
The free mountaineer and his bonny
    blue bonnet
    Have oft gone as far as the regular's
    .hat.

    We laugh at their taunting,
    For all we are wanting
Is licence our life for our country to give.
    Off with it merrily,
    Horse, foot, and artillery,
Each loyal Volunteer, long may he live!

'Tis not us alone, boys—the Army and
    Navy
    Have each got a slap 'mid their
    politic pranks;
CORNWALLIS cashier'd, that watch'd
    winters to save ye,
    And the Cape called a bauble un-
    worthy of thanks.
    But vain is their taunt,
    No soldier shall want
The thanks that his country to valour
    can give:
    Come, boys,
    Drink it off merrily,—
SIR DAVID and POPHAM, and long
    may they live!

And then our revenue—Lord knows
    how they view'd it,
    While each petty statesman talk'd
    lofty and big;
But the beer tax was weak, as if Whit-
    bread had brew'd it,
    And the pig-iron duty a shame to a
    pig.
    In vain is their vaunting,
    Too surely there's wanting,
What judgment, experience, and steadi-
    ness give:
    Come, boys,
    Drink about merrily,—
Health to sage MELVILLE, and long
    may he live!

Our King, too—our Princess—I dare
    not say more, sir,—
May Providence watch them with
    mercy and might!
While there's one Scottish hand that
    can wag a claymore, sir,
    They shall ne'er want a friend to
    stand up for the right.
    Be damn'd he that dare not,—
    For my part, I'll spare not

To beauty afflicted a tribute to give:
    Fill it up steadily,
    Drink it off readily—
Here's to the Princess, and long may
    she live!

And since we must not set Auld Reekie
    in glory,
    And make her brown visage as light
      as her heart;
Till each man illumine his own upper
    story,
    Nor law-book nor lawyer shall force
      us to part.
      In GRENVILLE and SPENCER,
      And some few good men, sir,
High talents we honour, slight differ-
    ence forgive;
      But the Brewer we'll hoax,
      Tallyho to the FOX,
And drink MELVILLE for ever, as long
    as we live!

———◆———

EPILOGUE TO THE APPEAL.*

SPOKEN BY MRS. HENRY SIDDONS,
FEB. 16, 1818.

A CAT of yore (or else old Æsop lied)
Was changed into a fair and blooming
    bride,
But spied a mouse upon her marriage-
    day,
Forgot her spouse, and seized upon her
    prey;
Even thus my bridegroom lawyer, as
    you saw,
Threw off poor me, and pounced upon
    papa.
His neck from Hymen's mystic knot
    made loose,
He twisted round my sire's the literal
    noose.
Such are the fruits of our dramatic labour
Since the New Jail became our next-
    door neighbour.

———

* *The Appeal*, a Tragedy, by John Galt, the
celebrated author of the *Annals of the Parish*,
and other novels, was played for four nights at
this time in Edinburgh.

Yes, times *are* changed; for, in your
    fathers' age,
The lawyers were the patrons of the
    stage;
However high advanced by future fate,
There stands the bench (*points to the
    Pit*) that first received their weight.
The future legal sage, 't was ours to see,
Doom though unwigg'd, and plead
    without a fee.

But now, astounding each poor mimic
    elf,
Instead of lawyers comes the law herself;
Tremendous neighbour, on our right she
    dwells,
Builds high her towers and excavates
    her cells;
While on the left she agitates the town
With the tempestuous question, Up or
    down?
'Twixt Scylla and Charybdis thus stand
    we,
Law's final end, and law's uncertainty.
But, soft! who lives at Rome the Pope
    must flatter,
And jails and lawsuits are no jesting
    matter.
Then—just farewell! We wait with
    serious awe
Till your applause or censure gives the
    law.
Trusting our humble efforts may assure
    ye,
We hold you Court and Counsel, Judge
    and Jury.

———◆———

EPILOGUE.

1824.

THE sages—for authority, pray look
Seneca's morals, or the copy-book—
The sages to disparage woman's power,
Say beauty is a fair but fading flower;—
I cannot tell—I 've small philosophy—
Yet, if it fades, it does not surely die,
But, like the violet, when decay'd in
    bloom,
Survives through many a year in rich
    perfume.

Witness our theme to-night, two ages
　　gone,
A third wanes fast, since Mary filled
　　the throne.
Brief was her bloom, with scarce one
　　sunny day,
'Twixt Pinkie's field and fatal Fother-
　　ingay :
But when, while Scottish hearts and
　　blood you boast,
Shall sympathy with Mary's woes be
　　lost?
O'er Mary's mem'ry the learned quarrel,
By Mary's grave the poet plants his
　　laurel,
Time's echo, old tradition, makes her
　　name
The constant burden of his falt'ring
　　theme ;
In each old hall his grey-hair'd heralds
　　tell
Of Mary's picture, and of Mary's cell,
And show—my fingers tingle at the
　　thought—
The loads of tapestry which that poor
　　Queen wrought.
In vain did Fate bestow a double dower
Of ev'ry ill that waits on rank and pow'r,
Of ev'ry ill on beauty that attends—
False ministers, false lovers, and false
　　friends.
Spite of three wedlocks so completely
　　curst,
They rose in ill from bad to worse, and
　　worst,
In spite of errors—I dare not say more,
For Duncan Targe lays hand on his
　　claymore.
In spite of all, however humours vary,
There is a talisman in that word Mary,
That unto Scottish bosoms all and some
Is found the genuine *open sesamum !*
In history, ballad, poetry, or novel,
It charms alike the castle and the hovel,
Even you—forgive me—who, demure
　　and shy,
Gorge not each bait, nor stir at every fly,
Must rise to this, else in her ancient reign
The Rose of Scotland has survived in
　　vain.

SONG.

Joy to the victors ! the sons of old
　　Aspen ! 　　　　　　[scar !
Joy to the race of the battle and
Glory's proud garland triumphantly
　　grasping ; 　　　　　[war.
Generous in peace, and victorious in
　　Honour acquiring,
　　Valour inspiring,
Bursting, resistless, through foemen
　　they go :
　　War-axes wielding,
　　Broken ranks yielding,
Till from the battle proud Roderic
　　retiring, 　　　　　　[foe.
Yields in wild rout the fair palm to his
Joy to each warrior, true follower of
　　Aspen ! 　　　　　[bold day !
Joy to the heroes that gained the
Health to our wounded, in agony gasp-
　　ing ; 　　　　　　[fray !
Peace to our brethren that fell in the
　　Boldly this morning,
　　Roderic's power scorning,
Well for their chieftain their blades
　　did they wield :
　　Joy blest them dying,
　　As Maltingen flying,
Low laid his banners, our conquest
　　adorning,
Their death-clouded eyeballs descried
　　on the field !

Now to our home, the proud mansion
　　of Aspen, 　　　　[away ;
Bend we, gay victors, triumphant
There each fond damsel, her gallant
　　youth clasping,
Shall wipe from his forehead the
　　stains of the fray.
　　Listening the prancing
　　Of horses advancing ;
E'en now on the turrets our maidens
　　appear.
　　Love our hearts warming,
　　Songs the night charming,
Round goes the grape in the goblet
　　gay dancing ;
Love, wine, and song, our blithe even-
　　ing shall cheer '

Songs and Poems from Waverley.

"On receiving intelligence of his commission as captain of a troop of horse in Colonel Gardiner's regiment, his tutor, Mr. Pembroke, picked up about Edward's room some fragments of irregular verse, which he appeared to have composed under the influence of the agitating feelings occasioned by this sudden page being turned up to him in the book of life."—*Waverley, Chap.* v.

LATE, when the autumn evening fell
On Mirkwood-Mere's romantic dell,
The lake return'd, in chasten'd gleam,
The purple cloud, the golden beam:
Reflected in the crystal pool,
Headland and bank lay fair and cool;
The weather-tinted rock and tower,
Each drooping tree, each fairy flower,
So true, so soft, the mirror gave,
As if there lay beneath the wave,
Secure from trouble, toil, and care,
A world than earthly world more fair.

But distant winds began to wake,
And roused the Genius of the Lake!
He heard the groaning of the oak,
And donn'd at once his sable cloak,
As warrior, at the battle cry,
Invests him with his panoply:
Then, as the whirlwind nearer press'd,
He 'gan to shake his fôamy crest
O'er furrow'd brow and blacken'd cheek,
And bade his surge in thunder speak.
In wild and broken eddies whirl'd,
Flitted that fond ideal world;
And, to the shore in tumult tost,
The realms of fairy bliss were lost.

Yet, with a stern delight and strange,
I saw the spirit-stirring change.
As warr'd the wind with wave and wood,
Upon the ruin'd tower I stood,
And felt my heart more strongly bound,
Responsive to the lofty sound,
While, joying in the mighty roar,
I mourn'd that tranquil scene no more.

So, on the idle dreams of youth
Breaks the loud trumpet-call of truth,

Bids each fair vision pass away,
Like landscape on the lake that lay,
As fair, as flitting, and as frail,
As that which fled the autumn gale—
For ever dead to fancy's eye
Be each gay form that glided by,
While dreams of love and lady's charms
Give place to honour and to arms!

DAVIE GELLATLEY'S SONGS.

"He (Daft Davie Gellatley) sung with great earnestness, and not without some taste, a fragment of an old Scotch ditty :"

FALSE love, and hast thou play'd me this
　In summer among the flowers?
I will repay thee back again
　In winter among the showers.
Unless again, again, my love,
　Unless you turn again;
As you with other maidens rove,
　I'll smile on other men.

THE Knight's to the mountain
　His bugle to wind;
The Lady's to greenwood
　Her garland to bind.
The bower of Burd Ellen
　Has moss on the floor,
That the step of Lord William
　Be silent and sure.

Chap. ix.

"The stamping of horses was now heard in the court, and Davie Gellatley's voice singing to the two large deer greyhounds."

HIE away, hie away,
Over bank and over brae,
Where the copsewood is the greenest,
Where the fountains glisten sheenest,
Where the lady-fern grows strongest,
Where the morning dew lies longest,
Where the black-cock sweetest sips it,
Where the fairy latest trips it:
Hie to haunts right seldom seen,
Lovely, lonesome, cool, and green,
Over bank and over brae,
Hie away, hie away.

Chap. xii.

YOUNG men will love thee more fair and
    more fast;
  Heard ye so merry the little bird sing?
Old men's love the longest will last,
  And the throstle-cock's head is under his
    wing.

The young man's wrath is like light straw
  on fire;
  Heard ye so merry the little bird sing?
But like red-hot steel is the old man's ire,
  And the throstle-cock's head is under his
    wing.

The young man will brawl at the evening
  board;
  Heard ye so merry the little bird sing?
But the old man will draw at the dawning
  the sword,
  And the throstle-cock's head is under his
    wing.   *Chap.* XIV.

ST. SWITHIN'S CHAIR.

ON Hallow-Mass Eve, ere you boune ye
  to rest,
Ever beware that your couch be bless'd;
Sign it with cross, and sain it with bead,
Sing the Ave, and say the Creed.

For on Hallow-Mass Eve the Night-Hag
  will ride,
And all her nine-fold sweeping on by her
  side,
Whether the wind sing lowly or loud,
Sailing through moonshine or swath'd in
  the cloud.

The Lady she sate in St. Swithin's Chair,
The dew of the night has damp'd her hair:
Her cheek was pale—but resolved and high
Was the word of her lip and the glance
  of her eye.

She mutter'd the spell of Swithin bold,
When his naked foot traced the midnight
  wold,
When he stopp'd the Hag as she rode
  the night,
And bade her descend, and her promise
  plight.

He that dare sit on St. Swithin's Chair,
When the Night-Hag wings the troubled
  air,
Questions three, when he speaks the spell,
He may ask, and she must tell.

The Baron has been with King Robert his
  liege,
These three long years in battle and siege;
News are there none of his weal or his
  woe,
And fain the Lady his fate would know.

She shudders and stops as the charm she
  speaks;—
Is it the moody owl that shrieks?
Or is that sound, betwixt laughter and
  scream,
The voice of the Demon who haunts the
  stream?

The moan of the wind sunk silent and
  low,
And the roaring torrent had ceased to
  flow;
The calm was more dreadful than raging
  storm,
When the cold grey mist brought the
  ghastly form!
   *   *   *   *

            Chap. XIII.

FLORA MACIVOR'S SONG.

THERE is mist on the mountain, and night
  on the vale,
But more dark is the sleep of the sons of
  the Gael.
A stranger commanded—it sunk on the
  land,
It has frozen each heart, and benumb'd
  every hand!

The dirk and the target lie sordid with
  dust,
The bloodless claymore is but redden'd
  with rust;
On the hill or the glen if a gun should
  appear,
It is only to war with the heath-cock or
  deer,

The deeds of our sires if our bards should rehearse,
Let a blush or a blow be the meed of their verse!
Be mute every string, and be hush'd every tone,
That shall bid us remember the fame that is flown.

But the dark hours of night and of slumber are past,
The morn on our mountains is dawning at last;
Glenaladale's peaks are illumed with the rays,
And the streams of Glenfinnan leap bright in the blaze.

O high-minded Moray!—the exiled—the dear!—
In the blush of the dawning the STANDARD uprear!
Wide, wide on the winds of the north let it fly,
Like the sun's latest flash when the tempest is nigh!

Ye sons of the strong, when that dawning shall break,
Need the harp of the aged remind you to wake?
That dawn never beam'd on your forefathers' eye,
But it roused each high chieftain to vanquish or die.

O sprung from the Kings who in Islay kept state,
Proud chiefs of Clan-Ranald, Glengary, and Sleat!
Combine like three streams from one mountain of snow,
And resistless in union rush down on the foe.

True son of Sir Evan, undaunted Lochiel,
Place thy targe on thy shoulder and burnish thy steel!
Rough Keppoch, give breath to thy bugle's bold swell,
Till far Coryarrich resound to the knell!

Stern son of Lord Kenneth, high chief of Kintail,
Let the stag in thy standard bound wild in the gale!
May the race of Clan-Gillian, the fearless and free,
Remember Glenlivat, Harlaw, and Dundee!

Let the clan of grey Fingon, whose offspring has given
Such heroes to earth, and such martyrs to heaven,
Unite with the race of renown'd Rorri More,
To launch the long galley, and stretch to the oar.

How Mac-Shimei will joy when their chief shall display
The yew-crested bonnet o'er tresses of grey!
How the race of wrong'd Alpine and murder'd Glencoe
Shall shout for revenge when they pour on the foe!

Ye sons of brown Dermid, who slew the wild boar,
Resume the pure faith of the great Callum-More!
Mac-Niel of the Islands, and Moy of the Lake,
For honour, for freedom, for vengeance awake!

Awake on your hills, on your islands awake,
Brave sons of the mountain, the frith, and the lake!
'Tis the bugle—but not for the chase is the call;
'Tis the pibroch's shrill summons—but not to the hall.

'Tis the summons of heroes for conquest or death,
When the banners are blazing on mountain and heath;
They call to the dirk, the claymore, and the targe,
To the march and the muster, the line and the charge.

Be the brand of each chieftain like Fin's
    in his ire!
May the blood through his veins flow like
    currents of fire!
Burst the base foreign yoke as your sires
    did of yore!
Or die, like your sires, and endure it no
    more!   *Chap.* xxii.

TO AN OAK TREE,

*In the Churchyard of ———, in the High-
lands of Scotland, said to mark the grave
of Captain Wogan, killed in 1649.*

EMBLEM of England's ancient faith,
    Full proudly may thy branches wave,
Where loyalty lies low in death,
    And valour fills a timeless grave.

And thou, brave tenant of the tomb!
    Repine not if our clime deny,
Above thine honour'd sod to bloom,
    The flowrets of a milder sky.

These owe their birth to genial May;
    Beneath a fiercer sun they pine,
Before the winter storm decay—
    And can their worth be type of thine?

No! for, 'mid storms of Fate opposing,
    Still higher swell'd thy dauntless heart,
And, while Despair the scene was closing,
    Commenced thy brief but brilliant part.

'Twas then thou sought'st on Albyn's
    hill,
    (When England's sons the strife re-
    sign'd,)
A rugged race resisting still,
    And unsubdued though unrefined.

Thy death's hour heard no kindred wail,
    No holy knell thy requiem rung;
Thy mourners were the plaided Gael,
    Thy dirge the clamorous pibroch sung.

Yet who, in Fortune's summer-shine
    To waste life's longest term away,
Would change that glorious dawn of
    thine,
    Though darken'd ere its noontide day?

Be thine the Tree whose dauntless boughs
    Brave summer's drought and winter's
    gloom!
Rome bound with oak her patriots' brows,
    As Albyn shadows Wogan's tomb.
           Chap. xxix.

FAREWELL TO MACKENZIE,
HIGH CHIEF OF KINTAIL.

FROM THE GAELIC.

1815.

The original verses are arranged to a beautiful Gaelic air, of which the chorus is adapted
to the double pull upon the oars of a galley,
and which is therefore distinct from the
ordinary jorrams, or boat-songs. They were
composed by the Family Bard upon the departure of the Earl of Seaforth, who was
obliged to take refuge in Spain, after an un-
successful effort at insurrection in favour of
the Stuart family, in the year 1718.

FAREWELL to Mackenneth, great Earl
    of the North,
The Lord of Lochcarron, Glenshiel, and
    Seaforth;
To the Chieftain this morning his course
    who began,
Launching forth on the billows his bark
    like a swan.
For a far foreign land he has hoisted his
    sail,
Farewell to Mackenzie, High Chief of
    Kintail!

O swift be the galley, and hardy her crew,
May her captain be skilful, her mariners
    true,
In danger undaunted, unwearied by toil,
Though the whirlwind should rise, and
    the ocean should boil:
On the brave vessel's gunnel I drank his
    bonail,*
And farewell to Mackenzie, High Chief
    of Kintail!

---

* Bonail, or Bonallez, the old Scottish
phrase for a feast at parting with a friend.

Awake in thy chamber, thou sweet south-
    land gale!
Like the sighs of his people, breathe soft
    on his sail;
Be prolong'd as regret, that his vassals
    must know,
Be fair as their faith, and sincere as their
    woe:
Be so soft, and so fair, and so faithful,
    sweet gale,
Wafting onward Mackenzie, High Chief
    of Kintail!

Be his pilot experienced, and trusty, and
    wise,
To measure the seas and to study the
    skies:
May he hoist all his canvass from streamer
    to deck,
But O! crowd it higher when wafting
    him back—
Till the cliffs of Skooroora, and Conan's
    glad vale,
Shall welcome Mackenzie, High Chief of
    Kintail!

WAR-SONG OF LACHLAN,

HIGH CHIEF OF MACLEAN.

FROM THE GAELIC.

1815.

This song appears to be imperfect, or, at
least, like many of the early Gaelic poems,
makes a rapid transition from one subject to
another; from the situation, namely, of one
of the daughters of the clan, who opens the
song by lamenting the absence of her lover,
to an eulogium over the military glories of
the Chieftain. The translator has endeavoured
to imitate the abrupt style of the original.

A WEARY month has wander'd o'er
Since last we parted on the shore;
Heaven! that I saw thee, Love, once
    more,
    Safe on that shore again!—
'Twas valiant Lachlan gave the word:
Lachlan, of many a galley lord:
He call'd his kindred bands on board,
    And launch'd them on the main.

Clan-Gillian is to ocean gone,
Clan-Gillian, fierce in foray known;
Rejoicing in the glory won
    In many a bloody broil:
For wide is heard the thundering fray,
The rout, the ruin, the dismay,
When from the twilight glens away
    Clan-Gillian drives the spoil.

Woe to the hills that shall rebound
Our banner'd bag-pipes' maddening
    sound;
Clan-Gillian's onset echoing round,
    Shall shake their inmost cell.
Woe to the bark whose crew shall gaze,
Where Lachlan's silken streamer plays!
The fools might face the lightning's blaze
    As wisely and as well!

SAINT CLOUD.

Paris, 5th September, 1815.

SOFT spread the southern summer night
    Her veil of darksome blue;
Then thousand stars combined to light
    The terrace of Saint Cloud.

The evening breezes gently sigh'd,
    Like breath of lover true,
Bewailing the deserted pride
    And wreck of sweet Saint Cloud.

The drum's deep roll was heard afar,
    The bugle wildly blew
Good-night to Hulan and Hussar,
    That garrison Saint Cloud.

The startled Naiads from the shade
    With broken urns withdrew,
And silenced was that proud cascade,
    The glory of Saint Cloud.

We sate upon its steps of stone,
    Nor could its silence rue,
When waked, to music of our own,
    The echoes of Saint Cloud.

Slow Seine might hear each lovely note
    Fall light as summer dew,
While through the moonless air they
    float,
    Prolong'd from fair Saint Cloud.

And sure a melody more sweet
  His waters never knew,
Though music's self was wont to meet
  With Princes at Saint Cloud.

Nor then, with more delighted ear,
  The circle round her drew,
Than ours, when gather'd round to hear
  Our songstress at Saint Cloud.

Few happy hours poor mortals pass,—
  Then give those hours their due,
And rank among the foremost class
  Our evenings at Saint Cloud.

THE DANCE OF DEATH.

1815.

I.

NIGHT and morning were at meeting
  Over Waterloo;
Cocks had sung their earliest greeting;
  Faint and low they crew,
For no paly beam yet shone
On the heights of Mount Saint John;
Tempest-clouds prolonged the sway
Of timeless darkness over day;
Whirlwind, thunder-clap, and shower,
Mark'd it a predestined hour.
Broad and frequent through the night
Flash'd the sheets of levin-light;
Muskets, glancing lightnings back,
Show'd the dreary bivouac
  Where the soldier lay,
Chill and stiff, and drench'd with rain,
Wishing dawn of morn again,
  Though death should come with day.

II.

'Tis at such a tide and hour,
Wizard, witch, and fiend have power,
And ghastly forms through mist and
  shower
  Gleam on the gifted ken;
And then the affrighted prophet's ear
Drinks whispers strange of fate and fear
Presaging death and ruin near
  Among the sons of men;—
Apart from Albyn's war-array,
'Twas then grey Allan sleepless lay;

Grey Allan, who, for many a day,
  Had follow'd stout and stern,
Where, through battle's rout and reel,
Storm of shot and hedge of steel,
Led the grandson of Lochiel,
  Valiant Fassiefern.
Through steel and shot he leads no more,
Low laid 'mid friends' and foemen's gore—
But long his native lake's wild shore,
And Sunart rough and high Ardgower,
  And Morven long shall tell,
And proud Bennevis hear with awe,
How, upon bloody Quatre-Bras,
Brave Cameron heard the wild hurra
  Of conquest as he fell.

III.

'Lone on the outskirts of the host,
The weary sentinel held post,
And heard, through darkness far aloof,
The frequent clang of courser's hoof,
Where held the cloak'd patrol their
  course,
And spurr'd 'gainst storm the swerving
  horse;
But there are sounds in Allan's ear,
Patrol nor sentinel may hear,
And sights before his eye aghast
Invisible to them have pass'd,
  When down the destined plain,
'Twixt Britain and the bands of France,
Wild as marsh-borne meteor's glance,
Strange phantoms wheel'd a revel dance,
  And doom'd the future slain.—
Such forms were seen, such sounds were
  heard
When Scotland's James his march pre-
  pared
For Flodden's fatal plain;
Such, when he drew his ruthless sword,
As Choosers of the Slain, adored
  The yet unchristen'd Dane.
An indistinct and phantom band,
They wheel'd their ring-dance hand in
  hand,
  With gestures wild and dread;
The Seer, who watch'd them ride the
  storm,
Saw through their faint and shadowy form
  The lightning's flash more red;

And still their ghastly roundelay
Was of the coming battle-fray,
  And of the destined dead.

IV.

Song.

Wheel the wild dance
While lightnings glance,
  And thunders rattle loud,
And call the brave
To bloody grave,
  To sleep without a shroud.

Our airy feet,
So light and fleet,
  They do not bend the rye
That sinks its head when whirlwinds
    rave,
And swells again in eddying wave,
  As each wild gust blows by;
But still the corn,
At dawn of morn,
  Our fatal steps that bore,
At eve lies waste,
A trampled paste
  Of blackening mud and gore.

V.

Wheel the wild dance
While lightnings glance,
  And thunders rattle loud,
And call the brave
To bloody grave,
  To sleep without a shroud.

Wheel the wild dance!
Brave sons of France,
  For you our ring makes room;
Make space full wide
For martial pride,
  For banner, spear, and plume.
Approach, draw near,
Proud Cuirassier!
  Room for the men of steel!
Through crest and plate
The broadsword's weight
  Both head and heart shall feel.

VI.

Wheel the wild dance!
While lightnings glance,
  And thunders rattle loud,

And call the brave
To bloody grave,
  To sleep without a shroud.

Sons of the Spear!
You feel us near
  In many a ghastly dream;
With fancy's eye
Our forms you spy,
  And hear our fatal scream.
With clearer sight
Ere falls the night,
  Just when to weal or woe
Your disembodied souls take flight
On trembling wing—each startled
    sprite
  Our choir of death shall know.

VII.

Wheel the wild dance
While lightnings glance,
  And thunders rattle loud,
And call the brave
To bloody grave,
  To sleep without a shroud.

Burst, ye clouds, in tempest showers,
Redder rain shall soon be ours—
  See the east grows wan—
Yield we place to sterner game,
Ere deadlier bolts and direr flame
Shall the welkin's thunders shame;
Elemental rage is tame
  To the wrath of man.

VIII.

At morn, grey Allan's mates with awe
Heard of the vision'd sights he saw,
  The legend heard him say;
But the Seer's gifted eye was dim,
Deafen'd his ear, and stark his limb,
  Ere closed that bloody day—
He sleeps far from his Highland heath,—
But often of the Dance of Death
  His comrades tell the tale,
On picquet-post, when ebbs the night,
And waning watch-fires glow less bright,
  And dawn is glimmering pale.

ROMANCE OF DUNOIS.*

FROM THE FRENCH.

1815.

The original of this little Romance makes part of a manuscript collection of French Songs, (probably compiled by some young officer,) which was found on the field of Waterloo, so much stained with clay and with blood, as sufficiently to indicate the fate of its late owner. The song is popular in France, and is rather a good specimen of the style of composition to which it belongs. The translation is strictly literal.

IT was Dunois, the young and brave, was
  bound for Palestine,
But first he made his orisons before St.
  Mary's shrine :
" And grant, immortal Queen of Heaven,"
  was still the Soldier's prayer,
" That I may prove the bravest knight,
  and love the fairest fair."

His oath of honour on the shrine he
  graved it with his sword,
And follow'd to the Holy Land the banner of his Lord ;
Where, faithful to his noble vow, his
  war-cry fill'd the air,
" Be honour'd aye the bravest knight,
  beloved the fairest fair.

They owed the conquest to his arm,
  and then his Liege-Lord said,
" The heart that has for honour beat by
  bliss must be repaid.—
My daughter Isabel and thou shall be a
  wedded pair,
For thou art bravest of the brave, she
  fairest of the fair."

And then they bound the holy knot
  before Saint Mary's shrine,
That makes a paradise on earth, if hearts
  and hands combine ;

---

* " Partant pour la Syrie " was written and the air composed by Queen Hortense of Holland, the daughter of Josephine, and the mother of Napoleon III. It has become the national air of France.

And every lord and lady bright, that
  were in chapel there,
Cried, " Honour'd be the bravest knight,
  beloved the fairest fair !"

THE TROUBADOUR.

FROM THE SAME COLLECTION.

Also Composed and Written by Queen Hortense.

1815.

GLOWING with love, on fire for fame,
  A Troubadour that hated sorrow,
Beneath his Lady's window came,
  And thus he sung his last good-morrow:
" My arm it is my country's right,
  My heart is in my true-love's bower ;
Gaily for love and fame to fight
  Befits the gallant Troubadour."

And while he march'd with helm on head
  And harp in hand, the descant rung,
As, faithful to his favourite maid,
  The minstrel-burden still he sung :
" My arm it is my country's right,
  My heart is in my lady's bower ;
Resolved for love and fame to fight,
  I come, a gallant Troubadour."

Even when the battle-roar was deep,
  With dauntless heart he hew'd his way,
'Mid splintering lance and falchion-sweep,
  And still was heard his warrior-lay :
" My life it is my country's right,
  My heart is in my lady's bower ;
For love to die, for fame to fight,
  Becomes the valiant Troubadour."

Alas ! upon the bloody field
  He fell beneath the foeman's glaive,
But still reclining on his shield,
  Expiring sung the exulting stave :—
" My life it is my country's right,
  My heart is in my lady's bower ;
For love and fame to fall in fight
  Becomes the valiant Troubadour."

FROM THE FRENCH.

1815.

IT chanced that Cupid on a season,
By Fancy urged, resolved to wed,
But could not settle whether Reason
Or Folly should partake his bed.

What does he then?—Upon my life,
'Twas bad example for a deity—
He takes me Reason for a wife,
And Folly for his hours of gaiety.

Though thus he dealt in petty treason,
He loved them both in equal measure;
Fidelity was born of Reason,
And Folly brought to bed of Pleasure.

———◆———

SONG.

*On the lifting of the banner of the House
of Buccleuch, at a great foot-ball match
on Carterhaugh.*

1815.

FROM the brown crest of Newark its
summons extending,
Our signal is waving in smoke and in
flame;
And each forester blithe, from his mountain descending,
Bounds light o'er the heather to join in
the game.

CHORUS.

*Then up with the Banner, let forest winds
fan her,
She has blazed over Ettrick eight ages
and more;
In sport we'll attend her, in battle defend
her,
With heart and with hand, like our
fathers before.*

When the Southern invader spread waste
and disorder,
At the glance of her crescents he
paused and withdrew,

For around them were marshall'd the
pride of the Border,
The Flowers of the Forest, the bands
of BUCCLEUCH.
Then up with the Banner, &c.

A Stripling's weak hand to our revel has
borne her,
No mail-glove has grasp'd her, no spearmen surround;
But ere a bold foeman should scathe or
should scorn her,
A thousand true hearts would be cold
on the ground.
Then up with the Banner, &c.

We forget each contention of civil dis-
sension,
And hail, like our brethren, HOME,
DOUGLAS, and CAR:
And ELLIOT and PRINGLE in pastime
shall mingle,
As welcome in peace as their fathers in
war.
Then up with the Banner, &c.

Then strip, lads, and to it, though sharp
be the weather,
And if, by mischance, you should hap-
pen to fall,
There are worse things in life than a
tumble on heather,
And life is itself but a game at foot-ball.
Then up with the Banner, &c.

And when it is over, we'll drink a blithe
measure
To each Laird and each Lady that
witness'd our fun,
And to every blithe heart that took part
in our pleasure,
To the lads that have lost and the lads
that have won.
Then up with the Banner, &c.

May the Forest still flourish, both Bo-
rough and Landward,
From the hall of the Peer to the Herd's
ingle-nook;
And huzza! my brave hearts, for BUC-
CLEUCH and his standard,
For the King and the Country, the Clan
and the Duke!

Then up with the Banner, let forest winds fan her,
  She has blazed over Ettrick eight ages and more;
In sport we'll attend her, in battle defend her,
  With heart and with hand, like our fathers before.

LULLABY OF AN INFANT CHIEF.

AIR—*Cadul gu lo.*

1815.

I.

O, HUSH thee, my babie, thy sire was a knight,
Thy mother a lady, both lovely and bright;
The woods and the glens, from the towers which we see,
They all are belonging, dear babie, to thee.
        O ho ro, i ri ri, cadul gu lo,
        O ho ro, i ri ri, &c.

II.

O, fear not the bugle, though loudly it blows,
It calls but the warders that guard thy repose;
Their bows would be bended, their blades would be red,
Ere the step of a foeman draws near to thy bed.
        O ho ro, i ri ri, &c.

III.

O, hush thee, my babie, the time soon will come,
When thy sleep shall be broken by trumpet and drum;
Then hush thee, my darling, take rest while you may,
For strife comes with manhood, and waking with day.
        O ho ro, i ri ri, &c.

SONGS OF MEG MERRILIES

FROM GUY MANNERING.

1815.

"TWIST YE, TWINE YE."

TWIST ye, twine ye! even so,
Mingle shades of joy and woe,
Hope, and fear, and peace, and strife,
In the thread of human life.

While the mystic twist is spinning,
And the infant's life beginning,
Dimly seen through twilight bending,
Lo, what varied shapes attending!

Passions wild, and follies vain,
Pleasures soon exchanged for pain;
Doubt, and jealousy, and fear,
In the magic dance appear.

Now they wax, and now they dwindle,
Whirling with the whirling spindle.
Twist ye, twine ye! even so,
Mingle human bliss and woe.—
                    Vol. 1, *Chap.* iii.

THE DYING GIPSY'S DIRGE.

WASTED, weary, wherefore stay,
Wrestling thus with earth and clay?
From the body pass away;—
        Hark! the mass is singing.

From thee doff thy mortal weed,
Mary Mother be thy speed,
Saints to help thee at thy need;—
        Hark! the knell is ringing.

Fear not snow-drift driving fast,
Sleet, or hail, or levin blast;
Soon the shroud shall lap thee fast,
And the sleep be on thee cast
        That shall ne'er know waking.

Haste thee, haste thee, to be gone,
Earth flits fast, and time draws on,—
Gasp thy gasp, and groan thy groan,
        Day is near the breaking.

THE RETURN TO ULSTER.

1816.

ONCE again,—but how changed since my
    wand'rings began—
I have heard the deep voice of the Lagan
    and Bann,
And the pines of Clanbrassil resound to
    the roar
That wearies the echoes of fair Tullamore.
Alas! my poor bosom, and why shouldst
    thou burn?
With the scenes of my youth can its
    raptures return?
Can I live the dear life of delusion again,
That flow'd when these echoes first mix'd
    with my strain?

It was then that around me, though poor
    and unknown,
High spells of mysterious enchantment
    were thrown;
The streams were of silver, of diamond
    the dew,
The land was an Eden, for fancy was new.
I had heard of our bards, and my soul
    was on fire
At the rush of their verse, and the sweep
    of their lyre:
To me 'twas not legend, nor tale to
    the ear,
But a vision of noontide, distinguish'd and
    clear.

Ultonia's old heroes awoke at the call,
And renew'd the wild pomp of the chase
    and the hall;
And the standard of Fion flash'd fierce
    from on high,
Like a burst of the sun when the tempest
    is nigh.
It seem'd that the harp of green Erin
    once more
Could renew all the glories she boasted of
    yore.—
Yet why at remembrance, fond heart,
    shouldst thou burn?
They were days of delusion, and cannot
    return.

But was she, too, a phantom, the Maid
    who stood by,
And listed my lay, while she turn'd from
    mine eye?
Was she, too, a vision, just glancing to
    view,
Then dispersed in the sunbeam, or melted
    to dew?
Oh! would it had been so,—Oh! would
    that her eye
Had been but a star-glance that shot
    through the sky,
And her voice that was moulded to
    melody's thrill,
Had been but a zephyr, that sigh'd and
    was still!

Oh! would it had been so,—not then
    this poor heart
Had learn'd the sad lesson, to love and to
    part;
To bear, unassisted, its burthen of care,
While I toil'd for the wealth I had no
    one to share.
Not then had I said, when life's summer
    was done,
And the hours of her autumn were fast
    speeding on,
" Take the fame and the riches ye brought
    in your train,
And restore me the dream of my spring-
    tide again."

———

JOCK OF HAZELDEAN.

AIR—*A Border Melody.*

1816.

The first stanza of this ballad is ancient.
The others were written for Mr. Campbell's
Albyn's Anthology.

I.

" WHY weep ye by the tide, ladie?
    Why weep ye by the tide?
I'll wed ye to my youngest son,
    And ye sall be his bride
And ye sall be his bride, ladie,
    Sae comely to be seen"—
But aye she loot the tears down fa'
    For Jock of Hazeldean.

II.

" Now let this wilfu' grief be done,
    And dry that cheek so pale;
Young Frank is chief of Errington,
    And lord of Langley-dale;
His step is first in peaceful ha',
    His sword in battle keen"—
But aye she loot the tears down fa'
    For Jock of Hazeldean.

III.

" A chain of gold ye sall not lack,
    Nor braid to bind your hair;
Nor mettled hound, nor managed hawk,
    Nor palfrey fresh and fair;
And you, the foremost o' them a',
    Shall ride our forest queen"—
But aye she loot the tears down fa'
    For Jock of Hazeldean.

IV.

The kirk was deck'd at morning-tide,
    The tapers glimmer'd fair;
The priest and bridegroom wait the bride,
    And dame and knight are there.
They sought her baith by bower and ha';
    The ladie was not seen!
She's o'er the Border, and awa'
    Wi' Jock of Hazeldean.

PIBROCH OF DONALD DHU.*

AIR—" *Piobair of Donuil Dhuidh.*"

1816.

This is a very ancient pibroch belonging to
Clan Macdonald, and supposed to refer to the
expedition of Donald Balloch, who, in 1431,
launched from the Isles with a considerable
force, invaded Lochaber, and at Inverlochy
defeated and put to flight the Earls of Mar
and Caithness, though at the head of an army
superior to his own. The words of the set,
theme, or melody, to which the pipe variations
are applied, run thus in Gaelic:—

Piobaireachd Dhonuil Dhuidh, piobaireachd
    Dhonuil;
Piobaireachd Dhonuil Dhuidh, piobaireachd
    Dhonuil;

---

* *Dhu*—the Black.

Piobaireachd Dhonuil Dhuidh, piobaireachd
    Dhonuil;
Piob agus bratach air faiche Inverlochi.
The pipe-summons of Donald the Black,
The pipe-summons of Donald the Black,
The war-pipe and the pennon are on the
    gathering place at Inverlochy.

Pibroch of Donuil Dhu,
    Pibroch of Donuil,
Wake thy wild voice anew,
    Summon Clan-Conuil.
Come away, come away,
    Hark to the summons!
Come in your war array,
    Gentles and commons.

Come from deep glen, and
    From mountain so rocky,
The war-pipe and pennon
    Are at Inverlocky.
Come every hill-plaid, and
    True heart that wears one,
Come every steel blade, and
    Strong hand that bears one.

Leave untended the herd,
    The flock without shelter;
Leave the corpse uninterr'd,
    The bride at the altar;
Leave the deer, leave the steer,
    Leave nets and barges:
Come with your fighting gear,
    Broadswords and targes.

Come as the winds come, when
    Forests are rended,
Come as the waves come, when
    Navies are stranded:
Faster come, faster come,
    Faster and faster,
Chief, vassal, page and groom,
    Tenant and master.

Fast they come, fast they come;
    See how they gather!
Wide waves the eagle plume,
    Blended with heather.
Cast your plaids, draw your blades,
    Forward each man set!
Pibroch of Donuil Dhu,
    Knell for the onset!

NORA'S VOW.

AIR—*Cha teid mis a chaoidh.**

WRITTEN FOR ALBYN'S ANTHOLOGY.

1816.

In the original Gaelic, the Lady makes protestations that she will not go with the Red Earl's son, until the swan should build in the cliff, and the eagle in the lake—until one mountain should change place with another, and so forth. It is but fair to add, that there is no authority for supposing that she altered her mind—except the vehemence of her protestation.

I.

HEAR what Highland Nora said—
" The Earlie's son I will not wed,
Should all the race of nature die,
And none be left but he and I.
For all the gold, for all the gear,
And all the lands both far and near,
That ever valour lost or won,
I would not wed the Earlie's son."—

II.

" A maiden's vows," old Callum spoke,
" Are lightly made and lightly broke;
The heather on the mountain's height
Begins to bloom in purple light;
The frost-wind soon shall sweep away
That lustre deep from glen and brae;
Yet Nora, ere its bloom be gone,
May blithely wed the Earlie's son."—

III.

" The swan," she said, " the lake's clear breast
May barter for the eagle's nest;
The Awe's fierce stream may backward turn,
Ben-Cruaichan fall, and crush Kilchurn;
Our kilted clans, when blood is high,
Before their foes may turn and fly;
But I, were all these marvels done,
Would never wed the Earlie's son."

IV.

Still in the water-lily's shade
Her wonted nest the wild-swan made;
Ben-Cruaichan stands as fast as ever,
Still downward foams the Awe's fierce river;
To shun the clash of foeman's steel,
No Highland brogue has turned the heel;
But Nora's heart is lost and won,
—She's wedded to the Earlie's son!

MACGREGOR'S GATHERING.

AIR—*Thain' a Grigalach.**

WRITTEN FOR ALBYN'S ANTHOLOGY.

1816.

These verses are adapted to a very wild, yet lively gathering-tune, used by the MacGregors. The severe treatment of this Clan, their outlawry, and the proscription of their very name, are alluded to in the Ballad.

THE moon's on the lake, and the mist's on the brae,
And the Clan has a name that is nameless by day;
  Then gather, gather, gather Grigalach!
  Gather, gather, gather, &c.

Our signal for fight, that from monarchs we drew,
Must be heard but by night in our vengeful haloo!
  Then haloo, Grigalach! haloo, Grigalach!
  Haloo, haloo, haloo, Grigalach, &c.

Glen Orchy's proud mountains, Coalchuirn and her towers,
Glenstrae and Glenlyon no longer are ours;
  We're landless, landless, landless, Grigalach!
  Landless, landless, landless, &c.

---

* " I will never go with him."   † " The MacGregor is come."

But doom'd and devoted by vassal and
    lord,
Macgregor has still both his heart and his
    sword!
  Then courage, courage, courage, Gri-
    galach!
  Courage, courage, courage, &c.

If they rob us of name, and pursue us
    with beagles,
Give their roofs to the flame, and their
    flesh to the eagles!
  Then vengeance, vengeance, vengeance,
    Grigalach!
  Vengeance, vengeance, vengeance, &c.

While there's leaves in the forest, and
    foam on the river,
MacGregor, despite them, shall flourish
    for ever!
  Come then, Grigalach, come then,
    Grigalach,
  Come then, come then, come then, &c.

Through the depths of Loch Katrine the
    steed shall career,
O'er the peak of Ben-Lomond the galley
    shall steer,
And the rocks of Craig-Royston like
    icicles melt,
Ere our wrongs be forgot, or our ven-
    geance unfelt!
  Then gather, gather, gather, Grigalach!
  Gather, gather, gather, &c.

━━━━━━

Songs from the Antiquary.

1816.

TIME.

" WHY sit'st thou by that ruin'd hall,
    Thou aged carle so stern and grey?
  Dost thou its former pride recal,
    Or ponder how it pass'd away!"—

" Know'st thou not me!" the Deep
    Voice cried;
  " So long enjoy'd, so oft misused—
Alternate, in thy fickle pride,
  Desired, neglected, and accused!

" Before my breath, like blazing flax,
    Man and his marvels pass away!
And changing empires wane and wax,
    Are founded, flourish, and decay.

" Redeem mine hours—the space is
    brief—
  While in my glass the sand-grains
    shiver,
And measureless thy joy or grief,
    When TIME and thou shalt part for
    ever!"

                                Chap. x.

ELSPETH'S BALLAD.

THE herring loves the merry moon-light,
  The mackerel loves the wind,
But the oyster loves the dredging sang,
  For they come of a gentle kind.

Now haud your tongue, baith wife and
    carle,
  And listen great and sma',
And I will sing of Glenallan's Earl
  That fought on the red Harlaw.

The cronach's cried on Bennachie,
  And doun the Don and a',
And hieland and lawland may mournfu'
    be
  For the sair field of Harlaw.——

They saddled a hundred milk-white
    steeds,
  They hae bridled a hundred black,
With a chafron of steel on each horse's
    head,
  And a good knight upon his back.

They hadna ridden a mile, a mile,
  A mile but barely ten,
When Donald came branking down the
    brae
  Wi' twenty thousand men.

Their tartans they were waving wide,
  Their glaives were glancing clear,
The pibrochs rung frae side to side,
  Would deafen ye to hear.

The great Earl in his stirrups stood,
  That Highland host to see:
" Now here a knight that's stout and
    good
May prove a jeopardie:

" What would'st thou do, my squire so
    gay,
That rides beside my reyne,—
Were ye Glenallan's Earl the day,
  And I were Roland Cheyne?

" To turn the rein were sin and shame,
  To fight were wond'rous peril,—
What would ye do now, Roland Cheyne,
  Were ye Glenallan's Earl?"—

" Were I Glenallan's Earl this tide,
  And ye were Roland Cheyne,
The spur should be in my horse's side,
  And the bridle upon his mane.

" If they hae twenty thousand blades,
  And we twice ten times ten,
Yet they hae but their tartan plaids,
  And we are mail-clad men.

" My horse shall ride through ranks sae
    rude,
  As through the moorland fern,—
Then ne'er let the gentle Norman blude
  Grow cauld for Highland kerne."

  *   *   *   *   *   *
  *   *   *   *   *   *

He turn'd him right and round a-ain,
  Said, Scorn na at my mither;
Light loves I may get mony a ane,
  But minnie ne'er anither.
                 Chap, xl.

MOTTOES

IN THE ANTIQUARY.

I KNEW Anselmo. He was shrewd and
  prudent,
Wisdom and cunning had their shares of
  him;
But he was shrewish as a wayward child,

And pleased again by toys which child-
  hood please;
As—book of fables graced with print of
  wood,
Or else the jingling of a rusty medal,
Or the rare melody of some old ditty,
That first was sung to please King
  Pepin's cradle.

CHAP. IX.

" Be brave," she cried, " you yet may
  be our guest,
Our haunted room was ever held the best :
If, then, your valour can the fight sustain
Of rustling curtains, and the clinking
  chain;
If your courageous tongue have powers
  to talk,
When round your bed the horrid ghost
  shall walk
If you dare ask it why it leaves its tomb,
I'll see your sheets well air'd, and show
  the room."—*True Story.*

CHAP. XI.

Sometimes he thinks that Heaven this
  vision sent,
And order'd all the pageants as they went;
Sometimes that only 'twas wild Fancy's
  play,—
The loose and scatter'd relics of the day.

CHAP. XII.

Beggar!—the only freemen of your
  Commonwealth!
Free above Scot-free, that observe no
  laws,
Obey no governor, use no religion
But what they draw from their own
  ancient customs,
Or constitute themselves, yet they are no
  rebels.—*Brome.*

CHAP. XIX.

Here has been such a stormy encounter,
Betwixt my cousin Captain, and this
  soldier,

About I know not what—nothing, in-
deed;
Competitions, degrees, and comparatives
Of soldiership!—*A Faire Quarrel.*

CHAP. XX.

—— If you fail honour here,
Never presume to serve her any more;
Bid farewell to the integrity of arms,
And the honourable name of soldier
Fall from you, like a shiver'd wreath of
laurel
By thunder struck from a desertlesse fore-
head.—*A Faire Quarrel.*

CHAP. XXI.

—— The Lord Abbot had a soul
Subtile and quick, and searching as the
fire:
By magic stairs he went as deep as hell,
And if in devils' possession gold be kept,
He brought some sure from thence—'tis
hid in caves,
Known, save to me, to none——
The Wonder of a Kingdome.

CHAP. XXVII.

—— Many great ones
Would part with half their states, to have
the plan
And credit to beg in the first style.—
Beggar's Bush.

CHAP. XXX.

Who is he?—One that for the lack of
land
Shall fight upon the water—he hath chal-
lenged
Formerly the grand whale; and by his
titles
Of Leviathan, Behemoth, and so forth.
He tilted with a sword-fish—Marry, sir,
Th' aquatic had the best—the argument
Still galls our champion's breech.—
Old Play.

CHAP. XXXI.

Tell me not of it, friend—when the young
weep,
Their tears are lukewarm brine;—from
our old eyes
Sorrow falls down like hail-drops of the
North,
Chilling the furrows of our wither'd cheeks,
Cold as our hopes, and harden'd as our
feeling—
Theirs, as they fall, sink sightless—ours
recoil,
Heap the fair plain, and bleaken all before
us.—*Old Play.*

CHAP. XXXIII.

Remorse—she ne'er forsakes us!—
A bloodhound stanch—she tracks our
rapid step
Through the wild labyrinth of youthful
frenzy,
Unheard, perchance, until old age hath
tamed us;
Then in our lair, when Time hath chill'd
our joints,
And maim'd our hope of combat, or of
flight,
We hear her deep-mouth'd bay, announcing all
Of wrath and woe and punishment that
bides us.—*Old Play.*

CHAP. XXXIV.

Still in his dead hand clench'd remain the
strings
That thrill his father's heart—e'en as the
limb,
Lopp'd off and laid in grave, retains, they
tell us,
Strange commerce with the mutilated
stump,
Whose nerves are twinging still in maim'd
existence.—*Old Play.*

CHAP. XXXV.

—— Life, with you,
Glows in the brain and dances then
arteries;

'Tis like the wine some joyous guest hath
   quaff'd,
That glads the heart and elevates the
   fancy:—
Mine is the poor residuum of the cup,
Vapid, and dull, and tasteless, only soiling
With its base dregs the vessel that con-
   tains it.—*Old Play.*

CHAP. XXXVII.

Yes! I love Justice well—as well as you
   do—
But, since the good dame's blind, she shall
   excuse me,
If, time and reason fitting, I prove
   dumb;—
The breath I utter now shall be no means
To take away from me my breath in
   future.—*Old Play.*

CHAP. XXXVIII.

Well, well, at worst, 'tis neither theft nor
   coinage,
Granting I knew all that you charge me
   with.
What, tho' the tomb hath born a second
   birth,
And given the wealth to one that knew
   not on't,
Yet fair exchange was never robbery,
Far less pure bounty.—*Old Play.*

CHAP. XL.

Life ebbs from such old age, unmark'd
   and silent,
As the slow neap-tide leaves yon stranded
   galley—
Late she rock'd merrily at the least im-
   pulse
That wind or wave could give; but now
   her keel
Is settling on the sand, her mast has ta'en
An angle with the sky, from which it
   shifts not.
Each wave receding shakes her less and
   less,
Till, bedded on the strand, she shall remain
Useless as motionless.—*Old Play.*

CHAP. XLI.

So, while the Goose, of whom the fable
   told,
Incumbent, brooded o'er her eggs of gold,
With hand outstretch'd, impatient to
   destroy,
Stole on her secret nest the cruel Boy,
Whose gripe rapacious changed her
   splendid dream,
For wings vain fluttering, and for dying
   scream.—
     The Loves of the Sea-Weeds.

CHAP. XLII.

Let those go see who will—I like it not—
For, say he was a slave to rank and pomp,
And all the nothings he is now divorced
   from
By the hard doom of stern necessity;
Yet is it sad to mark his alter'd brow,
Where Vanity adjusts her flimsy veil
O'er the deep wrinkles of repentant An-
   guish.—*Old Play.*

CHAP. XLIII.

Fortune, you say, flies from us—She but
   circles,
Like the fleet sea-bird round the fowler's
   skiff,—
Lost in the mist one moment, and the
   next
Brushing the white sail with her whiter
   wing,
As if to court the aim.—Experience
   watches,
And has her on the wheel.—*Old Play.*

CHAP. XLIV.

Nay, if she love me not, I care not for her:
Shall I look pale because the maiden
   blooms?
Or sigh because she smiles—and smiles
   on others?
Not I, by Heaven!—I hold my peace too
   dear,
To let it, like the plume upon her cap,
Shake at each nod that her caprice shall
   dictate.—*Old Play.*

From the Black Dwarf.

1816.

CHAP. XVI.

—— 'Twas time and griefs
That framed him thus: Time, with his
    fairer hand,
Offering the fortunes of his former days,
The former man may make him—Bring
    us to him,
And chance it as it may.—*Old Play.*

* * *

From Old Mortality.

1816.

MAJOR BELLENDEN'S SONG.

And what though winter will pinch severe
    Through locks of grey and a cloak that's
    old,
Yet keep up thy heart, bold cavalier,
    For a cup of sack shall fence the cold.

For time will rust the brightest blade,
    And years will break the strongest bow;
Was never wight so starkly made,
    But time and years would overthrow!
                              Chap. xix.

VERSES FOUND IN BOTHWELL'S POCKET-BOOK.

Thy hue, dear pledge, is pure and bright,
As in that well-remember'd night,
When first thy mystic braid was wove,
And first my Agnes whisper'd love.

Since then how often hast thou press'd
The torrid zone of this wild breast,
Whose wrath and hate have sworn to
    dwell
With the first sin which peopled hell.
A breast whose blood's a troubled ocean,
Each throb the earthquake's wild com-
    motion!—
O, if such clime thou canst endure,
Yet keep thy hue unstain'd and pure,

What conquest o'er each erring thought
Of that fierce realm had Agnes wrought!
I had not wander'd wild and wide,
With such an angel for my guide;
Nor heaven nor earth could then reprove
    me,
If she had lived, and lived to love me.

Not then this world's wild joys had been
To me one savage hunting scene,
My sole delight the headlong race,
And frantic hurry of the chase;
To start, pursue, and bring to bay,
Rush in, drag down, and rend my prey,
Then—from the carcass turn away!
Mine ireful mood had sweetness tamed,
And sooth'd each wound which pride
    inflamed!
Yes, God and man might now approve me,
If thou hadst lived, and lived to love me.
                              Chap. xxiii.

MOTTOES

FROM OLD MORTALITY.

CHAP. XIV.

My hounds may a' rin masterless,
    My hawks may fly frae tree to tree,
My lord may grip my vassal lands,
    For there again maun I never be!
                              Old Ballad.

CHAP. XXXIV.

Sound, sound the clarion, fill the fife!
    To all the sensual world proclaim,
One crowded hour of glorious life
    Is worth an age without a name.
                              Anonymous.

* * *

THE SEARCH AFTER HAPPI-NESS;

OR, THE QUEST OF SULTAUN SOLIMAUN.

1817.

I.

Oh for a glance of that gay Muse's eye,
    That lighten'd on Bandello's laughing
    tale,

And twinkled with a lustre shewd and
  sly,
When Giam Battista bade her vision
  hail!—
Yet fear not, ladies, the *naïve* detail
Given by the natives of that land cano-
  rous;
Italian license loves to leap the pale,
We Britons have the fear of shame be-
  fore us,
And, if not wise in mirth, at least must
  be decorous.

II.

In the far eastern clime, no great while since,
Lived Sultaun Solimaun, a mighty prince,
Whose eyes, as oft as they perform'd their
  round,
Beheld all others fix'd upon the ground;
Whose ears received the same unvaried
  phrase,
"Sultaun! thy vassal hears, and he obeys!"
All have their tastes—this may the fancy
  strike
Of such grave folks as pomp and grandeur
  like;
For me, I love the honest heart and warm
Of Monarch who can amble round his farm,
Or, when the toil of state no more annoys,
In chimney corner seek domestic joys—
I love a prince will bid the bottle pass,
Exchanging with his subjects glance and
  glass;
In fitting time, can, gayest of the gay,
Keep up the jest, and mingle in the lay—
Such Monarchs best our free-born hu-
  mours suit,
But Despots must be stately, stern, and
  mute.

III.

This Solimaun, Serendib had in sway—
And where's Serendib? may some critic
  say.—
Good lack, mine honest friend, consult
  the chart,
Scare not my Pegasus before I start!
If Rennell has it not, you'll find, mayhap,
The isle laid down in Captain Sinbad's
  map,—

Famed mariner! whose merciless nar-
  rations
Drove every friend and kinsman out of
  patience,
Till, fain to find a guest who thought them
  shorter,
He deign'd to tell them over to a porter—
The last edition see, by Long. and Co.,
Rees, Hurst, and Orme, our fathers in
  the Row.

IV.

Serendib found, deem not my tale a
  fiction—
This Sultaun, whether lacking contradic-
  tion—
(A sort of stimulant which hath its uses,
To raise the spirits and reform the juices,
—Sovereign specific for all sorts of cures
In my wife's practice, and perhaps in
  yours,)
The Sultaun lacking this same wholesome
  bitter,
Or cordial smooth for prince's palate
  fitter—
Or if some Mollah had hag-rid his dreams
With Degial, Ginnistan, and such wild
  themes
Belonging to the Mollah's subtle craft,
I wot not—but the Sultaun never laugh'd,
Scarce ate or drank, and took a melancholy,
That scorn'd all remedy—profane or holy;
In his long list of melancholies, mad,
Or mazed, or dumb, hath Burton none so
  bad.*

V.

Physicians soon arrived, sage, ware, and
  tried,
  As e'er scrawl'd jargon in a darken'd
    room;
With heedful glance the Sultaun's tongue
  they eyed,
Peep'd in his bath, and God knows where
  beside,
  And then in solemn accent spoke their
    doom.

* See Burton, *Anatomy of Melancholy.*

" His Majesty is very far from well."
Then each to work with his specific fell:
The Hakim Ibrahım *instanter* brought
His unguent Mahazzim al Zerdukkaut,
While Roompot, a practitioner more wily,
Relied on his Munaskıf al fillfily.
More and yet more ın deep array appear,
And some the front assail, and some the
    rear ;
Their remedies to reinforce·and vary,
Came surgeon eke, and eke apothecary ;
Till the tired Monarch, though of words
    grown chary,
Yet dropt, to recompense their fruitless
    labour,
Some hint about a bowstring or a sabre. ·
There lack'd, I promıse you, no longer
    speeches
To rid the palace of those learned leeches.

VI.

Then was the council call'd—by their
    advice,
(They deem'd the matter ticklish all, and
    nice,
    And sought to shift it off from their own
      shoulders,)
Tartars and couriers in all speed were sent,
To call a sort of Eastern Parliament
Of feudatory chieftains and freeholders —
Such have the Persians at this very day,
My gallant Malcolm calls them *cou-
    roultai ;—*
I'm not prepared to show in this slight
    song
That to Serendib the same forms belong,—
E'en let the learn'd go search, and tell me
    if I'm wrong.

VII.

The Omrahs, each with hand on scymitar,
Gave, like Sempronius, still their voice for
    war—
" The sabre of the Sultaun in its sheath
Too long has slept, nor own'd the work
    of death ;
Let the Tambourgi bid his signal rattle,
Bang the loud gong, and raise the shout
    of battle !

This dreary cloud that dims our sove-
    reign's day,
Shall from hıs kindled bosom flit away,
When the bold Lootie wheels his courser
    round,
And the arm'd elephant shall shake the
    ground.
Each noble pants to own the glorious
    summons—
And for the charges—Lo! your faithful
    Commons !"
The Riots who attended in their places
    (Serendib language calls a farmer Riot)
Look'd ruefully in one another's faces,
    From this oration auguring much dis-
      quiet,
Double assessment, forage, and free
    quarters ;
And fearing these as China-men the
    Tartars,
Or as the whisker'd vermin fear the
    mousers,
Each fumbled in the pocket of his
    trowsers.

VIII.

And next came forth the reverend Con-
    vocation,
    Bald heads, white beards, and many a
      turban green,
Imaum and Mollah there of every station,
    Santon, Fakir, and Calendar were seen.
Their votes were various—some advised a
    Mosque
    With fitting revenues should be erected,
With seemly gardens and with gay
    Kiosque,
    To recreate a band of priests selected ;
Others opined that through the realms a
    dole
    Be made to holy men, whose prayers
      might profit
The Sultaun's weal in body and in soul.
    But their long-headed chief, the Sheik
      Ul-Sofit,
More closely touch'd the point :—" Thy
    studious mood,"
Quoth he, " O Prince! hath thicken'd all
    thy blood,

And dull'd thy brain with labour beyond
measure;
Wherefore relax a space and take thy
pleasure,
And toy with beauty, or tell o'er thy
treasure;
From all the cares of state, my Liege,
enlarge thee,
And leave the burden to thy faithful
clergy."

IX.

These counsels sage availed not a whit,
And so the patient (as is not uncommon
Where grave physicians lose their time
and wit)
Resolved to take advice of an old
woman;
His mother she, a dame who once was
beauteous,
And still was called so by each subject
duteous.
Now, whether Fatima was witch in earnest,
Or only made believe, I cannot say—
But she profess'd to cure disease the
sternest,
By dint of magic amulet or lay;
And, when all other skill in vain was shown,
She deem'd it fitting time to use her own.

X.

" *Sympathia magica* hath wonders done,"
(Thus did old Fatima bespeak her son,)
" It works upon the fibres and the pores,
And thus, insensibly, our health restores,
And it must help us here.—Thou must
endure
The ill, my son, or travel for the cure.
Search land and sea, and get, where'er
you can,
The inmost vesture of a happy man,
I mean his SHIRT, my son; which, taken
warm
And fresh from off his back, shall chase
your harm,
Bid every current of your veins rejoice,
And your dull heart leap light as shep-
herd-boy's."
Such was the counsel from his mother
came;—
I know not if she had some under-game,

As Doctors have, who bid their patients
roam
And live abroad, when sure to die at
home;
Or if she thought, that, somehow or
another,
Queen-Regent sounded better than Queen-
Mother;
But, says the Chronicle (who will go
look it,)
That such was her advice—the Sultaun
took it.

XI.

All are on board—the Sultaun and his
train,
In gilded galley prompt to plough the
main.
The old Rais* was the first who ques-
tioned, " Whither?"
They paused—" Arabia," thought the
pensive Prince,
" Was call'd The Happy many ages
since—
For Mokha, Rais."—And they came
safely thither.
But not in Araby, with all her balm,
Not where Judea weeps beneath her
palm,
Not in rich Egypt, not in Nubian waste,
Could there the step of happiness be
traced.
One Copt alone profess'd to have seen
her smile,
When Bruce his goblet fill'd at infant
Nile:
She bless'd the dauntless traveller as he
quaff'd,
But vanish'd from him with the ended
draught.

XII.

" Enough of turbans," said the weary
King,
" These dolimans of ours are not the
thing;

---

* Sea captain.

Try we the Giaours, these men of coat
   and cap, I
Incline to think some of them must be
   happy;
At least, they have as fair a cause as any
   can,
They drink good wine and keep no
   Ramazan.
Then northward, ho!"—The vessel cuts
   the sea,
And fair Italia lies upon her lee.—
But fair Italia, she who once unfurl'd
Her eagle banners o'er a conquer'd world,
Long from her throne of domination
   tumbled,
Lay, by her quondam vassals, sorely
   humbled;
The Pope himself look'd pensive, pale,
   and lean,
And was not half the man he once had
   been.
" While these the priest and those the
   noble fleeces,
Our poor old boot," they said, " is torn
   to pieces.
Its tops the vengeful claws of Austria feel,
And the Great Devil is rending toe and
   heel.
If happiness you seek, to tell you truly,
We think she dwells with one Giovanni
   Bulli;
A tramontane, a heretic,—the buck,
Poffaredio! still has all the luck;
By land or ocean never strikes his flag—
And then—a perfect walking money-
   bag."
Off set our Prince to seek John Bull's
   abode,
But first took France—it lay upon the
   road.

XIII.

Monsieur Baboon, after much late com-
   motion,
Was agitated like a settling ocean,
Quite out of sorts, and could not tell
   what ail'd him,
Only the glory of his house had fail'd
   him;

Besides, some tumours on his noddle
   biding,
Gave indication of a recent hiding.
Our Prince, though Sultauns of such
   things are heedless,
Thought it a thing indelicate and needless
   To ask, if at that moment he was happy.
And Monsieur, seeing that he was *comme
   il faut*, a
Loud voice muster'd up, for "*Vive le
   Roi!*"
  Then whisper'd, " Ave you any news
   of Nappy?"
The Sultaun answer'd him with a cross
   question,—
" Pray, can you tell me aught of one
   John Bull,
That dwells somewhere beyond your
   herring-pool?"
The query seem'd of difficult digestion,
The party shrugg'd, and grinn'd, and
   took his snuff,
And found his whole good-breeding
   scarce enough.

XIV.

Twitching his visage into as many puckers
As damsels wont to put into their tuckers,
(Ere liberal Fashion damn'd both lace
   and lawn,
And bade the veil of modesty be drawn,)
Replied the Frenchman, after a brief
   pause,
" Jean Bool!—I vas not know him—Yes,
   I vas—
I vas remember dat, von year or two,
I saw him at von place call'd Vaterloo—
Ma foi! il s'est tres joliment battu,
Dat is for Englishman,—m'entendez-
   vous?
But den he had wit him one damn son-
   gun,
Rogue I no like—dey call him Vellington."
Monsieur's politeness could not hide his
   fret,
So Solimaun took leave, and cross'd the
   strait.

XV.

John Bull was in his very worst of moods,
Raving of sterile farms and unsold goods;

His sugar-loaves and bales about he
  threw,
And on his counter beat the devil's tattoo.
His wars were ended, and the victory
  won,
But then, 'twas reckoning-day with
  honest John;
And authors vouch, 'twas still this
  Worthy's way,
" Never to grumble till he came to pay;
And then he always thinks, his temper's
  such,
The work too little, and the pay too
  much."

Yet, grumbler as he is, so kind and
  hearty,
That when his mortal foe was on the floor,
And past the power to harm his quiet
  more,
  Poor John had wellnigh wept for
  Bonaparte!
Such was the wight whom Solimaun
  salam'd,—
" And who are you," John answer'd,
  " and be d—d!"

XVI.

" A stranger, come to see the happiest
  man,—
So, signior, all avouch,—in Frangistan."—
" Happy? my tenants breaking on my
  hand;
Unstock'd my pastures, and untill'd my
  land;
Sugar and rum a drug, and mice and
  moths
The sole consumers of my good broad-
  cloths—
Happy?—Why, cursed war and racking
  tax
Have left us scarcely raiment to our
  backs."—
" In that case, signior, I may take my
  leave;
I came to ask a favour—but I grieve"——
" Favour?" said John, and eyed the
  Sultaun hard,
" It's my belief you come to break the
  yard!—

But, stay, you look like some poor
  foreign sinner,—
Take that to buy yourself a shirt and
  dinner."—
With that he chuck'd a guinea at his
  head;
But, with due dignity, the Sultaun said,
" Permit me, sir, your bounty to decline;
A *shirt* indeed I seek, but none of thine.
Signior, I kiss your hands, so fare you
  well."—
" Kiss and be d—d," quoth John, " and
  go to hell!"

XVII.

Next door to John there dwelt his sister
  Peg,
Once a wild lass as ever shook a leg
When the blithe bagpipe blew—but,
  soberer now,
She *doucely* span her flax and milk'd her
  cow.
And whereas erst she was a needy slattern,
Nor now of wealth or cleanliness a pattern,
Yet once a-month her house was partly
  swept,
And once a-week a plenteous board she
  kept.
And whereas, eke, the vixen used her
  claws
  And teeth, of yore, on slender provo-
  cation,
She now was grown amenable to laws,
  A quiet soul as any in the nation;
The sole remembrance of her warlike
  joys
Was in old songs she sang to please her
  boys.
John Bull, whom, in their years of early
  strife,
She wont to lead a cat-and-doggish life,
Now found the woman, as he said, a
  neighbour,
Who look'd to the main chance, declined
  no labour,
Loved a long grace, and spoke a northern
  jargon,
And was d—d close in making or a
  bargain.

XVIII.

The Sultaun enter'd, and he made his leg,
And with decorum curtsy'd sister Peg;
(She loved a book, and knew a thing or
     two,
And guess'd at once with whom she had
     to do.)
She bade him " Sit into the fire," and
     took
Her dram, her cake, her kebbuck from
     the nook;
Ask'd him " about the news from Eastern
     parts;
And of her absent bairns, puir Highland
     hearts!
If peace brought down the price of tea
     and pepper,
And if the *nitmugs* were grown *ony*
     cheaper;—
Were there nae *speerings* of our Mungo
     Park—
Ye'll be the gentleman that wants the
     sark!
If ye wad buy a web o' auld wife's
     spinnin',
I'll warrant ye it's a weel-wearing linen."

XIX.

Then up got Peg, and round the house
     'gan scuttle
In search of goods her customer to nail,
Until the Sultaun strain'd his princely
     throttle,
     And hollo'd—" Ma'am, that is not
     what I ail.
Pray, are you happy, ma'am, in this snug
     glen?"—
" Happy?" said Peg; " What for d'ye
     want to ken?
Besides, just think upon this by-gane year,
     Grain wadna pay the yoking of the
     pleugh."—
" What say you to the present?"—
     " Meal's sae dear,
     To mak' their *brose* my bairns have
     scarce aneugh."—
" The devil take the shirt," said Solimaun,
" I think my quest will end as it began.—

Farewell, ma'am; nay, no ceremony, I
     beg"——
" Ye'll no be for the linen then?" said
     Peg.

XX.

Now, for the land of verdant Erin,
The Sultaun's royal bark is steering,
The Emerald Isle, where honest Paddy
     dwells,
The cousin of John Bull, as story tells.
For a long space had John, with words
     of thunder,
Hard looks, and harder knocks, kept
     Paddy under,
Till the poor lad, like boy that's flogg'd
     unduly,
Had gotten somewhat restive and unruly.
Hard was his lot and lodging, you'll
     allow,
A wigwam that would hardly serve a
     sow;
His landlord, and of middle-men two
     brace,
Had screw'd his rent up to the starving-
     place;
His garment was a top-coat, and an old
     one,
His meal was a potato, and a cold one;
But still for fun or frolic, and all that,
In the round world was not the match of
     Pat.

XXI.

The Sultaun saw him on a holiday,
Which is with Paddy still a jolly day:
When mass is ended, and his load of sins
Confess'd, and Mother Church hath from
     her binns
Dealt forth a bonus of imputed merit,
Then is Pat's time for fancy, whim, and
     spirit!
To jest, to sing, to caper fair and free,
And dance as light as leaf upon the tree.
" By Mahomet," said Sultaun Solimaun,
" That ragged fellow is our very man!
Rush in and seize him—do not do him
     hurt,
But, will he nill he, let me have his *shirt*."—

XXII.

Shilela their plan was wellnigh after
    baulking,
(Much less provocation will set it a-walk-
    ing,)
But the odds that foil'd Hercules foil'd
    Paddy Whack;
They seized, and they floor'd, and they
    stripp'd him—Alack !
Up-bubboo! Paddy had not——a shirt
    to his back ! ! !
And the King, disappointed, with sorrow
    and shame,
Went back to Serendib as sad as he came.

THE SUN UPON THE WEIRD-LAW HILL.

1817.

THE sun upon the Weirdlaw Hill,
    In Ettrick's vale, is sinking sweet ;
The westland wind is hush and still,
    The lake lies sleeping at my feet.
Yet not the landscape to mine eye
    Bears those bright hues that once it
      bore ;
Though evening, with her richest dye,
    Flames o'er the hills of Ettrick's shore.

With listless look along the plain,
    I see Tweed's silver current glide,
And coldly mark the holy fane
    Of Melrose rise in ruin'd pride.
The quiet lake, the balmy air,
    The hill, the stream, the tower, the
      tree,—
Are they still such as once they were?
    Or is the dreary change in me ?

Alas, the warp'd and broken board,
    How can it bear the painter's dye !
The harp of strain'd and tuneless chord,
    How to the minstrel's skill reply !
To aching eyes each landscape lowers,
    To feverish pulse each gale blows chill;
And Araby's or Eden's bowers
    Were barren as this moorland hill.

THE MONKS OF BANGOR'S MARCH.

AIR—" *Ymdaith Mionge.*"

WRITTEN FOR MR. GEORGE THOMSON'S
WELSH MELODIES.

1817.

ETHELFRID or OLFRID, King of Northumberland, having besieged Chester in 613, and
BROCKMAEL, a British Prince, advancing to
relieve it, the religious of the neighbouring
Monastery of Bangor marched in procession,
to pray for the success of their countrymen.
But the British being totally defeated, the
heathen victor put the monks to the sword,
and destroyed their monastery. The tune to
which these verses are adapted is called the
Monks' March, and is supposed to have been
played at their ill-omened procession.

WHEN the heathen trumpet's clang
Round beleaguer'd Chester rang,
Veiled nun and friar grey
March'd from Bangor's fair Abbaye;
High their holy anthem sounds,
Cestria's vale the hymn rebounds,
Floating down the silvan Dee,
        O miserere, Domine !

On the long procession goes,
Glory round their crosses glows,
And the Virgin-mother mild
In their peaceful banner smiled;
Who could think such saintly band
Doom'd to feel unhallow'd hand ?
Such was the Divine decree,
        O miserere, Domine !

Bands that masses only sung,
Hands that censers only swung,
Met the northern bow and bill,
Heard the war-cry wild and shrill:
Woe to Brockmael's feeble hand,
Woe to Olfrid's bloody brand,
Woe to Saxon cruelty,
        O miserere, Domine !

Weltering amid warriors slain,
Spurn'd by steeds with bloody mane,

Slaughter'd down by heathen blade,
Bangor's peaceful monks are laid ;
Word of parting rest unspoke,
Mass unsung, and bread unbroke;
For their souls for charity,
     Sing, *O miserere, Domine!*

Bangor! o'er the murder wail!
Long thy ruins told the tale,
Shatter'd towers and broken arch
Long recall'd the woful march :*
On thy shrine no tapers burn,
Never shall thy priests return ;
The pilgrim sighs, and sings for thee,
     O miserere Domine!

MOTTOES FROM ROB ROY.

CHAP. X.

In the wide pile, by others heeded not,
Hers was one sacred solitary spot,
Whose gloomy aisles and bending shelves contain,
For moral hunger food, and cures for moral pain.—*Anonymous.*

CHAP. XIII.

Dire was his thought, who first in poison steep'd
The weapon form'd for slaughter—direr his,
And worthier of damnation, who instill'd
The mortal venom in the social cup,
To fill the veins with death instead of life.—*Anonymous.*

CHAP. XXII.

Look round thee, young Astolpho : Here's the place
Which men (for being poor) are sent to starve in,—
Rude remedy, I trow, for sore disease.

Within these walls, stifled by damp and stench,
Doth Hope's fair torch expire : and at the snuff,
Ere yet 'tis quite extinct, rude, wild, and wayward,
The desperate revelries of wild despair,
Kindling their hell-born cressets, light to deeds
That the poor captive would have died ere practised,
Till bondage sunk his soul to his condition.—*The Prison, Scene* iii. *Act* i.

CHAP. XXVII.

Far as the eve could reach no tree was seen,
Earth, clad in russet, scorn'd the lively green ;
No birds, except as birds of passage, flew;
No bee was heard to hum, no dove to coo ;
No streams, as amber smooth, as amber clear,
Were seen to glide, or heard to warble here.—*Prophecy of Famine.*

CHAP. XXXI.

"Woe to the vanquish'd !" was stern Brenno's word,
When sunk proud Rome beneath the Gallic sword—
"Woe to the vanquish'd !" when his massive blade
Bore down the scale against her ransom weigh'd,
And on the field of foughten battle still,
Who knows no limit save the victor's will.—*The Gaulliad.*

CHAP. XXXII.

And be he safe restored ere evening set,
Or, if there's vengeance in an injured heart,
And power to wreak it in an arm'd hand,
Your land shall ache for't.—*Old Play.*

---

* In William of Malmsbury's time the ruins of Bangor still attested the cruelty of the Northumbrians.

CHAP. XXXVI.

Farewell to the land where the clouds love
to rest,
Like the shroud of the dead on the mountain's cold breast;
To the cataract's roar where the eagles
reply,
And the lake her lone bosom expands to
the sky.

———

MACKRIMMON'S LAMENT.
1818.

AIR—"*Cha till mi tuille.*"

Mackrimmon, hereditary piper to the Laird
of Macleod, is said to have composed this
Lament when the Clan was about to depart
upon a distant and dangerous expedition.
The Minstrel was impressed with a belief,
which the event verified, that he was to be
slain in the approaching feud; and hence the
Gaelic words, "*Cha till mi tuille; ged thillis
Macleod, cha till Mackrimmon,*" "I shall
never return; although Macleod returns, yet
Mackrimmon shall never return!" The
piece is but too well known, from its being
the strain with which the emigrants from the
West Highlands and Isles usually take leave
of their native shore.

MACLEOD'S wizard flag from the grey
castle sallies,
The rowers are seated, unmoor'd are the
galleys;
Gleam war-axe and broadsword, clang
target and quiver,
As Mackrimmon sings, "Farewell to
Dunvegan for ever!
Farewell to each cliff, on which breakers
are foaming;
Farewell each dark glen, in which red-
deer are roaming;
Farewell, lonely Skye, to lake, mountain,
and river,
Macleod may return, but Mackrimmon
shall never!

"Farewell the bright clouds that on
Quillan are sleeping;
Farewell the bright eyes in the Dun that
are weeping;

To each minstrel delusion, farewell!—and
for ever—
Mackrimmon departs, to return to you
never!
The *Banshee's* wild voice sings the death-
dirge before me,
The pall of the dead for a mantle hangs
o'er me;
But my heart shall not flag, and my
nerves shall not shiver,
Though devoted I go—to return again
never!

"Too oft shall the notes of Mackrim-
mon's bewailing
Be heard when the Gael on their exile are
sailing;
Dear land! to the shores, whence un-
willing we sever,
Return—return—return shall we never!
Cha till, cha till, cha till sin tuille!
Cha till, cha till, cha till sin tuille,
Cha till, cha till, cha till sin tuille,
Ged thillis Macleod, cha till Mack-
rimmon!"

———

DONALD CAIRD'S COME AGAIN.

AIR—"*Malcolm Caird's come again.*"

1818.

CHORUS.

DONALD CAIRD'S *come again!*
Donald Caird's come again!
Tell the news in brugh and glen,
Donald Caird's come again!

Donald Caird can lilt and sing,
Blithely dance the Highland fling,
Drink till the gudeman be blind,
Fleech till the gudewife be kind;
Hoop a leglin, clout a pan,
Or crack a pow wi' ony man;
Tell the news in brugh and glen,
Donald Caird's come again.

Donald Caird's come again!
Donald Caird's come again!
Tell the news in brugh and glen,
Donald Caird's come again.

Donald Caird can wire a maukin,
Kens the wiles o' dun-deer staukin',
Leisters kipper, makes a shift
To shoot a muir-fowl in the drift;
Water-bailiffs, rangers, keepers,
He can wauk when they are sleepers;
Not for bountith or reward
Dare ye mell wi' Donald Caird.

 Donald Caird's come again!
 Donald Caird's come again!
 Gar the bagpipes hum amain,
 Donald Caird's come again.

Donald Caird can drink a gill
Fast as hostler-wife can fill;
Ilka ane that sells gude liquor
Kens how Donald bends a bicker;
When he's fou he's stout and saucy,
Keeps the cantle o' the cawsey;
Hieland chief and Lawland laird
Maun gie room to Donald Caird!

 Donald Caird's come again!
 Donald Caird's come again!
 Tell the news in brugh and glen,
 Donald Caird's come again.

Steek the amrie, lock the kist,
Else some gear may weel be mis't;
Donald Caird finds orra things
Where Allan Gregor fand the tings;
Dunts of Kebbuck, taits o' woo,
Whiles a hen and whiles a sow,
Webs or duds frae hedge or yard—
'Ware the wuddie, Donald Caird!

 Donald Caird's come again!
 Donald Caird's come again
 Dinna let the Shirra ken
 Donald Caird's come again.

On Donald Caird the doom was stern,
Craig to tether, legs to airn;
But Donald Caird, wi' mickle study,
Caught the gift to cheat the wuddie;
Rings of airn, and bolts of steel,
Fell like ice frae hand and heel!
Watch the sheep in fauld and glen,
Donald Caird's come again!

 Donald Caird's come again!
 Donald Caird's come again!
 Dinna let the Justice ken
 Donald Caird's come again.

---

from the Heart of Mid-Lothian.

1818.

MADGE WILDFIRE'S SONGS.

When the gledd's in the blue cloud,
 The lavrock lies still;
When the hound's in the green-wood,
 The hind keeps the hill.

O sleep ye sound, Sir James, she said,
 When ye suld rise and ride?
There's twenty men, wi' bow and blade,
 Are seeking where ye hide.

Hey for cavaliers, ho for cavaliers,
 Dub a dub, dub a dub;
 Have at old Beëlzebub,—
Oliver's running for fear.—

I glance like the wildfire through country
 and town;
I'm seen on the causeway—I'm seen on
 the down;
The lightning that flashes so bright and
 so free,
Is scarcely so blithe or so bonny as me.

What did ye wi' the bridal ring—bridal
 ring—bridal ring?
What did ye wi' your wedding ring, ye
 little cutty quean, O?
I gied it till a sodger, a sodger, a sodger,
I gied it till a sodger, an auld true love o'
 mine, O.

Good even, good fair moon, good even to
 thee;
I prithee, dear moon, now show to me
The form and the features, the speech and
 degree,
Of the man that true lover of mine shall be.

It is the bonny butcher lad,
　That wears the sleeves of blue,
He sells the flesh on Saturday,
　On Friday that he slew.

———

There's a bloodhound ranging Tinwald
　Wood,
　There's harness glancing sheen;
There's a maiden sits on Tinwald brae,
　And she sings loud between.

———

Up in the air,
On my bonnie grey mare,
And I see, and I see, and I see her yet.

———

In the bonnie cells of Bedlam,
　Ere I was ane and twenty,
I had hempen bracelets strong,
　And merry whips, ding-dong,
　And prayers and fasting plenty.

———

My banes are buried in yon kirk-yard
　Sae far ayont the sea,
And it is but my blithsome ghaist
　That's speaking now to thee.

———

I'm Madge of the country, I'm Madge of
　the town,
And I'm Madge of the lad I am blithest
　to own—
The Lady of Beever in diamonds may
　shine,
But has not a heart half so lightsome as
　mine.

———

I am Queen of the Wake, and I'm Lady
　of May,
And I lead the blithe ring round the May-
　pole to-day;
The wild-fire that flashes so fair and so
　free
Was never so bright, or so bonnie as me.

———

Our work is over—over now,
The goodman wipes his weary brow,
The last long wain wends slow away,
And we are free to sport and play.

The night comes on when sets the sun,
And labour ends when day is done.
When Autumn's gone, and Winter's
　come,
We hold our jovial harvest-home.

———

When the fight of grace is fought,—
When the marriage vest is wrought,—
When Faith has chased cold Doubt
　away,—
And Hope but sickens at delay,—
When Charity, imprisoned here,
Longs for a more expanded sphere;
Doff thy robe of sin and clay;
Christian, rise, and come away.

———

Cauld is my bed, Lord Archibald,
　And sad my sleep ot sorrow:
But thine sall be as sad and cauld,
　My fause true-love! to-morrow.

And weep ye not, my maidens free,
　Though death your mistress borrow;
For he for whom I die to-day,
　Shall die for me to-morrow.

———

Proud Maisie is in the wood,
　Walking so early;
Sweet Robin sits on the bush,
　Singing so rarely.

" Tell me, thou bonny bird,
　When shall I marry me?"—
" When six braw gentlemen
　Kirkward shall carry ye."

" Who makes the bridal bed,
　Birdie, say truly?"—
" The grey-headed sexton
　That delves the grave duly.

" The glow-worm o'er grave and stone
　Shall light thee steady.
The owl from the steeple sing,
　' Welcome, proud lady.'"

———

From the Bride of Lammermoor.

1819.

LUCY ASHTON'S SONG.

LOOK not thou on beauty's charming,—
Sit thou still when kings are arming,—
Taste not when the wine-cup glistens,—
Speak not when the people listens,—
Stop thine ear against the singer,——
From the red gold keep thy finger,—
Vacant heart, and hand, and eye,
Easy live and quiet die.—*Chap.* iii.

NORMAN THE FORESTER'S SONG.

THE monk must arise when the matins
    ring,
    The abbot may sleep to their chime;
But the yeoman must start when the
    bugles sing,
    'Tis time, my hearts, 'tis time.

There's bucks and raes on Billhope braes,
    There's a herd on Shortwood Shaw;
But a lily white doe in the garden goes,
    She's fairly worth them a'.—*Chap.* iii.

MOTTOES.

CHAP. XIV.

As, to the Autumn breeze's bugle-sound,
Various and vague the dry leaves dance
    their round;
Or, from the garner-door, on æther borne,
The chaff flies devious from the winnow'd
    corn;
So vague, so devious, at the breath of
    heaven,
From their fix'd aim are mortal counsels
    driven.—*Anonymous.*

CHAP. XVII.

—— Here is a father now,
Will truck his daugher for a foreign ven-
    ture,
Make her a stop-gap to some canker'd
    feud,

Or fling her o'er, like Jonah, to the fishes,
To appease the sea at highest.—
                                Anonymous.

CHAP. XVIII.

Sir, stay at home and take an old man's
    counsel;
Seek not to bask you by a stranger's hearth;
Our own blue smoke is warmer than their
    fire.
Domestic food is wholesome, though 'tis
    homely,
And foreign dainties poisonous, though
    tasteful.—*The French Courtezan.*

CHAP. XXV.

True-love, an' thou be true,
    Thou hast ane kittle part to play,
For fortune, fashion, fancy, and thou
    Maun strive for many a day.

I've kend by mony friend's tale,
    Far better by this heart of mine,
What time and change of fancy avail
    A true love-knote to untwine.—
                                Hendersoun.

CHAP. XXVII.

Why, now I have Dame Fortune by the
    forelock,
And if she 'scapes my grasp, the fault is
    mine;
He that hath buffeted with stern adversity,
Best knows to shape his course to favour-
    ing breezes.—*Old Play.*

From the Legend of Montrose.

ANNOT LYLE'S SONGS.

I.

BIRDS of omen dark and foul,
Night-crow, raven, bat, and owl,
Leave the sick man to his dream—
All night long he heard you scream.
Haste to cave and ruin'd tower,
Ivy tod, or dingled-bower,

There to wink and mope, for, hark!
In the mid air sings the lark.

II.

Hie to moorish gills and rocks,
Prowling wolf and wily fox,—
Hie ye fast, nor turn your view,
Though the lamb bleats to the ewe.
Couch your trains, and speed your flight,
Safety parts with parting night;
And on distant echo borne,
Comes the hunter's early horn.

III.

The moon's wan crescent scarcely gleams,
Ghost-like she fades in morning beams;
Hie hence, each peevish imp and fay
That scare the pilgrim on his way.—
Quench, kelpy! quench, in fog and fen,
Thy torch, that cheats benighted men;
Thy dance is o'er, thy reign is done,
For Benyieglo hath seen the sun.

IV.

Wild thoughts, that, sinful, dark, and deep,
O'erpower the passive mind in sleep,
Pass from the slumberer's soul away:
Like night-mists from the brow of day:
Foul hag, whose blasted visage grim
Smothers the pulse, unnerves the limb,
Spur thy dark palfrey, and begone!
Thou darest not face the godlike sun.
Chap. vi.

THE ORPHAN MAID.

NOVEMBER's hail-cloud drifts away,
November's sun-beam wan
Looks coldly on the castle grey,
When forth comes Lady Anne.

The orphan by the oak was set,
Her arms, her feet, were bare;
The hail-drops had not melted yet,
Amid her raven hair.

"And, dame," she said, "by all the ties
That child and mother know,
Aid one who never knew these joys,—
Relieve an orphan's woe."

The lady said, "An orphan's state
Is hard and sad to bear;
Yet worse the widow'd mother's fate,
Who mourns both lord and heir.

"Twelve times the rolling year has sped,
Since, while from vengeance wild
Of fierce Strathallan's chief I fled,
Forth's eddies whelm'd my child."—

"Twelve times the year its course has borne,"
The wandering maid replied;
"Since fishers on St. Bridget's morn
Drew nets on Campsie side.

"St. Bridget sent no scaly spoil;
An infant, well-nigh dead,
They saved, and rear'd in want and toil,
To beg from you her bread."

That orphan maid the lady kiss'd,—
"My husband's looks you bear;
Saint Bridget and her morn be bless'd!
You are his widow's heir."

They've robed that maid, so poor and pale,
In silk and sendals rare;
And pearls, for drops of frozen hail,
Are glistening in her hair.—*Chap.* ix.

From Ivanhoe.

THE CRUSADER'S RETURN.

I.

HIGH deeds achieved of knightly fame,
From Palestine the champion came;
The cross upon his shoulders borne,
Battle and blast had dimm'd and torn.
Each dint upon his batter'd shield
Was token of a foughten field;
And thus, beneath his lady's bower,
He sung, as fell the twilight hour:

II.

"Joy to the fair!—thy knight behold,
Return'd from yonder land of gold;

No wealth he brings, no wealth can need,
Save his good arms and battle-steed;
His spurs to dash against a foe,
His lance and sword to lay him low;
Such all the trophies of his toil,
Such—and the hope of Tekla's smile!

III.

" Joy to the fair! whose constant knight
Her favour fired to feats of might!
Unnoted shall she not remain
Where meet the bright and noble train;
Minstrel shall sing, and herald tell—
' Mark yonder maid of beauty well,
'Tis she for whose bright eyes was won
The listed field of Ascalon!

IV.

" ' Note well her smile!—it edged the blade
Which fifty wives to widows made,
When, vain his strength and Mahound's spell,
Iconium's turban'd Soldan fell.
See'st thou her locks, whose sunny glow
Half shows, half shades, her neck of snow?
Twines not of them one golden thread,
But for its sake a Paynim bled.'

V.

" Joy to the fair!—my name unknown,
Each deed, and all its praise, thine own;
Then, oh! unbar this churlish gate,
The night-dew falls, the hour is late.
Inured to Syria's glowing breath,
I feel the north breeze chill as death;
Let grateful love quell maiden shame,
And grant him bliss who brings thee fame."
                                    Chap. xviii.

THE BAREFOOTED FRIAR.

I.

I'LL give thee, good fellow, a twelvemonth or twain,
To search Europe through from Byzantium to Spain;
But ne'er shall you find, should you search till you tire,
So happy a man as the Barefooted Friar.

II.

Your knight for his lady pricks forth in career,
And is brought home at even-song prick'd through with a spear;
I confess him in haste—for his lady desires
No comfort on earth save the Barefooted Friar's.

III.

Your monarch!—Pshaw! many a prince has been known
To barter his robes for our cowl and our gown;
But which of us e'er felt the idle desire
To exchange for a crown the grey hood of a Friar?

IV.

The Friar has walk'd out, and where'er he has gone,
The land and its fatness is mark'd for his own;
He can roam where he lists, he can stop where he tires,
For every man's house is the Barefooted Friar's.

V.

He's expected at noon, and no wight, till he comes,
May profane the great chair, or the porridge of plums;
For the best of the cheer, and the seat by the fire,
Is the undenied right of the Barefooted Friar.

VI.

He's expected at night, and the pasty's made hot,
They broach the brown ale, and they fill the black pot;
And the good-wife would wish the goodman in the mire,
Ere he lack'd a soft pillow, the Barefooted Friar.

VII.

Long flourish the sandal, the cord, and
 the cope,
The dread of the devil and trust of the
 Pope!
For to gather life's roses unscathed by
 the briar
Is granted alone to the Barefooted Friar.
     Chap. xviii.

SAXON WAR-SONG.

I.

WHET the bright steel,
Sons of the White Dragon!
Kindle the torch,
Daughter of Hengist!
The steel glimmers not for the carving of
 the banquet,
It is hard, broad, and sharply pointed;
The torch goeth not to the bridal chamber,
It steams and glitters blue with sulphur.
Whet the steel, the raven croaks!
Light the torch, Zernebock is yelling!
Whet the steel, sons of the Dragon!
Kindle the torch, daughter of Hengist!

II.

The black clouds are low over the thane's
 castle:
The eagle screams—he rides on their
 bosom.
Scream not, grey rider of the sable cloud,
Thy banquet is prepared!
The maidens of Valhalla look forth,
The race of Hengist will send them guests.
Shake your black tresses, maidens of
 Valhalla!
And strike your loud timbrels for joy!
Many a haughty step bends to your halls,
Many a helmed head.

III.

Dark sits the evening upon the thane's
 castle,
The black clouds gather round;
Soon shall they be red as the blood of the
 valiant!
The destroyer of forests shall shake his
 red crest against them;

He, the bright consumer of palaces,
Broad waves he his blazing banner,
Red, wide, and dusky,
Over the strife of the valiant;
His joy is in the clashing swords and
 broken bucklers;
He loves to lick the hissing blood as it
 bursts warm from the wound!

IV.

All must perish!
The sword cleaveth the helmet;
The strong armour is pierced by the lance:
Fire devoureth the dwelling of princes,
Engines break down the fences of the
 battle.
All must perish!
The race of Hengist is gone—
The name of Horsa is no more!
Shrink not then from your doom, sons of
 the sword!
Let your blades drink blood like wine;
Feast ye in the banquet of slaughter,
By the light of the blazing halls!
Strong be your swords while your blood
 is warm,
And spare neither for pity nor fear,
For vengeance hath but an hour;
Strong hate itself shall expire!
I also must perish.

Note.—" It will readily occur to the antiquary, that these verses are intended to imitate
the antique poetry of the Scalds—the minstrels of the old Scandinavians—the race, as the
Laureate so happily terms them,

" Stern to inflict, and stubborn to endure,
 Who smiled in death."

The poetry of the Anglo-Saxons, after their
civilization and conversion, was of a different
and softer character; but, in the circumstances of Ulrica, she may be not unnaturally
supposed to return to the wild strains which
animated her forefathers during the times of
Paganism and untamed ferocity."
     Chap. xxxii.

REBECCA'S HYMN.

WHEN Israel, of the Lord beloved,
 Out from the land of bondage came,

Her fathers' God before her moved,
  An awful guide in smoke and flame.
By day, along the astonish'd lands
  The clouded pillar glided slow;
By night, Arabia's crimson'd sands
  Return'd the fiery column's glow.

There rose the choral hymn of praise,
  And trump and timbrel answer'd keen,
And Zion's daughters pour'd their lays,
  With priest's and warrior's voice between.
No portents now our foes amaze,
  Forsaken Israel wanders lone:
Our fathers would not know THY ways,
  And THOU hast left them to their own.

But present still, though now unseen!
  When brightly shines the prosperous day,
Be thoughts of THEE a cloudy screen
  To temper the deceitful ray.
And oh, when stoops on Judah's path
  In shade and storm the frequent night,
Be THOU, long-suffering, slow to wrath,
  A burning and a shining light!

Our harps we left by Babel's streams,
  The tyrant's jest, the Gentile's scorn;
No censer round our altar beams,
  And mute are timbrel, harp, and horn.
But THOU hast said, The blood of goat,
  The flesh of rams I will not prize;
A contrite heart, a humble thought,
  Are mine accepted sacrifice.—*Chap.* xl.

THE BLACK KNIGHT'S SONG
OR VIRELAI.

ANNA-MARIE, love, up is the sun,
Anna-Marie, love, morn is begun,
Mists are dispersing, love, birds singing free,
Up in the morning, love, Anna-Marie.
Anna-Marie, love, up in the morn,
The hunter is winding blithe sounds on his horn,
The echo rings merry from rock and from tree.
'Tis time to arouse thee, love, Anna-Marie.

WAMBA.

O Tybalt, love, Tybalt, awake me not yet,
Around my soft pillow while softer dreams flit;
For what are the joys that in waking we prove,
Compared with these visions, O Tybalt! my love?
Let the birds to the rise of the mist carol shrill,
Let the hunter blow out his loud horn on the hill,
Softer sounds, softer pleasures, in slumber I prove,
But think not I dream'd of thee, Tybalt, my love.—*Chap.* xli.

SONG.

DUET BETWEEN THE BLACK KNIGHT AND WAMBA.

THERE came three merry men from south, west, and north,
  Ever more sing the roundelay;
To win the Widow of Wycombe forth,
  And where was the widow might say them nay?

The first was a knight, and from Tynedale he came,
  Ever more sing the roundelay;
And his fathers, God save us, were men of great fame,
  And where was the widow might say him nay?

Of his father the laird, of his uncle the squire,
  He boasted in rhyme and in roundelay;
She bade him go bask by his sea-coal fire,
  For she was the widow would say him nay.

WAMBA.

The next that came forth, swore by blood and by nails,
  Merrily sing the roundelay;
Hur's a gentleman, God wot, and hur's lineage was of Wales,
  And where was the widow might say him nay?

Sir David ap Morgan ap Griffith ap Hugh
  Ap Tudor ap Rhice, quoth his roun-
    delay;
She said that one widow for so many was
  too few,
And she bade the Welshman wend his
  way.

But then next came a yeoman, a yeoman
  of Kent,
  Jollily singing his roundelay;
He spoke to the widow of living and
  rent,
And where was a widow could say him
  nay.

BOTH.

So the knight and the squire were both
  left in the mire,
  There for to sing their roundelay;
For a yeoman of Kent, with his yearly
  rent,
  There ne'er was a widow could say him
nay.—*Chap.* xli.

FUNERAL HYMN.

DUST unto dust,
To this all must;
  The tenant has resign'd
The faded form
To waste and worm—
  Corruption claims her kind.

Through paths unknown
Thy soul hath flown,
  To seek the realms of woe,
Where fiery pain
Shall purge the stain
  Of actions done below.

In that sad place,
By Mary's grace,
  Brief may thy dwelling be;
Till prayers and alms,
And holy psalms,
  Shall set the captive free.
            Chap. xliii.

MOTTOES

CHAP. XXXI.

APPROACH the chamber, look upon his
  bed.
His is the passing of no peaceful ghost,
Which, as the lark arises to the sky,
'Mid morning's sweetest breeze and softest
  dew,
Is wing'd to heaven by good men's sighs
  and tears!
Anselm parts otherwise.—*Old Play.*

CHAP. XXXIII.

Trust me, each state must have its policies:
Kingdoms have edicts, cities have their
  charters;
Even the wild outlaw, in his forest-walk,
Keeps yet some touch of civil discipline.
For not since Adam wore his verdant
  apron,
Hath man with man in social union dwelt,
But laws were made to draw the union
  closer.—*Old Play.*

CHAP. XXXVI.

Arouse the tiger of Hyrcanian deserts,
Strive with the half-starved lion for his
  prey;
Lesser the risk, than rouse the slumbering
  fire
Of wild Fanaticism.—*Anonymous.*

CHAP. XXXVII.

Say not my art is fraud—all live by
  seeming.
The beggar begs with it, and the gay
  courtier
Gains land and title, rank and rule, by
  seeming:
The clergy scorn it not, and the bold soldier
Will eke with it his service.—All admit it,
All practise it; and he who is content
With showing what he is, shall have small
  credit
In church, or camp, or state.—So wags
  the world.—*Old Play.*

CHAP. XXXVIII.

Stern was the law which bade its vot'ries
     leave
At human woes with human hearts to
     grieve;
Stern was the law, which at the winning
     wile
Of frank and harmless mirth forbade to
     smile;
But sterner still, when high the iron rod
Of tyrant power she shook, and call'd that
     power of God."—*The Middle Ages.*

From the Monastery.

1820.

SONGS OF THE WHITE LADY
OF AVENEL.

ON TWEED RIVER.

I.

MERRILY swim we, the moon shines
     bright,
Both current and ripple are dancing in
     light.
We have roused the night raven, I heard
     him croak,
As we plashed along beneath the oak
That flings its broad branches so far and
     so wide,
Their shadows are dancing in midst of
     the tide.
" Who wakens my nestlings?" the raven,
     he said,
" My beak shall ere morn in his blood be
     red !
For a blue swollen corpse is a dainty meal,
And I'll have my share with the pike and
     the eel."

II.

Merrily swim we, the moon shines bright,
There's a golden gleam on the distant
     height :
There's a silver shower on the alders
     dank,
And the drooping willows that wave on
     the bank.

I see the Abbey, both turret and tower,
It is all astir for the vesper hour;
The Monks for the chapel are leaving each
     cell,
But where 's Father Philip should toll the
     bell ?

III.

Merrily swim we, the moon shines bright,
Downward we drift through shadow and
     light ;
Under yon rock the eddies sleep,
Calm and silent, dark and deep.
The Kelpy has risen from the fathomless
     pool,
He has lighted his candle of death and of
     dool :
Look, Father, look, and you'll laugh to see
How he gapes and glares with his eyes on
     thee !

IV.

Good luck to your fishing, whom watch
     ye to-night ?
A man of mean or a man of might ?
Is it layman or priest that must float in
     your cove,
Or lover who crosses to visit his love ?
Hark ! heard ye the Kelpy reply as we
     pass'd,—
" God's blessing on the warder, he lock'd
     the bridge fast !
All that come to my cove are sunk,
Priest or layman, lover or monk."

Landed—landed ! the black book hath
     won,
Else had you seen Berwick with morning
     sun !
Sain ye, and save ye, and blithe mot ye be,
For seldom they land that go swimming
     with me.—*Chap.* v.

TO THE SUB-PRIOR.

GOOD evening, Sir Priest, and so late as
     you ride,
With your mule so fair, and your mantle
     so wide;

But ride you through valley, or ride you
    o'er hill,
There is one that has warrant to wait on
    you still.
      Back, back,
      The volume black!
I have a warrant to carry it back.

What, ho! Sub-Prior, and came you but
    here
To conjure a book from a dead woman's
    bier?
Sain you, and save you, be wary and wise,
Ride back with the book, or you'll pay
    for your prize.
      Back, back,
      There's death in the track!
In the name of my master, I bid thee bear
    back.

"In the name of MY Master," said the
astonished Monk, "that name before
which all things created tremble, I conjure thee to say what thou art that
hauntest me thus?"

  The same voice replied,—

That which is neither ill nor well,
That which belongs not to heaven nor to
    hell,
A wreath of the mist, a bubble of the
    stream,
'Twixt a waking thought and a sleeping
    dream;
      A form that men spy
      With the half-shut eye
In the beams of the setting sun, am I.

Vainly, Sir Prior, wouldst thou bar me
    my right!
Like the star when it shoots, I can dart
    through the night;
I can dance on the torrent, and ride on
    the air,
And travel the world with the bonny
    night-mare.
      Again, again,
      At the crook of the glen,
Where bickers the burnie, I'll meet thee
    again.

Men of good are bold as sackless,*
Men of rude are wild and reckless,
    Lie thou still
    In the nook of the hill,
For those be before thee that wish thee ill.
          Chap. ix.

HALBERT'S INVOCATION.

  THRICE to the holly brake—
    Thrice to the well:—
I bid thee awake,
    White Maid of Avenel!

Noon gleams on the Lake—
    Noon glows on the Fell—
Wake thee, O wake,
    White Maid of Avenel.

TO HALBERT.

YOUTH of the dark eye, wherefore didst
    thou call me?
Wherefore art thou here, if terrors can
    appal thee?
He that seeks to deal with us must know
    nor fear nor failing;
To coward and churl our speech is dark,
    our gifts are unavailing.
The breeze that brought me hither now
    must sweep Egyptian ground,
The fleecy cloud on which I ride for
    Araby is bound:
The fleecy cloud is drifting by, the breeze
    sighs for my stay,
For I must sail a thousand miles before
    the close of day.

      ———

What I am I must not show—
What I am thou couldst not know—
Something betwixt heaven and hell—
Something that neither stood nor fell—
Something that through thy wit or will
May work thee good—may work thee ill.
Neither substance quite, nor shadow,
Haunting lonely moor and meadow,
Dancing by the haunted spring,
Riding on the whirlwind's wing;

---

* *Sackless*—Innocent.

Aping in fantastic fashion
Every change of human passion,
While o'er our frozen minds they pass,
Like shadows from the mirror'd glass.
Wayward, fickle, is our mood,
Hovering betwixt bad and good,
Happier than brief-dated man,
Living ten times o'er his span;
Far less happy, for we have
Help nor hope beyond the grave!
Man awakes to joy or sorrow;
Ours the sleep that knows no morrow.
This is all that I can show—
This is all that thou may'st know.

———

Ay! and I taught thee the word and the spell,
To waken me here by the Fairies' Well.
But thou hast loved the heron and hawk,
More than to seek my haunted walk;
And thou hast loved the lance and the sword,
More than good text and holy word;
And thou hast loved the deer to track,
More than the lines and the letters black;
And thou art a ranger of moss and wood,
And scornest the nurture of gentle blood.

———

Thy craven fear my truth accused,
Thine idlehood my trust abused;
He that draws to harbour late,
Must sleep without, or burst the gate.
There is a star for thee which burn'd,
Its influence wanes, its course is turn'd;
Valour and constancy alone
Can bring thee back the chance that's flown.

———

Within that awful volume lies
The mystery of mysteries!
Happiest they of human race,
To whom God has granted grace
To read, to fear, to hope, to pray,
To lift the latch, and force the way;
And better had they ne'er been born,
Who read to doubt, or read to scorn.

———

Many a fathom dark and deep
I have laid the book to sleep;

Ethereal fires around it glowing—
Ethereal music ever flowing—
The sacred pledge of Heav'n
All things revere,
Each in his sphere,
Save man for whom 'twas giv'n:
Lend thy hand, and thou shalt spy
Things ne'er seen by mortal eye.

———

Fearest thou to go with me?
Still it is free to thee
A peasant to dwell;
Thou may'st drive the dull steer,
And chase the king's deer,
But never more come near
This haunted well.

———

Here lies the volume thou boldly hast sought;
Touch it, and take it, 'twill dearly be bought.

———

Rash thy deed,
Mortal weed
To immortal flames applying;
Rasher trust
Has thing of dust,
On his own weak worth relying:
Strip thee of such fences vain,
Strip, and prove thy luck again.

———

Mortal warp and mortal woof
Cannot brook this charmed roof;
All that mortal art hath wrought
In our cell returns to nought.
The molten gold returns to clay,
The polish'd diamond melts away;
All is altered, all is flown,
Nought stands fast but truth alone.
Not for that thy quest give o'er:
Courage! prove thy chance once more.

———

Alas! alas!
Not ours the grace
These holy characters to trace;
Idle forms of painted air,
Not to us is given to share
The boon bestow'd on Adam's race.

With patience bide,
Heaven will provide
The fitting time, the fitting guide.—
Chap. xii.

SONGS

IN HALBERT'S SECOND INTERVIEW WITH
THE WHITE LADY OF AVENEL.

THIS is the day when the fairy kind
Sit weeping alone for their hopeless lot,
And the wood-maiden sighs to the sighing
    wind,
And the mermaiden weeps in her crystal
    grot;
For this is a day that the deed was wrought,
In which we have neither part nor share,
For the children of clay was salvation
    bought,
But not for the forms of sea or air!
And ever the mortal is most forlorn,
Who meeteth our race on the Friday morn.

Daring youth! for thee it is well,
Here calling me in haunted dell,
    That thy heart has not quail'd,
    Nor thy courage fail'd,
    And that thou couldst brook
    The angry look
    Of Her of Avenel.
    Did one limb shiver,
    Or an eyelid quiver,
    Thou wert lost for ever.

Though I'm form'd from the ether blue,
And my blood is of the unfallen dew,
And thou art framed of mud and dust,
'Tis thine to speak, reply I must.

A mightier wizard far than I
Wields o'er the universe his power;
Him owns the eagle in the sky,
    The turtle in the bower.
Changeful in shape, yet mightiest still,
He wields the heart of man at will,
From ill to good, from good to ill,
    In cot and castle-tower.

Ask thy heart, whose secret cell
Is fill'd with Mary Avenel!

Ask thy pride, why scornful look
In Mary's view it will not brook?
Ask it, why thou seek'st to rise
Among the mighty and the wise,—
Why thou spurn'st thy lowly lot,—
Why thy pastimes are forgot,—
Why thou wouldst in bloody strife
Mend thy luck or lose thy life?
Ask thy heart, and it shall tell,
Sighing from its secret cell,
'Tis for Mary Avenel.

Do not ask me;
On doubts like these thou canst not task me.
We only see the passing show
Of human passions' ebb and flow;
And view the pageants idle glance
As mortals eye the northern dance,
When thousand streamers, flashing bright,
Career it o'er the brow of night,
And gazers mark their changeful gleams,
But feel no influence from their beams.

By ties mysterious link'd, our fated race
Holds strange connection with the sons
    of men.
The star that rose upon the House of
    Avenel,
When Norman Ulric first assumed the
    name,
That star, when culminating in its orbit,
Shot from its sphere a drop of diamond
    dew,
And this bright font received it—and a
    Spirit
Rose from the fountain, and her date of life
Hath co-existence with the House of
    Avenel
And with the star that rules it.

Look on my girdle—on this thread of
    gold—
'Tis fine as web of lightest gossamer,
And, but there is a spell on't, would not
    bind,
Light as they are, the folds of my thin
    robe.
But when 'twas donn'd, it was a massive
    chain,

Such as might bind the champion of the
Jews,
Even when his locks were longest—it
hath dwindled,
Hath 'minish'd in its substance and its
strength,
As sunk the greatness of the House of
Avenel.
When this frail thread gives way, I to the
elements
Resign the principles of life they lent me.
Ask me no more of this!—the stars
forbid it.

———

Dim burns the once bright star of Avenel,
Dim as the beacon when the morn is nigh,
And the o'er-wearied warder leaves the
light-house;
There is an influence sorrowful and fearful,
That dogs its downward course. Disas-
trous passion,
Fierce hate and rivalry, are in the aspect
That lowers upon its fortunes.

———

Complain not of me, child of clay,
If to thy harm I yield the way.
We, who soar thy sphere above,
Know not aught of hate or love;
As will or wisdom rules thy mood.
My gifts to evil turn or good.

            Chap. xvii.

THE WHITE LADY TO MARY AVENEL.

MAIDEN, whose sorrows wail the Living
Dead,
Whose eyes shall commune with the
Dead Alive,
Maiden, attend! Beneath my foot lies hid
The Word, the Law, the Path which
thou dost strive
To find, and canst not find.—Could
Spirits shed
Tears for their lot, it were my lot to weep,
Showing the road which I shall never tread,
Though my foot points it.—Sleep,
eternal sleep,
Dark, long, and cold forgetfulness my lot!—
But do not thou at human ills repine;

Secure there lies full guerdon in this spot
For all the woes that wait frail Adam's
line—
Stoop then and make it yours,—I may
not make it mine!—*Chap.* xxx.

THE WHITE LADY TO EDWARD GLENDINNING.

THOU who seek'st my fountain lone,
With thoughts and hopes thou dar'st not
own;
Whose heart within leap'd wildly glad,
When most his brow seem'd dark and sad;
Hie thee back, thou find'st not here
Corpse or coffin, grave or bier;
The Dead Alive is gone and fled—
Go thou, and join the Living Dead!

The Living Dead, whose sober brow
Oft shrouds such thoughts as thou hast
now,
Whose hearts within are seldom cured
Of passions by their vows abjured;
Where, under sad and solemn show,
Vain hopes are nursed, wild wishes glow.
Seek the convent's vaulted room,
Prayer and vigil be thy doom;
Doff the green, and don the grey,
To the cloister hence away!—

            Chap. xxxii.

THE WHITE LADY'S FAREWELL.

FARE THEE WELL, thou Holly green!
Thou shalt seldom now be seen,
With all thy glittering garlands bending,
As to greet my slow descending,
Startling the bewilder'd hind,
Who sees thee wave without a wind.

Farewell, Fountain! now not long
Shalt thou murmur to my song,
While thy crystal bubbles glancing,
Keep the time in mystic dancing,
Rise and swell, are burst and lost,
Like mortal schemes by fortune cross'd

The knot of fate at length is tied,
The Churl is Lord, the Maid is Bride.

Vainly did my magic sleight
Send the lover from her sight;
Wither bush, and perish well,
Fall'n is lofty Avenel!—*Chap.* xxxvii.

BORDER BALLAD.

I.

March, march, Ettrick and Teviotdale,
Why the deil dinna ye march forward
in order?
March, march, Eskdale and Liddesdale,
All the Blue Bonnets are bound for
the Border.
Many a banner spread,
Flutters above your head,
Many a crest that is famous in story.
Mount and make ready then,
Sons of the mountain glen,
Fight for the Queen and our old Scottish
glory.

II.

Come from the hills where your hirsels
are grazing,
Come from the glen of the buck and
the roe;
Come to the crag where the beacon is
blazing,
Come with the buckler, the lance, and
the bow.
Trumpets are sounding,
War-steeds are bounding,
Stand to your arms, and march in good
order,
England shall many a day
Tell of the bloody fray,
When the Blue Bonnets came over the
Border.—*Chap.* xxv.

MOTTOES.

CHAP. I.

O ay! the Monks, the Monks, they did
the mischief!
Theirs all the grossness, all the super-
stition
Of a most gross and superstitious age.—
May HE be praised that sent the health-
ful tempest,
And scatter'd all these pestilential vapours;
But that we owed them *all* to yonder
Harlot
Throned on the seven hills with her cup
of gold,
I will as soon believe, with kind Sir Roger,
That old Moll White took wing with
cat and broomstick,
And raised the last night's thunder.
                              Old Play.

CHAP. II.

In yon lone vale his early youth was bred.
Not solitary then—the bugle-horn
Of fell Alecto often waked its windings,
From where the brook joins the majest.c
river,
To the wild northern bog, the curlew's
haunt,
Where oozes forth its first and feeble
streamlet.—*Old Play.*

CHAP. VIII.

Nay, dally not with time, the wise man's
treasure,
Though fools are lavish on't—the fatal
Fisher
Hooks souls, while we waste moments.
                              Old Play.

CHAP. XI.

You call this education, do you not?
Why, 'tis the forced march of a herd of
bullocks
Before a shouting drover. The glad van
Move on at ease, and pause a while to
snatch
A passing morsel from the dewy green-
sward,
While all the blows, the oaths, the in-
dignation,
Fall on the croupe of the ill-fated laggard
That cripples in the rear.—*Old Play.*

CHAP. XII.

There's something in that ancient superstition,
Which, erring as it is, our fancy loves.
The spring that, with its thousand crystal
bubbles,

Bursts from the bosom of some desert
    rock
In secret solitude, may well be deem'd
The haunt of something purer, more re-
    fined,
And mightier than ourselves.—*Old Play.*

CHAP. XIV.

Nay, let me have the friends who eat my
    victuals,
As various as my dishes. The feast's
    naught,
Where one huge plate predominates.—
    John Plaintext,
He shall be mighty beef, our English
    staple;
The worthy Alderman, a butter'd dump-
    ling;
Yon pair of whisker'd Cornets, ruffs and
    reeves;
Their friend the Dandy, a green goose in
    sippets.
And so the board is spread at once and
    fill'd
On the same principle—Variety.
                            New Play.

CHAP. XV.

He strikes no coin, 'tis true, but coins
    new phrases,
And vends them forth as knaves vend
    gilded counters,
Which wise men scorn, and fools accept
    in payment.—*Old Play.*

CHAP. XIX.

Now choose thee, gallant, betwixt wealth
    and honour;
There lies the pelf, in sum to bear thee
    through
The dance of youth, and the turmoil of
    manhood,
Yet leave enough for age's chimney-
    corner;
But an thou grasp to it, farewell Ambition!
Farewell each hope of bettering thy con-
    dition,
And raising thy low rank above the churls
That till the earth for bread! - *Old Play.*

CHAP. XXI.

Indifferent, but indifferent—pshaw! he
    doth it not
Like one who is his craft's master—ne'er-
    theless
I have seen a clown confer a bloody cox-
    comb
On one who was a master of defence.
                            Old Play.

CHAP. XXII.

Yes, life hath left him — every busy
    thought,
Each fiery passion, every strong affection,
The sense of outward ill and inward
    sorrow,
Are fled at once from the pale trunk
    before me;
And I have given that which spoke and
    moved,
Thought, acted, suffer'd, as a living man,
To be a ghastly form of bloody clay,
Soon the foul food for reptiles.—*Old Play.*

CHAP. XXIII.

'Tis when the wound is stiffening with
    the cold,
The warrior first feels pain—'tis when the
    heat
And fiery fever of his soul is past,
The sinner feels remorse.—*Old Play.*

CHAP. XXIV.

I'll walk on tiptoe; arm my eye with
    caution,
My heart with courage, and my hand with
    weapon
Like him who ventures on a lion's den.
                            Old Play.

CHAP. XXVII.

Now, by Our Lady, Sheriff, 'tis hard
    reckoning,
That I, with every odds of birth and
    barony,
Should be detain'd here for the casual
    death
Of a wild forester, whose utmost having

Is but the brazen buckle of the belt
In which he sticks his hedge-knife.—
Old Play

CHAP. XXX.

You call it an ill angel—it may be so;
But sure I am, among the ranks which
fell,
'Tis the first fiend e'er counsell'd man to
rise,
And win the bliss the sprite himself had
forfeited.—*Old Play.*

CHAP. XXXI.

At school I knew him—a sharp-witted
youth,
Grave, thoughtful, and reserved amongst
his mates,
Turning the hours of sport and food to
labour,
Starving his body to inform his mind.
Old Play.

CHAP. XXXIII.

Now on my faith this gear is all entangled,
Like to the yarn-clew of the drowsy
knitter,
Dragg'd by the frolic kitten through the
cabin,
While the good dame sits nodding o'er
the fire—
Masters, attend; 'twill crave some skill to
clear it.—*Old Play.*

CHAP. XXXIV.

It is not texts will do it—Church artillery
Are silenced soon by real ordnance,
And canons are but vain opposed to cannon.
Go, coin your crosier, melt your church
plate down,
Bid the starved soldiers banquet in your
halls,
And quaff your long-saved hogsheads—
Turn them out
Thus primed with your good cheer, to
guard your wall,
And they will venture for 't.—*Old Play.*

From the Abbot.

1820.

MOTTOES.

CHAP. V.

——In the wild storm,
The seaman hews his mast down, and the
merchant
Heaves to the billows wares he once
deem'd precious:
So prince and peer, 'mid popular conten-
tions,
Cast off their favourites.—*Old Play.*

CHAP. VI.

Thou hast each secret of the household,
Francis.
I dare be sworn thou hast been in the
buttery
Steeping thy curious humour in fat ale,
And in the butler's tattle—ay, or chatting
With the glib waiting-woman o'er her
comfits—
These bear the key to each domestic
mystery.—*Old Play.*

CHAP. VIII.

The sacred tapers' lights are gone,
Grey moss has clad the altar stone,
The holy image is o'erthrown,
    The bell has ceased to toll.
The long ribb'd aisles are burst and shrunk,
The holy shrines to ruin sunk,
Departed is the pious monk,
    God's blessing on his soul!
Rediviva.

CHAP. XI.

Life hath its May, and all is mirthful then:
The woods are vocal, and the flowers all
odour;
Its very blast has mirth in't,—and the
maidens,
The while they don their cloaks to skreen
their kirtles,
Laugh at the rain that wets them.
Old Play.

CHAP. XII.

Nay, hear me, brother—I am elder, wiser,
And holier than thou; and age, and
   wisdom,
And holiness, have peremptory claims,
And will be listen'd to.—*Old Play.*

CHAP. XIV.

Not the wild billow, when it breaks its
   barrier—
Not the wild wind, escaping from its
   cavern—
Not the wild fiend, that mingles both together,
And pours their rage upon the ripening
   harvest,
Can match the wild freaks of this mirthful meeting—
Comic, yet fearful—droll, and yet destructive.—*The Conspiracy.*

CHAP. XVI.

Youth! thou wear'st to manhood now,
Darker lip and darker brow,
Statelier step, more pensive mien,
In thy face and gait are seen:
Thou must now brook midnight watches,
Take thy food and sport by snatches!
For the gambol and the jest,
Thou wert wont to love the best,
Graver follies must thou follow,
But as senseless, false, and hollow.
        Life, a Poem.

CHAP. XIX.

It is and is not—'tis the thing I sought for,
Have kneel'd for, pray'd for, risk'd my
   fame and life for,
And yet it is not—no more than the shadow
Upon the hard, cold, flat, and polish'd
   mirror,
Is the warm, graceful, rounded, living
   substance
Which it presents in form and lineament.
        Old Play.

CHAP. XXIII.

Give me a morsel on the greensward
   rather,
Coarse as you will the cooking—Let the
   fresh spring
Bubble beside my napkin—and the free
   birds,
Twittering and chirping, hop from bough
   to bough.
To claim the crumbs I leave for per-
   quisites—
Your prison-feasts I like not.
        The Woodman, a Drama.

CHAP. XXIV.

'Tis a weary life this——
Vaults overhead, and grates and bars
   around me,
And my sad hours spent with as sad
   companions,
Whose thoughts are brooding o'er their
   own mischances,
Far, far too deeply to take part in mine.
        The Woodsman.

CHAP. XXV.

And when Love's torch hath set the heart
   in flame,
Comes Seignor Reason, with his saws and
   cautions,
Giving such aid as the old grey-beard
   Sexton,
Who from the church-vault drags his
   crazy engine,
To ply its dribbling ineffectual streamlet
Against a conflagration.—*Old Play.*

CHAP. XXVIII.

Yes, it is she whose eyes look'd on thy
   childhood
And watch'd with trembling hope thy
   dawn of youth,
That now, with these same eye-balls,
   dimm'd with age,
And dimmer yet with tears, sees thy dishonour.—*Old Play.*

CHAP. XXX.

In some breasts passion lies conceal'd and
    silent,
Like war's swart powder in a castle vault,
Until occasion, like the linstock, lights it;
Then comes at once the lightning and the
    thunder,
And distant echoes tell that all is rent
    asunder.—*Old Play.*

———

From Kenilworth.

1821.

GOLDTHRED'S SONG.

Of all the birds on bush or tree,
    Commend me to the owl,
Since he may best ensample be
    To those the cup that trowl.
For when the sun hath left the west,
He chooses the tree that he loves the best,
And he whoops out his song, and he
    laughs at his jest.
Then, though hours be late, and weather
    foul,
We'll drink to the health of the bonny,
    bonny owl.

The lark is but a bumpkin fowl,
    He sleeps in his nest till morn;
But my blessing upon the jolly owl,
    That all night blows his horn.
Then up with your cup till you stagger
    in speech,
And match me this catch, till you swagger
    and screech,
And drink till you wink, my merry men
    each;
For, though hours be late, and weather
    be foul,
We'll drink to the health of the bonny,
    bonny owl.—*Chap.* ii.

MOTTOES.

CHAP. IV.

Not serve two masters?—Here's a youth
    will try it—

Would fain serve God, yet give the devil
    his due;
Says grace before he doth a deed of vil-
    lany,
And returns his thanks devoutly when 'tis
    acted.—*Old Play.*

CHAP. VII.

———— This is He
Who rides on the court-gale; controls its
    tides;
Knows all their secret shoals and fatal
    eddies;
Whose frown abases, and whose smile
    exalts.
He shines like any rainbow—and, per-
    chance,
His colours are as transient.—*Old Play.*

CHAP. XIV.

This is rare news thou tell'st me, my good
    fellow;
There are two bulls fierce battling on the
    green
For one fair heifer—if the one goes down,
The dale will be more peaceful, and the
    herd,
Which have small interest in their brulzie-
    ment,
May pasture there in peace.—*Old Play.*

CHAP. XXIII.

Now God be good to me in this wild pil-
    grimage!
All hope in human aid I cast behind me.
Oh, who would be a woman? who that
    fool,
A weeping, pining, faithful, loving woman?
She hath hard measure still where she
    hopes kindest,
And all her bounties only make ingrates.
        Love's Pilgrimage.

CHAP. XXV.

Hark! the bells summon, and the bugle
    calls,
But she the fairest answers not; the tide
Of nobles and of ladies throngs the halls,
But she the loveliest must in secret hide.

What eyes were thine, proud Prince,
    which in the gleam
Of yon gay meteors lost that better sense,
That o'er the glow-worm doth the star
    esteem,
And merit's modest blush o'er courtly
    insolence?—*The Glass Slipper.*

CHAP. XXVIII.

What, man, ne'er lack a draught, when
    the full can
Stands at thine elbow, and craves empty-
    ing!—
Nay, fear not me, for I have no delight
To watch men's vices, since I have my-
    self
Of virtue nought to boast of.—I'm a
    striker,
Would have the world strike with me,
    pell-mell, all.—*Pandæmonium.*

CHAP. XXXII.

The wisest sovereigns err like private men,
And royal hand has sometimes laid the
    sword
Of chivalry upon a worthless shoulder,
Which better had been branded by the
    hangman.
What then? Kings do their best,—and
    they and we
Must answer for the intent, and not the
    event.—*Old Play.*

CHAP. XL.

High o'er the eastern steep the sun is
    beaming,
And darkness flies with her deceitful
    shadows;
So truth prevails o'er falsehood.
                    Old Play.

———

From the Pirate.
1821.
THE SONG OF THE TEMPEST.

I.

STERN eagle of the far north-west,
Thou that bearest in thy grasp the thun-
    derbolt,

Thou whose rushing pinions stir ocean
    to madness,
Thou the destroyer of herds, thou the
    scatterer of navies,
Amidst the scream of thy rage,
Amidst the rushing of thy onward wings,
Though thy scream be loud as the cry
    of a perishing nation,
Though the rushing of thy wings be like
    the roar of ten thousand waves,
Yet hear, in thine ire and thy haste,
Hear thou the voice of the Reim-kennar.

II.

Thou hast met the pine-trees of Dron-
    theim,
Their dark green heads lie prostrate
    beside their uprooted stems;
Thou hast met the rider of the ocean,
The tall, the strong bark of the fearless
    rover,
And she has struck to thee the topsail
That she had not vail'd to a royal armada.
Thou hast met the tower that bears its
    crest among the clouds,
The battled massive tower of the Jarl of
    former days,
And the cope-stone of the turret
Is lying upon its hospitable hearth;
But thou too shalt stoop, proud compeller
    of clouds,
When thou hearest the voice of the
    Reim-kennar.

III.

There are verses that can stop the stag
    in the forest,
Ay, when the dark-colour'd dog is
    opening on his track;
There are verses can make the wild hawk
    pause on the wing,
Like the falcon that wears the hood and
    the jesses,
And who knows the shrill whistle of the
    fowler.
Thou who canst mock at the scream of
    the drowning mariner,
And the crash of the ravaged forest,
And the groan of the overwhelmed
    crowds,

When the church hath fallen in the
  moment of prayer;
There are sounds which thou also must
  list,
When they are chanted by the voice of
  the Reim-kennar.

IV.

Enough of woe hast thou wrought on
  the ocean,
The widows wring their hands on the
  beach;
Enough of woe hast thou wrought on
  the land,
The husbandman folds his arms in de-
  spair;
Cease thou the waving of thy pinions,
Let the ocean repose in her dark strength;
Cease thou the flashing of thine eye,
Let the thunderbolt sleep in the armoury
  of Odin;
Be thou still at my bidding, viewless
  racer of the north-western heaven,—
Sleep thou at the voice of Norna the
  Reim-kennar.

V.

Eagle of the far north-western waters,
Thou hast heard the voice of the Reim-
  kennar,
Thou hast closed thy wide sails at her
  bidding,
And folded them in peace by thy side.
My blessing be on thy retiring path;
When thou stoopest from thy place on
  high,
Soft be thy slumbers in the caverns of
  the unknown ocean,
Rest till destiny shall again awaken thee;
Eagle of the north-west, thou hast heard
  the voice of the Reim-kennar.
                              Chap. vi.

CLAUD HALCRO'S SONG.

MARY.

FAREWELL to Northmaven,
  Grey Hillswicke, farewell!
To the calms of thy haven,
  The storms on thy fell—

To each breeze that can vary
  The mood of thy main,
And to thee, bonny Mary!
  We meet not again!

Farewell the wild ferry,
  Which Hacon could brave,
When the peaks of the Skerry
  Were white in the wave.
There's a maid may look over
  These wild waves in vain,—
For the skiff of her lover—
  He comes not again!

The vows thou hast broke,
  On the wild currents fling them;
On the quicksand and rock
  Let the mermaidens sing them.
New sweetness they'll give her
  Bewildering strain;
But there's one who will never
  Believe them again.

O were there an island,
  Though ever so wild,
Where woman could smile, and
  No man be beguiled—
Too tempting a snare
  To poor mortals were given;
And the hope would fix there,
  That should anchor in heaven.
                              Chap. xii.

THE SONG OF HAROLD HARFAGER.

THE sun is rising dimly red,
The wind is wailing low and dread;
From his cliff the eagle sallies,
Leaves the wolf his darksome valleys;
In the midst the ravens hover,
Peep the wild dogs from the cover,
Screaming, croaking, baying, yelling,
Each in his wild accents telling,
" Soon we feast on dead and dying,
Fair-hair'd Harold's flag is flying."

Many a crest on air is streaming,
Many a helmet darkly gleaming,
Many an arm the axe uprears,
Doom'd to hew the wood of spears,
All along the crowded ranks
Horses neigh and armour clanks;

Chiefs are shouting, clarions ringing,
Louder still the bard is singing,
" Gather footmen, gather horsemen,
To the field, ye valiant Norsemen !

" Halt ye not for food or slumber,
View not vantage, count not number:
Jolly reapers, forward still,
Grow the crop on vale or hill,
Thick or scatter'd, stiff or lithe,
It shall down before the scythe.
Forward with your sickles bright,
Reap the harvest of the fight.—
Onward footmen, onward horsemen,
To the charge ye gallant Norsemen !

" Fatal Choosers of the Slaughter,
O'er you hovers Odin's daughter ;
Hear the choice she spreads before ye,—
Victory, and wealth, and glory;
Or old Valhalla's roaring hail,
Her ever-circling mead and ale,
Where for eternity unite
The joys of wassail and of fight.
Headlong forward, foot and horsemen,
Charge and fight, and die like Norse-
    men !"—*Chap*. xv.

SONG OF THE MERMAIDS AND MERMEN.

MERMAID.

FATHOMS deep beneath the wave,
    Stringing beads of glistering pearl,
Singing the achievements brave
    Of many an old Norwegian earl;
Dwelling where the tempest's raving,
    Falls as light upon our ear,
As the sigh of lover, craving
    Pity from his lady dear,
Children of wild Thule, we,
From the deep caves of the sea,
As the lark springs from the lea,
Hither come, to share your glee.

MERMAN.

From reining of the water-horse,
    That bounded till the waves were
        foaming,
Watching the infant tempest's course,
    Chasing the sea-snake in his roaming ;

From winding charge-notes on the shell,
    When the huge whale and sword-fish
        duel,
Or tolling shroudless seamen's knell,
    When the winds and waves are cruel ;
Children of wild Thule, we
Have plough'd such furrows on the sea,
As the steer draws on the lea,
And hither we come to share your glee.

MERMAIDS AND MERMEN.

We heard you in our twilight caves,
    A hundred fathom deep below,
For notes of joy can pierce the waves,
    That drown each sound of war and
        woe.
Those who dwell beneath the sea
    Love the sons of Thule well;
Thus, to aid your mirth, bring we
    Dance, and song, and sounding shell.
Children of dark Thule, know,
Those who dwell by haaf and voe,
Where your daring shallops row,
Come to share the festal show.—
                        Chap. xvi.

NORNA'S SONG.

FOR leagues along the watery way,
    Through gulf and stream my course
        has been ;
The billows know my Runic lay,
    And smooth their crests to silent green.

The billows know my Runic lay,—
    The gulf grows smooth, the stream is
        still ;
But human hearts, more wild than they,
    Know but the rule of wayward will.

One hour is mine, in all the year,
    To tell my woes,—and one alone ;
When gleams this magic lamp, 'tis here,—
    When dies the mystic light, 'tis gone.

Daughters of northern Magnus, hail !
    The lamp is lit, the flame is clear,—
To you I come to tell my tale,
    Awake, arise, my tale to hear !
                        Chap. xix.

CLAUD HALCRO AND NORNA.

CLAUD HALCRO.

MOTHER darksome, Mother dread,
Dweller of the Fitful-head,
Thou canst see what deeds are done
Under the never-setting sun.
Look through sleet, and look through frost,
Look to Greenland's caves and coast,—
By the ice-berg is a sail
Chasing of the swarthy whale ;
Mother doubtful, Mother dread,
Tell us, has the good ship sped?

NORNA.

The thought of the aged is ever on gear,—
On his fishing, his furrow, his flock, and
    his steer;
But thrive may his fishing, flock, furrow,
    and herd,
While the aged for anguish shall tear his
    grey beard.
The ship, well-laden as bark need be,
Lies deep in the furrow of the Iceland
    sea ;—
The breeze for Zetland blows fair and soft,
And gaily the garland is fluttering aloft :
Seven good fishes have spouted their last,
And their jaw-bones are hanging to yard
    and mast ;
Two are for Lerwick, and two for Kirk-
    wall,—
Three for Burgh Westra, the choicest of
    all.

CLAUD HALCRO.

Mother doubtful, Mother dread !
Dweller of the Fitful-head,
Thou hast conn'd full many a rhyme,
That lives upon the surge of time :
Tell me, shall my lays be sung,
Like Hacon's of the golden tongue,
Long after Halcro's dead and gone ?
Or, shall Hialtland's minstrel own
One note to rival glorious John ?

NORNA.

The infant loves the rattle's noise ;
Age, double childhood, hath its toys ;
But different far the descant rings,
As strikes a different hand the strings.

The eagle mounts the polar sky—
The Imber-goose, unskill'd to fly,
Must be content to glide along,
Where seal and sea-dog list his song.

CLAUD HALCRO.

Be mine the Imber-goose to play,
And haunt lone cave and silent bay ;
The archer's aim so shall I shun—
So shall I 'scape the levell'd gun—
Content my verses' tuneless jingle,
With Thule's sounding tides to mingle,
While, to the ear of wondering wight,
Upon the distant headland's height,
Soften'd by murmur of the sea,
The rude sounds seems like harmony !

*   *   *   *   *

Mother doubtful, Mother dread,
Dweller of the Fitful-head,
A gallant bark from far abroad,
Saint Magnus hath her in his road,
With guns and firelocks not a few—
A silken and a scarlet crew,
Deep stored with precious merchandise,
Of gold, and goods of rare device—
What interest hath our comrade bold
In bark and crew, in goods and gold ?

NORNA.

Gold is ruddy, fair, and free,
Blood is crimson, and dark to see ;—
I look'd out on Saint Magnus Bay,
And I saw a falcon that struck her prey,—
A gobbet of flesh in her beak she bore,
And talons and singles are dripping with
    gore ;—
Let he that asks after them look on his
    hand,
And if there is blood on't, he's one of
    their band.

CLAUD HALCRO.

Mother doubtful, Mother dread,
Dweller of the Fitful-head,
Well thou know'st it is thy task
To tell what Beauty will not ask :—
Then steep thy words in wine and milk,
And weave a doom of gold and silk,—
For we would know, shall Brenda prove
In love, and happy in her love ?

NORNA.

Untouch'd by love, the maiden's breast
Is like the snow on Rona's crest,
High seated in the middle sky,
In bright and barren purity;
But by the sunbeam gently kiss'd,
Scarce by the gazing eye 'tis miss'd,
Ere, down the lonely valley stealing,
Fresh grass and growth its course revealing,
It cheers the flock, revives the flower,
And decks some happy shepherd's bower.

MAGNUS TROIL.

Mother, speak, and do not tarry,
Here's a maiden fain would marry,
Shall she marry, ay or not?
If she marry, what's her lot?

NORNA.

Untouch'd by love, the maiden's breast
Is like the snow on Rona's crest;
So pure, so free from earthly dye,
It seems, whilst leaning on the sky,
Part of the heaven to which 'tis nigh;
But passion, like the wild March rain,
May soil the wreath with many a stain.
We gaze—the lovely vision's gone—
A torrent fills the bed of stone,
That hurrying to destruction's shock,
Leaps headlong from the lofty rock.

Chap. xxi.

SONG OF THE ZETLAND FISHERMAN.

FAREWELL, merry maidens, to song, and to laugh,
For the brave lads of Westra are bound to the Haaf;
And we must have labour, and hunger, and pain,
Ere we dance with the maids of Dunrossness again.

For now, in our trim boats of Noroway deal,
We must dance on the waves, with the porpoise and seal;
The breeze it shall pipe, so it pipe not too high,
And the gull be our songstress whene'er she flits by.

Sing on, my brave bird, while we follow, like thee,
By bank, shoal, and quicksand, the swarms of the sea;
And when twenty-score fishes are straining our line,
Sing louder, brave bird, for their spoils shall be thine.

We'll sing while we bait, and we'll sing while we haul,
For the deeps of the Haaf have enough for us all:
There is torsk for the gentle, and skate for the carle,
And there's wealth for bold Magnus, the son of the earl.

Huzza! my brave comrades, give way for the Haaf,
We shall sooner come back to the dance and the laugh;
For life without mirth is a lamp without oil;
Then, mirth and long life to the bold Magnus Troil!—*Chap.* xxii.

CLEVELAND'S SONGS.

I.

LOVE wakes and weeps
While Beauty sleeps!
O for Music's softest numbers,
To prompt a theme,
For Beauty's dream,
Soft as the pillow of her slumbers

II.

Through groves of palm
Sigh gales of balm,
Fire-flies on the air are wheeling;
While through the gloom
Comes soft perfume,
The distant beds of flowers revealing.

III.

O wake and live!
No dream can give
A shadow'd bliss, the real excelling;
No longer sleep,
From lattice peep,
And list the tale that Love is telling.

FAREWELL! farewell! the voice you hear,
  Has left its last soft tone with you,—
Its next must join the seaward cheer,
  And shout among the shouting crew.

The accents which I scarce could form
  Beneath your frown's controlling check,
Must give the word, above the storm,
  To cut the mast, and clear the wreck.

The timid eye I dared not raise,—
  The hand, that shook when press'd to thine,
Must point the guns upon the chase—
  Must bid the deadly cutlass shine.

To all I love, or hope, or fear,—
  Honour, or own, a long adieu!
To all that life has soft and dear,
  Farewell! save memory of you!
                  Chap. xxiii.

CLAUD HALCRO'S VERSES.

AND you shall deal the funeral dole;
  Ay, deal it, mother mine,
To weary body, and to heavy soul,
  The white bread and the wine.

And you shall deal my horses of pride;
  Ay, deal them, mother mine;
And you shall deal my lands so wide,
  And deal my castles nine.

But deal not vengeance for the deed,
  And deal not for the crime;
The body to its place, and the soul to Heaven's grace,
  And the rest in God's own time.

NORNA'S INCANTATIONS.

CHAMPION, famed for warlike toil,
Art thou silent, Ribolt Troil?
Sand, and dust, and pebbly stones,
Are leaving bare thy giant bones.
Who dared touch the wild bear's skin
Ye slumber'd on, while life was in?—
A woman now, or babe, may come
And cast the covering from thy tomb.

Yet be not wrathful, Chief, nor blight,
Mine eyes or ears with sound or sight!

I come not, with unhallow'd tread,
To wake the slumbers of the dead,
Or lay thy giant reliques bare;
But what I seek thou well canst spare.
Be it to my hand allow'd
To shear a merk's weight from thy shroud;
Yet leave thee sheeted lead enough
To shield thy bones from weather rough.

See, I draw my magic knife—
Never, while thou wert in life,
Laidst thou still for sloth or fear,
When point and edge were glittering near;
See, the cerements now I sever—
Waken now, or sleep for ever!
Thou wilt not wake—the deed is done!—
The prize I sought is fairly won.

Thanks, Ribolt, thanks,—for this the sea
Shall smooth its ruffled crest for thee—
And while afar its billows foam,
Subside to peace near Ribolt's tomb.
Thanks, Ribolt, thanks—for this the might
Of wild winds raging at their height,
When to thy place of slumber nigh,
Shall soften to a lullaby.

She, the dame of doubt and dread,
Norna of the Fitful-head,
Mighty in her own despite,—
Miserable in her might;
In despair and frenzy great,
In her greatness desolate;
Wisest, wickedest who lives,--
Well can keep the word she gives.
                  Chap. xxv.

[HER INTERVIEW WITH MINNA.]

Thou, so needful, yet so dread,
With cloudy crest, and wing of red;
Thou, without whose genial breath
The North would sleep the sleep of death;
Who deign'st to warm the cottage hearth,
Yet hurlst proud palaces to earth,—
Brightest, keenest of the Powers,
Which form and rule this world of ours,
With my rhyme of Runic, I
Thank thee for thy agency.

Old Reim-kennar, to thy art
Mother Hertha sends her part;
She, whose gracious bounty gives
Needful food for all that lives.
From the deep mine of the North
Came the mystic metal forth,
Doom'd amidst disjointed stones,
Long to cere a champion's bones,
Disinhumed my charms to aid—
Mother Earth, my thanks are paid.

Girdle of our islands dear,
Element of Water, hear!
Thou whose power can overwhelm
Broken mounds and ruin'd realm
  On the lowly Belgian strand;
All thy fiercest rage can never
Of our soil a furlong sever
  From our rock-defended land;
Play then gently thou thy part,
To assist old Norna's art.

Elements, each other greeting,
Gifts and power attend your meeting:

Thou, that over billows dark,
Safely send'st the fisher's bark,—
Giving him a path and motion
Through the wilderness of ocean;
Thou, that when the billows brave ye,
O'er the shelves canst drive the navy,—
Didst thou chafe as one neglected,
While thy brethren were respected?
To appease thee, see, I tear
This full grasp of grizzled hair;
Oft thy breath hath through it sung,
Softening to my magic tongue,—
Now, 'tis thine to bid it fly
Through the wide expanse of sky,
'Mid the countless swarms to sail
Of wild-fowl wheeling on thy gale;
Take thy portion and rejoice,—
Spirit, thou hast heard my voice!

She who sits by haunted well,
Is subject to the Nixies' spell;
She who walks on lonely beach,
To the Mermaid's charmed speech;
She who walks round ring of green,
Offends the peevish Fairy Queen;

And she who takes rest in the Dwarfie's
  cave,
A weary weird of woe shall have.

By ring, by spring, by cave, by shore,
Minna Troil has braved all this and more;
And yet hath the root of her sorrow and ill,
A source that's more deep and more
  mystical still.—
Thou art within a demon's hold,
More wise than Heims, more strong than
  Trold.
No siren sings so sweet as he,—
No fay springs lighter on the lea;
No elfin power hath half the art
To soothe, to move, to wring the heart,—
Life-blood from the cheek to drain,
Drench the eye and dry the vein.
Maiden, ere we farther go,
Dost thou note me, ay or no?

MINNA.

I mark thee, my mother, both word, look,
  and sign;
Speak on with thy riddle—to read it be
  mine.

NORNA.

Mark me! for the word I speak
Shall bring the colour to thy cheek.
This leaden heart, so light of cost,
The symbol of a treasure lost,
Thou shalt wear in hope and in peace,
That the cause of your sickness and
  sorrow may cease,
When crimson foot meets crimson hand
In the Martyr's Aisle, and in Orkney
  land.—

Be patient, be patient; for Patience hath
  power
To ward us in danger, like mantle in
  shower;
A fairy gift you best may hold
In a chain of fairy gold;—
The chain and the gift are each a true
  token,
That not without warrant old Norna has
  spoken;

But thy nearest and dearest must never
behold them,
Till time shall accomplish the truths I
have told them.—*Chap.* xxviii.

MOTTOES.

CHAP. II.

'TIS not alone the scene—the man, An-
selmo,
The man finds sympathies in these wild
wastes,
And roughly tumbling seas, which fairer
views
And smoother waves deny him.
Ancient Drama.

CHAP. VII.

She does no work by halves, yon raving
ocean ;
Engulphing those she strangles, her wild
womb
Affords the mariners whom she hath dealt
on,
Their death at once, and sepulchre.
Old Play.

CHAP. IX.

This is a gentle trader, and a prudent—
He's no Autolycus, to blear your eye,
With quips of worldly gauds and game-
someness ;
But seasons all his glittering merchandise
With wholesome doctrine suited to the use,
As men sauce goose with sage and rose-
mary.—*Old Play.*

CHAP. XIV.

We'll keep our customs—what is law
itself,
But old establish'd custom ? What religion,
(I mean, with one-half of the men that
use it,)
Save the good use and wont that carries
them
To worship how and where their fathers
worshipp'd ?
All things resolve in custom—we'll keep
ours.—*Old Play.*

CHAP. XXIX.

See yonder woman, whom our swains
revere,
And dread in secret, while they take her
counsel
When sweetheart shall be kind, or when
cross dame shall die ;
Where lurks the thief who stole the silver
tankard,
And how the pestilent murrain may be
cured ;—
This sage adviser's mad, stark mad, my
friend ;
Yet, in her madness, hath the art and
cunning
To wring fools' secrets from their inmost
bosoms,
And pay inquirers with the coin they gave
her.—*Old Play.*

CHAP. XXX.

What ho, my jovial mates! come on !
we'll frolic it
Like fairies frisking in the merry moonshine,
Seen by the curtal friar, who, from some
christening,
Or some blithe bridal, hies belated cel-
ward—
He starts, and changes his bold bottle
swagger
To churchman's pace professional,—and,
ransacking
His treacherous memory for some holy
hymn,
Finds but the roundel of the midnight
catch.—*Old Play.*

CHAP. XXXIII.

Parental love, my friend, has power o'er
wisdom,
And is the charm, which, like the falconer's
lure,
Can bring from heaven the highest soaring spirits.—
So, when famed Prosper doff'd his magic
robe,
It was Miranda pluck'd it from his
shoulders.—*Old Play.*

CHAP. XXXVII.

Over the mountains, and under the waves,
Over the fountains, and under the graves,
    Under floods that are deepest,
    Which Neptune obey,
    Over rocks that are steepest,
    Love will find out the way.
                  Old Song.

ON ETTRICK FOREST'S MOUNTAINS DUN.

1822.

ON Ettrick Forest's mountains dun,
'Tis blithe to hear the sportsman's gun,
And seek the heath-frequenting brood
Far through the noonday solitude;
By many a cairn and trenched mound,
Where chiefs of yore sleep lone and sound,
And springs, where grey-hair'd shepherds tell,
That still the fairies love to dwell.

Along the silver streams of Tweed,
'Tis blithe the mimic fly to lead,
When to the hook the salmon springs,
And the line whistles through the rings;
The boiling eddy see him try,
Then dashing from the current high,
Till watchful eye and cautious hand
Have led his wasted strength to land.

'Tis blithe along the midnight tide,
With stalwart arm the boat to guide;
On high the dazzling blaze to rear,
And heedful plunge the barbed spear;
Rock, wood, and scaur, emerging bright,
Fling on the stream their ruddy light,
And from the bank our band appears
Like Genii, arm'd with fiery spears.

'Tis blithe at eve to tell the tale,
How we succeed, and how we fail,
Whether at Alwyn's* lordly meal,
Or lowlier board of Ashestiel;
While the gay tapers cheerly shine,
Bickers the fire, and flows the wine—

---

* *Alwyn*, the seat of the Lord Somerville.

Days free from thought, and nights from care,
My blessing on the Forest fair!

FAREWELL TO THE MUSE.

1822.

ENCHANTRESS, farewell, who so oft has decoy'd me,
  At the close of the evening through woodlands to roam,
Where the forester, lated, with wonder espied me,
  Explore the wild scenes he was quitting for home.
Farewell, and take with thee thy numbers wild speaking
  The language alternate of rapture and woe:
Oh! none but some lover, whose heart-strings are breaking,
  The pang that I feel at our parting can know.

Each joy thou couldst double, and when there came sorrow,
  Or pale disappointment to darken my way,
What voice was like thine, that could sing of to-morrow,
  Till forgot in the strain was the grief of to-day!
But when friends drop around us in life's weary waning,
  The grief, Queen of Numbers, thou canst not assuage;
Nor the gradual estrangement of those yet remaining,
  The languor of pain, and the chillness of age.

'Twas thou that once taught me, in accents bewailing,
  To sing how a warrior lay stretch'd on the plain,
And a maiden hung o'er him with aid unavailing,
  And held to his lips the cold goblet in vain;

As vain thy enchantments, O Queen of
  wild Numbers,
    To a bard when the reign of his fancy
    is o'er,
And the quick pulse of feeling in apathy
  slumbers—
    Farewell, then, Enchantress! I meet
    thee no more!

THE MAID OF ISLA.

AIR—*The Maid of Isla.*

WRITTEN FOR MR. GEORGE THOMSON'S
SCOTTISH MELODIES.

1822.

OH, Maid of Isla, from the cliff,
  That looks on troubled wave and sky,
Dost thou not see yon little skiff
  Contend with ocean gallantly?
Now beating 'gainst the breeze and surge,
  And steep'd her leeward deck in foam,
Why does she war unequal urge?—
  Oh, Isla's maid, she seeks her home.

Oh, Isla's maid, yon sea-bird mark,
  Her white wing gleams through mist
  and spray,
Against the storm-cloud, lowering dark,
  As to the rock she wheels away;—
Where clouds are dark and billows rave,
  Why to the shelter should she come
Of cliff, exposed to wind and wave?—
  Oh, maid of Isla, 'tis her home!

As breeze and tide to yonder skiff,
  Thou'rt adverse to the suit I bring,
And cold as is yon wintry cliff,
  Where sea-birds close their wearied
  wing.
Yet cold as rock, unkind as wave,
  Still, Isla's maid, to thee I come;
For in thy love, or in his grave,
  Must Allan Vourich find his home.

CARLE, NOW THE KING'S COME.*

BEING NEW WORDS TO AN AULD SPRING.

1822.

THE news has flown frae mouth to mouth,
The North for ance has bang'd the South;
The deil a Scotsman's die o' drouth,
    Carle, now the King's come!

CHORUS.

Carle, now the King's come!
Carle, now the King's come!
Thou shalt dance, and I will sing,
    Carle, now the King's come!

Auld England held him lang and fast;
And Ireland had a joyfu' cast;
But Scotland's turn is come at last—
    Carle, now the King's come!

Auld Reekie, in her rokelay grey,
Thought never to have seen the day;
He's been a weary time away—
    But, Carle, now the King's come!

She's skirling frae the Castle-hill;
The Carline's voice is grown sae shrill,
Ye'll hear her at the Canon-mill—
    Carle, now the King's come!

"Up, bairns!" she cries, "baith grit and
  sma',
And busk ye for the weapon-shaw!
Stand by me, and we'll bang them a'—
    Carle, now the King's come!

" Come from Newbattle's ancient spires,
Bauld Lothian, with your knights and
  squires,
And match the mettle of your sires—
    Carle, now the King's come!

" You're welcome hame, my Montagu!
Bring in your hand the young Buccleuch;
I'm missing some that I may rue—
    Carle, now the King's come!

---

* An imitation of an old Jacobite ditty,
written on the arrival of George IV. in Scotland, August, 1822, and printed as a broad-
side.

"Come, Haddington, the kind and gay,
You've graced my causeway mony a day;
I'll weep the cause if you should stay—
    Carle, now the King's come!

"Come, premier Duke,* and carry doun
Frae yonder craig his ancient croun;
It's had a lang sleep and a soun'—
    But, Carle, now the King's come!

"Come, Athole, from the hill and wood,
Bring down your clansmen like a clud;
Come, Morton, show the Douglas'
    blood,—
    Carle, now the King's come!

"Come, Tweeddale, true as sword to
    sheath,
Come, Hopetoun, fear'd on fields of
    death;
Come, Clerk,† and give your bugle breath;
    Carle, now the King's come!

"Come, Wemyss, who modest merit aids;
Come, Rosebery, from Dalmeny shades;
Breadalbane, bring your belted plaids;
    Carle, now the King's come!

"Come, stately Niddrie, auld and true,
Girt with the sword that Minden knew;
We have o'er few such lairds as you—
    Carle, now the King's come!

"King Arthur's grown a common crier,
He's heard in Fife and far Cantire,—
'Fie, lads, behold my crest of fire!'
    Carle, now the King's come!

"Saint Abb roars out, 'I see him pass,
Between Tantallon and the Bass!'
Calton, get out your keeking-glass—
    Carle, now the King's come!"

The Carline stopp'd; and, sure I am,
For very glee had ta'en a dwam,
But Oman‡ help'd her to a dram.—
    Cogie, now the King's come!

Cogie, now the King's come!
Cogie, now the King's come!
I'se be fou and ye's be toom,§
    Cogie, now the King's come!

PART SECOND.

A Hawick gill of mountain dew,
Heised up Auld Reekie's heart, I trow,
It minded her of Waterloo—
    Carle, now the King's come!

Again I heard her summons swell,
For, sic a dirdum and a yell,
It drown'd Saint Giles's jowing bell—
    Carle, now the King's come!

"My trusty Provost, tried and tight,
Stand forward for the Good Town's right,
There's waur than you been made a
    knight∥—
    Carle, now the King's come!

"My reverend Clergy, look ye say
The best of thanksgivings ye ha'e,
And warstle for a sunny day—
    Carle, now the King's come!

"My Doctors, look that you agree,
Cure a' the town without a fee;
My Lawyers, dinna pike a plea—
    Carle, now the King's come!

"Come forth each sturdy Burgher's bairn,
That dints on wood or clanks on airn,
That fires the o'en, or winds the pirn—
    Carle, now the King's come!

"Come forward with the Blanket Blue,¶
Your sires were loyal men and true,
As Scotland's foemen oft might rue—
    Carle, now the King's come!

"Scots downa loup, and rin and rave,
We're steady folks and something grave,

---

* The Duke of Hamilton, the premier duke of Scotland.

† The Baron of Pennycuik, bound by his tenure to meet the sovereign whenever he or she visits Edinburgh at the Harestone, and there blow three blasts on a horn.

‡ The landlord of the Waterloo Hotel.

§ Empty.

∥ The Lord Provost had the agreeable surprise of hearing his health proposed, at the civic banquet given to George IV. in the Parliament-House, as "Sir William Arbuthnot, Bart."

¶ A Blue Blanket is the standard of the incorporated trades of Edinburgh.

We'll keep the causeway firm and brave—
   Carle, now the King's come!

"Sir Thomas,* thunder from your rock,
Till Pentland dinnles wi' the shock,
And lace wi' fire my snood o' smoke—
   Carle, now the King's come!

"Melville, bring out your bands of blue,
A' Louden lads, baith stout and true,
With Elcho, Hope, and Cockburn, too—
   Carle, now the King's come!

"And you, who on yon bluidy braes
Compell'd the vanquish'd Despot's praise,
Rank out—rank out—my gallant Greys†—
   Carle, now the King's come!

"Cock o' the North, my Huntly bra',
Where are you with the Forty-twa?
Ah! wae's my heart that ye're awa'—
   Carle, now the King's come!

"But yonder come my canty Celts,
With durk and pistols at their belts,
Thank God, we've still some plaids and
   kilts—
   Carle, now the King's come!

"Lord, how the pibrochs groan and yell!
Macdonnell's ta'en the field himsell,
Macleod comes branking o'er the fell—
   Carle, now the King's come!

"Bend up your bow each Archer spark,
For you're to guard him light and dark;
Faith, lads, for ance ye've hit the mark—
   Carle, now the King's come!

"Young Errol, take the sword of state,
The sceptre, Panie-Morarchate;
Knight Mareschal, see ye clear the gate—
   Carle, now the King's come!

"Kind cummer, Leith, ye've been mis-
   set,
But dinna be upon the fret—
Ye'se hae the handsel of him yet,
   Carle, now the King's come!

"My daughters, come with een sae blue,
Your garlands weave, your blossoms strew;
He ne'er saw fairer flowers than you—
   Carle, now the King's come!

"What shall we do for the propine—
We used to offer something fine,
But ne'er a groat's in pouch of mine—
   Carle, now the King's come!

"Deil care—for that I'se never start,
We'll welcome him with Highland heart;
Whate'er we have he's get a part—
   Carle, now the King's come!

"I'll show him mason-work this day—
Nane of your bricks of Babel clay,
But towers shall stand till Time's away—
   Carle, now the King's come!

"I'll show him wit, I'll show him lair,
And gallant lads and lasses fair,
And what wad kind heart wish for mair?—
   Carle, now the King's come!

"Step out, Sir John,‡ of projects rife,
Come win the thanks of an auld wife,
And bring him health and length of life—
   Carle, now the King's come!"

From the Fortunes of Nigel.

1822.

MOTTOES.

CHAP. XIX.

By this good light, a wench of matchless
   mettle!
This were a leaguer-lass to love a soldier,
To bind his wounds, and kiss his bloody
   brow,
And sing a roundel as she help'd to arm
   him,
Though the rough foeman's drums were
   beat so nigh,
They seem'd to bear the burden.
   Old Play.

---

* Sir Thomas Bradford, then commander of
the forces in Scotland.
   † The Scots Greys.

‡ Sir John Sinclair, Bart., father of the celebrated writer Catherine Sinclair.

CHAP. XXII.

Chance will not do the work—Chance
   sends the breeze ;
But if the pilot slumber at the helm,
The very wind that wafts us towards the
   port
May dash us on the shelves.—The steers-
   man's part is vigilance,
Blow it or rough or smooth.—*Old Play.*

CHAP. XXIV.

This is the time—heaven's maiden-sentinel
Hath quited her high watch—the lesser
   spangles
Are paling one by one ; give me the
   ladder
And the short lever—bid Anthony
Keep with his carabine the wicket-gate ;
And do thou bare thy knife and follow
   me,
For we will in and do it—darkness like
   this
Is dawning of our fortunes.—*Old Play.*

CHAP. XXV.

Death finds us 'mid our playthings—
   snatches us,
As a cross nurse might do a wayward
   child,
From all our toys and baubles. His
   rough call
Unlooses all our favourite ties on earth ;
And well if they are such as may be answer'd
In yonder world, where all is judged of
   truly.—*Old Play.*

CHAP. XXIX

How fares the man on whom good men
   would look
With eyes where scorn and censure com-
   bated,
But that kind Christian love hath taught
   the lesson—
That they who merit most contempt and
   hate,
Do most deserve our pity.—*Old Play.*

CHAP. XXXI.

Marry, come up, sir, with your gentle
   blood !
Here's a red stream beneath this coarse
   blue doublet,
That warms the heart as kindly as if
   drawn
From the far source of old Assyrian kings,
Who first made mankind subject to their
   sway.—*Old Play.*

CHAP. XXXV.

We are not worse at once—the course of
   evil
Begins so slowly, and from such slight
   source,
An infant's hand might stem its breach
   with clay ;
But let the stream get deeper, and philo-
   sophy—
Ay, and religion too—shall strive in vain
To turn the headlong torrent.—*Old Play.*

From Peveril of the Peak.

1823.

MOTTOES.

CHAP. II.

Why then, we will have bellowing of
   beeves,
Broaching of barrels, brandishing of
   spigots ;
Blood shall flow freely, but it shall be gore
Of herds and flocks, and venison and
   poultry,
Join'd to the brave heart's-blood of John-
   a-Barleycorn !—*Old Play.*

CHAP. IV.

No, sir,—I will not pledge—I'm one of
   those
Who think good wine needs neither bush
   nor preface
To make it welcome. If you doubt my
   word,
Fill the quart-cup, and see if I will choke
   on't.—*Old Play.*

CHAP. XVI.

Ascasto. Can she not speak?
Oswald. If speech be only in accented
    sounds,
Framed by the tongue and lips, the
    maiden's dumb;
But if by quick and apprehensive look,
By motion, sign, and glance, to give each
    meaning,
Express as clothed in language, be term'd
    speech,
She hath that wondrous faculty; for her
    eyes,
Like the bright stars of heaven, can hold
    discourse,
Though it be mute and soundless.
                        Old Play.

CHAP. XVII.

This is a love meeting? See the maiden
    mourns,
And the sad suitor bends his looks on
    earth.
There's more hath pass'd between them
    than belongs
To Love's sweet sorrows.—*Old Play.*

CHAP. XIX.

Now, hoist the anchor, mates—and let
    the sails
Give their broad bosom to the buxom
    wind,
Like lass that wooes a lover.—*Anon.*

CHAP. XXV.

The course of human life is changeful
    still
As is the fickle wind and wandering rill;
Or, like the light dance which the wild-
    breeze weaves
Amidst the faded race of fallen leaves;
Which now its breath bears down, now
    tosses high,
Beats to the earth, or wafts to middle sky.
Such, and so varied, the precarious play
Of fate with man, frail tenant of a day!
                      Anonymous.

CHAP. XXVI.

Necessity—thou best of peacemakers,
As well as surest prompter of invention—
Help us to composition!—*Anonymous.*

CHAP. XXVII.

——This is some creature of the
    elements
Most like your sea-gull. He can wheel
    and whistle
His screaming song, e'en when the storm
    is loudest—
Take for his sheeted couch the restless
    foam
Of the wild wave-crest—slumber in the
    calm,
And dally with the storm. Yet 'tis a gull,
An arrant gull, with all this.—*The Chieftain.*

CHAP. XXXI.

I fear the devil worst when gown and
    cassock,
Or, in the lack of them, old Calvin's
    cloak,
Conceals his cloven hoof.—*Anonymous.*

From Quentin Durward.

1823.

SONG—COUNTY GUY.

AH! County Guy, the hour is nigh,
    The sun has left the lea,
The orange flower perfumes the bower,
    The breeze is on the sea.
The lark, his lay who thrill'd all day,
    Sits hush'd his partner nigh;
Breeze, bird, and flower, confess the
    hour,
    But where is County Guy?—

The village maid steals through the shade,
    Her shepherd's suit to hear;
To beauty shy, by lattice high,
    Sings high-born Cavalier.
The star of Love, all stars above,
    Now reigns o'er earth and sky;
And high and low the influence know—
    But where is County Guy!—*Chap.* iv.

MOTTOES.

CHAP. XII.

This is a lecturer so skill'd in policy,
That (no disparagement to Satan's cun-
ning)
He well might read a lesson to the devil,
And teach the old seducer new tempta-
tions.—*Old Play.*

CHAP. XIV.

I see thee yet, fair France—thou favour'd
land
Of art and nature—thou art still before me:
Thy sons, to whom their labour is a sport,
So well thy grateful soil returns its
tribute;
Thy sun-burnt daughters, with their
laughing eyes
And glossy raven-locks. But, favour'd
France,
Thou hast had many a tale of woe to tell,
In ancient times as now.—*Anonymous.*

CHAP. XV.

He was a son of Egypt, as he told me,
And one descended from those dread
magicians,
Who waged rash war, when Israel dwelt
in Goshen,
With Israel and her Prophet—matching
rod
With his the sons of Levi's—and en-
countering
Jehovah's miracles with incantations,
Till upon Egypt came the avenging Angel,
And those proud sages wept for their
first-born,
As wept the unletter'd peasant.
Anonymous.

CHAP. XXIV.

Rescue or none, Sir Knight, I am your
captive;
Deal with me what your nobleness
suggests—
Thinking the chance of war may one day
place you
Where I must now be reckon'd—i' the
roll
Of melancholy prisoners.—*Anonymous.*

CHAP. XXV.

No human quality is so well wove
In warp and woof, but there's some flaw
in it;
I've known a brave man fly a shepherd's
cur,
A wise man so demean him, drivelling
idiocy
Had well nigh been ashamed on't. For
your crafty,
Your worldly-wise man, he, above the
rest,
Weaves his own snares so fine, he's often
caught in them.—*Old Play.*

CHAP. XXVI.

When Princes meet, astrologers may
mark it
An ominous conjunction, full of boding,
Like that of Mars with Saturn.—*Old Play.*

CHAP. XXIX.

Thy time is not yet out—the devil thou
servest
Has not as yet deserted thee. He aids
The friends who drudge for him, as the
blind man
Was aided by the guide, who lent his
shoulder
O'er rough and smooth, until he reach'd
the brink
Of the fell precipice—then hurl'd him
downward.—*Old Play.*

CHAP. XXX.

Our counsels waver like the unsteady
bark,
That reels amid the strife of meeting
currents.—*Old Play.*

CHAP. XXXI.

Hold fast thy truth, young soldier.—
Gentle maiden,
Keep you your promise plight—leave age
its subtleties,
And gray-hair'd policy its maze of false-
hood;
But be you candid as the morning sky,
Ere the high sun sucks vapours up to
stain it.—*The Trial.*

From St. Ronan's Well.

1823.

MOTTOES.

CHAP. III.

THERE must be government in all society—
Bees have their Queen, and stag herds have their leader;
Rome had her Consuls, Athens had her Archons,
And we, sir, have our Managing Committee.— *The Album of St. Ronan's.*

CHAP. XI.

Nearest of blood should still be next in love;
And when I see these happy children playing,
While William gathers flowers for Ellen's ringlets,
And Ellen dresses flies for William's angle,
I scarce can think, that in advancing life,
Coldness, unkindness, interest, or suspicion,
Will e'er divide that unity so sacred,
Which Nature bound at birth.
Anonymous.

CHAP. XXXII.

It comes—it wrings me in my parting hour,
The long-hid crime—the well-disguised guilt.
Bring me some holy priest to lay the spectre!—*Old Play.*

CHAP. XXXV.

Sedet post equitem atra cura——

Still though the headlong cavalier,
O'er rough and smooth, in wild career,
Seems racing with the wind;
His sad companion—ghastly pale,
And darksome as a widow's veil,
CARE—keeps her seat behind.
Horace.

CHAP. XXXVIII.

What sheeted ghost is wandering through the storm?
For never did a maid of middle earth
Choose such a time or spot to vent her sorrows.—*Old Play.*

CHAP. XXXIX.

Here come we to our close—for that which follows
Is but the tale of dull, unvaried misery.
Steep crags and headlong lins may court the pencil
Like sudden haps, dark plots, and strange adventures;
But who would paint the dull and fog-wrapt moor,
In its long tract of sterile desolation?
Old Play.

From Redgauntlet.

1824.

As lords their labourers' hire delay,
  Fate quits our toil with hopes to come,
Which, if far short of present pay,
  Still owns a debt and names a sum.

Quit not the pledge, frail sufferer, then,
  Although a distant date be given;
Despair is treason towards man,
  And blasphemy to Heaven.

From the Betrothed.

1825.

SONG—SOLDIER, WAKE.

I.

SOLDIER, wake—the day is peeping,
Honour ne'er was won in sleeping,
Never when the sunbeams still
Lay unreflected on the hill:
'Tis when they are glinted back
From axe and armour, spear and jack,

That they promise future story
Many a page of deathless glory.
Shields that are the foeman's terror,
Ever are the morning's mirror.

II.

Arm and up—the morning beam
Hath call'd the rustic to his team,
Hath call'd the falc'ner to the lake,
Hath call'd the huntsman to the brake;
The early student ponders o'er
His dusty tomes of ancient lore.
Soldier, wake—thy harvest, fame;
Thy study, conquest; war, thy game.
Shield, that would be foeman's terror,
Still should gleam the morning's mirror.

III.

Poor hire repays the rustic's pain;
More paltry still the sportsman's gain:
Vainest of all the student's theme
Ends in some metaphysic dream:
Yet each is up, and each has toil'd
Since first the peep of dawn has smiled;
And each is eagerer in his aim
Than he who barters life for fame.
Up, up, and arm thee, son of terror!
Be thy bright shield the morning's mirror.
Chap. xiv.

SONG—THE TRUTH OF WOMAN.

I.

WOMAN's faith, and woman's trust—
Write the characters in dust;
Stamp them on the running stream,
Print them on the moon's pale beam,
And each evanescent letter
Shall be clearer, firmer, better,
And more permanent, I ween,
Than the thing those letters mean.

II.

I have strain'd the spider's thread
'Gainst the promise of a maid;
I have weigh'd a grain of sand
'Gainst her plight of heart and hand;

I told my true love of the token,
How her faith proved light, and her word
　　was broken:
Again her word and truth she plight,
And I believed them again ere night.
Chap. xx.

MOTTOES.

CHAP. II.

IN Madoc's tent the clarion sounds,
　　With rapid clangour hurried far;
Each hill and dale the note rebounds,
　　But when return the sons of war!
Thou, born of stern Necessity,
Dull Peace! the valley yields to thee,
　　And owns thy melancholy sway.
Welsh Poem.

CHAP. VII.

O, sadly shines the morning sun
　　On leaguer'd castle wall,
When bastion, tower and battlement,
　　Seem nodding to their fall.—*Old Ballad.*

CHAP. XII.

Now all ye ladies of fair Scotland,
　　And ladies of England that happy
　　　would prove,
Marry never for houses, nor marry for land,
　　Nor marry for nothing but only love.
Family Quarrels.

CHAP. XIII.

Too much rest is rust,
　　There's ever cheer in changing;
We tyne by too much trust,
　　So we'll be up and ranging.—*Old Song.*

CHAP. XVII.

Ring out the merry bells, the bride approaches;
The blush upon her check has shamed
　　the morning,
For that is dawning palely. Grant, good
　　saints,
These clouds betoken nought of evil omen!
Old Play.

CHAP. XXVII.

Julia. —— Gentle sir,
You are our captive—but we'll use you so,
That you shall think your prison joys may
  match
Whate'er your liberty hath known of
  pleasure.
  Roderick. No, fairest, we have trifled
  here too long;
And, lingering to see your roses blossom,
I've let my laurels wither.—*Old Play.*

————

From the Talisman.

1825.

AHRIMAN.

DARK Ahriman, whom Irak still
Holds origin of woe and ill!
  When, bending at thy shrine,
We view the world with troubled eye,
Where see we 'neath the extended sky,
  An empire matching thine!

If the Benigner Power can yield
A fountain in the desert field,
  Where weary pilgrims drink;
Thine are the waves that lash the rock,
Thine the tornado's deadly shock,
  Where countless navies sink!

Or if He bid the soil dispense
Balsams to cheer the sinking sense,
  How few can they deliver
From lingering pains, or pang intense,
Red Fever, spotted Pestilence,
  The arrows of thy quiver!

Chief in Man's bosom sits thy sway,
And frequent, while in words we pray
  Before another throne,
Whate'er of specious form be there,
The secret meaning of the prayer
  Is, Ahriman, thine own.

Say, hast thou feeling, sense, and form,
Thunder thy voice, thy garments storm,
  As Eastern Magi say;

With sentient soul of hate and wrath,
And wings to sweep thy deadly path,
  And fangs to tear thy prey?

Or art thou mixed in Nature's source,
An ever operating force,
  Converting good to ill;
An evil principle innate
Contending with our better fate,
  And oh! victorious still?

Howe'er it be, dispute is vain.
On all without thou hold'st thy reign,
  Nor less on all within;
Each mortal passion's fierce career,
Love, hate, ambition, joy, and fear,
  Thou goadest into sin.

Whene'er a sunny gleam appears,
To brighten up our vale of tears,
  Thou art not distant far;
'Mid such brief solace of our lives,
Thou whett'st our very banquet-knives
  To tools of death and war.—

Thus, from the moment of our birth,
Long as we linger on the earth,
  Thou rul'st the fate of men;
Thine are the pangs of life's last hour,
And—who dare answer?—is thy power,
  Dark Spirit! ended THEN?
  Chap. iii.

————

SONG OF BLONDEL—THE BLOODY VEST.

'TWAS near the fair city of Benevent,
When the sun was setting on bough and
  bent,
And knights were preparing in bower and
  tent,
On the eve of the Baptist's tournament;
When in Lincoln green a stripling gent,
Well seeming a page by a princess sent,
Wander'd the camp, and, still as he went,
Enquired for the Englishman, Thomas a
  Kent.

Far hath he fared, and farther must fare,
Till he finds his pavilion nor stately nor
  rare,—

Little save iron and steel was there;
And, as lacking the coin to pay armourer's
care,
With his sinewy arms to the shoulders
bare,
The good knight with hammer and file
did repair
The mail that to-morrow must see him
wear,
For the honour of Saint John and his lady
fair.

"Thus speaks my lady," the page said he,
And the knight bent lowly both head and
knee,
"She is Benevent's Princess so high in
degree,
And thou art as lowly as knight may well
be—
He that would climb so lofty a tree,
Or spring such a gulf as divides her from
thee,
Must dare some high deed, by which all
men may see
His ambition is back'd by his high chi-
valrie.

"Therefore thus speaks my lady," the fair
page he said,
And the knight lowly louted with hand
and with head,
"Fling aside the good armour in which
thou art clad,
And don thou this weed of her night-gear
instead,
For a hauberk of steel, a kirtle of thread:
And charge, thus attired, in the tournament dread,
And fight as thy wont is where most
blood is shed,
And bring honour away, or remain with
the dead."

Untroubled in his look, and untroubled in
his breast,
The knight the weed hath taken, and
reverently hath kiss'd:
"Now bless'd be the moment, the messenger be blest!

Much honour'd do I hold me in my lady's
high behest;
And say unto my lady, in this dear night-
weed dress'd,
To the best arm'd champion I will not
vail my crest;
But if I live and bear me well 'tis her turn
to take the test."
Here, gentles, ends the foremost fytte of
the Lay of the Bloody Vest.

FYTTE SECOND.

The Baptist's fair morrow beheld gallant
feats—
There was winning of honour, and losing
of seats—
There was hewing with falchions, and
splintering of staves,
The victors won glory, the vanquish'd
won graves.
O, many a knight there fought bravely
and well,
Yet one was accounted his peers to excel,
And 'twas he whose sole armour on body
and breast,
Seem'd the weed of a damsel when boune
for her rest.

There were some dealt him wounds that
were bloody and sore,
But others respected his plight, and forebore.
"It is some oath of honour," they said,
"and I trow
'Twere unknightly to slay him achieving
his vow."
Then the Prince, for his sake, bade the
tournament cease,
He flung down his warder, the trumpets
sung peace;
And the judges declare, and competitors
yield,
That the Knight of the Night-gear was
first in the field.

The feast it was nigh, and the mass it was
nigher,
When before the fair Princess low louted
a squire,

And deliver'd a garment unseemly to view,
With sword-cut and spear-thrust, all
   hack'd and pierced through;
All rent and all tatter'd, all clotted with
   blood,
With foam of the horses, with dust, and
   with mud,
Not the point of that lady's small finger,
   I ween,
Could have rested on spot was unsullied
   and clean.

"This token my master, Sir Thomas a
   Kent,
Restores to the Princess of fair Benevent:
He that climbs the tall tree has won right
   to the fruit,
He that leaps the wide gulf should prevail
   in his suit;
Through life's utmost peril the prize J
   have won,
And now must the faith of my mistress
   be shown:
For she who prompts knight on such
   danger to run,
Must avouch his true service in front of
   the sun.

"'I restore,' says my master, 'the garment I've worn,
And I claim of the Princess to don it in
   turn;
For its stains and its rents she should prize
   it the more,
Since by shame 'tis unsullied, though
   crimson'd with gore.'"
Then deep blush'd the Princess—yet kiss'd
   she and press'd
The blood-spotted robes to her lips and
   her breast.
"Go tell my true knight, church and
   chamber shall show,
If I value the blood on this garment or no."

And when it was time for the nobles to
   pass,
In solemn procession to minster and mass,
The first walk'd the Princess in purple
   and pall,
But the blood-besmear'd night-robe she
   wore over all;

And eke, in the hall, where they all sat at
   dine
When she knelt to her father and proffer'd
   the wine,
Over all her rich robes and state jewels
   she wore,
That wimple unseemly bedabbled with
   gore.

Then lords whisper'd ladies, as well you
   may think,
And ladies replied, with nod, titter, and
   wink;
And the Prince, who in anger and shame
   had look'd down,
Turn'd at length to his daughter, and
   spoke with a frown:
"Now since thou hast publish'd thy folly
   and guilt,
E'en atone with thy hand for the blood
   thou hast spilt;
Yet sore for your boldness you both will
   repent,
When you wander as exiles from fair
   Benevent."

Then out spoke stout Thomas, in hall
   where he stood,
Exhausted and feeble, but dauntless of
   mood:
"The blood that I lost for this daughter
   of thine,
I pour'd forth as freely as flask gives its
   wine;
And if for my sake she brooks penance
   and blame,
Do not doubt I will save her from suffering and shame;
And light will she reck of thy princedom
   and rent,
When I hail her, in England, the Countess of Kent."—*Chap.* xxvi.

MOTTOES.

CHAP. IX.

THIS is the Prince of Leeches; fever,
   plague,

Cold rheum, and hot podagra, do but look
     on him,
And quit their grasp upon the tortured
     sinews.—*Anonymous.*

CHAP. XIII.

You talk of Gaiety and Innocence!
The moment when the fatal fruit was
     eaten,
They parted ne'er to meet again; and
     Malice
Has ever since been playmate to light
     Gaiety,
From the first moment when the smiling
     infant
Destroys the flower or butterfly he toys
     with,
To the last chuckle of the dying miser,
Who on his deathbed laughs his last to
     hear
His wealthy neighbour has become a bank-
     rupt.—*Old Play.*

CHAP. XVI.

'Tis not her sense—for sure, in that
     There's nothing more than common;
And all her wit is only chat,
     Like any other woman.—*Song.*

CHAP. XVII.

Were every hair upon his head a life,
And every life were to be supplicated
By numbers equal to those hairs quad-
     rupled,
Life after life should out like waning stars
Before the daybreak—or as festive lamps,
Which have lent lustre to the midnight
     revel,
Each after each are quench'd when guests
     depart!—*Old Play.*

CHAP. XX.

When beauty leads the lion in her toils,
Such are her charms, he dare not raise his
     mane,
Far less expand the terror of his fangs.
So great Alcides made his club a distaff,
And spun to please fair Omphale.
                Anonymous.

CHAP. XXIII.

'Mid these wild scenes Enchantment waves
     her hand
To change the face of the mysterious
     land,
Till the bewildering scenes around us seem
The vain productions of a feverish
     dream.—*Astolpho, a Romance.*

CHAP. XXVI.

The tears I shed must ever fall!
     I weep not for an absent swain,
For time may happier hours recall,
     And parted lovers meet again.

I weep not for the silent dead,
     Their pains are past, their sorrows o'er,
And those that loved their steps must
     tread,
     When death shall join to part no more.

But worse than absence, worse than death,
     She wept her lover's sullied fame,
And, fired with all the pride of birth,
     She wept a soldier's injured name.
                Ballad.

RHEIN-WEIN LIED.

WHAT makes the troopers' frozen
     courage muster?
     The grapes of juice divine.
Upon the Rhine, upon the Rhine they
     cluster:
     Oh, blessed be the Rhine!

Let fringe and furs, and many a rabbit
     skin, sirs,
     Bedeck your Saracen;
He'll freeze without what warms our
     hearts within, sirs,
     When the night-frost crusts the fen.

But on the Rhine, but on the Rhine
     they cluster,
     The grapes of juice divine,
That make our troopers' frozen courage
     muster;
     Oh, blessed be the Rhine!

WAR-SONG OF THE ROYAL EDINBURGH LIGHT DRAGOONS.—1797.

To horse! to horse! the standard flies,
  The bugles sound the call;
The Gallic navy stems the seas,
The voice of battle's on the breeze,
  Arouse ye, one and all!

From high Dunedin's towers we come,
  A band of brothers true;
Our casques the leopard's spoils sur-
    round,
With Scotland's hardy thistle crown'd;
  We boast the red and blue.

Though tamely crouch to Gallia's
    frown
  Dull Holland's tardy train;
Their ravish'd toys though Romans
    mourn;
Though gallant Switzers vainly spurn,
  And, foaming, gnaw the chain;

Oh! had they mark'd the avenging call
  Their brethren's murder gave,
Disunion ne'er their ranks had mown,
Nor patriot valour, desperate grown,
  Sought freedom in the grave!

Shall we, too, bend the stubborn head
  In Freedom's temple born,
Dress our pale cheek in timid smile,
To hail a master in our isle,
  Or brook a victor's scorn?

No! though destruction o'er the land
  Came pouring as a flood,
The sun that sees our falling day
Shall mark our sabres' deadly sway,
  And set that night in blood.

For gold let Gallia's legions fight,
  Or plunder's bloody gain;
Unbribed, unbought, our swords we
    draw,
To guard our king, to fence our law,
  Nor shall their edge be vain.

If ever breath of British gale
  Shall fan the tricolor,

Or footstep of invader rude,
With rapine foul, and red with blood,
  Pollute our happy shore,—

Then farewell home! and farewell
    friends!
  Adieu each tender tie!
Resolved, we mingle in the tide,
Where charging squadrons furious ride,
  To conquer or to die.

To horse! to horse! the sabres gleam;
  High sounds our bugle-call;
Combined by honour's sacred tie,
Our word is *Laws and Liberty!*
  March forward one and all!

———◇———

LINES TO SIR CUTHBERT SHARP.

1827.

FORGET thee? No! my worthy fere!
Forget blithe mirth and gallant cheer!
Death sooner stretch me on my bier!
  Forget thee? No.

Forget the universal shout *
When "canny Sunderland" spoke out—
A truth which knaves affect to doubt—
  Forget thee? No.

Forget you? No—though now-a-day
I've heard your knowing people say,
Disown the debt you cannot pay,
You'll find it far the thriftiest way—
  But I?—O no.

Forget your kindness found for all room,
In what, though large, seem'd still a
    small room.
Forget my *Surtees* in a ball-room—
  Forget you? No.

Forget your sprightly dumpty-diddles,
And beauty tripping to the fiddles,
Forget my lovely friends the *Liddells*—
  Forget you? No.

* An allusion to the enthusiastic reception
of the Duke of Wellington at Sunderland.—
ED.

THE DEATH OF KEELDAR.

These stanzas were written for Hood's "Gem," 1828, and accompanied an engraving from Cooper's painting of the Death of Keeldar.

UP rose the sun o'er moor and mead ;
Up with the sun rose Percy Rede ;
Brave Keeldar, from his couples freed,
　　Career'd along the lea ;
The palfrey sprung with sprightly
　　bound,
As if to match the gamesome hound ;
His horn the gallant huntsman wound:
　　They were a jovial three !

Man, hound, or horse, of higher fame,
To wake the wild deer never came,
Since Alnwick's Earl pursued the game
　　On Cheviot's rueful day ;
Keeldar was matchless in his speed,
Than Tarras, ne'er was stauncher steed,
A peerless archer, Percy Rede :
　　And right dear friends were they.

The chase engross'd their joys and
　　woes,
Together at the dawn they rose,
Together shared the noon's repose,
　　By fountain or by stream ;
And oft, when evening skies were red,
The heather was their common bed,
Where each, as wildering fancy led,
　　Still hunted in his dream.

Now is the thrilling moment near,
Of sylvan hope and sylvan fear,
Yon thicket holds the harbour'd deer,
　　The signs the hunters know ;—
With eyes of flame, and quivering ears,
The brake sagacious Keeldar nears ;
The restless palfrey paws and rears ;
　　The archer strings his bow.

The game's afoot !—Halloo ! Halloo !
Hunter, and horse, and hound
　　pursue :—
But woe the shaft that erring flew—
　　That e'er it left the string !
And ill betide the faithless yew !
The stag bounds scathless o'er the dew,
And gallant Keeldar's life-blood true
　　Has drench'd the grey-goose wing.

The noble hound—he dies, he dies,
Death, death has glazed his fixed eyes,
Stiff on the bloody heath he lies,
　　Without a groan or quiver.
Now day may break and bugle sound,
And whoop and hallow ring around,
And o'er his couch the stag may bound
　　But Keeldar sleeps for ever.

Dilated nostrils, staring eyes,
Mark the poor palfrey's mute surprise,
He knows not that his comrade dies,
　　Nor what is death—but still
His aspect hath expression drear
Of grief and wonder, mix'd with fear,
Like startled children when they hear
　　Some mystic tale of ill.

But he that bent the fatal bow,
Can well the sum of evil know,
And o'er his favourite, bending low,
　　In speechless grief recline ;
Can think he hears the senseless clay
In unreproachful accents say,
" The hand that took my life away,
　　Dear master, was it thine ?

" And if it be, the shaft be bless'd,
Which sure some erring aim address'd,
Since in your service prized, caress'd
　　I in your service die ;
And you may have a fleeter hound,
To match the dun-deer's merry bound,
But by your couch will ne'er be found
　　So true a guard as I."

And to his last stout Percy rued
The fatal chance ; for when he stood
'Gainst fearful odds in deadly feud,
　　And fell amid the fray,
E'en with his dying voice he cried,
" Had Keeldar but been at my side,
Your treacherous ambush had been
　　spied—
　　I had not died to-day !"

Remembrance of the erring bow
Long since had joined the tides which
　　flow,
Conveying human bliss and woe
　　Down dark oblivion's river :

But Art can Time's stern doom arrest,
And snatch his spoil from Lethe's breast,
And, in her Cooper's colours drest,
    The scene shall live for ever.

THE RESOLVE.

IN IMITATION OF AN OLD ENGLISH POEM.

Published in the "Edinburgh Annual Register."

1808.

MY wayward fate I needs must plain,
    Though bootless be the theme :
I loved, and was beloved again,
    Yet all was but a dream ;
For, as her love was quickly got,
    So it was quickly gone ;
No more I'll bask in flame so hot,
    But coldly dwell alone.

Not maid more bright than maid was e'er
    My fancy shall beguile,
By flattering word or feigned tear,
    By gesture, look, or smile :
No more I'll call the shaft fair shot,
    Till it has fairly flown,
Nor scorch me at a flame so hot ;—
    I'll rather freeze alone.

Each ambush'd Cupid I'll defy,
    In cheek, or chin, or brow,
And deem the glance of woman's eye
    As weak as woman's vow :
I'll lightly hold the lady's heart,
    That is but lightly won ;
I'll steel my breast to beauty's art,
    And learn to live alone.

The flaunting torch soon blazes out,
    The diamond's ray abides ;
The flame its glory hurls about,
    The gem its lustre hides :
Such gem I fondly deem'd was mine,
    And glowed a diamond stone,
But, since each eye may see it shine,
    I'll darkling dwell alone.

No waking dream shall tinge my thought
    With dyes so bright and vain,
No silken net, so slightly wrought,
    Shall tangle me again :
No more I'll pay so dear for wit,
    I'll live upon mine own ;
Nor shall wild passion trouble it,—
    I'll rather dwell alone.

And thus I'll hush my heart to rest,--
    " Thy loving labour's lost ;
Thou shalt no more be wildly blest,
    To be so strangely crost ;
The widow'd turtles mateless die,
    The phœnix is but one ;
They seek no loves—no more will I—
    I'll rather dwell alone."

MR. KEMBLE'S FAREWELL ADDRESS,

ON TAKING LEAVE OF THE EDINBURGH STAGE.

1817.

As the worn war-horse, at the trumpet's sound,
Erects his mane, and neighs, and paws the ground—
Disdains the ease his generous lord assigns,
And longs to rush on the embattled lines,
So I, your plaudits ringing on mine ear,
Can scarce sustain to think our parting near ;
To think my scenic hour for ever past,
And that these valued plaudits are my last.
Why should we part, while still some powers remain,
That in your service strive not yet in vain ?
Cannot high zeal the strength of youth supply,
And sense of duty fire the fading eye ;

And all the wrongs of age remain
subdued
Beneath the burning glow of gratitude ?
Ah no!—the taper, wearing to its
close,
Oft for a space in fitful lustre glows ;
But all too soon the transient gleam is
past—
It cannot be renew'd, and will not last ;
Even duty, zeal, and gratitude, can
wage
But short-lived conflict with the frosts
of age.

Yes ! it were poor, remembering what
I was,
To live a pensioner on your applause,
To drain the dregs of your endurance
dry,
And take, as alms, the praise I once
could buy ;
Till every sneering youth around in-
quires,
" Is this the man who once could
please our sires ?"
And scorn assumes compassion's
doubtful mien,
To warn me off from the encumber'd
scene.
This must not be ;—and higher duties
crave
Some space between the theatre and
the grave,
That like the Roman in the Capitol,
I may adjust my mantle ere I fall :
My life's brief act in public service
flown,
The last, the closing scene, must be
my own.

Here, then, adieu ! while yet some
well-graced parts
May fix an ancient favourite in your
hearts,
Not quite to be forgotten, even when
You look on better actors, younger
men :
And if your bosoms own this kindly
debt
Of old remembrance, how shall mine
forget—

O, how forget !—how oft I hither came
In anxious hope, how oft return'd with
fame !
How oft around your circle this weak
hand
Has waved immortal Shakspeare's
magic wand,
Till the full burst of inspiration came,
And I have felt, and you have fann'd
the flame !
By mem'ry treasured, while her reign
endures,
Those hours must live—and all their
charms are yours.

O favour'd Land, renown'd for arts
and arms,
For manly talent, and for female
charms,
Could this full bosom prompt the
sinking line,
What fervent benedictions now were
thine!
But my last part is play'd, my knell is
rung,
When e'en your praise falls faltering
from my tongue ;
And all that you can hear, or I can
tell,
Is—Friends and Patrons, hail ! and
FARE YOU WELL !

———

LINES,

WRITTEN FOR MISS SMITH.

1817.

WHEN the lone pilgrim views afar
The shrine that is his guiding star,
With awe his footsteps print the road
Which the loved saint of yore has
trod.
As near he draws, and yet more near
His dim eye sparkles with a tear ;
The Gothic fanes unwonted show,
The choral hymn, the tapers' glow,
Oppress his soul ; while they delight
And chasten rapture with affright.

No longer dare he think his toil
Can merit aught his patron's smile;
Too light appears the distant way,
The chilly eve, the sultry day—
All these endured no favour claim,
But murmuring forth the sainted name,
He lays his little offering down,
And only deprecates a frown.

We, too, who ply the Thespian art,
Oft feel such bodings of the heart,
And, when our utmost powers are strain'd,
Dare hardly hope your favour gain'd.
She, who from sister climes has sought
The ancient land where Wallace fought—
Land long renown'd for arms and arts,
And conquering eyes and dauntless hearts,—
She, as the flutterings *here* avow,
Feels all the pilgrim's terrors *now;*
Yet sure on Caledonian plain
The stranger never sued in vain.
'Tis yours the hospitable task
To give the applause she dare not ask;
And they who bid the pilgrim speed,
The pilgrim's blessing be their meed.

EPILOGUE

TO THE DRAMA FOUNDED ON
" ST. RONAN'S WELL."

1824.

" After the play, the following humorous address (ascribed to an eminent literary character) was spoken with infinite effect by Mr. Mackay in the character of MEG DODS."—*Edinburgh Weekly Journal, 9th June,* 1824.

Enter MEG DODS, *encircled by a crowd of unruly boys, whom a Town's Officer is driving off.*

THAT'S right, friend—drive the gaitlings back,
And lend yon muckle ane a whack;
Your Embro' bairns are grown a pack
    Sae proud and saucy,

They scarce will let an auld wife walk
    Upon your causey.

I've seen the day they would been scaur'd
Wi' the Tolbooth, or wi' the Guard.
Or maybe wud hae some regard
    For Jamie Laing[1]—
The Water-hole[2] was right well wared
    On sic a gang.

But whar's the gude Tolbooth[3] gane now?
Whar's the auld Claught,[4] wi' red and blue?
Whar's Jamie Laing? and whar's John Doo?[5]   [house?
            And whar's the Weigh-
Deil hae't I see but what is new,
    Except the Playhouse.

Yoursells are changed frae head to heel;
There's some that gar the causeway reel
With clashing hufe and rattling wheel,
            And horses canterin',
Wha's father's daunder'd hame as weel
    Wi' lass and lantern.

Mysell being in the public line,
I look for howfs I kenn'd lang syne,
Whar gentles used to drink gude wine,
            And eat cheap dinners;
But deil a soul gangs there to dine,
    Of saunts or sinners!

Fortune's[6] and Hunter's gane, alas!
And Bayle's is lost in empty space;
And now, if folk would splice a brace,
    Or crack a bottle,
They gang to a new-fangled place
            They ca' a Hottle.

---

[1] Jamie Laing, head of the Edinburgh Police at that time.
[2] Watch-hole.
[3] The Tolbooth was the great Edinburgh Jail, pulled down in 1817.
[4] The Claught was the old Town Guard.
[5] John Doo, one of the Guard or Police.
[6] Fortune's, Hunter's, and Bayle's were taverns.

The deevil hottle them for Meg !
They are sae greedy and sae gleg,
That if ye're served but wi' an egg,
      (And that's puir pickin',)
In comes a chiel, and makes a leg,
      And charges chicken !

" And wha may ye be," gin ye speer,
" That brings your auld-warld clavers
    here !"
Troth, if there's onybody near
      That kens the roads,
I'll haud ye Burgundy to beer,
      He kens Meg Dods.

I came a piece frae west o' Currie ;
And, since I see you're in a hurry,
Your patience I'll nae langer worry,
      But be sae crouse
As speak a word for ane Will Murray,
      That keeps this house.[1]

Plays are auld-fashion'd things, in
    truth,
And ye've seen wonders mair uncouth;
Yet actors shouldna suffer drouth,
      Or want of dramock,
Although they speak but wi' their
    mouth,
      Not with their stamock.

But ye take care of a' folk's pantry ;
And surely to hae stooden sentry
Ower this big house (that's far frae
    rent free,)
      For a lone sister,
Is claim as gude's to be a ventri²—
      How'st ca'd—loquister.

Weel, sirs, gude-e'en, and have a care
The bairns mak fun o' Meg nae mair ;
For gin they do, she tells you fair,
      And without failzie,
As sure as ever ye sit there,
      She'll tell the Bailee.

---

[1] The Edinburgh Theatre.
[2] An allusion to the recent performances of
Alexandre, the ventriloquist.

THE FORAY.

1830.

THE last of our steers on our board
    has been spread,
And the last flask of wine in our goblet
    is red ;
Up ! up, my brave kinsmen ! belt
    swords, and begone !—
There are dangers to dare, and there's
    spoil to be won.

The eyes, that so lately mix'd glances
    with ours,
For a space must be dim, as they gaze
    from the towers,
And strive to distinguish through tem-
    pest and gloom,
The prance of the steed, and the toss
    of the plume.

The rain is descending, the wind rises
    loud ;
And the moon her red beacon has
    veil'd with a cloud ;
'Tis the better, my mates ! for the
    warder's dull eye
Shall in confidence slumber, nor dream
    we are nigh.

Our steeds are impatient ! I hear my
    blithe Grey !
There is life in his hoof-clang, and
    hope in his neigh ;
Like the flash of a meteor, the glance
    of his mane
Shall marshal your march through the
    darkness and rain.

The drawbridge has dropped, the bugle
    has blown ;
One pledge is to quaff yet—then mount
    and begone !—
To their honour and peace, that shall
    rest with the slain !
To their health and their glee, that see
    Teviot again !

LINES,

ADDRESSED

TO MONSIEUR ALEXANDRE,[1]
THE CELEBRATED VENTRILOQUIST.

1824.

OF yore, in old England, it was not
    thought good
To carry two visages under one hood;
What should folk say to *you?* who
    have faces such plenty,
That from under one hood, you last
    night showed us twenty!
Stand forth, arch deceiver, and tell us
    in truth,
Are you handsome or ugly, in age or
    in youth?
Man, woman, or child—a dog or a
    mouse?
Or are you, at once, each live thing in
    the house?
Each live thing did I ask?—each dead
    implement, too,
A workshop in your person, — saw,
    chisel, and screw!
Above all, are you one individual? I
    know
You must be at least Alexandre and Co.
But I think you're a troop—an assem-
    blage—a mob,
And that I, as the Sheriff, should take
    up the job;
And instead of rehearsing your won-
    ders in verse,
Must read you the Riot Act, and bid
    you disperse.

---

[1] "When Monsieur Alexandre, the celebrated ventriloquist, was in Scotland, in 1824,
he paid a visit to Abbotsford, where he entertained his distinguished host and the other
visitors with his unrivalled imitations. Next
morning, when he was about to depart, Sir
Walter felt a good deal embarrassed as to the
sort of acknowledgment he should offer; but
at length, resolving that it would probably be
most agreeable to the young foreigner to be
paid in professional coin, if in any, he stepped
aside for a few minutes, and, on returning,
presented him with this epigram." The lines
were published in the *Edinburgh Annual
Register* for 1824.

EPITAPH ON MRS. ERSKINE.

1819.

PLAIN, as her native dignity of mind,
Arise the tomb of her we have resign'd;
Unflaw'd and stainless be the marble
    scroll,
Emblem of lovely form and candid soul.
But, oh! what symbol may avail, to tell
The kindness, wit, and sense, we loved
    so well!
What sculpture show the broken ties
    of life,
Here buried with the parent, friend,
    and wife!
Or on the tablet stamp each title dear
By which thine urn, EUPHEMIA, claims
    the tear!
Yet taught, by thy meek sufferance, to
    assume
Patience in anguish, hope beyond the
    tomb,
Resign'd though sad, this votive verse
    shall flow,
And brief, alas! as thy brief span
    below.

INSCRIPTION

FOR THE MONUMENT OF THE
REV. GEORGE SCOTT.

1830.

TO youth, to age, alike, this tablet pale
Tells the brief moral of its tragic tale.
Art thou a parent?—Reverence this
    bier—
The parents' fondest hopes lie buried
    here.
Art thou a youth, prepared on life to
    start,
With opening talents and a generous
    heart,
Fair hopes and flattering prospects all
    thine own!—
Lo! here their end—a monumental
    stone!
But let submission tame each sorrow-
    ing thought,
Heaven crown'd its champion ere the
    fight was fought.

MOTTOES FROM "WOODSTOCK."

CHAP. II.

Come forth, old man—Thy daughter's side
Is now the fitting place for thee:
When time hath quell'd the oak's bold pride,
 The youthful tendril yet may hide
  The ruins of the parent tree.

CHAP. IV.

  Yon path of greensward
Winds round by sparry grot and gay pavilion:
There is no flint to gall thy tender foot,
There's ready shelter from each breeze or shower.—
But duty guides not that way—see her stand,
With wand entwined with amaranth, near yon cliffs.
Oft where she leads thy blood must mark thy footsteps,
Oft where she leads thy head must bear the storm,
And thy shrunk form endure heat, cold, and hunger;
But she will guide thee up to noble heights,
Which he who gains seems native of the sky,
While earthly things lie stretch'd beneath his feet,
Diminish'd, shrunk, and valueless——
     Anonymous.

CHAP. X.

  Here we have one head
Upon two bodies—your two-headed bullock
Is but an ass to such a prodigy.
These two have but one meaning, thought, and counsel;
And when the single noddle has spoke out,
The four legs scrape assent to it.
     Old Play.

CHAP. XIV.

  Deeds are done on earth
Which have their punishment ere the earth closes
Upon the perpetrators. Be it the working
Of the remorse-stirr'd fancy, or the vision,
Distinct and real, of unearthly being,
All ages witness, that beside the couch
Of the fell homicide oft stalks the ghost
Of him he slew, and shows the shadowy wound.—*Old Play.*

CHAP. XXIV.

The deadliest snakes are those which, twined 'mongst flowers,
Blend their bright colouring with the varied blossoms,
Their fierce eyes glittering like the spangled dewdrop;
In all so like what nature has most harmless,
That sportive innocence, which dreads no danger,
Is poison'd unawares.—*Old Play.*

GLEE FOR KING CHARLES.

Bring the bowl which you boast,
 Fill it up to the brim;
'Tis to him we love most,
 And to all who love him.
Brave gallants, stand up,
 And avaunt, ye base carles!
Were there death in the cup,
 Here's a health to King Charles!

Though he wanders through dangers,
 Unaided, unknown,
Dependent on strangers,
 Estranged from his own;
Though 'tis under our breath,
 Amidst forfeits and perils,
Here's to honour and faith,
 And a health to King Charles!

Let such honours abound
  As the time can afford,
The knee on the ground,
  And the hand on the sword ;
But the time shall come round,
  When, 'mid Lords, Dukes, and Earls,
The loud trumpets shall sound,
  Here's a health to King Charles !
                    Chap. xx.

ONE HOUR WITH THEE.

AN hour with thee !—When earliest day
Dapples with gold the eastern grey,
Oh, what can frame my mind to bear
The toil and turmoil, cark and care,
New griefs, which coming hours unfold
And sad remembrance of the old ?
                    One hour with thee !

One hour with thee ! When burning June
Waves his red flag at pitch of noon ;
What shall repay the faithful swain,
His labour on the sultry plain ;
And more than cave or sheltering bough,
Cool feverish blood, and throbbing
  brow ?—
                    One hour with thee !

One hour with thee !—When sun is set,
O, what can teach me to forget
The thankless labours of the day ;
The hopes, the wishes, flung away ;
The increasing wants and lessening
  gains,
The master's pride, who scorns my
  pains ?—
                    One hour with thee !
                    Chap. xxvi.

MOTTOES FROM "THE FAIR MAID OF PERTH."

CHAP. I.

" BEHOLD the Tiber !" the vain Roman
  cried,
Viewing the ample Tay from Baiglie's
  side ;
But where's the Scot that would the
  vaunt repay,
And hail the puny Tiber for the Tay ?
                    Anonymous.

THE LAY OF POOR LOUISE.

AH, poor Louise ! The livelong day
She roams from cot to castle gay ;
And still her voice and viol say,
Ah, maids, beware the woodland way,
                    Think on Louise.

Ah, poor Louise ! The sun was high,
It smirch'd her cheek, it dimm'd her
  eye.
The woodland walk was cool and nigh,
Where birds with chiming streamlets vie
                    To cheer Louise.

Ah, poor Louise ! The savage bear
Made ne'er that lovely grove his lair ;
The wolves molest not paths so fair—
But better far had such been there
                    For poor Louise.

Ah, poor Louise ! In woody wold
She met a huntsman fair and bold ;
His baldric was of silk and gold,
And many a witching tale he told
                    To poor Louise.

Ah, poor Louise ! Small cause to pine
Hadst thou for treasures of the mine ;
For peace of mind, that gift divine,
And spotless innocence, were thine,
                    Ah, poor Louise !

Ah, poor Louise ! Thy treasure's reft !
I know not if by force or theft,
Or part by violence, part by gift ;
But misery is all that's left
                    To poor Louise.

Let poor Louise some succour have !
She will not long your bounty crave,
Or tire the gay with warning stave—
For Heaven has grace, and earth a
  grave
                    For poor Louise.
                    Chap. x.

CHANT OVER THE DEAD.

VIEWLESS Essence, thin and bare,
Wellnigh melted into air ;
Still with fondness hovering near
The earthly form thou once didst wear.

Pause upon thy pinion's flight,
Be thy course to left or right;
Be thou doom'd to soar or sink,
Pause upon the awful brink.

To avenge the deed expelling
Thee untimely from thy dwelling,
Mystic force thou shalt retain
O'er the blood and o'er the brain.

When the form thou shalt espy
That darken'd on thy closing eye;
When the footstep thou shalt hear,
That thrill'd upon thy dying ear;

Then strange sympathies shall wake,
The flesh shall thrill, the nerves shall
    quake;
The wounds renew their clotter'd flood,
And every drop cry blood for blood.
                    Chap. xxii.

YES, THOU MAYST SIGH.

YES, thou mayst sigh,
And look once more at all around,
At stream and bank, and sky and
    ground,
Thy life its final course has found,
And thou must die.

Yes, lay thee down,
And while thy struggling pulses flutter,
Bid the grey monk his soul mass
    mutter,
And the deep bell its death-tone utter—
Thy life is gone.

Be not afraid.
'Tis but a pang, and then a thrill,
A fever fit, and then a chill;
And then an end of human ill,
For thou art dead.   *Chap*. xxx.

OH, BOLD AND BLUE.

OH, Bold and True,
In bonnet blue,
That fear or falsehood never knew;
Whose heart was loyal to his word,
Whose hand was faithful to his sword—
Seek Europe wide from sea to sea,
But bonny Blue-cap still for me!

I've seen Almain's proud champions
    prance—
Have seen the gallant knights of France,
Unrivall'd with the sword and lance—
Have seen the sons of England true
Wield the brown bill, and bend the yew,
Search France the fair and England
    free,
But bonny Blue-cap still for me!
                    Chap. xxxii.

MOTTOES FROM "ANNE OF GEIERSTEIN."

CHAP. V.

—— I was one
Who loved the greenwood bank and
    lowing herd,
The russet prize, the lowly peasant's life,
Season'd with sweet content, more than
    the halls
Where revellers feast to fever-height.
    Believe me,
There ne'er was poison mix'd in maple
bowl.—*Anonymous*.

CHAP. X.

We know not when we sleep nor when
    we wake.
Visions distinct and perfect cross our
    eye,
Which to the slumberer seem realities;
And while they waked, some men have
    seen such sights
As set at nought the evidence of sense,
And left them well persuaded they were
    dreaming.—*Anonymous*.

CHAP. XI.

These be the adept's doctrines—every
    element
Is peopled with its separate race of
    spirits.
The airy Sylphs on the blue ether float;
Deep in the earthy cavern skulks the
    Gnome;
The sea-green Naiad skims the ocean
    billow,
And the fierce fire is yet a friendly home
To its peculiar sprite—the Salamander.
                    Anonymous.

CHAP. XXII.

Tell me not of it—I could ne'er abide
The mummery of all that forced
  civility.
"Pray, seat yourself, my lord." With
  cringing hams
The speech is spoken, and, with bended
  knee,
Heard by the smiling courtier.—
  "Before you, sir?
It must be on the earth then." Hang
  it all!
The pride which cloaks itself in such
  poor fashion
Is scarcely fit to swell a beggar's bosom.
                Old Play.

CHAP. XXX.

Ay, this is he who wears the wreath of
  bays
Wove by Apollo and the Sisters Nine,
Which Jove's dread lightning scathes
  not. He hath doft.
The cumbrous helm of steel, and flung
  aside
The yet more galling diadem of gold;
While, with a leafy circlet round his
  brows,
He reigns the King of Lovers and of
  Poets.

CHAP. XXXI.

      —— Want you a man
Experienced in the world and its
  affairs?
Here he is for your purpose. He's a
  monk.
He hath forsworn the world and all
  its work
The rather that he knows it passing
  well,
Special the worst of it; for he's a monk.
                Old Play.

CHAP. XXXIII.

  Toll, toll the bell!
  Greatness is o'er,
    The heart has broke,
    To ache no more;
An unsubstantial pageant all—
Drop o'er the scene the funeral-pall.
                Old Poem.

CHAP. XXXV.

    —— Here's a weapon now,
Shall shake a conquering general in
  his tent,
A monarch on his throne, or reach a
  prelate,
However holy be his offices,
E'en while he serves the altar.
                Old Play.

SONG OF THE JUDGES OF THE SECRET TRIBUNAL.

MEASURERS of good and evil,
Bring the square, the line, the level,—
Rear the altar, dig the trench.
Blood both stone and ditch shall drench
Cubits six, from end to end,
Must the fatal bench extend,—
Cubits six, from side to side,
Judge and culprit must divide.
On the east the Court assembles,
On the west the Accused trembles—
Answer, brethren, all and one,
Is the ritual rightly done?

Answer.

On life and soul, on blood and bone,
One for all, and all for one,
We warrant this is rightly done.

Judges.

How wears the night?—Doth morning
  shine
In early radiance on the Rhine?
What music floats upon his tide?
Do birds the tardy morning chide?
Brethren, look out from hill and height
And answer true, How wears the night?

Answer.

The night is old; on Rhine's broad
  breast
Glance drowsy stars which long to rest.
    No beams are twinkling in the
    east.
There is a voice upon the flood,
The stern still call of blood for blood:
  'Tis time we listen the behest.

Chorus.

Up, then, up ! When day's at rest,
 'Tis time that such as we are
  watchers ;
Rise to judgment, brethren, rise !
Vengeance knows not sleepy eyes,
 He and night are matchers.
      Chap. xx.

MOTTOES FROM
"COUNT ROBERT OF PARIS."

CHAP. VI.

VAIN man, thou mayst esteem thy love
 as fair
As fond hyperboles suffice to raise.
She may be all that's matchless in her
 person,
And all-divine in soul to match her
 body ;
But take this from me—thou shalt
 never call her
Superior to her sex, while *one* survives,
And I am her true votary.—*Old Play.*

CHAP. XVI.

Strange ape of man ! who loathes thee
 while he scorns thee ;
Half a reproach to us and half a jest.
What fancies can be ours ere we have
 pleasure
In viewing our own form, our pride
 and passions,
Reflected in a shape grotesque as
 thine !—*Anonymous.*

CHAP. XVII.

'Tis strange that, in the dark sulphureous mine,
Where wild ambition piles its ripening
 stores
Of slumbering thunder, Love will
 interpose
His tiny torch, and cause the stern
 explosion
To burst, when the deviser's least
 aware.—*Anonymous.*

CHAP. XXV.

Heaven knows its time ; the bullet has
 its billet.
Arrow and javelin each its destined
 purpose ;
The fated beasts of Nature's lower
 strain
Have each their separate task.
      Old Play.

MOTTOES FROM
"CASTLE DANGEROUS."

CHAP. XI.

WHERE is he ? Has the deep earth
 swallow'd him ?
Or hath he melted like some airy
 phantom
That shuns the approach of morn and
 the young sun ?
Or hath he wrapt him in Cimmerian
 darkness,
And passed beyond the circuit of the
 sight
With things of the night's shadows ?
      Anonymous.

CHAP. XIV.

The way is long, my children, long and
 rough—
The moors are dreary and the woods
 are dark ;
But he that creeps from cradle on to
 grave,
Unskilled save in the velvet course of
 fortune,
Hath missed the discipline of noble
 hearts.—*Old Play.*

CHAP. XVIII.

His talk was of another world—his
 bodiments
Strange, doubtful, and mysterious ;
 those who heard him
Listen'd as to a man in feverish dreams,
Who speaks of other objects than the
 present,
And mutters like to him who sees a
 vision.—*Old Play.*

PHAROS LOQUITUR.*

FAR in the bosom of the deep,
O'er these wild shelves my watch I
  keep,
A ruddy gem of changeful light,
Bound on the dusky brow of night,
The seaman bids my lustre hail,
And scorns to strike his timorous sail.

LETTER IN VERSE.

TO HIS GRACE THE DUKE OF BUC-
CLEUCH, ETC., ETC.

Lighthouse Yacht in the Sound of Lerwick,
    Zetland, 8th August, 1814.

HEALTH to the chieftain from his
  clansmen true !
From her true minstrel, health to fair
  Buccleuch !
Health from the isles, where dewy
  morning weaves
Her chaplet with the tints that Twilight
  leaves ;
Where late the sun scarce vanish'd
  from the sight,
And his bright pathway graced the
  short-lived night,
Though darker now as autumn's
  shades extend,
The north winds whistle and the mists
  ascend !
Health from the land where eddying
  whirlwinds toss
The storm-rocked *cradle* of the Cape
  of Noss ;
On outstretch'd cords the giddy engine
  slides,
His own strong arm the bold adventurer guides,

And he that lists such desperate feat
  to try,
May, like the sea-mew, skim 'twixt surf
  and sky,
And feel the mid-air gales around him
  blow,
And see the billows rage five hundred
  feet below.

Here, by each stormy peak and desert
  shore,
The hardy isleman tugs the daring oar,
Practised alike his venturous course to
  keep
Through the white breakers or the
  pathless deep,
By ceaseless peril and by toil to gain
A wretched pittance from the niggard
  main.
And when the worn-out drudge old
  ocean leaves,
What comfort greets him, and what
  hut receives ?
Lady ! the worst your presence ere has
  cheer'd
(When want and sorrow fled as you
  appear'd)
Were to a Zetlander as the high dome
Of proud Drumlanrig to my humble
  home.
Here rise no groves, and here no gar-
  dens blow,
Here even the hardy heath scarce
  dares to grow ;
But rocks on rocks, in mist and storm
  array'd,
Stretch far to sea their giant colonnade,
With many a cavern seam'd, the dreary
  haunt
Of the dun seal and swarthy cormo-
  rant.

---

* "On the 30th July, 1814, Mr. Hamilton,[1]
Mr. Erskine,[2] and Mr. Duff,[3] Commissioners,
along with Mr. (now Sir) Walter Scott, and
the writer, visited the Lighthouse ; the Commissioners being then on one of their voyages
of Inspection, noticed in the Introduction.
They breakfasted in the Library, when Sir
Walter, at the entreaty of the party, upon in-
scribing his name in the Album, added these
interesting lines."—STEVENSON's *Account of*
the Bell-Rock Lighthouse, 1824. Scott's Diary
of the Voyage is now published in his *Life.*

---

[1] The late Robert Hamilton, Esq., Advocate, long Sheriff-Depute of Lanarkshire, and
afterwards one of the Principal Clerks of
Session in Scotland—died in 1831.
[2] Afterwards Lord Kinnedder.
[3] The late Adam Duff, Esq., Sheriff-Depute
of the county of Edinburgh.

Wild round their rifted brows, with
    frequent cry
As of lament, the gulls and gannets fly,
And from their sable base, with sullen
    sound,
In sheets of whitening foam the waves
    rebound.

Yet even these coasts a touch of envy
    gain
From those whose land has known
    oppression's chain;
For here the industrious Dutchman
    comes once more
To moor his fishing craft by Bressay's
    shore;
Greets every former mate and brother
    tar,
Marvels how Lerwick 'scaped the rage
    of war,
Tells many a tale of Gallic outrage
    done,
And ends by blessing God and Wel-
    lington.
Here too the Greenland tar, a fiercer
    guest,
Claims a brief hour of riot, not of
    rest;
Proves each wild frolic that in wine
    has birth,
And wakes the land with brawls and
    boisterous mirth.
A sadder sight on yon poor vessel's
    prow
The captive Norseman sits in silent
    woe,
And eyes the flags of Britain as they
    flow.
Hard fate of war, which bade her
    terrors sway
His destined course, and seize so mean
    a prey;
A bark with planks so warp'd and
    seams so riven,
She scarce might face the gentlest airs
    of heaven:
Pensive he sits, and questions oft if
    none
Can list his speech, and understand
    his moan;

In vain—no Islesman now can use the
    tongue
Of the bold Norse, from whom their
    lineage sprung.
Not thus of old the Norsemen hither
    came,
Won by the love of danger or of fame;
On every storm-beat cape a shapeless
    tower
Tells of their wars, their conquests, and
    their power;
For ne'er for Grecia's vales, nor Latian
    land,
Was fiercer strife than for this barren
    strand;
A race severe—the isle and ocean lords,
Loved for its own delight the strife of
    swords;
With scornful laugh the mortal pang
    defied,
And blest their gods that they in battle
    died.

Such were the sires of Zetland's simple
    race,
And still the eye may faint resemblance
    trace
In the blue eye, tall form, proportion
    fair,
The limbs athletic, and the long light
    hair—
(Such was the mien, as Scald and
    Minstrel sings,
Of fair-hair'd Harold, first of Norway's
    Kings);
But their high deeds to scale these crags
    confined,
Their only warfare is with waves and
    wind.

Why should I talk of Mousa's castled
    coast?
Why of the horrors of the Sumburgh
    Rost?
May not these bald disjointed lines
    suffice,
Penn'd while my comrades whirl the
    rattling dice—
While down the cabin skylight lessening
    shine

The rays, and eve is chased with mirth
and wine?
Imagined while down Mousa's desert
bay
Our well-trimmed vessel urged her
nimble way,
While to the freshening breeze she
lean'd her side,
And bade her bowsprit kiss the foamy
tide.

Such are the lays that Zetland Isles
supply;
Drench'd with the drizzly spray and
dropping sky,
Weary and wet, a sea-sick minstrel I.
W. SCOTT.

POSTSCRIPTUM.

Kirkwall, Orkney, Aug. 13, 1814.

IN respect that your Grace has com-
mision'd a Kraken,
You will please be inform'd that they
seldom are taken;
It is January two years, the Zetland
folks say,
Since they saw the last Kraken in Scal-
loway bay;
He lay in the offing a fortnight or more,
But the devil a Zetlander put from the
shore,
Though bold in the seas of the North
to assail
The morse and the sea-horse, the
grampus and whale.
If your Grace thinks I'm writing the
thing that is not,
You may ask at a namesake of ours,
Mr. Scott—
(He's not from our clan, though his
merits deserve it,
But springs, I'm inform'd, from the
Scotts of Scotstarvet);*

---

* The Scotts of Scotstarvet, and other families of the name in Fife and elsewhere,
claim no kindred with the great clan of the
Border—and their armorial bearings are different.

He question'd the folks who beheld it
with eyes,
But they differ'd confoundedly as to
its size.
For instance, the modest and diffident
swore
That it seem'd like the keel of a ship,
and no more—
Those of eyesight more clear, or of
fancy more high,
Said it rose like an island 'twixt ocean
and sky—
But all of the hulk had a steady opinion
That 't was sure a *live* subject of Nep-
tune's dominion—
And I think, my Lord Duke, your
Grace hardly would wish
To cumber your house, such a kettle of
fish.
Had your order related to night-caps
or hose,
Or mittens of worsted, there's plenty of
those.
Or would you be pleased but to fancy
a whale?
And direct me to send it—by sea or by
mail?
The season, I'm told, is nigh over, but
still
I could get you one fit for the lake at
Bowhill.
Indeed, as to whales, there's no need
to be thrifty,
Since one day last fortnight two hun-
dred and fifty,
Pursued by seven Orkneymen's boats
and no more,
Betw'xt Truffness and Luffness were
drawn on the shore!
You'll ask if I saw this same wonder-
ful sight;
I own that I did not, but easily might,
For this mighty shoal of leviathans
lay
On our lee-beam a mile, in the loop of
the bay,
And the islemen of Sanda were all at
the spoil,
And *flinching* (so term it) the blubber
to boil;

(Ye spirits of lavender, drown the reflection
That awakes at the thoughts of this
  odorous dissection.)
To see this huge marvel full fain would
  we go,
But Wilson, the wind, and the current
  said no.
We have now got to Kirkwall, and
  needs I must stare
When I think that in verse I have once
  call'd it *fair*:
'Tis a base little borough, both dirty
  and mean—
There's nothing to hear, and there's
  nought to be seen,
Save a church, where of old times a
  prelate harangued,
And a palace that's built by an earl
  that was hang'd.
But, farewell to Kirkwall—aboard we
  are going,
The anchor's a-peak, and the breezes
  are blowing;
Our Commodore calls all his band to
  their places,
And 'tis time to release you—good
  night to your Graces!

LETTER

TO HIS GRACE THE DUKE OF BUC-
CLEUCH, DRUMLANRIG CASTLE,

Sanquhar, 2 o'clock, July 30, 1817.

FROM Ross, where the clouds on Ben-
  lomond are sleeping—
From Greenock, where Clyde to the
  Ocean is sweeping—
From Largs, where the Scotch gave the
  Northmen a drilling—
From Ardrossan, whose harbour cost
  many a shilling—
From Old Cumnock, where beds are as
  hard as a plank, sir—
From a chop and green pease, and a
  chicken in Sanquhar,
This eve, please the Fates, at Drum-
  lanrig we anchor.   W. S.

IMITATION OF THE FARE-
WELL TO MACKENZIE.*

(AT PAGE 470.)

So sung the old Bard, in the grief of
  his heart,
When he saw his loved Lord from his
  people depart.
Now mute on thy mountains, O Albyn,
  are heard,
Nor the voice of the song, nor the harp
  of the bard;
Or its strings are but waked by the
  stern winter gale,
As they mourn for Mackenzie, last
  Chief of Kintail.

From the far Southland Border a Min-
  strel came forth,
And he waited the hour that some
  Bard of the north
His hand on the harp of the ancient
  should cast,
And bid its wild numbers mix high
  with the blast;
But no bard was there left in the land
  of the Gael
To lament for Mackenzie, last Chief of
  Kintail.

And shalt thou then sleep, did the Minstrel exclaim,
Like the son of the lowly, unnoticed
  by fame?
No, son of Fitzgerald! in accents of
  woe
The song thou hast loved o'er thy coffin
  shall flow,
And teach thy wild mountains to join
  in the wail
That laments for Mackenzie, last Chief
  of Kintail.

------

* These verses were written shortly after
the death of Lord Seaforth, the last male representative of his illustrious house. He was
a nobleman of extraordinary talents, who must
have made for himself a lasting reputation,
had not his political exertions been checked
by the painful natural infirmities alluded to in
the fourth stanza.—See *Life of Scott.*

In vain, the bright course of thy talents
   to wrong,
Fate deaden'd thine ear and imprison'd
   thy tongue;
For brighter o'er all her obstructions
   arose
The glow of the genius they could not
   oppose;
And who in the land of the Saxon or
   Gael
Might match with Mackenzie, High
   Chief of Kintail?

Thy sons rose around thee in light and
   in love,
All a father could hope, all a friend
   could approve;
What 'vails it the tale of thy sorrows
   to tell,—
In the spring-time of youth and of promise they fell!
Of the line of Fitzgerald remains not a
   male
To bear the proud name of the Chief
   of Kintail.

And thou, gentle Dame, who must bear,
   to thy grief,
For thy clan and thy country the cares
   of a Chief,
Whom brief rolling moons in six
   changes have left,
Of thy husband, and father, and brethren bereft,
To thine ear of affection, how sad is
   the hail
That salutes thee the Heir of the line
   of Kintail!*

MY AUNT MARGARET'S MIRROR.

THERE are times
When Fancy plays her gambols, in
   despite
Even of our watchful senses, when in
   sooth

---

* The Honourable Lady Hood, daughter
of the last Lord Seaforth, widow of Admiral
Sir Samuel Hood, afterwards Mrs. Stewart
Mackenzie of Seaforth and Glasserton.—1833.

Substance seems shadow, shadow sub-
   stance seems,
When the broad, palpable, and marked
   partition
'Twixt that which is and is not, seems
   dissolved,
As if the mental eye gain'd power to
   gaze
Beyond the limits of the existing world.
Such hours of shadowy dreams I better
   love
Than all the gross realities of life.

VERSES,

COMPOSED FOR THE OCCASION, ADAPTED
TO HADYN'S AIR,

"*God Save the Emperor Francis,*"

AND SUNG BY A SELECT BAND AFTER THE
DINNER GIVEN BY THE LORD PROVOST OF
EDINBURGH TO THE

GRAND-DUKE NICHOLAS OF RUSSIA,

AND HIS SUITE, 19TH DECEMBER, 1816.

GOD protect brave ALEXANDER,
Heaven defend the noble Czar,
Mighty Russia's high Commander,
First in Europe's banded war;
For the realms he did deliver
From the tyrant overthrown,
Thou, of every good the Giver,
Grant him long to bless his own!
Bless him, 'mid his land's disaster,
For her rights who battled brave,
Of the land of foemen master,
Bless him who their wrongs forgave.

O'er his just resentment victor,
Victor over Europe's foes,
Late and long supreme director,
Grant in peace his reign may close.
Hail! then, hail! illustrious stranger!
Welcome to our mountain strand;
Mutual interests, hopes, and danger,
Link us with thy native land.

Freemen's force, or false beguiling,
Shall that union ne'er divide.
Hand in hand while peace is smiling,
And in battle side by side.*

THE BANNATYNE CLUB.†

I.

ASSIST me, ye friends of Old Books and
    Old Wine,
To sing in the praises of sage Bannatyne,
Who left such a treasure of old Scottish
    lore
As enables each age to print one volume
    more.
        One volume more, my friends, one
        volume more,
        We'll ransack old Banny for one
        volume more.

II.

And first, Allan Ramsay, was eager to
    glean
From Bannatyne's *Hortus* his bright
    Evergreen ;
Two light little volumes (intended for
    four)
Still leave us the task to print one
    volume more.
        One volume more, &c.

III.

His ways were not ours, for he cared
    not a pin
How much he left out, or how much he
    put in ;
The truth of the reading he thought was
    a bore,
So this accurate age calls for one volume
    more.
        One volume more, &c.

IV.

Correct and sagacious, then came my
    Lord Hailes,   [scales,
And weigh'd every letter in critical
But left out some brief words, which
    the prudish abhor,
And castrated Banny in one volume
    more.
        One volume more, my friends, one
        volume more ;
        We'll restore Banny's manhood in
        one volume more.

V.

John Pinkerton next, and I'm truly
    concern'd   [learn'd ;
I can't call that worthy so candid as
He rail'd at the plaid and blasphemed
    the claymore,
And set Scots by the ears in his one
    volume more.
        One volume more, my friends, one
        volume more,
        Celt and Goth shall be pleased
        with one volume more.

VI.

As bitter as gall, and as sharp as a razor,
And feeding on herbs as a Nebuchad-
    nezzar,
His diet too acid, his temper too sour,
Little Ritson came out with his two
    volumes more.
        But one volume, my friends, one
        volume more,
        We'll dine on roast-beef and print
        one volume more.

VII.

The stout Gothic yeditur, next on the
    roll,
With his beard like a brush and as
    black as a coal ;
And honest Greysteel, that was true to
    the core,
Lent their hearts and their hands each
    to one volume more.
        One volume more, &c.

* Mr., afterwards Sir William Arbuthnot,
the Lord Provost of Edinburgh, who had the
honour to entertain the Grand-Duke, afterwards Emperor of Russia, was a personal
friend of Sir Walter Scott's ; and these
Verses, with their heading, are now given
from the newspapers of 1816.

† Instituted in 1822 for the reprint and publication of rare works relating to the history
and antiquities of Scotland. Sir Walter Scott
was the first President of the Club, and wrote
these verses for the anniversary dinner of
March, 1823.

VIII.

Since by these single champions what
wonders were done,
What may not be achieved by our
Thirty and One?
Law, Gospel, and Commerce, we count
in our corps,
And the Trade and the Press join for
one volume more.
One volume more, &c.

IX.

Ancient libels and contraband books,
I assure ye,
We'll print as secure from Exchequer
or Jury;
Then hear your Committee and let them
count o'er
The Chiels they intend in their three
volumes more.
Three volumes more, &c.

X.

They'll produce you King Jamie, the
sapient and Sext,
And the Rob of Dumblane and her
Bishops come next;
One tome miscellaneous they'll add to
your store,
Resolving next year to print four volumes
more.
Four volumes more, my friends,
four volumes more;
Pay down your subscriptions for
four volumes more.

TO J. G. LOCKHART, ESQ.

ON THE COMPOSITION OF MAIDA'S
EPITAPH.

1824.

"Maidæ Marmorea dormis sub imagine
Maida!
Ad januam domini sit tibi terra levis."
See *Life of Scott.*

"DEAR JOHN,—I some time ago wrote
to inform his
Fat worship of *jaces,* misprinted for
dormis;

But that several Southrons assured me
the *januam*
Was a twitch to both ears of Ass
Priscian's cranium.
You, perhaps, may observe that one
Lionel Berguer,
In defence of our blunder appears a
stout arguer:
But at length I have settled, I hope,
all these clatters,
By a *rowt* in the papers—fine place for
such matters.
I have, therefore, to make it for once
my command, sir,
That my gudeson shall leave the whole
thing in my hand, sir,
And by no means accomplish what
James says you threaten,
Some banter in Blackwood to claim
your dog-Latin.
I have various reasons of weight, on
my word, sir,
For pronouncing a step of this sort were
absurd, sir.—
Firstly, erudite sir, 'twas against your
advising
I adopted the lines this monstrosity
lies in;
For you modestly hinted my English
translation
Would become better far such a digni-
fied station.
Second—how, in God's name, would
my bacon be saved,
By not having writ what I clearly en-
graved?
On the contrary, I, on the whole, think
it better
To be whipped as the thief, than his
'ousy resetter.
Thirdly—don't you perceive that I
don't care a boddle,
Although fifty false metres were flung
at my noddle,
For my back is as broad and as hard
as Benlomon's,
And I treat as I please both the Greeks
and the Romans;
Whereas the said heathens might rather
look serious

At a kick on their drum from the scribe
　　of Valerius.
And, fourthly and lastly—it is my good
　　pleasure
To remain the sole source of that mur-
　　derous measure.
So *stet pro ratione voluntas*—be tractile.
Invade not, I say, my own dear little
　　dactyl ;
If you do, you 'll occasion a breach in
　　our intercourse.
To-morrow will see me in town for the
　　winter-course,
But not at your door, at the usual hour,
　　sir,
My own pye-house daughter's good
　　prog to devour, sir.
Egro—peace !—on your duty, your
　　squeamishness throttle,
And we 'll soothe Priscian's spleen with
　　a canny third bottle.
A fig for all dactyls, a fig for all spondees,
A fig for all dunces and dominie
　　Grundys ;
A fig for dry thrapples, south, north,
　　east, and west, sir,
Speates and raxes* ere five for a
　　famishing guest, sir ;
And as Fatsman† and I have some
　　topics for haver, he 'll
Be invited, I hope, to meet me and
　　Dame Peveril,
Upon whom, to say nothing of Oury
　　and Anne, you a
Dog shall be deemed if you fasten your
　　Janua.

LIFE OF NAPOLEON.

JUNE, 1825.

"The rapid accumulation of books and
MSS. for the Life of Napoleon was at once
flattering and alarming ; and one of his
notes to me, about the middle of June, had
these rhymes by way of postscript :—

WHEN with Poetry dealing
　　Room enough in a shieling :

* See *Scotts Essays.*
† A nickname for James Ballantyne.

Neither cabin nor hovel
Too small for a novel :
Though my back I should rub
On Diogenes' tub,
How my fancy could prance
In a dance of romance !
But my house I must swap
With some Brobdignag chap,
Ere I grapple, God bless me ! with
　　Emperor Nap."
　　　　　　　　Scott's Life.

JUVENILE LINES.

FROM VIRGIL.

1782.—ÆTAT. 11.

"Scott's autobiography tells us that his
translations in verse from Horace and Virgil
were often approved by Dr. Adams [Rector
of the High School, Edinburgh]. One of
these little pieces, written in a weak boyish
scrawl, within pencilled marks still visible,
had been carefully preserved by his mother ;
it was found folded up in a cover, inscribed
by the old lady—"*My Walter's first lines,*
1782."—LOCKHART, *Life of Scott.*

IN awful ruins Ætna thunders nigh,
And sends in pitchy whirlwinds to the
　　sky
Blacks clouds of smoke, which, still as
　　they aspire,
From their dark sides there bursts the
　　glowing fire ;
At other times huge balls of fire are
　　toss'd,
That lick the stars, and in the smoke
　　are lost :
Sometimes the mount, with vast con-
　　vulsions torn,
Emits huge rocks, which instantly are
　　borne
With loud explosions to the starry skies,
The stones made liquid as the huge
　　mass flies,
Then back again with greater weight
　　recoils,
While Ætna thundering from the bot-
　　tom boils.

ON A THUNDER STORM.

1783.—ÆT. 12.

LOUD o'er my head though awful thunders roll,
And vivid lightnings flash from pole to
 pole,
Yet 'tis thy voice, my God, that bids
 them fly,
Thy arm directs those lightnings
 through the sky.

Then let the good thy mighty name
 revere,
And harden'd sinners thy just vengeance fear.

ON THE SETTING SUN.

1783.

THOSE evening clouds, that setting ray,
And beauteous tints, serve to display
 Their great Creator's praise;
Then let the short-lived thing call'd
 man,
Whose life's comprised within a span,
 To him his homage raise.

We often praise the evening clouds,
 And tints so gay and bold,
But seldom think upon our God,
 Who tinged these clouds with gold! *

---

* "It must, I think, be allowed that these lines, though * * * * * not to
be compared with the efforts of Pope, still less of Cowley at the same period, show, nevertheless, praiseworthy dexterity for a boy of twelve."—LOCKHART, *Life of Scott.*

HALIDON HILL;

A DRAMATIC SKETCH FROM SCOTTISH HISTORY.

PREFACE.

Though the Public seldom feel much interest in such communications, (nor is there any reason why they should,) the Author takes the liberty of stating, that these scenes were commenced with the purpose of contributing to a miscellany projected by a much-esteemed friend.* But instead of being confined to a scene or two, as intended, the work gradually swelled to the size of an independent publication. It is designed to illustrate military antiquities, and the manners of chivalry. The drama (if it can be termed one) is, in no particular, either designed or calculated for the stage.

The subject is to be found in Scottish history; but not to overload so slight a publication with antiquarian research, or quotations from obscure chronicles, may be sufficiently illustrated by the following passage from Pinkerton's *History of Scotland*, vol. i. p. 72.

"The Governor (anno 1402) dispatched a considerable force under Murdac, his eldest son: the Earls of Angus and Moray also joined Douglas, who entered England with an army of ten thousand men, carrying terror and devastation to the walls of Newcastle.

"Henry IV. was now engaged in the Welsh war against Owen Glendour; but the Earl of Northumberland, and his son, the Hotspur Percy, with the Earl of March, collected a numerous array, and awaited the return of the Scots, impeded with spoil, near Milfield, in the north part of Northumberland. Douglas had reached Wooler, in his return; and, perceiving the enemy, seized a strong post between the two armies, called Homildon-hill. In this method he rivalled his predecessor at the battle of Otterburn, but not with like success. The English advanced to the assault, and Henry Percy was about to lead them up the hill, when March caught his bridle, and advised him to advance no farther, but to pour the dreadful shower of English arrows into the enemy. This advice was followed by the usual fortune; for in all ages the bow was the English instrument of victory; and though the Scots, and perhaps the French, were superior in the use of the spear, yet this weapon was useless after the distant bow had decided the combat. Robert the Great, sensible of this at the battle of Bannockburn, ordered a prepared detachment of cavalry to rush among the English archers at the commencement, totally to disperse them, and stop the deadly effusion. But Douglas now used no such precaution; and the consequence was, that his people, drawn up on the face of the hill, presented one general mark to the enemy, none of whose arrows descended in vain. The Scots fell without fight, and unrevenged, till a spirited knight, Swinton, exclaimed aloud, 'O my brave countrymen! what fascination has seized you to-day, that you stand like deer to be shot, instead of indulging your ancient courage, and meeting your enemies hand to hand? Let those who will, descend with me, that we may gain victory, or life, or fall like men.' This being heard by Adam Gordon, between whom and Swinton there remained an ancient deadly feud, attended with the mutual slaughter of many followers, he instantly fell on his knees before Swinton, begged his pardon, and desired to be dubbed a knight by him whom he must now regard as the wisest and the boldest of that order in Britain. The ceremony performed, Swinton and Gordon descended the hill, accompanied only by one hundred men; and a desperate valour led the whole body to death. Had a similar spirit been shown by the Scottish army, it is probable that the event of the day would have been different. Douglas, who was certainly deficient in the most important

---

* Mrs. Joanna Baillie.

qualities of a general, seeing 'his army begin to disperse, at length attempted to descend the hill; but the English archers, retiring a little, sent a flight of arrows so sharp and strong, that no armour could withstand; and the Scottish leader himself, whose panoply was of remarkable temper, fell under five wounds, though not mortal. The English men-at-arms, knights, or squires, did not strike one blow, but remained spectators of the rout, which was now complete. Great numbers of the Scots were slain, and near five hundred perished in the river Tweed upon their flight. Among the illustrious captives was Douglas, whose chief wound deprived him of an eye; Murdac, son of Albany; the Earls of Moray and Angus; and about twenty-four gentlemen of eminent rank and power. The chief slain were, Swinton, Gordon, Livingston of Calendar, Ramsay of Dalhousie, Walter Sinclair, Roger Gordon, Walter Scott, and others. Such was the issue of the unfortunate battle of Homildon."

It may be proper to observe, that the scene of action has, in the following pages, been transferred from Homildon to Halidon Hill. For this there was an obvious reason;—for who would again venture to introduce upon the scene the celebrated Hotspur, who commanded the English at the former battle? There are, however, several coincidences which may reconcile even the severer antiquary to the substitution of Halidon Hill for Homildon. A Scottish army was defeated by the English on both occasions, and under nearly the same circumstances of address on the part of the victors, and mismanagement on that of the vanquished, for the English long-bow decided the day in both cases. In both cases, also, a Gordon was left on the field of battle; and at Halidon, as at Homildon, the Scots were commanded by an ill-fated representative of the great house of Douglas. He of Homildon was surnamed *Tineman, i.e., Loseman,* from his repeated defeats and miscarriages; and, with all the personal valour of his race, seems to have enjoyed so small a portion of their sagacity, as to be unable to learn military experience from reiterated calamity. I am far, however, from intimating, that the traits of imbecility and envy attributed to the Regent in the following sketch, are to be historically ascribed either to the elder Douglas of Halidon Hill, or to him called *Tineman,* who seems to have enjoyed the respect of his countrymen, notwithstanding that, like the celebrated Anne de Montmorency, he was either defeated, or wounded, or made prisoner, in every battle which he fought. The Regent of the sketch is a character purely imaginary.

The tradition of the Swinton family, which still survives in a lineal descent, and to which the author has the honour to be related, avers. that the Swinton who fell at Homildon in the manner related in the preceding extract, had slain Gordon's father; which seems sufficient ground for adopting that circumstance into the following dramatic sketch, though it is rendered improbable by other authorities.

If any reader will take the trouble of looking at Froissart, Fordun, or other historians of the period, he will find, that the character of the Lord of Swinton, for strength, courage, and conduct, is by no means exaggerated.

W. S.

ABBOTSFORD, 1822.

DRAMATIS PERSONÆ.

SCOTTISH.

THE REGENT OF SCOTLAND.

GORDON,
SWINTON,
LENNOX,
SUTHERLAND, } *Scottish Chiefs and*
ROSS, *Nobles.*
MAXWELL,
JOHNSTONE,
LINDESAY,

ADAM DE VIPONT, *a Knight Templar.*
THE PRIOR OF MAISON-DIEU.
REYNALD, *Swinton's Squire.*
HOB HATTELY, *a Border Moss-Trooper.*
Heralds.

ENGLISH.

KING EDWARD III.
CHANDOS, }
PERCY, } *English and Norman*
RIBAUMONT, } *Nobles.*
THE ABBOT OF WALTHAMSTOW.

ACT I.—SCENE I.

*The northern side of the eminence of Halidon.
The back Scene represents the summit of
the ascent, occupied by the Rear-guard of
the Scottish army. Bodies of armed Men
appear as advancing from different points,
to join the main Body.*

Enter DE VIPONT *and the* PRIOR OF
MAISON-DIEU.

VIP. No farther, Father—here I need
  no guidance—
I have already brought your peaceful step
Too near the verge of battle.

  PRI. Fain would I see you join some
    Baron's banner,
Before I say farewell. The honour'd sword
That fought so well in Syria, should not
  wave
Amid the ignoble crowd.

  VIP. Each spot is noble in a pitched field,
So that a man has room to fight and fall
  on't.
But I shall find out friends. 'Tis scarce
  twelve years
Since I left Scotland for the wars of Pa-
  lestine,
And then the flower of all the Scottish
  nobles
Were known to me; and I, in my degree,
Not all unknown to them.

  PRI. Alas! there have been changes
    since that time !
The Royal Bruce, with Randolph, Dou-
  glas, Grahame,
Then shook in field the banners which
  now moulder
Over their graves i' the chancel.

  VIP. And thence comes it,
That while I look'd on many a well-known
  crest
And blazon'd shield, as hitherward we
  came,
The faces of the Barons who displayed
  them
Were all unknown to me. Brave youths
  they seem'd ;
Yet, surely, fitter to adorn the tilt-yard,
Than to be leaders of a war. Their fol-
  lowers.

Young like themselves, seem like themselves unpractised—
Look at their battle-rank.

  PRI. I cannot gaze on't with undazzled
    eye,
So thick the rays dart back from shield
  and helmet,
And sword and battle-axe, and spear and
  pennon.
Sure 'tis a gallant show! The Bruce
  himself
Hath often conquer'd at the head of fewer
And worse appointed followers.

  VIP. Ay, but 'twas Bruce that led
    them. Reverend Father,
'Tis not the falchion's weight decides a
  combat ;
It is the strong and skilful hand that
  wields it.
Ill fate, that we should lack the noble
  King,
And all his champions now! Time call'd
  them not,
For when I parted hence for Palestine,
The brows of most were free from grizzled
  hair.

  PRI. Too true, alas! But well you
    know, in Scotland
Few hairs are silver'd underneath the
  helmet ;
'Tis cowls like mine which hide them.
  'Mongst the laity,
War's the rash reaper, who thrusts in his
  sickle
Before the grain is white. In threescore
  years
And ten, which I have seen, I have out-
  lived
Wellnigh two generations of our nobles.
The race which holds yon summit is the
  third.

  VIP. Thou mayst outlive them also.
  PRI.   Heaven forfend !
My prayer shall be, that Heaven will
  close my eyes,
Before they look upon the wrath to come.

  VIP. Retire, retire, good Father !—
    Pray for Scotland—
Think not on me. Here comes an ancient
  friend,

Brother in arms, with whom to-day I'll
   join me.
Back to your choir, assemble all your
   brotherhood,
And weary Heaven with prayers for
   victory.
   PRI. Heaven's blessing rest with thee,
Champion of Heaven, and of thy suffering country!

     [*Exit* PRIOR. VIPONT *draws a
     little aside and lets down the
     beaver of his helmet.*

Enter SWINTON, *followed by* REYNALD
  *and others, to whom he speaks as he
  enters.*

   SWI. Halt here, and plant my pennon,
   till the Regent
Assign our band its station in the host.
   REY. That must be by the Standard.
   We have had
That right since good Saint David's reign
   at least.
Fain would I see the Marcher would dis-
   pute it.
   SWI. Peace, Reynald! Where the
   general plants the soldier,
There is his place of honour, and there only
His valour can win worship. Thou'rt of
   those,
Who would have war's deep art bear the
   wild semblance
Of some disorder'd hunting, where, pell-
   mell,
Each trusting to the swiftness of his horse,
Gallants press on to see the quarry fall.
Yon steel-clad Southrons, Reynald, are
   no deer;
And England's Edward is no stag at bay.
   VIP. (*advancing.*) There needed not,
   to blazon forth the Swinton,
His ancient burgonet, the sable Boar
Chain'd to the gnarl'd oak,—nor his proud
   step,
Nor giant stature, nor the ponderous mace,
Which only he, of Scotland's realm, can
   wield:
His discipline and wisdom mark the leader,
As doth his frame the champion. Hail,
   brave Swinton!

   SWI. Brave Templar, thanks! Such
   your cross'd shoulder speaks you;
But the closed visor, which conceals your
   features
Forbids more knowledge. Umfraville,
   perhaps—
   VIP. (*unclosing his helmet.*) No; one
   less worthy of our sacred Order.
Yet, unless Syrian suns have scorch'd my
   features
Swart as my sable visor, Alan Swinton
Will welcome Symon Vipont.
   SWI. (*embracing him.*) As the blithe
   reaper
Welcomes a practised mate, when the
   ripe harvest
Lies deep before him, and the sun is high!
Thou'lt follow yon old pennon, wilt thou
   not?
'Tis tatter'd since thou saw'st it, and the
   Boar-heads
Look as if brought from off some Christ-
   mas board,
Where knives had notch'd them deeply.
   VIP. Have with them, ne'ertheless.
   The Stuart's Chequer,
The Bloody Heart of Douglas, Ross's
   Lymphads,
Sutherland's Wild-cats, nor the royal
   Lion,
Rampant in golden tressure, wins me from
   them.
We'll back the Boar-heads bravely. I
   see round them
A chosen band of lances—some well
   known to me.
Where's the main body of thy followers?
   SWI. Symon de Vipont, thou dost see
   them all
That Swinton's bugle-horn can call to
   battle,
However loud it rings. There's not a boy
Left in my halls, whose arm has strength
   enough
To bear a sword—there's not a man be-
   hind,
However old, who moves without a staff.
Striplings and greybeards, every one is here,
And here all should be—Scotland needs
   them all;

And more and better men, were each a
    Hercules,
And yonder handful centuplied.

  Vip. A thousand followers—such, with
    friends and kinsmen,
Allies and vassals, thou wert wont to lead—
A thousand followers shrunk to sixty
    lances
In twelve years' space?—And thy brave
    sons, Sir Alan?
Alas! I fear to ask.

  Swi. All slain, De Vipont. In my empty
    home
A puny babe lisps to a widow'd mother,
" Where is my grandsire! wherefore do
    you weep?"
But for that prattler, Lyulph's house is
    heirless.
I'm an old oak, from which the foresters
Have hew'd four goodly boughs, and left
    beside me
Only a sapling, which the fawn may crush
As he springs over it.

  Vip. All slain?—alas!

  Swi. Ay, all, De Vipont. And their
    attributes,
John with the Long Spear—Archibald
    with the Axe—
Richard the Ready—and my youngest
    darling,
My Fair-hair'd William—do but now
    survive
In measures which the grey-hair'd min-
    strels sing,
When they make maidens weep.

  Vip. These wars with England, they
    have rooted out
The flowers of Christendom. Knights,
    who might win
The sepulchre of Christ from the rude
    heathen,
Fall in unholy warfare!

  Swi. Unholy warfare? ay, well hast
    thou named it;
But not with England—would her cloth-
    yard shafts
Had bored their cuirasses! Their lives
    had been
Lost like their grandsire's, in the bold
    defence

Of their dear country—but in private
    feud
With the proud Gordon, fell my Long-
    spear'd John,
He with the Axe, and he men call'd the
    Ready,
Ay, and my Fair-hair'd Will—the Gor-
    don's wrath
Devour'd my gallant issue.

  Vip. Since thou dost weep, their death
    is unavenged?

  Swi. Templar, what think'st thou me?
    See yonder rock,
From which the fountain gushes—is it less
Compact of adamant, though waters flow
    from it?
Firm hearts have moister eyes.—They *are*
    avenged;
I wept not till they were—till the proud
    Gordon
Had with his life-blood dyed my father's
    sword,
In guerdon that he thinn'd my father's
    lineage,
And then I wept my sons; and, as the
    Gordon
Lay at my feet, there was a tear for him,
Which mingled with the rest. We had
    been friends,
Had shared the banquet and the chase to-
    gether,
Fought side by side,—and our first cause
    of strife,
Woe to the pride of both, was but a light
    one!

  Vip. You are at feud, then, with the
    mighty Gordon?

  Swi. At deadly feud. Here in this
    Border-land,
Where the sire's quarrels descend upon
    the son,
As due a part of his inheritance,
As the strong castle and the ancient blazon,
Where private Vengeance holds the scales
    of justice,
Weighing each drop of blood as scrupu-
    lously
As Jews or Lombards balance silver pence,
Not in this land, 'twixt Solway and Saint
    Abb's,

Rages a bitterer feud than mine and theirs,
The Swinton and the Gordon.

VIP. You, with some threescore lances
—and the Gordon
Leading a thousand followers.

SWI. You rate him far too low. Since
you sought Palestine,
He hath had grants of baronies and lord-
ships
In the far-distant North. A thousand
horse
His southern friends and vassals always
number'd.
Add Badenoch kerne, and horse from
Dey and Spey,
He'll count a thousand more.—And now,
De Vipont,
If the Boar-heads seem in your eyes less
worthy
For lack of followers—seek yonder stan-
dard—
The bounding Stag, with a brave host
around it;
There the young Gordon makes his
earliest field,
And pants to win his spurs. His father's
friend,
As well as mine, thou wert—go, join his
pennon,
And grace him with thy presence.

VIP. When you were friends, I was
the friend of both,
And now I can be enemy to neither;
But my poor person, though but slight
the aid,
Joins on this field the banner of the two
Which hath the smallest following.

SWI. Spoke like the generous Knight,
who gave up all,
Leading and lordship, in a heathen land
To fight, a Christian soldier! Yet, in
earnest,
I pray, De Vipont, you would join the
Gordon
In this high battle. 'Tis a noble youth,—
So fame doth vouch him,—amorous,
quick, and valiant;
Takes knighthood, too, this day, and well
may use
His spurs too rashly in the wish to win them.

A friend like thee beside him in the fight,
Were worth a hundred spears, to rein his
valour
And temper it with prudence:—'tis the
aged eagle
Teaches his brood to gaze upon the sun,
With eye undazzled.

VIP. Alas! brave Swinton! Would'st
thou train the hunter
That soon must bring thee to the bay?
Your custom,
Your most unchristian, savage, fiend-like
custom,
Binds Gordon to avenge his father's death.

SWI. Why, be it so! I look for no-
thing else:
My part was acted when I slew his father,
Avenging my four sons—Young Gordon's
sword,
If it should find my heart, can ne'er in-
flict there
A pang so poignant as his father's did.
But I would perish by a noble hand,
And such will his be if he bear him nobly,
Nobly and wisely on this field of Halidon.

Enter a PURSUIVANT.

PUR. Sir Knights, to council!—'tis
the Regent's order,
That knights and men of leading meet
him instantly
Before the royal standard. Edward's army
Is seen from the hill-summit.

SWI. Say to the Regent, we obey his
orders. [*Exit* PURSUIVANT.
[*To* REYNALD.] Hold thou my casque,
and furl my pennon up
Close to the staff. I will not show my
crest,
Nor standard, till the common foe shall
challenge them.
I'll wake no civil strife, nor tempt the
Gordon
With aught that's like defiance.

VIP. Will he not know your features?

SWI. He never saw me. In the distant
North,
Against his will, 'tis said, his friends de-
tain'd him

During his nurture—caring not, belike,
To trust a pledge so precious near the
Boar-tusks.
It was a natural but needless caution
I wage no war with children, for I think
Too deeply on mine own.

VIP. I have thought on it, and will
see the Gordon
As we go hence to council. I do bear
A cross, which binds me to be Christian
priest,
As well as Christian champion. God
may grant,
That I, at once his father's friend and
yours,
May make some peace betwixt you.

SWI. When that your priestly zeal, and
knightly valour,
Shall force the grave to render up the dead.
[*Exeunt severally.*

SCENE II.

*The Summit of Halidon Hill, before the Re-
gent's Tent. The Royal Standard of Scotland is seen in the back-ground, with the
Pennons and Banners of the principal
Nobles around it.*

Council of Scottish Nobles and Chiefs. SUTH-
ERLAND, ROSS, LENNOX, MAXWELL, *and
other Nobles of the highest rank, are close
to the* REGENT'S *person, and in the act of
keen debate.* VIPONT *with* GORDON *and
others, remain grouped at some distance on
the right hand of the Stage. On the left,
standing also apart, is* SWINTON, *alone
and bare-headed. The Nobles are dressed
in Highland or Lowland habits, as historical costume requires.* Trumpets, Heralds,
&c. are in attendance.

LEN. Nay, Lordings, put no shame
upon my counsels.
I did but say, if we retired a little,
We should have fairer field and better
vantage.
I've seen King Robert—ay, The Bruce
himself—
Retreat six leagues in length, and think
no shame on't.

REG. Ay, but King Edward sent a
haughty message,

Defying us to battle on this field,
This very hill of Halidon ; if we leave it
Unfought withal, it squares not with our
honour.

SWI. (*apart.*) A perilous honour that
allows the enemy,
And such an enemy as this same Edward,
To choose our field of battle! He knows
how
To make our Scottish pride betray its
master
Into the pitfall.
[*During this speech the debate among
the Nobles is continued.*

SUTH. (*aloud.*) We will not back one
furlong—not one yard,
No, nor one inch; where'er we find the foe,
Or where the foe finds us, there will we
fight him.
Retreat will dull the spirit of our followers,
Who now stand prompt for battle.

ROSS. My Lords, methinks great
Morarchat* has doubts,
That, if his Northern clans once turn the
seam
Of their check'd hose behind, it will be
hard
To halt and rally them.

SUTH. Say'st thou, Mac Donnell?—
Add another falsehood,
And name when Morarchat was coward
or traitor ?
Thine island race, as chronicles can tell,
Were oft affianced to the Southron cause:
Loving the weight and temper of their
gold,
More than the weight and temper of their
steel.

REG. Peace, my Lords, ho.

ROSS. (*throwing down his glove.*)
MacDonnell will not peace! There lies
my pledge,
Proud Morarchat, to witness thee a liar

MAX. Brought I all Nithsdale from
the Western Border;
Left I my towers exposed to foraying
England,

---

* Morarchate is the ancient Gaelic designa-
tion of the Earls of Sutherland.

And thieving Annandale, to see such misrule?

JOHN. Who speaks of Annandale?
Dare Maxwell slander
The gentle House of Lochwood?*

REG. Peace, Lordings, once again.
We represent
The Majesty of Scotland—in our presence
Brawling is treason.

SUTH. Were it in presence of the King himself,
What should prevent my saying——

Enter LINDESAY.

LIN. You must determine quickly.
Scarce a mile
Parts our vanguard from Edward's. On the plain
Bright gleams of armour flash through clouds of dust,
Like stars through frost-mist—steeds neigh, and weapons clash—
And arrows soon will whistle—the worst sound
That waits on English war.—You must determine.

REG. We are determined. We will spare proud Edward
Half of the ground that parts us.—Onward, Lords;
Saint Andrew strike for Scotland! We will lead
The middle ward ourselves, the Royal Standard
Display'd beside us; and beneath its shadow
Shall the young gallants, whom we knight this day,
Fight for their golden spurs.—Lennox, thou'rt wise,
And wilt obey command—lead thou the rear.

LEN. The rear?—why I the rear?
The van were fitter
For him who fought abreast with Robert Bruce.

SWI. (*apart.*) Discretion hath forsaken Lennox too!

The wisdom he was forty years in gathering
Has left him in an instant. 'Tis contagious
Even to witness frenzy.

SUTH. The Regent hath determined well. The rear
Suits him the best who counsell'd our retreat.

LEN. Proud Northern Thane, the van were soon the rear,
Were thy disorder'd followers planted there.

SUTH. Then, for that very word I make a vow,
By my broad Earldom, and my father's soul,
That, if I have not leading of the van,
I will not fight to-day!

ROSS. Morarchat! thou the leading of the van!
Not whilst MacDonnell lives.

SWI. (*apart.*) Nay, then a stone would speak.
[*Addresses the* REGENT.] May't please your Grace,
And you, great Lords, to hear an old man's counsel,
That hath seen fights enow. These open bickerings
Dishearten all our host. If that your Grace,
With these great Earls and Lords, must needs debate,
Let the closed tent conceal your disagreement;
Else 'twill be said, ill fares it with the flock,
If shepherds wrangle, when the wolf is nigh.

REG. The old Knight counsels well.
Let every Lord
Or Chief, who leads five hundred men or more,
Follow to council—others are excluded—
We'll have no vulgar censurers of our conduct— [*Looking at* SWINTON.
Young Gordon, your high rank and numerous following
Give you a seat with us, though yet unknighted

---

* Lochwood Castle was the ancient seat of the Johnstones, Lords of Annandale.

GORDON. I pray you, pardon me. My
  youth's unfit
To sit in council, when that Knight's
  grey hairs
And wisdom wait without.

  REG. Do as you will; we deign not
  bid you twice.

  [*The* REGENT, ROSS, SUTHER-
    LAND, LENNOX, MAXWELL,
    *&c. enter the Tent. The rest re-
    main grouped about the Stage.*

  GOR. (*observing* SWI.) That helmetless
old Knight, his giant stature,
His awful accents of rebuke and wisdom,
Have caught my fancy strangely. He
  doth seem
Like to some vision'd form which I have
  dream'd of,
But never saw with waking eyes till now.
I will accost him.

  VIP. Pray you, do not so;
Anon I'll give you reason why you should
  not.
There's other work in hand——

  GOR. I will but ask his name. There's
  in his presence
Something that works upon me like a spell,
Or like the feeling made my childish ear
Dote upon tales of superstitious dread,
Attracting while they chill'd my heart
  with fear.
Now, born the Gordon, I do feel right
  well
I'm bound to fear nought earthly—and I
  fear nought.
I'll know who this man is——

  [*Accosts* SWINTON.
Sir Knight, I pray you, of your gentle
  courtesy,
To tell your honour'd name. I am
  ashamed,
Being unknown in arms, to say that mine
Is Adam Gordon.

  SWINTON (*shows emotion, but instantly
    subdues it.*) It is a name that
  soundeth in my ear
Like to a death-knell—ay, and like the call
Of the shrill trumpet to the mortal lists;
Yet, 'tis a name which ne'er hath been
  dishonour'd,

And never will, I trust—most surely
  never
By such a youth as thou.

  GOR. There's a mysterious courtesy in
  this,
And yet it yields no answer to my question.
I trust you hold the Gordon not unworthy
To know the name he asks?

  SWI. Worthy of all that openness and
  honour
May show to friend or foe—but, for my
  name,
Vipont will show it you; and, i it sound
Harsh in your ear, remember that it knells
  there
But at your own request. This day, at
  least,
Though seldom wont to keep it in con-
  cealment,
As there's no cause I should, *you* had not
  heard it.

  GOR. This strange——
  VIP. The mystery is needful. Follow
  me. [*They retire behind the side scene*
  SWI. (*looking after them.*) 'Tis a brave
  youth. How blush'd his noble cheek,
While youthful modesty, and the embar-
  rassment
Of curiosity, combined with wonder,
And half suspicion of some slight intended,
All mingled in the flush: but soon 'twill
  deepen
Into revenge's glow. How slow is
  Vipont!—
I wait the issue, as I've seen spectators
Suspend the motion even of the eyelids,
When the slow gunner, with his lighted
  match,
Approach'd the charged cannon, in the
  act
To waken its dread slumbers.—Now 'tis
  out;
He draws his sword, and rushes towards
  me,
Who will nor seek nor shun him.

Enter GORDON, *withheld by* VIPONT.

  VIP. Hold, for the sake of Heaven!
  O, for the sake

Of your dear country, hold!—Has
Swinton slain your father,
And must you, therefore, be yourself a
parricide,
And stand recorded as the selfish traitor,
Who in her hour of need, his country's
cause
Deserts, that he may wreak a private
wrong?
Look to yon banner—that is Scotland's
standard;
Look to the Regent—he is Scotland's
general;
Look to the English—they are Scotland's
foemen!
Bethink thee, then, thou art a son of
Scotland,
And think on nought beside.

GOR. He hath come here to brave me!
—Off! unhand me!—
Thou canst not be my father's ancient
friend,
That stand'st 'twixt me and him who
slew my father.

VIP. You know not Swinton. Scarce
one passing thought
Of his high mind was with you; now, his
soul
Is fix'd on this day's battle. You might
slay him
At unawares before he saw your blade
drawn.—
Stand still, and watch him close.

Enter MAXWELL *from the tent.*

SWI. How go our councils, Maxwell,
may I ask?

MAX. As wild, as if the very wind and
sea
With every breeze and every billow
battled
For their precedence.

SWI. Most sure they are possess'd!
Some evil spirit,
To mock their valour, robs them of dis-
cretion.

Fie, fie upon 't!—O, that Dunfermline's
tomb
Could render up The Bruce! that Spain's
red shore

Could give us back the good Lord James
of Douglas!
Or that fierce Randolph, with his voice
of terror,
Were here, to awe these brawlers to submission!

VIP. *to* GOR. Thou hast perused him
at more leisure now.

GOR. I see the giant form which all
men speak of,
The stately port—but not the sullen eye,
Not the bloodthirsty look, that should
belong
To him that made me orphan. I shall
need
To name my father twice ere I can strike
At such grey hairs, and face of such com-
mand;
Yet my hand clenches on my falchion hilt,
In token he shall die.

VIP. Need I again remind you, that the
place
Permits not private quarrel?

GOR. I'm calm. I will not seek—
nay, I will shun it—
And yet methinks that such debate's the
fashion.
You've heard how taunts, reproaches, and
the lie,
The lie itself, have flown from mouth to
mouth;
As if a band of peasants were disputing
About a foot-ball match, rather than
Chiefs
Were ordering a battle. I am young,
And lack experience: tell me, brave De
Vipont,
Is such the fashion of your wars in Pales-
tine?

VIP. Such it at times hath been; and
then the Cross
Hath sunk before the Crescent. Heaven's
cause
Won us not victory where wisdom was
not.—
Behold yon English host come slowly on,
With equal front, rank marshall'd upon
rank,
As if one spirit ruled one moving body;
The leaders, in their places, each prepared

To charge, support, and rally, as the fortune
Of changeful battle needs: then look on
  ours,
Broken, disjointed, as the tumbling surges
Which the winds wake at random. Look
  on both,
And dread the issue; yet there might be
  succour.

GOR. We're fearfully o'ermatch'd in
  discipline;
So even my inexperienced eye can judge.
What succour save in Heaven?

VIP. Heaven acts by human means.
  The artist's skill
Supplies in war, as in mechanic crafts,
Deficiency of tools. There's courage,
  wisdom,
And skill enough, live in one leader here,
As, flung into the balance, might avail
To counterpoise the odds 'twixt that ruled
  host
And our wild multitude.—I must not
  name him.

GOR. I guess, but dare not ask.—What
  band is yonder,
Arranged as closely as the English discipline
Hath marshall'd their best files?

VIP. Know'st thou not the pennon?
One day, perhaps, thou'lt see it all too
  closely;—
It is Sir Alan Swinton's.

GOR. These, then, are his,—the relics
  of his power;
Yet worth an host of ordinary men.—
And I must slay my country's sagest
  leader,
And crush by numbers that determined
  handful,
When most my country needs their
  practised aid,
Or men will say, "There goes degenerate
  Gordon;
His father's blood is on the Swinton's
  sword,
And his is in his scabbard!"   [Muses.

VIP. (apart.) High blood and mettle,
  mix'd with early wisdom,
Sparkle in this brave youth. If he survive
This evil-omen'd day, I pawn my word,

That, in the ruin which I now forebode,
Scotland has treasure left.—How close he
  eyes
Each look and step of Swinton! Is it
  hate,
Or is it admiration, or are both
Commingled strangely in that steady gaze!
    [SWINTON and MAXWELL return
      from the bottom of the stage.

MAX. The storm is laid at length
  amongst these counsellors;
See, they come forth.

SWI. And it is more than time;
For I can mark the vanguard archery
Handling their quivers—bending up their
  bows.

Enter the REGENT *and Scottish Lords.*

REG. Thus shall it be, then, since we
  may no better,
And, since no Lord will yield one jot of
  way
To this high urgency, or give the vanguard
Up to another's guidance, we will abide
  them
Even on this bent; and as our troops are
  rank'd,
So shall they meet the foe. Chief, nor
  Thane,
Nor Noble, can complain of the precedence
Which chance has thus assign'd him.

SWI. (apart.) O, sage discipline,
That leaves to chance the marshalling of
  a battle!

GOR. Move him to speech, De Vipont.

VIP. Move *him!*—Move whom?

GOR. Even him, whom, but brief space
  since,
My hand did burn to put to utter silence.

VIP. I'll move it to him.—Swinton,
  speak to them,
They lack thy counsel sorely.

SWI. Had I the thousand spears which
  once I led,
I had not thus been silent. But men's
  wisdom
Is rated by their means. From the poor
  leader
Of sixty lances, who seeks words of
  weight?

GOR. (*steps forward.*) Swinton, there's that of wisdom on thy brow,
And valour in thine eye, and that of peril
In this most urgent hour, that bids me say,—
Bids me, thy mortal foe, say,—Swinton, speak,
For King and Country's sake!

SWI. Nay, if that voice commands me, speak I will;
It sounds as if the dead lays charge on me.

REG. (*To* LENNOX, *with whom he has been consulting.*) 'Tis better than you think. This broad hill-side
Affords fair compass for our power's display,
Rank above rank rising in seemly tiers;
So that the rearward stands as fair and open——

SWI. As e'er stood mark before an English archer.

REG. Who dares to say so?—Who is't dare impeach
Our rule of discipline?

SWI. A poor Knight of these Marches, good my Lord;
Alan of Swinton, who hath kept a house here,
He and his ancestry, since the old days
Of Malcolm, called the Maiden.

REG. You have brought here, even to this pitched field,
In which the Royal Banner is display'd,
I think some sixty spears, Sir Knight of Swinton;
Our musters name no more.

SWI. I brought each man I had; and Chief, or Earl,
Thane, Duke, or dignitary, brings no more:
And with them brought I what may here be useful—
An aged eye; which, what in England, Scotland,
Spain, France, and Flanders, hath seen fifty battles,
And ta'en some judgment of them; a stark hand too,

Which plays as with a straw with this same mace,—
Which if a young arm here can wield more lightly,
I never more will offer word of counsel.

LEN. Hear him, my Lord; it is the noble Swinton—
He hath had high experience.

MAX.   He is noted
The wisest warrior 'twixt the Tweed and Solway,—
I do beseech you, hear him.

JOHN. Ay, hear the Swinton—hear stout old Sir Alan;
Maxwell and Johnstone both agree for once.

REG. Where's your impatience now.
Late you were all for battle, would not hear
Ourself pronounce a word—and now you gaze
On yon old warrior, in his antique armour,
As if he were arisen from the dead,
To bring us Bruce's counsel for the battle.

SWI. 'Tis a proud word to speak; but he who fought
Long under Robert Bruce, may something guess,
Without communication with the dead,
At what he would have counsell'd.—Bruce had bidden ye
Review your battle-order, marshall'd broadly
Here on the bare hill-side, and bidden you mark
Yon clouds of Southron archers, bearing down
To the green meadow-lands which stretch beneath—
The Bruce had warn'd you, not a shaft to-day
But shall find mark within a Scottish bosom,
If thus our field be order'd. The callow boys,
Who draw but four-foot bows, shall gall our front,
While on our mainward, and upon the rear,

The cloth-yard shafts shall fall like
　　death's own darts,
And, though blind men discharge them,
　　find a mark.
Thus shall we die the death of slaughter'd
　　deer,
Which, driven into the toils, are shot at
　　ease
By boys and women, while they toss aloft
All idly and in vain their branchy horns,
As we shall shake our unavailing spears.
　　REG. Tush, tell not me! if their shot
　　fall like hail,
Our men have Milan coats to bear it out.
　　SWI. Never did armourer temper steel
　　on stithy
That made sure fence against an English
　　arrow;
A cobweb gossamer were guard as good
Against a wasp-sting.
　　REG. Who fears a wasp-sting?
　　SWI.　　　　I, my Lord, fear none;
Yet should a wise man brush the insect off,
Or he may smart for it.
　　REG. We'll keep the hill; it is the
　　vantage-ground
When the main battle joins.
　　SWI. It ne'er will join, while their light
　　archery
Can foil our spearmen and our barbed
　　horse.
To hope Plantagenet would seek close
　　combat
When he can conquer riskless, is to deem,
Sagacious Edward simpler than a babe
In battle-knowledge. Keep the hill, my
　　Lord,
With the main body, if it is your plea-
　　sure;
But let a body of your chosen horse
Make execution on yon waspish archers.
I've done such work before, and love it
　　well;
If 'tis your pleasure to give me the leading,
The dames of Sherwood, Inglewood, and
　　Weardale,
Shall sit in widowhood and long for veni-
　　son,
And long in vain. Whoe'er remembers
　　Bannockburn,—

And when shall Scotsman, till the last
　　loud trumpet,
Forget that stirring word!—knows *that*
　　great battle
Even thus was fought and won.
　　LEN. This is the shortest road to bandy
　　blows;
For when the bills step forth and bows go
　　back,
Then is the moment that our hardy spear-
　　men,
With their strong bodies, and their stub-
　　born hearts,
And limbs well knit by mountain exer-
　　cise,
At the close tug shall foil the short-
　　breath'd Southron,
　　SWI. I do not say the field will thus be
　　won;
The English host is numerous, brave, and
　　loyal;
Their Monarch most accomplish'd in war's
　　art,
Skill'd, resolute, and wary——
　　REG. And if your scheme secure not
　　victory,
What does it promise us?
　　SWI.　　　　This much at least,—
Darkling we shall not die: the peasant's
　　shaft,
Loosen'd perchance without an aim or
　　purpose,
Shall not drink up the life-blood we derive
From those famed ancestors, who made
　　their breasts
This frontier's barrier for a thousand
　　years.
We'll meet these Southron bravely hand
　　to hand,
And eye to eye, and weapon against wea-
　　pon;
Each man who falls shall see the foe who
　　strikes him.
While our good blades are faithful to the
　　hilts,
And our good hands to these good blades
　　are faithful,
Blow shall meet blow, and none fall un-
　　avenged—
We shall not bleed alone.

Reg. And this is all
Your wisdom hath devised?

Swi. Not all; for I would pray you,
noble Lords,
(If one, among the guilty guiltiest, might,)
For this one day to charm to ten hours'
rest
The never-dying worm of deadly feud,
That gnaws our vexed hearts—think no
one foe
Save Edward and his host:—days will
remain,
Ay, days by far too many will remain,
To avenge old feuds or struggles for prece-
dence;—
Let this one day be Scotland's.—For my-
self,
If there is any here may claim from me
(As well may chance) a debt of blood and
hatred,
My life is his to-morrow unresisting,
So he to-day will let me do the best
That my old arm may achieve for the dear
country
That's mother to us both.

[Gordon *shows much emotion
during this and the preceding
speech of* Swinton.

Reg. It is a dream—a vision!—if one
troop
Rush down upon the archers, all will
follow,
And order is destroy'd—we'll keep the
battle-rank
Our fathers wont to do. No more on't.—
Ho!
Where be those youths seek knighthood
from our sword?

Her. Here are the Gordon, Somerville,
and Hay,
And Hepburn, with a score of gallants
more.

Reg. Gordon, stand forth.

Gor. I pray your Grace forgive me.

Reg. How! seek you not for knighthood?

Gor. I do thirst for't.
But, pardon me—'tis from another sword.

Reg. It is your Sovereign's—seek you
for a worthier?

Gor. Who would drink purely, seeks
the secret fountain,
How small soever—not the general stream,
Though it be deep and wide. My Lord,
I seek
The boon of knighthood from the honour'd
weapon
Of the best knight, and of the sagest
leader,
That ever graced a ring of chivalry.
—Therefore, I beg the boon on bended
knee,
Even from Sir Alan Swinton. [*Kneels.*

Reg. Degenerate boy! Abject at once
and insolent!—
See, Lords, he kneels to him that slew his
father!

Gor. (*starting up.*) Shame be on him
who speaks such shameful word!
Shame be on him, whose tongue would
sow dissension,
When most the time demands that native
Scotsmen
Forget each private wrong!

Swi. (*interrupting him*). Youth, since
you crave me
To be your sire in chivalry, I remind you
War has its duties, Office has its reve-
rence;
Who governs in the Sovereign's name is
Sovereign;
Crave the Lord Regent's pardon.

Gor. You task me justly, and I crave
his pardon, [*Bows to the Regent.*
His and these noble Lords'; and pray
them all
Bear witness to my words.—Ye noble
presence,
Here I remit unto the Knight of Swinton
All bitter memory of my father's slaugh-
ter,
All thoughts of malice, hatred, and re-
venge;
By no base fear or composition moved,
But by the thought, that in our country's
battle
All hearts should be as one. I do forgive
him
As freely as I pray to be forgiven,

And once more kneel to him to sue for knighthood.

SWI. (*affected, and drawing his sword.*)
Alas! brave youth, 'tis I should kneel to you,
And, tendering thee the hilt of the fell sword
That made thee fatherless, bid thee use the point
After thine own discretion. For thy boon—
Trumpets be ready—In the Holiest name,
And in Our Lady's and Saint Andrew's name,
[*Touching his shoulder with his sword.*
I dub thee Knight!—Arise, Sir Adam Gordon!
Be faithful, brave, and O, be fortunate,
Should this ill hour permit!
　　　　[*The trumpets sound; the Heralds cry "Largesse," and the Attendants shout "A Gordon! A Gordon!"*

REG. Beggars and flatterers! Peace, peace, I say!
We'll to the Standard; knights shall there be made
Who will with better reason crave your clamour.

LEN. What of Swinton's counsel?
Here's Maxwell and myself think it worth noting.

REG. (*with concentrated indignation.*)
Let the best knight, and let the sagest leader—
So Gordon quotes the man who slew his father,—
With his old pedigree and heavy mace,
Essay the adventure if it pleases him,
With his fair threescore horse. As for ourselves,
We will not peril aught upon the measure.

GOR. Lord Regent, you mistake; for if Sir Alan
Shall venture such attack, each man who calls
The Gordon chief, and hopes or fears from him
Or good or evil, follows Swinton's banner
In this achievement.

REG. Why, God ha' mercy! This is of a piece.
Let young and old e'en follow their own counsel,
Since none will list to mine.

ROSS. The Border cockerel fain would be on horseback;
'Tis safe to be prepared for fight or flight:
And this comes of it to give Northern lands
To the false Norman blood.

GOR. Hearken, proud Chief of Isles! Within my stalls
I have two hundred horse; two hundred riders
Mount guard upon my castle, who would tread
Into the dust a thousand of your Red-shanks,
Nor count it a day's service.

SWI. 　　　　　　　Hear I this
From thee, young man, and on the day of battle?
And to the brave MacDonnell?

GOR. 'Twas he that urged me; but I am rebuked.

REG. He crouches like a leash-hound to his master!*

SWI. Each hound must do so that would head the deer—
'Tis mongrel curs that snatch at mate or master.

REG. Too much of this. Sirs, to the Royal Standard!
I bid you, in the name of good King David.
Sound trumpets—sound for Scotland and King David!
　　　　[*The REGENT and the rest go off, and the Scene closes. Manent GORDON, SWINTON, and VIPONT, with REYNALD and followers. LENNOX follows the REGENT; but returns, and addresses SWINTON.*

LEN. O, were my western horsemen but come up,
I would take part with you!

---

* The laws of chivalry demanded this submission to a father in chivalry.

Swi. Better that you remain;
They lack discretion; such grey head as
yours
May best supply that want.
Lennox, mine ancient friend, and
honour'd lord,
Farewell, I think, for ever!

Len. Farewell, brave friend!—and
farewell, noble Gordon,
Whose sun will be eclipsed even as it
rises!—
The Regent will not aid you.

Swi. We will so bear us, that as soon
the bloodhound
Shall halt, and take no part, what time his
comrade
Is grappling with the deer, as he stand still,
And see us overmatch'd.

Len. Alas! thou dost not know how
mean his pride is,
How strong his envy.

Swi. Then we will die, and leave the
shame with him. [*Exit* Lennox.

Vip. (*to* Gordon.) What ails thee,
noble youth? What means this
pause?
Thou dost not rue thy generosity?

Gor. I have been hurried on by strong
impulse,
Like to a bark that scuds before the storm,
Till driven upon some strange and distant
coast,
Which never pilot dream'd of.—Have I
not forgiven?
And am I not still fatherless?

Swi. Gordon, no;
For while we live I am a father to thee.

Gor. Thou, Swinton?—no!—that cannot, cannot be.

Swi. Then change the phrase, and say,
that while we live,
Gordon shall be my son. If thou art
fatherless,
Am I not childless too? Bethink thee,
Gordon,
Our death-feud was not like the house-
hold fire,
Which the poor peasant hides among its
embers.

To smoulder on, and wait a time for
waking.
Ours was the conflagration of the forest,
Which, in its fury, spares nor sprout nor
stem,
Hoar oak, nor sapling—not to be extin-
guish'd,
Till Heaven, in mercy, sends down all
her waters;
But, once subdued, its flame is quench'd
for ever;
And spring shall hide the tract of devastation,
With foliage and with flowers.—Give me
thy hand.

Gor. My hand and heart!—And freely
now!—to fight!

Vip. How will you act? [*To* Swinton.]
The Gordon's band and thine
Are in the rearward left, I think, in
scorn—
Ill post for them who wish to charge the
foremost!

Swi. We'll turn that scorn to vantage,
and descend
Sidelong the hill—some winding path
there must be—
O, for a well-skill'd guide!
[Hob Hattely *starts up from a*
thicket.

Hob. So here he stands.—An ancient
friend, Sir Alan.
Hob Hattely, or, if you like it better,
Hob of the Heron Plume. here stands
your guide.

Swi. An ancient friend?—a most no-
torious knave,
Whose throat I've destined to the
dodder'd oak
Before my castle, these ten months and
more.
Was it not you who drove from Simprim-
mains,
And Swinton-quarter, sixty head of
cattle?

Hob. What then, if now I lead your
sixty lances
Upon the English flank, where they'll
find spoil
Is worth six hundred beeves?

Swi. Why, thou canst do it, knave.
    I would not trust thee
With one poor bullock; yet would risk
    my life,
And all my followers, on thine honest
    guidance.
    Hob. There is a dingle, and a most
        discreet one,
(I've trod each step by star-light,) that
    sweeps round
The rearward of this hill, and opens
    secretly
Upon the archers' flank.—Will not that
    serve
Your present turn, Sir Alan?
    Swi.   Bravely, bravely!
    Gor. Mount, sirs, and cry my slogan.
Let all who love the Gordon follow me!
    Swi. Ay, let all follow—but in silence
        follow;
Scare not the hare that's couchant on her
    form—
The cushat from her nest—brush not, if
    possible,
The dew-drop from the spray—
Let no one whisper, until I cry, "Havoc!"
Then shout as loud's ye will.—On, on,
    brave Hob;
On, thou false thief, but yet most faithful
    Scotsman!   [Exeunt.

ACT II.—Scene I.

*A rising Ground immediately in front of
the Position of the English Main Body.*
Percy, Chandos, Ribaumont, *and other
English and Norman Nobles, are grouped
on the Stage.*

    Per. The Scots still keep the hill—the
        sun grows high;
Would that the charge would sound.
    Cha. Thou scent'st the slaughter,
        Percy.—Who comes here?

Enter the Abbot of Walthamstow.

Now, by my life, the holy priest of
    Walthamstow,
Like to a lamb among a herd of wolves!
See, he's about to bleat.
    Ab. The King, methinks, delays the
        onset long.

Cha. Your general, Father, like your
    rat-catcher,
Pauses to bait his traps, and set his snares.
    Ab. The metaphor is decent.
    Cha.   Reverend sir,
I will uphold it just. Our good King
    Edward
Will presently come to this battle-field,
And speak to you of the last tilting match,
Or of some feat he did a twenty years since;
But not a word of the day's work before him.
Even as the artist, sir, whose name offends
    you,
Sits prosing o'er his can, until the trap fall,
Announcing that the vermin are secured,
And then 'tis up, and on them.
    Per. Chandos, you give your tongue
        too bold a licence.
    Cha. Percy, I am a necessary evil.
King Edward would not want me, if he
    could,
And could not, if he would. I know
    my value.
My heavy hand excuses my light tongue.
So men wear weighty swords in their de-
    fence,
Although they may offend the tender shin,
When the steel-boot is doff'd.
    Ab.   My Lord of Chandos,
This is but idle speech on brink of battle,
When Christian men should think upon
    their sins;
For as the tree falls, so the trunk must lie,
Be it for good or evil. Lord, bethink thee,
Thou hast withheld from our most reve-
    rend house,
The tithes of Everingham and Settleton;
Wilt thou make satisfaction to the Church,
Before her thunders strike thee? I do
    warn thee
In most paternal sort.
    Cha. I thank you, Father, filially.
Though but a truant son of Holy Church,
I would not choose to undergo her cen-
    sures,
When Scottish blades are waving at my
    throat.
I'll make fair composition.
    Ab. No composition; I'll have all, or
        none.

CHA. None, then—'tis soonest spoke.
I'll take my chance,
And trust my sinful soul to Heaven's
mercy,
Rather than risk my worldly goods with
thee—
My hour may not be come.
 AB. Impious—impenitent—
 PER. Hush!—the King—the King!

Enter KING EDWARD, *attended by*
BALIOL *and others.*

KING (*apart to* CHA.) Hark hither,
Chandos! — Have the Yorkshire
archers
Yet join'd the vanguard?
 CHA. They are marching thither.
 K. ED. Bid them make haste, for
shame—send a quick rider.
The loitering knaves! were it to steal my
venison,
Their steps were light enough.—How
now, Sir Abbot?
Say, is your Reverence come to study
with us
The princely art of war?
 AB. I've had a lecture from my Lord
of Chandos,
In which he term'd your Grace a rat-
catcher.
 K. ED. Chandos, how's this?
 CHA. O, I will prove it, sir!—These
skipping Scots
Have changed a dozen times 'twixt Bruce
and Baliol,
Quitting each House when it began to
totter;
They're fierce and cunning, treacherous,
too, as rats,
And we, as such, will smoke them in
their fastnesses.
 K. ED. These rats have seen your back,
my Lord of Chandos,
And noble Percy's too.
 PER. Ay; but the mass which now
lies weltering
On yon hill side, like a Leviathan
That's stranded on the shallows, then had
soul in't,
Order and discipline, and power of action.

Now 'tis a headless corpse, which only
shows,
By wild convulsions, that some life re-
mains in't.
 K. ED. True, they had once a head;
and 'twas a wise,
Although a rebel head.
 AB. (*bowing to the* KING.) Would he
were here! we should find one to
match him.
 K. ED. There's something in that
wish which wakes an echo
Within my bosom. Yet it is as well,
Or better, that The Bruce is in his grave.
We have enough of powerful foes on
earth,—
No need to summon them from other
worlds.
 PER. Your Grace ne'er met The Bruce?
 K. ED. Never himself; but in my
earliest field
I did encounter with his famous captains,
Douglas and Randolph. Faith! they
press'd me hard.
 AB. My Liege, if I might urge you
with a question,
Will the Scots fight to-day?
 K. ED. (*sharply.*) Go look your breviary.
 CHA. (*apart.*) The Abbot has it—
Edward will not answer
On that nice point. We must observe
his humour.—
 [*Addresses the* KING.
Your first campaign, my Liege?—That
was in Weardale,
When Douglas gave our camp yon mid-
night ruffle,
And turn'd men's beds to biers.
 K. ED. Ay, by Saint Edward!—I
escaped right nearly.
I was a soldier then for holidays,
And slept not in mine armour: my safe
rest
Was startled by the cry of " Douglas!
Douglas!"
And by my couch, a grisly chamberlain,
Stood Alan Swinton, with his bloody
mace.
It was a churchman saved me—my stout
chaplain,

Heaven quit his spirit! caught a weapon up,
And grappled with the giant.—How now,
   Louis?

Enter an Officer, who whispers the KING.

K. ED. Say to him,—thus—and thus—
                 [*Whispers.*
AB. That Swinton's dead. A monk
   of ours reported,
Bound homeward from St. Ninian's pil-
   grimage,
The Lord of Gordon slew him.
   PER. Father, and if your house stood
   on our borders,
You might have cause to know that
   Swinton lives,
And is on horseback yet.
   CHA.   He slew the Gordon,
That's all the difference—a very trifle.
   AB. Trifling to those who wage a war
   more noble
Than with the arm of flesh.
   CHA. (*apart.*) The Abbot's vexed, I'll
   rub the sore for him.—
 (*Aloud.*) I have seen priests that used
   that arm of flesh,
And used it sturdily.—Most reverend
   Father,
What say you to the chaplain's deed of
   arms
In the King's tent at Weardale?
   AB. It was most sinful, being against
   the canon
Prohibiting all churchmen to bear
   weapons;
And as he fell in that unseemly guise,
Perchance his soul may rue it.
   K. ED. (*overhearing the last words.*)
   Who may rue?
And what is to be rued?
   CHA. (*apart.*) I'll match his Reverence
for the tithes of Everingham.
—The Abbot says, my Liege, the deed
   was sinful,
By which your chaplain, wielding secular
   weapons,
Secured your Grace's life and liberty,
And that he suffers for 't in purgatory.
   K. ED. (*to the* ABBOT.) Say'st thou
   my chaplain is in purgatory?

AB. It is the canon speaks it, good my
   Liege.
   K. ED. In purgatory! thou shalt pray
   him out on't,
Or I will make thee wish thyself beside
   him.
   AB. My Lord, perchance his soul is
   past the aid
Of all the Church may do—there is a
   place
From which there's no redemption.
   K. ED. And if I thought my faithful
   chaplain there,
Thou shouldst there join him, priest!—
   Go, watch, fast, pray,
And let me have such prayers as will
   storm Heaven—
None of your maim'd and mutter'd hunt-
   ing masses.
   AB. (*apart to* CHA.) For God's sake
   take him off.
   CHA. Wilt thou compound, then,
The tithes of Everingham?
   K. ED. I tell thee, if thou bear'st the
   keys of Heaven,
Abbot, thou shalt not turn a bolt with
   them
'Gainst any well-deserving English sub-
   ject.
   AB. (*to* CHA.) We will compound,
   and grant thee, too, a share
I' the next indulgence. Thou dost need
   it much,
And greatly 'twill avail thee.
   CHA. Enough—we're friends, and
   when occasion serves,
I will strike in.——
   [*Looks as if towards the Scottish Army.*
   K. ED. Answer, proud Abbot; is my
   chaplain's soul,
If thou knowest aught on't, in the evil
   place?
   CHA. My Liege, the Yorkshire men
   have gain'd the meadow.
I see the pennon green of merry Sherwood.
   K. ED. Then give the signal instant!
   We have lost
But too much time already.
   AB. My Liege, your holy chaplain's
   blessed soul—

K. ED. To hell with it and thee! Is
this a time
To speak of monks and chaplains?
  [*Flourish of Trumpets, answered by
  a distant sound of Bugles.*
See, Chandos, Percy—Ha, Saint George!
Saint Edward!
See it descending now, the fatal hail-
shower,
The storm of England's wrath—sure,
swift, resistless,
Which no mail-coat can brook.—Brave
English hearts!
How close they shoot together!—as one
eye
Had aim'd five thousand shafts—as if one
hand
Had loosed five thousand bow-strings!
PER.   The thick volley
Darkens the air, and hides the sun from us.
  K. ED. It falls on those shall see the
sun no more.
The winged, the resistless plague is with
them.
How their vex'd host is reeling to and fro,
Like the chafed whale with fifty lances
in him,
They do not see, and cannot shun the
wound.
The storm is viewless as death's sable
wing,
Unerring as his scythe.
  PER. Horses and riders are going
down together.
'Tis almost pity to see nobles fall,
And by a peasant's arrow.
  BAL.   I could weep them,
Although they are my rebels.
  CHA. (*aside to* PER.) His conquerors,
he means, who cast him out
From his usurped kingdom.—(*Aloud.*)
'Tis the worst of it,
That knights can claim small honour in
the field
Which archers win, unaided by our lances.
  K. ED. The battle is not ended.
            [*Looks towards the field.*
Not ended?—scarce begun! What
horse are these,
Rush from the thicket underneath the hill?

PER. They're Hainaulters, the fol-
lowers of Queen Isabel.
  K. ED. (*hastily.*) Hainaulters!—thou
art blind—wear Hainaulters
Saint Andrew's silver cross?—or would
they charge
Full on our archers, and make havoc of
them?—
Bruce is alive again — ho, rescue!
rescue!—
Who was't survey'd the ground?
  RIBA. Most royal Liege—
  K. ED. A rose hath fallen from thy
chaplet,* Ribaumont.
  RIBA. I'll win it back, or lay my head
beside it   [*Exit.*
  K. ED. Saint George! Saint Edward!
Gentlemen, to horse,
And to the rescue!—Percy, lead the bill-
men;
Chandos, do thou bring up the men-at-
arms.—
If yonder numerous host should now
bear down
Bold as their vanguard, (*to the Abbot,*)
thou mayst pray for us,
We may need good men's prayers.—To
the rescue,
Lords, to the rescue! ha, Saint George!
Saint Edward!   [*Exeunt*

SCENE II.

*A part of the Field of Battle betwixt the two
Main Armies. Tumults behind the scenes;
alarums, and cries of "Gordon! a Gordon!" "Swinton!" &c.*

*Enter, as victorious over the English
vanguard,* VIPONT, REYNALD, *and
others.*

  VIP. 'Tis sweet to hear these war-cries
sound together,—
Gordon and Swinton.

---

* The well-known expression by which
Robert Bruce censured the negligence of Randolph, for permitting an English body of
cavalry to pass his flank on the day preceding
the battle of Bannockburn.

Rey. 'Tis passing pleasant, yet 'tis
strange withal.
Faith, when at first I heard the Gordon's
slogan
Sounded so near me, I had nigh struck
down
The knave who cried it.

Enter Swinton *and* Gordon.

Swi. Pitch down my pennon in yon
holly bush.
Gor. Mine in the thorn beside it ; let
them wave,
As fought this morn their masters, side
by side.
Swi. Let the men rally, and restore
their ranks
Here in this vantage-ground—disorder'd
chase
Leads to disorder'd flight ; we have done
our part,
And if we're succour'd now, Plantagenet
Must turn his bridle southward.—
Reynald, spur to the Regent with the
basnet
Of stout De Grey, the leader of their
vanguard ;
Say, that in battle-front the Gordon slew
him,
And by that token bid him send us
succour.
Gor. And tell him that when Selby's
headlong charge
Had wellnigh borne me down, Sir Alan
smote him.
I cannot send his helmet, never nutshell
Went to so many shivers. — Harkye,
grooms ! [*To those behind the scenes.*
Why do you let my noble steed stand
stiffening
After so hot a course ?
Swi. Ay, breathe your horses, they'll
have work anon,
For Edward's men-at-arms will soon be
on us,
The flower of England, Gascony, and
Flanders ;
But with swift succour we will bide them
bravely.—
De Vipont, thou look'st sad.

Vip. It is because I hold a Templar's
sword
Wet to the crossed hilt with Christian
blood.—
Swi. The blood of English archers—
what can gild
A Scottish blade more bravely ?
Vip. Even therefore grieve I for those
gallant yeomen,
England's peculiar and appropriate sons,
Known in no other land. Each boasts
his hearth
And field as free as the best lord his
barony,
Owing subjection to no human vassalage,
Save to their King and law   Hence are
they resolute,
Leading the van on every day of battle,
As men who know the blessings they
defend.
Hence are they frank and generous in
peace,
As men who have their portion in its
plenty.
No other kingdom shows such worth and
happiness
Veil'd in such low estate—therefore I
mourn them.
Swi. I'll keep my sorrow for our
native Scots,
Who, spite of hardship, poverty, oppres-
sion,
Still follow to the field their Chieftain's
banner,
And die in the defence on't.
Gor. And if I live and see my halls
again,
They shall have portion in the good they
fight for.
Each hardy follower shall have his field,
His household hearth and sod-built
home, as free
As ever Southron had. They shall be
happy !—
And my Elizabeth shall smile to see it !—
I have betray'd myself.
Swi.   Do not believe it.—
Vipont, do thou look out from yonder
height,
And see what motion in the Scottish host,

And in King Edward's.— [*Exit* VIPONT.
Now will I counsel thee;
The Templar's ear is for no tale of love,
Being wedded to his Order. But I tell
thee,
The brave young knight that hath no
lady-love
Is like a lamp unlighted; his brave deeds,
And its rich painting, do seem then most
glorious,
When the pure ray gleams through
them.—
Hath thy Elizabeth no other name?
GOR. Must I then speak of her to you,
Sir Alan?
The thought of thee, and of thy matchless
strength,
Hath conjured phantoms up amongst her
dreams.
The name of Swinton hath been spell
sufficient
To chase the rich blood from her lovely
cheek,
And wouldst thou now know hers?
SWI. I would, nay must.
Thy father in the paths of chivalry,
Should know the load-star thou dost rule
thy course by.
GOR. Nay, then, her name is—hark—
[*Whispers.*
SWI. I know it well, that ancient
northern house.
GOR. O, thou shalt see its fairest grace
and honour
In my Elizabeth. And if music touch
thee——
SWI. It did, before disasters had un-
tuned me.
GOR. O, her notes
Shall hush each sad remembrance to ob-
livion,
Or melt them to such gentleness of feeling,
That grief shall have its sweetness. Who,
but she,
Knows the wild harpings of our native
land?
Whether they lull the shepherd on his
hill,
Or wake the knight to battle; rouse to
merriment,

Or soothe to sadness; she can touch each
mood.
Princes and statesmen, chiefs renown'd in
arms,
And grey-hair'd bards, contend which
shall the first
And choicest homage render to the en-
chantress.
SWI. You speak her talent bravely.
GOR. Though you smile,
I do not speak it half. Her gift creative,
New measures adds to every air she
wakes;
Varying and gracing it with liquid sweet-
ness,
Like the wild modulation of the lark;
Now leaving, now returning to the strain!
To listen to her, is to seem to wander
In some enchanted labyrinth of romance,
Whence nothing but the lovely fairy's
will,
Who wove the spell, can extricate the
wanderer.
Methinks I hear her now!—
SWI. Bless'd privilege
Of youth! There's scarce three minutes
to decide
'Twixt death and life, 'twixt triumph and
defeat,
Yet all his thoughts are in his lady's bower,
List'ning her harping! [*Enter* VIPONT.
Where are thine, De Vipont?
VIP. On death—on judgment—on
eternity!
For time is over with us.
SWI. There moves not, then, one pen-
non to our aid,
Of all that flutter yonder!
VIP. From the main English host come
rushing forward
Pennons enow—ay, and their Royal
Standard.
But ours stand rooted, as for crows to
roost on.
SWI. (*to himself.*) I'll rescue him at
least.—Young Lord of Gordon,
Spur to the Regent—show the instant
need——
GOR. I penetrate thy purpose; but I
go not.

Swi. Not at my bidding? I, thy sire
in chivalry—

Thy leader in the battle?—I command
thee!

Gor. No, thou wilt not command me
seek my safety,—

For such is thy kind meaning—at the
expense

Of the last hope which Heaven reserves
for Scotland.

While I abide, no follower of mine

Will turn his rein for life; but were I
gone,

What power can stay them? and, our
band dispersed,

What sword shall for an instant stem yon
host,

And save the latest chance for victory?

Vip. The noble youth speaks truth;
and were he gone,

There will not twenty spears be left with
us.

Gor. No, bravely as we have begun the
field,

So let us fight it out. The Regent's eyes,

More certain than a thousand messages,

Shall see us stand, the barrier of his host

Against yon bursting storm. If not for
honour,

If not for warlike rule, for shame at least

He must bear down to aid us.

Swi.   Must it be so?

And am I forced to yield the sad consent,

Devoting thy young life? O, Gordon,
Gordon!

I do it as the patriarch doom'd his issue;

I at my country's, he at Heaven's command;

But I seek vainly some atoning sacrifice,

Rather than such a victim :—(*Trumpets.*)
Hark, they come!

That music sounds not like thy lady's lute.

Gor. Yet shall my lady's name mix
with it gaily.—

Mount, vassals, couch your lances, and
cry, "Gordon!

Gordon for Scotland and Elizabeth!"

[*Exeunt. Loud Alarums.*

SCENE III.

*Another part of the Field of Battle, adjacent
to the former Scene.*

Alarums. Enter Swinton, *followed
by* Hob Hattely.

Swi. Stand to it yet! The man who
flies to-day,

May bastards warm them at his household hearth!

Hob. That ne'er shall be my curse.
My Magdalen

Is trusty as my broadsword.

Swi.   Ha, thou knave,

Art thou dismounted too?

Hob.   I know, Sir Alan,

You want no homeward guide; so threw
my reins

Upon my palfrey's neck, and let him loose.

Within an hour he stands before my gate;

And Magdalen will need no other token

To bid the Melrose Monks say masses for
me.

Swi. Thou art resolved to cheat the
halter, then?

Hob.   It is my purpose,

Having lived a thief, to die a brave man's
death;

And never had I a more glorious chance
for't.

Swi. Here lies the way to it, knave.—
Make in, make in,

And aid young Gordon!

[*Exeunt. Loud and long Alarums.
After which the back Scene rises,
and discovers* Swinton *on the
ground,* Gordon *supporting
him; both much wounded.*

Swi. All are cut down—the reapers
have pass'd o'er us,

And hie to distant harvest.—My toil's
over;

There lies my sickle. [*Dropping his
sword.*] Hand of mine again

Shall never, never wield it!

Gor. O valiant leader, is thy light ex-
tinguish'd!

That only beacon-flame which promised
safety

In this day's deadly wrack!

Swi. My lamp hath long been dim!
But thine, young Gordon,
Just kindled, to be quench'd so suddenly,
Ere Scotland saw its splendour !—

Gor. Five thousand horse hung idly
on yon hill,
Saw us o'erpower'd, and no one stirr'd to
aid us !

Swi. It was the Regent's envy.—Out!
—alas !

Why blame I him !—It was our civil dis-
cord,
Our selfish vanity, our jealous hatred,
Which framed this day of dole for our
poor country.—
Had thy brave father held yon leading
staff,
As well his rank and valour might have
claim'd it,
We had not fall'n unaided.—How, O how
Is he to answer it, whose deed pre-
vented——

Gor. Alas! alas! the author of the
death-feud,
He has his reckoning too! for had your sons
And num'rous vassals lived, we had lack'd
no aid.

Swi. May God assoil the dead, and him
who follows !
We've drank the poison'd beverage which
we brew'd :
Have sown the wind, and reap'd the tenfold whirlwind !—
But thou, brave youth, whose nobleness
of heart
Pour'd oil upon the wounds our hate inflicted ;
Thou, who hast done no wrong, need'st
no forgiveness,—
Why should'st thou share our punishment !

Gor. All need forgiveness—[*distant
alarums.*]——Hark, in yonder shout
Did the main battles counter !

Swi. Look on the field, brave Gordon,
if thou canst,
And tell me how the day goes.—But I guess,
Too surely do I guess——

Gor. All's lost! all's lost!—Of the
main Scottish host,

Some wildly fly, and some rush wildly
forward ;
And some there are who seem to turn
their spears
Against their countrymen.

Swi. Rashness, and cowardice, and
secret treason,
Combine to ruin us ; and our hot valour,
Devoid of discipline, is madmen's strength,
More fatal unto friends than enemies !
I'm glad that these dim eyes shall see no
more on't.—
Let thy hands close them, Gordon—I will
dream
My fair-hair'd William renders me that
office !   [*Dies.*

Gor. And, Swinton, I will think I do
that duty
To my dead father.

Enter De Vipont.

Vip. Fly, fly, brave youth !—A hand-
ful of thy followers,
The scatter'd gleaning of this desperate day,
Still hover yonder to essay thy rescue—
O linger not !—I'll be your guide to them.

Gor. Look there, and bid me fly !—
The oak has fall'n ;
And the young ivy bush, which learn'd to
climb
By its support, must needs partake its fall.

Vip. Swinton ? Alas ! the best, the
bravest, strongest,
And sagest of our Scottish chivalry !
Forgive one moment, if to save the living,
My tongue should wrong the dead.—
Gordon, bethink thee,
Thou dost but stay to perish with the
corpse
Of him who slew thy father.

Gor. Ay, but he was my sire in
chivalry !
He taught my youth to soar above the
promptings
Of mean and selfish vengeance ; gave my
youth
A name that shall not die even on this
death-spot.
Records shall tell this field had not been
lost,

37

Had all men fought like Swinton and like
  Gordon.   [*Trumpets.*

Save thee, De Vipont.—Hark! the
  Southron trumpets.

VIP. Nay, without thee I stir not.

Enter EDWARD, CHANDOS, PERCY,
    BALIOL, &c.

GOR. Ay, they come on—the Tyrant
  and the Traitor,

Workman and tool, Plantagenet and
  Baliol.—

O for a moment's strength in this poor
  arm,

To do one glorious deed !
    [*He rushes on the English, but is
      made prisoner wit., VIPONT.*

K. ED. Disarm them—harm them not;
  though it was they

Made havoc on the archers of our vanguard,

They and that bulky champion. Where
  is he ?

CHA. Here lies the giant ! Say his
  name, young Knight ?

GOR. Let it suffice, he was a man
  this morning.

CHA. I question'd thee in sport. I do
  not need

Thy information, youth. Who that has
  fought

Through all these Scottish wars, but
  knows his crest ?

The sable boar chain'd to the leafy oak,

And that huge mace still seen where war
  was wildest!

K. ED. 'Tis Alan Swinton!

Grim Chamberlain, who in my tent at
  Weardale,

Stood by my startled couch with torch
  and mace,

When the Black Douglas' war-cry waked
  my camp.

GOR. (*sinking down.*) If thus thou
  know'st him.

Thou wilt respect his corpse.

K. ED. As belted Knight and crowned
  King, I will.

GOR. And let mine

Sleep at his side, in token that our death
Ended the feud of Swinton and of Gordon.

K. ED It is the Gordon!—Is there
  aught besid:

Edward can do to honour bravery,
Even in an enemy ?

GOR. Nothing but this:

Let not base Baliol, with his touch or look,
Profane my corpse or Swinton's. I've
  some breath still,

Enough to say—Scotland—Elizabeth !
              [*Dies.*

CHA. Baliol, I would not brook such
  dying looks,

To buy the crown you aim at.

K. ED. (*to* VIP.) Vipont, thy crossed
  shield shows ill in warfare

Against a Christian king.

VIP. That Christian King is warring
  upon Scotland.

I was a Scotsman ere I was a Templar,
Sworn to my country ere I knew my
  Order.

K. ED. I will but know thee as a Christian champion,

And set thee free unransom'd.

Enter ABBOT OF WALTHAMSTOW.

AB. Heaven grant your Majesty

Many such glorious days as this has been !

K. ED. It is a day of much and high
  advantage ;

Glorious it might have been, had all our
  foes

Fought like these two brave champions.
  —Strike the drums,

Sound trumpets, and pursue the fugitives,
Till the Tweed's eddies whelm them,
  Berwick's render'd—

These wars, I trust, will soon find lasting
  close.

MACDUFF'S CROSS.

INTRODUCTION.

THESE few scenes had the honour to be included in a Miscellany, published in the year 1823, by Mrs. Joanna Baillie, and are here reprinted, to unite them with the trifles of the same kind which owe their birth to the author. The singular history of the Cross and Law of Clan MacDuff is given, at length enough to satisfy the keenest antiquary, in *The Minstrelsy of the Scottish Border.** It is here only necessary to state that the Cross was a place of refuge to any person related to MacDuff, within the ninth degree, who, having committed homicide in sudden quarrel, should reach this place, prove his descent from the Thane of Fife, and pay a certain penalty.

The shaft of the Cross was destroyed at the Reformation. The huge block of stone which served for its pedestal is still in existence near the town of Newburgh, on a kind of pass which commands the county of Fife to the southward, and to the north, the windings of the magnificent Tay and fertile country of Angusshire. The Cross bore an inscription, which is transmitted to us in an unintelligible form by Sir Robert Sibbald.

ABBOTSFORD, *January*, 1830.

DRAMATIS PERSONÆ.

NINIAN,
WALDHAVE, } *Monks of Lindores.*

LINDESAY, } *Scottish*
MAURICE BERKELEY, } *Barons.*

TO

MRS. JOANNA BAILLIE,

AUTHORESS OF

"THE PLAYS ON THE PASSIONS."

PRELUDE.

NAY, smile not, Lady, when I speak of witchcraft,
And say that still there lurks amongst our glens
Some touch of strange enchantment.—
Mark that fragment,

I mean that rough-hewn block of massive stone,
Placed on the summit of this mountain-pass,
Commanding prospect wide o'er field and fell,
And peopled village and extended moorland,
And the wide ocean and majestic Tay,
To the far distant Grampians.—Do not deem it
A loosen'd portion of the neighbouring rock,
Detach'd by storm and thunder,—'t was the pedestal
On which, in ancient times, a Cross was rear'd,
Carved o'er with words which foil'd philologists;
And the events it did commemorate
Were dark, remote, and undistinguishable,
As were the mystic characters it bore.

---

* Vol. iv. p. 266, in the Appendix to Lord Soulis, "Law of Clan McDuff."

But, mark,—a wizard, born on Avon's bank,

Tuned but his harp to this wild northern theme,

And, lo ! the scene is hallow'd. None shall pass,

Now, or in after days, beside that stone,

But he shall have strange visions; thoughts and words,

That shake, or rouse, or thrill the human heart,

Shall rush upon his memory when he hears

The spirit-stirring name of this rude symbol ;—

Oblivious ages, at that simple spell,

Shall render back their terrors with their woes,

Alas ! and with their crimes—and the proud phantoms

Shall move with step familiar to his eye,

And accents which, once heard, the ear forgets not,

Though ne'er again to list them. Siddons, thine,

Thou matchless Siddons ! thrill upon our ear ;

And on our eye thy lofty Brother's form

Rises as Scotland's monarch.—But, to thee,

Joanna, why to thee speak of such visions?

Thine own wild wand can raise them.

Yet since thou wilt an idle tale of mine,

Take one which scarcely is of worth enough

To give or to withhold.—Our time creeps on,

Fancy grows colder as the silvery hair

Tells the advancing winter of our life.

But if it be of worth enough to please,

That worth it owes to her who set the task ;

If otherwise, the fault rests with the author.

SCENE 1.

The summit of a Rocky Pass near to New-burgh, about two miles from the ancient Abbey of Lindores, in Fife. In the centre is MacDuff's Cross, an antique Monument, and, at a small distance, on one side, a Chapel, with a Lamp burning.

Enter, as having ascended the Pass, NINIAN and WALDHAVE, Monks of Lindores. NINIAN crosses himself, and seems to recite his devotions, WALDHAVE stands gazing on the prospect, as if in deep contemplation.

NIN. Here stands the Cross, good brother, consecrated

By the bold Thane unto his patron saint

Magridius, once a brother of our house.

Canst thou not spare an ave or a creed?

Or hath the steep ascent exhausted you?

You trode it stoutly, though 'twas rough and toilsome.

WAL. I have trode a rougher.

NIN.   On the Highland hills—

Scarcely within our sea-girt province here,

Unless upon the Lomonds or Bennarty.

WAL. I spoke not of the literal path, good father,

But of the road of life which I have travell'd,

Ere I assumed this habit; it was bounded,

Hedged in, and limited by earthly prospects,

As ours beneath was closed by dell and thicket.

Here we see wide and far, and the broad sky,

With wide horizon, opens full around,

While earthly objects dwindle. Brother Ninian,

Fain would I hope that mental elevation

Could raise me equally o'er worldly thoughts,

And place me nearer heaven.

NIN. 'T is good morality.—But yet forget not,

That though we look on heaven from this high eminence,
Yet doth the Prince of all the airy space,
Arch-foe of man, possess the realms between.

WAL. Most true, good brother; and men may be farther
From the bright heaven they aim at, even because
They deem themselves secure on 't.

NIN. (*after a pause*). You do gaze—
Strangers are wont to do so—on the prospect.
Yon is the Tay roll'd down from Highland hills,
That rests his waves, after so rude a race,
In the fair plains of Gowrie—farther westward,
Proud Stirling rises—yonder, to the east,
Dundee, the gift of God, and fair Montrose,
And still more northward lie the ancient towers——

WAL. Of Edzell.

NIN. How? know you the towers of Edzell?

WAL. I 've heard of them.

NIN. Then have you heard a tale
Which when he tells, the peasant shakes his head,
And shuns the mouldering and deserted walls.

WAL. Why, and by whom, deserted?

NIN. Long the tale—
Enough to say that the last Lord of Edzell,
Bold Louis Lindesay, had a wife, and found——

WAL. Enough is said, indeed—since a weak woman,
Ay, and a tempting fiend, lost Paradise,
When man was innocent.

NIN. They fell at strife,
Men say, on slight occasion: that fierce Lindesay
Did bend his sword against De Berkeley's breast,

And that the lady threw herself between:
That then De Berkeley dealt the Baron's death-wound.
Enough, that from that time De Berkeley bore
A spear in foreign wars. But, it is said,
He hath return'd of late; and, therefore, brother,
The Prior hath ordain'd our vigil here,
To watch the privilege of the sanctuary,
And rights of Clan MacDuff.

WAL. What rights are these?

NIN. Most true! you are but newly come from Rome,
And do not know our ancient usages.
Know then, when fell Macbeth beneath the arm
Of the predestined knight, unborn of woman,
Three boons the victor ask'd, and thrice did Malcolm,
Stooping the sceptre by the Thane restored,
Assent to his request. And hence the rule,
That first when Scotland's King assumes the crown,
MacDuff's descendant rings his brow with it:
And hence, when Scotland's King calls forth his host,
MacDuff's descendant leads the van in battle:
And last, in guerdon of the crown restored,
Red with the blood of the usurping tyrant,
The right was granted in succeeding time,
That if a kinsman of the Thane of Fife
Commit a slaughter on a sudden impulse,
And fly for refuge to this Cross MacDuff,
For the Thane's sake he shall find sanctuary;
For here must the avenger's step be stayed,

And here tne panting homicide find
   safety.
  WAL. And here a brother of your
   order watches,
To see the custom of the place ob-
   sᵣrved?
  NIN. Even so;—such is our convent's holy right,
Since Saint Magridius—blessed be his
   memory!—
Did by a vision warn the Abbot Ead-
   mir.—
And chief we watch, when there is
   bickering
Among the neighbouring nobles, now
   most likely
From this return of Berkeley from
   abroad,
Having the Lindesay's blood upon his
   hand.
  WAL. The Lindesay, then, was loved
   among his friends?
  NIN. Honour'd and fear'd he was—
   but little loved;
For even his bounty bore a show of
   sternness;
And when his passions waked, he was
   a Sathan
Of wrath and injury.
  WAL. How now, Sir Priest! (*fiercely*)
  —Forgive me (*recollecting him-
  self*)—I was dreaming
Of an old baron, who did bear about
   him
Some touch of your Lord Reynold.
  NIN. Lindesay's name, my brother,
Indeed was Reynold;—and methinks,
   moreover,
That, as you spoke even now, he would
   have spoken.
I brought him a petition from our con-
   vent:
He granted straight, but in such tone
   and manner,
By my good saint! I thought myself
   scarce safe
Till Tay roll'd broad between us. I
   must now
Unto the chapel—meanwhile the watch
   is thine;

And, at thy word, the hurrying fugitive
Should such arrive, must here find
   sanctuary;
And, at thy word, the fiery-paced
   avenger
Must stop his bloody course—e'en as
   swoln Jordan
Controll'd his waves, soon as they
   touch'd the feet
Of those who bore the ark.
  WAL.   Is this my charge?
  NIN. Even so; and I am near,
   should chance require me.
At midnight I relieve you on your
   watch,
When we may taste together some re-
   freshment:
I have cared for it; and for a flask of
   wine—
There is no sin, so that we drink it not
Until the midnight hour, when lauds
   have toll'd.
Farewell a while, and peaceful watch
   be with you!
          [*Exit towards the Chapel.*
  WAL. It is not with me, and alas!
   alas!
I know not where to seek it. This
   monk's mind
Is with his cloister match'd, nor lacks
   more room.
Its petty duties, formal ritual,
Its humble pleasures and its paltry
   troubles,
Fill up his round of life; even as some
   reptiles,
They say, are moulded to the very
   shape,
And all the angles of the rocky crevice,
In which they live and die. But for
   myself,
Retired in passion to the narrow cell,
Couching my tired limbs in its recesses,
So ill adapted am I to its limits,
That every attitude is agony.——
How now! what brings him back?

        Re-enter NINIAN.

  NIN. Look to your watch, my brother; horsemen come:

I heard their tread when kneeling in
the chapel.

WAL. (*looking to a distance*). My
thoughts have rapt me more than
thy devotion,
Else had I heard the tread of distant
horses
Farther than thou couldst hear the
sacring bell;
But now in truth they come : flight and
pursuit
Are sights I 've been long strange to.

NIN. See how they gallop down the
opposing hill!
Yon grey steed bounding down the
headlong path,
As on the level meadow; while the
black,
Urged by the rider with his naked
sword,
Stoops on his prey, as I have seen the
falcon
Dashing upon the heron.—Thou dost
frown
And clench thy hand, as if it grasp'd a
weapon?

WAL. 'T is but for shame to see a
man fly thus
While only one pursues him. Coward,
turn!—
Turn thee, I say! thou art as stout as
he,
And well mayst match thy single sword
with his—
Shame, that a man should rein a steed
like thee,
Yet fear to turn his front against a
foe!—
I am ashamed to look on them.

NIN. Yet look again; they quit their
horses now,
Unfit for the rough path : the fugitive
Keeps the advantage still.—They strain
towards us.

WAL. I 'll not believe that ever the
bold Thane
Rear'd up his Cross to be a sanctuary
To the base coward, who shunn'd an
equal combat.—

How 's this?—that look—that mien—
mine eyes grow dizzy!—

NIN. He comes!—thou art a novice
on this watch,—
Brother, I 'll take the word and speak
to him.
Pluck down thy cowl; know, that we
spiritual champions
Have honour to maintain, and must
not seem
To quail before the laity.

[WALDHAVE *lets down his cowl,
and steps back.*

Enter MAURICE BERKELEY.

NIN. Who art thou, stranger? speak
thy name and purpose.

BER. I claim the privilege of Clan
MacDuff.
My name is Maurice Berkeley, and my
lineage
Allies me nearly with the Thane of
Fife.

NIN. Give us to know the cause of
sanctuary?

BER. Let him show it,
Against whose violence I claim the
privilege.

Enter LINDESAY, *with his sword
drawn. He rushes at* BERKELEY;
NINIAN *interposes.*

NIN. Peace, in the name of Saint
Magridius!
Peace, in our Prior's name, and in the
name
Of that dear symbol, which did pur-
chase peace
And good-will towards man! I do
command thee
To sheathe thy sword, and stir no con-
test here.

LIN. One charm I 'll try first,
To lure the craven from the enchanted
circle
Which he hath harbour'd in.—Hear
you, De Berkeley,
This is my brother's sword—the hand
it arms

Is weapon'd to avenge a brother's
death :—
If thou hast heart to step a furlong off,
And change three blows,—even for so
short a space
As these good men may say an ave-
marie,—
So, Heaven be good to me! I will for-
give thee
Thy deed and all its consequences.

BER. Were not my right hand fetter'd
by the thought
That slaying thee were but a double
guilt
In which to steep my soul, no bridegroom ever
Stepp'd forth to trip a measure with
his bride
More joyfully than I, young man, would
rush
To meet thy challenge.

LIN. He quails, and shuns to look
upon my weapon,
Yet boasts himself a Berkeley!

BER. Lindesay, and if there were no
deeper cause
For shunning thee than terror of thy
weapon,
That rock-hewn Cross as soon should
start and stir,
Because a shepherd-boy blew horn beneath it,
As I for brag of thine.

NIN. I charge you both, and in the
name of Heaven,
Breathe no defiance on this sacred
spot,
Where Christian men must bear them
peacefully,
On pain of the Church thunders.
Calmly tell
Your cause of difference; and, Lord
Lindesay, thou
Be first to speak them.

LIN. Ask the blue welkin, ask the
silver Tay,
The northern Grampians—all things
know my wrongs;
But ask not me to tell them, while the
villain

Who wrought them stands and listens
with a smile.

NIN. It is said—
Since you refer us thus to general
fame—
That Berkeley slew thy brother, the
Lord Louis,
In his own halls at Edzell——

LIN. Ay, in his hall.
In his own halls, good father, that's
the word;
In his own halls he slew him, while the
wine
Pass'd on the board between. The
gallant Thane,
Who wreak'd Macbeth's inhospitable
murder,
Rear'd not yon Cross to sanction deeds
like these.

BER. Thou say'st I came a guest! I
came a victim,
A destined victim, train'd on to the
doom
His frantic jealousy prepared for me.
He fix'd a quarrel on me, and we fought.
Can I forget the form that came be-
tween us,
And perish'd by his sword? 'T was
then I fought
For vengeance; until then I guarded
life,
But then I sought to take it, and pre-
vail'd.

LIN. Wretch! thou didst first dishonour to thy victim,
And then didst slay him!

BER. There is a busy fiend tugs at
my heart,
But I will struggle with it. Youthful
knight,
My heart is sick of war, my hand of
slaughter;
I come not to my lordships, or my land,
But just to seek a spot in some cold
cloister,
Which I may kneel on living, and,
when dead,
Which may suffice to cover me.
Forgive me that I caused your brother's
death,

And I forgive thee the injurious terms
With which thou taxest me.

LIN. Take worse and blacker. Murderer, adulterer !
Art thou not moved yet?

BER.   Do not press me further.
The hunted stag, even when he seeks
the thicket,
Compell'd to stand at bay, grows dangerous.
Most true thy brother perish'd by my
hand,
And if you term it murder I must bear
it.
Thus far my patience can ; but if thou
brand
The purity of yonder martyr'd saint
Whom then my sword but poorly did
avenge,
With one injurious word, come to the
valley,
And I will show thee how it shall be
answer'd.

NIN. This heat, Lord Berkeley, doth
but ill accord
With thy late pious patience.

BER. Father, forgive, and let me
stand excused
To Heaven and thee, if patience brooks
no more.
I loved this lady fondly, truly loved ;
Loved her, and was beloved, ere yet
her father
Conferr'd her on another. While she
lived
Each thought of her was to my soul as
hallow'd
As those I send to heaven ; and on
her grave,
Her bloody early grave, while this poor
hand
Can hold a sword, shall no one cast a
scorn.

LIN. Follow me. Thou shalt hear
me call the adulteress
By her right name ; I 'm glad there 's
yet a spur
Can rouse thy sluggard mettle.

BER. Make then obeisance to the
blessed Cross,

For it shall be on earth thy last devotion.   [*They are going off.*
WAL. (*rushing forward*). Madmen,
stand !
Stay but one second, answer but one
question :
There, Maurice Berkeley, canst thou
look upon
That blessed sign, and swear thou 'st
spoken truth ?

BER. I swear by Heaven,
And by the memory of that murder'd
innocent,
Each seeming charge against her was
as false
As our bless'd Lady 's spotless. Hear,
each saint !
Hear me, thou holy rood ! Hear me
from heaven,
Thou martyr'd excellence ! Hear me
from penal fire
(For sure not yet thy guilt is expiated),
Stern ghost of her destroyer !——
WAL. (*throws back his cowl*). He
hears ! he hears ! Thy spell hath
raised the dead.

LIN. My brother ! and alive !
WAL. Alive—but yet, my Richard,
dead to thee,
No tie of kindred binds me to the
world ;
All were renounced when, with reviving
life,
Came the desire to seek the sacred
cloister.
Alas, in vain ! for to that last retreat,
Like to a pack of bloodhounds in full
chase,
My passion and my wrongs have follow'd me,
Wrath and remorse ; and, to fill up the
cry,
Thou hast brought vengeance hither.

LIN.   I but sought
To do the act and duty of a brother.
WAL. I ceased to be so when I left
the world ;
But if he can forgive as I forgive,
God sends me here a brother in mine
enemy.

To pray for me and with me. If thou
canst,
De Berkeley, give thine hand.
  BER. (*gives his hand*). It is the will
Of Heaven, made manifest in thy pre-
servation,
To inhibit further bloodshed ; for De
Berkeley,
The votary Maurice lays the title down.
Go to his halls, Lord Richard, where a
maiden,
Kin to his blood, and daughter in affec-
tion,
Heirs his broad lands. If thou canst
love her, Lindesay,
Woo her, and be successful.

THE DOOM OF DEVORGOIL.

~~~~~~~~~~~~~~~~~~

PREFACE.

THE first of these dramatic pieces* was long since written, for the purpose of obliging the late Mr. Terry, then Manager of the Adelphi Theatre, for whom the Author had a particular regard. The manner in which the mimic goblins of Devorgoil are intermixed with the supernatural machinery was found to be objectionable, and the production had other faults, which rendered it unfit for representation.† I have called the piece a Melodrama, for want of a better name; but, as I learn from the unquestionable authority of Mr. Colman's "Random Records" that one species of the drama is termed an *extravaganza*, I am sorry I was not sooner aware of a more appropriate name than that which I had selected for Devorgoil.

The Author's Publishers thought it advisable that the scenes, long condemned to oblivion, should be united to similar attempts of the same kind; and as he felt indifferent on the subject, they are printed in the same volume with Halidon Hill and MacDuff's Cross, and thrown off in a separate form, for the convenience of those who possess former editions of the Author's Poetical Works

The general story of the Doom of Devorgoil is founded on an old Scottish tradition, the scene of which lies in Galloway. The crime supposed to have occasioned the misfortunes of this devoted house is similar to that of a Lord Herries of Hoddam Castle, who is the principal personage of Mr. Charles Kirkpatrick Sharpe's interesting ballad, in the Minstrelsy of the Scottish Border, vol iv. p. 307. In remorse for his crime, he built the singular monument called the Tower of Repentance. In many cases the Scottish superstitions allude to the fairies, or those who, for sins of a milder description, are permitted to wander with the "rout that never rest," as they were termed by Dr. Leyden. They imitate human labour and human amusements, but their toil is useless and without any advantageous result, and their gaiety is unsubstantial and hollow. The phantom of Lord Erick is supposed to be a spectre of this character.

The story of the Ghostly Barber is told in many countries; but the best narrative founded on the passage is the tale called Stumme Liebe, among the legends of Musæus. I think it has been introduced upon the English stage in some pantomime, which was one objection to bringing it upon the scene a second time.

ABBOTSFORD, *April,* 1830.

---

* "The Doom of Devorgoil" and "Auchindrane" were published together in an octavo volume, in the spring of 1830.

† Mr. Daniel Terry, the comedian, distinguished for a very peculiar style of humour on the stage, and, moreover, by personal accomplishments of various sorts not generally shared by members of his profession, was, during many years, on terms of intimacy with Sir Walter Scott. Terry died 22nd June, 1829.

DRAMATIS PERSONÆ.

OSWALD OF DEVORGOIL, *a decayed Scottish Baron.*

LEONARD, *a Ranger.*

DURWARD, *a Palmer.*

LANCELOT BLACKTHORN, *a Companion of* LEONARD, *in love with* KATLEEN.

GULLCRAMMER, *a conceited Student.*

OWLSPIEGLE *and,* COCKLEDEMOY, *Maskers, represented by* BLACKTHORN *and* KATLEEN.

SPIRIT OF LORD ERICK OF DEVORGOIL.

Peasants, Shepherds, and Vassals of inferior rank.

ELEANOR, *Wife of Oswald, descended of obscure parentage.*

FLORA, *Daughter of* OSWALD.

KATLEEN, *Niece of* ELEANOR.

ACT I.—SCENE I.

The Scene represents a wild and hilly but not a mountainous Country, in a frontier district of Scotland. The flat Scene exhibits the Castle of Devorgoil, decayed and partly ruinous, situated upon a Lake, and connected with the land by a drawbridge, which is lowered. Time—Sunset.

FLORA *enters from the Castle, looks timidly around, then comes forward and speaks.*

He is not here—those pleasures are not ours
Which placid evening brings to all things else.

SONG.*

The sun upon the lake is low,
The wild birds hush their song,

-----

* The author thought of omitting this song, which was, in fact, abridged into one in "Quentin Durward," termed County Guy. It seemed, however, necessary to the sense, that the original stanzas should be retained here.

The hills have evening's deepest glow,
Yet Leonard tarries long.
Now all whom varied toil and care
From home and love divide,
In the calm sunset may repair
Each to the loved one's side.

The noble dame, on turret high,
Who waits her gallant knight,
Looks to the western beam to spy
The flash of armour bright.
The village maid, with hand on brow,
The level ray to shade,
Upon the footpath watches now
For Colin's darkening plaid.

Now to their mates the wild swans row,
By day they swam apart,
And to the thicket wanders slow
The hind beside the hart.
The woodlark at his partner's side
Twitters his closing song—
All meet whom day and care divide,
But Leonard tarries long.

[KATLEEN *has come out of the Castle while* FLORA *was singing, and speaks when the Song is ended.*

KAT. Ah, my dear coz !—if that your mother's niece
May so presume to call your father's daughter—
All these fond things have got some home of comfort
To tempt their rovers back—the lady's bower,
The shepherdess's hut, the wild swan's couch
Among the rushes, even the lark's low nest,
Has that of promise which lures home a lover,—
But we have nought of this.

FLO. How call you, then, this castle of my sire,
The towers of Devorgoil?

KAT. Dungeons for men, and palaces for owls ;
Yet no wise owl would change a farmer's barn
For yonder hungry hall -- our latest mouse,

Our last of mice, I tell you, has been
  found
Starved in the pantry; and the reverend
  spider,
Sole living tenant of the baron's halls,
Who, train'd to abstinence, lived a whole
  summer
Upon a single fly, he's famish'd too;
The cat is in the kitchen-chimney seated
Upon our last of fagots, destined soon
To dress our last of suppers, and, poor
  soul,
Is starved with cold, and mewling mad
  with hunger.

  FLO. D'ye mock our misery, Katleen?
  KAT. No, but I'm hysteric on the
  subject,
So I must laugh or cry, and laughing's
  lightest.
  FLO. Why stay you with us, then,
  my merry cousin?
From you my sire can ask no filial duty.
  KAT. No, thanks to Heaven!
No noble in wide Scotland, rich or
  poor,
Can claim an interest in the vulgar
  blood
That dances in my veins; and I might
  wed
A forester to-morrow, nothing fearing
The wrath of high-born kindred, and
  far less
That the dry bones of lead-lapp'd an-
  cestors
Would clatter in their cerements at the
  tidings.
  FLO. My mother, too, would gladly
  see you placed
Beyond the verge of our unhappiness,
Which, like a witch's circle, blights and
  taints
Whatever comes within it.
  KAT.   Ah! my good aunt!
She is a careful kinswoman and pru-
  dent,
In all but marrying a ruin'd baron,
When she could take her choice of
  honest yeomen;
And now, to balance this ambitious
  error,

She presses on her daughter's love the
  suit
Of one, who hath no touch of noble-
  ness,
In manners, birth, or mind, to recom-
  mend him,—
Sage Master Gullcrammer, the new-
  dubb'd preacher.
  FLO. Do not name him, Katleen!
  KAT. Ay, but I must, and with some
  gratitude.
I said but now, I saw our last of fagots
Destined to dress our last of meals, but
  said not
That the repast consisted of choice
  dainties,
Sent to our larder by that liberal suitor,
The kind Melchisedek.
  FLO.   Were famishing the word,
I'd famish ere I tasted them—the fop,
The fool, the low-born, low-bred, pedant
  coxcomb!
  KAT. There spoke the blood of long-
  descended sires!
My cottage wisdom ought to echo
  back,—
O the snug parsonage! the well-paid
  stipend!
The yew-hedged garden! beehives, pigs,
  and poultry!
But, to speak honestly, the peasant
  Katleen,
Valuing these good things justly, still
  would scorn
To wed, for such, the paltry Gull-
  crammer,
As much as Lady Flora.
  FLO. Mock me not with a title, gentle
  cousin,
Which poverty has made ridiculous.—
                [Trumpets far off.
Hark! they have broken up the weapon-
  shawing;
The vassals are dismiss'd, and marching
  homeward.
  KAT. Comes your sire back to-night?
  FLO.   He did purpose
To tarry for the banquet. This day
  only,
Summon'd as a king's tenant, he resumes

The right of rank his birth assigns to
him,
And mingles with the proudest.

KAT.   To return
To his domestic wretchedness to-mor-
row—
I envy not the privilege. Let us go
To yonder height, and see the marks-
men practise ;
They shoot their match down in the
dale beyond,
Betwixt the Lowland and the Forest
district,
By ancient custom, for a tun of wine.
Let us go see which wins.

FLO.   That were too forward.
KAT. Why, you may drop the screen
before your face,
Which some chance breeze may haply
blow aside
Just when a youth of special note takes
aim.
It chanced even so that memorable
morning,
When, nutting in the woods, we met
young Leonard ;—
And in good time here comes his sturdy
comrade,
The rough Lance Blackthorn.

Enter LANCELOT BLACKTHORN, *a
Forester, with the carcass of a deer
on his back, and a gun in his hand.*

BLA.   Save you, damsels !
KAT. Godden, good yeoman.—Come
you from the Weaponshaw?
BLA. Not I, indeed ; there lies the
mark I shot at.
                          [*Lays down the deer.*
The time has been I had not miss'd the
sport,
Although Lord Nithsdale's self had
wanted venison ;
But this same mate of mine, young
Leonard Dacre,
Makes me do what he lists ;—he'll win
the prize, though :
The Forest district will not lose its
honour,

And that is all I care for—(*some shouts
are heard.*) Hark ! they're at it.
I'll go see the issue.

FLO.   Leave not here
The produce of your hunting.
BLA.   But I must, though.
This is his lair to-night, for Leonard
Dacre   [goil ;
Charged me to leave the stag at Devor-
Then show me quickly where to stow
the quarry,
And let me to the sports—(*more shots.*)
Come, hasten, damsels !

FLO. It is impossible —we dare not
take it.
BLA. There let it lie, then, and I'll
wind my bugle,
That all within these tottering walls
may know
That here lies venison, whoso likes to
lift it.   [*About to blow.*
KAT. (*to* FLO.) He will alarm your
mother ; and, besides,
Our Forest proverb teaches, that no
question
Should ask where venison comes from.
Your careful mother, with her wonted
prudence,
Will hold its presence plead its own
apology.—
Come, Blackthorn, I will show you
where to stow it.
    [*Exeunt* KATLEEN *and* BLACK-
    THORN *into the Castle—more
    shooting— then a distant shout
    —Stragglers, armed in dif-
    ferent ways, pass over the
    stage, as if from the Wea-
    ponshaw.*
FLO. The prize is won ; that general
shout proclaim'd it.
The marksmen and the vassals are dispersing.   [*She draws back.*
FIRST VASSAL (*a Peasant*). Ay, ay,
—'t is lost and won,—the Forest
have it.
'T is they have all the luck on 't.
SECOND VAS. (*a Shepherd*). Luck,
sayst thou, man ? 'T is practice,
skill, and cunning.

THIRD VAS. 'T is no such thing.—I had hit the mark precisely,

But for this cursed flint; and, as I fired,

A swallow cross'd mine eye too. Will you tell me

That that was but a chance, mine honest shepherd?

FIRST VAS. Ay, and last year, when Lancelot Blackthorn won it,

Because my powder happen'd to be damp,

Was there no luck in that?—The worse luck mine.

SECOND VAS. Still I say 't was not chance; it might be witchcraft.

FIRST VAS. Faith, not unlikely, neighbours; for these foresters

Do often haunt about this ruin'd castle.

I 've seen myself this spark,—young Leonard Dacre,—

Come stealing like a ghost ere break of day,

And after sunset too, along this path;

And well you know the haunted towers of Devorgoil

Have no good reputation in the land.

SHEP. That have they not. I 've heard my father say,—

Ghosts dance as lightly in its moonlight halls

As ever maiden did at Midsummer

Upon the village green.

FIRST VAS. Those that frequent such spirit-haunted ruins

Must needs know more than simple Christians do.—

See, Lance this blessed moment leaves the castle,

And comes to triumph o'er us.

[BLACKTHORN *enters from the Castle, and comes forward while they speak.*

THIRD VAS. A mighty triumph! What is 't, after all,

Except the driving of a piece of lead,—

As learned Master Gullcrammer defined it,—

Just through the middle of a painted board?

BLA. And if he so define it, by your leave,

Your learned Master Gullcrammer's an ass.

THIRD VAS. (*angrily*). He is a preacher, huntsman, under favour.

SECOND VAS. No quarrelling, neighbours—you may both be right.

Enter a FOURTH VASSAL, *with a gallon stoup of wine.*

FOURTH VAS. Why stand you brawling here? Young Leonard Dacre

Has set abroach the tun of wine he gain'd,

That all may drink who list. Blackthorn, I sought you;

Your comrade prays you will bestow this flagon

Where you have left the deer you kill'd this morning.

BLA. And that I will; but first we 'll take toll

To see if it 's worth carriage. Shepherd, thy horn.

There must be due allowance made for leakage,

And that will come about a draught apiece.

Skink it about, and, when our throats are liquor'd,

We 'll merrily trowl our song of weaponshaw.

[*They drink about out of the* SHEPHERD'S *horn, and then sing.*

SONG.

We love the shrill trumpet, we love the drum's rattle,

They call us to sport, and they call us to battle;

And old Scotland shall laugh at the threats of a stranger,

While our comrades in pastime are comrades in danger.

If there 's mirth in our house, 't is our neighbour that shares it—

If peril approach, 't is our neighbour that dares it;

And when we lead off to the pipe and the tabor,

The fair hand we press is the hand of a neighbour.

Then close your ranks, comrades, the bands
  that combine them,
Faith, friendship, and brotherhood, join'd to
  entwine them ;
And we 'll laugh at the threats of each insolent
  stranger,
While our comrades in sport are our comrades
  in danger.

BLACK. Well, I must do mine errand.
  Master flagon (*shaking it*)
Is too consumptive for another bleed-
  ing.
SHEP. I must to my fold.
THIRD VAS. I 'll to the butt of wine,
And see if that has given up the ghost
  yet.
FIRST VAS. Have with you, neigh-
  bour.

> [BLACKTHORN *enters the Castle,
> the rest exeunt severally.*
> MELCHISEDEK GULLCRAM-
> MER *watches them off the
> stage, and then enters from the
> side-scene. His costume is a
> Geneva cloak and band, with
> a high-crowned hat; the rest
> of his dress in the fashion of
> James the First's time. He
> looks to the windows of the
> Castle, then draws back as if
> to escape observation, while he
> brushes his cloak, drives the
> white threads from his waist-
> coat with his wetted thumb,
> and dusts his shoes, all with
> the air of one who would not
> willingly be observed engaged
> in these offices. He then ad-
> justs his collar and band,
> comes forward and speaks.*

GULL. Right comely is thy garb,
  Melchisedek ;
As well beseemeth one, whom good
  Saint Mungo,
The patron of our land and univer-
  sity,
Hath graced with license both to teach
  and preach.
Who dare opine thou hither plod'st on
  foot ?

Trim sits thy cloak, unruffled is thy
  band,
And not a speck upon thine outward
  man
Bewrays the labour of thy weary sole.

> [*Touches his shoe, and smiles
> complacently.*

Quaint was that jest and pleasant !—
  Now will I
Approach and hail the dwellers of this
  fort ;
But specially sweet Flora Devorgoil,
Ere her proud sire return. He loves
  me not,
Mocketh my lineage, flouts at mine
  advancement—
Sour as the fruit the crab-tree furnishes,
And hard as is the cudgel it sup-
  plies ;
But Flora—she 's a lily on the lake,
And I must reach her, though I risk a
  ducking.

> [*As* GULLCRAMMER *moves to-
> wards the drawbridge,* BAUL-
> DIE DURWARD *enters, and
> interposes himself betwixt him
> and the Castle.* GULLCRAM-
> MER *stops and speaks.*

Whom have we here ?—that ancient
  fortune-teller,
Papist and sorcerer, and sturdy beggar,
Old Bauldie Durward ! Would I were
  well past him !

> [DURWARD *advances, partly in
> the dress of a Palmer, partly
> in that of an old Scottish
> mendicant, having coarse blue
> cloak and badge, white beard,
> &c.*

DUR. The blessing of the evening
  on your worship,
And on your taff'ty doublet. Much I
  marvel
Your wisdom chooseth such trim garb,
  when tempests
Are gathering to the bursting.
GULLCRAMMER (*looks to his dress,
  and then to the sky, with some apprehension*). Surely, Bauldie,

Thou dost belie the evening—in the
 west
The light sinks down as lovely as this
 band
Drops o'er this mantle. Tush, man!
 't will be fair.
 DUR. Ay, but the storm I bode is
  big with blows,
Horsewhips for hailstones, clubs for
 thunderbolts;
And for the wailing of the midnight
 wind,
The unpitied howling of a cudgell'd
 coxcomb.
Come, come, I know thou seek'st fair
 Flora Devorgoil.
 GUL. And if I did, I do the damsel
  grace.
Her mother thinks so, and she has
 accepted
At these poor hands gifts of some con-
 sequence,
And curious dainties for the evening
 cheer,
To which I am invited. She respects
 me.
 DUR. But not so doth her father,
  haughty Oswald.
Bethink thee, he's a baron——
 GUL.   And a bare one;
Construe me that, old man!—The
 crofts of Mucklewhame—
Destined for mine so soon as heaven
 and earth
Have shared my uncle's soul and bones
 between them—
The crofts of Mucklewhame, old man,
 which nourish
Three scores of sheep, three cows, with
 each follower,
A female palfrey eke—I will be candid,
She is of that meek tribe whom, in
 derision,
Our wealthy southern neighbours nick-
 name donkeys——
 DUR. She hath her follower too,—
  when thou art there.
 GUL. I say to thee, these crofts of
  Mucklewhame,   [produce,
In the mere tything of their stock and

Outvie whatever patch of land re-
 mains
To this old rugged castle and its owner.
Well, therefore, may Melchisedek Gull-
 crammer,
Younger of Mucklewhame, for such I
 write me,
Master of Arts, by grace of good Saint
 Andrew,
Preacher, in brief expectance of a kirk,
Endow'd with ten score Scottish pounds
 per annum,
Being eight pounds seventeen eight in
 sterling coin—
Well then, I say, may this Melchisedek,
Thus highly graced by fortune—and
 by nature
E'en gifted as thou seest—aspire to
 woo
The daughter of the beggar'd Devor-
 goil.
 DUR. Credit an old man's word,
  kind Master Gullcrammer,
You will not find it so.—Come, sir, I 've
 known
The hospitality of Mucklewhame;
It reach'd not to profuseness—yet, in
 gratitude
For the pure water of its living well,
And for the barley loaves of its fair
 fields,
Wherein chopp'd straw contended with
 the grain
Which best should satisfy the appetite,
I would not see the hopeful heir of
 Mucklewhame
Thus fling himself on danger.
 GUL. Danger! what danger?—
  Know'st thou not, old Oswald
This day attends the muster of the
 shire,
Where the crown-vassals meet to show
 their arms,
And their best horse of service?—
  'T was good sport
(An if a man had dared but laugh at it)
To see old Oswald with his rusty
 morion,
And huge two-handed sword, that
 might have seen

The field of Bannockburn or Chevy-
 Chase,
Without a squire or vassal, page or
 groom,
Or e'en a single pikeman at his heels,
Mix with the proudest nobles of the
 county,
And claim precedence for his tatter'd
 person
O'er armours double gilt and ostrich
 plumage.
 DUR. Ay! 'twas the jest at which
 fools laugh the loudest,
The downfall of our old nobility—
Which may forerun the ruin of a king-
 dom.
I've seen an idiot clap his hands, and
 shout
To see a tower like yon (*points to a
 part of the Castle*) stoop to its
 base
In headlong ruin; while the wise look'd
 round,
And fearful sought a distant stance to
 watch
What fragment of the fabric next should
 follow;
For when the turrets fall, the walls are
 tottering.
 GUL. (*after pondering*). If that
 means aught, it means thou saw'st
 old Oswald
Expell'd from the assembly.
 DUR.   Thy sharp wit
Hath glanced unwittingly right nigh
 the truth.
Expell'd he was not, but, his claim
 denied
At some contested point of cere-
 mony,
He left the weaponshaw in high dis-
 pleasure,
And hither comes—his wonted bitter
 temper
Scarce sweeten'd by the chances of
 the day.
'T were much like rashness should you
 wait his coming,
And thither tends my counsel.
 GUL.   And I'll take it;

Good Bauldie Durward, I will take thy
 counsel,
And will requite it with this minted
 farthing,
That bears our sovereign's head in
 purest copper.
 DUR. Thanks to thy bounty. Haste
 thee, good young master;
Oswald, besides the old two-handed
 sword,
Bears in his hand a staff of potency,
To charm intruders from his castle
 purlieus.
 GUL. I do abhor all charms, nor will
 abide
To hear or see, far less to feel their use.
Behold I have departed. [*Exit hastily.*

Manent DURWARD.

 DUR. Thus do I play the idle part
 of one
Who seeks to save the moth from
 scorching him
In the bright taper's flame. And Flora's
 beauty
Must, not unlike that taper, waste
 away,
Gilding the rugged walls that saw it
 kindled.
This was a shard-born beetle, heavy,
 drossy,
Though boasting his dull drone and
 gilded wing.
Here comes a flutterer of another
 stamp,
Whom the same ray is charming to his
 ruin.

Enter LEONARD, *dressed as a Huntsman; he pauses before the Tower,
and whistles a note or two at intervals—drawing back, as if fearful of
observation—yet waiting, as if expecting some reply.* DURWARD,
*whom he had not observed, moves
round, so as to front* LEONARD *unexpectedly.*

 LEON. I am too late—it was no easy
 task

To rid myself from yonder noisy revellers.

Flora!—I fear she's angry—Flora—
Flora!

SONG.

Admire not that I gain'd the prize
 From all the village crew;
How could I fail with hand or eyes,
 When heart and faith were true?

And when in floods of rosy wine
 My comrades drown'd their cares,
I thought but that thy heart was mine,
 My own leapt light as theirs.

My brief delay then do not blame,
 Nor deem your swain untrue;
My form but linger'd at the game,
 My soul was still with you.

She hears not!

DUR. But a friend hath heard—
Leonard, I pity thee.

LEON. (*starts, but recovers himself*).
Pity, good father, is for those in
want,
In age, in sorrow, in distress of mind,
Or agony of body. I'm in health—
Can match my limbs against the stag
in chase,
Have means enough to meet my simple
wants,
And am so free of soul that I can
carol
To woodland and to wild in notes as
lively
As are my jolly bugle s.

DUR. Even therefore dost thou need
my pity, Leonard,   [thee,
And therefore I bestow it, proff'ring
Before thou feel'st the need, my mite
of pity.
Leonard, thou lovest; and in that little
word
There lies enough to claim the sympathy
Of men who wear such hoary locks as
mine,
And know what misplaced love is sure
to end in.

LEON. Good father, thou art old, and
even thy youth,

As thou hast told me, spent in cloister'd
cells,
Fits thee but ill to judge the passions
Which are the joy and charm of social
life.
Press me no further, then, nor waste
those moments
Whose worth thou canst not estimate.
    [*As turning from him.*

DUR. (*detains him*). Stay, young
man!
'T is seldom that a beggar claims a
debt;
Yet I bethink me of a gay young stripling,
That owes to these white locks and
hoary beard
Something of reverence and of gratitude
More than he wills to pay.

LEON. Forgive me, father. Often
hast thou told me
That in the ruin of my father's house
You saved the orphan Leonard in his
cradle;
And well I know, that to thy care
alone—
Care seconded by means beyond thy
seeming—
I owe whate'er of nurture I can boast.

DUR. Then for thy life preserved,
And for the means of knowledge I have
furnish'd,
(Which lacking, man is levell'd with
the brutes),
Grant me this boon: — Avoid these
fatal walls!
A curse is on them, bitter, deep, and
heavy,
Of power to split the massiest tower
they boast
From pinnacle to dungeon vault. It
rose
Upon the gay horizon of proud Devor-
goil,
As unregarded as the fleecy cloud,
The first forerunner of the hurri-
cane,
Scarce seen amid the welkin's shade-
less blue.

Dark grew it, and more dark, and still
  the fortunes
Of this doomed family have darken'd
  with it.
It hid their sovereign's favour, and
  obscured
The lustre of their service, gender'd
  hate
Betwixt them and the mighty of the
  land ;
Till by degrees the waxing tempest
  rose,
And stripp'd the goodly tree of fruit
  and flowers,
And buds, and boughs, and branches.
  There remains
A rugged trunk, dismember'd and un-
  sightly,
Waiting the bursting of the final bolt
To splinter it to shivers. Now, go
  pluck
Its single tendril to enwreath thy
  brow,
And rest beneath its shade—to share
  the ruin !
  LEON. This anathema,
Whence should it come?—how me-
  rited ?—and when ?
  DUR. 'T was in the days
Of Oswald's grandsire, — 'mid Galwe-
  gian chiefs
The fellest foe, the fiercest champion.
His blood-red pennons scared the
  Cumbrian coasts,
And wasted towns and manors mark'd
  his progress.
His galleys stored with treasure, and
  their decks
Crowded with English captives, who
  beheld,
With weeping eyes, their native shores
  retire,
He bore him homeward ; but a tem-
  pest rose——
  LEON. So far I 've heard the tale,
And spare thee the recital.—The grim
  chief,
Marking his vessels labour on the sea,
And loth to lose his treasure, gave
  command

To plunge his captives in the raging
  deep.
  DUR. There sunk the lineage of a
  noble name,
And the wild waves boom'd over sire
  and son,
Mother and nurseling, of the house of
  Aglionby,
Leaving but one frail tendril.—Hence
  the fate
That hovers o'er th se turrets,—hence
  the peasant,
Belated, hieing homewards, dreads to
  cast
A glance upon that portal, lest he
  see
The unshrouded spectres of the mur-
  der'd dead ;
Or the avenging Angel, with his
  sword,
Waving destruction ; or the grisly
  phantom
Of that fell Chief, the doer of the
  deed,
Which still, they say, roams through
  his empty halls,
And mourns their wasteness and their
  lonelihood.
  LEON. Such is the dotage
Of superstition, father, ay, and the
  cant
Of hoodwink'd prejudice. — Not for
  atonement
Of some foul deed done in the ancient
  warfare,
When war was butchery, and men were
  wolves,
Doth Heaven consign the innocent to
  suffering.
I tell thee, Flora's virtues might
  atone
For all the massacres her sires have
  done,
Since first the Pictish race their stained
  limbs
Array'd in wolf's skin.
  DUR. Leonard, ere yet this beggar's
  scrip and cloak
Supplied the place of mitre and of
  crosier,

Which in these alter'd lands must not
be worn,
I was superior of a brotherhood
Of holy men,—the Prior of Lanercost.
Nobles then sought my footstool many
a league,
There to unload their sins—questions
of conscience
Of deepest import were not deem'd too
nice
For my decision, youth.—But not even
then,
With mitre on my brow, and all the
voice
Which Rome gives to a father of her
Church,
Dared I pronounce so boldly on the
ways
Of hidden Providence, as thou, young
man,
Whose chiefest knowledge is to track
a stag,
Or wind a bugle, hast presumed to do.
    LEON. Nay, I pray forgive me,
Father; thou know'st I meant not to
presume——
    DUR. Can I refuse thee pardon?—
Thou art all
That war and change have left to the
poor Durward.
Thy father, too, who lost his life and
fortune
Defending Lanercost, when its fair
aisles
Were spoil'd by sacrilege — I bless'd
his banner,
And yet it prosper'd not. But—all I
could—
Thee from the wreck I saved, and for
thy sake
Have still dragg'd on my life of pil-
grimage
And penitence upon the hated shores
I else had left for ever. Come with
me,
And I will teach thee there is healing
in
The wounds which friendship gives.
                    [*Exeunt.*

SCENE II.

*The Scene changes to the interior of the
Castle. An Apartment is discovered, in
which there is much appearance of present
poverty, mixed with some relics of former
grandeur. On the wall hangs, amongst
other things, a suit of ancient armour,
by the table is a covered basket, behind,
and concealed by it, the carcass of a roe
deer. There is a small latticed window,
which, appearing to perforate a wall of
great thickness, is supposed to look out
towards the drawbridge. It is in the shape
of a loophole for musketry; and, as is not
unusual in old buildings, is placed so high
up in the wall, that it is only approached
by five or six narrow stone steps.*
    ELEANOR, *the wife of* OSWALD *of* DE-
VORGOIL, FLORA *and* KATLEEN, *her
Daughter and Niece, are discovered at
work. The former spins, the latter are
embroidering.* ELEANOR *quits her own
labour to examine the manner in which*
FLORA *is executing her task, and shakes
her head as if dissatisfied.*

    ELE. Fie on it, Flora! this botch'd
work of thine
Shows that thy mind is distant from
thy task.
The finest tracery of our old cathedral
Had not a richer, freer, bolder pattern,
Than Flora once could trace. Thy
thoughts are wandering.
    FLO. They're with my father. Broad
upon the lake
The evening sun sunk down; huge
piles of clouds,
Crimson and sable, rose upon his disk,
And quench'd him ere his setting, like
some champion
In his last conflict, losing all his glory.
Sure signals those of storm. And if
my father
Be on his homeward road——
    ELE. But that he will not.
Baron of Devorgoil, this day at least
He banquets with the nobles, who the
next
Would scarce vouchsafe an alms to
save his household.

From want or famine. Thanks to a friend,
For one brief space we shall not need their aid.
FLO. (*joyfully*). What! knew you then his gift?
How silly I that would, yet durst not tell it!
I fear my father will condemn us both,
That easily accepted such a present.
KAT. Now, here's the game a bystander sees better
Than those who play it.—My good aunt is pondering
On the good cheer which Gullcrammer has sent us,
And Flora thinks upon the forest venison. [*Aside.*
ELE. (*to* FLO.) Thy father need not know on't—'t is a boon
Comes timely, when frugality, nay, abstinence,
Might scarce avail us longer. I had hoped
Ere now a visit from the youthful donor,
That we might thank his bounty; and perhaps
My Flora thought the same, when Sunday's kerchief
And the best kirtle were sought out, and donn'd
To grace a work-day evening.
FLO. Nay, mother, that is judging all too close!
My work-day gown was torn— my kerchief sullied;
And thus — But, think you, will the gallant come?
ELE. He will, for with these dainties came a message
From gentle Master Gullcrammer, to intimate——
FLO. (*greatly disappointed*). Gullcrammer?
KAT. There burst the bubble—down fell house of cards,
And cousin's like to cry for't! [*Aside.*
ELE. Gullcrammer? ay, Gullcrammer —thou scorn'st not at him?

'T were something short of wisdom in a maiden,
Who, like the poor bat in the Grecian fable,
Hovers betwixt two classes in the world,
And is disclaim'd by both the mouse and bird.
KAT. I am the poor mouse.
And may go creep into what hole I list, [word
And no one heed me. Yet I'll waste a
Of counsel on my betters.—Kind my aunt,
And you, my gentle cousin, were't not better
We thought of dressing this same gear for supper,
Than quarrelling about the worthless donor?
ELE. Peace, minx!
FLO. Thou hast no feeling, cousin Katleen.
KAT. Soh! I have brought them both on my poor shoulders,
So meddling peace-makers are still rewarded:
E'en let them to't again, and fight it out.
FLO. Mother, were I disclaim'd of every class,
I would not therefore so disclaim myself,
As even a passing thought of scorn to waste
On cloddish Gullcrammer.
ELE. List to me, love, and let adversity
Incline thine ear to wisdom. Look around thee—
Of the gay youths who boast a noble name,
Which will incline to wed a dowerless damsel?
And of the yeomanry, who, think'st thou, Flora,
Would ask to share the labours of his farm
An high-born beggar? — This young man is modest——

FLO. Silly, good mother; sheepish, if you will it.

ELE. E'en call it what you list—the softer temper,
The fitter to endure the bitter sallies
Of one whose wit is all too sharp for mine.

FLO. Mother, you cannot mean it as you say;
You cannot bid me prize conceited folly?

ELE. Content thee, child—each lot has its own blessings.
This youth, with his plain-dealing honest suit,
Proffers thee quiet, peace, and competence,
Redemption from a home o'er which fell Fate
Stoops like a falcon.—O, if thou couldst choose
(As no such choice is given) 'twixt such a mate
And some proud noble!—Who, in sober judgment,
Would like to navigate the heady river,
Dashing in fury from its parent mountain,
More than the waters of the quiet lake?

KAT. Now can I hold no longer. Lake, good aunt?
Nay, in the name of truth, say mill-pond, horse-pond;
Or if there be a pond more miry,
More sluggish, mean-derived, and base than either,
Be such Gullcrammer's emblem—and his portion!

FLO. I would that he or I were in our grave,
Rather than thus his suit should goad me!—Mother,
Flora of Devorgoil, though low in fortunes,
Is still too high in mind to join her name
With such a base-born churl as Gullcrammer.

ELE. You are trim maidens both!
(*To* FLORA). Have you forgotten,
Or did you mean to call to *my* remembrance
Thy father chose a wife of peasant blood?

FLO. Will you speak thus to me, or think the stream
Can mock the fountain it derives its source from?
My venerated mother, in that name
Lies all on earth a child should chiefest honour;
And with that name to mix reproach or taunt,
Were only short of blasphemy to Heaven.

ELE. Then listen, Flora, to that mother's counsel,
Or rather profit by that mother's fate.
Your father's fortunes were but bent, not broken,
Until he listen'd to his rash affection.
Means were afforded to redeem his house,
Ample and large—the hand of a rich heiress
Awaited, almost courted, his acceptance;
He saw my beauty—such it then was call'd,
Or such at least he thought it—the wither'd bush,
Whate'er it now may seem, had blossoms then,—
And he forsook the proud and wealthy heiress,
To wed with me and ruin——

KAT. (*aside*). The more fool,
Say I, apart, the peasant maiden then,
Who might have chose a mate from her own hamlet.

ELE. Friends fell off,
And to his own resources, his own counsels,
Abandon'd, as they said, the thoughtless prodigal,
Who had exchanged rank, riches, pomp, and honour,
For the mean beauties of a cottage maid.

FLO. It was done like my father,

Who scorn'd to sell what wealth can
   never buy—
True love and free affections. And he
   loves you !
If you have suffer'd in a weary world,
Your sorrows have been jointly borne,
   and love
Has made the load sit lighter.

   ELE. Ay, but a misplaced match
   hath that deep curse in 't,
That can embitter e'en the purest
   streams
Of true affection. Thou hast seen me
   seek,
With the strict caution early habits
   taught me,
To match our wants and means—hast
   seen thy father
With aristocracy's **high brow** of
   scorn,
Spurn at economy, the cottage virtue,
As best befitting her whose sires were
   peasants ;
Nor can I, when I see my lineage
   scorn'd,
Always conceal in what contempt I
   hold
The fancied claims of rank he clings to
   fondly.

   FLO. Why will you do so ?—well you
   know it chafes him.

   ELE. Flora, thy mother is but mortal
   woman,
Nor can at all times check an eager
   tongue.

   KAT. (aside). That's no new tidings
   to her niece and daughter.

   ELE. O, mayst thou never know the
   spited feelings
That gender discord in adversity
Betwixt the dearest friends and truest
   lovers !
In the chill damping gale of poverty,
If Love's lamp go not out, it gleams but
   palely,
And twinkles in the socket.

   FLO. But tenderness can screen it
   with her veil
Till it revive again. By gentleness,
   good mother.

How oft I've seen you soothe my
   father's mood !

   KAT. Now there speak youthful hope
   and fantasy !   [Aside.

   ELE. That is an easier task in youth
   than age ;
Our temper hardens, and our charms
   decay,
And both are needed in that art of
   soothing.

   KAT. And there speaks sad experience.   [Aside.

   ELE. Besides, since that our state
   was utter desperate,
Darker his brow, more dangerous grow
   his words.
Fain would I snatch thee from the woe
   and wrath
Which darken'd long my life, and soon
   must end it.
     [A knocking without; ELEANOR
     shows alarm.
It was thy father's knock, haste to the
   gate.
     [Exeunt FLORA and KATLEEN.
What can have happ'd ?—he thought
   to stay the night.
This gear must not be seen.
     [As she is about to remove the
     basket, she sees the body of the
     roe-deer.
What have we here ? a roe-deer !—as
   I fear it,
This was the gift of which poor Flora
   thought.
The young and handsome hunter ;—
   but time presses.
     [She removes the basket and the
     roe into a closet. As she has
     done—

Enter OSWALD *of* DEVORGOIL, FLORA,
   and KATLEEN.

[He is dressed in a scarlet cloak, which should
   seem worn and old—a headpiece, and old-
   fashioned sword—the rest of his dress that
   of a peasant. His countenance and manner
   should express the moody and irritable
   haughtiness of a proud man involved in
   calamity, and who has been exposed to
   recent insult.

Osw. (*addressing his Wife*). The sun hath set—why is the drawbridge lower'd?

Ele. The counterpoise has fail'd, and Flora's strength,
Katleen's, and mine united, could not raise it.

Osw. Flora and thou! A goodly garrison
To hold a castle, which, if fame say true,
Once foil'd the King of Norse and all his rovers.

Ele. It might be so in ancient times, but now——

Osw. A herd of deer might storm proud Devorgoil.

Kat. (*aside to* Flo.) You, Flora, know full well one deer already
Has enter'd at the breach; and, what is worse,
The escort is not yet march'd off, for Blackthorn
Is still within the castle.

Flo. In Heaven's name, rid him out on 't, ere my father
Discovers he is here! Why went he not
Before?

Kat. Because I staid him on some little business;
I had a plan to scare poor paltry Gull-crammer
Out of his paltry wits.

Flo. Well, haste ye now,
And try to get him off.

Kat. I will not promise that.
I would not turn an honest hunter's dog,
So well I love the woodcraft, out of shelter
In such a night as this—far less his master:
But I 'll do this, I 'll try to hide him for you.

Osw. (*whom his Wife has assisted to take off his cloak and feathered cap*). Ay, take them off, and bring my peasant's bonnet
And peasant's plaid—I 'll noble it no further.

Let them erase my name from honour's lists,
And drag my scutcheon at their horses' heels;
I have deserved it all, for I am poor,
And poverty hath neither right of birth,
Nor rank, relation, claim, nor privilege,
To match a new-coin'd viscount, whose good grandsire,
The Lord be with him! was a careful skipper,
And steer'd his paltry skiff 'twixt Leith and Campvere—
Marry, sir, he could buy Geneva cheap,
And knew the coast by moonlight.

Flo. Mean you the Viscount Ellondale, my father?
What strife has been between you?

Osw. Oh, a trifle!
Not worth a wise man's thinking twice about—
Precedence is a toy—a superstition
About a table's end, joint-stool, and trencher.
Something was once thought due to long descent,
And something to Galwegia's oldest baron,—
But let that pass—a dream of the old time.

Ele. It is indeed a dream.

Osw. (*turning upon her rather quickly*). Ha! said ye? let me hear these words more plain.

Ele. Alas! they are but echoes of your own.
Match'd with the real woes that hover o'er us,
What are the idle visions of precedence,
But, as you term them, dreams, and toys, and trifles,
Not worth a wise man's thinking twice upon?

Osw. Ay, 't was for you I framed that consolation,
The true philosophy of clouted shoe
And linsey-woolsey kirtle. I know, that minds
Of nobler stamp receive no dearer motive

Than what is link'd with honour.
    Ribands, tassels,
Which are but shreds of silk and span-
    gled tinsel—
The right of place, which in itself is
    momentary—
A word, which is but air—may in them-
    selves,
And to the nobler file, be steep'd so
    richly
In that elixir, honour, that the lack
Of things so very trivial in themselves
Shall be misfortune. One shall seek
    for them
O'er the wild waves—one in the deadly
    breach
And battle's headlong front—one in the
    paths
Of midnight study; and, in gaining
    these
Emblems of honour, each will hold
    himself
Repaid for all his labours, deeds, and
    dangers.
What then should he think, knowing
    them his own,
Who sees what warriors and what sages
    toil for,
The formal and establish'd marks of
    honour,
Usurp'd from him by upstart insolence?
  ELE. (*who has listened to the last
    speech with some impatience*). This
  is but empty declamation, Oswald.
The fragments left at yonder full-spread
    banquet,
Nay, even the poorest crust swept from
    the table,
Ought to be far more precious to a
    father,   [boast,
Whose family lacks food, than the vain
He sate at the board-head.
  OSW. Thou'lt drive me frantic!—I
    will tell thee, woman—
Yet why to thee? There is another ear
Which that tale better suits, and he
  shall hear it.
    [*Looks at his sword, which he
    has unbuckled, and addresses
    the rest of the speech to it.*

Yes, trusty friend, my father knew thy
    worth,
And often proved it—often told me of
    it—
Though thou and I be now held lightly
    of,
And want the gilded hatchments of the
    time,
I think we both may prove true metal
    still.
'T is thou shalt tell this story, right this
    wrong :
Rest thou till time is fitting.
             [*Hangs up the sword.*

    [*The Women look at each other with
    anxiety during this speech, which
    they partly overhear. They both
    approach* OSWALD.

  ELE. Oswald—my dearest husband!
  FLO.   My dear father!
  OSW. Peace, both!—we speak no
    more of this. I go
To heave the drawbridge up.   [*Exit.*

KATLEEN *mounts the steps towards the
    loophole, looks out, and speaks.*

The storm is gathering fast : broad,
    heavy drops
Fall plashing on the bosom of the lake,
And dash its inky surface into circles ;
The distant hills are hid in wreaths of
    darkness.
'T will be a fearful night.

OSWALD *re-enters, and throws himself
    into a seat.*

  ELE.   More dark and dreadful
Than is our destiny, it cannot be.
  OSW. (*to* FLO.) Such is Heaven's
    will—it is our part to bear it.
We're warranted, my child, from ancient
    story
And blessed writ, to say, that song
    assuages
The gloomy cares that prey upon our
    reason,
And wake a strife betwixt our better
    feelings
And the fierce dictates of the headlong
    passions.

Sing, then, my love; for if a voice have
  influence
To mediate peace betwixt me and my
  destiny,
Flora, it must be thine.
FLO.   My best to please you!

SONG.

When the tempest's at the loudest,
  On its gale the eagle rides;
When the ocean rolls the proudest,
  Through the foam the sea-bird glides—
All the rage of wind and sea
Is subdued by constancy.

Gnawing want and sickness pining,
  All the ills that men endure;
Each their various pangs combining,
  Constancy can find a cure—
Pain, and Fear, and Poverty
Are subdued by constancy.

Bar me from each wonted pleasure,
  Make me abject, mean, and poor;
Heap on insults without measure,
  Chain me to a dungeon floor—
I'll be happy, rich, and free,
If endow'd with constancy.

ACT II.—SCENE I.

*A Chamber in a distant part of the Castle.
A large window in the flat Scene, supposed to look on the Lake. which is occasionally illuminated by lightning. There
is a couch-bed in the room, and an antique
cabinet.*

Enter KATLEEN, *introducing* BLACK-
THORN.

KAT. This was the destined scene of
  action, Blackthorn,
And here our properties. But all in
  vain,
For of Gullcrammer we'll see nought
  to-night,
Except the dainties that I told you of.
  BLA. O, if he's left that same hog's
  face and sausages,
He will try back upon them, never fear
  it.
The cur will open on the trail of bacon,
Like my old brach-hound.

KAT. And should that hap, we'll
  play our comedy,—
Shall we not, Blackthorn? Thou shalt
  be Owlspiegle——
  BLA. And who may that hard-named
  person be?
  KAT. I've told you nine times over.
  BLA. Yes, pretty Katleen, but my
  eyes were busy
In looking at you all the time you were
  talking,
And so I lost the tale.
  KAT. Then shut your eyes, and let
  your goodly ears
Do their good office.
  BLA.   That were too hard penance.
Tell but thy tale once more, and I will
  hearken
As if I were thrown out, and listening
  for
My bloodhound's distant bay.
  KAT.   A civil simile!
Then, for the tenth time, and the last—
  be told,
Owlspiegle was of old the wicked
  barber
To Erick, wicked Lord of Devorgoil.
  BLA. The chief who drown'd his cap-
  tives in the Solway—
We all have heard of him.
  KAT. A hermit hoar, a venerable
  man—
So goes the legend—came to wake re-
  pentance
In the fierce lord, and tax'd him with
  his guilt;
But he, heart-harden'd, turn'd into de-
  rision
The man of heaven, and, as his dignity
Consisted much in a long reverend
  beard,
Which reach'd his girdle, Erick caused
  his barber,
This same Owlspiegle, violate its
  honours
With sacrilegious razor, and clip his
  hair
After the fashion of a roguish fool.
  BLA. This was reversing of our an-
  cient proverb,

And shaving for the devil's, not for
　God's sake.
　　KAT. True, most grave Blackthorn;
　　　and in punishment
Of this foul act of scorn, the barber's
　ghost
Is said to have no resting after death,
But haunts these halls, and chiefly this
　same chamber,
Where the profanity was acted, trim-
　ming
And clipping all such guests as sleep
　within it.
Such is at least the tale our elders tell,
With many others, of this haunted
　castle.
　　BLA. And you would have me take
　　this shape of Owlspiegle,
And trim the wise Melchisedek!—I
　wonnot.
　　KAT. You will not !
　　BLA. 　No—unless you bear a part.
　　KAT. What ! can you not alone play
　　such a farce?
　　BLA. Not I—I'm dull. Besides, we
　foresters
Still hunt our game in couples. Look
　you, Katleen,
We danced at Shrovetide—then you
　were my partner ;
We sung at Christmas—you kept time
　with me ;
And if we go a-mumming in this busi-
　ness,
By heaven, you must be one, or Master
　Gullcrammer
Is like to rest unshaven——
　　KAT. 　　　　Why, you fool,
What end can this serve?
　　BLA. 　　　　Nay, I know not, I.
But if we keep this wont of being part-
　ners,
Why, use makes perfect—who knows
　what may happen?
　　KAT. Thou art a foolish patch. But
　sing our carol,
As I have alter'd it, with some few
　words
To suit the characters, and I will
　bear—— 　　　　　[*Gives a paper.*

　　BLA. Part in the gambol. I'll go
　　study quickly.
Is there no other ghost, then, haunts
　the castle,
But this same barber shave-a-penny
　goblin?
I thought they glanced in every beam
　of moonshine,
As frequent as the bat.
　　KAT. I've heard my aunt's high hus-
　　band tell of prophecies,
And fates impending o'er the house of
　Devorgoil ;
Legends first coin'd by ancient super-
　stition,
And rendered current by credulity
And pride of lineage. Five years have
　I dwelt, 　　　　　　[chievous
And ne'er saw anything more mis-
Than what I am myself.
　　BLA. And that is quite enough, I
　　warrant you.
But, stay, where shall I find a dress
To play this—what d'ye call him—
　Owlspiegle?
　　KAT. (*takes dresses out of the cabinet*).
　　Why, there are his own clothes,
Preserved with other trumpery of the
　sort,
For we have kept nought but what is
　good for nought.
　　　[*She drops a cap as she draws
　　　　out the clothes.* BLACKTHORN
　　　　lifts it, and gives it to her.
Nay, keep it for thy pains—it is a cox-
　comb ;
So call'd in ancient times, in ours a
　fool's cap ;
For you must know they kept a Fool at
　Devorgoil
In former days ; but now are well con-
　tented
To play the fool themselves, to save
　expenses ;
Yet give it me, I'll find a worthy use
　for't.
I'll take this page's dress, to play the
　page
Cockledemoy, who waits on ghostly
　Owlspiegle ;

And yet 't is needless, too, for Gull-
    crammer
Will scarce be here to-night.
    BLA. I tell you that he will—I will
    uphold
His plighted faith and true allegiance
Unto a sous'd sow's face and sausages,
And such the dainties that you say he
    sent you
Against all other likings whatsoever,
Except a certain sneaking of affection,
Which makes some folks I know of
    play the fool,
To please some other folks.
    KAT. Well, I do hope he 'll come—
    there 's first a chance
He will be cudgell'd by my noble
    uncle—
I cry his mercy—by my good aunt's
    husband,
Who did vow vengeance, knowing
    nought of him
But by report, and by a limping sonnet
Which he had fashion'd to my cousin's
    glory,
And forwarded by blind Tom Long the
    carrier;
So there 's the chance, first of a hearty
    beating,
Which failing, we 've this after-plot of
    vengeance.
    BLA. Kind damsel, how considerate
    and merciful !
But how shall we get off, our parts
    being play'd ?
    KAT. For that we are well fitted ;
    here 's a trap-door
Sinks with a counterpoise—you shall
    go that way.
I 'll make my exit yonder—'neath the
    window,
A balcony communicates with the tower
That overhangs the lake.
    BLA. 'T were a rare place, this house
    of Devorgoil,
To play at hide-and-seek in—shall we
    try,
One day, my pretty Katleen?
    KAT. Hands off, rude ranger ! I 'm
    no managed hawk

To stoop to lure of yours.—But bear
    you gallantly ;
This Gullcrammer hath vex'd my cousin
    much,
I fain would have some vengeance.
    BLA. I 'll bear my part with glee ;—
    he spoke irreverently
Of practice at a mark !
    KAT.   That cries for vengeance.
But I must go ; I hear my aunt's shrill
    voice !
My cousin and her father will scream
    next.
    ELE. (*at a distance*). Katleen ! Kat-
    leen !
    BLA.   Hark to old Sweetlips !
Away with you before the full cry
    open—
But stay, what have you there ?
    KAT. (*with a bundle she has taken
    from the wardrobe*). My dress, my
    page's dress—let it alone.
    BLA. Your tiring-room is not, I hope,
    far distant ;
You 're inexperienced in these new
    habiliments—
I am most ready to assist your toilet.
    KAT. Out, you great ass ! was ever
    such a fool !   [*Runs off.*

            BLA. (*sings.*)

O, Robin Hood was a bowman good,
    And a bowman good was he,
And he met with a maiden in merry Sherwood,
    All under the greenwood tree.

Now give me a kiss, quoth bold Robin Hood,
    Now give me a kiss, said he,   [wood,
For there never came maid into merry Sher-
    But she paid the forester's fee.

I 've coursed this twelvemonth this sly
    puss, young Katleen,
And she has dodged me, turn'd beneath
    my nose,
And flung me out a score of yards at
    once ;
If this same gear fadge right, I 'll cote
    and mouth her,
And then ! whoop ! dead ! dead ! dead !
    —She is the metal

To make a woodsman's wife of!——
            [*Pauses a moment.*
Well—I can find a hare upon her form
With any man in Nithsdale—stalk a
            deer,
Run Reynard to the earth for all his
            doubles,
Reclaim a haggard hawk that's wild
            and wayward,
Can bait a wild cat,—sure the devil's
            in't
But I can match a woman. I'll to study.
            [*Sits down on the couch to examine
            the paper.*

SCENE II.

*Scene changes to the inhabited Apartment of
the Castle, as in the last Scene of the preceding Act. A fire is kindled. by which
OSWALD sits in an attitude of deep and
melancholy thought, without paying attention to what passes around him. ELEANOR
is busy in covering a table ; FLORA goes
out and re enters, as if busied in the kitchen. There should be some by-play—
the Women whispering together and
watching the state of OSWALD ; then se-
parating and seeking to avoid his observation when he casually raises his head and
drops it again. This must be left to taste
and management. The Women, in the
first part of the scene, talk apart, and as
if fearful of being overheard ; the by-play
of stopping occasionally, and attending to
OSWALD s movements, will give liveliness
to the scene.*

ELE. Is all prepared?
FLO.   Ay ; but I doubt the issue
Will give my sire less pleasure than
        you hope for.
ELE. Tush, maid—I know thy
        father's humour better.
He was high-bred in gentle luxuries ;
And when our griefs began, I 've wept
        apart,
While lordly cheer and high-fill'd cups
        of wine
Were blinding him against the woe to
        come.

He has turn'd his back upon a princely
        banquet ;
We will not spread his board — this
        night at least,
Since chance hath better furnish'd—
        with dry bread,
And water from the well.

*Enter KATLEEN, and hears the last
        speech.*

KAT. (*aside*). Considerate aunt ! she
        deems that a good supper
Were not a thing indifferent even to
        him
Who is to hang to-morrow. Since she
        thinks so,
We must take care the venison has due
        honour—
So much I owe the sturdy knave, Lance
        Blackthorn.
FLO. Mother, alas ! when Grief turns
        reveller,
Despair is cupbearer. What shall hap
        to-morrow ?
ELE. I have learn'd carelessness
        from fruitless care.
Too long I 've watch'd to-morrow ; let
        it come
And cater for itself. Thou hear'st the
        thunder.
            [*Low and distant thunder.*
This is a gloomy night—within, alas !
            [*Looking at her Husband.*
Still gloomier and more threatening.
        Let us use
Whatever means we have to drive it
        o'er,
And leave to Heaven to-morrow. Trust
        me, Flora,
'T is the philosophy of desperate want
To match itself but with the present
        evil,
And face one grief at once.
Away, I wish thine aid, and not thy
        counsel.
            [*As FLORA is about to go off,
            GULLCRAMMER'S voice is
            heard behind the flat Scene, as
            if from the drawbridge.*

GUL. *(behind.)* Hillo—hilloa—hilloa —hoa—hoa !

[OSWALD *raises himself and listens ;* ELEANOR *goes up the steps, and opens the window at the loophole ;* GULLCRAM- MER'S *voice is then heard more distinctly.*

GUL. Kind Lady Devorgoil—sweet Mistress Flora !—

The night grows fearful, I have lost my way, [with me,
And wander'd till the road turned round
And brought me back—for Heaven's sake give me shelter !

KAT. *(aside).* Now, as I live, the voice of Gullcrammer !

Now shall our gambol be played off with spirit ;
I 'll swear I am the only one to whom
That screech-owl whoop was e'er acceptable.

OSW. What bawling knave is this that takes our dwelling
For some hedge inn, the haunt of lated drunkards ?

ELE. What shall I say ?—Go, Katleen, speak to him.

KAT. *(aside).* The game is in my hands—I will say something
Will fret the baron's pride—and then he enters.

(She speaks from the window). Good sir, be patient !

We are poor folks—it is but six Scotch miles
To the next borough town, where your Reverence
May be accommodated to your wants ;
We are poor folks, an't please your Reverence,
And keep a narrow household—there's no tra k
To lead your steps astray——

GUL. Nor none to lead them right.— You kill me, lady,
If you deny me harbour. To budge from hence,
And in my weary plight, were sudden death.

Interment, funeral-sermon, tombstone, epitaph.

OSW. Who's he that is thus clamorous without ?
(To ELE *)* Thou know'st him ?

ELE. *(confused).* I know him ?—no —yes—'t is a worthy clergyman
Benighted on his way ;—but think not of him.

KAT. The morn will rise when that the tempest's past.
And if he miss the marsh, and can avoid
The crags upon the left, the road is plain.

OSW. Then this is all your piety !— to leave
One whom the holy duties of his office
Have summon'd over moor and wilderness,
To pray beside some dying wretch's bed,
Who (erring mortal) still would cleave to life,
Or wake some stubborn sinner to repentance,—
To leave him, after offices like these,
To choose his way in darkness 'twixt the marsh
And dizzy precipice?

ELE. What can I do ?

OSW. Do what thou canst — the wealthiest do no more—
And if so much, 't is well. These crumbling walls,
While yet they bear a roof, shall now, as ever,
Give shelter to the wanderer. Have we food?
He shall partake it—have we none ? the fast
Shall be accounted with the good man's merits,
And our misfortunes——

[*He goes to the loophole while he speaks, and places himself there in room of his Wife, who comes down with reluctance.*

GUL. *(without).* Hillo—hoa—hoa !

By my good faith, I cannot plod it
   farther ;
The attempt were death.

   OSW. (*speaks from the window*). Patience, my friend. I come to lower
the drawbridge.

                [*Descends and exit.*

   ELE. O, that the screaming bittern
   had his couch
Where he deserves it, in the deepest
   marsh !

   KAT. I would not give this sport for
   all the rent
Of Devorgoil, when Devorgoil was
   richest !
(*To* ELE.) But now you chided me, my
   dearest aunt,
For wishing him a horse-pond for his
   portion.

   ELE. Yes, saucy girl ; but, an it
   please you, then
He was not fretting me ; if he had sense
   enough
And skill to bear him as some casual
   stranger,—
But he is dull as earth, and every hint
Is lost on him, as hail-shot on the cormorant,
Whose hide is proof except to musket-
   bullets !

   FLO. (*apart*). And yet to such a one
would my kind mother,
Whose chiefest fault is loving me too
   fondly,
Wed her poor daughter !

Enter GULLCRAMMER, *his dress da-
maged by the storm;* ELEANOR *runs
to meet him, in order to explain to
him that she wished him to behave
as a stranger.* GULLCRAMMER,
*mistaking her approach for an in-
vitation to familiarity, advances
with the air of pedantic conceit belonging to his character, when*
OSWALD *enters.—*ELEANOR *recovers
herself, and assumes an air of distance.* — GULLCRAMMER *is confounded, and does not know what to
make of it.*

   OSW. The counterpoise has clean
   given way ; the bridge
Must e'en remain unraised, and leave
   us open,
For this night's course at least, to passing visitants.—
What have we here ? — is this the
   reverend man ?

      [*He takes up the candle, and sur-
       veys* GULLCRAMMER, *who
       strives to sustain the inspec-
       tion with confidence, while
       fear obviously contends with
       conceit and desire to show
       himself to the best advantage.*

   GUL. Kind sir—or, good my lord—
   my band is ruffled,
But yet 't was fresh this morning. This
   fell shower
Hath somewhat smirch'd my cloak,
   but you may note
It rates five marks per yard ; my
   doublet
Hath fairly 'scaped—'t is three-piled
   taffeta.

      [*Opens his cloak, and displays
       doublet.*

   OSW. A goodly inventory. Art thou
   a preacher ?

   GUL. Yea—I laud Heaven and good
   Saint Mungo for it.

   OSW. 'T is the time's plague, when
   those that should weed follies
Out of the common field, have their
   own minds
O'errun with foppery—Envoys 'twixt
   heaven and earth,
Example should with precept join, to
   show us
How we may scorn the world with all
   its vanities.

   GUL. Nay, the high heavens forefend that I were vain !
When our learn'd Principal such sounding laud
Gave to mine Essay on the hidden
   qualities
Of the sulphuric mineral, I disclaim'd
All self-exaltment. And (*turning to
   the Women*) when at the dance,

The lovely Saccharissa Kirkencroft,
Daughter to Kirkencroft of Kirkencroft,
Graced me with her soft hand, credit
me, ladies,
That still I felt myself a mortal man,
Though beauty smiled on me.

OSW. Come, sir, enough of this.
That you 're our guest to-night, thank
the rough heavens,
And all our worser fortunes; be con-
formable
Unto my rules ; these are no Saccha-
rissas
To gild with compliments. There 's in
your profession,
As the best grain will have its piles of
chaff,
A certain whiffler, who hath dared to
bait
A noble maiden with love tales and
sonnets ;
And if I meet him, his Geneva cap
May scarce be proof to save his ass's
ears.

KAT. (*aside*). Umph—I am strongly
tempted,
And yet I think I will be generous,
And give his brains a chance to save
his bones.
Then there 's more humour in our gob-
lin plot,
Than in a simple drubbing.

ELE. (*apart to* FLO.) What shall we
do? If he discover him,
He 'll fling him out at window.

FLO. My father's hint to keep himself unknown
Is all too broad, I think, to be neglected.

ELE. But yet the fool, if we produce
his bounty,
May claim the merit of presenting it ;
And then we 're but lost women for
accepting
A gift our needs made timely.

KAT. Do not produce them.
E'en let the fop go supperless to bed,
And keep his bones whole.

OSW. (*to his Wife*). Hast thou aught
To place before him ere he seek repose?

ELE. Alas ! too well you know our
needful fare
Is of the narrowest now, and knows no
surplus.

OSW. Shame us not with thy niggard
housekeeping ;
He is a stranger—were it our last crust,
And he the veriest coxcomb e'er wore
taffeta,
A pitch he 's little short of—he must
share it,
Though all should want to-morrow.

GUL. (*partly overhearing what passes
between them*). Nay, I am no lover
of your sauced dainties :
Plain food and plenty is my motto
still.
Your mountain air is bleak, and brings
an appetite ;
A soused sow's face, now, to my modest
thinking,
Has ne'er a fellow. What think these
fair ladies
Of a sow's face and sausages?
[*Makes signs to* ELEANOR.

FLO. Plague on the vulgar hind, and
on his courtesies,
The whole truth will come out !

OSW. What should they think, but
that you 're like to lack
Your favourite dishes, sir, unless perchance
You bring such dainties with you.

GUL. No, not *with* me; not, indeed,
Directly *with* me. But — aha ! fair
ladies ! [*Makes signs again.*

KAT. He 'll draw the beating down,
were that the worst.
Heaven's will be done ! [*Aside.*

OSW. (*apart*). What can he mean?
this is the veriest dog-whelp.
Still he 's a stranger, and the latest act
Of hospitality in this old mansion
Shall not be sullied.

GUL. Troth, sir, I think, under the
ladies' favour,
Without pretending skill in second
sight,
Those of my cloth being seldom con-
jurors——

Osw. I 'll take my Bible-oath that
thou art none.   [*Aside.*

Gul. I do opine, still with the ladies'
favour,

That I could guess the nature of our
supper.

I do not say in such and such precedence

The dishes will be placed—housewives,
as you know,

On such forms have their fancies—but,
I say still,

That a sow's face and sausages——

Osw.   Peace, sir !

O'er-driven jests (if this be one) are
insolent.

Flo. (*apart, seeing her Mother un-
easy*). The old saw still holds true
—a churl's benefits,

Sauced with his lack of feeling, sense,
and courtesy,

Savour like injuries.

[*A horn is winded without; then
a loud knocking at the gate.*

Leo. (*without*). Ope, for the sake of
love and charity !

[Oswald *goes to the loophole.*

Gul. Heaven's mercy ! should there
come another stranger,

And he half starved with wandering on
the wolds,

The sow's face boasts no substance, nor
the sausages,

To stand our reinforced attack ! I
judge, too,

By this starved baron's language,
there's no hope

Of a reserve of victuals.

Flo. Go to the casement, cousin.

Kat.   Go yourself,

And bid the gallant who that bugle
winded

Sleep in the storm-swept waste; as
meet for him

As for Lance Blackthorn. Come, I 'll
not distress you,

I 'll get admittance for this second
suitor,

And we 'll play out this gambol at cross
purposes.

But see, your father has prevented
me.

Osw. (*seems to have spoken with those
without, and answers*). Well, I will
ope the door ; one guest already,

Driven by the storm, has claim'd my
hospitality,

And you, if you were fiends, were scarce
less welcome

To this my mouldering roof, than empty
ignorance

And rank conceit—I hasten to admit
you.   [*Exit.*

Ele. (*to* Flo.) The tempest thickens.
By that winded bugle,

I guess the guest that next will honour
us.

Little deceiver, that didst mock my
troubles,

'T is now thy turn to fear !

Flo. Mother, if I knew less or more
of this

Unthought-of and most perilous visita-
tion,

I would your wishes were fulfill'd on
me,

And I were wedded to a thing like yon,

Gul. (*approaching*). Come, ladies,
now you see the jest is thread-
bare,

And you must own that same sow's face
and sausages——

Re-enter Oswald *with* Leonard,
supporting Bauldie Durward.
Oswald *takes a view of them, as
formerly of* Gullcrammer, *then
speaks.*

Osw. (*to* Leo.) By thy green cassock,
hunting-spear, and bugle,

I guess thou art a huntsman ?

Leo. (*bowing with respect*). A ranger
of the neighbouring royal forest,

Under the good Lord Nithsdale ; huntsman, therefore,

In time of peace, and when the land
has war,

To my best powers a soldier.

Osw. Welcome, as either. I have
loved the chase.

And was a soldier once. This aged
man,
What may he be?
  DUR. (*recovering his breath*). Is but
    a beggar, sir, an humble mendicant,
Who feels it passing strange, that from
    this roof,
Above all others, he should now crave
    shelter.
  OSW. Why so? You're welcome
    both—only the word
Warrants more courtesy than our pre-
    sent means
Permit us to bestow. A huntsman and
    a soldier
May be a prince's comrade, much more
    mine;
And for a beggar—friend, there little
    lacks,
Save that blue gown and badge, and
    clouted pouches,
To make us comrades too; then wel-
    come both,
And to a beggar's feast. I fear brown
    bread,
And water from the spring, will be the
    best on 't;
For we had cast to wend abroad this
    evening,
And left our larder empty.
  GUL.   Yet, if some kindly fairy,
In our behalf, would search its hid
    recesses.
(*Apart*). We'll not go supperless now,
    we're three to one;
Still do I say, that a soused face and
    sausages——
  OSW. (*looks sternly at him, then at
    his Wife*). There's something under
    this, but that the present
Is not a time to question. (*To* ELE.)
    Wife, my mood
Is at such height of tide, that a turn'd
    feather
Would make me frantic now, with mirth
    or fury!
Tempt me no more—but if thou hast
    the things
This carrion crow so croaks for, bring
    them forth;

For, by my father's beard, if I stand
    caterer
'T will be a fearful banquet!
  ELE. Your pleasure be obey'd. Come,
    aid me, Flora.   [*Exeunt.*
      [*During the following speeches
        the Women place dishes on
        the table.*
  OSW. (*to* DUR.) How did you lose
    your path?
  DUR. E'en when we thought to find
    it, a wild meteor
Danced in the moss, and led our feet
    astray.
I give small credence to the tales of
    old,
Of Friar's-lantern told, and Will-o'-
    wisp,
Else would I say that some malicious
    demon
Guided us in a round; for to the moat,
Which we had pass'd two hours since,
    were we led,
And there the gleam flicker'd and dis-
    appear'd,
Even on your drawbridge. I was so
    worn down,
So broke with labouring through marsh
    and moor,
That, wold I nold I, here my young
    conductor
Would needs implore for entrance:
    else, believe me,
I had not troubled you.
  OSW. And why not, father? Have
    you e'er heard aught,
Or of my house or me, that wanderers,
Whom or their roving trade or sudden
    circumstance
Oblige to seek a shelter, should avoid
The house of Devorgoil?
  DUR.   Sir, I am English born,
Native of Cumberland. Enough is said
Why I should shun those bowers, whose
    lords were hostile
To English blood, and unto Cumber-
    land
Most hostile and most fatal.
  OSW. Ay, father. Once my grand-
    sire plough'd, and harrow'd

And sow'd with salt, the streets of your
  fair towns ;
But what of that? you have the 'vantage
  now.
  DUR. True, Lord of Devorgoil, and
  well believe I,
That not in vain we sought these towers
  to-night,
So strangely guided, to behold their
  state.
  OSW. Ay, thou wouldst say, 't was fit
  a Cumbrian beggar
Should sit an equal guest in his proud
  halls,
Whose fathers beggar'd Cumberland.
  Greybeard, let it be so,
I 'll not dispute it with thee.
     [*To* LEO., *who was speaking to*
      FLORA, *but, on being surprised,*
      occupied himself with the suit
      of armour.
What makest thou there, young man?
  LEO. I marvell'd at this harness ; it
  is larger
Than arms of modern days. How
  richly carved
With gold inlaid on steel ! how close
  the rivets !
How justly fit the joints ! I think the
  gauntlet
Would swallow twice my hand.
     [*He is about to take down some*
      part of the armour; OSWALD
      interferes.
OSW.   Do not displace it.
My grandsire, Erick, doubled human
  strength,
And also human size—and human
  knowledge,
And human vice, and human virtue
  also,
As storm or sunshine chanced to oc-
  cupy
His mental hemisphere. After a fatal
  deed,
He hung his armour on the wall, for-
  bidding
It e'er should be ta'en down. There is
  a prophecy,
That of itself 't will fall, upon the night

When, in the fiftieth year from his
  decease,
Devorgoil's feast is full. This is the era;
But, as too well you see, no meet occa-
  sion
Will do the downfall of the armour
  justice,
Or grace it with a feast. There let it
  bide,
Trying its strength with the old walls
  it hangs
Which shall fall soonest.
  DUR. (*looking at the trophy with a*
    mixture of feeling). Then there
    stern Erick's harness hangs un-
    touch'd,
Since his last fatal raid on Cumber-
  land?
  OSW. Ay, waste and want, and
  recklessness—a comrade
Still yoked with waste and want—have
  stripp'd these walls
Of every other trophy. Antler'd skulls,
Whose branches vouch'd the tales old
  vassals told
Of desperate chases, partisans and
  spears,
Knights' barred helms and shields, the
  shafts and bows,
Axes and breastplates of the hardy
  yeomanry,
The banners of the vanquish'd—signs
  these arms
Were not assumed in vain—have dis-
  appear'd,
Yes, one by one they all have disap-
  pear'd ;
And now Lord Erick's armour hangs
  alone,
'Midst implements of vulgar husbandry
And mean economy ; as some old
  warrior,
Whom want hath made an inmate of
  an alms-house,
Shows 'mid the beggar'd spendthrifts,
  base mechanics,
And bankrupt pedlars, with whom fate
  has mix'd him.
  DUR. Or rather like a pirate, whom
  the prison-house,

Prime leveller next the grave, hath for
    the first time
Mingled with peaceful captives, low in
    fortunes,
But fair in innocence.

    Osw. (*looking at* Dur. *with sur-
    prise*). Friend, thou art bitter !

    Dur. Plain truth, sir, like the vulgar
    copper coinage,
Despised amongst the gentry, still finds
    value
And currency with beggars.

    Osw.   Be it so.
I will not trench on the immunities
I soon may claim to share. Thy fea-
    tures, too,
Though weatherbeaten, and thy strain
    of language,
Relish of better days. Come hither,
    friend,   [*They speak apart.*
And let me ask thee of thine occupa-
    tion.

    [Leonard *looks round, and,
    seeing* Oswald *engaged with*
    Durward, *and* Gullcram-
    mer *with* Eleanor, *ap-
    proaches towards* Flora, *who
    must give him an opportunity
    of doing so, with obvious in-
    tention on her part to give it
    the air of chance. The by-
    play here will rest with the
    Lady, who must engage the
    attention of the audience by
    playing off a little female hy-
    pocrisy and simple coquetry.*

    Leo. Flora——

    Flo. Ay, gallant huntsman, may she
    deign to question
Why Leonard came not at the ap-
    pointed hour,
Or why he came at midnight?

    Leo. Love has no certain loadstar,
    gentle Flora,
And oft gives up the helm to wayward
    pilotage.
To say the sooth—A beggar forced me
    hence,
And Will-o'-wisp did guide us back
    again.

    Flo. Ay, ay, your beggar was the
    faded spectre
Of Poverty, that sits upon the thresh-
    old
Of these our ruin'd walls. I've been
    unwise,
Leonard, to let you speak so oft with
    me ;
And you a fool to say what you have
    said.
E'en let us here break short ; and, wise
    at length,
Hold each our separate way through
    life's wide ocean.

    Leo. Nay, let us rather join our
    course together,
And share the breeze or tempest, doub-
    ling joys,
Relieving sorrows, warding evils off
With mutual effort, or enduring them
With mutual patience.

    Flo. This is but flattering counsel
    —sweet and baneful ;
But mine had wholesome bitter in 't.

    Kat. Ay, ay ; but like the sly apo-
    thecary,
You 'll be the last to take the bitter
    drug
That you prescribe to others.

    [*They whisper.* Eleanor *ad-
    vances to interrupt them, fol-
    lowed by* Gullcrammer.

    Ele. What, maid, no household
    cares? Leave to your elders
The task of filling passing strangers'
    ears
With the due notes of welcome.

    Gul.   Be it thine,
O Mistress Flora, the more useful
    talent
Of filling strangers' stomachs with sub-
    stantials ;
That is to say,—for learn'd commen-
    tators
Do so expound substantials in some
    places,—
With a sous'd bacon-face and sau-
    sages.

    Flo. (*apart*). Would thou wert sous'd,
    intolerable pedant,

Base, greedy, perverse, interrupting
    coxcomb!

KAT. Hush, coz, for we'll be well
    avenged on him,
And ere this night goes o'er, else wo-
    man's wit
Cannot o'ertake her wishes.
      [*She proceeds to arrange seats.*
      OSWALD *and* DURWARD *come*
      forward in conversation.

OSW. I like thine humour well.—So
    all men beg——

DUR. Yes—I can make it good by
    proof. Your soldier
Begs for a leaf of laurel, and a line
In the Gazette. He brandishes his
    sword
To back his suit, and is a sturdy
    beggar.
The courtier begs a riband or a star,
And, like our gentler mumpers, is pro-
    vided
With false certificates of health and
    fortune
Lost in the public service. For your
    lover,
Who begs a sigh, a smile, a lock of
    hair,
A buskin-point, he maunds upon the
    pad,
With the true cant of pure mendicity,
" The smallest trifle to relieve a Chris-
    tian,
And if it like your Ladyship!"——
      [*In a begging tone.*

KAT. (*apart*). This is a cunning
    knave, and feeds the humour
Of my aunt's husband, for I must not
    say
Mine honour'd uncle. I will try a
    question.—
Your man of merit though, who serves
    the commonwealth,
Nor asks for a requital?——
      [*To* DURWARD.

DUR.   Is a dumb beggar,
And lets his actions speak like signs
    for him,
Challenging double guerdon.—Now
    I'll show

How your true beggar has the fair
    advantage
O'er all the tribes of cloak'd mendicity
I have told over to you.—The soldier's
    laurel,
The statesman's riband, and the lady's
    favour,
Once won and gain'd, are not held
    worth a farthing
By such as longest, loudest, canted for
    them;
Whereas your charitable halfpenny,
Which is the scope of a true beggar's
    suit,
Is worth *two* fathings, and, in times of
    plenty,
Will buy a crust of bread.

FLO. (*interruping him, and address-
    ing her Father*). Sir, let me be a
    beggar with the time,
And pray you come to supper.

ELE. (*to* OSWALD, *apart*). Must he
    sit with us?
      [*Looking at* DURWARD.

OSW. Ay, ay, what else—since we
    are beggars all?
When cloaks are ragged, sure their
    worth is equal
Whether at first they were of silk or
    woollen.

ELE. Thou art scarce consistent:
This day thou didst refuse a princely
    banquet,
Because a new-made lord was placed
    above thee;
And now——

OSW. Wife, I have seen, at public
    executions,
A wretch that could not brook the hand
    of violence
Should push him from the scaffold,
    pluck up courage,
And, with a desperate sort of cheerful-
    ness,
Take the fell plunge himself.
Welcome then, beggars, to a beggar's
    feast.

GUL. (*who has in the meanwhile
    seated himself*). But this is more.—
    A better countenance—

Fair fall the hands that sous'd it !—
    than this hog's,
Or prettier provender than these same
    sausages
(By what good friend sent hither, shall
    be nameless,
Doubtless some youth whom love hath
    made profuse),
        [*Smiling significantly at* ELEA-
            NOR *and* FLORA.
No prince need wish to peck at. Long,
    I ween,
Since that the nostrils of this house (by
    metaphor,
I mean the chimneys) smell'd a steam
    so grateful.
By your good leave I cannot dally
    longer.   [*Helps himself.*
    Osw. (*places* DURWARD *above* GULL-
CRAMMER). Meanwhile, sir,
Please it your faithful learning to give
    place
To grey hairs and to wisdom ; and,
    moreover,
If you had tarried for the benedic-
    tion——
    GUL. (*somewhat abashed*). I said
grace to myself.
    Osw. (*not minding him*). And waited
for the company of others,
It had been better fashion.   Time has
    been,
I should have told a guest at Devor-
    goil,
Bearing himself thus forward, he was
    saucy.
        [*He seats himself, and helps the
        company and himself in dumb
        show. There should be a con-
        trast betwixt the precision of
        his aristocratic civility, and
        the rude under-breeding of*
        GUILCRAMMER.
    Osw. (*having tasted the dish next
    him*). Why, this is venison, Elea-
nor !
    GUL. Eh? What? Let's see—
        [*Pushes across* OSWALD *and
        helps himself.*
            It may be venison—

I'm sure 't is not beef, veal, mutton,
    lamb, or pork.
Eke am I sure, that be it what it will,
It is not half so good as sausages,
Or as a sow's face sous'd.
    Osw. Eleanor, whence all this ?——
    ELE.   Wait till to-morrow,
You shall know all. It was a happy
    chance
That furnish'd us to meet so many
    guests.   [*Fills wine.*
Try if your cup be not as richly garnish'd
As is your trencher.
    KAT. (*apart*). My aunt adheres to
    the good cautious maxim
Of—" Eat your pudding, friend, and
    hold your tongue."
    Osw. (*tastes the wine*). It is the
    grape of Bordeaux.
Such dainties, once familiar to my
    board,
Have been estranged from 't long.
        [*He again fills his glass, and
        continues to speak as he holds
        it up.*
Fill round, my friends—here is a
    treacherous friend now
Smiles in your face, yet seeks to steal
    the jewel,
Which is distinction between man and
    brute—
I mean our reason—this he does, and
    smiles.
But are not all friends treacherous ?—
    one shall cross you
Even in your dearest interests—one
    shall slander you—
This steal your daughter, that defraud
    your purse ;
But this gay flask of Bordeaux will but
    borrow
Your sense of mortal sorrows for a
    season,
And leave, instead, a gay delirium.
Methinks my brain, unused to such gay
    visitants,
The influence feels already !—we will
    revel !—   [*last.*
Our banquet shall be loud !—it is our
Katleen, thy song.

KAT. Not now, my lord—I mean to
    sing to night
For this same moderate, grave, and
    reverend clergyman ;
I 'll keep my voice till then.
    ELE. Your round refusal shows but
    cottage breeding.
    KAT. Ay, my good aunt, for I was
    cottage-nurtured,
And taught, I think, to prize my own
    wild will
Above all sacrifice to compliment.
Here is a huntsman—in his eyes I read
    it,
He sings the martial song my uncle
    loves,
What time fierce Claver'se with his
    Cavaliers,
Abjuring the new change of govern-
    ment,
Forcing his fearless way through timor-
    ous friends,
And enemies as timorous, left the
    capital
To rouse in James's cause the distant
    Highlands.
Have you ne'er heard the song, my
    noble uncle?
    Osw. Have I not heard, wench?—It
    was I rode next him,
'T is thirty summers since—rode by his
    rein
We marched on through the alarm'd
    city,
As sweeps the osprey through a flock
    of gulls,
Who scream and flutter, but dare no
    resistance
Against the bold sea-empress. They
    did murmur,
The crowds before us, in their sullen
    wrath,
And those whom we had pass'd,
    gathering fresh courage,
Cried havoc in the rear—we minded
    them
E'en as the brave bark minds the
    bursting billows,
Which, yielding to her bows, burst on
    her sides

And ripple in her wake.—Sing me that
    strain,   [To LEONARD.
And thou shalt have a meed I seldom
    tender,
Because they 're all I have to give—
    my thanks.
    LEO. Nay, if you 'll bear with what
    I cannot help,
A voice that 's rough with holloaing to
    the hounds,
I 'll sing the song even as old Rowland
    taught me.

SONG.

AIR—"*The Bonnets of Bonny Dundee.*"

To the Lords of Convention 't was Claver'se
    who spoke,
" Ere the King's crown shall fall there are
    crowns to be broke ;
So let each Cavalier who loves honour and me,
Come follow the bonnet of Bonny Dundee.

    "Come fill up my cup, come fill up my can,
    Come saddle your horses, and call up your
        men ;
    Come open the West Port, and let me gang
        free,
    And it 's room for the bonnets of Bonny
        Dundee !"

Dundee he is mounted, he rides up the street,
The bells are rung backward, the drums they
    are beat ;
But the Provost, douce man, said, "Just e'en
    let him be,
The Gude Town is weel quit of that Deil of
    Dundee."
        Come fill up my cup, &c.

As he rode down the sanctified bends of the
    Bow,
Ilk carline was flyting and shaking her pow ;
But the young plants of grace they look'd
    couthie and slee,
Thinking, luck to thy bonnet, thou Bonny
    Dundee !
        Come fill up my cup, &c.

With sour-featured Whigs the Grassmarket
    was cramm'd,
As if half the West had set tryst to be hang'd ;
There was spite in each look, there was fear
    in each e'e,
As they watch'd for the bonnets of Bonny
    Dundee.
        Come fill up my cup &c.

These cowls of Kilmarnock had spits and had
    spears,
And lang-hafted gullies to kill Cavaliers;
But they shrunk to close-heads, and the cause-
    way was free,
At the toss of the bonnet of Bonny Dundee.
    Come fill up my cup, &c.

He spurr'd to the foot of the proud Castle rock,
And with the gay Gordon he gallantly spoke:
"Let Mons Meg and her marrows speak twa
    words or three,
For the love of the bonnet of Bonny Dundee."
    Come fill up my cup, &c.

The Gordon demands of him which way he
    goes—
"Where'er shall direct me the shade of Mont-
    rose!
Your Grace in short space shall hear tidings
    of me,
Or that low lies the bonnet of Bonny Dundee.
    Come fill up my cup, &c.

"There are hills beyond Pentland, and lands
    beyond Forth,
If there's lords in the Lowlands, there's chiefs
    in the North;
There are wild Duniwassals three thousand
    times three,
Will cry *hoigh!* for the bonnet of Bonny
    Dundee.
    Come fill up my cup, &c.

"There's brass on the target of barken'd bull-
    hide;
There's steel in the scabbard that dangles
    beside:
The brass shall be burnish'd, the steel shall
    flash free,
At a toss of the bonnet of Bonny Dundee.
    Come fill up my cup, &c.

"Away to the hills, to the caves, to the rocks—
Ere I own an usurper, I'll couch with the fox;
And tremble, false Whigs, in the midst of your
    glee,
You have not seen the last of my bonnet and
    me!"
    Come fill up my cup, &c.

He waved his proud hand, and the trumpets
    were blown,
The kettle-drums clash'd, and the horsemen
    rode on,
Till on Ravelston's cliffs and on Clermiston's
    lee
Died away the wild war-notes of Bonny Dundee.
    Come fill up my cup, come fill up my can,
    Come saddle the horses and call up the men,
    Come open your gates, and let me gae free,
    For it's up with the bonnets of Bonny
    Dundee!

ELE. Katleen, do thou sing now. Thy
    uncle's cheerful;
We must not let his humour ebb again
    KAT. But I'll do better, aunt, than if
    I sung,
For Flora can sing blithe; so can this
    huntsman,
As he has shown e'en now; let them
    duet it.
    OSW. Well, huntsman, we must give
    to freakish maiden
The freedom of her fancy.—Raise the
    carol,
And Flora, if she can, will join the
    measure.

SONG.

When friends are met o'er merry cheer,
And lovely eyes are laughing near,
And in the goblet's bosom clear
    The cares of day are drown'd;
When puns are made, and bumpers quaff'd
And wild Wit shoots his roving shaft,
And Mirth his jovial laugh has laugh'd,
    Then is our banquet crown'd,
        Ah gay,
    Then is our banquet crown'd.

When glees are sung, and catches troll'd,
And bashfulness grows bright and bold,
And beauty is no longer cold,
    And age no longer dull;
When chimes are brief, and cocks do crow,
To tell us it is time to go,
Yet how to part we do not know,
    Then is our feast at full,
        Ah gay,
    Then is our feast at full.

OSW. (*rises with the cup in his hand*).
    Devorgoil's feast is full—
Drink to the pledge!
    [*A tremendous burst of thunder
    follows these words of the song;
    and the lightning should seem
    to strike the suit of black ar-
    mour, which falls with a crash.
    All rise in surprise and fear
    except* GULLCRAMMER, *who
    tumbles over backwards, and
    lies still.*

OSW. That sounded like the judgment
    peal—the roof
Still trembles with the volley.

Dur.   Happy those
Who are prepared to meet such fearful
   summons.—
Leonard, what dost thou there?
   Leo. (*supporting* Flo.) The duty of
   a man—
Supporting innocence. Were it the
   final call,
I were not misemploy'd.
   Osw. The armour of my grandsire
   hath fall'n down,
And old saws have spoke truth.—
   (*Musing.*) The fiftieth year—
Devorgoil's feast at fullest! What to
   think of it——
   Leo. (*lifting a scroll which had fallen
   with the armour*). This may inform
   us.
   [*Attempts to read the manuscript,
      shakes his head, and gives it
      to* Oswald.
But not to eyes unlearn'd it tells its
   tidings.
   Osw. Hawks, hounds, and revelling
   consumed the hours
I should have given to study.
         [*Looks at the manuscript.*
These characters I spell not more than
   thou.
They are not of our day, and, as I
   think,
Not of our language.—Where's our
   scholar now,
So forward at the banquet? Is he laggard
Upon a point of learning?
   Leo. Here is the man of letter'd
   dignity,
E'en in a piteous case.
         [*Drags* Gullcrammer *forward.*
   Osw. Art waking. craven? canst thou
   read this scroll?
Or art thou only learn'd in sousing
   swine's flesh,
And prompt in eating it?
   Gul. Eh—ah!—oh—ho!—have you
   no better time
To tax a man with riddles, than the
   moment
When he scarce knows whether he's
   dead or living?

   Osw. Confound the pedant!—can
   you read the scroll,
Or can you not, sir? If you *can*, pro-
   nounce
Its meaning speedily.
   Gul.   *Can* I read it, quotha!
When at our learned University,
I gain'd first premium for Hebrew
   learning,—
Which was a pound of high-dried Scot-
   tish snuff,
And half a peck of onions, with a bushel
Of curious oatmeal,—our learn'd Prin-
   cipal
Did say, "Melchisedek, thou canst do
   anything!"
Now comes he with his paltry scroll of
   parchment,
And "*Can* you read it?"—After such
   affront,
The point is, if I *will*.
   Osw.   A point soon solved,
Unless you choose to sleep among the
   frogs;
For look you, sir, there is the chamber
   window,
Beneath it lies the lake.
   Ele. Kind Master Gullcrammer, be-
   ware my husband,
He brooks no contradiction—'t is his
   fault,
And in his wrath he's dangerous.
   Gul. (*looks at the scroll, and mutters
   as if reading.*) Hashgaboth hotch-
   potch—
A simple matter this to make a rout
   of—
*Ten rashersen bacon, mish-mash veni-
   son,*
Sausagian soused-face.—'T is a simple
   catalogue
Of our small supper—made by the
   grave sage
Whose prescience knew this night that
   we should feast
On venison, hash'd sow's face, and
   sausages,
And hung his steel coat for a supper
   bell.
E'en let us to our provender again,

For it is written we shall finish it,
And bless our stars the lightning left
   it us.
  Osw. This must be impudence or
   ignorance !—   [me,
The spirit of rough Erick stirs within
And I will knock thy brains out if thou
  palterest !
Expound the scroll to me !
  Gul.   You 're over hasty ;
And yet you may be right too—'T is
  Samaritan,
Now I look closer on 't, and I did take it
For simple Hebrew.
  Dur. 'T is Hebrew to a simpleton,
That we see plainly, friend. Give me
  the scroll.
  Gul. Alas, good friend ! what would
  you do with it ?
  Dur. (*takes it from him*). My best
  to read it, sir. The character is
  Saxon,
Used at no distant date within this
  district ;
And thus the tenor runs—nor in Sama-
  ritan
Nor simple Hebrew, but in wholesome
  English :—

Devorgoil, thy bright moon waneth,
And the rust thy harness staineth ;
Servile guests the banquet soil
Of the once proud Devorgoil.
But should Black Erick's armour fall,
Look for guests shall scare you all !
They shall come ere peep of day,—
Wake and watch, and hope and pray.

  Kat. (*to* Flo.) Here is fine foolery
   —an old wall shakes
At a loud thunder-clap—down comes a
  suit
Of ancient armour, when its wasted
  braces
Were all too rotten to sustain its
  weight—
A beggar cries out, Miracle ! and your
  father,
Weighing the importance of his name
  and lineage,
Must needs believe the dotard !

  Flo. Mock not, I pray you ; this
  may be too serious.
  Kat. And if I live till morning, I
  will have
The power to tell a better tale of wonder
Wrought on wise Gulcrammer. I 'll
  go prepare me.   [*Exit*
  Flo. I have not Katleen's spirit, yet
  I hate
This Gullcrammer too heartily, to stop
Any disgrace that 's hasting towards
  him.
  Osw. (*to whom the Beggar has been
  again reading the scroll*). 'T is a
  strange prophecy ! The silver
  moon,
Now waning sorely, is our ancient
  bearing ;
Strange and unfitting guests——
  Gul. (*interrupting him*). Ay, ay,
  the matter
Is, as you say, all moonshine in the
  water.
  Osw. How mean you, sir?
                [*Threatening.*
  Gul.   To show that I can rhyme
With yonder bluegown. Give me
  breath and time,
I will maintain, in spite of his pretence,
Mine exposition had the better sense :
It spoke good victuals and increase of
  cheer,
And his more guests to eat what we
  have here ;
An increment right needless.
  Osw.   Get thee gone ;
To kennel, hound !
  Gul. The hound will have his bone.
    [*Takes up the platter of meat
     and a flask.*
  Osw. Flora, show him his chamber
  —take him hence,
Or, by the name I bear, I 'll see his
  brains.
  Gul. Ladies, good night. I spare
  you, sir, the pains.
    [*Exit, lighted by* Flora *with a
     lamp.*
  Osw. The owl is fled. I 'll not to
  bed to-night ;

There is some change impending o'er
    this house,
For good or ill. I would some holy
    man
Were here, to counsel us what we
    should do !
Yon witless thin-faced gull is but a
    cassock
Stuffed out with chaff and straw.

    DUR. *(assuming an air of dignity).*
                    I have been wont,
In other days, to point to erring mortals
The rock which they should anchor on.
    [*He holds up a Cross—the rest
    take a posture of devotion, and
    the Scene closes.*

ACT III.—SCENE I.

A ruinous Ante-room in the Castle. Enter
KATLEEN, *fantastically dressed to play
the character of* COCKLEDEMOY, *with the
visor in her hand.*

    KAT. I 've scarce had time to glance
    at my sweet person,
Yet this much could I see, with half a
    glance,
My elfish dress becomes me ; I 'll not
    mask me
Till I have seen Lance Blackthorn.
    Lance, I say !   [*Calls.*
Blackthorn, make haste !

Enter BLACKTHORN, *half dressed as*
OWLSPIEGLE.

    BLA. Here am I—Blackthorn in the
    upper half,
Much at your service ; but my nether
    parts
Are goblinized and Owlspiegled. I
    had much ado
To get these trankums on. I judge
    Lord Erick
Kept no good house, and starved his
    quondam barber.
    KAT. Peace, ass, and hide you—
    Gullcrammer is coming ;
He left the hall before, but then took
    fright,

And e'en sneak'd back. The Lady
    Flora lights him—
Trim occupation for her ladyship !
Had you seen Leonard, when she left
    the hall
On such fine errand !
    BLA. This Gullcrammer shall have
    a bob extraordinary
For my good comrade's sake. But,
    tell me, Katleen,
What dress is this of yours ?
    KAT. A page's, fool !
    BLA. I'm accounted no great scholar,
But 'tis a page that I would fain peruse
A little closer.   [*Approaches her.*
    KAT. Put on your spectacles,
And try if you can read it at this
    distance,
For you shall come no nearer.
    BLA. But is there nothing, then, save
    rank imposture,
In all these tales of goblinry at Devor-
    goil ?
    KAT. My aunt's grave lord thinks
    otherwise, supposing
That his great name so interests the
    Heavens,
That miracles must needs bespeak its
    fall.
I would that I were in a lowly cottage
Beneath the greenwood, on its walls no
    armour
To court the levin-bolt——
    BLA. And a kind husband, Katleen,
To ward such dangers as must needs
    come nigh.
My father's cottage stands so low and
    lone,
That you would think it solitude itself ;
The greenwood shields it from the
    northern blast,
And, in the woodbine round its latticed
    casement,
The linnet 's sure to build the earliest
    nest
In all the forest.
    KAT.   Peace, you fool, they come.

FLORA *lights* GULLCRAMMER *across
the Stage.*

KAT. (*when they have passed*). Away
  with you !
On with your cloak—be ready at the
  signal.
  BLA. And shall we talk of that same
    cottage, Katleen,
At better leisure ? I have much to say
In favour of my cottage.
  KAT.   If you will be talking,
You know I can't prevent you.
  BLA.   That's enough.
(*Aside.*) I shall have leave, I see, to
  spell the page
A little closer, when the due time comes.

SCENE II.

Scene changes to GULLCRAMMER'S *Sleeping
Apartment. He enters, ushered in by*
FLORA, *who sets on the table a flask, with
the lamp.*

  FLO. A flask, in case your reverence
    be athirsty ;
A light, in case your reverence be
  afear'd—
And so sweet slumber to your reverence.
  GUL. Kind Mistress Flora, will you?
    eh? eh? eh?
  FLO. Will I what?
  GUL. Tarry a little?
  FLO. (*smiling*). Kind Master Gull-
    crammer,
How can you ask me aught so unbe-
  coming?
  GUL. Oh, fie, fie, fie ! Believe me,
    Mistress Flora,
'T is not for that ; but being guided
  through
Such dreary galleries, stairs, and suites
  of rooms,
To this same cubicle, I'm somewhat
  loth
To bid adieu to pleasant company.
  FLO. A flattering compliment ! In
    plain truth you are frighten'd.
  GUL. What, frighten'd ? I—I—am
    not timorous.
  FLO. Perhaps you've heard this is
    our haunted chamber?

But then it is our best. Your reverence
  knows,
That in all tales which turn upon a
  ghost,
Your traveller belated has the luck
To enjoy the haunted room—it is a
  rule.
To some it were a hardship, but to
  you
Who are a scholar, and not timo
  rous——
  GUL. I did not say I was not timo-
    rous,
I said I was not temerarious.
I'll to the hall again.
  FLO.   You'll do your pleasure.
But you have somehow moved my
  father's anger,
And you had better meet our playful
  Owlspiegle—
So is our goblin call'd—then face Lord
  Oswald.
  GUL.   Owlspiegle?
It is an uncouth and outlandish name,
And in mine ear sounds fiendish.
  FLO. Hush, hush, hush !
Perhaps he hears us now. (*In an
  undertone*). A merry spirit ;
None of your elves that pinch folks
    black and blue,
For lack of cleanliness.
  GUL.   As for that, Mistress Flora,
My taffeta doublet hath been duly
  brush'd,
My shirt hebdomadal put on this
  morning.
  FLO. Why, you need fear no goblins.
    But this Owlspiegle
Is of another class, yet has his frolics :
Cuts hair, trims beards, and plays amid
  his antics
The office of a sinful mortal barber.
Such is, at least, the rumour.
  GUL. He will not cut my clothes?
    or scar my face?
Or draw my blood?
  FLO.   Enormities like these
Were never charged against him.
  GUL. And, Mistress Flora, would you
    smile on me,

If, prick'd by the fond hope of your
　　approval,
I should endure this venture?
　　Flo.　　　　　　I do hope
I shall have cause to smile.
　　Gul.　　　Well! in that hope
I will embrace the achievement for thy
　　sake.　　　　　　[*She is going.*
Yet stay, stay, stay! — on second
　　thoughts I will not—
I 've thought on it, and will the mortal
　　cudgel
Rather endure than face the ghostly
　　razor!
Your crab-tree's tough but blunt,—
　　your razor's polish'd,
But, as the proverb goes, 't is cruel
　　sharp;
I 'll to thy father, and unto his pleasure
Submit these destined shoulders.
　　Flo.　　　　　But you shall not,
Believe me, sir, you shall not; he is
　　desperate,
And better far be trimm'd by ghost or
　　goblin
Than by my sire in anger; there are
　　stores
Of hidden treasure, too, and Heaven
　　knows what,
Buried among these ruins—you shall
　　stay.
(*Apart*). And if indeed there be such
　　sprite as Owlspiegle,
And, lacking him, that thy fear plague
　　thee not
Worse than a goblin, I have miss'd my
　　purpose,
Which else stands good in either case.
　　—Good night, sir!
　　　　[*Exit, and double-locks the door.*
Gul. Nay, hold ye, hold!—Nay, gentle
　　Mistress Flora,
Wherefore this ceremony?—She has
　　lock'd me in,
And left me to the goblin!—(*Listen-
　　ing*).—So, so, so!
I hear her light foot trip to such a dis-
　　tance,
That I believe the castle's breadth
　　divides me

From human company. I 'm ill at
　　ease—
But if this citadel (*laying his hand on
　　his stomach*) were better victual'd,
It would be better mann'd.
　　　　　　　　　[*Sits down and drinks.*
She has a footstep light and taper
　　ankle.　　　　　　[*Chuckles.*
Aha! that ankle! yet, confound it too.
But for those charms Melchisedek had
　　been
Snug in his bed at Mucklewhame—.
　　say,
Confound her footstep, and her instep
　　too,
To use a cobbler's phrase.—There I
　　was quaint.
Now, what to do in this vile circum-
　　stance,
To watch or go to bed, I can't de-
　　termine;
Were I abed, the ghost might catch
　　me napping,
And if I watch, my terrors will increase
As ghostly hours approach. I 'll to my
　　bed
E'en in my taffeta doublet, shrink my
　　head
Beneath the clothes—leave the lamp
　　burning there, [*Sets it on the table.*
And trust to fate the issue.
　　　　[*He lays aside his cloak and
　　　　brushes it, as from habit, start-
　　　　ing at every moment; ties a
　　　　napkin over his head; then
　　　　shrinks beneath the bed-clothes.
　　　　He starts once or twice, and
　　　　at length seems to go to sleep.
　　　　A bell tolls* ONE. *He leaps up
　　　　in his bed.*
　　Gul. I had just coax'd myself to
　　sweet forgetfulness,
And that confounded bell—I hate all
　　bells,
Except a dinner bell—and yet I lie,
　　too—
I love the bell that soon shall tell the
　　parish
Of Gabblegoose, Melchisedek's in-
　　cumbent.

And shall the future minister of Gabble-
goose,
Whom his parishioners will soon re-
quire
To exorcise their ghosts, detect their
witches,
Lie shivering in his bed for a pert
goblin,
Whom, be he switch'd or cocktail'd,
horn'd or poll'd,
A few tight Hebrew words will soon
send packing?
Tush! I will rouse the parson up with-
in me,
And bid defiance——(*A distant noise.*)
In the name of Heaven,
What sounds are these? Oh, Lord!
this comes of rashness!
[*Draws his head down under the
bed-clothes.*

Duet without, between OWLSPIEGLE
and COCKLEDEMOY.

OWLSPIEGLE.
Cockledemoy!
My boy, my boy—

COCKLEDEMOY.
Here, father, here.

OWLSPIEGLE.
Now the pole-star's red and burning,
And the witch's spindle turning,
Appear, appear!

GUL. (*who has again raised himself,
and listened with great terror to
the duet*). I have heard of the
devil's dam before,
But never of his child. Now, Heaven
deliver me! [there;
The Papists have the better of us
They have their Latin prayers, cut and
dried, [think
And pat for such occasion—I can
On nought but the vernacular.

OWLSPIEGLE.
Cockledemoy!
My boy, my boy,
We'll sport us here—

COCKLEDEMOY.
Our gambols play,
Like elve and fay;

OWLSPIEGLE.
And domineer,

BOTH.
Laugh, frolic, and frisk, till the morning
appear.

COCKLEDEMOY.
Lift latch—open clasp—
Shoot bolt—and burst hasp!
[*The door opens with violence.*

Enter BLACKTHORN *as* OWSPIEGLE,
*fantastically dressed as a Spanish
Barber, tall, thin, emaciated, and
ghostly;* KATLEEN, *as* COCKLEDE-
MOY, *attends as his Page. All their
manners, tones, and actions are fantastic, as those of Goblins. They
make two or three times the circuit
of the room, without seeming to see*
GULLCRAMMER. *They then resume
their Chant or Recitative.*

OWLSPIEGLE.
Cockledemoy!
My boy, my boy,
What wilt thou do that will give thee
joy?
Wilt thou ride on the midnight owl?

COCKLEDEMOY.
No; for the weather is stormy and foul.

OWLSPIEGLE.
Cockledemoy!
My boy, my boy,
What wilt thou do that can give thee
joy?
With a needle for a sword, and a thimble
for a hat,
Wilt thou fight a traverse with the
castle cat?

COCKLEDEMOY.
Oh, no! she has claws, and I like not
that.

GUL. I see the devil is a doting
father,

And spoils his children—'t is the surest
    way
To make cursed imps of them. They
    see me not;
What will they think on next? It must
    be own'd   [tions.
They have a dainty choice of occupa-

OWLSPIEGLE.
    Cockledemoy!
    My boy, my boy,
What shall we do that can give thee
    joy?
Shall we go seek for a cuckoo's nest?

COCKLEDEMOY.
    That's best, that's best!

BOTH.
    About, about
    Like an elvish scout,
The cuckoo's a gull, and we'll soon
    find him out.

*[They search the room with mops
and mows. At length* COCK-
LEDEMOY *jumps on the bed.*
GULLCRAMMER *raises himself
half up, supporting himself by
his hands.* COCKLEDEMOY
*does the same and grins at him,
then skips from the bed and
runs to* OWLSPIEGLE.

COCKLEDEMOY.
    I've found the nest,
    And in it a guest,
With a sable cloak and a taffeta vest;
He must be wash'd, and trimm'd, and
    dress'd,
To please the eyes he loves the best.

OWLSPIEGLE.
    That's best, that's best!

BOTH.
He must be shaved, and trimm'd, and
    dress'd,
To please the eyes he loves the best.

*[They arrange shaving things
on the table, and sing as they
prepare them.*

BOTH.
Know that all of the humbug, the bite,
    and the buz,
Of the make-believe world, becomes
    forfeit to us.

OWLSPIEGLE (*sharpening his razor*).
The sword this is made of was lost in a
    fray
By a fop, who first bullied and then
    ran away;
And the strap from the hide of a lame
    racer, sold
By Lord Match to his friend, for some
    hundreds in gold.

BOTH.
For all of the humbug, the bite, and
    the buz,
Of the make-believe world, becomes
    forfeit to us.

COCKLEDEMOY (*placing the napkin*).
And this cambric napkin, so white and
    so fair,
At an usurer's funeral I stole from the
    heir.
    *[Drops something from a vial,
    as going to make suds.*
This dewdrop I caught from one eye of
    his mother,
Which wept while she ogled the parson
    with t'other.

BOTH.
For all of the humbug, the bite, and
    the buz,
Of the make-believe world, becomes
    forfeit to us.

OWLSPIEGLE (*arranging the lather and
the basin*).
My soap-ball is of the mild alkali made,
Which the soft dedicator employs in
    his trade;
And it froths with the pith of a promise
    that's sworn   [morn.
By a lover at night, and forgot on the

BOTH.
For all of the humbug, the bite, and
    the buz,
Of the make-believe world, becomes
    forfeit to us.

Halloo, halloo,
  The blackcock crew,
Thrice shriek'd hath the owl, thrice
  croak'd hath the raven,
Here, ho! Master Gullcrammer, rise
  and be shaven!
      Da capo.

GUL. (*who has been observing them*).
  I 'll pluck a spirit up; they're merry
    goblins,
And will deal mildly. I will soothe
  their humour;
Besides, my beard lacks trimming.
    [*He rises from his bed, and ad-
      vances with great symptoms
      of trepidation, but affecting an
      air of composure. The Gob-
      lins receive him with fantastic
      ceremony.*

Gentlemen, 't is your will I should be
  trimm'd—
E'en do your pleasure.
    [*They point to a seat; he sits.*
        Think, howsoe'er,
Of me as one who hates to see his
  blood;
Therefore I do beseech you, signior,
Be gentle in your craft. I know those
  barbers,
One would have harrows driven across
  his visnomy,
Rather than they should touch it with
  a razor.

OWLSPIEGLE *shaves* GULLCRAMMER,
  while COCKLEDEMOY *sings*—
Father never started hair,
Shaved too close, or left too bare—
Father's razor slips as glib
As from courtly tongue a fib.
Whiskers, mustache, he can trim in
Fashion meet to please the women;
Sharp's his blade, perfumed his lather;
Happy those are trimm'd by father!

GUL. That's a good boy. I love to
  hear a child
Stand for his father, if he were the
  devil. [*He motions to rise.*

Craving your pardon, sir.—What! sit
  again?
My hair lacks not your scissors.
    [OWLSPIEGLE *insists on his sitting.*
Nay, if you 're peremptory, I 'll ne'er
  dispute it,
Nor eat the cow and choke upon the
  tail—
E'en trim me to your fashion.
    [OWLSPIEGLE *cuts his hair, and
      shaves his head, ridiculously.*

COCKLEDEMOY (*sings as before*)—
Hair-breadth 'scapes, and hair-breadth
  snares,
Hair-brain'd follies, ventures, cares,
Part when father clips your hairs.
If there is a hero frantic,
Or a lover too romantic;
If threescore seeks second spouse,
Or fourteen lists lover's vows,
Bring them here—for a Scotch boddle,
Owlspiegle shall trim their noddle.

    [*They take the napkin from about
      GULLCRAMMER'S neck. He
      makes bows of acknowledg-
      ment, which they return fan-
      tastically, and sing*—

Thrice crow'd hath the blackcock,
  thrice croak'd hath the raven,
And Master Melchisedek Gullcrammer 's shaven!

GUL. My friends, you are too musical for me;
But though I cannot cope with you in
  song,
I would, in humble prose, inquire of
  you,
If that you will permit me to ac-
  quit
Even with the barber's pence the barber's service?
    [*They shake their heads.*
Or if there is aught else that I can do
  for you,
Sweet Master Owlspiegle, or your
  loving child,
The hopeful Cockle'moy?

COCKLEDEMOY.

Sir, you have been trimm'd of late,
Smooth's your chin, and bald your
    pate ;
Lest cold rheums should work you
    harm,
Here's a cap to keep you warm.

GUL. Welcome, as Fortunatus' wish-
    ing cap,
For 't was a cap that I was wishing for.
(There I was quaint in spite of mortal
    terror.)
    [*As he puts on the cap, a pair of
    ass's ears disengage themselves.*
Upon my faith, it is a dainty head-dress,
And might become an alderman !—
Thanks, sweet monsieur,
Thou 'rt a considerate youth.
    [*Both Goblins bow with cere-
    mony to* GULLCRAMMER,
    who returns their salutation.
    OWLSPIEGLE *descends by the
    trap-door.* COCKLEDEMOY
    springs out at window.

SONG (*without*).
OWLSPIEGLE.

Cockledemoy, my hope, my care,
Where art thou now, O tell me where ?

COCKLEDEMOY.

    Up in the sky,
On the bonny dragonfly,
Come, father, come you too—
She has four wings and strength enow,
And her long body has room for two.

GUL. Cockledemoy now is a naughty
    brat—
Would have the poor old stiff-rump'd
    devil, his father
Peril his fiendish neck.   All boys are
    thoughtless.

SONG.
OWLSPIEGLE.
Which way didst thou take ?

COCKLEDEMOY.

I have fall'n in the lake—
Help, father, for Beëlzebub's sake.

GUL. The imp is drown'd—a strange
    death for a devil,—
Oh, may all boys take warning and be
    civil ;
Respect their loving sires, endure a
    chiding,
Nor roam by night on dragonflies a-
    riding !

COCKLEDEMOY (*sings*).
Now merrily, merrily, row I to
    shore,
My bark is a bean-shell, a straw
    for an oar.

OWLSPIEGLE (*sings*).
    My life, my joy,
    My Cockledemoy !

GUL. I can bear this no longer—thus
    children are spoil'd.
    [*Strikes into the tune.*
Master Owlspiegle, hoy !
He deserves to be whipp'd little Cockle-
    demoy !
    [*Their voices are heard as if
    dying away.*
GUL. They 're gone !—Now, am I
    scared, or am I not ?
I think the very desperate ecstasy
Of fear has given me courage.   This is
    strange, now.
When they were here, I was not half
    so frighten'd
As now they 're gone—they were a sort
    of company.
What a strange thing is use !   A horn,
    a claw,
The tip of a fiend's tail, was wont to
    scare me.
Now am I with the devil hand and
    glove ;
His soap hath lather'd and his razor
    shaved me ;
I 've joined him in a catch, kept time
    and tune,
Could dine with him, nor ask for a long
    spoon ;
And if I keep not better company,
What will become of me when I shall
    die?   [*Exit.*

SCENE III.

A Gothic Hall, waste and ruinous. The moonlight is at times seen through the shafted windows. Enter KATLEEN *and* BLACKTHORN. *They have thrown off the more ludicrous parts of their disguise.*

KAT. This way—this way; was ever fool so gull'd !

BLA. I played the barber better than I thought for.
Well, I 've an occupation in reserve,
When the long-bow and merry musket fail me.—
But, hark ye, pretty Katleen.

KAT. What should I hearken to ?

BLA. Art thou not afraid,
In these wild halls while playing feigned goblins,
That we may meet with real ones ?

KAT. Not a jot
My spirit is too light, my heart too bold,
To fear a visit from the other world.

BLA. But is not this the place, the very hall
In which men say that Oswald's grandfather,
The Black Lord Erick, walks his penance round ?
Credit me, Katleen, these half-moulder'd columns
Have in their ruin something very fiendish,
And, if you 'll take an honest friend's advice,
The sooner that you change their shatter'd splendour
For the snug cottage that I told you of,
Believe me, it will prove the blither dwelling.

KAT. If I e'er see that cottage, honest Blackthorn, [tive
Believe me, it shall be from other mo-
Than fear of Erick's spectre.
   [*A rustling sound is heard.*

BLA.   I heard a rustling sound—
Upon my life, there 's something in the hall,
Katleen, besides us two !

KAT.   A yeoman thou,
A forester, and frightened ! I am sorry
I gave the fool's-cap to poor Gull-crammer,
And let thy head go bare.
  [*The same rushing sound is repeated.*

BLA. Why, are you mad, or hear you not the sound ?

KAT. And if I do, I take small heed of it.
Will you allow a maiden to be bolder
Than you, with beard on chin and sword at girdle ?

BLA. Nay, if I had my sword, I would not care ;
Though I ne'er heard of master of defence
So active at his weapon as to brave
The devil, or a ghost—See ! see ! see yonder.
  [*A Figure is imperfectly seen between two of the pillars.*

KAT. There 's something moves, that 's certain, and the moonlight,
Chased by the flitting gale, is too imperfect
To show its form ; but, in the name of God,
I 'll venture on it boldly.

BLA.   Wilt thou so ?
Were I alone, now, I were strongly tempted
To trust my heels for safety ; but with thee,
Be it fiend or fairy, I 'll take risk to meet it.

KAT. It stands full in our path, and we must pass it,
Or tarry here all night.

BLA.   In its vile company ?
  [*As they advance towards the Figure, it is more plainly distinguished, which might, I think, be contrived by raising successive screens of crape. The Figure is wrapped in a long robe, like the mantle of a Hermit or Palmer.*

PAL. Ho ! ye who thread by night these wildering scenes,

In garb of those who long have slept
   in death,
Fear ye the company of those you
   imitate?
BLA. This is the devil, Katleen, let
   us fly!   [*Runs off.*
KAT. I will not fly—why should I?
   My nerves shake
To look on this strange vision, but my
   heart
Partakes not the alarm.—If thou dost
   come in Heaven's name,
In Heaven's name art thou welcome!
   PAL. I come, by Heaven permitted.
   Quit this castle:
There is a fate on 't—if for good or evil,
Brief space shall soon determine. In
   that fate,
If good, by lineage thou canst nothing
   claim;
If evil, much mayest suffer.—Leave
   these precincts.
   KAT. Whate'er thou art, be answer'd.
   Know, I will not
Desert the kinswoman who train'd my
   youth;
Know, that I will not quit my friend,
   my Flora;
Know, that I will not leave the aged
   man
Whose roof has shelter'd me. This is
   my resolve—
If evil come, I aid my friends to bear it;
If good, my part shall be to see them
   prosper,
A portion in their happiness from which
No fiend can bar me.
   PAL.   Maid, before thy courage,
Firm built on innocence, even beings
   of nature
More powerful far than thine, give
   place and way;
Take then this key, and wait the event
   with courage.
   [*He drops the key. He disap-*
    pears gradually—the moon-
    light failing at the same time.
   KAT. (*after a pause*). Whate'er it
   was, 'tis gone! My head turns
   round—

The blood that lately fortified my heart
Now eddies in full torrent to my brain,
And makes wild work with reason. I
   will haste,
If that my steps can bear me so far safe,
To living company. What if I meet it
Again in the long aisle, or vaulted
   passage?
And if I do, the strong support that
   bore me
Through this appalling interview, again
Shall strengthen and uphold me.
   [*As she steps forward she*
    stumbles over the key.
What's this? The key! there may be
   mystery in 't.
I'll to my kinswoman, when this dizzy
   fit
Will give me leave to choose my way
   aright. [*She sits down exhausted.*

Re-enter BLACKTHORN, *with a drawn*
    sword and torch.

   BLA. Katleen! What, Katleen!
   What a wretch was I
To leave her! Katleen, I am weapon'd
   now,
And fear nor dog nor devil. She re-
   plies not!
Beast that I was—nay, worse than
   beast; the stag,
As timorous as he is, fights for his hind.
What's to be done? I'll search this
   cursed castle
From dungeon to the battlements; if
   I find her not,
I'll fling me from the highest pinna-
   cle——
   KATLEEN (*who has somewhat ga-*
    thered her spirits, in consequence
    of his entrance, comes behind and
    touches him; he starts). Brave sir,
I'll spare you that rash leap. You're
   a bold woodsman!
Surely I hope that from this night
   henceforward
You'll never kill a hare, since you're
   akin to them—
Oh, I could laugh, but that my head's
   so dizzy.

BLA. Lean on me, Katleen. By my
honest word,
I thought you close behind. I was
surprised,
Not a jot frighten'd.

KAT. Thou art a fool to ask me to
thy cottage,
And then to show me at what slight
expense
Of manhood I might master thee and it.

BLA. I 'll take the risk of that. This
goblin business
Came rather unexpected: the best horse
Will start at sudden sights. Try me
again,
And if I prove not true to bonny Katleen,
Hang me in mine own bowstring.
[*Exeunt.*

SCENE IV.

*The Scene returns to the Apartment at the
beginning of Act Second.* OSWALD *and*
DURWARD *are discovered with* ELEANOR,
FLORA, *and* LEONARD. DURWARD
*shuts a prayer-book, which he seems to
have been reading.*

DUR. 'T is true—the difference be-
twixt the churches,
Which zealots love to dwell on, to the
wise
Of either flock are of far less importance
Than those great truths to which all
Christian men
Subscribe with equal reverence.

OSW. We thank thee, father, for the
holy office,
Still best performed when the pastor's
tongue
Is echo to his breast; of jarring creeds
It ill beseems a layman's tongue to
speak.—
Where have you stow'd yon prater?
[*To* FLORA.

FLO. Safe in the goblin chamber.

ELE. The goblin chamber!
Maiden, wert thou frantic?—if his
Reverence
Have suffer'd harm by waspish Owl-
spiegle,
Be sure thou shalt abye it.

FLO. Here he comes,
Can answer for himself!

Enter GULLCRAMMER, *in the fashion
in which* OWLSPIEGLE *had put him:
having the fool's-cap on his head, and
towel about his neck, &c. His manner through the scene is wild and
extravagant, as if the fright had a
little affected his brain.*

DUR. A goodly spectacle!—Is there
such a goblin,
(*To* OSW.) Or has sheer terror made
him such a figure?

OSW. There is a sort of wavering
tradition
Of a malicious imp who teased all
strangers;
My father wont to call him Owlspiegle.

GUL. Who talks of Owlspiegle?
He is an honest fellow for a devil,
So is his son, the hopeful Cockle'moy.

(*Sings.*)
"My hope, my joy,
My Cockledemoy!"

LEO. The fool's bewitch'd—the goblin hath furnish'd him
A cap which well befits his reverend
wisdom.

FLO. If I could think he had lost his
slender wits,
I should be sorry for the trick they
play'd him.

LEO. O, fear him not; it were a foul
reflection
On any fiend of sense and reputation,
To filch such petty wares as his poor
brains.

DUR. What saw'st thou, sir? What
heard'st thou?

GUL. What was't I saw and heard?
That which old greybeards,
Who conjure Hebrew into Anglo-
Saxon,
To cheat starved barons with, can little
guess at.

FLO. If he begin so roundly with my
father,

His madness is not like to save his
   bones.

GUL. Sirs, midnight came, and with
   it came the goblin.
I had reposed me after some brief
   study;
But as the soldier, sleeping in the
   trench,
Keeps sword and musket by him, so I
   had
My little Hebrew manual prompt for
   service.

FLO. *Sausagian sous'd-face;* that
   much of your Hebrew
Even I can bear in memory.

GUL.   We counter'd,
The goblin and myself, even in mid-
   chamber,
And each stepp'd back a pace, as 'twere
   to study
The foe he had to deal with!—I be-
   thought me,
Ghosts ne'er have the first word, and
   so I took it,   [him.
And fired a volley of round Greek at
He stood his ground, and answer'd in
   the Syriac;
I flank'd my Greek with Hebrew, and
   compell'd him—   [*A noise heard.*

OSW. Peace, idle prater!—Hark—
   what sounds are these?
Amid the growling of the storm without,
I hear strange notes of music, and the
   clash
Of coursers' trampling feet.

VOICES (*without*).

We come, dark riders of the night,
And flit before the dawning light;
Hill and valley, far aloof,
Shake to hear our chargers' hoof;
But not a foot-stamp on the green
At morn shall show where we have
   been.

OSW. These must be revellers be-
   lated—   [Devorgoil
Let them pass on; the ruin'd halls of
Open to no such guests.—
    [*Flourish of trumpets at a dis-
    tance, then nearer*

They sound a summons;
What can they lack at this dead hour
   of night?
Look out, and see their number, and
   their bearing.

LEO. (*goes up to the window*). 'T is
   strange—one single shadowy form
   alone
Is hovering on the drawbridge—far
   apart
Flit through the tempest banners,
   horse, and riders,
In darkness lost, or dimly seen by
   lightning.—
Hither the figure moves—the bolts revolve—
The gate uncloses to him.

ELE.   Heaven protect us!

The PALMER *enters—*GULLCRAMMER
    runs off.

OSW. Whence and what art thou?
   for what end come hither?

PAL. I come from a far land, where
   the storm howls not,
And the sun sets not, to pronounce to
   thee,
Oswald of Devorgoil, thy house's fate.

DUR. I charge thee, in the name we
   late have kneel'd to——

PAL. Abbot of Lanercost, I bid thee
   peace;
Uninterrupted let me do mine errand:
Baron of Devorgoil, son of the bold, the
   proud,
The warlike and the mighty, wherefore
   wear'st thou
The habit of a peasant? Tell me,
   wherefore
Are thy fair halls thus waste—thy
   chambers bare—
Where are the tapestries, where the
   conquer'd banners,
Trophies, and gilded arms, that deck'd
   the walls
Of once proud Devorgoil?
    [*He advances, and places himself
    where the armour hung, so
    as to be nearly in the centre of
    the scene.*

Dur. Whoe'er thou art, if thou dost
know so much,
Needs must thou know——
  Osw. Peace! I will answer here—
to me he spoke.
Mysterious stranger, briefly I reply:
A peasant's dress befits a peasant's
fortune;
And 't were vain mockery to array these
walls
In trophies, of whose memory nought
remains,
Save that the cruelty outvied the valour
Of those who wore them.
  Pal.   Degenerate as thou art,
Knowst thou to whom thou say'st this?
  [*He drops his mantle, and is
discovered armed as nearly as
may be to the suit which hung
on the wall; all express terror.*
  Osw. It is himself—the spirit of
mine ancestor!
  Eri. Tremble not, son, but hear me.
  [*He strikes the wall; it opens,
and discovers the Treasure-
Chamber.*

             There lies piled
The wealth I brought from wasted
Cumberland,
Enough to reinstate thy ruin'd for-
tunes,
Cast from thine high-born brows that
peasant bonnet,
Throw from thy noble grasp the pea-
sant's staff;
O'er all, withdraw thine hand from
that mean mate,
Whom in an hour of reckless despera-
tion
Thy fortunes cast thee on. This do
And be as great as ere was Devorgoil,
When Devorgoil was richest!
  Dur. Lord Oswald, thou are tempted
by a fiend,
Who doth assail thee on thy weakest
side——
Thy pride of lineage, and thy love of
grandeur;
Stand fast—resist—contemn his fatal
offers.

  Ele. Urge him not, father; if the
sacrifice
Of such a wasted woe-worn wretch as
I am,
Can save him from the abyss of
misery,
Upon whose verge he's tottering, let
me wander
An unacknowledged outcast from his
castle,
Even to the humble cottage I was born
in.
  Osw. No, Ellen, no! It is not thus
they part,
Whose hearts and souls, disasters borne
in common
Have knit together, close as summer
saplings
Are twined in union by the eddying
tempest.
Spirit of Erick, while thou bear'st his
shape,
I'll answer with no ruder conjuration
Thy impious counsel, other than with
these words,
Depart, and tempt me not!
  Eri. Then fate will have her course.
Fall, massive grate,
Yield them the tempting view of these
rich treasures,
But bar them from possession!
  [*A portcullis falls before the door
of the Treasure-Chamber.*
             Mortals, hear!
No hand may ope that grate, except the
Heir
Of plunder'd Aglionby, whose mighty
wealth,
Ravish'd in evil hour, lies yonder piled;
And not his hand prevails without the
key
Of Black Lord Eric; brief space is
given
To save proud Devorgoil.—So wills
high Heaven.
      [*Thunder; he disappears.*
  Dur. Gaze not so wildly; you have
stood the trial
That his commission bore, and Heaven
designs,

If I may spell his will, to rescue De-
vorgoil
Even by the Heir of Aglionby. Behold
him
In that young forester, unto whose hand
Those bars shall yield the treasures of
his house,
Destined to ransom yours.—Advance,
young Leonard,
And prove the adventure.

LEO. (*advances and attempts the
grate*).   It is fast
As is the tower, rock-seated.

OSW. We will fetch other means, and
prove its strength,
Nor starve in poverty with wealth before
us.

DUR. Think what the vision spoke ;
The key—the fated key—

Enter GULLCRAMMER.

GUL. A key?—I say a quay is what
we want,
Thus by the learn'd orthographized—
Q, u, a, y.
The lake is overflow'd !—A quay, a boat,
Oars, punt, or sculler, is all one to me !—
We shall be drown'd, good people ! ! !

Enter KATLEEN *and* BLACKTHORN.

KAT.   Deliver us !
Haste, save yourselves—the lake is
rising fast.

BLA. 'T has risen my bow's height
in the last five minutes,
And still is swelling strangely.

GUL. (*who has stood astonished upon
seeing them*). We shall be drown'd
without your kind assistance.
Sweet Master Owlspiegle, your dragonfly—
Your straw, your bean-stalk, gentle
Cockle'moy !

LEO. (*looking from the shot-hole*).
'T is true, by all that 's fearful ! The
proud lake   [bounds,
Peers, like ambitious tyrant, o'er his
And soon will whelm the castle—even
the drawbridge
Is under water now.

KAT. Let us escape ! Why stand you
gazing there ?

DUR. Upon the opening of that fatal
grate
Depends the fearful spell that now en-
traps us,
The key of Black Lord Erick—ere we
find it,
The castle will be whelm'd beneath the
waves,
And we shall perish in it !

KAT. (*giving the key*). Here, prove
this ;
A chance most strange and fearful gave
it me.

[OSW. *puts it into the lock, and
attempts to turn it—a loud
clap of thunder.*

FLO. The lake still rises faster.—
Leonard, Leonard,
Canst thou not save us ?

[LEONARD *tries the lock—it opens
with a violent noise, and the
portcullis rises. A loud strain
of wild music.—There may be
a Chorus here.*

[OSWALD *enters the apartment,
and brings out a scroll.*

LEO. The lake is ebbing with as
wondrous haste
As late it rose—the drawbridge is left
dry !

OSW. This may explain the cause.—
(GULLCRAMMER *offers to take it.*) But
soft you, sir,
We 'll not disturb your learning for the
matter ;
Yet, since you 've borne a part in this
strange drama,
You shall not go unguerdon'd. Wise
or learn'd,
Modest or gentle, Heaven alone can
make thee,
Being so much otherwise ; but from
this abundance
Thou shalt have that shall gild thine
ignorance,
Exalt thy base descent, make thy presumption

Seem modest confidence, and find thee
hundreds
Ready to swear that same fool's-cap of
thine
Is reverend as a mitre.

GUL. Thanks, mighty baron, now no
more a bare one!—   [*Aside.*
I will be quaint with him, for all quips.

OSW. Nor shall kind Katleen lack
Her portion in our happiness.

KAT. Thanks, my good lord, but
Katleen's fate is fix'd.
There is a certain valiant forester,
Too much afear'd of ghosts to sleep
anights
In his lone cottage, without one to guard
him.—

LEO. If I forget my comrade's faithful friendship,
May I be lost to fortune, hope, and
love!

DUR. Peace, all! and hear the blessing which this scroll
Speaks unto faith, and constancy, and
virtue.

No more this castle's troubled guest,
Dark Erick's spirit hath found rest.
The storms of angry Fate are past—
For Constancy defies their blast.
Of Devorgoil the daughter free
Shall wed the Heir of Aglionby ·
Nor ever more dishonour soil
The rescued house of Devorgoil!

AUCHINDRANE; OR, THE AYRSHIRE TRAGEDY.

Cur aliquid vidi? cur noxia lumina feci?
Cur imprudenti cognitæ culpa mihi est?
Ovidii Tristium, Liber Secundus.

PREFACE.

There is not, perhaps, upon record, a tale of horror which gives us a more perfect picture than is afforded by the present, of the violence of our ancestors, or the complicated crimes into which they were hurried, by what their wise, but ill-enforced, laws termed the heathenish and accursed practice of Deadly Feud. The author has tried to extract some dramatic scenes out of it; but he is conscious no exertions of his can increase the horror of that which is in itself so iniquitous. Yet, if we look at modern events, we must not too hastily venture to conclude that our own times have so much the superiority over former days as we might at first be tempted to infer. One great object has indeed been obtained: the power of the laws extends over the country universally, and if criminals at present sometimes escape punishment, this can only be by eluding justice,—not, as of old by defying it.

But the motives which influence modern ruffians to commit actions at which we pause with wonder and horror, arise, in a great measure, from the thirst of gain. For the hope of lucre, we have seen a wretch seduced to his fate, under the pretext that he was to share in amusement and conviviality; and, for gold, we have seen the meanest of wretches deprived of life, and their miserable remains cheated of the grave.

The loftier if equally cruel, feelings of pride, ambition, and love of vengeance, were the idols of our forefathers, while the caitiffs of our day bend to Mammon, the meanest of the spirits who fell. The criminals, therefore, of former times, drew their hellish inspiration from a loftier source than is known to modern villains. The fever of unsated ambition, the frenzy of ungratified revenge, the *perfervidum ingenium Scotorum*, stigmatized by our jurists and our legislators, held life but as passing breath; and such enormities as now sound like the acts of a madman, were then the familiar deeds of every offended noble. With these observations we proceed to our story.

John Muir, or Mure, of Auchindrane, the contriver and executer of the following cruelties, was a gentleman of an ancient family and good estate in the west of Scotland; bold, ambitious, treacherous to the last degree, and utterly unconscientious,—a Richard the Third in private life, inaccessible alike to pity and to remorse. His view was to raise the power and extend the grandeur of his own family. This gentleman had married the daughter of Sir Thomas Kennedy of Barganie, who was, excepting the Earl of Cassilis, the most important person in all Carrick, the district of Ayrshire which he inhabited, and where the name of Kennedy held so great a sway as to give rise to the popular rhyme,—

> " 'Twixt Wigton and the town of Air,
> Portpatrick and the Cruives of Cree,
> No man need think for to bide there,
> Unless he court Saint Kennedie."

Now, Mure of Auchindrane, who had promised himself high advancement by means of his father-in-law, Barganie, saw, with envy and resentment, that his influence remained second and inferior to the house of Cassilis, chief of all the Kennedys. The Earl was indeed a minor, but his authority was maintained, and his affairs well managed by his uncle, Sir Thomas Kennedy of Cullayne, the brother of the deceased Earl, and tutor and guardian to the present. This worthy gentleman supported his nephew's dignity and the credit of the house so effectually, that Barganie's consequence was much thrown into the shade, and the ambitious Auchindrane, his son-in-law, saw no better remedy than to remove so formidable a rival as Cullayne by violent means.

For this purpose, in the year of God 1597, he came with a party of followers to the town of Maybole (where Sir Thomas Kennedy of Cullayne then resided), and lay in ambush in an orchard, through which he knew his destined victim was to pass, in returning homewards from a house where he was engaged to sup. Sir Thomas Kennedy came alone and unattended, when he was suddenly fired upon by Auchindrane and his accomplices, who, having missed their aim, drew their swords, and rushed upon him to slay him. But the party thus assailed at disadvantage had the good fortune to hide himself for that time in a ruinous house, where he lay concealed till the inhabitants of the place came to his assistance.

Sir Thomas Kennedy prosecuted Mure for this assault, who, finding himself in danger from the law, made a sort of apology and agreement with the Lord of Cullayne, to whose daughter he united his eldest son, in testimony of the closest friendship in future. This agreement was sincere on the part of Kennedy, who, after it had been entered into, showed himself Auchindrane's friend and assistant on all occasions. But it was most false and treacherous on that of Mure, who continued to nourish the purpose of murdering his new friend and ally on the first opportunity.

Auchindrane's first attempt to effect this was by means of the young Gilbert Kennedy of Barganie (for old Barganie, Auchindrane's father-in-law, was dead), whom he persuaded to brave the Earl of Cassilis, as one who usurped an undue influence over the rest of the name. Accordingly, this hotheaded youth, at the instigation of Auchindrane, rode past the gate of the Earl of Cassilis, without waiting on his chief, or sending him any message of civility. This led to mutual defiance, being regarded by the Earl, according to the ideas of the time, as a personal insult. Both parties took the field with their followers, at the head of about 250 men on each side. The action which ensued was shorter and less bloody than might have been expected. Young Barganie, with the rashness of headlong courage, and Auchindrane, fired by deadly enmity to the house of Cassilis, made a precipitate attack on the Earl, whose men were strongly posted and under cover. They were received by a heavy fire. Barganie was slain. Mure of Auchindrane, severely wounded in the thigh, became unable to sit his horse, and, the leaders thus slain or disabled, their party drew off without continuing the action. It must be particularly observed that Sir Thomas Kennedy remained neuter in this quarrel, considering his connexion with Auchindrane as too intimate to be broken even by his desire to assist his nephew.

For this temperate and honourable conduct he met a vile reward; for Auchindrane, in resentment of the loss of his relative Barganie, and the downfall of his ambitious hopes, continued his practices against the life of Sir Thomas of Cullayne, though totally innocent of contributing to either. Chance favoured his wicked purpose.

The Knight of Cullayne, finding himself obliged to go to Edinburgh on a particular day, sent a message by a servant to Mure, in which he told him, in the most unsuspecting confidence, the purpose of his journey, and named the road which he proposed to take, inviting Mure to meet him at Duppill, to the west of the town of Ayr, a place appointed, for the purpose of giving him any commissions which he might have for Edinburgh, and assuring his treacherous ally he would attend to any business which he might have in the Scottish metropolis as anxiously as to his own. Sir Thomas Kennedy's message was carried to the town of Maybole, where his messenger, for some trivial reason, had the import committed to writing by a schoolmaster in that town, and despatched it to its destination by means of a poor student, named Dalrymple, instead of carrying it to the house of Auchindrane in person.

This suggested to Mure a diabolical plot. Having thus received tidings of Sir Thomas Kennedy's motions, he conceived the infernal purpose of having the confiding friend who sent the information waylaid and murdered at the place appointed to meet with him, not only in friendship, but for the purpose of rendering him service. He dismissed the messenger Dalrymple, cautioning the lad to carry back the letter to Maybole, and to say that he had not found him, Auchindrane, in his house. Having taken this precaution, he proceeded to instigate the brother of the slain Gilbert of Barganie, Thomas Kennedy of Drumurghie by name, and Walter Mure of Cloncaird, a kinsman of his own, to take this opportunity of revenging Barganie's death. The fiery young men were easily induced to undertake the crime. They waylaid the unsuspecting Sir Thomas of Cullayne at the place appointed to meet the traitor Auchindrane, and the murderers having in company five or six servants, well mounted and armed, assaulted and cruelly murdered him with many wounds. They then plundered the dead corpse of his purse, containing a thousand merks in gold, cut off the gold buttons which he wore on his coat, and despoiled the body of some valuable rings and jewels.

The revenge due for his uncle's murder was keenly pursued by the Earl of Cassilis. As the murderers fled from trial, they were declared outlaws; which doom, being pronounced by three blasts of a horn, was called "being put to the horn, and declared the king's rebel." Mure of Auchindrane was strongly suspected of having been the instigator of the crime. But he conceived there could be no evidence to prove his guilt if he could keep the boy Dalrymple out of the way, who delivered the letter which made him acquainted with Cullayne's journey, and the place at which he meant to halt. On the contrary, he saw that if the lad could be produced at the trial, it would afford ground of fatal presumption, since it could be then proved that persons so nearly connected with him as Kennedy and Cloncaird had left his house, and committed the murder at the very spot which Cullayne had fixed for their meeting.

To avoid this imminent danger, Mure brought Dalrymple to his house, and detained him there for several weeks. But the youth tiring of this confinement, Mure sent him to reside with a friend, Montgomery of Skellmorly, who maintained him under a borrowed name, amid the desert regions of the then almost savage Island of Arran. Being confident in the absence of this material witness, Auchindrane, instead of flying, like his agents Drumurghie and Cloncaird, presented himself boldly at the bar, demanded a fair trial, and offered his person in combat to the death against any of Lord Cassilis' friends who might impugn his innocence. This audacity was successful, and he was dismissed without trial.

Still, however, Mure did not consider himself safe, so long as Dalrymple was within the realm of Scotland; and the danger grew more pressing when he learned that the lad had become impatient of the restraint which he sustained in the Island of Arran, and returned to some of his friends in Ayrshire. Mure no sooner heard of this than he again obtained possession of the boy's person, and a second time concealed him at Auchindrane, until he found an opportunity to transport him to the Low Countries, where he contrived to have him enlisted in Buccleuch's regiment; trusting, doubtless, that some one of the numerous chances of war might destroy the poor young man, whose life was so dangerous to him.

But after five or six years' uncertain safety, bought at the expense of so much violence and cunning, Auchindrane's fears were exasperated into frenzy when he found this dangerous witness, having escaped from all the perils of climate and battle, had left, or been discharged from, the Legion of Borderers, and had again accomplished his return to Ayrshire. There is ground to suspect that Dalrymple knew the nature of the hold which he possessed over Auchindrane, and was desirous of extorting from his fears some better provision than he had found either in Arran or the Netherlands. But if so, it was a fatal experiment to tamper with the fears of such a man as Auchindrane, who determined to rid himself effectually of this unhappy young man.

Mure now lodged him in a house of his own, called Chapeldonan, tenanted by a vassal and connexion of his called James Bannatyne. This man he commissioned to meet him at ten o'clock at night on the sea-sands near Girvan, and bring with him the unfortunate Dalrymple, the object of his fear and dread. The victim seems to have come with Bannatyne without the least suspicion, though such might have been raised by the time and place appointed for the meeting. When Bannatyne and Dalrymple came to the appointed spot, Auchindrane met them, accompanied by his eldest son, James. Old Auchindrane, having taken Bannatyne aside, imparted his bloody purpose of ridding himself of Dalrymple for ever, by murdering him on the spot. His own life and honour were, he said, endangered by the manner in which this inconvenient witness repeatedly thrust himself back into Ayrshire, and nothing could secure his safety but taking the lad's life, in which action he requested James Bannatyne's assistance. Bannatyne felt some compunction, and remonstrated against the cruel expedient, saying it would be better to transport Dalrymple to Ireland, and take precautions against his return. While old Auchindrane seemed disposed to listen to this proposal, his son concluded that the time was come for accomplishing the purpose of their meeting, and, without waiting the termination of his father's conference with Bannatyne, he rushed suddenly on Dalrymple, beat him to the ground, and, kneeling down on him, with his father's assistance accomplished the crime, by strangling the unhappy object of their fear and jealousy. Bannatyne, the witness, and partly the accomplice, of the murder, assisted them in their attempt to make a hole in the sand, with a spade which they had brought on purpose, in order to conceal the dead body. But as the tide was coming in, the holes which they made filled with water before they could get the body buried, and the ground seemed to their terrified consciences to refuse to be accessory to concealing their crime. Despairing of hiding the corpse in the manner they proposed, the murderers carried it out into the sea as deep as they dared wade, and there abandoned it to the billows, trusting that a wind, which was blowing off the shore, would drive these remains of their crime out to sea, where they would never more be heard of. But the sea, as well as the land, seemed unwilling to conceal their cruelty. After floating for some hours, or days, the dead body was, by the wind and tide, again driven on shore, near the very spot where the murder had been committed.

This attracted general attention, and when the corpse was known to be that of the same William Dalrymple whom Auchindrane had so often spirited out of the country, or concealed when he was in it, a strong and general suspicion arose that this young person had met with foul play from the bold bad man who had shown himself so much interested in his absence. It was always said or supposed that the dead body had bled at the approach of a grandchild of Mure of Auchindrane, a girl who, from curiosity, had come to look at a sight which others crowded to see. The bleeding of a murdered corpse at the touch of the murderer, was a thing at that time so much believed, that it was admitted as a proof of guilt; but I know no case, save that of Auchindrane, in which the phenomenon was supposed to be extended to the approach of the innocent kindred; nor do I think that the fact itself, though mentioned by ancient lawyers, was ever admitted to proof in the proceedings against Auchindrane.

It is certain, however, that Auchindrane found himself so much the object of suspicion from this new crime, that he resolved to fly from justice, and suffer himself to be declared a rebel and outlaw rather than face a trial. But his conduct in preparing to cover his flight with another motive than the real one, is a curious picture of the men and manners of the times. He knew well that if he were to shun his trial for the murder of Dalrymple, the whole country would consider him as a man guilty of a mean and disgraceful crime in putting to death an obscure lad, against whom he had no personal quarrel. He knew, besides, that his powerful friends, who would have interceded for him had his offence been merely burning a house, or killing a neighbour, would not plead for or stand by him in so pitiful a concern as the slaughter of this wretched wanderer.

Accordingly Mure sought to provide himself with some ostensible cause for avoiding the law, with which the feelings of his kindred and friends might sympathize ; and none occurred to him so natural as an assault upon some friend and adherent of the Earl of Cassilis. Should he kill such a one, it would be indeed an unlawful action, but so far from b ing infamous, would be accounted the natural consequence of the avowed quarrel between the families. With this purpose, Mure, with the assistance of a relative, of whom he seems always to have had some ready to execute his worst purposes, beset Hugh Kennedy of Garriehorne, a follower of the Earl's, against whom they had especial ill-will, fired their pistols at him, and used other means to put him to death. But Garriehorne, a stout-hearted man. and well armed, defended himself in a very different manner from the unfortunate Knight of Cullayne, and beat off the assailants, wounding young Auchindrane in the right hand, so that he wellnigh lost the use of it.

But though Auchindrane's purpose did not entirely succeed, he availed himself of it to circulate a report, that if he could obtain a pardon for firing upon his feudal enemy with pistols, weapons declared unlawful by Act of Parliament, he would willingly stand his trial for the death of Dalrymple, respecting which he protested his total innocence. The King, however, was decidedly of opinion that the Mures, both father and son, were alike guilty of both crimes, and used intercession with the Earl of Abercorn, as a person of power in those western counties, as well as in Ireland, to arrest and transmit them prisoners to Edinburgh. In consequence of the Earl's exertions, old Auchindrane was made prisoner, and lodged in the tolbooth of Edinburgh.

Young Auchindrane no sooner heard that his father was in custody, than he became as apprehensive of Bannatyne, the accomplice in Dalrymple's murder, telling tales, as ever his father had been of Dalrymple. He, therefore, hastened to him, and prevailed on him to pass over for a while to the neighbouring coast of Ireland, finding him money and means to accomplish the voyage, and engaging in the meantime to take care of his affairs in Scotland. Secure as they thought in this precaution, old Auchindrane persisted in his innocence, and his son found security to stand his trial. Both appeared with the same confidence at the day appointed, and braved the public justice, hoping to be put to a formal trial, in which Auchindrane reckoned upon an acquittal for want of the evidence which he had removed. This trial was, however, postponed, and Mure the elder was dismissed, under high security, to return when called for.

But King James, being convinced of the guilt of the accused, ordered young Auchindrane, instead of being sent to trial, to be examined under the force of torture, in order to compel him to tell whatever he knew of the things charged against him. He was accordingly severely tortured ; but the result only served to show that such examinations are as useless as they are cruel. A man of weak resolution, or of a nervous habit, would probably have assented to any confession, however false, rather than have endured the extremity of fear and pain to which Mure was subjected. But young Auchindrane, a strong and determined ruffian, endured the torture with the utmost firmness, and by the constant audacity with which, in spite of the intolerable pain, he continued to assert his innocence, he spread so favourable an opinion of his case, that the detaining him in prison, instead of bringing him to open trial, was censured as severe and oppressive. James, however, remained firmly persuaded of his guilt, and by an exertion of authority quite inconsistent with our present laws, commanded young Auchindrane to be still detained in close custody till further light could be thrown on these dark proceedings. He was detained accordingly by the King's express personal command, and against the opinion even of his privy councillors. This exertion of authority was much murmured against.

In the meanwhile old Auchindrane being, as we have seen, at liberty on pledges, skulked about in the west, feeling how little security he had gained by Dalrymple's murder, and that he had placed himself by that crime in the power of Bannatyne, whose evidence concerning the death of Dalrymple could not be less fatal than what Dalrymple might have told concerning Auchindrane's accession to the conspiracy against Sir Thomas Kennedy of Cullayne. But though the event had shown the error of his wicked policy, Auchindrane could think of no better mode in this case than that which had failed in relation to Dalrymple. When any man's life became inconsistent with his own safety, no idea seems to have occurred to this inveterate ruffian, save to murder the person by whom he might himself be in any way endangered. He therefore attempted the life of James Bannatyne by more agents than one. Nay, he had nearly ripened a plan, by which one Pennycuke was to be employed to slay Bannatyne, while, after the deed was done, it was devised that Mure of Auchnull, a connexion of Bannatyne, should be instigated to slay Pennycuke; and thus close up this train of murders by one, which, flowing in the ordinary cause of deadly feud, should have nothing in it so particular as to attract much attention.

But the justice of Heaven would bear this complicated train of iniquity no longer. Bannatyne, knowing with what sort of men he had to deal, kept on his guard, and, by his caution, disconcerted more than one attempt to take his life, while another miscarried by the remorse of Pennycuke, the agent whom Mure employed. At length Bannatyne, tiring of this state of insecurity, and in despair of escaping such repeated plots, and also feeling remorse for the crime to which he had been accessory, resolved rather to submit himself to the severity of the law, than remain the object of the principal criminal practices. He surrendered himself to the Earl of Abercorn, and was transported to Edinburgh, where he confessed before the King and council all the particulars of the murder of Dalrymple, and the attempt to hide his body by committing it to the sea.

When Bannatyne was confronted with the two Mures before the Privy Council, they denied with vehemence every part of the evidence he had given, and affirmed that the witness had been bribed to destroy them by a false tale. Bannatyne's behaviour seemed sincere and simple, that of Auchindrane more resolute and crafty. The wretched accomplice fell upon his knees, invoking God to witness that all the land in Scotland could not have bribed him to bring a false accusation against a master whom he had served, loved, and followed in so many dangers, and calling upon Auchindrane to honour God by confessing the crime he had committed. Mure the elder, on the other hand, boldly replied that he hoped God would not so far forsake him as to permit him to confess a crime of which he was innocent, and exhorted Bannatyne in his turn to confess the practices by which he had been induced to devise such falsehoods against him.

The two Mures, father and son, were therefore put upon their solemn trial, along with Bannatyne, in 1611, and, after a great deal of evidence had been brought in support of Bannatyne's confession, all three were found guilty. The elder Auchindrane was convicted of counselling and directing the murder of Sir Thomas Kennedy of Cullayne, and also of the actual murder of the lad Dalrymple. Bannatyne and the younger Mure were found guilty of the latter crime, and all three were sentenced to be beheaded. Bannatyne, however, the accomplice, received the King's pardon, in consequence of his voluntary surrender and confession. The two Mures were both executed. The younger was affected by the remonstrances of the clergy who attended him, and he confessed the guilt of which he was accused. The father, also, was at length brought to avow the fact, but in other respects died as impenitent as he had lived;—and so ended this dark and extraordinary tragedy.

The Lord Advocate of the day, Sir Thomas Hamilton, afterwards successively Earl of Melrose and of Haddington, seems to have busied himself much in drawing up a statement of this foul transaction, for the purpose of vindicating to the people of Scotland the severe course of justice observed by King James VI. He assumes the task in a high tone of prerogative law, and, on the whole, seems at a loss whether to attribute to Providence, or to his most sacred Majesty, the greatest share in bringing to light these mysterious villanies, but rather inclines to the latter opinion. There is, I believe, no printed copy of the intended tract, which seems never to have been published; but the curious will be enabled to judge of it, as it appears in the next *fasciculus* of Mr. Robert Pitcairn's very interesting publications from the Scottish Criminal Record.

The family of Auchindrane did not become extinct on the death of the two homicides. The last descendant existed in the eighteenth century, a poor and distressed man. The following anecdote shows that he had a strong feeling of his situation.

There was in front of the old castle a huge ash-tree, called the Dule-tree (*mourning-tree*) of Auchindrane, probably because it was the place where the baron executed the criminals who fell under his jurisdiction. It is described as having been the finest tree of the neighbourhood. This last representative of the family of Auchindrane had the misfortune to be arrested for payment of a small debt, and, unable to discharge it, was prepared to accompany the messenger (bailiff) to the jail of Ayr. The servant of the law had compassion for his prisoner, and offered to accept of this remarkable tree as of value adequate to the discharge of the debt. "What!" said the debtor, "sell the Dule-tree of Auchindrane! I will sooner die in the worst dungeon of your prison." In this luckless character the line of Auchindrane ended. The family, blackened with the crimes of its predecessors, became extinct, and the estate passed into other hands.

DRAMATIS PERSONÆ.

JOHN MURE OF AUCHINDRANE, *an Ayrshire Baron. He has been a follower of the Regent, Earl of Morton, during the Civil Wars, and hides an oppressive, ferocious, and unscrupulous disposition under some pretences to strictness of life and doctrine, which, however, never influence his conduct. He is in danger from the law, owing to his having been formerly active in the assassination of the Earl of Cassilis.*

PHILIP MURE, *his Son, a wild, debauched Profligate, professing and practising a contempt for his Father's hypocrisy, while he is as fierce and licentious as* AUCHINDRANE *himself.*

GIFFORD, *their Relation, a Courtier.*

QUENTIN BLANE, *a Youth, educated for a Clergyman, but sent by* AUCHINDRANE *to serve in a Band of Auxiliaries in the Wars of the Netherlands, and lately employed as Clerk or Comptroller to the Regiment—disbanded, however, and on his return to his native country. He is of a mild, gentle, and rather feeble character, liable to be influenced by any person of stronger mind who will take the trouble to direct him. He is somewhat of a nervous temperament, varying from sadness to gaiety, according to the impulse of the moment; an amiable hypochondriac.*

HILDEBRAND, *a stout old Englishman, who, by feats of courage, has raised himself to the rank of Sergeant-Major (then of greater consequence than at present). He, too, has been disbanded, but cannot bring himself to believe that he has lost his command over his regiment.*

ABRAHAM, WILLIAMS, JENKIN, *and others.* *Privates dismissed from the same regiment in which* QUENTIN *and* HILDEBRAND *had served. These are mutinous, and are much disposed to remember former quarrels with their late Officers.*

NIEL MACLELLAN, *Keeper of Auchindrane Forest and Game.*

EARL OF DUNBAR, *commanding an Army as Lieutenant of* JAMES VI., *for execution of Justice on Offenders.*

Guards, Attendants, &c., &c.

MARION, *Wife of* NIEL MACLELLAN.

ISABEL, *their Daughter, a Girl of six years old.*

Other Children and Peasant Women.

ACT I.—SCENE 1.

A rocky Bay on the Coast of Carrick, in Ayrshire, not far from the Point of Turnberry. The sea comes in upon a bold rocky shore. The remains of a small half-ruined Tower are seen on the right hand, overhanging the sea. There is a Vessel at a distance in the offing. A Boat at the bottom of the Stage lands eight or ten persons, dressed like disbanded, and in one or two cases like disabled, Soldiers. They come straggling forward with their knapsacks and bundles. HILDEBRAND, *the Sergeant belonging to the party, a stout elderly man, stands by the boat, as if superintending the disembarkation.* QUENTIN *remains apart.*

ABRAHAM. Farewell, the flats of Holland, and right welcome
The cliffs of Scotland! Fare thee well, black beer
And Schiedam gin! and welcome two-penny,
Oatcakes, and usquebaugh!
  WILLIAMS (*who wants an arm*). Farewell, the gallant field, and "Forward, pikemen!"
For the bridge-end, the suburb, and the lane;
And, "Bless your honour, noble gentleman,
Remember a poor soldier!"
  ABR. My tongue shall never need to smooth itself
To such poor sounds, while it can boldly say,
"Stand and deliver!"
  WIL. Hush, the sergeant hears you!
  ABR. And let him hear; he makes a bustle yonder,
And dreams of his authority, forgetting
We are disbanded men, o'er whom his halberd
Has not such influence as the beadle's baton.
We are no soldiers now, but every one
The lord of his own person.
  WIL. A wretched lordship—and our freedom such

As that of the old cart-horse, when the owner
Turns him upon the common. I for one
Will still continue to respect the sergeant,
And the comptroller too,—while the cash lasts.
  ABR. I scorn them both. I am too stout a Scotsman
To bear a Southron's rule an instant longer
Than discipline obliges; and for Quentin,
Quentin the quillman, Quentin the comptroller,
We have no regiment now; or, if we had,
Quentin's no longer clerk to it.
  WIL. For shame! for shame! What, shall old comrades jar thus,
And on the verge of parting, and for ever?—
Nay, keep thy temper, Abraham, though a bad one.—
Good Master Quentin, let thy song last night
Give us once more our welcome to old Scotland.
  ABR. Ay, they sing light whose task is telling money,
When dollars clink for chorus.
  QUE. I've done with clinking silver, honest Abraham,
As thou, I fear, with pouching thy small share on 't.
But lend your voices, lads, and I will sing
As blithely yet as if a town were won;
As if upon a field of battle gain'd,
Our banners waved victorious.
  [*He sings, and the rest bear chorus.*

SONG.

Hither we come,
Once slaves to the drum,
But no longer we list to its rattle;
Adieu to the wars,
With their slashes and scars,
The march, and the storm, and the battle.

There are some of us maim'd,
And some that are lamed,
And some of old aches are complaining;
But we'll take up the tools,
Which we flung by like fools,
'Gainst Don Spaniard to go a-campaigning.

Dick Hathorn doth vow
To return to the plough,
Jack Steele to his anvil and hammer;
The weaver shall find room
At the wight-wapping loom,
And your clerk shall teach writing and grammar.

ABR. And this is all that thou canst do, gay Quentin?
To swagger o'er a herd of parish brats,
Cut cheese or dibble onions with thy poniard,
And turn the sheath into a ferula?
QUE. I am the prodigal in holy writ;
I cannot work,—to beg I am ashamed.
Besides, good mates, I care not who may know it,
I'm e'en as fairly tired of this same fighting,
As the poor cur that's worried in the shambles
By all the mastiff dogs of all the butchers;   [petronel,
Wherefore, farewell sword, poniard,
And welcome poverty and peaceful labour.
ABR. Clerk Quentin, if of fighting thou art tired,
By my good word, thou'rt quickly satisfied,
For thou'st seen but little on't.
WIL. Thou dost belie him—I have seen him fight
Bravely enough for one in his condition.
ABR. What, he? that counter-casting, smock-faced boy?
What was he but the colonel's scribbling drudge,
With men of straw to stuff the regiment roll;
With cipherings unjust to cheat his comrades,

And cloak false musters for our noble captain?
He bid farewell to sword and petronel!
He should have said, farewell my pen and standish.
These, with the rosin used to hide erasures,
Were the best friends he left in camp behind him.
QUE. The sword you scoff at is not far, but scorns
The threats of an unmanner'd mutineer.
SER. (*interposes*). We'll have no brawling. Shall it e'er be said,
That being comrades six long years together,
While gulping down the frowsy fogs of Holland,
We tilted at each other's throats so soon
As the first draught of native air refresh'd them?
No! by Saint Dunstan, I forbid the combat.
You all, methinks, do know this trusty halberd;
For I opine, that every back amongst you
Hath felt the weight of the tough ashen staff,
Endlong or overthwart. Who is it wishes
A remembrancer now?
                    [*Raises his halberd.*
ABR.   Comrades, have you ears
To hear the old man bully? Eyes to see
His staff rear'd o'er your heads, as o'er the hounds
The huntsman cracks his whip?
WIL. Well said—stout Abraham has the right on't.—
I tell thee, sergeant, we do reverence thee,
And pardon the rash humours thou hast caught,
Like wiser men, from thy authority.
'Tis ended, howsoe'er, and we'll not suffer
A word of sergeantry, or halberd-staff,
Nor the most petty threat of discipline.
If thou wilt lay aside thy pride of office,

And drop thy wont of swaggering and
commanding,
Thou art our comrade still for good or
evil.
Else take thy course apart, or with the
clerk there—
A sergeant thou, and he being all thy
regiment.

SER. Is't come to this, false knaves?
And think you not,
That if you bear a name o'er other
soldiers,
It was because you follow'd to the charge
One that had zeal and skill enough to
lead you
Where fame was won by danger?

WIL. We grant thy skill in leading,
noble sergeant ;
Witness some empty boots and sleeves
amongst us,
Which else had still been tenanted with
limbs
In the full quantity ; and for the argu-
ments
With which you used to back our resolution,
Our shoulders do record them. At a
word,
Will you conform, or must we part our
company?

SER. Conform to you? Base dogs !
I would not lead you
A bolt-flight farther to be made a general.
Mean mutineers ! when you swill'd off
the dregs
Of my poor sea-stores, it was, "Noble
sergeant—
Heaven bless old Hildebrand—we 'll
follow him,
At least, until we safely see him lodged
Within the merry bounds of his own
England !"

WIL. Ay, truly, sir ; but, mark, the
ale was mighty,
And the Geneva potent. Such stout
liquor
Makes violent protestations. Skink it
round,
If you have any left, to the same tune,
And we may find a chorus for it still.

ABR. We lose our time.—Tell us at
once, old man,
If thou wilt march with us, or stay with
Quentin?

SER. Out, mutineers ! Dishonour
dog your heels !

ABR. Wilful will have his way.
Adieu, stout Hildebrand !

[*The Soldiers go off laughing,
and taking leave with mockery of the* SERGEANT *and*
QUENTIN, *who remain on the
Stage.*

SER. (*after a pause*). Fly you not
with the rest? fail you to follow
Yon goodly fellowship and fair example?
Come, take you wild-goose flight. I
know you Scots,
Like your own sea-fowl, seek your
course together.

QUE. Faith, a poor heron I, who
wing my flight
In loneliness, or with a single partner :
And right it is that I should seek for
solitude,
Bringing but evil luck on them I herd
with.

SER. Thou 'rt thankless. Had we
landed on the coast,
Where our course bore us, thou wert
far from home ;
But the fierce wind that drove us round
the island,
Barring each port and inlet that we
aim'd at,
Hath wafted thee to harbour ; for I
judge
This is thy native land we disembark
on.

QUE. True, worthy friend. Each
rock, each stream I look on,
Each bosky wood, and every frowning
tower,
Awakens some young dream of infancy.
Yet such is my hard hap, I might more
safely
Have look'd on Indian cliffs, or Afric's
desert,
Than on my native shores. I 'm like a
babe,

Doom'd to draw poison from my nurse's
  bosom.
  SER. Thou dream'st, young man.
    Unreal terrors haunt,
As I have noted, giddy brains like
  thine—
Flighty, poetic, and imaginative—
To whom a minstrel whim gives idle
  rapture,
And, when it fades, fantastic misery.
  QUE. But mine is not fantastic. I
    can tell thee,
Since I have known thee still my faith-
  ful friend,
In part at least the dangerous plight I
  stand in.
  SER. And I will hear thee willingly,
    the rather
That I would let these vagabonds
  march on,
Nor join their troop again. Besides,
  good sooth,
I'm wearied with the toil of yester-
  day,
And revel of last night.—And I may
  aid thee,
Yes, I may aid thee, comrade, and per-
  chance
Thou may st advantage me.
  QUE. May it prove well for both!—
    But note, my friend,
I can but intimate my mystic story.
Some of it lies so secret,—even the
  winds
That whistle round us must not know
  the whole—
An oath!—an oath!——
  SER. That must be kept, of course;
I ask but that which thou mayst freely
  tell.
  QUE. I was an orphan boy, and first
    saw light
Not far from where we stand—my
  lineage low,
But honest in its poverty. A lord,
The master of the soil for many a mile,
Dreaded and powerful, took a kindly
  charge
For my advance in letters, and the
  qualities

Of the poor orphan lad drew some
  applause.
The knight was proud of me, and, in
  his halls,
I had such kind of welcome as the
  great
Give to the humble, whom they love to
  point to
As objects not unworthy their protec-
  tion,
Whose progress is some honour to their
  patron—
A cure was spoken of, which I might
  serve,
My manners, doctrine, and acquire-
  ments fitting.
  SER. Hitherto thy luck
Was of the best, good friend. Few
  lords had cared
If thou couldst read thy grammar or
  thy psalter.
Thou hadst been valued couldst thou
  scour a harness,
And dress a steed distinctly.
  QUE.   My old master
Held different doctrine, at least it
  seem'd so,
But he was mix'd in many a deadly
  feud—
And here my tale grows mystic. I
  became,
Unwitting and unwilling, the deposi-
  tary
Of a dread secret, and the knowledge
  on't
Has wreck'd my peace for ever. It
  became
My patron's will, that I, as one who
  knew
More than I should, must leave the
  realm of Scotland,
And live or die within a distant land.
  SER. Ah! thou hast done a fault in
    some wild raid,
As you wild Scotsmen call them.
  QUE.   Comrade, nay;
Mine was a peaceful part, and happ'd
  by chance.
I must not tell you more. Enough, my
  presence

Brought danger to my benefactor's
house.
Tower after tower conceal'd me, willing
still
To hide my ill-omen'd face with owls
and ravens,
And let my patron's safety be the pur-
chase
Of my severe and desolate captivity.
So thought I, when dark Arran, with
its walls
Of native rock, enclosed me. There I
lurk'd,
A peaceful stranger amid armed clans,
Without a friend to love or to defend
me,
Where all beside were link'd by close
alliances.
At length I made my option to take
service
In that same legion of auxiliaries
In which we lately served the Belgian.
Our leader, stout Montgomery, hath
been kind
Through full six years of warfare, and
assign'd me
More peaceful tasks than the rough
front of war,
For which my education little suited
me.
  SER. Ay, therein was Montgomery
kind indeed ;
Nay, kinder than you think, my simple
Quentin.
The letters which you brought to the
Montgomery,
Pointed to thrust thee on some desperate
service,
Which should most likely end thee.
  QUE. Bore I such letters?—Surely,
comrade, no.
Full deeply was the writer bound to aid
me.
Perchance he only meant to prove my
mettle ;
And it was but a trick of my bad fortune
That gave his letters ill interpretation.
  SER. Ay, but thy better angel wrought
for good,
Whatever ill thy evil fate designed thee,

Montgomery pitied thee, and changed
thy service
In the rough field for labour in the tent,
More fit for thy green years and peaceful
habits.
  QUE. Even there his well-meant kind-
ness injured me.
My comrades hated, undervalued me,
And whatsoe'er of service I could do
them,
They guerdon'd with ingratitude and
envy—
Such my strange doom, that if I serve
a man
At deepest risk, he is my foe for ever!
  SER. Hast thou worse fate than others
if it were so?
Worse even than me, thy friend, thine
officer,
Whom yon ungrateful slaves have
pitch'd ashore,
As wild waves heap the sea-weed on
the beach,
And left him here, as if he had the
pest
Or leprosy, and death were in his com-
pany?
  QUE. They think at least you have
the worst of plagues,
The worst of leprosies,—they think you
poor.
  SER. They think like lying villains
then, I 'm rich,
And they, too, might have felt it. I 've
a thought—
But stay—what plans your wisdom for
yourself?
  QUE. My thoughts are wellnigh desperate. But I purpose
Return to my stern patron—there to
tell him
That wars, and winds, and waves, have
cross'd his pleasure,
And cast me on the shore from whence
he banish'd me.
Then let him do his will, and destine
for me
A dungeon or a grave.
  SER. Now, by the rood, thou art a
simple fool !

I can do better for thee. Mark me,
    Quentin.
I took my license from the noble
    regiment,
Partly that I was worn with age and
    warfare,
Partly that an estate of yeomanry,
Of no great purchase, but enough to
    live on,
Has call'd me owner since a kinsman's
    death.
It lies in merry Yorkshire, where the
    wealth
Of fold and furrow, proper to Old
    England,
Stretches by streams which walk no
    sluggish pace,
But dance as light as yours. Now,
    good friend Quentin,
This copyhold can keep two quiet in-
    mates,
And I am childless. Wilt thou be my
    son ?
    QUE. Nay, you can only jest, my
        worthy friend !
What claim have I to be a burden to
    you ?
    SER. The claim of him that wants,
        and is in danger,
On him that has, and can afford pro-
    tection :
Thou wouldst not fear a foeman in my
    cottage,
Where a stout mastiff slumber'd on the
    hearth,
And this good halberd hung above the
    chimney ?
But come—I have it—thou shalt earn
    thy bread
Duly, and honourably, and usefully.
Our village schoolmaster hath left the
    parish,
Forsook the ancient schoolhouse with
    its yew-trees,
That lurk'd beside a church two cen-
    turies older—
So long devotion took the lead of
    knowledge ;
And since his little flock are shepherd-
    less.

'T is thou shalt be promoted in his
    room—
And rather than thou wantest scholars,
    man,
Myself will enter pupil. Better late,
Our proverb says, than never to do well.
And look you, on the holydays I 'd tell
To all the wondering boors and gaping
    children,
Strange tales of what the regiment did
    in Flanders,
And thou shouldst say Amen, and be
    my warrant,
That I speak truth to them.
    QUE. Would I might take thy offer !
        But, alas !
Thou art the hermit who compell'd a
    pilgrim,
In name of Heaven and heavenly
    charity,
To share his roof and meal, but found
    too late
That he had drawn a curse on him and
    his,
By sheltering a wretch foredoom'd of
    Heaven !
    SER. Thou talk'st in riddles to me.
    QUE.   If I do,
'T is that I am a riddle to myself.
Thou know'st I am by nature born a
    friend
To glee and merriment—can make
    wild verses ;
The jest or laugh has never stopp'd
    with me,
When once 't was set a-rolling.
    SER.   I have known thee
A blithe companion still, and wonder
    now
Thou shouldst become thus crestfallen.
    QUE. Does the lark sing her descant
        when the falcon
Scales the blue vault with bolder wing
    than hers,
And meditates a stoop? The mirth
    thou 'st noted
Was all deception, fraud—hated enough
For other causes. I did veil my feelings
Beneath the mask of mirth—laugh'd,
    sung, and caroll'd,

To gain some interest in my comrades' bosoms,
Although mine own was bursting.
 SER.   Thou'rt a hypocrite
Of a new order.
 QUE. But harmless as the innoxious snake,
Which bears the adder's form, lurks in his haunts,
Yet neither hath his fang-teeth nor his poison.
Look you, kind Hildebrand, I would seem merry,
Lest other men should, tiring of my sadness,
Expel me from them, as the hunted wether
Is driven from the flock.
 SER. Faith, thou hast borne it bravely out.
Had I been ask'd to name the merriest fellow
Of all our muster-roll—that man wert thou.
 QUE. See'st thou, my friend, yon brook dance down the valley,
And sing blithe carols over broken rock
And tiny waterfall, kissing each shrub
And each gay flower it nurses in its passage?—
Where, think'st thou, is its source, the bonny brook?—
It flows from forth a cavern, black and gloomy,
Sullen and sunless, like this heart of mine,
Which others see in a false glare of gaiety,
Which I have laid before you in its sadness.
 SER. If such wild fancies dog thee, wherefore leave
The trade where thou wert safe 'midst others' dangers,
And venture to thy native land, where fate
Lies on the watch for thee? Had old Montgomery
Been with the regiment, thou hadst had no congé.

 QUE. No, 'tis most likely. But I had a hope,
A poor vain hope, that I might live obscurely
In some far corner of my native Scotland,
Which, of all others, splintered into districts,
Differing in manners, families, even language,
Seem'd a safe refuge for the humble wretch,
Whose highest hope was to remain unheard of.
But fate has baffled me—the winds and waves,
With force resistless, have impell'd me hither—
Have driven me to the clime most dang'rous to me;
And I obey the call, like the hurt deer,
Which seeks instinctively his native lair,
Though his heart tells him it is but to die there.
 SER. 'Tis false, by Heaven, young man! This same despair,
Though showing resignation in its banner,
Is but a kind of covert cowardice.
Wise men have said, that though our stars incline,
They cannot force us. Wisdom is the pilot,
And if he cannot cross, he may evade them.
You lend an ear to idle auguries,
The fruits of our last revels—still most sad
Under the gloom that follows boisterous mirth,
As earth looks blackest after brilliant sunshine.
 QUE. No, by my honest word. I join'd the revel,
And aided it with laugh, and song, and shout,
But my heart revell'd not; and, when the mirth
Was at the loudest, on yon galliot's prow

I stood unmark'd, and gazed upon the land,
My native land—each cape and cliff I knew.
"Behold me now," I said, "your destined victim!"
So greets the sentenced criminal the headsman,
Who slow approaches with his lifted axe.
"Hither I come," I said, "ye kindred hills,
Whose darksome outline in a distant land
Haunted my slumbers; here I stand, thou ocean,
Whose hoarse voice, murmuring in my dreams, required me;
See me now here, ye winds, whose plaintive wail,
On yonder distant shores, appear'd to call me—
Summon'd, behold me." And the winds and waves,
And the deep echoes of the distant mountain
Made answer—"Come, and die!"

SER. Fantastic all! Poor boy, thou art distracted
With the vain terrors of some feudal tyrant,
Whose frown hath been from infancy thy bugbear.
Why seek his presence?

QUE.   Wherefore does the moth
Fly to the scorching taper? Why the bird,
Dazzled by lights at midnight, seek the net?
Why does the prey, which feels the fascination
Of the snake's glaring eye, drop in his jaws?

SER. Such wild examples but refute themselves.
Let bird, let moth, let the coil'd adder's prey
Resist the fascination, and be safe.
Thou goest not near this baron—if thou goest,

I will go with thee. Known in many a field,
Which he, in a whole life of petty feud
Has never dream'd of, I will teach the knight
To rule him in this matter—be thy warrant,
That far from him, and from his petty lordship,
You shall henceforth tread English land, and never
Thy presence shall alarm his conscience more.

QUE. 'Twere desperate risk for both. I will far rather
Hastily guide thee through this dangerous province,
And seek thy school, thy yew-trees, and thy churchyard;
The last, perchance, will be the first I find.

SER. I would rather face him,
Like a bold Englishman that knows his right,
And will stand by his friend. And yet 't is folly—
Fancies like these are not to be resisted;
'T is better to escape them. Many a presage,
Too rashly braved, becomes its own accomplishment.
Then let us go—but whither? My old head
As little knows where it shall lie to-night,
As yonder mutineers that left their officer,
As reckless of his quarters as these billows,
That leave the withered sea-weed on the beach,
And care not where they pile it.

QUE. Think not for that, good friend. We are in Scotland,
And if it is not varied from its wont,
Each cot that sends a curl of smoke to heaven,   [night,
Will yield a stranger quarters for the
Simply because he needs them,

SER. But are there none within an easy walk
Give lodgings here for hire? for I have left
Some of the Don's piastres (though I kept
The secret from yon gulls), and I had rather
Pay the fair reckoning I can well afford,
And my host takes with pleasure, than I'd cumber,
Some poor man's roof with me and all my wants,
And tax his charity beyond discretion.

QUE. Some six miles hence there is a town and hostelry—
But you are wayworn, and it is most likely
Our comrades must have fill'd it.

SER.   Out upon them!
Were there a friendly mastiff who would lend me
Half of his supper, half of his poor kennel,
I would help Honesty to pick his bones,
And share his straw, far rather than I'd sup
On jolly fare with these base varlets.

QUE. We'll manage better, for our Scottish dogs,
Though stout and trusty, are but ill-instructed
In hospitable rights. Here is a maiden,
A little maid, will tell us of the country,
And sorely it is changed since I have left it,
If we should fail to find a harbourage.

Enter ISABEL MACLELLAN, *a girl of about six years old, bearing a milk-pail on her head; she stops on seeing the* SERGEANT *and* QUENTIN.

QUE. There's something in her look that doth remind me—
But 't is not wonder I find recollections
In all that here I look on. Pretty maid——
SER. You're slow, and hesitate; I will be spokesman,

Good even, my prétty maiden. Canst thou tell us,
Is there a Christian house would render strangers,
For love or guerdon, a night's meal and lodging?
ISA. Full surely, sir. We dwell in yon old house
Upon the cliff, they call it Chapeldonan.
                    [*Points to the building.*
Our house is large enough, and if our supper
Chance to be scant, you shall have half of mine—
For, as I think, sir, you have been a soldier.
Up yonder lies our house; I'll trip before,
And tell my mother she has guests a-coming:
The path is something steep, but you shall see
I'll be there first. I must chain up the dogs, too;
Nimrod and Bloodylass are cross to strangers,
But gentle when you know them.
          [*Exit, and is seen partially as-cending to the Castle.*
SER.   You have spoke
Your country folk aright, both for the dogs
And for the people. We had luck to light
On one too young for cunning and for selfishness.
He's in a reverie—a deep one sure,
Since the gibe on his country wakes him not.
Bestir thee, Quentin!
QUE. 'T was a wondrous likeness!
SER. Likeness! of whom? I'll warrant thee of one
Whom thou hast loved and lost. Such fantasies
Live long in brains like thine, which fashion visions
Of woe and death when they are cross'd in love,
As most men are or have been,

QUE. Thy guess hath touch'd me,
   though it is but slightly,
'Mongst other woes: I knew, in former
   days,
A maid that view'd me with some glance
   of favour,
But my fate carried me to other shores,
And she has since been wedded. I did
   think on 't,
But as a bubble burst, a rainbow
   vanish'd;
It adds no deeper shade to the dark
   gloom
Which chills the springs of hope and
   life within me.
Our guide hath got a trick of voice and
   feature
Like to the maid I spoke of—that is
   all.

  SER. She bounds before us like a
   gamesome doe,
Or rather as the rock-bred eaglet soars
Up to her nest, as if she rose by will
Without an effort. Now a Nether-
   lander,
One of our Frogland friends, viewing
   the scene,
Would take his oath that tower, and
   rock, and maiden,
Were forms too light and lofty to be
   real,
And only some delusion of the fancy,
Such as men dream at sunset. I myself
Have kept the level ground so many
   years,
I have wellnigh forgot the art to climb,
Unless assisted by thy younger arm.
    [*They go off as if to ascend to
    the Tower, the* SERGEANT
    leaning upon QUENTIN.

SCENE II.

Scene changes to the front of the old Tower.
ISABEL *comes forward with her Mother,*
—MARION *speaking as they advance.*

  MAR. I blame thee not, my child,
   for bidding wanderers
Come share our food and shelter, if
   thy father

Were here to welcome them; but,
   Isabel,
He waits upon his lord at Auchindrane,
And comes not home to-night.
  ISA.   What, then, mother?
The travellers do not ask to see my
   father;
Food, shelter, rest, is all the poor men
   want,
And we can give them these without
   my father.
  MAR. Thou canst not understand,
   nor I explain,
Why a lone female asks not visitants
What time her husband's absent.—
   (*Apart.*) My poor child,
And if thou 'rt wedded to a jealous
   husband,
Thou 'lt know too soon the cause.
  ISA. (*partly overhearing what her
   Mother says*). Ay, but I know
   already—Jealousy
Is, when my father chides, and you sit
   weeping.
  MAR. Out, little spy! thy father
   never chides;
Or, if he does, 't is when his wife
   deserves it.—
But to our strangers; they are old
   men, Isabel,
That seek this shelter? are they not?
  ISA.   One is old—
Old as this tower of ours, and worn
   like that,
Bearing deep marks of battles long
   since fought.
  MAR. Some remnant of the wars;
   he's welcome, surely,
Bringing no quality along with him
Which can alarm suspicion.—Well, the
   other?
  ISA. A young man, gentle-voiced and
   gentle-eyed,
Who looks and speaks like one the
   world has frown'd on;
But smiles when you smile, seeming
   that he feels
Joy in your joy, though he himself is
   sad.
Brown hair, and downcast looks.

MAR. (*alarmed*). 'T is but an idle
thought—it cannot be! [*Listens.*
I hear his accents. It is all too true—
My terrors were prophetic!
　　　　　　I 'll compose myself,
And then accost him firmly. Thus it
　must be.
　　[*She retires hastily into the
　　　Tower. The voices of the
　　　SERGEANT and* QUENTIN *are
　　　heard ascending behind the
　　　scenes.*
QUE. One effort more—we stand upon
　the level.
I 've seen thee work thee up glacis and
　cavalier
Steeper than this ascent, when cannon,
　culverine,
Musket, and hackbut, shower'd their
　shot upon thee,
And form'd, with ceaseless blaze, a fiery
　garland
Round the defences of the post you
　storm'd.
　　[*They come on the Stage, and at
　　　the same time* MARION *re-
　　　enters from the Tower.*
SER. Truly thou speak'st. I am the
　tardier,
That I, in climbing hither, miss the fire,
Which wont to tell me there was death
　in loitering.—
Here stands, methinks, our hostess.
　　[*He goes forward to address*
　　　MARION. QUENTIN, *struck
　　　on seeing her, keeps back.*
SER. Kind dame, yon little lass hath
　brought you strangers,
Willing to be a trouble, not a charge to
　you.
We are disbanded soldiers, but have
　means
Ample enough to pay our journey home-
　ward.
MAR. We keep no house of general
　entertainment,
But know our duty, sir, to locks like
　yours,
Whiten'd and thinn'd by many a long
　campaign.

Ill chances tnat my husband should be
　absent—
(*Apart*)—Courage alone can make me
　struggle through it—
For in your comrade, though he hath
　forgot me,
I spy a friend whom I have known in
　school-days,
And whom I think MacLellan well
　remembers.
　　　　　[*She goes up to* QUENTIN.
You see a woman's memory
Is faithfuller than yours; for Quentin
　Blane
Hath not a greeting left for Marion
　Harkness.
QUE. (*with effort*). I seek, indeed,
　my native land, good Marion,
But seek it like a stranger. All is
　changed.
And thou thyself——
　　MAR. You left a giddy maiden,
And find, on your return, a wife and
　mother.
Thine old acquaintance, Quentin, is my
　mate—
Stout Niel MacLellan, ranger to our
　lord,
The Knight of Auchindrane. He 's
　absent now,
But will rejoice to see his former com-
　rade,
If, as I trust, you tarry his return.
(*Apart*). Heaven grant he understand
　my words by contraries!
He must remember Niel and he were
　rivals;
He must remember Niel and he were
　foes;
He must remember Niel is warm of
　temper,
And think, instead of welcome, I would
　blithely
Bid him God speed you. But he is as
　simple
And void of guile as ever.
　QUE. Marion, I gladly rest within
　your cottage,
And gladly wait return of Niel Mac-
　Lellan,

To clasp his hand, and wish him happiness.
Some rising feelings might perhaps prevent this—
But 't is a peevish part to grudge our friends
Their share of fortune because we have miss'd it;
I can wish others joy and happiness,
Though I must ne'er partake them.

MAR. But if it grieve you——

QUE. No! do not fear. The brightest gleams of hope
That shine on me are such as are reflected
From those which shine on others.

[_The_ SERGEANT _and_ QUENTIN _enter the Tower with the little Girl._

MAR. (_comes forward, and speaks in agitation_). Even so! the simple youth has miss'd my meaning.
I shame to make it plainer, or to say,
In one brief word, Pass on. Heaven guide the bark,
For we are on the breakers!

[_Exit into the Tower._

ACT II.—SCENE I.

A Withdrawing Apartment in the Castle of Auchindrane. Servants _place a table, with a flask of wine and drinking-cups._

Enter MURE _of_ AUCHINDRANE, _with_ ALBERT GIFFORD, _his Relation and Visitor. They place themselves by the table after some complimentary ceremony. At some distance is heard the noise of revelling._

AUCH. We're better placed for confidential talk,
Than in the hall fill'd with disbanded soldiers,
And fools and fiddlers gather'd on the highway,—
The worthy guests whom Philip crowds my hall with,
And with them spends his evening.

GIF. But think you not, my friend, that your son Philip
Should be participant of these our counsels,
Being so deeply mingled in the danger,
Your house's only heir—your only son?

AUCH. Kind cousin Gifford, if thou lack'st good counsel
At race, at cockpit, or at gambling-table,
Or any freak by which men cheat themselves
As well of life as of the means to live,
Call for assistance upon Philip Mure:
But in all serious parley spare invoking him.

GIF. You speak too lightly of my cousin Philip;
All name him brave in arms.

AUCH.   A second Bevis;
But I, my youth bred up in graver fashions,
Mourn o'er the mode of life in which he spends,
Or rather dissipates, his time and substance.
No vagabond escapes his search—The soldier
Spurn'd from the service, henceforth to be ruffian
Upon his own account, is Philip's comrade;
The fiddler, whose crack'd crowd has still three strings on 't;
The balladeer, whose voice has still two notes left;
Whate'er is roguish and whate'er is vice,
Are welcome to the board of Auchindrane,
And Philip will return them shout for shout,
And pledge for jovial pledge, and song for song,
Until the shamefaced sun peep at our windows,
And ask, "What have we here?"

GIF. You take such revel deeply—we are Scotsmen,
Far known for rustic hospitality,

That mind not birth or titles in our
    guests ;
The harper has his seat beside our
    hearth,
The wanderer must find comfort at our
    board,
His name unask'd, his pedigree un-
    known ;
So did our ancestors, and so must we.
  AUCH. All this is freely granted,
    worthy kinsman ;
And prithee do not think me churl
    enough
To count how many sit beneath my
    salt.
I 've wealth enough to fill my father's
    hall
Each day at noon, and feed the guests
    who crowd it ;
I am near mate with those whom men
    call Lord,
Though a rude western knight. But
    mark me, cousin,
Although I feed wayfaring vagabonds,
I make them not my comrades. Such
    as I,
Who have advanced the fortunes of
    my line,
And swell'd a baron's turret to a palace,
Have oft the curse awaiting on our
    thrift,
To see, while yet we live, the things
    which must be
At our decease—the downfall of our
    family,
The loss of land and lordship, name
    and knighthood,
The wreck of the fair fabric we have
    built,
By a degenerate heir. Philip has that
Of inborn meanness in him, that he
    loves not
The company of betters, nor of equals ;
Never at ease, unless he bears the
    bell,
And crows the loudest in the company.
He 's mesh'd, too, in the snares of every
    female
Who deigns to cast a passing glance
    on him—

Licentious, disrespectful, rash, and pro-
    fligate.
  GIF. Come, my good coz, think we
    too have been young,
And I will swear that in your father's
    lifetime
You have yourself been trapp'd by toys
    like these.
  AUCH. A fool I may have been—
    but not a madman ;
I never play'd the rake among my
    followers,
Pursuing this man's sister, that man's
    wife ;
And therefore never saw I man of
    mine,
When summon'd to obey my hest,
    grow restive,
Talk of his honour, of his peace de-
    stroy'd,
And, while obeying, mutter threats of
    vengeance.
But now the humour of an idle youth,
Disgusting trusted followers, sworn
    dependants,
Plays football with his honour and my
    safety.
  GIF. I 'm sorry to find discord in
    your house,
For I had hoped, while bringing you
    cold news,
To find you arm'd in union 'gainst the
    danger.
  AUCH. What can man speak that I
    would shrink to hear ?
And where the danger I would deign
    to shun ?   [*He rises.*
What should appal a man inured to
    perils,
Like the bold climber on the crags of
    Ailsa ?
Winds whistle past him, billows rage
    below,
The sea-fowl sweep around, with shriek
    and clang ;
One single slip, one unadvised pace,
One qualm of giddiness—and peace be
    with him !
But he whose grasp is sure, whose step
    is firm,

Whose brain is constant—he makes
one proud rock
The means to scale another, till he
stand
Triumphant on the peak.

GIF.   And so I trust
Thou wilt surmount the danger now
approaching,
Which scarcely can I frame my tongue
to tell you,
Though I rode here on purpose.

AUGH. Cousin, I think thy heart was
never coward,
And strange it seems thy tongue should
take such semblance.
I've heard of many a loud-mouth'd
noisy braggart,
Whose hand gave feeble sanction to
his tongue;
But thou art one whose heart can think
bold things,
Whose hand can act them, but who
shrinks to speak them.

GIF. And if I speak them not, 't is
that I shame
To tell thee of the calumnies that load
thee.
Things loudly spoken at the city Cross,
Things closely whisper'd in our Sove-
reign's ear,
Things which the plumed lord and
flat-capp'd citizen
Do circulate amid their different ranks,
Things false, no doubt; but, falsehoods
while I deem them,
Still honouring thee, I shun the odious
topic.

AUCH. Shun it not, cousin; 't is a
friend's best office
To bring the news we hear unwillingly.
The sentinel who tells the foe's approach,
And wakes the sleeping camp, does but
his duty:
Be thou as bold in telling me of danger,
As I shall be in facing danger told of.

GIF. I need not bid thee recollect
the death-feud
That raged so long betwixt thy house
and Cassilis;
I need not bid thee recollect the league.

When royal James himself stood me-
diator
Between thee and Earl Gilbert.

AUCH. Call you these news? You
might as well have told me
That old King Coil is dead, and graved
at Kylesfeld.
I'll help thee out: King James com-
manded us
Henceforth to live in peace—made us
clasp hands too.
Oh, sir, when such an union hath been
made,
In heart and hand conjoining mortal
foes,
Under a monarch's royal mediation,
The league is not forgotten. And with
this
What is there to be told? The King
commanded—
" Be friends." No doubt we were so—
Who dare doubt it?

GIF. You speak but half the tale.

AUCH. By good Saint Trimon, but
I'll tell the whole!
There is no terror in the tale for me—
Go speak of ghosts to children!—This
Earl Gilbert
(God sain him) loved Heaven's peace
as well as I did,
And we were wondrous friends when-
e'er we met
At church or market, or in burrows
town.
'Midst this, our good Lord Gilbert, Earl
of Cassilis,
Takes purpose he would journey forth
to Edinburgh.
The King was doling gifts of abbey-
lands,
Good things that thrifty house was
wont to fish for.
Our mighty Earl forsakes his sea-
wash'd castle,
Passes our borders some four miles
from hence;
And, holding it unwholesome to be
fasters
Long after sunrise, lo! the Earl and
train

Dismount, to rest their nags and eat
their breakfast.

The morning rose, the small birds
caroll'd sweetly—

The corks were drawn, the pasty
brooks incision—

His lordship jests, his train are choked
with laughter,

When,—wondrous change of cheer,
and most unlook'd-for,

Strange epilogue to bottle and to baked
meat !—

Flash'd from the greenwood half a score
of carabines

And the good Earl of Cassilis, in his
breakfast,

Had nooning, dinner, supper, all at
once,

Even in the morning that he closed his
journey ;

And the grim sexton, for his chamberlain,

Made him the bed which rests the head
for ever.

GIF. Told with much spirit, cousin—
some there are

Would add, and in a tone resembling
triumph.

And would that with these long establish'd facts

My tale began and ended ! I must tell
you,

That evil-deeming censures of the
events,

Both at the time and now, throw blame
on thee—

Time, place, and circumstance, they
say, proclaim thee,

Alike, the author of that morning's
ambush.

AUCH. Ay, 't is an old belief in
Carrick here,

Where natives do not always die in bed,

That if a Kennedy shall not attain

Methuselah's last span, a Mure has
slain him.

Such is the general creed of all their
clan.

Thank Heaven, that they're bound to
prove the charge

They are so prompt in making. They
have clamour'd

Enough of this before, to show their
malice.

But what said these coward pickthanks
when I came

Before the King, before the Justicers,

Rebutting all their calumnies, and
daring them

To show that I knew aught of Cassilis'
journey—

Which way he meant to travel—where
to halt—

Without which knowledge I possess'd
no means

To dress an ambush for him? Did I
not

Defy the assembled clan of Kennedys

To show, by proof direct or inferen-
tial,

Wherefore they slander'd me with this
foul charge?

My gauntlet rung before them in the
court,

And I did dare the best of them to lift
it,

And prove such charge a true one—
Did I not?

GIF. I saw your gauntlet lie before
the Kennedys,

Who look'd on it as men do on an
adder,

Longing to crush, and yet afraid to
grasp it.

Not an eye sparkled—not a foot advanced—

No arm was stretch'd to lift the fatal
symbol.

AUCH. Then wherefore do the hild-
ings murmur now?

Wish they to see again, how one bold
Mure

Can baffle and defy their assembled
valour?

GIF. No ; but they speak of evidence
suppress'd.

AUCH. Suppress'd !—what evidence?
by whom suppress'd?

What Will-'o-wisp—what idiot of a
witness,

Is he to whom they trace an empty
  voice,
But cannot show his person?
  GIF.   They pretend,
With the King's leave, to bring it to a
  trial;
Averring that a lad, named Quentin
  Blane,
Brought thee a letter from the murder'd
  Earl,
With friendly greetings, telling of his
  journey,
The hour which he set forth, the place
  he halted at
Affording thee the means to form the
  ambush,
Of which your hatred made the applica-
  tion.
  AUCH. A prudent Earl, indeed, if
  such his practice,
When dealing with a recent enemy!
And what should he propose by such
  strange confidence
In one who sought it not?
  GIF. His purposes were kindly, say
  the Kennedys—
Desiring you would meet him where he
  halted,
Offering to undertake whate'er com-
  missions
You listed trust him with, for court or
  city;
And, thus apprised of Cassilis' purposed
  journey,
And of his halting-place, you placed
  the ambush,
Prepared the homicides——
  AUCH. They're free to say their
  pleasure. They are men
Of the new court—and I am but a
  fragment
Of stout old Morton's faction. It is
  reason
That such as I be rooted from the earth,
That they may have full room to spread
  their branches.
No doubt, 'tis easy to find strolling
  vagrants
To prove whate'er they prompt. This
  Quentin Blane—

Did you not call him so?—why comes
  he now?
And wherefore not before? This must
  be answer'd—(*abruptly*)—
Where is he now?
  GIF. Abroad—they say—kidnapp'd,
By you kidnapp'd, that he might die in
  Flanders.
But orders have been sent for his dis-
  charge,
And his transmission hither.
  AUCH. (*assuming an air of com-
  posure*). When they produce such
  witness, cousin Gifford,
We'll be prepared to meet it. In the
  meanwhile,
The King doth ill to throw his royal
  sceptre
In the accuser's scale, ere he can know
How justice shall incline it.
  GIF.   Our sage prince
Resents, it may be, less the death of
  Cassilis,
Than he is angry that the feud should
  burn
After his royal voice had said "Be
  quench'd;"
Thus urging prosecution less for
  slaughter,
Than that, being done against the
  King's command,
Treason is mix'd with homicide.
  AUCH. Ha! ha! most true, my cousin.
Why, well consider'd, 'tis a crime so
  great
To slay one's enemy, the King forbid-
  ding it,
Like parricide, it should be held im-
  possible.
'Tis just as if a wretch retain'd the
  evil,
When the King's touch had bid the sores
  be heal'd—
And such a crime merits the stake at
  least.
What! can there be within a Scottish
  bosom
A feud so deadly, that it kept its ground
When the King said be friends? It is
  not credible.

Were I King James, I never would
believe it ;

I'd rather think the story all a dream,

And that there was no friendship, feud,
nor journey,

No halt, no ambush, and no Earl of
Cassilis,

Than dream anointed Majesty has
wrong.

GIF. Speak within door, coz.

AUCH. O, true—(*aside*)—I shall betray myself

Even to this half-bred fool. I must
have room,

Room for an instant, or I suffocate.—

Cousin, I prithee call our Philip hither ;

Forgive me, 't were more meet I summon'd him

Myself—but then the sight of yonder
revel

Would chafe my blood, and I have
need of coolness.

GIF. I understand thee—I will bring
him straight.   [*Exit.*

AUCH. And if thou dost, he's lost
his ancient trick

To fathom, as he wont, his five-pint
flagons.

This space is mine—O for the power
to fill it,

Instead of senseless rage and empty
curses,

With the dark spell which witches learn
from fiends,

That smites the object of their hate afar,

Nor leaves a token of its mystic action,

Stealing the soul from out the unscathed body,

As lightning melts the blade, nor harms
the scabbard.

'T is vain to wish for it. Each curse
of mine

Falls to the ground as harmless as the
arrows

Which children shoot at stars. The
time for thought,

If thought could aught avail me, melts
away,

Like to a snowball in a schoolboy's
hand,

That melts the faster the more close he
grasps it.

If I had time, this Scottish Solomon,

Whom some call son of David the
musician,

Might find it perilous work to march to
Carrick.

There's many a feud still slumbering
in its ashes,

Whose embers are yet red. Nobles we
have

Stout as old Graysteel, and as hot as
Bothwell ;

Here too are castles look from crags as
high,   [King—

On seas as wide as Logan's. So the

Pshaw ! He is here again.

Enter GIFFORD.

GIF.   I heard you name

The King, my kinsman ; know, he
comes not hither.

AUCH. (*affecting indifference*). Nay,
then we need not broach our
barrels, cousin,

Nor purchase us new jerkins. Comes
not Philip ?

GIF. Yes, sir. He tarries but to
drink a service

To his good friends at parting.

AUCH. Friends for the beadle or the
sheriff-officer.

Well, let it pass. Who comes, and
how attended,

Since James designs not westward ?

GIF. O, you shall have, instead, his
fiery functionary,

George Home that was, but now Dun,
bar's great Earl ;

He leads a royal host, and comes to
show you

How he distributes justice on the
Border,

Where judge and hangman oft reverse
their office,

And the noose does its work before the
sentence.   [worst.

But I have said my tidings best and

None but yourself can know what
course the time

Ana peril may demand.   To lift your
    banner,
If I might be a judge, were desperate
    game :
Ireland and Galloway offer you conve-
    nience
For flight, if flight be thought the better
    remedy ;
To face the court requires the conscious-
    ness
And confidence of innocence.   You
    alone
Can judge if you possess these attri-
    butes. [*A noise behind the scenes.*

AUCH. Philip, I think, has broken
    up his revels ;   [them,
His ragged regiment are dispersing
Well liquor'd, doubtless. They 're dis-
    banded soldiers,
Or some such vagabonds.—Here comes
    the gallant.
            [*Enter* PHILIP. *He has a buff
            coat and headpiece, wears a
            sword and dagger, with pis-
            tols at his girdle. He ap-
            pears to be affected by liquor,
            but to be by no means in-
            toxicated.*

AUCH. You scarce have been made
    known to one another,
Although you sate together at the
    board.
Son Philip, know and prize our cousin
    Gifford.

PHI. (*tastes the wine on the table*).
    If you had prized him, sir, you had
    been loth
To have welcomed him in bastard Ali-
    cant ;
I 'll make amends, by pledging his good
    journey
In glorious Burgundy.   The stirrup-
    cup, ho !   [court.
And bring my cousin's horses to the

AUCH. (*draws him aside*). The stirrup-
    cup !   He doth not ride to-night—
Shame on such churlish conduct to a
    kinsman !

PHI. (*aside to his Father*). I 've
    news of pressing import.

Send the fool off—stay, I will start him
    for you.
(*To* GIF.) Yes, my kind cousin, Bur-
    gundy is better
On a night ride, to those who thread
    our moors,
And we may deal it freely to our
    friends,
For we came freely by it.   Yonder
    ocean
Rolls many a purple cask upon our
    shore,
Rough with embossed shells and
    shagged sea-weed,
When the good skipper and his care-
    ful crew
Have had their latest earthly draught
    of brine.
And gone to quench or to endure their
    thirst,
Where nectar's plenty, or even water's
    scarce,
And filter'd to the parched crew by
    dropsfull.

AUCH. Thou'rt mad, son Philip !
    Gifford's no intruder,
That we should rid him hence by such
    wild rants :
My kinsman hither rode at his own
    danger,
To tell us that Dunbar is hasting to us,
With a strong force, and with the King's
    commission,
To enforce against our house a hateful
    charge,
With every measure of extremity.

PHI. And is this all that our good
    cousin tells us ?
I can say more, thanks to the ragged
    regiment,
With whose good company you have
    upbraided me,
On whose authority, I tell thee, cousin,
Dunbar is here already.

GIF.   Already ?

PHI. Yes, gentle coz.   And you, my
    sire, be hasty
In what you think to do.

AUCH. I think thou darest not jest
    on such a subject.

Where hadst thou these fell tidings?
 PHI. Where you, too, might have
  heard them, noble father,
Save that your ears, nail'd to our kins-
  man's lips,
Would list no coarser accents. O, my
  soldiers,
My merry crew of vagabonds, for ever!
Scum of the Netherlands, and wash'd
  ashore
Upon this coast like unregarded sea-
  weed,
They had not been two hours on Scottish
  land,
When, lo! they met a military friend,
An ancient fourier, known to them of
  old,
Who, warm'd by certain stoups of
  searching wine,
Inform'd his old companions that
  Dunbar
Left Glasgow yesterday, comes here to-
  morrow;
Himself, he said, was sent a spy be-
  fore,
To view what preparations we were
  making.
 AUCH. (*to* GIF.) If this be sooth,
  good kinsman, thou must claim
To take a part with us for life and death,
Or speed from hence, and leave us to
  our fortune.
 GIF. In such dilemma,
Believe me, friend, I'd choose upon the
  instant—
But I lack harness, and a steed to
  charge on,
For mine is overtired, and, save my
  page,
There's not a man to back me. But
  I'll hie
To Kyle, and raise my vassals to your
  aid.
 PHI. 'T will be when the rats,
That on these tidings fly this house of
  ours,
Come back to pay their rents. (*Apart.*)
 AUCH. Courage, cousin—
Thou goest not hence ill mounted for
  thy need.

Full forty coursers feed in my wide
  stalls,
The best of them is yours to speed your
  journey.
 PHI. Stand not on ceremony, good
  our cousin,
When safety signs to shorten courtesy.
 GIF.(*to* AUCH.) Farewell, then, cousin,
  for my tarrying here
Were ruin to myself, small aid to
  you;
Yet loving well your name and family,
I'd fain——
 PHI. Be gone?—that is our object,
  too.
Kinsman, adieu.
   [*Exit* GIFFORD. PHILIP *calls
    after him.*
    You yeoman of the stable,
Give Master Gifford there my fleetest
  steed,
Yon cut-tail'd roan that trembles at a
  spear.
   [*Tramping of the horse heard
    going off.*
Hark! he departs. How swift the
  dastard rides,
To shun the neighbourhood of jeopardy!
   [*He lays aside the appearance of
    levity which he has hitherto
    worn, and says very seriously.*
    And now, my father——
 AUCH. And now, my son—thou'st
  ta'en a perilous game
Into thine hands, rejecting elder coun-
  sel,—
How dost thou mean to play it?
 PHI. Sir, good gamesters play not
Till they review the cards which fate
  has dealt them,
Computing thus the chances of the
  game;
And wofully they seem to weigh against
  us.
 AUCH. Exile's a passing ill, and may
  be borne;
And when Dunbar and all his myrmi-
  dons
Are eastward turn'd, we'll seize our
  own again.

PHI. Would that were all the risk
we had to stand to !

But more and worse,—a doom of treason, forfeiture,

Death to ourselves, dishonour to our
house,

Is what the stern Justiciary menaces ;

And, fatally for us, he hath the
means

To make his threatenings good.

AUCH. It cannot be. I tell thee,
there's no force

In Scottish law to raze a house like
mine,

Coeval with the time the Lords of
Galloway

Submitted them unto the Scottish
sceptre,

Renouncing rights of Tanistry and
Brehon.

Some dreams they have of evidence ;
some suspicion.

But old Montgomery knows my purpose well,

And long before their mandate reach
the camp

To crave the presence of this mighty
witness,

He will be fitted with an answer to it.

PHI. Father, what we call great, is
often ruin'd

By means so ludicrously disproportion'd,

They make me think upon the gunner's
linstock,

Which, yielding forth a light about the
size

And semblance of the glowworm, yet
applied

To powder, blew a palace into atoms,

Sent a young King—a young Queen's
mate at least—

Into the air, as high as e'er flew night-
hawk,

And made such wild work in the realm
of Scotland

As they can tell who heard,—and you
were one

Who saw, perhaps, the night-flight
which began it.

AUCH. If thou hast nought to speak
but drunken folly,

I cannot listen longer.

PHI. I will speak brief and sudden.
—There is one

Whose tongue to us has the same
perilous force

Which Bothwell's powder had to Kirk
of Field ;

One whose least tones, and those but
peasant accents,

Could rend the roof from off our father's
castle,

Level its tallest turret with its base ;

And he that doth possess this wondrous
power

Sleeps this same night not five miles
distant from us.

AUCH. (*who had looked on* PHILIP
*with much appearance of astonish-
ment and doubt, exclaims*). Then
thou art mad indeed ! Ha ! ha !
I'm glad on't.

I'd purchase an escape from what I
dread,

Even by the frenzy of my only son !

PHI. I thank you, but agree not to
the bargain.

You rest on what yon civet cat has
said.

Yon silken doublet stuff'd with rotten
straw,

Told you but half truth, and knew no
more.

But my good vagrants had a perfect
tale ;

They told me, little judging the importance

That Quentin Blane had been discharged with them.

They told me that a quarrel happ'd at
landing,

And that the youngster and an ancient
sergeant

Had left their company and taken
refuge

In Chapeldonan, where our ranger
dwells ;

They saw him scale the cliff on which
it stands,

Ere they were out of sight; the old
    man with him.
And therefore laugh no more at me as
    mad;
But laugh, if thou hast list for merri-
    ment,
To think he stands on the same land
    with us,
Whose absence thou wouldst deem were
    cheaply purchased
With thy soul's ransom and thy body's
    danger.
    AUCH. 'Tis then a fatal truth! Thou
    art no yelper
To open rashly on so wild a scent;
Thou 'rt the young bloodhound, which
    careers and springs,
Frolics and fawns, as if the friend of
    man,
But seizes on his victim like a tiger.
    PHI. No matter what I am. I 'm as
    you bred me;
So let that pass till there be time to
    mend me,
And let us speak like men and to the
    purpose.
This object of our fear, and of our
    dread,
Since such our pride must own him,
    sleeps to-night
Within our power—to-morrow in Dun-
    bar's,
And we are then his victims.
    AUCH. He is in *ours* to-night.
    PHI. He is. I 'll answer that Mac-
    Lellan 's trusty.
    AUCH. Yet he replied to you to-day
    full rudely.
    PHI. Yes! The poor knave has got
    a handsome wife,
And is gone mad with jealousy.
    AUCH. Fool! When we need the ut-
    most faith, allegiance,
Obedience, and attachment in our
    vassals,
Thy wild intrigues pour gall into their
    hearts,
And turn their love to hatred!
    PHI. Most reverend sire, you talk of
    ancient morals,

Preach'd on by Knox, and practised by
    Glencairn;
Respectable, indeed, but somewhat
    musty
In these our modern nostrils. In our
    days,
If a young baron chance to leave his
    vassal
The sole possessor of a handsome wife,
'T is sign he loves his follower; and, if
    not,
He loves his follower's wife, which often
    proves
The surer bond of patronage. Take
    either case:
Favour flows in, of course, and vassals
    rise.
    AUCH. Philip, this is infamous,
And, what is worse, impolitic. Take
    example:
Break not God's laws or man's for each
    temptation
That youth and blood suggest. I am
    a man—
A weak and erring man; full well thou
    know'st
That I may hardly term myself a
    pattern
Even to my son: yet thus far will I say,
I never swerved from my integrity,
Save at the voice of strong necessity,
Or such o'erpowering view of high ad-
    vantage
As wise men liken to necessity,
In strength and force compulsive. No
    one saw me
Exchange my reputation for my
    pleasure,
Or do the Devil's work without his
    wages.
I practised prudence, and paid tax to
    virtue,
By following her behests, save where
    strong reason
Compell'd a deviation. Then, if
    preachers
At times look'd sour, or elders shook
    their heads,
They could not term my walk irregular;
For I stood up still for the worthy cause,

A pillar, though a flaw'd one, of the altar,
Kept a strict walk, and led three hundred horse.
  PHI. Ah, these three hundred horse in such rough times
Were better commendation to a party
Than all your efforts at hypocrisy,
Betray'd so oft by avarice and ambition,
And dragg'd to open shame. But, righteous father,
When sire and son unite in mutual crime,
And join their efforts to the same enormity,
It is no time to measure other's faults,
Or fix the amount of each. Most moral father,
Think if it be a moment now to weigh
The vices of the Heir of Auchindrane,
Or take precaution that the ancient house
Shall have another heir than the sly courtier
That 's gaping for the forfeiture.
  AUCH. We'll disappoint him, Philip,
We 'll disappoint him yet. It is a folly,
A wilful cheat, to cast our eyes behind
When time, and the fast flitting opportunity,
Call loudly—nay, compel us—to look forward.
Why are we not already at MacLellan's,
Since there the victim sleeps?
  PHI.   Nay, soft, I pray thee.
I had not made your piety my confessor,
Nor enter'd in debate on these sage counsels,
Which you 're more like to give than I to profit by,
Could I have used the time more usefully;
But first an interval must pass between
The fate of Quentin and the little artifice
That shall detach him from his comrade,
The stout old soldier that I told you of.
  AUCH. How work a point so difficult
—so dangerous?
  PHI. 'T is cared for. Mark, my father, the convenience

Arising from mean company. My agents
Are at my hand, like a good workman's tools,
And if I mean a mischief, ten to one
That they anticipate the deed and guilt.
Well knowing this, when first the vagrant's tattle
Gave me the hint that Quentin was so near us,
Instant I sent MacLellan, with strong charges
To stop him for the night, and bring me word,
Like an accomplish'd spy, how all things stood,
Lulling the enemy into security.
  AUCH. There was a prudent general!
  PHI. MacLellan went and came within the hour.
The jealous bee, which buzzes in his nightcap,
Had humm'd to him, this fellow, Quentin Blane,
Had been in schoolboy days an humble lover
Of his own pretty wife—
  AUCH.   Most fortunate!
The knave will be more prompt to serve our purpose.
  PHI. No doubt on 't. 'Mid the tidings he brought back
Was one of some importance. The old man
Is flush of dollars; this I caused him tell
Among his comrades, who became as eager
To have him in their company, as e'er
They had been wild to part with him. And in brief space,
A letter 's framed by an old hand amongst them,
Familiar with such feats. It bore the name
And character of old Montgomery,
Whom he might well suppose at no great distance,
Commanding his old Sergeant Hildebrand.

By all the ties of late authority,
Conjuring him by ancient soldiership,
To hasten to his mansion instantly,
On business of high import, with a charge
To come alone——
 AUCH. Well, he sets out, I doubt it not,—what follows?
 PHI. I am not curious into others' practices,—
So far I'm an economist in guilt,
As you my sire advise. But on the road
To old Montgomery's he meets his comrades,
They nourish grudge against him and his dollars,
And things may hap, which counsel, learn'd in law,
Call Robbery and Murder. Should he live,
He has seen nought that we would hide from him.
 AUCH. Who carries the forged letter to the veteran?
 PHI. Why, Niel MacLellan, who return'd again
To his own tower, as if to pass the night there.
They pass'd on him, or tried to pass, a story, [pany,
As if they wish'd the sergeant's com-
Without the young comptroller's—that is Quentin's,
And he became an agent of their plot,
That he might better carry on our own.
 AUGH. There's life in it—yes, there is life in't;
And we will have a mounted party ready
To scour the moors in quest of the banditti
That kill'd the poor old man—they shall die instantly.
Dunbar shall see us use sharp justice here
As well as he in Teviotdale. You are sure
You gave no hint nor impulse to their purpose?

 PHI. It needed not. The whole pack oped at once
Upon the scent of dollars.—But time comes
When I must seek the tower, and act with Niel
What further's to be done.
 AUCH. Alone with him thou goest not. He bears grudge—
Thou art my only son, and on a night
When such wild passions are so free abroad,
When such wild deeds are doing, 't is but natural
I guarantee thy safety.—I'll ride with thee.
 PHI. E'en as you will, my lord. But, pardon me,—
If you will come, let us not have a word
Of conscience, and of pity, and forgiveness;
Fine words to-morrow, out of place to-night.
Take counsel, then, leave all this work to me;
Call up your household, make fit preparation,
In love and peace, to welcome this Earl Justiciar,
As one that's free of guilt. Go, deck the castle
As for an honour'd guest. Hallow the chapel
(If they have power to hallow it) with thy prayers.
Let me ride forth alone, and ere the sun
Comes o'er the eastern hill, thou shalt accost him:
" Now do thy worst, thou oft-returning spy,
Here's nought thou canst discover."
 AUCH. Yet goest thou not alone with that MacLellan !
He deems thou bearest will to injure him,
And seek'st occasion suiting to such will.
Philip, thou art irreverent, fierce, ill-nurtured,

Stain'd with low vices, which disgust a
  father;
Yet ridest thou not alone with yonder
  man,—
Come weal come woe, myself will go
  with thee.

  [*Exit, and calls to horse behind
    the scene.*

  PHI. (*alone*). Now would I give my
    fleetest horse to know
What sudden thought roused this pa-
  ternal care,
And if 't is on his own account or mine:
'T is true, he hath the deepest share in
  all
That's likely now to hap, or which has
  happen'd   [reign
Yet strong through Nature's universal
The link which binds the parent to the
  offspring—
The she-wolf knows it, and the tigress
  owns it;
So that dark man, who, shunning what
  is vicious,
Ne'er turn'd aside from an atrocity,
Hath still some care left for his hapless
  offspring.
Therefore 't is meet, though wayward,
  light, and stubborn,
That I should do for him all that a son
Can do for sire—and his dark wisdom
  join'd
To influence my bold courses, 't will be
  hard
To break our mutual purpose. Horses,
  there!   [*Exit.*

ACT III.—SCENE I.

*It is moonlight. The Scene is the Beach
  beneath the Tower which was exhibited in
  the first Scene; the vessel is gone from her
  anchorage.* AUCHINDRANE *and* PHILIP,
  *as if dismounted from their horses, come
  forward cautiously.*

  PHI. The nags are safely stow'd.
    Their noise might scare him;
Let them be safe, and ready when we
  need them,

The business is but short. We'll call
  MacLellan,
To wake him, and in quiet bring him
  forth,
If he be so disposed, for here are waters
Enough to drown, and sand enough to
  cover him.
But if he hesitate, or fear to meet us,
By Heaven I'll deal on him in Chapel-
  donan
With my own hand!
  AUCH. Too furious boy! alarm or
    noise undoes us,
Our practice must be silent as 't is
  sudden.
Bethink thee that conviction of this
  slaughter
Confirms the very worst of accusations
Our foes can bring against us. Where-
  fore should we,
Who by our birth and fortune mate
  with nobles,
And are allied with them, take this lad's
  life—
His peasant life—unless to quash his
  evidence;
Taking such pains to rid him from the
  world,
Who would, if spared, have fix'd a crime
  upon us?
  PHI. Well, I do own me one of those
    wise folks
Who think that when a deed of fate is
  plann'd,
The execution cannot be too rapid.
But do we still keep purpose? Is't
  determined
He sails for Ireland, and without a
  wherry?
Salt water is his passport—is it not so?
  AUCH. I would it could be otherwise.
Might he not go there while in life and
  limb,
And breathe his span out in another
  air?
Many seek Ulster never to return—
Why might this wretched youth not
  harbour there?
  PHI. With all my heart. It is small
    honour to me

To be the agent in a work like this.
Yet this poor caitiff, having thrust him-
　　self
Into the secrets of a noble house,
And twined himself so closely with our
　　safety,
That we must perish, or that he must
　　die,
I 'll hesitate as little on the action,
As I would do to slay the animal
Whose flesh supplies my dinner. 'T is
　　as harmless,
That deer or steer, as is this Quentin
　　Blane,
And not more necessary is its death
To our accommodation—so we slay it
Without a moment's pause or hesita-
　　tion.
　　AUCH. 'T is not, my son, the feeling
　　call'd remorse,
That now lies tugging at this heart of
　　mine,
Engendering thoughts that stop the
　　lifted hand.
Have I not heard John Knox pour
　　forth his thunders
Against the oppressor and the man of
　　blood,
In accents of a minister of vengeance?
Were not his fiery eyeballs turn'd on
　　me,
As if he said expressly, " Thou 'rt the
　　man ! "
Yet did my solid purpose, as I listen'd,
Remain unshaken as that massive rock.
　　PHI. Well, then, I 'll understand 't is
　　not remorse,—
As 't is a foible little known to thee,—
That interrupts thy purpose. What,
　　then, is it?
Is 't scorn, or is 't compassion? One
　　thing 's certain,
Either the feeling must have free in-
　　dulgence,
Or fully be subjected to your reason—
There is no room for these same trea-
　　cherous courses,
Which men call moderate measures.
We must confide in Quentin, or must
　　slay him.

　　AUCH. In Ireland he might live afar
　　from us.
　　PHI. Among Queen Mary's faithful
　　partisans,
Your ancient enemies, the haughty
　　Hamiltons,
The stern MacDonnells, the resentful
　　Græmes—
With these around him, and with
　　Cassilis' death
Exasperating them against you, think,
　　my father,
What chance of Quentin's silence.
　　AUCH. Too true—too true. He is a
　　silly youth, too,
Who had not wit to shift for his own
　　living—
A bashful lover, whom his rivals laugh'd
　　at—
Of pliant temper, which companions
　　play'd on—
A moonlight waker, and a noontide
　　dreamer—
A torturer of phrases into sonnets,—
Whom all might lead that chose to
　　praise his rhymes.
　　PHI. I marvel that your memory has
　　room
To hold so much on such a worthless
　　subject.
　　AUCH. Base in himself, and yet so
　　strangely link'd
With me and with my fortunes, that
　　I 've studied
To read him through and through, as
　　I would read
Some paltry rhyme of vulgar prophecy,
Said to contain the fortunes of my
　　house ;
And, let me speak him truly—he is
　　grateful,
Kind, tractable, obedient—a child
Might lead him by a thread. He shall
　　not die !
　　PHI. Indeed !—then have we had
　　our midnight ride
To wondrous little purpose.
　　AUCH.　　　　By the blue heaven,
Thou shalt not murder him, cold selfish
　　sensualist !

Yon pure vault speaks it—yonder summer moon,
With its ten million sparklers, cries, Forbear!
The deep earth sighs it forth: thou shalt not murder!
Thou shalt not mar the image of thy Maker!
Thou shalt not from thy brother take the life,
The precious gift which God alone can give!

PHI. Here is a worthy guerdon now, for stuffing
His memory with old saws and holy sayings!
They come upon him in the very crisis,
And when his resolution should be firmest,
They shake it like a palsy. Let it be,
He'll end at last by yielding to temptation,
Consenting to the thing which must be done,
With more remorse the more he hesitates.

[*To his Father, who has stood fixed after his last speech.*

Well, sir, 't is fitting you resolve at last.
How the young clerk shall be disposed upon;
Unless you would ride home to Auchindrane,
And bid them rear the Maiden in the courtyard,
That when Dunbar comes he have nought to do
But bid us kiss the cushion and the headsman.

AUCH. It is too true. There is no safety for us
Consistent with the unhappy wretch's life.
In Ireland he is sure to find my enemies.
Arran I've proved, the Netherlands I've tried,
But wilds and wars return him on my hands.

PHI. Yet fear not, father, we'll make surer work:

The land has caves, the sea has whirlpools,
Where that which they suck in returns no more.

AUCH. I will know nought of it, hard-hearted boy!

PHI. Hard-hearted! Why, my heart is soft as yours.
But then they must not feel remorse at once,
We can't afford such wasteful tenderness.
I can mouth forth remorse as well as you;
Be executioner, and I'll be chaplain,
And say as mild and moving things as you can—
But one of us must keep his steely temper.

AUCH. Do thou the deed—I cannot look on it.

PHI. So be it—walk with me—MacLellan brings him.
The boat lies moor'd within that reach of rock,
And 't will require our greatest strength combined
To launch it from the beach. Meantime, MacLellan
Brings our man hither. See the twinkling light
That glances in the tower.

AUCH. Let us withdraw, for should he see us suddenly,
He may suspect us, and alarm the family.

PHI. Fear not—MacLellan has his trust and confidence,
Bought with a few sweet words and welcomes home.

AUCH. But think you that the ranger may be trusted?

PHI. I'll answer for him. Let's go float the shallop.

[*They go off, and as they leave the Stage,* MACLELLAN *is seen descending from the Tower with* QUENTIN. *The former bears a dark lantern. They come upon the Stage.*

MAC. (*showing the light*). So—
bravely done—that's the last ledge
of rocks,
And we are on the sands. I have broke
your slumbers
Somewhat untimely.

QUE.   Do not think so, friend.
These six years past I have been used
to stir
When the réveille rung; and that,
believe me,
Chooses the hours for rousing me at
random,
And, having given its summons, yields
no license
To indulge a second slumber. Nay,
more, I'll tell thee,
That, like a pleased child, I was e'en
too happy
For sound repose.

MAC.   The greater fool were you.
Men should enjoy the moments given
to slumber;
For who can tell how soon may be the
waking,
Or where we shall have leave to sleep
again?

QUE. The God of Slumber comes
not at command.
Last night the blood danced merry
through my veins:
Instead of finding this our land of
Carrick
The dreary waste my fears had appre-
hended,
I saw thy wife, MacLellan, and thy
daughter,
And had a brother's welcome; saw
thee, too,
Renew'd my early friendship with you
both,
And felt once more that I had friends
and country.
So keen the joy that tingled through
my system,
Join'd with the searching powers of
yonder wine,   [lair,
That I am glad to leave my feverish
Although my hostess smooth'd my
couch herself,

To cool my brow upon this moonlight
beach,
Gaze on the moonlight dancing on the
waves.
Such scenes are wont to soothe me into
melancholy;
But such the hurry of my spirits now,
That everything I look on makes me
laugh.

MAC. I've seen but few so gamesome, Master Quentin,
Being roused from sleep so suddenly as
you were.

QUE. Why, there's the jest on't.
Your old castle's haunted.
In vain the host—in vain the lovely
hostess,
In kind addition to all means of rest,
Add their best wishes for our sound
repose,
When some hobgoblin brings a press-
ing message:
Montgomery presently must see his
sergeant,
And up gets Hildebrand, and off he
trudges.
I can't but laugh to think upon the
grin
With which he doff'd the kerchief he
had twisted
Around his brows, and put his morion
on—
Ha! ha! ha! ha!

MAC. I'm glad to see you merry,
Quentin.

QUE. Why, faith, my spirits are but
transitory,
And you may live with me a month or
more,
And never see me smile. Then some
such trifle
As yonder little maid of yours would
laugh at,
Will serve me for a theme of merriment—
Even now, I scarce can keep my
gravity;
We were so snugly settled in our
quarters,
With full intent to let the sun be high

Ere we should leave our beds—and
    first the one
And then the other's summon'd briefly
    forth,
To the old tune, "Black Bandsmen, up
    and march!

MAC. Well! you shall sleep anon—
    rely upon it,
And make up time misspent. Mean-
    time, methinks,
You are so merry on your broken
    slumbers,
You ask'd not why I call'd you.

QUE.   I can guess.
You lack my aid to search the weir for
    seals,
You lack my company to stalk a
    deer.
Think you I have forgot your sylvan
    tasks,
Which oft you have permitted me to
    share,
Till days that we were rivals?

MAC.   You have memory
Of that too?—

QUE. Like the memory of a dream,
Delusion far too exquisite to last.

MAC. You guess not then for what
    I call you forth;
It was to meet a friend——

QUE. What friend? Thyself ex-
    cepted,
The good old man who's gone to see
    Montgomery,
And one to whom I once gave dearer
    title,
I know not in wide Scotland man or
    woman
Whom I could name a friend.

MAC.   Thou art mistaken,
There is a baron, and a powerful
    one——

QUE. There flies my fit of mirth.
    You have a grave
And alter'd man before you.

MAC. Compose yourself, there is no
    cause for fear,—
He will and must speak with you.

QUE. Spare me the meeting, Niel, I
    cannot see him.

Say, I'm just landed on my native
    earth;
Say, that I will not cumber it a day;
Say, that my wretched thread of poor
    existence
Shall be drawn out in solitude and exile,
Where never memory of so mean a thing
Again shall cross his path—but do not
    ask me
To see or speak again with that dark
    man!

MAC. Your fears are now as foolish
    as your mirth.
What should the powerful Knight of
    Auchindrane
In common have with such a man as
    thou?

QUE. No matter what—Enough, I
    will not see him.

MAC. He is thy master, and he
    claims obedience.

QUE. My master? Ay, my task-
    master. Ever since
I could write man, his hand hath been
    upon me,
No step I've made but cumber'd with
    his chain,
And I am weary on't—I will not see
    him.

MAC. You must and shall—there is
    no remedy.

QUE. Take heed that you compel me
    not to find one.
I've seen the wars since we had strife
    together;
To put my late experience to the test
Were something dangerous—Ha, I am
    betray'd!

    [*While the latter part of this
    dialogue is passing,* AUCHIN-
    DRANE *and* PHILIP *enter on
    the Stage from behind, and
    suddenly present themselves.*

AUCH. What says the runagate?

QUE (*laying aside all appearance of
    resistance*). Nothing, you are my
    fate;
And in a shape more fearfully resistless
My evil angel could not stand before
    me.

AUCH. And so you scruple, slave, at my command,
To meet me when I deign to ask thy presence?
QUE. No, sir; I had forgot—I am your bond-slave
But sure a passing thought of independence,
For such I 've seen whole nations doing battle,
Was not, in one wh' has so long enjoy'd it,
A crime beyond forgiveness.
  AUCH.   We shall see :
Thou wert my vassal, born upon my land,
Bred by my bounty—It concern'd me highly,
Thou know'st it did—and yet against my charge
Again I find thy worthlessness in Scotland.
  QUE. Alas ! the wealthy and the powerful know not
How very dear to those who have least in 't
Is that sweet word of country ! The poor exile
Feels, in each action of the varied day,
His doom of banishment. The very air
Cools not his brow as in his native land ;
The scene is strange, the food is loathly to him ;
The language, nay, the music jars his ear.
Why should I, guiltless of the slightest crime,
Suffer a punishment which, sparing life,
Deprives that life of all which men hold dear?
  AUCH. Hear ye the serf I bred, begin to reckon
Upon his rights and pleasure ! Who am I—
Thou abject, who am I, whose will thou thwartest?
  PHI. Well spoke, my pious sire. There goes remorse !

Let once thy precious pride take fire, and then,
MacLellan, you and I may have small trouble.
  QUE. Your words are deadly, and your power resistless ;
I 'm in your hands—but, surely, less than life
May give you the security you seek,
Without commission of a mortal crime.
  AUCH. Who is 't would deign to think upon thy life ?
I but require of thee to speed to Ireland,
Where thou mayst sojourn for some little space,
Having due means of living dealt to thee,
And, when it suits the changes of the times,
Permission to return.
  QUE.   Noble my lord
I am too weak to combat with your pleasure ;
Yet, O, for mercy's sake, and for the sake
Of that dear land which is our common mother,
Let me not part in darkness from my country !
Pass but an hour or two, and every cape,
Headland, and bay, shall gleam with new-born light,
And I 'll take boat as gaily as the bird
That soars to meet the morning.
Grant me but this—to show no darker thoughts
Are on your heart than those your speech expresses !
  PHI. A modest favour, friend, is this you ask !
Are we to pace the beach like watermen,
Waiting your worship's pleasure to take boat?
No, by my faith ! you go upon the instant.
The boat lies ready, and the ship receives you

Near to the point of Turnberry.—
　　Come, we wait you;
Bestir you!
　　QUE.　　I obey.—Then farewell
　　　Scotland,
And Heaven forgive my sins, and
　　grant that mercy
Which mortal man deserves not!
　　AUCH. (*speaks aside to his Son*).
　　　What signal
Shall let me know 't is done?
　　PHI.　　When the light is quench'd,
Your fears for Quentin Blane are at an
　　end.
(*To* QUE.) Come, comrade, come, we
　　must begin our voyage.
　　QUE.　But when, O, when to end it?
　　　[*He goes off reluctantly with*
　　　PHILIP *and* MACLELLAN.
　　　AUCHINDRANE *stands look-*
　　　ing after them. The moon
　　　becomes overclouded, and the
　　　Stage dark. AUCHINDRANE,
　　　who has gazed fixedly and
　　　eagerly after those who have
　　　left the Stage, becomes ani-
　　　mated, and speaks.
　　AUCH. It is no fallacy!—The night
　　　is dark,
The moon has sunk before the deepen-
　　ing clouds;
I cannot on the murky beach distin-
　　guish
The shallop from the rocks which lie
　　beside it;
I cannot see tall Philip's floating plume,
Nor trace the sullen brow of Niel
　　MacLellan;
Yet still that caitiff's visage is before
　　me,
With chattering teeth, mazed look, and
　　bristling hair,
As he stood here this moment!—Have
　　I changed
My human eyes for those of some night
　　prowler,
The wolf's, the tiger-cat's, or the hoarse
　　bird's
That spies its prey at midnight? I can
　　see him—

Yes, I can see him, seeing no one
　　else,—
And well it is I do so. In his absence
Strange thoughts of pity mingled with
　　my purpose,
And moved remorse within me—but
　　they vanish'd
Whene'er he stood a living man before
　　me;
Then my antipathy awaked within
　　me,
Seeing its object close within my
　　reach,
Till I could scarce forbear him.—How
　　they linger!
The boat's not yet to sea!—I ask my-
　　self,
What has the poor wretch done to wake
　　my hatred—
Docile, obedient, and in sufferance
　　patient?—
As well demand what evil has the
　　hare
Done to the hound that courses her in
　　sport.
Instinct infallible supplies the reason,
And that must plead my cause.—The
　　vision's gone!
Their boat now walks the waves; a
　　single gleam,
Now seen, now lost, is all that marks
　　her course;
That soon shall vanish too—then all is
　　over!—
Would it were o'er, for in this moment
　　lies
The agony of ages!—Now 't is gone—
And all is acted!—no—she breasts
　　again
The opposing wave, and bears the tiny
　　sparkle
Upon her crest—(*a faint cry heard as
　　from seaward.*) Ah! there was
　　fatal evidence,
All's over now, indeed!—The light is
　　quench'd,
And Quentin, source of all my fear,
　　exists not.—
The morning tide shall sweep his corpse
　　to sea,

And hide all memory of this stern
night's work.

> [*He walks in a slow and deeply
> meditative manner towards
> the side of the Stage, and sud-
> denly meets* MARION, *the wife
> of* MACLELLAN, *who has de-
> scended from the Castle.*

Now, how to meet Dunbar—Heaven
guard my senses !
Stand ! who goes there?—Do spirits
walk the earth
Ere yet they've left the body?

MAR.   Is it you,
My lord, on this wild beach at such an
hour ?

AUCH. It is MacLellan's wife, in
search of him,
Or of her lover—of the murderer,
Or of the murder'd man.—Go to, Dame
Marion,
Men have their hunting-gear to give an
eye to,
Their snares and trackings for their
game. But women
Should shun the night air. A young
wife also,
Still more a handsome one, should keep
her pillow
Till the sun gives example for her
wakening.
Come, dame, go back—back to your
bed again.

MAR. Hear me, my lord ! there have
been sights and sounds
That terrified my child and me—
Groans, screams,
As if of dying seamen, came from
ocean—
A corpse-light danced upon the crested
waves
For several minutes' space, then sunk
at once.
When we retired to rest we had two
guests,
Besides my husband Niel—I'll tell
your lordship
Who the men were——

AUCH. Pshaw, woman, can you think
That I have any interest in your gossips?

Please your own husband, and that you
may please him,
Get thee to bed, and shut up doors,
good dame.
Were I MacLellan, I should scarce be
satisfied
To find thee wandering here in mist
and moonlight,
When silence should be in thy habitation,
And sleep upon thy pillow.

MAR.   Good my lord,
This is a holyday.—By an ancient
custom
Our children seek the shore at break of
day,
And gather shells, and dance, and play,
and sport them
In honour of the ocean. Old men say
The custom is derived from heathen
times. Our Isabel
Is mistress of the feast, and you may
think
She is awake already, and impatient
To be the first shall stand upon the
beach,
And bid the sun good morrow.

AUCH.   Ay, indeed ?
Linger such dregs of heathendom
among you?
And hath Knox preach'd, and Wishart
died, in vain ?
Take notice, I forbid these sinful practices,
And will not have my followers mingle
in them.

MAR. If such your honour's pleasure,
I must go
And lock the door on Isabel ; she is
wilful,
And voice of mine will have small
force to keep her
From the amusement she so long has
dream'd of.
But I must tell your honour, the old
people,
That were survivors of the former race,
Prophesied evil if this day should pass
Without due homage to the mighty
ocean,

AUCH. Folly and Papistry! Perhaps the ocean
Hath had his morning sacrifice already;
Or can you think the dreadful element,
Whose frown is death, whose roar the dirge of navies,
Will miss the idle pageant you prepare for?
I've business for you, too—the dawn advances—
I'd have thee lock thy little child in safety,
And get to Auchindrane before the sun rise;
Tell them to get a royal banquet ready,
As if a king were coming there to feast him.

MAR. I will obey your pleasure. But my husband——

AUCH. I wait him on the beach, and bring him in
To share the banquet.

MAR.   But he has a friend,
Whom it would ill become him to intrude
Upon your hospitality.

AUCH. Fear not; his friend shall be made welcome too,
Should he return with Niel.

MAR. He must—he will return—he has no option.

AUCH. (apart). Thus rashly do we deem of others' destiny—
He has indeed no option—but he comes not.
Begone on thy commission—I go this way
To meet thy husband.

[MARION goes to her Tower, and after entering it, is seen to come out, lock the door, and leave the Stage, as if to execute AUCHINDRANE'S commission. He, apparently going off in a different direction, has watched her from the side of the Stage, and on her departure speaks.

AUCH. Fare thee well, fond woman,
Most dangerous of spies—thou prying, prating,

Spying, and telling woman! I've cut short
Thy dangerous testimony—hated word!
What other evidence have we cut short,
And by what fated means, this dreary morning!—
Bright lances here and helmets?—I must shift
To join the others.   [Exit.

Enter from the other side the SER-
GEANT, accompanied with an
OFFICER and two PIKEMEN.

SER. 'Twas in good time you came; a minute later
The knaves had ta'en my dollars and my life.

OFF. You fought most stoutly. Two of them were down
Ere we came to your aid.

SER.   Gramercy, halberd!
And well it happens, since your leader seeks
This Quentin Blane, that you have fall'n on me;
None else can surely tell you where he hides,
Being in some fear, and bent to quit this province.

OFF. 'Twill do our Earl good service. He has sent   [tin.
Despatches into Holland for this Quen-
SER. I left him two hours since in yonder tower,
Under the guard of one who smoothly spoke,
Although he look'd but roughly—I will chide him
For bidding me go forth with yonder traitor.

OFF. Assure yourself 't was a concerted stratagem.
Montgomery's been at Holyrood for months,
And can have sent no letter—'t was a plan
On you and on your dollars, and a base one,
To which this ranger was most likely privy;

Such men as he hang on our fiercer
   barons,
The ready agents of their lawless will ;
Boys of the belt, who aid their master's
   pleasures,
And in his moods ne'er scruple his
   injunctions.
But haste, for now we must unkennel
   Quentin ;
I 've strictest charge concerning him.
   SER. Go up, then, to the tower.
You 've younger limbs than mine—
   there shall you find him
Lounging and snoring, like a lazy cur
Before a stable door ; it is his practice.
   [*The* OFFICER *goes up to the
      Tower, and after knocking
      without receiving an answer,
      turns the key which* MARION
      had left in the lock, and enters;
      ISABEL, *dressed as if for her
      dance, runs out and descends
      to the Stage; the* OFFICER
      follows.
   OFF. There 's no one in the house,
      this little maid
Excepted——
   ISA. And for me, I 'm there no longer,
And will not be again for three hours
   good :   [sands.
I 'm gone to join my playmates on the
   OFF. (*detaining her*). You shall, when
   you have told to me distinctly
Where are the guests who slept up
   there last night.
   ISA. Why, there is the old man, he
      stands beside you,
The merry old man, with the glistening
   hair ;
He left the tower at midnight, for my
   father
Brought him a letter.
   SER.   In ill hour I left you,
I wish to Heaven that I had stay'd with
   you ;
There is a nameless horror that comes
   o'er me.—
Speak, pretty maiden, tell us what
   chanced next,
And thou shalt have thy freedom.

   ISA. After you went last night, my
      father
Grew moody, and refused to doff his
   clothes,
Or go to bed, as sometimes he will
   do
When there is aught to chafe him.
   Until past midnight
He wander'd to and fro, then call'd the
   stranger,
The gay young man, that sung such
   merry songs,
Yet ever look'd most sadly whilst he
   sung them,
And forth they went together.
   OFF.   And you 've seen
Or heard nought of them since ?
   ISA. Seen surely nothing, and I can-
      not think
That they have lot or share in what I
   heard.
I heard my mother praying, for the
   corpse-lights
Were dancing on the waves ; and at
   one o'clock,
Just as the abbey steeple toll'd the
   knell,
There was a heavy plunge upon the
   waters,
And some one cried aloud for mercy !
   —mercy !
It was the water-spirit, sure, which
   promised
Mercy to boat and fisherman, if we
Perform'd to-day's rites duly. Let me
   go—
I am to lead the ring.
   OFF. (*to* SER.) Detain her not. She
      cannot tell us more ;
To give her liberty is the sure way
To lure her parents homeward. —
   Strahan, take two men,
And should the father or the mother
   come,
Arrest them both, or either. Auchin-
   drane
May come upon the beach ; arrest him
   also,
But do not state a cause. I 'll back
   again,

And take directions from my Lord
 Dunbar. [eye
Keep you upon the beach, and have an
To all that passes here.
                    [*Exeunt separately.*

SCENE II.

*Scene changes to a remote and rocky part of
the Sea-beach.*

Enter AUCHINDRANE *meeting*
PHILIP.

AUCH. The devil's brought his legions
 to this beach,
That wont to be so lonely ; morions,
 lances,
Show in the morning beam as thick as
 glowworms
At summer midnight.
    PHI.   I 'm right glad to see them,
Be they whoe'er they may, so they are
 mortal ;
For I 've contended with a lifeless foe,
And I have lost the battle. I would
 give
A thousand crowns to hear a mortal
 steel
Ring on a mortal harness.
    AUCH. How now !—Art mad, or hast
 thou done the turn—
The turn we came for, and must live
 or die by ?
    PHI. 'T is done, if man can do it ;
 but I doubt
If this unhappy wretch have Heaven's
 permission
To die by mortal hands.
    AUCH. Where is he ?—where's Mac-
 Lellan ?
    PHI.   In the deep—
Both in the deep, and what 's immortal
 of them
Gone to the judgment-seat, where we
 must meet them.
    AUCH. MacLellan dead, and Quen-
 tin too ?—So be it
To all that menace ill to Auchindrane,
Or have the power to injure him !—
 Thy words

Are full of comfort, but thine eye and
 look
Have in this pallid gloom a ghastliness,
Which contradicts the tidings of thy
 tongue.
    PHI. Hear me, old man—there *is* a
 heaven above us,
As you have heard old Knox and Wishart preach,
Though little to your boot. The dreaded witness
Is slain and silent. But his misused
 body
Comes right ashore, as if to cry for
 vengeance ;
It rides the waters like a living thing,
Erect, as if he trode the waves which
 bear him.
    AUCH. Thou speakest frenzy, when
 sense is most required.
    PHI. Hear me yet more !—I say I
 did the deed
With all the coolness of a practised
 hunter
When dealing with a stag. I struck
 him overboard,
And with MacLellan's aid I held his
 head
Under the waters, while the ranger
 tied
The weights we had provided to his
 feet.
We cast him loose when life and body
 parted,
And bid him speed for Ireland. But
 even then,
As in defiance of the words we spoke,
The body rose upright behind our stern,
One half in ocean, and one half in air,
And tided after as in chase of us.
    AUCH. It was enchantment !—Did
 you strike at it ?
    PHI. Once and again. But blows
 avail'd no more
Than on a wreath of smoke, where
 they may break
The column for a moment, which
 unites
And is entire again. Thus the dead
 body

Sunk down before my oar, but rose un-
     harm'd,
And dogg'd us closer still, as in defiance.
     AUCH. 'Twas Hell's own work!——
     PHI.   MacLellan then grew restive
And desperate in his fear, blasphemed
     aloud,
Cursing us both as authors of his
     ruin.
Myself was wellnigh frantic while pur-
     sued
By this dead shape, upon whose ghastly
     features
The changeful moonbeam spread a
     grisly light;
And, baited thus, I took the nearest
     way
To ensure his silence, and to quell his
     noise;
I used my dagger, and I flung him
     overboard,
And half expected his dead carcass
     also
Would join the chase—but he sunk
     down at once.
     AUCH. He had enough of mortal sin
     about him
To sink an argosy.
     PHI. But now resolve you what de-
     fence to make,
If Quentin's body shall be recognised;
For 't is ashore already; and he bears
Marks of my handiwork; so does
     MacLellan.
     AUCH. The concourse thickens still
     —Away, away!
We must avoid the multitude.
                    [*They rush out.*

SCENE III.

Scene changes to another part of the Beach.
CHILDREN *are seen dancing, and*
VILLAGERS *looking on.* ISABEL *seems
to take the management of the dance.*

VIL. WOM. How well she queens it,
     the brave little maiden!
VIL. Ay, they all queen it from their
     very cradle,

These willing slaves of haughty Auchin-
     drane.
But now I hear the old man's reign is
     ended ;—
'T is well—he has been tyrant long
     enough.
     SECOND VIL. Finlay, speak low, you
     interrupt the sports.
     THIRD VIL. Look out to sea—There's
     something coming yonder,
Bound for the beach, will scare us from
     our mirth.
     FOURTH VIL. Pshaw, it is but a sea-
     gull on the wing,
Between the wave and sky.
     THIRD VIL.   Thou art a fool,
Standing on solid land—'tis a dead
     body.
     SECOND VIL. And if it be, he bears
     him like a live one,
Not prone and weltering like a drown-
     ed corpse,
But bolt erect, as if he trode the waters,
And used them as his path.
     FOURTH VIL.   It is a merman,
And nothing of this earth, alive or dead.
     [*By degrees all the Dancers break
          off from their sport, and stand
          gazing to seaward, while an
          object, imperfectly seen, drifts
          towards the beach, and at
          length arrives among the rocks
          which border the tide.*
     THIRD VIL. Perhaps it is some
     wretch who needs assistance ;
Jasper, make in and see.
     SECOND VIL.   Not I, my friend ;
E'en take the risk yourself you'd put
     on others.
          [HILDEBRAND *has entered and
               heard the two last words.*
     SER. What, are you men?
Fear ye to look on what you must be
     one day?
I, who have seen a thousand dead and
     dying
Within a flight-shot square, will teach
     you how in war
We look upon the corpse when life has
     left it.

[He goes to the back scene, and seems attempting to turn the body, which has come ashore with its face downwards.

Will none of you come aid to turn the body?

ISA. You're cowards all.—I'll help thee, good old man.

[She goes to the aid of the SERGEANT with the body, and presently gives a cry and faints. HILDEBRAND comes forward. All crowd round him; he speaks with an expression of horror.

SER. 'T is Quentin Blane! Poor youth, his gloomy bodings
Have been the prologue to an act of darkness;
His feet are manacled, his bosom stabb'd, [knight
And he is foully murder'd. The proud
And his dark ranger must have done this deed,
For which no common ruffian could have motive.

A PEA. Caution were best, old man. Thou art a stranger,
The knight is great and powerful.

SER.   Let it be so.
Call'd on by Heaven to stand forth an avenger,
I will not blench for fear of mortal man.
Have I not seen that when that inno-
cent   [murder'd body,
Had placed her hands upon the
His gaping wounds, that erst were soak'd with brine,   [cloud
Burstforth with blood as ruddy as the
Which now the sun doth rise on?

PEA. What of that?

SER. Nothing that can affect the innocent child,
But murder's guilt attaching to her father,   [veins
Since the blood musters in the victim's
At the approach of what holds lease from him
Of all that parents can transmit to children.

And here comes one to whom I'll vouch the circumstance.

[The EARL OF DUNBAR enters with Soldiers and others, having AUCHINDRANE and PHILIP prisoners.

DUN. Fetter the young ruffian and his trait'rous father!

[They are made secure.

AUCH. 'T was a lord spoke it—I have known a knight,
Sir George of Home, who had not dared to say so.

DUN. 'T is Heaven, not I, decides upon your guilt.   [power,
A harmless youth is traced within your
Sleeps in your ranger's house—his friend at midnight
Is spirited away. Then lights are seen,
And groans are heard, and corpses come ashore
Mangled with daggers, while (*to* PHILIP)
your dagger wears
The sanguine livery of recent slaughter.
Here, too, the body of a murder'd victim,   [remove,)
(Whom none but you had interest to
Bleeds on a child's approach, because the daughter
Of one the abettor of the wicked deed.
All this, and other proofs corroborative,
Call on us briefly to pronounce the doom
We have in charge to utter.

AUCH. If my house perish, Heaven's will be done!
I wish not to survive it; but, O Philip,
Would one could pay the ransom for us both!

PHI. Father, 'tis fitter that we both should die,
Leaving no heir behind.—The piety
Of a bless'd saint, the morals of an anchorite,
Could not atone thy dark hypocrisy,
Or the wild profligacy I have practised.
Ruin'd our house, and shatter'd be our towers,
And with them end the curse our sins have merited.

APPENDIX.

THE LAY OF THE LAST MINSTREL.

NOTE 1.

The feast was over in Branksome tower.—P. 4.

IN the reign of James I., Sir William Scott of Buccleuch, chief of the clan bearing that name, exchanged, with Sir Thomas Inglis of Manor, the estate of Murdiestone, in Lanarkshire, for one-half of the barony of Branksome, or Brankholm, lying upon the Teviot, about three miles above Hawick. He was probably induced to this transaction from the vicinity of Branksome to the extensive domain which he possessed in Ettrick Forest, and in Teviotdale. In the former district he held by occupancy the estate of Buccleuch, and much of the forest land on the river Ettrick. In Teviotdale, he enjoyed the barony of Eckford, by a grant from Robert II. to his ancestor, Walter Scott of Kirkurd, for the apprehending of Gilbert Ridderford, confirmed by Robert III. 3rd May, 1424. Tradition imputes the exchange betwixt Scott and Inglis to a conversation, in which the latter—a man, it would appear, of a mild and forbearing nature—complained much of the injuries to which he was exposed from the English Borderers, who frequently plundered his lands of Branksome. Sir William Scott instantly offered him the estate of Murdiestone, in exchange for that which was subject to such egregious inconvenience. When the bargain was completed, he dryly remarked, that the cattle in Cumberland were as good as those of Teviotdale; and proceeded to commence a system of reprisals upon the English, which was regularly pursued by his successors. In the next reign, James II. granted to Sir Walter Scott of Branksome, and to Sir David, his son, the remaining half of the barony of Branksome, to be held in blanche for the payment of a red rose. The cause assigned for the grant is, their brave and faithful exertions in favour of the King against the house of Douglas, with whom James had been recently tugging for the throne of Scotland. This charter is dated the 2nd February, 1443; and, in the same month, part of the barony of Langholm, and many lands in Lanarkshire, were conferred upon Sir Walter and his son by the same monarch.

NOTE 2.

*Nine-and-twenty knights of fame
Hung their shields in Branksome Hall.*—P. 4.

The ancient barons of Buccleuch, both from feudal splendour and from their frontier situation, retained in their household at Branksome, a number of gentlemen of their own name, who held lands from their chief, for the military service of watching and warding his castle.

NOTE 3.

— with Jedwood-axe at saddlebow.—P. 5.

"Of a truth," says Froissart, "the Scottish cannot boast great skill with the bow, but rather bear axes, with which, in time of need, they give heavy strokes." The Jedwood-axe was a sort of partisan, used by horsemen, as appears from the arms of Jedburgh, which bear a cavalier mounted, and armed with this weapon. It is also called a Jedwood or Jeddart staff.

NOTE 4.

*They watch, against Southern force and guile,
Lest Scroop, or Howard, or Percy's powers,
Threaten Branksome's lordly towers,
From Warkworth, or Naworth, or merry
Carlisle.*—P. 5.

Branksome Castle was continually exposed to the attacks of the English, both from its situation and the restless military disposition of its inhabitants, who were seldom on good terms with their neighbours.

NOTE 5.

Bards long shall tell,
How Lord Walter fell.—P. 5.

Sir Walter Scott of Buccleuch succeeded to
his grandfather, Sir David, in 1492. He was
a brave and powerful baron, and Warden of
the West Marches of Scotland. His death
was the consequence of a feud betwixt the
Scotts and Kerrs.

NOTE 6.

While Cessford owns the rule of Carr,
  While Ettrick boasts the line of Scott,
The slaughter'd chiefs, the mortal jar,
The havock of the feudal war,
  Shall never, never be forgot!—P. 5.

Among other expedients resorted to for
stanching the feud betwixt the Scotts and the
Kerrs, there was a bond executed in 1529,
between the heads of each clan, binding themselves to perform reciprocally the four principal pilgrimages of Scotland, for the benefit
of the souls of those of the opposite name
who had fallen in the quarrel. But either this
indenture never took effect, or else the feud
was renewed shortly afterwards.

NOTE 7.

With Carr in arms had stood.—P. 5.

The family of Ker, Kerr, or Carr,* was
very powerful on the Border. Their influence
extended from the village of Preston-Grange,
in Lothian, to the limits of England. Cessford Castle, now in ruins, the ancient baronial
residence of the family, is situated near the
village of Morebattle, within two or three
miles of the Cheviot Hills. Tradition affirms
that it was founded by Halbert, or Habby
Kerr, a gigantic warrior, concerning whom
many stories are current in Roxburghshire.
The Duke of Roxburgh represents Ker of
Cessford.

NOTE 8.

Lord Cranstoun.—P. 5.

The Cranstouns are an ancient Border
family, whose chief seat was at Crailing, in
Teviotdale. They were at this time at feud
with the clan of Scott; for it appears that
the Lady of Buccleuch, in 1557, beset the
Laird of Cranstoun, seeking his life. Nevertheless, the same Cranstoun, or perhaps his

son, was married to a daughter of the same
lady.

NOTE 9.

Of Bethune's line of Picardie.—P. 6.

The Bethunes were of French origin, and
derived their name from a small town in
Artois. There were several distinguished
families of the Bethunes in the neighbouring
province of Picardy; they numbered among
their descendants the celebrated Duc de Sully,
and the name was accounted among the most
noble in France, while aught noble remained
in that country.† The family of Bethune, or
Beatoun, in Fife, produced three learned and
dignified prelates, namely, Cardinal Beaton,
and two successive Archbishops of Glasgow,
all of whom flourished about the date of the
romance. Of this family was descended Dame
Janet Beaton, Lady Buccleuch, widow of Sir
Walter Scott of Branksome. She was a
woman of masculine spirit, as appeared from
her riding at the head of her son's clan, after
her husband's murder. She was believed by
the superstition of the vulgar to possess
supernatural knowledge. With this was
mingled, by faction, the foul accusation of
her having influenced Queen Mary to the
murder of her husband. One of the pla-
cards, preserved in Buchanan's Detection,
accuses of Darnley's murder "the Erle
of Bothwell, Mr. James Balfour, the persoun
of Fliske, Mr. David Chalmers, black Mr.
John Spens, who was principal deviser of the
murder; and the Queen, assenting thairto,
throw the persuasion of the Erle Bothwell,
and *the witchcraft of Lady Buckleuch.*"

NOTE 10.

He learned the art that none may name,
  In Padua, far beyond the sea.—P. 6.

Padua was long supposed by the Scottish
peasants to be the principal school of necromancy. The Earl of Gowrie, slain at Perth,
in 1600, pretended, during his studies in Italy,
to have acquired some knowledge of the
cabala.—See the examination of Wemyss of
Bogie, before the Privy Council, concerning
Gowrie's Conspiracy.

NOTE 11.

His form no darkening shadow traced
  Upon the sunny wall.—P. 6.

The shadow of a necromancer is indepen-

---

* The name is spelt differently by the various
families who bear it. Carr is selected, not as the
most correct, but as the most poetical reading.

† This expression and sentiment were dictated by
the situation of France, in the year 1803, when the
poem was originally written. 1821.

dent of the sun. Glycas informs us that Simon Magus caused his shadow to go before him, making people believe it was an attendant spirit.—HEYWOOD's *Hierarchie*, p. 475. A common superstition was that when a class of students had made a certain progress in their mystic studies, they were obliged to run through a subterranean hall, where the devil literally caught the hindmost in the race, unless he crossed the hall so speedily that the arch-enemy could only grasp his shadow. Hence the old Scotch proverb, "De'il take the hindmost." Sorcerers were often fabled to have given their shadows to the fiend.

NOTE 12.

By wily turns, by desperate bounds,
Had baffled Percy's best blood-hounds.—P. 7.

The kings and heroes of Scotland, as well as the Border-riders, were sometimes obliged to study how to evade the pursuit of bloodhounds. Barbour informs us that Robert Bruce was repeatedly tracked by sleuth-dogs. On one occasion, he escaped by wading a bow-shot down a brook, and ascending into a tree by a branch which overhung the water; thus, leaving no trace on land of his footsteps, he baffled the scent.

A sure way of stopping the dog was to spill blood upon the track, which destroyed the discriminating fineness of his scent. A captive was sometimes sacrificed on such occasions. Henry the Minstrel tells a romantic story of Wallace, founded on this circumstance :—The hero's little band had been joined by an Irishman, named Fawdoun, or Fadzean, a dark, savage, and suspicious character. After a sharp skirmish at Black-Erne Side, Wallace was forced to retreat with only sixteen followers, the English pursuing with a Border blood-hound.

In the retreat, Fawdoun, tired, or affecting to be so, would go no farther, and Wallace, having in vain argued with him, in hasty anger, struck off his head, and continued the retreat. When the English came up, their hound stayed upon the dead body :—

"The sleuth stopped at Fawdon, still she stood,
Nor farther would, fra time she fund the blood."

NOTE 13.

But when Melrose he reach'd 'twas silence all ;
He meetly stabled his steed in stall,
And sought the convent's lonely wall.—P. 9.

The ancient and beautiful monastery of Melrose was founded by King David I. Its ruins afford the finest specimen of Gothic

architecture and Gothic sculpture which Scotland can boast. The stone of which it is built, though it has resisted the weather for so many ages, retains perfect sharpness, so that even the most minute ornaments seem as entire as when newly wrought.

NOTE 14.

When buttress and buttress, alternately,
Seem framed of ebon and ivory ;
When silver edges the imagery,
And the scrolls that teach thee to live and die.
. . . . .
Then view St. David's ruin'd pile.—P. 9.

The buttresses ranged along the sides of the ruins of Melrose Abbey, are, according to the Gothic style, richly carved and fretted, containing niches for the statues of saints, and labelled with scrolls, bearing appropriate texts of Scripture. Most of these statues have been demolished.

David I. of Scotland, purchased the reputation of sanctity, by founding, and liberally endowing, not only the monastery of Melrose, but those of Kelso, Jedburgh, and many others ; which led to the well-known observation of his successor, that he was a *sore saint for the crown.*

NOTE 15.

And there the dying lamps did burn,
Before thy low and lonely urn,
O gallant Chief of Otterburne!—P. 11.

The famous and desperate battle of Otterburne was fought 15th August, 1388, betwixt Henry Percy, called Hotspur, and James, Earl of Douglas. Both these renowned rival champions were at the head of a chosen body of troops. The Earl of Douglas was slain in the action. He was buried at Melrose, beneath the high altar.

NOTE 16.

—— Dark Knight of Liddesdale.—P. 11.

William Douglas, called the Knight of Liddesdale, flourished during the reign of David II., and was so distinguished by his valour, that he was called the Flower of Chivalry. Nevertheless, he tarnished his renown by the cruel murder of Sir Alexander Ramsay of Dalhousie, originally his friend and brother in arms. The King had conferred upon Ramsay the sheriffdom of Teviotdale, to which Douglas pretended some claim. In revenge of this preference, the

Knight of Liddesdale came down upon Ramsay, while he was administering justice at Hawick, seized and carried him off to his remote and inaccessible castle of Hermitage, where he threw his unfortunate prisoner, horse and man, into a dungeon, leaving him to perish of hunger.

NOTE 17.

—— *The wondrous Michael Scott.*—P. 11.

Sir Michael Scott of Balwearie flourished during the 13th century, and was one of the ambassadors sent to bring the Maid of Norway to Scotland upon the death of Alexander III. By a poetical anachronism, he is here placed in a later era. He was a man of much learning, chiefly acquired in foreign countries. He wrote a commentary upon Aristotle, printed at Venice in 1496 ; and several treatises upon natural philosophy, from which he appears to have been addicted to the abstruse studies of judicial astrology, alchymy, physiognomy, and chiromancy. Hence he passed among his contemporaries for a skilful magician. Dempster informs us that he remembers to have heard in his youth that the magic books of Michael Scott were still in existence, but could not be opened without danger, on account of the malignant fiends who were thereby invoked.

Tradition varies concerning the place of his burial ; some contend for Home Coltrame, in Cumberland ; others for Melrose Abbey. But all agree that his books of magic were interred in his grave, or preserved in the convent where he died.

NOTE 18.

The words that cleft Eildon hills in three.— P. 11.

Michael Scott was, once upon a time, much embarrassed by a spirit, for whom he was under the necessity of finding constant employment. He commanded him to build a *cauld*, or dam-head, across the Tweed at Kelso ; it was accomplished in one night, and still does honour to the infernal architect. Michael next ordered that Eildon hill, which was then a uniform cone, should be divided into three. Another night was sufficient to part its summit into the three picturesque peaks which it now bears. At length the enchanter conquered this indefatigable demon, by employing him in the hopeless and endless task of making ropes out of sea-sand.

NOTE 19.

The Baron's Dwarf his courser held.—P. 14.

The idea of Lord Cranstoun's Goblin Page is taken from a being called Gilpin Horner, who appeared, and made some stay, at a farm-house among the Border mountains.

NOTE 20.

All was delusion, naught was truth.—P. 17.

Glamour, in the legends of Scottish superstition, means the magic power of imposing on the eyesight of the spectators, so that the appearance of an object shall be totally different from the reality. To such a charm the ballad of Johnny Fa' imputes the fascination of the lovely Countess, who eloped with that gipsy leader :—

"Sae soon as they saw her weel-far'd face,
They cast the *glamour* o'er her."

NOTE 21.

Until they came to a woodland brook,
The running stream dissolved the spell.—
P. 17.

It is a firm article of popular faith, that no enchantment can subsist in a living stream. Nay, if you can interpose a brook betwixt you and witches, spectres, or even fiends, you are in perfect safety. Burns's inimitable *Tam o' Shanter* turns entirely upon such a superstition.

NOTE 22.

He never counted him a man,
Would strike below the knee.—P. 18.

To wound an antagonist in the thigh or leg was reckoned contrary to the law of arms. In a tilt betwixt Gawain Michael, an English squire, and Joachim Cathore, a Frenchman, "they met at the speare poyntes rudely ; the French squyer justed right pleasantly ; the Englishman ran too lowe, for he strak the Frenchman depe into the thigh. Wherewith the Erle of Buckingham was right sore displeased, and so were all the other lords, and sayde how it was shamefully done."—FROIS-SART, vol. i. chap. 366.

NOTE 23.

On many a cairn's grey pyramid,
Where urns of mighty chiefs lie hid.—
P. 20.

The cairns, or piles of loose stones, which

crown the summit of most of our Scottish hills, and are found in other remarkable situations, seem usually, though not universally, to have been sepulchral monuments. Six flat stones are commonly found in the centre, forming a cavity of greater or smaller dimensions, in which an urn is often placed. The author is possessed of one, discovered beneath an immense cairn at Roughlee, in Liddesdale. It is of the most barbarous construction ; the middle of the substance alone having been subjected to the fire, over which, when hardened, the artist had laid an inner and outer coat of unbaked clay, etched with some very rude ornaments, his skill apparently being inadequate to baking the vase when completely finished. The contents were bones and ashes, and a quantity of beads made of coal. This seems to have been a barbarous imitation of the Roman fashion of sepulture.

NOTE 24.

For pathless marsh and mountain cell,
The peasant left his lowly shed.—P. 21.

The morasses were the usual refuge of the Border herdsmen on the approach of an English army.—(*Minstrelsy of the Scottish Border*, vol. i. p. 393.) Caves, hewed in the most dangerous and inaccessible places, also afforded an occasional retreat. Such caverns may be seen in the precipitous banks of the Teviot at Sunlaws, upon the Ale at Ancram, upon the Jed at Hundalee, and in many other places upon the Border. The banks of the Eske, at Gorton and Hawthornden, are hollowed into similar recesses.

NOTE 25.

Watt Tinlinn.—P. 21.

This person was, in my younger days, the theme of many a fireside tale. He was a retainer of the Buccleuch family, and held for his Border service a small tower on the frontiers of Liddesdale. Watt was by profession a *sutor*, but by inclination and practice an archer and warrior. Upon occasion, the captain of Bewcastle, military governor of that wild district of Cumberland, is said to have made an incursion into Scotland, in which he was defeated, and forced to fly. Watt Tinlinn pursued him closely through a dangerous morass ; the captain, however, gained the firm ground ; and, seeing Tinlinn dismounted and floundering in the bog, used these words of insult :—"Sutor Watt, ye cannot sew your boots ; the heels *risp*, and the seams *rive*."*

---

* *Risp*, creak.—*Rive*. tear.

—"If I cannot sew," retorted Tinlinn, discharging a shaft, which nailed the captain's thigh to the saddle, "if I cannot sew I can *yerk*."†

NOTE 26.

Belted Will Howard.—P. 22.

Lord William Howard, third son of Thomas, Duke of Norfolk, succeeded to Naworth Castle, and a large domain annexed to it, in right of his wife Elizabeth, sister of George Lord Dacre, who died without heirs male, in the 11th of Queen Elizabeth. By a poetical anachronism, he is introduced into the romance a few years earlier than he actually flourished. He was warden of the Western Marches : and, from the rigour with which he repressed the Border excesses, the name of Belted Will Howard is still famous in our traditions.

NOTE 27.

Lord Dacre.—P. 22.

The well-known name of Dacre is derived from the exploits of one of their ancestors at the siege of Acre, or Ptolemais, under Richard Cœur de Lion.

NOTE 28.

The German hackbut-men.—P. 22.

In the wars with Scotland, Henry VIII. and his successors employed numerous bands of mercenary troops. At the battle of Pinky, there were in the English army six hundred hackbutters on foot, and two hundred on horseback, composed chiefly of foreigners. On the 27th of September, 1549, the Duke of Somerset, Lord Protector, writes thus to the Lord Dacre, warden of the West Marches :—"The Almains, in number two thousand, very valiant soldiers, shall be sent to you shortly from Newcastle, together with Sir Thomas Holcroft, and with the force of your wardenry, (which we would were advanced to the most strength of horsemen that might be,) shall make the attempt to Loughmaben, being of no such strength but that it may be skailed with ladders, whereof, beforehand, we would you caused secretly some number to be provided ; or else undermined with the pyke-axe, and só taken : either to be kept for the King's Majesty, or otherwise to be defaced, and taken from the profits of the enemy. And in like manner the house of Carlaverock to be

---

† *Yerk*, to twitch, as shoemakers do, in securing the stitches of their work.

used."—*History of Cumberland*, vol. i. Introd. p. lxi.

NOTE 29.

" Ready, aye ready," for the field.—P. 22.

Sir John Scott of Thirlestane flourished in the reign of James V., and possessed the estates of Thirlestane, Gamescleuch, &c., lying upon the river of Ettrick, and extending to St. Mary's Loch, at the head of Yarrow. It appears that when James had assembled his nobility and their feudal followers, at Fala, with the purpose of invading England, and was, as is well known, disappointed by the obstinate refusal of his peers, this baron alone declared himself ready to follow the King wherever he should lead. In memory of his fidelity, James granted to his family a charter of arms, entitling them to bear a border of fleurs-de-luce, similar to the tressure in the royal arms, with a bundle of spears for the crest ; motto, *Ready, aye ready.*

NOTE 30.

Their gathering word was Bellenden.—P. 24.

Bellenden is situated near the head of Borthwick water, and being in the centre of the possessions of the Scotts, was frequently used as their place of rendezvous and gathering word.

NOTE 31.

That he may suffer march-treason pain.— P. 26.

Several species of offences, peculiar to the Border, constituted what was called march-treason. Among others, was the crime of riding, or causing to ride, against the opposite country during the time of truce. Thus, in an indenture made on the 25th day of March, 1334, betwixt noble lords Sirs Henry Percy, Earl of Northumberland, and Archibald Douglas, Lord of Galloway, a truce is agreed upon until the 1st day of July ; and it is expressly accorded, "Gif ony stellis authir on the ta part, or on the tothyr, that he shall be hanget or heofdit ; and gif ony company stellis any gudes within the trieux beforesayd, ane of that company sall be hanget or heofdit, and the remnant sall restore the gudys stolen in the dubble."— *History of Westmoreland and Cumberland*, Introd. p. xxxix.

NOTE 32.

Knighthood he took of Douglas' sword.—P. 26.

The dignity of knighthood, according to the original institution, had this peculiarity, that it did not flow from the monarch, but could be conferred by one who himself possessed it, upon any squire who, after due probation, was found to merit the honour of chivalry. Latterly, this power was confined to generals who were wont to create knights bannerets after or before an engagement.

NOTE 33.

When English blood swell'd Ancram's ford.— P. 26.

The battle of Ancram Moor, or Penielheuch, was fought A.D. 1545. The English, commanded by Sir Ralph Evers, and Sir Brian Latoun, were totally routed, and both their leaders slain in the action. The Scottish army was commanded by Archibald Douglas, Earl of Angus, assisted by the Laird of Buccleuch and Norman Lesley.

NOTE 34.

For who, in field or foray slack,
Saw the blanche lion e'er fall back.—P. 27.

This was the cognizance of the noble house of Howard in all its branches. The crest, or bearing, of a warrior, was often used as a *nomme de guerre.*

NOTE 35.

The Bloody Heart blazed in the van,
Announcing Douglas, dreaded name.—
P. 29.

The chief of this potent race of heroes, about the date of the poem, was Archibald Douglas, seventh Earl of Angus, a man of great courage and activity. The Bloody Heart was the well-known cognizance of the House of Douglas, assumed from the time of good Lord James, to whose care Robert Bruce committed his heart, to be carried to the Holy Land.

NOTE 36.

And Swinton laid the lance in rest,
That tamed of yore the sparkling crest
Of Clarence's Plantagenet.—P. 29.

At the battle of Beaugé, in France, Thomas, Duke of Clarence, brother to Henry V., was unhorsed by Sir John Swinton of Swinton, who distinguished him by a coronet set with precious stones, which he wore around his helmet. The family of Swinton is one of the most ancient in Scotland, and produced many celebrated warriors.

NOTE 37.

And shouting still, A Home! a Home!—P. 30.

The Earls of Home, as descendants of the Dunbars, ancient Earls of March, carried a lion rampant, argent; but, as a difference, changed the colour of the shield from gules to vert, in allusion to Greenlaw, their ancient possession. The slogan, or war-cry, of this powerful family, was, "A Home! a Home!" It was anciently placed in an escrol above the crest. The helmet is armed with a lion's head erased gules, with a cap of state gules, turned up ermine.

The Hepburns, a powerful family in East Lothian, were usually in close alliance with the Homes. The chief of this clan was Hepburn, Lord of Hailes; a family which terminated in the too famous Earl of Bothwell.

NOTE 38.

*'Twixt truce and war, such sudden change
Was not infrequent, nor held strange,
In the old Border-day.*—P. 30.

Notwithstanding the constant wars upon the Borders, and the occasional cruelties which marked the mutual inroads, the inhabitants on either side do not appear to have regarded each other with that violent and personal animosity which might have been expected. On the contrary, like the outposts of hostile armies, they often carried on something resembling friendly intercourse, even in the middle of hostilities; and it is evident, from various ordinances against trade and intermarriages, between English and Scottish Borderers, that the governments of both countries were jealous of their cherishing too intimate a connexion.

NOTE 39.

*—— on the darkening plain,
Loud hollo, whoop, or whistle ran,
As bands, their stragglers to regain,
Give the shrill watchword of their clan.*—
P. 30.

Patten remarks, with bitter censure, the disorderly conduct of the English Borderers, who attended the Protector Somerset on his expedition against Scotland.

NOTE 40.

She wrought not by forbidden spell.—P. 36.

Popular belief, though contrary to the doc-trines of the Church, made a favourable distinction betwixt magicians, and necromancers, or wizards; the former were supposed to command the evil spirits, and the latter to serve, or at least to be in league and compact with, those enemies of mankind. The arts of subjecting the demons were manifold; sometimes the fiends were actually swindled by the magicians.*

NOTE 41.

*A merlin sat upon her wrist,
Held by a leash of silken twist.*—P. 36.

A merlin, or sparrow-hawk, was actually carried by ladies of rank, as a falcon was, in time of peace, the constant attendant of a knight or baron. See LATHAM *on Falconry.*—Godscroft relates, that when Mary of Lorraine was regent, she pressed the Earl of Angus to admit a royal garrison into his Castle of Tantallon. To this he returned no direct answer; but, as if apostrophizing a goss-hawk, which sat on his wrist, and which he was feeding during the Queen's speech, he exclaimed, "The devil's in this greedy glede, she will never be full."—HUME's *History of the House of Douglas,* 1743, vol. ii. p. 131. Barclay complains of the common and indecent practice of bringing hawks and hounds into churches.

NOTE 42.

*And princely peacock's gilded train,
And o'er the boar-head garnish'd brave.*—
P. 36.

The peacock, it is well known, was considered, during the times of chivalry, not merely as an exquisite delicacy, but as a dish of peculiar solemnity. After being roasted, it was again decorated with its plumage, and a sponge, dipped in lighted spirits of wine, was placed in its bill. When it was introduced on days of grand festival, it was the signal for the adventurous knights to take upon them vows to do some deed of chivalry, "before the peacock and the ladies."

The boar's head was also a usual dish of feudal splendour. In Scotland it was sometimes surrounded with little banners, displaying the colours and achievements of the baron at whose board it was served.—PINKERTON's *History,* vol. i. p. 432.

---

* There are some amusing German and Irish stories to that effect.

NOTE 43.

Smote, with his gauntlet, stout Hunthill.—
P. 37.

The Rutherfords of Hunthill were an ancient race of Border Lairds, whose names occur in history, sometimes as defending the frontier against the English, sometimes as disturbing the peace of their own country. Dickon Draw-the-sword was son to the ancient warrior, called in tradition the Cock of Hunthill, remarkable for leading into battle nine sons, gallant warriors, all sons of the aged champion.

NOTE 44.

*—— bit his glove.—*P. 37.

To bite the thumb, or the glove, seems not to have been considered, upon the Border, as a gesture of contempt, though so used by Shakspeare, but as a pledge of mortal revenge. It is yet remembered, that a young gentleman of Teviotdale, on the morning after a hard drinking-bout, observed that he had bitten his glove. He instantly demanded of his companion with whom he had quarrelled? And, learning that he had had words with one of the party, insisted on instant satisfaction, asserting that though he remembered nothing of the dispute, yet he was sure he never would have bit his glove unless he had received some unpardonable insult. He fell in the duel, which was fought near Selkirk, in 1721.

NOTE 45.

—— old Albert Græme,
*The Minstrel of that ancient name.—*P. 37.

"John Græme, second son of *Malice*, Earl of *Monteith*, commonly sirnamed *John with the Bright Sword*, upon some displeasure risen against him at court, retired with many of his clan and kindred into the English Borders, in the reign of King Henry the Fourth, where they seated themselves; and many of their posterity have continued ever since. Mr. Sandford, speaking of them, says, (which indeed was applicable to most of the Borderers on both sides,) 'They were all stark moss-troopers, and arrant thieves: Both to England and Scotland outlawed; yet sometimes connived at, because they gave intelligence forth of Scotland, and would raise 400 horse at any time upon a raid of the English into Scotland. A saying is recorded of a mother to her son, (which is now become proverbial,) *Ride, Rowley, hough's i' the pot:* that is, the last piece of beef was in the pot, and therefore it was high time for him to go and fetch more.'"—*Introduction to the History of Cumberland.*

NOTE 46.

*Who has not heard of Surrey's fame ?—*P. 38.

The gallant and unfortunate Henry Howard, Earl of Surrey, was unquestionably the most accomplished cavalier of his time; and his sonnets display beauties which would do honour to a more polished age. He was beheaded on Tower-hill in 1546; a victim to the mean jealousy of Henry VIII., who could not bear so brilliant a character near his throne.

The song of the supposed bard is founded on an incident said to have happened to the Earl in his travels. Cornelius Agrippa, the celebrated alchemist, showed him in a looking-glass the lovely Geraldine, to whose service he had devoted his pen and his sword. The vision represented her as indisposed, and reclining upon a couch, reading her lover's verses by the light of a waxen taper.

~~~~~~~~~~~~~~~~

MARMION.

NOTE 1.

As when the Champion of the Lake
Enters Morgana's fated house,
Or in the Chapel Perilous,
Despising spells and demons' force,
*Holds converse with the unburied corse.—*P. 50.

The romance of the Morte Arthur contains a sort of abridgment of the most celebrated adventures of the Round Table; and, being written in comparatively modern language, gives the general reader an excellent idea of what romances of chivalry actually were. It has also the merit of being written in pure old English; and many of the wild adventures which it contains are told with a simplicity bordering upon the sublime. Several of these are referred to in the text ; and I would have illustrated them by more full extracts, but as this curious work is about to be republished, I confine myself to the tale of the Chapel Perilous, and of the quest of Sir Launcelot after the Sangreal.

"Right so Sir Launcelot departed, and when he came to the Chapell Perilous, he alighted downe, and tied his horse to a little gate. And as soon as he was within the churchyard, he saw, on the front of the chapell, many faire rich shields turned upside downe ; and many of the shields Sir Launcelot had seene knights have before ; with that he saw stand by him thirtie great knights, more, by a yard, than any man that ever he had seene, and all those grinned and gnashed at Sir Launcelot; and when he saw their countenance, hee dread them sore, and so put his shield afore him, and tooke his sword in his hand, ready to doe battaile ; and they were all armed in black harneis, ready, with their shields and swords drawn. And when Sir Launcelot would have gone through them, they scattered on every side of him, and gave him the way ; and therewith he waxed all bold, and entered into the chapell, and then hee saw no light but a dimme lampe burning, and then was he ware of a corps covered with a cloath of silke ; then Sir Launcelot stooped downe, and cut a piece of that cloth away, and then it fared under him as the earth had quaked a little, whereof he was afeard, and then hee saw a faire sword lye by the dead knight, and that he gat in his hand, and hied him out of the chappell. As soon as he was in the chappell-yerd, all the knights spoke to him with a grimly voice, and said, ' Knight, Sir Launcelot, lay that sword from thee, or else thou shalt die.'—' Whether I live or die,' said Sir Launcelot, ' with no great words get yee it againe, therefore fight for it and yee list.' Therewith he passed through them ; and, beyond the chappell-yerd, there met him a faire damosell, and said, ' Sir Launcelot, leave that sword behind thee, or thou wilt die for it.'—' I will not leave it,' said Sir Launcelot, ' for no threats.'—' No ?' said she ; ' and ye did leave that sword, Queen Guenever should ye never see.'—' Then were I a fool and I would leave this sword,' said Sir Launcelot. ' Now, gentle knight,' said the damosell, ' I require thee to kiss me once.'—' Nay,' said Sir Launcelot, ' that God forbid !'—' Well, sir,' said she, ' and thou haddest kissed me thy life dayes had been done, but now, alas !' said she, ' I have lost all my labour ; for I ordeined this chappell for thy sake, and for Sir Gawaine : and once I had Sir Gawaine within

it ; and at that time he fought with that knight which there lieth dead in yonder chappell, Sir Gilbert the bastard, and at that time hee smote off Sir Gilbert the bastard's left hand. And so, Sir Launcelot, now I tell thee, that I have loved thee these seaven yeare ; but there may no woman have thy love but Queene Guenever ; but sithen I may not rejoyice thee to have thy body alive, I had kept no more joy in this world but to have had thy dead body ; and I would have balmed it and served, and so have kept it in my life daies, and daily I should have clipped thee, and kissed thee, in the despite of Queen Guenever.' —' Yee say well,' said Sir Launcelot ; ' Jesus preserve me from your subtill craft.' And therewith he took his horse, and departed from her."

NOTE 2.

A sinful man, and unconfess'd,
He took the Sangreal's holy quest,
And, slumbering, saw the vision high,
He might not view with waking eye.—P. 50.

One day, when Arthur was holding a high feast with his Knights of the Round Table, the Sangreal, or vessel out of which the last passover was eaten, (a precious relic, which had long remained concealed from human eyes, because of the sins of the land,) suddenly appeared to him and all his chivalry. The consequence of this vision was, that all the knights took on them a solemn vow to seek the Sangreal. But alas ! it could only be revealed to a knight at once accomplished in earthly chivalry, and pure and guiltless of evil conversation. All Sir Launcelot's noble accomplishments were therefore rendered vain by his guilty intrigue with Queen Guenever, or Ganore ; and in his holy quest he encountered only such disgraceful disasters as that which follows :—

"But Sir Launcelot rode overthwart and endlong in a wild forest, and held no path but as wild adventure led him ; and at the last he came unto a stone crosse, which departed two wayes, in wast land ; and, by the crosse, was a stone that was of marble ; but it was so dark, that Sir Launcelot might not well know what it was. Then Sir Launcelot looked by him, and saw an old chappell, and there he wend to have found people. And so Sir Launcelot tied his horse to a tree, and there he put off his shield, and hung it upon a tree, and then hee went unto the chappell doore, and found it wasted and broken. And within he found a faire altar, full richly arrayed with cloth of silk, and there stood a faire candlestick which beare six great candles, and the candlesticke was of silver. And when Sir Launcelot saw this light, hee had a great will for to enter into the chappell, but he could find no place where hee might enter. Then was hee passing heavie and dismaied. Then he returned, and came againe to his horse, and tooke off his saddle and his bridle, and let him pasture, and unlaced his helme, and ungirded his sword, and laid him downe to sleepe upon his shield, before the crosse.

"And so hee fell on sleepe ; and, halfe waking and halfe sleeping, he saw come by him two palfreys, both faire and white, the which beare a litter, therein lying a sicke knight. And when he was nigh the crosse, he there abode still. All this Sir Launcelot saw and beheld, for hee slept not verily, and hee heard him say, 'O sweete Lord,' when shall this sorrow leave me, and when shall the holy vessell come by me, where through I shall be blessed, for I have endured thus long for little trespasse !' And thus a great while complained the knight, and alwaies Sir Launcelot heard it. With that Sir Launcelot saw the candlesticke, with the fire tapers, come before the crosse ; but he could see nobody that brought it. Also there came a table of silver, and the holy vessell of the Sancgreall, the which Sir Launcelot had seen before that time in King Petchour's house. And therewithall the sicke knight set him upright, and held up both his hands, and said, 'Faire sweete Lord, which is here within the holy vessell, take heede to mee, that I may bee hole of this great malady !' And therewith upon his hands, and upon his knees, he went so nigh, that he touched the holy vessell, and kissed it : And anon he was hole, and then he said, 'Lord God, I thank thee, for I am healed of this malady.' Soo when the holy vessell had been there a great while, it went into the chappelle againe, with the candlesticke and the light, so that Sir Launcelot wist not where it became, for he was overtaken with sinne, that hee had no power to arise against the holy vessell, wherefore afterward many men said of him shame. But he tooke repentance afterward. Then the sicke knight dressed him upright, and kissed the crosse. Then anon his squire brought him his armes, and asked his lord how he did. 'Certainly,' said hee, 'I thanke God right heartily, for through the holy vessell I am healed : But I have right great mervaile of this sleeping knight, which hath had neither grace nor power to awake during the time that this holy vessell hath beene here present.'—'I dare it right well say,' said the squire, 'that this same knight is defouled with some manner of deadly sinne, whereof

he has never confessed.'—' By my faith,' said the knight, 'whatsoever he be, he is unhappie ; for, as I deeme, hee is of the fellowship of the Round Table, the which is entered into the quest of the Sancgreall.'—' Sir,' said the squire, 'here I have brought you all your armes, save your helme and your sword; and, therefore, by mine assent, now may ye take this knight's helme and his sword ;' and so he did. And when he was cleane armed, he took Sir Launcelot's horse, for he was better than his owne, and so they departed from the crosse.

"Then anon Sir Launcelot awaked, and set himselfe upright, and he thought him what hee had there seene, and whether it were dreames or not ; right so he heard a voice that said, ·Sir Launcelot, more hardy than is the stone, and more bitter than is the wood, and more naked and bare than is the liefe of the fig-tree, therefore go thou from hence, and withdraw thee from this holy place;' and when Sir Launcelot heard this, he was passing heavy, and wist not what to doe. And so he departed sore weeping, and cursed the time that he was borne; for then he deemed never to have had more worship ; for the words went unto his heart, till that he knew wherefore that hee was so called."

NOTE 3.

And Dryden, in immortal strain,
Had raised the Table Round again.—P. 50.

Dryden's melancholy account of his projected Epic Poem, blasted by the selfish and sordid parsimony of his patrons, is contained in an "Essay on Satire," addressed to the Earl of Dorset, and prefixed to the Translation of Juvenal. After mentioning a plan of supplying machinery from the guardian angels of kingdoms, mentioned in the Book of Daniel, he adds,—

"Thus, my lord, I have, as briefly as I could, given your lordship, and by you the world, a rude draught of what I have been long labouring in my imagination, and what I had intended to have put in practice ; (though far unable for the attempt of such a poem ;) and to have left the stage, to which my genius never much inclined me, for a work which would have taken up my life in the performance of it. This, too, I had intended chiefly for the honour of my native country, to which a poet is particularly obliged. Of two subjects, both relating to it, I was doubtful whether I should choose that of King Arthur conquering the Saxons, which, being farther distant in time, gives the greater scope to my invention; or that of Edward the Black Prince, in subduing Spain, and restoring it to the lawful prince, though a great tyrant, Don Pedro the Cruel; which, for the compass of time, including only the expedition of one year, for the greatness of the action, and its answerable event, for the magnanimity of the English hero, opposed to the ingratitude of the person whom he restored, and for the many beautiful episodes which I had interwoven with the principal design, together with the characters of the chiefest English persons, (wherein, after Virgil and Spenser, I would have taken occasion to represent my living friends and patrons of the noblest families, and also shadowed the events of future ages in the succession of our imperial line,) —with these helps, and those of the machines which I have mentioned, I might perhaps have done as well as some of my predecessors, or at least chalked out a way for others to amend my errors in a like design; but being encouraged only with fair words by King Charles II., my little salary ill paid, and no prospect of a future subsistence, I was then discouraged in the beginning of my attempt; and now age has overtaken me, and want, a more insufferable evil, through the change of the times, has wholly disabled me."

NOTE 4.

Their theme the merry minstrels made,
*Of Ascapart, and Bevis bold.—*P. 50.

The "History of Bevis of Hampton" is abridged by my friend Mr. George Ellis, with that liveliness which extracts amusement even out of the most rude and unpromising of our old tales of chivalry. Ascapart, a most important personage in the romance, is thus described in an extract:—

> " This geaunt was mighty and strong,
> And full thirty foot was long.
> He was bristled like a sow;
> A foot he had between each brow;
> His lips were great, and hung aside;
> His eyen were hollow, his mouth was wide;
> Lothly he was to look on than,
> And liker a devil than a man.
> His staff was a young oak,
> Hard and heavy was his stroke."

Specimens of Metrical Romances, vol. ii. p. 136.

I am happy to say, that the memory of Sir Bevis is still fragrant in his town of Southampton; the gate of which is sentinelled by the effigies of that doughty knight-errant and his gigantic associate.

NOTE 5.

Day set on Norham's castled steep,
And Tweed's fair river, broad and deep, &c.
P. 51.

The ruinous castle of Norham (anciently called Ubbanford) is situated on the southern bank of the Tweed, about six miles above Berwick, and where that river is still the boundary between England and Scotland. The extent of its ruins, as well as its historical importance, shows it to have been a place of magnificence, as well as strength. Edward I. resided there when he was created umpire of the dispute concerning the Scottish succession. It was repeatedly taken and retaken during the wars between England and Scotland; and, indeed, scarce any happened, in which it had not a principal share. Norham Castle is situated on a steep bank, which overhangs the river. The repeated sieges which the castle had sustained rendered frequent repairs necessary. In 1164, it was almost rebuilt by Hugh Pudsey, Bishop of Durham, who added a huge keep, or donjon; notwithstanding which, King Henry II., in 1174, took the castle from the bishop, and committed the keeping of it to William de Neville. After this period it seems to have been chiefly garrisoned by the King, and considered as a royal fortress. The Greys of Chillingham Castle were frequently the castellans, or captains of the garrison: yet, as the castle was situated in the patrimony of St. Cuthbert, the property was in the see of Durham till the Reformation. After that period it passed through various hands. At the union of the crowns, it was in the possession of Sir Robert Carey (afterwards Earl of Monmouth), for his own life, and that of two of his sons. After King James's accession, Carey sold Norham Castle to George Home, Earl of Dunbar, for 6000*l.* See his curious Memoirs, published by Mr. Constable of Edinburgh.

According to Mr. Pinkerton there is, in the British Museum, Cal. B. 6. 216, a curious memoir of the Dacres on the state of Norham Castle in 1522, not long after the battle of Flodden. The inner ward, or keep, is represented as impregnable:—" The provisions are three great vats of salt eels, forty-four kine, three hogsheads of salted salmon, forty quarters of grain, besides many cows and four hundred sheep, lying under the castlewall nightly; but a number of the arrows wanted feathers, and a good *Fletcher* [*i.e.* maker of arrows) was required."—*History of Scotland,* vol. ii. p. 201, note.

The ruins of the castle are at present considerable, as well as picturesque. They consist of a large shattered tower, with many vaults, and fragments of other edifices enclosed within an outward wall of great circuit.

NOTE 6.

The battled towers, the donjon keep.—P. 51.

It is perhaps unnecessary to remind my readers that the *donjon*, in its proper signification, means the strongest part of a feudal castle; a high square tower, with walls of tremendous thickness, situated in the centre of the other buildings, from which, however, it was usually detached. Here, in case of the outward defences being gained, the garrison retreated to make their last stand. The donjon contained the great hall, and principal rooms of state for solemn occasions, and also the prison of the fortress; from which last circumstance we derive the modern and restricted use of the word *dungeon*. Ducange (*voce* DUNJO) conjectures plausibly, that the name is derived from these keeps being usually built upon a hill, which in Celtic is called DUN. Borlase supposes the word came from the darkness of the apartments in these towers, which were thence figuratively called Dungeons; thus deriving the ancient word from the modern application of it.

NOTE 7.

Well was he arm'd from head to heel,
In mail and plate of Milan steel.—P. 52.

The artists of Milan were famous in the Middle Ages for their skill in armoury, as appears from the following passage, in which Froissart gives an account of the preparations made by Henry, Earl of Hereford, afterwards Henry IV., and Thomas, Duke of Norfolk, Earl Marischal, for their proposed combat in the lists at Coventry:—"These two lords made ample provision of all things necessary for the combat; and the Earl of Derby sent off messengers to Lombardy, to have armour from Sir Galeas, Duke of Milan. The Duke complied with joy, and gave the knight, called Sir Francis, who had brought the message, the choice of all his armour for the Earl of Derby. When he had selected what he wished for in plated and mail armour, the Lord of Milan, out of his abundant love for the Earl, ordered four of the best armourers in Milan to accompany the knight to England, that the Earl of Derby might be more completely armed."—JOHNES' *Froissart*, vol. iv. p. 597.

NOTE 8.

Who checks at me, to death is dight.—P. 52.

The crest and motto of Marmion are borrowed from the following story:—Sir David de Lindsay, first Earl of Crauford, was, among other gentlemen of quality, attended, during a visit to London, in 1390, by Sir William Dalzell, who was, according to my authority, Bower, not only excelling in wisdom, but also of a lively wit. Chancing to be at the court, he there saw Sir Piers Courtenay, an English knight, famous for skill in tilting, and for the beauty of his person, parading the palace, arrayed in a new mantle, bearing for device an embroidered falcon, with this rhyme,—

> "I bear a falcon, fairest of flight,
>> Whoso pinches at her, his death is dight*
>>> In graith."†

The Scottish knight, being a wag, appeared next day in a dress exactly similar to that of Courtenay, but bearing a magpie instead of the falcon, with a motto ingeniously contrived to rhyme to the vaunting inscription of Sir Piers:—

> "I bear a pie picking at a piece,
>> Whoso picks at her, I shall pick at his nese,‡
>>> In faith."

This affront could only be expiated by a just with sharp lances. In the course, Dalzell left his helmet unlaced, so that it gave way at the touch of his antagonist's lance, and he thus avoided the shock of the encounter. This happened twice: in the third encounter the handsome Courtenay lost two of his front teeth. As the Englishman complained bitterly of Dalzell's fraud in not fastening his helmet, the Scottishman agreed to run six courses more, each champion staking in the hand of the King two hundred pounds, to be forfeited, if, on entering the lists, any unequal advantage should be detected. This being agreed to, the wily Scot demanded that Sir Piers, in addition to the loss of his teeth, should consent to the extinction of one of his eyes, he himself having lost an eye in the fight of Otterburn. As Courtenay demurred to this equalization of optical powers, Dalzell demanded the forfeit; which, after much altercation, the King appointed to be paid to him, saying, he surpassed the English both in wit and valour. This must appear to the reader a singular specimen of the humour of that time. I suspect the Jockey Club would have given a different decision from Henry IV.

---

* Prepared.　† Armour.　‡ Nose.

NOTE 9.

They hail'd Lord Marmion:
They hail'd him Lord of Fontenayc,
Of Lutterward, and Scrivelbaye,
Of Tamworth tower and town.—P. 53.

Lord Marmion, the principal character of the present romance, is entirely a fictitious personage. In earlier times, indeed, the family of Marmion, Lords of Fontenay, in Normandy, was highly distinguished. Robert de Marmion, Lord of Fontenay, a distinguished follower of the Conqueror, obtained a grant of the castle and town of Tamworth, and also of the manor of Scrivelby, in Lincolnshire. One or both of these noble possessions was held by the honourable service of being the Royal Champion, as the ancestors of Marmion had formerly been to the Dukes of Normandy. But after the castle and demesne of Tamworth had passed through four successive barons from Robert, the family became extinct in the person of Philip de Marmion, who died in 20th Edward I. without issue male. He was succeeded in his castle of Tamworth by Alexander de Freville, who married Mazera, his grand-daughter. Baldwin de Freville, Alexander's descendant, in the reign of Richard II., by the supposed tenure of his castle of Tamworth, claimed the office of Royal Champion, and to do the service appertaining; namely, on the day of coronation, to ride, completely armed, upon a barbed horse, into Westminster Hall, and there to challenge the combat against any who would gainsay the King's title. But this office was adjudged to Sir John Dymoke, to whom the manor of Scrivelby had descended by another of the co-heiresses of Robert de Marmion; and it remains in that family, whose representative is Hereditary Champion of England at the present day. The family and possessions of Freville have merged in the Earls of Ferrars. I have not, therefore, created a new family, but only revived the titles of an old one in an imaginary personage.

It was one of the Marmion family, who, in the reign of Edward II., performed that chivalrous feat before the very castle of Norham, which Bishop Percy has woven into his beautiful ballad, "The Hermit of Warkworth."—The story is thus told by Leland:—

"The Scottes cam yn to the marches of England, and destroyed the castles of Werk and Herbotel, and overran much of Northumberland marches.

"At this tyme, Thomas Gray and his friendes defended Norham from the Scottes.

"It were a wonderful processe to declare, what mischefes cam by hungre and asseges by the space of xi years in Northumberland; for the Scottes became so proude, after they had got Berwick, that they nothing esteemed the Englishmen.

"About this tyme there was a great feste made yn Lincolnshir, to which came many gentlemen and ladies; and amonge them one lady brought a heaulme for a man of were, with a very riche creste of gold, to William Marmion, knight, with a letter of commandement of her lady, that he should go into the daungerest place in England, and ther to let the heaulme be seene and known as famous. So he went to Norham; whither, within 4 days of cumming, cam Philip Moubray, guardian of Berwicke, having yn his bande 40 men of armes, the very flour of men of the Scottish marches.

"Thomas Gray, capitayne of Norham, seynge this, brought his garison afore the barriers of the castel, behind whom cam William, richly arrayed, as al glittering in gold, and wearing the heaulme, his lady's present.

"Then said Thomas Gray to Marmion, 'Sir Knight, ye be cum hither to fame your helmet: mount up on yowr horse, and ride lyke a valiant man to yowr foes even here at hand, and I forsake God if I rescue not thy body deade or alyve, or I myself wyl dye for it.'

"Whereupon he toke his cursere, and rode among the throng of ennemyes; the which layed sore stripes on him, and pulled him at the last out of his sadel to the grounde.

"Then Thomas Gray, with al the hole garison, lette prick yn among the Scottes, and so wondid them and their horses, that they were overthrowan; and Marmion, sore beten, was horsid agayn, and, with Gray, persewed the Scottes yn chase. There were taken fifty horse of price; and the women of Norham brought them to the foote men to follow the chase."

NOTE 10.

Sir Hugh the Heron bold,
Baron of Twisel, and of Ford,
And Captain of the Hold.—P. 53.

Were accuracy of any consequence in a fictitious narrative, this castellan's name ought to have been William; for William Heron of Ford was husband to the famous Lady Ford, whose siren charms are said to have cost our James IV. so dear. Moreover, the said William Heron was, at the time supposed, a prisoner in Scotland, being surrendered by

Henry VIII., on account of his share in the slaughter of Sir Robert Ker of Cessford. His wife, represented in the text as residing at the Court of Scotland, was, in fact, living in her own Castle at Ford.—See Sir RICHARD HERON'S curious *Genealogy of the Heron Family.*

NOTE II.

James back'd the cause of that mock prince,
Warbeck, that Flemish counterfeit,
Who on the gibbet paid the cheat.
Then did I march with Surrey's power,
What time we razed old Ayton tower.—P. 54.

The story of Perkin Warbeck, or Richard, Duke of York, is well known. In 1496 he was received honourably in Scotland; and James IV., after conferring upon him in marriage his own relation, the Lady Catharine Gordon, made war on England in behalf of his pretensions. To retaliate an invasion of England, Surrey advanced into Berwickshire at the head of considerable forces, but retreated, after taking the inconsiderable fortress of Ayton.

NOTE 12.

—— *I trow,*
Norham can find you guides enow;
For here be some have pricked as far,
On Scottish ground, as to Dunbar;
Have drunk the monks of St. Bothan's ale,
And driven the beeves of Lauderdale;
Harried the wives of Greenlaw's goods,
And given them light to set their hoods.—
P. 54.

The garrisons of the English castles of Wark, Norham, and Berwick, were, as may be easily supposed, very troublesome neighbours to Scotland. Sir Richard Maitland of Ledington wrote a poem, called "The Blind Baron's Comfort;" when his barony of Blythe, in Lauderdale, was *harried* by Rowland Foster, the English captain of Wark, with his company, to the number of 300 men. They spoiled the poetical knight of 5000 sheep, 200 nolt, 30 horses and mares; the whole furniture of his house of Blythe, worth 100 pounds Scots (8*l.* 6*s.* 8*d.*), and everything else that was portable.

NOTE 13.

The priest of Shoreswood—he could rein
The wildest war-horse in your train.—
P. 55.

This churchman seems to have been akin to Welsh, the vicar of St. Thomas of Exeter,

a leader among the Cornish insurgents in 1549. "This man," says Holinshed, "had many good things in him. He was of no great stature, but well set, and mightilie compact. He was a very good wrestler; shot well, both in the longbow and also in the crossbow; he handled his hand-gun and peece very well; he was a very good woodman, and a hardie, and such a one as would not give his head for the polling, or his beard for the washing. He was a companion in any exercise of activitie, and of a courteous and gentle behaviour. He descended of a good honest parentage, being borne at Peneverin in Cornwall; and yet, in this rebellion, an arch-captain and a principal doer."—Vol. iv. p. 958, 4to edition. This model of clerical talents had the misfortune to be hanged upon the steeple of his own church.

NOTE 14.

—— *that Grot where Olives nod,*
Where, darling of each heart and eye,
From all the youth of Sicily,
Saint Rosalie retired to God.—P. 55.

"Santa Rosalia was of Palermo, and born of a very noble family, and when very young abhorred so much the vanities of this world, and avoided the converse of mankind, resolving to dedicate herself wholly to God Almighty, that she, by Divine inspiration, forsook her father's house, and never was more heard of till her body was found in that cleft of a rock, on that almost inaccessible mountain, where now the chapel is built; and they affirm she was carried up there by the hands of angels; for that place was not formerly so accessible (as now it is) in the days of the Saint; and even now it is a very bad, and steepy, and breakneck way. In this frightful place, this holy woman lived a great many years, feeding only on what she found growing on that barren mountain, and creeping into a narrow, and dreadful cleft in a rock, which was always dropping wet, and was her place of retirement as well as prayer; having worn out even the rock with her knees in a certain place, which is now open'd on purpose to show it to those who come here. This chapel is very richly adorn'd; and on the spot where the Saint's dead body was discover'd, which is just beneath the hole in the rock, which is opened on purpose, as I said, there is a very fine statue of marble, representing her in a lying posture, railed in all about with fine iron and brass work; and the altar, on which they say mass, is built just over it."—*Voyage to Sicily and Malta,* by Mr. John Dryden (son to the poet), p. 107.

NOTE 15.

Friar John —
Himself still sleeps before his beads
Have marked ten aves, and two creeds.—
P. 56.

Friar John understood the soporific virtue of his beads and breviary as well as his namesake in Rabelais. "But Gargantua could not sleep by any means, on which side soever he turned himself. Whereupon the monk said to him, 'I never sleep soundly but when I am at sermon or prayers. Let us therefore begin, you and I, the seven penitential psalms, to try whether you shall not quickly fall asleep.' The conceit pleased Gargantua very well ; and beginning the first of these psalms, as soon as they came to *Beati quorum*, they fell asleep, both the one and the other."

NOTE 16.

The summon'd Palmer came in place.—P. 56.

A *Palmer*, opposed to a *Pilgrim*, was one who made it his sole business to visit different holy shrines ; travelling incessantly, and subsisting by charity : whereas the Pilgrim retired to his usual home and occupations, when he had paid his devotions at the particular spot which was the object of his pilgrimage. The Palmers seem to have been the *Questionarii* of the ancient Scottish canons 1242 and 1296.

NOTE 17.

To fair St. Andrews bound,
Within the ocean-cave to pray,
Where good Saint Rule his holy lay,
From midnight to the dawn of day,
Sung to the billows' sound.—P. 57.

St. Regulus (*Scottice*, St. Rule), a monk of Patræ, in Achaia, warned by a vision, is said, A.D. 370, to have sailed westward, until he landed at St. Andrews in Scotland, where he founded a chapel and tower. The latter is still standing ; and, though we may doubt the precise date of its foundation, is certainly one of the most ancient edifices in Scotland. A cave, nearly fronting the ruinous castle of the Archbishops of St. Andrews, bears the name of this religious person. It is difficult of access : and the rock in which it is hewn is washed by the German Ocean. It is nearly round, about ten feet in diameter, and the same in height. On one side is a sort of stone altar ; on the other an aperture into an inner den, where the miserable ascetic, who in-

habited this dwelling, probably slept. At full tide, egress and regress are hardly practicable. As Regulus first colonized the metropolitan see of Scotland, and converted the inhabitants in the vicinity, he has some reason to complain, that the ancient name of Killrule (*Cella Reguli*) should have been superseded, even in favour of the tutelar saint of Scotland. The reason of the change was, that St. Rule is said to have brought to Scotland the relics of Saint Andrew.

NOTE 18.

—— Saint Fillan's blessed well,
Whose spring can frenzied dreams dispel,
And the crazed brain restore.—P. 57.

St. Fillan was a Scottish saint of some reputation. Although Popery is, with us, matter of abomination, yet the common people still retain some of the superstitions connected with it. There are in Perthshire several wells and springs dedicated to St. Fillan, which are still places of pilgrimage and offerings, even among the Protestants. They are held powerful in cases of madness ; and, in some of very late occurrence, lunatics have been left all night bound to the holy stone, in confidence that the saint would cure and unloose them before morning.

NOTE 19.

The scenes are desert now, and bare,
Where flourish'd once a forest fair.—P. 57.

Ettrick Forest, now a range of mountainous sheep-walks, was anciently reserved for the pleasure of the royal chase. Since it was disparked, the wood has been, by degrees, almost totally destroyed, although, wherever protected from the sheep, copses soon arise without any planting. When the King hunted there, he often summoned the array of the country to meet and assist his sport. Thus, in 1528, James V. "made proclamation to all lords, barons, gentlemen, landwardmen, and freeholders, that they should compear at Edinburgh, with a month's victuals, to pass with the King where he pleased, to danton the thieves of Tiviotdale, Annandale, Liddisdale, and other parts of that country ; and also warned all gentlemen that had good dogs to bring them, that he might hunt in the said country as he pleased : The whilk the Earl of Argyle, the Earl of Huntley, the Earl of Athole, and so all the rest of the gentlemen of the Highland, did, and brought their hounds with them in like manner, to hunt with the King, as he pleased.

"The second day of June the King past

out of Edinburgh to the hunting, with many of the nobles and gentlemen of Scotland with him, to the number of twelve thousand men ; and then past to Meggitland, and hounded and hawked all the country and bounds ; that is to say, Crammat, Pappertlaw, St. Mary-laws, Carlavrick, Chapel, Ewindoores, and Longhope. I heard say, he slew, in these bounds, eighteen score of harts."*

These huntings had, of course, a military character, and attendance upon them was a part of the duty of a vassal. The act for abolishing ward or military tenures in Scot-land, enumerates the services of hunting, hosting, watching, and warding, as those which were in future to be illegal.

Taylor, the water-poet, has given an account of the mode in which these huntings were conducted in the Highlands of Scotland, in the seventeenth century, having been present at Braemar upon such an occasion :—

"There did I find the truly noble and right honourable lords, John Erskine, Earl of Mar ; James Stewart, Earl of Murray ; George Gordon, Earl of Engye, son and heir to the Marquis of Huntley ; James Erskine, Earl of Buchan ; and John, Lord Erskine, son and heir to the Earl of Mar, and their Countesses, with my much honoured, and my last assured and approved friend, Sir William Murray, knight of Abercarney, and hundreds of others, knights, esquires, and their followers ; all and every man, in general, in one habit, as if Ly-curgus had been there, and made laws of equality ; for once in the year, which is the whole month of August, and sometimes part of September, many of the nobility and gentry of the kingdom (for their pleasure) do come into these Highland countries to hunt ; where they do conform themselves to the habit of the Highlandmen, who, for the most part, speak nothing but Irish ; and, in former time, were those people which were called the *Red-shanks.* Their habit is—shoes, with but one sole a-piece ; stockings (which they call short hose,) made of a warm stuff of divers colours, which they call tartan ; as for breeches, many of them, nor their forefathers, never wore any, but a jerkin of the same stuff that their hose is of ; their garters being bands or wreaths of hay or straw ; with a plaid about their shoulders ; which is a mantle of divers colours, much finer and lighter stuff than their hose ; with blue flat caps on their heads ; a handkerchief, knit with two knots, about their necks : and thus are they attired. Now their weapons are —long bowes and forked arrows, swords, and

targets, harquebusses, muskets, durks, and Lochaber axes. With these arms I found many of them armed for the hunting. As for their attire, any man, of what degree soever, that comes amongst them, must not disdain to wear it ; for, if they do, then they will dis-dain to hunt, or willingly to bring in their dogs ; but if men be kind unto them, and be in their habit, then are they conquered with kindness, and the sport will be plentiful. This was the reason that I found so many noblemen and gentlemen in those shapes. But to pro-ceed to the hunting :—

"My good Lord of Marr having put me into that shape, I rode with him from his house, where I saw the ruins of an old castle, called the Castle of Kindroghit. It was built by King Malcolm Canmore (for a hunting-house), who reigned in Scotland, when Edward the Confessor, Harold, and Norman William, reigned in England. I speak of it, because it was the last house I saw in those parts ; for I was the space of twelve days after, before I saw either house, corn-field, or habitation for any creature but deer, wild horses, wolves, and such like creatures,—which made me doubt that I should never have seen a house again.

"Thus, the first day, we travelled eight miles, where there were small cottages, built on purpose to lodge in, which they call Lon-quhards. I thank my good Lord Erskine, he commanded that I should always be lodged in his lodging : the kitchen being always on the side of a bank : many kettles and pots boiling, and many spits turning and winding, with great variety of cheer,—as venison baked ; sodden, rost, and stewed beef ; mutton, goats, kid, hares, fresh salmon, pigeons, hens, ca-pons, chickens, partridges, muir-coots, heath-cocks, caperkellies, and termagants ; good ale, sacke, white and claret, tent (or allegant), with most potent aquavitæ.

"All these, and more than these, we had continually in superfluous abundance, caught by falconers, fowlers, fishers, and brought by my lord's tenants and purveyors to victual our camp, which consisteth of fourteen or fifteen hundred men and horses. The manner of the hunting is this : Five or six hundred men do rise early in the morning, and they do disperse themselves divers ways, and seven, eight, or ten miles compass, they do bring, or chase in, the deer in many herds, (two, three, or four hundred in a herd,) to such or such a place, as the noblemen shall appoint them ; then, when day is come, the lords and gentlemen of their companies do ride or go to the said places, sometimes wading up to the middles, through burns and rivers ; and then, they being come to the place, do lie down on the ground, till those foresaid scouts, which are called the Tinkhell, do bring down the deer; but, as the proverb says of the bad cook, so these tinkhell men do lick their own fingers; for, besides their bows and arrows, which they carry with them, we can hear, now and then, a harquebuss or a musket go off, which they do seldom discharge in vain. Then, after we had staid there three hours, or thereabouts, we might perceive the deer appear on the hills round about us (their heads making a show like a wood,) which, being followed close by the tinkhell, are chased down into the valley where we lay; then all the valley, on each side, being way-laid with a hundred couple of strong Irish greyhounds, they are all let loose, as occasion serves, upon the herd of deer, that with dogs, guns, arrows, durks, and daggers, in the space of two hours, fourscore fat deer were slain; which after are disposed of, some one way, and some another, twenty and thirty miles, and more than enough left for us, to make merry withall, at our rendezvous."

NOTE 20.

By lone Saint Mary's silent lake.—P. 59.

This beautiful sheet of water forms the reservoir from which the Yarrow takes its course. It is connected with a smaller lake, called the Loch of the Lowes, and surrounded by mountains. In the winter, it is still frequented by flights of wild swans; hence my friend Mr. Wordsworth's lines :—

> "The swan on sweet St. Mary's lake
> Floats double, swan and shadow."

Near the lower extremity of the lake, are the ruins of Dryhope tower, the birth-place of Mary Scott, daughter of Philip Scott of Dryhope, and famous by the traditional name of the Flower of Yarrow. She was married to Walter Scott of Harden, no less renowned for his depredations, than his bride for her beauty. Her romantic appellation was, in later days, with equal justice, conferred on Miss Mary Lilias Scott, the last of the elder branch of the Harden family. The author well remembers the talent and spirit of the latter Flower of Yarrow, though age had then injured the charms which procured her the name. The words usually sung to the air of "Tweedside," beginning, "What beauties does Flora disclose," were composed in her honour.

NOTE 21.

—— in feudal strife, a foe,
Hath laid Our Lady's chapel low.—P. 59.

The chapel of St. Mary of the Lowes (*de lacubus*) was situated on the eastern side of the lake, to which it gives name. It was injured by the clan of Scott, in a feud with the Cranstouns; but continued to be a place of worship during the seventeenth century. The vestiges of the building can now scarcely be traced; but the burial ground is still used as a cemetery. A funeral, in a spot so very retired, has an uncommonly striking effect. The vestiges of the chaplain's house are yet visible. Being in a high situation, it commanded a full view of the lake, with the opposite mountain of Bourhope, belonging, with the lake itself, to Lord Napier. On the left hand is the tower of Dryhope, mentioned in a preceding note.

NOTE 22.

—— the Wizard's grave;
That Wizard Priest's, whose bones are thrust
From company of holy dust.—P. 60.

At one corner of the burial ground of the demolished chapel, but without its precincts, is a small mound, called *Binram's Corse*, where tradition deposits the remains of a necromantic priest, the former tenant of the chaplainry.

NOTE 23.

Some ruder and more savage scene,
Like that which frowns round dark Loch-skene.
P. 60.

Loch-skene is a mountain lake, of considerable size, at the head of the Moffat-water. The character of the scenery is uncommonly savage; and the earn, or Scottish eagle, has, for many ages, built its nest yearly upon an islet in the lake. Loch-skene discharges itself into a brook, which, after a short and precipitate course, falls from a cataract of immense height, and gloomy grandeur, called, from its appearance, the "Grey Mare's Tail." The "Giant's Grave," afterwards mentioned, is a sort of trench, which bears that name, a little way from the foot of the cataract. It has the appearance of a battery, designed to command the pass.

NOTE 24.

—— St. Cuthbert's Holy Isle.—P. 60.

Lindisfarne, an isle on the coast of Northumberland, was called Holy Island, from the sanctity of its ancient monastery, and from its having been the episcopal seat of the see of Durham during the early ages of British Christianity. A succession of holy men held that office: but their merits were swallowed up in the superior fame of St. Cuthbert. who was sixth Bishop of Durham, and who bestowed the name of his "patrimony" upon the extensive property of the see. The ruins of the monastery upon Holy Island betoken great antiquity. The arches are, in general, strictly Saxon; and the pillars which support them, short, strong, and massy. In some places, however, there are pointed windows, which indicate that the building has been repaired at a period long subsequent to the original foundation. The exterior ornaments of the building, being of a light sandy stone, have been wasted, as described in the text. Lindisfarne is not properly an island, but rather, as the venerable Bede has termed it, a semi-isle; for, although surrounded by the sea at full tide, the ebb leaves the sands dry between it and the opposite coast of Northumberland, from which it is about three miles distant.

NOTE 25.

—— in their convent cell
A Saxon princess once did dwell,
*The lovely Edelfled—*P. 63.

She was the daughter of King Oswy, who, in gratitude to Heaven for the great victory which he won in 655, against Penda, the Pagan King of Mercia, dedicated Edelfleda, then but a year old, to the service of God, in the monastery of Whitby, of which St. Hilda was then abbess. She afterwards adorned the place of her education with great magnificence.

NOTE 26.

—— of thousand snakes, each one
Was changed into a coil of stone,
When holy Hilda pray'd;
They told, how sea-fowls' pinions fail,
*As over Whitby's towers they sail.—*P. 63.

These two miracles are much insisted upon by all ancient writers who have occasion to mention either Whitby or St. Hilda. The relics of the snakes which infested the precincts of the convent, and were, at the abbess's prayer, not only beheaded, but petrified, are still found about the rocks, and are termed by Protestant fossilists, *Ammonitæ.*

The other miracle is thus mentioned by Camden: "It is also ascribed to the power of her sanctity, that these wild geese, which, in the winter, fly in great flocks to the lakes and rivers unfrozen in the southern parts, to the great amazement of every one, fall down suddenly upon the ground, when they are in their flight over certain neighbouring fields herebouts : a relation I should not have made, if

I had not received it from several credible men. But those who are less inclined to heed superstition attribute it to some occult quality in the ground, and to somewhat of antipathy between it and the geese, such as they say is betwixt wolves and scylla roots: For that such hidden tendencies and aversions, as we call sympathies and antipathies, are implanted in many things by provident Nature for the preservation of them, is a thing so evident that everybody grants it." Mr. Charlton, in his History of Whitby, points out the true origin of the fable, from the number of sea-gulls that, when flying from a storm, often alight near Whitby; and from the woodcocks, and other birds of passage, who do the same upon their arrival on shore, after a long flight.

NOTE 27.

His body's resting-place, of old,
How oft their Patron changed, they told.—
P. 63.

St. Cuthbert was, in the choice of his sepulchre, one of the most mutable and unreasonable saints in the Calendar. He died A.D. 688, in a hermitage upon the Farne Islands, having resigned the bishopric of Lindisfarne, or Holy Island, about two years before. His body was brought to Lindisfarne, where it remained until a descent of the Danes, about 793, when the monastery was nearly destroyed. The monks fled to Scotland with what they deemed their chief treasure, the relics of St. Cuthbert. The Saint was, however, a most capricious fellow-traveller; which was the more intolerable, as, like Sinbad's Old Man of the Sea, he journeyed upon the shoulders of his companions. They paraded him through Scotland for several years, and came as far west as Whithern, in Galloway, whence they attempted to sail for Ireland, but were driven back by tempests. He at length made a halt at Norham ; from thence he went to Melrose, where he remained stationary for a short time, and then caused himself to be launched upon the Tweed in a stone coffin, which landed him at Tilmouth, in Northumberland.

The resting-place of the remains of this Saint is not now matter of uncertainty. So recently as 17th May, 1827, 1139 years after his death, their discovery and disinterment were effected. Under a blue stone, in the middle of the shrine of St. Cuthbert, at the eastern extremity of the choir of Durham Cathedral, there was then found a walled grave, containing the coffins of the Saint. The first, or outer one, was ascertained to be that of 1541, the second of 1041 ; the third, or inner one, answering in every particular to the description of that of 698, was found to contain, not indeed, as had been averred then, and even until 1539, the incorruptible body, but the entire skeleton of the Saint; the bottom of the grave being perfectly dry, free from offensive smell, and without the slightest symptom that a human body had ever undergone decomposition within its walls. The skeleton was found swathed in five silk robes of emblematical embroidery, the ornamental parts laid with gold leaf, and these again covered with a robe of linen. Beside the skeleton were also deposited several gold and silver *insignia*, and other relics of the Saint.

[Speaking of the burial of Cuthbert, Mr. Hartshorne says, "Aldhune was at that time bishop of the, previously for a long period, wandering See of Lindisfarne. But we now hear no more of that ancient name as the seat of Episcopacy. A cathedral church, such as it was . . . . was speedily erected upon the hill of Durham. This church was consecrated, with much magnificence and solemnity, in the year 999."—*History of Northumberland*, p. 227.]

NOTE 28.

Even Scotland's dauntless king and heir, &c. Before his standard fled.—P. 64.

Every one has heard, that when David I., with his son Henry, invaded Northumberland in 1136, the English host marched against them under the holy banner of St. Cuthbert; to the efficacy of which was imputed the great victory which they obtained in the bloody battle of Northallerton, or Cutonmoor. The conquerors were at least as much indebted to the jealousy and intractability of the different tribes who composed David's army; among whom, as mentioned in the text, were the Galwegians, the Britons of Strath-Clyde, the men of Teviotdale and Lothian, with many Norman and German warriors, who asserted the cause of the Empress Maud. See CHALMER'S *Caledonia*, vol. i. p. 622; a most laborious, curious, and interesting publication, from which considerable defects of style and manner ought not to turn aside the Scottish antiquary.

NOTE 29.

'*Twas he, to vindicate his reign, Edged Alfred's falchion on the Dane, And turn'd the Conqueror back again.*—
P. 64.

Cuthbert, we have seen, had no great reason to spare the Danes, when opportunity offered. Accordingly, I find, in Simeon of Durham, that the Saint appeared in a vision

to Alfred, when lurking in the marshes of Glastonbury, and promised him assistance and victory over his heathen enemies; a consolation which, as was reasonable, Alfred, after the victory of Ashendown, rewarded by a royal offering at the shrine of the Saint. As to William the Conqueror, the terror spread before his army, when he marched to punish the revolt of the Northumbrians, in 1096, had forced the monks to fly once more to Holy Island with the body of the Saint. It was, however, replaced before William left the north; and, to balance accounts, the Conqueror having intimated an indiscreet curiosity to view the Saint's body, he was, while in the act of commanding the shrine to be opened, seized with heat and sickness, accompanied with such a panic terror, that, notwithstanding there was a sumptuous dinner prepared for him, he fled without eating a morsel, (which the monkish historian seems to have thought no small part both of the miracle and the penance), and never drew his bridle till he got to the river Tees.

NOTE 30.

Saint Cuthbert sits, and toils to frame The sea-born beads that bear his name.—P. 64.

Although we do not learn that Cuthbert was, during his life, such an artificer as Dunstan, his brother in sanctity, yet, since his death, he has acquired the reputation of forging those *Entrochi* which are found among the rocks of Holy Island, and pass there by the name of St. Cuthbert's Beads. While at this task, he is supposed to sit during the night upon a certain rock, and use another as his anvil. This story was perhaps credited in former days; at least the Saint's legend contains some not more probable.

NOTE 31.

Old Colwulf.—P. 64.

Ceolwulf, or Colwulf, King of Northumberland, flourished in the eighth century. He was a man of some learning; for the venerable Bede dedicates to him his "Ecclesiastical History." He abdicated the throne about 738, and retired to Holy Island, where he died in the odour of sanctity. Saint as Colwulf was, however, I fear the foundation of the penance vault does not correspond with his character; for it is recorded among his *memorabilia*, that, finding the air of the island raw and cold, he indulged the monks, whose rule had hitherto confined them to milk or water, with the comfortable privilege of using wine or ale. If any rigid antiquary insists on this objection, he is welcome to suppose the penance-vault was intended, by the founder, for the more genial purposes of a cellar.

NOTE 32.

Tynemouth's haughty Prioress.—P. 65.

That there was an ancient priory at Tynemouth is certain. Its ruins are situated on a high rocky point; and, doubtless, many a vow was made to the shrine by the distressed mariners who drove towards the iron-bound coast of Northumberland in stormy weather. It was anciently a nunnery; for Virca, abbess of Tynemouth, presented St. Cuthbert (yet alive) with a rare winding-sheet, in emulation of a holy lady called Tuda, who had sent him a coffin: But, as in the case of Whitby, and of Holy Island, the introduction of nuns at Tynemouth in the reign of Henry VIII. is an anachronism. The nunnery at Holy Island is altogether fictitious. Indeed, St. Cuthbert was unlikely to permit such an establishment; for, notwithstanding his accepting the mortuary gifts above-mentioned, and his carrying on a visiting acquaintance with the Abbess of Coldingham, he certainly hated the whole female sex; and, in revenge of a slippery trick played to him by an Irish princess, he, after death, inflicted severe penances on such as presumed to approach within a certain distance of his shrine.

NOTE 33.

On those the wall was to enclose,
Alive within the tomb.—P. 66.

It is well known that the religious, who broke their vows of chastity, were subjected to the same penalty as the Roman vestals in a similar case. A small niche, sufficient to enclose their bodies, was made in the massive wall of the convent; a slender pittance of food and water was deposited in it, and the awful words, VADE IN PACE, were the signal for immuring the criminal. It is not likely that, in latter times, this punishment was often resorted to; but among the ruins of the Abbey of Coldingham were some years ago discovered the remains of a female skeleton, which, from the shape of the niche and position of the figure, seemed to be that of an immured nun.

NOTE 34.

The village inn.—P. 71.

The accommodations of a Scottish hostelrie, or inn, in the 16th century, may be collected from Dunbar's admirable tale of "The Friars of Berwick." Simon Lawder, "the gay ostler," seems to have lived very comfortably; and his wife decorated her person with a scarlet kirtle, and a belt of silk and silver, and rings upon her fingers; and feasted her paramour with rabbits, capons, partridges, and Bordeaux wine. At least, if the Scottish inns were not good, it was not for want of encouragement from the legislature; who, so early as the reign of James I., not only enacted that in all boroughs and fairs there be hostellaries, having stables and chambers, and provision for man and horse, but by another statute ordained that no man, travelling on horse or foot, should presume to lodge anywhere except in these hostellaries; and that no person, save innkeepers, should receive such travellers, under the penalty of forty shillings, for exercising such hospitality. But, in spite of these provident enactments, the Scottish hostels are but indifferent, and strangers continue to find reception in the houses of individuals.

NOTE 35.

The death of a dear friend.—P. 73.

Among other omens to which faithful credit is given among the Scottish peasantry, is what is called the "dead-bell," explained by my friend James Hogg to be that tinkling in the ears which the country people regard as the secret intelligence of some friend's decease.

NOTE 36.

The Goblin-Hall.—P. 74.

A vaulted hall under the ancient castle of Gifford or Yester, (for it bears either name indifferently,) the construction of which has from a very remote period been ascribed to magic. The statistical Account of the Parish of Garvald and Baro gives the following account of the present state of this castle and apartment:—" Upon a peninsula, formed by the water of Hopes on the east, and a large rivulet on the west, stands the ancient castle of Yester. Sir David Dalrymple, in his Annals, relates, that 'Hugh Giffon de Yester died in 1267; that in his castle there was a capacious cavern, formed by magical art, and called in the country Bo-Hall, *i.e.* Hobgoblin Hall.' A staircase of twenty-four steps led down to this apartment, which is a large and spacious hall, with an arched roof; and though it hath stood for so many centuries, and been exposed to the external air for a period of fifty or sixty years, it is still as firm and entire as if it had only stood a few years.

From the floor of this hall, another staircase of thirty-six steps leads down to a pit which hath a communication with Hopes-water. A great part of the walls of this large and ancient castle are still standing. There is a tradition that the castle of Yester was the last fortification, in this country, that surrendered to General Gray, sent into Scotland by Protector Somerset."—*Statistical Account*, vol. xiii. I have only to add, that, in 1737, the Goblin Hall was tenanted by the Marquis of Tweeddale's falconer, as I learn from a poem by Boyse, entitled "Retirement," written upon visiting Yester. It is now rendered inaccessible by the fall of the stair.

NOTE 37.

There floated Haco's banner trim
Above Norweyan warriors grim.—P. 75.

In 1263, Haco, King of Norway, came into the Frith of Clyde with a powerful armament, and made a descent at Largs, in Ayrshire. Here he was encountered and defeated, on the 2nd October, by Alexander III. Haco retreated to Orkney, where he died soon after this disgrace to his arms. There are still existing, near the place of battle, many barrows, some of which, having been opened, were found, as usual, to contain bones and urns.

NOTE 38.

Upon his breast a pentacle.—P. 75.

"A pentacle is a piece of fine linen, folded with five corners, according to the five senses, and suitably inscribed with characters. This the magician extends towards the spirits which he invokes, when they are stubborn and rebellious, and refuse to be conformable unto the ceremonies and rites of magic."—See the Discourses, &c., in Reginald Scott's *Discovery of Witchcraft*, ed. 1665, p. 66.

NOTE 39.

As born upon that blessed night,
When yawning graves and dying groan
Proclaimed Hell's empire overthrown.—
P. 75.

It is a popular article of faith that those who are born on Christmas, or Good Friday, have the power of seeing spirits, and even of commanding them. The Spaniards imputed the haggard and downcast looks of their Philip II. to the disagreeable visions to which this privilege subjected him.

NOTE 40.

Yet still the knightly spear and shield
The Elfin warrior doth wield
Upon the brown hill's breast.—P. 76.

The following extract from the Essay upon the Fairy superstitions, in the "Minstrelsy of the Scottish Border," vol. ii., will show whence many of the particulars of the combat between Alexander III. and the Goblin Knight are derived :—

Gervase of Tilbury *Otia Imperial. ap. Script. rer. Brunsvic.* (vol. i. p. 797) relates the following popular story concerning a fairy knight : "Osbert, a bold and powerful baron, visited a noble family in the vicinity of Wandlebury, in the bishopric of Ely. Among other stories related in the social circle of his friends, who, according to custom, amused each other by repeating ancient tales and traditions, he was informed, that if any knight, unattended, entered an adjacent plain by moonlight, and challenged an adversary to appear, he would be immediately encountered by a spirit in the form of a knight. Osbert resolved to make the experiment, and set out, attended by a single squire, whom he ordered to remain without the limits of the plain, which was surrounded by an ancient entrenchment. On repeating the challenge, he was instantly assailed by an adversary, whom he quickly unhorsed, and seized the reins of his steed. During this operation, his ghostly opponent sprung up, and darting his spear, like a javelin, at Osbert, wounded him in the thigh. Osbert returned in triumph with the horse, which he committed to the care of his servants. The horse was of a sable colour, as well as his whole accoutrements, and apparently of great beauty and vigour. He remained with his keeper till cock-growing, when, with eyes flashing fire, he reared, spurned the ground, and vanished. On disarming himself, Osbert perceived that he was wounded, and that one of his steel boots was full of blood." Gervase adds, that "as long as he lived, the scar of his wound opened afresh on the anniversary of the eve on which he encountered the spirit." Less fortunate was the gallant Bohemian knight, who, travelling by night with a single companion, "came in sight of a fairy host, arrayed under displayed banners. Despising the remonstrances of his friend, the knight pricked forward to break a lance with a champion, who advanced from the ranks apparently in defiance. His companion beheld the Bohemian overthrown, horse and man, by his aërial adversary; and returning to the spot next morning, he found the mangled corpse of the knight and steed."—*Hierarchy of Blessed Angels*, p. 554.

Besides these instances of Elfin chivalry above quoted, many others might be alleged in support of employing fairy machinery in this manner. The forest of Glenmore, in the North Highlands, is believed to be haunted by a spirit called *Lham-dearg*, in the array of an ancient warrior, having a bloody hand, from which he takes his name. He insists upon those with whom he meets doing battle with him; and the clergyman who makes up an account of the district, extant in the Macfarlane MS. in the Advocates' Library, gravely assures us, that, in his time, *Lham-dearg* fought with three brothers, whom he met in his walk, none of whom long survived the ghostly conflict. Barclay, in his "Euphormion," gives a singular account of an officer who had ventured, with his servant, rather to intrude upon a haunted house in a town in Flanders, than to put up with worse quarters elsewhere. After taking the usual precautions of providing fires, lights, and arms, they watched till midnight, when behold ! the severed arm of a man dropped from the ceiling; this was followed by the legs, the other arm, the trunk, and the head of the body, all separately. The members rolled together, united themselves in the presence of the astonished soldiers, and formed a gigantic warrior, who defied them both to combat. Their blows, although they penetrated the body and amputated the limbs of their strange antagonist, had, as the reader may easily believe, little effect on an enemy who possessed such powers of self-union; nor did his efforts make more effectual impression upon them. How the combat terminated I do not exactly remember, and have not the book by me ; but I think the spirit made to the intruders on his mansion the usual proposal, that they should renounce their redemption ; which being declined, he was obliged to retract.

The northern champions of old were accustomed peculiarly to search for, and delight in, encounters with such military spectres. See a whole chapter on the subject, in BARTHOLINUS, *De Causis contemptæ Mortis a Danis*, p. 253.

NOTE 41.

Close to the hut, no more his own,
Close to the aid he sought in vain,
The morn may find the stiffen'd swain.
                                    P. 79.

I cannot help here mentioning, that, on the night in which these lines were written, suggested as they were, by a sudden fall of snow,

beginning after sunset, an unfortunate man perished exactly in the maner here described, and his body was next morning found close to his own house. The accident happened within five miles of the farm of Ashestiel.

NOTE 42.

—— *Forbes.*—P. 79.

Sir William Forbes of Pitsligo, Baronet ; unequalled, perhaps, in the degree of individual affection entertained for him by his friends, as well as in the general respect and esteem of Scotland at large. His "Life of Beattie," whom he befriended and patronized in life, as well as celebrated after his decease, was not long published, before the benevolent and affectionate biographer was called to follow the subject of his narrative. This melancholy event very shortly succeeded the marriage of the friend, to whom this introduction is addressed, with one of Sir William's daughters.

NOTE 43.

Friar Rush.—P. 80.

Alias "Will o' the Wisp." This personage is a strolling demon, or *esprit follet*, who, once upon a time, got admittance into a monastery as a scullion, and played the monks many pranks. He was also a sort of Robin Goodfellow, and Jack o' Lanthorn. It is in allusion to this mischievous demon that Milton's clown speaks,

"She was pinched, and pulled, she said,
And he by *Friar's lanthorn* led."

"The History of Friar Rush" is of extreme rarity, and, for some time, even the existence of such a book was doubted, although it is expressly alluded to by Reginald Scott, in his "Discovery of Witchcraft." I have perused a copy in the valuable library of my friend Mr. Heber ; and I observe, from Mr. Beloe's "Anecdotes of Literature," that there is one in the excellent collection of the Marquis of Stafford.

NOTE 44.

Sir David Lindesay of the Mount,
Lord Lion King-at-arms.—P. 82.

The late elaborate edition of Sir David Lindsay's Works, by Mr. George Chalmers, has probably introduced him to many of my readers. It is perhaps to be regretted, that the learned Editor had not bestowed more pains in elucidating his author, even although he should have omitted, or at least reserved, his disquisitions on the origin of the language used by the poet : But, with all its faults, his work is an acceptable present to Scottish antiquaries. Sir David Lindesay was well known for his early efforts in favour of the Reformed doctrines ; and, indeed, his play, coarse as it now seems, must have had a powerful effect upon the people of his age. I am uncertain if I abuse poetical licence, by introducing Sir David Lindesay in the character of Lion-Herald, sixteen years before he obtained that office. At any rate, I am not the first who has been guilty of the anachronism ; for the author of "Flodden Field" despatches *Dallamount*, which can mean nobody but Sir David de la Mont, to France, on the message of defiance from James IV. to Henry VIII. It was often an office imposed on the Lion King-at-arms, to receive foreign ambassadors ; and Lindesay himself did this honour to Sir Ralph Sadler, in 1539-40. Indeed, the oath of the Lion, in its first article, bears reference to his frequent employment upon royal messages and embassies.

The office of heralds, in feudal times, being held of the utmost importance, the inauguration of the Kings-at-arms, who presided over their colleges, was proportionally solemn. In fact, it was the mimicry of a royal coronation, except that the unction was made with wine instead of oil. In Scotland, a namesake and kinsman of Sir David Lindesay, inaugurated in 1592, "was crowned by King James with the ancient crown of Scotland, which was used before the Scottish kings assumed a close crown;" and, on occasion of the same solemnity, dined at the King's table, wearing the crown. It is probable that the coronation of his predecessor was not less solemn. So sacred was the herald's office, that, in 1515, Lord Drummond was by Parliament declared guilty of treason, and his lands forfeited, because he had struck with his fist the Lion King-at-arms, when he reproved him for his follies. Nor was he restored, but at the Lion's earnest solicitation.

NOTE 45.

Crichtoun Castle.—P. 82.

A large ruinous castle on the banks of the Tyne, about ten miles from Edinburgh. As indicated in the text, it was built at different times, and with a very differing regard to splendour and accommodation. The oldest part of the building is a narrow keep, or tower, such as formed the mansion of a lesser Scottish baron ; but so many additions have been made to it, that there is now a large court-yard, surrounded by buildings of different ages. The eastern front of the court is raised above a portico, and decorated with entablatures, bearing anchors. All the stones of this front are cut into diamond facets, the angular projections of which have an uncommonly rich appearance. The inside of this part of the building appears to have contained a gallery of great length, and uncommon elegance. Access was given to it by a magnificent staircase, now quite destroyed. The soffits are ornamented with twining cordage and rosettes; and the whole seems to have been far more splendid than was usual in Scottish castles. The castle belonged originally to the Chancellor, Sir William Crichton, and probably owed to him its first enlargement, as well as its being taken by the Earl of Douglas, who imputed to Crichton's counsels the death of his predecessor, Earl William, beheaded in Edinburgh Castle, with his brother, in 1440. It is said to have been totally demolished on that occasion ; but the present state of the ruin shows the contrary. In 1483, it was garrisoned by Lord Crichton, then its proprietor, against King James III., whose displeasure he had incurred by seducing his sister Margaret, in revenge, it is said, for the Monarch having dishonoured his bed. From the Crichton family the castle passed to that of the Hepburns, Earls of Bothwell; and when the forfeitures of Stewart, the last Earl of Bothwell, were divided, the barony and castle of Crichton fell to the share of the Earl of Buccleuch. They were afterwards the property of the Pringles of Clifton, and are now that of Sir John Callander, Baronet. It were to be wished the proprietor would take a little pains to preserve these splendid remains of antiquity, which are at present used as a fold for sheep, and wintering cattle ; although, perhaps, there are very few ruins in Scotland which display so well the style and beauty of ancient castle-architecture. The castle of Crichton has a dungeon vault, called the *Massey Mole.* The epithet, which is not uncommonly applied to the prisons of other old castles in Scotland, is of Saracenic origin. It occurs twice in the "*Epistolæ Itinerariæ*" of Tollius, "*Carcer subterraneus, sive, ut Mauri appellant,* MAZMORRA*,*" p. 147; and again, "*Coguntur omnes Captivi sub noctem in ergastula subterranea, quæ Turcæ Algezerani vocant* MAZMORRAS," p. 243. The same word applies to the dungeons of the ancient Moorish castles in Spain, and serves to show from what nation the Gothic style of castle-building was originally derived.

Note 46.

Earl Adam Hepburn.—P. 83.

He was the second Earl of Bothwell, and fell in the field of Flodden, where, according to an ancient English poet, he distinguished himself by a furious attempt to retrieve the day:—

"Then on the Scottish part, right proud,
　The Earl of Bothwell then out brast,
And stepping forth, with stomach good,
　Into the enemies' throng he thrast;
And *Bothwell! Bothwell!* cried bold,
　To cause his souldiers to ensue,
But there he caught a wellcome cold,
　The Englishmen straight down him threw.
Thus Haburn through his hardy heart
　His fatal fine in conflict found, &c.

　　　　　Flodden Field, a Poem; edited by
　　　　　　　H. Weber.　Edin. 1808.

Adam was grandfather to James, Earl of Bothwell, too well known in the history of Queen Mary.

Note 47.

*For that a messenger from heaven,
In vain to James had counsel given,
Against the English war.*—P. 83.

This story is told by Pitscottie with characteristic simplicity:—"The King, seeing that France could get no support of him for that time, made a proclamation, full hastily, through all the realm of Scotland both east and west, south and north, as well in the isles as in the firm land, to all manner of men, between sixty and sixteen years, that they should be ready, within twenty days, to pass with him, with forty days' victual, and to meet at the Burrow-muir of Edinburgh, and there to pass forward where he pleased. His proclamations were hastily obeyed, contrary the Council of Scotland's will ; but every man loved his prince so well that they would on no ways disobey him; but every man caused make his proclamation so hastily, conform to the charge of the King's proclamation.

"The King came to Lithgow, where he happened to be for the time at the Council, very sad and dolorous, making his devotion to God, to send him good chance and fortune in his voyage. In this meantime there came a man, clad in a blue gown, in at the kirk door, and belted about him in a roll of linen cloth ; a pair of brotikings on his feet, to the great of his legs ; with all other hose and clothes conform thereto : but he had nothing on his head,

but syde red yellow hair behind, and on his haffets, which wan down to his shoulders; but his forehead was bald and bare. He seemed to be a man of two-and-fifty years, with a great pike-staff in his hand, and came first forward among the lords, crying and speiring for the King, saying, he desired to speak with him. While, at the last, he came where the King was sitting in the desk at his prayers ; but when he saw the King, he made him little reverence or salutation, but leaned down groffling on the desk before him, and said to him in this manner, as after follows:—
'Sir King, my mother hath sent me to you, desiring you not to pass, at this time, where thou art purposed ; for if thou does, thou wilt not fare well in thy journey, nor none that passeth with thee. Further, she bade thee mell with no woman, nor use their counsel, nor let them touch thy body, nor thou theirs ; for, if thou do it, thou wilt be confounded and brought to shame.'

"By this man had spoken thir words unto the King's grace, the evening song was near done, and the King paused on thir words, studying to give him an answer; but, in the meantime, before the King's eyes, and in the presence of all the lords that were about him for the time, this man vanished away, and could no ways be seen or comprehended, but vanished away as he had been a blink of the sun, or a whip of the whirlwind, and could no more be seen. I heard say, Sir David Lindesay Lyon-herauld, and John Inglis the marshal, who were, at that time, young men, and special servants to the King's grace, were standing presently beside the King, who thought to have laid hands on this man, that they might have speired further tidings at him: But all for nought; they could not touch him; for he vanished away betwixt them, and was no more seen."

Note 48.

The wild buckbells.—P. 84.

I am glad of an opportunity to describe the cry of the deer by another word than *braying,* although the latter has been sanctified by the use of the Scottish metrical translation of the Psalms. *Bell* seems to be an abbreviation of bellow. This sylvan sound conveyed great delight to our ancestors, chiefly, I suppose, from association. A gentle knight in the reign of Henry VIII., Sir Thomas Wortley, built Wantley Lodge, in Wancliffe Forest, for the pleasure (as an ancient inscription testifies) of "listening to the hart's *bell.*"

NOTE 49.

June saw his father's overthrow.—P. 84.

The rebellion against James III. was signalized by the cruel circumstance of his son's presence in the hostile army. When the King saw his own banner displayed against him, and his son in the faction of his enemies, he lost the little courage he had ever possessed, fled out of the field, fell from his horse as it started at a woman and water-pitcher, and was slain, it is not well understood by whom. James IV., after the battle, passed to Stirling, and hearing the monks of the chapel-royal deploring the death of his father, their founder, he was seized with deep remorse, which manifested itself in severe penances. (See a following Note on stanza ix. of canto v.) The battle of Sauchie-burn, in which James III. fell, was fought 18th June, 1488.

NOTE 50.

The Borough-moor.—P. 86.

The Borough, or Common Moor of Edinburgh, was of very great extent, reaching from the southern walls of the city to the bottom of Braid Hills. It was anciently a forest; and, in that state, was so great a nuisance, that the inhabitants of Edinburgh had permission granted to them of building wooden galleries, projecting over the street, in order to encourage them to consume the timber, which they seem to have done very effectually. When James IV. mustered the array of the kingdom there, in 1513, the Borough-moor was, according to Hawthornden, "afield spacious, and delightful by the shade of many stately and aged oaks." Upon that, and similar occasions, the royal standard is traditionally said to have been displayed from the Hare-Stane, a high stone, now built into the wall, on the left hand of the high-way leading towards Braid, not far from the head of Burntsfield Links. The Hare-Stane probably derives its name from the British word *Har*, signifying an army.

NOTE 51.

—— *in proud Scotland's royal shield,* *The ruddy lion ramp'd in gold.*—P. 87.

The well-known arms of Scotland. If you will believe Boethius and Buchanan, the double tressure round the shield, mentioned, *counter fleur-de-lysed or lingued and armed azure*, was first assumed by Echaius, King of Scotland, contemporary of Charlemagne, and founder of the celebrated League with France; but later antiquaries make poor Eochy, or

Achy, little better than a sort of King of Brentford, whom old Grig (who has also swelled into Gregorius Magnus) associated with himself in the important duty of governing some part of the north-eastern coast of Scotland.

NOTE 52.

—— *Caledonia's Queen is changed.*—P. 89.

The Old Town of Edinburgh was secured on the north side by a lake, now drained, and on the south by a wall, which there was some attempt to make defensible even so late as 1745. The gates, and the greater part of the wall, have been pulled down, in the course of the late extensive and beautiful enlargement of the city. My ingenious and valued friend, Mr. Thomas Campbell, proposed to celebrate Edinburgh under the epithet here borrowed. But the "Queen of the North" has not been so fortunate as to receive from so eminent a pen the proposed distinction.

NOTE 53.

The cloth-yard arrows.—P. 91.

This is no poetical exaggeration. In some of the counties of England, distinguished for archery, shafts of this extraordinary length were actually used. Thus, at the battle of Blackheath, between the troops of Henry VII., and the Cornish insurgents, in 1496, the bridge of Dartford was defended by a picked band of archers from the rebel army, "whose arrows," says Holinshed, "were in length a full cloth yard." The Scottish, according to Ascham, had a proverb, that every English archer carried under his belt twenty-four Scots, in allusion to his bundle of unerring shafts.

NOTE 54.

He saw the hardy burghers there *March arm'd on foot with faces bare.*—P. 91.

The Scottish burgesses were, like yeomen, appointed to be armed with bows and sheaves, sword, buckler, knife, spear, or a good axe instead of a bow, if worth 100*l.* : their armour to be of white or bright harness. They wore *white hats*, i.e., bright steel caps, without crest or visor. By an act of James IV. their *weapon-schawings* are appointed to be held four times a year, under the aldermen or bailiffs.

NOTE 55.

On foot the yeomen too—— *Each at his back (a slender store)* *His forty days' provision bore,* *His arms were halbert, axe, or spear.*—P. 91.

Bows and quivers were in vain recommended

to the peasantry of Scotland, by repeated statutes; spears and axes seem universally to have been used instead of them. Their defensive armour was the plate-jack, hauberk, or brigantine; and their missile weapons crossbows and culverins. All wore swords of excellent temper, according to Patten; and a voluminous handkerchief round their neck, "not for cold, but for cutting." The mace also was much used in the Scottish army. The old poem on the battle of Flodden mentions a band—

> "Who manfully did meet their foes,
> With leaden mauls, and lances long."

When the feudal array of the kingdom was called forth, each man was obliged to appear with forty days' provision. When this was expended, which took place before the battle of Flodden, the army melted away of course. Almost all the Scottish forces, except a few knights, men-at-arms, and the Border-prickers, who formed excellent light cavalry, acted upon foot.

NOTE 56.

A banquet rich, and costly wines,
To Marmion and his train.—P. 92.

In all transactions of great or petty importance, and among whomsoever taking place, it would seem that a present of wine was a uniform and indispensable preliminary. It was not to Sir John Falstaff alone that such an introductory preface was necessary, however well judged and acceptable on the part of Mr. Brook; for Sir Ralph Sadler, while on an embassy to Scotland in 1539-40, mentions, with complacency, "the same night came Rothesay (the herald so called) to me again, and brought me wine from the King, both white and red."—*Clifford's Edition,* p. 39.

NOTE 57.

—— his iron-belt,
That bound his breast in penance pain,
In memory of his father slain.—P. 93.

Few readers need to be reminded of this belt, to the weight of which James added certain ounces every year that he lived. Pitscottie founds his belief, that James was not slain in the battle of Flodden, because the English never had this token of the iron-belt to show to any Scottishman. The person and character of James are delineated according to our best historians. His romantic disposition, which led him highly to relish gaiety, approaching to license, was, at the same time, tinged with enthusiastic devotion. These propensities sometimes formed a strange contrast.

He was wont, during his fits of devotion, to assume the dress, and conform to the rules, of the order of Franciscans; and when he had thus done penance for some time in Stirling, to plunge again into the tide of pleasure. Probably, too, with no unusual inconsistency, he sometimes laughed at the superstitious observances to which he at other times subjected himself.

NOTE 58.

Sir Hugh the Heron's wife.—P. 93.

It has been already noticed (see note to stanza xiii. of canto i.) that King James's acquaintance with Lady Heron of Ford did not commence until he marched into England. Our historians impute to the King's infatuated passion the delays which led to the fatal defeat of Flodden. The author of "The Genealogy of the Heron Family" endeavours, with laudable anxiety, to clear the Lady Ford from the scandal; that she came and went, however, between the armies of James and Surrey is certain. See PINKERTON'S *History,* and the authorities he refers to, vol. ii. p. 99.

NOTE 59.

The fair Queen of France
Sent him a turquois ring and glove,
And charged him, as her knight and love,
For her to break a lance.—P. 94.

"Also the Queen of France wrote a love-letter to the King of Scotland, calling him her love, showing him that she had suffered much rebuke in France for the defending of his honour. She believed surely that he would recompense her again with some of his kingly support in her necessity; that is to say, that he would raise her an army, and come three foot of ground on English ground, for her sake. To that effect she sent him a ring off her finger, with fourteen thousand French crowns to pay his expenses." PITSCOTTIE, p. 110.—A turquois ring; probably this fatal gift is, with James's sword and dagger, preserved in the College of Heralds, London.

NOTE 60.

Archibald Bell-the-Cat.—P. 95.

Archibald Douglas, Earl of Angus, a man remarkable for strength of body and mind, acquired the popular name of *Bell-the-Cat,* upon the following remarkable occasion :— James the Third, of whom Pitscottie complains that he delighted more in music, and "policies of building," than in hunting hawking, and other noble exercises, was so ill advised as to make favourites of his architects and musicians, whom the same historian irreverently terms masons and fiddlers. His nobility, who did not sympathize in the King's respect for the fine arts, were extremely incensed at the honours conferred on those persons, particularly on Cochrane, a mason, who had been created Earl of Mar ; and, seizing the opportunity, when, in 1482, the King had convoked the whole array of the country to march against the English, they held a midnight council in the church of Lauder, for the purpose of forcibly removing these minions from the King's person. When all had agreed on the propriety of this measure, Lord Gray told the assembly the apologue of the Mice, who had formed a resolution that it would be highly advantageous to their community to tie a bell round the cat's neck, that they might hear her approach at a distance ; but which public measure unfortunately miscarried, from no mouse being willing to undertake the task of fastening the bell. " I understand the moral," said Angus, "and, that what we propose may not lack execution, I will *bell-the-cat.*"

NOTE 61.

Against the war had Angus stood,
And chafed his royal Lord.—P. 96.

Angus was an old man when the war against England was resolved upon. He earnestly spoke against that measure from its commencement ; and, on the eve of the battle of Flodden, remonstrated so freely upon the impolicy of fighting, that the King said to him, with scorn and indignation, "if he was afraid he might go home." The Earl burst into tears at this insupportable insult, and retired accordingly, leaving his sons George, Master of Angus, and Sir William of Glenbervie, to command his followers. They were both slain in the battle, with two hundred gentlemen of the name of Douglas. The aged Earl, broken-hearted at the calamities of his house and his country, retired into a religious house, where he died about a year after the field of Flodden.

NOTE 62.

Tantallon hold.—P. 96.

The ruins of Tantallon Castle occupy a high rock projecting into the German Ocean, about two miles east of North Berwick. The building formed a principal castle of the Douglas family, and when the Earl of Angus was banished, in 1527, it continued to hold out against James V. The King went in person against it, and for its reduction, borrowed from the Castle of Dunbar, then belonging to the Duke of Albany, two great cannons, " Thrawn-mouth'd Meg and her Marrow ;" also, " two great botcards, and two moyan, two double falcons, and four quarter falcons." Yet, notwithstanding all this apparatus, James was forced to raise the siege, and only afterwards obtained possession of Tantallon by treaty with the governor, Simon Panango. When the Earl of Angus returned from banishment, upon the death of James, he again obtained possession of Tantallon, and it actually afforded refuge to an English ambassador, under circumstances similar to those described in the text. This was no other than the celebrated Sir Ralph Sadler, who resided there for some time under Angus's protection, after the failure of his negotiation for matching the infant Mary with Edward VI.

NOTE 63.

Their motto on his blade.—P. 96.

A very ancient sword, in possession of Lord Douglas, bears, among a great deal of flourishing, two hands pointing to a heart, which is placed betwixt them, and the date 1329, being the year in which Bruce charged the Good Lord Douglas to carry his heart to the Holy Land.

NOTE 64.

—— *Martin Swart.*—P. 98.

A German general, who commanded the auxiliaries sent by the Duchess of Burgundy with Lambert Simnel. He was defeated and killed at Stokefield. The name of this German general is preserved by that of the field of battle, which is called, after him, Swartmoor.—There were songs about him long current in England.—See Dissertation prefixed to RITSON'S *Ancient Songs*, 1792, p. lxi.

NOTE 65.

—— *The Cross.*—P. 99.

The Cross of Edinburgh was an ancient and curious structure. The lower part was an octagonal tower, sixteen feet in diameter, and about fifteen feet high. At each angle there was a pillar, and between them an arch, of the Grecian shape. Above these was a projecting battlement, with a turret at each corner, and medallions, of rude but curious workmanship, between them. Above this rose the proper Cross, a column of one stone, upwards of twenty feet high, surmounted with a unicorn. This pillar is preserved in the grounds of the property of Drum, near Edinburgh.

NOTE 66.

This awful summons came.—P. 99.

This supernatural citation is mentioned by all our Scottish historians. It was, probably, like the apparition at Linlithgow, an attempt, by those averse to the war, to impose upon the superstitious temper of James IV.

NOTE 67.

One of his own ancestry,
Drove the Monks forth of Coventry.—P. 101.

This relates to the catastrophe of a real Robert de Marmion, in the reign of King Stephen, whom William of Newbury describes with some attributes of my fictitious hero: *Homo bellicosus, ferocia, et astucia, fere nullo suo tempore impar.*" This Baron, having expelled the Monks from the church of Coventry, was not long of experiencing the divine judgment, as the same monks, no doubt, termed his disaster. Having waged a feudal war with the Earl of Chester, Marmion's horse fell, as he charged in the van of his troop, against a body of the Earl's followers: the rider's thigh being broken by the fall, his head was cut off by a common foot-soldier, ere he could receive any succour. The whole story is told by William of Newbury.

NOTE 68.

—— The savage Dane
At Iol more deep the mead did drain.—P. 103.

The Iol of the heathen Danes (a word still applied to Christmas in Scotland) was solemnized with great festivity. The humour of the Danes at table displayed itself in pelting each other with bones; and Torfæus tells a long and curious story, in the History of Hrolfe Kraka, of one Hottus, an inmate of the Court of Denmark, who was so generally assailed with these missiles, that he constructed, out of the bones with which he was overwhelmed, a very respectable intrenchment, against those who continued the raillery.

NOTE 69.

Who lists may in their mumming see
Traces of ancient mystery.—P. 103.

It seems certain, that the *Mummers* of England, who (in Northumberland at least)

used to go about in disguise to the neighbouring houses, bearing the then useless ploughshare; and the *Guisards* of Scotland, not yet in total disuse, present, in some indistinct degree, a shadow of the old mysteries, which were the origin of the English drama. In Scotland, (*me ipso teste,*) we were wont, during my boyhood, to take the characters of the apostles, at least of Peter, Paul, and Judas Iscariot; the first had the keys, the second carried a sword, and the last the bag, in which the dole of our neighbours' plum-cake was deposited. One played a champion, and recited some traditional rhymes; another was

. . . . "Alexander, King of Macedon,
Who conquer'd all the world but Scotland alone."

These, and many such verses, were repeated, but by rote, and unconnectedly. There was also, occasionally, I believe, a Saint George. In all, there was a confused resemblance of the ancient mysteries, in which the characters of Scripture, the Nine Worthies, and other popular personages, were usually exhibited.

NOTE 70.

The Highlander ——
Will, on a Friday morn, look pale,
If ask'd to tell a fairy tale.—P. 104.

The *Daoine shi'*, or *Men of Peace,* of the Scottish Highlanders, rather resemble the Scandinavian *Duergar* than the English Fairies. Notwithstanding their name, they are, if not absolutely malevolent, at least peevish, discontented, and apt to do mischief on slight provocation. The belief of their existence is deeply impressed on the Highlanders, who think they are particularly offended at mortals who talk of them, who wear their favourite colour green, or in any respect interfere with their affairs. This is especially to be avoided on Friday, when, whether as dedicated to Venus, with whom, in Germany, this subterraneous people are held nearly connected, or for a more solemn reason, they are more active, and possessed of greater power. Some curious particulars concerning the popular superstitions of the Highlanders may be found in Dr. Graham's Picturesque Sketches of Perthshire.

NOTE 71.

The last lord of Franchémont.—P. 105.

The journal of the friend to whom the Fourth Canto of the Poem is inscribed, furnished me with the following account of a striking superstition.

'Passed the pretty little village of Franchémont, (near Spaw), with the romantic ruins of
the old castle of the Counts of that name.
The road leads through many delightful vales
on a rising ground ; at the extremity of one
of them stands the ancient castle, now the
subject of many superstitious legends. It is
firmly believed by the neighbouring peasantry, that the last Baron of Franchémont
deposited, in one of the vaults of the castle,
a ponderous chest, containing an immense
treasure in gold and silver, which, by some
magic spell, was intrusted to the care of the
Devil, who is constantly found sitting on the
chest in the shape of a huntsman. Any one
adventurous enough to touch the chest is instantly seized with the palsy. Upon one occasion, a priest of noted piety was brought to
the vault : he used all the arts of exorcism to
persuade his infernal majesty to vacate his
seat, but in vain ; the huntsman remained
immovable. At last, moved by the earnestness of the priest, he told him that he would
agree to resign the chest, if the exorciser
would sign his name with blood. But the
priest understood his meaning, and refused,
as by that act he would have delivered over
his soul to the Devil Yet if any body can
discover the mystic words used by the person
who deposited the treasure, and pronounce
them, the fiend must instantly decamp.   I
had many stories of a similar nature from a
peasant, who had himself seen the Devil in
the shape of a great cat."

NOTE 72.

—— *the huge and sweeping brand*
Which wont of yore, in battle fray,
His foeman's limbs to shred away,
As wood-knife lops the sapling spray.—P. 109.

The Earl of Angus had strength and personal activity corresponding to his courage.
Spens of Kilspindie, a favourite of James IV.,
having spoken of him lightly, the Earl met
him while hawking, and, compelling him to
single combat, at one blow cut asunder his
thigh-bone, and killed him on the spot. But
ere he could obtain James's pardon for this
slaughter, Angus was obliged to yield his
castle of Hermitage, in exchange for that of
Bothwell, which was some diminution to the
family greatness. The sword with which he
struck so remarkable a blow, was presented
by his descendant James, Earl of Morton,
afterwards Regent of Scotland, to Lord Lindesay of the Byres, when he defied Bothwell to single combat on Carberry Hill. See
Introduction to the *Minstrelsy of the Scottish
Border*

NOTE 73.

And hopest thou hence unscathed to go ?—
No ! by St. Bride of Bothwell, no !
*Up drawbridge, grooms !—What, Warder,
ho !*
Let the portcullis fall.—P. 110.

This ebullition of violence in the potent
Earl of Angus is not without its example in
the real history of the house of Douglas,
whose chieftains possessed the ferocity, with
the heroic virtues of a savage state. The
most curious instance occurred in the case of
Maclellan, Tutor of Bombay, who, having
refused to acknowledge the pre-eminence
claimed by Douglas over the gentlemen and
Barons of Galloway, was seized and imprisoned by the Earl, in his castle of the
Thrieve, on the borders of Kirkcudbright-
shire. Sir Patrick Gray, commander of King
James the Second's guard, was uncle to the
Tutor of Bombay, and obtained from the
King a "sweet letter of supplication," praying the Earl to deliver his prisoner into Gray's
hand. When Sir Patrick arrived at the
castle, he was received with all the honour
due to a favourite servant of the King's household ; but while he was at dinner, the Earl,
who suspected his errand, caused his prisoner
to be led forth and beheaded. After dinner,
Sir Patrick presented the King's letter to the
Earl, who received it with great affectation of
reverence ; "and took him by the hand, and
led him forth to the green, where the gentleman was lying dead, and showed him the
manner, and said, 'Sir Patrick, you are come
a little too late ; yonder is your sister's son
lying, but he wants the head : take his body,
and do with it what you will.'—Sir Patrick
answered again, with a sore heart, and said,
'My lord, if ye have taken from him his
head, dispone upon the body as ye please ;'
and with that called for his horse, and leaped
thereon ; and when he was on horseback, he
said to the Earl on this manner, 'My lord, if
I live you shall be rewarded for your labours
that you have used at this time, according to
your demerits.'

"At this saying the Earl was highly
offended, and cried for horse. Sir Patrick,
seeing the Earl's fury, spurred his horse, but
he was chased near Edinburgh ere they left
him ; and had it not been his led horse was so
tried and good, he had been taken."—PIT-
SCOTTIE'S *History*, p. 39.

NOTE 74.

A letter forged !—Saint Jude to speed !
Did ever knight so foul a deed !—P. 110.

Lest the reader should partake of the Earl's

astonishment, and consider the crime as inconsistent with the manners of the period, I have to remind him of the numerous forgeries (partly executed by a female assistant) devised by Robert of Artois, to forward his suit against the Countess Matilda ; which, being detected, occasioned his flight into England, and proved the remote cause of Edward the Third's memorable wars in France. John Harding, also, was expressly hired by Edward I. to forge such documents as might appear to establish the claim of fealty asserted over Scotland by the English monarchs.

NOTE 75.

Twisel bridge.—P. 112.

On the evening previous to the memorable battle of Flodden, Surrey's head-quarters were at Barmoor Wood, and King James held an inaccessible position on the ridge of Flodden-hill, one of the last and lowest eminences detached from the ridge of Cheviot. The Till, a deep and slow river, winded between the armies. On the morning of the 9th September 1513, Surrey marched in a north-westerly direction, and crossed the Till, with his van and artillery, at Twiselbridge, nigh where that river joins the Tweed, his rear-guard column passing about a mile higher, by a ford. This movement had the double effect of placing his army between King James and his supplies from Scotland, and of striking the Scottish monarch with surprise, as he seems to have relied on the depth of the river in his front. But as the passage, both over the bridge and through the ford, was difficult and slow, it seems possible that the English might have been attacked to great advantage while struggling with these natural obstacles. I know not if we are to impute James's forbearance to want of military skill, or to the romantic declaration which Pitscottie puts in his mouth, "that he was determined to have his enemies before him on a plain field," and therefore would suffer no interruption to be given, even by artillery, to their passing the river.

NOTE 76.

Hence might they see the full array,
Of either host, for deadly fray.—P. 113.

The reader cannot here expect a full account of the battle of Flodden ; but, so far as is necessary to understand the romance, I beg to remind him, that, when the English army, by their skilful countermarch, were fairly placed between King James and his own country, the Scottish monarch resolved to fight ; and, setting fire to his tents, descended from the ridge of Flodden to secure the neighbouring eminence of Brankstone, on which that village is built. Thus the two armies met, almost without seeing each other, when, according to the old poem, of "Flodden Field,"

> " The English line stretch'd east and west,
> And southward were their faces set ;
> The Scottish northward proudly prest,
> And manfully their foes they met."

The English army advanced in four divisions. On the right, which first engaged, were the sons of Earl Surrey, namely, Thomas Howard, the Admiral of England, and Sir Edmund, the Knight Marshal of the army. Their divisions were separated from each other ; but, at the request of Sir Edmund, his brother's battalion was drawn very near to his own. The centre was commanded by Surrey in person ; the left wing by Sir Edward Stanley, with the men of Lancashire, and of the palatinate of Chester. Lord Dacres, with a large body of horse, formed a reserve. When the smoke, which the wind had driven between the armies, was somewhat dispersed, they perceived the Scots, who had moved down the hill in a similar order of battle and in deep silence. The Earls of Huntley and of Home commanded their left wing, and charged Sir Edmund Howard with such success as entirely to defeat his part of the English right wing. Sir Edmund's banner was beaten down, and he himself escaped with difficulty to his brother's division. The Admiral, however, stood firm ; and Dacre advancing to his support with the reserve of cavalry, probably between the interval of the divisions commanded by the brothers Howard, appears to have kept the victors in effectual check. Home's men, chiefly Borderers, began to pillage the baggage of both armies ; and their leader is branded by the Scottish historians with negligence or treachery. On the other hand, Huntley, on whom they bestow many encomiums, is said by the English historians to have left the field after the first charge. Meanwhile the Admiral, whose flank these chiefs ought to have attacked, availed himself of their inactivity, and pushed forward against another large division of the Scottish army in his front, headed by the Earls of Crawford and Montrose, both of whom were slain, and their forces routed. On the left, the success of the English was yet more decisive ; for the Scottish right wing, consisting of undisciplined Highlanders, commanded by Lennox and Argyle, was unable to sustain the charge of Sir Edward Stanley, and especially the severe execution of the Lancashire archers. The King and Surrey, who commanded the respective centres of their armies, were meanwhile engaged in close and dubious conflict. James, surrounded by the flower of his kingdom, and impatient of the galling discharge of arrows, supported also by his reserve under Bothwell, charged with such fury, that the standard of Surrey was in danger. At that critical moment, Stanley, who had routed the left wing of the Scottish, pursued his career of victory, and arrived on the right flank, and in the rear of James's division, which, throwing itself into a circle, disputed the battle till night came on. Surrey then drew back his forces; for the Scottish centre not having been broken, and their left wing being victorious, he yet doubted the event of the field. The Scottish army, however, felt their loss, and abandoned the field of battle in disorder, before dawn. They lost, perhaps, from eight to ten thousand men; but that included the very prime of their nobility, gentry, and even clergy. Scarce a family of eminence but has an ancestor killed at Flodden; and there is no province in Scotland, even at this day, where the battle is mentioned without a sensation of terror and sorrow. The English lost also a great number of men, perhaps within one-third of the vanquished, but they were of inferior note.

NOTE 77.

—— Brian Tunstall, stainless knight.
P. 113.

Sir Brian Tunstall, called in the romantic language of the time, Tunstall the Undefiled, was one of the few Englishmen of rank slain at Flodden. He figures in the ancient English poem, to which I may safely refer my readers; as an edition, with full explanatory notes, has been published by my friend, Mr. Henry Weber. Tunstall, perhaps, derived his epithet of *undefiled* from his white armour and banner, the latter bearing a white cock, about to crow, as well as from his unstained loyalty and knightly faith. His place of residence was Thurland Castle.

NOTE 78.

Reckless of life, he desperate fought,
And fell on Flodden plain :
And well in death his trusty brand,
Firm clench'd within his manly hand,
Beseem'd the monarch slain.—P. 117.

There can be no doubt that King James fell in the battle of Flodden. He was killed, says the curious French Gazette, within a lance's length of the Earl of Surrey; and the same account adds, that none of his division were made prisoners, though many were killed; a circumstance that testifies the desperation of their resistance. The Scottish historians record many of the idle reports which passed among the vulgar of their day. Home was accused, by the popular voice, not only of failing to support the King, but even of having carried him out of the field, and murdered him. And this tale was revived in my remembrance, by an unauthenticated story of a skeleton, wrapped in a bull's hide, and surrounded with an iron chain, said to have been found in the well of Home Castle; for which, on inquiry, I could never find any better authority than the sexton of the parish having said, that, *if the well were cleaned out, he would not be surprised at such a discovery.* Home was the chamberlain of the King, and his prime favourite; he had much to lose (in fact did lose all) in consequence of James's death, and nothing earthly to gain by that event: but the retreat, or inactivity of the left wing which he commanded, after defeating Sir Edmund Howard, and even the circumstance of his returning unhurt, and loaded with spoil, from so fatal a conflict, rendered the propagation of any calumny against him easy and acceptable. Other reports gave a still more romantic turn to the King's fate, and averred that James, weary of greatness, after the carnage among his nobles, had gone on a pilgrimage, to merit absolution for the death of his father, and the breach of his oath of amity to Henry. In particular, it was objected to the English, that they could never show the token of the iron belt; which, however, he was likely enough to have laid aside on the day of battle, as encumbering his personal exertions. They produce a better evidence, the monarch's sword and dagger, which are still preserved in the Heralds' College in London. Stowe has recorded a degrading story of the disgrace with which the remains of the unfortunate monarch were treated in his time. An unhewn column marks the spot where James fell, still called the King's Stone.

NOTE 79.

The fair cathedral storm'd and took.
P. 118.

This storm of Lichfield cathedral, which had been garrisoned on the part of the King, took place in the Great Civil War. Lord Brook, who, with Sir John Gill, commanded the assailants, was shot with a musket-ball through the vizor of his helmet. The royalists remarked, that he was killed by a shot fired from St. Chad's cathedral, and upon St. Chad's Day, and received his death-wound in the very eye with which, he had said, he hoped to see the ruin of all the cathedrals in England. The magnificent church in question suffered cruelly upon this, and other occasions; the principal spire being ruined by the fire of the besiegers.

THE LADY OF THE LAKE.

NOTE 1.

> —— *the heights of Uam-Var,*
> *And roused the cavern, where, 'tis told,*
> *A giant made his den of old.*—P. 124.

Ua-var, as the name is pronounced, or more properly *Uaighmor*, is a mountain to the north-east of the village of Callender in Menteith, deriving its name, which signifies the great den, or cavern, from a sort of retreat among the rocks on the south side, said, by tradition, to have been the abode of a giant. In latter times, it was the refuge of robbers and banditti, who have been only extirpated within these forty or fifty years. Strictly speaking, this stronghold is not a cave, as the name would imply, but a sort of small enclosure, or recess, surrounded with large rocks, and open above head.

NOTE 2.

> *Two dogs of black Saint Hubert's breed,*
> *Unmatch'd for courage, breath, and speed.*
> P. 124.

"The hounds which we call Saint Hubert's hounds, are commonly all blacke, yet neuertheless, the race is so mingled at these days, that we find them of all colours. These are the hounds which the abbots of St. Hubert haue always kept some of their race or kind, in honour or remembrance of the saint, which was a hunter with S. Eustace. Whereupon we may conceiue that (by the grace of God) all good huntsmen shall follow them into paradise."—*The Noble Art of Venerie or Hunting, translated and collected for the Use of all Noblemen and Gentlemen.* Lond. 1611, 4to, p. 15.

NOTE 3.

> *For the death-wound and death-halloc,*
> *Muster'd his breath, his whinyard drew.*
> P. 125.

When the stag turned to bay, the ancient hunter had the perilous task of going in upon, and killing or disabling the desperate animal. At certain times of the year this was held particularly dangerous, a wound received from a stag's horn being then deemed poisonous, and more dangerous than one from the tusks of a boar, as the old rhyme testifies :—

> "If thou be hurt with hart, it brings thee to thy bier,
> But barber's hand will boar's hurt heal, therefore thou need'st not fear."

At all times, however, the task was dangerous, and to be adventured upon wisely and warily, either by getting behind the stag while he was gazing on the hounds, or by watching an opportunity to gallop roundly in upon him, and kill him with the sword.

NOTE 4.

> *And now to issue from the glen,*
> *No pathway meets the wanderer's ken,*
> *Unless he climb, with footing nice,*
> *A far projecting precipice.*—P. 126.

Until the present road was made through the romantic pass which I have presumptuously attempted to describe in the preceding stanzas, there was no mode of issuing out of the defile called the Trosachs, excepting by a sort of ladder, composed of the branches and roots of trees.

NOTE 5.

> *To meet with Highland plunderers here,*
> *Were worse than loss of steed or deer.*—P. 127.

The clans who inhabited the romantic regions in the neighbourhood of Loch Katrine, were, even until a late period, much addicted to predatory excursions upon their Lowland neighbours.

NOTE 6.

A grey-hair'd sire, whose eye intent,
Was on the vision'd future bent.—P. 128.

If force of evidence could authorise us to believe facts inconsistent with the general laws of nature, enough might be produced in favour of the existence of the Second-sight. It is called in Gaelic *Taishitaraugh*, from *Taish*, an unreal or shadowy appearance ; and those possessed of the faculty are called *Taish-atrin*, which may be aptly translated visionaries. Martin, a steady believer in the second-sight, gives the following account of it :—

"The second-sight is a singular faculty, of seeing an otherwise invisible object, without any previous means used by the person that used it for that end ; the vision makes such a lively impression upon the seers, that they neither see, nor think of anything else, except the vision, as long as it continues ; and then they appear pensive or jovial, according to the object that was represented to them.

"At the sight of a vision, the eyelids of the person are erected, and the eyes continue staring until the object vanish. This is obvious to others who are by, when the persons happen to see a vision, and occurred more than once to my own observation, and to others that were with me.

"If a woman is seen standing at a man's left hand, it is a presage that she will be his wife, whether they be married to others, or unmarried at the time of the apparition.

"To see a spark of fire fall upon one's arm or breast, is a forerunner of a dead child to be seen in the arms of those persons ; of which there are several fresh instances.

"To see a seat empty at the time of one's sitting in it, is a presage of that person's death soon after."—MARTIN's *Description of the Western Islands*, 1716, 8vo, p. 300, *et seq.*

To these particulars innumerable examples might be added, all attested by grave and credible authors. But, in despite of evidence which neither Bacon, Boyle, nor Johnson were able to resist, the *Taisch*, with all its visionary properties, seems to be now universally abandoned to the use of poetry. The exquisitely beautiful poem of Lochiel will at once occur to the recollection of every reader.

NOTE 7.

Here, for retreat in dangerous hour,
Some chief had framed a rustic bower.
P. 129.

The Celtic chieftains, whose lives were continually exposed to peril, had usually, in the most retired spot of their domains, some place of retreat for the hour of necessity, which, as circumstances would admit, was a tower, a cavern, or a rustic hut, in a strong and secluded situation. One of these last gave refuge to the unfortunate Charles Edward, in his perilous wanderings after the battle of Culloden.

NOTE 8.

My sire's tall form might grace the part
Of Ferragus or Ascabart.—P. 130.

These two sons of Anak flourished in romantic fable. The first is well known to the admirers of Ariosto, by the name of Ferrau. He was an antagonist of Orlando, and was at length slain by him in single combat.

Ascapart, or Ascabart, makes a very material figure in the History of Bevis of Hampton, by whom he was conquered. His effigies may be seen guarding one side of a gate at Southampton, while the other is occupied by Sir Bevis himself.

NOTE 9.

Though all unask'd his birth and name.
P. 130.

The Highlanders, who carried hospitality to a punctilious excess, are said to have considered it as churlish, to ask a stranger his name or lineage, before he had taken refreshment. Feuds were so frequent among them, that a contrary rule would in many cases have produced the discovery of some circumstance, which might have excluded the guest from the benefit of the assistance he stood in need of.

NOTE 10.

Morn's genial influence roused a minstrel grey.
—— *Allan Bane.*—P. 132.

The Highland chieftains retained in their service the bard, as a family officer, to a late period.

NOTE 11.

—— *The Græme.*—P. 133.

The ancient and powerful family of Graham (which, for metrical reasons, is here spelt after the Scottish pronunciation) held extensive possessions in the counties of Dumbarton and Stirling. Few families can boast of more historical renown, having claim to three of the most remarkable characters in the Scottish annals. Sir John the Græme, the faithful and undaunted partaker of the labours and patriotic warfare of Wallace, fell in the unfortunate field of Falkirk, 1298. The celebrated

Marquis of Montrose, in whom De Retz saw realized his abstract idea of the heroes of antiquity, was the second of these worthies. And, notwithstanding the severity of his temper, and the rigour with which he executed the oppressive mandates of the princes whom he served, I do not hesitate to name as a third, John Græme of Claverhouse, Viscount of Dundee, whose heroic death in the arms of victory may be allowed to cancel the memory of his cruelty to the nonconformists, during the reigns of Charles II. and James II.

NOTE 12.

This harp, which erst Saint Modan sway'd.
P. 133.

I am not prepared to show that Saint Modan was a performer on the harp. It was, however, no unsaintly accomplishment ; for Saint Dunstan certainly did play upon that instrument, which retaining, as was natural, a portion of the sanctity attached to its master's character, announced future events by its spontaneous sound.

NOTE 13.

Ere Douglasses, to ruin driven,
Were exiled from their native heaven.
P. 134.

The downfall of the Douglasses of the house of Angus during the reign of James V. is the event alluded to in the text.

NOTE 14.

In Holy-Rood a knight he slew.—P. 135.

This was by no means an uncommon occurrence in the Court of Scotland ; nay, the presence of the sovereign himself scarcely restrained the ferocious and inveterate feuds which were the perpetual source of bloodshed among the Scottish nobility. The murder of Sir William Stuart of Ochiltree, called *The Bloody*, by the celebrated Francis, Earl of Bothwell, may be mentioned among many others.—Johnstoni *Historia Rerum Britannicarum*, ab anno 1572 ad annum 1628. Amstelodami, 1655. fol. p. 135.

NOTE 15.

The Douglas, like a stricken deer,
Disown'd by every noble peer.—P. 135.

The exile state of this powerful race is not exaggerated in this and subsequent passages. The hatred of James against the race of Doug-las was so inveterate, that numerous as their allies were, and disregarded as the regal authority had usually been in similar cases, their nearest friends, even in the most remote parts of Scotland, durst not entertain them, unless under the strictest and closest disguise.

NOTE 16.

—— *Maronnan's cell.*—P. 135.

The parish of Kilmaronock, at the eastern extremity of Loch Lomond, derives its name from a cell or chapel, dedicated to St. Maronock, or Marnock, or Maronnan, about whose sanctity very little is now remembered. There is a fountain devoted to him in the same parish ; but its virtues, like the merits of its patron, have fallen into oblivion.

NOTE 17.

—— *Bracklinn's thundering wave.*—P. 135.

This is a beautiful cascade made by a mountain stream called the Keltie, at a place called the Bridge of Bracklinn, about a mile from the village of Callender in Menteith.

NOTE 18.

For Tine-man forged by fairy lore.—P. 135.

Archibald, the third Earl of Douglas, was so unfortunate in all his enterprises, that he acquired the epithet of Tineman, because he *tined*, or lost, his followers in every battle which he fought.

NOTE 19.

Did, self-unscabbarded, foreshow
The footstep of a secret foe.—P. 136.

The ancient warriors, whose hope and confidence rested chiefly in their blades, were accustomed to deduce omens from them, especially from such as were supposed to have been fabricated by enchanted skill, of which we have various instances in the romances and legends of the time.

NOTE 20.

Those thrilling sounds that call the might
Of old Clan-Alpine to the fight.—P. 136.

The connoisseurs in pipe-music affect to discover in a well-composed pibroch, the imitative sounds of march, conflict, flight, pursuit, and all the "current of a heady fight."

NOTE 21.

Roderigh Vich Alpine dhu, ho! ieroe!
P. 137.

Besides his ordinary name and surname, which were chiefly used in the intercourse with the Lowlands, every Highland chief had an epithet expressive of his patriarchal dignity as head of the clan, and which was common to all his predecessors and successors, as Pharaoh to the kings of Egypt, or Arsaces to those of Parthia. This name was usually a patronymic, expressive of his descent from the founder of the family. Thus the Duke of Argyle is called MacCallum More, or the *son of Colin the Great*.

NOTE 22.

And while the Fiery Cross glanced, like a meteor, round.—P. 143.

When a chieftain designed to summon his clan, upon any sudden or important emergency, he slew a goat, and making a cross of any light wood, seared its extremities in the fire, and extinguished them in the blood of the animal. This was called the *Fiery Cross*, also *Crean Tarigh*, or the *Cross of Shame*, because disobedience to what the symbol implied, inferred infamy. It was delivered to a swift and trusty messenger, who ran full speed with it to the next hamlet, where he presented it to the principal person, with a single word, implying the place of rendezvous. He who received the symbol was bound to send it forward, with equal dispatch, to the next village; and thus it passed with incredible celerity through all the district which owed allegiance to the chief, and also among his allies and neighbours, if the danger was common to them. At sight of the Fiery Cross, every man, from sixteen years old to sixty, capable of bearing arms, was obliged instantly to repair, in his best arms and accoutrements, to the place of rendezvous. He who failed to appear, suffered the extremities of fire and sword, which were emblematically denounced to the disobedient by the bloody and burnt marks upon this warlike signal. During the civil war of 1745-6, the Fiery Cross often made its circuit; and upon one occasion it passed through the whole district of Breadalbane, a tract of thirty-two miles, in three hours.

NOTE 23.

That monk, of savage form and face.—P. 143.

The state of religion in the middle ages afforded considerable facilities for those whose mode of life excluded them from regular worship, to secure, nevertheless, the ghostly assistance of confessors, perfectly willing to adapt the nature of their doctrine to the necessities and peculiar circumstances of their flock. Robin Hood, it is well known, had his celebrated domestic chaplain, Friar Tuck.

NOTE 24.

Of Brian's birth strange tales were told.
P. 143.

The legend which follows is not of the author's invention. It is possible he may differ from modern critics, in supposing that the records of human superstition, if peculiar to, and characteristic of, the country in which the scene is laid, are a legitimate subject of poetry. He gives, however, a ready assent to the narrower proposition which condemns all attempts of an irregular and disordered fancy to excite terror, by accumulating a train of fantastic and incoherent horrors, whether borrowed from all countries, and patched upon a narrative belonging to one which knew them not, or derived from the author's own imagination. In the present case, therefore, I appeal to the record which I have transcribed, with the variation of a very few words, from the geographical collections made by the Laird of Macfarlane. I know not whether it be necessary to remark, that the miscellaneous concourse of youths and maidens on the night and on the spot where the miracle is said to have taken place, might, even in a credulous age, have somewhat diminished the wonder which accompanied the conception of Gilli-Doir-Magrevollich.

"There is bot two myles from Inverloghie, the church of Kilmalee, in Lochyeld. In ancient tymes there was ane church builded upon ane hill, which was above this church, which doeth now stand in this toune; and ancient men doeth say, that there was a battell foughten on ane litle hill not the tenth part of a myle from this church, be certaine men which did not know what they were. And long tyme thereafter, certaine herds of that toune, and of the next toune, called Unnatt, both wenches and youthes, did on a tyme conveen with others on that hill; and the day being somewhat cold, did gather the bones of the dead men that were slayne long tyme before in that place, and did make a fire to warm them. At last they did all remove from the fire, except one maid or wench, which was verie cold, and she did remaine there for a space. She being quyetlie her alone, without anie other companie, took up her cloaths above her knees, or thereby to warm her ; a wind did come and caste the ashes upon her, and she was conceived of ane man-chyld. Severall tymes thereafter she was verie sick, and at last she was knowne to be with chyld. And then her parents did ask at her the matter heiroff, which the wench could not weel answer which way to satisfie them. At last she resolved them with ane answer. As fortune fell upon her concerning this marvellous miracle, the chyld being borne, his name was called *Gili-doir Maghrevollich*, that is to say, the *Black Child, Son to the Bones.* So called, his grandfather sent him to school, and so he was a good schollar, and godlie. He did build this church which doeth now stand in Lochyeld, called Kilmalie."—MACFARLANE, *ut supra,* ii. 188.

NOTE 25.

Yet ne'er again to braid her hair
The Virgin snood did Alice wear.—P. 144.

The *snood,* or riband, with which a Scottish lass braided her hair, had an emblematical signification, and applied to her maiden character. It was exchanged for the *curch, toy,* or coif, when she passed, by marriage, into the matron state. But if the damsel was so unfortunate as to lose pretensions to the name of maiden, without gaining a right to that of matron, she was neither permitted to use the snood, nor advanced to the graver dignity of the curch. In old Scottish songs there occur many sly allusions to such misfortune ; as in the old words to the popular tune of "Ower the muir amang the heather."

" Down amang the broom, the broom,
   Down amang the broom, my dearie,
 The lassie lost her silken snood,
   That gard her greet till she was wearie."

NOTE 26.

The fatal Ben-Shie's boding scream.—P. 144.

Most great families in the Highlands were supposed to have a tutelar, or rather a domestic spirit, attached to them, who took an interest in their prosperity, and intimated, by its wailings, any approaching disaster. A superstition of the same kind is, I believe, universally received by the inferior ranks of the native Irish.

NOTE 27.

Sounds, too, had come in midnight blast,
Of charging steeds, careering fast
Along Benharrow's shingly side,
Where mortal horsemen ne'er might ride.—
                                                    P. 144.

A presage of the kind alluded to in the text, is still believed to announce death to the ancient Highland family of M'Lean of Lochbuy. The spirit of an ancestor slain in battle is heard to gallop along a stony bank, and then to ride thrice around the family residence, ringing his fairy bridle, and thus intimating the approaching calamity.

NOTE 28.

—— *the dun deer's hide*
On fleeter foot was never tied.—P. 146.

The present *brogue* of the Highlanders is made of half-dried leather, with holes to admit and let out the water; for walking the moors dry-shod is a matter altogether out of the question. The ancient buskin was still ruder, being made of undressed deer's hide, with the hair outwards; a circumstance which procured the Highlanders the well-known epithet of *Red-shanks.*

NOTE 29.

The dismal coronach.—P. 146.

The *Coronach* of the Highlanders, like the *Ululatus* of the Romans, and the *Ululoo* of the Irish, was a wild expression of lamentation, poured forth by the mourners over the body of a departed friend. When the words of it were articulate, they expressed the praises of the deceased, and the loss the clan would sustain by his death.

NOTE 30.

Not faster o'er thy heathery braes,
Balquidder, speeds the midnight blaze.
                                                    P. 149.

It may be necessary to inform the southern reader, that the heath on the Scottish moorlands is often set fire to, that the sheep may have the advantage of the young herbage produced, in room of the tough old heather plants. This custom (execrated by sportsmen) produces occasionally the most beautiful nocturnal appearances, similar almost to the discharge of a volcano. This simile is not new to poetry. The charge of a warrior, in the fine ballad of Hardyknute, is said to be "like fire to heather set."

NOTE 31.

—— by many a bard, in Celtic tongue,
Has Coir-nan-Uriskin been sung.—P. 149.

This is a very steep and most romantic hollow in the mountain of Benvenue, overhanging the south-eastern extremity of Loch Katrine. It is surrounded with stupendous rocks, and overshadowed with birch-trees, mingled with oaks, the spontaneous production of the mountain, even where its cliffs appear denuded of soil.

NOTE 32.

The Taghairm call'd; by which, afar,
Our sires foresaw the events of war.—P 152.

The Highlanders, like all rude people, had various superstitious modes of inquiring into futurity. One of the most noted was the *Taghairm*, mentioned in the text. A person was wrapped up in the skin of a newly-slain bullock, and deposited beside a waterfall, or at the bottom of a precipice, or in some other strange, wild, and unusual situation, where the scenery around him suggested nothing but objects of horror. In this situation, he revolved in his mind the question proposed; and whatever was impressed upon him by his exalted imagination, passed for the inspiration of the disembodied spirits, who haunt the desolate recesses.

NOTE 33.

—— that huge cliff, whose ample verge
Tradition calls the Hero's Targe.—P. 152.

There is a rock so named in the Forest of Glenfinlas, by which a tumultuary cataract takes its course. This wild place is said in former times to have afforded refuge to an outlaw, who was supplied with provisions by a woman, who lowered them down from the brink of the precipice above. His water he procured for himself, by letting down a flagon tied to a string, into the black pool beneath the fall.

NOTE 34.

Which spills the foremost foeman's life,
That party conquers in the strife.—P. 153.

Though this be in the text described as a response of the Taghairm, or Oracle of the Hide, it was of itself an augury frequently attended to. The fate of the battle was often anticipated in the imagination of the combatants, by observing which party first shed blood. It is said that the Highlanders under Montrose were so deeply imbued with this notion, that, on the morning of the battle of Tippermoor, they murdered a defenceless herdsman, whom they found in the fields, merely to secure an advantage of so much consequence to their party.

NOTE 35.

Why sounds yon stroke on beech and oak,
Our moonlight circle's screen?
Or who comes here to chase the deer,
Beloved of our Elfin Queen?—P. 155.

Fairies, if not positively malevolent, are capricious, and easily offended. They are, like other proprietors of the forests, peculiarly jealous of their rights of *vert* and *venison*. This jealousy was also an attribute of the northern *Duergar*, or dwarfs; to many of whose distinctions the fairies seem to have succeeded, if, indeed, they are not the same class of beings.

NOTE 36.

—— who may dare on wold to wear
The fairies' fatal green?—P. 155.

As the *Daoine Shi'*, or Men of Peace, wore green habits, they were supposed to take offence when any mortals ventured to assume their favourite colour. Indeed, from some reason which has been, perhaps, originally a general superstition, *green* is held in Scotland to be unlucky to particular tribes and counties. The Caithness men, who hold this belief, allege as a reason, that their bands wore that colour when they were cut off at the battle of Flodden; and for the same reason they avoid crossing the Ord on a Monday, being the day of the week on which their ill-omened array set forth. Green is also disliked by those of the name of Ogilvy; but more especially is it held fatal to the whole clan of Grahame. It is remembered of an aged gentleman of that name, that when his horse fell in a fox-chase, he accounted for it at once by observing, that the whipcord attached to his lash was of this unlucky colour.

NOTE 37.

For thou wert christen'd man.—P. 155.

The elves were supposed greatly to envy the privileges acquired by Christian initiation, and they gave to those mortals who had fallen into their power a certain precedence, founded upon this advantageous distinction. Tamlane, in the old ballad, describes his own rank in the fairy procession:—

"For I ride on a milk-white steed,
    And aye nearest the town;
Because I was a christen'd knight,
    They give me that renown."

NOTE 38.

Who ever reck'd, where, how, or when,
The prowling fox was trapp'd or slain?
P. 161.

St. John actually used this illustration when engaged in confuting the plea of law proposed for the unfortunate Earl of Strafford: "It was true we gave laws to hares and deer, because they are beasts of chase; but it was never accounted either cruelty or foul play to knock foxes or wolves on the head as they can be found, because they are beasts of prey. In a word, the law and humanity were alike; the one being more fallacious, and the other more barbarous, than in any age had been vented in such an authority."—CLARENDON'S *History of the Rebellion.* Oxford, 1702, fol. vol. p. 183.

NOTE 39.

—— his Highland cheer,
The harden'd flesh of mountain-deer.—P. 161.

The Scottish Highlanders in former times, had a concise mode of cooking their venison, or rather of dispensing with cooking it, which appears greatly to have surprised the French whom chance made acquainted with it. The Vidame of Charters, when a hostage in England, during the reign of Edward VI., was permitted to travel into Scotland, and penetrated as far as to the remote Highlands (*au fin fond des Sauvages*). After a great hunting party, at which a most wonderful quantity of game was destroyed, he saw these *Scottish Savages* devour a part of their venison raw, without any farther preparation than compressing it between two batons of wood, so as to force out the blood, and render it extremely hard. This they reckoned a great delicacy; and when the Vidame partook of it, his compliance with their taste rendered him extremely popular.

NOTE 40.

Not then claim'd sovereignty his due
While Albany, with feeble hand,
Held borrow'd truncheon of command.—
P. 163.

There is scarcely a more disorderly period in Scottish history than that which succeeded the battle of Flodden, and occupied the minority of James V. Feuds of ancient standing broke out like old wounds, and every quarrel among the independent nobility, which occurred daily, and almost hourly, gave rise to fresh bloodshed.

NOTE 41.

—— I only meant
To show the reed on which you leant,
Deeming this path you might pursue
Without a pass from Roderick Dhu.—P. 164.

This incident, like some other passages in the poem, illustrative of the character of the ancient Gael, is not imaginary, but borrowed from fact. The Highlanders, with the inconsistency of most nations in the same state, were alternately capable of great exertions of generosity, and of cruel revenge and perfidy.

NOTE 42.

On Bochastle the mouldering lines,
Where Rome, the Empress of the world,
Of yore her eagle-wings unfurl'd.—P. 165.

The torrent which discharges itself from Loch Vennachar, the lowest and eastmost of the three lakes which forms the scenery adjoining to the Trosachs, sweeps through a flat and extensive moor, called Bochastle. Upon a small eminence, called the *Dun* of Bochastle, and indeed on the plain itself, are some intrenchments, which have been thought Roman. There is, adjacent to Callender, a sweet villa, the residence of Captain Fairfoul, entitled the Roman Camp.

NOTE 43.

See, here, all vantageless I stand,
Arm'd, like thyself, with single brand.
P. 165.

The duellists of former times did not always stand upon those punctilios respecting equality of arms, which are now judged essential to fair combat. It is true, that in former combats in the lists, the parties were, by the judges of the field, put as nearly as possible in the same circumstances. But in private duel it was often otherwise.

NOTE 44.

Ill fared it then with Roderick Dhu,
That on the field his targe he threw,
For train'd abroad his arms to wield,
Fitz-James's blade was sword and shield.
P. 166.

A round target of light wood, covered with

strong leather, and studded with brass or iron, was a necessary part of a Highlander's equipment. In charging regular troops, they received the thrust of the bayonet in this buckler, twisted it aside, and used the broadsword against the encumbered soldier. In the civil war of 1745, most of the front rank of the clans were thus armed : and Captain Grose informs us, that, in 1747, the privates of the 42nd regiment, then in Flanders, were, for the most part, permitted to carry targets. —*Military Antiquities*, vol. i. p. 164.

NOTE 45.

The burghers hold their sports to-day.
P. 168.

Every burgh of Scotland, of the least note, but more especially the considerable towns, had their solemn *play*, or festival, when feats of archery were exhibited, and prizes distributed to those who excelled in wrestling, hurling the bar, and the other gymnastic exercises of the period. Stirling, a usual place of royal residence, was not likely to be deficient in pomp upon such occasions, especially since James V. was very partial to them. His ready participation in these popular amusements was one cause of his acquiring the title of King of the Commons, or *Rex Plebeiorum*, as Lesley has latinized it. The usual prize to the best shooter was a silver arrow. Such a one is preserved at Selkirk and at Peebles.

NOTE 46.

*Robin Hood.—*P. 68.

The exhibition of this renowned outlaw and his band was a favourite frolic at such festivals as we are describing. This sporting, in which kings did not disdain to be actors, was prohibited in Scotland upon the Reformation, by a statute of the 6th Parliament of Queen Mary, c. 61, A.D. 1555, which ordered, under heavy penalties, that "na manner of person be chosen Robert Hude, nor Little John, Abbot of Unreason, Queen of May, nor otherwise." But in 1561, the "rascal multitude," says John Knox, "were stirred up to make a Robin Hude, whilk enormity was of many years left and damned by statute and act of Parliament; yet would they not be forbidden." Accordingly, they raised a very serious tumult, and at length made prisoners the magistrates who endeavoured to suppress it, and would not release them till they extorted a formal promise that no one should be punished for his share of the disturbance. It

would seem, from the complaints of the General Assembly of the Kirk, that these profane festivities were continued down to 1592.

NOTE 47.

Prize of the wrestling match, the King
*To Douglas gave a golden ring.—*P. 169.

The usual prize of a wrestling was a ram and a ring, but the animal would have embarrassed my story. Thus, in the Cokes Tale of Gamelyn, ascribed to Chaucer:

"There happed to be there beside
    Tryed a wrestling;
  And therefore there was y-setten
    A ram and als a ring."

NOTE 48.

These drew not for their fields the sword
Like tenants of a feudal lord,
Nor own'd the patriarchal claim
Of Chieftain in their leader's name;
*Adventurers they.—*P. 172.

The Scottish armies consisted chiefly of the nobility and barons, with their vassals, who held lands under them, for military service by themselves and their tenants. The patriarchal influence exercised by the heads of clans in the Highlands and Borders was of a different nature, and sometimes at variance with feudal principles. It flowed from the *Patria Potestas*, exercised by the chieftain as representing the original father of the whole name, and was often obeyed in contradiction to the feudal superior.

NOTE 49.

Thou now hast glee-maiden and harp !
Get thee an ape, and trudge the land,
*The leader of a juggler band.—*P. 174.

The jongleurs, or jugglers, used to call in the aid of various assistants, to render these performances as captivating as possible. The glee-maiden was a necessary attendant. Her duty was tumbling and dancing; and therefore the Anglo-Saxon version of Saint Mark's Gospel states Herodias to have vaulted or tumbled before King Herod.

NOTE 50.

That stirring air that peals on high,
O'er Dermid's race our victory.—
*Strike it !—*P. 176.

There are several instances, at least in tradition, of persons so much attached to particular tunes, as to require to hear them on their deathbed. Such an anecdote is mentioned by the late Mr. Riddel of Glenriddel, in his collection of Border tunes, respecting an air called the "Dandling of the Bairns," for which a certain Gallovidian laird is said to have evinced this strong mark of partiality. It is popularly told of a famous freebooter, that he composed the tune known by the name of Macpherson's Rant, while under sentence of death, and played it at the gallows-tree. Some spirited words have been adapted to it by Burns. A similar story is recounted of a Welsh bard, who composed and played on his deathbed the air called *Dafyddy Garregg Wen.*

NOTE 51.

Battle of Beal' an Duine.—P. 176.

A skirmish actually took place at a pass thus called in the Trosachs, and closed with the remarkable incident mentioned in the text. It was greatly posterior in date to the reign of James V.

NOTE 52.

And Snowdoun's Knight is Scotland's King. P. 181.

This discovery will probably remind the reader of the beautiful Arabian tale of *Il Bondocani.* Yet the incident is not borrowed from that elegant story, but from Scottish tradition. James V., of whom we are treating, was a monarch whose good and benevolent intentions often rendered his romantic freaks venial, if not respectable, since, from his anxious attention to the interests of the lower and most oppressed class of his subjects, he was, as we have seen, popularly termed the *King of the Commons.* For the purpose of seeing that justice was regularly administered, and frequently from the less justifiable motive of gallantry, he used to traverse the vicinage of his several palaces in various disguises. The two excellent comic songs, entitled, "The Gaberlunzie man," and "We'll gae nae mair a roving," are said to have been founded upon the success of his amorous adventures when travelling in the disguise of a beggar. The latter is perhaps the best comic ballad in any language.

NOTE 53.

—— *Stirling's tower* *Of yore the name of Snowdoun claims.* P. 181.

William of Worcester, who wrote about the middle of the fifteenth century, calls Stirling Castle Snowdoun. Sir David Lindsay bestows the same epithet upon it in his complaint of the Papingo:

"Adieu, fair Snawdoun, with thy towers high,
Thy chaple-royal, park, and table round;
May, June, and July, would I dwell in thee,
Were I a man, to hear the birdis sound,
Whilk doth againe thy royal rock rebound."

THE VISION OF DON RODERICK.

NOTE 1.

And Cattreath's glens with voice of triumph rung, *And mystic Merlin harp'd, and grey-hair'd Llywarch sung!*—P. 186.

THIS locality may startle those readers who do not recollect that much of the ancient poetry preserved in Wales refers less to the history of the Principality to which that name is now limited, than to events which happened in the north-west of England and south-west of Scotland, where the Britons for a long time made a stand against the Saxons. The battle of Cattreath, lamented by the celebrated Aneu-rin, is supposed, by the learned Dr. Leyden, to have been fought on the skirts of Ettrick Forest. It is known to the English reader by the paraphrase of Gray, beginning,

"Had I but the torrent's might,
With headlong rage and wild affright," &c.

NOTE 2.

—— *Minchmore's haunted spring.*—P. 186.

A belief in the existence and noctural revels of the fairies still lingers among the vulgar in Selkirkshire. A copious fountain upon the ridge of Minchmore, called the Cheesewell, is supposed to be sacred to these fanciful spirits, and it was customary to propitiate them by throwing in something upon passing it. A pin was the usual oblation; and the ceremony is still sometimes practised, though rather in jest than earnest.

NOTE 3.

—— *the rude villager, his labour done,*
In verse spontaneous chants some favour'd
name.—P. 186.

The flexibility of the Italian and Spanish languages, and perhaps the liveliness of their genius, renders these countries distinguished for the talent of improvvisation, which is found even among the lowest of the people. It is mentioned by Baretti and other travellers.

NOTE 4.

—— *kindling at the deeds of Græme.*
P. 186.

Over a name sacred for ages to heroic verse, a poet may be allowed to exercise some power. I have used the freedom, here and elsewhere, to alter the orthography of the name of my gallant countryman, in order to apprize the Southern reader of its legitimate sound;— Grahame being, on the other side of the Tweed, usually pronounced as a dissyllable.

NOTE 5.

What! will Don Roderick here till morning
stay,
To wear in shrift and prayer the night away?
And are his hours in such dull penance past,
For fair Florinda's plunder'd charms to pay?
P. 188.

Almost all the Spanish historians, as well as the voice of tradition, ascribe the invasion of the Moors to the forcible violation committed by Roderick upon Florinda, called by the Moors, Caba or Cava. She was the daughter of Count Julian, one of the Gothic monarch's principal lieutenants, who, when the crime was perpetrated, was engaged in the defence of Ceuta against the Moors. In his indignation at the ingratitude of his sovereign, and the dishonour of his daughter, Count Julian forgot the duties of a Christian and a patriot, and, forming an alliance with Musa, then the Caliph's lieutenant in Africa, he countenanced the invasion of Spain by a body of Saracens and Africans, commanded by the celebrated Tarik; the issue of which was the defeat and death of Roderick, and the occupation of almost the whole peninsula by the Moors. Voltaire, in his General History, expresses his doubts of this popular story, and Gibbon gives him some countenance; but the universal tradition is quite sufficient for the purposes of poetry. The Spaniards, in detestation of Florinda's memory, are said, by Cervantes, never to bestow that name on any human female, reserving it for their dogs.

NOTE 6.

The Tecbir war-cry and the Lelie's yell.
P. 191.

The Tecbir (derived from the words *Alla acbar,* God is most mighty,) was the original war-cry of the Saracens. It is celebrated by Hughes in the Siege of Damascus:—

" We heard the Tecbir; so these Arabs call
Their shout of onset, when, with loud appeal,
They challenge Heaven, as if demanding conquest."

The *Lelie,* well known to the Christians during the crusades, is the shout of *Alla illa Alla,* the Mahomedan confession of faith. It is twice used in poetry by my friend Mr. W. Stewart Rose, in the romance of Partenopex, and in the Crusade of St. Lewis.

NOTE 7.

By Heaven, the Moors prevail! the Christians
yield!—
Their coward leader gives for flight the
sign!
The sceptred craven mounts to quit the field—
Is not yon steed Orelia?—Yes, 'tis mine!
P. 191.

Count Julian, the father of the injured Florinda, with the connivance and assistance of Oppas, Archbishop of Toledo, invited, in 713, the Saracens into Spain. A considerable army arrived under the command of Tarik, or Tarif, who bequeathed the well-known name of Gibraltar (*Gibel al Tarik,* or the mountain of Tarik) to the place of his landing. He was joined by Count Julian, ravaged Andalusia, and took Seville. In 714, they returned with a still greater force, and Roderick marched into Andalusia at the head of a great army, to give them battle. The field was chosen near Xeres. [Roderick was defeated, and fled from the field of battle on his favourite steed Orelia. This famous and matchless charger was found riderless on the banks of the river Guadelite, with the King's upper garment, buskins, &c. It was supposed that in trying to swim the river he was drowned. But wild legends as to his after fate long prevailed in Spain.—*See* SOUTHEY'S "Don Roderick." ED.]

NOTE 8.

When for the light bolero ready stand,
The mozo blithe, with gay muchacha met.

P. 193.

The bolero is a very light and active dance, much practised by the Spaniards, in which castanets are always used. *Mozo* and *muchacha* are equivalent to our phrase of lad and lass.

NOTE 9.

While trumpets rang, and heralds cried,
*"Castile!"—*P. 195.

The heralds, at the coronation of a Spanish monarch, proclaim his name three times, and repeat three times the word *Castilla, Castilla, Castilla;* which, with all other ceremonies, was carefully copied in the mock inauguration of Joseph Bonaparte.

NOTE 10.

*High blazed the war, and long, and far, and wide.—*P. 196.

Those who were disposed to believe that mere virtue and energy are able of themselves to work forth the salvation of an oppressed people, surprised in a moment of confidence, deprived of their officers, armies, and fortresses, who had every means of resistance to seek in the very moment when they were to be made use of, and whom the numerous treasons among the higher orders deprived of confidence in their natural leaders,—those who entertained this enthusiastic but delusive opinion may be pardoned for expressing their disappointment at the protracted warfare in the Peninsula. There are, however, another class of persons, who, having themselves the highest dread or veneration, or something allied to both, for the power of the modern Attila, will nevertheless give the heroical Spaniards little or no credit for the long, stubborn, and unsubdued resistance of three years to a power before whom their former well-prepared, well-armed, and numerous adversaries fell in the course of as many months. While these gentlemen plead for deference to Bonaparte, and crave

" Respect for his great place, and bid the devil
Be duly honoured for his burning throne,"

it may not be altogether unreasonable to claim some modification of censure upon those who have been long and to a great extent successfully resisting this great enemy of mankind. That the energy of Spain has not uniformly been directed by conduct equal to its vigour, has

been too obvious; that her armies, under their complicated disadvantages, have shared the fate of such as were defeated after taking the field with every possible advantage of arms and discipline, is surely not to be wondered at. But that a nation, under the circumstances of repeated discomfiture, internal treason, and the mismanagement incident to a temporary and hastily adopted government, should have wasted, by its stübborn, uniform, and prolonged resistance, myriads after myriads of those soldiers who had overrun the world— that some of its provinces should, like Galicia, after being abandoned by their allies, and overrun by their enemies, have recovered their freedom by their own unassisted exertions ; that others, like Catalonia, undismayed by the treason which betrayed some fortresses, and the force which subdued others, should not only have continued their resistance, but have attained over their victorious enemy a superiority, which is even now enabling them to besiege and retake the places of strength which had been wrested from them, is a tale hitherto untold in the revolutionary war.

NOTE 11.

*They won not Zaragoza, but her children's bloody tomb.—*P. 197.

The interesting account of Mr. Vaughan has made most readers acquainted with the first siege of Zaragoza. The last and fatal siege of that gallant and devoted city is detailed with great eloquence and precision in the "Edinburgh Annual Register" for 1809, —a work in which the affairs of Spain have been treated of with attention corresponding to their deep interest, and to the peculiar sources of information open to the historian. The following are a few brief extracts from this splendid historical narrative :—

"A breach was soon made in the mud walls, and then, as in the former siege, the war was carried on in the streets and houses ; but the French had been taught by experience, that in this species of warfare the Zaragozans derived a superiority from the feeling and principle which inspired them, and the cause for which they fought. The only means of conquering Zaragoza was to destroy it house by house, and street by street ; and upon this system of destruction they proceeded. Three companies of miners, and eight companies of sappers, carried on this subterraneous war ; the Spaniards, it is said, attempted to oppose them by countermines ; these were operations to which they were wholly unused, and, according to the French statement, their miners were every day discovered and suffocated. Meantime, the bombardment was incessantly kept up. 'Within the last forty-eight hours,' said Palafox in a letter to his friend General Doyle, '6000 shells have been thrown in. Two-thirds of the town are in ruins, but we shall perish under the ruins of the remaining third rather than surrender.' In the course of the siege, above 17,000 bombs were thrown at the town; the stock of powder with which Zaragoza had been stored was exhausted; they had none at last but what they manufactured day by day; and no other cannon-balls than those which were shot into the town, and which they collected and fired back upon the enemy."

In the midst of these horrors and privations, the pestilence broke out in Zaragoza. To various causes, enumerated by the annalist, he adds, "scantiness of food, crowded quarters, unusual exertion of body, anxiety of mind, and the impossibility of recruiting their exhausted strength by needful rest, in a city which was almost incessantly bombarded, and where every hour their sleep was broken by the tremendous explosion of mines. There was now no respite, either by day or night, for this devoted city; even the natural order of light and darkness was destroyed in Zaragoza; by day it was involved in a red sulphureous atmosphere of smoke, which hid the face of heaven; by night, the fire of cannons and mortars, and the flames of burning houses, kept it in a state of terrific illumination.

"When once the pestilence had begun, it was impossible to check its progress, or confine it to one quarter of the city. Hospitals were immediately established,—there were above thirty of them; as soon as one was destroyed by the bombardment, the patients were removed to another, and thus the infection was carried to every part of Zaragoza. Famine aggravated the evil; the city had probably not been sufficiently provided at the commencement of the siege, and of the provisions which it contained, much was destroyed in the daily ruin which the mines and bombs had effected. Had the Zaragozans and their garrison proceeded according to military rules, they would have surrendered before the end of January; their batteries had then been demolished, there were open breaches in many parts of their weak walls, and the enemy were already within the city. On the 30th, above sixty houses were blown up, and the French obtained possession of the monasteries of the Augustines and Las Monicas, which adjoined each other, two of the last defensible places left. The enemy forced their way into the church; every column, every chapel, every

altar, became a point of defence, which was repeatedly attacked, taken, and retaken; the pavement was covered with blood, the aisles and body of the church strewed with the dead, who were trampled under foot by the combatants. In the midst of this conflict, the roof, shattered by repeated bombs, fell in; the few who were not crushed, after a short pause, which this tremendous shock, and their own unexpected escape, occasioned, renewed the fight with rekindled fury: fresh parties of the enemy poured in; monks and citizens, and soldiers, came to the defence, and the contest was continued upon the ruins, and the bodies of the dead and the dying."——

Yet, seventeen days after sustaining these extremities, did the heroic inhabitants of Zaragoza continue their defence; nor did they then surrender until their despair had extracted from the French generals a capitulation, more honourable than has been granted to fortresses of the first order.

Who shall venture to refuse the Zaragozans the eulogium conferred upon them by the eloquence of Wordsworth!—"Most gloriously have the citizens of Zaragoza proved that the true army of Spain, in a contest of this nature, is the whole people. The same city has also exemplified a melancholy, yea, a dismal truth, yet consolatory and full of joy,—that when a people are called suddenly to fight for their liberty, and are sorely pressed upon, their best field of battle is the floors upon which their children have played; the chambers where the family of each man has slept, (his own or his neighbours';) upon or under the roofs by which they have been sheltered; in the gardens of their recreation; in the street, or in the market-place; before the altars of their temples, and among their congregated dwellings, blazing or uprooted.

"The government of Spain must never forget Zaragoza for a moment. Nothing is wanting to produce the same effects everywhere, but a leading mind, such as that city was blessed with. In the latter contest this has been proved; for Zaragoza contained, at that time, bodies of men from almost all parts of Spain. The narrative of those two sieges should be the manual of every Spaniard. He may add to it the ancient stories of Numantia and Saguntum; let him sleep upon the book as a pillow, and, if he be a devout adherent to the religion of his country, let him wear it in his bosom for his crucifix to rest upon."— WORDSWORTH *on the Convention of Cintra.*

NOTE 12.

The Vault of Destiny.—P. 199.

Before finally dismissing the enchanted

cavern of Don Roderick, it may be noticed, that the legend occurs in one of Calderon's plays, entitled *La Virgin del Sagrario.* The scene opens with the noise of the chase, and Recisundo, a predecessor of Roderick upon the Gothic throne, enters pursuing a stag. The animal assumes the form of a man, and defies the king to enter the cave, which forms the bottom of the scene, and engage with him in single combat. The king accepts the challenge, and they engage accordingly, but without advantage on either side, which induces the Genie to inform Recisundo, that he is not the monarch for whom the adventure of the enchanted cavern is reserved, and he proceeds to predict the downfall of the Gothic monarchy, and of the Christian religion, which shall attend the discovery of its mysteries. Recisundo, appalled by these prophecies, orders the cavern to be secured by a gate and bolts of iron. In the second part of the same play, we are informed that Don Roderick had removed the barrier, and transgressed the prohibition of his ancestor, and had been apprized by the prodigies which he discovered of the approaching ruin of his kingdom.

NOTE 13.

While downward on the land his legions press,
Before them it was rich with vine and flock,
   And smiled like Eden in her summer dress ;—
Behind their wasteful march, a reeking wilderness.—P. 200.

I have ventured to apply to the movements of the French army that sublime passage in the prophecies of Joel, which seems applicable to them in more respects than that I have adopted in the text. One would think their ravages, their military appointments, the terror which they spread among invaded nations, their military discipline, their arts of political intrigue and deceit, were distinctly pointed out in the following verses of Scripture :—

"2. A day of darknesse and of gloominesse, a day of clouds and of thick darknesse, as the morning spread upon the mountains ; a great people and a strong, there hath not been ever the like, neither shall be any more after it, even to the yeares of many generations. 3. A fire devoureth before them, and behind them a flame burneth ; the land is as the garden of Eden before them, and behinde them a desolate wilderness, yea, and nothing shall escape them. 4. The appearance of them is as the appearance of horses ; and as horsemen, so shall they runne. 5. Like the

noise of chariots on the tops of mountains, shall they leap, like the noise of a flame of fire that devoureth the stubble, as a strong people set in battel array. 6. Before their face shall the people be much pained ; all faces shall gather blacknesse. 7. They shall run like mighty men, they shall climb the wall like men of warre, and they shall march every one in his wayes, and they shall not break their ranks. 8. Neither shall one thrust another, they shall walk every one in his path : and when they fall upon the sword, they shall not be wounded. 9. They shall run to and fro in the citie ; they shall run upon the wall, they shall climbe up upon the houses: they shall enter in at the windows like a thief. 10. The earth shall quake before them, the heavens shall tremble, the sunne and the moon shall be dark, and the starres shall withdraw their shining."

In verse 20th also, which announces the retreat of the northern army, described in such dreadful colours, into a "land barren and desolate," and the dishonour with which God afflicted them for having "magnified themselves to do great things," there are particulars not inapplicable to the retreat of Massena ;— Divine Providence having, in all ages, attached disgrace as the natural punishment of cruelty and presumption.

NOTE 14.

The rudest sentinel, in Britain born,
   With horror paused to view the havoc done,
Gave his poor crust to feed some wretch forlorn.—P. 201.

Even the unexampled gallantry of the British army in the campaign of 1810-11, although they never fought but to conquer, will do them less honour in history than their humanity, attentive to soften to the utmost of their power the horrors which war, in its mildest aspect, must always inflict upon the defenceless inhabitants of the country in which it is waged, and which, on this occasion, were tenfold augmented by the barbarous cruelties of the French. Soup-kitchens were established by subscription among the officers, wherever the troops were quartered for any length of time. The commissaries contributed the heads, feet, &c. of the cattle slaughtered for the soldiery; rice, vegetables, and bread, where it could be had, were purchased by the officers. Fifty or sixty starving peasants were daily fed at one of these regimental establishments, and carried home the relics to their famished households. The emaciated wretches, who could not crawl from weakness, were speedily employed in pruning their vines. While pursuing Massena, the soldiers evinced the same spirit of humanity, and in many instances, when reduced themselves to short allowance, from having out-marched their supplies, they shared their pittance with the starving inhabitants, who had ventured back to view the ruins of their habitations, burnt by the retreating enemy, and to bury the bodies of their relations whom they had butchered. Is it possible to know such facts without feeling a sort of confidence, that those who so well deserve victory are most likely to attain it?—It is not the least of Lord Wellington's military merits, that the slightest disposition towards marauding meets immediate punishment. Independently of all moral obligation, the army which is most orderly in a friendly country, has always proved most formidable to an armed enemy.

NOTE 15.

Vain-glorious fugitive!—P. 201.

The French conducted this memorable retreat with much of the *fanfaronnade* proper to their country, by which they attempt to impose upon others, and perhaps on themselves, a belief that they are triumphing in the very moment of their discomfiture. On the 30th March 1811, their rear-guard was overtaken near Pega by the British cavalry. Being well posted, and conceiving themselves safe from infantry, (who were indeed many miles in the rear,) and from artillery, they indulged themselves in parading their bands of music, and actually performed "God save the King." Their minstrelsy was, however, deranged by the undesired accompaniment of the British horse-artillery, on whose part in the concert they had not calculated. The surprise was sudden, and the rout complete; for the artillery and cavalry did execution upon them for about four miles, pursuing at the gallop as often as they got beyond the range of the guns.

NOTE 16.

Vainly thy squadrons hide Assuava's plain, And front the flying thunders as they roar, With frantic charge and tenfold odds, in vain!—P. 201.

In the severe action of Fuentes d'Honoro, upon 5th May, 1811, the grand mass of the French cavalry attacked the right of the British position, covered by two guns of the horse-artillery, and two squadrons of cavalry. After suffering considerably from the fire of the guns, which annoyed them in every at-

tempt at formation, the enemy turned their wrath entirely towards them, distributed brandy among their troopers, and advanced to carry the field-pieces with the desperation of drunken fury. They were in nowise checked by the heavy loss which they sustained in this daring attempt, but closed, and fairly mingled with the British cavalry, to whom they bore the proportion of ten to one. Captain Ramsay, (let me be permitted to name a gallant countryman,) who commanded the two guns, dismissed them at the gallop, and putting himself at the head of the mounted artillerymen, ordered them to fall upon the French, sabre-in-hand. This very unexpected conversion of artillerymen into dragoons, contributed greatly to the defeat of the enemy already disconcerted by the reception they had met from the two British squadrons; and the appearance of some small reinforcements, notwithstanding the immense disproportion of force, put them to absolute rout. A colonel or major of their cavalry, and many prisoners, (almost all intoxicated,) remained in our possession. Those who consider for a moment the difference of the services, and how much an artilleryman is necessarily and naturally led to identify his own safety and utility with abiding by the tremendous implement of war, to the exercise of which he is chiefly, if not exclusively, trained, will know how to estimate the presence of mind which commanded so bold a manœuvre, and the steadiness and confidence with which it was executed.

NOTE 17.

And what avails thee that, for Cameron slain, Wild from his plaided ranks the yell was given.—P. 201.

The gallant Colonel Cameron was wounded mortally during the desperate contest in the streets of the village called Fuentes d'Honoro. He fell at the head of his native Highlanders, the 71st and 79th, who raised a dreadful shriek of grief and rage. They charged, with irresistible fury, the finest body of French grenadiers ever seen, being a part of Bonaparte's selected guard. The officer who led the French, a man remarkable for stature and symmetry, was killed on the spot. The Frenchman who stepped out of his rank to take aim at Colonel Cameron was also bayoneted, pierced with a thousand wounds, and almost torn to pieces by the furious Highlanders, who, under the command of Colonel Cadogan, bore the enemy out of the contested ground at the point of the bayonet. Massena pays my countrymen a singular compliment in his account of the attack and defence of this village, in which he says the British lost many officers, *and Scotch.*

NOTE 18.

O who shall grudge him Albuera's bays,
  Who brought a race regenerate to the field,
Roused them to emulate their fathers' praise,
  Temper'd their headlong rage, their courage
    steel'd,
And raised fair Lusitania's fallen shield.
                                P. 202.

Nothing during the war of Portugal seems, to a distinct observer, more deserving of praise, than the self-devotion of Field-Marshal Beresford, who was contented to undertake all the hazard of obloquy which might have been founded upon any miscarriage in the highly important experiment of training the Portuguese troops to an improved state of discipline. In exposing his military reputation to the censure of imprudence from the most moderate, and all manner of unutterable calumnies from the ignorant and malignant, he placed at stake the dearest pledge which a military man had to offer, and nothing but the deepest conviction of the high and essential importance attached to success can be supposed an adequate motive. How great the chance of miscarriage was supposed, may be estimated from the general opinion of officers of unquestioned talents and experience, possessed of every opportunity of information; how completely the experiment has succeeded, and how much the spirit and patriotism of our ancient allies had been underrated, is evident, not only from those victories in which they have borne a distinguished share, but from the liberal and highly honourable manner in which these opinions have been retracted. The success of this plan, with all its important consequences, we owe to the indefatigable exertions of Field-Marshal Beresford.

NOTE 19.

—— a race renown'd of old,
Whose war-cry oft has waked the battle-
    swell.

—— the conquering shout of Græme.—P. 203.

This stanza alludes to the various achievements of the warlike family of Græme, or Grahame. They are said, by tradition, to have descended from the Scottish chief, under whose command his countrymen stormed the wall built by the Emperor Severus between the Friths of Forth and Clyde, the fragments of which are still popularly called Græme's Dyke. Sir John the Græme, "the hardy, wight, and wise," is well known as the friend of Sir William Wallace. Alderne, Kilsythe, and Tibbermuir, were scenes of the victories of the heroic Marquis of Montrose. The pass of Killycrankie is famous for the action between King William's forces and the Highlanders in 1689,

"Where glad Dundee in faint huzzas expired."

It is seldom that one line can number so many heroes, and yet more rare when it can appeal to the glory of a living descendant in support of its ancient renown.

The allusions to the private history and character of General Grahame may be illustrated by referring to the eloquent and affecting speech of Mr. Sheridan, upon the vote of thanks to the Victors of Barossa.

ROKEBY.

NOTE 1.

On Barnard's towers, and Tees's stream, &c.
                                P. 207.

"BARNARD'S CASTLE," saith old Leland, "standeth stately upon Tees." It is founded upon a very high bank, and its ruins impend over the river, including within the area a circuit of six acres and upwards. This once magnificent fortress derives its name from its founder, Barnard Baliol, the ancestor of the short and unfortunate dynasty of that name, which succeeded to the Scottish throne under the patronage of Edward I. and Edward III. Baliol's Tower, afterwards mentioned in the poem, is a round tower of great size, situated at the western extremity of the building. It bears marks of great antiquity, and was remarkable for the curious construction of its vaulted roof, which has been lately greatly injured by the operations of some persons, to whom the tower has been leased for the purpose of making patent shot! The prospect from the top of Baliol's Tower commands a rich and magnificent view of the wooded valley of the Tees.

NOTE 2.

—— *no human ear,*
Unsharpen'd by revenge and fear,
Could e'er distinguish horse's clank.—P. 208.

I have had occasion to remark, in real life, the effect of keen and fervent anxiety in giving acuteness to the organs of sense. My gifted friend, Miss Joanna Baillie, whose dramatic works display such intimate acquaintance with the operations of human passion, has not omitted this remarkable circumstance:—

"*De Montfort.* (*Off his guard.*) 'Tis Rezenvelt: I heard his well-known foot,
From the first staircase mounting step by step.
   Freb. How quick an ear thou hast for distant sound!
I heard him not.
   (*De Montfort looks embarrassed, and is silent.*)"

NOTE 3.

The morion's plumes his visage hide,
And the buff-coat, an ample fold,
Mantles his form's gigantic mould.—P. 208.

The use of complete suits of armour was fallen into disuse during the Civil War, though they were still worn by leaders of rank and importance. "In the reign of King James I.," says our military antiquary, "no great alterations were made in the article of defensive armour, except that the buff-coat, or jerkin, which was originally worn under the cuirass, now became frequently a substitute for it, it having been found that a good buff leather would of itself resist the stroke of a sword; this, however, only occasionally took place among the light-armed cavalry and infantry, complete suits of armour being still used among the heavy horse. Buff-coats continued to be worn by the city trained-bands till within the memory of persons now living, so that defensive armour may, in some measure, be said to have terminated in the same materials with which it began, that is, the skins of animals, or leather."—GROSE'S *Military Antiquities.* Lond. 1801, 4to, vol. ii. p. 323.

Of the buff-coats, which were worn over the corslets, several are yet preserved; and Captain Grose has given an engraving of one which was used in the time of Charles I. by Sir Francis Rhodes, Bart. of Balbrough-Hall, Derbyshire.

NOTE 4.

On his dark face a scorching clime,
And toil, had done the work of time.

. . . .

Death had he seen by sudden blow,
By wasting plague, by tortures slow.—P. 208.

In this character, I have attempted to sketch one of those West Indian adventurers, who, during the course of the seventeenth century, were popularly known by the name of Bucaniers. The successes of the English in the predatory incursions upon Spanish America, during the reign of Elizabeth, had never been forgotten; and, from that period downward, the exploits of Drake and Raleigh were imitated, upon a smaller scale indeed, but with equally desperate valour, by small bands of pirates, gathered from all nations, but chiefly French and English. The engrossing policy of the Spaniards tended greatly to increase the number of these freebooters, from whom their commerce and colonies suffered, in the issue, dreadful calamity.

NOTE 5.

—— *On Marston heath*
Met, front to front, the ranks of death.
P. 209.

The well-known and desperate battle of Long-Marston Moor, which terminated so unfortunately for the cause of Charles, commenced under very different auspices. Prince Rupert had marched with an army of 20,000 men for the relief of York, then besieged by Sir Thomas Fairfax, at the head of the Parliamentary army, and the Earl of Leven, with the Scottish auxiliary forces. In this he so completely succeeded, that he compelled the besiegers to retreat to Marston Moor, a large open plain, about eight miles distant from the city. Thither they were followed by the Prince, who had now united to his army the garrison of York, probably not less than ten thousand men strong, under the gallant Marquis (then Earl) of Newcastle. Whitelocke has recorded, with much impartiality, the following particulars of this eventful day:—"The right wing of the Parliament was commanded by Sir Thomas Fairfax, and consisted of all his horse, and three regiments of the Scots horse; the left wing was commanded by the Earl of Manchester and Colonel Cromwell. One body of their foot was commanded by Lord Fairfax, and consisted of his foot, and two brigades of the Scots foot for reserve; and the main body of the rest of the foot was commanded by General Leven.

"The right wing of the Prince's army was commanded by the Earl of Newcastle; the left wing by the Prince himself ; and the main body by General Goring, Sir Charles Lucas, and Major-General Porter. Thus were both sides drawn up into battalia.

"July 3rd, 1644. In this posture both armies faced each other, and about seven o'clock in the morning the fight began between them. The Prince, with his left wing, fell on the Parliament's right wing, routed them, and pursued them a great way ; the like did General Goring, Lucas, and Porter, upon the Parliament's main body. The three generals, giving all for lost, hasted out of the field, and many of their soldiers fled, and threw down their arms ; the King's forces too eagerly following them, the victory, now almost achieved by them, was again snatched out of their hands. For Colonel Cromwell, with the brave regiment of his countrymen, and Sir Thomas Fairfax, having rallied some of his horse, fell upon the Prince's right wing, where the Earl of Newcastle was, and routed them ; and the rest of their companions rallying, they fell altogether upon the divided bodies of Rupert and Goring, and totally dispersed them, and obtained a complete victory, after three hours' fight.

"From this battle and the pursuit, some reckon were buried 7000 Englishmen ; all agree that above 3000 of the Prince's men were slain in the battle, besides those in the chase, and 3000 prisoners taken, many of their chief officers, twenty-five pieces of ordnance, forty-seven colours, 10,000 arms, two waggons of carabins and pistols, 130 barrels of powder, and all their bag and baggage."
—WHITELOCKE'S *Memoirs*, fol. p. 89. Lond. 1682.

NOTE 6.

Monckton and Mitton told the news,
How troops of Roundheads choked the Ouse,
And many a bonny Scot, aghast,
Spurring his palfrey northward, past,
Cursing the day when zeal or meed
First lured their Lesley o'er the Tweed.

P. 212.

Monckton and Mitton are villages near the river Ouse, and not very distant from the field of battle. The particulars of the action were violently disputed at the time ; but the following extract, from the Manuscript History of the Baronial House of Somerville, is decisive as to the flight of the Scottish general, the Earl of Leven. The details are given by the author of the history on the authority of his father, then the representative of the family. This curious manuscript was published by consent of Lord Somerville.

"The order of this great battell, wherin both armies was neer of ane equall number, consisting, to the best calculatione, neer to three score thousand men upon both sydes, I shall not take upon me to discryve ; albeit, from the draughts then taken upon the place, and information I receaved from this gentleman, who being then a volunteer, as having no command, had opportunitie and libertie to ryde from the one wing of the armie to the other, to view all ther several squadrons of horse and battallions of foot, how formed, and in what manner drawn up, with every other circumstance relating to the fight, and that both as to the King's armies and that of the Parliament's, amongst whom, untill the engadgment, he went from statione to statione to observe ther order and forme ; but that the descriptione of this battell, with the various success on both sides at the beginning, with the loss of the royal armie, and the sad effects that followed that misfortune as to his Majestie's interest, hes been so often done already by English authors, little to our commendatione, how justly I shall not dispute, seing the truth is, as our principal generall fled that night neer fourtie mylles from the place of the fight, that part of the armie where he commanded being totallie routed ; but it is as true, that much of the victorie is attributed to the good conduct of David Lesselie, lievetennent-generall of our horse. Cromwell himself, that minione of fortune, but the rod of God's wrath, to punish eftirward three rebellious nations, disdained not to take orders from him, albeit then in the same qualitie of command for the Parliament, as being lievetennent-general to the Earl of Manchester's horse, whom, with the assistance of the Scots horse, haveing routed the Prince's right wing, as he had done that of the Parliament's. These two commanders of the horse upon that wing wisely restrained the great bodies of their horse from persuing these brocken troups, but, wheelling to the left-hand, falls in upon the naked flanks of the Prince's main battallion of foot, carrying them doune with great violence ; nether mett they with any great resistance untill they came to the Marques of Newcastle his battallione of White Coats, who, first peppering them soundly with ther shott, when they came to charge, stoutly bore them up with their picks that they could not enter to break them. Here the Parliament's horse of that wing receaved ther greatest losse, and a stop for sometyme putt to ther hoped-for victorie ; and that only by the stout resistance of this gallant battallione, which consisted neer of four thousand foot, until at length a Scots regiment of dragouns, commanded by Collonell Frizeall, with other two, was brought to open them upon some hand, which at length they did, when all the ammunitione was spent. Having refused quarters, every man fell in the same order and ranke wherein he had foughten.

"Be this execution was done, the Prince returned from the persuite of the right wing of the Parliament's horse, which he had beatten and followed too farre, to the losse of the battell, which certanely, in all men's opinions, he might have caryed if he had not been too violent upon the pursuite; which gave his enemies upon the left-hand opportunitie to disperse and cut doune his infantrie, who, haveing cleared the field of all the standing bodies of foot, wer now, with many [foot soldiers] of their oune, standing ready to receave the charge of his allmost spent horses, if he should attempt it; which the Prince observeing, and seeing all lost, he retreated to Yorke with two thousand horse. Notwithstanding of this, ther was that night such a consternation in the Parliament armies, that it's believed by most of those that wer there present, that if the Prince, haveing so great a body of horse inteire, had made ane onfall that night, or the ensueing morning be-tyme, he had carryed the victorie out of ther hands; for it's certane by the morning's light, he had rallyed a body of ten thousand men, wherof ther was neer three thousand gallant horse. These, with the assistance of the toune and garrisoune of Yorke, might have done much to have recovered the victory, for the loss of this battell in effect lost the King and his interest in the three kingdomes; his Majestie never being able eftir this to make head in the north, but lost his garrisons every day.

"As for Generall Lesselie, in the beginning of this flight haveing that part of the army quite brocken, whare he had placed himself, by the valour of the Prince, he imagined, and was confermed by the opinione of others then upon the place with him, that the battell was irrecoverably lost, seeing they wer fleeing upon all hands; theirfore they humblie intreated his excellence to reteir and wait his better fortune, which, without farder advyseing, he did; and never drew bridle untill he came the lenth of Leads, having ridden all that night with a cloak of *drap de berrie* about him, belonging to this gentleman of whom I write, then in his retinue, with many other officers of good qualitie. It was neer twelve the next day befor they had the certanety who was master of the field, when at length ther

arryves ane expresse, sent by David Lesselie, to acquaint the General they had obtained a most glorious victory, and that the Prince, with his brocken troupes, was fled from Yorke. This intelligence was somewhat amazeing to these gentlemen that had been eye-witnesses to the disorder of the armie before ther retearing, and had then accompanyed the General in his flight; who, being much wearyed that evening of the battell with ordering of his armie, and now quite spent with his long journey in the night, had casten himselfe doune upon a bed to rest, when this gentleman comeing quyetly into his chamber, he awoke, and hastily cryes out, 'Lievetennent-collonell, what news?'—'All is safe, may it please your Excellence; the Parliament's armie hes obtained a great victory;' and then delyvers the letter. The Generall, upon the hearing of this, knocked upon his breast, and sayes, 'I would to God I had died upon the place!' and then opens the letter, which, in a few lines, gave ane account of the victory, and in the close pressed his speedy returne to the armie, which he did the next day, being accompanyed some mylles back by this gentleman, who then takes his leave of him, and receaved at parting many expressions of kyndenesse, with promises that he would never be unmyndful of his care and respect towards him; and in the end he intreats him to present his service to all his friends and acquaintances in Scotland. Thereftir the Generall sets forward in his journey for the armie,

. . . .

in order to his transportatione for Scotland, where he arryved sex dayes eftir the fight of Mestoune Muir, and gave the first true account and descriptione of that great battell, wherein the Covenanters then gloryed soe much, that they impiously boasted the Lord had now signally appeared for his cause and people; it being ordinary for them, dureing the whole time of this warre, to attribute the greatnes of their success to the goodnes and justice of ther cause, untill Divine Justice trysted them with some crosse dispensatione, and then you might have heard this language from them, 'That it pleases the Lord to give his oune the heavyest end of the tree to bear, that the saints and the people of God must still be sufferers while they are here away, that the malignant party was God's rod to punish them for ther unthankfullnesse, which in the end he will cast into the fire;' with a thousand other expressions and scripture citations, prophanely and blasphemously uttered by them, to palliate ther villainie and rebellion."—*Memoires of the Somervilles.*—Edin, 1815.

NOTE 7.

With his barb'd horse, fresh tidings say,
Stout Cromwell has redeem'd the day.—P. 212.

Cromwell, with his regiment of cuirassiers, had a principal share in turning the fate of the day at Marston Moor; which was equally matter of triumph to the Independents, and of grief and heart-burning to the Presbyterians and to the Scottish.

NOTE 8.

Do not my native dales prolong
Of Percy Rede, the tragic song,
Train'd forward to his bloody fall,
By Girsonfield, that treacherous Hall?
P. 212.

In a poem, entitled "The Lay of the Reedwater Minstrel," Newcastle, 1809, this tale, with many others peculiar to the valley of the Reed, is commemorated :—"The particulars of the traditional story of Parcy Reed of Troughend, and the Halls of Girsonfield, the author had from a descendant of the family of Reed. From his account, it appears that Percival Reed, Esquire, a keeper of Reedsdale, was betrayed by the Halls (hence denominated the false-hearted Halls) to a band of moss-troopers of the name of Crosier, who slew him at Batinghope, near the source of the Reed.

"The Halls were, after the murder of Parcy Reed, held in such universal abhorrence and contempt by the inhabitants of Reedsdale, for their cowardly and treacherous behaviour, that they were obliged to leave the country." In another passage, we are informed that the ghost of the injured Borderer is supposed to haunt the banks of a brook called the Pringle. These Reeds of Troughend were a very ancient family, as may be conjectured from their deriving their surname from the river on which they had their mansion. An epitaph on one of their tombs affirms, that the family held their lands of Troughend, which are situated on the Reed, nearly opposite to Otterburn, for the incredible space of nine hundred years.

NOTE 9.

And near the spot that gave me name,
The moated mound of Risingham,
Where Reed upon her margin sees
Sweet Woodburne's cottages and trees,
Some ancient sculptor's art has shown
An outlaw's image on the stone.—P. 212.

Risingham, upon the river Reed, near the beautiful hamlet of Woodburn, is an ancient Roman station, formerly called Habitancum. Camden says, that in his time the popular account bore, that it had been the abode of a deity, or giant, called Magon; and appeals, in support of this tradition, as well as to the etymology of Risingham, or Reisenham, which signifies, in German, the habitation of the giants, to two Roman altars taken out of the river, inscribed, DEO MOGONTI CADENORUM. About half a mile distant from Risingham, upon an eminence covered with scattered birch-trees, and fragments of rock, there is cut upon a large rock, in *alto relievo*, a remarkable figure, called Robin of Risingham, or Robin of Reedsdale. It presents a hunter, with his bow raised in one hand, and in the other what seems to be a hare. There is a quiver at the back of the figure, and he is dressed in a long coat, or kirtle, coming down to the knees, and meeting close, with a girdle bound round him. Dr. Horsley, who saw all monuments of antiquity with Roman eyes, inclines to think this figure a Roman archer: and certainly the bow is rather of the ancient size than of that which was so formidable in the hand of the English archers of the Middle Ages. But the rudeness of the whole figure prevents our founding strongly upon mere inaccuracy of proportion. The popular tradition is, that it represents a giant, whose brother resided at Woodburn, and he himself at Risingham. It adds, that they subsisted by hunting, and that one of them, finding the game become too scarce to support them, poisoned his companion, in whose memory the monument was engraved. What strange and tragic circumstance may be concealed under this legend, or whether it is utterly apocryphal, it is now impossible to discover.

NOTE 10.

—— Do thou revere
The statutes of the Bucanier.—P. 212.

The "statutes of the Bucaniers" were, in reality, more equitable than could have been expected from the state of society under which they had been formed. They chiefly related, as may readily be conjectured, to the distribution and the inheritance of their plunder.

When the expedition was completed, the fund of prize-money acquired was thrown together, each party taking his oath that he had retained or concealed no part of the common stock. If any one transgressed in this important particular, the punishment was, his being set ashore on some desert key or island, to shift for himself as he could. The owners of the vessel had then their share assigned for the expenses of the outfit. These were generally old pirates, settled at Tobago, Jamaica, St. Domingo, or some other French or English settlement. The surgeon's and carpenter's salaries, with the price of provisions and ammunition, were also defrayed. Then followed the compensation due to the maimed and wounded, rated according to the damage they had sustained; as six hundred pieces of eight, or six slaves, for the loss of an arm or leg, and so in proportion.

"After this act of justice and humanity, the remainder of the booty was divided into as many shares as there were Bucaniers. The commander could only lay claim to a single share, as the rest; but they complimented him with two or three, in proportion as he had acquitted himself to their satisfaction. When the vessel was not the property of the whole company, the persons who had fitted it out, and furnished it with necessary arms and ammunition, were entitled to a third of all the prizes. Favour had never any influence in the division of the booty, for every share was determined by lot. Instances of such rigid justice as this are not easily met with, and they extended even to the dead. Their share was given to the man who was known to be their companion when alive, and therefore their heir. If the person who had been killed had no intimate, his part was sent to his relations, when they were known. If there were no friends nor relations, it was distributed in charity to the poor and to churches, which were to pray for the person in whose name these benefactions were given, the fruits of inhuman, but necessary piratical plunder."—RAYNAL'S *History of European Settlements in the East and West Indies, by Justamond.* Lond. 1776, 8vo, iii. p. 41.

NOTE 11.

The course of Tees.—P. 216.

The view from Barnard Castle commands the rich and magnificent valley of Tees. Immediately adjacent to the river, the banks are very thickly wooded; at a little distance they are more open and cultivated; but, being interspersed with hedge-rows, and with isolated trees of great size and age, they still retain the richness of woodland scenery. The river itself flows in a deep trench of solid rock, chiefly limestone and marble. The finest view of its romantic course is from a handsome modern-built bridge over the Tees, by the late Mr. Morritt of Rokeby. In Leland's time, the marble quarries seem to have been of some value, "Hard under the cliff by Eglis-

ton, is found on eche side of Tese very fair marble, wont to be taken up booth by marbelers of Barnardes Castelle and of Egliston, and partly to have been wrought by them, and partly sold onwrought to others."—*Itinerary.* Oxford, 1768, 8vo, p. 88.

NOTE 12.

Egliston's grey ruins.—P. 217.

The ruins of this abbey, or priory, (for Tanner calls it the former, and Leland the latter,) are beautifully situated upon the angle formed by a little dell called Thorsgill, at its junction with the Tees.

NOTE 13.

—— *the mound,*
Raised by that Legion long renown'd,
Whose votive shrine asserts their claim,
Of pious, faithful, conquering fame.
P. 217.

Close behind the George Inn at Greta Bridge, there is a well-preserved Roman encampment, surrounded with a triple ditch, lying between the river Greta and a brook called the Tutta. The four entrances are easily to be discerned. Very many Roman altars and monuments have been found in the vicinity, most of which are preserved at Rokeby by my friend Mr. Morritt.

NOTE 14.

Rokeby's turrets high—P. 217.

This ancient manor long gave name to a family by whom it is said to have been possessed from the Conquest downward, and who are at different times distinguished in history. It was the Baron of Rokeby who finally defeated the insurrection of the Earl of Northumberland, *tempore Hen. IV.* The Rokeby, or Rokesby family, continued to be distinguished until the great Civil War, when, having embraced the cause of Charles I., they suffered severely by fines and confiscations. The estate then passed from its ancient possessors to the family of the Robinsons, from whom it was purchased by the father of my valued friend, the present proprietor.

NOTE 15.

A stern and lone, yet lovely road,
As e'er the foot of Minstrel trode.
P. 217.

What follows is an attempt to describe the romantic glen or rather ravine, through which the Greta finds a passage between Rokeby and Mortham ; the former situated upon the left bank of Greta, the latter on the right bank, about half a mile nearer to its junction with the Tees.

NOTE 16.

—— *tell*

. . . .
How whistle rash bids tempests roar.
P. 219.

That this is a general superstition is well known to all who have been on ship-board, or who have conversed with seamen. The most formidable whistler that I remember to have met with was the apparition of a certain Mrs. Leakey, who, about 1636, resided, we are told, at Mynehead, in Somerset, where her only son drove a considerable trade between that port and Waterford, and was owner of several vessels. This old gentlewoman was of a social disposition, and so acceptable to her friends, that they used to say to her and to each other, it were a pity such an excellent good-natured old lady should die ; to which she was wont to reply, that whatever pleasure they might find in her company just now, they would not greatly like to see or converse with her after death, which nevertheless she was apt to think might happen. Accordingly, after her death and funeral, she began to appear to various persons by night and by noon-day, in her own house, in the town and fields, at sea and upon shore. So far had she departed from her former urbanity, that she is recorded to have kicked a doctor of medicine for his impolite negligence in omitting to hand her over a stile. It was also her humour to appear upon the quay, and call for a boat. But especially as soon as any of her son's ships approached the harbour, "this ghost would appear in the same garb and likeness as when she was alive, and, standing at the mainmast, would blow with a whistle, and though it were never so great a calm, yet immediately there would arise a most dreadful storm, that would break, wreck, and drown ship and goods." When she had thus proceeded until her son had neither cash to freight a vessel, nor could have procured men to sail in it, she began to attack the persons of his family, and actually strangled their only child in the cradle. The rest of her story, showing how the spectre looked over the shoulder of her daughter-in-law, while dressing her hair in the looking-glass, and how Mrs. Leaky the younger took courage to address her, and how the beldame despatched her to an Irish prelate, famous for his crimes

and misfortunes, to exhort him to repentance, and to apprize him that otherwise he would be hanged, and how the bishop was satisfied with replying that if he was born to be hanged, he should not be drowned ;—all these, with many more particulars, may be found at the end of one of John Dunton's publications, called Athenianism, London, 1710, where the tale is engrossed under the title of The Apparition Evidence.

NOTE 17.

Of Erick's cap and Elmo's light.—P. 219.

"This Ericus, King of Sweden, in his time was held second to none in the magical art; and he was so familiar with the evil spirits, which he exceedingly adored, that which way soever he turned his cap, the wind would presently blow that way. From this occasion he was called Windy Cap; and many men believed that Regnerus, King of Denmark, by the conduct of this Ericus, who was his nephew, did happily extend his piracy into the most remote parts of the earth, and conquered many countries and fenced cities by his cunning, and at last was his coadjutor; that by the consent of the nobles, he should be chosen King of Sweden, which continued a long time with him very happily, until he died of old age."— OLAUS, *ut supra*, p. 40.

NOTE 18.

The Demon frigate.—P. 219.

This is an allusion to a well-known nautical superstition concerning a fantastic vessel, called by sailors the Flying Dutchman, and supposed to be seen about the latitude of the Cape of Good Hope. She is distinguished from earthly vessels by bearing a press of sail when all others are unable, from stress of weather, to show an inch of canvas. The cause of her wandering is not altogether certain; but the general account is, that she was originally a vessel loaded with great wealth, on board of which some horrid act of murder and piracy had been committed; that the plague broke out among the wicked crew who had perpetrated the crime, and that they sailed in vain from port to port, offering, as the price of shelter, the whole of their ill-gotten wealth; that they were excluded from every harbour, for fear of the contagion which was devouring them ; and that, as a punishment of their crimes, the apparition of the ship still continues to haunt those seas in which the catastrophe took place, and is considered by the mariners as the worst of all possible omens.

NOTE 19.

—— *by some desert isle or key.*—P. 219.

What contributed much to the security of the Bucaniers about the Windward Islands, was the great number of little islets, called in that country *keys.* These are small sandy patches, appearing just above the surface of the ocean, covered only with a few bushes and weeds, but sometimes affording springs of water, and, in general, much frequented by turtle. Such little uninhabited spots afforded the pirates good harbours, either for refitting or for the purpose of ambush; they were occasionally the hiding-place of their treasure, and often afforded a shelter to themselves. As many of the atrocities which they practised on their prisoners were committed in such spots, there are some of these keys which even now have an indifferent reputation among seamen, and where they are with difficulty prevailed on to remain ashore at night, on account of the visionary terrors incident to places which have been thus contaminated.

NOTE 20.

Before the gate of Mortham stood.—P. 220.

The castle of Mortham, which Leland terms " Mr. Rokesby's Place, in *ripa citer.*, scant a quarter of a mile from Greta Bridge, and not a quarter of a mile beneath into Tees," is a picturesque tower, surrounded by buildings of different ages, now converted into a farm-house and offices.

The situation is eminently beautiful, occupying a high bank, at the bottom of which the Greta winds out of the dark, narrow, and romantic dell, which the text has attempted to describe, and flows onward through a more open valley to meet the Tees about a quarter of a mile from the castle. Mortham is surrounded by old trees, happily and widely grouped with Mr. Morritt's new plantations.

NOTE 21.

There dig, and tomb your precious heap,
And bid the dead your treasure keep.
P. 221.

If time did not permit the Bucaniers to lavish away their plunder in their usual debaucheries, they were wont to hide it, with many superstitious solemnities, in the desert islands and keys which they frequented, and where much treasure, whose lawless owners perished without reclaiming it, is still supposed to be concealed. The most cruel of mankind are often the most superstitious; and these pirates are said to have had recourse to a horrid ritual, in order to secure an unearthly guardian to their treasures. They killed a Negro or Spaniard, and buried him with the treasure, believing that his spirit would haunt the spot, and terrify away all intruders. I cannot produce any other authority on which this custom is ascribed to them than that of maritime tradition, which is, however, amply sufficient for the purposes of poetry.

NOTE 22.

The power . . . .
. . . . . .
That unsubdued and lurking lies
To take the felon by surprise,
And force him, as by magic spell,
In his despite his guilt to tell.—P. 221.

All who are conversant with the administration of criminal justice, must remember many occasions in which malefactors appear to have conducted themselves with a species of infatuation, either by making unnecessary confidences respecting their guilt, or by sudden and involuntary allusions to circumstances by which it could not fail to be exposed. A remarkable instance occurred in the celebrated case of Eugene Aram. A skeleton being found near Knaresborough, was supposed, by the persons who gathered around the spot, to be the remains of one Clarke, who had disappeared some years before, under circumstances leading to a suspicion of his having been murdered. One Houseman, who had mingled in the crowd, suddenly said, while looking at the skeleton, and hearing the opinion which was buzzed around, " That is no more Dan Clarke's bone than it is mine !"—a sentiment expressed so positively, and with such peculiarity of manner, as to lead all who heard him to infer that he must necessarily know where the real body had been interred. Accordingly, being apprehended, he confessed having assisted Eugene Aram to murder Clarke, and to hide his body in Saint Robert's Cave. It happened to the author himself, while conversing with a person accused of an atrocious crime, for the purpose of rendering him professional assistance upon his trial, to hear the prisoner, after the most solemn and reiterated protestations that he was guiltless, suddenly, and, as it were, involuntarily, in the course of his communications, make such an admission as was altogether incompatible with innocence.

NOTE 23.

—— *Brackenbury's dismal tower.*—P. 223.

This tower has been already mentioned. It

Is situated near the north-eastern extremity of the wall which encloses Barnard Castle, and is traditionally said to have been the prison. By an odd coincidence, it bears a name which we naturally connect with imprisonment, from its being that of Sir Robert Brackenbury, lieutenant of the Tower of London under Edward IV. and Richard III.

NOTE 24.

Nobles and knights, so proud of late,
Must fine for freedom and estate.

. . . .

Right heavy shall his ransom be,
Unless that maid compound with thee.

P. 224.

After the battle of Marston Moor, the Earl of Newcastle retired beyond sea in disgust, and many of his followers laid down their arms, and made the best composition they could with the Committees of Parliament. Fines were imposed upon them in proportion to their estates and degrees of delinquency, and these fines were often bestowed upon such persons as had deserved well of the Commons. In some circumstances it happened, that the oppressed cavaliers were fain to form family alliances with some powerful person among the triumphant party.

NOTE 25.

The Indian, prowling for his prey,
Who hears the settlers track his way.

P. 224.

The patience, abstinence, and ingenuity, exerted by the North American Indians, when in pursuit of plunder or vengeance, is the most distinguished feature in their character; and the activity and address which they display in their retreat is equally surprising.

NOTE 26.

In Redesdale his youth had heard,
Each art her wily dalesmen dared,
When Rooken-edge, and Redswair high,
To bugle rung and bloodhound's cry.

P. 224.

"What manner of cattle-stealers they are that inhabit these valleys in the marches of both kingdoms, John Lesley, a Scotche man himself, and Bishop of Ross, will inform you. They sally out of their own borders in the night, in troops, through unfrequented by-ways and many intricate windings. All the day-time they refresh themselves and their horses in lurking holes they had pitched upon before, till they arrive in the dark in those places they have a design upon. As soon as they have seized upon the booty, they, in like manner, return home in the night, through blind ways, and fetching many a compass. The more skilful any captain is to pass through those wild deserts, crooked turnings, and deep precipices, in the thickest mists, his reputation is the greater, and he is looked upon as a man of an excellent head. And they are so very cunning, that they seldom have their booty taken from them, unless sometimes when, by the help of blood-hounds following them exactly upon the track, they may chance to fall into the hands of their adversaries. When being taken, they have so much persuasive eloquence, and so many smooth insinuating words at command, that if they do not move their judges, nay, and even their adversaries, (notwithstanding the severity of their natures,) to have mercy, yet they incite them to admiration and compassion."—CAMDEN'S *Britannia*.

The inhabitants of the valleys of Tyne and Reed were, in ancient times, so inordinately addicted to these depredations, that in 1564, the Incorporated Merchant-adventurers of Newcastle made a law that none born in these districts should be admitted apprentice. The inhabitants are stated to be so generally addicted to rapine, that no faith should be reposed in those proceeding from "such lewde and wicked progenitors." This regulation continued to stand unrepealed until 1771. A beggar, in an old play, describes himself as "born in Redesdale, in Northumberland, and come of a wight-riding surname, called the Robsons, good honest men and true, *saving a little shifting for their living, God help them!*"—a description which would have applied to most Borderers on both sides.

Reidswair, famed for a skirmish to which it gives name, [see Border Minstrelsy, vol. ii. p. 15,] is on the very edge of the Carter-fell, which divides England from Scotland. The Rooken is a place upon Reedwater. Bertram, being described as a native of these dales, where the habits of hostile depredation long survived the union of the crowns, may have been, in some degree, prepared by education for the exercise of a similar trade in the wars of the Bucaniers.

NOTE 27.

Hiding his face, lest foemen spy,
The sparkle of his swarthy eye.

P. 225.

After one of the recent battles, in which the Irish rebels were defeated, one of their most active leaders was found in a bog, in which he was immersed up to the shoulders, while his head was concealed by an impending ledge of turf. Being detected and seized, notwithstanding his precaution, he became solicitous to know how his retreat had been discovered. "I caught," answered the Sutherland Highlander, by whom he was taken, "the sparkle of your eye." Those who are accustomed to mark hares upon their form usually discover them by the same circumstance.

NOTE 28.

*Here stood a wretch, prepared to change
His soul's redemption for revenge!*—P. 226.

It is agreed by all the writers upon magic and witchcraft, that revenge was the most common motive for the pretended compact between Satan and his vassals.

NOTE 29.

*Of my marauding on the clowns
Of Calverley and Bradford downs.*
P. 227.

The troops of the King, when they first took the field, were as well disciplined as could be expected from circumstances. But as the circumstances of Charles became less favourable, and his funds for regularly paying his forces decreased, habits of military licence prevailed among them in greater excess. Lacy the player, who served his master during the Civil War, brought out, after the Restoration, a piece called The Old Troop, in which he seems to have commemorated some real incidents which occurred in his military career. The names of the officers of the Troop sufficiently express their habits. We have Fleaflint Plunder-master-General, Captain Ferretfarm, and Quarter-master Burn-drop. The officers of the Troop are in league with these worthies, and connive at their plundering the country for a suitable share in the booty. All this was undoubtedly drawn from the life, which Lacy had an opportunity to study. The moral of the whole is comprehended in a rebuke given to the lieutenant, whose disorders in the country are said to prejudice the King's cause more than his courage in the field could recompense. The piece is by no means void of farcical humour.

NOTE 30.

—*Brignall's woods, and Scargill's, wave,
E'en now, o'er many a sister cave.*—P. 228.

The banks of the Greta, below Rutherford Bridge, abound in seams of greyish slate, which are wrought in some places to a very great depth under ground, thus forming artificial caverns, which, when the seam has been exhausted, are gradually hidden by the underwood which grows in profusion upon the romantic banks of the river. In times of public confusion, they might be well adapted to the purposes of banditti.

NOTE 31.

When Spain waged warfare with our land.
P. 230.

There was a short war with Spain in 1625-6, which will be found to agree pretty well with the chronology of the poem. But probably Bertram held an opinion very common among the maritime heroes of the age, that "there was no peace beyond he Line." The Spanish *guarda-costas* were constantly employed in aggressions upon the trade and settlements of the English and French; and, by their own severities, gave room for the system of bucaniering, at first adopted in self-defence and retaliation, and afterwards persevered in from habit and thirst of plunder.

NOTE 32.

—*our comrades' strife.*—P. 230.

The laws of the Bucaniers, and their successors the Pirates, however severe and equitable, were, like other laws, often set aside by the stronger party. Their quarrels about the division of the spoil fill their history, and they as frequently arose out of mere frolic, or the tyrannical humour of their chiefs. An anecdote of Teach, (called Blackbeard), shows that their habitual indifference for human life extended to their companions, as well as their enemies and captives.

"One night, drinking in his cabin with Hands, the pilot, and another man, Blackbeard, without any provocation, privately draws out a small pair of pistols, and cocks them under the table, which, being perceived by the man, he withdrew upon deck, leaving Hands, the pilot, and the captain together. When the pistols were ready, he blew out the candles, and, crossing his hands, discharged them at his company. Hands, the master, was shot through the knee, and lamed for life; the other pistol did no execution."—JOHNSON's *History of Pirates.* Lond. 1733, 8vo, vol. i. p. 38.

NOTE 33.

Song.—Adieu for evermore.—P. 232.

The last verse of this song is taken from the fragment of an old Scottish ballad, of which

I only recollected two verses when the first edition of Rokeby was published. Mr. Thomas Sheridan kindly pointed out to me an entire copy of this beautiful song, which seems to express the fortunes of some followers of the Stuart family :—

> " It was a' for our rightful king
> That we left fair Scotland's strand,
> It was a' for our rightful king
> That we e'er saw Irish land,
>   My dear,
> That we e'er saw Irish land.
>
> "Now all is done that man can do
> And all is done in vain!
> My love! my native land, adieu!
> For I must cross the main,
>   My dear,
> For I must cross the main.
>
> " He turned him round and right about,
> All on the Irish shore,
> He gave his bridle-reins a shake,
> With, Adieu for evermore,
>   My dear !
> Adieu for evermore !
>
> "The soldier frae the war returns,
> And the merchant frae the main,
> But I hae parted wi' my love,
> And ne'er to meet again,
>   My dear,
> And ne'er to meet again.
>
> " When day is gone and night is come,
> And a' are boun' to sleep,
> I think on them that's far awa'
> The lee-lang night, and weep,
>   My dear,
> The lee-lang night, and weep."

NOTE 34.

Rere-cross on Stanmore.—P. 232.

This is a fragment of an old cross, with its pediment, surrounded by an intrenchment, upon the very summit of the waste ridge of Stanmore, near a small house of entertainment. The situation of the cross, and the pains taken to defend it, seem to indicate that it was intended for a land-mark of importance.

NOTE 35.

Hast thou lodged our deer ?—P. 233.

The duty of the ranger, or pricker, was first to lodge or harbour the deer ; *i.e.* to discover his retreat, and then to make his report to his prince or master.

NOTE 36.

*When Denmark's raven soar'd on high,
Triumphant through Northumbrian sky,
Till, hovering near, her fatal croak
Bade Reged's Britons dread the yoke.*—
P. 233.

About the year of God 866, the Danes, under their celebrated leaders Inguar (more properly Agnar), and Hubba, sons, it is said, of the still more celebrated Regnar Lodbrog, invaded Northumberland, bringing with them the magical standard, so often mentioned in poetry, called REAFEN, or Rumfan, from its bearing the figure of a raven :—

> " Wrought by the sisters of the Danish king,
> Of furious Ivar in a midnight hour :
> While the sick moon at their enchanted song
> Wrapt in pale tempest, labour'd through the
>   clouds,
> The demons of destruction then, they say,
> Were all abroad, and mixing with the woof
> Their baleful power : The sisters ever sung,
> 'Shake, standard, shake this ruin on our foes.' "
>
> THOMSON *and* MALLET'S *Alfred.*

The Danes renewed and extended their incursions, and began to colonize, establishing a kind of capital at York, from which they spread their conquests and incursions in every direction. Stanmore, which divides the mountains of Westmoreland and Cumberland, was probably the boundary of the Danish kingdom in that direction. The district to the west, known in ancient British history by the name of Reged, had never been conquered by the Saxons, and continued to maintain a precarious independence until it was ceded to Malcolm, King of Scots, by William the Conqueror, probably on account of its similarity in language and manners to the neighbouring British kingdom of Strath-Clyde.

Upon the extent and duration of the Danish sovereignty in Northumberland, the curious may consult the various authorities quoted in the *Gesta et Vestigia Danorum extra Daniam*, tom ii. p. 40. The most powerful of their Northumbrian leaders seems to have been Ivar, called, from the extent of his conquests, *Widfam*, that is, *The Strider*.

NOTE 37.

*Beneath the shade the Northmen came,
Fix'd on each vale a Runic name.*

P. 233.

The heathen Danes have left several traces of their religion in the upper part of Teesdale. Balder-garth, which derives its name from the unfortunate son of Odin, is a tract of waste land on the very ridge of Stanmore ; and a brook, which falls into the Tees near Barnard Castle, is named after the same deity. A field upon the banks of the Tees is also termed Woden-Croft, from the supreme deity of the Edda.

NOTE 38.

Who has not heard how brave O'Neale
In English blood imbrued his steel?

P. 234.

The O'Neale here meant, for more than one succeeded to the chieftainship during the reign of Elizabeth, was Hugh, the grandson of Con O'Neale, called Con Bacco, or the Lame. His father, Matthew O'Kelly, was illegitimate, and, being the son of a blacksmith's wife, was usually called Matthew the Blacksmith. His father, nevertheless, destined his succession to him; and he was created, by Elizabeth, Baron of Dungannon. Upon the death of Con Bacco, this Matthew was slain by his brother. Hugh narrowly escaped the same fate, and was protected by the English. Shane O'Neale, his uncle, called Shane Dymas, was succeeded by Turlough Lynogh O'Neale; after whose death Hugh, having assumed the chieftainship, became nearly as formidable to the English as any by whom it had been possessed. He rebelled repeatedly, and as often made submissions, of which it was usually a condition that he should not any longer assume the title of O'Neale; in lieu of which he was created Earl of Tyrone. But this condition he never observed longer than until the pressure of superior force was withdrawn. His baffling the gallant Earl of Essex in the field, and overreaching him in a treaty, was the induction to that nobleman's tragedy. Lord Mountjoy succeeded in finally subjugating O'Neale; but it was not till the succession of James, to whom he made personal submission, and was received with civility at court.

NOTE 39.

But chief arose his victor pride,
When that brave Marshal fought and died.

P. 235.

The chief victory which Tyrone obtained over the English was in a battle fought near Blackwater, while he besieged a fort garrisoned by the English, which commanded the passes into his country.

Tyrone is said to have entertained a personal animosity against the knight-marshal, Sir Henry Bagnal, whom he accused of detaining the letters which he sent to Queen Elizabeth, explanatory of his conduct, and offering terms of submission. The river, called by the English, Blackwater, is termed in Irish, Avon-Duff, which has the same signification. Both names are mentioned by Spenser in his "Marriage of the Thames and the Medway." But I understand that his verses relate not to the Blackwater of Ulster, but to a river of the same name in the south of Ireland:—

> "Swift Avon-Duff, which of the Englishmen
> Is called Blackwater."

NOTE 40.

The Tanist he to great O'Neale.—P. 235.

"*Eudox.* What is that which you call Tanist and Tanistry? These be names and terms never heard of nor known to us.

"*Iren.* It is a custom amongst all the Irish, that presently after the death of one of their chiefe lords or captaines, they doe presently assemble themselves to a place generally appointed and knowne unto them, to choose another in his stead, where they do nominate and elect, for the most part not the eldest sonne, nor any of the children of the lord deceased, but the next to him in blood, that is, the eldest and worthiest, as commonly the next brother unto him, if he have any, or the next cousin, or so forth, as any is elder in that kindred or sept; and then next to them doe they choose the next of the blood to be Tanist, who shall next succeed him in the said captainry, if he live thereunto.

"*Eudox.* Do they not use any ceremony in this election, for all barbarous nations are commonly great observers of ceremonies and superstitious rites?

"*Iren.* They use to place him that shall be their captaine upon a stone, always reserved to that purpose, and placed commonly upon a hill. In some of which I have seen formed and engraven a foot, which they say was the measure of their first captaine's foot; whereon hee standing, receives an oath to preserve all the ancient former customes of the countrey inviolable, and to deliver up the succession peaceably to his Tanist, and then hath a wand delivered unto him by some whose proper office that is; after which, descending from the stone, he turneth himself round, thrice forwards and thrice backwards.

"*Eudox.* But how is the Tanist chosen?

"*Iren.* They say he setteth but one foot upon the stone, and receiveth the like oath that the captaine did."—SPENSER'S *View of the State of Ireland,* apud *Works,* Lond. 1805, 8vo, vol. viii. p. 306.

The Tanist, therefore, of O'Neale, was the heir-apparent of his power. This kind of succession appears also to have regulated, in very remote times, the succession to the crown of Scotland. It would have been imprudent, if not impossible, to have asserted a minors' right of succession in those stormy days, when the principles of policy were summed up in my friend Mr. Wordsworth's lines:—

> "—— the good old rule
> Sufficeth them; the simple plan,
> That they should take who have the power,
> And they should keep who can."

NOTE 41.

With wild majestic port and tone,
Like envoy of some barbarous throne.
P. 235.

The Irish chiefs, in their intercourse with the English, and with each other, were wont to assume the language and style of independent royalty.

NOTE 42.

His foster-father was his guide.—P. 236.

There was no tie more sacred among the Irish than that which connected the foster-father, as well as the nurse herself, with the child they brought up.

NOTE 43.

Great Nial of the Pledges Nine.—P. 237.

Neal Naighvallach, or Of the Nine Hostages, is said to have been Monarch of all Ireland, during the end of the fourth or beginning of the fifth century. He exercised a predatory warfare on the coast of England and of Bretagne, or Armorica; and from the latter country brought off the celebrated Saint Patrick, a youth of sixteen, among other captives, whom he transported to Ireland. Neal derived his epithet from nine nations, or tribes, whom he held under his subjection, and from whom he took hostages.

NOTE 44.

Shane-Dymas wild.—P. 237.

This Shane-Dymas, or John the Wanton, held the title and power of O'Neale in the earlier part of Elizabeth's reign, against whom he rebelled repeatedly.

"This chieftain is handed down to us as the most proud and profligate man on earth. He was immoderately addicted to women and wine. He is said to have had 200 tuns of wine at once in his cellar at Dandram, but usquebaugh was his favourite liquor. He spared neither age nor condition of the fair sex. Altho' so illiterate that he could not write, he was not destitute of address, his understanding was strong, and his courage daring. He had 600 men for his guard; 4000 foot, 1000 horse for the field. He claimed superiority over all the lords of Ulster, and called himself king thereof."—CAMDEN.

When reduced to extremity by the English, and forsaken by his allies, this Shane-Dymas fled to Clandeboy, then occupied by a colony of Scottish Highlanders of the family of Mac-Donell. He was at first courteously received; but by degrees they began to quarrel about the slaughter of some of their friends whom Shane-Dymas had put to death, and advancing from words to deeds, fell upon him with their broad-swords, and cut him to pieces. After his death a law was made that none should presume to take the name and title of O'Neale.

NOTE 45.

—— Geraldine.—P. 237.

The O'Neales were closely allied with this powerful and warlike family; for Henry Owen O'Neale married the daughter of Thomas Earl of Kildare, and their son Con-More married his cousin-german, a daughter of Gerald Earl of Kildare. This Con-More cursed any of his posterity who should learn the English language, sow corn, or build houses, so as to invite the English to settle in their country. Others ascribe this anathema to his son Con-Bacco. Fearflatha O'Gnive, bard to the O'Neales of Clannaboy, complains in the same spirit of the towers and ramparts with which the strangers had *disfigured* the fair sporting fields of Erin.—See WALKER'S *Irish Bards*, p. 140.

NOTE 46.

—— his page, the next degree
In that old time to chivalry.—P. 237.

Originally, the order of chivalry embraced three ranks:—1. The Page; 2. The Squire; 3. The Knight;—a gradation which seems to have been imitated in the mystery of freemasonry. But, before the reign of Charles I., the custom of serving as a squire had fallen into disuse, though the order of the page was still, to a certain degree, in observance. This state of servitude was so far from inferring anything degrading, that it was considered as the regular school for acquiring every quality necessary for future distinction.

NOTE 47.

Seem'd half abandon'd to decay.—P. 243.

The ancient castle of Rokeby stood exactly upon the site of the present mansion, by which a part of its walls is enclosed. It is surrounded by a profusion of fine wood, and the park in which it stands is adorned by the junction of the Greta and of the Tees. The title of Baron Rokeby of Armagh was, in 1777, conferred on the Right Reverend Richard Robinson, Primate of Ireland, descended of the Robinsons, formerly of Rokeby, in Yorkshire.

NOTE 48.

—— The Felon Sow.—P. 245.

The ancient minstrels had a comic as well as a serious strain of romance; and although the examples of the latter are by far the most numerous, they are, perhaps, the less valuable. The comic romance was a sort of parody upon the usual subjects of minstrel poetry. If the latter described deeds of heroic achievement, and the events of the battle, the tourney, and the chase, the former, as in the Tournament of Tottenham, introduced a set of clowns debating in the field, with all the assumed circumstances of chivalry. One of the very best of these mock romances, and which has no small portion of comic humour, is the Hunting of the Felon Sow of Rokeby by the Friars of Richmond.

NOTE 49.

The Filea of O'Neale was he.—P. 245.

The Filea, or Ollamh Re Dan, was the proper bard, or, as the name literally implies, poet. Each chieftain of distinction had one or more in his service, whose office was usually hereditary. The late ingenious Mr. Cooper Walker, has assembled a curious collection of particulars concerning this order of men, in his Historical Memoirs of the Irish Bards. There were itinerant bards of less elevated rank, but all were held in the highest veneration.

NOTE 50.

Ah, Clandeboy! thy friendly floor
Slieve-Donard's oak shall light no more.
P. 245.

Clandeboy is a district of Ulster, formerly possessed by the sept of the O'Neales, and Slieve-Donard a romantic mountain in the same province. The clan was ruined after Tyrone's great rebellion, and their places of abode laid desolate. The ancient Irish, wild and uncultivated in other respects, did not yield even to their descendants in practising the most free and extended hospitality.

NOTE 51.

On Marwood Chase and Toller Hill.—P. 246.

Marwood Chase is the old Park extending

along the Durham side of the Tees, attached to Barnard Castle. Toller hill is an eminence on the Yorkshire side of the river, commanding a full view of the ruins.

NOTE 52.

The ancient English minstrel's dress.
P. 247.

Among the entertainments presented to Elizabeth at Kenilworth Castle, was the introduction of a person designed to represent a travelling minstrel, who entertained her with a solemn story out of the Acts of King Arthur. Of this person's dress and appearance Mr. Laneham has given us a very accurate account, transferred by Bishop Percy to the preliminary Dissertation on Minstrels, prefixed to The Reliques of Ancient Poetry, vol. i.

NOTE 53.

Littlecote Hall.—P. 250.

This Ballad is founded on a fact:—the horrible murder of an infant by Wild Dayrell, as he was called. He gave the house and lands as a bribe to the judge (Popham) in order to save his life. A few months after Dayrell broke his neck by a fall from his horse.—EDITOR.

NOTE 54.

As thick a smoke these hearths have given
At Hallow-tide, or Christmas-even.
P. 252.

Such an exhortation was, in similar circumstances, actually given to his followers by a Welsh chieftain.

NOTE 55.

O'er Hexham's altar hung my glove.—P. 260.

This custom among the Redesdale and Tynedale Borderers is mentioned in the interesting Life of Barnard Gilpin.

"It happened that a quarrel of this kind was on foot when Mr. Gilpin was at Rothbury, in those parts. During the two or three first days of his preaching, the contending parties observed some decorum, and never appeared at church together. At length, however, they met. One party had been early at church, and just as Mr. Gilpin began his sermon, the other entered. They stood not long silent. Inflamed at the sight of each other, they began to clash their weapons, for they were all armed with javelins and swords, and mutually approached. Awed, however, by the sacredness of the place, the tumult in some degree ceased. Mr. Gilpin proceeded: when again the combatants began to brandish their weapons, and draw towards each other. As a fray seemed near, Mr. Gilpin stepped from the pulpit, went between them, and addressed the leaders, put an end to the quarrel, for the present, but could not effect an entire reconciliation. They promised him, however, that till the sermon was over they would make no more disturbance. He then went again into the pulpit, and spent the rest of the time in endeavouring to make them ashamed of what they had done. His behaviour and discourse affected them so much, that, at his farther entreaty, they promised to forbear all acts of hostility while he continued in the country. And so much respected was he among them, that whoever was in fear of his enemy used to resort where Mr. Gilpin was, esteeming his presence the best protection.

"One Sunday morning, coming to a church in those parts, before the people were assembled, he observed a glove hanging up, and was informed by the sexton, that it was meant as a challenge to any one who should take it down. Mr. Gilpin ordered the sexton to reach it to him; but upon his utterly refusing to touch it, he took it down himself, and put it into his breast. When the people were assembled, he went into the pulpit, and, before he concluded his sermon, took occasion to rebuke them severely for these inhuman challenges. 'I hear,' saith he, 'that one among you hath hanged up a glove, even in this sacred place, threatening to fight any one who taketh it down: see, I have taken it down;' and, pulling out the glove, he held it up to the congregation, and then showed them how unsuitable such savage practices were to the profession of Christianity, using such persuasives to mutual love as he thought would most affect them."—*Life of Barnard Gilpin.* Lond. 1753, 8vo, p. 177.

NOTE 56.

A horseman arm'd, at headlong speed.— P. 264.

This, and what follows, is taken from a real achievement of Major Robert Philipson, called from his desperate and adventurous courage, Robin the Devil.

THE BRIDAL OF TRIERMAIN.

NOTE 1.

The Baron of Triermain.—P. 273.

Triermain was a fief of the Barony of Gilsland, in Cumberland ; it was possessed by a Saxon family at the time of the Conquest, but, "after the death of Gilmore, Lord of Tryermaine and Torcrossock, Hubert Vaux gave Tryermaine and Torcrossock to his second son, Ranulph Vaux ; which Ranulph afterwards became heir to his elder brother Robert, the founder of Lanercost, who died without issue. Ranulph, being Lord of all Gilsland, gave Gilmore's lands to his younger son, named Roland, and let the Barony descend to his eldest son Robert, son of Ranulph. Ronald had issue Alexander, and he Ranulph, after whom succeeded Robert, and they were named Rolands successively, that were lords thereof, until the reign of Edward the Fourth. That house gave for arms, Vert, a bend dexter, chequy, or and gules,"—BURNS's *Antiquities of Westmoreland and Cumberland,* vol. ii. p. 482.

NOTE 2.

He pass'd red Penrith's Table Round.—P. 274.

A circular intrenchment, about half a mile from Penrith, is thus popularly termed. The circle within the ditch is about one hundred and sixty paces in circumference, with openings, or approaches, directly opposite to each other. As this ditch is on the inner side, it could not be intended for the purpose of defence, and it has reasonably been conjectured, that the enclosure was designed for the solemn exercise of feats of chivalry, and the embankment around for the convenience of the spectators.

NOTE 3.

Mayburgh's mound.—P. 274.

Higher up the river Eamont than Arthur's Round Table, is a prodigious enclosure of great antiquity, formed by a collection of stones upon the top of a gently sloping hill, called Mayburgh. In the plain which it encloses there stands erect an unhewn stone of twelve feet in height. Two similar masses are said to have been destroyed during the memory of man. The whole appears to be a monument of Druidical times.

NOTE 4.

The sable tarn.—P. 275.

The small lake called Scales-tarn lies so deeply embosomed in the recesses of the huge mountain called Saddleback, more poetically Glaramara, is of such great depth, and so completely hidden from the sun, that it is said its beams never reach it, and that the reflection of the stars may be seen at mid-day.

NOTE 5.

The terrors of Tintadgel's spear.—P. 277.

Tintadgel Castle, in Cornwall, is reported to have been the birth-place of King Arthur.

NOTE 6.

Scattering a shower of fiery dew.—P. 280.

The author has an indistinct recollection of an adventure, somewhat similar to that which is here ascribed to King Arthur, having befallen one of the ancient Kings of Denmark. The horn in which the burning liquor was presented to that Monarch, is said still to be preserved in the Royal Museum at Copenhagen.

NOTE 7.

The Monarch, breathless and amazed,
Back on the fatal castle gazed—
Nor tower nor donjon could he spy,
Darkening against the morning sky.
P. 280.

— "We now gained a view of the Vale of St. John's, a very narrow dell, hemmed in by mountains, through which a small brook makes many meanderings, washing little enclosures of grass-ground, which stretch up the rising of the hills. In the widest part of the dale you are struck with the appearance of an ancient ruined castle, which seems to stand upon the summit of a little mount, the mountains around forming an amphitheatre. The massive bulwark shows a front of various towers, and makes an awful, rude, and Gothic appearance, with its lofty turrets and rugged battlements; we traced the galleries, the bending arches, the buttresses. The greatest antiquity stands characterized in its architecture; the inhabitants near it assert it is an antediluvian structure.

"The traveller's curiosity is roused, and he prepares to make a nearer approach, when that curiosity is put upon the rack, by his being assured, that, if he advances, certain genii who govern the place, by virtue of their supernatural art and necromancy, will strip it of all its beauties, and by enchantment, transform the magic walls. The vale seems adapted for the habitation of such beings; its gloomy recesses and retirements look like the haunts of evil spirits. There was no delusion in the report; we were soon convinced of its truth: for this piece of antiquity, so venerable and noble in its aspect, as we drew near, changed its figure, and proved no other than a shaken massive pile of rocks, which stand in the midst of this little vale, disunited from the adjoining mountains, and have so much the real form and resemblance of a castle, that they bear the name of the Castle Rocks of St. John."—HUTCHINSON'S *Excursion to the Lakes,* p. 121.

NOTE 8.

Twelve bloody fields, with glory fought.
P. 280.

Arthur is said to have defeated the Saxons in twelve pitched battles, and to have achieved the other feats alluded to in the text.

NOTE 9.

The flower of chivalry.
There Galaad sat with manly grace,
Yet maiden meekness in his face;
There Morolt of the iron mace,
And love-lorn Tristrem there.
P. 281.

The characters named in the stanza are all of them more or less distinguished in the romances which treat of King Arthur and his Round Table, and their names are strung together, according to the established custom of minstrels upon such occasions; for example, in the ballad of the Marriage of Sir Gawaine:—

"Sir Lancelot, Sir Stephen bolde,
  They rode with him that daye,
And foremost of the companye,
  There rode the stewarde Kaye.

"Soe did Sir Banier, and Sir Bore,
  And eke Sir Garratte keen,
Sir Tristrem too, that gentle knight,
  To the forest fresh and greene."

NOTE 10.

—— *Lancelot that ever more,*
Look'd stol'n-wise on the Queen.
P. 281.

Upon this delicate subject hear Richard Robinson, citizen of London, in his Assertion of King Arthur :—"But as it is a thing sufficiently apparent that she (Guenever, wife of King Arthur) was beautiful, so it is a thing doubted whether she was chaste, yea or no. Truly, so far as I can with honestie, I would spare the impayred honour of noble women. But yet the truth of the historie pluckes me by the eare, and willeth not onely, but commandeth me to declare what the ancients have deemed of her. To wrestle or contend with so great authoritie were indeed unto me a controversie, and that greate."—*Assertion of King Arthure.* Imprinted by John Wolfe, London, 1582.

NOTE 11.

There were two who loved their neighbour's wives,
And one who loved his own.—P. 282.

" In our forefathers' tyme, when Papistrie, as a standyng poole covered and overflowed all England, fewe books were read in our tongue, savying certaine bookes of chevalrie, as they said, for pastime and pleasure ; which, as some say, were made in the monasteries, by idle monks or wanton chanons. As one, for example, La Morte d'Arthure ; the whole pleasure of which book standeth in two special poyntes, in open manslaughter and bold bawdrye ; in which booke they be counted the noblest knightes that do kill most men without any quarrell, and commit foulest adulteries by subtlest shiftes ; as Sir Launcelot, with the wife of King Arthur, his master ; Sir Tristram, with the wife of King Marke, his uncle ; Sir

Lamerocke, with the wife of King Lote, that was his own aunt. This is good stuff for wise men to laugh at ; or honest men to take pleasure at : yet I know when God's Bible was banished the Court, and La Morte d'Arthure received into the Prince's chamber."—AS-CHAM'S *Schoolmaster.*

NOTE 12.

Who won the cup of gold.—P. 282.

See the comic tale of the Boy and the Mantle, in the third volume of Percy's Reliques of Ancient Poetry, from the Breton or Norman original of which Ariosto is supposed to have taken his Tale of the Enchanted Cup.

NOTE 13.

Whose logic is from Single-speech.—P. 286.

See "Parliamentary Logic, &c.," by the Hon. W. G. Hamilton (1808), commonly called "Single-Speech Hamilton."

NOTE TO THE POEM.

Scott composed this poem with the intention that the public should attribute it to his friend Mr. Erskine (Lord Kinedder). The joke succeeded ; but on the third edition being published, Lord Kinedder avowed the true author, the deception having gone further than either he or Scott intended. We mention this fact in order to explain the preface.—ED.

THE LORD OF THE ISLES.

NOTE 1.

Thy rugged halls, Artornish! rung.—P. 304.

THE ruins of the Castle of Artornish are situated upon a promontory, on the Morven, or mainland side of the Sound of Mull, a name given to the deep arm of the sea, which divides that island from the continent. The situation is wild and romantic in the highest degree, having on the one hand a high and precipitous chain of rocks overhanging the sea, and on the other the narrow entrance to the beautiful salt-water lake, called Loch Alline, which is in many places finely fringed with copsewood. The ruins of Artornish are not now very considerable, and consist chiefly of the remains of an old keep, or tower, with fragments of outward defences. But, in for-

mer days, it was a place of great consequence, being one of the principal strongholds, which the Lords of the Isles, during the period of their stormy independence, possessed upon the mainland of Argyleshire. It is almost opposite to the Bay of Aros, in the Island of Mull, where there was another castle, the occasional residence of the Lords of the Isles.

NOTE 2.

Rude Heiskar's seal through surges dark,
Will long pursue the minstrel's bark.

P. 304.

The seal displays a taste for music, which could scarcely be expected from his habits and local predilections. They will long follow a boat in which any musical instrument is played, and even a tune simply whistled has attractions for them. The Dean of the Isles says of Heiskar, a small uninhabited rock, about twelve (Scottish) miles from the Isle of Uist, that an infinite slaughter of seals takes place there.

NOTE 3.

—— a turret's airy head,
Slender and steep, and battled round,
O'erlook'd, dark Mull! thy mighty Sound.

P. 305.

The Sound of Mull, which divides that island from the continent of Scotland, is one of the most striking scenes which the Hebrides afford to the traveller. Sailing from Oban to Aros, or Tobermory, through a narrow channel, yet deep enough to bear vessels of the largest burden, he has on his left the bold and mountainous shores of Mull; on the right those of that district of Argyleshire, called Morven, or Morvern, successively indented by deep salt-water lochs, running up many miles inland. To the south-eastward arise a prodigious range of mountains, among which Cruachan-Ben is pre-eminent. And to the north-east is the no less huge and picturesque range of the Ardnamurchan hills. Many ruinous castles, situated generally upon cliffs overhanging the ocean, add interest to the scene.

NOTE 4.

The heir of mighty Somerled.—P. 305.

Somerled was thane of Argyle and Lord of the Isles, about the middle of the twelfth century. He seems to have exercised his authority in both capacities, independent of the crown of Scotland, against which he often stood in hostility. He made various incursions upon the western lowlands during the reign of Malcolm IV., and seems to have made peace with him upon the terms of an independent prince, about the year 1157. In 1164, he resumed the war against Malcolm, and invaded Scotland with a large, but probably a tumultuary army, collected in the isles, in the mainland of Argyleshire, and in the neighbouring provinces of Ireland. He was defeated and slain in an engagement with a very inferior force, near Renfrew.

NOTE 5.

Lord of the Isles.—P. 305.

The representative of this independent principality, for such it seems to have been, though acknowledging occasionally the pre-eminence of the Scottish crown, was, at the period of the poem, Angus, called Angus Og; but the name has been, *euphoniæ gratia*, exchanged for that of Ronald, which frequently occurs in the genealogy. Angus was a protector of Robert Bruce, whom he received in his Castle of Dunnaverty, during the time of his greatest distress.

NOTE 6.

—— The House of Lorn.—P. 306.

The House of Lorn, as we oberved in a former note, was, like the Lord of the Isles, descended from a son of Somerled, slain at Renfrew, in 1164. This son obtained the succession of his mainland territories, comprehending the greater part of the three districts of Lorn, in Argyleshire, and of course might rather be considered as petty princes than feudal barons. They assumed the patronymic appellation of MacDougal, by which they are distinguished in the history of the Middle Ages.

NOTE 7.

Awaked before the rushing prow,
The mimic fires of ocean glow,
Those lightnings of the wave.

P. 308.

The phenomenon called by sailors Sea-fire, is one of the most beautiful and interesting which is witnessed in the Hebrides. At times the ocean appears entirely illuminated around the vessel, and a long train of lambent coruscations are perpetually bursting upon the sides of the vessel, or pursuing her wake through the darkness.

NOTE 8.

That keen knight, De Argentine.—P. 311.

Sir Egidius, or Giles de Argentine, was one of the most accomplished knights of the period. He had served in the wars of Henry of Luxemburg with such high reputation, that he was, in popular estimation, the third worthy of the age. Those to whom fame assigned precedence over him were, Henry of Luxemburg himself, and Robert Bruce. Argentine had warred in Palestine, encountered thrice with the Saracens, and had slain two antagonists in each engagement:—an easy matter, he said, for one Christian knight to slay two Pagan dogs.

NOTE 9.

"*Fill me the mighty cup!*" he said,
"*Erst own'd by royal Somerled.*"

P. 311.

A Hebridean drinking cup, of the most

ancient and curious workmanship, has been long preserved in the castle of Dunvegan, in Skye, the romantic seat of Mac-Leod of Mac-Leod, the chief of that ancient and powerful clan. The horn of Rorie More, preserved in the same family, and recorded by Dr. Johnson, is not to be compared with this piece of antiquity, which is one of the greatest curiosities in Scotland.

NOTE 10.

—— *the rebellious Scottish crew,*
Who to Rath-Erin's shelter drew,
With Carrick's outlaw'd Chief.
P. 313.

It must be remembered by all who have read the Scottish history, that after he had slain Comyn at Dumfries, and asserted his right to the Scottish crown, Robert Bruce was reduced to the greatest extremity by the English and their adherents. He was crowned at Scone by the general consent of the Scottish barons, but his authority endured but a short time. According to the phrase said to have been used by his wife, he was for that year "a summer king, but not a winter one."

NOTE 11.

The Broach of Lorn—P. 313.

It has been generally mentioned in the preceding notes, that Robert Bruce, after his defeat at Methven, being hard pressed by the English, endeavoured, with the dispirited remnant of his followers, to escape from Breadalbane and the mountains of Perthshire into the Argyleshire Highlands. But he was encountered and repulsed, after a very severe engagement, by the Lord of Lorn. Bruce's personal strength and courage were never displayed to greater advantage than in this conflict. There is a tradition in the family of the Mac-Dougals of Lorn, that their chieftain engaged in personal battle with Bruce himself, while the latter was employed in protecting the retreat of his men; that Mac-Dougal was struck down by the king, whose strength of body was equal to his vigour of mind, and would have been slain on the spot, had not two of Lorn's vassals, a father and son, whom tradition terms Mac-Keoch, rescued him, by seizing the mantle of the monarch, and dragging him from above his adversary. Bruce rid himself of these foes by two blows of his redoubted battle-axe, but was so closely pressed by the other followers of Lorn, that he was forced to abandon the mantle, and broach which fastened it, clasped in the dying grasp of the Mac-Keochs. A studded broach, said to have

been that which King Robert lost upon this occasion, was long preserved in the family of Mac-Dougal, and was lost in a fire which consumed their temporary residence.

NOTE 12.

When Comyn fell beneath the knife
Of that fell homicide The Bruce.—P. 310.

Vain Kirkpatrick's bloody dirk,
Making sure of murder's work.—P. 313.

Every reader must recollect that the proximate cause of Bruce's asserting his right to the crown of Scotland, was the death of John, called the Red Comyn. The causes of this act of violence, equally extraordinary from the high rank both of the perpetrator and sufferer, and from the place where the slaughter was committed, are variously related by the Scottish and English historians, and cannot now be ascertained. The fact that they met at the high altar of the Minorites, or Greyfriars' Church in Dumfries, that their difference broke out into high and insulting language, and that Bruce drew his dagger and stabbed Comyn, is certain. Rushing to the door of the church, Bruce met two powerful barons, Kirkpatrick of Closeburn, and James de Lindsay, who eagerly asked him what tidings? "Bad tidings," answered Bruce; "I doubt I have slain Comyn."—"Doubtest thou?" said Kirkpatrick; "I make sicker," (*i. e.* sure.) With these words, he and Lindsay rushed into the church, and despatched the wounded Comyn. The Kirkpatricks of Closeburn assumed, in memory of this deed, a hand holding a dagger, with the memorable words, "I make sicker."

NOTE 13.

Barendown fled fast away,
Fled the fiery De la Haye.—P. 313.

These knights are enumerated by Barbour among the small number of Bruce's adherents, who remained in arms with him after the battle of Methven.

NOTE 14.

Was't not enough to Ronald's bower,
I brought thee, like a paramour.—P. 316.

It was anciently customary in the Highlands to bring the bride to the house of the husband. Nay, in some cases the complaisance was stretched so far, that she remained there upon trial for a twelvemonth; and the bridegroom, even after this period of cohabitation, retained an option of refusing to fulfil his engagement. It is said that a desperate feud ensued between the clans of Mac-Donald of Sleate and Mac-Leod, owing to the former chief having availed himself of this licence to send back to Dunvegan a sister, or daughter of the latter. Mac-Leod, resenting the indignity, observed, that since there was no wedding bonfire, there should be one to solemnize the divorce. Accordingly, he burned and laid waste the territories of Mac-Donald, who retaliated, and a deadly feud, with all its accompaniments, took place in form

NOTE 15.

Since matchless Wallace first had been,
In mock'ry crown'd with wreaths of green.
P. 317.

Stow gives the following curious account of the trial and execution of this celebrated patriot :—" William Wallace, who had oft-times set Scotland in great trouble, was taken and brought to London, with great numbers of men and women wondering upon him. He was lodged in the house of William Delect, a citizen of London, in Fenchurch-street. On the morrow, being the eve of St. Bartholomew, he was brought on horseback to Westminster. John Legrave and Geffrey, knights, the mayor, sheriffs, and aldermen of London, and many others, both on horseback and on foot, accompanying him ; and in the great hall at Westminster, he being placed on the south bench, crowned with laurel, for that he had said in times past that he ought to bear a crown in that hall, as it was commonly reported ; and being appeached for a traitor by Sir Peter Malorie, the king's justice, he answered, that he was never traitor to the King of England ; but for other things whereof he was accused, he confessed them ; and was after headed and quartered."—STOW, *Chr.* p. 209. There is something singularly doubtful about the mode in which Wallace was taken. That he was betrayed to the English is indubitable ; and popular fame charges Sir John Menteith with the indelible infamy. " Accursed," says Arnold Blair, " be the day of nativity of John de Menteith, and may his name be struck out of the book of life." But John de Menteith was all along a zealous favourer of the English interest, and was governor of Dumbarton Castle by commission from Edward the First ; and therefore, as the accurate Lord Hailes has observed, could not be the friend and confidant of Wallace, as tradition states him to be. The truth seems to be, that Menteith, thoroughly engaged in the English interest, pursued Wallace closely, and made him prisoner through the treachery of an attendant, whom Peter

Langtoft calls Jack Short. The infamy of seizing Wallace must rest, therefore, between a degenerate Scottish nobleman, the vassal of England, and a domestic, the obscure agent of his treachery ; between Sir John Menteith, son of Walter, Earl of Menteith, and the traitor Jack Short.

NOTE 16.

Was not the life of Athole shed,
To soothe the tyrant's sicken'd bed.
P. 317.

John de Strathbogie, Earl of Athole, had attempted to escape out of the kingdom, but a storm cast him upon the coast, when he was taken, sent to London, and executed, with circumstances of great barbarity, being first half strangled, then let down from the gallows while yet alive, barbarously dismembered, and his body burnt. It may surprise the reader to learn, that this was a *mitigated* punishment ; for in respect that his mother was a grand-daughter of King John, by his natural son Richard, he was not drawn on a sledge to execution, "that point was forgiven," and he made the passage on horseback. Matthew of Westminster tells us that King Edward, then extremely ill, received great ease from the news that his relative was apprehended. " *Quo audito, Rex Angliæ, etsi gravissimo morbo tunc langueret, levius tamen tulit dolorem.*" To this singular expression the text alludes.

NOTE 17.

While I the blessed cross advance,
And expiate this unhappy chance,
In Palestine, with sword and lance.
P. 318.

Bruce uniformly professed, and probably felt, compunction for having violated the sanctuary of the church by the slaughter of Comyn; and finally, in his last hours, in testimony of his faith, penitence, and zeal, he requested James Lord Douglas to carry his heart to Jerusalem, to be there deposited in the Holy Sepulchre.

NOTE 18.

De Bruce! I rose with purpose dread
To speak my curse upon thy head.
P. 318.

So soon as the notice of Comyn's slaughter reached Rome, Bruce and his adherents were excommunicated. It was published first by the Archbishop of York, and renewed at different times, particularly by Lambyrton, Bishop of St. Andrews, in 1308; but it does not appear to have answered the purpose which the English monarch expected. Indeed, for reasons which it may be difficult to trace, the thunders of Rome descended upon the Scottish mountains with less effect than in more fertile countries. Probably the comparative poverty of the benefices occasioned that fewer foreign clergy settled in Scotland ; and the interests of the native churchmen were linked with that of their country. Many of the Scottish prelates, Lambyrton the primate particularly, declared for Bruce, while he was yet under the ban of the church, although he afterwards again changed sides.

NOTE 19.

*A hunted wanderer on the wild,
On foreign shores a man exiled.*

P. 318.

This is not metaphorical. The echoes of Scotland did actually

" —— ring
With the bloodhounds that bayed for her fugitive king."

A very curious and romantic tale is told by Barbour upon this subject, which may be abridged as follows :—

When Bruce had again got footing in Scotland in the spring of 1306, he continued to be in a very weak and precarious condition, gaining, indeed, occasional advantages, but obliged to fly before his enemies whenever they assembled in force. Upon one occasion, while he was lying with a small party in the wilds of Cumnock, in Ayrshire, Aymer de Valence, Earl of Pembroke, with his inveterate foe John of Lorn, came against him suddenly with eight hundred Highlanders, besides a large body of men-at-arms. They brought with them a slough-dog, or bloodhound, which, some say, had been once a favourite with the Bruce himself, and therefore was least likely to lose the trace.

Bruce, whose force was under four hundred men, continued to make head against the cavalry, till the men of Lorn had nearly cut off his retreat. Perceiving the danger of his situation, he acted as the celebrated and ill-requited Mina is said to have done in similar circumstances. He divided his force into three parts, appointed a place of rendezvous, and commanded them to retreat by different routes. But when John of Lorn arrived at the spot where they divided, he caused the hound to be put upon the trace, which immediately directed him to the pursuit of that party which Bruce headed. This, therefore, Lorn pursued with his whole force, paying no attention to the others. The king again sub-

divided his small body into three parts, and with the same result, for the pursuers attached themselves exclusively to that which he led in person. He then caused his followers to disperse, and retained only his foster-brother in his company. The slough-dog followed the trace, and, neglecting the others, attached himself and his attendants to the pursuit of the king. Lorn became convinced that his enemy was nearly in his power, and detached five of his most active attendants to follow him, and interrupt his flight. They did so with all the agility of mountaineers. "What aid wilt thou make ?" said Bruce to his single attendant, when he saw the five men gain ground on him. "The best I can," replied his foster-brother. "Then," said Bruce, "here I make my stand." The five pursuers came up fast. The king took three to himself, leaving the other two to his foster-brother. He slew the first who encountered him ; but observing his foster-brother hard pressed, he sprung to his assistance, and despatched one of his assailants. Leaving him to deal with the survivor, he returned upon the other two, both of whom he slew before his foster-brother had despatched his single antagonist. When this hard encounter was over, with a courtesy, which in the whole work marks Bruce's character, he thanked his foster-brother for his aid. "It likes you to say so," answered his follower ; "but you yourself slew four of the five."—"True," said the king, "but only because I had better opportunity than you. They were not apprehensive of me when they saw me encounter three, so I had a moment's time to spring to thy aid, and to return equally unexpectedly upon my own opponents."

In the meanwhile Lorn's party approached rapidly, and the king and his foster-brother betook themselves to a neighbouring wood. Here they sat down, for Bruce was exhausted by fatigue, until the cry of the slough-hound came so near, that his foster-brother entreated Bruce to provide for his safety by retreating further. "I have heard," answered the king, "that whosoever will wade a bow-shot length down a running-stream, shall make the slough-hound lose scent.—Let us try the experiment, for were yon devilish hound silenced, I should care little for the rest."

Lorn in the meanwhile advanced, and found the bodies of his slain vassals, over whom he made his moan, and threatened the most deadly vengeance. Then he followed the hound to the side of the brook down which the king had waded a great way. Here the hound was at fault, and John of Lorn, after long attempting in vain to recover Bruce's trace, relinquished the pursuit.

"Others," says Barbour, "affirm, that upon this occasion the king's life was saved by an excellent archer who accompanied him, and who perceiving they would be finally taken by means of the blood-hound hid himself in a thicket, and shot him with an arrow. In which way," adds the metrical biographer, "this escape happened I am uncertain, but at that brook the king escaped from his pursuers."

NOTE 20.

" Alas! dear youth, the unhappy time,"
Answer'd the Bruce, " must bear the crime,
Since, guiltier far than you,
Even I"—he paused ; for Falkirk's woes
*Upon his conscious soul arose.--*P. 320.

I have followed the vulgar and inaccurate tradition, that Bruce fought against Wallace, and the array of Scotland, at the fatal battle of Falkirk. The story, which seems to have no better authority than that of Blind Harry, bears, that having made much slaughter during the engagement, he sat down to dine with the conquerors without washing the filthy witness from his hands.

"Fasting he was, and had been in great need,
Blooded were all his weapons and his weed;
Southeron lords scorn'd him in terms rude,
And said, Behold yon Scot eats his own blood.

"Then rued he sore, for reason bad be known,
That blood and land alike should be his own;
With them he long was, ere he got away,
But contrair Scots he fought not from that day."

The account given by most of our historians, of the conversation between Bruce and Wallace over the Carron river, is equally apocryphal. There is full evidence that Bruce was not at that time on the English side, nor present at the battle of Falkirk ; nay, that he acted as a guardian of Scotland, along with John Comyn, in the name of Baliol, and in opposition to the English.

NOTE 21.

These are the savage wilds that lie
North of Strathnardill and Dunskye.
P. 321.

The extraordinary piece of scenery which I have here attempted to describe is, I think, unparalleled in any part of Scotland, at least in any which I have happened to visit. It lies just upon the frontier of the Laird of Mac-Leod's country, which is thereabouts divided from the estate of Mr. Mac-Allister of Strath-Aird, called Strathnardill by the Dean of the Isles.

NOTE 22.

And mermaid's alabaster grot,
Who bathes her limbs in sunless well,
Deep in Strathaird's enchanted cell.
P. 326.

Imagination can hardly conceive anything more beautiful than the extraordinary grotto discovered not many years since upon the estate of Alexander Mac-Allister, Esq., of Strathaird. It has since been much and deservedly celebrated, and a full account of its beauties has been published by Dr. Mac-Leay of Oban. The general impression may perhaps be gathered from the following extract from a journal, which, written under the feelings of the moment, is likely to be more accurate than any attempt to recollect the impressions then received:—"The first entrance to this celebrated cave is rude and unpromising; but the light of the torches, with which we were provided, was soon reflected from the roof, floor, and walls, which seem as if they were sheeted with marble, partly smooth, partly rough with frost-work and rustic ornaments, and partly seeming to be wrought into statuary. The floor forms a steep and difficult ascent, and might be fancifully compared to a sheet of water, which, while it rushed whitening and foaming down a declivity, had been suddenly arrested and consolidated by the spell of an enchanter. Upon attaining the summit of this ascent, the cave opens into a splendid gallery, adorned with the most dazzling crystallizations, and finally descends with rapidity to the brink of a pool of the most limpid water, about four or five yards broad. There opens beyond this pool a portal arch, formed by two columns of white spar, with beautiful chasing upon the sides, which promises a continuation of the cave. One of our sailors swam across, for there is no other mode of passing, and informed us (as indeed we partly saw by the light he carried) that the enchantment of Mac-Allister's cave terminates with this portal, a little beyond which there was only a rude cavern, speedily choked with stones and earth. But the pool, on the brink of which we stood, surrounded by the most fanciful mouldings, in a substance resembling white marble, and distinguished by the depth and purity of its waters, might have been the bathing grotto of a naiad. The groups of combined figures projecting, or embossed, by which the pool is surrounded, are exquisitely elegant and fanciful. A statuary might catch beautiful hints from the singular and romantic disposition of those stalactites. There is scarce a form or group on which active fancy may not trace figures or grotesque ornaments, which have been gradually moulded in this cavern by the dropping of the calcareous water hardening into petrifactions. Many of those fine groups have been injured by the senseless rage of appropriation of recent tourists; and the grotto had lost, (I am informed,) through the smoke of torches, something of that vivid silver tint which was originally one of its chief distinctions. But enough of beauty remains to compensate for all that may be lost."—Mr. Mac-Allister of Strathaird has, with great propriety, built up the exterior entrance to this cave, in order that strangers may enter properly attended by a guide, to prevent any repetition of the wanton and selfish injury which this singular scene has already sustained.

NOTE 23.

Yet to no sense of selfish wrongs,
Bear witness with me, Heaven, belongs
My joy o'er Edward's bier.—P. 328.

The generosity which does justice to the character of an enemy, often marks Bruce's sentiments, as recorded by the faithful Barbour. He seldom mentions a fallen enemy without praising such good qualities as he might possess. I shall only take one instance. Shortly after Bruce landed in Carrick, in 1306, Sir Ingram Bell, the English governor of Ayr, engaged a wealthy yeoman, who had hitherto been a follower of Bruce, to undertake the task of assassinating him. The king learned this treachery, as he is said to have done other secrets of the enemy, by means of a female with whom he had an intrigue. Shortly after he was possessed of this information, Bruce, resorting to a small thicket at a distance from his men, with only a single page to attend him, met the traitor, accompanied by two of his sons. They approached him with their wonted familiarity, but Bruce, taking his page's bow and arrow, commanded them to keep at a distance. As they still pressed forward with professions of zeal for his person and service, he, after a second warning, shot the father with the arrow; and being assaulted successively by the two sons, despatched first one, who was armed with an axe, then as the other charged him with a spear, avoided the thrust, struck the head from the spear, and cleft the skull of the assassin with a blow of his two-handed sword.

NOTE 24.

And Ronin's mountains dark have sent
Their hunters to the shore.—P. 330.

Ronin (popularly called Rum, a name which a poet may be pardoned for avoiding if possible) is a very rough and mountainous island, adjacent to those of Eigg and Cannay. There is almost no arable ground upon it, so that, except in the plenty of the deer, which of course are now nearly extirpated, it still deserves the description bestowed by the archdean of the Isles. "Ronin, sixteen myle north-west from the ile of Coll, lyes ane ile callit Ronin Ile, of sixteen myle long, and six in bredthe in the narrowest, ane forest of heigh mountains, and abundance of little deir in it, quhilk deir will never be slane dounewith, but the principal saittis man be in the height of the hill, because the deir will be callit upwart ay be the tainchell or without tynchel they will pass upwart perforce. In this ile will be gotten about Britane als many wild nests upon the plane mure as men pleasis to gadder, and yet by resson the fowls has few to start them except deir. This ile lyes from the west to the eist in lenth, and pertains to M'Kenabrey of Colla. Many solan geese are in this ile."—MONRO'S *Description of the Western Isles,* p. 18

NOTE 25.

On Scooreigg next a warning light
Summon'd her warriors to the fight;
A numerous race, ere stern Macleod
O'er their bleak shores in vengeance strode.
P. 330.

These, and the following lines of the stanza, refer to a dreadful tale of feudal vengeance, of which unfortunately there are relics that still attest the truth. Scoor-Eigg is a high peak in the centre of the small Isle of Eigg, or Egg. It is well known to mineralogists, as affording many interesting specimens, and to others whom chance or curiosity may lead to the island, for the astonishing view of the mainland and neighbouring isles, which it commands.

26th August, 1814.—At seven this morning we were in the Sound which divides the Isle of Rum from that of Eigg. The latter, although hilly and rocky, and traversed by a remarkably high and barren ridge, called Scoor-Rigg, has, in point of soil, a much more promising appearance. Southward of both lies the Isle of Muich, or Muck, a low and fertile island, and though the least, yet probably the most valuable of the three. We manned the boat and rowed along the shore of Egg in quest of a cavern, which had been the memorable scene of a horrid feudal vengeance. We had rounded more than half the island, admiring the entrance of many a bold natural cave, which its rocks exhibited, without finding that which we sought, until we procured a guide. Nor, indeed, was it surprising that it should have escaped the search of strangers, as there are no outward indications more than might distinguish the entrance of a fox-earth. This noted cave has a very narrow opening, through which one can hardly creep on his knees and hands. It rises steep and lofty within, and runs into the bowels of the rock to the depth of 255 measured feet; the height at the entrance may be about three feet, but rises within to eighteen or twenty, and the breadth may vary in the same proportion. The rude and stony bottom of this cave is strewed with the bones of men, women, and children, the sad relics of the ancient inhabitants of the island, 200 in number, who were slain on the following occasion: —The Mac-Donalds of the Isle of Egg, a people dependent on Clan-Ranald, had done some injury to the Laird of Mac-Leod. The tradition of the isle says, that it was by a personal attack on the chieftain, in which his back was broken. But that of the other isles bears, more probably, that the injury was offered to two or three of the Mac-Leods, who, landing upon Eigg, and using some freedom with the young women, were seized by the islanders, bound hand and foot, and turned adrift in a boat, which the winds and waves safely conducted to Skye. To avenge the offence given, Mac-Leod sailed with such a body of men as rendered resistance hopeless. The natives, fearing his vengeance, concealed themselves in this cavern, and, after a strict search, the Mac-Leods went on board their galleys, after doing what mischief they could, concluding the inhabitants had left the isle, and betaken themselves to the Long Island, or some of Clan-Ranald's other possessions. But next morning they espied from the vessels a man upon the island, and immediately landing again, they traced his retreat by the marks of his footsteps, a light snow being unhappily on the ground. Mac-Leod then surrounded the cavern, summoned the subterranean garrison, and demanded that the individuals who had offended him should be delivered up to him. This was peremptorily refused. The chieftain then caused his people to divert the course of a rill of water, which, falling over the entrance of the cave, would have prevented his purposed vengeance. He then kindled at the entrance of the cavern a huge fire, composed of turf and fern, and maintained it with unrelenting assiduity, until all within were destroyed by suffocation. The date of this dreadful deed must have been recent, if one may judge from the fresh appearance of those relics. I brought off, in spite of the prejudice of our sailors, a skull from among the numerous specimens of mortality which the cavern afforded. Before re-embarking we visited another cave, opening to the sea, but of a character entirely different, being a large open vault, as high as that of a cathedral, and running back a great way into the rock at the same height. The height and width of the opening gives ample light to the whole. Here, after 1745, when the Catholic priests were scarcely tolerated, the priest of Eigg used to perform the Roman Catholic service, most of the islanders being of that persuasion. A huge ledge of rocks rising about half-way up one side of the vault, served for altar and pulpit; and the appearance of a priest and Highland congregation in such an extraordinary place of worship, might have engaged the pencil of Salvator."

NOTE 26.

Scenes sung by him who sings no more.

P. 331.

The ballad, entitled "Macphail of Colonsay, and the Mermaid of Corrievrekin." [See Border Minstrelsy, vol. iv. p. 285] was composed by John Leyden, from a tradition which he found while making a tour through the Hebrides about 1801, soon before his fatal departure for India, where, after having made farther progress in Oriental literature than any man of letters who had embraced those studies, he died a martyr to his zeal for knowledge, in the island of Java, immediately after the landing of our forces near Batavia, in August, 1811.

NOTE 27.

Up Tarbat's western lake they bore,
Then dragg'd their bark the isthmus o'er.

P. 331.

The peninsula of Cantire is joined to South Knapdale by a very narrow isthmus; formed by the western and eastern Loch of Tarbat. These two saltwater lakes, or bays, encroach so far upon the land, and the extremities come so near to each other, that there is not above a mile of land to divide them.

NOTE 28.

The sun, ere yet he sunk behind
Ben-Ghoil, " the Mountain of the Wind,"
Gave his grim peaks a greeting kind,
And bade Loch Ranza smile.—P. 331.

Loch Ranza is a beautiful bay, on the northern extremity of Arran, opening towards East Tarbat Loch. It is well described by Pennant :—"The approach was magnificent; a fine bay in front, about a mile deep, having a ruined castle near the lower end, on a low far projecting neck of land, that forms another harbour, with a narrow passage ; but within has three fathom of water, even at the lowest ebb. Beyond is a little plain watered by a stream, and inhabited by the people of a small village. The whole is environed with a theatre of mountains ; and in the background the serrated crags of Grianan-Athol soar above."—PENNANT'S *Tour to the Western Isles*, pp. 191-2. Ben-Ghaoil, " the mountain of the winds," is generally known by its English, and less poetical name, of Goatfield.

NOTE 29.

Each to Loch Ranza's margin spring;
That blast was winded by the King!

P. 333.

The passage in Barbour, describing the landing of Bruce, and his being recognised by Douglas and those of his followers who had preceded him, by the sound of his horn, is in the original singularly simple and affecting.— The King arrived in Arran with thirty-three small row-boats. He interrogated a female if there had arrived any warlike men of late in that country. "Surely, sir," she replied, " I can tell you of many who lately came hither, discomfited the English governor, and blockaded his castle of Brodick. They maintain themselves in a wood at no great distance." The king, truly conceiving that this must be Douglas and his followers, who had lately set forth to try their fortune in Arran, desired the woman to conduct him to the wood. She obeyed.

> " The king then blew his horn on high;
> And girt his men that were him by,
> Hold them still, and all privy ;
> And syne again his horn blew he.
> James of Dowglas heard him blow,
> And at the last alone gan know,
> And said, ' Soothly yon is the king ;
> I know long while since his blowing.'
> The third time therewithall he blew,
> And then Sir Robert Boid it knew ;
> And said, ' Yon is the king, but dread,
> Go we forth till him, better speed.'
> Then went they till the king in hye,
> And him inclined courteously.
> And blithly welcomed them the king,
> And was joyful of their meeting,
> And kissed them ; and speared syne
> How they had fared in hunting ?
> And they him told all, but lesing :
> Syne laud they God of their meeting.
> Syne with the king till his harbourye
> Went both joyfu' and jolly."

BARBOUR'S *Bruce*, Book v. p. 115, 116.

NOTE 30.

—— his brother blamed,
But shared the weakness, while ashamed,
With haughty laugh his head he turn'd,
And dashed away the tear he scorn'd.

P. 333.

The kind, and yet fiery character of Edward Bruce, is well painted by Barbour, in the account of his behaviour after the battle of Bannockburn. Sir Walter Ross, one of the very few Scottish nobles who fell in that battle, was so dearly beloved by Edward, that he wished the victory had been lost, so Ross had lived.

NOTE 31.

Thou heard'st a wretched female plain
In agony of travail-pain,
And thou didst bid thy little band
Upon the instant turn and stand,
And dare the worst the foe might do,
Rather than, like a knight untrue,
Leave to pursuers merciless
A woman in her last distress.—P. 335.

This incident, which illustrates so happily the chivalrous generosity of Bruce's character, is one of the many simple and natural traits recorded by Barbour. It occurred during the expedition which Bruce made to Ireland, to support the pretensions of his brother Edward to the throne of that kingdom.

NOTE 32.

O'er chasms he passed, where fractures wide
Craved wary eye and ample stride.—P. 338.

The interior of the island of Arran abounds with beautiful Highland scenery. The hills, being very rocky and precipitous, afford some cataracts of great height, though of inconsiderable breadth. There is one pass over the river Machrai, renowned for the dilemma of a poor woman, who, being tempted by the narrowness of the ravine to step across, succeeded in making the first movement, but took fright when it became necessary to move the other foot, and remained in a posture equally ludicrous and dangerous, until some chance passenger assisted her to extricate herself. It is said she remained there some hours.

NOTE 33.

Old Brodick's gothic towers were seen ;
From Hastings, late their English Lord,
Douglas had won them by the sword.

P. 338.

Brodick or Brathwick Castle, in the Isle of Arran, is an ancient fortress, near an open roadstead called Brodick-Bay, and not far distant from a tolerable harbour, closed in by the Island of Lamlash. This important place had been assailed a short time before Bruce's arrival in the island. James Lord Douglas, who accompanied Bruce to his retreat in Rachrine, seems, in the spring of 1306, to have tired of his abode there, and set out accordingly, in the phrase of the times, to see what adventure God would send him. Sir Robert Boyd accompanied him; and his knowledge of the localities of Arran appears to have directed his course thither. They landed in the island privately, and appear to have laid an ambush for Sir John Hastings, the English governor of Brodwick, and surprised a considerable supply of arms and provisions, and nearly took the castle itself. Indeed, that they actually did so, has been generally averred by historians, although it does not appear from the narrative of Barbour. On the contrary, it would seem that they took shelter within a fortification of the ancient inhabitants . . . . The castle is now much modernized, but has a dignified appearance, being surrounded by flourishing plantations.

NOTE 34.

Oft, too, with unaccustom'd ears,
A language much unmeet he hears.

P. 338.

Barbour, with great simplicity, gives an anecdote, from which it would seem that the vice of profane swearing, afterwards too general among the Scottish nation, was, at this time, confined to military men. As Douglas, after Bruce's return to Scotland, was roving about the mountainous country of Tweeddale, near the water of Line, he chanced to hear some persons in a farm-house say *"the devil."* Concluding, from this hardy expression, that the house contained warlike guests, he immediately assailed it, and had the good fortune to make prisoners Thomas Randolph, afterwards the famous Earl of Murray, and Alexander Stuart, Lord Bonkle. Both were then in the English interest, and had come into that country with the purpose of driving out Douglas. They afterwards ranked among Bruce's most zealous adherents.

NOTE 35.

Now ask you whence that wondrous light,
Whose fairy glow beguiled their sight!
It ne'er was known.—P. 341.

The following are the words of an ingenious correspondent, to whom I am obliged for much information respecting Turnberry and its neighbourhood. "The only tradition now

remembered of the landing of Robert the Bruce in Carrick, relates to the fire seen by him from the Isle of Arran. It is still generally reported, and religiously believed by many, that this fire was really the work of supernatural power, unassisted by the hand of any mortal being; and it is said, that, for several centuries, the flame rose yearly on the same hour of the same night of the year, on which the king first saw it from the turrets of Brodick Castle; and some go so far as to say, that if the exact time were known, it would be still seen. That this superstitious notion is very ancient, is evident from the place where the fire is said to have appeared, being called the Bogles' Brae, beyond the remembrance of man. In support of this curious belief, it is said that the practice of burning heath for the improvement of land was then unknown; that a spunkie (Jack o'lanthorn) could not have been seen across the breadth of the Forth of Clyde, between Ayrshire and Arran; and that the courier of Bruce was his kinsman, and never suspected of treachery."—Letter from Mr. Joseph Train, of Newton Stewart.

NOTE 36.

The Bruce hath won his father's hall!

P. 345.

I have followed the flattering and pleasing tradition, that the Bruce, after his descent upon the coast of Ayrshire, actually gained possession of his maternal castle. But the tradition is not accurate. The fact is, that he was only strong enough to alarm and drive in the outposts of the English garrison, then commanded, not by Clifford, as assumed in the text, but by Percy. Neither was Clifford slain upon this occasion, though he had several skirmishes with Bruce. He fell afterwards in the battle of Bannockburn. Bruce, after alarming the castle of Turnberry, and surprising some part of the garrison, who were quartered without the walls of the fortress, retreated into the mountainous part of Carrick, and there made himself so strong, that the English were obliged to evacuate Turnberry, and at length the Castle of Ayr. Many of his benefactions and royal gifts attest his attachment to the hereditary followers of his house, in this part of the country.

NOTE 37.

When Bruce's banner had victorious flow'd,
O'er Loudoun's mountain, and in Ury's vale.

P. 346.

The first important advantage gained by Bruce, after landing at Turnberry, was over

Aymer de Valence, Earl of Pembroke, the same by whom he had been defeated near Methven. They met, as has been said, by appointment, at Loudonhill, in the west of Scotland. Pembroke sustained a defeat; and from that time Bruce was at the head of a considerable flying army. Yet he was subsequently obliged to retreat into Aberdeenshire, and was there assailed by Comyn, Earl of Buchan, desirous to avenge the death of his relative, the Red Comyn, and supported by a body of English troops under Philip de Mowbray. Bruce was ill at the time of a scrofulous disorder, but took horse to meet his enemies, although obliged to be supported on either side. He was victorious, and it is said that the agitation of his spirits restored his health.

NOTE 38.

When English blood oft deluged Douglas-dale.
P. 346.

The "good Lord James of Douglas," during these commotions, often took from the English his own castle of Douglas, but being unable to garrison it, contented himself with destroying the fortifications, and retiring into the mountains. As a reward to his patriotism, it is said to have been prophesied, that how often soever Douglas Castle should be destroyed, it should always again arise more magnificent from its ruins. Upon one of these occasions he used fearful cruelty, causing all the store of provisions, which the English had laid up in his castle, to be heaped together, bursting the wine and beer casks among the wheat and flour, slaughtering the cattle upon the same spot, and upon the top of the whole cutting the throats of the English prisoners. This pleasantry of the "good Lord James" is commemorated under the name of the *Douglas's Larder.*

NOTE 39.

And fiery Edward routed stout St. John.
P. 346.

"John de St. John, with 15,000 horsemen, had advanced to oppose the inroad of the Scots. By a forced march he endeavoured to surprise them, but intelligence of his motions was timeously received. The courage of Edward Bruce, approaching to temerity, frequently enabled him to achieve what men of more judicious valour would never have attempted. He ordered the infantry, and the meaner sort of his army, to intrench themselves in strong narrow ground. He himself, with fifty horsemen well harnessed, issued forth under cover of a thick mist, surprised the English on their march, attacked and dis-

persed them." — DALRYMPLE's *Annals of Edinburgh*, quarto, Edinburgh, 1779, p. 25.

NOTE 40.

When Randolph's war-cry swell'd the southern gale.—P. 346.

Thomas Randolph, Bruce's sister's son, a renowned Scottish chief, was in the early part of his life not more remarkable for consistency than Bruce himself. He espoused his uncle's party when Bruce first assumed the crown, and was made prisoner at the fatal battle of Methven, in which his relative's hopes appeared to be ruined. Randolph accordingly not only submitted to the English, but took an active part against Bruce; appeared in arms against him; and in the skirmish where he was so closely pursued by the bloodhound, it is said his nephew took his standard with his own hand. But Randolph was afterwards made prisoner by Douglas in Tweeddale, and brought before King Robert. Some harsh language was exchanged between the uncle and nephew, and the latter was committed for a time to close custody. Afterwards, however, they were reconciled, and Randolph was created Earl of Moray about 1312. After this period he eminently distinguished himself, first by the surprise of Edinburgh Castle, and afterwards by many similar enterprises, conducted with equal courage and ability.

NOTE 41.

—— *Stirling's towers,*
Beleaguer'd by King Robert's powers;
And they took term of truce.—P. 347.

When a long train of success, actively improved by Robert Bruce, had made him master of almost all Scotland, Stirling Castle continued to hold out. The care of the blockade was committed by the king to his brother Edward, who concluded a treaty with Sir Philip Mowbray, the governor, that he should surrender the fortress, if it were not succoured by the King of England before St. John the Baptist's day. The king severely blamed his brother for the impolicy of a treaty, which gave time to the King of England to advance to the relief of the castle with all his assembled forces, and obliged himself either to meet them in battle with an inferior force, or to retreat with dishonour. "Let all England come," answered the reckless Edward; "we will fight them were they more." The consequence was, of course, that each kingdom mustered its strength for the expected battle; and as the space agreed upon reached from Lent to Midsummer, full time was allowed for that purpose.

NOTE 24.

And Cambria, but of late subdued,
Sent forth her mountain multitude.
P. 347.

Edward the First, with the usual policy of a conqueror, employed the Welsh, whom he had subdued, to assist him in his Scottish wars, for which their habits, as mountaineers, particularly fitted them. But this policy was not without its risks. Previous to the battle of Falkirk, the Welsh quarrelled with the English men-at-arms, and after bloodshed on both parts, separated themselves from his army, and the feud between them, at so dangerous and critical a juncture, was reconciled with difficulty. Edward II. followed his father's example in this particular, and with no better success. They could not be brought to exert themselves in the cause of their conquerors. But they had an indifferent reward for their forbearance. Without arms, and clad only in scanty dresses of linen cloth, they appeared naked in the eyes even of the Scottish peasantry; and after the rout of Bannockburn, were massacred by them in great numbers, as they retired in confusion towards their own country. They were under command of Sir Maurice de Berkeley.

NOTE 43.

And Connoght pour'd from waste and wood
Her hundred tribes, whose sceptre rude
Dark Eth O'Connor sway'd.—P. 347.

There is in the Fœdera an invitation to Eth O'Connor, chief of the Irish of Connaught, setting forth that the king was about to move against his Scottish rebels, and therefore requesting the attendance of all the force he could muster, either commanded by himself in person, or by some nobleman of his race. These auxiliaries were to be commanded by Richard de Burgh, Earl of Ulster.

NOTE 44.

The monarch rode along the van.—P. 350.

The English vanguard, commanded by the Earls of Gloucester and Hereford, came in sight of the Scottish army upon the evening of the 23rd of June. Bruce was then riding upon a little palfrey, in front of his foremost line, putting his host in order. It was then that the personal encounter took place betwixt him and Sir Henry de Bohun, a gallant English knight, the issue of which had a great effect upon the spirits of both armies.

NOTE 45.

Responsive from the Scottish host,
Pipe-clang and bugle-sound were toss'd.
P. 352.

There is an old tradition, that the well-known Scottish tune of "Hey, tutti, taitti," was Bruce's march at the battle of Bannockburn. The late Mr. Ritson, no granter of propositions, doubts whether the Scots had any martial music, quotes Froissart's account of each soldier in the host bearing a little horn, on which, at the onset, they would make such a horrible noise, as if all the devils of hell had been among them. He observes, that these horns are the only music mentioned by Barbour, and concludes, that it must remain a moot point whether Bruce's army were cheered by the sound even of a solitary bagpipe.—*Historical Essay prefixed to Ritson's Scottish Songs.*—It may be observed in passing, that the Scottish of this period certainly observed some musical cadence, even in winding their horns, since Bruce was at once recognised by his followers from his mode of blowing. See Note 29, p. 333. But the tradition, true or false, has been the means of securing to Scotland one of the finest lyrics in the language, the celebrated war-song of Burns,—"Scots, wha hae wi' Wallace bled."

NOTE 46.

See where yon bare-foot Abbot stands,
And blesses them with lifted hands.—P. 352.

"Maurice, abbot of Inchaffray, placing himself on an eminence, celebrated mass in sight of the Scottish army. He then passed along the front bare-footed, and bearing a crucifix in his hands, and exhorting the Scots, in few and forcible words, to combat for their rights and their liberty. The Scots kneeled down. 'They yield,' cried Edward; 'see, they implore mercy.'—'They do,' answered Ingelram de Umfraville, 'but not ours. On that field they will be victorious, or die.'"—*Annals of Scotland*, vol. ii. p. 47.

NOTE 47.

Forth, Marshal, on the peasant foe!
We'll tame the terrors of their bow,
And cut the bow-string loose!
P. 353.

The English archers commenced the attack with their usual bravery and dexterity. But against a force, whose importance he had learned by fatal experience, Bruce was provided. A small but select body of cavalry were detached from the right, under command of Sir Robert Keith. They rounded, as I conceive, the marsh called Milton bog, and, keeping the firm ground, charged the left flank and rear of the English archers. As the bowmen had no spears nor long weapons fit to defend themselves against horse, they were instantly thrown into disorder, and spread through the whole English army a confusion from which they never fairly recovered.

Although the success of this manœuvre was evident, it is very remarkable that the Scottish generals do not appear to have profited by the lesson. Almost every subsequent battle which they lost against England, was decided by the archers, to whom the close and compact array of the Scottish phalanx afforded an exposed and unresisting mark. The bloody battle of Halidoun-hill, fought scarce twenty years afterwards, was so completely gained by the archers, that the English are said to have lost only one knight, one esquire, and a few foot-soldiers. At the battle of Neville's Cross, in 1346, where David II. was defeated and made prisoner, John de Graham, observing the loss which the Scots sustained from the English bowmen, offered to charge and disperse them, if a hundred men-at-arms were put under his command. "*But*, to confess the truth," says Fordun, "he could not procure a single horseman for the service proposed." Of such little use is experience in war, where its results are opposed by habit or prejudice.

NOTE 48.

Each braggart churl could boast before,
Twelve Scottish lives his baldrick bore.

P. 353.

Roger Ascham quotes a similar Scottish proverb, "whereby they give the whole praise of shooting honestly to Englishmen, saying thus, 'that every English archer beareth under his girdle twenty-four Scottes.' Indeed Toxophilus says before, and truly of the Scottish nation, 'The Scottes surely be good men of warre in theyre owne feates as can be; but as for shootinge, they can neither use it to any profite, nor yet challenge it for any praise.'" —*Works of Ascham, edited by Bennet,* 4to, p. 110.

It is said, I trust incorrectly, by an ancient English historian, that the "good Lord James of Douglas" dreaded the superiority of the English archers so much, that when he made any of them prisoner, he gave him the option of losing the forefinger of his right hand, or his right eye, either species of mutilation ren-

dering him incapable to use the bow. I have mislaid the reference to this singular passage.

NOTE 49.

Down! down! in headlong overthrow,
Horseman and horse, the foremost go.

P. 353.

It is generally alleged by historians, that the English men-at-arms fell into the hidden snare which Bruce had prepared for them. Barbour does not mention the circumstance. According to his account, Randolph, seeing the slaughter made by the cavalry on the right wing among the archers, advanced courageously against the main body of the English, and entered into close combat with them. Douglas and Stuart, who commanded the Scottish centre, led their division also to the charge, and the battle becoming general along the whole line, was obstinately maintained on both sides for a long space of time; the Scottish archers doing great execution among the English men-at-arms, after the bowmen of England were dispersed.

NOTE 50.

And steeds that shriek in agony.—P. 353.

I have been told that this line requires an explanatory note; and, indeed, those who witness the silent patience with which horses submit to the most cruel usage, may be permitted to doubt, that, in moments of sudden and intolerable anguish, they utter a most melancholy cry. Lord Erskine, in a speech made in the House of Lords, upon a bill for enforcing humanity towards animals, noticed this remarkable fact, in language which I will not mutilate by attempting to repeat it. It was my fortune, upon one occasion, to hear a horse, in a moment of agony, utter a thrilling scream, which I still consider the most melancholy sound I ever heard.

NOTE 51.

Lord of the Isles, my trust in thee
Is firm as Ailsa Rock!
Rush on with Highland sword and targe,
I, with my Carrick spearmen charge.

P. 354.

When the engagement between the main bodies had lasted some time, Bruce made a decisive movement, by bringing up the Scottish reserve. It is traditionally said, that at this crisis, he addressed the Lord of the Isles in a phrase used as a motto by some of his descendants, "My trust is constant in thee." Barbour intimates, that the reserve "assembled on one field," that is, on the same line with the Scottish forces already engaged; which leads Lord Hailes to conjecture that the Scottish ranks must have been much thinned by slaughter, since, in that circumscribed ground, there was room for the reserve to fall into the line. But the advance of the Scottish cavalry must have contributed a good deal to form the vacancy occupied by the reserve.

NOTE 52.

To arms they flew,—axe, club, or spear,—
And mimic ensigns high they rear.—P. 355.

The followers of the Scottish camp observed, from the Gillies' Hill in the rear, the impression produced upon the English army by the bringing up of the Scottish reserve, and, prompted by the enthusiasm of the moment, or the desire of plunder, assumed, in a tumultuary manner, such arms as they found nearest, fastened sheets to tent-poles and lances, and showed themselves like a new army advancing to battle.

The unexpected apparition, of what seemed a new army, completed the confusion which already prevailed among the English, who fled in every direction, and were pursued with immense slaughter.

THE FIELD OF WATERLOO.

NOTE 1.

The peasant, at his labour blithe,
Plies the hook'd staff and shorten'd scythe.
P. 361.

The reaper in Flanders carries in his left hand a stick with an iron hook, with which he collects as much grain as he can cut at one sweep with a short scythe, which he holds in his right hand. They carry on this double process with great spirit and dexterity.

NOTE 2.

Pale Brussels! then what thoughts were thine.
P. 363.

It was affirmed by the prisoners of war, that Bonaparte had promised his army, in case of victory, twenty-four hours' plunder of the city of Brussels.

NOTE 3.

"On! On!" was still his stern exclaim.
P. 363.

The characteristic obstinacy of Napoleon was never more fully displayed than in what we may be permitted to hope will prove the last of his fields. He would listen to no advice, and allow of no obstacles. An eye-witness has given the following account of his demeanour towards the end of the action:—

"It was near seven o'clock; Bonaparte, who till then had remained upon the ridge of the hill whence he could best behold what passed, contemplated with a stern countenance, the scene of this horrible slaughter. The more that obstacles seemed to multiply, the more his obstinacy seemed to increase. He became indignant at these unforeseen difficulties; and, far from fearing to push to extremities an army whose confidence in him was boundless, he ceased not to pour down fresh troops, and to give orders to march forward—to charge with the bayonet—to carry by storm. He was repeatedly informed, from different points, that the day went against him, and that the troops seemed to be disordered; to which he only replied,—'*En avant! En avant!*'

"One general sent to inform the Emperor that he was in a position which he could not maintain, because it was commanded by a battery, and requested to know, at the same time, in what way he should protect his division from the murderous fire of the English artillery. 'Let him storm the battery,' replied Bonaparte, and turned his back on the aide-de-camp who brought the message."—*Rélation de la Bataille de Mont-St.-Jean. Par un Témoin Oculaire.* Paris, 1815, 8vo, p. 51.

NOTE 4.

The fate their leader shunn'd to share.
P. 363.

It has been reported that Bonaparte charged at the head of his guards, at the last period of this dreadful conflict. This, however, is not accurate. He came down indeed to a hollow part of the high road, leading to Charleroi, within less than a quarter of a mile of the farm of La Haye Sainte, one of the points most fiercely disputed. Here he harangued the guards, and informed them that his preceding operations had destroyed the British infantry and cavalry, and that they had only to support the fire of the artillery, which they were to attack with the bayonet. This exhortation was received with shouts of *Vive l'Empereur*, which were heard over all our line, and led to an idea that Napoleon was charging in person. But the guards were led on by Ney; nor did Bonaparte approach nearer the scene of action than the spot already mentioned, which the rising banks on each side rendered secure from all such balls as did not come in a straight line. He witnessed the earlier part of the battle from places yet more remote, particularly from an observatory which had been placed there by the King of the Netherlands, some weeks before, for the purpose of surveying the country.* It is not meant to infer from these particulars that Napoleon showed, on that memorable occasion, the least deficiency in personal courage; on the contrary, he evinced the greatest composure and presence of mind during the whole action. But it is no less true that report has erred in ascribing to him any desperate efforts of valour for recovery of the battle; and it is remarkable, that during the whole carnage, none of his suite were either killed or wounded, whereas scarcely one of the Duke of Wellington's personal attendants escaped unhurt.

NOTE 5.

England shall tell the fight.—P. 363.

In riding up to a regiment which was hard pressed,† the Duke called to the men, "Soldiers, we must never be beat,—what will they say in England?" It is needless to say how this appeal was answered.

NOTE 6.

As plies the smith his clanging trade.—P. 364.

A private soldier of the 95th regiment compared the sound which took place immediately upon the British cavalry mingling with those of the enemy, to "*a thousand tinkers at work mending pots and kettles.*"

NOTE 7.

The British shock of levell'd steel.—P. 364.

No persuasion or authority could prevail upon the French troops to stand the shock of the bayonet. The Imperial Guards, in particular, hardly stood till the British were within thirty yards of them, although the French author, already quoted, has put into their mouths the magnanimous sentiment, "The Guards never yield—they die." The same author has covered the plateau, or eminence, of St. Jean, which formed the British position, with redoubts and retrenchments which never

had an existence. As the narrative, which is in many respects curious, was written by an eye-witness, he was probably deceived by the appearance of a road and ditch which run along part of the hill. It may be also mentioned, in criticizing this work, that the writer mentions the Chateau of Hougomont to have been carried by the French, although it was resolutely and successfully defended during the whole action. The enemy, indeed, possessed themselves of the wood by which it is surrounded, and at length set fire to the house itself; but the British (a detachment of the Guards, under the command of Colonel Macdonnell, and afterwards of Colonel Home) made good the garden, and thus preserved, by their desperate resistance, the post which covered the return of the Duke of Wellington's right flank.

NOTE 8.

What bright careers 'twas thine to close.
P. 366.

Sir Thomas Picton, Sir William Ponsonby, Sir William de Lancy, and numberless gallant officers.

NOTE 9.

Laurels from the hand of Death.—P. 366.

Colonel Sir William de Lancy had married the beautiful Miss Hall only two months before the battle of Waterloo.

NOTE 10.

Gallant Miller's failing eye.—P. 366.

Colonel Miller of the Guards, when lying mortally wounded in the attack on the Bois de Bossa, desired to see once more the colours of his regiment. They were waved about his head, and he died declaring that he was satisfied.

NOTE 11.

And Cameron, in the shock of steel.—P. 366.

Colonel Cameron fell at Quatre Bras, heading a charge of the 92nd Highlanders.

NOTE 12.

And generous Gordon.—P. 366.

"Generous Gordon"—brother to the Earl of Aberdeen—who fell by the side of the Duke in the heat of the action.

NOTE 13.

Fair Hougomont.—P. 367.

"Hougomont"—a chateau with a garden and wood round it. A post of great importance, valiantly held by the Guards during the battle.

---

* The mistakes concerning this observatory have been mutual. The English supposed it was erected for the use of Bonaparte: and a French writer affirms it was constructed by the Duke of Wellington.

† The 95th. The Duke's words were—"Stand fast, 95th—what will they say in England?"

GLENFINLAS.

NOTE 1.

How blazed Lord Ronald's beltane-tree.
P. 408.

THE fires lighted by the Highlanders, on the 1st of May, in compliance with a custom derived from the Pagan times, are termed *The Beltane-tree.* It is a festival celebrated with various superstitious rites, both in the north of Scotland and in Wales.

NOTE 2.

The seer's prophetic spirit found.—P. 408.

I can only describe the second sight, by adopting Dr. Johnson's definition, who calls it "An impression, either by the mind upon the eye, or by the eye upon the mind, by which things distant and future are perceived and seen as if they were present." To which I would only add, that the spectral appearances, thus presented, usually presage misfortune; that the faculty is painful to those who suppose they possess it; and that they usually acquire it while themselves under the pressure of melancholy.

NOTE 3.

Will good St. Oran's rule prevail?—P. 409.

St. Oran was a friend and follower of St. Columba, and was buried at Icolmkill. His pretensions to be a saint were rather dubious. According to the legend, he consented to be buried alive, in order to propitiate certain demons of the soil, who obstructed the attempts of Columba to build a chapel. Columba caused the body of his friend to be dug up, after three days had elapsed; when Oran, to the horror and scandal of the assistants, declared, that there was neither a God, a judgment, nor a future state! He had no time to make further discoveries, for Columba caused the earth once more to be shovelled over him with the utmost despatch. The chapel, however, and the cemetery, was called *Relig Ouran;* and, in memory of his rigid celibacy, no female was permitted to pay her devotions, or be buried in that place. This is the rule alluded to in the poem.

NOTE 4.

And thrice St. Fillan's powerful prayer.
P. 411.

St. Fillan has given his name to many chapels, holy fountains, &c., in Scotland. He was, according to Camerarius, an Abbot of Pittenweem, in Fife; from which situation he retired, and died a hermit in the wilds of Glenurchy, A.D. 649. While engaged in transcribing the Scriptures, his left hand was observed to send forth such a splendour, as to afford light to that with which he wrote; a miracle which saved many candles to the convent, as St. Fillan used to spend whole nights in that exercise. The 9th of January was dedicated to this saint, who gave his name to Kilfillan, in Renfrew, and St. Phillans, or Forgend, in Fife. Lesley, lib. 7, tells us, that Robert the Bruce was possessed of Fillan's miraculous and luminous arm, which he enclosed in a silver shrine, and had it carried at the head of his army. Previous to the Battle of Bannockburn, the king's chaplain, a man of little faith, abstracted the relic, and deposited it in a place of security, lest it should fall into the hands of the English. But, lo! while Robert was addressing his prayers to the empty casket, it was observed to open and shut suddenly; and, on inspection, the saint was found to have himself deposited his arm in the shrine as an assurance of victory. Such is the tale of Lesley. But though Bruce little needed that the arm of St. Fillan should assist his own, he dedicated to him, in gratitude, a priory at Killin, upon Loch Tay.

In the Scots Magazine for July, 1802, there is a copy of a very curious crown grant, dated 11th July, 1487, by which James III. confirms, to Malice Doire, an inhabitant of Strathfillan, in Perthshire, the peaceable exercise and enjoyment of a relic of St. Fillan, being apparently the head of a pastoral staff called the Quegrich, which he and his predecessors are said to have possessed since the days of Robert Bruce. As the Quegrich was used to cure diseases, this document is probably the most ancient patent ever granted for a quack medicine. The ingenious correspondent, by whom it is furnished, farther observes, that additional particulars, concerning St. Fillan, are to be found in BELLENDEN'S *Boece*, Book 4, folio ccxiii., and in PENNANT'S *Tour in Scotland*, 1772, pp. 11, 15.

THE EVE OF ST. JOHN.

NOTE 1.

BATTLE OF ANCRAM MOOR.—P. 412.

LORD EVERS, and Sir Brian Latoun, during the year 1544, committed the most dreadful ravages upon the Scottish frontiers, compelling most of the inhabitants, and especially the men of Liddesdale, to take assurance under the King of England. Upon the 17th November, in that year, the sum total of their depredations stood thus, in the bloody ledger of Lord Evers :—

Towns, towers, barnekynes, paryshe churches, bastill houses, burned and destroyed, 192
Scots slain 403
Prisoners taken 816
Nolt (cattle) 10,386
Shepe 12,492
Nags and geldings . . . 1296
Gayt 200
Bolls of corn 850
Insight gear, &c. (furniture) an incalculable quantity.

MURDIN'S *State Papers*, vol. i. p. 51.

For these services Sir Ralph Evers was made a Lord of Parliament. See a strain of exulting congratulation upon his promotion poured forth by some contemporary minstrel, in vol. i. p. 417.

The King of England had promised to these two barons a feudal grant of the country, which they had thus reduced to a desert ; upon hearing which, Archibald Douglas, the seventh earl of Angus, is said to have sworn to write the deed of investiture upon their skins, with sharp pens and bloody ink, in resentment for their having defaced the tombs of his ancestors at Melrose.—*Godscroft.* In 1545, Lord Evers and Latoun again entered Scotland, with an army consisting of 3000 mercenaries, 1500 English Borderers, and 700 assured Scottish men, chiefly Armstrongs, Turnbulls, and other broken clans. In this second incursion, the English generals even exceeded their former cruelty. Evers burned the tower of Broomhouse, with its lady (a noble and aged woman, says Lesley), and her whole family. The English penetrated as far as Melrose, which they had destroyed last year, and which they now again pillaged. As they returned towards Jedburgh, they were followed by Angus at the head of 1000 horse, who was shortly after joined by the famous Norman Lesley, with a body of Fife-men. The

English being probably unwilling to cross the Teviot while the Scots hung upon their rear, halted upon Ancram Moor, above the village of that name ; and the Scottish general was deliberating whether to advance or retire, when Sir Walter Scott* of Buccleuch came up at full speed with a small but chosen body of his retainers, the rest of whom were near at hand. By the advice of this experienced warrior (to whose conduct Pitscottie and Buchanan ascribe the success of the engagement), Angus withdrew from the height which he occupied, and drew up his forces behind it, upon a piece of low flat ground, called Panier-heugh, or Paniel-heugh. The spare horses being sent to an eminence in their rear, appeared to the English to be the main body of the Scots in the act of flight. Under this persuasion, Evers and Latoun hurried precipitately forward, and having ascended the hill, which their foes had abandoned, were no less dismayed than astonished to find the phalanx of Scottish spearmen drawn up, in firm array upon the flat ground below. The Scots, in their turn became the assailants. A heron, roused from the marshes by the tumult, soared away betwixt the encountering armies : "O !" exclaimed Angus, "that I had here my white goss-hawk, that we might all yoke at once !" —*Godscroft.* The English, breathless and fatigued, having the setting sun and wind full in their faces, were unable to withstand the resolute and desperate charge of the Scottish lances. No sooner had they begun to waver, than their own allies, the assured Borderers, who had been waiting the event, threw aside their red crosses, and, joining their countrymen, made a most merciless slaughter among the English fugitives, the pursuers calling upon each other to "remember Broomhouse !"—LESLEY, p. 478.

---

* The Editor has found no instance upon record of this family having taken assurance with England. Hence, they usually suffered dreadfully from the English forays. In August, 1544 (the year preceding the battle), the whole lands belonging to Buccleuch, in West Teviotdale, were harried by Evers ; the outworks, or barmkin, of the tower of Branxholm burned ; eight Scots slain, thirty made prisoners, and an immense prey of horses, cattle, and sheep carried off. The lands upon Kale Water, belonging to the same chieftain, were also plundered, and much spoil obtained ; 30 Scots slain, and the Moss Tower (a fortress near Eskford) *smokd verey sore.* Thus Buccleuch had a long account to settle at Ancram Moor.—MURDIN'S *State Papers,* pp. 45, 46.

In the battle fell Lord Evers, and his son, together with Sir Brian Latoun, and 800 Englishmen, many of whom were persons of rank. A thousand prisoners were taken. Among these was a patriotic alderman of London, Read by name, who, having contumaciously refused to pay his portion of a benevolence, demanded from the city by Henry VIII., was sent by royal authority to serve against the Scots. These, at settling his ransom, he found still more exorbitant in their exactions than the monarch.—REDPATH'S *Border History*, p. 563.

Evers was much regretted by King Henry, who swore to avenge his death upon Angus, against whom he conceived himself to have particular grounds of resentment, on account of favours received by the earl at his hands. The answer of Angus was worthy of a Douglas: "Is our brother-in-law offended,"* said he, "that I, as a good Scotsman, have avenged my ravaged country, and the defaced tombs of my ancestors, upon Ralph Evers? They were better men than he, and I was bound to do no less. And will he take my life for that? Little knows King Henry the skirts of Kirnetable :† I can keep myself there against all his English host."—GODSCROFT.

Such was the noted battle of Ancram Moor. The spot on which it was fought, is called Lilyard's Edge, from an Amazonian Scottish woman of that name, who is reported, by tradition, to have distinguished herself in the same manner as Squire Witherington.‡ The old people point out her monument, now broken and defaced. The inscription is said to have been legible within this century, and to have run thus :

"Fair maiden Lylliard lies under this stane,
Little was her stature, but great was her fame ;
Upon the English louns she laid mony thumps,
And, when her legs were cutted off, she fought
upon her stumps."

Vide *Account of the Parish of Melrose.*

It appears, from a passage in Stowe, that an ancestor of Lord Evers held also a grant of Scottish lands from an English monarch. "I have seen," says the historian, "under the broad-seale of the said King Edward I., a manor, called Ketnes, in the county of Forfare, in Scotland, and neere the furthest part of the same nation northward, given to John Ure and his heires, ancestor to the Lord Ure

* Angus had married the widow of James IV., sister to King Henry VIII.
† Kirnetable, now called Cairntable, is a mountainous tract at the head of Douglasdale.
‡ See *Chevy Chase.*

that now is, for his service done in these partes, with market, &c., dated at Lanercost, the 20th day of October, anno regis 34."—STOWE'S *Annals*, p. 210. This grant, like that of Henry, must have been dangerous to the receiver.

NOTE 2.

A covering on her wrist.—P. 415.

There is an old and well-known Irish tradition, that the bodies of certain spirits and devils are scorchingly hot, so that they leave upon anything they touch an impress as if of red-hot iron. It is related of one of Melancthon's relations, that a devil seized hold of her hand, which bore the mark of a burn to her dying day. The incident in the poem is of a similar nature—the ghost's hands "scorch'd like a fiery brand," leaving a burning impress on the table and the lady's wrist. Another class of fiends are reported to be icy-cold, and to freeze the skin of any one with whom they come in contact.

NOTE 3.

That nun who ne'er beholds the day.—P. 415.

The circumstance of the nun, "who never saw the day," is not entirely imaginary. About fifty years ago, an unfortunate female wanderer took up her residence in a dark vault, among the ruins of Dryburgh Abbey, which, during the day, she never quitted. When night fell, she issued from this miserable habitation, and went to the house of Mr. Haliburton of Newmains, the Editor's great-grandfather, or to that of Mr. Erskine of Sheilfield, two gentlemen of the neighbourhood. From their charity she obtained such necessaries as she could be prevailed upon to accept. At twelve, each night, she lighted her candle, and returned to her vault, assuring her friendly neighbours, that, during her absence, her habitation was arranged by a spirit, to whom she gave the uncouth name of *Fat lips;* describing him as a little man, wearing heavy iron shoes, with which he trampled the clay floor of the vault, to dispel the damps. This circumstance caused her to be regarded, by the well-informed, with compassion, as deranged in her understanding ; and, by the vulgar, with some degree of terror. The cause of her adopting this extraordinary mode of life she would never explain. It was, however, believed to have been occasioned by a vow, that, during the absence of a man to whom she was attached, she would never look upon the sun. Her lover never returned. He fell during the civil war of 1745-6,* and she never more would behold the light of day.

The vault, or rather dungeon, in which this unfortunate woman lived and died, passes still by the name of the supernatural being, with which its gloom was tenanted by her disturbed imagination, and few of the neighbouring peasants dare enter it by night.

CADYOW CASTLE.

NOTE 1.

—— *sound the pryse!*—P. 418.

Pryse.—The note blown at the death of the game.—*In Caledonia olim frequens erat sylvestris quidam bos, nunc vero rarior, qui, colore candidissimo, jubam densam et demissam instar leonis gestat, truculentus ac ferus ab humano genere abhorrens, ut quæcunque homines vel manibus contrectârint, vel halitu perflaverint, ab iis multos post dies omnino abstinuerunt. Ad hoc tanta audacia huic bovi indita erat, ut non solum irritatus equites furenter prosterneret, sed ne tantillum lacessitus omnes promiscue homines cornibus ac ungulis peterit; ac canum, qui apud nos ferocissimi sunt, impetus plane contemneret. Ejus sarnes cartilaginosæ, sed saporis suavissimi. Erat is olim per illam vastissimam Caledoniæ sylvam frequens, sed humana ingluvie jam assumptus tribus tantum locis est reliquus, Strivilingii, Cumbernaldiæ, et Kincarniæ.—* LESLÆUS, Scotiæ Descriptio, p. 13.

NOTE 2.

Stern Claud replied.—P. 418.

Lord Claud Hamilton, second son of the Duke of Chatelherault, and commendator of the Abbey of Paisley, acted a distinguished part during the troubles of Queen Mary's reign, and remained unalterably attached to the cause of that unfortunate princess. He led the van of her army at the fatal battle of Langside, and was one of the commanders at the Raid of Stirling, which had so nearly given complete success to the Queen's faction. He was ancestor of the present Marquis of Abercorn.

NOTE 3.

Woodhouselee.—P. 418.

This barony, stretching along the banks of the Esk, near Auchendinny, belonged to Bothwellhaugh, in right of his wife. The ruins of the mansion, from whence she was expelled in the brutal manner which occasioned her death, are still to be seen in a hollow glen beside the river. Popular report tenants them with the restless ghost of the Lady Bothwellhaugh; whom, however, it confounds with Lady Anne Bothwell, whose *Lament* is so popular. This spectre is so tenacious of her rights, that, a part of the stones of the ancient edifice having been employed in building or repairing the present Woodhouselee, she has deemed it a part of her privilege to haunt that house also; and, even of very late years, has excited considerable disturbance and terror among the domestics. This is a more remarkable vindication of the *rights of ghosts* as the present Woodhouselee, which gives his title to the Honourable Alexander Fraser Tytler, a senator of the College of Justice, is situated on the slope of the Pentland hills, distant at least four miles from her proper abode. She always appears in white, and with her child in her arms.

NOTE 4.

Drives to the leap his jaded steed.—P. 418.

Birrel informs us, that Bothwellhaugh, being closely pursued, "after that spur and wand had failed him, he drew forth his dagger, and strocke his horse behind, whilk caused the horse to leap a very brode stanke [*i.e.* ditch,] by whilk means he escapit, and gat away from all the rest of the horses."—BIRREL'S *Diary*, p. 18.

NOTE 5.

From the wild Border's humbled side.—P. 418.

Murray's death took place shortly after an expedition to the Borders; which is thus commemorated by the author of his Elegy:

"So having stablischt all things in this sort,
　To Liddisdaill agane he did resort,
Throw Ewisdail, Eskdail, and all the daills rode he,
And also lay three nights in Cannabie,
Whair na prince lay thir hundred yeiris before.
Nae thief durst stir. they did him feir sa sair;

And, that they suld na mair thair thift allege,
Threescore and twelf he brocht of thame in
 pledge,
Syne wardit thame, whilk maid the rest keep
 ordour;
Than mycht the rasch-bus keep ky on the
 Border."

    Scottish Poems, 16th century, p. 232.

NOTE 6.

With hackbut bent.—P. 419.

Hackbut bent—Gun cock'd. The carbine, with which the Regent was shot, is preserved at Hamilton Palace. It is a brass piece, of a middling length, very small in the bore, and, what is rather extraordinary, appears to have been rifled or indented in the barrel. It had a matchlock, for which a modern firelock has been injudiciously substituted.

NOTE 7.

The wild Macfarlane's plaided clan.—P. 419.

This clan of Lennox Highlanders were attached to the Regent Murray. Holinshed, speaking of the battle of Langside, says, "In this batayle the vallancie of an Heiland gentleman, named Macfarlane, stood the Regent's part in great steede; for, in the hottest brunte of the fighte, he came up with two hundred of his friendes and countrymen, and so manfully gav' in upon the flankes of the Queen's people, that he was a great cause of the disordering of them. This Macfarlane had been lately before, as I have heard, condemned to die, for some outrage by him committed, and obtayning pardon through suyte of the Countess of Murray, he recompensed that clemencie by this piece of service now at this batayle." Calderwood's account is less favourable to the Macfarlanes. He states that "Macfarlane, with his Highlandmen, fled from the wing where they were set. The Lord Lindsay, who stood nearest to them in the Regent's battle, said, 'Let them go! I shall fill their place better:' and so, stepping forward, with a com-

pany of fresh men, charged the enemy, whose spears were now spent, with long weapons, so that they were driven back by force, being before almost overthrown by the avaunt-guard and harquebusiers, and so were turned to flight."—CALDERWOOD'S *MS. apud* KEITH, p. 80. Melville mentions the flight of the vanguard, but states it to have been commanded by Morton, and composed chiefly of commoners of the barony of Renfrew.

NOTE 8.

Glencairn and stout Parkhead were nigh.
         P. 419.

The Earl of Glencairn was a steady adherent of the Regent. George Douglas of Parkhead was a natural brother of the Earl of Morton, whose horse was killed by the same ball by which Murray fell.

NOTE 9.

—— *haggard Lindesay's iron eye,*
That saw fair Mary weep in vain.—P. 419.

Lord Lindsay of the Byres was the most ferocious and brutal of the Regent's faction, and, as such, was employed to extort Mary's signature to the deed of resignation presented to her in Lochleven castle. He discharged his commission with the most savage rigour; and it is even said, that when the weeping captive in the act of signing, averted her eyes from the fatal deed, he pinched her arm with the grasp of his iron glove.

NOTE 10.

So close the minions crowded nigh.—P. 419.

Not only had the Regent notice of the intended attempt upon his life, but even of the very house from which it was threatened. With that infatuation at which men wonder, after such events have happened, he deemed it would be a sufficient precaution to ride briskly past the dangerous spot. But even this was prevented by the crowd: so that Bothwellhaugh had time to take a deliberate aim.—SPOTTISWOODE, p. 233. BUCHANAN.

~~~~~~~~~

THE GRAY BROTHER.

NOTE 1.

By blast of bugle free.—P. 421.

THE barony of Pennycuik, the property of Sir George Clerk, Bart., is held by a singular

tenure; the proprietor being bound to sit upon a large rocky fragment called the Buckstane, and wind three blasts of a horn, when the King shall come to hunt on the Borough Muir, near Edinburgh. Hence the family have adopted as their crest a demi-forester proper, winding a horn, with the motto, *Free for a Blast.* The beautiful mansion-house of Pennycuik is much admired, both on account of the architecture and surrounding scenery.

NOTE 2.

To Auchendinny's hazel shade.—P. 421.

Auchendinny, situated upon the Eske below Pennycuik, the present residence of the ingenious H. Mackenzie, Esq., author of the *Man of Feeling, &c.*—Edition 1803.

NOTE 3.

Melville's beechy grove.—P. 421.

Melville Castle, the seat of the Right Honourable Lord Melville, to whom it gives the title of Viscount, is delightfully situated upon the Eske, near Lasswade.

NOTE 4.

Roslin's rocky glen.—P. 421.

The ruins of Roslin Castle, the baronial residence of the ancient family of St. Clair. The Gothic chapel, which is still in beautiful preservation, with the romantic and woody dell in which they are situated, belong to the Right Honourable the Earl of Rosslyn, the representative of the former Lords of Roslin.

NOTE 5.

Dalkeith, which all the virtues love.—P. 421.

The village and castle of Dalkeith belonged of old to the famous Earl of Morton, but is now the residence of the noble family of Buccleuch. The park extends along the Eske, which is there joined by its sister stream of the same name.

NOTE 6.

Classic Hawthornden.—P. 421.

Hawthornden, the residence of the poet Drummond. A house of more modern date is enclosed, as it were, by the ruins of the ancient castle, and overhangs a tremendous precipice upon the banks of the Eske, perforated by winding caves, which in former times were a refuge to the oppressed patriots of Scotland. Here Drummond received Ben Jonson, who journeyed from London on foot in order to visit him.